The Apostles' Bible

GENERAL EDITOR: PAUL W. ESPOSITO

ISBN NUMBER: 978-0-6151-8079-3

What is the Apostles' Bible?

The Apostles' Bible is a revision of Sir Lancelot C.L. Brenton's (1807-1862) original translation of the Greek Septuagint, which was first published in London in 1851.

What I have done, is updated this great work to make it more readable, in today's English, while leaving it absolutely "literal", as it was originally translated.

Perhaps someone might ask, "Why? Why are you doing this?"

My answer is simple: What was the Apostles' Bible like? What would it look like?

Wouldn't you want a copy of the Apostles' Bible, if you could get one? The Septuagint eliminates all possible controversy that exists today over the New Testament, and the manuscripts that were used to translate it, because the Lord Himself, as well as the apostolic writers, quoted from it, thus authenticating it.

The Apostles' Bible is an absolute must for any serious Bible student, as well as for anybody who desires to see the types of manuscripts that were around, and quoted from, in Jesus' day. You'll be amazed at the different readings in here.

Paul W. Esposito

Stauros Ministries

The Apostles' Bible

THE BOOK OF GENESIS

The History of Creation

[1] In the beginning God made the heaven and the earth.

[2] But the earth was unsightly and unfurnished, and darkness was over the deep, and the Spirit of God moved over the water.

[3] And God said, "Let there be light"; and there was light.

[4] And God saw the light that it was good, and God divided the light from the darkness.

[5] And God called the light Day, and the darkness He called Night, and there was evening and there was morning, the first day.

[6] And God said, "Let there be a firmament in the midst of the water, and let it be a division between water and water"; and it was so.

[7] And God made the firmament, and God divided between the water which was under the firmament and the water which was above the firmament.

[8] And God called the firmament Heaven, and God saw that it was good, and there was evening and there was morning, the second day.

[9] And God said, "Let the water which is under the heaven be gathered into one place, and let the dry land appear"; and it was so. And the water which was under the heaven was gathered into its places, and the dry land appeared.

[10] And God called the dry land Earth, and the gathering of the waters He called Seas; and God saw that it was good.

[11] And God said, "Let the earth bring forth the herb of grass-bearing seed according to its kind and according to its likeness, and the fruit tree bearing fruit whose seed is in it, according to its kind on the earth"; and it was so.

[12] And the earth brought forth the herb of grass-bearing seed according to its kind and according to its likeness, and the fruit tree bearing fruit whose seed is in it, according to its kind on the earth; and God saw that it was good.

[13] And there was evening and there was morning, the third day.

[14] And God said, "Let there be lights in the firmament of the heaven to give light upon the earth, to divide between day and night, and let them be for signs and for seasons and for days and for years.

[15] And let them be for light in the firmament of the heaven, so as to shine upon the earth"; and it was so.

[16] And God made two great lights, the greater light to rule the day, and the lesser light to rule the night; *He made* the stars also.

[17] And God set them in the firmament of the heaven, so as to shine upon the earth,

[18] and to rule over *the* day and *the* night, and to divide between the light and the darkness. And God saw that it was good.

[19] And there was evening and there was morning, the fourth day.

[20] And God said, "Let the waters bring forth reptiles having life, and winged creatures flying above the earth in the firmament of heaven"; and it was so.

[21] And God made great whales, and every living reptile, which the waters brought forth according to their kinds, and every creature that flies with wings according to its kind; and God saw that they were good.

[22] And God blessed them saying, "Increase and multiply, and fill the waters in the seas, and let the creatures that fly be multiplied on the earth."

[23] And there was evening and there was morning, the fifth day.

[24] And God said, "Let the earth bring forth the living creature according to its kind, cattle and reptiles and wild beasts of the earth according to their kind"; and it was so.

[25] And God made the wild beasts of the earth according to their kind, and cattle according to their kind, and all the reptiles of the earth according to their kind, and God saw that they were good.

[26] And God said, "Let Us make man according to Our image and likeness, and let them have dominion over the fish of the sea, and over the birds of the sky, and over the cattle and all the earth, and over all the reptiles that move upon the earth."

[27] And God made man, according to the image of God He made him, male and female He made them.

[28] And God blessed them, saying, "Increase and multiply, and fill the earth and subdue it, and have dominion over the fish of the seas, and the birds of the sky, and all the cattle and all the earth, and all the reptiles that move on the earth."

[29] And God said, "Behold, I have given to you every plant-yielding seed which is upon all the earth, and every tree with seed in its fruit; to you it shall be for food.

[30] And to all the wild beasts of the earth, and to all the birds of the sky, and to every reptile that creeps on the earth, which has in itself the breath of life, even every green plant for food"; and it was so.

[31] And God saw everything that He had made, and behold, they were very good. And there was evening and there was morning, the sixth day.

GENESIS CHAPTER 2

[1] Thus the heavens and the earth were finished, and the whole host of them.

[2] And God finished on the sixth day His works which He made, and He ceased on the seventh day from all His works which He made.

[3] And God blessed the seventh day and sanctified it, because in it He ceased from all His works which God began to do.

Another Account of Creation

[4] This is the book of the generations of heaven and earth, when they were made, in the day in which the Lord God made the heaven and the earth,

[5] and every herb of the field before it was on the earth, and all the grass of the field before it sprang up, for God had not sent rain upon the earth, and there was no man to cultivate it.

[6] But there rose up a fountain out of the earth, and it watered the whole face of the earth.

[7] And God formed the man of the dust of the earth, and breathed into his nostrils the breath of life, and man became a living soul.

[8] And God planted a garden eastward in Eden, and He placed the man there whom He had formed.

[9] And God caused to spring up also out of the earth every tree beautiful to the eye and good for food, and the tree of life in the midst of the garden, and the tree of the knowledge of good and evil.

[10] And a river proceeded out of Eden to water the garden, and it divided itself there into four heads.

[11] The name of the one *is* Pishon, this is that which encircles the whole land of Havilah, where there is gold.

[12] And the gold of that land is good, there also is carbuncle and emerald.

[13] And the name of the second river is Gihon, this is that which encircles the whole land of Ethiopia.

[14] And the third river is Tigris, this is that which flows forth over against the Assyrians. And the fourth river is Euphrates.

[15] And the Lord God took the man whom He had formed, and placed him in the garden of Eden, to cultivate and keep it.

[16] And the Lord God commanded Adam, saying, "Of every tree which is in the garden you may freely eat,

[17] but of the tree of the knowledge of good and evil—of it you shall not eat, for in the day that you eat of it, you shall surely die."

[18] And the Lord God said, "*It is* not good that the man should be alone, let Us make for him a helper suitable to him."

[19] And God formed yet farther out of the earth all the wild beasts of the field, and all the birds of the sky, and He brought them to Adam, to see what he would call them, and whatever Adam called any living creature, that was its name.

[20] And Adam gave names to all the cattle and to all the birds of the sky, and to all the wild beasts of the field, but for Adam there was not found a helper comparable to himself.

[21] And God brought a trance upon Adam, and he slept, and He took one of his ribs, and closed up the flesh in its place.

[22] And God formed the rib which he took from Adam into a woman, and brought her to Adam.

[23] And Adam said, "This now is bone of my bones, and flesh of my flesh; she shall be called [1]Woman, because she was taken out of Man."

[24] Therefore shall a man leave his father and his mother and shall cleave to his wife, and the two shall become one flesh.

[25] And the two were naked, both Adam and his wife, and were not ashamed.

GENESIS CHAPTER 3

The Temptation and Fall of Man

[1] Now the serpent was the most crafty of all the brutes on the earth, which the Lord God had made. And the serpent said to the woman, "Has God truly said, 'Eat not of every tree of the garden'?"

[2] And the woman said to the serpent, "We may eat of the fruit of the trees of the garden,

[3] but of the fruit of the tree which is in the midst of the garden, God said, 'You shall not eat of it, neither shall you touch it, lest you die.' "

[4] And the serpent said to the woman, "You shall not surely die!

[5] For God knew that in whatever day you should eat of it, your eyes would be opened, and you would be as gods, knowing good and evil."

[6] And the woman saw that the tree was good for food, and that it was pleasant to the eyes to look upon and beautiful to contemplate, and having taken of its fruit she ate, and she gave to her husband also with her, and they ate.

[7] And the eyes of both of them were opened, and they perceived that they were naked, and they sewed fig leaves together, and made themselves coverings to go around them.

[8] And they heard the voice of the Lord God walking in the garden in the cool of the day; and both Adam and his wife hid themselves from the face of the Lord God in the midst of the trees of the garden.

[9] And the Lord God called Adam and said to him, "Adam, where are you?"

[10] And he said to Him, "I heard Your voice as You walked in the garden, and I feared because I was naked and I hid myself."

[11] And God said to him, "Who told you that you were naked, unless you have eaten of the tree of which I commanded you not to eat?"

[12] And Adam said, "The woman whom You gave to be with me—she gave me of the tree, and I ate."

[13] And the Lord God said to the woman, "Why have you done this?" And the woman said, "The serpent deceived me, and I ate."

[14] And the Lord God said to the serpent, "Because you have done this, you are cursed above all cattle and all the brutes

---

[1] Or wife.

of the earth; on your breast and belly you shall go, and you shall eat dust all the days of your life.

¹⁵ And I will put enmity between you and the woman and between your seed and her Seed, He shall bruise your head, and you shall bruise His heel."

¹⁶ And to the woman He said, "I will greatly multiply your pains and your groanings; in pain you shall bring forth children, and your submission shall be to your husband, and he shall rule over you."

¹⁷ And to Adam He said, "Because you have listened to the voice of your wife, and eaten of the tree of which I commanded you not to eat of it—of that you have eaten, cursed is the ground in your labors, in pain shall you eat of it all the days of your life.

¹⁸ Thorns and thistles shall it bring forth to you, and you shall eat the herb of the field.

¹⁹ In the sweat of your face shall you eat your bread until you return to the ground out of which you were taken, for dust you are, and to dust you shall return."

²⁰ And Adam called the name of his wife Eve, because she was the mother of all living.

²¹ And the Lord God made garments of skin for Adam and his wife, and clothed them.

²² And God said, "Behold, Adam has become like one of Us, knowing good and evil; and now, lest at any time he stretch forth his hand, and take of the tree of life and eat, and so he shall live forever"—

²³ so the Lord God sent him forth out of the garden of Eden, to cultivate the ground out of which he was taken.

²⁴ And He cast out Adam and caused him to dwell outside of the garden of Eden, and stationed the cherubim and the fiery sword that turns about to keep the way of the tree of life.

GENESIS CHAPTER 4

Cain Murders Abel

¹ Now Adam Abel knew Eve his wife, and she conceived and brought forth Cain and said, "I have gained a man through God."

² And she again bore his brother Abel. And Abel was a keeper of sheep, but Cain was a tiller of the ground.

³ And it was so after some time that Cain brought a sacrifice to the Lord of the fruits of the earth.

⁴ And Abel also brought of the firstborn of his sheep and of his fatlings. And God looked upon Abel and his gifts,

⁵ but Cain and his sacrifices He regarded not, and Cain was exceedingly sorrowful and his countenance fell.

⁶ And the Lord God said to Cain, "Why are you downcast, and why has your countenance fallen?

⁷ Have you not sinned if you have brought it rightly, but not rightly divided it? Be still, to you shall be his submission, and you shall rule over him."

⁸ And Cain said to Abel his brother, "Let us go out into the plain." And it came to pass, that when they were in the plain, Cain rose up against Abel his brother, and killed him.

⁹ And the Lord God said to Cain, "Where is Abel your brother?" And he said, "I do not know—am I my brother's keeper?"

¹⁰ And the Lord said, "What have you done? The voice of your brother's blood cries *out* to Me from the ground.

¹¹ And now you *are* cursed from the earth which has opened her mouth to receive your brother's blood from your hand.

¹² When you till the earth, then it shall not continue to give its strength to you: you shall be groaning and trembling on the earth."

¹³ And Cain said to the Lord God, "My crime is too great for me to be forgiven.

¹⁴ If You cast me out this day from the face of the earth, and I shall be hidden from Your presence, and I shall be groaning and trembling upon the earth, then it will be that anyone that finds me shall kill me."

¹⁵ And the Lord God said to him, "Not so; anyone that slays Cain shall suffer a seven-fold vengeance." And the Lord God set a mark upon Cain, so that no one that found him would kill him.

The Beginnings of Civilization

¹⁶ So Cain went forth from the presence of God, and dwelt in the land of Nod over against Eden.

¹⁷ And Cain knew his wife, and having conceived she bore Enoch; and he built a city; and he named the city after the name of his son, Enoch.

¹⁸ And to Enoch was born Irad; and Irad fathered Mehujael; and Mehujael fathered Methushael; and Methushael fathered Lamech.

¹⁹ And Lamech took to himself two wives; the name of the one was Adah, and the name of the second *was* Zillah.

²⁰ And Adah bore Jabal; he was the father of those that dwell in tents, feeding cattle.

²¹ And the name of his brother was Jubal; it was he who invented the psaltery and harp.

²² And Zillah also bore Tubal-Cain; he was a smith, a manufacturer both of brass and iron; and the sister of Tubal-Cain was Naamah.

²³ And Lamech said to his wives, Adah and Zillah, "Hear my voice, you wives of Lamech, consider my words, because I have slain a man to my sorrow and a youth to my grief.

²⁴ Because vengeance has been exacted seven times on Cain's behalf, on Lamech's *it shall be* seventy times seven."

²⁵ And Adam knew Eve his wife, and she conceived and bore a son, and called his name Seth, saying, "For God has raised up to me another offspring in place of Abel, whom Cain killed."

²⁶ And Seth had a son, and he called his name Enosh; he hoped to call on the name of the Lord God.

GENESIS CHAPTER 5

Adam's Descendants to Noah and His Sons

[1] This is the genealogy of men in the day in which God made Adam; in the image of God He made him:

[2] male and female He made them, and blessed them; and He called his name Adam, in the day in which He made them.

[3] And Adam lived two hundred and thirty years, and fathered *a son* in his *own* likeness, and after his own image, and he called his name Seth.

[4] And the days of Adam, which he lived after he fathered Seth, were seven hundred years; and he had sons and daughters.

[5] Thus all the days that Adam lived were nine hundred and thirty years, and he died.

[6] Now Seth lived two hundred and five years, and fathered Enosh. [7] And Seth lived seven hundred and seven years after he had Enosh, and he fathered *other* sons and daughters.

[8] And all the days of Seth were nine hundred and twelve years, and he died.

[9] And Enosh lived one hundred and ninety years, and fathered Cainan.

[10] And Enosh lived seven hundred and fifteen years after he had Cainan, and he fathered *other* sons and daughters.

[11] And all the days of Enosh were nine hundred and five years, and he died.

[12] And Cainan lived one hundred and seventy years, and he fathered Mahalalel.

[13] And Cainan lived seven hundred and forty years after he had Mahalalel, and he fathered *other* sons and daughters.

[14] And all the days of Cainan were nine hundred and ten years, and he died.

[15] And Mahalalel lived one hundred and sixty five years, and he fathered Jared.

[16] And Mahalalel lived seven hundred and thirty years after his begetting *of* Jared, and he fathered *other* sons and daughters.

[17] And all the days of Mahalalel were eight hundred and ninety-five years, and he died.

[18] And Jared lived one hundred and sixty-two years, and fathered Enoch:

[19] and Jared lived eight hundred years after he had Enoch, and he fathered *other* sons and daughters.

[20] And all the days of Jared were nine hundred and sixty-two years, and he died.

[21] And Enoch lived one hundred and sixty-five years, and fathered Methuselah.

[22] And Enoch was well-pleasing to God. After he had Methuselah, *He walked with God* two hundred years, and he fathered *other* sons and daughters.

[23] And all the days of Enoch were three hundred and sixty-five years.

[24] And Enoch was well-pleasing to God, and was not found, for God translated him.

[25] And Methuselah lived one hundred and sixty-seven years, and fathered Lamech.

[26] And Methuselah lived eight hundred and two years after he had Lamech, and fathered *other* sons and daughters.

[27] And all the days of Methuselah, which he lived, were nine hundred and sixty-nine years, and he died.

[28] And Lamech lived one hundred and eighty-eight years, and fathered a son.

[29] And he called his name Noah, saying, "This one will cause us to cease from our works, and from the toils of our hands, and from the earth, which the Lord God has cursed."

[30] And Lamech lived five hundred and sixty-five years after he had Noah, and fathered *other* sons and daughters.

[31] And all the days of Lamech were seven hundred and fifty-three years, and he died.

[32] And Noah was five hundred years old, and he fathered three sons: Shem, Ham, and Japheth.

GENESIS CHAPTER 6

The Wickedness and Judgment of Man

[1] And it came to pass when men began to be numerous upon the earth, and daughters were born to them,

[2] that the sons of God, having seen the daughters of men, that they were beautiful, took to themselves wives of all whom they chose.

[3] And the Lord God said, "My Spirit shall by no means remain with these men forever, for they are flesh, but their days shall be one hundred and twenty years."

[4] Now the giants were upon the earth in those days; and after that when the sons of God came in to the daughters of men, they bore *children* to them, those were the giants of old, the men of renown.

[5] And the Lord God, having seen that the wicked actions of men were multiplied upon the earth, and that everyone in his heart was meditating on evil continually,

[6] that God took it to heart that He had made man upon the earth, and He pondered it deeply.

[7] And God said, "I will blot out man whom I have made from the face of the earth, even man and beast, and reptiles, along with the birds of the sky, for I am grieved that I have made them."

[8] But Noah found grace before the Lord God.

Noah Pleases God

[9] And these are the generations of Noah. Noah was a just man; being perfect in his generation; Noah was well pleasing to God.

[10] And Noah fathered three sons: Shem, Ham, and Japheth.

[11] But the earth was corrupt before God, and the earth was filled with unrighteousness.

[12] And the Lord God saw the earth, that it was corrupt; for all flesh had corrupted its way upon the earth.

The Preparation of the Ark

[13] And the Lord God said to Noah, "The end of all flesh has come before Me; for the earth has been filled with unrighteousness by them, and behold, I shall destroy them and the earth.

[14] Therefore make for yourself an ark of square timber; you shall make the ark in compartments, and you shall pitch it inside and out with pitch.

[15] And thus shall you make the ark: the length of the ark shall be three hundred cubits, its breadth fifty cubits, and its height thirty cubits.

[16] You shall narrow the ark as you make it, and in a cubit above you shall finish it, and the door of the ark you shall make on the side; with lower, second, and third stories you shall make it.

[17] And behold, I shall bring a flood of water upon the earth, to destroy all flesh in which is the breath of life under heaven, and whatsoever things are upon the earth shall die.

[18] And I will establish My covenant with you, and you shall enter into the ark, and your sons and your wife, and your sons' wives with you.

[19] And of all cattle and of all reptiles and of all wild beasts, even of all flesh, you shall bring by pairs into the ark, so that you may feed them with yourself: male and female they shall be.

[20] Of all winged birds after their kind, and of all cattle after their kind, and of all reptiles creeping upon the earth after their kind, pairs of all shall come in to you, male and female, to be fed with you.

[21] And you shall take to yourself of all kinds of food which you eat, and you shall gather them to yourself, and it shall be for you and them to eat."

[22] And Noah did everything that the Lord God commanded him.

GENESIS CHAPTER 7

The Great Flood

[1] And the Lord God said to Noah, "Enter into the ark, you and all your family, for I have seen *that* you *are* righteous before Me in this generation.

[2] You shall take with you seven each of every clean animal, male and female, and of the unclean animals *take* two each, male and female.

[3] And also seven each of *the* clean birds of the sky, male and female, and also pairs of all unclean birds, male and female, to maintain seed on all the earth.

[4] For after seven more days I shall bring rain upon the earth *for* forty days and forty nights, and I shall blot out every offspring which I have made from the face of all the earth."

[5] And Noah *did* all things, whatever the Lord God commanded him.

[6] And Noah was six hundred years old when the flood of water came upon the earth.

[7] And then Noah, his sons, his wife, and his sons' wives, went into the ark, because of the water of the flood.

[8] And of the clean birds and the unclean birds, and of the clean cattle and the unclean cattle, and of all the things that creep upon the earth,

[9] by pairs they went in to Noah into the ark, male and female, as God had commanded Noah.

[10] And it came to pass after seven days that the floodwaters came upon the earth.

[11] In the six hundredth year of the life of Noah, in the second month, on the twenty-seventh day of the month, on this day all the fountains of the abyss were broken up, and the flood gates of heaven were opened.

[12] And the rain *fell* upon the earth *for* forty days and forty nights.

[13] On that very day Noah, his sons Shem, Ham, Japheth, and Noah's wife, and the three wives of his sons, entered into the ark.

[14] And all the wild beasts after their kind, and all the cattle after their kind, and all the reptiles after their kind, and every flying bird after its kind,

[15] went in to Noah into the ark, by pairs, *both* male and female of all flesh in which is the breath of life.

[16] And those that entered went in male and female of all flesh, as God commanded Noah, and the Lord God shut the door behind him.

[17] And the flood was upon the earth forty days and forty nights, and the water increased greatly and raised up the ark, and it was lifted up high from off of the earth.

[18] And the water prevailed and abounded exceedingly upon the earth, and the ark floated upon the water.

[19] And the water prevailed exceedingly upon the earth, and covered all the high mountains which were under heaven.

[20] Fifteen cubits upwards was the water raised, and it covered all the high mountains.

[21] And all flesh that moved upon the earth died; of the birds and cattle, and of the wild beasts, and every reptile moving upon the earth, and every man.

[22] And all things which have the breath of life, and whatever was on the dry land, died.

[23] And *God* blotted out every living thing which was upon the face of the earth, both man and beast, and reptiles, and birds of the sky, and they were blotted out from the earth, and Noah was left alone, and those that were with him in the ark.

[24] And the water was raised over the earth one hundred and fifty days.

GENESIS CHAPTER 8

The Flood Subsides

[1] And God remembered Noah, and all the wild beasts, and all the cattle, and all the birds, and all the reptiles that creep, as many as were with him in the ark, and God brought a wind upon the earth, and the water subsided.

² And the fountains of the deep were closed up, and the flood gates of heaven, and the rain from heaven was withheld.

³ And the water subsided, and went off the earth, and after one hundred and fifty days the water was diminished, and the ark rested in the seventh month, on the twenty-seventh day of the month, on the mountains of Ararat.

⁴ And the water continued to decrease until the tenth month.

⁵ And in the tenth month, on the first day of the month, the heads of the mountains were visible.

⁶ And it came to pass after forty days, that Noah opened the window of the ark which he had made.

⁷ And he sent forth a raven; and it went out, and did not return until the water was dried from off of the earth.

⁸ And he sent a dove after it, to see if the water had ceased from off of the earth.

⁹ And the dove, not having found rest for her feet, returned to him into the ark, because the water was upon all the face of the earth, and he stretched out his hand and took her *in*, and brought her to himself into the ark.

¹⁰ And waiting yet another seven days, he again sent forth the dove from the ark.

¹¹ And the dove returned to him in the evening, and had an olive leaf in her mouth; and Noah knew that the water had ceased from off the earth.

¹² And waiting yet another seven days, he again sent forth the dove, and she did not return to him again anymore.

¹³ And it came to pass in the six hundred and first year of the life of Noah, in the first month, on the first day of the month, that the water subsided from off of the earth, and Noah opened the covering of the ark which he had made, and he saw that the water had subsided from the face of the earth.

¹⁴ And in the second month the earth had dried, on the twenty-seventh day of the month.

¹⁵ And the Lord God spoke to Noah, saying,

¹⁶ "Come out from the ark, you and your wife and your sons, and your sons' wives with you.

¹⁷ And all the wild beasts, as many as are with you, and all flesh, both of birds and beasts, and every reptile moving upon the earth, bring forth with you: be fruitful, and multiply upon the earth."

¹⁸ And Noah came forth, and his wife and his sons, and his sons' wives with him.

¹⁹ And all the wild beasts and all the cattle and every bird, and every reptile creeping upon the earth after their kind, came forth out of the ark.

God's Covenant with Man

²⁰ And Noah built an altar to the Lord, and took of all clean beasts, and of all clean birds, and offered a burnt offering upon the altar.

²¹ And the Lord God smelled a sweet aroma. And the Lord God, having considered *all things*, said, "I will never again curse the earth, due to the works of men, because the imagination of man is intently bent upon evil things from his youth, I will never again destroy all living flesh as I have done.

²² "All the days of the earth, seed and harvest, cold and heat, summer and spring, shall not cease by day or night."

GENESIS CHAPTER 9

God's Covenant with Noah

¹ And God blessed Noah and his sons, and said to them, "Be fruitful and multiply, and fill the earth and have dominion over it.

² And the dread and the fear of you shall be upon all the wild beasts of the earth, on all the birds of the sky, and on all things moving upon the earth, and upon all the fish of the sea, I have placed them under your power.

³ And every living reptile shall be to you for food, I have given all things to you as the green herbs.

⁴ But flesh with its lifeblood you shall not eat.

⁵ For your lifeblood shall I require at the hand of all wild beasts, and I shall require a man's life at the hand of his fellow man.

⁶ He that sheds man's blood, instead of that blood shall his own be shed, for in the image of God I made man.

⁷ But as for you, be fruitful and multiply, and fill the earth, and have dominion over it."

⁸ And God spoke to Noah, and to his sons with him, saying,

⁹ "Behold, I establish My covenant with you, and with your seed after you,

¹⁰ and with every living creature with you, of birds and of beasts, and with all the wild beasts of the earth, as many as are with you, of all that came out of the ark.

¹¹ And I will establish My covenant with you: never again shall all flesh die by the water of the flood, and never again shall there be a flood of water to destroy all the earth."

¹² And the Lord God said to Noah, "This is the sign of the covenant which I set between Me and you, and between every living creature which is with you for all generations:

¹³ I set My rainbow in the cloud, and it shall be a sign of the covenant between Me and the earth.

¹⁴ And it shall be when I gather clouds upon the earth, that My rainbow shall be seen in the cloud.

¹⁵ And I shall remember My covenant, which is between Me and you, and between every living soul in all flesh, and there shall no longer be water for a deluge, so as to blot out all flesh.

¹⁶ And My rainbow shall be in the cloud, and I will look at it and remember the everlasting covenant between Me and the earth, and between every living soul in all flesh, which is upon the earth."

¹⁷ And God said to Noah, "This is the sign of the covenant, which I have made between Me and all flesh, which is upon the earth."

Noah and His Sons

¹⁸ Now the sons of Noah which came out of the ark were Shem, Ham, and Japheth. And Ham was the father of Canaan.

¹⁹ These three are the sons of Noah, of these were men scattered over all the earth.

²⁰ And Noah began to be a farmer, and he planted a vineyard.

²¹ And he drank of the wine, and was drunk, and was naked in his house.

²² And Ham the father of Canaan saw the nakedness of his father, and he went out and told his two brothers outside.

²³ And Shem and Japheth, having taken a garment, put it on both their backs and went backwards, and covered the nakedness of their father; and their face *was* backward, and they did not see the nakedness of their father.

²⁴ And Noah recovered from the wine, and knew all that his younger son had done to him.

²⁵ And he said, "Cursed be the servant Canaan, a slave shall he be to his brothers."

²⁶ And he said, "Blessed be the Lord God of Shem, and Canaan shall be his servant.

²⁷ "May God make room for Japheth, and let him dwell in the habitations of Shem, and let Canaan be his servant."

²⁸ And Noah lived after the flood three hundred and fifty years.

²⁹ And all the days of Noah were nine hundred and fifty years, and he died.

GENESIS CHAPTER 10

Nations Descended from Noah

¹ Now these *are* the generations of the sons of Noah: Shem, Ham, and Japheth; and sons were born to them after the flood.

² The sons of Japheth *were* Gomer, Magog, Madai, Javan, Elisa, Tubal, Meshech, and Tiras.

³ And the sons of Gomer *were* Ashkenaz, Riphath, and Togarmah.

⁴ And the sons of Jovan *were* Elishah, Tarshish, Kittim, and Dodanim.

⁵ From these were the islands of the Gentiles divided in their land, each according to his tongue, in their tribes and in their nations.

⁶ And the sons of Ham *were* Cush, Mizraim, Put, and Canaan.

⁷ And the sons of Cush *were* Seba, Havilah, Sabtah, Raamah, and Sabtechah. And the sons of Raamah *were* Sheba and Dedan.

⁸ And Cush fathered Nimrod: he began to be a giant upon the earth.

⁹ He was a mighty hunter before the Lord God; therefore they said, "Like Nimrod the mighty hunter before the Lord."

¹⁰ And the beginning of his kingdom was Babylon, Erech, Accad, and Calneh, in the land of Shinar.

¹¹ Out of that land he came to Assyria, and built Nineveh, and the city Rehoboth Ir, and Calah,

¹² and Resen between Nineveh and Calah: this is the great city.

¹³ And Mizraim fathered the Ludim, and the Naphtuhim, and the Enemetim, and the Lehabim,

¹⁴ and the Pathrusim, and the Casluhim (from whom came forth the Philistine) and the Caphtorim.

¹⁵ And Canaan fathered Sidon his firstborn, and the Hittite,

¹⁶ and the Jebusite, and the Amorite, and the Girgashite,

¹⁷ and the Hivite, and the Arkite, and the Senite,

¹⁸ and the Aradian, and the Samarean, and the Amathite; and after this the tribes of the Canaanites were dispersed.

¹⁹ And the boundaries of the Canaanites were from Sidon till one comes to Gerar and Gaza, till one comes to Sodom and Gomorrah, Admah and Zeboiim, as far as Lasha.

²⁰ These *were* the sons of Ham in their tribes according to their tongues, in their countries, and in their nations.

²¹ And to Shem himself also were children born, the father of all the sons of Eber, the brother of Japheth the elder.

²² The sons of Shem *were* Elam, Asshur, Arphaxad, Lud, Aram, and Cainan.

²³ The sons of Aram *were* Uz, Hul, Gether, and Mesech.

²⁴ And Arphaxad fathered Cainan, and Cainan fathered Salah, and Salah fathered Eber.

²⁵ And to Eber were born two sons, the name of the one *was* Peleg, because in his days the earth was divided, and the name of his brother *was* Joktan.

²⁶ And Joktan fathered Almodad, Sheleph, Sarmoth, Jerah,

²⁷ Hadoram, Uzal, Diklah,

²⁸ Ebal, Abimael, Sheba,

²⁹ Ophir, Havila, and Jobab. All these were the sons of Joktan.

³⁰ And their dwelling was from Mesha, till one comes to Sephar, a mountain of the east.

³¹ These were the sons of Shem in their tribes, according to their tongues, in their countries, and in their nations.

³² These are the tribes of the sons of Noah, according to their generations, according to their nations: of them were the islands of the Gentiles scattered over the earth after the flood.

GENESIS CHAPTER 11

The Tower of Babel

¹ And all the earth had one language, and one speech.

² And it came to pass as they moved from the east, that they found a plain in the land of Shinar, and they dwelt there.

³ And a man said to his neighbor, "Come, let us make bricks and bake them with fire." And the brick was to them for stone, and their mortar was asphalt.

⁴ And they said, "Come, let us build for ourselves a city and tower, whose top shall be to heaven, and let us make for

ourselves a name, before we are scattered abroad upon the face of the whole earth."

⁵ And the Lord came down to see the city and the tower, which the sons of men had built.

⁶ And the Lord said, "Behold, they are one people, and they have one language between them, and they have begun to do this, and now nothing shall fail from them of all that they have purposed to do.

⁷ Come, let Us go down and confound their language, that they may not understand each the voice of his neighbor."

⁸ And the Lord scattered them from there over the face of all the earth, and they left off building the city and the tower.

⁹ On this account its name was called Babel, because there the Lord confounded the languages of all the earth, and then the Lord scattered them upon the face of all the earth.

The Descendants of Shem

¹⁰ And these are the generations of Shem: and Shem was one hundred years old when he fathered Arphaxad, the second year after the flood.

¹¹ And Shem lived five hundred years after he had fathered Arphaxad, and fathered *other* sons and daughters, and died.

¹² And Arphaxad lived one hundred and thirty-five years, and fathered Cainan.

¹³ And Arphaxad lived four hundred years after he had fathered Cainan, and fathered *other* sons and daughters, and died. And Cainan lived one hundred and thirty years and fathered Salah; and Canaan lived three hundred and thirty years after he had fathered Salah, and fathered *other* sons and daughters, and died.

¹⁴ And Salah lived one hundred and thirty years, and fathered Heber.

¹⁵ And Salah lived three hundred and thirty years after he had fathered Eber, and fathered *other* sons and daughters, and died.

¹⁶ And Eber lived one hundred and thirty-four years, and fathered Peleg.

¹⁷ And Eber lived two hundred and seventy years after he had fathered Peleg, and fathered *other* sons and daughters, and died.

¹⁸ And Peleg lived one hundred and thirty years, and fathered Reu.

¹⁹ And Peleg lived two hundred and nine years after he had fathered Reu, and fathered *other* sons and daughters, and died.

²⁰ And Reu lived one hundred and thirty-two years, and fathered Serug.

²¹ And Reu lived two hundred and seven years after he had fathered Serug, and fathered *other* sons and daughters, and died.

²² And Serug lived one hundred and thirty years, and fathered Nahor.

²³ And Serug lived two hundred years after he had fathered Nahor, and fathered *other* sons and daughters, and died.

²⁴ And Nahor lived one hundred and seventy-nine years, and fathered Terah.

²⁵ And Nahor lived one hundred and twenty-five years after he had fathered Terah, and fathered *other* sons and daughters, and he died.

²⁶ And Terah lived seventy years and fathered Abram, Nahor, and Haran.

The Descendants of Terah

²⁷ And these are the generations of Terah: Terah fathered Abram, Nahor, and Haran; and Haran fathered Lot.

²⁸ And Haran died in the presence of Terah his father, in the land in which he was born, in the country of the Chaldees.

²⁹ And Abram and Nahor took to themselves wives; the name of Abram's wife was Sarai, and the name of Nachor's wife *was* Milcah, daughter of Haran, and he was the father of Milcah, *and* the father of Iscah.

³⁰ And Sarai was barren, and had no children.

³¹ And Terah took Abram his son, and Lot his grandson, the son of Haran, and Sarai his daughter-in-law, the wife of Abram his son, and led them forth out of the land of the Chaldees, to go into the land of Canaan, and they came as far as Haran, and dwelt there.

³² And all the days of Terah in the land of Haran were two hundred and five years, and Terah died in Haran.

GENESIS CHAPTER 12

The Call of Abram

¹ And the Lord said to Abram, "Go forth out of your land, and out from your family, and out of the house of your father, into the land which I will show you.

² "And I will make you a great nation, and I will bless you and magnify your name, and you shall be blessed.

³ "And I will bless those that bless you, and curse those that curse you, and in you all the tribes of the earth shall be blessed."

⁴ So Abram went, as the Lord had told him, and Lot went with him. And Abram was seventy-five years old when he departed from Haran.

⁵ And Abram took Sarai his wife, and Lot the son of his brother, and all their possessions that they had gathered, and every soul which they had acquired in Haran, and they departed to go into the land of Canaan.

⁶ And Abram traveled the land lengthwise as far as Shechem, to the terebinth tree of Moreh. And the Canaanites then inhabited the land.

⁷ Then the Lord appeared to Abram, and said to him, "I will give this land to your descendants." And Abram built an altar there to the Lord who appeared to him.

⁸ And he departed from there to the mountain east of Bethel, and there he pitched his tent in Bethel near the sea, and Ai toward the east, and there he built an altar to the Lord, and called on the name of the Lord.

⁹ And Abram departed and went and encamped in the wilderness.

Abram and Sarai in Egypt

¹⁰ Now there was a famine in the land, and Abram went down to Egypt to sojourn there, because the famine prevailed in the land.

¹¹ And it came to pass when Abram approached Egypt, that he said to Sarai his wife, "I know that you are a beautiful woman.

¹² It shall come to pass then, that when the Egyptians shall see you, that they shall say, 'This is his wife,' and they shall kill me, but they shall keep you alive.

¹³ Therefore say to them, 'I am his sister,' that it may be well with me on account of you, and my soul shall live because of you."

¹⁴ And it came to pass when Abram entered into Egypt—the Egyptians having seen his wife that she was very beautiful—

¹⁵ that the princes of Pharaoh saw her, and praised her to Pharaoh, and brought her into Pharaoh's house.

¹⁶ And they treated Abram well on her account, and he had sheep, calves, donkeys, male and female servants, mules, and camels.

¹⁷ And God afflicted Pharaoh and his house with great and severe afflictions, because of Sarai, Abram's wife.

¹⁸ And Pharaoh, having called Abram, said, "What is this you have done to me, that you did not tell me that she was your wife?

¹⁹ Why then did you say, 'She is my sister?' And I took her for a wife to myself; and now, behold, your wife is before you, take her and go away immediately."

²⁰ And Pharaoh commanded *his* men concerning Abram, to join in sending him forward, and his wife, and all that he had.

GENESIS CHAPTER 13

Abram and Lot Separate

¹ And Abram went up out of Egypt, he and his wife, and all that he had, and Lot with him, into the wilderness.

² And Abram was very rich in cattle, and silver, and gold.

³ And he went *to the place* where he came, into the wilderness as far as Bethel, as far as the place where his tent was before, between Bethel and Ai,

⁴ to the place of the altar, which he built there at first, and Abram there called on the name of the Lord.

⁵ And Lot, who went out with Abram, had sheep, oxen, and tents.

⁶ And the land was not large enough for them to live together, because their possessions were great; and the land was not large enough for them to live together.

⁷ And there was strife between the herdsmen of Abram's cattle, and the herdsmen of Lot's cattle, and the Canaanites and the Perizzites then inhabited the land.

⁸ And Abram said to Lot, "Let there not be strife between me and you, and between my herdsmen and your herdsmen, for we are brothers.

⁹ Behold, is not the whole land before you? Separate yourself from me; if you *go* to the left, I will go to the right, and if you go to the right, I will go to the left."

¹⁰ And Lot, having lifted up his eyes, observed all the country round about the Jordan, that it was all watered, before God overthrew Sodom and Gomorrah, as the garden of the Lord, and as the land of Egypt, until you come to Zoar.

¹¹ And Lot chose for himself all the country surrounding the Jordan, and Lot went from the east, and they were separated each from his brother. And Abram dwelt in the land of Canaan.

¹² And Lot dwelt in a city of the neighboring people, and pitched his tent in Sodom.

¹³ But the men of Sodom were evil, and exceedingly sinful before God.

¹⁴ And God said to Abram after Lot was separated from him, "Look up with your eyes, and behold from the place where you now are northward and southward, and eastward and westward;

¹⁵ for all the land which you see, I will give to you and to your descendants forever.

¹⁶ And I will make your descendants like the dust of the earth; if anyone is able to number the dust of the earth, then shall your descendants be numbered.

¹⁷ Arise, walk in the land, both in its length and in its breadth; for to you will I give it, and to your descendants forever."

¹⁸ And Abram, having removed his tent, came and dwelt by the oak of Mamre, which was in Hebron, and there he built an altar to the Lord.

GENESIS CHAPTER 14

Lot's Captivity and Rescue

¹ And it came to pass in the reign of Amraphel king of Shinar, and Arioch king of Ellasar, that Chedorlaomer king of Elam, and Tidal king of nations,

² made war with Bera king of Sodom, and with Birsha king of Gomorrah, and with Shinab, king of Adamah, and with Shemeber king of Zeboiim and the king of Bela, (that is, Zoar).

³ All these met with one accord at the Salt Valley; this is now the Salt Sea.

⁴ Twelve years they served Chedorlaomer, and the thirteenth year they revolted.

⁵ And in the fourteenth year Chedorlaomer came, and the kings with him, and they cut to pieces the giants in Ashteroth, and Karnaim, and strong nations with them, and the Emim in the city of Shaveh Kiriathaim.

⁶ And the Horites in the mountains of Seir, to the terebinth tree of El Paran, which is in the desert.

⁷ And having turned back, they came to the Well of Judgment; this is Kadesh, and they cut to pieces all the princes of Amalek, and the Amorites dwelling in Hazezon Tamar.

⁸ And the king of Sodom, the king of Gomorrhah, the king of Admah, the king of Zeboiim, and the king of Bela, (that is, Zoar) went out, and they set themselves in battle array against them for war in the Salt Valley,

⁹ against Chedorlaomer king of Elam, Tidal king of nations, Amraphel king of Shinar, and Arioch king of Ellasar, the four kings against the five.

¹⁰ Now the Salt Valley consists of slime pits. And the king of Sodom fled and the king of Gomorrah, and they fell in there. And those that were left fled to the mountain country.

¹¹ And they took all the cavalry of Sodom and Gomorrah, and all their provisions, and departed.

¹² And they also took Lot, the son of Abram's brother, and his possessions, and departed, for he dwelt in Sodom.

¹³ And one of them that had been rescued came and told Abram the Hebrew; and he dwelt by the oak of Mamre the Amorite, the brother of Eschol, and the brother of Aner, who were confederates of Abram.

¹⁴ And Abram, having heard that Lot his nephew had been taken captive, numbered his own home-born servants, three hundred and eighteen, and pursued after them to Dan.

¹⁵ And he came upon them by night, he and his servants, and he struck them, and pursued them as far as Hobah, which is north of Damascus.

¹⁶ And he recovered all the cavalry of Sodom, and he recovered Lot his nephew, and all his possessions, and the women and the people.

¹⁷ And the king of Sodom went out to meet him, after he returned from the slaughter of Chedorlaomer, and the kings with him, to the valley of Shaveh; this was the plain of the kings.

Abram and Melchizedek

¹⁸ And Melchizedek king of Salem brought forth loaves and wine, and he was the priest of the Most High God.

¹⁹ And he blessed Abram, and said, "Blessed be Abram of the Most High God, who made heaven and earth,

²⁰ and blessed be the Most High God, who delivered your enemies into your power." And Abram gave him a tenth of everything.

²¹ And the king of Sodom said to Abram, "Give me the men, and take the horses to yourself."

²² And Abram said to the king of Sodom, "I will stretch out my hand to the Lord, the Most High God, who made the heaven and the earth,

²³ that I will not take from all your goods, from a string to a sandal strap, lest you should say, 'I have made Abram rich.'

²⁴ Except what things the young men have eaten, and the portion of the men that went with me, Eschol, Aner, Mamre, these shall take a portion."

GENESIS CHAPTER 15

God's Covenant with Abram

¹ And after these things the word of the Lord came to Abram in a vision, saying, "Do not fear, Abram, *for I am* your shield. Your reward shall be very great."

² And Abram said, "Master and Lord, what shall You give me? Seeing I am departing without a child, but the son of Masek my home-born female slave, this Eliezer of Damascus *is my heir*."

³ And Abram said, "*I am grieved* since You have given me no offspring, but my home-born servant shall succeed me."

⁴ And immediately the voice of the Lord came to him, saying, "This shall not be your heir; but he that shall come out of you shall be your heir."

⁵ And He brought him out and said to him, "Look up now to heaven, and count the stars, if you shall be able to number them fully." And He said, "So shall your descendants be."

⁶ And Abram believed God, and it was credited to him as righteousness.

⁷ And He said to him, "I am God that brought you out of the land of the Chaldeans, so as to give you this land to inherit."

⁸ And he said, "Master and Lord, how shall I know that I shall inherit it?"

⁹ And He said to him, "Take for Me a heifer in her third year, and a female goat in her third year, and a ram in his third year, and a dove and a pigeon."

¹⁰ So he took to Him all these things, and divided them in the midst, and set them opposite to each other, but the birds he did not divide.

¹¹ And birds came down upon the carcasses, upon the divided parts of them, and Abram sat down by them.

¹² And about sunset, a deep sleep came on Abram, and behold, fear and great darkness pressed upon him.

¹³ And *God* said to Abram, "You shall surely know that your descendants shall be sojourners in a land not their own, and they shall enslave them, and afflict them, and humble them four hundred years.

¹⁴ And the nation whom they shall serve I will judge; and after this, they shall come forth with much property.

¹⁵ But you shall depart to your fathers in peace, nourished in a good old age.

¹⁶ And in the fourth generation they shall return here, for the sins of the Amorites are not yet filled up, even until now."

¹⁷ And when the sun was about to set, there was a flame, and behold, a smoking furnace and lamps of fire, which passed between the divided pieces.

¹⁸ In that day the Lord made a covenant with Abram, saying, "To your descendants I will give this land, from the river of Egypt to the great river Euphrates.

¹⁹ The Kenites, the Kenezzites, the Kadmonites,

²⁰ the Hittites, the Perizzites, the Rephaim,

²¹ the Amorites, the Canaanites, the Hivites, the Girgashites, and the Jebusites."

GENESIS CHAPTER 16

Hagar and Ishmael

¹ Now Sarai, Abram's wife, bore him no children; and she had an Egyptian maid, whose name was Hagar.

² And Sarai said to Abram, "Behold, the Lord has prevented me from bearing children; go therefore in to my maid, that I may obtain children for myself through her." And Abram listened to the voice of Sarai.

³ So Sarai, Abram's wife, having taken Hagar the Egyptian her maid, after Abram had dwelt ten years in the land of Canaan, gave her to Abram her husband as a wife.

⁴ And he went in to Hagar, and she conceived. And when she saw that she was pregnant, her mistress was dishonored before her.

⁵ Then Sarai said to Abram, "You have hurt me! I gave my maid into your arms, and when I saw that she was pregnant, I was dishonored before her. The Lord judge between me and you!"

⁶ And Abram said to Sarai, "Behold your maid is in your hands, use her as it may seem good to you." And Sarai afflicted her, and she fled from before her.

⁷ And the Angel of the Lord found her by the fountain of water in the wilderness, by the fountain in the way to Shur.

⁸ And the Angel of the Lord said to her, "Hagar, Sarai's maid, from where do you come, and where are you going?" And she said, "I am fleeing from the face of my mistress Sarai."

⁹ And the Angel of the Lord said to her, "Return to your mistress, and submit yourself to her authority."

¹⁰ And the Angel of the Lord said to her, "I will surely multiply your descendants, so that they shall be too many to count."

¹¹ And the Angel of the Lord said to her, "Behold, you are pregnant, and shall bear a son, and you shall call his name Ishmael, for the Lord has *seen* your humiliation.

¹² He shall be a wild man, his hands shall be against all, and the hands of all shall be against him, and he shall dwell in the presence of all his brothers."

¹³ And she called the name of the Lord God who spoke to her, "You are the God who sees"; for she said, "For I have openly seen Him that appeared to me."

¹⁴ Therefore she called the well Beer Lahai Roi; behold it is between Kadesh and Bered.

¹⁵ And Hagar bore a son to Abram; and Abram called the name of his son which Hagar bore to him, Ishmael.

¹⁶ And Abram was eighty-six years old when Hagar bore Ishmael to Abram.

GENESIS CHAPTER 17

The Sign of the Covenant

¹ When Abram was ninety-nine years old, the Lord appeared to Abram and said to him, "I am your God, be well-pleasing before Me, and be blameless.

² And I will establish My covenant between Me and you, and I will multiply you exceedingly."

³ And Abram fell upon his face, and God spoke to him, saying,

⁴ "And I, behold! My covenant is with you, and you shall be a father of many nations.

⁵ And your name shall no longer be called Abram, but your name shall be Abraham, for I have made you a father of many nations.

⁶ And I will increase you very exceedingly, and I will make nations of you, and kings shall come out of you.

⁷ "And I will establish My covenant between you and your descendants after you, to their generations, for an everlasting covenant, to be your God, and the God of your descendants after you.

⁸ And I will give to you and to your descendants after you the land in which you sojourn, even all the land of Canaan for an everlasting possession, and I will be to them a God."

⁹ And God said to Abraham, "You also shall fully keep My covenant, you and your descendants after you for their generations.

¹⁰ And this is the covenant which you shall fully keep between Me and you, and between your descendants after you for their generations; every male of you shall be circumcised.

¹¹ And you shall be circumcised in the flesh of your foreskin, and it shall be for a sign of a covenant between Me and you.

¹² And he that is eight days old shall be circumcised by you, every male throughout your generations, and the servant born in the house and he that is bought with money, of every son of a stranger, who is not of your offspring.

¹³ He that is born in your house, and he that is bought with money shall surely be circumcised, and My covenant shall be in your flesh for an everlasting covenant.

¹⁴ And the uncircumcised male, who shall not be circumcised in the flesh of his foreskin on the eighth day, that soul shall be utterly destroyed from his family, for he has broken My covenant."

¹⁵ And God said to Abraham, "Sarai, your wife—her name shall not be called Sarai, *but* Sarah shall be her name.

¹⁶ And I will bless her, and give you a son by her, and I will bless him, and he shall become nations, and kings of nations shall *decend* from him."

¹⁷ And Abraham fell upon his face and laughed; and said in his heart, "Shall there be a child to one who is a hundred years old, and shall Sarah, who is ninety years old, bear *a child*?"

¹⁸ And Abraham said to God, "Let this Ismael live before You."

¹⁹ And God said to Abraham, "Behold, Sarah your wife shall bear you a son, and you shall call his name Isaac; and I will establish My covenant with him, for an everlasting covenant, to be a God to him and to his descendants after him.

²⁰ And concerning Ishmael, behold, I have heard you, and behold, I have blessed him, and will increase him and

multiply him exceedingly; twelve nations shall he father, and I will make him a great nation.

²¹ But I will establish My covenant with Isaac, whom Sarah shall bear to you at this time next year."

²² And He left off speaking with him, and God went up from Abraham.

²³ And Abraham took Ishmael his son, and all his home-born servants, and all those bought with money, and every male of the men in the house of Abraham, and he circumcised their foreskins in the time of that day, according as God spoke to him.

²⁴ And Abraham was ninety-nine years old, when he was circumcised in the flesh of his foreskin.

²⁵ And Ishmael his son was thirteen years old when he was circumcised in the flesh of his foreskin.

²⁶ And at the period of that day, Abraham was circumcised, and Ishmael his son,

²⁷ and all the men of his house, both those born in the house, and those bought with money among the foreign nations.

GENESIS CHAPTER 18

A Son Promised to Abraham and Sarah

¹ And God appeared to him by the oak of Mamre, as he sat by the door of his tent in the heat of the day.

² And he lifted up his eyes and looked, and behold, three men stood before him; and having seen them, he ran to meet them from the door of his tent, and bowed himself to the ground.

³ And he said, "Lord, if indeed I have found grace in Your sight, do not pass by Your servant.

⁴ Let water now be brought, and let them wash your feet, and refresh yourselves under the tree.

⁵ And I will bring bread, and you shall eat, and after this you shall depart on your journey, on account of which refreshment you have turned aside to your servant." And He said, "Do as you have said."

⁶ And Abraham hastened to the tent to Sarah, and said to her, "Quickly, knead three measures of fine flour, and make cakes."

⁷ And Abraham ran to the herd, and took a young calf, tender and good, and gave it to his servant, and he hastened to prepare it.

⁸ And he took butter and milk, and the calf which he had prepared; and he set them before them, and they ate, and he stood by them under the tree.

⁹ And He said to him, "Where is Sarah your wife?" And he answered and said, "There, in the tent."

¹⁰ And He said, "I will return and come to you at the appointed time, and Sarah your wife shall have a son." And Sarah was listening at the tent door, being behind him.

¹¹ And Abraham and Sarah were old, advanced in days, and the custom of women had ceased with Sarah.

¹² And Sarah laughed within herself, saying, "The thing has not as yet happened to me, even until now, and my lord is old."

¹³ And the Lord said to Abraham, "Why did Sarah laugh, saying, 'Shall I indeed bear *a child*? But I have grown old.'

¹⁴ Shall anything be impossible with the Lord? At the appointed time I shall return to you, and Sarah shall have a son."

¹⁵ But Sarah denied *it*, saying, "I did not laugh," for she was afraid. And He said to her, "No, but you did laugh!"

Judgment Pronounced on Sodom

¹⁶ And the men rose up from there, and looked towards Sodom and Gomorrah. And Abraham went with them, attending to them on their journey.

¹⁷ And the Lord said, "Shall I hide from Abraham My servant what I intend to do?

¹⁸ But Abraham shall become a great and populous nation, and in him shall all the nations of the earth be blessed.

¹⁹ For I know that he will order his sons, and his house after him, and they will keep the ways of the Lord, to do justice and judgment, that the Lord may bring upon Abraham all things whatsoever He has spoken to him."

²⁰ And the Lord said, "The cry of Sodom and Gomorrah has reached My *ears*, and their sins are very great.

²¹ I will therefore go down and see, if they completely correspond with the cry which comes to Me, and if not, I will know."

²² And the men, having departed from there, came to Sodom. And the Lord stood before Abraham.

²³ And Abraham drew near and said, "Would You destroy the righteous with the wicked, and shall the righteous be as the wicked?

²⁴ Should there be fifty righteous in the city, will You destroy them? Will You not spare the whole place for the sake of the fifty righteous, if they be in it?

²⁵ Far be it from You to do such at thing, so as to destroy the righteous with the wicked, so that the righteous shall be as the wicked: far be it from You! Shall not the Judge of all the earth do right?"

²⁶ And the Lord said, "If there should be in Sodom fifty righteous people, I will spare the whole city, and the whole place for their sakes."

²⁷ And Abraham answered and said, "Now I have begun to speak to my Lord, and I am *but* dust and ashes.

²⁸ But if the fifty righteous should be diminished to forty-five, will You destroy the whole city because of the five that are lacking?" And He said, "I will not destroy it, if I should find there forty-five."

²⁹ And he continued to speak to Him still, and said, "But if there should be found there forty?" And He said, "I will not destroy it for the forty's sake."

³⁰ And he said, "Will there be anything against me, Lord, if I shall speak? But if there be found there thirty?" And He said, "I will not destroy it for the thirty's sake."

³¹ And he said, "Since I am able to speak to the Lord, what if there should be found there twenty?" And He said, "I will not destroy it, if I should find there twenty."

³² And he said, "Will there be anything against me, Lord, if I speak yet once *more*? But if there should be found there ten?" And He said, "I will not destroy it for the sake of the ten."

³³ And the Lord departed, when He left off speaking to Abraham, and Abraham returned to his place.

GENESIS CHAPTER 19

The Depravity of Sodom

¹ And the two angels came to Sodom at evening. And Lot sat by the gate of Sodom. And Lot, having seen them, rose up to meet them, and he bowed down with his face to the ground, and said,

² "Wait, My lords, turn aside to the house of your servant, and rest from your journey, and wash your feet. Rise early in the morning to depart on your journey." And they said, "No, but we will lodge in the street."

³ And he constrained them, and they turned aside to him, and they entered into his house. And he made a feast for them, and baked unleavened cakes for them, and they ate.

⁴ But before they went to sleep, the men of the city, the Sodomites, surrounded the house, both young and old, all the people together.

⁵ And they called out Lot, and said to him, "Where are the men that came to you this night? Bring them out to us, that we may be with them."

⁶ And Lot went out to them to the porch, and he shut the door behind him,

⁷ and said to them, "By no means, brothers, do not act so wickedly.

⁸ But I have two daughters, who have not known a man. I will bring them out to you, and you may do with them as you wish, only do not harm these men, since this is the reason they have come under the shelter of my roof."

⁹ And they said to him, "Stand back! You came here to sojourn, was it also to judge? Now then we would harm you more than them!" And they pressed hard against the man Lot, and they drew near to break down the door.

¹⁰ And the men stretched forth their hands, and they pulled Lot inside the house, and shut the door.

¹¹ And they struck the men that were at the door of the house with blindness, both small and great, and they were wearied with seeking the door.

Sodom and Gomorrah Destroyed

¹² And the men said to Lot, "Have you anyone else here? Son-in-law, or sons or daughters, or if you have any other friend in the city, bring them out of this place.

¹³ For we are going to destroy this place; for their cry has risen up before the Lord, and the Lord has sent us to destroy it."

¹⁴ And Lot went out, and spoke to his sons-in-law who had married his daughters, and said, "Rise up, and depart out of this place, for the Lord is about to destroy the city"; but he seemed to be speaking foolishly before his sons-in-law.

¹⁵ But when it was morning, the angels urged Lot, saying, "Arise and take your wife, and your two daughters, and go forth; lest you also be destroyed with the iniquities of the city."

¹⁶ And they were troubled, and the angels laid hold on his hand, and the hand of his wife, and the hands of his two daughters, in that the Lord spared him.

¹⁷ And it came to pass when they brought them out, that they said, "By all means save your own life; do not look behind you, nor stay in this surrounding country, *but* escape to the mountains, lest perhaps you be overtaken together with them."

¹⁸ And Lot said to them, "I beseech you, my lords,

¹⁹ since your servant has found mercy before you, and you have magnified your righteousness, in that you have spared my life, but I shall not be able to escape to the mountains, lest perhaps the calamity overtake me and I die.

²⁰ Behold, this city is near for me to escape to, which is a small one, and there shall I be preserved, is it not little? And my soul shall live because of you."

²¹ And he said to him, "Behold, I have had respect to you also about this thing, that I should not overthrow the city of which you have spoken.

²² Hurry then to escape there, for I shall not be able to do anything until you arrive there." Therefore he called the name of that city, Zoar.

²³ *Now* the sun had risen upon the earth when Lot entered into Zoar.

²⁴ And the Lord rained on Sodom and Gomorrah brimstone and fire out of heaven.

²⁵ And He overthrew these cities, and all the surrounding countryside, and all the inhabitaints of the cities, and the plants which grew of the ground.

²⁶ And his wife looked back, and she became a pillar of salt.

²⁷ And Abraham rose up early to go to the place where he had stood before the Lord.

²⁸ And he looked towards Sodom and Gomorrah, and towards the neighboring countryside, and behold, he saw a flame going up from the earth, like the smoke from a furnace.

²⁹ And it came to pass, that when God had destroyed all the cities of the region round about, that God remembered Abraham, and sent Lot out of the midst of the overthrow, when the Lord overthrew those cities in which Lot dwelt.

The Shameful Origin of Moab and Ammon

³⁰ And Lot went up out of Zoar, and dwelt in the mountain, he and his two daughters with him, for he feared to dwell in Zoar; and he dwelt in a cave, he and his two daughters with him.

³¹ And the elder said to the younger, "Our father is old, and there is no one on the earth who shall come in to us, as it is fit in all the earth.

³² Come, let us make our father drink wine, and let us sleep with him, and let us raise up offspring from our father."

³³ So they made their father drink wine in that night, and the elder went in and lay with her father that night, and he knew not when he slept and when he rose up.

³⁴ And it came to pass on the next day, that the elder said to the younger, "Behold, I slept last night with our father, let us make him drink wine tonight as well, and you go in and sleep with him, and let us raise up offspring from our father."

³⁵ So they made their father drink wine in that night also, and the younger went in and slept with her father, and he knew not when he slept, nor when he arose.

³⁶ And the two daughters of Lot conceived by their father.

³⁷ And the elder bore a son and called his name Moab, saying, "*He is* of my father." This is the father of the Moabites to this day.

³⁸ And the younger also bore a son, and called his name Ammon, saying, "The son of my family." This is the father of the Ammonites to this day.

GENESIS CHAPTER 20

Abraham and Sarah at Gerar

¹ And Abraham journeyed from there to the southern country, and dwelt between Kadesh and Shur, and sojourned in Gerar.

² And Abraham said concerning Sarah his wife, "She is my sister," for he feared to say, "She is my wife," lest at any time the men of the city should kill him for her sake. So Abimelech king of Gerar sent and took Sarah.

³ And God came to Abimelech by night in his sleep, and said, "Behold, you shall die for the woman whom you have taken, for she has a husband."

⁴ But Abimelech had not touched her, and he said, "Lord, will You destroy an ignorantly *sinning* and just nation?

⁵ Did he not say to me, 'She is my sister', and she, even she herself said, 'He is my brother'? With a pure heart and in the righteousness of my hands have I done this."

⁶ And God said to him in his sleep, "Yes, I knew that you did this with a pure heart, and I spared you, so that you should not sin against Me, therefore I did not let you touch her.

⁷ But now return the man his wife; for he is a prophet, and *he* shall pray for you, and you shall live; but if you do not restore her *to him*, know that you and all yours shall die."

⁸ And Abimelech rose early in the morning, and called all his servants, and he spoke all these words in their ears, and all the men feared exceedingly.

⁹ And Abimelech called Abraham and said to him, "What is this you have done to us? Have we sinned against you, that you have brought upon me and upon my kingdom *this* great sin? You have done a deed to me which no one ought to do."

¹⁰ And Abimelech said to Abraham, "What have you seen in me that you have done this?"

¹¹ And Abraham said, "Because I *thought*, 'Surely there is not the worship of God in this place, and they will slay me because of my wife.'

¹² For truly she is my sister by my father, but not by my mother, and she became my wife."

¹³ And it came to pass when God brought me forth out of the house of my father, that I said to her, "This righteousness you shall perform to me, in every place into which we may enter, say of me, 'He is my brother.'"

¹⁴ And Abimelech took a thousand pieces of silver, and sheep, and calves, and servants, and maid servants, and gave them to Abraham, and he returned Sarah his wife to him.

¹⁵ And Abimelech said to Abraham, "Behold, my land is before you, dwell wherever it may please you."

¹⁶ And to Sarah he said, "Behold, I have given your brother a thousand pieces of silver, those shall be to you for the price of your countenance, and to all the women with you, and speak the truth in all things."

¹⁷ And Abraham prayed to God, and God healed Abimelech, and his wife, and his women servants, and they bore children.

¹⁸ Because the Lord had closed up all the wombs of the house of Abimelech, because of Sarah, Abraham's wife.

GENESIS CHAPTER 21

The Birth of Isaac

¹ And the Lord visited Sarah, as He said, and the Lord did to Sarah as He spoke.

² And she conceived and bore to Abraham a son in his old age, at the appointed time according as the Lord spoke to him.

³ And Abraham called the name of his son that was born to him, whom Sarah bore to him, Isaac.

⁴ And Abraham circumcised Isaac on the eighth day, as God commanded him.

⁵ And Abraham was one hundred years old when his son Isaac was born to him.

⁶ And Sarah said, "The Lord has made laughter for me, for whoever shall hear shall rejoice with me."

⁷ And she said, "Who shall say to Abraham that Sarah nurses a child? For I have born a child in my old age."

Hagar and Ishmael Sent Away

⁸ And the child grew and was weaned, and Abraham made a great feast the day that his son Isaac was weaned.

⁹ And Sarah, having seen the son of Hagar the Egyptian, who was born to Abraham, sporting with Isaac her son,

¹⁰ that she said to Abraham, "Cast out this bondwoman and her son, for the son of this bondwoman shall not inherit with my son Isaac."

11 But the word appeared very distressing before Abraham concerning his son.

12 But God said to Abraham, "Let it not be distressing before you concerning the child, and concerning the bondwoman; whatever Sarah shall say to you, listen to her voice, for in Isaac shall your seed be called.

13 And moreover, I will make the son of this bondwoman a great nation, because he is your offspring."

14 And Abraham rose up in the morning and took loaves and a skin of water, and gave them to Hagar, and he put the child on her shoulder, and sent her away, and she, having departed, wandered in the wilderness near the Well of the Oath.

15 And the water failed out of the skin, and she cast the child under a fir tree.

16 And she departed, and sat down opposite him at a distance, as it were about a bowshot, for she said, "Surely I cannot see the death of my child." And she sat opposite him, and the child cried aloud and wept.

17 And God heard the voice of the child from the place where he was, and an angel of God called to Hagar out of heaven, and said to her, "What is it, Hagar? Do not fear, for God has heard the voice of the child from the place where he is.

18 Rise up, and take the child, and hold him in your hand, for I will make him a great nation."

19 And God opened her eyes, and she saw a well of springing water; and she went and filled the skin with water, and gave the child a drink.

20 And God was with the child, and he grew and dwelt in the wilderness, and became an archer.

21 And he dwelt in the wilderness, and his mother took for him a wife out of Paran of Egypt.

Abraham and Abimelech Make a Covenant

22 And it came to pass at that time that Abimelech, and Ochozath his friend, and Phichol the chief captain of his army, spoke to Abraham, saying, "God is with you in all things, in all that you do.

23 Now therefore, swear to me by God that you will not injure me, nor my offspring, nor my name, but according to the righteousness which I have performed with you, you shall deal with me, and with the land in which you have sojourned."

24 And Abraham said, "I will swear."

25 And Abraham reproved Abimelech because of the wells of water, which the servants of Abimelech took away.

26 And Abimelech said to him, "I know not who has done this thing to you, neither did you tell it to me, neither did I hear it until today."

27 And Abraham took sheep and calves, and gave them to Abimelech, and they both made a covenant.

28 And Abraham set seven ewe lambs by themselves.

29 And Abimelech said to Abraham, "What are these seven ewe lambs which you have set alone?"

30 And Abraham said, "You shall receive the seven ewe lambs from me, that they may be for me as a witness, that I dug this well."

31 Therefore he named the name of that place, The Well of the Oath, for there they both swore.

32 And they made a covenant at the Well of the Oath. And there rose up Abimelech, Ochozath his friend, and Phichol the commander-in-chief of his army, and they returned to the land of the Philistines.

33 And Abraham planted a field at the Well of the Oath, and called there on the name of the Lord, the Everlasting God.

34 And Abraham sojourned in the land of the Philistines many days.

GENESIS CHAPTER 22

The Testing of Abraham's Faith

1 And it came to pass after these things that God tested Abraham, and said to him, "Abraham, Abraham"; and he said, "Behold! I am here."

2 And He said, "Take your son, the beloved one, whom you have loved—Isaac, and go into the high land, and offer him there for a burnt offering on one of the mountains of which I will tell you."

3 And Abraham rose up in the morning and saddled his donkey, and he took two servants with him, and Isaac his son, and having split wood for a burnt offering, he arose and departed, and came to the place of which God spoke to him.

4 On the third day Abraham, having lifted up his eyes, saw the place afar off.

5 And Abraham said to his servants, "Sit here with the donkey, and I and the lad will proceed thus far, and having worshipped, we will return to you."

6 And Abraham took the wood of the burnt offering, and laid it on Isaac his son, and he took into his hands both the fire and the knife, and the two went together.

7 And Isaac said to Abraham his father, "Father." And he said, "What is it, son?" And he said, "Behold the fire and the wood, but where is the sheep for a burnt offering?"

8 And Abraham said, "God will provide for Himself a sheep for a burnt offering, my son." And both, having gone together,

9 came to the place which God spoke to him of; and there Abraham built the altar, and laid the wood on it, and having bound the feet of Isaac his son together, he laid him on the altar upon the wood.

10 And Abraham stretched forth his hand to take the knife to kill his son.

11 But the Angel of the Lord called to him out of heaven, and said, "Abraham, Abraham." And he said, "Behold, I *am here*."

12 And He said, "Do not lay your hand upon the child, neither do anything to him, for now I know that you fear God, and for My sake you have not spared your beloved son."

¹³ And Abraham lifted up his eyes and beheld, and lo! A ram caught by his horns in a plant of Sabek; and Abraham went and took the ram, and offered him up for a burnt offering in the place of Isaac his son.

¹⁴ And Abraham called the name of that place, The Lord Has Seen; that they might say today, In the mount the Lord was seen.

¹⁵ Then the Angel of the Lord called Abraham the second time out of heaven, saying,

¹⁶ "I have sworn by Myself," says the Lord, "because you have done this thing, and on My account have not spared your beloved son,

¹⁷ surely blessing I will bless you, and multiplying I will multiply your descendants as the stars of heaven, and as the sand which is on the seashore, and your descendants shall inherit the cities of their enemies.

¹⁸ And in your descendants shall all the nations of the earth be blessed, because you have obeyed My voice."

¹⁹ And Abraham returned to his servants, and they arose and went together to the Well of the Oath; and Abraham dwelt at the Well of the Oath.

The Family of Nahor

²⁰ And it came to pass after these things, that it was reported to Abraham, saying, "Behold, Milcah herself too has born sons to Nahor your brother."

²¹ Huz the firstborn, and Buz his brother, and Kemuel the father of the Syrians, and Chesed,

²² Hazo, Pildash, Jidlaph, Bethuel, and Bethuel fathered Rebecca. ²³ These are eight sons which Milcah bore to Nahor, the brother of Abraham.

²⁴ And his concubine, whose name was Reumah, she also bore Tebah, Gaham, Thahash, and Maachah.

GENESIS CHAPTER 23

The Death of Sarah

¹ And the life of Sarah was one hundred and twenty-seven years.

² And Sarah died in Kirjath Arba, which is in the valley, this is Hebron in the land of Canaan; and Abraham came to lament for Sarah and to mourn.

³ And Abraham stood up from before his dead; and Abraham spoke to the sons of Heth, saying,

⁴ "I am a sojourner and a stranger among you. Therefore give me possession of a burial place among you, and I will bury my dead away from me."

⁵ And the sons of Heth answered Abraham, saying, "Not so, sir,

⁶ but hear us; you are in the midst of us a prince of God; bury your dead in our choice tombs, for none of us will by any means withhold his tomb from you, so that you should not bury your dead there."

⁷ And Abraham rose up and bowed himself to the people of the land, to the sons of Heth.

⁸ And Abraham spoke to them, saying, "If you have it in your mind that I should bury my dead out of my sight, listen to me, and speak to Ephron the son of Zohar for me.

⁹ And let him give me the double cave which he has, which is in a part of his field, let him give it to me for the money it is worth for possession of a burial place among you."

¹⁰ Now Ephron was sitting in the midst of the children of Heth, and Ephron the Hittite answered Abraham and spoke in the hearing of the sons of Heth, and of all who entered the city, saying,

¹¹ "Attend to me, my lord, and hear me, I give to you the field and the cave which is in it; I have given it to you before all my countrymen; bury your dead."

¹² And Abraham bowed down before the people of the land.

¹³ And he said in the ears of Ephron before the people of the land, "Since you are on my side, hear me; take the price of the field from me, and I will bury my dead there."

¹⁴ But Ephron answered Abraham, saying,

¹⁵ "No, my lord, I have heard indeed, the land *is worth* four hundred silver shekels, but what can this be between me and you? So bury your dead."

¹⁶ And Abraham listened to Ephron, and Abraham rendered to Ephron the money, which he mentioned in the ears of the sons of Heth, four hundred shekels of silver approved with merchants.

¹⁷ And the field of Ephron, which was in Double Cave, which is opposite Mamre, the field and the cave, which was in it, and every tree which was in the field, and whatever is in its borders round about, were deeded

¹⁸ to Abraham for a possession, before the sons of Heth, and all that entered into the city.

¹⁹ After this Abraham buried Sarah his wife in the Double Cave of the field, which is opposite Mamre, this is Hebron in the land of Canaan.

²⁰ So the field and the cave which was in it were deeded to Abraham for possession of a burying place, by the sons of Heth.

GENESIS CHAPTER 24

The Marriage of Isaac and Rebekah

¹ And Abraham was old, advanced in days, and the Lord blessed Abraham in all things.

² And Abraham said to his servant the elder of his house, who had rule over all his possessions, "Put your hand under my thigh,

³ and I will make you swear by the Lord, the God of heaven, and the God of the earth, that you do not take a wife for my son Isaac from the daughters of the Canaanites, with whom I dwell, in the midst of them.

⁴ But you shall go instead to my country, where I was born, and to my tribe, and you shall take from there a wife for my son Isaac."

5 And the servant said to him, "Shall I carry back your son to the land from which you came from, if the woman should not be willing to return happily with me to this land?"

6 And Abraham said to him, "See that you do not carry my son back there.

7 The Lord, the God of heaven, and the God of the earth, who took me out of my father's house, and out of the land from which I sprang, who spoke to me, and who swore to me, saying, 'I will give this land to you and to your descendants', He shall send His angel before you, and you shall take a wife to my son from there.

8 And if the woman should not be willing to come with you into this land, you shall be clear from my oath, only do not carry my son there again."

9 And the servant put his hand under the thigh of his master Abraham, and swore to him concerning this matter.

10 And the servant took ten camels from among his master's herds, and *he took* of all the goods of his master with him, and he arose and went into Mesopotamia to the city of Nahor.

11 And he rested his camels outside the city by the well of water towards evening, when women go forth to draw water.

12 And he said, "O Lord God of my master Abraham, prosper my way before me today, and deal mercifully with my master Abraham.

13 Behold, I stand by the well of water, and the daughters of them that inhabit the city come forth to draw water.

14 And it shall be, the virgin to whomsoever I shall say, Let down your water pot, that I may drink, and she shall say, 'Drink, and I will give your camels a drink, until they have finished drinking'—even this one You have prepared for Your servant Isaac, and hereby shall I know that You have dealt mercifully with my master Abraham."

15 And it came to pass before he had done speaking in his mind, that behold, Rebecca the daughter of Bethuel, the son of Milcah, the wife of Nahor, Abraham's brother, came forth, having a water pot on her shoulders.

16 And the virgin was very beautiful in appearance, she was a virgin, a man had not known her; and she went down to the well, and filled her water pot, and came up.

17 And the servant ran up to meet her, and said, "Give me a little water to drink out of your pitcher";

18 and she said, "Drink, sir"; and she quickly let down the pitcher upon her arm, and gave him to drink, till he ceased drinking.

19 And she said, "I will also draw water for your camels, till they shall all have drunk."

20 And she quickly emptied the water pot into the trough, and ran to the well to draw again, and drew water for all the camels.

21 And the man took great notice of her, and remained silent to know whether the Lord had made his way prosperous or not.

22 And it came to pass when all the camels ceased drinking, that the man took golden earrings, each weighing half a shekel, and he put two bracelets on her hands, their weight was ten pieces of gold.

23 And he asked her, and said, "Whose daughter are you? Tell me if there is room for us to lodge with your father."

24 And she said to him, "I am the daughter of Bethuel the son of Milcah, whom she bore to Nahor."

25 And she said to him, "We have both straw and much feed, and a place for resting."

26 And the man, being well pleased, worshipped the Lord,

27 and said, "Blessed be the Lord, the God of my master Abraham, who has not allowed His righteousness to fail, nor His truth from my master, and the Lord has brought me prosperously to the house of the brother of my lord."

28 And the woman ran and reported to the house of her mother according to these words.

29 And Rebecca had a brother whose name was Laban; and Laban ran out to meet the man, by the well.

30 And it came to pass when he saw the earrings and the bracelets on the hands of his sister, and when he heard the words of Rebecca his sister, saying, "Thus the man spoke to me," that he went to the man, as he stood by the camels at the well.

31 And he said to him, "Come in here, you blessed of the Lord, why do you stand outside, whereas I have prepared the house and a place for the camels?"

32 And the man entered into the house, and unloaded the camels, and gave the camels straw and feed, and water to wash his feet, and the feet of the men that were with him.

33 And he set before them loaves to eat; but he said, "I will not eat, until I have told my errand." And he said, "Speak on."

34 And he said, "I am a servant of Abraham;

35 and the Lord has blessed my master greatly, and he has become great; and He has given him sheep, calves, silver, gold, male and female servants, camels, and donkeys.

36 And Sarah my master's wife bore one son to my master after he had grown old; and he gave him whatever he had.

37 And my master caused me to swear, saying, 'You shall not take a wife to my son of the daughters of the Canaanites, among whom I sojourn in their land.

38 But you shall go to the house of my father, and to my tribe, and you shall take from there a wife for my son.'

39 And I said to my master, Perhaps the woman will not happily go with me.

40 And he said to me, 'The Lord God Himself, to whom I have been acceptable in His presence, shall send out His angel with you, and shall prosper your journey, and you shall take a wife for my son of my tribe, and of the house of my father.

41 Then shall you be clear from my oath, for whenever you have come to my tribe, and they shall not give her to you, then shall you be clear from my oath.'

42 And having come this day to the well, I said, 'Lord God of my master Abraham, if You prosper my journey on which I am now going,

[43] behold, I stand by the well of water, and the daughters of the men of the city come forth to draw water, and it shall be that the woman to whom I shall say, 'Give me a little water to drink out of your pitcher',

[44] and she shall say to me, 'Drink, and I will draw water for your camels', also; this *shall be* the wife whom the Lord has prepared for His own servant Isaac; and hereby shall I know that You have shown mercy to my master Abraham.'"

[45] "And it came to pass before I had done speaking in my mind, that Rebecca came forth, having her pitcher on her shoulders; and she went down to the well, and drew water; and I said to her, 'Give me a drink'.

[46] And she quickly let down her pitcher on her arm from her head, and said, 'Drink, and I will give your camels a drink, also'; and I drank, and she gave the camels a drink.

[47] And I asked her, and said, 'Whose daughter are you? Tell me'; and she said, 'I am the daughter of Bethuel the son of Nahor, whom Milcah bore to him'; and I put on her the earrings, and the bracelets on her hands.

[48] And being well-pleased, I worshipped the Lord, and I blessed the Lord, the God of my master Abraham, who has prospered me in a true way, so that I should take the daughter of my master's brother for his son.

[49] If then you *will* deal mercifully and justly with my lord, *tell me*, and if not, tell me, that I may turn to the right hand or to the left."

[50] And Laban and Bethuel answered and said, "This matter has come forth from the Lord, we shall not be able to answer you bad or good.

[51] Behold, Rebecca is before you, take her and go away, and let her be the wife to the son of your master, as the Lord has said."

[52] And it came to pass when the servant of Abraham heard these words, he *worshipped* the Lord, bowing down to the earth.

[53] And the servant, having brought forth jewels of silver and gold and clothing, gave them to Rebecca, and gave gifts to her brother, and to her mother.

[54] And both he and the men with him ate and drank and went to sleep. And he arose in the morning and said, "Send me away, that I may go to my master."

[55] And her brothers and her mother said, "Let the virgin remain with us about ten days, and after that she shall depart."

[56] But he said to them, "Do not delay me, for the Lord has prospered my journey for me; send me away, that I may depart to my master."

[57] And they said, "Let us call the woman, and ask her personally." [58] And they called Rebecca, and said to her, "Will you go with this man?" And she said, "I will go."

[59] So they sent forth Rebecca their sister, and her goods, and the servant of Abraham, and his attendants.

[60] And they blessed Rebecca, and said to her, "You are our sister; *may* you become *the mother* of thousands and thousands, and let your descendants possess the cities of their enemies."

[61] And Rebecca rose up, *both she* and her maidens, and they mounted the camels and went with the man. And the servant, having taken up Rebecca, departed.

[62] And Isaac went through the wilderness to the Well of the Vision, and he dwelt in the land toward the south.

[63] And Isaac went forth into the plain toward evening to meditate; and having lifted up his eyes, he saw camels coming.

[64] And Rebecca lifted up her eyes, and saw Isaac; and she dismounted at once from off of the camel,

[65] and said to the servant, "Who is that man that walks in the plain to meet us?" And the servant said, "This is my master"; and she took her veil and covered herself.

[66] And the servant told Isaac all that he had done.

[67] And Isaac went into the house of his mother, and took Rebecca, and she became his wife, and he loved her; and Isaac was comforted over Sarah his mother.

GENESIS CHAPTER 25

Abraham Marries Keturah

[1] And Abraham again took a wife, whose name was Keturah.

[2] And she bore to him Zimran, Jokshan, Medan, Midian, Ishbak, and Shuah.

[3] And Jokshan fathered Sheba and Dedan. And the sons of Dedan were the Assurians, the Letushim, and the Leummim.

[4] And the sons of Midian were Ephah, Epher, Hanoch, Abidah, and Eldaah; all these were sons of Keturah.

[5] But Abraham gave all his possessions to Isaac his son.

[6] But to the sons of his concubines Abraham gave gifts, and he sent them away from his son Isaac, while he was yet living, to the country of the east.

The Death of Abraham

[7] And these *were* the years of the days of the life of Abraham, as many as he lived, one hundred and seventy-five years.

[8] Then Abraham breathed his last, and died in a good old age, an old man and full of days, and was added to his people.

[9] And Isaac and Ishmael his sons buried him in the double cave, in the field of Ephron the son of Zohar the Hittite, which is over against Mamre,

[10] *even* the field and the cave which Abraham bought from the sons of Heth; there they buried Abraham and Sarah his wife.

[11] And it came to pass after Abraham was dead, that God blessed Isaac his son, and Isaac dwelt by the Well of the Vision.

Ishmael's Descendants

¹² And these are the generations of Ishmael the son of Abraham, whom Hagar the Egyptian, the maid of Sarah, bore to Abraham.

¹³ And these are the names of the sons of Ismael, according to the names of their generations: the firstborn of Ishmael *was* Nabajoth, then Kedar, Adbeel, Mibsam,

¹⁴ Mishma, Dumah, Massa,

¹⁵ Hadar, Tema, Jetur, Naphish, and Kedemah.

¹⁶ These are the sons of Ishmael, and these are their names by their towns and in their camps, twelve princes according to their nations.

¹⁷ And these are the years of the life of Ishmael, one hundred and thirty-seven years; and he breathed his last and died, and was added to his fathers.

¹⁸ And he dwelt from Havilah to Shur, which is opposite Egypt, until one comes to the Assyrians; he dwelt in the presence of all his brothers.

Esau and Jacob

¹⁹ And these are the generations of Isaac the son of Abraham:

²⁰ Abraham fathered Isaac. And Isaac was forty years old when he took Rebecca as wife, daughter of Bethuel the Syrian, out of Syrian Mesopotamia, sister of Laban the Syrian.

²¹ Now Isaac prayed to the Lord concerning Rebecca his wife, because she was barren; and the Lord heard him, and his wife Rebecca conceived in her womb.

²² And the babes leaped within her; and she said, "If it is thus, why is this *happening* to me?" And she went to inquire of the Lord.

²³ And the Lord said to her, "There are two nations in your womb, and two peoples shall be separated from your body, and one people shall be stronger than the other, and the older shall serve the younger."

²⁴ And the days were fulfilled that she should be delivered, and she had twins in her womb.

²⁵ And the first came out red, hairy all over like a garment; and she called his name Esau.

²⁶ And after this his brother came forth, and his hand took hold of the heel of Esau; and she called his name Jacob. And Isaac was sixty years old when Rebecca bore them.

²⁷ And the boys grew; and Esau was a man skilled in hunting, dwelling in the country, and Jacob a simple man, dwelling in a house.

²⁸ And Isaac loved Esau, because his venison was his food, but Rebecca loved Jacob.

²⁹ And Jacob cooked a stew, and Esau came from the plain, and he *was* weary.

³⁰ And Esau said to Jacob, "Let me taste of that red stew, because I am fainting"; therefore his name was called Edom.

³¹ And Jacob said to Esau, "Sell me this day your birthright."

³² And Esau said, "Behold, I am going to die, and for what good does this birthright *belong* to me?"

³³ And Jacob said to him, "Swear to me this day"; and he swore to him; and Esau sold his birthright to Jacob.

³⁴ And Jacob gave bread to Esau, and a stew of lentiles; and he ate and drank, and he arose and departed; thus Esau despised his birthright.

GENESIS CHAPTER 26

Isaac and Abimelech

¹ And there was a famine in the land, besides the former famine, which was in the time of Abraham; and Isaac went to Abimelech the king of the Philistines to Gerar.

² And the Lord appeared to him and said, "Do not go down to Egypt, but dwell in the land which I shall tell you of.

³ And sojourn in this land; and I will be with you, and bless you, for I will give to you and to your descendants all this land; and I will establish My oath which I swore to your father Abraham.

⁴ And I will multiply your descendants as the stars of heaven; and I will give to your descendants all this land, and all the nations of the earth shall be blessed in your descendants.

⁵ Because Abraham your father obeyed My voice, and kept My injunctions, My commandments, My ordinances, and My statutes."

⁶ And Isaac dwelt in Gerar.

⁷ And the men of the place questioned him concerning Rebecca his wife, and he said, "She is my sister" (for he feared to say, "She is my wife," lest at any time the men of the place should kill him because of Rebecca, because she was beautiful).

⁸ And he remained there a long time, and Abimelech the king of Gerar leaned to look through the window, and saw Isaac sporting with Rebecca his wife.

⁹ And Abimelech called Isaac, and said to him, "Is she then your wife? Why have you said, 'She is my sister?'" And Isaac said to him, "*I did so,* for I said, 'Lest at any time I should die on her account.'"

¹⁰ And Abimelech said to him, "Why have you done this to us? One of my kindred might soon have lain with your wife, and you would have brought a sin of ignorance upon us."

¹¹ And Abimelech charged all his people, saying, "Every man that touches this man and his wife shall be liable to death."

¹² And Isaac sowed in that land, and he found barley in that year, and reaped one hundred fold, and the Lord blessed him.

¹³ And the man prospered, and continued prospering, till he became very great.

¹⁴ And he had herds of sheep, and herds of oxen, and many tilled lands, and the Philistines envied him.

[15] And all the wells which the servants of his father had dug in the time of his father, the Philistines had stopped them, and filled them with earth.

[16] And Abimelech said to Isaac, "Depart from us, for you have become much greater than us."

[17] And Isaac departed from there, and rested in the valley of Gerar, and dwelt there.

[18] And Isaac dug again the wells of water, which the servants of his father Abraham had dug, and the Philistines had stopped them up, after the death of his father Abraham; and he gave them names, according to the names by which his father named them.

[19] And the servants of Isaac dug in the valley of Gerar, and they found there a well of living water.

[20] And the shepherds of Gerar quarreled with the shepherds of Isaac, saying that the water was theirs; and they called the name of the well, Injury, for they injured him.

[21] And having departed from there he dug another well, and they fought for that one also; and he named the name of it, Enmity.

[22] And he departed from there and dug another well; and they did not quarrel about that *one*; and he named the name of it, Room, saying, "Because now the Lord has made room for us, and has increased us upon the earth."

[23] And he went up from there to the Well of the Oath.

[24] And the Lord appeared to him in that night and said, "I am the God of Abraham your father; fear not, for I am with you, and I will bless you, and multiply your descendants for the sake of Abraham your father."

[25] And he built an altar there, and called on the name of the Lord, and there he pitched his tent, and there the servants of Isaac dug a well in the valley of Gerar.

[26] And Abimelech came to him from Gerar, and so did Ahuzzath his friend, and Phichol the commander of his army.

[27] And Isaac said to them, "Why have you come to me? Seeing *that* you hated me, and sent me away from you."

[28] And they said, "We have surely seen that the Lord was with you, and we said, 'Let there be an oath between us and you, and we will make a covenant with you,

[29] that you shall do us no harm, as we have not abhorred you, and since we have treated you well, and have sent you forth peaceably; and now you are blessed of the Lord.'"

[30] And he made a feast for them, and they ate and drank.

[31] And they arose in the morning, and swore each to his neighbor; and Isaac sent them forth, and they departed from him in safety.

[32] And it came to pass in that day, that the servants of Isaac came and told him of the well which they had dug; and they said, "We have not found water."

[33] And he called it, Oath: therefore he called the name of that city, the Well of Oath, until this day.

[34] And Esau was forty years old; and he took as wives Judith the daughter of Beeri the Hittite, and Basemath, daughter of Elon the Hittite.

[35] And they brought grief to Isaac and Rebecca.

GENESIS CHAPTER 27

Isaac Blesses Jacob

[1] And it came to pass after Isaac was old, that his eyes were dimmed so that he could not see; and he called Esau, his older son, and said to him, "My son"; and he said, "Behold, I *am here*."

[2] And he said, "Behold, I have grown old, and I do not know the day of my death.

[3] Now then take the weapons, both your quiver and your bow, and go into the plain, and get me some venison,

[4] and prepare some meats for me, as I like them, and bring them to me that I may eat, that my soul may bless you before I die."

[5] And Rebecca heard Isaac speaking to Esau his son; and Esau went to the plain to procure venison for his father.

[6] And Rebecca said to Jacob her younger son, "Behold, I heard your father speaking to Esau your brother, saying,

[7] 'Bring me some venison, and prepare some meats for me, that I may eat and bless you before the Lord, before I die.'

[8] Now then, my son, listen to me, as I command you.

[9] Go now to the cattle and bring me from there two choice kids, tender and good, and I will prepare the meats for your father, as he likes.

[10] And you shall bring them in to your father, and he shall eat, that your father may bless you before he dies."

[11] And Jacob said to his mother Rebecca, "Esau my brother is a hairy man, and I am a smooth-*skinned* man.

[12] Perhaps my father may feel me, and I shall be before him as one ill-intentioned, and I shall bring upon me a curse, and not a blessing."

[13] And his mother said to him, "On me be your curse, *my* son; only listen to my voice, and go and bring *them* for me."

[14] So he went and took and brought them to his mother; and his mother prepared the meats, as his father liked *them*.

[15] And Rebecca, having taken the fine clothing of her elder son Esau which was with her in the house, put it on Jacob her younger son.

[16] And she put on his arms the skins of the kids of the goats, and on the bare parts of his neck.

[17] And she gave the meats, and the loaves which she had prepared, into the hands of Jacob her son.

[18] And he brought *them* to his father, and said, "Father"; and he said, "Behold I *am here*; who are you, son?"

[19] And Jacob said to his father, "I, Esau your firstborn, have done as you told me: come, sit and eat of my venison, that your soul may bless me."

[20] And Isaac said to his son, "What is this which you have quickly found?" And he said, "That which the Lord your God presented before me."

[21] And Isaac said to Jacob, "Come close to me, and I will feel you, son, if you are my son Esau or not."

22 And Jacob came close to his father Isaac, and he felt him, and said, "The voice is Jacob's voice, but the hands are the hands of Esau."

23 And he did not recognize him, for his hands were as the hands of his brother Esau, hairy; and he blessed him,

24 and he said, "Are you my son Esau?" And he said, "I *am*."

25 And he said, "Bring *it* near to me, and I will eat of your venison, *my* son, that my soul may bless you." And he brought it near to him, and he ate, and he brought him wine, and he drank.

26 And Isaac his father said to him, "Come close to me, and kiss me, *my* son."

27 And he came close and kissed him, and smelled the smell of his garments, and blessed him, and said, "Behold, the smell of my son is as the smell of an abundant field, which the Lord has blessed.

28 And may God give you of the dew of heaven, and of the fatness of the earth, and abundance of grain and wine.

29 And let nations serve you, and princes bow down to you, and be master over your brother, and the sons of your father shall reverence you; accursed is he that curses you, and blessed is he that blesses you."

Esau's Lost Blessing

30 And it came to pass after Isaac had ceased blessing his son Jacob, just when Jacob had gone out from the presence of Isaac his father, that Esau his brother came in from his hunting.

31 And he also had prepared meats and brought them to his father; and he said to his father, "Let my father arise and eat of his son's venison, that your soul may bless me."

32 And Isaac his father said to him, "Who are you?" And he said, "I am Esau, your firstborn son."

33 And Isaac was amazed with very great amazement, and said, "Who then is it that has procured venison for me and brought it to me? And I have eaten all of it before you came, and I have blessed him, and he shall be blessed."

34 And it came to pass when Esau heard the words of his father Isaac, he cried out with a great and very bitter cry, and said, "Bless me—me also, father!"

35 And he said to him, "Your brother has come with deceit, and has taken away your blessing."

36 And he said, "Rightly was his name called Jacob, for behold, this second time has he supplanted me; he has both taken my birthright, and now he has taken my blessing!" And Esau said to his father, "Have you not a blessing left for me, father?"

37 And Isaac answered and said to Esau, "If I have made him your master, and have made all his brothers his servants, and have strengthened him with grain and wine, what then shall I do for you, son?"

38 And Esau said to his father, "Have you *only* one blessing, father? Bless me—me also, O my father!" And Isaac being troubled, Esau cried aloud and wept.

39 And Isaac his father answered and said to him, "Behold, your dwelling shall be of the fatness of the earth, and of the dew of heaven from above.

40 And you shall live by your sword, and shall serve your brother; and there shall be *a time* when you shall break and loosen his yoke from off your neck."

Jacob Escapes Esau's Fury

41 And Esau was angry with Jacob because of the blessing, with which his father blessed him; and Esau said in his mind, "Let the days of my father's mourning draw near, that I may kill my brother Jacob."

42 And the words of Esau her elder son were reported to Rebecca, and she sent and called Jacob her younger son, and said to him, "Behold, Esau your brother threatens you, to kill you.

43 Now then, my son, hear my voice, and rise and depart quickly into Mesopotamia to Laban my brother, into Haran.

44 And dwell with him certain days, until your brother's anger

45 and rage toward you departs, and he forget what you have done to him; and I will send and bring you from there, lest at any time I should be bereaved of you both in one day."

46 And Rebecca said to Isaac, "I am weary of my life, because of the daughters of the sons of Heth; if Jacob shall take a wife of the daughters of this land, where then should I live?"

GENESIS CHAPTER 28

1 And Isaac, having called for Jacob, blessed him, and charged him, saying, "You shall not take a wife of the daughters of the Canaanites.

2 Rise and depart quickly into Mesopotamia, to the house of Bethuel the father of your mother, and take to yourself a wife of the daughters of Laban, your mother's brother.

3 And may my God bless you, and increase you, and multiply you, and you shall become an assembly of nations.

4 And may He give you the blessing of my father Abraham, even to you and to your descendants after you, to inherit the land of your sojourning, which God gave to Abraham."

5 So Isaac sent Jacob away, and he went into Mesopotamia, to Laban the son of Bethuel the Syrian, the brother of Rebecca the mother of Jacob and Esau.

Esau Marries Ishmael's Daughter

6 And Esau saw that Isaac blessed Jacob, and sent him away to Mesopotamia of Syria as he blessed him, to take to himself a wife from there, and *that* he charged him, saying, "You shall not take a wife of the daughters of the Canaanites";

7 and *that* Jacob listened to his father and his mother, and went to Mesopotamia of Syria.

8 And Esau, also having seen that the daughters of Canaan were evil before his father Isaac,

9 went to Ishmael, and took Mahalath the daughter of Ishmael, the son of Abraham, the sister of Nebajoth, for a wife, in addition to his *other* wives.

Jacob's Dream at Bethel

10 And Jacob went forth from the Well of the Oath, and departed into Haran.

11 So he came to a certain place and slept there, for the sun had gone down; and he took one of the stones of the place, and put it at his head, and lay down to sleep in that place,

12 and dreamed. And behold, a ladder fixed on the earth, whose top reached to heaven, and the angels of God ascended and descended on it.

13 And the Lord stood upon it, and said, "I am the God of your father Abraham, and the God of Isaac; fear not, the land on which you lie I will give to you and to your descendants.

14 And your descendants shall be as the sand of the earth; and it shall spread abroad to the sea, and the south, and the north, and to the east; and in you and in your descendants shall all the tribes of the earth be blessed.

15 And behold, I am with you, to preserve you continually wherever you shall go; and I will bring you back to this land; for I will not desert you, until I have done all that I have said to you."

16 And Jacob awakened out of his sleep, and said, "The Lord is in this place, and I did not know it."

17 And he was afraid, and said, "How fearful is this place! This is none other than the house of God, and this is the gate of heaven!"

18 And Jacob rose up in the morning, and took the stone he *had* laid there by his head, and he set it up as a pillar, and poured oil on the top of it.

19 And he called the name of that place, the House of God; and the name of the city before was Luz.

20 And Jacob vowed a vow, saying, "If the Lord God will be with me, and guard me throughout on this journey, on which I am going, and give me bread to eat, and clothing to put on,

21 and bring me back in safety to the house of my father, then shall the Lord be my God.

22 And this stone, which I have set up for a pillar, shall be to me a house of God; and of everything You shall give me, I will tithe a tenth to You."

GENESIS CHAPTER 29

Jacob Meets Rachel

1 So Jacob started on his journey and came to the land of the east to Laban, the son of Bethuel the Syrian, and the brother of Rebecca, mother of Jacob and Esau.

2 And he looked, and behold, a well in the plain; and there were three flocks of sheep resting at it, for out of that well they watered the flocks, but there was a great stone at the mouth of the well.

3 And there were all the flocks gathered, and they used to roll away the stone from the mouth of the well, and water the flocks, and set the stone again in its place on the mouth of the well.

4 And Jacob said to them, "Brothers, where are you from?" And they said, "We are from Haran."

5 And he said to them, "Do you know Laban, the son of Nahor?" And they said, "We know him."

6 And he said to them, "Is he well?" And they said, "He is well." And behold Rachel his daughter came with the sheep.

7 And Jacob said, "It is yet high day, it is not yet time that the flocks be gathered together. Water the flocks, and go and feed them."

8 And they said, "We shall not be able, until all the shepherds are gathered together, and they shall roll away the stone from the mouth of the well, then we will water the flocks."

9 While he was yet speaking to them, behold, Rachel the daughter of Laban came with her father's sheep, for she fed the sheep of her father.

10 And it came to pass when Jacob saw Rachel the daughter of Laban, his mother's brother, and the sheep of Laban, his mother's brother, that Jacob came and rolled away the stone from the mouth of the well, and watered the sheep of Laban, his mother's brother.

11 And Jacob kissed Rachel, and cried with a loud voice and wept. 12 And he told Rachel that he was the near relative of her father, and the son of Rebecca; and she ran and reported to her father according to these words.

13 And it came to pass when Laban heard the name of Jacob, his sister's son, he ran to meet him, and embraced and kissed him, and brought him into his house; and he told Laban all these sayings.

14 And Laban said to him, "You are of my bones and of my flesh"; and he was with him a full month.

Jacob Marries Laban's Daughters

15 And Laban said to Jacob, "Surely you shall not serve me for nothing, because you are my brother; tell me what your reward is to be."

16 Now Laban had two daughters, the name of the elder was Leah, and the name of the younger was Rachel.

17 And the eyes of Leah were weak, but Rachel was beautiful in appearance, and exceedingly fair in countenance.

18 And Jacob loved Rachel, and said, "I will serve you seven years for your younger daughter Rachel."

19 And Laban said to him, "It is better that I should give her to you, than that I should give her to another man; dwell with me."

20 And Jacob served for Rachel seven years, and they seemed *only* a few days, because of the love that he had for her.

²¹ And Jacob said to Laban, "Give me my wife, for my days are fulfilled, that I may go in to her."

²² And Laban gathered together all the men of the place, and made a marriage feast.

²³ And so it was, that he took his daughter Leah, and brought her in to Jacob, and Jacob went in to her.

²⁴ And Laban gave his maid Zilpah to his daughter Leah, as a maid for her.

²⁵ So it came to pass in the morning, that behold, it was Leah; and Jacob said to Laban, "What is this that you have done to me? Did I not serve you for Rachel? And why have you deceived me?"

²⁶ And Laban answered, "It is not done thus in our country, to give the younger before the elder.

²⁷ Fulfill then her week, and I will give her to you also in return for your service, which you serve with me, yet seven other years."

²⁸ And Jacob did so, and fulfilled her week; and Laban gave him his daughter Rachel as wife also.

²⁹ And Laban gave his maid Bilhah to his daughter as a maid to her.

³⁰ And he went in to Rachel; and he loved Rachel more than Leah; and he served him seven other years.

³¹ And when the Lord God saw that Leah was hated, He opened her womb; but Rachel was barren.

³² And Leah conceived and bore a son to Jacob; and she called his name Reuben, saying, "Because the Lord has looked on my humiliation, and has given me a son, now then my husband will love me."

³³ And she conceived again, and bore a second son to Jacob; and she said, "Because the Lord has heard that I am hated, He has given to me this one also"; and she called his name Simeon.

³⁴ And she conceived yet again, and bore a son, and said, "In the present time my husband will be with me, for I have born him three sons"; therefore she called his name Levi.

³⁵ And having conceived yet again, she bore a son, and said, "Now yet again this time will I give thanks to the Lord"; therefore she called his name, Judah; and ceased bearing.

GENESIS CHAPTER 30

¹ And Rachel, having perceived that she bore Jacob no children, was jealous of her sister; and said to Jacob, "Give me children; and if not, I shall die."

² And Jacob was angry with Rachel, and said to her, "Am I in the place of God, who has deprived you of the fruit of the womb?"

³ And Rachel said to Jacob, "Behold my maid Bilhah, go in to her, and she shall bear upon my knees, and I also shall have children by her."

⁴ And she gave him Bilhah her maid, for a wife to him; and Jacob went in to her.

⁵ And Bilhah, Rachel's maid, conceived, and bore Jacob a son.

⁶ And Rachel said, "God has given judgment for me, and heard my voice, and has given me a son"; therefore she called his name Dan.

⁷ And Bilhah, Rachel's maid, conceived yet again, and bore a second son to Jacob.

⁸ And Rachel said, "God has helped me, and I contended with my sister and prevailed"; and she called his name Naphtali.

⁹ And Leah saw that she ceased from bearing, and she took Zilpah her maid, and gave her to Jacob for a wife; and he went in to her.

¹⁰ And Zilpah Leah's maid conceived, and bore Jacob a son.

¹¹ And Leah said, "It is happily"; and she called his name Gad.

¹² And Zilpah Leah's maid conceived yet again, and bore Jacob a second son.

¹³ And Leah said, "I am blessed, for the women will pronounce me blessed"; and she called his name Asher.

¹⁴ And Reuben went in the day of barley harvest, and found apples of mandrakes in the field, and brought them to his mother Leah; and Rachel said to Leah her sister, "Give me *some* of your son's mandrakes."

¹⁵ And Leah said, "*Is it* not enough for you that you have taken my husband, will you also take my son's mandrakes?" And Rachel said, "Not so: let him lie with you tonight for your son's mandrakes."

¹⁶ And Jacob came in out of the field in the evening; and Leah went forth to meet him, and said, "You shall come in to me this day, for I have hired you for my son's mandrakes"; and he lay with her that night.

¹⁷ And God listened to Leah, and she conceived, and bore Jacob a fifth son.

¹⁸ And Leah said, "God has given me my reward, because I gave my maid to my husband"; and she called his name Issachar, which is, Reward.

¹⁹ And Leah conceived again, and bore Jacob a sixth son.

²⁰ And Leah said, "God has given me a good gift in this time; my husband will choose me, for I have born him six sons"; and she called his name Zebulun.

²¹ And after this she bore a daughter; and she called her name Dinah.

²² And God remembered Rachel, and God listened to her, and He opened her womb.

²³ And she conceived, and bore Jacob a son; and Rachel said, "God has taken away my reproach."

²⁴ And she called his name Joseph, saying, "Let God add to me another son."

Jacob Prospers at Laban's Expense

²⁵ And it came to pass when Rachel had born Joseph, Jacob said to Laban, "Send me away, that I may go to my place and to my land.

26 Restore my wives and my children, for whom I have served you, that I may depart, for you know the service with which I have served you."

27 And Laban said to him, "If I have found grace in your sight, for I have learned by experience that the Lord has blessed me at your coming in.

28 Name me your wages, and I will give *them*."

29 And Jacob said, "You know in what things I have served you, and how many livestock of yours is with me.

30 For what you had was little before my time, and it is increased to a multitude, and the Lord God has blessed you since my coming; now then, when shall I set up also my own house?"

31 And Laban said to him, "What shall I give you?" And Jacob said to him, "You shall not give me anything; if you will do this thing for me, I will again tend your flocks and keep them.

32 Let all your sheep pass by today, and separate from there every gray sheep among the rams, and everyone that is speckled and spotted among the goats—*this* shall be my reward.

33 And my righteousness shall answer for me in the morning, for it is my reward before you: whatever shall not be spotted and speckled among the goats, and gray among the rams, shall be considered stolen if *it is* with me."

34 And Laban said to him, "Let it be according to your word."

35 And he separated in that day the spotted and speckled male goats, and all the spotted and speckled female goats, and all those that were gray among the rams, and everyone that was white among them, and he gave them into the hand of his sons.

36 And he set a distance of a three days' journey between them and Jacob. And Jacob tended the cattle of Laban that were left behind.

37 And Jacob took to himself rods of green poplar, and walnut and plane tree; and Jacob peeled white strips in them; and as he drew off the green, the white strips which he had made appeared alternate on the rods.

38 And he laid the rods which he had peeled in the hollows of the watering troughs, so that whenever the cattle should come to drink, they might conceive at the rods.

39 So the cattle conceived before the rods, and the cattle brought forth young speckled, streaked and spotted with ash-colored *spots*.

40 And Jacob separated the lambs, and set before the sheep a speckled ram, and every streaked one among the lambs, and he separated flocks for himself alone, and did not mingle them with Laban's sheep.

41 And it came to pass in the time that whenever the cattle became pregnant, that Jacob put the rods before the cattle in the troughs, that they might conceive by the rods.

42 But he did not put them in *indiscriminately* whenever the cattle happened to bring forth, but the unmarked ones were Laban's, and the marked ones were Jacob's.

43 And the man became very rich, and he had many cattle and oxen, and male and female servants, and camels and donkeys.

GENESIS CHAPTER 31

Jacob Flees from Laban

1 And Jacob heard the words of the sons of Laban, saying, "Jacob has taken all that was our father's, and of our father's property has he gotten all this glory."

2 And Jacob saw the countenance of Laban, and behold it was not *favorable* toward him as before.

3 And the Lord said to Jacob, "Return to the land of your father, and to your family, and I will be with you."

4 And Jacob sent and called Leah and Rachel to the plain where the flocks were.

5 And he said to them, "I see the countenance of your father, that it is not *favorable* toward me as before, but the God of my father was with me.

6 And you too know that with all my might I have served your father.

7 But your father deceived me, and changed my wages for the ten lambs, yet God did not give him the *power* to hurt me.

8 If he should say thus, 'The speckled shall be your reward,' then all the cattle would bear speckled; and if he should say, 'The white shall be your reward,' then would all the cattle bear white.

9 So God has taken away all the cattle of your father, and given them to me.

10 And it came to pass when the cattle conceived and were with young, that I beheld with my eyes and saw in a dream, and behold, the male goats and the rams leaping on the sheep and the female goats, speckled and streaked and spotted with ash-colored spots.

11 And the Angel of God said to me in a dream, 'Jacob'; and I said, 'What is it'?

12 And He said, 'Look up with your eyes, and behold the male goats and the rams leaping on the sheep and the female goats, speckled and streaked and spotted with ash-colored spots; for I have seen all things that Laban does to you.

13 I am God that appeared to you in the place of God where you anointed a pillar to Me, and vowed to Me there a vow; now then arise and depart out of this land, depart into the land of your nativity, and I will be with you.'"

14 And Rachel and Leah answered and said to him, "Have we yet a part or inheritance in the house of our father?

15 Are we not considered strangers by him? For he has sold us, and quite devoured our money.

16 All the wealth and the glory which God has taken from our father, it shall be ours, and our children's; now then do whatever God has said to you."

17 And Jacob arose and took his wives and his children up on the camels;

18 and he took away all his possessions and all his store, which he had gotten in Mesopotamia, and all that belonged to him, to depart to Isaac his father in the land of Canaan.

19 And Laban went to shear his sheep; and Rachel stole her father's idols.

20 And Jacob hid *the matter from* Laban the Syrian, so as not to tell him that he ran away.

21 And he departed, himself and all that belonged to him, and passed over the river, and went into the mountain of Gilead.

Laban Pursues Jacob

22 But it was told to Laban the Syrian on the third day that Jacob had fled.

23 And having taken his brothers with him, he pursued after him seven days' journey, and overtook him on Mount Gilead.

24 And God came to Laban the Syrian in sleep by night, and said to him, "Take heed to yourself that you do not speak evil things to Jacob at any time."

25 And Laban overtook Jacob; and Jacob pitched his tent in the mountain; and Laban stationed his brothers in the mountains of Gilead.

26 And Laban said to Jacob, "What have you done? Why did you run away secretly, and pillage me, and lead away my daughters as captives taken with the sword?

27 If you had told me, I would have sent you away with joy, and with songs, with timbrel and harp.

28 And I was not counted worthy to embrace my children and my daughters. Now then you have done foolishly.

29 And now my hand has the power to hurt you; but the God of your father spoke to me yesterday, saying, 'Take heed to yourself that you speak no evil words to Jacob.'

30 Now then go on your way, for you have earnestly desired to depart to the house of your father; *but* why have you stolen my gods?"

31 And Jacob answered and said to Laban, "Because I was afraid; for I said, Lest at any time you should take away your daughters from me, and all my possessions."

32 And Jacob said, "With whomever you shall find your gods, he shall not live in the presence of our brothers; take notice of what I have of your property, and take it"; and he observed nothing with him, but Jacob did not know that his wife Rachel had stolen them.

33 And Laban went in and searched in the house of Leah, and did not found *them*; and he went out of the house of Leah, and searched in the house of Jacob, and in the house of the two maid-servants, and did not found *them*; and he went also into the house of Rachel.

34 And Rachel took the idols, and cast them among the camel's packs, and sat upon them.

35 And she said to her father, "Do not be angry, Sir; I cannot rise up before you, for it is with me according to the manner of women." Laban searched in all the house, and did not find the images.

36 And Jacob was angry, and contended with Laban; and Jacob answered and said to Laban, "What is my injustice, and what *is* my sin, that you have pursued after me,

37 and that you have searched all the furniture of my house? What have you found of all the furniture of your house? Set it here between your relations and my relations, and let them decide between us two.

38 These twenty years have I been with you; your sheep, and your female goats have not failed in bearing; and I have not eaten the rams of your cattle.

39 That which was torn of beasts I did not bring to you; I made good of myself the thefts of the day, and the thefts of the night.

40 I was parched with heat by day, and *chilled* with frost by night, and my sleep departed from my eyes.

41 These twenty years have I been in your house; I served you fourteen years for your two daughters, and six years among your sheep, and you falsely changed my wages for ten lambs.

42 Unless the God of my father, the God of Abraham and the Fear of Isaac, had been with me, surely now you would have sent me away empty-handed; *but* God saw my humiliation, and the labor of my hands, and rebuked you yesterday."

Laban's Covenant with Jacob

43 And Laban answered and said to Jacob, "The daughters are my daughters, and the sons my sons, and the cattle are my cattle, and all things which you see are mine, and *the property* of my daughters; what shall I do to them today, or their children which they bore?

44 Now then come, let me make a covenant, both you and I, and it shall be for a witness between me and you"; and he said to him, "Behold, there is no one with us; behold, God is witness between me and you."

45 And Jacob, having taken a stone, set it up for a pillar.

46 And Jacob said to his kinsmen, "Gather stones"; and they gathered stones and made a heap, and ate there upon the heap; and Laban said to him, "This heap witnesses between me and you this day."

47 And Laban called it, the Heap of Testimony; and Jacob called it, the Witness Heap.

48 And Laban said to Jacob, "Behold this heap, and the pillar, which I have set between me and you; this heap witnesses, and this pillar witnesses; therefore its name was called, The Heap Witnesses.

49 And the vision of which he said, Let God look to it between me and you, because we are about to depart from each other.

50 If you shall humble my daughters, if you should take wives in addition to my daughters, see, there is no one with us looking on. God is witness between me and you."

51 And Laban said to Jacob, "Behold, this heap and this pillar are a witness.

⁵² For if I should not cross over unto you, neither should you cross over to me, for mischief beyond this heap and this pillar.

⁵³ The God of Abraham and the God of Nahor judge between us"; and Jacob swore by the Fear of his father Isaac.

⁵⁴ And he offered a sacrifice in the mountain, and called his kinsmen, and they ate and drank, and slept in the mountain.

⁵⁵ And Laban rose up in the morning, and kissed his sons and his daughters, and blessed them; and Laban, having turned back, departed to his place.

GENESIS CHAPTER 32

Esau Comes to Meet Jacob

¹ And Jacob departed for his journey; and having looked up, he saw the host of God encamped; and the angels of God met him.

² And Jacob said, when he saw them, "This is the Camp of God"; and he called the name of that place, Encampments.

³ And Jacob sent messengers before him to Esau his brother to the land of Seir, to the country of Edom.

⁴ And he charged them, saying, "Thus shall you say to my lord Esau: Thus says your servant Jacob; 'I have sojourned with Laban and stayed there until now.

⁵ And there were born to me oxen, donkeys, sheep, male and female servants; and I sent to tell my lord Esau, that your servant might find grace in your sight.'"

⁶ And the messengers returned to Jacob, saying, "We came to your brother Esau, and behold, he is coming to meet you, and four hundred men with him."

⁷ And Jacob was greatly terrified, and was perplexed; and he divided the people that was with him, and the cows, and the camels, and the sheep, into two camps.

⁸ And Jacob said, "If Esau should come to one camp and strike it, the other camp shall be in safety."

⁹ And Jacob said, "God of my father Abraham, and God of my father Isaac, O Lord, You are He that said to me, 'Depart quickly to the land of your birth, and I will do you good.'

¹⁰ Let there be to me a sufficiency of all the justice and all the truth which You have wrought with Your servant; for with this my staff I passed over this Jordan, and now I have become two camps.

¹¹ Deliver me from the hand of my brother, from the hand of Esau, for I am afraid of him, lest he should come and attack me, and the mother with the children.

¹² But You said, 'I will do you good, and will make your descendants as the sand of the sea, which shall not be numbered for multitude.'"

¹³ And he slept there that night, and took of the gifts which he carried *with him*, and sent out to Esau his brother

¹⁴ two hundred female goats, twenty male goats, two hundred sheep, twenty rams,

¹⁵ thirty milk camels with their foals, forty cows, ten bulls, twenty donkeys, and ten colts.

¹⁶ And he delivered them to his servants, every drove by itself; and he said to his servants, "Go on before me, and put a space between successive droves."

¹⁷ And he charged the first, saying, "If Esau my brother meets you, and he asks you, saying, 'To whom do you belong? And where are you going, and whose are these possessions in front of you?'

¹⁸ You shall say, 'Your servant Jacob's; he has sent gifts to my lord Esau, and behold, he is behind us.'"

¹⁹ And he charged the first, the second, and the third, and all that went before him after these flocks, saying, "Thus shall you speak to Esau when you find him;

²⁰ and you shall say, 'Behold your servant Jacob comes after us.'" For he said, "I will appease him with the gifts going before his presence, and afterwards I will behold his face, perhaps he will accept me."

²¹ So the presents went on before him, but he himself lodged that night in the camp.

Jacob Wrestles with God

²² And he rose up in that night, and took his two wives and his two maids, and his eleven children, and crossed over the ford of Jabbok.

²³ And he took them, and passed over the brook, and brought over all his possessions.

²⁴ And Jacob was left alone; and a Man wrestled with him till the morning.

²⁵ And He saw that He did not prevail against him; and He touched the broad part of his thigh, and the broad part of Jacob's thigh was numbed in his wrestling with Him.

²⁶ And He said to him, "Let Me go, for the day has dawned"; but he said, "I will not let You go, except You bless me."

²⁷ And He said to him, "What is your name?" And he answered, "Jacob."

²⁸ And He said to him, "Your name shall no longer be called Jacob, but Israel shall be your name; for you have prevailed with God, and shall be mighty with men."

²⁹ And Jacob asked and said, "Tell me Your name"; and He said, "Why is it that you ask about My name?" And He blessed him there.

³⁰ And Jacob called the name of that place Peniel; for, *he said*, "I have seen God face to face, and my life was preserved."

³¹ And the sun rose upon him, when he passed Peniel; and he limped upon his thigh.

³² Therefore the children of Israel will by no means eat of the sinew which was numbed, which is on the broad part of the thigh, until this day, because *the Angel* touched the broad part of Jacob's thigh—*even* the sinew which was numbed.

GENESIS CHAPTER 33

Jacob and Esau Meet

1 And Jacob lifted up his eyes and beheld, and lo, Esau his brother *was* coming, and four hundred men with him. And Jacob divided the children to Leah and to Rachel, and the two maidservants.

2 And he put the two maidservants and their children with the first, and Leah and her children behind, and Rachel and Joseph last.

3 But he advanced himself before them, and bowed himself to the ground seven times, until he drew near to his brother.

4 And Esau ran on to meet him, and embraced him, and fell on his neck, and kissed him; and they both wept.

5 And Esau looked up and saw the women and the children, and said, "What are these to you?" And he said, "The children with which God has mercifully blessed your servant."

6 And the maidservants and their children drew near and bowed down.

7 And Leah and her children drew near and bowed down; and after Rachel and Joseph drew near, and bowed down.

8 And he said, "What are these things to you, all these companies that I have met?" And he said, "That your servant might find grace in your sight, my lord."

9 And Esau said, "I have much, my brother; keep your own."

10 And Jacob said, "If I have found grace in your sight, receive the gifts through my hands; therefore have I seen your face, as if anyone should see the face of God, and you shall be well-pleased with me.

11 Receive my blessings, which I have brought you, because God has had mercy on me, and I have all things"; and he urged him, and he took *them*.

12 And he said, "Let us depart, and proceed onward."

13 And he said to him, "My lord knows, that the children are very tender, and the flocks and the herds with me are with young; if then I shall drive them hard one day, all the cattle will die.

14 Let my lord go on before his servant, and I shall have strength on the road according to the ease of the journey before me, and according to the strength of the children, until I come to my lord to Seir."

15 And Esau said, "I will leave with you some of the people who are with me." And he said, "Why so? It is enough that I have found favor before you, my lord."

16 And Esau returned on that day on his journey to Seir.

17 And Jacob departed to his tents; and he made for himself a house there, and for his cattle he made booths; therefore he called the name of that place, Succoth.

18 And Jacob came to Salem, a city of Shechem, which is in the land of Canaan, when he departed out of Mesopotamia of Syria, and took up a position in front of the city.

19 And he bought the portion of the field, where he pitched his tent, of Hamor the father of Shechem, for a hundred lambs.

20 And he set up an altar there, and called on the God of Israel.

GENESIS CHAPTER 34

The Rape of Dinah

1 And Dinah, the daughter of Leah, whom she bore to Jacob, went forth to observe the daughters of the inhabitants.

2 And Shechem the son of Hamor the Hivite, the ruler of the land, saw her, he took her and lay with her, and violated her.

3 And he was strongly attracted to Dinah the daughter of Jacob, and he loved the young woman, and he spoke kindly to the young woman.

4 Shechem spoke to Hamor his father, saying, "Take for me this young woman for a wife."

5 And Jacob heard that the son of Hamor had defiled Dinah his daughter (now his sons were with his herds in the plain). And Jacob was silent until they came.

6 And Hamor the father of Shechem went out to Jacob, to speak with him.

7 And the sons of Jacob came from the plain; and when they heard, the men were deeply pained, and it was very grievous to them, because *the man* had done a disgraceful thing in Israel, having lain with the daughter of Jacob, which ought not to be done.

8 And Hamor spoke to them, saying, "Shechem my son has chosen your daughter in his heart; therefore give her to him for a wife,

9 and intermarry with us. Give us your daughters, and take our daughters for your sons.

10 And dwell in the midst of us; and behold, the land is spacious before you; dwell in it, and trade, and acquire possessions in it."

11 And Shechem said to her father and to her brothers, "I seek grace before you, and will give whatever you shall name.

12 Multiply *your demand of* dowry very much, and I will give accordingly as you shall say to me, only you shall give to me this young woman for a wife."

13 And the sons of Jacob answered to Shechem and Hamor his father craftily, and spoke to them, because they had defiled Dinah their sister.

14 And Simeon and Levi, the brothers of Dinah, said to them, "We shall not be able to do this thing, to give our sister to a man who is uncircumcised, for it is a reproach to us.

15 Only on these terms will we conform to you, and dwell among you, if you also will be as we are, in that every male of you be circumcised.

16 And we will give our daughters to you, and we will take of your daughters for wives to us, and we will dwell with you, and we will be as one race.

17 But if you will not heed us and be circumcised, we will take our daughter and depart."

¹⁸ And the words pleased Hamor and Shechem, Hamor's son.

¹⁹ And the young man did not delay to do this thing, for he was much attached to Jacob's daughter, and he was the most honorable of all in his father's house.

²⁰ And Hamor and Shechem his son came to the gate of their city, and spoke to the men of their city, saying,

²¹ "These men are peaceable, let them dwell with us upon the land, and let them trade in it, and behold the land is extensive before them; we will take their daughters to us for wives, and we will give them our daughters.

²² Only on these terms will the men conform to us to dwell with us so as to be one people, if every male of us be circumcised, as they also are circumcised.

²³ And shall not their cattle and their herds, and their possessions, be ours? Only in this let us conform to them, and they will dwell with us."

²⁴ And all that went in at the gate of their city hearkened to Hamor and Shechem his son, and they were circumcised in the flesh of their foreskin, every male.

Dinah's Brothers Avenge Their Sister

²⁵ And it came to pass on the third day, when they were in pain, that the two sons of Jacob, Simeon and Levi, Dinah's brothers, each man took his sword, and came upon the city securely, and killed every male.

²⁶ And they killed Hamor and Shechem his son with the edge of the sword, and took Dinah out of the house of Shechem, and went forth.

²⁷ But the sons of Jacob came upon the wounded, and ravaged the city in which they had defiled Dinah their sister.

²⁸ And they took their sheep, their oxen, and their donkeys, and all things that were in the city, and were in the plain.

²⁹ And they took captive all their people, and all their store, and their wives, and plundered both whatever things there were in the city, and whatever things there were in the houses.

³⁰ And Jacob said to Simeon and Levi, "You have made me hateful so that I should be evil to all the inhabitants of the land, both among the Canaanites and the Perizzites, and I am few in number; they will gather themselves against me and cut me in pieces, and I shall be utterly destroyed, and my house."

³¹ And they said, "No, but shall they treat our sister as a harlot?"

GENESIS CHAPTER 35

Jacob Returns to Bethel

¹ And God said to Jacob, "Arise, go up to Bethel, and dwell there; and make there an altar to the God that appeared to you, when you fled from the face of Esau your brother."

² And Jacob said to his house, and to all that were with him, "Remove the foreign gods that are with you from the midst of you, and purify yourselves, and change your clothes.

³ And let us rise and go up to Bethel, and let us there make an altar to God who listened to me in the day of calamity, who was with me, and preserved me throughout in the journey, by which I went."

⁴ And they gave to Jacob the foreign gods, which were in their hands, and the earrings which were in their ears, and Jacob hid them under the terebinth tree which is in Shechem, and destroyed them to this day.

⁵ So Israel departed from Shechem, and the fear of God was upon the cities round about them, and they did not pursue after the children of Israel.

⁶ And Jacob came to Luz, which is in the land of Canaan, which is Bethel, he and all the people that were with him.

⁷ And he built there an altar, and called the name of the place Bethel; for there God appeared to him, when he fled from the face of his brother Esau.

⁸ And Deborah, Rebecca's nurse, died, and was buried below Bethel under the oak; and Jacob called its name, The Oak of Mourning.

⁹ And God appeared to Jacob once more in Luz, when he came out of Mesopotamia of Syria, and God blessed him.

¹⁰ And God said to him, "Your name shall not be called Jacob, but Israel shall be your name"; and He called his name Israel.

¹¹ And God said to him, "I am your God; be fruitful and multiply; for nations and gatherings of nations shall proceed from you, and kings shall come out of your loins.

¹² And the land which I gave to Abraham and Isaac, I have given to you; and it shall come to pass that I will give this land also to your descendants after you."

¹³ And God went up from him from the place where He spoke with him.

¹⁴ And Jacob set up a pillar in the place where God spoke with him, *even* a pillar of stone; and offered a drink offering upon it, and poured oil upon it.

¹⁵ And Jacob called the name of the place in which God spoke with him, Bethel.

The Death of Rachel

¹⁶ (And Jacob journeyed from Bethel, and pitched his tent beyond the tower of Gader,) and it came to pass when he drew near to Habratha, to enter into Ephratha, Rachel labored *in childbirth*; and she had hard labor.

¹⁷ And it came to pass in her hard labor, that the midwife said to her, "Be of good courage, for you shall also have this son."

¹⁸ And it came to pass in her giving up the ghost (for she was dying), that she called his name, The son of my pain; but his father called his name Benjamin.

¹⁹ So Rachel died, and was buried in the way of the course of Ephratha, (that is, Bethlehem.)

²⁰ And Jacob set up a pillar on her tomb; this is the pillar on the tomb of Rachel, until this day.

²¹ (This verse omitted in LXX)

22 And it came to pass when Israel dwelt in that land, that Reuben went and lay with Bilhah, the concubine of his father Jacob; and Israel heard, and the thing appeared grievous before him.

Jacob's Twelve Sons

Now the sons of Jacob were twelve:

23 The sons of Leah *were* Reuben, Jacob's firstborn; Simeon, Levi, Judah, Issachar, and Zebulun.

24 And the sons of Rachel *were* Joseph and Benjamin.

25 And the sons of Bilhah, Rachel's maidservant, *were* Dan and Naphtali.

26 And the sons of Zilpah, Leah's maidservant, *were* Gad and Asher. These are the sons of Jacob, which were born to him in Mesopotamia of Syria.

The Death of Isaac

27 And Jacob came to Isaac his father, to Mamre, to a city of the plain; this is Hebron in the land of Canaan, where Abraham and Isaac sojourned.

28 And the days of Isaac which he lived were one hundred and eighty years.

29 And Isaac gave up the ghost and died, and was gathered to his people, old and full of days; and Esau and Jacob his sons buried him.

GENESIS CHAPTER 36

The Descendants of Esau

1 And these are the generations of Esau, who is Edom.

2 And Esau took to himself wives of the daughters of the Canaanites; Adah, the daughter of Elon the Hittite; and Oholibamah, daughter of Anah, the son of Zibeon, the Hivite;

3 and Basemath, daughter of Ishmael, sister of Nabajoth.

4 And Adah bore to him Eliphaz; and Basemath bore Reuel.

5 And Oholibamah bore Jeush, Jaalam, and Korah; these are the sons of Esau, which were born to him in the land of Canaan.

6 And Esau took his wives, and his sons, and his daughters, and all the persons of his house, and all his possessions, and all his cattle, and all that he had gotten, and all things whatsoever that he had acquired in the land of Canaan; and Esau went forth from the land of Canaan, from the face of his brother Jacob.

7 For their possessions were too great for them to dwell together; and the land of their sojourning could not bear them, because of the abundance of their possessions.

8 And Esau dwelt in Mount Seir; Esau is Edom.

9 And these are the generations of Esau, the father of the Edomites in Mount Seir.

10 And these are the names of the sons of Esau: Eliphaz, the son of Adah, the wife of Esau; and Reuel, the son of Basemath, wife of Esau.

11 And the sons of Eliphaz were Teman, Omar, Zepho, Gatam, and Kenaz.

12 And Timna was a concubine of Eliphaz, the son of Esau; and she bore Amalek to Eliphaz. These are the sons of Adah, the wife of Esau.

13 And these are the sons of Reuel; Nahath, Zerah, Shammah, and Mizzah. These were the sons of Basemath, wife of Esau.

14 And these are the sons of Oholibamah, the daughter of Anah, the son of Sebegon, the wife of Esau; and she bore to Esau: Jeush, Jaalam, and Korah.

15 These are the chiefs of the son of Esau, even the sons of Eliphaz, the firstborn of Esau; Chief Teman, Chief Omar, Chief Zepho, Chief Kenaz,

16 Chief Korah, Chief Gatam, and Chief Amalek. These are the chiefs of Eliphaz, in the land of Edom; these are the sons of Adah.

17 And these are the sons of Reuel, the son of Esau: Chief Nahath, Chief Zerah, Chief Shammah, and Chief Mizzah. These are the chiefs of Reuel, in the land of Edom; these are the sons of Basemath, wife of Esau.

18 And these are the sons of Oholibamah, wife of Esau; Chief Jeush, Chief Jaalam, and Chief Korah. These are the chiefs of Oholibamah, daughter of Anah, wife of Esau.

19 These are the sons of Esau, who is Edom, and these are the chiefs. .

20 And these are the sons of Seir, the Horite, who inhabited the land: Lotan, Shobal, Zibeon, Anah,

21 Dishon, Ezer, and Dishan. These are the chiefs of the Horites, the son of Seir, in the land of Edom.

22 And the sons of Lotan were Hori and Heman; and the sister of Lotan was Timna.

23 And these are the sons of Shobal: Alvan, Manahath, Ebal, Shepho, and Onam.

24 And these are the sons of Zibeon: Ajah, and Anah; this is the Anah who found Jamin in the wilderness, when he tended the beasts of his father Zibeon.

25 And these are the children of Anah: Dishon and Oholibamah the daughter of Anah.

26 And these are the sons of Dishon: Hemdan, Eshban, Ithran, and Cheran.

27 And these are the sons of Ezer: Bilhan, Zaavan, and Akan.

28 And these are the sons of Dishan: Uz and Aran.

29 And these are the chiefs of Horri: Chief Lotan, Chief Shobai, Chief Zibeon, Chief Anah,

30 Chief Dishon, Chief Ezer, and Chief Dishon. These are the chiefs of Horri, in their principalities in the land of Edom.

31 Now these are the kings which reigned in Edom, before a king reigned in Israel:

32 Bela, son of Beor reigned in Edom; and the name of his city was Dinhabah.

33 And Bela died; and Jobab, son of Zerah, from Bozrah reigned in his place.

[34] When Jobab died, Husham, from the land of the Temanites reigned in his place.

[35] And when Husham died, Hadad son of Bedad, who cut off Midian in the plain of Moab, ruled in his place; and the name of his city was Avith.

[36] When Hadad died, Samlah of Masrekah reigned in his place.

[37] And when Samlah died, Saul of Rehoboth-by-the River reigned in his place.

[38] When Saul died, Baal-Hanan the son of Achbor reigned in his place.

[39] And when Baal-Hanan the son of Achbor died, Hadar the son of Barad reigned in his place; and the name of his city was Pau; and the name of his wife was Mehetabel, daughter of Matred, son of Mezahab.

[40] These are the names of the chiefs of Esau, in their tribes, according to their place, in their countries, and in their nations; Chief Timnah, Chief Alvah, Chief Jetheth,

[41] Chief Oholibamah, Chief Elah, Chief Pinon,

[42] Chief Kenaz, Chief Teman, Chief Mibzar,

[43] Chief Magdiel, and Chief Iram. These are the chiefs of Edom in their dwelling places in the land of their possession; this is Esau, the father of Edom.

GENESIS CHAPTER 37

Joseph's Dream of Greatness

[1] And Jacob dwelt in the land where his father sojourned, in the land of Canaan.

[2] And these are the generations of Jacob. And Joseph was seventeen years old, feeding the sheep of his father with his brothers, being young; with the sons of Bilhah, and with the sons of Zilpah, the wives of his father; and Joseph brought a bad report of them to Israel their father.

[3] And Jacob loved Joseph more than all his sons, because he was to him the son of his old age; and he made for him a coat of many colors.

[4] And his brothers, seeing that his father loved him more than all his sons, hated him, and could not speak anything peaceable to him.

[5] And Joseph dreamed a dream, and told it to his brothers.

[6] And he said to them, "Hear this dream which I have dreamed.

[7] I thought you were binding sheaves in the middle of the field, and my sheaf stood up and was erected, and your sheaves turned round, and bowed down to my sheaf."

[8] And his brothers said to him, "Shall you indeed reign over us, or shall you indeed be lord over us?" And they hated him all the more for his dreams and for his words.

[9] And he dreamed another dream, and told it to his father, and to his brothers, and said, "Behold, I have dreamed another dream: and this time, the sun and the moon and the eleven stars bowed down to me."

[10] And his father rebuked him, and said to him, "What is this dream which you have dreamed? Shall indeed both I and your mother and your brothers come and bow before you to the earth?"

[11] And his brothers envied him; but his father observed the saying.

Joseph Sold by His Brothers

[12] And his brothers went to feed the sheep of their father in Shechem.

[13] And Israel said to Joseph, "Do not your brothers feed their flock in Shechem? Come, I will send you to them"; and he said to him, Behold, I *am here*.

[14] And Israel said to him, "Go and see if your brothers and the sheep are well, and bring me word." So he sent him out of the valley of Hebron, and he came to Shechem.

[15] And a man found him wandering in the field; and the man asked him, saying, "What are you seeking?"

[16] And he said, "I am seeking my brothers; tell me where they feed *their flocks.*"

[17] And the man said to him, "They have departed from here, for I heard them saying, Let us go to Dothan"; and Joseph went after his brothers, and found them in Dothan.

[18] And they spied him from a distance before he came near them, and they wickedly took counsel to kill him.

[19] And each said to his brother, "Look, here comes that dreamer!

[20] Now then come, let us kill him, and cast him into one of the pits; and we will say, 'An evil wild beast has devoured him'; and we shall see what his dreams will be."

[21] And Reuben, having heard it, rescued him out of their hands, and said, "Let us not kill him."

[22] And Reuben said to them, "Shed no blood; cast him into one of these pits in the wilderness, but do not lay *your* hand upon him; that he might rescue him out of their hands, and restore him to his father."

[23] And it came to pass, when Joseph came to his brothers, that they stripped Joseph of his tunic that was upon him, *the tunic* of many colors.

[24] And they took him and cast him into the pit; and the pit was empty, it had no water.

[25] And they sat down to eat bread. And having lifted up their eyes they beheld, and lo, Ishmaelite travelers came from Gilead, and their camels were heavily loaded with spices, and resin, and myrrh; and they were on their way to bring them to Egypt.

[26] And Judah said to his brothers, "What profit is it if we slay our brother, and conceal his blood?

[27] Come, let us sell him to these Ishmaelites, but let not our hands be upon him, because he is our brother and our flesh"; and his brothers listened.

[28] And the men, the merchants of Midian, went by, and they reached down and lifted Joseph out of the pit, and sold Joseph to the Ishmaelites for twenty pieces of gold; and they brought Joseph down into Egypt.

[29] And Reuben returned to the pit, and did not see Joseph in the pit; and he tore his clothes.

[30] And he returned to his brothers and said, "The boy is no *more*; and I, where shall I go?"

[31] And having taken the coat of Joseph, they killed a kid of the goats, and stained the coat with the blood.

[32] And they sent the coat of many colors, and they brought it to their father, and said, "We have found this: Do you know if it is your son's coat or not?"

[33] And he recognized it, and said, "It is my son's coat, an evil wild beast has devoured him; a wild beast has carried off Joseph."

[34] And Jacob tore his clothes, and put sackcloth on his loins, and mourned for his son many days.

[35] And all his sons and his daughters gathered themselves together, and came to comfort him; but he would not be comforted, saying, "I will go down to my son mourning to Hades"; and his father wept for him.

[36] And the Midianites sold Joseph into Egypt; to Potiphar, Pharaoh's eunuch, the captain of the guard.

GENESIS CHAPTER 38

Judah and Tamar

[1] And it came to pass at that time, that Judah went down from his brothers, and came as far as to a certain man of Adullam, whose name was Hirah.

[2] And Judah saw there the daughter of a Canaanite man, whose name was Shua; and he took her, and went in to her.

[3] And she conceived and bore a son, and called his name Er.

[4] And she conceived and bore a son again, and called his name Onan.

[5] And she again bore a son, and called his name Shelah; and she was in Chezib when she bore them.

[6] And Judah took a wife for Er his firstborn, whose name was Tamar.

[7] And Er, the firstborn of Judah, was wicked before the Lord; and God killed him.

[8] And Judah said to Onan, "Go in to your brother's wife, and marry her as her brother-in-law, and raise up descendants to your brother."

[9] And Onan, knowing that the descendants would not be his—and it came to pass when he went in to his brother's wife, that he spilled it upon the ground, so that he should not give seed to his brother's wife.

[10] And his doing this appeared evil before God; and He killed him also.

[11] And Judah said to Tamar, his daughter-in-law, "Remain a widow in the house of your father-in-law, until Shelah my son is grown"; for he said, "lest he also die as his brothers"; and Tamar departed, and sat in the house of her father.

[12] And the days were fulfilled, and Shua, Judah's wife, died; and Judah, being comforted, went to them that sheared his sheep, himself and Hirah the Adullamite, to Timna.

[13] And it was told Tamar his daughter-in-law, saying, Behold, your father-in-law is going up to Timna, to shear his sheep.

[14] And having taken off the garments of her widowhood from her, she put on a veil, and adorned her face, and sat by the gates of Aenan, which is in the way to Timna, for she saw that Shelah was grown; but she was not given to him as a wife.

[15] And when Judah saw her, he thought her to be a harlot; for she covered her face, and he did not recognize her.

[16] And he went out of his way to her, and said to her, "Let me come in to you." (For he did not know that she was his daughter-in-law). And she said, "What will you give me if you should come in to me?"

[17] And he said, "I will send you a kid of the goats from my flock." And she said, "Well, if you will give me a pledge, until you send it."

[18] And he said, "What is the pledge that I shall give you?" And she said, "Your ring, and your bracelet, and the staff in your hand." And he gave them to her, and went in to her, and she conceived by him.

[19] And she arose and departed, and took off her veil, and put on the garments of her widowhood.

[20] And Judah sent the kid of the goats by the hand of his shepherd the Adullamite, to receive the pledge from the woman; but he did not find her.

[21] And he asked the men of the place, "Where is the harlot who was in Aenan by the way side?" And they said, "There was no harlot here."

[22] And he returned to Judah, and said, "I have not found her; and the men of the place say, There is no harlot here."

[23] And Judah said, "Let her have them, but let us not be ridiculed; I sent this kid, but you have not found her."

[24] And it came to pass after three months, that it was told Judah, saying, "Tamar your daughter-in-law has grievously played the harlot, and behold she is with child by harlotry." And Judah said, "Bring her out, and let her be burned."

[25] And as they were bringing her, she sent to her father-in-law, saying, "I am with child by the man whose these things are." And she said, "See whose ring this is, and bracelet and staff."

[26] And Judah acknowledged them, and said, "Tamar is more righteous than I, because I did not give her to Shelah my son"; and he never knew her again.

[27] And it came to pass when she was in labor, that she also had twins in her womb.

[28] And it came to pass as she was bringing forth, one thrust forth his hand, and the midwife, having taken hold of it, bound upon his hand a scarlet thread, saying, "This one shall come out first."

[29] And when he drew back his hand, then immediately came forth his brother; and she said, "Why has the barrier been cut through because of you?" And she called his name Perez.

30 And after this came forth his brother, on whose hand was the scarlet thread; and she called his name Zerah.

GENESIS CHAPTER 39

Joseph a Slave in Egypt

1 And Joseph was brought down to Egypt. And Potiphar, Pharaoh's eunuch, the captain of the guard, an Egyptian, bought him from the hands of the Ishmaelites, who brought him down there.

2 And the Lord was with Joseph, and he was a prosperous man; and he was in the house with his master the Egyptian.

3 And his master knew that the Lord was with him, and that the Lord prospered in his hands all that he did.

4 And Joseph found grace in the presence of his master, and was well-pleasing to him; and he set him over his house; and all that he had, he gave into the hand of Joseph.

5 And it came to pass after that he was set over his house, and over all that he had, that the Lord blessed the house of the Egyptian for Joseph's sake; and the blessing of the Lord was on all his possessions in the house, and in his field.

6 And he committed all that he had into the hands of Joseph; and he knew not of anything that belonged to him, except the bread which he himself ate. And Joseph was handsome in form, and exceedingly beautiful in countenance.

7 And it came to pass after these things, that his master's wife cast her eyes upon Joseph, and said, "Lie with me."

8 But he would not; but said to his master's wife, "If because of me my master knows nothing in his house, and has given into my hands all things that belong to him;

9 and in this house there is nothing above me, nor has anything been kept back from me, but you, because you are his wife—how then shall I do this wicked thing, and sin against God?"

10 So it was, as she talked with Joseph day by day, that he did not heed her, to sleep with her, or to be with her.

11 But it came to pass on a certain day, that Joseph went into the house to do his business, and there was no one of the household inside.

12 And she caught hold of him by his clothes, and said, "Lie with me." And having left his clothes in her hands, he fled, and ran outside.

13 And it came to pass, when she saw that he had left his clothes in her hands and fled, and ran outside,

14 that she called those that were of her house, and spoke to them, saying, "See, he has brought in to us a Hebrew servant to mock us—he came in to me, saying, 'Lie with me,' and I cried with a loud voice.

15 And when he heard that I lifted up my voice and cried, having left his clothes with me, he fled, and went outside."

16 So she left his clothes by her, until his master came home.

17 And she spoke to him according to these words, saying, "The Hebrew servant, whom you brought in to us, came in to me to mock me, and said to me, 'I will lie with you.'

18 And when he heard that I lifted up my voice and cried, having left his clothes with me, he fled outside."

19 And it came to pass, when his master heard all the words of his wife, that she spoke to him, saying, "Thus did your servant to me," that he was very angry.

20 And his master took Joseph, and cast him into the prison, into the place where *all* the king's prisoners are kept. *And he was* there in the prison.

21 And the Lord was with Joseph, and poured down mercy upon him; and He gave him favor in the sight of the chief keeper of the prison.

22 And the chief keeper of the prison gave the prison into the hand of Joseph, and all the prisoners, as many as were in the prison; and all things whatsoever they do there, he did them.

23 Because of him the chief keeper of the prison knew nothing, for all things were in the hands of Joseph, because the Lord was with him; and whatever things he did, the Lord made them to prosper in his hands.

GENESIS CHAPTER 40

The Prisoners' Dreams

1 And it came to pass after these things, that the chief cupbearer of the king of Egypt and the chief baker trespassed against their lord, the king of Egypt.

2 And Pharaoh was angry with his two eunuchs, with his chief cupbearer, and with his chief baker.

3 So he put them in custody, into the prison, into the place where Joseph was confined.

4 And the chief keeper of the prison committed them to Joseph, and he served them; and they were some days in the prison.

5 And they both had a dream in one night; and the vision of the dream of the chief cupbearer and chief baker, who belonged to the king of Egypt, who were in the prison, was this:

6 Joseph went in to them in the morning, and saw them, and they had been troubled.

7 So he asked the eunuchs of Pharaoh who were with him in the prison with his master, saying, "Why is it that you look so sad today?"

8 And they said to him, "We have seen a dream, and there is no interpreter of it." And Joseph said to them, "Is not the interpretation of them with God? Therefore tell them to me."

9 And the chief cupbearer related his dream to Joseph, and said, "In my dream a vine was before me.

10 And in the vine were three stems; and its budding shot forth blossoms; the clusters of grapes were ripe.

11 And the cup of Pharaoh was in my hand; and I took the bunch of grapes, and squeezed it into the cup, and gave the cup into Pharaoh's hand."

12 And Joseph said to him, "This is the interpretation of it. The three stems are three days.

13 Yet three days and Pharaoh shall remember your position, and he shall restore you to your place of chief cupbearer, and you shall give Pharaoh's cup into his hand, according to your former high place, as you were his cupbearer.

14 But remember me when it is well with you, and you shall deal mercifully with me, and you shall make mention of me to Pharaoh, and you shall bring me forth out of this dungeon.

15 For surely I was stolen away out of the land of the Hebrews, and here I have done nothing, but they have cast me into this pit."

16 And the chief baker saw that he interpreted correctly; and he said to Joseph, "I also saw a dream, and *in it* I took up on my head three baskets of bread.

17 And in the upper basket there was the work of the baker of every kind *of bread* which Pharaoh eats; and the birds of the air ate them out of the basket that was on my head."

18 And Joseph answered and said to him, "This is the interpretation of it; The three baskets are three days.

19 Yet three days, and Pharaoh shall lift up your head from off you, and shall hang you from a tree, and the birds of the sky shall eat your flesh from off of you."

20 And it came to pass on the third day that it was Pharaoh's birthday, and he made a banquet for all his servants, and he remembered the office of the cupbearer and the office of the baker in the midst of his servants.

21 And he restored the chief cupbearer to his office, and he gave the cup into Pharaoh's hand.

22 And he hanged the chief baker, as Joseph interpreted to them.

23 Yet the chief cupbearer did not remember Joseph, but forgot him.

GENESIS CHAPTER 41

Pharaoh's Dreams

1 And it came to pass after two full years that Pharaoh had a dream. He thought he stood upon *the bank of* the river.

2 And behold, there came up out of the river seven cows, fair in appearance, and choice of flesh, and they fed in the meadow.

3 Then behold, seven other cows came up after these out of the river, ill-favored and lean-fleshed, and fed by the other cows on the bank of the river.

4 And the seven ill-favored and lean cows devoured the seven well-favored and choice-fleshed cows. So Pharaoh awoke.

5 And he dreamed again. And behold, seven heads of grain came up on one stalk, choice and good.

6 And behold, seven thin heads, blasted by the wind, grew up after them.

7 And the seven thin heads blasted with the wind devoured the seven choice and full heads. And Pharaoh awoke, and indeed, it was a dream.

8 And it was morning, and his soul was troubled. And he sent and called all the interpreters of Egypt, and all the wise men; and Pharaoh related to them his dream, and there was no one to interpret it to Pharaoh.

9 And the chief cupbearer spoke to Pharaoh, saying, "This day I remember my fault:

10 when Pharaoh was angry with his servants, and put us in prison in the house of the captain of the guard, both me and the chief baker.

11 And we both had a dream in one night, *both* he and I; we saw, each according to his dream.

12 And there was there with us a young man, a Hebrew servant of the captain of the guard; and we related to him *our dreams*, and he interpreted *them* to us.

13 And it came to pass, as he interpreted them to us, so also it happened, both that I was restored to my office, and that he was hanged."

14 And Pharaoh, having sent, called Joseph; and they brought him out from the prison, and shaved him, and changed his clothes, and he came to Pharaoh.

15 And Pharaoh said to Joseph, "I have seen a vision, and there is no one to interpret it; but I have heard it said concerning you that you can hear dreams and interpret them."

16 And Joseph answered Pharaoh and said, "Without God an answer of safety shall not be given to Pharaoh."

17 And Pharaoh spoke to Joseph, saying, "In my dream, I stood by the bank of the river.

18 Suddenly seven cows came up out of the river, well-favored and choice-fleshed, and they fed in the meadow.

19 And behold, seven other cows came up after them out of the river, evil and ill-favored and lean-fleshed, such that I never saw worse in all the land of Egypt.

20 And the seven ill-favored and thin cows ate up the seven first good and choice cows.

21 And they went into their bellies; and it was not perceptible that they had gone into their bellies, and their appearance was ill-favored, as also at the beginning. And after I awoke, I slept,

22 and I saw again in my sleep, and seven heads came up on one stem, full and good.

23 Then behold, seven heads, thin and blasted with the wind, sprang up close to them.

24 And the seven thin and blasted heads devoured the seven fine and full heads: so I spoke to the interpreters, and there was no one to explain it to me."

25 And Joseph said to Pharaoh, "The dream of Pharaoh is one; God has shown Pharaoh what He is about to do.

26 The seven good cows are seven years, and the seven good heads are seven years; the dream of Pharaoh is one.

27 And the seven thin cows that came up after them are seven years; and the seven thin and blasted heads are seven years; there shall be seven years of famine.

28 And as for the word which I have told Pharaoh, God has shown Pharaoh what He is about to do.

29 Behold, for seven years there is coming great plenty in all the land of Egypt.

30 But there shall come seven years of famine after these, and they shall forget the plenty that shall be in all Egypt, and the famine shall consume the land.

31 And the plenty shall not be known in the land by reason of the famine that shall be after this, for it shall be very grievous.

32 And concerning the repetition of the dream to Pharaoh twice, it is because the saying which is from God shall be true, and God will hasten to accomplish it.

33 Now then, select a wise and prudent man, and set him over the land of Egypt.

34 And let Pharaoh make and appoint local governors over the land; and let them take up a fifth part of all the produce of the land of Egypt for the seven years of the plenty.

35 And let them gather all the food of these seven good years that are coming, and let the grain be gathered under the hand of Pharaoh; let food be kept in the cities.

36 And the stored food shall be for the land against the seven years of famine, which shall be in the land of Egypt; and the land shall not be utterly destroyed by the famine."

Joseph's Rise to Power

37 And the word was pleasing in the sight of Pharaoh, and in the sight of all his servants.

38 And Pharaoh said to all his servants, "Shall we find such a man as this, who has the Spirit of God in him?"

39 And Pharaoh said to Joseph, "Since God has shown you all these things, there is not a wiser or more prudent man than you. 40 You shall be over my house, and all my people shall be obedient to your word; only in the throne will I excel you."

41 And Pharaoh said to Joseph, "Behold, I set you this day over all the land of Egypt."

42 And Pharaoh took his ring off his hand, and put it on the hand of Joseph, and put on him a robe of fine linen, and put a necklace of gold about his neck.

43 And he mounted him on the second of his chariots, and a herald made proclamation before him; and he set him over all the land of Egypt.

44 And Pharaoh said to Joseph, "I am Pharaoh; without you no one shall lift up his hand on all the land of Egypt."

45 And Pharaoh called the name of Joseph Zaphnath-Paaneah; and he gave him Asenath, the daughter of Poti-Pherah, priest of Heliopolis, as a wife.

46 And Joseph was thirty years old when he stood before Pharaoh, king of Egypt. And Joseph went out from the presence of Pharaoh, and went through all the land of Egypt.

47 And the land produced, in the seven years of plenty, *whole* handfuls *of grain*.

48 And he gathered all the food of the seven years, in which was the plenty in the land of Egypt; and he laid up the food in the cities; the food of the fields of a city round about it he laid up in it.

49 And Joseph gathered very much grain as the sand of the sea, until it could not be numbered, for there was no number of it.

50 And to Joseph were born two sons, before the seven years of famine came, which Asenath, the daughter of Poti-Pherah, priest of Heliopolis, bore to him.

51 And Joseph called the name of the firstborn, Manasseh; "For God," *he said*, "has made me forget all my toils, and all my father's house."

52 And he called the name of the second, Ephraim; "For God," *he said*, "has increased me in the land of my humiliation."

53 And the seven years of plenty passed away, which were in the land of Egypt.

54 And the seven years of famine began to come, as Joseph said; and there was a famine in all the land; but in all the land of Egypt there was bread.

55 And all the land of Egypt was hungry; and the people cried to Pharaoh for bread. And Pharaoh said to all the Egyptians, "Go to Joseph, and do whatever he shall say to you."

56 And the famine was upon the face of the whole earth; and Joseph opened all the granaries, and sold to all the Egyptians.

57 And all countries came to Egypt to buy from Joseph, for the famine prevailed in all the earth.

GENESIS CHAPTER 42

Joseph's Brothers Go to Egypt

1 And Jacob, having seen that there was a sale *of grain* in Egypt, said to his sons, "Why do look at one another?

2 Behold, I have heard that there is grain in Egypt; now go down there, and buy for us a little food, that we may live, and not die!"

3 And the ten brothers of Joseph went down to buy grain out of Egypt.

4 But Jacob did not send Joseph's brother Benjamin with his brothers; for he said, "Lest some calamity befall him."

5 And the sons of Israel came to buy with those that journeyed, for the famine was in the land of Canaan.

6 Now Joseph was ruler over the land; and he sold to all the people of the land. And the brothers of Joseph, having come, bowed down to him, with their faces to the ground.

7 And when Joseph saw his brothers, he knew them, and estranged himself from them, and spoke harsh words to them; and said to them, "Where do you come from?" And they said, "Out of the land of Canaan, to buy food."

8 And Joseph knew his brothers, but they did not know him.

9 And Joseph remembered his dream, which he saw; and he said to them, "You are spies! You have come to see the exposed parts of the land!"

10 But they said, "No, my lord, we your servants have come to buy food;

11 we are all sons of one man; we are peaceable; your servants are not spies."

12 And he said to them, "No, but you have come to see the exposed parts of the land."

13 And they said, "We your servants are twelve brothers, in the land of Canaan; and, behold, the youngest is with our father today, but the other one is not."

14 And Joseph said to them, "This is what I mean when I spoke to you, saying, 'you are spies.'

15 In this manner shall you be tested; by the life of Pharaoh, you shall not depart from here, unless your younger brother comes here.

16 Send one of you, and take your brother; and you shall be kept in prison, until your words may be tested, whether you speak the truth or not; but, if not, by the life of Pharaoh, surely you are spies."

17 And he put them in prison for three days.

18 And he said to them on the third day, "Do this, and you shall live, for I fear God.

19 If you are peaceable, let one of your brothers be detained in prison; but go, and carry back the grain you have purchased.

20 And bring your younger brother to me, and your words shall be believed; but, if not, you shall die." And they did so.

21 And each said to his brother, "Yes indeed, for we are to blame concerning our brother, when we disregarded the anguish of his soul, when he pleaded with us, and we would not hear him; therefore has this affliction come upon us."

22 And Reuben answered them, saying, "Did I not speak to you, saying, 'Do not hurt the boy, and you would not listen? Therefore behold, his blood is now required of us."

23 But they did not know that Joseph understood them; for there was an interpreter between them.

24 And Joseph turned away from them and wept; and again he came to them, and spoke to them; and he took Simeon from them, and bound him before their eyes.

Joseph's Brothers Return to Canaan

25 And Joseph gave orders to fill their vessels with grain, and to return their money to each into his sack, and to give them provisions for the way; and it was so done to them.

26 And having put the grain on the donkeys, they departed from there.

27 And one *of them*, having opened his sack to feed his donkeys, at the place where they rested, saw also his bundle of money, for it was on the mouth of his sack.

28 And he said to his brothers, "My money has been restored to me, and behold it is in my sack!" And their hearts sank, and they were troubled, saying one to another, "What is this that God has done to us?"

29 And they came to their father Jacob, into the land of Canaan, and reported to him all that had happened to them, saying,

30 "The man, the lord of the land, spoke harshly to us, and put us in prison as spies of the land.

31 And we said to him, 'We are men of peace, we are not spies.

32 We are twelve brothers, sons of our father; one is not, and the youngest is with his father today in the land of Canaan.'

33 And the man, the lord of the land, said to us, 'By this shall I know that you are peaceable: leave one brother here with me, and having taken the grain you have purchased for your family, depart.

34 And bring to me your younger brother; then I shall know that you are not spies, but that you are men of peace; and I will restore you your brother, and you shall trade in the land.'"

35 And it came to pass as they were emptying their sacks, there was each man's bundle of money in his sack; and they and their father saw their bundles of money, and they were afraid.

36 And their father Jacob said to them, "You have bereaved me. Joseph is no *more*, Simeon is no *more*, and will you take Benjamin *as well*? All these things have come against me!"

37 And Reuben spoke to his father, saying, "Kill my two sons if I do not bring him *back* to you; give him into my hand, and I will bring him back to you."

38 But he said, "My son shall not go down with you, because his brother is dead, and only he has been left; and *suppose* it shall come to pass that he is afflicted by the way by which you go, then you shall bring down my old age with sorrow to Hades."

GENESIS CHAPTER 43

Joseph's Brothers Return with Benjamin

1 Now the famine prevailed in the land.

2 And it came to pass, when they had finished eating the grain which they had brought out of Egypt, that their father said to them, "Go again; buy us a little food."

3 And Judah spoke to him, saying, "The man, the lord of the country, positively testified to us, saying, 'You shall not see my face, unless your younger brother is with you.

4 If, then, you send our brother with us, we will go down, and buy you food;

5 but if you do not send our brother with us, we will not go: for the man spoke to us, saying, 'You shall not see my face, unless your younger brother is with you.'"

6 And Israel said, "Why did you harm me, inasmuch as you told the man that you had a brother?"

7 And they said, "The man closely questioned us about our family also, saying, 'Does your father yet live, and have you

a brother?' And we answered him according to this question: did we know that he would say to us, 'Bring your brother?'"

[8] And Judah said to his father Israel, "Send the boy with me, and we will arise and go, that we may live and not die, both we and you, and our store.

[9] And I myself will be a surety for him; at my hand you shall require him; if I do not bring him to you, and place him before you, I shall be guilty toward you forever.

[10] For if we had not lingered, we would have returned twice by now."

[11] And Israel their father said to them, "If it be so, do this; take of the fruits of the earth in your vessels, and carry down to the man presents of balm and honey, frankincense and myrrh, pistachio nuts and walnuts.

[12] And take double money in your hands, and the money that was returned in your sacks, carry back with you, lest perhaps it was a mistake.

[13] And take your brother; and arise, go down to the man.

[14] And may God give you favor in the sight of the man, and send away your other brother, and Benjamin, for I accordingly, as I have been bereaved, am bereaved."

[15] And the men, having taken these presents, and the double money, took Benjamin in their hands; and they rose up and went down to Egypt, and stood before Joseph.

[16] And Joseph saw them and his brother Benjamin, born of the same mother; and he said to the steward of his household, "Bring the men into the house, and slaughter an animal and make ready, for the men are to eat bread with me at noon."

[17] And the man did as Joseph said; and he brought the men into the house of Joseph.

[18] And the men, when they perceived that they were brought into the house of Joseph, said, "We have been brought in because of the money that was returned in our sacks in the beginning; to make a case against us, and lay it to our charge; to take us for servants, and our donkeys."

[19] And having approached the man who was over the house of Joseph, they spoke to him in the porch of the house,

[20] saying, "O Sir; we came down at first to buy food.

[21] And it came to pass, when we came to the encampment, that we opened our sacks; and *there*, in our sacks, *was* each man's money. We have now brought back our money, in full weight, in our hands.

[22] And we have brought other money with us to buy food; we know not who put the money into our sacks."

[23] And he said to them, "*God deal* mercifully with you; be not afraid; your God, and the God of your fathers, has given you treasures in your sacks, and I have enough of your good money." And he brought Simeon out to them.

[24] And he brought water to wash their feet, and gave feed to their donkeys.

[25] And they prepared their gifts, until Joseph came at noon, for they heard that he was going to dine there.

[26] And Joseph entered into the house, and they brought him the gifts which they had in their hands, into the house; and they bowed down before him with their faces to the ground.

[27] And he asked them, "How are you?" And he said to them, "Is your father, the old man of whom you spoke, well? Does he still live?"

[28] And they said, "Your servant our father is well; he is still alive." And he said, "Blessed be that man by God"—and they bowed, and prostrated themselves.

[29] And Joseph lifted up his eyes, and saw his brother Benjamin, born of the same mother; and he said, "Is this your younger brother, whom you spoke of bringing to me?" And he said, "God have mercy on you, my son."

[30] And Joseph was troubled, for his heart yearned over his brother, and he wanted to weep; and he went into his chamber, and wept there.

[31] And he washed his face and came out, and refrained himself, and said, "Set out bread."

[32] And they set out *bread* for him alone, and for them by themselves, and for the Egyptians feasting with him by themselves, for the Egyptians could not eat bread with the Hebrews, for it is an abomination to the Egyptians.

[33] And they sat before him, the firstborn according to his seniority, and the younger according to his youth; and the men looked with amazement, everyone at his brother.

[34] And they took their portions from him to themselves; but Benjamin's portion was five times as much as the portions of *the others*. And they drank and were merry with him.

GENESIS CHAPTER 44

Joseph Detains Benjamin

[1] And Joseph charged the manager of his house, saying, "Fill the men's sacks with food, as much as they can carry, and put the money of each in the mouth of his sack.

[2] And put my silver cup into the sack of the youngest, and the price of his grain." And it was done according to the word of Joseph, as he said.

[3] The morning dawned, and the men were sent away, they and their donkeys.

[4] And when they had gone out of the city, and were not far off, then Joseph said to his manager, "Arise, and pursue after the men; and you shall overtake them, and say to them, 'Why have you returned evil for good?

[5] Why have you stolen my silver cup? Is it not this out of which my lord drinks? And he practices divination with it. You have accomplished evil in that which you have done.'"

[6] And he found them, and spoke to them according to these words.

[7] And they said to him, "Why does our lord speak according to these words? Far be it from your servants to do according to this word!

[8] If we brought back to you out of the land of Canaan the money which we found in our sacks, why should we steal silver or gold out of the house of your lord?

9 With whomever of your servants you shall find the cup, let him die; and moreover, we will be servants to our lord."

10 And he said, "Now then it shall be as you say; with whomever the cup shall be found, he shall be my servant, and you shall be blameless."

11 And they made haste, and took down every man his sack on the ground, and they opened every man's sack.

12 And he searched, beginning from the eldest, until he came to the youngest; and he found the cup in Benjamin's sack.

13 And they tore their clothes, and laid each man's sack on his donkey, and returned to the city.

14 And Judah and his brothers came in to Joseph, while he was yet there, and fell on the ground before him.

15 And Joseph said to them, "What is this thing you have done? Did you not know that a man such as I can certainly practice divination?"

16 And Judah said, "What shall we answer to our lord, or what shall we say, or how shall we clear ourselves? God has discovered the unrighteousness of your servants; behold, we are slaves to our lord, both we and he with whom the cup has been found."

17 And Joseph said, "Far be it from me to do this thing; the man with whom the cup has been found, he shall be my servant. But as for you, go up with safety to your father."

Judah Intercedes for Benjamin

18 And Judah drew near him, and said, "I beseech you, Sir, let your servant speak a word before you, and be not angry with your servant, for you are next to Pharaoh.

19 Sir, you asked your servants, saying, 'Have you a father or a brother?'

20 And we said to my lord, 'We have a father, an old man, and he has a son of his old age, a young one, and his brother is dead, and he alone has been left behind to his mother, and his father loves him.'

21 And you said to your servants, 'Bring him down to me, and I will take care of him.'

22 And we said to my lord, 'The child will not be able to leave his father; but if he should leave his father, he will die.'

23 But you said to your servants, 'Except your younger brother come down with you, you shall not see my face again.'

24 And it came to pass, when we went up to your servant our father, we reported to him the words of our lord.

25 And our father said, 'Go again, and buy us a little food.'

26 And we said, 'We shall not be able to go down; but if our younger brother go down with us, we will go down; for we shall not be able to see the man's face if our younger brother is not with us.'

27 And your servant our father said to us, 'You know that my wife bore me two sons;

28 and one is departed from me; and you said that he was devoured by wild beasts, and I have not seen him until now.

29 If then you take this one also from my presence, and an affliction happen to him by the way, then shall you bring down my old age with sorrow to the grave.'

30 Now then, if I should go in to your servant, and our father, and the boy should not be with us, (and his life depends on this *lad's* life)

31 —it shall even come to pass, when he sees the boy is not with us, *that* he will die, and your servants will bring down the old age of your servant, and our father, with sorrow to the grave.

32 For your servant has received the boy in charge from his father, saying, 'If I don't bring him to you, and place him before you, I shall be guilty towards my father forever.'

33 Now then, I will remain a servant with you instead of the lad, a slave of my lord; but let the lad go up with his brothers.

34 For how shall I go up to my father, *if* the lad is not with us? Lest I behold the evils which will befall my father."

GENESIS CHAPTER 45

Joseph Reveals Himself to His Brothers

1 And Joseph could not refrain himself when all were standing by him, but said, "Dismiss everyone from before me"; and no one stood near Joseph, when he made himself known to his brothers.

2 And he uttered his voice with weeping; and all the Egyptians heard, and it was reported to the house of Pharaoh.

3 And Joseph said to his brothers, "I am Joseph; does my father yet live?" And his brothers could not answer him, for they were troubled.

4 And Joseph said to his brothers, "Draw near to me"; and they drew near; and he said, "I am your brother Joseph, whom you sold into Egypt.

5 Now then, do not be grieved or angry with yourselves because you sold me here, for God sent me before you to preserve life.

6 For this second year there is famine on the earth, and there are yet five years remaining, in which there is to be neither plowing, nor mowing.

7 For God sent me before you, that there might be left to you a remnant upon the earth, even to nourish a great remnant of you.

8 Now then, you did not send me here, but God; and He has made me as a father to Pharaoh, and lord of all his house, and ruler of all the land of Egypt.

9 Hurry, therefore, and go up to my father, and say to him, 'Thus says your son Joseph: God has made me lord of all the land of Egypt; come down therefore to me, and do not delay.

10 And you shall dwell in the land of Goshen of Arabia; and you shall be near me, you and your sons, and your sons' sons, your sheep and your oxen, and whatever things are yours.

¹¹ And I will provide for you there: for the famine is yet for five years; lest you be consumed, and your sons, and all your possessions.

¹² Behold, your eyes see, and the eyes of my brother Benjamin, that it is my mouth that speaks to you.'

¹³ Therefore report to my father all my glory in Egypt, and all things that you have seen, and make haste and bring my father down here."

¹⁴ And he fell on his brother Benjamin's neck, and wept on him; and Benjamin wept on his neck.

¹⁵ And he kissed all his brothers, and wept on them; and after these things his brothers spoke to him.

¹⁶ And the report was carried into the house of Pharaoh, saying, "Joseph's brothers have come"; and Pharaoh was glad, and his household.

¹⁷ And Pharaoh said to Joseph, "Say to your brothers, Do this; fill your wagons, and depart into the land of Canaan.

¹⁸ And take up your father, and your possessions, and come to me; and I will give you of all the goods of Egypt, and you shall eat the fat of the land.

¹⁹ And do charge them thusly: that they should take for themselves wagons out of the land of Egypt, for your little ones, and for your wives; and take up your father, and come.

²⁰ And be not sparing in regard to your property, for all the best of Egypt shall be yours."

²¹ And the children of Israel did so; and Joseph gave to them wagons, according to the words spoken by King Pharaoh; and he gave them provision for the journey.

²² And he gave to them all two sets of clothing apiece; but to Benjamin he gave three hundred pieces of gold, and five changes of clothing.

²³ And to his father he sent *presents* at the same rate, and ten donkeys, bearing some of all the good things of Egypt, and ten mules, bearing bread for his father for the journey.

²⁴ And he sent away his brothers, and they went; and he said to them, "Be not angry by the way."

²⁵ And they went up out of Egypt, and came into the land of Canaan, to Jacob their father.

²⁶ And they reported to him, saying, "Your son Joseph is living, and he is ruler over all the land of Egypt." And Jacob was amazed, for he did not believe them.

²⁷ But they spoke to him all the words uttered by Joseph, whatsoever he said to them; and having seen the chariots which Joseph sent to take him up, the spirit of Jacob their father revived.

²⁸ And Israel said, "It is a great thing for me if Joseph my son is yet alive. I will go and see him before I die."

GENESIS CHAPTER 46

Jacob's Journey to Egypt

¹ And Israel departed, he and all that he had, and came to the Well of the Oath; and he offered a sacrifice to the God of his father Isaac.

² And God spoke to Israel in a night vision, saying, "Jacob, Jacob"; and he said, "What is it?"

³ And He said to him, "I am the God of your fathers; do not fear to go down into Egypt, for I will make of you a great nation there.

⁴ And I will go down with you into Egypt, and I will bring you up at the end; and Joseph shall put his hands on your eyes."

⁵ And Jacob rose up from the Well of the Oath; and the sons of Israel took up their father, and the baggage, and their wives on the wagons, which Joseph sent to take them.

⁶ And they took up their goods, and all their property, which they had gotten in the land of Canaan, and they came into the land of Egypt—Jacob, and all his descendants with him.

⁷ His sons, and his grandsons with him; his daughters, and his granddaughters *as well*; and he brought all of his family into Egypt.

⁸ And these are the names of the sons of Israel that went into Egypt with their father Jacob—Jacob and his sons. The firstborn of Jacob *was* Reuben.

⁹ And the sons of Reuben *were* Hanoch, Pallu, Hezron, and Carmi.

¹⁰ And the sons of Simeon *were* Jemuel, Jamin, Ohad, Jachin, Zohar, and Shaul, the son of a Canaanite woman.

¹¹ And the sons of Levi *were* Gershon, Kohath, and Merari.

¹² And the sons of Judah *were* Er, Onan, Shelah, Perez, and Zerah (but Er and Onan died in the land of Canaan).

¹³ And the sons of Perez *were* Esron, and Jemuel. And the sons of Issachar *were* Tola, Puvah, Job, and Shimron.

¹⁴ And the sons of Zebulun *were* Sered, Elon, and Jahleel.

¹⁵ These are the sons of Leah, which she bore to Jacob in Mesopotamia of Syria, with Dinah his daughter; all the persons, sons and daughters, *were* thirty-three.

¹⁶ And the sons of Gad *were* Ziphion, Haggi, Shuni, Ezbron, Eri, Arodi, and Areli.

¹⁷ And the sons of Asher *were* Jimnah, Ishuah, Isui, Beriah, and Serah, their sister. And the sons of Beriah *were* Heber and Malchiel.

¹⁸ These are the sons of Zilpah, whom Laban gave to his daughter Leah, who bore these to Jacob, sixteen persons.

¹⁹ And the sons of Rachel, the wife of Jacob, *were* Joseph and Benjamin.

²⁰ And there were sons born to Joseph in the land of Egypt, whom Asenath, the daughter of Poti-Pherah, priest of Heliopolis, bore to him, even Manasseh and Ephraim. And there were sons born to Manasseh, which the Syrian concubine bore to him, *even* Machir. And Machir fathered Gilead. And the sons of Ephraim, the brother of Manasseh *were* Sutalaam, and Taam. And the son of Sutalaam *was* Edom.

²¹ And the sons of Benjamin *were* Belah, Becher, and Ashbel. And the sons of Belah *were* Gera, Naaman, Ehi, Rosh, and Muppim. And Gera fathered Ard.

²² These are the sons of Rachel, which she bore to Jacob; eighteen persons in all.

²³ The son of Dan *was* Hushim.

24 And the sons of Naphtali *were* Jahzeel, Guni, Jezer, and Shillem.

25 These are the sons of Bilhah, whom Laban gave to his daughter Rachel, who bore these to Jacob; seven persons in all.

26 And all the souls that came with Jacob into Egypt, who came out of his loins, besides the wives of the sons of Jacob, were sixty-six persons in all.

27 And the sons of Joseph, who were born to him in the land of Egypt were nine persons. All the persons of the house of Jacob who came with Joseph into Egypt were seventy-five persons.

Jacob Settles in Goshen

28 And he sent Judah before him to Joseph, to meet him at the City of Heroes, into the land of Rameses.

29 And Joseph, having made ready his chariots, went up to meet Israel his father, at the City of Heroes; and having appeared to him, he fell on his neck, and wept with abundant weeping.

30 And Israel said to Joseph, "After this I will *gladly* die, since I have seen your face, and you are still alive!"

31 And Joseph said to his brothers, "I will go up and tell Pharaoh, and will say to him, 'My brothers, and my father's house, who were in the land of Canaan, have come to me.

32 And the men are shepherds; for they have been feeders of cattle, and they have brought with them their cattle, and their cows, and all their property.'

33 If then Pharaoh calls you, and says to you, 'What is your occupation?'

34 You shall say, 'We your servants are herdsmen from our youth until now, both we and our fathers'; that you may dwell in the land of Goshen of Arabia, for every shepherd is an abomination to the Egyptians."

GENESIS CHAPTER 47

1 And Joseph came and told Pharaoh, *saying*, "My father, my brothers, their cattle, their oxen, and all their possessions have come out of the land of Canaan, and behold, they are in the land of Goshen."

2 And he took five men from among his brothers, and set them before Pharaoh.

3 And Pharaoh said to Joseph's brothers, "What is your occupation?" And they said to Pharaoh, "Your servants are shepherds, both we and our father."

4 And they said to Pharaoh, "We have come to sojourn in the land, for there is no pasture for the flocks of your servants, for the famine has prevailed in the land of Canaan. Now then, we will dwell in the land of Goshen." And Pharaoh said to Joseph, "Let them dwell in the land of Goshen; and if you know that there are among them able men, make them overseers of my cattle." So Jacob and his sons came into Egypt, to Joseph; and Pharaoh, king of Egypt, heard *of it.*

5 And Pharaoh spoke to Joseph, saying, "Your father and your brothers have come to you.

6 Behold, the land of Egypt is before you; settle your father and your brothers in the best land."

7 And Joseph brought in Jacob his father, and set him before Pharaoh; and Jacob blessed Pharaoh.

8 And Pharaoh said to Jacob, "How old are you?"

9 And Jacob said to Pharaoh, "The days of the years of my life, wherein I sojourn, are one hundred and thirty years; few and evil have been the days of the years of my life, they have not attained to the days of the life of my fathers, in which days they sojourned."

10 And Jacob blessed Pharaoh, and departed from him.

11 And Joseph settled his father and his brothers, and gave them a possession in the land of Egypt, in the best land, in the land of Rameses, as Pharaoh commanded.

12 And Joseph gave provision to his father, and his brothers, and to all the house of his father, bread for each person.

The Famine in Egypt

13 And there was no bread in all the land, for the famine prevailed greatly; and the land of Egypt and the land of Canaan fainted on account of the famine.

14 And Joseph gathered all the money that was found in the land of Egypt, and the land of Canaan, *in return for* the grain which they bought, and he distributed grain to them; and Joseph brought all the money into the house of Pharaoh.

15 And all the money failed out of the land of Egypt, and out of the land of Canaan. And all the Egyptians came to Joseph, saying, "Give us bread, and why do we die in your presence? For our money is spent."

16 And Joseph said to them, "Bring your cattle, and I will give you bread for your cattle, if your money is spent."

17 And they brought their cattle to Joseph; and Joseph gave them bread in return for their horses, and for their sheep, and for their oxen, and for their donkeys; and Joseph maintained them with bread for all their cattle in that year.

18 And that year passed, and they came to him in the second year, and said to him, "Must we then be consumed from before our lord? For if our money has failed, and our possessions, and our cattle, *brought* to you our lord, and there has not been left to us before our lord more than our own bodies and our land, *we are indeed destitute.*

19 In order then that we die not before you, and the land be made desolate, buy us and our land for bread, and we and our land will be servants to Pharaoh: give seed that we may sow, and live and not die, so our land shall not be made desolate."

20 And Joseph bought all the land of the Egyptians for Pharaoh, for the Egyptians sold their land to Pharaoh; for the famine prevailed against them, and the land became Pharaoh's.

21 And he brought the people into bondage to him, for servants, from one extremity of Egypt to the other,

22 except for the land of the priests; Joseph did not buy this, for Pharaoh gave a portion in the way of a gift to the priests, and they ate their portion which Pharaoh gave them; therefore they did not sell their land.

23 And Joseph said to all the Egyptians, "Behold, I have bought you and your land this day for Pharaoh; take seed for yourselves, and sow the land.

24 And there shall be the fruits of it; and you shall give the fifth part to Pharaoh, and the four *remaining* parts shall be for yourselves, for seed for the earth, and for food for yourselves, and all that are in your houses."

25 And they said, "You have saved us; we have found favor before our lord, and we will be servants to Pharaoh."

26 And Joseph appointed it to them for an ordinance until this day; to reserve a fifth part for Pharaoh, of the land of Egypt, except for the land of the priests, that was not Pharaoh's.

The Last Days of Jacob

27 And Israel dwelt in Egypt, in the land of Goshen, and they gained an inheritance upon it; and they increased and multiplied very greatly.

28 And Jacob survived seventeen years in the land of Egypt; and Jacob's days of the years of his life were one hundred and forty-seven years.

29 And the days of Israel drew near for him to die. And he called his son Joseph, and said to him, "If I have found favor before you, put your hand under my thigh, and you shall execute mercy and truth toward me, so as not to bury me in Egypt.

30 But I will sleep with my fathers, and you shall carry me up out of Egypt, and bury me in their tomb." And he said, "I will do according to your word."

31 And he said, "Swear to me"; and he swore to him. And Israel bowed down, leaning on the top of his staff.

GENESIS CHAPTER 48

Jacob Blesses Joseph's Sons

1 And it came to pass after these things, that it was reported to Joseph, "Behold, your father is ill." And having taken his two sons, Manasseh and Ephraim, he came to Jacob.

2 And it was reported to Jacob, saying, "Behold, your son Joseph has come to you." And Israel, having strengthened himself, sat up upon the bed.

3 And Jacob said to Joseph, "My God appeared to me in Luz, in the land of Canaan, and blessed me,

4 and said to me, 'Behold, I will increase you, and multiply you, and will make of you a multitude of nations; and I will give this land to you, and to your descendants after you, for an everlasting possession.'

5 Now then your two sons, Ephraim and Manasseh, who were born to you in the land of Egypt, before I came to you in Egypt, are mine; as Reuben and Simeon they shall be mine.

6 And the children which you shall beget hereafter, shall be in the name of their brothers; they shall be named after their inheritances.

7 And as for me, when I came out of Mesopotamia of Syria, Rachel, your mother, died in the land of Canaan, as I drew near to the horse course of Cabratha of the land *of Canaan*, so as to come to Ephratha; and I buried her by the road of the course; which is Bethlehem."

8 And when Israel saw the sons of Joseph, he said, "Who are these to you?"

9 And Joseph said to his father, "They are my sons, whom God gave me here." And Jacob said, "Bring them to me, that I may bless them."

10 Now the eyes of Israel were dim with age, and he could not see; and he brought them near to him, and he kissed them, and embraced them.

11 And Israel said to Joseph, "Behold, I have not been deprived of *seeing* your face, and lo! God has shown me your children also." 12 And Joseph brought them out from *between* his knees, and they bowed down to him, with their face to the ground.

13 And Joseph took his two sons, both Ephraim in his right hand, but on the left of Israel, and Manasseh on his left hand, but on the right of Israel, and brought them near to him.

14 But Israel, having stretched out his right hand, laid it on the head of Ephraim, and he was the younger; and his left hand on the head of Manasseh *guiding* his hands crosswise.

15 And he blessed them and said, "The God in whose sight my fathers were well pleasing, *even* Abraham and Isaac, the God who continues to feed me from my youth until this day;

16 the angel who delivers me from all evils, bless these boys, and my name shall be called upon them, and the name of my fathers, Abraham and Isaac; and let them be increased to a great multitude on the earth."

17 And Joseph, having seen that his father put his right hand on the head of Ephraim—it seemed grievous to him; and Joseph took hold of the hand of his father, to remove it from the head of Ephraim to the head of Manasseh.

18 And Joseph said to his father, "Not so, father; for this is the firstborn; lay your right hand upon his head."

19 And he would not, but said, "I know it, son, I know it; he also shall be a people, and he shall be exalted, but his younger brother shall be greater than he, and his descendants shall become a multitude of nations."

20 And he blessed them in that day, saying, "In you shall Israel be blessed," saying, "God make you as Ephraim and Manasseh"; and he set Ephraim before Manasseh.

21 And Israel said to Joseph, "Behold, I die; and God shall be with you, and restore you to the land of your fathers.

22 And I give to you Sicima, a select portion above your brothers, which I took out of the hand of the Amorites with my sword and bow."

GENESIS CHAPTER 49

Jacob's Last Words to His Sons

[1] And Jacob called his sons, and said to them,

[2] "Assemble yourselves, that I may tell you what shall happen to you in the last days. Gather yourselves together, and hear me, *you* sons of Jacob; hear Israel, hear your father.

[3] Reuben, you *are* my firstborn, you my strength, and the first of my children, hard to be endured, *hard and* self-willed.

[4] You were insolent like water, burst not forth with violence, for you went up to the bed of your father; then you defiled the couch, whereupon you went up.

[5] Simeon and Levi, brothers, accomplished the injustice of their cutting off.

[6] Let not my soul come into their counsel, and let not my inward parts contend in their conspiracy, for in their wrath they slew men, and in their passion they hamstrung a bull.

[7] Cursed be their wrath, for it was willful, and their anger, for it was cruel: I will divide them in Jacob, and scatter them in Israel.

[8] Judah, your brothers have praised you, and your hands shall be on the back of your enemies; your father's sons shall bow down before you.

[9] Judah is a lion's whelp: from the tender plant, my son, you have gone up. Having couched, you lie down like a lion, and as a whelp; who shall stir him up?

[10] A ruler shall not fail from Judah, nor a prince from his loins, until there come the things stored up for him; and He is the expectation of nations.

[11] Binding his foal to the vine, and the foal of his donkey to the branch of it, he shall wash his robe in wine, and his garment in the blood of the grape.

[12] His eyes shall be more cheering than wine, and his teeth whiter than milk.

[13] Zebulun shall dwell on the coast, and he *shall be* by a haven of ships, and shall extend to Sidon.

[14] Issachar has desired that which is good; resting between the inheritances.

[15] And having seen the resting place that it was good, and the land that it was fertile, he subjected his shoulder to labor, and became a farmer.

[16] Dan shall judge his people, as one of the tribes of Israel.

[17] And let Dan be a serpent in the way, besetting the path, biting the heel of the horse (and the rider shall fall backward),

[18] waiting for the salvation of the Lord.

[19] Gad, a plundering troop shall plunder him; but he shall plunder him, *pursuing him* closely.

[20] Asher, his bread *shall be* fat; and he shall yield dainties to princes.

[21] Naphtali is a spreading stem, bestowing beauty on its fruit.

[22] Joseph is a son increased; my dearly loved son is increased; my youngest son, turn to me.

[23] Against whom men taking evil counsel reproached *him*, and the archers pressed hard upon him.

[24] But their bow and arrows were mightily consumed, and the sinews of their arms were slackened by the hand of the Mighty One of Jacob; this is he that strengthened Israel from the God of your father;

[25] and my God helped you, and He blessed you with the blessing of heaven from above, and the blessing of the earth possessing all things, because of the blessing of the breasts and of the womb,

[26] the blessings of your father and your mother—it has prevailed above the blessing of the lasting mountains, and beyond the blessings of the everlasting hills; they shall be upon the head of Joseph, and upon the head of the brothers of whom he took the lead.

[27] Benjamin, as a ravening wolf, shall eat still in the morning, and at evening he gives food."

[28] All these are the twelve sons of Jacob; and their father spoke these words to them, and he blessed them; he blessed each of them according to his blessing.

Jacob's Death and Burial

[29] And he said to them, "I am added to my people; you shall bury me with my fathers in the cave, which is in the field of Ephron the Hittite,

[30] in the double cave which is opposite Mamre, in the land of Canaan, the cave which Abraham bought from Ephron the Hittite for a possession, for a tomb.

[31] There they buried Abraham and Sarah his wife; there they buried Isaac, and Rebecca his wife; there they buried Leah;

[32] in the portion of the field, and of the cave that was in it, *purchased* from the sons of Heth."

[33] And Jacob ceased giving charges to his sons; and having lifted up his feet on the bed, he died, and was gathered to his people.

GENESIS CHAPTER 50

[1] And Joseph fell upon his father's face, and wept on him, and kissed him.

[2] And Joseph commanded his servants the embalmers to embalm his father; and the embalmers embalmed Israel.

[3] And they fulfilled forty days for him, for so are the days of embalming numbered; and Egypt mourned for him seventy days.

[4] And when the days of mourning were past, Joseph spoke to the princes of Pharaoh, saying, "If I have found favor in your sight, speak concerning me in the ears of Pharaoh, saying,

[5] 'My father adjured me, saying, 'In the tomb which I dug for myself in the land of Canaan, there you shall bury me'; now then I will go up and bury my father, and return again.'"

[6] And Pharaoh said to Joseph, "Go up, bury your father, as he made you to swear."

7 So Joseph went up to bury his father; and all the servants of Pharaoh went up with him, and the elders of his house, and all the elders of the land of Egypt.

8 And all the household of Joseph, and his brothers, and all the house of his father, and his kindred; and they left behind the sheep and the oxen in the land of Goshen.

9 And there went up with him also chariots and horsemen; and there was a very great company.

10 And they came to the threshing floor of Atad, which is beyond the Jordan; and they bewailed him with a great and very sore lamentation; and he made a mourning for his father seven days.

11 And the inhabitants of the land of Canaan saw the mourning at the floor of Atad, and said, "This is a great mourning to the Egyptians; therefore he called its name, The Mourning of Egypt, which is beyond the Jordan."

12 And thus his sons did to him.

13 So his sons carried him up into the land of Canaan, and buried him in the double cave which Abraham bought for possession of a burying place from Ephrom the Hittite, before Mamre.

14 And Joseph returned to Egypt, he and his brothers, and those that had gone up with him to bury his father.

Joseph Forgives His Brothers

15 And when Joseph's brothers saw that their father was dead, they said, "*Let us take heed*, lest at any time Joseph remember evil against us, and recompense to us all the evils which we have done against him."

16 And they came to Joseph, and said, "Your father adjured us before his death, saying,

17 'Thus you shall say to Joseph, 'Forgive them their injustice and their sin, forasmuch as they have done you evil; and now pardon the injustice of the servants of the God of your father.'" And Joseph wept while they spoke to him.

18 And they came to him and said, "We, these *persons*, are your servants."

19 And Joseph said to them, "Do not fear, for I am God's.

20 You took counsel against me for evil, but God took counsel for me for good, that the matter might be as it is today, and many people might be fed."

21 And he said to them, "Do not fear, I will maintain you, and your families. And he comforted them, and spoke kindly to them.

The Death of Joseph

22 And Joseph dwelt in Egypt, he and his brothers, and all the family of his father; and Joseph lived one hundred and ten years.

23 And Joseph saw the children of Ephraim to the third generation; and the sons of Machir, the son of Manasseh were borne on the sides of Joseph.

24 And Joseph spoke to his brothers, saying, "I die, and God will surely visit you, and will bring you out of this land to the land concerning which God swore to our fathers, Abraham, Isaac, and Jacob."

25 And Joseph adjured the sons of Israel, saying, "At the visitation with which God shall visit you, then you shall carry up my bones from here with you."

26 And Joseph died, being one hundred and ten years; and they prepared his body, and put him in a coffin in Egypt.

THE BOOK OF EXODUS

Israel's Suffering In Egypt

1 These are the names of the sons of Israel that came into Egypt, together with Jacob their father. They came in each with their whole family.

2 Reuben, Simeon, Levi, Judah,

3 Issachar, Zebulun, Benjamin,

4 Dan, Naphtali, Gad and Asher.

5 But Joseph was in Egypt. And all the souls born of Jacob were seventy-five.

6 And Joseph died, and all his brothers, and all that generation.

7 And the children of Israel increased and multiplied, and became numerous and grew exceedingly strong, and the land multiplied them.

8 And there arose up another king over Egypt, who did not know Joseph.

9 And he said to his nation, "Behold, the race of the children of Israel is a great multitude, and is stronger than us!

10 Come then, let us deal craftily with them, lest at any time they be increased, and whenever war shall happen to us, these also shall be added to our enemies, and having prevailed against us in war, they will depart out of the land."

11 And he set over them taskmasters, who afflicted them in their works; and they built strong cities for Pharaoh, both Pithom, and Raamses, and On, which is Heliopolis.

12 But as they humbled them, by so much they multiplied, and grew exceedingly strong. And the Egyptians greatly abhorred the children of Israel.

13 And the Egyptians tyrannized over the children of Israel by force.

14 And they embittered their life by hard labors, in the clay and in brick-making, and all the works in the plains, according to all the works, wherein they caused them to serve with violence.

15 And the king of the Egyptians spoke to the midwives of the Hebrews. The name of the one was Shiphrah, and the name of the second *was* Puah.

16 And he said, "When you do the duties of midwife to the Hebrew women, and they are about to be delivered, if the baby is a male, kill it; but if a female, save it."

17 But the midwives feared God, and did not do as the king of Egypt appointed them; and they saved the male children alive.

¹⁸ And the king of Egypt called the midwives, and said to them, "Why is it that you have done this thing, and saved the male children alive?"

¹⁹ And the midwives said to Pharaoh, "The Hebrew women are not as the women of Egypt, for they are delivered before the midwives go in to them." So they bore children.

²⁰ And God blessed the midwives, and the people multiplied, and grew very strong.

²¹ And as the midwives feared God, they established for themselves families.

²² And Pharaoh charged all his people, saying, "Whatever male *child* shall be born to the Hebrews, cast into the river; and every female, save it alive."

EXODUS CHAPTER 2

The Birth of Moses

¹ And there was a certain man of the tribe of Levi, who took to wife one of the daughters of Levi.

² And she conceived, and bore a male child; and having seen that he was fair, they hid him three months.

³ And when they could no longer hide him, his mother took an ark, covered it with pitch, and put the child into it, and put it in the reeds by the river.

⁴ And his sister was watching from a distance, to see what would happen to him.

⁵ And the daughter of Pharaoh came down to the river to bathe. And her maids walked by the riverside, and having seen the ark in the reeds, she sent her maid, and took it up.

⁶ And having opened it, she saw the babe weeping in the ark. And the daughter of Pharaoh had compassion on it, and said, "This *is one* of the Hebrew's children."

⁷ And his sister said to the daughter of Pharaoh, "Do you will that I call for you a nurse from the Hebrews, and shall she nurse the child for you?"

⁸ And the daughter of Pharaoh said, "Go." And the young woman went, and called the mother of the child.

⁹ And the daughter of Pharaoh said to her, "Take care of this child, and nurse it for me, and I will give *you* your wages." And the woman took the child, and nursed it.

¹⁰ And when the boy was grown, she brought him to the daughter of Pharaoh, and he became her son; and she called his name Moses, saying, "I took him out of the water."

Moses Flees to Midian

¹¹ And it came to pass after some time, that Moses, having grown, went out to his brothers, the sons of Israel. And having noticed their distress, he saw an Egyptian striking a certain Hebrew from among his brothers, the children of Israel.

¹² And having looked around this way and that, he saw no one. And he killed the Egyptian, and hid him in the sand.

¹³ And having gone out the second day, he saw two Hebrew men fighting; and he said to the injurer, "Why do you strike your neighbor?"

¹⁴ And he said, "Who made you a ruler and a judge over us? Will you slay me as you slew the Egyptian yesterday?" Then Moses was alarmed, and said, "If *it be* thus, this matter has become known."

¹⁵ And Pharaoh heard this matter, and sought to kill Moses. And Moses departed from the presence of Pharaoh, and dwelt in the land of Midian. And having come into the land of Midian, he sat on the well.

¹⁶ And the priest of Midian had seven daughters, feeding the flock of their father Jethro. And they came and drew water until they filled their pitchers, to water the flock of their father Jethro.

¹⁷ And the shepherds came, and were driving them away; and Moses rose up and rescued them, and drew water for them, and watered their sheep.

¹⁸ And they came to Reuel their father; and he said to them, "Why have you come so quickly today?"

¹⁹ And they said, "An Egyptian delivered us from the shepherds, and drew water for us and watered our sheep."

²⁰ And he said to his daughters, "And where is he? And why have you left the man? Call him, that he may eat bread."

²¹ And Moses was established with the man, and he gave Zipporah his daughter to Moses for a wife.

²² And the woman conceived and bore a son, and Moses called his name Gershom, saying, "I am a sojourner in a strange land."

²³ And in those days, after some time, the king of Egypt died. And the children of Israel groaned because of their tasks, and cried, and their cry because of their tasks went up to God.

²⁴ And God heard their groanings, and God remembered His covenant *that He* made with Abraham, Isaac and Jacob.

²⁵ And God looked upon the children of Israel, and acknowledged them.

EXODUS CHAPTER 3

Moses at the Burning Bush

¹ And Moses was feeding the flock of Jethro his father-in-law, the priest of Midian. And he brought the sheep close to the wilderness, and came to the mount of Horeb.

² And the Angel of the Lord appeared to him in flaming fire out of the bush, and he saw that the bush burned with fire, but the bush was not consumed.

³ And Moses said, "I will go near and see this great sight, why the bush is not consumed."

⁴ And when the Lord saw that he drew near to see, the Lord called him out of the bush, saying, "Moses, Moses." And he said, "What is it?"

⁵ And He said, "Draw no closer! Loose your sandals from off your feet, for the place on which you stand is holy ground."

⁶ And He said, "I am the God of your father—the God of Abraham, and the God of Isaac, and the God of Jacob." And Moses turned away his face, for he was afraid to gaze at God.

7 And the Lord said to Moses, "I have surely seen the affliction of My people that is in Egypt, and I have heard their cry *caused* by their taskmasters; for I know their affliction.

8 And I have come down to deliver them out of the hand of the Egyptians, and to bring them out of that land, and to bring them into a good and wide land, into a land flowing with milk and honey, into the place of the Canaanites and the Hittites and the Amorites and the Perizzites and Girgashites and Hivites and Jebusites.

9 And now behold, the cry of the children of Israel has come to Me, and I have seen the affliction with which the Egyptians afflict them.

10 And now come, I will send you to Pharaoh, king of Egypt, and you shall bring out My people the children of Israel from the land of Egypt."

11 And Moses said to God, "Who am I, that I should go to Pharaoh king of Egypt, and that I should bring out the children of Israel from the land of Egypt?"

12 And God spoke to Moses, saying, "I will be with you, and this shall be the sign to you that I shall send you forth: when you bring out My people out of Egypt, then you shall serve God in this mountain."

The Divine Name Revealed

13 And Moses said to God, "Behold, I shall go forth to the children of Israel, and shall say to them, 'The God of our fathers has sent me to you'; and they will ask me, 'What is His name?' What shall I say to them?"

14 And God spoke to Moses, saying, "I am THE BEING." And He said, "Thus shall you say to the children of Israel, THE BEING has sent me to you."

15 And God said again to Moses, "Thus shall you say to the sons of Israel: 'The Lord God of our fathers, the God of Abraham, and the God of Isaac, and the God of Jacob, has sent me to you: this is My name forever, and My memorial to all generations.'

16 Go then and gather the elders of the children of Israel, and you shall say to them, 'The Lord God of our fathers has appeared to me, the God of Abraham, and the God of Isaac, and the God of Jacob, saying, 'I have surely looked upon you, and upon all the things which have happened to you in Egypt.'"

17 And He said, "I will bring you up out of the affliction of the Egyptians to the land of the Canaanites and the Hittites and the Amorites and the Perizzites and the Girgashites and the Hivites and the Jebusites, to a land flowing with milk and honey.

18 And they shall hearken to your voice, and you and the elders of Israel shall go in to Pharaoh, king of Egypt, and you shall say to him, 'The God of the Hebrews has called us. We will go then a journey of three days into the wilderness, that we may sacrifice to our God.'

19 But I know that Pharaoh king of Egypt will not let you go, except by a mighty hand;

20 and I will stretch out My hand, and strike the Egyptians with all My wonders, which I shall work among them, and after that he will send you forth.

21 And I will give this people favor in the sight of the Egyptians, and whenever you shall escape, you shall not depart empty.

22 But every woman shall ask of her neighbor and fellow lodger, articles of gold and silver, and apparel; and you shall put them upon your sons and upon your daughters. So you shall plunder the Egyptians."

EXODUS CHAPTER 4

Moses' Miraculous Power

1 And Moses answered and said, "If they do not believe me, and do not listen to my voice (for they will say, 'God has not appeared to you'), what shall I say to them?"

2 And the Lord said to him, "What is this thing that is in your hand?" And he said, "A rod."

3 And He said, "Cast it on the ground." And he cast it on the ground, and it became a serpent, and Moses fled from it.

4 And the Lord said to Moses, "Stretch forth your hand, and take hold of its tail (and he stretched forth his hand and took hold of the tail,

5 and it became a rod in his hand), that they may believe you, that the God of your fathers has appeared to you, the God of Abraham, and the God of Isaac, and the God of Jacob."

6 And the Lord said again to him, "Put your hand into your bosom." And he put his hand into his bosom, and brought his hand out of his bosom, and his hand became *leprous*, as snow.

7 And He said again, "Put your hand into your bosom." And he put his hand into his bosom, and brought his hand out of his bosom, and it was again restored to the complexion of the rest of his flesh.

8 *And God said,* "And if they will not believe you, nor heed the message of the first sign, they will believe you because of the message of the second sign.

9 And it shall come to pass if they will not believe you for these two signs, and will not heed your voice, that you shall take of the water of the river and pour it upon the dry land, and the water which you shall take from the river shall be blood upon the dry land."

10 And Moses said to the Lord, "I pray, O Lord, I have not been sufficient in former times, neither from the time that You have begun to speak to Your servant: I am weak in speech, and slow of tongue."

11 And the Lord said to Moses, "Who has given a mouth to man, and who has made the very hard of hearing, and the deaf, the seeing and the blind? Have not I, God?

12 And now go, and I will open your mouth, and will instruct you in what you shall say."

13 And Moses said, "O Lord, I pray, appoint another able person whom You shall send."

14 And the Lord was greatly angered against Moses, and said, "Lo! Is not Aaron the Levite your brother? I know that he will surely speak to you. And behold, he will come forth to meet you, and beholding you, he will rejoice within himself.

15 And you shall speak to him; and you shall put My words into his mouth, and I will open your mouth and his mouth, and I will instruct you in what you shall do.

16 And he shall speak for you to the people, and he shall be your mouth, and you shall be for him in things pertaining to God.

17 And this rod that was turned into a serpent you shall take in your hand, with which you shall work miracles."

Moses Returns to Egypt

18 And Moses went and returned to Jethro his father-in-law, and said, "I will go and return to my brothers in Egypt, and will see if they are yet living." And Jethro said to Moses, "Go in health." And in those days after some time, the king of Egypt died.

19 And the Lord said to Moses in Midian, "Go, depart into Egypt, for all that sought your life are dead."

20 And Moses took his wife and his children, and mounted them on the beasts, and returned to Egypt. And Moses took the rod of God in his hand.

21 And the Lord said to Moses, "When you go and return to Egypt, see—all the miracles I have charged you with, you shall work before Pharaoh. And I will harden his heart, and he shall certainly not send away the people.

22 And you shall say to Pharaoh, 'Thus says the Lord: Israel is My firstborn.

23 And I said to you, Send away My people, that they may serve Me: now if you will not send them away, see, I will kill your firstborn son.'"

24 And it came to pass that the Angel of the Lord met him by the way in the inn, and sought to kill him.

25 And Zipporah, having taken a stone, cut off the foreskin of her son, and fell at his feet and said, "The blood of the circumcision of my son is established!"

26 And he departed from him, because she said, "The blood of the circumcision of my son is established."

27 And the Lord said to Aaron, "Go into the wilderness to meet Moses." And he went and met him in the mount of God, and they kissed each other.

28 And Moses reported to Aaron all the words of the Lord, which He sent, and all the things which He charged him.

29 And Moses and Aaron went and gathered the elders of the children of Israel.

30 And Aaron spoke all these words, which God spoke to Moses, and worked the miracles before the people.

31 And the people believed and rejoiced, because God visited the children of Israel, and because He saw their affliction. And the people bowed down and worshipped.

EXODUS CHAPTER 5

Bricks Without Straw

1 And after this Moses and Aaron went in to Pharaoh, and they said to him, "Thus says the Lord God of Israel: Let My people go, that they may keep a feast to Me in the wilderness."

2 And Pharaoh said, "Who is He that I should listen to His voice, so that I should send away the children of Israel? I do not know the Lord, and I will not let Israel go."

3 And they said to him, "The God of the Hebrews has called us to Him: we will go, therefore, on a three days' journey into the wilderness, that we may sacrifice to the Lord our God, lest at any time death or slaughter happen to us."

4 And the king of Egypt said to them, "Why do you, Moses and Aaron, turn the people from their works? Depart, each of you, to your works."

5 And Pharaoh said, "Behold now, the people are very numerous; let us not then give them rest from their work."

6 And Pharaoh gave orders to the taskmasters of the people and the accountants, saying,

7 "You shall no longer give straw to the people for brick-making as yesterday and the third day; but let them go themselves, and collect straw for themselves.

8 And you shall impose on them daily the rate of brick-making which they perform: you shall not reduce anything, for they are idle. Therefore have they cried, saying, 'Let us arise and do sacrifice to our God.'

9 Let the works of these men be made grievous, and let them care for these things, and not care for vain words."

10 And the taskmasters and the accountants hastened them, and they spoke to the people, saying, "Thus says Pharaoh: I will give you straw no longer.

11 Go yourselves, get for yourselves straw wherever you can find it, for nothing is diminished from your rate."

12 So the people were dispersed in all the land of Egypt, to gather stubble for straw.

13 And the taskmasters hastened them, saying, "Fulfill your regular daily tasks, even as when straw was given to you."

14 And the accountants of the race of the children of Israel, who were set over them by the masters of Pharaoh, were scourged, *and were asked*, "Why have you not fulfilled your rates of brickwork as yesterday and the third day, *and* today also?"

15 And the accountants of the children of Israel went in and cried to Pharaoh, saying, "Why do you act thus to your servants?

16 Straw is not given to your servants, and they tell us to make bricks; and behold, your servants have been scourged; therefore you will injure your people."

17 And he said to them, "You are idle, you are idlers. Therefore you say, 'Let us go and do sacrifice to our God.'

18 Now then go and work, for straw shall not be given to you, yet you shall return the rate of bricks."

19 And the accountants of the children of Israel saw themselves in an evil plight, *for* men *were* saying, "You shall not fail to deliver the daily rate of the brick-making."

²⁰ And they met Moses and Aaron coming forth to meet them, as they came forth from Pharaoh.

²¹ And they said to them, "The Lord look upon you and judge you, for you have made our scent abominable before Pharaoh, and before his servants, to put a sword into his hands to kill us."

²² And Moses turned to the Lord and said, "I pray, O Lord, why have You afflicted this people? And why have You sent me?

²³ For from the time that I went to Pharaoh to speak in Your name, he has afflicted this people, and You have not delivered Your people."

EXODUS CHAPTER 6

Israel's Deliverance Assured

¹ And the Lord said to Moses, "Now you shall see what I will do to Pharaoh; for he shall send them forth with a mighty hand, and with a high arm shall he cast them out of his land."

² And God spoke to Moses and said to him, "I am the Lord.

³ And I appeared to Abraham and Isaac and Jacob, being their God, but I did not manifest My name LORD to them.

⁴ And I established My covenant with them, to give them the land of the Canaanites, the land in which they sojourned, in which also they dwelt as strangers.

⁵ And I heard the groaning of the children of Israel (the affliction with which the Egyptians enslave them) and I remembered the covenant with you.

⁶ Go, speak to the children of Israel, saying, 'I am the Lord; and I will lead you forth from the tyranny of the Egyptians, and I will deliver you from bondage, and I will ransom you with a high arm, and great judgment.

⁷ And I will take you to Me as a people unto Myself, and I will be your God; and you shall know that I am the Lord your God, who brought you out from the tyranny of the Egyptians.

⁸ And I will bring you into the land concerning which I stretched out My hand to give it to Abraham and Isaac and Jacob, and I will give it to you for an inheritance: I am the Lord.'"

⁹ And Moses spoke thus to the sons of Israel, and they did not listen to Moses, on account of *their* faint-heartedness, and because of their hard tasks.

¹⁰ And the Lord spoke to Moses, saying,

¹¹ "Go in, speak to Pharaoh king of Egypt, that he send forth the children of Israel out of his land."

¹² And Moses spoke before the Lord, saying, "Behold, the children of Israel do not listen to me, and how shall Pharaoh hearken to me? And I am not eloquent."

¹³ And the Lord spoke to Moses and Aaron, and gave them a charge to Pharaoh king of Egypt, that he should send forth the children of Israel out of the land of Egypt.

The Families of Moses and Aaron

¹⁴ And these are the heads of the houses of their families: the sons of Reuben the firstborn of Israel *were* Hanoch, Pallu, Hezron, and Carmi. These are the families of Reuben.

¹⁵ And the sons of Simeon *were* Jemuel, Jamin, Ohad, Jachin, Zohar and Shaul the son of a Phoenician woman. These are the families of the sons of Simeon.

¹⁶ And these are the names of the sons of Levi according to their families: Gershon, Kohath, and Merari. And the years of the life of Levi were one hundred and thirty-seven.

¹⁷ And these are the sons of Gershon: Libni and Shimi, according to their family. And the sons of Kohath *were*

¹⁸ Amram, Izhar, Hebron, and Uzziel. And the years of the life of Kohath were one hundred and thirty-three years.

¹⁹ And the sons of Merari *were* Mahli and Mushi. These are the houses of the families of Levi, according to their families.

²⁰ And Amram took Jochabed for a wife, the daughter of his father's brother, and she bore to him both Aaron and Moses, and Miriam their sister. And the years of the life of Amram were one hundred and thirty-two years.

²¹ And the sons of Izhar *were* Korah, Nepheg, and Zichri.

²² And the sons of Uzziel *were* Mishael, Elzaphan, and Zithri.

²³ And Aaron took for himself Elisabeth, daughter of Aminadab sister of Naasson, as a wife, and she bore to him Nadab, Abihu, Eleazar and Ithamar.

²⁴ And the sons of Korah *were* Asir, Elkanah, and Abiasaph. These are the generations of Korah.

²⁵ And Eleazar the son of Aaron took for himself one of the daughters of Putiel as wife, and she bore to him Phinehas. These are the heads of the family of the Levites, according to their generations.

²⁶ This is Aaron and Moses, whom God told to bring out the children of Israel out of the land of Egypt with their forces.

²⁷ These are they that spoke with Pharaoh, king of Egypt, and Aaron himself and Moses brought out the children of Israel from the land of Egypt,

²⁸ in the day in which the Lord spoke to Moses in the land of Egypt.

Moses and Aaron Obey God's Commands

²⁹ Then the Lord spoke to Moses, saying, "I am the Lord. Speak to Pharaoh king of Egypt whatsoever I say to you."

³⁰ And Moses said before the Lord, "Behold, I am not able in speech, and how shall Pharaoh hearken unto me?"

EXODUS CHAPTER 7

¹ And the Lord spoke to Moses, saying, "Behold, I have made you a god to Pharaoh, and Aaron your brother shall be your prophet.

² And you shall say to him all things that I command you, and Aaron your brother shall speak to Pharaoh, that he should send forth the children of Israel out of his land.

³ And I will harden the heart of Pharaoh, and I will multiply My signs and wonders in the land of Egypt.

⁴ And Pharaoh will not listen to you, and I will lay My hand upon Egypt; and I will bring out My people, the children of Israel, with My power out of the land of Egypt with great vengeance.

⁵ And all the Egyptians shall know that I am the Lord, stretching out My hand upon Egypt, and I will bring out the children of Israel from the midst of them."

⁶ And Moses and Aaron did as the Lord commanded them.

⁷ And Moses was eighty years old, and Aaron his brother was eighty-three years old, when he spoke to Pharaoh.

Aaron's Miraculous Rod

⁸ And the Lord spoke to Moses and Aaron, saying,

⁹ "Now if Pharaoh should speak to you, saying, 'Give us a sign or a wonder,' then shall you say to your brother Aaron, 'Take your rod and cast it upon the ground before Pharaoh, and before his servants, and it shall become a serpent.'"

¹⁰ So Moses and Aaron went in before Pharaoh, and *before* his servants, and they did as the Lord commanded them. And Aaron cast down his rod before Pharaoh, and before his servants, and it became a serpent.

¹¹ But Pharaoh called together the wise men of Egypt, and the sorcerers, and the charmers, also of the Egyptians, *and they* did likewise with their sorceries.

¹² And they each cast down their rods, and they became serpents, but the rod of Aaron swallowed up their rods.

¹³ And the heart of Pharaoh was hardened, and he would not listen to them, as the Lord had said.

The First Plague: Water Turned to Blood

¹⁴ And the Lord said to Moses, "The heart of Pharaoh is made hard, so that he should not let the people go.

¹⁵ Go to Pharaoh early in the morning—behold, he goes forth to the water; and you shall meet him on the bank of the river, and you shall take in your hand the rod that was turned into a serpent.

¹⁶ And you shall say to him, 'The Lord God of the Hebrews has sent me to you, saying, 'Let My people go, that they may serve Me in the wilderness; but indeed, until now you have not heard!'

¹⁷ Thus says the Lord: By this you shall know that I am the Lord: behold, I will strike the water which is in the river with the rod that is in my hand, and it shall turn to blood.

¹⁸ And the fish that are in the river shall die, and the river shall stink, and the Egyptians shall not be able to drink water from the river."

¹⁹ And the Lord said to Moses, "Say to your brother Aaron, 'Take your rod in your hand, and stretch forth your hand over the waters of Egypt, and over their rivers, and over their canals, and over their ponds, and over all their standing water, and it shall become blood. And there was blood in all the land of Egypt, both in vessels of wood and of stone.'"

²⁰ And Moses and Aaron did so, as the Lord commanded them. And Aaron, having lifted up *his hand* with his rod, struck the water in the river before Pharaoh and before his servants, and changed all the water in the river into blood.

²¹ And the fish in the river died, and the river stank; and the Egyptians could not drink water from the river, and the blood was in all the land of Egypt.

²² And the charmers also of the Egyptians did so with their sorceries; and the heart of Pharaoh was hardened, and he did not listen to them, even as the Lord had said.

²³ And Pharaoh turned and entered into his house, and paid no attention to this thing.

²⁴ And all the Egyptians dug round about the river, so as to drink water, for they could not drink water from the river.

²⁵ And seven days were fulfilled after the Lord had struck the river.

EXODUS CHAPTER 8

The Second Plague: Frogs

¹ And the Lord said to Moses, "Go in to Pharaoh, and you shall say to him, 'Thus says the Lord: Let My people go, that they may serve Me.

² And if you will not send them forth, behold, I afflict all your borders with frogs.

³ And the river shall be filled with frogs, and they shall go up and enter into your houses, and into your bedrooms, and upon your beds, and upon the houses of your servants, and of your people and on your dough, and on your ovens.

⁴ And upon you, and upon your servants, and upon your people, shall the frogs come up.'"

⁵ And the Lord said to Moses, "Say to Aaron your brother, 'Stretch forth your hand with your rod over the rivers, and over the canals, and over the pools, and bring up the frogs.'"

⁶ And Aaron stretched forth his hand over the waters of Egypt, and brought up the frogs. And the frogs were brought up, and covered the land of Egypt.

⁷ And the charmers of the Egyptians also did likewise with their sorceries, and brought up the frogs on the land of Egypt.

⁸ And Pharaoh called Moses and Aaron, and said, "Pray to the Lord for me, and let Him take away the frogs from me and from my people; and I will send them away, and they shall sacrifice to the Lord."

⁹ And Moses said to Pharaoh, "Appoint me *a time* when I shall pray for you, and for your servants, and for your people, to cause the frogs to disappear from you, and from your people, and from your houses; only in the river shall they be left behind."

¹⁰ And he said, "Tomorrow." Therefore he said, "As you have said, that you may know, that there is no other *God* but the Lord.

¹¹ And the frogs shall be removed away from you, and from your houses and from the villages, and from your servants, and from your people; only in the river they shall be left."

12 And Moses and Aaron went forth from Pharaoh, and Moses cried to the Lord concerning the restriction of the frogs, as Pharaoh appointed him.

13 And the Lord did as Moses had requested, and the frogs died out of the houses, and out of the villages, and out of the fields.

14 And they gathered them together in heaps, and the land stank.

15 And when Pharaoh saw that there was relief, his heart was hardened, and he did not listen to them, as the Lord said.

The Third Plague: Lice

16 And the Lord said to Moses, "Say to Aaron, 'Stretch forth your rod with your hand and strike the dust of the earth; and there shall be lice upon both man and beast, and in all the land of Egypt.'"

17 So Aaron stretched out his rod with his hand, and struck the dust of the earth; and the lice were on men and beasts, and in all the dust of the earth there were lice.

18 And the charmers tried to bring forth the lice with their sorceries, but they could not. And the lice were both on the men and on the beasts.

19 So the charmers said to Pharaoh, "This is the finger of God." But the heart of Pharaoh was hardened, and he did not listen to them, as the Lord said.

The Fourth Plague: Flies

20 And the Lord said to Moses, "Rise up early in the morning, and stand before Pharaoh, and behold, he will go forth to the water, and you shall say to him, 'Thus says the Lord: Let My people go, that they may serve Me in the wilderness.

21 And if you will not let My people go, behold, I send upon you, and upon your servants, and upon your people, and upon your houses, the dog-fly. And the houses of the Egyptians shall be filled with the dog-fly, even throughout the land upon which they are.

22 And I will distinguish marvelously in that day the land of Goshen, on which My people dwell, in which the dog-fly shall not be, so that you may know that I am the Lord, the God of all the earth.

23 And I will put a difference between My people and your people, and tomorrow shall this be on the land.'" And the Lord did thus.

24 And the dog-fly came in abundance into the houses of Pharaoh, and into the houses of his servants, and into all the land of Egypt. And the land was destroyed by the dog-fly.

25 And Pharaoh called Moses and Aaron, saying, "Go and sacrifice to the Lord your God in the land."

26 And Moses said, "It cannot be so, for we would be sacrificing to the Lord our God the abominations of the Egyptians; for if we sacrifice the abominations of the Egyptians before them, we shall be stoned.

27 We will go a journey of three days into the wilderness, and we will sacrifice to the Lord our God, as the Lord has said to us."

28 And Pharaoh said, "I *will* let you go and sacrifice to your God in the wilderness, but do not go very far away—pray then to the Lord for me."

29 And Moses said, "I then will go forth from you and pray to God, and the dog-fly shall depart both from your servants, and from your people tomorrow. However do not deceive again, Pharaoh, so as not to send the people away, that they may sacrifice to the Lord."

30 And Moses went out from Pharaoh, and prayed to God.

31 And the Lord did as Moses had requested, and removed the dog-fly from Pharaoh, and from his servants, and from his people, and there was not one left.

32 And Pharaoh hardened his heart, even on this occasion, and he would not send the people away.

EXODUS CHAPTER 9

The Fifth Plague: Livestock Diseased

1 And the Lord said to Moses, "Go in to Pharaoh, and you shall say to him, 'Thus says the Lord God of the Hebrews: Let My people go, that they may serve Me.

2 If, however, you refuse to let My people go, but yet detain them—

3 behold, the hand of the Lord shall be upon your cattle in the fields, on the horses, on the donkeys, on the camels, on the oxen and on the sheep—a very great pestilence.

4 And I will make a marvelous distinction in that time between the livestock of the Egyptians and the livestock of the children of Israel: nothing shall die of all that belongs to the children of Israel.'"

5 And God fixed a limit, saying, "Tomorrow the Lord will do this thing on the land."

6 And the Lord did this thing on the next day, and all the livestock of the Egyptians died, but of the livestock of the children of Israel not one of them died.

7 And when Pharaoh saw that of all the livestock of the children of Israel, that not one had died, the heart of Pharaoh was hardened, and he did not let the people go.

The Sixth Plague: Boils

8 And the Lord spoke to Moses and Aaron, saying, "Take for yourselves handfuls of ashes from the furnace, and let Moses scatter it toward heaven before Pharaoh, and before his servants.

9 And let it become dust over all the land of Egypt, and there shall be sore boils breaking forth upon men and upon beasts, in all the land of Egypt."

10 So he took ashes from the furnace before Pharaoh, and Moses scattered it toward heaven, and it became sore boils breaking forth both on men and on beasts.

11 And the sorcerers could not stand before Moses because of the sores, for the sores were on the sorcerers, and in all the land of Egypt.

12 And the Lord hardened Pharaoh's heart, and he did not listen to them, as the Lord appointed.

The Seventh Plague: Hail

13 And the Lord said to Moses, "Rise up early in the morning, and stand before Pharaoh; and you shall say to him, 'Thus says the Lord God of the Hebrews: Let My people go, that they may serve Me.

14 For at this present time I will send forth all My plagues into your heart, and the heart of your servants and of your people; that you may know that there is not another such as I in all the earth.

15 For now I will stretch forth My hand and strike you and kill your people, and you shall be consumed from off of the earth.

16 And for this purpose have you been preserved, that I might display My strength in you, and that My name might be declared in all the earth.

17 Do you then yet exert yourself to hinder My people, so as not to let them go?

18 Behold, tomorrow at this hour I will rain a very great hail, such as has not been in Egypt from the time it was created until this day.

19 Now then hasten to gather your livestock, and all that you have in the fields, for all the men and the livestock, as many as shall be found in the fields, and shall not enter into a house, (but the hail shall fall upon them,) shall die.'"

20 He who feared the word of the Lord among Pharaoh's servants gathered his cattle into the houses.

21 And he that did not attend in his mind to the word of the Lord left the cattle in the fields.

22 And the Lord said to Moses, "Stretch out your hand toward heaven, and there shall be hail on all the land of Egypt, both on the men and on the cattle, and on all the herbs on the land."

23 And Moses stretched forth his hand toward heaven, and the Lord sent thunder and hail; and the fire ran along upon the ground, and the Lord rained hail on all the land of Egypt.

24 So there was hail and flaming fire mingled with hail; and the hail was very great, such as was not in Egypt from the time there was a nation upon it.

25 And the hail struck both man and beast in all the land of Egypt, and the hail struck all the grass in the field, and the hail broke in pieces all the trees in the field.

26 Only in the land of Goshen, where the children of Israel were, was there not hail.

27 And Pharaoh sent and called for Moses and Aaron, and said to them, "I have sinned this time: the Lord is righteous, and I and my people are wicked.

28 Pray then for me to the Lord, and let Him cause the thundering of God to cease, and the hail and the fire, and I will send you forth and you shall remain no longer."

29 And Moses said to him, "When I have departed from the city, I will stretch out my hands to the Lord, and the thundering shall cease, and the hail and the rain shall be no longer, so that you may know that the earth is the Lord's.

30 But as for you and your servants, I know that you have not yet feared the Lord."

31 Now the flax and the barley were struck, for the barley was advanced, and the flax was seeding.

32 But the wheat and the rye were not struck, for they were late.

33 And Moses went forth from Pharaoh out of the city, and stretched out his hands to the Lord, and the thunders ceased and the hail, and the rain did not drop on the earth.

34 And when Pharaoh saw that the rain and the hail and the thunders had ceased, he continued to sin; and *he* hardened his heart, and the heart of his servants. And the heart of Pharaoh was hardened, and he did not send forth the children of Israel, as the Lord said to Moses.

EXODUS CHAPTER 10

The Eighth Plague: Locusts

1 And the Lord spoke to Moses, saying, "Go in to Pharaoh; for I have hardened his heart and the heart of his servants, that these signs may come upon them; in order

2 that you may relate in the ears of your children, and to your children's children, in how many things I have mocked the Egyptians, and My wonders which I wrought among them; and you shall know that I am the Lord."

3 And Moses and Aaron went in before Pharaoh, and they said to him, "Thus says the Lord God of the Hebrews: 'How long do you refuse to reverence Me? Let My people go, that they may serve Me.

4 But if you will not send My people away, behold, at this hour tomorrow I will bring an abundance of locusts upon all your coasts.

5 And they shall cover the face of the earth, and you shall not be able to see the earth; and they shall devour all that is left of the abundance of the earth, which the hail has left you, and shall devour every tree that grows for you on the land.

6 And your houses shall be filled, and the houses of your servants, and all the houses in all the land of the Egyptians; things which your fathers have never seen, nor their forefathers, from the day that they were upon the earth until this day.'" And Moses turned away and departed from Pharaoh.

7 And Pharaoh's servants said to him, "How long shall this be a snare to us? Send the men away, that they may serve their God; don't you know that Egypt is destroyed?"

8 And they brought back both Moses and Aaron to Pharaoh; and he said to them, "Go and serve the Lord your God; but who are they that are going with you?"

9 And Moses said, "We will go with the young and the old, with our sons and daughters, and our sheep and oxen; for it is a feast to the Lord."

10 And he said to them, "So let the Lord be with you. As I *will* send you away, *must I send away* your little ones also? Beware, for evil is before you."

11 "Not so, but let the men go and serve God, for this you yourselves seek." And they cast them out from the presence of Pharaoh.

12 And the Lord said to Moses, "Stretch out your hand over the land of Egypt, and let the locust come up on the land, and it shall devour every herb of the land, and all the fruit of the trees, which the hail left."

13 And Moses lifted up his rod towards heaven, and the Lord brought a south wind upon the earth, all that day and all that night. The morning dawned, and the south wind brought up the locusts,

14 and brought them up over all the land of Egypt. And they rested in very great abundance over all the borders of Egypt. Before them there were not such locusts, neither after them shall there be.

15 And they covered the face of the earth, and the land was wasted, and they devoured every herb of the land, and all the fruit of the trees, which was left by the hail: there was no green thing left on the trees, nor on all the herbs of the field, in all the land of Egypt.

16 And Pharaoh hastened to call Moses and Aaron, saying, "I have sinned before the Lord your God, and against you.

17 Therefore pardon my sin yet this time, and pray to the Lord your God, and let Him take away from me this death."

18 And Moses went forth from Pharaoh, and prayed to God.

19 And the Lord brought in the opposite direction a strong wind from the sea, and took up the locusts and cast them into the Red Sea, and there was not one locust left in all the land of Egypt.

20 And the Lord hardened the heart of Pharaoh, and he did not send away the children of Israel.

The Ninth Plague: Darkness

21 And the Lord said to Moses, "Stretch out your hand toward heaven, and let there be darkness over the land of Egypt—darkness that may be felt."

22 And Moses stretched out his hand toward heaven, and there was darkness, very black, even a storm over all the land of Egypt three days.

23 And for three days no man saw his brother, and no man rose up from his bed for three days. But all the children of Israel had light in all the places where they were.

24 And Pharaoh called Moses and Aaron, saying, "Go, serve the Lord your God, only leave your sheep and your oxen, and let your little ones depart with you."

25 And Moses said, "No, but you shall give to us burnt offerings and sacrifices, which we will sacrifice to the Lord our God.

26 And our livestock shall go with us, and we will not leave a hoof behind, for of them we will take to serve the Lord our God; but we know not in what manner we shall serve the Lord our God until we arrive there."

27 But the Lord hardened the heart of Pharaoh, and he would not let them go.

28 And Pharaoh said, "Depart from me! Beware of seeing my face again, for in what day you shall appear before me, you shall die!"

29 And Moses said, "You have spoken *well*. I will not appear in your presence again."

EXODUS CHAPTER 11

Tenth Plague Announced

1 And the Lord said to Moses, "I will yet bring one plague upon Pharaoh and upon Egypt, and after that he will send you forth from here; and whenever he sends you forth with everything, he will indeed cast you out *altogether*.

2 Therefore speak secretly in the ears of the people, and let everyone ask of his neighbor jewels of silver and gold, and clothing."

3 And the Lord gave His people favor in the sight of the Egyptians, and they lent to them; and the man Moses was very great before the Egyptians, and before Pharaoh, and before his servants.

4 And Moses said, "Thus says the Lord: 'About midnight I will go forth into the midst of Egypt.

5 And every firstborn in the land of Egypt shall die, from the firstborn of Pharaoh that sits on the throne, even to the firstborn of the female servant that is by the mill, and to the firstborn of all cattle.

6 And there shall be a great cry throughout all the land of Egypt, such as never before, the *likes of* which shall not be repeated again.

7 But among all the children of Israel shall not a dog snarl with his tongue, either at man or beast; that you may know how wide a distinction the Lord will make between the Egyptians and Israel.'

8 And all these your servants shall come down to me, and reverence me, saying, 'Go forth, you and all the people over whom you presided, and afterwards I will go forth."

9 And Moses went forth from Pharaoh with great anger. And the Lord said to Moses, "Pharaoh will not heed you, that I may greatly multiply My signs and wonders in the land of Egypt."

10 And Moses and Aaron did all these signs and wonders in the land of Egypt before Pharaoh; and the Lord hardened the heart of Pharaoh, and he did not hearken to send forth the children of Israel out of the land of Egypt.

EXODUS CHAPTER 12

The Passover Instituted

[1] And the Lord spoke to Moses and Aaron in the land of Egypt, saying,

[2] "This month *shall be* to you the beginning of months: it is the first to you among the months of the year.

[3] Speak to all the congregation of the children of Israel, saying, 'On the tenth of this month let each man take for himself a lamb according to the houses of their families, every man a lamb for his household.

[4] And if there be few in a household, so that there are not enough for the lamb, he shall take with himself his neighbor that lives near to him, as to the number of persons, everyone according to each man's need you shall make a reckoning for the lamb.

[5] It shall be to you a lamb unblemished, a male of a year old. You shall take it from the lambs or from the goats.

[6] And it shall be kept by you till the fourteenth of this month, and all the multitude of the congregation of the children of Israel shall kill it toward evening.

[7] And they shall take of the blood, and shall put it on the two doorposts, and on the lintel, in the houses wherever they shall eat them.

[8] And they shall eat the flesh in this night roasted with fire, and they shall eat unleavened bread with bitter herbs.

[9] You shall not eat of it raw nor boiled in water, but only roasted with fire, the head with its legs and its entrails.

[10] Nothing shall be left of it till the morning, and a bone of it you shall not break; but that which is left of it till the morning you shall burn with fire.

[11] And thus shall you eat it: your loins girded, and your sandals on your feet, and your staff in your hand, and you shall eat it in haste. It is a Passover to the Lord.

[12] And I will go throughout the land of Egypt in that night, and I will strike every firstborn in the land of Egypt, both man and beast, and on all the gods of Egypt will I execute vengeance: I am the Lord.

[13] And the blood shall be for a sign to you on the houses in which you are, and I will see the blood, and I will protect you, and there shall not be on you the plague of destruction, when I strike in the land of Egypt.

[14] And this day shall be to you a memorial, and you shall keep it a feast to the Lord through all your generations; you shall keep it a feast for a perpetual ordinance.

[15] Seven days you shall eat unleavened bread, and from the first day you shall utterly remove leaven from your houses: whoever shall eat leaven, that soul shall be utterly destroyed from Israel, from the first day until the seventh day.

[16] And the first day shall be called holy, and the seventh day shall be a holy convocation to you. You shall do no customary work on them, only as many things as is necessary shall be done by every soul, this only shall be done by you.

[17] And you shall keep this commandment, for on this day will I bring out your force out of the land of Egypt; and you shall make this day a perpetual ordinance for you throughout your generations.

[18] Beginning the fourteenth day of the first month, you shall eat unleavened bread from evening, till the twenty-first day of the month, till evening.

[19] Seven days leaven shall not be found in your houses; whosoever shall eat anything leavened, that soul shall be cut off from the congregation of Israel, both among the occupiers of the land and the original inhabitants.

[20] You shall eat nothing leavened, but in every habitation of yours you shall eat unleavened bread.'"

[21] Then Moses called all the elders of the children of Israel, and said to them, "Go away and take to yourselves a lamb according to your families, and slay the Passover *lamb*.

[22] And you shall take a bunch of hyssop, and having dipped it into some of the blood that is by the door, you shall touch the lintel, and *shall put it* upon both doorposts, even of the blood which is by the door; but none of you shall go out of the door of his house until morning.

[23] And the Lord shall pass by to strike the Egyptians, and shall see the blood upon the lintel, and upon the doorposts; and the Lord shall pass over the door, and shall not allow the destroyer to enter into your houses to kill you.

[24] And keep this thing as an ordinance for yourself and for your children forever.

[25] And if you should enter into the land which the Lord shall give you, as He has spoken, keep this service.

[26] And it shall come to pass, if your sons say to you, 'What is this service?'

[27] That you shall say to them, 'This Passover is a sacrifice to the Lord, as He defended the houses of the children of Israel in Egypt, when He struck the Egyptians, but delivered our houses.'"

[28] And the people bowed and worshipped. And the children of Israel departed and did as the Lord commanded Moses and Aaron, so did they.

The Tenth Plague: Death of the Firstborn

[29] And it came to pass at midnight that the Lord struck all the firstborn in the land of Egypt, from the firstborn of Pharaoh that sat on the throne, to the firstborn of the captive in the dungeon, and the firstborn of all cattle.

[30] And Pharaoh rose up by night, and his servants, and all the Egyptians. And there was a great cry in all the land of Egypt, for there was not a house in which there was not one dead.

The Exodus

[31] And Pharaoh called Moses and Aaron by night, and said to them, "Rise and depart from my people, both you and the children of Israel. Go and serve the Lord your God, even as you say.

³² And take with you your sheep, and your oxen: bless me also, I pray."

³³ And the Egyptians constrained the people, so that they cast them out of the land with haste, for they said, "We all shall die."

³⁴ And the people took their dough before their meal was leavened, bound up as it was in their garments, on their shoulders.

³⁵ And the children of Israel did as Moses commanded them, and they asked of the Egyptians articles of silver and gold and apparel.

³⁶ And the Lord gave His people favor in the sight of the Egyptians, and they lent to them; and they plundered the Egyptians.

³⁷ And the children Israel departed from Rameses to Succoth, *to the full number of* six hundred thousand footmen, even men, besides the baggage.

³⁸ And a great mixed *company* went up with them, and sheep and oxen and very much cattle.

³⁹ And they baked the dough which they brought out of Egypt, *and made* unleavened cakes, for it had not been leavened; for the Egyptians cast them out, and they could not remain, neither did they prepare provisions for themselves for the journey.

⁴⁰ And the sojourning of the children of Israel, while they sojourned in the land of Egypt and the land of Canaan, was four hundred and thirty years.

⁴¹ And it came to pass after the four hundred and thirty years, all the forces of the Lord came forth out of the land of Egypt by night.

⁴² It is a watch kept to the Lord, so that He should bring them out of the land of Egypt; that very night is a watch kept to the Lord, so that it should be to all the children of Israel to their generations.

Instructions Regarding the Passover

⁴³ And the Lord said to Moses and Aaron, "This is the law of the Passover: no stranger shall eat of it.

⁴⁴ And every slave or servant bought with money—him you shall circumcise, and then shall he eat of it.

⁴⁵ A sojourner or hireling shall not eat of it.

⁴⁶ In one house shall it be eaten, and you shall not carry of the flesh out from the house; and a bone of it you shall not break.

⁴⁷ All the congregation of the children of Israel shall keep it.

⁴⁸ And if any proselyte shall come to you to keep the Passover to the Lord, you shall circumcise every male of him, and then shall he approach to sacrifice it, and he shall be even as the original inhabitant of the land; no uncircumcised person shall eat of it.

⁴⁹ There shall be one law to the native, and to the proselyte coming among you."

⁵⁰ And the children of Israel did as the Lord commanded Moses and Aaron for them, so they did.

⁵¹ And it came to pass in that day that the Lord brought out the children of Israel from the land of Egypt with their forces.

EXODUS CHAPTER 13

The Firstborn Consecrated

¹ And the Lord spoke to Moses, saying,

² "Sanctify to Me every firstborn, first produced, opening every womb among the children of Israel, both of man and beast: it is Mine."

³ And Moses said to the people, "Remember this day in which you came forth out of the land of Egypt, out of the house of bondage, for with a strong hand the Lord brought you out from this *place*. No leavened bread shall be eaten.

⁴ For on this day you are going out, in the month of new *grain*.

⁵ And it shall come to pass when the Lord your God shall have brought you into the land of the Canaanites and the Hittites and the Amorites and the Hivites and the Jebusites and the Girgashites and the Perizzites, which He swore to your fathers to give you, a land flowing with milk and honey, that you shall perform this service in this month.

⁶ Six days you shall eat unleavened bread, and on the seventh day is a feast to the Lord.

⁷ Seven days shall you eat unleavened bread; nothing leavened shall be seen with you, neither shall you have leaven in all your borders.

⁸ And you shall tell your son in that day, saying, 'Therefore the Lord has dealt thus with me, as I was going out of Egypt.'

⁹ And it shall be unto you a sign upon your hand and a memorial before your eyes, that the law of the Lord may be in your mouth, for with a strong hand the Lord God has brought you out of Egypt.

¹⁰ And preserve this law according to the times of the seasons, from year to year.

The Law of the Firstborn

¹¹ And it shall come to pass when the Lord your God shall bring you into the land of the Canaanites, as He swore to your fathers, and shall give it you,

¹² that you shall set apart every *offspring* opening the womb, the males to the Lord, everyone that opens the womb out of the herds or among your cattle, as many as you shall have: you shall sanctify the males to the Lord.

¹³ Every *offspring* opening the womb of the donkey you shall change for a sheep; and if you will not change it, you shall redeem it. Every firstborn of man among your sons you shall redeem.

¹⁴ And if later on your son should ask you, saying, 'What is this?' Then you shall say to him, 'With a strong hand the Lord brought us out of Egypt, out of the house of bondage.'

¹⁵ And when Pharaoh hardened *his heart so as not* to send us away, He slew every firstborn in the land of Egypt, both

the firstborn of man and the firstborn of beast; therefore I sacrifice every *offspring* that opens the womb, the males to the Lord, and every firstborn of my sons I will redeem.

[16] And it shall be for a sign upon your hand, and immovable before your eyes, for with a strong hand the Lord has brought you out of Egypt."

The Pillars of Cloud and Fire

[17] And when Pharaoh sent forth the people, God did not lead them by the way of the land of the Philistines, because it was near; for God said, "Lest at any time the people repent when they see war, and return to Egypt."

[18] And God led the people round by the way to the wilderness, to the Red Sea. And in the fifth generation the children of Israel went up out of the land of Egypt.

[19] And Moses took the bones of Joseph with him, for he had solemnly adjured the children of Israel, saying, "God will surely visit you, and you shall carry up my bones from here with you."

[20] And the children of Israel departed from Succoth, and encamped in Etham by the wilderness.

[21] And God led them in the day by a pillar of cloud, to show them the way, and in the night by a pillar of fire.

[22] And the pillar of cloud did not fail by day, nor the pillar of fire by night, before all the people.

EXODUS CHAPTER 14

Crossing the Red Sea

[1] And the Lord spoke to Moses, saying,

[2] "Speak to the children of Israel, and let them turn and encamp before the village, between Migdol and the sea, opposite Baal Zephon: before them shall you encamp by the sea.

[3] And Pharaoh will say to his people, 'As for these children of Israel, they are wandering in the land, for the wilderness has shut them in.'

[4] And I will harden the heart of Pharaoh, and he shall pursue after them; and I will be glorified in Pharaoh, and in all his army, and all the Egyptians shall know that I am the Lord." And they did so.

[5] And it was reported to the king of the Egyptians that the people had fled. And the heart of Pharaoh was turned, and that of his servants against the people; and they said, "What is this that we have done, to let the children of Israel go, so that they should not serve us?"

[6] So Pharaoh yoked his chariots, and led off all his people with himself.

[7] Also he took six hundred chosen chariots, and all the cavalry of the Egyptians, and rulers over all.

[8] And the Lord hardened the heart of Pharaoh, king of Egypt, and of his servants, and he pursued after the children of Israel; and the children of Israel went forth with a high hand.

[9] And the Egyptians pursued after them and found them encamped by the sea; and all the cavalry and the chariots of Pharaoh, and the horsemen, and his host were before the village, over against Baal Zephon.

[10] And Pharaoh approached, and the children of Israel, having looked up, beheld, and the Egyptians encamped behind them. And they were very greatly terrified, and the children of Israel cried to the Lord,

[11] and said to Moses, "Because there were no graves in the land of Egypt have you brought us forth to slay us in the wilderness? What is this that you have done to us, having brought us out of Egypt?

[12] Is not this the word which we spoke to you in Egypt, saying, 'Let us alone that we may serve the Egyptians? For it is better for us to serve the Egyptians than to die in this wilderness.'"

[13] And Moses said to the people, "Be of good courage: stand still and see the salvation of the Lord, which He will work for us this day; for as you have seen the Egyptians today, you shall see them again no more forever.

[14] The Lord shall fight for you, and you shall hold your peace."

[15] And the Lord said to Moses, "Why do you cry to Me? Speak to the children of Israel, and let them proceed.

[16] But lift up your rod, and stretch forth your hand over the sea, and divide it, and let the children of Israel enter into the midst of the sea on the dry land.

[17] And behold, I will harden the heart of Pharaoh and of all the Egyptians, and they shall go in after them; and I will be glorified upon Pharaoh, and upon all his army, and on his chariots and his horses.

[18] And all the Egyptians shall know that I am the Lord, when I am glorified upon Pharaoh and upon his chariots and his horses."

[19] And the Angel of God that went before the camp of the children of Israel removed and went behind *them*, and the pillar of the cloud also removed from before them and stood behind them.

[20] And it went between the camp of the Egyptians and the camp of Israel, and stood; and there was darkness and blackness; and the night passed, and they did not come near to one another during the whole night.

[21] And Moses stretched forth his hand over the sea, and the Lord carried back the sea with a strong south wind the whole night long, and made the sea dry, and the water was divided.

[22] And the children of Israel went into the midst of the sea on the dry land, and the water of it was a wall on the right hand and on the left.

[23] And the Egyptians pursued them and went in after them, all of Pharaoh's horses, his chariots, and his horsemen, into the midst of the sea.

[24] And it came to pass in the morning watch that the Lord looked forth on the camp of the Egyptians through the pillar of fire and cloud, and troubled the camp of the Egyptians,

[25] and bound the axle-trees of their chariots, and caused them to go with difficulty; and the Egyptians said, "Let us flee from the face of Israel, for the Lord fights for them against the Egyptians."

[26] And the Lord said to Moses, "Stretch forth your hand over the sea, and let the water be turned back to its place, and let it cover the Egyptians, *coming* over both their chariots and their riders."

[27] And Moses stretched forth his hand over the sea, and the water returned to its place toward day; and the Egyptians fled from the water, and the Lord shook off the Egyptians in the midst of the sea.

[28] And the water returned and covered the chariots and the riders, and all the forces of Pharaoh, who entered after them into the sea; and there was not so much as one of them left.

[29] But the children of Israel went along dry land in the midst of the sea, and the water was to them a wall on the right hand, and on the left.

[30] So the Lord delivered Israel in that day from the hand of the Egyptians, and Israel saw the Egyptians dead by the shore of the sea.

[31] And Israel saw the mighty hand, the things which the Lord did to the Egyptians; and the people feared the Lord, and they believed God and Moses His servant.

EXODUS CHAPTER 15

The Song of Moses

[1] Then Moses and the children of Israel sang this song to God, and spoke, saying, "Let us sing to the Lord, for He is very greatly glorified: horse and rider He has thrown into the sea.

[2] He was to me a helper and protector for salvation: this is my God and I will glorify Him; my father's God, and I will exalt Him.

[3] The Lord brings wars to nought, the Lord is His name.

[4] He has cast the chariots of Pharaoh and his army into the sea, the chosen mounted captains: they were swallowed up in the Red Sea.

[5] He covered them with the sea: they sank to the depth like a stone.

[6] Your right hand, O God, has been glorified in strength; Your right hand, O God, has broken the enemies.

[7] And in the abundance of Your glory You have broken the adversaries to pieces. You have sent forth Your wrath, it devoured them as stubble.

[8] And by the breath of Your anger the waters were parted; the waters were congealed as a wall, the waves were congealed in the midst of the sea.

[9] The enemy said, 'I will pursue, I will overtake, I will divide the spoils; I will satisfy my soul, I will destroy with my sword, my hand shall have dominion.'

[10] You sent forth Your wind, the sea covered them; they sank like lead in the mighty water.

[11] Who is like You among the gods, O Lord? Who is like You? Glorified in holiness, marvelous in glories, working wonders.

[12] You stretched forth Your right hand, *and* the earth swallowed them up.

[13] You have guided in Your righteousness this Your people whom You have redeemed, by Your strength You have called them into Your holy resting place.

[14] The nations heard and were angry; pangs have seized among the inhabitants of the Philistines.

[15] Then the princes of Edom, and the chiefs of the Moabites hastened; trembling took hold upon them, all the inhabitants of Canaan melted away.

[16] Let trembling and fear fall upon them; by the greatness of Your arm, let them become as stone; till Your people pass over, O Lord, till this Your people pass over, whom You have purchased.

[17] Bring them in and plant them in the mountain of their inheritance, in Your prepared habitation, which You, O Lord, have prepared; the sanctuary, O Lord, which Your hands have made ready.

[18] The Lord reigns forever and ever!

[19] For the horse of Pharaoh went in with the chariots and horsemen into the sea, and the Lord brought upon them the water of the sea, but the children of Israel walked through dry land in the midst of the sea."

The Song of Miriam

[20] Then Miriam the prophetess, the sister of Aaron, having taken a timbrel in her hand, then there went forth all the women after her with timbrels and dances.

[21] And Miriam led them, saying, "Let us sing to the Lord, for He has been very greatly glorified: the horse and rider has He cast into the sea."

Bitter Water Made Sweet

[22] So Moses brought up the children of Israel from the Red Sea, and brought them into the Wilderness of Shur; and they went three days in the wilderness, and found no water to drink.

[23] And they came to Marah, and they could not drink *the water* of Marah, for it was bitter; therefore he named the name of that place, Bitterness.

[24] And the people murmured against Moses, saying, "What shall we drink?"

[25] And Moses cried to the Lord, and the Lord showed him a tree, and he cast it into the water, and the water was sweetened. There He established to him ordinances and judgments, and there He proved him,

[26] and said, "If you will indeed hear the voice of the Lord your God, and do the things pleasing before Him, and will heed His commands, and keep all His ordinances, no disease which I have brought upon the Egyptians will I bring upon you, for I am the Lord your God that heals you."

²⁷ And they came to Elim, where there were twelve fountains of water and seventy stems of palm trees; and they camped there by the waters.

EXODUS CHAPTER 16

Bread From Heaven

¹ And they departed from Elim, and all the congregation of the children of Israel came to the Wilderness of Sin, which is between Elim and Sinai; and on the fifteenth day, in the second month after their departure from the land of Egypt,

² all the congregation of the children of Israel murmured against Moses and Aaron.

³ And the children of Israel said to them, "If only we would have died smitten by the Lord in the land of Egypt, when we sat by the fleshpots, and ate bread to the full! For you have brought us out into this wilderness, to slay all this congregation with hunger."

⁴ And the Lord said to Moses, "Behold, I will rain bread upon you out of heaven; and the people shall go forth, and they shall gather their daily portion for the day, that I may test them, whether they will walk in My law or not.

⁵ And it shall come to pass on the sixth day that they shall prepare whatsoever they have brought in, and it shall be double of what they shall have gathered for the day, daily."

⁶ And Moses and Aaron said to all the congregation of the children of Israel, "At evening you shall know that the Lord has brought you out of the land of Egypt;

⁷ and in the morning you shall see the glory of the Lord, inasmuch as He hears your murmuring against God; and who are we, that you continue to murmur against us?"

⁸ And Moses said, "*This shall be* when the Lord gives you meat to eat in the evening, and bread in the morning to the full, because the Lord has heard your murmuring, which you murmur against us: and what are we? For your murmuring is not against us, but against God."

⁹ And Moses said to Aaron, "Say to all the congregation of the children of Israel, 'Come near before God; for He has heard your murmuring.'"

¹⁰ And when Aaron spoke to all the congregation of the children of Israel, and they turned toward the wilderness, then the glory of the Lord appeared in a cloud.

¹¹ And the Lord spoke to Moses, saying,

¹² "I have heard the murmuring of the children of Israel. Speak to them, saying, 'Towards evening you shall eat meat, and in the morning you shall be satisfied with bread; and you shall know that I am the Lord your God.'"

¹³ And it was evening, and quails came up and covered the camp. ¹⁴ In the morning it came to pass as the dew ceased round about the camp, that behold, on the face of the wilderness *was* a small thing like white coriander seed, as frost upon the earth.

¹⁵ And when the children of Israel saw it, they said one to another, "What is this?" For they did not know what it was; and Moses said to them,

¹⁶ "This *is* the bread which the Lord has given you to eat. This is that which the Lord has appointed; gather of it each man for his family, a homer for each person, according to the number of your souls, gather each of you with his fellow lodgers."

¹⁷ And the children of Israel did so and gathered, some much, and some less.

¹⁸ And having measured the homer *full*, he that gathered much had nothing *left* over, and he that had gathered less had no lack; each gathered according to the need of those who belonged to him.

¹⁹ And Moses said to them, "Let no man leave any of it till the morning."

²⁰ But they did not hearken to Moses, but some left of it till the morning; and it bred worms and stank. And Moses was irritated with them.

²¹ And they gathered it every morning, each man what he needed, and when the sun became hot it melted.

²² And it came to pass on the sixth day, they gathered double what was needed, two homers for one *man*; and all the chiefs of the synagogue went in and reported it to Moses.

²³ And Moses said to them, "Is not this the word which the Lord spoke? Tomorrow is the Sabbath, a holy rest to the Lord: bake what you will bake, and boil what you will boil, and all that is *left* over lay aside for tomorrow."

²⁴ And they left it aside till the morning, as Moses commanded them; and it did not stink, neither was there a worm in it.

²⁵ And Moses said, "Eat *that* today, for today is a Sabbath to the Lord: *it* shall not be found in the plain.

²⁶ Six days you shall gather it, and on the seventh day is a Sabbath, for there shall be none on that *day*."

²⁷ And it came to pass on the seventh day that some of the people went forth to gather, and found none.

²⁸ And the Lord said to Moses, "How long are you unwilling to heed My commands and My law?

²⁹ See, for the Lord has given you this day as the Sabbath, therefore He has given you on the sixth day the bread of two days. You shall sit each of you in your houses; let no one go forth from his place on the seventh day."

³⁰ And the people kept the Sabbath on the seventh day.

³¹ And the children of Israel called the name of it Manna; and it was as white coriander seed, and the taste of it as a wafer with honey.

³² And Moses said, "This is the thing which the Lord has commanded, Fill a homer with manna, to be laid up for your generations, that they may see the bread which you ate in the wilderness, when the Lord led you forth out of the land of Egypt."

³³ And Moses said to Aaron, "Take a golden pot, and cast into it one full homer of manna; and you shall lay it up before God, to be kept for your generations,"

³⁴ as the Lord commanded Moses. And Aaron laid it up before the testimony to be kept.

35 And the children of Israel ate manna for forty years, until they came to the land they ate the manna, until they came to the region of Phoenicia.

36 Now a homer was the tenth part of three measures.

EXODUS CHAPTER 17

Water from the Rock

1 And all the congregation of the children of Israel departed from the Wilderness of Sin, according to their encampments, by the word of the Lord; and they encamped in Rephidim. And there was no water for the people to drink.

2 And the people reviled Moses, saying, "Give us water, that we may drink!" And Moses said to them, "Why do you revile me, and why do you tempt the Lord?"

3 And the people thirsted there for water, and there the people murmured against Moses, saying, "Why is this? Have you brought us up out of Egypt to slay us and our children and our cattle with thirst?"

4 And Moses cried to the Lord, saying, "What shall I do to this people? Yet a little while and they will stone me."

5 And the Lord said to Moses, "Go before this people, and take with you some of the elders of the people; and the rod with which you struck the river, take in your hand, and you shall go.

6 Behold, I stand there before you, on the rock in Horeb, and you shall strike the rock, and water shall come out from it, and the people shall drink." And Moses did so before the sons of Israel.

7 And he called the name of that place, Temptation and Reviling, because of the reviling of the children of Israel, and because they tempted the Lord, saying, "Is the Lord among us or not?"

Amelek Attacks Israel and Is Defeated

8 And Amalek came and fought with Israel in Rephidim.

9 And Moses said to Joshua, "Choose out for yourself mighty men, and go forth and set the army in array against Amalek tomorrow; and behold, I *shall* stand on the top of the hill, and the rod of God *will be* in my hand."

10 And Joshua did as Moses said to him, and he went out and set the army in array against Amalek, and Moses and Aaron and Hur went up to the top of the hill.

11 And it came to pass, when Moses lifted up his hands, Israel prevailed; and when he let down his hands, Amalek prevailed.

12 But the hands of Moses were heavy, and they took a stone and put it under him, and he sat upon it; and Aaron and Hur supported his hands, one on this side and one on the other, and the hands of Moses were supported till sunset.

13 And Joshua routed Amalek and all his people with the edge of the sword.

14 And the Lord said to Moses, "Write this for a memorial in a book, and speak in the ears of Joshua; for I will utterly blot out the memorial of Amalek from under heaven."

15 And Moses built an altar to the Lord, and called the name of it, The Lord my Refuge.

16 For with a secret hand the Lord wages war upon Amalek to all generations.

EXODUS CHAPTER 18

Jethro's Advice

1 And Jethro the priest of Midian, the father-in-law of Moses, heard of all that the Lord did to His people Israel; for the Lord brought Israel out of Egypt.

2 And Jethro the father-in-law of Moses, took Zipporah the wife of Moses after she had been sent away,

3 and her two sons: the name of the one was Gershom, *his father* saying, "I was a sojourner in a strange land";

4 and the name of the second *was* Eliezer, saying, "For the God of my father is my helper, and He has rescued me out of the hand of Pharaoh."

5 And Jethro the father-in-law of Moses, and his sons and his wife, went forth to Moses into the wilderness, where he encamped on the mount of God.

6 And it was told Moses, saying, "Behold, your father-in-law Jethro is coming to you, and your wife and two sons with him."

7 And Moses went forth to meet his father-in-law, and bowed down and kissed him, and they embraced each other, and he brought them into the tent.

8 And Moses related to his father-in-law all things that the Lord had done to Pharaoh and all the Egyptians for Israel's sake, and all the labor that had come upon them along the way, and that the Lord had rescued them out of the hand of Pharaoh, and out of the hand of the Egyptians.

9 And Jethro was amazed at all the good things which the Lord had done to them, inasmuch as he rescued them out of the hand of the Egyptians and out of the hand of Pharaoh.

10 And Jethro said, "Blessed be the Lord, because He has rescued them out of the hand of the Egyptians and out of the hand of Pharaoh.

11 For now I know that the Lord is great above all gods, because of this, wherein they attacked them."

12 And Jethro the father-in-law of Moses took burnt offerings and sacrifices for God, for Aaron and all the elders of Israel came to eat bread with the father-in-law of Moses before God.

13 And it came to pass the next day that Moses sat to judge the people, and all the people stood by Moses from morning till evening.

14 And Jethro, having seen all that *Moses* did to the people, said, "What is this that you do to the people? Why do you alone sit, and all the people stand by you from morning till evening?"

¹⁵ And Moses said to his father-in-law, "Because the people come to me to seek judgment from God.

¹⁶ For whenever there is a dispute among them, and they come to me, I give judgment upon each, and I teach them the ordinances of God and His law."

¹⁷ And the father-in-law of Moses said to him, "The thing that you do is not good.

¹⁸ You will wear away with intolerable weariness, both you and all these people who are with you: this thing is hard, you will not be able to endure it by yourself.

¹⁹ Now then listen to me, and I will advise you, and God shall be with you: be all things to the people pertaining to God, and you shall bring their matters to God.

²⁰ And you shall testify to them the ordinances of God and His law, and you shall show to them the ways in which they shall walk, and the works which they shall do.

²¹ Also you shall select for yourself able men out of all the people, God fearing *men*, righteous men, hating pride, and you shall set over the people captains of thousands and captains of hundreds, and captains of fifties, and captains of tens.

²² And they shall judge the people at all times, and those matters too burdensome they shall bring to you, but they shall judge the smaller cases; so they shall relieve you and help you.

²³ If you will do this thing, God shall strengthen you, and you shall be able to endure, and all this people shall go into their own place with peace."

²⁴ And Moses listened to the voice of his father-in-law, and did all that he said to him.

²⁵ And Moses chose out able men out of all Israel, and he made them captains of thousands and captains of hundreds, and captains of fifties and captains of tens over the people.

²⁶ And they judged the people at all times; and every matter too burdensome they brought to Moses, but every light matter they judged themselves.

²⁷ And Moses dismissed his father-in-law, and he returned to his own land.

EXODUS CHAPTER 19

Israel at Mount Sinai

¹ And in the third month of the departure of the children of Israel out of the land of Egypt, on the same day, they came into the Wilderness of Sinai.

² And they departed from Rephidim, and came into the Wilderness of Sinai, and there Israel encamped before the mountain.

³ And Moses went up to the mount of God, and God called him out of the mountain, saying, "These things shall you say to the house of Jacob, and you shall report them to the children of Israel.

⁴ 'You have seen all that I have done to the Egyptians, and I took you up as upon eagles' wings, and I brought you near to Myself.

⁵ And now if you will indeed hear My voice, and keep My covenant, you shall be to Me a peculiar people above all nations; for the whole earth is Mine.

⁶ And you shall be to Me a royal priesthood and a holy nation.' These words shall you speak to the children of Israel."

⁷ And Moses came and called the elders of the people, and he set before them all these words, which God appointed them.

⁸ And all the people answered with one accord, and said, "All things that God has spoken, we will do and hearken to." And Moses reported these words to God.

⁹ And the Lord said to Moses, "Behold, I come to you in a pillar of a cloud, that the people may hear Me speaking to you, and may believe you forever." And Moses reported the words of the people to the Lord.

¹⁰ And the Lord said to Moses, "Go down and solemnly charge the people, and sanctify them today and tomorrow, and let them wash their garments.

¹¹ And let them be ready for the third day, for on the third day the Lord will descend upon Mount Sinai before all the people.

¹² And you shall separate the people round about, saying, 'Take heed to yourselves that you do not go up into the mountain, nor touch any part of it: *for* whoever touches the mountain shall surely die.

¹³ A hand shall not touch it, for *everyone that touches* shall be stoned with stones or shot through with a dart, whether beast or man, it shall not live; when the voices and trumpets and cloud depart from off the mountain, they shall come up on the mountain.'"

¹⁴ And Moses went down from the mountain to the people and sanctified them, and they washed their clothes.

¹⁵ And he said to the people, "Be ready: for three days do not come near to a woman.

¹⁶ And it came to pass on the third day, as the morning drew near, *that* there were voices and lightnings and a dark cloud on Mount Sinai. The voice of the trumpet sounded loud, and all the people in the camp trembled.

¹⁷ And Moses led the people forth out of the camp to meet God, and they stood by under the camp.

¹⁸ Now Mount Sinai was engulfed in smoke, because God had descended upon it in fire; and the smoke went up like the smoke of a furnace, and the people were exceedingly amazed.

¹⁹ And the sounds of the trumpet were growing much louder. *And* Moses spoke, and God answered him with a voice.

²⁰ And the Lord came down upon Mount Sinai on the top of the mountain; and the Lord called Moses to the top of the mountain, and Moses went up.

²¹ And God spoke to Moses, saying, "Go down, and solemnly charge the people, lest at any time they draw near to God to gaze, and many of them perish.

22 And let the priests that draw near to the Lord God sanctify themselves, lest He destroy some of them."

23 And Moses said to God, "The people cannot approach Mount Sinai, for You have solemnly charged us, saying, 'Set boundaries around the mountain and sanctify it.'"

24 And the Lord said to him, "Go down and then come up, you and Aaron with you; but let not the priests and the people force their way to come up to God, lest the Lord destroy some of them."

25 And Moses went down to the people, and spoke to them.

EXODUS CHAPTER 20

The Ten Commandments

1 And the Lord spoke all these words, saying:

2 "I am the Lord your God, who brought you out of the land of Egypt, out of the house of bondage.

3 You shall have no other gods beside Me.

4 "You shall not make for yourself an idol, nor likeness of anything, whatever things are in the heaven above, and whatever are in the earth beneath, and whatever are in the waters under the earth.

5 You shall not bow down to them, nor serve them; for I am the Lord your God, a jealous God, recompensing the sins of the fathers upon the children, to the third and fourth generation to them that hate Me,

6 and bestowing mercy on them that love Me, to *the* thousands *of them*, and on them that keep My commandments.

7 "You shall not take the name of the Lord your God in vain; for the Lord your God will not acquit him that takes His name in vain.

8 "Remember the Sabbath day, to keep it holy.

9 Six days you shall labor, and do all your work.

10 But on the seventh day is the Sabbath of the Lord your God; on it you shall do no work: you, nor your son, nor your daughter, your servant nor your maidservant, your ox, nor your donkey, nor any cattle of yours, nor the stranger that sojourns with you.

11 For in six days the Lord made the heaven and the earth, and the sea and all things in them, and rested on the seventh day; therefore the Lord blessed the seventh day, and sanctified it.

12 "Honor your father and your mother, that it may be well with you, and that you may live long on the good land, which the Lord your God gives to you.

13 "You shall not kill.

14 "You shall not commit adultery.

15 "You shall not steal.

16 "You shall not bear false witness against your neighbor.

17 "You shall not covet your neighbor's wife; you shall not covet your neighbor's house; nor his field, nor his servant, nor his maid, nor his ox, nor his donkey, nor any of his cattle, nor whatever belongs to your neighbor."

18 And all the people perceived the thundering, and the flashes, and the voice of the trumpet, and the mountain smoking; and all the people feared and stood afar off,

19 and said to Moses, "You speak to us, but let not God speak to us, lest we die."

20 And Moses said to them, "Be of good courage, for God has come to you to test you, that His fear may be among you, that you do not sin."

21 And the people stood afar off, and Moses went into the darkness where God was.

The Law Concerning the Altar

22 And the Lord said to Moses, "Thus shall you say to the house of Jacob, and you shall report it to the children of Israel: "You have seen that I have spoken to you from heaven.

23 You shall not make for yourselves gods of silver, and gods of gold you shall not make for yourselves.

24 You shall make to Me an altar of earth; and upon it you shall sacrifice your burnt offerings, and your peace offerings, and your sheep and your calves in every place, where I shall record My name; and I will come to you and bless you.

25 And if you will make to Me an altar of stones, you shall not build it of hewn *stones*; for if you have lifted up your tool upon them, then they are defiled.

26 You shall not go up to My altar by steps, that you may not uncover your nakedness upon it."

EXODUS CHAPTER 21

The Law Concerning Servants

1 "And these *are* the ordinances which you shall set before them:

2 If you buy a Hebrew servant, six years shall he serve you, and in the seventh year he shall go forth free for nothing.

3 If he should have come in alone, he shall also go forth alone; and if his wife should have gone in together with him, his wife also shall go out.

4 Moreover, if his master gives him a wife, and she has *born* him sons or daughters, the wife and the children shall be his master's; and he shall go forth alone.

5 And if the servant should answer and say, 'I love my master and wife and children, I will not go away free';

6 his master shall bring him to the judgment seat of God, and then shall he bring him to the door, to the doorpost, and his master shall bore his ear through with an awl, and he shall serve him forever.

7 "And if anyone sell his daughter as a domestic, she shall not depart as the maidservants depart.

8 If she be not pleasing to her master, after she has betrothed herself to him, he shall let her go free; but he is not at liberty to sell her to a foreign nation, because he has dealt deceitfully with her.

9 And if he should have betrothed her to his son, he shall do to her according to the right of daughters.

[10] And if he take another to himself, he shall not diminish her food, her clothing, and her companionship *with him*.

[11] And if he will not do these three things to her, she shall go out free without money.

The Law Concerning Violence

[12] "And if any man strike another and he dies, let him by all means be put to death.

[13] But as for him that did it not willingly, but God delivered him into his hands, I will give you a place where the slayer may flee to.

[14] "And if anyone lie in wait for his neighbor to slay him by craft, and he go for refuge, you shall take him from My altar to put him to death.

[15] "Whoever strikes his father or his mother, let him be certainly put to death.

[16] "Whosoever shall steal one of the children of Israel, and prevail over him and sell him, and he be found with him, let him certainly die.

[17] "He that reviles his father or his mother shall surely die.

[18] "And if two men contend with each other, and one strikes the other with a stone or with his fist, and he does not die, but is laid upon his bed;

[19] if the man arises and walks about with his staff, he that struck him shall be clear; only he shall pay for his loss of time, and for his healing.

[20] "And if a man beats his manservant or his maidservant with a rod, and *the party* dies under his hands, he shall be surely punished.

[21] But if *the servant* continues to live a day or two, let not *the master* be punished; for he is his property.

[22] "And if two men strive and strike a woman with child, and her child be born imperfectly formed, he shall be forced to pay a penalty: as the woman's husband may lay upon him, he shall pay with a valuation.

[23] But if it be perfectly formed, he shall give life for life,

[24] eye for eye, tooth for tooth, hand for hand, foot for foot,

[25] burning for burning, wound for wound, stripe for stripe.

[26] "And if one strike the eye of his manservant, or the eye of his maidservant, and put it out, he shall let them go free for their eye's sake.

[27] And if he should strike out the tooth of his manservant, or the tooth of his maidservant, he shall send them away free for their tooth's sake.

Laws Concerning Property

[28] "And if a bull gores a man or woman and they die, the bull shall be stoned with stones, and his flesh shall not be eaten; but the owner of the bull shall be clear.

[29] But if the bull was inclined to goring in the past, and men have told his owner, and he has not removed him, so that it has killed a man or a woman, the bull shall be stoned, and his owner shall die also.

[30] And if a ransom should be imposed on him, he shall pay for the ransom of his soul as much as they shall lay upon him.

[31] And if *the bull* gores a son or daughter, let them do to him according to this ordinance.

[32] And if the bull gores a manservant or maidservant, he shall pay to their master thirty silver shekels, and the bull shall be stoned.

[33] And if anyone opens a pit, or digs a pit and does not cover it, and an ox or a donkey fall in there,

[34] the owner of the pit shall make compensation; he shall give money to their owner, and the dead shall be his own.

[35] And if any man's bull gores the bull of his neighbor, and it dies, they shall sell the living bull and divide the money, and they shall divide the dead bull.

[36] But if the bull was known to have been given to goring in the past, and they have testified to his owner and he has not removed him, he shall repay bull for bull, but the dead shall be his own."

EXODUS CHAPTER 22

Laws of Restitution

[1] "And if one steals an ox or a sheep, and kills it or sells it, he shall pay five calves for a calf, and four sheep for a sheep.

[2] And if the thief is found breaking in, and he is struck so that he dies, there shall be no blood shed for him.

[3] But if the sun has risen upon him, he is guilty, *and* he shall die instead; and if a thief has nothing, let him be sold in compensation for what he has stolen.

[4] And if the thing stolen is left and is in his hand alive, whether ox or sheep, he shall restore them twofold.

[5] "And if anyone should feed down a field or a vineyard, and should send in his beast to feed down another field, he shall make compensation of his own field according to his produce; and if he shall have fed down the whole field, he shall pay for compensation the best of his own field and the best of his vineyard.

[6] "And if fire has gone forth and caught thorns, and should also set on fire threshing floors or ears of corn or a field, he that kindled the fire shall make compensation.

[7] "And if anyone gives to his neighbor money or goods to keep, and they are stolen out of the man's house, if the thief is found he shall repay double.

[8] But if the thief is not found, the master of the house shall come forward before God, and shall swear that surely he has not done wickedly in regard to any part of his neighbor's goods,

[9] according to every injury alleged, *whether it* concerns a calf, a donkey, a sheep, a garment, and every alleged loss, whatever in fact it may be—the judgment of both shall proceed before God, and he that is convicted by God shall repay to his neighbor double.

¹⁰ "And if anyone gives to his neighbor a calf, a sheep or any beast to keep, and it is wounded or dies or is taken, and no one know,

¹¹ an oath of God shall be between both, *each swearing* that he has by no means been guilty in the matter of his neighbor's goods; and so his master shall hold him guiltless, and he shall not make compensation.

¹² But if it is stolen from him, he shall make compensation to the owner.

¹³ And if it is seized by beasts, he shall bring him to *witness* the prey, and he shall not make compensation.

Social and Religious Laws

¹⁴ "And if anyone borrow from his neighbor, and it becomes wounded or dies or is carried away, and the owner of it is not with it, he shall make compensation.

¹⁵ But if the owner is with it, he shall not make compensation: but if it is a hired thing, there shall be *a compensation* to him instead of his hire.

¹⁶ "And if anyone deceive a virgin that is not betrothed, and lie with her, he shall surely endow her for a wife to himself.

¹⁷ And if her father positively refuses, and will not consent to give her to him for a wife, he shall pay compensation to her father according to the amount of the dowry of virgins.

¹⁸ "You shall not save the lives of sorcerers.

¹⁹ "Everyone that lies with a beast shall surely be put to death.

²⁰ "He that sacrifices to any gods but to the Lord alone, shall be destroyed by death.

²¹ "And you shall not hurt a stranger, nor afflict him; for you were strangers in the land of Egypt.

²² "You shall hurt no widow or orphan.

²³ And if you should afflict them by ill treatment, and they should cry aloud to Me, I will surely hear their voice.

²⁴ And I will be very angry, and will slay you with the sword, and your wives shall be widows and your children orphans.

²⁵ "And if you should lend money to your poor brother who is among you, you shall not be hard upon him—you shall not charge interest from him.

²⁶ And if you take your neighbor's garment for a pledge, you shall restore it to him before sunset.

²⁷ For this is his clothing, this is the only covering of his nakedness; how shall he sleep? If then he shall cry to Me, I will listen to him, for I am merciful.

²⁸ "You shall not revile God, nor curse a ruler of your people.

²⁹ "You shall not keep back the firstfruits of your threshing floor and press. The firstborn of your sons you shall give unto Me.

³⁰ So shall you do with your calf and your sheep and your donkey; seven days shall it be under the mother, and the eighth day you shall give it unto Me.

³¹ "And you shall be holy men to Me; and you shall not eat flesh taken from beasts, you shall cast it to the dogs."

EXODUS CHAPTER 23

Justice for All

¹ "You shall not receive a false report. You shall not agree with the unjust to become an unjust witness.

² You shall not associate with the multitude for evil. You shall not join yourself with a multitude to turn aside with the majority so as to shut out judgment.

³ And you shall not spare a poor man in judgment.

⁴ "And if you meet your enemy's ox or his donkey going astray, you shall turn them back and restore them to him.

⁵ And if you see your enemy's donkey fallen under its burden, you shall not pass by it, but you shall help to raise it with him.

⁶ "You shall not pervert the judgment of the poor in his cause.

⁷ You shall abstain from every unjust thing: you shall not slay the innocent and righteous, and you shall not justify the wicked for gifts.

⁸ And you shall not receive gifts; for gifts blind the eyes of the seeing, and corrupt just words.

⁹ And you shall not afflict a stranger, for you know the heart of a stranger; for you yourselves were strangers in the land of Egypt.

The Law of Sabbaths

¹⁰ "Six years you shall sow your land, and gather in the fruits of it.

¹¹ But in the seventh year you shall let it rest, and leave it, and the poor of your nation shall feed; and the wild beasts of the field shall eat that which remains; thus shall you do to your vineyard and to your olive grove.

¹² Six days shall you do your work, and on the seventh day there shall be rest, that your ox and your donkey may rest, and that the son of your maidservant and the stranger may be refreshed.

¹³ Observe all things whatsoever I have commanded you; and you shall make no mention of the name of other gods, neither shall they be heard out of your mouth.

Three Annual Feasts

¹⁴ "Three times you shall keep a feast to Me in the year.

¹⁵ Take heed to keep the Feast of Unleavened Bread: seven days you shall eat unleavened bread, as I commanded you at the season of the month of new *grain*, for in it you came out of Egypt. You shall not appear before Me empty.

¹⁶ And you shall keep the Feast of Harvest, the firstfruits of your labors, whatsoever you shall have sown in your field, and the Feast of Completion at the end of the year in the gathering of your fruits out of your field.

¹⁷ Three times in the year shall all your males appear before the Lord your God.

¹⁸ For when I shall have cast out the nations from before you, and shall have widened your borders, you shall not

offer the blood of My sacrifice with leaven, neither must the fat of My feast abide till the morning.

19 You shall bring the first offerings of the firstfruits of your land into the house of the Lord your God. You shall not boil a young lamb in its mother's milk.

The Conquest of Canaan Promised

20 "And behold, I send My Angel before your face, that He may keep you in the way, that He may bring you into the land which I have prepared for you.

21 Take heed to yourself and hearken to Him, and do not disobey Him; for He will not give way to you, for My name is in Him.

22 If you will indeed hear My voice, and if you will do all the things I shall command you, and keep My covenant, you shall be to Me a peculiar people above all nations. For the whole earth is Mine, and you shall be to Me a royal priesthood, and a holy nation. These words shall you speak to the children of Israel: 'If you shall indeed hear My voice, and do all the things I shall tell you, then I will be an enemy to your enemies, and an adversary to your adversaries.

23 For My Angel shall go as your leader, and shall bring you to the Amorites and the Hittites and the Perizzites and the Canaanites and the Gergesites and the Hivites and the Jebusites, and I will destroy them.

24 You shall not worship their gods, nor serve them. You shall not do according to their works, but you shall utterly destroy them, and break to pieces their pillars.

25 And you shall serve the Lord your God, and I will bless your bread and your wine and your water, and I will turn away sickness from you.

26 There shall not be one that is impotent or barren on your land. I will surely fulfill the number of your days.

27 "And I will send terror before you, and I will strike with amazement all the nations to which you shall come, and I will make all your enemies to flee.

28 And I will send hornets before you, and you shall cast out the Amorites and the Hivites and the Canaanites and the Hittites from you.

29 I will not cast them out in one year, lest the land become desolate, and the beasts of the field multiply against you.

30 By little *and little* I will cast them out from before you, until you shall be increased and inherit the earth.

31 And I will set your borders from the Red Sea to the sea of the Philistines, and from the wilderness to the great river Euphrates; and I will give into your hand those that dwell in the land, and will cast them out from you.

32 You shall make no covenant with them and their gods.

33 And they shall not dwell in your land, lest they cause you to sin against Me; for if you should serve their gods, these will be an offense to you."

EXODUS CHAPTER 24

The Blood of the Covenant

1 And to Moses he said, "Go up to the Lord, you and Aaron and Nadab and Abihu, and seventy of the elders of Israel: and they shall worship the Lord from a distance.

2 And Moses alone shall draw near to God; and they shall not draw near, and the people shall not come up with them."

3 And Moses went in and related to the people all the words of God and the ordinances; and all the people answered with one voice, saying, "All the words which the Lord has spoken, we will do and be obedient."

4 And Moses wrote all the words of the Lord; and Moses rose up early in the morning, and built an altar under the mountain, and *set up* twelve stones for the twelve tribes of Israel.

5 And he sent forth the young men of the children of Israel, and they offered burnt offerings, and they sacrificed young calves as a peace offering to God.

6 And Moses took half the blood and poured it into bowls, and half the blood he poured out upon the altar.

7 And he took the Book of the Covenant and read it in the ears of the people, and they said, "All things whatsoever the Lord has said we will do and be obedient."

8 And Moses took the blood and sprinkled it upon the people, and said, "Behold the blood of the covenant, which the Lord has made with you concerning all these words."

On the Mountain with God

9 And Moses went up, and Aaron, and Nadab and Abihu, and seventy of the elders of Israel.

10 And they saw the place where the God of Israel stood; and under His feet was as it were a work of sapphire slabs, and as it were the appearance of the firmament of heaven in its purity.

11 And of the chosen ones of Israel there was not even one missing, and they appeared in the place of God, and did eat and drink.

12 And the Lord said to Moses, "Come up to Me into the mountain, and be there; and I will give you the tablets of stone, the law and the commandments, which I have written to give them laws."

13 And Moses rose up and Joshua his attendant, and they went up into the mount of God.

14 And to the elders they said, "Rest there till we return to you; and behold, Aaron and Hur are with you: if any man have a cause to be tried, let them go to them."

15 And Moses and Joshua went up to the mountain, and the cloud covered the mountain.

16 And the glory of God came down upon Mount Sinai, and the cloud covered it six days; and the Lord called Moses on the seventh day out of the midst of the cloud.

17 And the appearance of the glory of the Lord was as burning fire on the top of the mountain, before the children of Israel.

18 And Moses went into the midst of the cloud, and went up to the mountain, and was there in the mountain forty days and forty nights.

EXODUS CHAPTER 25

Offerings for the Sanctuary

¹ And the Lord spoke to Moses, saying,

² "Speak to the children of Israel, and take *the* firstfruits from all, who may be disposed in their heart to give; and you shall take My firstfruits.

³ And this is the offering which you shall take of them: gold, silver and brass;

⁴ blue, purple, and double scarlet; fine spun linen, and goats' hair;

⁵ rams' skins dyed red, blue skins, and incorruptible wood;

⁶ and oil for the light, incense for anointing oil, for the composition of incense,

⁷ and sardius stones, and stones for the carved work of the breastplate, and the full-length robe.

⁸ And you shall make Me a sanctuary, and I will appear among you.

⁹ And you shall make for Me according to all things which I show you in the mountain; even the pattern of the tabernacle, and the pattern of all its furniture: so shall you make it.

The Ark of Testimony

¹⁰ "And you shall make the Ark of Testimony of incorruptible wood; the length of two cubits and a half, and the breadth of a cubit and a half, and the height of a cubit and a half.

¹¹ And you shall overlay it with pure gold, inside and out you shall overlay it; and you shall make for it golden wreaths twisted round about.

¹² And you shall cast for it four golden rings, and shall put them on the four sides; two rings on the one side, and two rings on the other side.

¹³ And you shall make poles *of* incorruptible wood, and shall overlay them with gold.

¹⁴ And you shall put the poles into the rings on the sides of the ark, to bear the ark with them.

¹⁵ The poles shall remain fixed in the rings of the ark.

¹⁶ And you shall put into the ark the testimonies which I shall give you.

¹⁷ And you shall make a mercy seat, a lid of pure gold; the length of two cubits and a half, and the breadth of a cubit and a half.

¹⁸ And you shall make two cherubim graven in gold, and you shall put them on both sides of the mercy seat.

¹⁹ They shall be made, one cherub on this side, and another cherub on the other side of the mercy seat; and you shall make the two cherubim on the two sides.

²⁰ The cherubim shall stretch forth their wings above, overshadowing the mercy seat with their wings; and their faces shall be toward each other, the faces of the cherubim shall be toward the mercy seat.

²¹ And you shall set the mercy seat on the ark above, and you shall put into the ark the testimonies which I shall give you.

²² And I will make Myself known to you from there, and I will speak to you from above the mercy seat between the two cherubim, which are upon the Ark of Testimony, even in all things which I shall charge you concerning the children of Israel.

The Table for the Showbread

²³ "And you shall make a golden table of pure gold, in length two cubits, and in breadth a cubit, and in height a cubit and a half.

²⁴ And you shall make for it golden wreaths twisted round about, and you shall make for it a crown of an handbreadth round about.

²⁵ And you shall make a twisted wreath for the crown round about.

²⁶ And you shall make four golden rings; and you shall put the four rings upon the four parts of its feet under the crown.

²⁷ And the rings shall be for bearings for the poles, that they may bear the table with them.

²⁸ And you shall make the poles of incorruptible wood, and you shall overlay them with pure gold; and the table shall be borne with them.

²⁹ And you shall make its dishes, its censers, its bowls, and its cups, with which you shall offer drink offerings. Of pure gold shall you make them.

³⁰ And you shall set upon the table showbread before Me continually.

The Gold Lampstand

³¹ "And you shall make a lampstand of pure gold; you shall make the lampstand of graven work: its stem and its branches, its bowls, its *ornamental* knobs, and its lilies shall be of one piece.

³² And six branches shall proceed out of its sides, three branches of the lampstand from one side of it, and three branches of the lampstand from the other side.

³³ And three bowls fashioned like almonds, on each branch a knob and a lily; so to the six branches proceeding from the lampstand,

³⁴ and in the lampstand four bowls fashioned like almonds, in each branch knobs and the flowers of the same.

³⁵ A knob under two branches out of it, and a knob under four branches out of it; so to the six branches proceeding from the lampstand; and in the lampstand four bowls fashioned like almonds.

³⁶ Let the knobs and the branches be of one piece, altogether graven of one piece of pure gold.

³⁷ And you shall make its seven lamps; and you shall set on *it* the lamps, and they shall shine from one front.

³⁸ And you shall make its wick-trimmers and its snuff-dishes of pure gold.

³⁹ All these articles *shall be* a talent of pure gold.

⁴⁰ See, you shall make them according to the pattern which was shown you on the mount."

The Tabernacle

¹ "And you shall make the tabernacle *with* ten curtains of fine spun linen, and blue and purple, and scarlet spun *with* cherubim; you shall make them with *the* work of a weaver.

² The length of one curtain shall be twenty-eight cubits, and one curtain shall be the breadth of four cubits: there shall be the same measure to all the curtains.

³ And the five curtains shall be joined one to another, and *the other* five curtains shall be closely connected the one with the other.

⁴ And you shall make for them loops of blue on the edge of one curtain, on one side for the coupling, and so shall you make on the edge of the outer curtain for the second coupling.

⁵ Fifty loops shall you make for one curtain, and fifty loops shall you make on the part of the curtain answering to the coupling of the second, opposite *each other*, corresponding to each other at each point.

⁶ And you shall make fifty golden rings; and you shall join the curtains to each other with the rings, and it shall be one tabernacle.

⁷ "And you shall make for a covering of the tabernacle skins with the hair on, you shall make them eleven skins.

⁸ The length of one skin thirty cubits, and the breadth of one skin four cubits. There shall be the same measure to the eleven skins.

⁹ And you shall join the five skins together, and the six skins together; and you shall double the sixth skin in front of the tabernacle.

¹⁰ And you shall make fifty loops on the border of one skin, which is in the midst for the joinings; and you shall make fifty loops on the edge of the second skin that joins it.

¹¹ And you shall make fifty bronze rings; and you shall join the rings by the loops, and you shall join the skins, and they shall be one.

¹² And you shall fix at the end that which is over in the skins of the tabernacle; the half of the skin that is left shall you fold over, according to the overplus of the skins of the tabernacle; you shall fold it over behind the tabernacle.

¹³ A cubit on this side, and a cubit on that side of that which remains of the skins, of the length of the skins of the tabernacle: it shall be folding over the sides of the tabernacle on this side and that side, that it may cover it.

¹⁴ And you shall make for a covering of the tabernacle rams' skins dyed red, and blue skins as coverings above.

¹⁵ And you shall make the posts of the tabernacle of incorruptible wood.

¹⁶ Of ten cubits shall you make one post, and the breadth of one post of a cubit and a half.

¹⁷ Two joints shall you make in one post, answering the one to the other: so shall you do to all the posts of the tabernacle.

¹⁸ And you shall make posts to the tabernacle, twenty posts on the north side.

¹⁹ And you shall make to the twenty posts forty silver sockets; two sockets to one post on both its sides, and two sockets to the other post on both its sides.

²⁰ And for the next side, toward the south, twenty posts,

²¹ and their forty silver sockets: two sockets to one post on both its sides, and two sockets to the other post on both its sides.

²² And on the back of the tabernacle at the part which is toward the *west* you shall make six posts.

²³ And you shall make two posts on the corners of the tabernacle behind.

²⁴ And it shall be equal below, they shall be equal toward the same part from the heads to one joining; so shall you make to both the two corners, let them be equal.

²⁵ And there shall be eight posts, and their sixteen silver sockets; two sockets to one post on both its sides, and two sockets to the other post.

²⁶ "And you shall make bars of incorruptible wood; five to one post on one side of the tabernacle,

²⁷ and five bars to one post on the second side of the tabernacle, and five bars to the hinder posts, on the side of the tabernacle toward the sea.

²⁸ And let the bar in the middle between the posts go through from the one side to the other side.

²⁹ And you shall overlay the posts with gold; and you shall make golden rings, into which you shall introduce the bars, and you shall overlay the bars with gold.

³⁰ And you shall set up the tabernacle according to the pattern shown to you on the mount.

³¹ "And you shall make a veil of blue and purple and scarlet woven, and fine linen spun: you shall make it cherubim *in* woven work.

³² And you shall set it upon four posts of incorruptible wood overlaid with gold; and their tops *shall be* of gold, and their four sockets *shall be* of silver.

³³ And you shall put the veil on the posts, and you shall carry the ark of the Testimony in there within the veil; and the veil shall make a separation for you between the holy *place*, and the Most Holy.

³⁴ And you shall screen with the veil the ark of the testimony in the Most Holy.

³⁵ And you shall set the table outside the veil, and the lampstand opposite the table on the south side of the tabernacle; and you shall put the table on the north side of the tabernacle.

³⁶ "And you shall make a screen for the door of the tabernacle of blue, purple, and spun scarlet and fine linen spun, the work of the embroiderer.

37 And you shall make for the veil five posts, and you shall overlay them with gold; and their hooks shall be gold; and you shall cast for them five bronze sockets."

EXODUS CHAPTER 27

The Altar of Burnt Offering

1 "And you shall make an altar of incorruptible wood, of five cubits in the length, and five cubits in the breadth; the altar shall be square, and the height of it shall be three cubits.

2 And you shall make the horns on the four corners; the horns shall be of the same piece, and you shall overlay them with brass.

3 And you shall make a rim for the altar; and its covering and its cups, and its flesh-hooks, and its fire-pan, and all its vessels shall you make of brass.

4 And you shall make for it a network of bronze; and you shall make for the network four bronze rings under the four sides.

5 And you shall put them below under the rim of the altar, and the network shall extend to the middle of the altar.

6 And you shall make for the altar poles of incorruptible wood, and you shall overlay them with brass.

7 And you shall put the poles into the rings; and let the poles be on the sides of the altar to carry it.

8 You shall make it hollow with boards. According to what was shown to you on the mount, so you shall make it.

The Court of the Tabernacle

9 "And you shall make a court for the tabernacle, curtains of the court of fine linen spun on the south side, the length of a hundred cubits for one side.

10 And their pillars twenty, and twenty bronze sockets for them, and their rings and their clasps of silver.

11 Thus *shall there be* to the side toward the north curtains of a hundred cubits in length; and their pillars twenty, and their sockets twenty of brass, and the rings and the clasps of the pillars, and their sockets overlaid with silver.

12 And in the breadth of the tabernacle toward the west curtains of fifty cubits, their pillars ten and their sockets ten.

13 And in the breadth of the tabernacle toward the south, curtains of fifty cubits; their pillars ten, and their sockets ten.

14 And the height of the curtains *shall be* of fifty cubits for the one side *of the gate*; their pillars three, and their sockets three.

15 And *for* the second side the height of the curtains *shall be* of fifteen cubits; their pillars three, and their sockets three.

16 "And a veil for the door of the court, the height *of it* twenty cubits of blue linen, and of purple, and spun scarlet, and of fine linen spun with the art of the embroiderer; their pillars four, and their sockets four.

17 All the pillars of the court round about overlaid with silver, and their hooks silver and their brass sockets.

18 And the length of the court *shall be* a hundred *cubits* on each side, and the breadth fifty on each side, and the height five cubits of fine linen spun, and their sockets of brass.

19 And all the furniture and all the instruments and the pins of the court *shall be* of brass.

The Oil for the Lamp

20 "And command the children of Israel, and let them take for you refined pure olive oil beaten to burn for light, that a lamp may burn continually

21 in the tabernacle of the testimony, outside the veil that is before the *ark of the* Covenant, shall Aaron and his sons burn it from evening until morning, before the Lord—it is a perpetual ordinance throughout your generations of the children of Israel."

EXODUS CHAPTER 28

Vestments for the Priesthood

1 "And take to yourself both Aaron your brother, and his sons, even *those* of the children of Israel; so that Aaron, Nadab, Abihu, Eleazar and Ithamar, Aaron's sons, may minister to Me.

2 And you shall make holy apparel for Aaron your brother, for honor and glory.

3 And speak to all those who are wise in understanding, whom I have filled with the spirit of wisdom and perception; and they shall make the holy apparel of Aaron for the sanctuary, in which he shall minister to Me as priest.

4 And these are the garments which they shall make: a breastplate, an ephod, a full-length robe, a tunic with a fringe, a turban, and a sash; and they shall make holy garments for Aaron and his sons to minister to Me as priests.

The Ephod

5 "And they shall take the gold, and the blue, and the purple, and the scarlet, and the fine linen.

6 And they shall make the ephod of fine linen spun, the woven work of the embroiderer.

7 It shall have two shoulder-pieces joined together, fastened on the two sides.

8 And the woven work of the ephod which is upon it shall be of one piece according to the work, of pure gold, blue, purple, and spun scarlet and fine twined linen.

9 And you shall take the two stones, the stones of emerald, and you shall engrave on them the names of the children of Israel.

10 Six names on the first stone, and the other six names on the second stone, according to their births.

11 *It shall be* the work of the stone engraver's art; as the engraving of a seal you shall engrave the two stones with the names of the children of Israel.

12 And you shall put the two stones on the shoulders of the ephod, for they are memorial stones for the children of

Israel; and Aaron shall bear the names of the children of Israel before the Lord on his two shoulders, as a memorial for them.

¹³ And you shall make settings of pure gold.

¹⁴ And you shall make two chains of pure gold like braided cords, and fasten the braided chains to the settings.

The Oracle of Judgment (Breastplate)

¹⁵ "And you shall make the oracle of judgment, the work of the embroiderer: in keeping with the ephod, you shall make it of gold, and blue and purple, of spun scarlet, and fine linen, spun.

¹⁶ You shall make it square: it shall be double; of the length of it a span, and the breadth of a span.

¹⁷ And you shall interweave with it a texture of four rows of stone; there shall be a row of stones: a sardius, a topaz, and an emerald: *this shall be* the first row.

¹⁸ And the second row *shall be* a turquoise, a sapphire, and a jasper.

¹⁹ And the third row a jacinth, an agate, and an amethyst.

²⁰ And the fourth row, a chrysolite, a beryl, and an onyx stone, set round with gold, bound together with gold: let them be according to their row.

²¹ And let the stones of the names of the children of Israel be twelve according to their names, engravings as of seals: let them be for the twelve tribes each according to the name.

²² And you shall make on the oracle woven fringes, a chain-work of pure gold."

²³ (This verse omitted in LXX).

²⁴ (This verse omitted in LXX).

²⁵ (This verse omitted in LXX).

²⁶ (This verse omitted in LXX).

²⁷ (This verse omitted in LXX).

²⁸ (This verse omitted in LXX).

²⁹ "And Aaron shall take the names of the children of Israel on the breastplate of judgment on his breast, a memorial before God for him as he goes into the sanctuary. And you shall put the fringes on the breastplate of judgment; you shall put the wreaths on both sides of the breastplate, and you shall put the two circlets on both the shoulders of the ephod in front.

³⁰ And you shall put the Manifestation and the Truth on the breastplate of judgment; and it shall be on the breast of Aaron, when he goes into the holy place before the Lord; and Aaron shall bear the judgments of the children of Israel on his breast before the Lord continually.

³¹ "And you shall make the full-length tunic all of blue.

³² And the opening of it shall be in the middle having a fringe round about the opening, the work of the weaver, woven together in the joining of the same piece so that it might not tear.

³³ "And under the fringe of the robe below you shall make as it were pomegranates of a flowering pomegranate tree, of blue, and purple, and spun scarlet, and fine linen spun, under the fringe of the robe round about: golden pomegranates of the same shape, and bells round about between these.

³⁴ A bell by the side of a golden pomegranate, and flower-work on the fringe of the robe round about.

³⁵ And the sound of Aaron shall be audible when he ministers, as he goes into the sanctuary before the Lord, and as he goes out, so that he does not die.

³⁶ "And you shall make a plate *of* pure gold, and you shall engrave on it *like* the engraving of a signet: HOLINESS TO THE LORD.

³⁷ And you shall put it on the spun blue cloth, and it shall be on the turban: it shall be in the front of the turban.

³⁸ And it shall be on the forehead of Aaron; and Aaron shall bear away the sins of their holy things, all that the children of Israel shall sanctify of every gift of their holy things, and it shall be on the forehead of Aaron continually acceptable for them before the Lord."

³⁹ "And the fringes of the garments *shall be* of fine linen; and you shall make a tire of fine linen, and you shall make a sash, the work of the embroiderer.

⁴⁰ "And for the sons of Aaron you shall make tunics and sashes, and you shall make headpieces for them for honor and glory.

⁴¹ And you shall put them on Aaron your brother, and his sons with him, and you shall anoint them and fill their hands; and you shall sanctify them, that they may minister to Me in the priest's office.

⁴² And you shall make for them linen trousers to cover the nakedness of their flesh; they shall reach from the loins to the thighs.

⁴³ And Aaron shall have them, and his sons, whenever they enter into the tabernacle of witness, or when they shall advance to the altar of the sanctuary to minister, so they shall not bring sin upon themselves, lest they die: *it is* a perpetual statute for him, and for his descendants after him."

EXODUS CHAPTER 29

Aaron and His Sons Consecrated

¹ "And these are the things which you shall do to them: you shall sanctify them, so that they shall serve Me in the priesthood; and you shall take one young calf from the herd, and two unblemished rams;

² and unleavened loaves kneaded with oil, and unleavened cakes anointed with oil: you shall make them of fine wheat flour.

³ And you shall put them on one basket, and you shall offer them on the basket, and the young calf and the two rams.

⁴ And you shall bring Aaron and his sons to the doors of the tabernacle of testimony, and you shall wash them with water.

⁵ And having taken the garments, you shall put on Aaron your brother the full-length robe, the ephod, and the oracle; and you shall join for him the oracle to the ephod.

6 And you shall put the turban on his head; and you shall put the plate, *even* the holy crown, on the turban.

7 And you shall take of the anointing oil, and you shall pour it on his head, and shall anoint him,

8 and you shall bring his sons, and put garments on them.

9 And you shall gird them with sashes, and put the hats upon them, and they shall have a priestly office unto Me forever; and you shall fill the hands of Aaron and the hands of his sons.

10 "And you shall bring the calf to the door of the tabernacle of witness; and Aaron and his sons shall lay their hands on the head of the calf, before the Lord, by the doors of the tabernacle of witness.

11 And you shall slay the calf before the Lord, by the doors of the tabernacle of witness.

12 And you shall take of the blood of the calf, and put it on the horns of the altar with your finger, but all the rest of the blood you shall pour out at the foot of the altar.

13 And you shall take all the fat that is on the belly, and the lobe of the liver, and the two kidneys, and the fat that is upon them, and shall put them upon the altar.

14 But the flesh of the calf, and his skin, and his dung, you shall burn with fire outside the camp; for it is a sin *offering*.

15 "And you shall take one ram, and Aaron and his sons shall lay their hands on the head of the ram.

16 And you shall kill it, and take the blood and pour it on the altar round about.

17 And you shall divide the ram by his several limbs, and you shall wash the inward parts and the feet with water, and you shall put them on the divided parts with the head.

18 And you shall offer the whole ram on the altar, a burnt offering to the Lord for a sweet-smelling aroma: it is an offering of incense to the Lord.

19 "And you shall take the second ram, and Aaron and his sons shall lay their hands on the head of the ram.

20 And you shall kill it, and take its blood, and put it on the tip of Aaron's right ear, and on the thumb of his right hand, and on the big toe of his right foot, and on the tips of the right ears of his sons, and on the thumbs of their right hands, and on the big toes of their right feet.

21 And you shall take of the blood from the altar, and of the anointing oil; and you shall sprinkle it upon Aaron and on his garments, and on his sons and on his sons' garments with him; and he and his garments shall be sanctified, and his sons and his sons' garments with him. But the blood of the ram you shall pour round about upon the altar.

22 And you shall take from the ram its fat, both the fat that covers the belly, and the lobe of the liver, and the two kidneys, and the fat that is upon them, and the right shoulder, for this is a consecration.

23 And one cake *made* with oil, and one cake from the basket of unleavened bread set forth before the Lord.

24 And you shall put them all on the hands of Aaron, and on the hands of his sons, and you shall separate them as a separate offering before the Lord.

25 And you shall take them from their hands, and shall offer them up on the altar as a burnt offering, for a sweet-smelling aroma before the Lord: it is an offering to the Lord.

26 And you shall take the breast from the ram of consecration which is Aaron's, and you shall separate it as a separate offering before the Lord, and it shall be to you for a portion.

27 And you shall sanctify the separated breast and the shoulder of removal which has been separated, and which has been removed from the ram of consecration, of the portion of Aaron and of his sons.

28 And it shall be a perpetual statute of the children of Israel to Aaron and his sons, for this is a separate offering; and it shall be a special offering from the children of Israel, from the peace offerings of the children of Israel, a special offering to the Lord.

29 "And the garments of the sanctuary which is Aaron's shall be his son's after him, for them to be anointed in them, and to fill their hands.

30 The priest (his successor from among his sons who shall go into the tabernacle of witness to minister in the holy *place*), shall put them on *for* seven days.

31 "And you shall take the ram of consecration, and you shall boil the flesh in the holy place.

32 And Aaron and his sons shall eat the flesh of the ram, and the loaves in the basket, by the doors of the tabernacle of witness.

33 They shall eat the offerings with which they were sanctified to fill their hands, to sanctify them; and a stranger shall not eat of them, for they are holy.

34 And if *any* is left of the flesh of the sacrifice of consecration and of the loaves until the morning, you shall burn the remainder with fire: it shall not be eaten, for it is a holy thing.

35 And thus shall you do for Aaron and for his sons according to all things that I have commanded you; seven days shall you fill their hands.

36 And you shall sacrifice the calf of the sin offering on the day of purification, and you shall purify the altar when you perform consecration upon it, and you shall anoint it so as to sanctify it.

37 Seven days shall you purify the altar and sanctify it; and the altar shall be most holy, everyone that touches the altar shall be hallowed.

The Daily Offerings

38 "And these are the offerings which you shall offer upon the altar; two unblemished lambs of a year old daily on the altar continually, a constant offering.

39 One lamb you shall offer in the morning, and the second lamb you shall offer in the evening.

40 And a tenth measure of fine flour mingled with the fourth part of a hin of pressed oil, and a drink offering the fourth part of a hin of wine for one lamb.

[41] And you shall offer the second lamb in the evening, after the manner of the morning offering, and according to the drink offering of the morning lamb; you shall offer it to the Lord for a sweet-smelling aroma,

[42] a perpetual sacrifice throughout your generations, at the door of the tabernacle of witness before the Lord; wherein I will be known to you from there, so as to speak to you.

[43] And from there I will give orders to the children of Israel, and I will be sanctified in My glory.

[44] And I will sanctify the tabernacle of testimony and the altar, and I will sanctify Aaron and his sons, to minister as priests to Me.

[45] And I will be called upon among the children of Israel, and will be their God.

[46] And they shall know that I am the Lord their God, who brought them forth out of the land of Egypt, to be called upon by them, and to be their God."

EXODUS CHAPTER 30

The Altar of Incense

[1] "And you shall make the altar of incense of incorruptible wood.

[2] And you shall make it a cubit in length, and a cubit in breadth: it shall be square; and the height of it shall be of two cubits, its horns shall be of the same piece.

[3] And you shall overlay its grate with pure gold, and its sides round about, and its horns; and you shall make for it a molding of gold round about.

[4] And you shall make under its molding two rings of pure gold; you shall make it to the two corners on the two sides, and they shall be holders for the poles, so as to bear it.

[5] And you shall make the poles of incorruptible wood, and shall overlay them with gold.

[6] And you shall set it before the veil that is over the ark of the Testimony, wherein I will make Myself known to you from there.

[7] And Aaron shall burn upon it fine compound incense every morning; whenever he trims the lamps he shall burn incense upon it.

[8] And when Aaron lights the lamps in the evening, he shall burn incense upon it; a constant incense offering always before the Lord for their generations.

[9] And you shall not offer strange incense upon it, *nor* and offering made by fire, *nor* a sacrifice; and you shall not pour a drink offering upon it.

[10] And once in the year Aaron shall make atonement on its horns, he shall purge it with the blood of purification for their generations: it is most holy to the Lord."

The Half-Shekel Ransom

[11] And the Lord spoke to Moses, saying,

[12] "When you take a census of the children of Israel for their number, then every man shall give a ransom for his soul to the Lord, then there shall not be among them a destruction in the visiting of them.

[13] And this is what they shall give, as many as pass the survey, half a shekel which is according to the shekel of the sanctuary (a shekel is twenty gerahs). The half-shekel *shall be* the offering to the Lord.

[14] Everyone that passes the survey from twenty years old and upwards shall give the offering to the Lord.

[15] The rich shall not give more, and the poor shall not give less than the half-shekel in giving the offering to the Lord, to make atonement for your souls.

[16] And you shall take the money of the offering from the children of Israel, and shall give it for the service of the tabernacle of testimony; and it shall be to the children of Israel a memorial before the Lord, to make atonement for your souls."

The Bronze Laver

[17] And the Lord spoke to Moses, saying,

[18] "Make a bronze laver, and a bronze base for it, for washing; and you shall put it between the tabernacle of witness and the altar, and you shall pour forth water into it.

[19] And Aaron and his sons shall wash their hands and their feet with water from it.

[20] Whenever they shall go into the tabernacle of witness, they shall wash themselves with water, so they shall not die, whenever they advance to the altar to do service and to offer the burnt offerings to the Lord.

[21] They shall wash their hands and feet with water, whenever they shall go into the tabernacle of witness; they shall wash themselves with water, that they die not; and it shall be for them a perpetual statute, for him and his posterity after him."

The Holy Anointing Oil

[22] And the Lord spoke to Moses, saying,

[23] "Also take for yourself sweet herbs, the flower of choice myrrh five hundred shekels, and the half of this two hundred and fifty shekels of sweet-smelling cinnamon, and two hundred and fifty shekels of sweet-smelling calamus,

[24] and of cassia five hundred shekels of the sanctuary, and a hin of olive oil.

[25] And you shall make it a holy anointing oil, a perfumed ointment *tempered* by the art of the perfumer: it shall be a holy anointing oil.

[26] And you shall anoint with it the tabernacle of witness, and the ark of the tabernacle of witness,

[27] and all its furniture, and the lampstand and all its utensils, and the altar of incense,

[28] and the altar of burnt offerings and all its utensils, and the table and all its utensils, and the laver.

[29] And you shall sanctify them, and they shall be most holy: everyone that touches them shall be hallowed.

[30] And you shall anoint Aaron and his sons, and sanctify them that they may minister to Me as priests.

³¹ And you shall speak to the children of Israel, saying, 'This shall be to you a holy anointing oil throughout your generations.

³² On man's flesh it shall not be poured, and you shall not make *any* for yourselves according to this composition: it is holy, and shall be holiness unto you.

³³ Whosoever shall make it in like manner, and whosoever shall give of it to a stranger, shall be destroyed from among his people.'"

The Incense

³⁴ And the Lord said to Moses, "Take for yourself sweet herbs, stacte, onycha, sweet galbanum, and transparent frankincense; there shall be and equal weight of each.

³⁵ And they shall make with it perfumed incense, tempered with the art of a perfumer, a pure holy work.

³⁶ And of these you shall beat some very fine, and you shall put it before the testimonies in the tabernacle of testimony, from where I will make Myself known to you: it shall be to you a most holy incense.

³⁷ You shall not make any for yourselves according to this composition; it shall be to you a holy thing for the Lord.

³⁸ Whosoever shall make any in like manner, so as to smell it, shall perish from his people."

EXODUS CHAPTER 31

Bezalel and Aholiab

¹ And the Lord spoke to Moses, saying,

² "Behold, I have called by name Bezalel the son of Uri, the son of Hur, of the tribe of Judah.

³ And I have filled him *with* a divine spirit of wisdom, and understanding, and knowledge, to invent in every work,

⁴ and to frame works, to labor in gold, silver, brass, blue, purple, and spun scarlet,

⁵ and works in stone, and for artificers' work in wood, to work at all works.

⁶ And I have appointed with him Aholiab the *son of* Ahisamach, of the tribe of Dan, and to everyone understanding in heart I have given understanding; and they shall make all things, as many as I have commanded you,

⁷ the tabernacle of witness, and the ark of the Covenant, and the mercy seat that is upon it, and the furniture of the tabernacle,

⁸ and the altars, and the table and all its furniture,

⁹ and the pure lampstand and all its utensils, and the laver and its base,

¹⁰ and Aaron's robes of ministry, and the robes of his sons to minister to Me as priests,

¹¹ and the anointing oil and the compound incense of the sanctuary; according to all that I have commanded you shall they make them."

The Sabbath Law

¹² And the Lord spoke to Moses, saying,

¹³ "Speak also to the children of Israel, saying, 'Take heed and keep My Sabbaths; *for* they are a sign between Me and you throughout your generations, that you may know that I am the Lord that sanctifies you.

¹⁴ And you shall keep the Sabbath, because this is holy to the Lord for you; he that profanes it shall surely be put to death: everyone who shall do a work on it, that soul shall be destroyed from the midst of his people.

¹⁵ Six days you shall work, but the seventh day is the Sabbath, a holy rest unto the Lord; everyone who shall do a work on the seventh day shall be put to death.

¹⁶ And the children of Israel shall keep the Sabbath, to observe them throughout their generations.

¹⁷ It is a perpetual covenant between Me and the children of Israel, it is a perpetual sign with Me; for in six days the Lord made the heaven and the earth, and on the seventh day He ceased, and rested.'"

¹⁸ And He gave to Moses, when He left off speaking to him in Mount Sinai, the two tablets of the Testimony, tablets of stone written by the finger of God.

EXODUS CHAPTER 32

The Golden Calf

¹ And when the people saw that Moses delayed to come down from the mountain, the people combined against Aaron, and said to him, "Arise and make us gods who shall go before us; for this Moses, the man who brought us forth out of the land of Egypt—we do not know what has become of him."

² And Aaron said to them, "Take off the golden earrings which are in the ears of your wives and daughters, and bring them to me."

³ And all the people took off the golden earrings that were in their ears, and brought them to Aaron.

⁴ And he received them from their hands, and formed them with an engraving tool; and he made the *people* a molded calf, and said, "These *are* your gods, O Israel, which have brought you up out of the land of Egypt."

⁵ And Aaron, having seen it, built an altar before it, and Aaron made a proclamation saying, "Tomorrow *is* a feast to the Lord."

⁶ And having risen early on the next day, he offered burnt offerings, and offered a peace offering; and the people sat down to eat and drink, and rose up to play.

⁷ And the Lord spoke to Moses, saying, "Go quickly, descend from here, for your people whom you brought out of the land of Egypt have transgressed;

⁸ they have quickly gone out of the way which you have commanded; they have made for themselves a calf, and worshipped it, and sacrificed to it, and said,

⁹ 'These are your gods, O Israel, who brought you up out of the land of Egypt.'

[10] Now therefore let Me alone, and I will be very angry with them and consume them, and I will make you a great nation."

[11] And Moses prayed before the Lord God, and said, "Why, O Lord, are You very angry with Your people, whom You have brought out of the land of Egypt with great strength, and with Your mighty arm?

[12] *Take heed* lest at any time the Egyptians speak, saying, 'With evil intent He brought them out to slay them in the mountains, and to consume them from off the earth'; cease from Your wrathful anger, and be merciful to the sin of Your people,

[13] remembering Abraham and Isaac and Jacob Your servants, to whom You have sworn by Yourself, and have spoken to them, saying, 'I will greatly multiply your descendants as the stars of heaven for multitude, and all this land which You spoke of to give to them, so that they shall possess it forever."

[14] And the Lord was prevailed upon to preserve His people.

[15] And Moses turned and went down from the mountain, and the two tablets of the Testimony were in his hands, tablets of stone written on both their sides: they were written within and without.

[16] And the tablets were the work of God, and the writing *was* the writing of God written on the tablets.

[17] And Joshua, having heard the voice of the people crying, said to Moses, "There is a noise of war in the camp."

[18] And *Moses* said, "It is not the voice of them that begin the battle, nor the voice of them that begin *the cry* of defeat, but the voice of them that begin *the banquet* of wine that I hear."

[19] And when he drew near to the camp, he saw the calf and the *people* dancing; and Moses, being very angry, cast the two tablets out of his hands and broke them to pieces under the mountain.

[20] And having taken the calf which they made, he consumed it with fire, and ground it very small, and scattered it on the water, and made the children of Israel to drink it.

[21] And Moses said to Aaron, "What have this people done to you, that you have brought such a great sin upon them?"

[22] And Aaron said to Moses, "Be not angry, *my* lord, for you know the impulsiveness of this people.

[23] For they said to me, 'Make us gods which shall go before us; as for this man Moses, who brought us out of Egypt, we do not know what has become of him.'

[24] And I said to them, 'If anyone has golden ornaments, take them off'; and they gave them to me, and I cast them into the fire, and this calf came out."

[25] And when Moses saw that the people were scattered (for Aaron *had* scattered them *so as to be* a rejoicing to their enemies)

[26] then Moses stood at the gate of the camp, and said, "Who is on the Lord's side? Let him come to me." Then all the sons of Levi came to him.

[27] And he said to them, "Thus says the Lord God of Israel: 'Let every man put his sword on his thigh, and go through and return from gate to gate through the camp, and kill every man his brother, and every man his neighbor, and every man that is nearest to him.'"

[28] And the sons of Levi did as Moses spoke to them, and there fell of the people in that day to the *number of* three thousand men.

[29] And Moses said to them, "You have filled your hands this day to the Lord, each one on his son or on his brother, so that blessing should be given to you."

[30] And it came to pass on the next day that Moses said to the people, "You have sinned a great sin; and now I will go up to God, that I may make atonement for your sin."

[31] And Moses returned to the Lord and said, "I pray, O Lord, this people have sinned a great sin, and they have made for themselves golden gods.

[32] And now if You will forgive their sin, forgive; and if not, blot me out of Your book, which You have written."

[33] And the Lord said to Moses, "If anyone has sinned against Me, I will blot them out of My book.

[34] And now go, descend *from here*, and lead this people into the place of which I spoke to you: behold, My Angel shall go before your face; and in the day when I shall visit I will bring upon them their sin."

[35] And the Lord struck the people for the making of the calf, which Aaron made.

EXODUS CHAPTER 33

The Command to Leave Sinai

[1] And the Lord said to Moses, "Go forward, go up from here, you and your people, whom you brought out of the land of Egypt, into the land which I swore to Abraham, Isaac, and Jacob, saying, I will give it to your descendants.

[2] And I will send at the same time My Angel before your face, and He shall cast out the Amorite and the Hittite and the Perizzite and the Girgashite and the Hivite and the Jebusite and the Canaanite.

[3] And I will bring you into a land flowing with milk and honey; for I will not go up with you, because you are a stiff-necked people, lest I consume you by the way."

[4] And the people, having heard this grievous saying, mourned in mourning apparel.

[5] For the Lord said to the children of Israel, "You are a stiff-necked people; take heed lest I bring on you another plague and destroy you: now then put off your glorious apparel, and *your* ornaments, and I will show you what I will do to you."

[6] So the sons of Israel took off their ornaments and their array at the mount of Horeb.

The Tent Outside the Camp

[7] And Moses took the tabernacle and pitched it outside the camp, at a distance from the camp; and it was called the Tabernacle of Testimony. And it came to pass *that* everyone

that sought the Lord went forth to the tabernacle which was outside the camp.

[8] And whenever Moses went into the tabernacle outside the camp, *that* all the people rose, everyone watching by the doors of his tent; and when Moses departed, they took notice until he entered into the tabernacle.

[9] And when Moses entered into the tabernacle, the pillar of cloud descended, and stood at the door of the tabernacle, and *God* talked to Moses.

[10] And all the people saw the pillar of the cloud standing by the door of the tabernacle, and all the people stood and worshipped, everyone at the door of his tent.

[11] And the Lord spoke to Moses face to face, as if one should speak to his friend; and he retired into the camp: but his servant Joshua the son of Nun, a young man, did not depart from the tabernacle.

Moses' Intercession

[12] And Moses said to the Lord, "See, You say to me, Lead on this people; but You have not shown me whom You will send with me, but You have said to me, 'I know you above all, and you have favor with Me.'

[13] If then I have found favor in Your sight, reveal Yourself to me, that I may see You; that I may find favor in Your sight, and that I may know that this great nation *is* Your people."

[14] And He said, "I Myself will go before you, and give you rest."

[15] Then he said to Him, "If You do not go up with us Yourself, do not bring me up from here.

[16] And how shall it be surely known, that both I and this people have found favor with You, except only if You go with us? So both I and Your people shall be glorified beyond all the nations, as many as are upon the earth."

[17] And the Lord said to Moses, "I will also do for you this thing which you have spoken; for you have found grace before Me, and I know you above all."

[18] And *Moses* said, "Manifest Yourself to me."

[19] And *God* said, "I will pass by before you with My glory, and I will call by My name, LORD, before you; and I will have mercy on whom I will have mercy, and I will have compassion on whom I will have compassion."

[20] And *God* said, "You shall not be able to see My face; for no man shall see My face and live."

[21] And the Lord said, "Behold, *there is* a place by Me: you shall stand upon the rock;

[22] and when My glory shall pass by, then I will put you into a hole of the rock; and I will cover you over with My hand, until I have passed by.

[23] And I will remove My hand, and then shall you see My back parts; but My face you shall not see."

EXODUS CHAPTER 34

Moses Makes New Tablets

[1] And the Lord said to Moses, "Hew for yourself two tablets of stone, like the first *ones* were, and come up to Me on the mountain; and I will write upon the tablets the words which were on the first tablets, which you broke.

[2] And be ready by the morning, and you shall go up to Mount Sinai, and you shall stand there before Me on the top of the mountain.

[3] And let no one go up with you, nor be seen in all the mountain; and let not the sheep and oxen feed near that mountain."

[4] And *Moses* cut out two tablets of stone, as also the first *ones* were; and Moses, having arisen early, went up to Mount Sinai, as the Lord appointed him; and Moses took the two tablets of stone.

[5] And the Lord descended in a cloud, and stood near him there, and called by the name of the Lord.

[6] And the Lord passed by before his face, and proclaimed, "The Lord God, gracious and merciful, longsuffering and very compassionate, and true,

[7] and keeping justice and mercy for thousands, taking away iniquity and unrighteousness and sins; and He will not clear the guilty; bringing the iniquity of the fathers upon the children, and to the children's children, to the third and fourth generation."

[8] So Moses hastened, and bowed to the earth and worshipped;

[9] and said, "If I have found grace in Your sight, let my Lord go with us; for the people are stiff-necked: and You shall take away our sins and our iniquities, and we shall be Yours."

The Covenant Renewed

[10] And the Lord said to Moses, "Behold, I establish a covenant with you in the presence of all your people. I will do glorious things which have not been done in all the earth, or in any nation; and all the people among you shall see the works of the Lord, that they are wonderful, which I will do with you.

[11] Take heed to all things whatsoever *that* I command you. Behold, I cast out before your face the Amorite and the Canaanite and the Perizzite and the Hittite and the Hivite and the Girgashite and the Jebusite.

[12] Take heed to yourself, lest at any time you make a covenant with the inhabitants of the land into which you are entering, lest it be to you a stumbling block among you.

[13] You shall destroy their altars, and break in pieces their pillars, and you shall cut down their groves, and the graven images of their gods you shall burn with fire.

[14] For you shall not worship strange gods, for the Lord God, whose name is Jealous, is a jealous God;

[15] lest at any time you make a covenant with the inhabitants of the land, and they whore after their gods, and sacrifice to their gods, and they call you, and you should eat of their feasts,

16 and you should take of their daughters to your sons, and you should give of your daughters to their sons; and your daughters should whore after their gods, and your sons should whore after their gods.

17 And you shall not make to yourself molded gods."

18 "And you shall keep the Feast of Unleavened Bread: seven days shall you eat unleavened bread, as I have commanded you, at the season in the month of *the* new *grain*; for in the month of *the* new *grain* you came out from Egypt.

19 The males *are* Mine, everything that opens the womb; every firstborn of oxen, and *every* firstborn of sheep.

20 And the firstborn of a donkey you shall redeem with a sheep, and if you will not redeem it you shall pay a price: every firstborn of your sons you shall redeem. You shall not appear before Me empty-handed."

21 "Six days you shall work, but on the seventh day you shall rest. *There shall be* rest in seed time and in harvest.

22 And you shall keep to Me the Feast of Weeks, the beginning of wheat-harvest; and the Feast of Ingathering in the middle of the year.

23 Three times in the year shall every male of yours appear before the Lord, the God of Israel.

24 For when I have cast out the nations from before your face, and have enlarged your coasts, no one shall desire your land, whenever you may go up to appear before the Lord your God, three times in the year."

25 "You shall not offer the blood of My sacrifices with leaven, neither shall the sacrifices of the Feast of the Passover remain till the morning.

26 The firstfruits of your land shall you put into the house of the Lord your God. You shall not boil a lamb in his mother's milk."

27 And the Lord said to Moses, "Write these words for yourself, for on these words I have established a covenant with you and with Israel."

28 And Moses was there before the Lord forty days and forty nights; he did not eat bread, and he did not drink water; and He wrote upon the tablets these words of the covenant, the Ten Commandments.

Moses' Face Shines

29 Now when Moses came down from the mountain (*there were* two tablets in Moses' hand as he came down from the mountain), Moses did not know that the appearance of his face was glorified, when God spoke to him.

30 And Aaron and all the elders of Israel saw Moses, and the appearance of his face was made glorious, and they feared to approach him.

31 And Moses called them, and Aaron and all the rulers of the synagogue turned towards him, and Moses spoke to them.

32 And afterwards all the children of Israel came to him, and he commanded them all things, whatsoever the Lord had commanded him in Mount Sinai.

33 And when he ceased speaking to them, he put a veil on his face.

34 And whenever Moses went in before the Lord to speak to Him, he took off the veil till he went out, and he went forth and spoke to all the children of Israel whatsoever the Lord commanded him.

35 And the children of Israel saw the face of Moses, that it was glorified; and Moses put the veil over his face, till he went in to speak with Him.

EXODUS CHAPTER 35

Sabbath Regulations

1 And Moses gathered all the congregation of the children of Israel together, and said, "These are the words which the Lord has spoken, for *you* to do them:

2 Six days shall you work, but on the seventh day *shall be* a rest—a holy Sabbath—a rest unto the Lord: everyone that does work on it, let him die.

3 You shall not burn a fire in any of your dwellings on the Sabbath day; I *am* the Lord."

Offerings for the Tabernacle

4 And Moses spoke to all the congregation of the children of Israel, saying, "This *is* the thing which the Lord has commanded, saying,

5 'Take of yourselves an offering for the Lord: everyone that engages in his heart shall bring the firstfruits to the Lord—gold, silver, brass,

6 blue, purple, double scarlet spun, fine linen spun, goats' hair,

7 rams' skins dyed red, skins *dyed* blue, incorruptible wood,

8 (This verse omitted in LXX).

9 sardine stones, and stones for engraving for the ephod and the full-length robe.

10 'And every man that is wise in heart among you, let him come and work all things whatsoever the Lord has commanded.

11 The tabernacle, the cords, the coverings, the rings, the bars, the posts,

12 the ark of the Testimony and its poles, its mercy seat, the veil, 13 the table and all its furniture,

14 also the lampstand for the light and all its utensils,

15 the incense, the anointing oil,

16 the altar and all its furniture;

17 the curtains of the court and its posts, the emerald stones,

18 (This verse omitted in LXX).

19 and the holy garments of Aaron the priest, and the garments in which they shall do service. And the garments of priesthood for the sons of Aaron and the anointing oil, and the compound incense.'"

20 And all the congregation of the children of Israel went out from Moses. And they brought, they whose heart prompted

them, and they to whomsoever it seemed good in their mind, an offering.

²¹ And they brought an offering to the Lord for all the works of the tabernacle of witness, and all its services, and for all the robes of the sanctuary.

²² And the men, even everyone to whom it seemed good in his heart, brought from the women, *they* brought seals and earrings, finger rings, necklaces and bracelets, every article of gold.

²³ And all as many as brought ornaments of gold to the Lord, and with whomsoever fine linen was found; and they brought skins *dyed* blue, and rams' skins dyed red.

²⁴ And everyone that offered an offering brought silver and brass, the offerings to the Lord; and *they* with whom was found incorruptible wood; and they brought *offerings* for all the works of the preparation.

²⁵ And every woman skilled in her heart to spin with her hands, brought spun *articles*, the blue, purple, scarlet and fine linen.

²⁶ And all the women to whom it seemed good in their heart in their wisdom, spun the goats' hair.

²⁷ And the rulers brought the emerald stones, and the stones for setting in the ephod, and the oracle,

²⁸ and the compounds both for the anointing oil, and the composition of the incense.

²⁹ And every man and woman whose mind inclined them to come in and do all the works as many as the Lord appointed them to do by Moses—*they* the children of Israel brought an offering to the Lord.

Bezalel and Aholiab

³⁰ And Moses said to the children of Israel, "Behold, God has called by name Bezalel the *son* of Uri the *son of* Hur, of the tribe of Judah,

³¹ and has filled him with a divine spirit of wisdom and understanding, and knowledge of all things,

³² to labor skillfully in all works of cunning workmanship to form the gold and the silver and the brass,

³³ and to work in stone, and to fashion the wood, and to work in every work of wisdom."

³⁴ And *God* gave increased understanding, both to him, and to Eliab the *son* of Ahisamach of the tribe of Dan.

³⁵ And *God* filled them with wisdom, understanding, *and* perception, to understand to work all the works of the sanctuary, and to weave the woven and embroidered work with scarlet and fine linen, to do all work of curious workmanship *and* embroidery.

EXODUS CHAPTER 36

¹ And Bezalel performed his work, and Eliab and everyone wise in understanding, to whom was given wisdom and knowledge, to understand how to do all the works according to the holy offices, according to all things which the Lord commanded.

² And Moses called Bezalel and Eliab, and all that had wisdom, to whom God gave knowledge in *their* heart, and all who were freely willing to come forward to the works, to perform them.

³ And they received from Moses all the offerings, which the children of Israel brought for all the works of the sanctuary, to do them; and they continued to receive the gifts brought, from those who brought them in the morning.

⁴ And there came all the wise men who wrought the works of the sanctuary, each according to his own work, which they performed. ⁵ And one said to Moses, "The people bring an abundance *too great* in proportion to all the works which the Lord has appointed *them* to do."

⁶ And Moses commanded, and proclaimed in the camp, saying, "Let neither man nor woman any longer labor for the offerings of the sanctuary"; and the people were restrained from bringing any more.

⁷ And they had materials sufficient for making the furniture, and they left some besides.

⁸ And every wise one among those that wrought made the robes of the holy places, which belong to Aaron the priest, as the Lord commanded Moses.

⁹ And he made the ephod of gold, blue, purple, and spun scarlet, and fine linen twined.

¹⁰ And the plates were divided, the threads of gold, so as to interweave with the blue and purple, and with the spun scarlet, and the fine linen twined, they made it a woven work;

¹¹ shoulder pieces joined from both sides, a work woven by mutual twisting of the parts into one another.

¹² They made it of the same material according to the making of it, of gold, blue, purple, and spun scarlet, and fine linen twined, as the Lord commanded Moses.

¹³ And they made the two emerald stones clasped together and set in gold, graven and cut after the cutting of a seal with the names of the children of Israel;

¹⁴ and he put them on the shoulder pieces of the ephod, *as* stones of memorial of the children of Israel, as the Lord commanded Moses.

¹⁵ And they made the oracle, a work woven with embroidery, according to the work of the ephod, of gold, blue, purple, and spun scarlet, and fine linen twined.

¹⁶ They made the oracle square *and* double, the length of a span, and the breadth of a span, double.

¹⁷ And there was interwoven with it a woven work of four rows of stones, a series of stones, the first row, a sardius and topaz and emerald;

¹⁸ and the second row a carbuncle and sapphire and jasper;

¹⁹ and the third row, a ligure and agate and amethyst;

²⁰ and the fourth row a chrysolite and beryl and onyx, set round about with gold, and fastened with gold.

²¹ And the stones were twelve according to the names of the children of Israel, graven according to their names like seals, each according to his own name for the twelve tribes.

22 And they made on the oracle turned wreaths, wreathen work, of pure gold,

23 and they made two golden circlets and two golden rings.

24 And they put the two golden rings on both the *upper* corners of the oracle;

25 and they put the golden wreaths on the rings on both sides of the oracle, and the two wreaths into the two couplings.

26 And they put them on the two circlets, and they put them on the shoulders of the ephod opposite *each other* in front.

27 And they made two golden rings, and put them on the two projections on the top of the oracle, and on the top of the hinder part of the ephod within.

28 And they made two golden rings, and put them on both the shoulders of the ephod under it, in front by the coupling above the connection of the ephod.

29 And he fastened the oracle by the rings that were on it to the rings of the ephod, which were fastened with *a string* of blue, joined together with the woven work of the ephod; that the oracle should not be loosed from the ephod, as the Lord commanded Moses.

30 And they made the tunic under the ephod, woven work, all of blue.

31 And the opening of the tunic in the midst woven closely together, the opening having a fringe round about, that it might not be torn.

32 And they made on the border of the tunic below pomegranates as of a flowering pomegranate tree, of blue, purple, spun scarlet, and fine linen twined.

33 And they made golden bells, and put the bells on the border of the tunic round about between the pomegranates:

34 a golden bell and a pomegranate on the border of the tunic round about, for the ministration, as the Lord commanded Moses.

35 And they made vestments of fine linen, a woven work, for Aaron and his sons,

36 and the tires of fine linen, and the turban of fine linen, and the drawers of fine linen twined;

37 and their sashes of fine linen, blue, purple, and scarlet spun, the work of an embroiderer, according as the Lord commanded Moses.

38 And they made the golden plate, a dedicated thing of the sanctuary, of pure gold;

39 and he wrote upon it graven letters *as* of a seal, Holiness to the Lord.

40 And they put it on the border of blue, so that it should be on the turban above, as the Lord commanded Moses.

EXODUS CHAPTER 37

The Tabernacle

1 And they made ten curtains for the tabernacle.

2 The length of one curtain was twenty-eight cubits: the same *measure* was to all, and the breadth of one curtain was four cubits.

3 And they made the veil of blue, purple, spun scarlet, and fine linen twined, the woven work with cherubim.

4 And they put it on four posts of incorruptible *wood* overlaid with gold; and their chapiters were gold, and their four sockets were silver.

5 And they made the veil of the door of the tabernacle of witness of blue, purple, spun scarlet, and fine linen twined, woven work with cherubim,

6 and their posts five, and the rings; and they gilded their chapiters and their clasps with gold, and they had five sockets of brass.

7 And they made the court toward the south; the curtains of the court of fine linen twined, a hundred *cubits* every way,

8 and their posts twenty, and their sockets twenty;

9 and on the north side a hundred every way, and on the south side a hundred every way, and their posts twenty and their sockets twenty.

10 And on the west side curtains of fifty cubits, their posts ten and their sockets ten.

11 And on the east side curtains of fifty cubits of fifteen cubits behind,

12 and their pillars three, and their sockets three.

13 And at the second back on this side and on that by the gate of the court, curtains of fifteen cubits, their pillars three and their sockets three;

14 all the curtains of the tabernacle of fine linen twined.

15 And the sockets of their pillars of brass, and their hooks of silver, and their chapiters overlaid with silver, and all the posts of the court overlaid with silver;

16 and the veil of the gate of the court, the work of an embroiderer of blue, purple, spun scarlet, and fine linen twined; the length of twenty cubits, and the height and the breadth of five cubits, made equal to the curtains of the court;

17 and their pillars four, and their sockets four of brass, and their hooks of silver, and their chapiters overlaid with silver.

18 And all the pins of the court round about of brass, and they *were* overlaid with silver.

The Tabernacle of Witness

19 And this was the construction of the tabernacle of witness, accordingly as it was commanded to Moses; so that the public service should belong to the Levites, through Ithamar the son of Aaron the priest.

20 And Bezalel the son of Uri of the tribe of Judah, did as the Lord commanded Moses.

21 And Eliab the son of Ahisamach of the tribe of Dan *was there*, who was chief artificer in the woven works and needle-works and embroideries, in weaving with the scarlet and fine linen.

EXODUS CHAPTER 38

The Construction of the Ark

1 And Bezalel made the ark,

² and overlaid it with pure gold within and without;

³ and he cast for it four golden rings, two on the one side, and two on the other,

⁴ wide *enough* for the poles, so that men should bear the ark with them.

⁵ And he made the mercy seat over the ark of pure gold,

⁶ and the two cherubim of gold;

⁷ one cherub on the one end of the mercy seat, and another cherub on the other end of the mercy seat,

⁸ overshadowing the mercy seat with their wings.

The Construction of the Table

⁹ And he made the set table of pure gold,

¹⁰ and cast for it four rings: two on the one side and two on the other side, broad, so that *men* should lift it with the poles in them.

¹¹ And he made the poles of the ark and of the table, and gilded them with gold.

¹² And he made the furniture of the table, both the dishes, and the censers, and the cups, and the bowls with which he should offer drink offerings, of gold.

¹³ And he made the lampstand which gives light of gold;

¹⁴ the stem solid, and the branches from both its sides;

¹⁵ and blossoms proceeding from its branches, three on this side, and three on the other, made equal to each other.

¹⁶ And *as to* their lamps, which are on the ends, knobs *proceeded* from them; and sockets proceeding from them, that the lamps might be upon them; and the seventh socket, on the top of the lampstand, on the summit above, entirely of solid gold.

¹⁷ And on the lampstand seven golden lamps, and its snuffers gold, and its funnels gold.

¹⁸ He overlaid the posts *with silver*, and cast for each post golden rings, and gilded the bars with gold; and he gilded the posts of the veil with gold, and made the hooks of gold.

¹⁹ He made also the rings of the tabernacle of gold; and the rings of the court, and the rings for drawing out the veil above of brass.

²⁰ He cast the silver chapiters of the tabernacle, and the bronze chapiters of the door of the tabernacle, and the gate of the court; and he made silver hooks for the posts, he overlaid them with silver on the posts.

²¹ He made the pins of the tabernacle and the pins of the court of brass.

The Bronze Altar

²² He made the bronze altar of the bronze censers, which belonged to the men engaged in sedition with the gathering of Core.

²³ He made all the vessels of the altar and its grate, its base, its bowls, and the bronze flesh-hooks.

²⁴ He made an appendage for the altar of network under the grate, beneath it as far as the middle of it; and he fastened to it four bronze rings on the four parts of the appendage of the altar, wide *enough* for the bars, so as to bear the altar with them.

²⁵ He made the holy anointing oil and the composition of the incense, the pure work of the perfumer.

²⁶ He made the bronze laver, and the bronze base of it of the mirrors of the women that fasted, who fasted by the doors of the tabernacle of witness, in the day in which he set it up.

²⁷ And he made the laver, that at it Moses and Aaron and his sons might wash their hands and their feet when they went into the tabernacle of witness, or whenever they should advance to the altar to do service, they washed at it, as the Lord commanded Moses.

EXODUS CHAPTER 39

¹ All the gold that was employed for the works according to all the fabrication of the holy things, was from the gold of the offerings, twenty-nine talents, and seven hundred and twenty shekels according to the holy shekel.

² And the offering of silver from the men that were numbered of the congregation *was* a hundred talents, and a thousand seven hundred and seventy-five shekels, one drachma apiece, even the half shekel, according to the holy shekel.

³ Everyone that passed the survey from twenty years old and upwards to the *number of* six hundred thousand, and three thousand five hundred and fifty.

⁴ And the hundred talents of silver went to the casting of the hundred chapiters of the tabernacle, and to the chapiters of the veil;

⁵ a hundred chapiters to the hundred talents, a talent to a chapiter.

⁶ And the thousand seven hundred and seventy-five shekels he formed into hooks for the pillars, and he overlaid their chapiters and adorned them.

⁷ And the brass of the offering *was* seventy talents, and a thousand five hundred shekels;

⁸ and they made of it the bases of the door of the tabernacle of witness,

⁹ and the bases of the court round about, and the bases of the gate of the court, and the pins of the tabernacle, and the pins of the court

¹⁰ round about; and the bronze appendage of the altar, and all the vessels of the altar, and all the instruments of the tabernacle of witness.

The Leftover Material

¹¹ And the children of Israel did as the Lord commanded Moses, so they did.

¹² And of the gold that remained of the offering they made vessels to minister with before the Lord.

¹³ And the blue that was left, and the purple, and the scarlet they made *into* garments of ministry for Aaron, so that he should minister with them in the sanctuary;

14 and they brought the garments to Moses, and the tabernacle, and its furniture, its bases and its bars and the posts;

15 and the ark of the Covenant, and its bearers, and the altar and all its furniture.

16 And they made the anointing oil, and the incense of composition, and the pure lampstand,

17 and its lamps, lamps for burning, and oil for the light,

18 and the table of showbread, and all its furniture, and the showbread upon it,

19 and the garments of the sanctuary which belong to Aaron, and the garments of his sons, for the priestly ministry;

20 and the curtains of the court, and the posts, and the veil of the door of the tabernacle, and the gate of the court,

21 and all the vessels of the tabernacle and all its instruments: and the skins, even rams' skins dyed red, and the blue coverings, and the coverings of the other things, and the ins, and all the instruments for the works of the tabernacle of witness.

22 Whatsoever things the Lord commanded Moses, so did the children of Israel make all the furniture.

23 And Moses saw all the works; and they had done them all as the Lord commanded Moses, so had they made them; and Moses blessed them.

Exodus Chapter 40

The Tabernacle Erected and Its Equipment Installed

1 And the Lord spoke to Moses, saying,

2 "On the first day of the first month, at the new moon, you shall set up the tabernacle of witness,

3 and you shall place *in it* the ark of the testimony, and shall cover the ark with the veil,

4 and you shall bring in the table and shall set forth that which is to be set forth on it; and you shall bring in the lampstand and place its lamps on it.

5 And you shall place the golden altar, to burn incense before the ark; and you shall put a covering of a veil on the door of the tabernacle of witness.

6 And you shall put the altar of burnt offerings by the doors of the tabernacle of witness, and you shall set up the tabernacle round about, and you shall sanctify all that belongs to it round about.

7 (This verse omitted in the LXX).

8 (This verse omitted in the LXX).

9 And you shall take the anointing oil, and shall anoint the tabernacle, and all things in it; and shall sanctify it, and all its furniture, and it shall be holy.

10 And you shall anoint the altar of burnt offerings, and all its furniture; and you shall sanctify the altar, and the altar shall be most holy.

11 (This verse omitted in LXX).

12 And you shall bring Aaron and his sons to the doors of the tabernacle of witness, and you shall wash them with water.

13 And you shall put on Aaron the holy garments, and you shall anoint him, and you shall sanctify him, and he shall minister to Me as priest.

14 And you shall bring up his sons, and shall put garments on them.

15 And you shall anoint them as you anointed their father, and they shall minister to Me as priests; and it shall be that they shall have an everlasting anointing of priesthood, throughout their generations."

16 And Moses did all things whatsoever the Lord commanded him, so did he.

17 And it came to pass in the first month, in the second year after their going forth out of Egypt, at the new moon, that the tabernacle was set up.

18 And Moses set up the tabernacle, and put on the chapiters, and put the bars into their places, and set up the posts.

19 And he stretched out the curtains over the tabernacle, and put the veil of the tabernacle on it above as the Lord commanded Moses.

20 And he took the testimonies, and put them into the ark; and he put the poles by the sides of the ark.

21 And he brought the ark into the tabernacle, and put on *it* the covering of the veil, and covered the ark of the Testimony, as the Lord commanded Moses.

22 And he put the table in the tabernacle of witness, on the north side without the veil of the tabernacle.

23 And he put on it the showbread before the Lord, as the Lord commanded Moses.

24 And he put the lampstand into the tabernacle of witness, on the side of the tabernacle toward the south.

25 And he put on it its lamps before the Lord, as the Lord had commanded Moses.

26 And he put the golden altar in the tabernacle of witness before the veil;

27 and he burned on it incense of composition, as the Lord commanded Moses.

28 (This verse omitted in the LXX).

29 And he put the altar of the burnt offerings by the doors of the tabernacle.

30 (This verse omitted in the LXX).

31 (This verse omitted in the LXX).

32 (This verse omitted in the LXX).

33 And he set up the court round about the tabernacle and the altar; and Moses accomplished all the works.

The Cloud and the Glory

34 And the cloud covered the tabernacle of witness, and the tabernacle was filled with the glory of the Lord.

35 And Moses was not able to enter into the tabernacle of testimony, because the cloud overshadowed it, and the tabernacle was filled with the glory of the Lord.

36 And when the cloud went up from the tabernacle, the children of Israel prepared to depart with their baggage.

37 And if the cloud went not up, they did not prepare to depart, till the day when the cloud went up.

38 For a cloud was on the tabernacle by day, and fire was on it by night before all Israel, in all their journeys.

THE BOOK OF LEVITICUS

The Burnt Offering

1 And the Lord called Moses again and spoke to him out of the tabernacle of witness, saying, "Speak to the children of Israel, and you shall say to them,

2 'If *any* man of you shall bring gifts to the Lord, you shall bring your gifts of the cattle and of the oxen and of the sheep.

3 'If his gift be a burnt offering, he shall bring an unblemished male of the herd to the door of the tabernacle of witness, he shall bring it as acceptable before the Lord.

4 And he shall lay his hand on the head of the burnt offering as a thing acceptable for him, to make atonement for him.

5 And they shall slay the calf before the Lord; and the sons of Aaron the priests shall bring the blood, and they shall pour the blood round about on the altar, which *is* at the doors of the tabernacle of witness.

6 And having skinned the burnt offering, they shall divide it by its limbs.

7 And the sons of Aaron the priests shall put fire on the altar, and shall pile wood on the fire.

8 And the sons of Aaron the priests shall pile up the divided parts, and the head, and the fat on the wood on the fire, *the wood* which is on the altar.

9 And the entrails and the feet they shall wash in water, and the priests shall put all on the altar; it is a burnt offering, a sacrifice, an aroma of sweet savor to the Lord.

10 'And if his gift *be* of the sheep to the Lord, or of the lambs, or of the kids for a burnt offering, he shall bring a male without blemish.

11 And he shall lay his hand on its head; and they shall kill it by the side of the altar, toward the north before the Lord, and the sons of Aaron the priests shall pour its blood on the altar round about.

12 And they shall divide it by its limbs, and its head and its fat, and the priests shall pile them up on the wood which is on the fire, on the altar.

13 And they shall wash the entrails and the feet with water, and the priest shall bring all the *parts* and put them on the altar: it is a burnt offering, a sacrifice, an aroma of sweet savor to the Lord.

14 'And if he bring his gift, a burnt offering to the Lord, of birds, then shall he bring his gift of doves or pigeons.

15 And the priest shall bring it to the altar, and shall wring off its head; and the priest shall put it on the altar, and shall wring out the blood at the bottom of the altar.

16 And he shall take away the crop with the feathers, and shall cast it forth by the altar toward the east, to the place of the ashes.

17 And he shall break it off from the wings and shall not separate it, and the priest shall put it on the altar on the wood which is on the fire: it is a burnt offering, a sacrifice, a sweet-smelling savor to the Lord.

LEVITICUS CHAPTER 2

The Grain Offering

1 'And if a soul bring a gift, a sacrifice to the Lord, his gift shall be fine flour; and he shall pour oil upon it, and shall put frankincense on it: it is a sacrifice.

2 And he shall bring it to the priests the sons of Aaron. And having taken from it a handful of the fine flour with the oil, and all its frankincense, then the priest shall put the memorial of it on the altar: *it is* a sacrifice, an aroma of sweet savor to the Lord.

3 And the remainder of the sacrifice shall be for Aaron and his sons, a most holy portion from the sacrifices of the Lord.

4 'And if he bring as a gift a sacrifice baked from the oven, a gift to the Lord of fine flour, *he shall bring* unleavened bread kneaded with oil, and unleavened cakes anointed with oil.

5 And if your gift *be* a sacrifice from a pan, it is fine flour mingled with oil, unleavened *offerings*.

6 And you shall break them into fragments and pour oil upon them: it is a sacrifice to the Lord.

7 'And if your gift be a sacrifice from the hearth, it shall be made of fine flour with oil.

8 And he shall offer the sacrifice which he shall make of these to the Lord, and shall bring it to the priest.

9 And the priest shall approach the altar, and shall take away from the sacrifice a memorial of it, and the priest shall place it on the altar: a burnt offering, an aroma of sweet savor to the Lord.

10 And that which is left of the sacrifice *shall be* for Aaron and his sons, most holy from the burnt offerings of the Lord.

11 'You shall not leaven any sacrifice which you shall bring to the Lord; for *as to* any leaven, or any honey, you shall not bring of it to offer a gift to the Lord.

12 You shall bring them in the way of fruits to the Lord, but they shall not be offered on the altar for a sweet-smelling savor to the Lord.

13 And every gift of your sacrifice shall be seasoned with salt; do not omit the salt of the covenant of the Lord from your sacrifices: on every gift of yours you shall offer salt to the Lord your God.

14 And if you would offer a sacrifice of firstfruits to the Lord, *it shall be* new grains ground *and* roasted for the Lord; so shall you bring the sacrifice of the firstfruits.

15 And you shall pour oil upon it, and shall put frankincense on it: it is a sacrifice.

16 And the priest shall offer the memorial of it *taken* from the grains with the oil, and all its frankincense: it is a burnt offering to the Lord.

LEVITICUS CHAPTER 3

The Peace Offering

1 'And if his gift to the Lord be a peace-offering, if he should bring it of the oxen, whether it be male or whether it be female, he shall bring it unblemished before the Lord.

2 And he shall lay his hands on the head of the gift, and shall slay it before the Lord, by the doors of the tabernacle of witness. And the priests the sons of Aaron shall pour the blood on the altar of burnt offerings round about.

3 And they shall bring of the peace-offering a burnt sacrifice to the Lord, the fat covering the belly, and all the fat on the belly;

4 and the two kidneys and the fat that is upon them; he shall take away that which is on the thighs, and the fatty lobe above the liver together with the kidneys.

5 And the priests the sons of Aaron shall offer them on the altar on the burnt offering, on the wood which is on the fire upon the altar: *it is* a burnt offering, an aroma of sweet savor to the Lord.

6 'And if his gift be of the sheep, a peace-offering to the Lord, male or female, he shall bring it unblemished.

7 If he bring a lamb for his gift, he shall bring it before the Lord.

8 And he shall lay his hands on the head of his offering, and shall slay it by the doors of the tabernacle of witness; and the priests, the sons of Aaron, shall pour out the blood on the altar round about.

9 And he shall bring of the peace-offering, a burnt sacrifice to the Lord: the fat and the hinder part unblemished he shall take away with the loins, and having taken away all the fat that covers the belly, and all the fat that is on the belly,

10 and both the kidneys and the fat that is upon them, *and* that which is on the thighs, and the fatty lobe which is on the liver with the kidneys,

11 the priest shall offer these on the altar: *it is* a sacrifice of sweet savor, a burnt offering to the Lord.

12 And if his offering be of the goats, then shall he bring it before the Lord.

13 And he shall lay his hands on its head; and they shall slay it before the Lord by the doors of the tabernacle of witness; and the priests, the sons of Aaron, shall pour out the blood on the altar round about.

14 And he shall offer of it a burnt offering to the Lord, *even* the fat that covers the belly, and all the fat that is on the belly.

15 And both the kidneys, and all the fat that is upon them, that which is upon the thighs, and the fatty lobe of the liver with the kidneys, shall he take away.

16 And the priest shall offer it upon the altar: *it is* a burnt offering, an aroma of sweet savor to the Lord. All the fat *belongs* to the Lord.

17 '*It is* a perpetual statute throughout your generations, in all your habitations; you shall eat no fat and no blood.'"

LEVITICUS CHAPTER 4

The Sin Offering

1 And the Lord spoke to Moses, saying,

2 "Speak to the children of Israel, saying, 'If a soul shall sin unwillingly before the Lord, in any of the commandments of the Lord concerning things which he ought not to do, and shall do some of them;

3 if the anointed priest should sin so as to cause the people to sin, then shall he bring for his sin, which he has sinned, an unblemished calf of the herd to the Lord for his sin.

4 And he shall bring the calf to the door of the tabernacle of witness before the Lord, and he shall put his hand on the head of the calf before the Lord, and shall slay the calf in the presence of the Lord.

5 And the anointed priest who has been consecrated, having received of the blood of the calf, shall then bring it into the tabernacle of witness.

6 And the priest shall dip his finger into the blood, and sprinkle of the blood seven times before the Lord, over against the holy veil.

7 And the priest shall put of the blood of the calf on the horns of the altar of the compound incense which is before the Lord, which is in the tabernacle of witness; and all the blood of the calf shall he pour out by the foot of the altar of burnt offerings, which is by the doors of the tabernacle of witness.

8 and all the fat of the calf of the sin-offering shall he take off from it; the fat that covers the inwards, and all the fat that is on the inwards,

9 and the two kidneys, and the fat that is upon them, which is on the thighs, and the fatty lobe that is on the liver with the kidneys, them shall he take away,

10 as he takes it away from the calf of the sacrifice of peace-offering, so shall the priest offer it on the altar of burnt offering.

11 And *they shall take* the skin of the calf, and all his flesh with the head and the extremities and the belly and the dung,

12 and they shall carry out the whole calf out of the camp into a clean place, where they pour out the ashes, and they shall consume it there on wood with fire: it shall be burned on the ashes poured out.

13 'And if the whole congregation of Israel should trespass ignorantly, and a thing should escape the notice of the congregation, and they should do one thing forbidden of any of the commands of the Lord, which ought not to be done, and should transgress;

¹⁴ and the sin in which they have sinned should become known to them, then shall the congregation bring an unblemished calf of the herd for a sin-offering, and they shall bring it to the doors of the tabernacle of witness.

¹⁵ And the elders of the congregation shall lay their hands on the head of the calf before the Lord, and they shall slay the calf before the Lord.

¹⁶ And the anointed priest shall bring in of the blood of the calf into the tabernacle of witness.

¹⁷ And the priest shall dip his finger into some of the blood of the calf, and shall sprinkle it seven times before the Lord, in front of the veil of the sanctuary.

¹⁸ And the priest shall put some of the blood on the horns of the altar of the incense of composition, which is before the Lord, which is in the tabernacle of witness; and he shall pour out all the blood at the bottom of the altar of burnt offerings, which is by the door of the tabernacle of witness.

¹⁹ And he shall take away all the fat from it, and shall offer it up on the altar.

²⁰ And he shall do to the calf as he did to the calf of the sin-offering, so shall it be done; and the priest shall make atonement for them, and the trespass shall be forgiven them.

²¹ And they shall carry forth the calf whole outside the camp, and they shall burn the calf as they burned the former calf: it is the sin-offering of the congregation.

²² 'And if a ruler should sin, and break one of all the commands of the Lord his God, *doing that* which ought not to be done, unwillingly, and shall sin and trespass,

²³ and his trespass in which he has sinned be known to him, then shall he offer for his gift a kid of the goats, a male without blemish.

²⁴ And he shall lay his hand on the head of the kid, and they shall kill it in the place were they kill the *victims for* burnt offerings before the Lord; it is a sin-offering.

²⁵ And the priest shall put some of the blood of the sin-offering with his finger on the horns of the altar of burnt offering; and he shall pour out all its blood by the bottom of the altar of burnt offerings.

²⁶ And he shall offer up all his fat on the altar, as the fat of the sacrifice of peace-offering; and the priest shall make atonement for him concerning his sin, and it shall be forgiven him.

²⁷ 'And if a soul of the people of the land should sin unwillingly, in doing a thing *contrary to* any of the commandments of the Lord, which ought not to be done, and shall transgress,

²⁸ and his sin should be known to him, in which he has sinned, then shall he bring a kid of the goats, a female without blemish shall he bring for his sin, which he has sinned.

²⁹ And he shall lay his hand on the head of his sin-offering, and they shall slay the kid of the sin-offering in the place where they slay the *victims for* burnt offerings.

³⁰ And the priest shall take of its blood with his finger, and shall put it on the horns of the altar of burnt offerings; and all its blood he shall pour forth by the foot of the altar.

³¹ And he shall take away all the fat, as the fat is taken away from the sacrifice of peace-offering, and the priest shall offer it on the altar for an aroma of sweet savor to the Lord; and the priest shall make atonement for him, and *his sin* shall be forgiven him.

³² And if he should offer a lamb for his sin-offering, he shall offer it a female without blemish.

³³ And he shall lay his hand on the head of the sin-offerings, and they shall kill it in the place where they kill the *victims for* burnt offerings.

³⁴ And the priest shall take of the blood of the sin-offering with his finger, and shall put it on the horns of the altar of burnt offerings, and he shall pour out all its blood by the bottom of the altar of burnt offering.

³⁵ And he shall take away all his fat, as the fat of the lamb of the sacrifice of peace-offering is taken away, and the priest shall put it on the altar for a burnt offering to the Lord; and the priest shall make atonement for him for the sin which he sinned, and it shall be forgiven him.

LEVITICUS CHAPTER 5

The Trespass Offering

¹ 'And if a soul sin, and hear the voice of swearing, and he is a witness or has seen or been conscious, if he does not report it, he shall bear his iniquity.

² That soul which shall touch any unclean thing, or carcass, or *that which is* unclean being taken of beasts, or the dead bodies of abominable *reptiles* which are unclean, or carcasses of unclean cattle,

³ or should touch the uncleanness of a man, or whatever kind, which he may touch and be defiled by, and it should have escaped him, but afterwards he should know, then he shall have transgressed.

⁴ That unrighteous soul, which determines with his lips to do evil or to do good according to whatsoever a man may determine with an oath, and it shall have escaped his notice, and he shall *afterwards* know *it*, and *so* he should sin in one of these things;

⁵ then shall he declare his sin in the things in which he has sinned by that sin.

⁶ And he shall bring for his transgressions against the Lord, for his sin which he has sinned, a ewe lamb of the flock, or a kid of the goats, for a sin-offering; and the priest shall make an atonement for him for his sin which he has sinned, and his sin shall be forgiven him.

⁷ 'And if he cannot afford a sheep, he shall bring for his sin which he has sinned, two turtle doves or two young pigeons to the Lord: one for a sin-offering, and the other for a burnt offering.

8 And he shall bring them to the priest, and the priest shall bring the sin-offering first; and the priest shall pinch off the head from the neck, and shall not divide the body.

9 And he shall sprinkle of the blood of the sin-offering on the side of the altar, but the rest of the blood he shall drop at the foot of the altar, for it is a sin-offering.

10 And he shall make the second a burnt offering, as it is fit; and the priest shall make atonement for his sin which he has sinned, and it shall be forgiven him.

11 'And if he cannot afford a pair of turtle doves, or two young pigeons, then shall he bring as his gift for his sin, the tenth part of an ephah of fine flour for a sin-offering; he shall not pour oil upon it, nor shall he put frankincense upon it, because it is a sin-offering.

12 And he shall bring it to the priest; and the priest, having taken a handful of it, shall lay the memorial of it on the altar of burnt offerings to the Lord: it is a sin-offering.

13 And the priest shall make atonement for him for his sin, which he has sinned in one of these things, and it shall be forgiven him; and that which is left shall be the priest's, as an offering of fine flour.'"

Offerings with Restitution

14 And the Lord spoke to Moses, saying,

15 "The soul which shall be really unconscious, and shall sin unwillingly in any of the holy things of the Lord, shall even bring to the Lord for his transgression, a ram of the flock without blemish, valued according to shekels of silver according to the shekel of the sanctuary, for his *transgression* in which he transgressed.

16 And he shall make compensation for that in which he has sinned in the holy things; and he shall add the fifth part to it, and give it to the priest; and the priest shall make atonement for him with the ram of transgression, and *his sin* shall be forgiven him.

17 "And the soul which shall sin, and do one thing *against* any of the commandments of the Lord, which it is not right to do, and has not known it, and shall have transgressed, and shall have contracted guilt,

18 he shall even bring a ram without blemish from the flock, *valued* at a price of silver for his transgression to the priest; and the priest shall make atonement for his trespass of ignorance, wherein he ignorantly trespassed, and he knew it not; and it shall be forgiven him.

19 For he has surely been guilty of transgression before the Lord."

LEVITICUS CHAPTER 6

Instructions Concerning Sacrifices

1 And the Lord spoke to Moses, saying,

2 "The soul which shall have sinned, and willfully overlooked the commandments of the Lord, and shall have dealt falsely in the affairs of his neighbor in the matter of a deposit, or concerning fellowship, or concerning plunder, or has in anything wronged his neighbor,

3 or has found that which was lost, and shall have lied concerning it, and shall have sworn unjustly concerning *any* one of all the things, whatsoever a man may do, so as to sin hereby;

4 it shall come to pass, whenever he shall have sinned, and transgressed, that he shall restore the plunder which he has seized, or *redress* the injury which he has committed, or restore the deposit which was entrusted to him, or the lost article which he has found of any kind, about which he swore unjustly, he shall even restore it in full; and he shall add to it a fifth part besides; he shall restore it to him whose it is in the day in which he happens to be convicted.

5 And he shall bring to the Lord for his trespass, a ram of the flock, without blemish, of value to the amount of the thing in which he trespassed.

6 And the priest shall make atonement for him before the Lord, and he shall be forgiven for any one of all the things which he did and trespassed in it."

7 And the Lord spoke to Moses, saying,

8 "Command Aaron and his sons, saying,

9 'This *is* the law of burnt offering; this is the burnt offering in its burning on the altar all the night till the morning; and the fire of the altar shall burn on it, it shall not be put out.

10 And the priest shall put on the linen tunic, and he shall put the linen drawers on his body; and shall take away that which has been thoroughly burned, which the fire shall have consumed, even the burnt offering from the altar, and he shall put it near the altar.

11 And he shall put off his robe, and put on another robe, and he shall take forth the offering that has been burned without the camp into a clean place.

12 And the fire on the altar shall be kept burning on it and shall not be extinguished; and the priest shall burn on it wood every morning, and shall heap on it the burnt offering, and shall lay on it the fat of the peace-offering.

13 And the fire shall always burn on the altar; it shall not be extinguished.

14 'This is the law of the sacrifice, which the sons of Aaron shall bring near before the Lord, before the altar.

15 And he shall take from it a handful of the fine flour of the sacrifice with its oil, and with all its frankincense, which are upon the sacrifice; and he shall offer up on the altar a burnt offering as a sweet-smelling savor, a memorial of it to the Lord.

16 And Aaron and his sons shall eat that which is left of it: it shall be eaten without leaven in a holy place, they shall eat it in the court of the tabernacle of witness.

17 It shall not be baked with leaven. I have given it as a portion to them of the burnt offerings of the Lord: it is most holy, as the offering for sin, and as the offering for trespass.

18 Every male of the priests shall eat it: it is a perpetual ordinance throughout your generations of the burnt offerings of the Lord; whosoever shall touch them shall be hallowed.'"

19 And the Lord spoke to Moses, saying,

20 "This is the gift of Aaron and of his sons, which they shall offer to the Lord in the day in which you shall anoint him; the tenth of an ephah of fine flour for a sacrifice continually, the half of it in the morning, and the half of it in the evening.

21 It shall be made with oil in a frying pan; he shall offer it kneaded *and* in rolls, an offering of fragments, an offering of a sweet savor unto the Lord.

22 The anointed priest who is in his place, *one* of his sons, shall offer it: it is a perpetual statute, it shall all be consumed.

23 And every sacrifice of a priest shall be thoroughly burned, and shall not be eaten."

24 And the Lord spoke to Moses, saying,

25 "Speak to Aaron and to his sons, saying, 'This is the law of the sin-offering: in the place where they slay the burnt offering, they shall slay the sin-offerings before the Lord: they are most holy.

26 The priest that offers it shall eat it; in a holy place it shall be eaten, in the court of the tabernacle of witness.

27 Everyone that touches the flesh of it shall be holy, and on whosoever's garment any of its blood shall have been sprinkled, whoever shall have it sprinkled, shall be washed in the holy place.

28 And the earthen vessel in which it is boiled shall be broken; and if it shall have been boiled in a bronze vessel, he shall scour it and wash it with water.

29 Every male among the priests shall eat it: it is most holy to the Lord.

30 And no offerings for sin, of whose blood there shall be brought any into the tabernacle of witness to make atonement in the holy place, shall be eaten: they shall be burned with fire.

LEVITICUS CHAPTER 7

The Law of the Trespass Offering

1 'And this *is* the law of the ram for the trespass-offering: it is most holy.

2 In the place where they slay the burnt offering, they shall slay the ram of the trespass-offering before the Lord, and he shall pour out the blood at the bottom of the altar round about.

3 And he shall offer all the fat from it; and the loins, and all the fat that covers the inwards, and all the fat that is upon the inwards,

4 and the two kidneys, and the fat that is upon them, that which is upon the thighs, and the fatty lobe upon the liver with the kidney, he shall take them away.

5 And the priest shall offer them on the altar, a burnt offering to the Lord: it is for trespass.

6 Every male of the priests shall eat them, in the holy place they shall eat them: they are most holy.

7 As the sin-offering, so also *is* the trespass-offering. There is one law of them; the priest who shall make atonement with it, his it shall be.

8 And *as for* the priest who offers a man's burnt offering, the skin of the burnt offering which he offers shall be his.

9 And every sacrifice which shall be prepared in the oven, and everyone which shall be prepared on the hearth, or on a frying-pan, it is the property of the priest that offers it: it shall be his.

10 And every sacrifice made up with oil, or not made up *with oil*, shall belong to the sons of Aaron, an equal portion to each.

The Law of Peace Offerings

11 'This *is* the law of the sacrifice of peace-offering, which they shall bring to the Lord.

12 If a man should offer it for praise, then shall he bring, for the sacrifice of praise, loaves of fine flour made up with oil, and unleavened cakes anointed with oil, and fine flour kneaded with oil.

13 With leavened bread he shall offer his gifts, with the peace-offering of praise.

14 And he shall bring one of all his gifts, a separate offering to the Lord; it shall belong to the priest who pours forth the blood of the peace-offering.

15 'And the flesh of the sacrifice of the peace-offering of praise shall be his, and it shall be eaten in the day in which it is offered; they shall not leave of it till the morning.

16 And if it be a vow, or he offer his gift of his own will, on whatsoever day he shall offer his sacrifice, it shall be eaten, and on the next day.

17 And that which is left of the flesh of the sacrifice till the third day, shall be consumed with fire.

18 And if he should eat of the flesh on the third day, it shall not be accepted for him that offers: it shall not be reckoned to him, it is pollution; and whatsoever soul shall eat of it, shall bear his iniquity.

19 'And whatsoever flesh shall have touched any unclean thing, it shall not be eaten, it shall be consumed with fire; everyone that is clean shall eat the flesh.

20 And whatsoever soul shall eat of the flesh of the sacrifice of the peace-offering which is the Lord's, and his uncleanness be upon him, that soul shall perish from his people.

21 And whatsoever soul shall touch any unclean thing, either of the uncleanness of a man, or of unclean quadrupeds, or any unclean abominable thing, and shall eat of the flesh of the sacrifice of the peace-offering, which is the Lord's, that soul shall perish from his people.'"

Fat and Blood May Not Be Eaten

22 And the Lord spoke to Moses, saying,

23 "Speak to the children of Israel, saying, 'You shall eat no fat of oxen or sheep or goats.

24 And the fat of such animals as have died of themselves, or have been seized of beasts, may be employed for any work; but it shall not be eaten for food.

25 Everyone that eats fat off the beasts, from which he will bring a burnt offering to the Lord—that soul shall perish from his people.

26 You shall eat no blood in all your habitations, either of beasts or of birds.

27 Every soul that shall eat blood, that soul shall perish from his people.'"

28 And the Lord spoke to Moses, saying,

29 "You shall also speak to the children of Israel, saying, 'He that offers a sacrifice of peace-offering, shall bring his gift to the Lord also from the sacrifice of peace-offering.

30 His hands shall bring the burnt offerings to the Lord; the fat which is on the breast and the lobe of the liver, he shall bring them, so as to set them for a gift before the Lord.

31 And the priest shall offer the fat upon the altar, and the breast shall be Aaron's and his sons,

32 and you shall give the right shoulder for a choice piece to the priest of your sacrifices of peace-offering.

33 He that offers the blood of the peace-offering, and the fat, of the sons of Aaron, his shall be the right shoulder for a portion.

34 For I have taken the wave-breast and shoulder of separation from the children of Israel from the sacrifices of your peace-offerings, and I have given them to Aaron the priest and his sons, a perpetual ordinance *due* from the children of Israel.'"

35 This is the anointing of Aaron, and the anointing of his sons, *their portion* of the burnt offerings of the Lord, in the day in which He brought them forward to minister as priests to the Lord,

36 as the Lord commanded to give to them in the day in which He anointed them of the sons of Israel, a perpetual statute through their generations.

37 This *is* the law of the burnt offerings, and of sacrifice, and of sin-offering, and of offering for transgression, and of the sacrifice of consecration, and of the sacrifice of peace-offering;

38 as the Lord commanded Moses on Mount Sinai, in the day in which He commanded the children of Israel to offer their gifts before the Lord in the Wilderness of Sinai.

LEVITICUS CHAPTER 8

The Rites of Ordination

1 And the Lord spoke to Moses, saying,

2 "Take Aaron and his sons, and his robes and the anointing oil, and the calf for the sin-offering, and the two rams, and the basket of unleavened bread,

3 and assemble the whole congregation at the door of the tabernacle of witness."

4 And Moses did as the Lord appointed him, and he assembled the congregation at the door of the tabernacle of witness.

5 And Moses said to the congregation, "This is the thing which the Lord has commanded you to do."

6 And Moses brought Aaron and his sons near, and washed them with water,

7 and put on him the coat, and girded him with the sash, and clothed him with the tunic, and put on him the ephod;

8 and girded him according to the make of the ephod, and clasped him closely with it; and put upon it the oracle, and put upon the oracle the Manifestation and the Truth.

9 And he put the turban on his head, and put upon the turban in front the golden plate, the most holy thing, as the Lord commanded Moses.

10 And Moses took of the anointing oil,

11 and sprinkled of it seven times on the altar; and anointed the altar, and hallowed it, and all things on it, and the laver and its foot, and sanctified them; and anointed the tabernacle and all its furniture, and hallowed it.

12 And Moses poured of the anointing oil on the head of Aaron; and he anointed him and sanctified him.

13 And Moses brought the sons of Aaron near, and put on them tunics and girded them with sashes, and put hats on them, as the Lord commanded Moses.

14 And Moses brought near the calf for the sin-offering, and Aaron and his sons laid their hands on the head of the calf of the sin-offering,

15 and he killed it. And Moses took of the blood, and put it on the horns of the altar round about with his finger; and he purified the altar, and poured out the blood at the bottom of the altar, and sanctified it, to make atonement upon it.

16 And Moses took all the fat that was upon the inwards, and the lobe on the liver, and both the kidneys, and the fat that was upon them, and Moses offered them on the altar.

17 But the calf, and his hide, and his flesh, and his dung, he burned with fire outside the camp, as the Lord commanded Moses.

18 And Moses brought near the ram for a burnt offering, and Aaron and his sons laid their hands on the head of the ram, and Moses killed the ram. And Moses poured the blood on the altar round about.

19 And he divided the ram by its limbs, and Moses offered the head, and the limbs, and the fat; and he washed the belly and the feet with water.

20 And Moses offered up the whole ram on the altar: it is a burnt offering for a sweet-smelling savor; it is a burnt offering to the Lord, as the Lord commanded Moses.

21 And Moses brought the second ram, the ram of consecration, and Aaron and his sons laid their hands on the head of the ram, and *he* slew him;

22 and Moses took of his blood, and put it upon the tip of Aaron's right ear, and on the thumb of his right hand, and on the big toe of his right foot.

²³ And Moses brought near the sons of Aaron; and Moses put of the blood on the tips of their right ears, and on the thumbs of their right hands, and on the big toes of their right feet, and Moses poured out the blood on the altar round about.

²⁴ And he took the fat, and the rump, and the fat on the belly, and the lobe of the liver, and the two kidneys, and the fat that is upon them, and the right shoulder.

²⁵ And from the basket of consecration, which was before the Lord, he also took one unleavened loaf, and one loaf made with oil, and one cake; and put *them* upon the fat, and the right shoulder;

²⁶ and put them all on the hands of Aaron, and upon the hands of his sons, and offered them up for a wave-offering before the Lord.

²⁷ And Moses took them at their hands, and Moses offered them on the altar, on the burnt offering of consecration, which is an aroma of sweet savor: it is a burnt offering to the Lord.

²⁸ And Moses took the breast, and separated it for a heave-offering before the Lord, from the ram of consecration; and it became Moses' portion, as the Lord commanded Moses.

²⁹ And Moses took of the anointing oil, and of the blood that was on the altar, and sprinkled it on Aaron, and on his garments, and his sons, and the garments of his sons with him.

³⁰ And he sanctified Aaron and his garments, and his sons, and the garments of his sons with him.

³¹ And Moses said to Aaron and to his sons, "Boil the flesh in the tent of the tabernacle of witness in the holy place; and there you shall eat it and the loaves in the basket of consecration, as it has been appointed me, *the Lord* saying, 'Aaron and his sons shall eat them.'

³² And that which is left of the flesh and of the loaves you shall burn with fire.

³³ And you shall not go out from the door of the tabernacle of witness for seven days, until the day be fulfilled, the day of your consecration; for in seven days shall he consecrate you,

³⁴ as he did in this day on which the Lord commanded me to do so, to make an atonement for you.

³⁵ And you shall remain seven days at the door of the tabernacle of witness, day and night; you shall observe the ordinances of the Lord, so that you do not die; for so has the Lord God commanded me."

³⁶ And Aaron and his sons performed all these commands which the Lord commanded Moses.

LEVITICUS CHAPTER 9

Aaron's Priesthood Inaugurated

¹ And it came to pass on the eighth day, that Moses called Aaron and his sons, and the elders of Israel,

² and Moses said to Aaron, "Take to yourself a young calf of the herd for a sin-offering, and a ram for a burnt offering, unblemished, and offer them before the Lord.

³ And speak to the elders of Israel, saying, 'Take one kid of the goats for a sin-offering, and a young calf, and a lamb of a year old for a burnt offering, spotless,

⁴ and a calf and a ram for a peace offering before the Lord, and fine flour mingled with oil, for today the Lord will appear among you.'"

⁵ And they took as Moses commanded them before the tabernacle of witness, and all the congregation drew near, and they stood before the Lord.

⁶ And Moses said, "This is the thing which the Lord has spoken: do *it*, and the glory of the Lord shall appear among you."

⁷ And Moses said to Aaron, "Draw near to the altar, and offer your sin-offering, and your burnt offering, and make atonement for yourself, and for your house; and offer the gifts of the people, and make atonement for them"; as the Lord commanded Moses.

⁸ And Aaron drew near to the altar, and killed the calf of his sin-offering.

⁹ And the sons of Aaron brought the blood to him, and he dipped his finger into the blood, and put it on the horns of the altar, and he poured out the blood at the bottom of the altar.

¹⁰ And he offered up on the altar the fat and the kidneys and the lobe of the liver of the sin-offering, according as the Lord commanded Moses.

¹¹ And the flesh and the hide he burned with fire outside of the camp.

¹² And he killed the burnt offering; and the sons of Aaron brought the blood to him, and he poured it on the altar round about.

¹³ And they brought the burnt offering, according to its pieces; them and the head he put upon the altar.

¹⁴ And he washed the belly and the feet with water, and he put them on the burnt offering on the altar.

¹⁵ And he brought the gift of the people, and took the goat of the sin-offering of the people, and slew it, and purified it as also the first.

¹⁶ And he brought the burnt offering, and offered it in due form. ¹⁷ And he brought the sacrifice and filled his hands with it, and laid it on the altar, besides the morning burnt offering.

¹⁸ And he killed the calf, and the ram of the sacrifice of peace-offering of the people; and the sons of Aaron brought the blood to him, and he poured it out on the altar round about.

¹⁹ And *he took* the fat of the calf, and the hind quarters of the ram, and the fat covering the belly, and the two kidneys, and the fat upon them, and the fatty lobe on the liver.

²⁰ And he put the fat on the breasts, and offered the fat on the altar.

21 And Aaron separated the breast and the right shoulder as a choice-offering before the Lord, as the Lord commanded Moses.

22 And Aaron lifted up his hands on the people and blessed them; and after he had offered the sin-offering, and the burnt offerings, and the peace-offerings, he came down.

23 And Moses and Aaron entered into the tabernacle of witness. And they came out and blessed all the people, and the glory of the Lord appeared to all the people.

24 And fire came forth from the Lord, and devoured the offerings on the altar, both the burnt offerings and the fat; and all the people saw, and were amazed, and fell upon their faces.

LEVITICUS CHAPTER 10

Nadab and Abihu Offer Profane Fire

1 And the two sons of Aaron, Nadab and Abihu, took each his censer, and put fire in it, and threw incense on it, and offered strange fire before the Lord, which the Lord did not command them,

2 and fire came forth from the Lord, and devoured them, and they died before the Lord.

3 And Moses said to Aaron, "This is the thing which the Lord spoke, saying, 'I will be sanctified among them that draw near to Me, and I will be glorified in the whole congregation.'" And Aaron was pricked *in his heart*.

4 And Moses called Mishael and Elisaphan, sons of Uzziel, sons of the brother of Aaron's father, and said to them, "Draw near and take your brothers from before the sanctuary out of the camp."

5 And they came near and took them in their coats out of the camp, as Moses said.

6 And Moses said to Aaron, and Eleazar and Ithamar his sons that were left, "You shall not uncover your heads, and you shall not tear your clothes, so that you do not die, and *so* there should be wrath on all the congregation. But your brothers, *even* all the house of Israel, shall lament for the burning, with which they were burned by the Lord.

7 And you shall not go forth from the door of the tabernacle of witness, that you do not die; for the Lord's anointing oil *is* upon you." And they did according to the word of Moses.

Priestly Conduct

8 And the Lord spoke to Aaron, saying,

9 "You shall not drink wine nor strong drink, you and your sons with you, whenever you enter into the tabernacle of witness, or when you approach the altar, so shall you not die; *it is* a perpetual statute for your generations,

10 to distinguish between sacred and profane, and between clean and unclean,

11 and to teach the children of Israel all the statutes, which the Lord spoke to them by Moses."

12 And Moses said to Aaron, and to Eleazar and Ithamar, the sons of Aaron who survived, "Take the sacrifice that is left of the burnt offerings of the Lord, and you shall eat unleavened bread by the altar: it is most holy.

13 And you shall eat it in the holy place; for this is a statute for you and a statute for your sons, of the burnt offerings to the Lord; for so it has been commanded me.

14 And you shall eat the breast of separation, and the shoulder of the choice-offering in the holy place, you and your sons and your house with you; for it has been given as an ordinance for you and an ordinance for your sons, of the sacrifices of peace-offering of the children of Israel.

15 They shall bring the shoulder of the choice-offering, and the breast of the separation upon the burnt offerings of the fat, to separate for a separation before the Lord; and it shall be a perpetual ordinance for you and your sons and your daughters with you, as the Lord commanded Moses."

16 And Moses diligently sought the goat of the sin-offering, but it had been consumed by fire; and Moses was angry with Eleazar and Ithamar the sons of Aaron that were left, saying, 17 "Why did you not eat the sin-offering in the holy place? For because it is most holy He has given you this to eat, that you might take away the sin of the congregation, and make atonement for them before the Lord.

18 For the blood of it was not brought into the holy place: you shall eat it inside, before *the Lord*, as the Lord commanded me."

19 And Aaron spoke to Moses, saying, "If they have brought near today their sin-offerings, and their burnt offerings before the Lord, and these events have happened to me, and *yet* I should eat today of the sin-offerings, would it be pleasing to the Lord?"

20 And Moses heard *it*, and it pleased him.

LEVITICUS CHAPTER 11

Clean and Unclean Foods

1 And the Lord spoke to Moses and Aaron, saying,

2 "Speak to the sons of Israel, saying, 'These are the beasts which you shall eat out of all beasts that are upon the earth.

3 Every beast parting the hoof and making divisions of two claws, and chewing the cud among beasts, these you shall eat.

4 But of these you shall not eat, of those that chew the cud, and of those that part the hoofs, and divide claws: the camel, because it chews the cud, but does not divide the hoof, this is unclean to you.

5 And the rabbit, because it chews the cud, but does not divide the hoof, this is unclean to you.

6 And the hare, because it does not chew the cud, and does not divide the hoof, this is unclean to you.

7 And the swine, because this *animal* divides the hoof, and makes claws of the hoof, and it does not chew the cud, is unclean to you.

8 You shall not eat of their flesh, and you shall not touch their carcasses; these are unclean to you.

9 'And these *are* what you shall eat of all that are in the waters: all things that have fins and scales in the waters, and in the seas, and in the brooks, these you shall eat.

10 And all things which have not fins or scales in the water, or in the seas, and in the brooks, of all which the waters produce, and of every soul living in the water, are an abomination; and they shall be abominations to you.

11 You shall not eat of their flesh, and you shall abhor their carcasses.

12 And all things that have not fins or scales of those that are in the waters, these are an abomination to you.

13 'And these are the things which you shall abhor of birds, an they shall not be eaten, they are an abomination: the eagle and the ossifrage, and the sea-eagle.

14 And the vulture, and the kite, and the like to it;

15 and the sparrow, and the owl, and the sea-mew, and the like to it;

16 and every raven, and the birds like it, and the hawk and his like,

17 and the night-raven and the cormorant and the stork,

18 and the red-bill, and the pelican, and swan,

19 and the heron, and the lapwing, and the like to it, and the hoopoe and the bat.

20 'And all winged creatures that creep, which go upon four feet, are abominations to you.

21 But these you shall eat of the creeping winged animals, which go upon four feet, which have legs above their feet, to leap with on the earth.

22 And these of them you shall eat: the caterpillar and his like, and the attacus and his like, and the cantharus and his like, and the locust and his like.

23 Every creeping thing from among the birds, which has four feet, is an abomination to you.

Unclean Animals

24 'And by these you shall be defiled; everyone that touches their carcasses shall be unclean till the evening.

25 And everyone that takes of their dead bodies shall wash his garments, and shall be unclean till the evening.

26 And whichever among the beasts divides the hoof and makes claws, and does not chew the cud, shall be unclean to you; everyone that touches their dead bodies shall be unclean till evening.

27 And everyone among all the wild beasts that moves upon its four feet, which goes on all four, is unclean to you; everyone that touches their dead bodies shall be unclean till evening.

28 And he that takes of their dead bodies shall wash his garments, and shall be unclean till evening: these are unclean to you.

29 'And these *are* unclean to you of reptiles upon the earth: the weasel, the mouse, the lizard,

30 the ferret, the chameleon, the evet, the newt, and the mole.

31 These are unclean to you of all the reptiles which are on the earth; everyone who touches their carcasses shall be unclean till evening.

32 And on whatsoever one of their dead bodies shall fall it shall be unclean; whatever wooden vessel, or garment, or skin, or sack it may be, every vessel in which work should be done, shall be dipped in water, and shall be unclean till evening; and *then* it shall be clean.

33 And every earthen vessel into which one of these things shall fall, whatsoever is inside it shall be unclean, and it shall be broken.

34 And all food that is eaten, on which water shall come *from such a vessel*, shall be unclean; and every beverage which is drunk in any *such* vessel shall be unclean.

35 And everything on which there shall fall of their dead bodies shall be unclean; ovens and stands for jars shall be broken down: these are unclean, and they shall be unclean to you.

36 Only *if the water be* of fountains of water, or a pool, or confluence of water, it shall be clean; but he that touches their carcasses shall be unclean.

37 And if one of their carcasses should fall upon any sowing seed which shall be sown, it shall be clean.

38 But if water be poured on any seed, and one of their dead bodies fall upon it, it is unclean to you.

39 'And if one of the cattle die, which it is lawful for you to eat, he that touches their carcasses shall be unclean till evening.

40 And he that eats of their carcasses shall wash his garments, and be unclean till evening; and he that carries any of their carcasses shall wash his garments, and bathe himself in water, and be unclean till evening.

41 'And every reptile that creeps on the earth, this shall be an abomination to you; it shall not be eaten.

42 And every *animal* that creeps on its belly, and everyone that goes on four *feet* continually, which abounds with feet among all the reptiles creeping upon the earth— you shall not eat it, for it is an abomination to you.

43 And you shall not defile your souls with any of the reptiles that creep upon the earth, and you shall not be polluted with them, and you shall not be unclean by them.

44 For I am the Lord your God; and you shall be sanctified, and you shall be holy, because I the Lord your God am holy; and you shall not defile your souls with any of the reptiles creeping upon the earth.

45 For I am the Lord who brought you up out of the land of Egypt to be your God; and you shall be holy, for I the Lord am holy.

46 This is the law concerning beasts and birds and every living creature moving in the water, and every living creature creeping on the earth;

47 to distinguish between the unclean and the clean; and between those that bring forth alive, such as should be eaten, and those that bring forth alive, such as should not be eaten.'"

LEVITICUS CHAPTER 12

Purification of Women After Childbirth

[1] And the Lord spoke to Moses, saying,

[2] "Speak to the children of Israel, and you shall say to them, 'Whatsoever woman shall have conceived and born a male child shall be unclean seven days, she shall be unclean according to the days of separation for her monthly courses.

[3] And on the eighth day she shall circumcise the flesh of his foreskin.

[4] And for thirty-three days she shall continue in her unclean blood; she shall touch nothing holy, and shall not enter the sanctuary, until the days of her purification be fulfilled.

[5] But if she should have born a female child, then she shall be unclean fourteen days, according to the time of her monthly courses; and for sixty-six days shall she remain in her unclean blood.

[6] 'And when the days of her purification shall have been fulfilled for a son or a daughter, she shall bring a lamb of a year old without blemish for a burnt offering, and a young pigeon or turtle dove for a sin-offering to the door of the tabernacle of witness, to the priest.

[7] And he shall present it before the Lord, and the priest shall make atonement for her, and shall purge her from the fountain of her blood; this is the law of her who bears a male or a female.

[8] And if she cannot afford a lamb, then shall she take two turtle doves or two young pigeons, one for a burnt offering, and one for a sin-offering; and the priest shall make atonement for her, and she shall be purified.'"

LEVITICUS CHAPTER 13

The Law Concerning Leprosy

[1] And the Lord spoke to Moses and Aaron, saying,

[2] "If any man should have in the skin of his flesh a bright clear spot, and there should be in the skin of his flesh a plague of leprosy, he shall be brought to Aaron the priest, or to one of his sons the priests.

[3] And the priest shall view the spot in the skin of his flesh; and *if* the hair in the spot be changed *to* white, and the appearance of the spot be below the skin of the flesh, it is a plague of leprosy; and the priest shall look upon it, and pronounce him unclean.

[4] But if the spot be clear and white in the skin of his flesh, yet the appearance of it be not deep below the skin, and its hair has not changed *itself for* white hair, but it is dark, then the priest shall separate *him that has* the spot for seven days;

[5] and the priest shall look on the spot the seventh day; and behold, *if* the spot remains before him, *if* the spot has not spread in the skin, then the priest shall separate him the second time for seven days.

[6] And the priest shall look upon him the second time on the seventh day. And behold, *if* the spot is dark, *and* the spot has not spread in the skin, then the priest shall pronounce him clean; for it is a *mere* mark, and the man shall wash his garments and be clean.

[7] But if the bright spot should have changed and spread in the skin, after the priest has seen him for the purpose of purifying him, then shall he appear the second time to the priest,

[8] and the priest shall look upon him; and behold, *if* the mark has spread in the skin, then the priest shall pronounce him unclean: it is leprosy.

[9] "And if a man should have a plague of leprosy, then he shall come to the priest;

[10] and the priest shall look, and behold, if it is a white spot in the skin, and it has changed the hair to white, and *there be* some of the sound part of the quick flesh in the sore—

[11] it is leprosy advancing in the skin of the flesh; and the priest shall pronounce him unclean, and shall separate him, because he is unclean.

[12] "And if the leprosy should have come out very evidently in the skin, and the leprosy should cover all the skin of the patient from the head to the feet, wherever the priest shall look;

[13] then the priest shall look, and behold, the leprosy has covered all the skin of the flesh; and the priest shall pronounce him clean of the plague, because it has changed all to white, it is clean.

[14] But on whatever day the quick flesh shall appear on him, he shall be pronounced unclean.

[15] And the priest shall look upon the sound flesh, and the sound flesh shall prove him to be unclean; for it is unclean, it is a leprosy.

[16] But if the sound flesh be restored and changed *to* white, then shall he come to the priest;

[17] and the priest shall see *him*, and behold, *if* the plague is turned white, then the priest shall pronounce the patient clean: he is clean.

[18] "And if the flesh should have become an ulcer in his skin, and should be healed,

[19] and there should be in the place of the ulcer a white sore, or *one* looking white and bright, or fiery, and it shall be seen by the priest;

[20] then the priest shall look, and behold, if the appearance be beneath the skin, and its hair has changed to white, then the priest shall pronounce him unclean; because it is leprosy, it has broken out in the ulcer.

[21] But if the priest look, and behold there is no white hair on it, and it is not below the skin of the flesh, and it is dark-colored; then the priest shall separate him for seven days.

[22] But if it manifestly spread over the skin, then the priest shall pronounce him unclean: it is a plague of leprosy; it has broken out in the ulcer.

23 But if the bright spot should remain in its place and not spread, it is the scar of the ulcer; and the priest shall pronounce him clean.

24 "And if his flesh is *in a state of* fiery inflammation, and there should be in his skin the part which is healed of the inflammation, bright, clear, and white, suffused with red or very white;

25 then the priest shall look upon him, and behold, *if* the hair being white is changed to a bright color, and its appearance is lower than the skin, it is a leprosy; it has broken out in the inflammation, and the priest shall pronounce him unclean: it is a plague of leprosy.

26 But if the priest should look, and behold, there is not in the bright spot any white hair, and it should not be lower than the skin, and it should be dark, then the priest shall separate him seven days.

27 And the priest shall look upon him on the seventh day; and if the spot has spread much in the skin, then the priest shall pronounce him unclean: it is a plague of leprosy, it has broken out in the ulcer.

28 But if the bright spot remain stationary, and has not spread in the skin, but *the sore* should be dark, it is a scar of inflammation; and the priest shall pronounce him clean, for it is the mark of the inflammation.

29 "And if a man or a woman have in them a plague of leprosy in the head or the beard,

30 then the priest shall look on the plague, and behold, *if* the appearance of it is beneath the skin, and in it there is thin yellowish hair, then the priest shall pronounce him unclean: it is a scurf, it is leprosy of the head, or leprosy of the beard.

31 And if the priest should see the plague of the scurf, and behold, the appearance of it is not beneath the skin, and there is no yellowish hair in it, then the priest shall set apart *him that has* the plague of the scurf for seven days.

32 And the priest shall look at the plague on the seventh day; and behold, *if* the scurf has not spread, and there is no yellowish hair on it, and the appearance of the scurf is not hollow under the skin;

33 then the skin shall be shaven, but the scurf shall not be shaven; and the priest shall set aside the person having the scurf the second time for seven days.

34 And the priest shall see the scurf on the seventh day; and behold, *if* the scurf is not spread in the skin after the man has been shaved, and the appearance of the scurf is not hollow beneath the skin, then the priest shall pronounce him clean; and he shall wash his garments, and be clean.

35 But if the scurf has indeed spread in the skin after he has been purified,

36 then the priest shall look, and behold, *if* the scurf has spread in the skin, the priest shall not examine concerning the yellow hair, for he is unclean.

37 But if the scurf remain before *him* in its place, and a dark hair should have arisen in it, the scurf is healed: he is clean, and the priest shall pronounce him clean.

38 "And if a man or woman should have in the skin of their flesh spots of a bright whiteness,

39 then the priest shall look; and behold, there *being* bright spots of a bright whiteness in the skin of their flesh, it is a tetter; it burst forth in the skin of his flesh; he is clean.

40 And if anyone's head should lose his hair, he is *only* bald, he is clean.

41 And if his head should lose the hair in front, he is forehead bald, he is clean.

42 And if there should be in his baldness of head, or his baldness of forehead, a white or fiery plague, it is leprosy in his baldness of head, or baldness of forehead.

43 And the priest shall look upon him, and behold, if the appearance of the plague is white or inflamed in his baldness of head or baldness in front, as the appearance of leprosy in the skin of his flesh,

44 *then* he is a leprous man; the priest shall surely pronounce him unclean, his plague is in his head.

45 And the leper in whom the plague is, let his garments be torn, and his head uncovered; and let him have a covering put upon his mouth, and he shall be called unclean.

46 All the days in which the plague shall be upon him, being unclean, he shall be *esteemed* unclean; he shall dwell apart, his place of sojourn shall be outside the camp.

The Law Concerning Leprous Clothing

47 "And if a garment have in it the plague of leprosy, a garment of wool, or a garment of flax,

48 either in the warp or in the woof, or in the linen, or in the woolen threads, or in a skin, or in any workmanship of skin,

49 and the plague is greenish or reddish in the skin, or in the garment, either in the warp, or in the woof, or in any utensil of skin, it is a plague of leprosy, and he shall show it to the priest.

50 And the priest shall look upon the plague, and the priest shall set apart *that which has* the plague for seven days.

51 And the priest shall look upon the plague on the seventh day. And if the plague has spread in the garment, either in the warp or in the woof, or in the skin, in whatsoever things skins may be used in their workmanship, the plague is a confirmed leprosy; it is unclean.

52 He shall burn the garment, either the warp or woof in woolen garments or in flaxen, or in any utensil of skin, in which there may be the plague; because it is a confirmed leprosy; it shall be burned with fire.

53 "And if the priest should see, and the plague has not spread in the garments, either in the warp or in the woof, or in any utensil of skin,

54 then the priest shall give directions, and *one* shall wash that on which there may have been the plague, and the priest shall set it aside a second time for seven days.

55 And the priest shall look upon it after the plague has been washed; and *if* this, even the plague, has not changed its appearance, and the plague does not spread, it is unclean; it

shall be burned with fire: it is fixed in the garment, in the warp, or in the woof.

56 And if the priest should look, and the spot is dark after it has been washed, he shall tear it off from the garment, either from the warp or from the woof, or from the skin.

57 And if it should still appear in the garment, either in the warp or in the woof, or in any article of skin, it is leprosy bursting forth: that in which is the plague shall be burned with fire.

58 And the garment, or the warp, or the woof, or any article of skin, which shall be washed, and the plague depart from it, shall also be washed again, and shall be clean.

59 This is the law of the plague of leprosy of a woolen or linen garment, either of the warp, or woof, or any leather article, to pronounce it clean or unclean."

LEVITICUS CHAPTER 14

Purification of Lepers and Leprous Houses

1 And the Lord spoke to Moses, saying,

2 "This is the law of the leper: in whatsoever day he shall have been cleansed, then shall he be brought to the priest.

3 And the priest shall come forth out of the camp, and the priest shall look, and behold, the plague of the leprosy is removed from the leper.

4 And the priest shall give directions, and they shall take for him that is cleansed two clean live birds, and cedar wood, and spun scarlet, and hyssop.

5 And the priest shall give direction, and they shall kill one bird over an earthen vessel over running water.

6 And as for the living bird he shall take it, and the cedar wood, and the spun scarlet, and the hyssop, and he shall dip them and the living bird into the blood of the bird that was slain over running water.

7 And he shall sprinkle seven times upon him that was cleansed of his leprosy, and he shall be clean; and he shall let go the living bird into the field.

8 And the man that has been cleansed shall wash his garments, and shall shave off all his hair, and shall wash himself in water, and shall be clean; and after that he shall go into the camp, and shall remain out of his house for seven days.

9 And it shall come to pass on the seventh day, he shall shave off all his hair, his head and his beard, and his eyebrows, even all his hair shall he shave; and he shall wash his garments, and wash his body with water, and shall be clean.

10 "And on the eighth day he shall take two lambs without spot of a year old, and one ewe lamb without spot of a year old, and three-tenths *of an ephah* of fine flour for sacrifice kneaded with oil, and one small cup of oil.

11 And the priest that cleanses shall present the man under purification, and these *offerings* before the Lord, at the door of the tabernacle of witness.

12 And the priest shall take one lamb, and offer him for a trespass-offering, and the cup of oil, and set them apart for a special offering before the Lord.

13 And they shall kill the lamb in the place where they kill the burnt offerings, and the sin-offerings, in the holy places; for it is a sin-offering: as the trespass-offering, it belongs to the priest, it is most holy.

14 And the priest shall take of the blood of the trespass-offering, and the priest shall put it on the tip of the right ear of the person under cleansing, and on the thumb of his right hand, and on the big toe of his right foot.

15 And the priest shall take of the cup of oil, and shall pour it upon his own left hand.

16 And he shall dip with the finger of his right hand *into* some of the oil that is in his left hand, and he shall sprinkle with his finger seven times before the Lord.

17 And the remaining oil that is in his hand, the priest shall put on the tip of the right ear of him that is under cleansing, and on the thumb of his right hand, and on the big toe of his right foot, on the place of the blood of the trespass-offering.

18 And the remaining oil that is on the hand of the priest, the priest shall put on the head of the cleansed *leper*, and the priest shall make atonement for him before the Lord.

19 And the priest shall sacrifice the sin-offering, and the priest shall make atonement for the person under purification *to cleanse him* from his sin, and afterwards the priest shall slay the burnt offering.

20 And the priest shall offer the burnt offering, and the sacrifice upon the altar before the Lord; and the priest shall make atonement for him, and he shall be cleansed.

21 "And if he should be poor, and cannot afford so much, he shall take one lamb for his transgression for a separate-offering, so as to make propitiation for him, and a tenth deal of fine flour mingled with oil for a sacrifice, and one cup of oil,

22 and two turtle doves, or two young pigeons, as he can afford; and the one shall be for a sin-offering, and the other for a burnt offering.

23 And he shall bring them on the eighth day, to purify him, to the priest, to the door of the tabernacle of witness before the Lord.

24 And the priest shall take the lamb of the trespass-offering, and the cup of oil, and place them for a set-offering before the Lord.

25 And he shall kill the lamb of the trespass-offering; and the priest shall take of the blood of the trespass-offering, and put it on the tip of the right ear of him that is under purification, and on the thumb of his right hand, and on the big toe of his right foot.

26 And the priest shall pour of the oil on his own left hand.

27 And the priest shall sprinkle with the finger of his right hand some of the oil that is in his left hand seven times before the Lord.

28 And the priest shall put of the oil that is on his hand on the tip of the right ear of him that is under purification, and

on the thumb of his right hand, and on the big toe of his right foot, on the place of the blood of the trespass-offering.

29 And that which is left of the oil which is on the hand of the priest he shall put on the head of him that is purged, and the priest shall make atonement for him before the Lord.

30 And he shall offer one of the turtle doves or of the young pigeons, as he can afford it,

31 the one for a sin-offering, the other for a burnt offering with the grain offering, and the priest shall make an atonement before the Lord for him that is under purification.

32 This is the law for him in whom is the plague of leprosy, and who cannot afford the offerings for his purification."

33 And the Lord spoke to Moses and Aaron, saying,

34 "Whenever you shall enter into the land of the Canaanites, which I give you for a possession, and I shall put the plague of leprosy in the houses of the land of your possession;

35 then the owner of the house shall come and report to the priest, saying, 'I have seen a plague in the house.'

36 And the priest shall give orders to remove the furniture of the house, before the priest comes in to see the plague, and *thus* none of the things in the house shall become unclean; and afterwards the priest shall go in to examine the house.

37 And he shall look on the plague, and behold, *if* the plague is in the walls of the house, *he will see* greenish or reddish cavities, and the appearance of them *will be* beneath the surface of the walls.

38 And the priest shall come out of the house to the door of the house, and the priest shall separate the house for seven days. 39 And the priest shall return on the seventh day and view the house. And behold, *if* the plague has spread in the walls of the house,

40 then the priest shall give orders, and they shall take away the stones in which the plague is, and shall cast them out of the city into an unclean place.

41 And they shall scrape the house inside round about, and shall pour out the dust scraped off outside the city into an unclean place.

42 And they shall take other scraped stones, and put them in the place of the *former* stones, and they shall take other plaster and plaster the house.

43 "And if the plague should return again, and break out in the house after they have taken away the stones and after the house is scraped, and after it has been plastered,

44 then the priest shall go in and see if the plague has spread in the house: it is a confirmed leprosy in the house, it is unclean.

45 And they shall take down the house, and its timbers and its stones, and they shall carry out all the mortar outside the city into an unclean place.

46 And he that goes into the house at any time, during its separation, shall be unclean until evening.

47 And he that sleeps in the house shall wash his garments, and be unclean until evening; and he that eats in the house shall wash his garments, and be unclean until evening.

48 "And if the priest shall arrive and enter and see, and behold the plague has not at all spread in the house after the house has been plastered, then the priest shall declare the house clean, because the plague is healed.

49 And he shall take to purify the house two clean living birds, and cedar wood, and spun scarlet, and hyssop.

50 And he shall kill one bird in an earthen vessel over running water.

51 And he shall take the cedar wood, and the spun scarlet, and the hyssop, and the living bird; and shall dip it into the blood of the bird slain over running water, and with them he shall sprinkle the house seven times.

52 And he shall purify the house with the blood of the bird, and with the running water, and with the living bird, and with the cedar wood, and with the hyssop, and with the spun scarlet.

53 And he shall let the living bird go out of the city into the field, and shall make atonement for the house, and it shall be clean.

54 "This *is* the law concerning every plague of leprosy and scurf,

55 and of the leprosy of a garment, and of a house,

56 and of a sore, and of a clear spot, and of a shining one,

57 and of declaring in what day it is unclean, and in what day it shall be purged: this *is* the law of the leprosy."

LEVITICUS CHAPTER 15

The Law Concerning Bodily Discharges

1 And the Lord spoke to Moses and Aaron, saying,

2 "Speak to the children of Israel, and you shall say to them, 'Whatever man shall have a discharge out of his body, his discharge is unclean.

3 And this *is* the law of his uncleanness: whoever has a discharge out of his body, this is his uncleanness in him by reason of the discharge, by which, his body is affected through the discharge. All the days of the discharge of his body, by which his body is affected through the discharge, there is his uncleanness.

4 Every bed on which he that has the discharge shall happen to lie, is unclean; and every seat on which he that has the discharge may happen to sit, shall be unclean.

5 And the man who shall touch his bed, shall wash his garments, and bathe himself in water, and shall be unclean till evening.

6 And whosoever sits on the seat on which he that has the discharge may have sat, shall wash his garments, and bathe himself in water, and shall be unclean until evening.

7 And he that touches the skin of him that has the discharge, shall wash his garments and bathe himself in water, and shall be unclean till evening.

8 And if he that has the discharge should spit upon one that is clean, *that person* shall wash his garments, and bathe himself in water, and be unclean until evening.

9 And every donkey's saddle, on which the man with the discharge shall have mounted, shall be unclean till evening.

10 And everyone that touches whatsoever shall have been under him shall be unclean until evening; and he that takes them up shall wash his garments, and bathe himself in water, and shall be unclean until evening.

11 And whomsoever he that has the discharge shall touch, if he has not rinsed his hands in water, he shall wash his garments, and bathe his body in water, and shall be unclean until evening.

12 And the earthen vessel which he that has the discharge shall happen to touch, shall be broken; and a wooden vessel shall be washed with water, and shall be clean.

13 'And if he that has the discharge should be cleansed of his issue, then shall he number to himself seven days for his purification; and he shall wash his garments, and bathe his body in water, and shall be clean.

14 And on the eighth day he shall take to himself two turtle doves or two young pigeons, and he shall bring them before the Lord to the doors of the tabernacle of witness, and shall give them to the priest.

15 And the priest shall offer them, one for a sin-offering, and the other for a burnt offering; and the priest shall make atonement for him before the Lord for his discharge.

16 'And the man whose seed of copulation shall happen to go forth from him, shall then wash his whole body, and shall be unclean until evening.

17 And every garment, and every skin on which there shall be the seed of copulation shall both be washed with water, and be unclean until evening.

18 And a woman, if a man shall lie with her with seed of copulation-- they shall both bathe themselves in water and shall be unclean until evening.

19 'And the woman whosoever shall have an issue of blood, when her issue shall be in her body, shall be seven days in her separation; everyone that touches her shall be unclean until evening.

20 And everywhere that she shall lie upon in her separation shall be unclean; and whatever she shall sit upon, shall be unclean.

21 And whosoever shall touch her bed shall wash his garments, and bathe his body in water, and shall be unclean until evening.

22 And everyone that touches any vessel on which she shall sit, shall wash his garments and bathe himself in water, and shall be unclean until evening.

23 And whether it be while she is on her bed, or on a seat which she may happen to sit upon when he touches her, he shall be unclean till evening.

24 And if anyone shall lie with her, and her uncleanness be upon him, he shall be unclean seven days; and every bed on which he shall have lain shall be unclean.

25 'And if a woman have an issue of blood many days, not in the time of her separation; if the blood should also flow after her separation, all the days of the issue of her uncleanness *shall be* as the days of her separation: she shall be unclean.

26 And every bed on which she shall lie all the days of her flux shall be to her as the bed of her separation, and every seat whereon she shall sit shall be unclean according to the uncleanness of her separation.

27 Everyone that touches it shall be unclean; and he shall wash his garments, and bathe his body in water, and shall be unclean till evening.

28 'But if she shall be cleansed from her flux, then she shall number to herself seven days, and afterwards she shall be esteemed clean.

29 And on the eighth day she shall take two turtle doves, or two young pigeons, and shall bring them to the priest, to the door of the tabernacle of witness.

30 And the priest shall offer one for a sin-offering, and the other for a burnt offering, and the priest shall make atonement for her before the Lord for her unclean flux.

31 'And you shall cause the children of Israel to beware of their uncleanness, so they shall not die for their uncleanness, in polluting My tabernacle that is among them.

32 This is the law of the man who has an issue, and if one discharge seed of copulation, so that he should be polluted by it.

33 And *this is the law* for her that has the issue of blood in her separation, and as to the person who has an issue of seed, in his issue: *it is a law* for the male and the female, and for the man who shall have lain with her that is set apart.'"

LEVITICUS CHAPTER 16

The Day of Atonement

1 And the Lord spoke to Moses after the two sons of Aaron died in bringing strange fire before the Lord, so they died.

2 And the Lord said to Moses, "Speak to Aaron your brother, and let him not come in at all times into the holy place within the veil before the mercy seat, which is upon the ark of the testimony, and he shall not die; for I will appear in a cloud on the mercy seat.

3 Thus shall Aaron enter into the holy place: with a calf of the herd for a sin-offering, and *having* a ram for a burnt offering.

4 And he shall put on the consecrated linen tunic, and he shall have on his flesh the linen drawers, and shall gird himself with a linen sash, and shall put on the linen cap, they are holy garments; and he shall bathe all his body in water, and shall put them on.

5 And he shall take of the congregation of the children of Israel two kids of the goats for a sin-offering, and one lamb for a burnt offering.

6 "And Aaron shall bring the calf for his own sin-offering, and shall make atonement for himself and for his house.

7 And he shall take the two goats, and place them before the Lord by the door of the tabernacle of witness.

8 And Aaron shall cast lots upon the two goats, one lot for the Lord, and the other for the scapegoat.

9 And Aaron shall bring forward the goat on which the lot for the Lord fell, and shall offer him for a sin-offering.

10 And the goat upon which the lot of the scapegoat came, he shall present alive before the Lord, to make atonement upon him, so as to send him away as a scapegoat, and he shall send him into the wilderness.

11 "And Aaron shall bring the calf for his sin, and he shall make atonement for himself and for his house, and he shall kill the calf for his sin-offering.

12 And he shall take his censer full of coals of fire off the altar, which is before the Lord; and he shall fill his hands with fine compound incense, and shall bring it inside the veil.

13 And he shall put the incense on the fire before the Lord, and the smoke of the incense shall cover the mercy seat over the tables of testimony, and he shall not die.

14 And he shall take of the blood of the calf, and sprinkle with his finger on the mercy seat eastward: before the mercy seat shall he sprinkle seven times of the blood with his finger.

15 "And he shall kill the goat for the sin-offering that is for the people, before the Lord. And he shall bring in of its blood within the veil, and shall do with its blood as he did with the blood of the calf, and shall sprinkle its blood on the mercy seat, in front of the mercy seat.

16 And he shall make atonement for the sanctuary on account of the uncleanness of the children of Israel, and for their trespasses in the matter of all their sins; and thus shall he do to the tabernacle of witness established among them in the midst of their uncleanness.

17 And there shall be no man in the tabernacle of witness, when he goes in to make atonement in the holy place, until he shall have come out; and he shall make atonement for himself, and for his house, and for all the congregation of the children of Israel.

18 And he shall come forth to the altar that is before the Lord, and he shall make atonement upon it; and he shall take of the blood of the calf, and of the blood of the goat, and shall put it on the horns of the altar round about.

19 And he shall sprinkle some of the blood upon it seven times with his finger, and shall purge it, and hallow it from the uncleanness of the children of Israel.

20 "And he shall finish making atonement for the sanctuary and for the tabernacle of witness, and for the altar, and he shall make a cleansing for the priests, and he shall bring the living goat;

21 and Aaron shall lay his hands on the head of the live goat, and he shall declare over him all the iniquities of the children of Israel, and all their unrighteousness, and all their sins; and he shall lay them upon the head of the live goat, and shall send him by the hand of a ready man into the wilderness.

22 And the goat shall bear their unrighteousnesses upon him into a desert land; and Aaron shall send away the goat into the wilderness.

23 "And Aaron shall enter into the tabernacle of witness, and shall put off the linen garment, which he had put on, as he entered into the holy place, and shall lay it by there.

24 And he shall bathe his body in water in the holy place, and shall put on his garments, and shall go out and offer the burnt offering for himself and the burnt offering for the people: and shall make atonement for himself and for his house, and for the people, as for the priests.

25 And he shall offer the fat for the sin-offering on the altar.

26 And he that sends forth the goat that has been set apart to be let go, shall wash his garments, and bathe his body in water, and afterwards shall enter into the camp.

27 And the calf for the sin-offering, and the goat for the sin-offering, whose blood was brought in to make atonement in the holy place, they shall carry forth out of the camp, and burn them with fire, even their skins and their flesh and their dung. 28 And he that burns them shall wash his garments, and bathe his body in water, and afterwards he shall enter into the camp.

29 "And this shall be a perpetual statute for you; in the seventh month, on the tenth day of the month, you shall humble your souls, and shall do no work, the native and the stranger who abides among you.

30 For in this day he shall make an atonement for you, to cleanse you from all your sins before the Lord, and you shall be purged.

31 This shall be to you a most holy Sabbath, a rest, and you shall humble your souls; it is a perpetual ordinance.

32 The priest whomsoever they shall anoint shall make atonement, and whomsoever they shall consecrate to exercise the priestly office after his father; and he shall put on the linen robe, the holy garment.

33 And he shall make atonement for the most holy place, and the tabernacle of witness; and he shall make atonement for the altar, and for the priests; and he shall make atonement for all the congregation.

34 And this shall be to you a perpetual statute to make atonement for the children of Israel for all their sins: it shall be done once in the year," as the Lord commanded Moses.

LEVITICUS CHAPTER 17

The Sanctity of Blood

1 And the Lord spoke to Moses, saying,

2 "Speak to Aaron and to his sons, and to all the children of Israel, and you shall say to them, 'This is the word which the Lord has commanded, saying,

3 'Every man of the children of Israel, or of the strangers abiding among you, who shall kill a calf, or a sheep, or a goat in the camp, or who shall kill it outside of the camp,

4 and shall not bring it to the door of the tabernacle of witness, so as to sacrifice it for a burnt offering or peace-

offering to the Lord to be acceptable for a sweet-smelling savor; and whosoever shall kill it outside the camp, and shall not bring it to the door of the tabernacle of witness, so as to offer it as a gift to the Lord before the tabernacle of the Lord; blood shall be imputed to that man, he has shed blood; that soul shall be cut off from his people.

5 That the children of Israel may offer their sacrifices, all that they shall kill in the fields, and bring them to the Lord, unto the doors of the tabernacle of witness to the priest, and they shall sacrifice them as a peace-offering to the Lord.

6 And the priest shall pour the blood on the altar round about before the Lord by the doors of the tabernacle of witness, and shall offer the fat for a sweet-smelling savor to the Lord.

7 And they shall no longer offer their sacrifices to vain *gods* after which they whore after; it shall be a perpetual statute to you for your generations.'

8 And you shall say to them, 'Whatever man of the children of Israel, or of the sons of the proselytes abiding among you, shall offer a burnt offering or a sacrifice,

9 and shall not bring it to the door of the tabernacle of witness to sacrifice it to the Lord, that man shall be destroyed from among his people.

10 'And whatever man of the children of Israel, or of the strangers abiding among you, shall eat any blood, I will even set My face against that soul that eats blood, and I will destroy *that soul* from *among* its people.

11 For the life of flesh is its blood, and I have given it to you on the altar to make atonement for your souls; for its blood shall make atonement for the soul.

12 Therefore I said to the children of Israel, 'No soul of you shall eat blood, and the stranger that abides among you shall not eat blood.

13 And whatever man of the children of Israel, or of the strangers abiding among you shall take any animal in hunting, beast, or bird, which is eaten, then shall he pour out the blood, and cover it in the dust.

14 For the blood of all flesh is its life; and I said to the children of Israel, 'You shall not eat the blood of any flesh, for the life of all flesh is its blood: everyone that eats it shall be destroyed.

15 'And every soul which eats that which has died of itself, or is taken of beasts, either among the natives or among the strangers, shall wash his garments, and bathe himself in water, and shall be unclean until evening: then shall he be clean.

16 But if he does not wash his garments, and does not bathe his body in water, then shall he bear his iniquity.'"

LEVITICUS CHAPTER 18

The Laws of Sexual Morality

1 And the Lord spoke to Moses, saying,

2 "Speak to the children of Israel, and you shall say to them, 'I *am* the Lord your God.

3 You shall not do according to what is done in Egypt, in which you dwelt: and according to what is done in the land of Canaan, into which I bring you, you shall not do; and you shall not walk in their ordinances.

4 You shall observe My judgments, and shall keep My ordinances, and shall walk in them: I *am* the Lord your God.

5 So you shall keep all My ordinances, and all My judgments, and do them; which if a man shall do, he shall live in them: I *am* the Lord your God.

6 'No man shall draw near to any of his relatives to uncover their nakedness; I *am* the Lord.

7 You shall not uncover the nakedness of your father, or the nakedness of your mother, for she is your mother; you shall not uncover her nakedness.

8 You shall not uncover the nakedness of your father's wife; it is your father's nakedness.

9 The nakedness of your sister by your father or by your mother, born at home or abroad, their nakedness you shall not uncover.

10 The nakedness of your son's daughter, or your daughter's daughter, their nakedness you shall not uncover; because it is your nakedness.

11 You shall not uncover the nakedness of the daughter of your father's wife; she is your sister by the same father: you shall not uncover her nakedness.

12 You shall not uncover the nakedness of your father's sister, for she is near akin to your father.

13 You shall not uncover the nakedness of your mother's sister, for she is near akin to your mother.

14 You shall not uncover the nakedness of your father's brother, and you shall not go in to his wife; for she is your relation.

15 You shall not uncover the nakedness of your daughter-in-law, for she is your son's wife, you shall not uncover her nakedness.

16 You shall not uncover the nakedness of your brother's wife: it is your brother's nakedness.

17 The nakedness of a woman and her daughter shall you not uncover; her son's daughter, and her daughter's daughter, shall you not take, to uncover their nakedness, for they are your kinswomen: it is impiety.

18 You shall not take a wife in addition to her sister, as a rival, to uncover her nakedness in opposition to her, while she is yet living.

19 'And you shall not go in to a woman under separation for her uncleanness, to uncover her nakedness.

20 And you shall not lie with your neighbor's wife, to defile yourself with her.

21 And you shall not give of your seed to serve a ruler; and you shall not profane My holy name; I *am* the Lord.

22 And you shall not lie with a man as with a woman, for it is an abomination.

23 Neither shall you lie with any animal, to mate with it, *and* be polluted by it: neither shall a woman present herself before any animal to mate with it; for it is an abomination.

²⁴ 'Do not defile yourselves with any of these things; for in all these things the nations are defiled, which I drove out before you,

²⁵ and the land is polluted; and I have recompensed their iniquity to them because of it, and the land is aggrieved with them that dwell upon it.

²⁶ And you shall keep all My statutes and all My ordinances, and you shall do none of these abominations; neither the native, nor the stranger that joins himself with you:

²⁷ (for all these abominations the men of the land did who were before you, and the land was defiled)

²⁸ and lest the land be enraged with you in your polluting it, as it was enraged with the nations before you.

²⁹ For whosoever shall do any of these abominations, the souls that do them shall be destroyed from among their people.

³⁰ And you shall keep My ordinances, that you may not do any of the abominable practices, which have taken place before your time; and you shall not be polluted in them; for I *am* the Lord your God.'"

LEVITICUS CHAPTER 19

Ritual and Moral Holiness

¹ And the Lord spoke to Moses, saying,

² "Speak to the congregation of the children of Israel, and you shall say to them, 'You shall be holy, for I the Lord your God *am* holy.

³ Let everyone of you reverence his father and his mother; and you shall keep My Sabbaths: I *am* the Lord your God.

⁴ You shall not follow idols, and you shall not make to yourselves molten gods: I *am* the Lord your God.

⁵ 'And if you will sacrifice a peace-offering to the Lord, you shall offer it acceptable from yourselves.

⁶ In whatever day you shall sacrifice it, it shall be eaten; and on the following day, and if any of it should be left till the third day, it shall be thoroughly burned with fire.

⁷ And if it should be at all eaten on the third day, it is unfit for sacrifice: it shall not be accepted.

⁸ And he that eats it shall bear his iniquity, because he has profaned the holy things of the Lord; and the souls that eat it shall be destroyed from among their people.

⁹ 'And when you reap the harvest of your land, you shall not complete the reaping of your field with exactness, and you shall not gather that which falls from your reaping.

¹⁰ And you shall not go over the gathering of your vineyard, neither shall you gather the remaining grapes of your vineyard: you shall leave them for the poor and the stranger: I am the Lord your God.

¹¹ 'You shall not steal, you shall not lie, neither shall one bear false witness as an informer against his neighbor.

¹² And you shall not swear unjustly by My name, and you shall not profane the holy name of your God: I am the Lord your God.

¹³ 'You shall not injure your neighbor, neither shall you rob *him*, neither shall the wages of your hireling remain with you until the morning.

¹⁴ You shall not revile the deaf, neither shall you put a stumbling block in the way of the blind; and you shall fear the Lord your God: I am the Lord your God.

¹⁵ 'You shall not act unjustly in judgment: you shall not be partial to the poor, nor honor the person of the mighty; with justice shall you judge your neighbor.

¹⁶ You shall not walk deceitfully among your people; you shall not rise up against the blood of your neighbor: I am the Lord your God.

¹⁷ 'You shall not hate your brother in your heart: you shall surely rebuke your neighbor, so you shall not bear sin on his account.

¹⁸ And your hand shall not avenge you; and you shall not be angry with the children of your people; and you shall love your neighbor as yourself; I am the Lord

¹⁹ 'You shall observe My law: you shall not let your cattle breed with one of a different kind, and you shall not sow your vineyard with diverse seed; and you shall not put upon yourself a mingled garment woven of two *materials*.

²⁰ And if anyone should lie carnally with a woman, and she should be a home-servant kept for a man, and she has not been ransomed, *and* her freedom has not been given to her, they shall be visited *with punishment*; but they shall not die, because she was not set at liberty.

²¹ And he shall bring for his trespass to the Lord, to the door of the tabernacle of witness, a ram for a trespass-offering.

²² And the priest shall make atonement for him with the ram of the trespass-offering, before the Lord, for the sin which he sinned; and the sin which he sinned shall be forgiven him.

²³ 'And whenever you shall enter into the land which the Lord your God gives you, and shall plant any fruit tree, then shall you purge away its uncleanness; its fruit shall be unclean to you for three years; it shall not be eaten.

²⁴ And in the fourth year all its fruit shall be holy, a subject of praise to the Lord.

²⁵ And in the fifth year you shall eat the fruit, its produce is an increase to you. I am the Lord your God.

²⁶ 'Do not eat on the mountains, nor shall you employ divination, nor divine by inspection of birds.

²⁷ You shall not make a round cutting of the hair of your head, nor disfigure your beard.

²⁸ And you shall not make cuttings in your body for a *dead* body, and you shall not inscribe on yourselves any marks. I am the Lord your God.

²⁹ 'You shall not profane your daughter to prostitute her; so the land shall not whore after, and the land be filled with iniquity.

³⁰ 'You shall keep My Sabbaths, and reverence My sanctuaries: I am the Lord.

³¹ 'You shall not attend to those who have in them divining spirits, nor attach yourselves to enchanters, to pollute yourselves with them: I am the Lord your God.

32 'You shall rise up before the gray-headed, and honor the face of the old man, and shall fear your God: I am the Lord your God.

33 'And if there should come to you a stranger in your land, you shall not afflict him.

34 The stranger that comes to you shall be among you as the native, and you shall love him as yourself; for you were strangers in the land of Egypt: I am the Lord your God.

35 'You shall not act unrighteously in judgment, in measures and weights and scales.

36 There shall be among you honest balances and honest weights and honest liquid measure. I am the Lord your God, who brought you out of the land of Egypt.

37 'And you shall keep all My laws and all My ordinances, and you shall do them: I am the Lord your God.'"

LEVITICUS CHAPTER 20

Penalties for Breaking the Law

1 And the Lord spoke to Moses, saying,

2 "You shall also say to the children of Israel, 'If *there shall be* any of the children of Israel, or of those who have become proselytes in Israel, who shall give of his seed to Moloch, let him be surely put to death; the nation upon the land shall stone him with stones.

3 And I will set My face against that man, and will cut him off from his people, because he has given of his seed to Moloch, to defile My sanctuary, and profane the name of them that are consecrated to Me.

4 And if the natives of the land should in anyway overlook that man in giving of his seed to Moloch, so as not to put him to death;

5 then will I set My face against that man and his family, and I will destroy him, and all who have consented with him, so that he should whore after the chief *gods* of their people.

6 'And the soul that shall follow those who have in them divining spirits, or enchanters, so as to whore after them; I will set My face against that soul, and will destroy it from among its people.

7 And you shall be holy, for I the Lord your God *am* holy.

8 'And you shall observe My ordinances, and do them: I *am* the Lord that sanctifies you.

9 Every man who shall speak evil of his father or of his mother, let him die the death; has he spoken evil of his father or his mother? He shall be guilty.

10 Whatever man shall commit adultery with the wife of a man, or whoever shall commit adultery with the wife of his neighbor, let them die the death, the adulterer and the adulteress.

11 And if anyone should lie with his father's wife, he has uncovered his father's nakedness: let them both die the death, they are guilty.

12 And if anyone should lie with his daughter-in-law, let them both be put to death; for they have committed perversion, they are guilty.

13 And whoever shall lie with a male as with a woman, they have both committed an abomination; let them die the death, they are guilty.

14 Whosoever shall take a woman and her mother, it is iniquity: they shall burn him and them with fire; so there shall not be iniquity among you.

15 And whosoever shall lie with a beast, let him die the death; and you shall kill the beast.

16 And whatever woman shall approach any beast, so as to mate with it, you shall kill the woman and the beast: let them die the death, they are guilty.

17 Whosoever shall take his sister by his father or by his mother, and shall see her nakedness, and she see his nakedness, it is a reproach: they shall be destroyed before the children of their family; he has uncovered his sister's nakedness, they shall bear their sin.

18 And whatever man shall lie with a woman that is set apart *for her impurity*, and shall uncover her nakedness, he has uncovered her fountain, and she has uncovered the flux of her blood: they shall both be destroyed from among their generation.

19 And you shall not uncover the nakedness of your father's sister, or of the sister of your mother; for that man has uncovered the nakedness of a close relative: they shall bear their iniquity.

20 Whosoever shall lie with his near kinswoman, has uncovered the nakedness of a close relataive: they shall die childless.

21 Whoever shall take his brother's wife, it is uncleanness; he has uncovered his brother's nakedness; they shall die childless.

22 'And keep all My ordinances, and My judgments; and you shall do them, and the land shall not be enraged with you, into which I bring you to dwell upon it.

23 And do not walk according to the customs of the nations which I drive out from before you; for they have done all these things, and I have abhorred them:

24 and I said to you, 'You shall inherit their land, and I will give it to you for a possession, a land flowing with milk and honey': I *am* the Lord your God, who has separated you from all people.

25 And you shall make a distinction between the clean and the unclean cattle, and between clean and unclean birds; and you shall not defile your souls with cattle, or with birds, or with any creeping things of the earth, which I have separated for you by reason of uncleanness.

26 And you shall be holy to Me; because I the Lord your God *am* holy, who separated you from all nations, to be Mine.

27 "And *as for* a man or woman whosoever of them shall have in them a divining spirit, or be an enchanter, let them both die the death: you shall stone them with stones, they are guilty."

LEVITICUS CHAPTER 21

The Holiness of Priests

[1] And the Lord spoke to Moses, saying, "Speak to the priests, the sons of Aaron, and you shall tell them *that* they shall not defile themselves in their nation for the dead,

[2] but *they may mourn* for a relative who is very near to them, for a father and mother, and sons and daughters, for a brother,

[3] and for a virgin sister that is near to him, that has no husband; for her he may defile himself.

[4] *Otherwise* he shall not defile himself suddenly among his people to profane himself.

[5] And you shall not shave your head for the dead with a baldness on the top; and they shall not shave their beard, neither shall they make gashes on their flesh.

[6] They shall be holy to their God, and they shall not profane the name of their God; for they offer the sacrifices of the Lord as the gifts of their God, and they shall be holy.

[7] They shall not take a woman who is a harlot and profaned, or a woman put away from her husband; for he is holy to the Lord his God.

[8] And you shall sanctify him; he offers the gifts of the Lord your God: he shall be holy, for I the Lord that sanctify them *is* holy.

[9] And if the daughter of a priest should profane herself by playing the harlot, she profanes the name of her father: she shall be burned with fire.

[10] "And the priest that is chief among his brothers, the oil having been poured upon the head of the anointed one, and he having been consecrated to put on the garments, shall not take the turban off his head, and shall not tear his clothes;

[11] neither shall he go in to any dead body, neither shall he defile himself for his father or his mother.

[12] And he shall not go forth out of the sanctuary, and he shall not profane the sanctuary of his God, because the holy anointing oil of God *is* upon him: I *am* the Lord.

[13] He shall take for a wife a virgin of his own tribe.

[14] But a widow, or one that is put away, or profaned, or a harlot, these he shall not take; but he shall take for a wife a virgin of his own people.

[15] And he shall not profane his seed among his people: I *am* the Lord that sanctifies him."

[16] And the Lord spoke to Moses, saying,

[17] "Say to Aaron, A man of your tribe throughout your generations, who shall have a blemish on him, shall not draw near to offer the gifts of his God.

[18] No man who has a blemish on him shall draw near; a man blind, lame, with his nose disfigured, or his ears cut,

[19] a man who has a broken hand or a broken foot,

[20] or hump-backed, or bleary-eyed, or that has lost his eyelashes, or a man who has a malignant ulcer, or tetter, or one that has lost a testicle.

[21] Whoever of the descendants of Aaron the priest has a blemish on him, shall not draw near to offer sacrifices to your God, because he has a blemish on him; he shall not draw near to offer the gifts of God.

[22] The gifts of God *are* most holy, and he shall eat of the holy things.

[23] Only he shall not approach the veil, and he shall not draw near to the altar, because he has a blemish; and he shall not profane the sanctuary of his God, for I am the Lord that sanctifies them."

[24] And Moses spoke to Aaron and his sons, and to all the children of Israel.

LEVITICUS CHAPTER 22

The Use of Holy Offerings

[1] And the Lord spoke to Moses, saying,

[2] "Speak to Aaron and to his sons, and let them take heed concerning the holy things of the children of Israel, so they shall not profane My holy name in any of the things which they consecrate to Me: I *am* the Lord.

[3] Say to them, 'Every man throughout your generations, whoever of all your descendants shall approach to the holy things, whatsoever the children of Israel shall consecrate to the Lord, while his uncleanness is upon him, that soul shall be cut off from Me: I *am* the Lord your God.

[4] And the man of the descendants of Aaron the priest, if he should have leprosy or issue of the reins, shall not eat of the holy things, until he be cleansed; and he that touches any uncleanness of a dead body, or the man whose seed of copulation shall have gone out from him,

[5] or whosoever shall touch any unclean reptile, which will defile him, or *who shall touch* a man, whereby he shall defile him according to all his uncleanness;

[6] whatsoever soul shall touch them shall be unclean until evening; he shall not eat of the holy things, unless he bathe his body in water,

[7] and the sun go down, and then he shall be clean; and then shall he eat of all the holy things, for they are his bread.

[8] He shall not eat that which dies of itself, or is taken of beasts, so that he should be polluted by them: I *am* the Lord.

[9] And they shall keep My ordinances, that they do not bear iniquity because of them, and die because of them, if they shall profane them: I *am* the Lord God that sanctifies them.

[10] 'And no stranger shall eat the holy things: one that sojourns with a priest, or a hireling, shall not eat the holy things.

[11] But if a priest should have a soul purchased for money, he shall eat of his bread; and they that are born in his house, they also shall eat of his bread.

[12] And if the daughter of a priest should marry a stranger, she shall not eat of the offerings of the sanctuary.

[13] And if the daughter of priest should be a widow, or put away, and have no descendants, she shall return to her father's house, as in her youth: she shall eat of her father's bread, but no stranger shall eat of it.

14 'And the man who shall ignorantly eat holy things, shall add the fifth part to it, and give the holy thing to the priest.

15 And they shall not profane the holy things of the children of Israel, which they offer to the Lord.

16 So should they bring upon themselves the iniquity of trespass in their eating their holy things: for I *am* the Lord that sanctifies them.'"

Acceptable Offerings

17 And the Lord spoke to Moses, saying,

18 "Speak to Aaron and his sons, and to all the congregation of Israel, and you shall say to them, 'Any man of the children of Israel, or of the strangers that abide among them in Israel, who shall offer his gifts according to all their confession and according to all their choice, whatsoever they may bring to the Lord for burnt offerings,

19 your freewill offerings *shall* be males without blemish of the herds, or of the sheep, or of the goats.

20 They shall not bring to the Lord anything that has a blemish in it, for it shall not be acceptable for you.

21 And whatsoever man shall offer a peace-offering to the Lord, discharging a vow, or in the way of freewill offering, or an offering in your feasts, of the herds or of the sheep, it shall be without blemish for acceptance: there shall be no blemish in it. 22 One that is blind, or broken, or has its tongue cut out, or is troubled with warts, or has a malignant ulcer, or tetters, they shall not offer these to the Lord; neither shall you offer any of them for a burnt offering on the altar of the Lord.

23 And a calf or a sheep with the ears cut off, or that has lost its tail, you shall kill them for yourself; but they shall not be accepted for your vow.

24 That which has broken testicles, or is crushed or gelded or mutilated—you shall not offer them to the Lord, neither shall you sacrifice them upon your land.

25 Neither shall you offer the gifts of your God of all these things by the hand of a stranger, because there is corruption in them, a blemish in them: these shall not be accepted for you.'"

26 And the Lord spoke to Moses, saying,

27 "As for a calf, or a sheep, or a goat, whenever it is born, then shall it be seven days under its mother; and on the eighth day and after they shall be accepted for sacrifices, a burnt offering to the Lord.

28 And a bullock and a ewe, it and its young, you shall not kill in one day.

29 And if you should offer a sacrifice, a vow of rejoicing to the Lord, you shall offer it so as to be accepted for you.

30 In that same day it shall be eaten; you shall not leave of the flesh till the morning: I am the Lord.

31 "And you shall keep My commandments and do them.

32 And you shall not profane the name of the Holy One, and I will be sanctified in the midst of the children of Israel. I *am* the Lord that sanctifies you,

33 who brought you out of the land of Egypt, to be your God: I *am* the Lord."

LEVITICUS CHAPTER 23

Feasts of the Lord

1 And the Lord spoke to Moses, saying,

2 "Speak to the children of Israel, and you shall say unto them, 'The feasts of the Lord which you shall call holy assemblies, these are My feasts.

The Sabbath

3 'Six days shall you do work, but on the seventh day is the Sabbath; a rest, a holy convocation to the Lord: you shall not do any work, it is a Sabbath to the Lord in all your dwellings.

The Passover and Unleavened Bread

4 'These *are* the feasts to the Lord, holy convocations, which you shall call in their seasons.

5 In the first month, on the fourteenth day of the month, between the evening times is the Lord's Passover.

6 And on the fifteenth day of this month is the Feast of Unleavened Bread to the Lord; seven days shall you eat unleavened bread.

7 And the first day shall be a holy convocation to you: you shall do no customary work.

8 And you shall offer burnt offerings to the Lord for seven days; and the seventh day shall be a holy convocation to you: you shall do no customary work.'"

The Feast of Firstfruits

9 And the Lord spoke to Moses, saying,

10 "Speak to the children of Israel, and you shall say to them, 'When you shall enter into the land which I give you, and reap the harvest of it, then shall you bring a sheaf, the firstfruits of your harvest, to the priest;

11 and he shall lift up the sheaf before the Lord, to be accepted for you. On the morning of the first day the priest shall lift it up.

12 And you shall offer on the day on which you bring the sheaf, a lamb without blemish of a year old for a burnt offering to the Lord.

13 And its grain offering two tenth portions of fine flour mingled with oil: it is a sacrifice to the Lord, an aroma of sweet savor to the Lord, and its drink offering the fourth part of a hin of wine.

14 And you shall not eat bread, or the new parched grain, until this same day, until you offer the sacrifices to your God: *it is* a perpetual statute throughout your generations in all your dwellings.

The Feast of Weeks

15 'And you shall number to yourselves from the day after the Sabbath, from the day on which you shall offer the sheaf of the heave-offering, seven full weeks:

16 until the day after the last week you shall number fifty days, and shall bring a new grain offering to the Lord.

17 You shall bring loaves from your dwelling *places*, as a heave offering, two loaves: they shall be of two tenth portions of fine flour, they shall be baked with leaven of the firstfruits to the Lord.

18 And you shall bring with the loaves seven unblemished lambs of a year old, and one calf of the herd, and two rams without blemish, and they shall be a burnt offering to the Lord. And their grain offerings and their drink offerings *shall be* a sacrifice, an aroma of sweet savor to the Lord.

19 And they shall sacrifice one kid of the goats for a sin offering, and two lambs of a year old for a peace offering, with the loaves of the firstfruits.

20 And the priest shall place them with the loaves of the firstfruits, an offering before the Lord with the two lambs, they shall be holy to the Lord, they shall belong to the priest that brings them.

21 And you shall call this day a convocation: it shall be holy to you; you shall do no customary work on it: it is a perpetual ordinance throughout your generations in all your habitations.

22 'And when you shall reap the harvest of your land, you shall not fully reap the remainder of the harvest of your field when you reap, and you shall not gather that which falls from your reaping; you shall leave it for the poor and the stranger: I *am* the Lord your God.'"

The Feast of Trumpets

23 And the Lord spoke to Moses, saying,

24 "Speak to the children of Israel, saying, 'In the seventh month, on the first day of the month, you shall have a rest, a memorial of trumpets: it shall be to you a holy convocation.

25 You shall do no customary work, and you shall offer a burnt offering to the Lord.'"

26 And the Lord spoke to Moses, saying,

27 "Also on the tenth day of this seventh month is the Day of Atonement: it shall be a holy convocation to you; and you shall humble your souls, and offer a burnt offering to the Lord.

28 You shall do no work on that same day; for this is the Day of Atonement for you, to make atonement for you before the Lord your God.

29 Every soul that shall not be humbled in that day, shall be cut off from among its people.

30 And every soul which shall do work on that day, that soul shall be destroyed from among its people.

31 You shall do no manner of work: it is a perpetual statute throughout your generations in all your habitations.

32 It shall be a holy Sabbath to you; and you shall humble your souls, from the ninth day of the month: from evening to evening you shall keep your Sabbaths."

33 And the Lord spoke to Moses, saying,

34 "Speak to the children of Israel, saying, 'On the fifteenth day of this seventh month, there shall be the Feast of Tabernacles, seven days to the Lord.

35 And on the first day shall be a holy convocation; you shall do no customary work.

36 Seven days shall you offer burnt offerings to the Lord, and the eighth day shall be a holy convocation to you; and you shall offer burnt offerings to the Lord: it is a time of release, you shall do no customary work.

37 These *are* the feasts to the Lord, which you shall call holy convocations, to offer burnt offerings to the Lord, burnt offerings and their grain offerings, and their drink offerings, that for each day on its day:

38 besides the Sabbaths of the Lord, and besides your gifts, and besides all your vows, and besides your freewill offerings, which you shall give to the Lord.

39 'And on the fifteenth day of this seventh month, when you shall have completely gathered in the fruits of the earth, you shall keep a feast to the Lord seven days; on the first day there shall be a rest, and on the eighth day a rest.

40 And on the first day you shall take the good fruit of beautiful trees, and branches of palm trees, and thick boughs of trees, and willows, and branches of osiers from the brook, to rejoice before the Lord your God seven days in the year.

41 *It is* a perpetual statute for your generations: in the seventh month you shall keep it.

42 Seven days you shall dwell in tabernacles: every native in Israel shall dwell in tents,

43 that your posterity may see, that I made the children of Israel to dwell in tents, when I brought them out of the land of Egypt: I *am* the Lord your God.'"

44 And Moses recounted the feasts of the Lord to the children of Israel.

LEVITICUS CHAPTER 24

The Lamp

1 And the Lord spoke to Moses, saying,

2 "Command the children of Israel, and let them take for you pure olive oil beaten for the light, to burn a lamp continually,

3 outside the veil in the tabernacle of witness; and Aaron and his sons shall burn it from evening until morning before the Lord continually, a perpetual statute throughout your generations.

4 You shall burn the lamps on the pure lampstand before the Lord till the morning.

The Bread for the Tabernacle

5 "And you shall take fine flour, and make of it twelve loaves; each loaf shall be of two tenth parts.

6 And you shall put them *in* two rows, each row *containing* six loaves, on the pure table before the Lord.

7 And you shall put on *each* row pure frankincense and salt; and *these things* shall be for loaves for a memorial, set forth before the Lord.

8 On the Sabbath day they shall be set forth before the Lord continually before the children of Israel, for an everlasting covenant.

9 And they shall be for Aaron and his sons, and they shall eat them in the holy place: for this is their most holy portion of the offerings made to the Lord, a perpetual statute."

Blasphemy and Its Punishment

10 And there went forth a son of an Israelite woman, and he was son of an Egyptian man among the sons of Israel; and they fought in the camp, the son of the Israelite woman, and a man who was an Israelite.

11 And the son of the Israelite woman named THE NAME and cursed; and they brought him to Moses. And his mother's name was Shelomith, daughter of Dibri, of the tribe of Dan.

12 And they put him in custody, to judge him by the command of the Lord.

13 And the Lord spoke to Moses, saying,

14 "Bring forth him that cursed outside the camp, and all who heard shall lay their hands upon his head, and all the congregation shall stone him.

15 And speak to the sons of Israel, and you shall say to them, 'Whosoever shall curse God shall bear his sin.

16 And he that names the name of the Lord, let him die the death: let all the congregation of Israel stone him with stones; whether he be a stranger or a native, let him die for naming the name of the Lord.

17 'And whosoever shall strike a man and he die, let him die the death.

18 And whosoever shall strike a beast, and it shall die, let him render life for life.

19 And whosoever shall inflict a blemish on his neighbor, as he has done to him, so shall it be done to himself in return;

20 bruise for bruise, eye for eye, tooth for tooth: as anyone may inflict a blemish on a man, so shall it be rendered to him.

21 Whosoever shall strike a man, and he shall die, let him die the death.

22 There shall be one judgment for the stranger and the native, for I *am* the Lord your God.'"

23 And Moses spoke to the children of Israel, and they brought him that had cursed out of the camp, and they stoned him with stones. And the children of Israel did as the Lord commanded Moses.

LEVITICUS CHAPTER 25

The Sabbatical Year

1 And the Lord spoke to Moses on Mount Sinai, saying,

2 "Speak to the children of Israel, and you shall say to them, 'When you come into the land which I give to you, then the land shall rest, to keep its Sabbaths to the Lord.

3 Six years you shall sow your field, and six years you shall prune your vine, and gather in its fruit.

4 But in the seventh year *shall be* a Sabbath, it shall be a rest to the land, a Sabbath unto the Lord: you shall not sow your field, and you shall not prune your vine.

5 And you shall not gather the spontaneous produce of your field, and you shall not gather fully the grapes of your dedication: it shall be a year of rest to the land.

6 And the Sabbaths of the land shall be food for you, and for your man servant, and for your maid servant, and your hireling, and the stranger that abides with you.

7 And for your cattle, and for the wild beats that are in your land, shall every fruit of it be for food.

The Year of Jubilee

8 'And you shall reckon to yourself seven Sabbaths of years, seven times seven years; and they shall be to you seven weeks of years, forty-nine years.

9 In the seventh month, on the tenth day of the month, you shall make a proclamation with the sound of a trumpet in all your land; on the Day of Atonement you shall make a proclamation with a trumpet in all your land.

10 And you shall sanctify the year, the fiftieth year, and you shall proclaim a release upon the land to all that inhabit it. It shall be given a year of release, a jubilee for you; and each one shall depart to his possession, and you shall go each to his family.

11 This is a jubilee of release, the year shall be to you the fiftieth year: you shall not sow, nor reap the produce that comes of itself from the land, neither shall you gather it dedicated fruits.

12 For it is a jubilee of release; it shall be holy to you, you shall eat its fruits off the fields.

13 'In the year of the release, *even* the jubilee of it, shall *each* one return to his possession.

14 And if you should sell a possession to your neighbor, or if you should buy of your neighbor, let not a man oppress his neighbor.

15 According to the number of years after the jubilee shall you buy of your neighbor, according to the number of years of the fruits shall he sell to you.

16 According as *there may be* a greater number of years he shall increase *the value of* his possession, and according as *there may be* a less number of years he shall lessen *the value of* his possession; for according to the number of his crops, so shall he sell to you.

17 Let not a man oppress his neighbor, and you shall fear the Lord your God: I am the Lord your God.

18 'And you shall keep all My ordinances, and all My judgments; and you shall observe them, and you shall keep them, and dwell securely in the land.

19 And the land shall yield her increase, and you shall eat to *your* fullness, and shall dwell securely in it.

20 And if you should say, 'What shall we eat in this seventh year, if we do not sow nor gather in our fruits?'

21 Then will I send My blessing upon you in the sixth year, and the land shall produce its fruits for three years.

22 And you shall sow in the eighth year, and eat old fruits till the ninth year: until its fruit come, you shall eat old fruits of the old.

Redemption of Property

23 'And the land shall not be sold permanently; for the land is Mine, because you are strangers and sojourners before Me.

24 And in every land of your possession, you shall allow ransoms for the land.

25 And if your brother who is with you is poor, and should have sold *part* of his possession, and his relative who is near to him should come, then he shall redeem the possession which his brother has sold.

26 And if one has no close relative, and he prospers with his hand, and he finds sufficient money, *even* his ransom;

27 then shall he calculate the years of his sale, and he shall give what is due to the man to whom he sold it, and he shall return to his possession.

28 But if his hand has not prospered sufficiently, so as that he should restore the money to him, then he that bought the possessions shall have them till the sixth year of the release; and it shall go out in the release, and the owner shall return to his possession.

29 And if anyone should sell an inhabited house in a walled city, then there shall be the ransom of it, until *the time* is fulfilled: its time of ransom shall be a full year.

30 And if it be not ransomed until there be completed of its time a full year, the house which is in the walled city shall be surely confirmed to him that bought it, throughout his generations; and it shall not go out in the release.

31 But the houses in the villages which have not a wall round about them, shall be reckoned as the fields of the country: they shall always be redeemable, and they shall go out in the release.

32 And the cities of the Levites, the houses of the cities in their possession, shall be always redeemable to the Levites.

33 And if anyone shall redeem a house of the Levites, then shall their sale of the houses of their possession go out in the release; because the houses of the cities of the Levites are their possession in the midst of the children of Israel.

34 And the lands set apart for their cities shall not be sold, because this is their perpetual possession.

Lending to the Poor

35 'And if your brother who is with you should become poor, and he fail in resources with you, you shall help him as a stranger and a sojourner, and your brother shall live with you.

36 You shall not receive from him interest, nor increase: and you shall fear your God: I *am* the Lord; and your brother shall live with you.

37 You shall not lend your money to him at interest, and you shall not lend your food to him to be returned with a profit.

38 I *am* the Lord your God, who brought you out of the land of Egypt, to give you the land of Canaan, so as to be your God.

The Law Concerning Slavery

39 'And if your brother by you should become poor, and be sold to you, he shall not serve you with the servitude of a slave.

40 He shall be with you as a hireling or a sojourner, he shall work for you till the year of release;

41 and he shall go out in the release, and his children with him; and he shall go to his family, he shall hasten back to his family.

42 Because these are My servants, whom I brought out of the land of Egypt; such a one shall not be sold as a *common* servant.

43 You shall not oppress him with labor, and shall fear the Lord your God.

44 And whatever number of men servants and maid servants you shall have, you shall purchase male and female servants from the nations that are round about you.

45 And of the sons of the sojourners that are among you, of these you shall buy and of their relations, all that shall be in your lands; let them be to you for a possession.

46 And you shall distribute them to your children after you, and they shall be to you permanent possessions forever. But of your brothers the children of Israel, one shall not oppress his brother in labors.

47 'And if a stranger or sojourner with you becomes rich, and your brother in distress be sold to the stranger or the sojourner that is with you, or to a proselyte by extraction;

48 after he is sold to him there shall be redemption for him, one of his brothers shall redeem him.

49 A brother of his father, or a son of his father's brother shall redeem him; or let one of his close relatives from among his tribe redeem him, and if he should be rich and redeem himself,

50 then shall he calculate with his purchaser from the year that he sold himself to him until the year of release: and the money of his purchase shall be as that of a hireling, he shall be with him from year to year.

51 And if any have a greater number of years *remaining*, according to these he shall pay his ransom out of his purchase money.

52 And if but a little time is left of the years to the year of release, then shall he reckon to him according to his years, and shall pay his ransom as a hireling.

53 He shall be with him from year to year; you shall not oppress him with labor before you.

54 And if he does not pay his ransom accordingly, he shall go out in the year of his release, he and his children with him.

55 For the children of Israel are My servants: they are My attendants, whom I brought out of the land of Egypt.'"

LEVITICUS CHAPTER 26

Rewards for Obedience

1 "I *am* the Lord your God: you shall not make to yourselves gods made with hands, or graven *images*; neither shall you rear up a pillar for yourselves, neither shall you set up a stone *for* an object in your land to worship it: I am the Lord your God.

2 You shall keep My Sabbaths, and reverence My sanctuaries: I am the Lord.

3 If you will walk in My ordinances, and keep My commandments, and do them,

4 then will I give you the rain in its season, and the land shall produce its fruits, and the trees of the field shall yield their fruit.

5 And your threshing time shall overtake the vintage, and your vintage shall overtake your seedtime; and you shall eat your bread to the full; and you shall dwell safely upon your land, and war shall not go through your land.

6 And I will give peace in your land, and you shall sleep, and none *shall* make you afraid; and I will destroy the evil beasts out of your land,

7 and you shall pursue your enemies, and they shall fall before you with slaughter.

8 And five of you shall chase a hundred, and a hundred of you shall chase tens of thousands; and your enemies shall fall before you by the sword.

9 'And I will look upon you, and increase you, and multiply you, and establish My covenant with you.

10 And you shall eat that which is old and very old, and bring forth the old to make way for the new.

11 And I will set My tabernacle among you, and My soul shall not abhor you;

12 and I will walk among you, and be your God, and you shall be My people.

13 I am the Lord your God, who brought you out of the land of Egypt, where you were slaves; and I broke the band of your yoke, and brought you forth openly.

14 'But if you will not hearken to Me, nor obey these My ordinances,

15 but disobey them, and your soul should loathe My judgments, so that you should not keep all My commands, so as to break My covenant,

16 then will I do thus to you: I will even bring upon you perplexity and the itch, and the fever that causes your eyes to waste away, and *disease* that consumes your life; and you shall sow your seeds in vain, and your enemies shall eat them.

17 And I will set My face against you, and you shall fall before your enemies, and they that hate you shall pursue you; and you shall flee, no one pursuing you.

18 'And if you still refuse to hearken to Me, then will I chasten you yet more, even seven times for your sins.

19 And I will break down the haughtiness of your pride; and I will make your heavens *like* iron, and your earth like brass.

20 And your strength shall be in vain; and your land shall not yield its seed, and the tree of your field shall not yield its fruit.

21 'And if after this you should walk perversely, and not be willing to obey Me, I will further bring upon you seven plagues according to your sins.

22 And I will send upon you the wild beasts of the land, and they shall devour you, and shall consume your cattle; and I will make you few in number, and your ways shall be desolate.

23 'And if hereupon you are not corrected, but walk perversely towards Me,

24 I also will walk with you with a perverse spirit, and I also will strike you seven times for your sins.

25 And I will bring upon you a sword avenging the cause of *My* covenant, and you shall flee for refuge to your cities; and I will send out death against you, and you shall be delivered into the hands of your enemies.

26 When I afflict you with famine of bread, then ten women shall bake your loaves in one oven, and they shall render your loaves by weight; and you shall eat, and not be satisfied.

27 'And if hereupon you will not obey Me, but walk perversely towards Me,

28 then will I walk contrary to you in fury, and I will chasten you seven-fold according to your sins.

29 And you shall eat the flesh of your sons, and the flesh of your daughters shall you eat.

30 And I will render your pillars desolate, and will utterly destroy your wooden *images* made with hands; and I will lay your carcasses on the carcasses of your idols, and My soul shall loathe you.

31 And I will lay your cities waste, and I will make your sanctuaries desolate, and I will not smell the savor of your sacrifices.

32 And I will lay your land desolate, and your enemies who dwell in it shall wonder at it.

33 And I will scatter you among the nations, and the sword shall come upon you and consume you; and your land shall be desolate, and your cities shall be desolate.

34 Then the land shall enjoy its Sabbaths all the days of its desolation.

35 And you shall be in the land of your enemies; then the land shall keep its Sabbaths, and the land shall enjoy its Sabbaths all the days of its desolation: it shall keep Sabbaths which it kept not among your Sabbaths, when you dwelt in it.

36 'And to those who are left of you I will bring bondage into their heart in the land of their enemies; and the sound of a shaken leaf shall chase them, and they shall flee as fleeing from war, and shall fall when none pursues them.

37 And brother shall disregard brother as in war, when none pursues; and you shall not be able to withstand your enemies.

38 And you shall perish among the Gentiles, and the land of your enemies shall devour you.

39 And those who are left of you shall perish, because of their sins, and because of the sins of their fathers: in the land of their enemies shall they consume away.

40 'And they shall confess their sins, and the sins of their fathers, that they have transgressed and neglected Me, and that they have walked perversely before Me,

41 and I walked with them with a perverse mind; and I will destroy them in the land of their enemies: then shall their uncircumcised heart be ashamed, and then shall they acquiesce in *the punishment of* their sins.

42 And I will remember the covenant of Jacob, and the covenant of Isaac, and the covenant of Abraham will I remember.

43 And I will remember the land, and the land shall be left of them; then the land shall enjoy her Sabbaths, when it is deserted through them; and they shall accept *the punishment of* their iniquities, because they neglected My judgments, and in their soul loathed My ordinances.

44 And yet not even thus, while they were in the land of their enemies, did I overlook them, nor did I loathe them so as to consume them, to break My covenant made with them; for I am the Lord their God.

45 And I will remember their former covenant, when I brought them out of the land of Egypt, out of the house of bondage before the nation, to be their God; I am the Lord.

46 'These are My judgments and My ordinances, and the law which the Lord gave between himself and the children of Israel, in Mount Sinai, by the hand of Moses.'"

LEVITICUS CHAPTER 27

Votive Offerings

1 And the Lord spoke to Moses, saying,

2 "Speak to the children of Israel, and you shall say to them, 'Whosoever shall vow a vow as the valuation of his soul for the Lord,

3 the valuation of a male from twenty years old to sixty years old shall be—his valuation shall be fifty shekels of silver by the standard of the sanctuary.

4 And the valuation of a female shall be thirty shekels.

5 And if it be from five years old to twenty, the valuation of a male shall be twenty shekels, and of a female ten shekels.

6 And from a month old to five years old, the valuation of a male shall be five shekels, and of a female, three shekels of silver.

7 And if from sixty years *old* and upward, if it be a male, his valuation shall be fifteen shekels of silver, and if a female, ten shekels.

8 And if the man is too poor for the valuation, he shall stand before the priest; and the priest shall value him: according to what the man who has vowed can afford, the priest shall value him.

9 'And if it be from the cattle that are offered as a gift to the Lord, whoever shall offer one of these to the Lord, it shall be holy.

10 He shall not change it, a good for a bad, or a bad for a good; and if he shall change it, a beast for a beast, it and the substitute shall be holy.

11 And if it be any unclean beast, of which none are offered as a gift to the Lord, he shall set the beast before the priest.

12 And the priest shall make a valuation between the good and the bad, and accordingly as the priest shall value it, so shall it stand.

13 And if *the worshipper* will at all redeem it, he shall add the fifth part to its value.

14 'And whatsoever man shall consecrate his house as holy to the Lord, the priest shall make a valuation of it between the good and the bad: as the priest shall value it, so shall it stand.

15 And if he that has sanctified it should redeem his house, he shall add to it the fifth part of the money of the valuation, and it shall be his.

16 'And if a man should set apart to the Lord a part of the field of his possession, then the valuation shall be according to its seed, fifty shekels of silver for a homer of barley.

17 And if he should set apart his field from the year of release, it shall stand according to his valuation.

18 And if he should set apart his field in the latter time after the release, the priest shall reckon to him the money for the remaining years, until the *next* year of release, and it shall be deducted as an equivalent from his full valuation.

19 And if he that set apart the field would redeem it, he shall add to its value the fifth part of the money, and it shall be his.

20 And if he does not redeem the field, but should sell the field to another man, he shall not afterwards redeem it.

21 But the field shall be holy to the Lord after the release, as separated land; the priest shall have possession of it.

22 And if he should consecrate to the Lord of a field which he has bought, which is not of the field of his possession,

23 the priest shall reckon to him the full valuation from the year of release, and he shall pay the valuation in that day *as* holy to the Lord.

24 And in the year of release the land shall be restored to the man of whom the other bought it, whose the possession of the land was.

25 And every valuation shall be by holy weights: the shekel shall be twenty gerahs.

26 'And every firstborn which shall be produced among your cattle shall be the Lord's, and no man shall sanctify it: whether calf or sheep, it is the Lord's.

27 But if he should redeem an unclean beast, according to its valuation, then he shall add the fifth part to it, and it shall be his; and if he redeem it not, it shall be sold according to its valuation.

28 'And every dedicated thing which a man shall dedicate to the Lord of all that he has, whether man or beast, or of the field of his possession, he shall not sell it, nor redeem it: every devoted thing shall be most holy to the Lord.

29 And whatever shall be dedicated of men, shall not be ransomed, but shall be surely put to death.

30 Every tithe of the land, both of the seed of the land, and of the fruit of trees, is the Lord's, holy to the Lord.

31 And if a man should at all redeem his tithe, he shall add the fifth part to it, and it shall be his.

32 And every tithe of oxen, and of sheep, and whatsoever may come in numbering under the rod, the tenth shall be holy to the Lord.

33 You shall not change a good for a bad, or a bad for a good; and if you should at all change it, its equivalent also shall be holy, it shall not be redeemed.'"

34 These are the commandments which the Lord commanded Moses for the sons of Israel on Mount Sinai.

THE BOOK OF NUMBERS

The First Census of Israel

1 And the Lord spoke to Moses in the Wilderness of Sinai, in the tabernacle of witness, on the first day of the second month, in the second year of their departure from the land of Egypt, saying,

2 "Take the sum of all the congregation of Israel according to their families, according to the houses of their fathers' families, according to their number by their names, according to their heads: every male

3 from twenty years old and upwards, everyone that goes forth in the forces of Israel, take account of them with their strength; you and Aaron take account of them.

4 And with you there shall be each one of the rulers according to the tribe of each: they shall be according to the houses of their families.

5 "And these are the names of the men who shall be present with you; of the tribe of Reuben, Elizur the son of Shedeur;

6 of Simeon, Shelumiel the son of Zuri-shaddai;

7 of Judah, Nahshon the son of Amminadab;

8 of Issachar, Nathanel the son of Zuar;

9 of Zebulun, Eliab the son of Helon;

10 of the sons of Joseph, of Ephraim, Elishama the son of Ammihud; of Manasseh, Gamalliel the son of Pedahzur;

11 of Benjamin, Abidan the son of Gideoni;

12 of Dan, Ahiezer the son of Ammishaddai;

13 of Asher, Pagiel the son of Ocran;

14 of Gad, Eliasaph the son of Deuel;

15 of Naphtali, Ahira the son of Enan."

16 These were famous men of the congregation, heads of the tribes according to their families: these are heads of thousands in Israel.

17 And Moses and Aaron took these men who were called by name.

18 And they assembled all the congregation on the first day of the month in the second year; and they registered them after their lineage, after their families, after the number of their names, from twenty years old and upwards, every male according to their number;

19 as the Lord commanded Moses, so they were numbered in the Wilderness of Sinai.

20 And the sons of Reuben the firstborn of Israel according to their families, according to their divisions, according to the houses of their families, according to the number of their names, according to their heads, were all males from twenty years old and upward, everyone that went out with the army.

21 The numbering of them of the tribe of Reuben was forty-six thousand four hundred.

22 For the children of Simeon according to their families, according to their divisions, according to the houses of their families, according to the number of their names, according to their polls, all males from twenty years old and upward, everyone that goes out with the army,

23 the numbering of them of the tribe of Simeon was fifty-nine thousand three hundred.

24 For the sons of Gad according to their families, according to their divisions, according to the houses of their families, according to the number of their names, according to their polls, all males from twenty years old and upward, everyone that goes forth with the army,

25 the numbering of them of the tribe of Gad was forty-five thousand six hundred and fifty.

26 For the sons of Judah according to their families, according to their divisions, according to the houses of their families, according to the number of their names, according to their polls, all males from twenty years old and upward, everyone that goes forth with the army,

27 the numbering of them of the tribe of Judah was seventy-four thousand six hundred.

28 For the sons of Issachar according to their families, according to their divisions, according to the houses of their families, according to the number of their names, according to their polls, all males from twenty years old and upward, everyone that goes forth with the army,

29 the numbering of them of the tribe of Issachar was fifty-four thousand four hundred.

30 For the sons of Zebulun according to their families, according to their divisions, according to the houses of their families, according to the number of their names, according to their polls, all males from twenty years old and upward, everyone that goes out with the army,

31 the numbering of them of the tribe of Zebulun was fifty-seven thousand four hundred.

32 For the sons of Joseph, the sons of Ephraim, according to their families, according to their divisions, according to the houses of their families, according to the number of their names, according to their polls, all males from twenty years old and upward, everyone that goes out with the army,

33 the numbering of them of the tribe of Ephraim was forty thousand five hundred.

34 For the sons of Manasseh according to their families, according to their divisions, according to the houses of their families, according to the number of their names, according to their polls, all males from twenty years old and upward, everyone that goes out with the army,

35 the numbering of them of the tribe of Manasseh was thirty-two thousand two hundred.

36 For the sons of Benjamin according to their families, according to their divisions, according to the houses of their families, according to the number of their names, according to their polls, every male from twenty years old and upward, everyone that goes forth with the army,

37 the numbering of them of the tribe of Benjamin was thirty-five thousand four hundred.

38 For the sons of Dan according to their families, according to their divisions, according to the houses of their families, according to the number of their names, according to their polls, all males from twenty years old and upward, everyone that goes forth with the army,

39 the numbering of them of the tribe of Dan was sixty-two thousand seven hundred.

40 For the sons of Asher according to their families, according to their divisions, according to the houses of their families, according to the number of their names, according to their polls, every male from twenty years old and upward, everyone that goes forth with the army,

41 the numbering of them of the tribe of Asher was forty-one thousand five hundred.

42 For the sons of Naphtali according to their families, according to their divisions, according to the houses of their families, according to the number of their names, according to their polls, every male from twenty years old and upward, everyone who goes forth with the army,

43 the numbering of them of the tribe of Naphtali was fifty-three thousand four hundred.

44 This is the numbering which Moses and Aaron and the rulers of Israel, being twelve men, conducted. There was a man for each tribe, they were according to the tribe of the houses of their family.

45 And the whole numbering of the children of Israel with their army from twenty years old and upward, everyone that goes out to set himself in battle array in Israel, came to

46 six hundred and three thousand, five hundred and fifty.

47 But the Levites of the tribe of their family were not counted among the children of Israel.

48 And the Lord spoke to Moses, saying,

49 "See, you shall not muster the tribe of Levi, and you shall not take their numbers, in the midst of the children of Israel.

50 And you shall set the Levites over the tabernacle of witness, and over all its furniture, and over all things that are in it; and they shall do service in it, and they shall encamp round about the tabernacle.

51 And in removing the tabernacle, the Levites shall take it down, and in pitching the tabernacle they shall set it up: and let the stranger that advances *to touch it* die.

52 And the children of Israel shall encamp, every man in his own order, and every man according to his company, with their army.

53 But let the Levites encamp round about the tabernacle of witness fronting it, and *so* there shall be no sin among the children of Israel; and the Levites themselves shall keep the guard of the tabernacle of witness."

54 And the children of Israel did according to all that the Lord commanded Moses and Aaron, so did they.

NUMBERS CHAPTER 2

The Order of Encampment and Marching

1 And the Lord spoke to Moses and Aaron, saying,

2 "Let the children of Israel encamp facing *each other*, every man keeping his own rank, according to *their* standards, according to the houses of their families; the children of Israel shall encamp round about the tabernacle of witness.

3 And they that encamp first toward the east *shall be* the order of the camp of Judah with their army, and the prince of the sons of Judah, Nahshon the son of Amminadab."

4 His forces that were numbered were seventy-four thousand six hundred.

5 "And they that encamp next *shall be* of the tribe of Issachar, and the prince of the sons of Issachar *shall be* Nathanel the son of Zuar."

6 His forces that were numbered were fifty-four thousand four hundred.

7 "And they that encamp next *shall be* of the tribe of Zebulun, and the prince of the sons of Zebulun *shall be* Eliab the son of Helon."

8 His forces that were numbered were fifty-seven thousand four hundred.

9 All that were numbered of the camp of Judah were one hundred and eighty-six thousand four hundred. "They shall move first with their forces.

10 "*This is* the order of the camp of Reuben: their forces *shall be* toward the south, and the prince of the children of Reuben *shall be* Elizur the son of Shedeur."

11 His forces that were numbered were forty-six thousand five hundred.

12 "And they that encamp next to him *shall be* of the tribe of Simeon, and the prince of the sons of Simeon *shall be* Shelumiel the son of Zuri-shaddai."

13 His forces that were numbered were fifty-nine thousand three hundred.

14 "And they that encamp next to them *shall be* the tribe of Gad; and the prince of the sons of Gad, Eliasaph the son of Deuel."

15 His forces that were numbered were forty-five thousand six hundred and fifty.

16 All who were numbered of the camp of Reuben were a hundred and fifty-one thousand four hundred and fifty. "They with their forces shall proceed in the second place.

17 And *then* the tabernacle of witness shall be set forward, and the camp of the Levites *shall be* between the camps; as they shall encamp, so also shall they commence their march, each one next in order to his fellow according to their companies.

18 "The station of the camp of Ephraim *shall be* westward with their forces, and the head of the children of Ephraim *shall be* Elishama the son of Ammihud."

19 His forces that were numbered are forty thousand five hundred.

20 "And they that encamp next *shall be* of the tribe of Manasseh, and the prince of the sons of Manasseh, Gamalliel the son of Pedahzur."

21 His forces that were numbered were thirty-two thousand two hundred.

22 "And they that encamp next *shall be* of the tribe of Benjamin, and the prince of the sons of Benjamin, Abidan the son of Gideoni."

23 His forces that were numbered were thirty-five thousand four hundred.

24 All that were numbered of the camp of Ephraim were one hundred and eight thousand one hundred. "They with their forces shall set out third.

25 "The order of the camp of Dan *shall be* northward with their forces; and the prince of the sons of Dan, Ahiezer the son of Ammishaddai."

26 His forces that were numbered were sixty-two thousand seven hundred.

27 "And they that encamp next to him *shall be* the tribe of Asher; and the prince of the sons of Asher, Pagiel the son of Ocran."

28 His forces that were numbered were forty-one thousand five hundred.

29 "And they that encamp next *shall be* of the tribe of Naphtali; and the prince of the children of Naphtali, Ahira son of Enan." 30 His forces that were numbered were fifty-three thousand four hundred.

31 All that were numbered of the camp of Dan, *were* a hundred and fifty-seven thousand six hundred. "They shall set out last according to their order."

32 This *is* the numbering of the children of Israel according to the houses of their families: all the numbering of the camps with their forces *was* six hundred and three thousand, five hundred and fifty.

33 But the Levites were not numbered with them, as the Lord commanded Moses.

34 And the children of Israel did all things that the Lord commanded Moses; thus they encamped in their order, and thus they began their march in succession each according to their divisions, according to the houses of their families.

NUMBERS CHAPTER 3

The Sons of Aaron

1 And these *are* the generations of Aaron and Moses, in the day in which the Lord spoke to Moses in Mount Sinai.

2 And these *are* the names of the sons of Aaron: Nadab the firstborn; and Abiud, Eleazar and Ithamar.

3 These *are* the names of the sons of Aaron, the anointed priests whom they consecrated to the priesthood.

4 And Nadab and Abiud died before the Lord, when they offered strange fire before the Lord, in the Wilderness of Sinai; and they had no children; and Eleazar and Ithamar ministered in the priests' office with Aaron their father.

The Duties of the Levites

5 And the Lord spoke to Moses, saying,

6 "Take the tribe of Levi, and you shall set them before Aaron the priest, and they shall minister to him,

7 and shall keep his charges, and the charges of the children of Israel, before the tabernacle of witness, to do the works of the tabernacle.

8 And they shall keep all the furniture of the tabernacle of witness, and the charges of the children of Israel as to all the works of the tabernacle.

9 And you shall give the Levites to Aaron, and to his sons the priests; they are given for a gift to Me of the children of Israel.

10 And you shall appoint Aaron and his sons over the tabernacle of witness; and they shall keep their charge of priesthood, and all things belonging to the altar, and within the veil; and the stranger that touches them shall die."

11 And the Lord spoke to Moses, saying,

12 "Behold, I have taken the Levites from the midst of the children of Israel, instead of every male that opens the womb from among the children of Israel: they shall be their ransom, and the Levites shall be Mine.

13 For every firstborn *is* Mine; in the day in which I struck every firstborn in the land of Egypt, I sanctified to Myself every firstborn in Israel: both of man and beast, they shall be Mine: I *am* the Lord."

A Census of the Levites

14 And the Lord spoke to Moses in the Wilderness of Sinai, saying,

15 "Take the number of the sons of Levi, according to the houses of their families, according to their divisions; and number every male from a month old and upwards."

16 And Moses and Aaron numbered them by the word of the Lord, as the Lord commanded them.

¹⁷ And these were the sons of Levi by their names: Gershon, Kohath, and Merari;

¹⁸ and these *are* the names of the sons of Gershon according to their families: Libni and Shimei;

¹⁹ and the sons of Kohath according to their families: Amram and Izehar, Hebron and Uzziel;

²⁰ and the sons of Merari according to their families: Mahli and Mushi; these are the families of the Levites according to the houses of their families.

²¹ To Gershon belongs the family of Libni, and the family of Shimei: these are the families of Gershon.

²² The numbering of them according to the number of every male from a month old and upwards, their numbering *was* seven thousand and five hundred.

²³ And the sons of Gershon shall encamp westward behind the tabernacle.

²⁴ And the ruler of the household of the family of Gershon *was* Eliasaph the son of Lael.

²⁵ And the charge of the sons of Gershon in the tabernacle of witness *was* the tent and the veil, and the covering of the door of the tabernacle of witness,

²⁶ and the curtains of the court, and the veil of the door of the court, which is by the tabernacle, and the remainder of all its works.

²⁷ To Kohath *belonged* one division, that of Amram, and another division, that of Izehar, and another division, that of Hebron, and another division, that of Uzziel: these are the divisions of Kohath, according to number.

²⁸ Every male from a month old and upward, eight thousand and six hundred, keeping the charges of the holy things.

²⁹ The families of the sons of Kohath shall encamp beside the tabernacle toward the south.

³⁰ And the chief of the house of the families of the divisions of Kohath *was* Elizaphan the son of Uzziel.

³¹ And their charge *was* the ark, and the table, and the lampstand, and the altars, and all the vessels of the sanctuary wherewith they do holy service, and the veil, and all their works.

³² And the chief over the chief of the Levites *was* Eleazar the son of Aaron the priest, appointed to keep the charges of the holy things.

³³ To Merari *belonged* the family of Mahli, and the family of Mushi: these are the families of Merari.

³⁴ The mustering of them according to their number, every male from a month old and upwards, *was* six thousand and fifty.

³⁵ And the head of the house of the families of the division of Merari was Zuriel the son of Abihail. They shall encamp by the side of the tabernacle northwards.

³⁶ The oversight of the charge of the sons of Merari *included* the boards of the tabernacle, and its bars, its pillars, its sockets and all their furniture, and their works,

³⁷ and the pillars of the court round about, and their bases, their pins, and their cords.

³⁸ They that encamp before the tabernacle of witness on the east *shall be* Moses and Aaron and his sons, keeping the charges of the sanctuary according to the charges of the children of Israel; and the stranger that touches them shall die.

³⁹ All the numbering of the Levites, whom Moses and Aaron numbered by the word of the Lord, according to their families, every male from a month old and upwards, *were* twenty-two thousand.

The Redemption of the Firstborn

⁴⁰ And the Lord spoke to Moses, saying, "Count every firstborn male of the children of Israel from a month old and upwards, and take the number by name.

⁴¹ And you shall take the Levites for Me—I *am* the Lord—instead of all the firstborn of the sons of Israel, and the cattle of the Levites instead of all the firstborn among the cattle of the children of Israel."

⁴² And Moses counted, as the Lord commanded him, every firstborn among the children of Israel.

⁴³ And all the male firstborn in number by name, from a month old and upwards, were according to their numbering twenty-two thousand two hundred and seventy-three.

⁴⁴ And the Lord spoke to Moses, saying,

⁴⁵ "Take the Levites instead of all the firstborn of the sons of Israel, and the cattle of the Levites instead of their cattle, and the Levites shall be Mine: I *am* the Lord.

⁴⁶ And for the ransoms of the two hundred and seventy-three which exceed the Levites in number of the firstborn of the sons of Israel,

⁴⁷ you shall even take five shekels a head; you shall take them according to the holy shekel, twenty gerahs to the shekel.

⁴⁸ And you shall give the money to Aaron and to his sons, the ransom of those who exceed in number among them."

⁴⁹ And Moses took the silver, the ransom of those that exceeded in number the redemption of the Levites.

⁵⁰ He took the silver from the firstborn of the sons of Israel, a thousand three hundred and sixty-five shekels, according to the holy shekel.

⁵¹ And Moses gave the ransom of them that were over to Aaron and his sons, by the word of the Lord, as the Lord commanded Moses.

NUMBERS CHAPTER 4

The Kohathites

¹ And the Lord spoke to Moses and Aaron, saying,

² "Take the sum of the children of Kohath from the midst of the sons of Levi, after their families, according to the houses of their fathers' households,

³ from twenty-five years old and upward until fifty years, everyone that goes in to minister, to do all the works in the tabernacle of witness.

⁴ "And these are the works of the sons of Kohath in the tabernacle of witness; it is most holy.

⁵ And Aaron and his sons shall go in, when the camp is about to move, and shall take down the shadowing veil, and they shall cover with it the ark of the Testimony.

⁶ And they shall put a cover on it of blue skin, a garment of all blue, and they shall put the poles through *the rings*.

⁷ And they shall put on the table set forth for showbread a cloth all of purple, and the dishes, and the censers, and the cups, and the vessels with which one offers drink offerings; and the continual loaves shall be upon it.

⁸ And they shall put upon it a scarlet cloth, and they shall cover it with a blue covering of skin, and they shall put the poles into it.

⁹ And they shall take a blue covering, and cover the lampstand that gives light, and its lamps, and its snuffers, and its funnels, and all the vessels of oil with which they minister.

¹⁰ And they shall put it, and all its vessels, into a blue skin cover; and they shall put it on bearers.

¹¹ And they shall put a blue cloth for a cover on the golden altar, and shall cover it with a blue skin cover, and put in its poles.

¹² And they shall take all the instruments of service, with which they minister in the sanctuary: and shall place them in a cloth of blue, and shall cover them with blue skin covering, and put them upon poles.

¹³ And he shall put the covering on the altar, and they shall cover it with a cloth all of purple.

¹⁴ And they shall put upon it all the vessels with which they minister upon it, and the firepans, and the flesh-hooks, and the cups, and the cover, and all the vessels of the altar; and they shall put on it a blue cover of skins, and shall put in its poles; and they shall take a purple cloth, and cover the laver and its foot, and they shall put it into a blue cover of skin, and put it on bars.

¹⁵ And Aaron and his sons shall finish covering the holy things, and all the holy vessels, when the camp begins to move; and afterwards the sons of Kohath shall go in to take up *the furniture*; but shall not touch the holy things, lest they die: these shall the sons of Kohath bear in the tabernacle of witness.

¹⁶ Eleazar the son of Aaron the priest is overseer—the oil of the light, and the incense of composition, and the daily grain offering and the anointing oil, are his charge; even the oversight of the whole tabernacle, and all things that are in it in the holy place, in all the works."

¹⁷ And the Lord spoke to Moses and Aaron, saying,

¹⁸ "You shall not destroy the family of Kohath from the tribe out of the midst of the Levites.

¹⁹ But do this in regard to them, and they shall live and not die, when they approach the holy of holies: Let Aaron and his sons advance, and they shall place them each in his post for bearing.

²⁰ And *so* they shall by no means go in to look suddenly upon the holy things, and die."

The Gershonites and Merarites

²¹ And the Lord spoke to Moses, saying,

²² "Take the sum of the children of Gershon, and these according to the houses of their lineage, according to there families.

²³ Take the number of them from twenty-five years old and upwards until the age of fifty, everyone that goes in to minister, to do his business in the tabernacle of witness.

²⁴ This *is* the public service of the family of Gershon, to minister and to bear.

²⁵ And they shall bear the skins of the tabernacle, and the tabernacle of witness, and its veil, and the blue cover that was on it above, and the cover of the door of the tabernacle of witness.

²⁶ And all the curtains of the court which were upon the tabernacle of witness, and the appendages, and all the vessels of service that they minister with they shall attend to.

²⁷ According to the direction of Aaron and his sons shall be the ministry of the sons of Gershon, in all their ministries, and in all their works; and you shall take account of them by name in all things borne by them.

²⁸ This is the service of the sons of Gershon in the tabernacle of witness, and their charge by the hand of Ithamar the son of Aaron the priest.

²⁹ "Take the number of the sons of Merari according to their families, according to the houses of their lineage.

³⁰ Take the number of them from twenty-five years old and upwards until fifty years old, everyone that goes in to perform the services of the tabernacle of witness.

³¹ And these are the charges of the things borne by them according to all their works in the tabernacle of witness: they shall bear the boards of the tabernacle, and the bars, and its pillars, and its sockets, and the veil, and *there shall be* their sockets, and their pillars, and the curtain of the door of the tabernacle.

³² And they shall bear the pillars of the court round about, and *there shall be* their sockets, and *they shall bear* the pillars of the veil of the door of the court, and their sockets and their pins, and their cords, and all their furniture, and all their instruments of service. And you shall take their number by name, and all the articles of the charge of the things borne by them.

³³ This is the ministration of the family of the sons of Merari in all their works in the tabernacle of witness, by the hand of Ithamar the son of Aaron the priest."

Census of the Levites

³⁴ And Moses and Aaron and the rulers of Israel took the number of the sons of Kohath according to their families, according to the houses of their lineage,

35 from twenty-five years old and upwards to the age of fifty years, everyone that goes in to minister and do service in the tabernacle of witness.

36 And the numbering of them according to their families was two thousand, seven hundred and fifty.

37 This is the numbering of the family of Kohath, everyone that ministers in the tabernacle of witness, as Moses and Aaron numbered them by the word of the Lord, by the hand of Moses.

38 And the sons of Gershon were numbered according to their families, according to the houses of their lineage,

39 from twenty-five years old and upward till fifty years old, everyone that goes in to minister and to do the services in the tabernacle of witness.

40 And the numbering of them according to their families, according to the houses of their lineage, was two thousand six hundred and thirty.

41 This is the numbering of the family of the sons of Gershon, everyone who ministers in the tabernacle of witness; whom Moses and Aaron numbered by the word of the Lord, by the hand of Moses.

42 And also the family of the sons of Merari were numbered according to their divisions, according to the house of their fathers;

43 from twenty-five years old and upward till fifty years old, everyone that goes in to minister in the services of the tabernacle of witness.

44 And the numbering of them according to their families, according to the houses of their lineage, was three thousand two hundred.

45 This is the numbering of the family of the sons of Merari, whom Moses and Aaron numbered by the word of the Lord, by the hand of Moses.

46 All that were numbered, whom Moses and Aaron and the rulers of Israel numbered, namely, the Levites, according to their families and according to the houses of their lineage,

47 from twenty-five years old and upward till fifty years old, everyone that goes in to the service of the works, and the charge of the things that are carried in the tabernacle of witness.

48 And they that were numbered were eight thousand five hundred and eighty.

49 He reviewed them by the word of the Lord by the hand of Moses, appointing each man severally over their respective work, and over their burdens; and they were numbered, as the Lord commanded Moses.

NUMBERS CHAPTER 5

Unclean Persons

1 And the Lord spoke to Moses, saying,

2 "Command the children of Israel, and let them send forth out of the camp every leper, and everyone who has a discharge, and everyone who is unclean from a dead body.

3 Whether male or female, send them forth out of the camp; and they shall not defile their camps in which I dwell among them."

4 And the children of Israel did so, and sent them out of the camp: as the Lord said to Moses, so did the children of Israel.

Confession and Restitution

5 And the Lord spoke to Moses, saying,

6 "Speak to the children of Israel, saying, Every man or woman who shall commit any sin that is common to man, or if that soul shall have neglected the commandment and transgressed,

7 that person shall confess the sin which he has committed, and shall make restitution for his trespass: he shall pay the principal, and shall add to it the fifth part, and shall make restoration to him against whom he has trespassed.

8 But if a man should have no close relative, so as to make satisfaction for his trespass to him, the trespass offering paid to the Lord shall be for the priest, besides the ram of atonement, by which he shall make atonement with it for him.

9 And every firstfruits in all the sanctified things among the children of Israel, whatsoever they shall offer to the Lord, shall be for the priest himself.

10 And the sanctified things of every man shall be his; and whatever man shall give anything to the priest, the gift shall be his."

Concerning an Unfaithful Wife

11 And the Lord spoke to Moses, saying,

12 "Speak to the children of Israel, and you shall say to them, 'If any man's wife shall transgress against him, and slight and despise him,

13 and supposing anyone shall lie with her carnally, and the thing shall be hid from the eyes of her husband, and she should conceal it and be herself defiled, and there be no witness with her, and she should not be taken;

14 and there should come upon him a spirit of jealousy, and he should be jealous of his wife, and she be defiled; or there should come upon him a spirit of jealousy, and he should be jealous of his wife, and she should not be defiled,

15 then shall the man bring his wife to the priest, and shall bring his gift for her, the tenth part of an ephah of barley meal. He shall not pour oil upon it, neither shall he put frankincense upon it; for it is a sacrifice of jealousy, a sacrifice of memorial, recalling sin to remembrance.

16 'And the priest shall bring her, and cause her to stand before the Lord.

17 And the priest shall take pure running water in an earthen vessel, and he shall take of the dust that is on the floor of the tabernacle of witness, and the priest, having taken it, shall cast it into the water.

18 And the priest shall cause the woman to stand before the Lord, and shall uncover the head of the woman, and shall

put into her hands the sacrifice of memorial, the sacrifice of jealousy; and in the hand of the priest shall be the water of this conviction that brings the curse.

19 And the priest shall adjure her, and shall say to the woman, 'If no one has lain with you, and if you have not transgressed so as to be polluted, being under the power of your husband, be free from this water of the conviction that causes the curse.

20 But if being a married woman you have transgressed, or been polluted, and anyone has lain with you, beside your husband,

21 then the priest shall adjure the woman by the oaths of this curse,' and the priest shall say to the woman, 'The Lord bring you into a curse and under an oath in the midst of your people, in that the Lord should cause your thigh to rot and your belly to swell;

22 and this water bringing the curse shall enter into your womb to cause your belly to swell, and your thigh to rot.' And the woman shall say, 'So be it, So be it.'

23 'And the priest shall write these curses in a book, and shall blot them out with the water of the conviction that brings the curse.

24 And he shall cause the woman to drink the water of the conviction that brings the curse; and the water of the conviction that brings the curse shall enter into her.

25 And the priest shall take from the hand of the woman the sacrifice of jealousy, and shall present the sacrifice before the Lord, and shall bring it to the altar.

26 And the priest shall take a handful of the sacrifice as a memorial of it, and shall offer it up upon the altar; and afterwards he shall cause the woman to drink the water.

27 And it shall come to pass, if she has been defiled, and has altogether escaped the notice of her husband, then the water of the conviction that brings the curse shall enter into her; and she shall swell in her belly, and her thigh shall rot, and the woman shall be for a curse in the midst of her people.

28 But if the woman has not been polluted, and is clean, then shall she be guiltless and shall conceive seed.

29 'This is the law of jealousy, in which a married woman should happen to transgress, and be defiled;

30 or in the case of a man on whomsoever the spirit of jealousy should come, and he should be jealous of his wife, and he should place his wife before the Lord, and the priest shall execute towards her all this law.

31 Then the man shall be clear from sin, and that woman shall bear her sin.'"

NUMBERS CHAPTER 6

The Nazarites

1 And the Lord spoke to Moses, saying,

2 "Speak to the children of Israel, and you shall say to them, 'Whatsoever man or woman shall specially vow a vow to separate oneself with purity to the Lord,

3 he shall purely abstain from wine and strong drink; and he shall drink no vinegar of wine or vinegar of strong drink; and whatever is made of the grape he shall not drink; neither shall he eat fresh grapes or raisins,

4 all the days of his vow: he shall eat none of the things that come from the vine, wine from the grape stones to the husk,

5 all the days of his separation—a razor shall not come upon his head, until the days be fulfilled which he vowed to the Lord. He shall be holy, cherishing the long hair of his head,

6 all the days of his vow to the Lord: he shall not come near to any dead body,

7 to his father or his mother, or to his brother or his sister; he shall not defile himself for them, when they have died, because the vow of God is upon him, on his head.

8 All the days of his vow he shall be holy unto the Lord.

9 'And if anyone should die suddenly by him, immediately the head of his vow shall be defiled; and he shall shave his head in whatever day he shall be purified: on the seventh day he shall be shaved.

10 And on the eighth day he shall bring two turtle doves, or two young pigeons, to the priest, to the doors of the tabernacle of witness.

11 And the priest shall offer one for a sin offering, and the other for a burnt offering; and the priest shall make atonement for him in the things in which he sinned respecting the dead body, and he shall sanctify his head in that day,

12 in which he was consecrated to the Lord, *all* the days of his vow. And he shall bring a lamb of a year old for a trespass offering; and the former days shall not be reckoned, because the head of his vow was polluted.

13 'And this is the law of him that has vowed: in whatever day he shall have fulfilled the days of his vow, he shall himself bring his gift to the doors of the tabernacle of witness.

14 And he shall bring his gift to the Lord; one male lamb of a year old without blemish for a burnt offering, and one ewe lamb of a year old without blemish for a sin offering, and one ram without blemish for a peace offering;

15 and a basket of unleavened bread of fine flour, *even* loaves kneaded with oil, and unleavened cakes anointed with oil, and their grain offering, and their drink offering.

16 And the priest shall bring them before the Lord, and shall offer his sin offering, and his burnt offering.

17 And he shall offer the ram as a sacrifice of peace offering to the Lord with the basket of unleavened bread; and the priest shall offer its grain offering and its drink offering.

18 And he that has vowed shall shave the head of his consecration by the doors of the tabernacle of witness, and shall put the hairs on the fire which is under the sacrifice of peace offering.

19 And the priest shall take the sodden shoulder of the ram, and one unleavened loaf from the basket, and one unleavened cake, and shall put them on the hands of the Nazirite after he has shaved off his holy hair.

20 And the priest shall present them as an offering before the Lord; it shall be the holy portion for the priest beside the breast of the heave offering and beside the shoulder of the wave offering: and afterwards the Nazirite shall drink wine.

21 'This is the law of the Nazirite who shall have vowed to the Lord his gift to the Lord, concerning his vow, besides what he may be able to afford according to the value of his vow, which he may have vowed according to the law of separation.'"

The Priestly Benediction

22 And the Lord spoke to Moses, saying,

23 "Speak to Aaron and to his sons, saying, 'Thus you shall bless the children of Israel, saying to them,

24 'The Lord bless you and keep you;

25 the Lord make His face to shine upon you, and have mercy upon you;

26 the Lord lift up His countenance upon you, and give you peace.'

27 And they shall put My name upon the children of Israel, and I the Lord will bless them."

NUMBERS CHAPTER 7

Offerings of the Leaders

1 And it came to pass in the day in which Moses finished the setting up of the tabernacle, that he anointed it, and consecrated it, and all its furniture, and the altar and all its furniture; he anointed them, and consecrated them.

2 And the princes of Israel brought *gifts*, twelve princes of their fathers' houses: these were ten heads of tribes, these are they that presided over the numbering.

3 And they brought their gift before the Lord: six covered wagons, and twelve oxen; a wagon from two princes, and a calf from each; and they brought them before the tabernacle.

4 And the Lord spoke to Moses, saying,

5 "Take of them, and they shall be for the works of the services of the tabernacle of witness; and you shall give them to the Levites, to each one according to his ministration."

6 And Moses took the wagons and the oxen, and gave them to the Levites.

7 And he gave two wagons and four oxen to the sons of Gershon, according to their ministrations.

8 And four wagons and eight oxen he gave to the sons of Merari according to their ministrations, by Ithamar the son of Aaron the priest.

9 But to the sons of Kohath he gave them not, because they have the ministrations of the sacred things: they shall bear them on their shoulders.

10 And the rulers brought *gifts* for the dedication of the altar, in the day in which he anointed it, and the rulers brought their gifts before the altar.

11 And the Lord said to Moses, "One chief each day, they shall offer their gifts, a chief each day, for the dedication of the altar."

12 And he that offered his gift on the first day was Nahshon the son of Amminadab, prince of the tribe of Judah.

13 And he brought his gift, one silver charger of a hundred and thirty shekels was its weight, one silver bowl of seventy shekels according to the holy shekel; both full of fine flour kneaded with oil for a grain offering.

14 One golden censer of ten shekels full of incense.

15 One calf of the herd, one ram, one male lamb of a year old for a burnt offering;

16 and one kid of the goats for a sin offering.

17 And for a sacrifice of peace offering, two heifers, five rams, five male goats, five ewe lambs of a year old: this *was* the gift of Nahshon the son of Amminadab.

18 On the second day Nathanel son of Zuar, the prince of the tribe of Issachar, brought *his offering*.

19 And he brought this gift: one silver charger, its weight a hundred and thirty shekels, one silver bowl of seventy shekels according to the holy shekel; both full of fine flour kneaded with oil for a grain offering.

20 One censer of ten golden shekels, full of incense.

21 One calf of the herd, one ram, one male lamb of a year old for a burnt offering,

22 and one kid of the goats for a sin offering.

23 And for a sacrifice, a peace offering, two heifers, five rams, five male goats, and five ewe lambs of a year old: this *was* the gift of Nathanel the son of Zuar.

24 On the third day the prince of the sons of Zebulun, Eliab the son of Helon *came*.

25 *He brought* his gift, one silver charger, its weight a hundred and thirty shekels, one silver bowl of seventy shekels according to the holy shekel; both full of fine flour kneaded with oil for a grain offering.

26 One golden censer of ten shekels, full of incense.

27 One calf of the herd, one ram, one male lamb of a year old for a burnt offering,

28 and one kid of the goats for a sin offering.

29 And for a sacrifice of peace offering, two heifers, five rams, five male goats, and five ewe lambs of a year old: this *was* the gift of Eliab the son of Helon.

30 On the fourth day Elisur the son of Sediur, the prince of the children of Reuben, *came*.

31 *He brought* his gift, one silver charger, its weight a hundred and thirty shekels, one silver bowl of seventy shekels according to the holy shekel; both full of fine flour kneaded with oil for a grain offering.

32 One golden censer of ten shekels full of incense.

33 One calf of the herd, one ram, one male lamb of a year old for a burnt offering,

34 and one kid of the goats for a sin offering.

35 And for a sacrifice of peace offering, two heifers, five rams, five male goats, and five ewe lambs of a year old: this *was* the gift of Elisur the son of Sediur.

36 On the fifth day *came* the prince of the children of Simeon, Shelumiel the son of Zuri-shaddai.

37 *He brought* his gift, one silver charger, its weight one hundred and thirty shekels, one silver bowl of seventy shekels according to the holy shekel; both full of fine flour kneaded with oil for a grain offering.

38 One golden censer of ten shekels, full of incense.

39 One calf of the herd, one ram, one male lamb of a year old for a burnt offering,

40 and one kid of the goats for a sin offering.

41 And for a sacrifice of peace offering, two heifers, five rams, five male goats, and five ewe lambs of a year old: this *was* the gift of Shelumiel the son of Zuri-shaddai.

42 On the sixth day the prince of the sons of Gad, Eliasaph the son of Deuel *came*.

43 *He brought* his gift, one silver charger, its weight a hundred and thirty shekels, one silver bowl of seventy shekels according to the holy shekel; both full of fine flour kneaded with oil for a grain offering.

44 One golden censer of ten shekels, full of incense.

45 One calf of the herd, one ram, one male lamb of a year old for a burnt offering,

46 and one kid of the goats for a sin offering.

47 And for a sacrifice of peace offering, two heifers, five rams, five male goats, and five ewe lambs of a year old: this *was* the gift of Eliasaph the son of Deuel.

48 On the seventh day the prince of the sons of Ephraim, Elishama the son of Ammihud *came*.

49 *He brought* his gift, one silver charger, its weight was a hundred and thirty shekels, one silver bowl of seventy shekels according to the holy shekel; both full of fine flour kneaded with oil for a grain offering.

50 One golden censer of ten shekels, full of incense.

51 One calf of the herd, one ram, one male lamb of a year old for a burnt offering,

52 and one kid of the goats for a sin offering.

53 And for a sacrifice of peace offering, two heifers, five rams, five male goats, and five ewe lambs of a year old: this *was* the gift of Elishama the son of Ammihud.

54 On the eighth day the prince of the sons of Manasseh, Gamalliel the son of Pedahzur *came*.

55 *He brought* his gift, one silver charger, its weight one hundred and thirty shekels, one silver bowl of seventy shekels according to the holy shekel; both full of fine flour mingled with oil for a grain offering.

56 One golden censer of ten shekels, full of incense.

57 One calf of the herd, one ram, one male lamb of a year old for a burnt offering,

58 and one kid of the goats for a sin offering.

59 And for a sacrifice of peace offering two heifers, five rams, five male goats, and five ewe lambs of a year old: this *was* the gift of Gamalliel the son of Pedahzur.

60 On the ninth day the prince of the sons of Benjamin, Abidan the son of Gideoni *came*.

61 *He brought* his gift, one silver charger, its weight a hundred and thirty *shekels*, one silver bowl of seventy shekels according to the holy shekel; both full of fine flour mingled with oil for a grain offering.

62 One golden censer of ten shekels, full of incense.

63 One calf of the herd, one ram, one male lamb of a year old for a burnt offering,

64 and one kid of the goats for a sin offering.

65 And for a sacrifice of peace offering, two heifers, five rams, five male goats, and five ewe lambs of a year old: this *was* the gift of Abidan the son of Gideoni.

66 On the tenth day the prince of the sons of Dan, Ahiezer the son of Ammishaddai *came*.

67 *He brought* his gift, one silver charger, its weight a hundred and thirty *shekels*, one silver bowl of seventy shekels according to the holy shekel; both full of fine flour kneaded with oil for a grain offering.

68 One golden censer of ten shekels, full of incense.

69 One calf of the herd, one ram, one male lamb of a year old for a burnt offering,

70 and one kid of the goats for a sin offering.

71 And for a sacrifice of peace offering, two heifers, five rams, five male goats, and five ewe lambs of a year old. This *was* the gift of Ahiezer the son of Ammishaddai.

72 On the eleventh day the prince of the sons of Asher, Phageel the son of Ocran *came*.

73 *He brought* his gift, one silver charger, its weight a hundred and thirty *shekels*, one silver bowl of seventy shekels according to the holy shekel; both full of fine flour mingled with oil for grain offering.

74 One golden censer of ten shekels, full of incense.

75 One calf of the herd, one ram, one male lamb of a year old for a burnt offering,

76 and one kid of the goats for a sin offering.

77 And for a sacrifice of peace offering, two heifers, five rams, five male goats, and five ewe lambs of a year old: this *was* the gift of Phageel the son of Ocran.

78 On the twelfth day the prince of the sons of Naphtali, Ahira the son of Enan *came*.

79 *He brought* his gift, one silver charger, its weight a hundred and thirty shekels; one silver bowl of seventy shekels according to the holy shekel; both full of fine flour mingled with oil for a grain offering.

80 One golden censer of ten shekels, full of incense.

81 One calf of the herd, one ram, one male lamb of a year old for a burnt offering,

82 and one kid of the goats for a sin offering.

83 And for a sacrifice of peace offering, two heifers, five rams, five male goats, and five ewe lambs of a year old: this *was* the gift of Ahira the son of Enan.

84 This was the dedication of the altar in the day in which *Moses* anointed it, by the princes of the sons of Israel; twelve silver chargers, twelve silver bowls, twelve golden censers:

85 each charger of a hundred and thirty shekels, and each bowl of seventy shekels: all the silver of the vessels *was* two thousand four hundred shekels, the shekels according to the holy shekel.

86 Twelve golden censers full of incense: all the gold of the shekels, a hundred and twenty shekels.

87 All the cattle for burnt offerings, twelve calves, twelve rams, twelve male lambs of a year old, and their grain offerings, and their drink offerings; and twelve kids of the goats for sin offering.

88 All the cattle for a sacrifice of peace offering, twenty-four heifers, sixty rams, sixty male goats of a year old, sixty ewe lambs of a year old without blemish; this is the dedication of the altar, after that *Moses* consecrated *Aaron*, and he anointed him.

89 When Moses went into the tabernacle of witness to speak to God, then he heard the voice of the Lord speaking to him from off the mercy seat, which is upon the ark of the Testimony, between the two cherubim; and He spoke to him.

NUMBERS CHAPTER 8

The Seven Lamps

1 And the Lord spoke to Moses, saying,

2 "Speak to Aaron, and you shall say to him, 'Whenever you shall set the lamps in order, the seven lamps shall give light opposite the lampstand.'"

3 And Aaron did so. On one side opposite the lampstand he lighted its lamps, as the Lord appointed Moses.

4 And this *is* the construction of the lampstand: *it is* solid, golden—its stem, and its lilies *were* all solid; according to the pattern which the Lord showed Moses, so he made the lampstand.

Consecration and Service of the Levites

5 And the Lord spoke to Moses, saying,

6 "Take the Levites out of the midst of the children of Israel, and you shall purify them.

7 And thus shall you perform their purification: you shall sprinkle them with the water of purification, and a razor shall come upon the whole of their body, and they shall wash their garments, and shall be clean.

8 And they shall take one calf of the herd, and its grain offering, fine flour mingled with oil; and you shall take a calf of a year old of the herd for a sin offering.

9 And you shall bring the Levites before the tabernacle of witness; and you shall assemble all the congregation of the sons of Israel.

10 And you shall bring the Levites before the Lord; and the sons of Israel shall lay their hands upon the Levites.

11 And Aaron shall separate the Levites for a gift before the Lord from the children of Israel; and they shall be prepared to perform the works of the Lord.

12 And the Levites shall lay their hands on the heads of the calves; and you shall offer one for a sin offering, and the other for a burnt offering to the Lord, to make atonement for them.

13 And you shall set the Levites before the Lord, and before Aaron, and before his sons; and you shall give them as a gift before the Lord.

14 And you shall separate the Levites from the midst of the sons of Israel, and they shall be Mine.

15 And afterwards the Levites shall go in to perform the works of the tabernacle of witness; and you shall purify them, and present them before the Lord.

16 For these are given to Me for a present out of the midst of the children of Israel: I have taken them to Myself instead of all the firstborn of the sons of Israel that open every womb.

17 For every firstborn among the children of Israel *is* Mine, whether of man or beast: in the day in which I struck every firstborn in the land of Egypt, I sanctified them to Myself.

18 And I took the Levites in the place of every firstborn among the children of Israel.

19 And I gave the Levites presented as a gift to Aaron and his sons out of the midst of the children of Israel, to do the service of the children of Israel in the tabernacle of witness, and to make atonement for the children of Israel; thus there shall be none among the sons of Israel to draw near to the holy things."

20 And Moses and Aaron, and all the congregation of the children of Israel did to the Levites as the Lord commanded Moses concerning the Levites, so the sons of Israel did to them.

21 So the Levites purified themselves and washed their garments, and Aaron presented them as a gift before the Lord, and Aaron made atonement for them, to purify them.

22 And afterwards the Levites went in to minister in their service in the tabernacle of witness before Aaron, and before his sons; as the Lord appointed Moses concerning the Levites, so they did to them.

23 And the Lord spoke to Moses, saying,

24 "This is the *ordinance* for the Levites: From twenty-five years old and upward, they shall go in to minister in the tabernacle of witness.

25 And from fifty years old *the Levites* shall cease from the ministry, and shall not work any longer.

26 And his brother shall serve in the tabernacle of witness to keep the charges, but he shall not do the works: so shall you do to the Levites in their charges."

NUMBERS CHAPTER 9

The Passover at Sinai

1 And the Lord spoke to Moses in the Wilderness of Sinai in the second year after they had gone forth from the land of Egypt, in the first month, saying,

2 "Speak, and let the children of Israel keep the Passover in its season.

[3] On the fourteenth day of the first month at evening, you shall keep it in its season; you shall keep it according to its law, and according to its ordinance."

[4] And Moses ordered the children of Israel to sacrifice the Passover,

[5] on the fourteenth day of the first month in the Wilderness of Sinai, as the Lord appointed Moses, so the children of Israel did.

[6] And there came men who were unclean by reason of a dead body, and they were not able to keep the Passover on that day; and they came before Moses and Aaron on that day.

[7] And those men said to Moses, "We are unclean by reason of the dead body of a man: shall we therefore fail to offer the gift to the Lord in its season in the midst of the children of Israel?"

[8] And Moses said to them, "Stand there, and I will hear what command the Lord will give concerning you."

[9] And the Lord spoke to Moses, saying,

[10] "Speak to the children of Israel, saying, 'Whatever man shall be unclean by reason of a dead body, or on a journey far off, among you, or among your posterity; he shall then keep the Passover to the Lord,

[11] in the second month, on the fourteenth day; in the evening they shall offer it, with unleavened bread and bitter herbs shall they eat it.

[12] They shall leave none of it until morning, and they shall not break a bone of it; they shall sacrifice it according to the ordinance of the Passover.

[13] And whatsoever man shall be clean, and is not far off on a journey, and shall fail to keep the Passover, that soul shall be cut off from his people, because he has not offered the gift to the Lord in its season; that man shall bear his iniquity.

[14] And if there should come to you a stranger in your land, and should keep the Passover to the Lord, he shall keep it according to the law of the Passover and according to its ordinance. There shall be one law for you, both for the stranger, and for the native of the land.'"

The Cloud and the Fire

[15] And in the day in which the tabernacle was pitched the cloud covered the tabernacle, the place of the testimony; and in the evening there was upon the tabernacle as the appearance of fire till the morning.

[16] So it was continually: the cloud covered it by day, and the appearance of fire by night.

[17] And when the cloud went up from the tabernacle, then after that the children of Israel departed; and in whatever place the cloud rested, there the children of Israel encamped.

[18] The children of Israel shall encamp by the command of the Lord, and by the command of the Lord they shall journey; all the days in which the cloud overshadows the tabernacle, the children of Israel shall encamp.

[19] And whenever the cloud shall be drawn over the tabernacle for many days, then the children of Israel shall keep the command of God, and they shall not journey.

[20] And it shall be, whenever the cloud overshadows the tabernacle a number of days, they shall encamp by the word of the Lord, and shall journey by the command of the Lord.

[21] And it shall come to pass, whenever the cloud shall remain from the evening till the morning, and in the morning the cloud shall go up, then shall they journey by day or by night.

[22] When the cloud continues a full month overshadowing the tabernacle, the children of Israel shall encamp, and shall not depart.

[23] For they shall depart by the command of the Lord: they kept the charge of the Lord by the command of the Lord by the hand of Moses.

NUMBERS CHAPTER 10

The Silver Trumpets

[1] And the Lord spoke to Moses, saying,

[2] "Make to yourself two silver trumpets: you shall make them of hammered work; and they shall be to you for the purpose of calling the assembly, and of removing the camps.

[3] And you shall sound with them, and all the congregation shall be gathered to the door of the tabernacle of witness.

[4] And if they shall sound with one, all the rulers, even the princes of Israel, shall come to you.

[5] And you shall sound an alarm, and the camps pitched eastward shall begin to move.

[6] And you shall sound a second alarm, and the camps pitched southward shall move; and you shall sound a third alarm, and the camps pitched westward shall move forward; and you shall sound a fourth alarm, and they that encamp toward the north shall move forward: they shall sound an alarm at their departure.

[7] And whenever you shall gather the assembly, you shall sound, but not an alarm.

[8] And the priests, the sons of Aaron, shall sound with the trumpets; and it shall be a perpetual ordinance for you throughout your generations.

[9] And if you shall go forth to war in your land against your enemies that are opposed to you, then shall you sound with the trumpets; and you shall be had in remembrance before the Lord, and you shall be saved from your enemies.

[10] And in the days of your gladness, and in your feasts, and in your new moons, you shall sound with the trumpets at your burnt offerings, and at the sacrifices of your peace offerings; and there shall be a memorial for you before your God: I *am* the Lord your God."

Departure from Sinai

[11] And it came to pass in the second year, in the second month, on the twentieth day of the month, that the cloud went up from the tabernacle of witness.

12 And the children of Israel set forward with their baggage in the Wilderness of Sinai; and the cloud rested in the Wilderness of Paran.

13 And the first rank departed by the word of the Lord by the hand of Moses.

14 And they first set in motion the order of the camp of the children of Judah with their host; and over their host *was* Nahshon, son of Amminadab.

15 And over the host of the tribe of the sons of Issachar *was* Nathanel son of Zuar.

16 And over the host of the tribe of the sons of Zebulun *was* Eliab the son of Helon.

17 And they shall take down the tabernacle, and the sons of Gershon shall set forward, and the sons of Merari, who bear the tabernacle.

18 And the order of the camp of Reuben set forward with their host; and over their host *was* Elisur the son of Sediur.

19 And over the host of the tribe of the sons of Simeon *was* Shelumiel son of Zuri-shaddai.

20 And over the host of the tribe of the children of Gad *was* Eliasaph the son of Deuel.

21 And the sons of Kohath shall set forward bearing the holy things, and *the others* shall set up the tabernacle until they arrive.

22 And the order of the camp of Ephraim shall set forward with their forces; and over their forces *was* Elishama the son of Sammihud.

23 And over the forces of the tribes of the sons of Manasseh *was* Gamalliel the *son* of Pedahzur.

24 And over the forces of the tribe of the children of Benjamin *was* Abidan the *son* of Gideoni.

25 And the order of the camp of the sons of Dan shall set forward the last of all the camps, with their forces: and over their forces *was* Ahiezer the son of Ammishaddai.

26 And over the forces of the tribe of the sons of Asher *was* Pagiel the son of Ocran.

27 And over the forces of the tribe of the sons of Naphtali *was* Ahira the son of Enan.

28 These *are* the armies of the children of Israel; and they set forward with their forces.

29 And Moses said to Hobab the son of Jethro the Midianite, the father-in-law of Moses, "We are going forward to the place concerning which the Lord said, 'This will I give to you': Come with us, and we will do you good, for the Lord has spoken good concerning Israel."

30 And he said to him, "I will not go, but *I will go* to my land and to my kindred."

31 And he said, "Do not leave us, because you have been with us in the wilderness, and you shall be an elder among us.

32 And it shall come to pass if you will go with us, it shall even come to pass that in whatsoever things the Lord shall do us good, we will also do you good."

33 And they departed from the mount of the Lord on a three days' journey; and the ark of the covenant of the Lord went before them, a three days' journey to provide rest for them.

34 And the cloud overshadowed them by day, when they departed from the camp.

35 And it came to pass when the ark set forward, that Moses said, "Arise, O Lord, and let Your enemies be scattered: let all that hate You flee."

36 And in the resting he said, "Turn again, O Lord, the thousands *and* tens of thousands in Israel."

NUMBERS CHAPTER 11

Complaining in the Desert

1 And the people murmured sinfully before the Lord; and the Lord heard *them* and was very angry; and fire was kindled among them from the Lord, and devoured a part of the camp.

2 And the people cried to Moses, and Moses prayed to the Lord, and the fire was quenched.

3 And the name of that place was called Burning; for a fire was kindled among them from the Lord.

4 And the mixed multitude among them lusted exceedingly; and they and the children of Israel sat down and wept and said, "Who shall give us meat to eat?

5 We remember the fish which we ate freely in Egypt; and the cucumbers, and the melons, and the leeks, and the garlic, and the onions.

6 But now our soul is dried up; our eyes *turn* to nothing but to the manna!"

7 Now the manna was like coriander seed, and the appearance of it was like bdellium.

8 And the people went through the field and gathered, and ground it in the mill, or pounded it in a mortar, and baked it in a pan, and made cakes of it; and the sweetness of it was as the taste *of* a wafer made with oil.

9 And when the dew came upon the camp by night, the manna came down upon it.

10 And Moses heard them weeping by their families, everyone in his door. And the Lord was very angry; and the thing was evil in the sight of Moses.

11 And Moses said to the Lord, "Why have You afflicted Your servant, and why have I not found grace in Your sight, that You should lay the weight of this people upon me?

12 Have I conceived all this people, or have I born them? That You say to me, Take them into your bosom, as a nurse would take her suckling, into the land which You swore to their fathers?

13 Where am I to get the meat to give to all these people? For they weep to me, saying, 'Give us meat, that we may eat.'

14 I shall not be able to bear these people alone, for this thing is too heavy for me.

15 And if You do thus to me, slay me utterly, if I have found favor with You, that I may not see my affliction."

The Seventy Elders

16 And the Lord said to Moses, "Gather Me seventy men from the elders of Israel, whom you yourself know that they are the elders of the people, and their scribes; and you shall bring them to the tabernacle of witness, and they shall stand there with you.

17 And I will go down, and speak there with you; and I will take of the spirit that is upon you, and will put it upon them; and they shall bear together with you the burden of the people, and you shall not bear them alone.

18 And to the people you shall say, 'Consecrate yourselves for tomorrow, and you shall eat meat; for you wept before the Lord, saying, 'Who shall give us meat to eat?' For it was well with us in Egypt: and the Lord shall allow you to eat meat, and you shall eat meat.

19 You shall not eat one day, nor two, nor five days, nor ten days, nor twenty days;

20 you shall eat for a full month, until *the meat* comes out of your nostrils; and it shall be loathsome unto you, because you disobeyed the Lord, who is among you, and wept before Him, saying, 'What had we to do to come out of Egypt?'"

21 And Moses said, "The people whom I am among are six hundred thousand footmen; and You said, 'I will give them meat to eat, and they shall eat a whole month.'

22 Shall sheep and oxen be slain for them, and shall it suffice them? Or shall all the fish of the sea be gathered together for them, and shall it suffice them?"

23 And the Lord said to Moses, "Shall not the hand of the Lord be fully sufficient? Now shall you know whether My word shall come to pass to you or not."

24 And Moses went out, and spoke the words of the Lord to the people. And he gathered seventy men of the elders of the people, and he set them round about the tabernacle.

25 And the Lord came down in a cloud, and spoke to him, and took of the spirit that was upon him, and put it upon the seventy men that were elders; and when the spirit rested upon them, they prophesied and ceased.

26 And there were two men left in the camp, the name of the one was Eldad, and the name of the other Medad; and the spirit rested upon them, and these were of the number of them that were enrolled, but they did not come to the tabernacle; and they prophesied in the camp.

27 And a young man ran and told Moses, and spoke, saying, "Eldad and Medad are prophesying in the camp!"

28 And Joshua the son of Nun, who attended on Moses, the chosen one, said, "*My* lord Moses, forbid them."

29 And Moses said to him, "Are you jealous on my account? I wish that all the Lord's people were prophets; whenever the Lord shall put His Spirit upon them."

30 And Moses departed into the camp, himself and the elders of Israel.

The Lord Sends Quail

31 And there went forth a wind from the Lord, and brought quails over from the sea; and it brought them down upon the camp a day's journey on this side, and a day's journey on that side, round about the camp, as it were two cubits from the earth.

32 And the people rose up all the day, and all the night, and all the next day, and gathered quails; he that gathered least gathered ten measures; and they refreshed themselves round about the camp.

33 The flesh was yet between their teeth, before it failed, when the Lord was angry with the people, and the Lord struck the people with a very great plague.

34 And the name of that place was called the Graves of Lust; for there they buried the people that lusted.

35 The people departed from the Graves of Lust to Asheroth; and the people halted at Asheroth.

NUMBERS CHAPTER 12

Aaron and Miriam Jealous of Moses

1 And Miriam and Aaron spoke against Moses, because of the Ethiopian woman whom Moses took; for he had taken an Ethiopian woman.

2 And they said, "Has the Lord spoken to Moses only? Has He not also spoken to us?" And the Lord heard it.

3 And the man Moses was very meek beyond all the men that were upon the earth.

4 And the Lord said immediately to Moses and Aaron and Miriam, "Come forth, all three of you, to the tabernacle of witness."

5 And the three came forth to the tabernacle of witness; and the Lord descended in a pillar of a cloud, and stood at the door of the tabernacle of witness. And Aaron and Miriam were called; and both came forth.

6 And He said to them, "Hear My words: If there should be a prophet of the Lord among you, I will be made known to him in a vision, and in sleep will I speak to him.

7 My servant Moses *is* not so; he is faithful in all My house.

8 I will speak plainly to him, mouth to mouth, and not in riddles; and he has seen the glory of the Lord; and why were you not afraid to speak against My servant Moses?"

9 And the great anger of the Lord *was* upon them, and He departed.

10 And the cloud departed from the tabernacle. And behold, Miriam became leprous, *white* as snow; and Aaron looked upon Miriam, and behold, she *was* leprous.

11 And Aaron said to Moses, "I beseech you, my lord, do not lay *this* sin upon us, for we were ignorant in which we have sinned.

12 Let her not be like death, as an abortion coming out of his mother's womb, when *the disease* devours the half of the flesh."

13 And Moses cried to the Lord, saying, "O God, I beseech You, heal her."

14 And the Lord said to Moses, "If her father had only spit in her face, would she not be ashamed seven days? Let her be set apart seven days outside the camp, and afterwards she shall come in."

15 And Miriam was separated outside the camp for seven days; and the people did not move forward until Miriam was cleansed.

16 And afterwards the people set forth from Asheroth, and encamped in the Wilderness of Paran.

NUMBERS CHAPTER 13

Spies Sent into Canaan

1 And the Lord spoke to Moses, saying,

2 "Send for yourself *some* men, and let them spy the land of the Canaanites, which I am giving to the sons of Israel for a possession—one man for a tribe, you shall send them away according to their families, everyone of them a prince."

3 And Moses sent them out of the Wilderness of Paran by the word of the Lord; all these *were* the princes of the sons of Israel.

4 And these *are* their names: of the tribe of Reuben, Samuel the son of Zachur.

5 Of the tribe of Simeon, Saphat the son of Suri.

6 Of the tribe of Judah, Caleb the son of Jephunneh.

7 Of the tribe of Issachar, Igal the son of Joseph.

8 Of the tribe of Ephraim, Oshea the son of Nun.

9 Of the tribe of Benjamin, Palti the son of Raphu.

10 Of the tribe of Zebulun, Gaddiel the son of Sudi.

11 Of the tribe of Joseph of the sons of Mannasseh, Gaddi the son of Susi.

12 Of the tribe of Dan, Ammiel the son of Gamalli.

13 Of the tribe of Asher, Sethur the son of Michael.

14 Of the tribe of Naphtali, Nahbi the son of Vophsi.

15 Of the tribe of Gad, Gaddiel the son of Macchi.

16 These *are* the names of the men whom Moses sent to spy out the land; and Moses called Oshea the son of Nun, Joshua.

17 And Moses sent them to spy out the land of Canaan, and said to them, "Go up by this wilderness; and you shall go up to the mountain,

18 and you shall see the land, what it is, and the people that dwell on it, whether *they* are strong or weak, or *whether* they are few or many.

19 And what the land is on which they dwell, *whether* it is good or bad; and what the cities are in which these dwell in, whether they dwell in walled or unwalled *cities*.

20 And what the land is, whether rich or poor; whether there are trees in it or not, and you shall persevere and take of the fruits of the land." Now the days *were* the days of spring, the forerunners of the grape.

21 And they went up and surveyed the land from the Wilderness of Zin to Rehob, as men go in to Hamath.

22 And they went up by the wilderness, and departed as far as Hebron; and there *was* Ahiman, Seshai, and Talmai, the descendants of Anak. Now Hebron was built seven years before Tanin of Egypt.

23 And they came to the Valley of the Cluster and surveyed it; and they cut down from there a bough and one cluster of grapes upon it, and carried it on poles, and *they took* of the pomegranates and the figs.

24 And they called that place, The Valley of the Cluster, because of the cluster which the children of Israel cut down from there.

25 And they returned from there, having surveyed the land, after forty days.

26 And they proceeded and came to Moses and Aaron and all the congregation of the children of Israel, to the Wilderness of Paran Kadesh; and they brought word to them and to all the congregation, and they showed the fruit of the land.

27 And they reported to him, and said, "We came into the land into which you sent us, a land flowing with milk and honey; and this is the fruit of it.

28 Only the nation that dwells upon it is bold, and they have very great and strong-walled towns, and we saw the children of Anak there.

29 And Amalek dwells in the land toward the south: and the Hittite and the Hivite, and the Jebusite, and the Amorite dwells in the hill country: and the Canaanite dwells by the sea, and by the River Jordan."

30 And Caleb quieted the people from speaking before Moses, and said to him, "No, but we will go up by all means, and will inherit it, for we shall surely prevail against them!"

31 But the men that went up together with him said, "We shall not go up! For we shall by no means be able to go up against the nation, for it is much stronger than we."

32 And they brought a fearful report of that land of which they surveyed unto the children of Israel, saying, "The land which we passed by to survey it, is a land that devours its inhabitants; and all the people whom we saw in it are men of extraordinary stature.

33 And we saw giants there; and we were as mere insects in our own sight, and so we were before them."

NUMBERS CHAPTER 14

The People Rebel

1 And all the congregation lifted up their voice and cried; and the people wept all that night.

2 And all the children of Israel murmured against Moses and Aaron; and all the congregation said to them,

3 "If only we would have died in the land of Egypt! Or if only we would have died in this wilderness! And why does the Lord bring us into this land to fall in war? Our wives and our children shall be for a prey: now then it is better to return into Egypt."

4 And they said to one another, "Let us select a leader and return into Egypt."

[5] And Moses and Aaron fell upon their face before all the congregation of the children of Israel.

[6] But Joshua the son of Nun, and Caleb the son of Jephunneh, of those that spied out the land, tore their clothes,

[7] and spoke to all the congregation of the children of Israel, saying, "The land which we surveyed is indeed very good.

[8] If the Lord delights in us, He will bring us into this land, and give it to us; a land which flows with milk and honey.

[9] Only do not depart from the Lord; and do not fear the people of the land, for they shall be as food to us; for the season *of prosperity* has departed from them, but the Lord *is* among us; do not fear them."

[10] And all the congregation said to stone them with stones; and the glory of the Lord appeared in the cloud on the tabernacle of witness to all the children of Israel.

Moses Intercedes for the People

[11] And the Lord said to Moses, "How long will these people provoke Me? And how long do they refuse to believe Me for all the signs which I have done among them?

[12] I will strike them with death, and destroy them; and I will make of you and of your father's house a great nation, and much greater than this."

[13] And Moses said to the Lord, "So Egypt shall hear, for You have brought up this people from them by Your might.

[14] Moreover all the inhabitants of this land have heard that You are Lord in the midst of this people, who, O Lord, are seen *by them* face to face, and Your cloud rests upon them, and You go before them by day in a pillar of cloud, and by night in a pillar of fire.

[15] And *if* You shall destroy this nation as one man; then all the nations that have heard Your name shall speak, saying,

[16] 'Because the Lord could not bring this people into the land which He swore to them, He has overthrown them in the wilderness.'

[17] And now, O Lord, let Your strength be exalted, as You spoke, saying,

[18] 'The Lord *is* longsuffering and merciful, and true, removing transgressions and iniquities and sins, and He shall by no means clear the guilty, visiting the sins of the fathers upon the children to the third and fourth generation.'

[19] Forgive this people their sin according to Your great mercy, as You were favorable to them from Egypt until now."

[20] And the Lord said to Moses, "I am gracious to them according to your word.

[21] But *as* I live, and as My name lives, so the glory of the Lord shall fill all the earth.

[22] For all the men who see My glory, and the signs which I have done in Egypt, and in the wilderness, and have tempted Me this tenth time, and have not hearkened to My voice,

[23] surely they shall not see the land which I swore to their fathers; but their children which are with Me here, as many as do not know good or evil, every inexperienced youth, to them shall I give the land; but none who have provoked Me shall see it.

[24] However My servant Caleb, because there was another spirit in him, and he has followed Me, I will bring him into the land into which he entered, and his descendants shall inherit it.

[25] Now Amalek and the Canaanite dwell in the valley. Tomorrow, turn and depart for the wilderness by the way of the Red Sea."

Death Sentence on the Rebels

[26] And the Lord spoke to Moses and Aaron, saying,

[27] "How long *shall I endure* this wicked congregation? I have heard their murmurings against Me, *even* the murmuring of the children of Israel, which they have murmured concerning you.

[28] Say to them, '*As* I live, says the Lord, surely as you spoke into My ears, so will I do to you.

[29] Your carcasses shall fall in this wilderness; and all of you that were reviewed, and those of you that were numbered from twenty years old and upward, all that murmured against Me,

[30] you shall not enter into the land for which I stretched out My hand to establish you upon it; except only Caleb the son of Jephunneh, and Joshua the son of Nun.

[31] And your little ones, who you said should be a prey, them will I bring into the land; and they shall inherit the land, which you have rejected.

[32] And your carcasses shall fall in this wilderness.

[33] And your sons shall be fed in the wilderness forty years, and they shall bear your fornication, until your carcasses are consumed in the wilderness.

[34] According to the number of the days during which you spied the land, forty days, a day for a year, you shall bear your sins forty years, and you shall know My fierce anger.

[35] I the Lord have spoken, Surely will I do thus to this evil congregation that has risen up together against Me. In this wilderness they shall be utterly consumed, and there they shall die."

[36] And the men whom Moses sent to spy out the land, and who came and murmured against it to the assembly, so as to bring out evil words concerning the land,

[37] the men that spoke evil reports against the land, died of the plague before the Lord.

[38] And Joshua the son of Nun and Caleb the son of Jephunneh *still* lived among those men that went to spy out the land.

An Attempted Invasion is Repulsed

[39] And Moses spoke these words to all the children of Israel; and the people mourned exceedingly.

[40] And they rose early in the morning and went up to the top of the mountain, saying, "Behold, we that are here will go up to the place of which the Lord has spoken, because we have sinned."

41 And Moses said, "Why do you transgress the word of the Lord? You shall not prosper.

42 Do not go up, for the Lord is not with you; so shall you fall before the face of your enemies.

43 For Amalek and the Canaanite *are* there before you, and you shall fall by the sword; because you have disobeyed the Lord and turned aside, and the Lord will not be among you."

44 And having forced their passage, they went up to the top of the mountain; but the ark of the covenant of the Lord and Moses did not leave the camp.

45 And Amalek and the Canaanite that dwelt in that mountain came down, and routed them, and destroyed them unto Herman; and they returned to the camp.

NUMBERS CHAPTER 15

Various Offerings

1 And the Lord spoke to Moses, saying,

2 "Speak to the children of Israel, and you shall say to them, 'When you have come into the land of your habitation, which I give to you,

3 and you will offer burnt offerings to the Lord, a burnt offering or a grain offering to perform a vow, or a freewill offering, or to offer in your feasts a sacrifice of sweet savor to the Lord, whether of the herd or the flock:

4 then he that offers his gift to the Lord shall bring a grain offering of fine flour, a tenth part of an ephah mingled with oil, even with the fourth part of a hin.

5 And for a drink offering you shall offer the fourth part of a hin on the burnt offering, or on the grain offering: for every lamb you shall offer so much, as a sacrifice, an aroma of sweet savor to the Lord.

6 And for a ram, when you offer it as a burnt offering or as a sacrifice, you shall prepare as a grain offering two tenths of fine flour mingled with oil, the third part of a hin.

7 And you shall offer for an aroma of sweet savor to the Lord wine for a drink offering, the third part of a hin.

8 And if you sacrifice *a young bull* from the herd for a burnt offering or for a sacrifice, to perform a vow or a peace offering to the Lord,

9 then *the worshipper* shall offer upon the calf a grain offering, three tenth deals of fine flour mingled with oil, the half of a hin. 10 And wine for a drink offering the half of a hin, a sacrifice for an aroma of sweet savor to the Lord.

11 Thus shall you do to one calf or to one ram, or to one lamb of the sheep or kid of the goats.

12 According to the number of what you shall offer, so shall you do to each one, according to their number.

13 Every native of the country shall do thus to offer such things as sacrifices for an aroma of sweet savor to the Lord.

14 And if there should be a stranger among you in your land, or one who should be born to you among your generations, and he will offer a sacrifice, an aroma of sweet savor to the Lord—as you do, so the *whole* congregation shall offer to the Lord.

15 There shall be one law for you and for the strangers abiding among you, a perpetual law for your generations: as you *are*, so shall the stranger be before the Lord.

16 There shall be one law and one ordinance for you, and for the stranger that abides among you.'"

17 And the Lord spoke to Moses, saying,

18 "Speak to the sons of Israel, and you shall say to them, 'When you are entering into the land, into which I bring you,

19 then it shall come to pass, when you shall eat of the bread of the land, you shall separate a heave offering, a special offering to the Lord, the firstfruits of your dough.

20 You shall offer your bread as a heave offering: as a heave offering from the threshing floor, so shall you separate it,

21 even the firstfruits of your dough, and you shall give the Lord a heave offering throughout your generations.

Laws Concerning Unintentional Sin

22 'But whenever you shall transgress, and not perform all these commands, which the Lord spoke to Moses;

23 as the Lord appointed you by the hand of Moses, from the day which the Lord appointed you and forward throughout your generations,

24 then it shall come to pass, if a trespass be committed unwillingly, unknown to the congregation, then shall all the congregation offer a calf of the herd without blemish for a burnt offering of sweet savor to the Lord, and its grain offering and its drink offering according to the ordinance, and one kid of the goats for a sin offering.

25 And the priest shall make atonement for all the congregation of the children of Israel, and *the trespass* shall be forgiven them, because it is involuntary; and they have brought their gift, a burnt offering to the Lord for their trespass before the Lord, even for their involuntary sins.

26 And it shall be forgiven as respects all the congregation of the children of Israel, and the stranger that is abiding among you, because *it is* involuntary to all the people.

27 'And if one soul sins unwillingly, he shall bring one female goat of a year old for a sin offering.

28 And the priest shall make atonement for the soul that committed the trespass unwillingly, and that sinned unwillingly before the Lord, to make atonement for him.

29 There shall be one law for the native among the children of Israel, and for the stranger that abides among them, whosoever shall commit a trespass unwillingly.

30 'And whatever soul either of the natives or of the strangers shall do anything with a presumptuous hand, he will provoke God; that soul shall be cut off from his people,

31 for he has despised the word of the Lord, and broken His commands; that soul shall be utterly destroyed, his sin *is* upon him.'"

Penalty for Violating the Sabbath

32 And the children of Israel were in the wilderness, and they found a man gathering sticks on the Sabbath day.

33 And they who found him gathering sticks on the Sabbath day brought him to Moses and Aaron, and to all the congregation of the children of Israel.

34 And they placed him in custody, for they had not *yet* determined what they should do to him.

35 And the Lord spoke to Moses, saying, "Let the man by all means be put to death: all the congregation shall stone him with stones."

36 And all the congregation brought him forth out of the camp; and all the congregation stoned him with stones outside the camp, as the Lord commanded Moses.

37 And the Lord spoke to Moses, saying,

38 "Speak to the children of Israel, and you shall tell them; and let them make for themselves fringes upon the borders of their garments throughout their generations; and you shall put blue lace upon the fringes of the borders.

39 And it shall be on your fringes, and you shall look on them, and you shall remember all the commands of the Lord, and do them. And you shall not turn back after your imaginations, and after *the sight of* your eyes in the things after which you whore after,

40 that you may remember and perform all My commands, and you shall be holy unto your God.

41 I *am* the Lord your God that brought you out of the land of Egypt, to be your God: I *am* the Lord your God."

NUMBERS CHAPTER 16

Rebellion Against Moses and Aaron

1 And Korah the son of Izhar the son of Kohath the son of Levi, and Dathan and Abiron, sons of Eliab, and On the son of Peleth the son of Reuben, spoke;

2 and rose up before Moses, and two hundred and fifty men of the sons of Israel, chiefs of the assembly, chosen counselors, and men of renown.

3 They rose up against Moses and Aaron, and said, "Let it be enough for you that all the congregation *is* holy, and the Lord *is* among them; and why do you set up yourselves against the congregation of the Lord?"

4 And when Moses heard it, he fell on his face.

5 And he spoke to Korah and all his assembly, saying, "God has visited and known those that are His and who are holy, and has brought them to Himself; and whom He has chosen for Himself, He has brought to Himself.

6 Therefore do this: take to yourselves censers, Korah and all his company;

7 and put fire on them, and put incense on them before the Lord tomorrow; and it shall come to pass that the man whom the Lord has chosen, he shall be holy: let it be enough for you, you sons of Levi!"

8 And Moses said to Korah, "Listen to me, you sons of Levi.

9 Is it a little thing for you, that the God of Israel has separated you from the congregation of Israel, and brought you near to Himself to minister in the services of the tabernacle of the Lord, and to stand before the tabernacle to minister for them?

10 And He has brought you near and all your brothers the sons of Levi with you, and do you seek to be priests also?

11 Thus *it is with* you and all your congregation which is gathered together against God: and who is Aaron, that you murmur against him?"

12 And Moses sent to call Dathan and Abiram sons of Eliab; and they said, "We will not go up.

13 Is it a little thing that you have brought us up to a land flowing with milk and honey, to kill us in the wilderness, *and* that you altogether rule over us?

14 You are a prince, and have you brought us into a land flowing with milk and honey, and have you given us an inheritance of land and vineyards? Would you have put out the eyes of those men? We will not go up!"

15 And Moses was exceeding indignant, and said to the Lord, "Take no heed to their offering; I have not taken away the desire of anyone of them, neither have I hurt anyone of them."

16 And Moses said to Korah, "Sanctify your company, and be ready before the Lord, you and Aaron and they, tomorrow.

17 And take each man his censer, and you shall put incense upon them, and shall bring each one his censer before the Lord, two hundred and fifty censers, and you and Aaron shall bring each his censer."

18 And each man took his censer, and they put fire on them, and laid incense on them; and Moses and Aaron stood by the doors of the tabernacle of witness.

19 And Korah raised up against them all his company by the door of the tabernacle of witness; and the glory of the Lord appeared to all the congregation.

20 And the Lord spoke to Moses and Aaron, saying,

21 "Separate yourselves from the midst of this congregation, and I will consume them at once."

22 And they fell on their faces, and said, "O God, the God of spirits and of all flesh, if one man has sinned, *shall* the wrath of the Lord *be* upon the whole congregation?"

23 And the Lord spoke to Moses, saying,

24 "Speak to the congregation, saying, 'Depart from the company of Korah round about.'"

25 And Moses rose up and went to Dathan and Abiram, and all the elders of Israel went with him.

26 And he spoke to the congregation, saying, "Separate yourselves from the tents of these stubborn men, and touch nothing that belongs to them, lest you be consumed with them in all their sin."

27 And they moved away from the tent of Korah round about; and Dathan and Abiram went forth and stood by the doors of their tents, and their wives and their children and their belongings.

28 And Moses said, "Hereby shall you know that the Lord has sent me to perform all these works, that *I have* not *done them* of myself.

29 If these men shall die according to the death of all men, if also their visitation shall be according to the visitation of all men, then the Lord has not sent me.

30 But if the Lord shall show by a wonder, and the earth shall open her mouth and swallow them up, and their houses, and their tents, and all that belongs to them, and they shall go down alive into Hades, then you shall know that these men have provoked the Lord."

31 And when he ceased speaking all these words, the ground split apart beneath them.

32 And the ground opened, and swallowed them up, and their houses, and all the men that were with Korah, and their cattle.

33 And they went down, *they* and all that they had, alive into Hades; and the ground covered them, and they perished from the midst of the congregation.

34 And all Israel round about them fled from the sound of them, for they said, "Lest the earth swallow us up, *too*!"

35 And fire went forth from the Lord, and devoured the two hundred and fifty men that offered incense.

36 And the Lord said to Moses,

37 and to Eleazar the son of Aaron the priest, "Take up the bronze censers out of the midst of the men that have been burned, and scatter the strange fire away from here, for they have sanctified the censers

38 of these sinners against their own souls, and make for them hammered plates as a covering for the altar, because they were brought before the Lord and hallowed; and they became a sign to the children of Israel."

39 So Eleazar the son of Aaron the priest took the bronze censers, which the men who had been burned brought near, and they put them as a covering on the altar,

40 a memorial to the children of Israel, that no stranger might draw near, who is not of the descendants of Aaron, to offer incense before the Lord; so he shall not be as Korah and as they that conspired with him, as the Lord spoke to him by the hand of Moses.

Complaints of the People

41 And the children of Israel murmured the next day against Moses and Aaron, saying, "You have killed the people of the Lord."

42 And it came to pass when the congregation had gathered against Moses and Aaron, that they ran quickly to the tabernacle of witness; and the cloud covered it, and the glory of the Lord appeared.

43 And Moses and Aaron entered the tabernacle of witness.

44 And the Lord spoke to Moses and Aaron, saying,

45 "Depart out of the midst of this congregation, and I will consume them at once." And they fell upon their faces.

46 And Moses said to Aaron, "Take a censer, and put on it fire from the altar, and put incense on it, and carry it away quickly into the camp, and make atonement for them, for wrath has gone forth from the presence of the Lord, and it has begun to destroy the people."

47 And Aaron did as Moses commanded him, and he ran among the congregation, for the plague had already begun among the people; and he put in the incense, and made atonement for the people.

48 And he stood between the dead and the living, and the plague ceased.

49 And those that died in the plague were fourteen thousand seven hundred, besides those that died on account of Korah.

50 And Aaron returned to Moses to the door of the tabernacle of witness, and the plague ceased.

NUMBERS CHAPTER 17

The Budding of Aaron's Rod

1 And the Lord spoke to Moses, saying,

2 "Speak to the children of Israel, and take rods from them, according to the houses of their families, a rod from all their princes, according to the houses of their families, twelve rods, and write the name of each on his rod.

3 And write the name of Aaron on the rod of Levi; for it is one rod *for each;* they shall give *them* according to the tribe of the house of their families.

4 And you shall put them in the tabernacle of witness, before the testimony, where I will be made known to you.

5 And it shall be, that the man whom I shall choose, his rod shall blossom; and I will remove from Me the murmuring of the children of Israel, which they murmur against you."

6 And Moses spoke to the children of Israel, and all their chiefs gave him a rod *each*, for one chief a rod, according to the house of their families, twelve rods; and the rod of Aaron *was* in the midst of the rods.

7 And Moses laid up the rods before the Lord in the tabernacle of witness.

8 And it came to pass on the next day, that Moses and Aaron went into the tabernacle of witness; and behold, the rod of Aaron for the house of Levi blossomed, and put forth a bud, and bloomed blossoms and produced almonds.

9 And Moses brought forth all the rods from before the Lord to all the sons of Israel; and they looked, and each one took his rod.

10 And the Lord said to Moses, "Lay up the rod of Aaron before the testimonies to be kept as a sign for the children of the disobedient; and let their murmuring cease from Me, and they shall not die."

11 And Moses and Aaron did as the Lord commanded Moses, so did they.

12 And the children of Israel spoke to Moses, saying, "Behold, we are cut off, we are destroyed, we are consumed.

13 Everyone that touches the tabernacle of the Lord, dies: shall we die utterly?"

NUMBERS CHAPTER 18

Duties of Priests and Levites

[1] And the Lord spoke to Aaron, saying, "You and your sons and your father's house shall bear the sins of the holy things, and you and your sons shall bear the iniquity of your priesthood.

[2] And take to yourself your brothers, the tribe of Levi, the family of your father, and let them be joined to you, and let them minister to you; and you and your sons with you *shall minister* before the tabernacle of witness.

[3] And they shall keep your charges, and the charges of the tabernacle; only they shall not approach the holy vessels and the altar, so both they and you shall not die.

[4] And they shall be joined to you, and shall keep the charges of the tabernacle of witness, in all the services of the tabernacle; and a stranger shall not approach to you.

[5] And you shall keep the charges of the holy things, and the charges of the altar, and *so* there shall not be anger among the children of Israel.

[6] And I have taken your brothers the Levites out of the midst of the children of Israel, a present given to the Lord, to minister in the services of the tabernacle of witness.

[7] And you and your sons after you shall keep up your priestly ministration, according to the whole manner of the altar, and that which is within the veil; and you shall minister in the services as the office of your priesthood; and the stranger that comes near shall die."

The Priests' Portion

[8] And the Lord said to Aaron, "Behold, I have given you the charge of the firstfruits of all things consecrated to Me by the children of Israel; and I have given them to you as an honor, and to your sons after you for a perpetual ordinance.

[9] And let this be to you from all the holy things that are consecrated *to Me, even* the burnt offerings, from all their gifts, and from all their sacrifices, and from every trespass offering of theirs, and from all their sin offerings, whatever things they give to Me of all their holy things, they shall be yours and your sons'.

[10] In the most holy place shall you eat them; every male shall eat them, you and your sons: they shall be holy to you.

[11] And this shall be to you of the firstfruits of their gifts, of all the wave offerings of the children of Israel; to you have I given them and to your sons and your daughters with you, a perpetual ordinance; every clean person in your house shall eat them.

[12] Every first offering of oil, and every first offering of wine, their firstfruits of grain, whatsoever they may give to the Lord, to you have I given them.

[13] All the firstfruits that are in their land, whatsoever they shall offer to the Lord, shall be yours: every clean person in your house shall eat them.

[14] Every devoted thing among the children of Israel shall be yours.

[15] And everything that opens the womb of all flesh, whatsoever they bring to the Lord, whether man or beast, shall be yours: only the firstborn of men shall be surely redeemed, and you shall redeem the firstborn of unclean cattle.

[16] And the redemption of them *shall be* from a month old; their valuation of five shekels—it is twenty gerahs according to the holy shekel.

[17] But you shall not redeem the firstborn of calves and the firstborn of sheep and the firstborn of goats; they are holy; and you shall pour their blood upon the altar, and you shall offer the fat as a burnt offering for an aroma of sweet savor to the Lord.

[18] And the flesh shall be yours, as also the breast of the wave offering and as the right shoulder, it shall be yours.

[19] Every special offering of the holy things, whatsoever the children of Israel shall specially offer to the Lord, I have given to you and to your sons and to your daughters with you, a perpetual ordinance; it is a covenant of salt forever before the Lord, for you and your descendants after you."

[20] And the Lord said to Aaron, "You shall have no inheritance in their land, neither shall you have any portion among them, for I *am* your portion and your inheritance in the midst of the children of Israel.

Tithes for Support of the Levites

[21] "And behold, I have given to the sons of Levi every tithe in Israel for an inheritance for their services, the work in which they perform in the tabernacle of witness.

[22] And the children of Israel shall no more draw near to the tabernacle of witness to incur fatal guilt.

[23] And the Levite himself shall perform the service of the tabernacle of witness; and they shall bear their iniquities, it is a perpetual statute throughout their generations; and in the midst of the children of Israel they shall not receive an inheritance.

[24] Because I have given as a distinct portion to the Levites for an inheritance the tithes of the children of Israel, whatsoever they shall offer to the Lord; therefore I said to them, In the midst of the children of Israel they shall have no inheritance."

The Tithe of the Levite

[25] And the Lord spoke to Moses, saying,

[26] "You shall also speak to the Levites, and shall say to them, 'If you take the tithe from the children of Israel, which I have given you from them for an inheritance, then shall you separate from it a heave offering to the Lord, a tenth of the tenth.

[27] And your heave offerings shall be reckoned to you as grain from the threshing floor, and an offering from the winepress.

28 So shall you also separate them from all the offerings of the Lord out of all your tithes, whatsoever you shall receive from the children of Israel; and you shall give to them of the Lord's offering, to Aaron the priest.

29 Of all your gifts you shall offer an offering to the Lord, and of every firstfruit the consecrated part from it.

30 And you shall say to them, 'When you shall offer the firstfruits from it, then shall it be reckoned to the Levites as produce from the threshing floor, and as produce from the winepress.

31 And you shall eat it in any place, you and your families; for this is your reward for your services in the tabernacle of witness.

32 And you shall not bear sin by reason of it, for you shall have offered an offering of firstfruits from it, and you shall not profane the holy things of the children of Israel, so that you shall not die.'"

NUMBERS CHAPTER 19

Laws of Purification

1 And the Lord spoke to Moses and Aaron, saying,

2 "This is the constitution of the law, as the Lord has commanded, saying, 'Speak to the sons of Israel, and let them take for you a red heifer without spot, and on which no yoke has been put.

3 And you shall give her to Eleazar the priest; and they shall bring her out of the camp into a clean place, and shall kill her before his face.

4 And Eleazar shall take of her blood, and sprinkle of her blood seven times in front of the tabernacle of witness.

5 And they shall burn her to ashes before him; and her skin and her flesh and her blood, with her dung, shall be consumed.

6 And the priest shall take cedar wood and hyssop and scarlet wool, and they shall cast them into the midst of the burning of the heifer.

7 And the priest shall wash his garments, and bathe his body in water, and afterwards he shall go into the camp, and the priest shall be unclean till evening.

8 And he that burns her shall wash his garments, and bathe his body, and shall be unclean till evening.

9 And a clean man shall gather up the ashes of the heifer, and lay them up in a clean place outside the camp; and they shall be for the congregation of the children of Israel to keep: it is the water of sprinkling, a purification.

10 And he that gathers up the ashes of the heifer shall wash his garments, and shall be unclean until evening; and it shall be a perpetual statute for the children of Israel and for the strangers joined to them.

11 'He that touches the dead body of any man, shall be unclean for seven days.

12 He shall be purified on the third day and the seventh day, and shall be clean; but if he is not purged on the third day and the seventh day, he shall not be clean.

13 Everyone that touches the body of a man who has died, and has not been purified, has defiled the tabernacle of the Lord: that soul shall be cut off from Israel, because the water of sprinkling has not been sprinkled upon him; he is unclean, his uncleanness is yet upon him.

14 'And this *is* the law; if a man dies in a house, everyone that goes into the house, and all things in the house, shall be unclean for seven days.

15 And every open vessel which has not a covering bound upon it, shall be unclean.

16 And everyone who shall touch a man slain by violence, or a corpse, or human bone, or tomb, shall be unclean for seven days.

17 And they shall take for the unclean of the burnt ashes of purification, and they shall pour upon them running water into a vessel.

18 And a clean man shall take hyssop, and dip it into the water, and sprinkle it upon the house, and the furniture, and all the souls that are in there, and upon him that touched the human bone, or the slain man, or the corpse, or the tomb.

19 And the clean man shall sprinkle *the water* on the unclean on the third day and on the seventh day, and on the seventh day he shall purify himself; and *the other* shall wash his garments, and bathe himself in water, and shall be unclean until evening.

20 'And whatever man shall be defiled and shall not purify himself, that soul shall be cut off from the midst of the congregation, because he has defiled the holy things of the Lord, because the water of sprinkling has not been sprinkled upon him; he is unclean.

21 And it shall be to you a perpetual statute; and he that sprinkles the water of sprinkling shall wash his garments; and he that touches the water of sprinkling shall be unclean until evening.

22 And whatsoever the unclean man shall touch shall be unclean, and the soul that touches it shall be unclean till evening.'"

NUMBERS CHAPTER 20

Moses' Error at Kadesh

1 And the children of Israel, *even* the whole congregation, came into the Wilderness of Zin, in the first month, and the people stayed in Kadesh. And Miriam died there, and was buried there.

2 And there was no water for the congregation. And they gathered themselves together against Moses and Aaron.

3 And the people reviled Moses, saying, "If only we had died in the destruction of our brothers before the Lord!

4 And why have you brought up the congregation of the Lord into this wilderness, to kill us and our cattle?

5 And why *is* this? You have brought us up out of Egypt, that we should come into this evil place; a place where there is no sowing, neither figs, nor vines, nor pomegranates, neither is there water to drink."

6 And Moses and Aaron went from before the assembly to the door of the tabernacle of witness, and they fell upon their faces; and the glory of the Lord appeared to them.

7 And the Lord spoke to Moses, saying,

8 "Take your rod, and call the assembly, you and Aaron your brother, and speak to the rock before them, and it shall give forth its waters; and you shall bring forth for them water out of the rock, and give drink to the congregation and their cattle."

9 And Moses took his rod which was before the Lord, as the Lord commanded.

10 And Moses and Aaron assembled the congregation before the rock, and said to them, "Hear me, you disobedient; must we bring you water out of this rock?"

11 And Moses lifted up his hand and struck the rock with his rod twice; and much water came forth, and the congregation drank, and their cattle.

12 And the Lord said to Moses and Aaron, "Because you have not believed Me to sanctify Me before the children of Israel, therefore you shall not bring this congregation into the land which I have given them."

13 This is the Water of Strife, because the children of Israel spoke insolently before the Lord, and He was sanctified in them.

Passage Through Edom Refused

14 And Moses sent messengers from Kadesh to the king of Edom, saying, "Thus says your brother Israel; 'You know all the distress that has come upon us.

15 And *how* our fathers went down into Egypt, and we sojourned in Egypt many days, and the Egyptians afflicted us and our fathers.

16 And we cried to the Lord, and the Lord heard our voice, and sent an angel and brought us out of Egypt; and now we are in the city of Kadesh, at the extremity of your coasts.

17 We will pass through your land. We will not go through the fields, nor through the vineyards, nor will we drink water out of your cistern; we will go by the king's highway; we will not turn aside to the right hand or to the left, until we have passed your borders.'"

18 And Edom said to him, "You shall not pass through me, and if otherwise, I will go forth to meet you in war."

19 And the children of Israel said to him, "We will pass by the mountain; and if I and my cattle drink of your water, I will pay you: but it is no matter of importance, we will go by the mountain."

20 And he said, "You shall not pass through me"; and Edom went forth to meet him with a great army, and a mighty hand. 21 So Edom refused to allow Israel to pass through his borders, and Israel turned away from him.

The Death of Aaron

22 And they departed from Kadesh; and the children of Israel, even the whole congregation, and came to Mount Hor.

23 And the Lord spoke to Moses and Aaron on Mount Hor, on the borders of the land of Edom, saying,

24 "Let Aaron be added to his people; for you shall certainly not go into the land which I have given the children of Israel, because you provoked Me at the Water of Strife.

25 Take Aaron, and Eleazar his son, and bring them up to Mount Hor before all the congregation;

26 and take Aaron's garment from off him, and put it on Eleazar his son: and let Aaron die there and be added to *his people*."

27 And Moses did as the Lord commanded him, and took him up to Mount Hor, before all the congregation.

28 And he took off Aaron's garments, and put them on Eleazar his son, and Aaron died on the top of the mountain. And Moses and Eleazar came down from the mountain.

29 And all the congregation saw that Aaron was dead. And all the house of Israel wept for Aaron thirty days.

NUMBERS CHAPTER 21

The Bronze Serpent

1 And Arad the Canaanite king who dwelt by the wilderness, heard that Israel came by the way of Atharim; and he made war against Israel, and carried off some of them as captives.

2 So Israel made a vow to the Lord, and said, "If you will deliver this people into my power, I will devote it and its cities *to You*."

3 And the Lord hearkened to the voice of Israel, and delivered the Canaanite into his power; and *Israel* devoted him and his cities, and they called the name of that place Anathema.

4 And having departed from Mount Hor by the way *leading* to the Red Sea, they compassed the land of Edom, and the people lost courage by the way.

5 And the people spoke against God and against Moses, saying, "Why is this? Have you brought us out of Egypt to slay us in the wilderness? For there is neither bread nor water, and our soul loathes this light bread."

6 And the Lord sent deadly serpents among the people, and they bit them, and many people of the children of Israel died.

7 And the people came to Moses and said, "We have sinned, for we have spoken against the Lord, and against you: pray therefore to the Lord, and let Him take away the serpent from us."

8 And Moses prayed to the Lord for the people; and the Lord said to Moses, "Make for yourself a serpent, and put it on a staff; and it shall come to pass that whenever a serpent shall bite a man, everyone *so* bitten that looks upon it shall live."

9 And Moses made a serpent of bronze, and put it upon a staff. And it came to pass that whenever a serpent bit a man, and he looked on the bronze serpent, he lived.

The Journey to Moab

10 And the children of Israel departed and encamped in Oboth. 11 And having departed from Oboth, they encamped

in Ije Abarim, on the farther side in the wilderness, which is opposite Moab, toward the east.

[12] And from there they departed, and encamped in the Valley of Zered.

[13] And they departed from there and encamped on the other side of the Arnon in the wilderness, *the country* which extends from the coasts of the Amorites; for the Arnon is the border of Moab, between Moab and the Amorites.

[14] Therefore it is said in a book, "A war of the Lord has set on fire Zoob, and the brooks of Arnon.

[15] And He has appointed brooks to reach Ar to dwell *there*; and it lies near to the coasts of Moab."

[16] And from there *they came to* the well; this *is* the well of which the Lord said to Moses, "Gather the people, and I will give them water to drink."

[17] Then Israel sang this song at the well: "*Sing* of the well;

[18] the princes dug it, the kings of the nations in their kingdom, in their lordship sank it in the rock." And *they went* from the well to Mattaniah,

[19] and from Mattaniah to Nahaliel, and from Nahaliel to Bamoth, and from Bamoth to Janen, which is in the plain of Moab *as seen* from the top of the quarried *rock* that looks toward the wilderness.

King Sihon Defeated

[20] And Moses sent ambassadors to Sihon, king of the Amorites, with peaceable words, saying,

[21] "We will pass through your land, we will go by the road; we will not turn aside to the field or to the vineyard.

[22] We will not drink water out of your well; we will go by the king's highway, until we have past your boundaries."

[23] And Sihon did not allow Israel to pass through his borders, and Sihon gathered all his people, and went out to set the battle in array against Israel into the wilderness; and he came to Jahaz, and set the battle in array against Israel.

[24] And Israel struck him with the slaughter of the sword, and they became possessors of his land, from Arnon to Jabbok, as far as the children of Ammon (for Jahaz is the border of the children of Ammon).

[25] And Israel took all their cities, and Israel dwelt in all the cities of the Amorites, in Heshbon, and in all cities belonging to it.

[26] For Heshbon is the city of Sihon, king of the Amorites; and he before fought against the king of Moab, and they took all his land, from Aroer to Arnon.

[27] Therefore those who speak in parables say, "Come to Heshbon, that the city of Sihon may be built and prepared.

[28] For a fire has gone forth from Heshbon, a flame from the city of Sihon, and has consumed as far as Moab, and devoured the pillars of Arnon.

[29] Woe to you, Moab! You are lost, O people of Chemosh! Their sons are sold for preservation, and their daughters are captives to Sihon king of the Amorites.

[30] And their descendants shall perish *from* Heshbon to Dibon; and their women have kindled a fire against Moab."

[31] And Israel dwelt in all the cities of the Amorites.

[32] And Moses sent to spy out Jazer; and they took it, and its villages, and cast out the Amorites that dwelt there.

King Og Defeated

[33] And having returned, they went up the road that leads to Bashan. And Og the king of Bashan went forth to meet them, and all his people, to war at Edrei.

[34] And the Lord said to Moses, "Do not fear him; for I have delivered him and all his people, and all his land, into your hands; and you shall do to him as you did to Sihon king of the Amorites, who dwelled in Heshbon."

[35] And he struck him and his sons, and all his people, until he left none of his to be taken alive; and they inherited his land.

NUMBERS CHAPTER 22

Balak Summons Balaam to Curse Israel

[1] And the children of Israel departed, and encamped on the west of Moab by the Jordan toward Jericho.

[2] And when Balak son of Zippor saw all that Israel did to the Amorites,

[3] then Moab feared the people exceedingly because they were many; and Moab was grieved before the face of the children of Israel.

[4] And Moab said to the elders of Midian, "Now shall this assembly lick up all that are round about us, as a calf would lick up the green *herbs* of the field." And Balak son of Zippor was king of Moab at that time.

[5] And he sent ambassadors to Balaam, the son of Beor, to Pethor, which is on a river of the land of the sons of his people, to call him, saying, "Behold, a people have come out of Egypt, and behold, they have covered the face of the earth, and have encamped close to me.

[6] And now come *here, and* curse this people for me, for they are stronger than us. Perhaps we may be able to strike some of them, and cast them out of the land; for I know that whomsoever you bless, they are blessed, and whomsoever you curse, they are cursed."

[7] And the elders of Moab went, and the elders of Midian, and their divining *instruments were* in their hands; and they came to Balaam, and spoke to him the words of Balak.

[8] And he said to them, "Tarry here the night, and I will answer you the things which the Lord shall say to me." And the princes of Moab stayed with Balaam.

[9] And God came to Balaam, and said to him, "Who are these men with you?"

[10] And Balaam said to God, "Balak son of Zippor, king of Moab, sent them to me, saying,

[11] 'Behold, a people has come forth out of Egypt, and has covered the face of the land, and they have encamped near to me; and now come, curse them for me, if indeed I shall be able to strike them, and cast them out of the land.'"

12 And God said to Balaam, "You shall not go with them, neither shall you curse the people, for they are blessed."

13 And Balaam rose up in the morning, and said to the princes of Balak, "Depart quickly to your master; God does not permit me to go with you."

14 And the princes of Moab rose, and came to Balak, and said, "Balaam will not come with us."

15 And Balak yet again sent more princes, and more honorable than they.

16 And they came to Balaam, and they said to him, "Thus says Balak the son of Zippor: 'I beseech you, do not delay to come to me.

17 For I will greatly honor you, and will do for you whatsoever you shall say; come then, curse this people for me.'"

18 And Balaam answered and said to the princes of Balak, "If Balak would give me his house full of silver and gold, I shall not be able to go beyond the word of the Lord God, to make it little or great in my mind.

19 And now, you also tarry here this night, and I shall know what the Lord will yet say to me."

20 And God came to Balaam by night, and said to him, "If these men have come to call you, rise and follow them; nevertheless the word which I shall speak to you, this shall you do."

21 And Balaam rose up in the morning, and saddled his donkey, and went with the princes of Moab.

Balaam, the Donkey, and the Angel

22 And God was very angry because he went. And the Angel of the Lord rose up to withstand him. Now he had mounted his donkey, and his two servants were with him.

23 And when the donkey saw the Angel of the Lord standing opposite *her* in the road, and His sword drawn in His hand, then the donkey turned aside out of the way, and went into the field. And *Balaam* struck the donkey with his staff to direct her *back* onto the road.

24 And the Angel of the Lord stood in the avenues of the vines, a fence *being* on this side and that.

25 And when the donkey saw the Angel of the Lord, she thrust herself against the wall, and crushed Balaam's foot against the wall, and he struck her again.

26 And the Angel of the Lord went farther, and came and stood in a narrow place where it was impossible to turn to the right or the left.

27 And when the donkey saw the Angel of God, she lay down under Balaam. And Balaam was angry, and struck the donkey with his staff.

28 And God opened the mouth of the donkey, and she said to Balaam, "What have I done to you, that you have struck me this third time?"

29 And Balaam said to the donkey, "Because you have mocked me; and if I had a sword in my hand, I would now have killed you."

30 And the donkey said to Balaam, "*Am* I not your donkey on which you have ridden since your youth, to this day? Did I ever do thus to you, utterly disregarding *you*?" And he said, "No."

31 And God opened the eyes of Balaam, and he saw the Angel of the Lord opposing *him* in the road, and His sword drawn in His hand, and he stooped down and worshipped on his face.

32 And the Angel of the Lord said to him, "Why have you struck your donkey this third time? Behold, I came out to stand against you, for your way is unseemly before Me. And when the donkey saw Me, she turned away from Me this third time.

33 And if she had not turned out of the way, surely I would have killed you, and I would have saved her alive."

34 And Balaam said to the Angel of the Lord, "I have sinned, for I did not know that You were standing opposite *me* in the road, to meet *me*; and now, if it is not pleasing to You *for me to go on*, I shall return."

35 And the Angel of the Lord said to Balaam, "Go with the men: nevertheless the word which I shall speak to you, you shall take heed to speak." And Balaam went with the princes of Balak.

36 And when Balak heard that Balaam had come, he went out to meet him, to a city of Moab, which is on the borders of the Arnon, which is on the *extreme* part of the borders.

37 And Balak said to Balaam, "Did I not send to you to call you? Why have you not come to me? Shall I not indeed be able to honor you?"

38 And Balaam said to Balak, "Behold, I have now come to you: shall I be able to say anything? The word which God shall put into my mouth, that I shall speak."

39 And Balaam went with Balak, and they came to the cities of streets.

40 And Balak offered sheep and calves, and sent to Balaam and to his princes who were with him.

Balaam's First Oracle

41 And it was morning; and Balak took Balaam, and brought him up to the pillar of Baal, and showed him from there the extent of the people.

NUMBERS CHAPTER 23

1 And Balaam said to Balak, "Build seven altars for me here, and prepare for me seven calves, and seven rams."

2 And Balak did as Balaam told him; and he offered up a calf and a ram on *every* altar.

3 And Balaam said to Balak, "Stand by your sacrifice, and I will go and see if God will appear to me and meet me, and the word which He shall show me, I will report to you." And Balak stood by his sacrifice.

4 And Balaam went to inquire of God; and he went straight forward, and God appeared to Balaam. And Balaam said to

Him, "I have prepared the seven altars, and I have offered a calf and a ram on *every* altar."

5 And God put a word into the mouth of Balaam, and said, "You shall return to Balak, and thus shall you speak."

6 And he returned to him, and moreover he stood over his burnt offerings, and all the princes of Moab with him; and the Spirit of God came upon him.

7 And he took up his parable, and said, "Balak king of Moab sent for me out of Mesopotamia, out of the mountains of the east, saying, 'Come, curse Jacob for me, and come, call for a curse upon Israel for me.'

8 How can I curse whom the Lord has not cursed? Or how can I denounce whom God has not denounced?

9 For from the top of the mountains I shall see him, and from the hills I shall observe him. Behold, the people shall dwell alone, and shall not be reckoned among the nations.

10 Who has calculated the descendants of Jacob, and who shall number the families of Israel? Let my soul die with the souls of the righteous, and let my descendants be as their descendants."

11 And Balak said to Balaam, "What have you done to me? I called you to curse my enemies, and behold, you have greatly blessed *them*!"

12 And Balaam said to Balak, "Whatsoever the Lord shall put into my mouth, shall I not take heed to speak this?"

Balaam's Second Oracle

13 And Balak said to him, "Come yet with me to another place where you shall not see the people, but you shall only see a part of them, and shall not see them all; and curse them for me from there."

14 And he took him to a high place of the field to the top of the quarried *rock*, and he built there seven altars, and offered a calf and a ram on *every* altar.

15 And Balaam said to Balak, "Stand by your sacrifice, and I will go to inquire of God."

16 And God met Balaam, and put a word into his mouth, and said, "Return to Balak, and thus shall you speak."

17 And he returned to him. And there he was, standing by his whole burnt sacrifice, and all the princes of Moab with him. And Balak said to him, "What has the Lord spoken?"

18 And he took up his parable, and said, "Rise up, Balak, and hear; hearken as a witness, you son of Zippor.

19 God is not as a man that He should waver, nor as a son of man that He should be threatened; shall He say and not perform? Shall He speak and not keep *His word*?

20 Behold, I have received a *commandment* to bless: so bless I will do, and I will not turn back.

21 There shall not be trouble in Jacob, neither shall sorrow be seen in Israel; the Lord his God *is* with him, the glories of rulers *are* in him.

22 It was God who brought him out of Egypt; he has the glory of a unicorn.

23 For there is no divination in Jacob, nor enchantment in Israel; in season it shall be told to Jacob and Israel what God shall perform.

24 Behold, the people shall rise up as a lion's whelp, and shall exalt himself as a lion; he shall not lie down till he has eaten the prey, and he shall drink the blood of the slain."

25 And Balak said to Balaam, "Neither curse the people at all for me, nor bless them at all."

26 And Balaam answered and said to Balak, "Did I not tell you, saying, 'Whatsoever thing God shall speak to me, that will I do?'"

Balaam's Third Oracle

27 And Balak said to Balaam, "Come, I will take you to another place, if it shall please God, and curse them for me from there."

28 And Balak took Balaam to the top of Peor, which extends to the wilderness.

29 And Balaam said to Balak, "Build seven altars for me here, and prepare for me seven calves, and seven rams."

30 And Balak did as Balaam told him, and offered a calf and a ram on *every* altar.

NUMBERS CHAPTER 24

1 Now when Balaam saw that it pleased God to bless Israel, he did not go according to his custom, to seek to use sorcery, but turned his face toward the wilderness.

2 And Balaam lifted up his eyes, and beheld Israel encamped by their tribes. And the Spirit of God came upon him.

3 And he took up his parable and said, "The utterance of Balaam son of Beor, the man whose eyes are truly open,

4 he who hears the oracle of the Mighty One, who saw a vision of God in sleep, his eyes were opened, says,

5 'How wonderful *are* your tents, O Jacob, and your dwellings, O Israel!

6 As shady groves, and as gardens by a river, and as tents which God pitched, and as cedars by the waters.

7 There shall come a man out of his descendants, and he shall rule over many nations; and the kingdom of God shall be exalted, and his kingdom shall be increased.

8 God led him out of Egypt; he has as it were the glory of a unicorn. He shall consume the nations of his enemies, and he shall drain their marrow, and with his darts he shall shoot through the enemy.

9 He lies down, he rests as a lion; and as a young lion, who shall rouse him? Those that bless you are blessed, and those that curse you are cursed.'"

10 And Balak was angry with Balaam, and clapped his hands together. And Balak said to Balaam, "I called you to curse my enemy, and behold you have decidedly blessed *him* this third time.

11 Now therefore flee to your place. I said, I will honor you, but now the Lord has deprived you of glory."

12 And Balaam said to Balak, "Did I not speak to your messengers also whom you sent to me, saying,

13 'If Balak should give me his house full of silver and gold, I shall not be able to transgress the word of the Lord, to make it good or bad by myself; whatsoever things God shall say, them will I speak.'

14 And now, behold, I return to my place; come, I will advise you of what this people shall do to your people in the last days."

Balaam's Fourth Oracle

15 And he took up his parable and said, "The utterance of Balaam the son of Beor, the man whose eyes are truly open, 16 who hears the oracles of God, who receives knowledge from the Most High, and has seen a vision of God in sleep; his eyes were opened.

17 I will point to Him, but not now; I bless Him, but He draws not near: a Star shall arise out of Jacob, a man shall spring forth out of Israel; and shall crush the princes of Moab, and shall spoil all the sons of Seth.

18 And Edom shall be an inheritance, and Esau his enemy shall be an inheritance *of Israel*, and Israel does valiantly.

19 And *One* shall arise out of Jacob, and destroy out of the city him that escapes."

20 And having seen Amalek, he took up his parable and said, "Amalek *is* the first of the nations; yet his descendants shall perish."

21 And having seen the Kenite, he took up his parable and said, "Your dwelling place *is* strong; yet though you should put your nest in a rock,

22 and though Beor should have a skillfully contrived hiding place, the Assyrians shall carry you away captive."

23 And he looked upon Og, and took up his parable and said, "Alas, who shall live, when God shall do these things?

24 And one shall come forth from the hands of the Cyprians, and shall afflict Asshur, and shall afflict the Hebrews, and they shall perish together."

25 And Balaam rose up and departed and returned to his place, and Balak went to his own home.

NUMBERS CHAPTER 25

Worship of Baal of Peor

1 And Israel sojourned in Acacia Grove, and the people profaned themselves by committing harlotry with the daughters of Moab.

2 And they called them to the sacrifices of their idols; and the people ate of their sacrifices, and worshipped their idols.

3 And Israel consecrated themselves to Baal of Peor; and the Lord was very angry with Israel.

4 And the Lord said to Moses, "Take all the princes of the people, and make them examples *of judgment* for the Lord in the face of the sun, and the anger of the Lord shall be turned away from Israel."

5 And Moses said to the tribes of Israel, "Every one of you kill his friend that is consecrated to Baal of Peor."

6 And behold, a man of the children of Israel came and brought his brother to a Midianite woman before Moses, and before all the congregation of the children of Israel; and they were weeping at the door of the tabernacle of witness.

7 And Phinehas the son of Eleazar, the son of Aaron the priest saw it, and rose out of the midst of the congregation, and took a javelin in his hand,

8 and went in after the Israelite man into the chamber, and pierced them both through, both the Israelite man and the woman through her womb; and the plague was stopped from the children of Israel.

9 And those that died in the plague were twenty-four thousand.

10 And the Lord spoke to Moses, saying,

11 "Phinehas the son of Eleazar the son of Aaron the priest has caused My wrath to cease from the children of Israel, when I was exceedingly jealous among them, and I did not consume the children of Israel in My jealousy.

12 Therefore say, 'Behold, I give to him My covenant of peace;

13 and he and his descendants after him shall have a perpetual covenant of priesthood, because he was zealous for his God, and made atonement for the children of Israel.'"

14 Now the name of the smitten Israelite man, who was smitten with the Midianite woman, *was* Zambri son of Salmon, prince of a house of the tribe of Simeon.

15 And the name of the Midianite woman who was smitten, *was* Cozbi, daughter of Zur, a prince of the nation of Hommoth: it is a chief house among the people of Midian.

16 And the Lord spoke to Moses, saying, "Speak to the children of Israel, saying,

17 'Harass the Midianites as enemies, and strike them,

18 for they are enemies to you by the treachery in which they ensnare you through Peor, and through Cozbi their sister, daughter of a prince of Midian, who was smitten in the day of the plague because of Peor.'"

NUMBERS CHAPTER 26

The Second Census of Israel

1 And it came to pass after the plague that the Lord spoke to Moses and Eleazar the priest, saying,

2 "Take the sum of all the congregation of the children of Israel, from twenty years old and upward, according to the houses of their lineage, everyone that goes forth to battle in Israel."

3 And Moses and Eleazar the priest spoke in Araboth of Moab at the Jordan by Jericho, saying,

4 "*This is the numbering* from twenty years old and upward as the Lord commanded Moses." And the sons of Israel that came out of Egypt *are as follows:*

5 Reuben *was* the firstborn of Israel: and the sons of Reuben, Enoch and the family of Hanoch; to Pallu belongs the family of the Palluites.

6 To Hezron, the family of the Hezronites: to Carmi, the family of Carmi.

7 These *are* the families of Reuben; and their numbering was forty-three thousand seven hundred and thirty.

8 And the son of Pallu *was* Eliab.

9 And the sons of Eliab *were* Nemuel, Dathan, and Abiram: these *are* renowned men of the congregation; these are they that rose up against Moses and Aaron in the gathering of Korah, in the rebellion against the Lord.

10 And the earth opened her mouth, and swallowed up them and Korah, when their assembly perished, when the fire devoured the two hundred and fifty, and they were made a sign.

11 But the sons of Korah did not die.

12 And the sons of Simeon according to their families *were*: of Nemuel, the family of the Nemuelites; to Jamin the family of the Jaminites; to Jachin the family of the Jachinites.

13 To Zerah the family of the Zarhites; to Saul the family of the Saulites.

14 These *are* the families of Simeon according to their numbering: twenty-two thousand two hundred.

15 The sons of Gad according to their families *were*: to Zephon, the family of the Zephonites; to Haggi, the family of the Haggites; to Shuni, the family of the Shunites;

16 to Ozni, the family of the Oznites; to Eri, the family of the Erites;

17 to Arodi, the family of the Arodites; to Ariel, the family of the Arielites.

18 These *are* the families of the children of Gad according to their numbering: forty-four thousand five hundred.

19 And the sons of Judah *were* Er and Onan; and Er and Onan died in the land of Canaan.

20 And these were the sons of Judah, according to their families: of Shelah, the family of the Shelanites; of Perez, the family of the Parzites; of Zerah, the family of the Zarhites.

21 And the sons of Perez were: to Hezron, the family of the Hezronites; to Hamul, the family of the Hamulites.

22 These *are* the families of Judah according to their numbering: seventy-six thousand five hundred.

23 And the sons of Issachar according to their families *were*: of Tola, the family of the Tolaites; of Puah, the family of the Punites.

24 Of Jashub, the family of the Jashubites; of Shimron, the family of the Shimronites.

25 These *are* the families of Issachar according to their numbering: sixty-four thousand four hundred.

26 The sons of Zebulun according to their families *were*: of Sered, the family of the Sardites; of Elon, the family of the Elonites; of Jahleel, the family of the Jahleelites.

27 These *are* the families of Zebulun according to their numbering: sixty thousand five hundred.

28 The sons of Joseph according to their families *were*: Mannasseh and Ephraim.

29 The sons of Mannasseh: of Machir the family of the Machirites; and Machir fathered Gilead: of Gilead, the family of the Gileadites.

30 And these *are* the sons of Galaad: of Abiezer, the family of the Abiezerites; of Helek, the family of the Helekites;

31 of Asriel, the family of the Asrielites; of Shechem, the family of the Shechemites;

32 of Shemida, the family of the Shemidaites; and of Hepher, the family of the Hepherites.

33 And to Zelophedad the son of Hopher there were no sons, but daughters: and these *were* the names of the daughters of Zelophedad: Mahlah, Noah, Hoglah, Milcha, and Tirzah.

34 These *are* the families of Mannasseh according to their numbering: fifty-two thousand seven hundred.

35 And these *are* the children of Ephraim: of Shuthelah, the family of the Shuthalhites; of Tanach, the family of the Tanachites.

36 These *are* the sons of Shuthelah: of Eran, the family of the Eranites.

37 These *are* the families of Ephraim according to their numbering: thirty-two thousand five hundred. These *are* the families of the children of Joseph according to their families.

38 The sons of Benjamin according to their families *were*: of Bela, the family of the Belaites; of Ashbel, the family of the Ashbelites; of Ahiram, the family of the Ahiramites;

39 of Sophan, the family of the Sophanites.

40 And the sons of Bela were Ard and Naaman; to Adar, the family of the Adarites; and to Naaman, the family of the Naamanites.

41 These *are* the sons of Benjamin by their families according to their numbering: thirty-five thousand five hundred.

42 And the sons of Dan according to their families: to Shuham, the family of the Shuhamites; these *are* the families of Dan according to their families.

43 All the families of Shuhamites according to their numbering *were* sixty-four thousand four hundred.

44 The sons of Asher according to their families *were*: to Jimna, the family of the Jimnites; to Jesui, the family of the Jesuites; to Beriah, the family of the Beriites.

45 To Hober, the family of the Hoberites; to Malchiel, the family of the Malchielites.

46 And the name of the daughter of Asher *was* Serah.

47 These *are* the families of Asher according to their numbering; forty-three thousand four hundred.

48 The sons of Naphtali according to their families *were*: to Jahziel, the family of the Jahzielites; to Guni, the family of the Gunites.

49 To Jezer, the family of the Jezerites; to Shillem, the family of the Shillemites.

50 These *are* the families of Naphtali, according to their numbering: forty thousand three hundred.

[51] This *is* the numbering of the children of Israel, six hundred and one thousand seven hundred and thirty.

[52] And the Lord spoke to Moses, saying,

[53] "To these the land shall be divided, so that they may inherit according to the number of the names.

[54] To the greater number you shall give the greater inheritance, and to the lesser number you shall give the lesser inheritance: to each one, as they have been numbered, shall their inheritance be given.

[55] The land shall be divided to the names by lot, they shall inherit according to the tribes of their families.

[56] You shall divide their inheritance by lot between the many and the few."

[57] And the sons of Levi according to their families; to Gershon, the family of the Gershonites; to Kohath, the family of the Kohathites; to Merari, the family of the Merarites.

[58] These *are* the families of the sons of Levi; the family of the Libnites, the family of the Hebronites, the family of the Korahites, and the family of the Musites; and Kohath fathered Amram.

[59] And the name of his wife *was* Jochabed, daughter of Levi, who bore these to Levi in Egypt, and she bore to Amram, Aaron and Moses, and Miriam their sister.

[60] And to Aaron were born both Nadab and Abiud, and Eleazar, and Ithamar.

[61] And Nadab and Abiud died when they offered strange fire before the Lord in the Wilderness of Sinai.

[62] And there were according to their numbering, twenty-three thousand, every male from a month old and upward; for they were not numbered among the children of Israel, because they have no inheritance in the midst of the children of Israel.

[63] And this *is* the numbering of Moses and Eleazar the priest, who numbered the children of Israel in Araboth of Moab, at the Jordan by Jericho.

[64] And among these there was not a man numbered by Moses and Aaron, whom, *even* the children of Israel, they numbered in the Wilderness of Sinai.

[65] For the Lord said to them, "They shall surely die in the wilderness"; and there was not left even one of them, except Caleb the son of Jephunneh, and Joshua the son of Nun.

NUMBERS CHAPTER 27

The Daughters of Zelophehad

[1] And the daughters of Zelophehad the son of Hopher, the son of Gilead, the son of Machir, of the tribe of Mannasseh, of the sons of Joseph, came near; and these were their names, Mahlah, Noah, Hoglah, Milcah, and Tirzah.

[2] And they stood before Moses, and before Eleazar the priest, and before the princes, and before all the congregation at the door of the tabernacle of witness, saying,

[3] "Our father died in the wilderness, and he was not in the midst of the congregation that rebelled against the Lord in the gathering of Korah; for he died for his own sin, and he had no sons. Let not the name of our father be blotted out of the midst of his people, because he has no son—give us an inheritance in the midst of our father's brothers."

[4] And Moses brought their case before the Lord.

[5] And the Lord spoke to Moses, saying,

[6] "The daughters of Zelophehad have spoken rightly: you shall surely give them a possession of inheritance in the midst of their father's brothers, and you shall assign their father's inheritance to them.

[7] And you shall speak to the children of Israel, saying,

[8] 'If a man dies and has no son, you shall assign his inheritance to his daughter.

[9] And if he has no daughter, you shall give his inheritance to his brother.

[10] And if he has no brother, you shall give his inheritance to his father's brother.

[11] And if there be no brother of his father, you shall give the inheritance to his nearest relation of his tribe, to inherit his possessions." And this shall be to the children of Israel an ordinance of judgment, as the Lord commanded Moses.

Joshua Appointed as Moses' Successor

[12] And the Lord said to Moses, "Go up to the mountain that is in the country beyond the Jordan, this Mount Nebo, and behold the land of Canaan, which I shall give to the sons of Israel for a possession.

[13] And you shall see it, and you also shall be added to your people, as Aaron your brother was added,

[14] because you transgressed My commandment in the Wilderness of Zin, when the congregation refused to hallow Me; you did not hallow Me at the water before them." (This is the water of Strife in Kadesh, in the Wilderness of Zin.)

[15] And Moses said to the Lord,

[16] "Let the Lord God of spirits and of all flesh look out for a man over this congregation,

[17] who shall go out before them, and who shall come in before them, and who shall lead them out, and who shall bring them in; so the congregation of the Lord shall not be as sheep without a shepherd.

[18] And the Lord spoke to Moses, saying, "Take to yourself Joshua the son of Nun, a man who has the Spirit in him, and you shall lay your hands upon him.

[19] And you shall set him before Eleazar the priest, and you shall give him a charge before all the congregation, and you shall give a charge concerning him before them.

[20] And you shall put of your glory upon him, that the children of Israel may hearken to him.

[21] And he shall stand before Eleazar the priest, and they shall ask of him before the Lord the judgment of the Urim. They shall go forth at his word, and at his word they shall come in, he and the children of Israel with one accord, and all the congregation."

²² And Moses did as the Lord commanded him; and he took Joshua, and set him before Eleazar the priest, and before all the congregation.
²³ And he laid his hands on him, and appointed him as the Lord ordered Moses.

NUMBERS CHAPTER 28

Daily Offerings

¹ And the Lord spoke to Moses, saying,
² "Command the children of Israel, and you shall speak to them, saying, 'You shall observe to offer My gifts to Me in My feasts, My presents, and My burnt offerings for a sweet-smelling savor.'
³ And you shall say to them, 'These are the burnt offerings, all that you shall bring to the Lord: two lambs of a year old without blemish daily, for a burnt offering, perpetually.
⁴ You shall offer one lamb in the morning, and you shall offer the second lamb towards evening.
⁵ And you shall offer the tenth part of an ephah of fine flour for a grain offering, mingled with oil, with the fourth part of a hin.
⁶ *It is* a perpetual burnt offering, a sacrifice offered in the Mount of Sinai for a sweet-smelling savor to the Lord.
⁷ And its drink offering, the fourth part of a hin to each lamb; in the holy place shall you pour strong drink as a drink offering to the Lord.
⁸ And the second lamb you shall offer toward evening; you shall offer it according to its grain offering and according to its drink offering for an aroma of sweet savor to the Lord.

Sabbath Offerings

⁹ 'And on the Sabbath day you shall offer two lambs of a year old without blemish, and two tenth deals of fine flour mingled with oil for a grain offering, and a drink offering.
¹⁰ *It is* a burnt offering of the Sabbaths on the Sabbath days, besides the continued burnt offering, and its drink offering.

Monthly Offerings

¹¹ 'And at the new moons you shall bring a burnt offering to the Lord, two calves of the herd, and one ram, seven lambs of a year old without blemish.
¹² Three tenth deals of fine flour mingled with oil for one calf, and two tenth deals of fine flour mingled with oil for one ram.
¹³ A tenth deal of fine flour mingled with oil for each lamb, as a grain offering, a sweet-smelling savor, a burnt offering to the Lord.
¹⁴ Their drink offering shall be the half of a hin for one calf; and the third of a hin for one ram; and the fourth part of a hin of wine for one lamb: this *is* the burnt offering monthly throughout the months of the year.

¹⁵ And *he shall offer* one kid of the goats for a sin offering to the Lord; it shall be offered beside the continual burnt offering and its drink offering.

Offerings at Passover

¹⁶ 'And in the first month, on the fourteenth day of the month *is* the Passover to the Lord.
¹⁷ And on the fifteenth day of this month *is* a feast; seven days you shall eat unleavened bread.
¹⁸ And the first day shall be to you a holy convocation; you shall do no customary work.
¹⁹ And you shall bring burnt offerings, a sacrifice to the Lord, two calves of the herd, one ram, seven lambs of a year old; they shall be to you without blemish.
²⁰ And their grain offering shall be fine flour mingled with oil; three tenth deals for one calf, and two tenth deals for one ram. ²¹ You shall offer a tenth for each lamb, for the seven lambs.
²² And *you shall offer* one kid of the goats for a sin offering, to make atonement for you.
²³ Beside the perpetual burnt offering in the morning, which is a whole burnt sacrifice for a continuance,
²⁴ these shall you thus offer daily for seven days, a gift, a sacrifice for a sweet-smelling savor to the Lord; beside the continual burnt offering, you shall offer its drink offering.
²⁵ And the seventh day shall be to you a holy convocation; you shall do no customary work in it.

Offerings at the Feast of Weeks

²⁶ 'And on the day of the new grain, when you shall offer a new sacrifice at the Feast of Weeks to the Lord, there shall be to you a holy convocation; you shall do no customary work,
²⁷ and you shall bring burnt offerings for a sweet-smelling savor to the Lord, two calves of the herd, one ram, seven lambs without blemish.
²⁸ Their grain offering *shall be* fine flour mingled with oil; there shall be three tenth deals for one calf, and two tenth deals for one ram.
²⁹ A tenth for each lamb separately, for the seven lambs; and a kid of the goats,
³⁰ for a sin offering, to make atonement for you; beside the perpetual burnt offering: and
³¹ you shall offer to Me their grain offering. They shall be to you unblemished, and you shall offer their drink offerings.

NUMBERS CHAPTER 29

Offerings at the Feast of Trumpets

¹ 'And in the seventh month, on the first day of the month, there shall be to you a holy convocation: you shall do no customary work: it shall be to you a day of blowing the trumpets.

2 And you shall offer burnt offerings for a sweet savor to the Lord, one calf of the herd, one ram, seven lambs of a year old without blemish.

3 Their grain offering shall be fine flour mingled with oil; three tenth deals for one calf, and two tenth deals for one ram:

4 a tenth deal for each several ram, for the seven lambs.

5 And one kid of the goats for a sin offering, to make atonement for you.

6 Beside the burnt offerings for the new moon, and their grain offerings, and their drink offerings, and their perpetual burnt offering; and their grain offerings and their drink offerings according to their ordinance for a sweet-smelling savor to the Lord.

Offerings on the Day of Atonement

7 'And on the tenth of this month there shall be to you a holy convocation; and you shall afflict your souls, and you shall do no work.

8 And you shall bring near burnt offerings for a sweet-smelling savor to the Lord; burnt sacrifices to the Lord, one calf of the herd, one ram, seven lambs of a year old; they shall be to you without blemish.

9 Their grain offering shall be fine flour mingled with oil; three tenth deals for one calf, and two tenth deals for one ram.

10 A tenth deal for each several lamb, for the seven lambs.

11 And one kid of the goats for a sin offering, to make atonement for you; beside the sin offering for atonement, and the continual burnt offering, its grain offering, and its drink offering according to its ordinance for an aroma of sweet savor, a burnt sacrifice to the Lord.

Offerings at the Feast of Tabernacles

12 'And on the fifteenth day of this seventh month you shall have a holy convocation; you shall do no customary work, and you shall keep it a feast to the Lord for seven days.

13 And you shall bring near burnt offerings, a sacrifice for an aroma of sweet savor to the Lord, on the first day thirteen calves of the herd, two rams, fourteen lambs of a year old; they shall be without blemish.

14 Their grain offerings *shall be* fine flour mingled with oil; there shall be three tenth deals for one calf, for the thirteen calves; and two tenth deals for one ram, for the two rams.

15 A tenth deal for every lamb, for the fourteen lambs.

16 And one kid of the goats for a sin offering; beside the continual burnt offering: there shall be their grain offerings and their drink offerings.

17 'And on the second day twelve calves, two rams, fourteen lambs of a year old without blemish.

18 Their grain offering and their drink offering shall be for the calves and the rams and the lambs according to their number, according to their ordinance.

19 And one kid of the goats for a sin offering; beside the perpetual burnt offering; their grain offerings and their drink offerings.

20 'On the third day eleven calves, two rams, fourteen lambs of a year old without blemish.

21 Their grain offering and their drink offering shall be to the calves and to the rams and to the lambs according to their number, according to their ordinance.

22 And one kid of the goats for a sin offering; beside the continual burnt offering; *there shall be* their grain offerings and their drink offerings.

23 'On the fourth day ten calves, two rams, fourteen lambs of a year old without spot.

24 There shall be their grain offerings and their drink offerings to the calves and the rams and the lambs according to their number, according to their ordinance.

25 And one kid of the goats for a sin offering; beside the continual burnt offering *there shall be* their grain offerings and their drink offerings.

26 'On the fifth day nine calves, two rams, fourteen lambs of a year old without spot.

27 Their grain offerings and their drink offerings *shall be* to the calves and the rams and the lambs according to their number, according to their ordinance.

28 And one kid of the goats for a sin offering; beside the perpetual burnt offering; *there shall be* their grain offerings and their drink offerings.

29 'On the sixth day eight calves, two rams, fourteen lambs of a year old without blemish.

30 There shall be their grain offerings and their drink offerings to the calves and rams and lambs according to their number, according to their ordinance.

31 And one kid of the goats for a sin offering; beside the perpetual burnt offering; *there shall be* their grain offerings and their drink offerings.

32 'On the seventh day seven calves, two rams, fourteen lambs of a year old without blemish.

33 Their grain offerings and their drink offerings shall be to the calves and the rams and the lambs according to their number, according to their ordinance.

34 And one kid of the goats for a sin offering; beside the continual burnt offering; *there shall be* their grain offerings and their drink offerings.

35 'And on the eighth day there shall be to you a release: you shall do no customary work in it.

36 And you shall offer burnt offerings *as* sacrifices to the Lord, one calf, one ram, seven lambs of a year old without spot.

37 *There shall be* their grain offerings and their drink offerings for the calf and the ram and the lambs according to their number, according to their ordinance.

38 And one kid of the goats for a sin offering; beside the continual burnt offering; *there shall be* their grain offerings and their drink offerings.

39 'These *sacrifices* shall you offer to the Lord in your feasts, besides your vows; and *you shall offer* your freewill offerings and your burnt offerings, and your grain offerings and your drink offerings, and your peace offerings.'"

40 And Moses spoke to the children of Israel according to all that the Lord commanded Moses.

NUMBERS CHAPTER 30

The Law Concerning Vows

1 And Moses spoke to the heads of the tribes of the children of Israel, saying, "This *is* the thing which the Lord has commanded:

2 "Any man that shall vow a vow to the Lord, or swear an oath, or bind himself with an obligation upon his soul, he shall not break his word; all that shall come out of his mouth he shall do.

3 'And if a woman shall vow a vow to the Lord, or bind herself with an obligation in her youth in her father's house; and her father should hear her vows and her obligations, wherewith she has bound her soul, and her father should hold his peace at her, then all her vows shall stand,

4 and all the obligations with which she has bound her soul shall remain to her.

5 But if her father should strictly forbid *her* in the day in which he shall hear all her vows and her obligations, which she has contracted upon her soul, they shall not stand; and the Lord shall hold her guiltless, because her father forbade her.

6 'But if she should be indeed married, and her vows be upon her according to the utterance of her lips, in respect of *the obligations* which she has contracted upon her soul,

7 and her husband should hear, and hold his peace at her in the day in which he should hear, then thus shall all her vows be binding, and her obligations, which she has contracted upon her soul shall stand.

8 But if her husband should strictly forbid *her* in the day in which he should hear her, none of her vows or obligations which she has contracted upon her soul shall stand, because her husband has disallowed her, and the Lord shall hold her guiltless.

9 'And the vow of a widow and of her that is put away, whatsoever she shall bind upon her soul, shall stand to her.

10 'And if her vow *be made* in the house of her husband, or the obligation upon her soul with an oath,

11 and her husband should hear, and hold his peace at her, and not disallow her, then all her vows shall stand, and all the obligations which she contracted against her soul, shall stand against her.

12 But if her husband should utterly cancel the vow in the day in which he shall hear it, none of the things which shall proceed out of her lips in her vows, and in the obligations *contracted* upon her soul, shall stand to her; her husband has canceled them, and the Lord shall hold her guiltless.

13 Every vow, and every binding oath to afflict her soul, her husband shall confirm it to her, or her husband shall cancel it.

14 But if he be wholly silent at her from day to day, then shall he bind upon her all her vows; and he shall confirm to her the obligations *which she has bound* upon herself, because he held his peace at her in the day in which he heard her.

15 And if her husband should in any way cancel *them* after the day in which he heard *them*, then he shall bear his iniquity.'"

16 These *are* the ordinances which the Lord commanded Moses, between a man and his wife, and between a father and daughter in *her* youth in the house of *her* father.

NUMBERS CHAPTER 31

War Against Midian

1 And the Lord spoke to Moses, saying,

2 "Avenge the wrongs of the children of Israel on the Midianites, and afterwards you shall be added to your people." 3 And Moses spoke to the people, saying, "Arm some of yourselves for war, and set yourselves in array before the Lord against Midian, to inflict vengeance on Midian from the Lord.

4 Send a thousand of each tribe from all the tribes of the children of Israel to set themselves in array."

5 And they numbered of the thousands of Israel a thousand of *each* tribe, twelve thousand; *these were* armed for war.

6 And Moses sent them away, a thousand of every tribe with their forces, and Phinehas the son of Eleazar the son of Aaron the priest. And the holy instruments, and the signal trumpets *were* in their hands.

7 And they set themselves in array against Midian, as the Lord commanded Moses; and they killed every male.

8 And they killed the kings of Midian together with their slain *subjects*; even Evi, Rekem, Zur, Hur, and Reba, the five kings of Midian; and they killed with the sword Balaam the son of Beor with their *other* slain.

9 And they made a prey of the women of Midian, and their little ones, and their cattle, and all their possessions; and they spoiled their forces.

10 And they burned with fire all their cities in the places of their habitation, and they burned their villages with fire.

11 And they took all their plunder, and all their spoils, both man and beast.

Return from the War

12 And they brought to Moses and to Eleazar the priest, and to all the children of Israel, the captives, and the spoils, and the plunder, to the camp to Araboth Moab, which is at the Jordan by Jericho.

13 And Moses and Eleazar the priest and all the rulers of the synagogue went forth out of the camp to meet them.

¹⁴ And Moses was angry with the captains of the army, the heads of thousands and the heads of hundreds who came from the battle array.

¹⁵ And Moses said to them, "Why have you saved every female alive?

¹⁶ For they were *the occasion* to the children of Israel by the word of Balaam of their revolting and despising the word of the Lord, because of Peor, and there was a plague in the congregation of the Lord.

¹⁷ Now then, kill every male in all the spoil, kill every woman who has known a man intimately.

¹⁸ And as for all the captivity of women who have not known a man intimately, keep them alive.

¹⁹ And you shall remain outside the camp for seven days; whoever has killed, and whoever has touched a dead body, shall be purified on the third day, and you and your captivity *shall purify yourselves* on the seventh day.

²⁰ And you shall purify every garment and every leather utensil, and all furniture of goat skin, and every wooden vessel."

²¹ And Eleazar the priest said to the men of the army that came from the battle array, "This *is* the ordinance of the law which the Lord has commanded Moses.

²² Beside the gold, the silver, the brass, the iron, the lead, and the tin,

²³ everything that shall pass through the fire shall so be clean, nevertheless it shall be purified with the water of sanctification; and whatsoever will not pass through the fire shall pass through water.

²⁴ And on the seventh day you shall wash your garments and be clean; and afterwards you shall come into the camp."

Division of the Plunder

²⁵ And the Lord spoke to Moses, saying,

²⁶ "Take the sum of the spoils of the captivity both of man and beast, you and Eleazar the priest, and the heads of the families of the congregation.

²⁷ And you shall divide the spoils between the warriors that went out to battle, and the whole congregation.

²⁸ And you shall take a tribute for the Lord from the warriors that went out to battle; one soul out of five hundred, from the men and from the cattle, even from the oxen, and from the sheep, and from the donkeys; and you shall take from their half.

²⁹ And you shall give *them* to Eleazar the priest *as* the firstfruits of the Lord.

³⁰ And from the half belonging to the children of Israel you shall take one in fifty from the men, and from the oxen, and from the sheep, and from the donkeys, and from all the cattle; and you shall give them to the Levites that keep the charges in the tabernacle of the Lord."

³¹ And Moses and Eleazar the priest did as the Lord commanded Moses.

³² And that which remained of the spoil which the warriors took was six hundred and seventy-five thousand, among the sheep,

³³ and oxen, seventy-two thousand;

³⁴ and donkeys, sixty-one thousand;

³⁵ and of women who had not known a man intimately *were* thirty-two thousand.

³⁶ And the half, *even* the portion of them that went out to war, from the number of the sheep, was three hundred and thirty-seven thousand five hundred.

³⁷ And the tribute to the Lord from the sheep was six hundred and seventy-five.

³⁸ And the oxen, thirty-six thousand, and the tribute to the Lord seventy-two.

³⁹ And donkeys, thirty thousand five hundred, and the tribute to the Lord *was* sixty-one.

⁴⁰ And the persons *were* sixteen thousand, and the tribute of them to the Lord *was* thirty-two souls.

⁴¹ And Moses gave the tribute to the Lord, the heave offering of God, to Eleazar the priest, as the Lord commanded Moses;

⁴² from the half belonging to the children of Israel, whom Moses separated from the men of war.

⁴³ And the half *taken* from the sheep, belonging to the congregation, was three hundred and thirty-seven thousand five hundred.

⁴⁴ And the oxen, thirty-six thousand;

⁴⁵ *and the* donkeys, thirty thousand five hundred;

⁴⁶ and persons, sixteen thousand.

⁴⁷ And Moses took of the half belonging to the children of Israel the fiftieth part, of men and of cattle, and he gave them to the Levites who keep the charges of the tabernacle of the Lord, as the Lord commanded Moses.

⁴⁸ And all those who were appointed to be officers of thousands of the army, captains of thousands and captains of hundreds, approached Moses, and said to Moses,

⁴⁹ "Your servants have taken the sum of the men of war with us, and not one is missing.

⁵⁰ And we have brought our gift to the Lord, *every* man who has found an article of gold, whether an armlet, or a chain, or a ring, or a bracelet, or a clasp for hair, to make atonement for us before the Lord."

⁵¹ And Moses and Eleazar the priest took the gold from them, even every fashioned ornament.

⁵² And all the gold, even the offering that they offered to the Lord, was sixteen thousand seven hundred and fifty shekels from the captains of thousands and the captains of hundreds.

⁵³ For the men of war took plunder, every man for himself.

⁵⁴ And Moses and Eleazar the priest took the gold from the captains of thousands and captains of hundreds, and brought the vessels into the tabernacle of witness, a memorial of the children of Israel before the Lord.

NUMBERS CHAPTER 32

The Tribes Settling East of the Jordan

[1] And the children of Reuben and the children of Gad had a multitude of cattle, very great. And they saw the land of Jazer, and the land of Gilead; and the place was a place for cattle.

[2] And the children of Reuben and the children of Gad came and spoke to Moses, and to Eleazar the priest, and to the princes of the congregation, saying,

[3] "Ataroth, Dibon, Jazer, Nimrah, Heshbon, Elealeh, Shebam, Nebo, and Beon,

[4] the land which the Lord has delivered up before the children of Israel, is pasture land, and your servants have cattle."

[5] And they said, "If we have found grace in your sight, let this land be given to your servants for a possession, and do not cause us to pass over the Jordan."

[6] And Moses said to the sons of Gad and the sons of Reuben, "Shall your brothers go to war, and shall you sit here?

[7] And why do you pervert the minds of the children of Israel, that they should not cross over into the land, which the Lord gives them?

[8] Did not your fathers do thus, when I sent them from Kadesh Barnea to spy out the land?

[9] And they went up to the Valley of Eshcol, and spied the land, and turned aside the heart of the children of Israel, that they should not go into the land, which the Lord gave them.

[10] And the Lord was very angry in that day, and swore, saying,

[11] 'Surely these men who came up out of Egypt from twenty years old and upward, who know good and evil, shall not see the land which I swore *to give* to Abraham and Isaac and Jacob, for they have not closely followed after Me;

[12] except Caleb the son of Jephunneh, who was set apart, and Joshua the son of Nun, for they closely followed after the Lord.'

[13] And the Lord was very angry with Israel; and for forty years He caused them to wander in the wilderness, until all the generation which did evil in the sight of the Lord was extinct.

[14] Behold, you have risen up in the room of your fathers, a combination of sinful men, to increase yet farther the fierce wrath of the Lord against Israel.

[15] For you will turn away from Him to desert Him yet once more in the wilderness, and you will sin against this whole congregation."

[16] And they came to him, and said, "We will build here folds for our cattle, and cities for our possessions;

[17] and we will arm ourselves and go as an advanced guard before the children of Israel, until we shall have brought them into their place; and our possessions shall remain in walled cities because of the inhabitants of the land.

[18] We will not return to our houses till the children of Israel have been distributed, each to his own inheritance.

[19] And we will not any longer inherit with them from the other side of the Jordan and onwards, because we have our full inheritance on the side beyond the Jordan eastward."

[20] And Moses said to them, "If you will do according to these words, if you will arm yourselves before the Lord for battle,

[21] and everyone of you will pass over the Jordan fully armed before the Lord, until his enemy be destroyed from before his face,

[22] and the land shall be subdued before the Lord, then afterwards you shall return, and be guiltless before the Lord, and as regards to Israel; and this land shall be to you for a possession before the Lord.

[23] But if you will not do so, you will sin against the Lord; and you shall know your sin, when afflictions shall come upon you.

[24] And you shall build for yourselves cities for your little ones, and folds for your cattle; and you shall do that which proceeds out of your mouth."

[25] And the sons of Reuben and the sons of Gad spoke to Moses, saying, "Your servants will do as our Lord commands.

[26] Our little ones, and our wives, and all our cattle shall be in the cities of Gilead.

[27] But your servants will go over all armed and set in order before the Lord to battle, as the Lord says."

[28] And Moses appointed to them *for judges* Eleazar the priest, and Joshua the son of Nun, and the chiefs of the families of the tribes of Israel.

[29] And Moses said to them, "If the sons of Reuben and the sons of Gad will pass over the Jordan with you, everyone armed for war before the Lord, and you shall subdue the land before you, then you shall give to them the land of Gilead for a possession.

[30] But if they will not pass over armed with you to war before the Lord, then shall you cause to pass over their possessions and their wives and their cattle before you into the land of Canaan, and they shall inherit with you in the land of Canaan."

[31] And the sons of Reuben and the sons of Gad answered, saying, "Whatsoever the Lord says to His servants, that will we do.

[32] We will go over armed before the Lord into the land of Canaan, and you shall give us our inheritance beyond the Jordan."

[33] And Moses gave to them, even to the sons of Gad and the sons of Reuben, and to the half tribe of Mannasseh of the sons of Joseph, the kingdom of Sihon king of the Amorites, and the kingdom of Og king of Bashan, the land and its cities with its coasts, the cities of the land round about.

[34] And the sons of Gad built Dibon, Ataroth, Aroer,

[35] Sophar, Jazer, and they set them up,

36 and Nimrah, and Beth Haran, strong cities, and folds for sheep.

37 And the sons of Reuben built Heshbon, Elealeh, and Kirjathaim,

38 and Baal Meon, surrounded *with walls*, and Shibma; and they called the names of the cities which they built, after their own names.

39 And a son of Machir the son of Mannasseh went to Gilead, and took it, and destroyed the Amorites who dwelt in it.

40 And Moses gave Gilead to Machir the son of Mannasseh, and he dwelt there.

41 And Jair the son of Mannasseh went and took their villages, and called them the villages of Jair.

42 And Nobah went and took Kohath and her villages, and called them Nobah after his name.

NUMBERS CHAPTER 33

The Stages of Israel's Journey from Egypt

1 And these are the stages of the children of Israel, as they went out from the land of Egypt with their armies by the hand of Moses and Aaron.

2 And Moses wrote their removals and their stages, by the word of the Lord: and these are the stages of their journeying.

3 They departed from Rameses in the first month, on the fifteenth day of the first month; on the day after the Passover the children of Israel went forth with a high hand before all the Egyptians.

4 And the Egyptians buried those that died of them, even all that the Lord struck, every firstborn in the land of Egypt; also the Lord executed vengeance on their gods.

5 And the children of Israel departed from Rameses, and encamped in Succoth;

6 and they departed from Succoth and encamped in Etham, which is a part of the wilderness.

7 And they departed from Etham and encamped at the mouth of Hahiroth, which is opposite Baal Zephon, and encamped opposite Migdol.

8 And they departed from before Hahiroth, and crossed the middle of the sea into the wilderness; and they went a journey of three days through the wilderness, and encamped in Marah.

9 And they departed from Marah, and came to Elim; and in Elim *were* twelve fountains of water, and seventy palm trees, and they encamped there by the water.

10 And they departed from Elim, and encamped by the Red Sea.

11 And they departed from the Red Sea, and encamped in the Wilderness of Zin.

12 And they departed from the wilderness of Zin, and encamped in Dophkah.

13 And they departed from Dophkah, and encamped in Alush.

14 And they departed from Alush, and encamped in Rephidim; and there was no water there for the people to drink.

15 And they departed from Rephidim, and encamped in the Wilderness of Sinai.

16 And they departed from the Wilderness of Sinai, and encamped at the Graves of Lust.

17 And they departed from the Graves of Lust, and encamped in Asheroth.

18 And they departed from Asheroth, and encamped in Rithmah.

19 And they departed from Rithmah, and encamped in Rimmon Perez.

20 And they departed from Rimmon Perez, and encamped in Libnah.

21 And they departed from Libnah, and encamped in Rissah.

22 And they departed from Rissah, and encamped in Kehelathah.

23 And they departed from Kehelathah, and encamped in Saphar.

24 And they departed from Saphar, and encamped in Haradah.

25 And they departed from Haradah, and encamped in Makheloth.

26 And they departed from Makheloth, and encamped in Tahath.

27 And they departed from Tahath, and encamped in Terah.

28 And they departed from Terah, and encamped in Mithkah.

29 And they departed from Mithkah, and encamped in Hashmonah.

30 And they departed from Hashmonah, and encamped in Moseroth.

31 And they departed from Moseroth, and encamped in Bene Jaakan.

32 And they departed from Bene Jaakan, and encamped in the Mount Hagidgad

33 And they departed from the Mount Hagidgad, and encamped in Jotbathah.

34 And they departed from Jotbathah, and encamped in Abronah.

35 And they departed from Abronah, and encamped in Ezion Geber.

36 And they departed from Ezion Geber, and encamped in the Wilderness of Zin; and they departed from the Wilderness of Zin, and encamped in the Wilderness of Paran; this is Kadesh.

37 And they departed from Kadesh, and encamped in Mount Hor near the land of Edom.

38 And Aaron the priest went up by the command of the Lord, and died there in the fortieth year of the departure of the children of Israel from the land of Egypt, in the fifth month, on the first *day* of the month.

39 And Aaron was a hundred and twenty-three years old, when he died in Mount Hor.

40 And Arad the Canaanite king, (he too dwelt in the land of Canaan) having heard when the children of Israel were entering *the land,*

41 then they departed from Mount Hor, and encamped in Zalmonah.

42 And they departed from Zalmonah, and encamped in Punon.

43 And they departed from Punon, and encamped in Oboth.

44 And they departed from Oboth, and encamped in Gai, on the other side, on the borders of Moab.

45 And they departed from Gai, and encamped in Dibon Gad.

46 And they departed from Dibon Gad, and encamped in Almon Diblathaim.

47 And they departed from Almon Diblathaim, and encamped on the mountains of Abarim, over against Nebo.

48 And they departed from the mountains of Abarim, and encamped on the west of Moab, at Jordan by Jericho.

49 And they encamped by Jordan between Jesimoth, as far as Belsa to the west of Moab.

Instructions for the Conquest of Canaan

50 And the Lord spoke to Moses at the west of Moab by Jordan at Jericho, saying,

51 "Speak to the children of Israel, and you shall say to them, 'You are to pass over the Jordan into the land of Canaan.

52 And you shall destroy all that dwell in the land before your face, and you shall abolish their high places, and all their molten images you shall destroy, and you shall demolish all their pillars.

53 And you shall destroy all the inhabitants of the land, and you shall dwell in it, for I have given their land to you for an inheritance.

54 And you shall inherit their land according to your tribes; to the greater number you shall give the larger possession, and to the smaller you shall give the less possession; to whatsoever *part* a man's name shall go forth *by lot,* there shall be his *property:* you shall inherit according to the tribes of your families.

55 But if you will not destroy the inhabitants of the land from before you, then it shall come to pass that whomsoever of them you shall leave shall be thorns in your eyes, and darts in your sides, and they shall be enemies to you on the land on which you shall dwell;

56 and it shall come to pass that as I had determined to do to them, so I will do to you.'"

NUMBERS CHAPTER 34

The Boundaries of Canaan

1 And the Lord spoke to Moses, saying,

2 "Command the children of Israel, and you shall say to them, 'You are entering into the land of Canaan: it shall be to you for an inheritance, the land of Canaan with its boundaries.

3 And your southern side shall be from the Wilderness of Zin to the border of Edom, and your border southward shall extend on the side of the Salt Sea eastward.

4 And your border shall go round you from the south to the Ascent of Akrabbim, and shall proceed by Ennac, and the going forth of it shall be southward to Kadesh Barnea, and it shall go forth to the village of Arad, and shall proceed by Azmon.

5 And the border shall compass from Azmon to the river of Egypt, and the sea shall be the boundary.

6 'And you shall have your border on the west, the great sea shall be the boundary; this shall be to you the border on the west.

7 And this shall be your northern border; from the great sea you shall measure to yourselves, by the side of the mountain.

8 And you shall measure to yourselves the mountain from Mount *Hor* at the entering in to Hamath, and the termination of it shall be the coasts of Zedad.

9 And the border shall go out to Ziphron, and its termination shall be at Hazar Enan; this shall be your border from the north.

10 'And you shall measure to yourselves the eastern border from Hazar Enan to Shepham.

11 And the border shall go down from Shepham to Bela eastward to the fountains, and the border shall go down from Bela behind the Sea Chinnereth eastward.

12 And the border shall go down to the Jordan, and the termination shall be the Salt Sea; this shall be your land and its borders round about.'"

13 And Moses charged the children of Israel, saying, "This *is* the land which you shall inherit by lot, even as the Lord commanded us, to give it to the nine tribes and the half-tribe of Mannasseh.

14 For the tribe of the children of Reuben, and the tribe of the children of Gad have received *their inheritance* according to their families; and the half-tribe of Mannasseh have received their inheritances.

15 Two tribes and half a tribe have received their inheritance beyond the Jordan by Jericho eastward, towards the sunrise."

16 And the Lord spoke to Moses, saying,

17 "These *are* the names of the men who shall divide the land to you for an inheritance: Eleazar the priest and Joshua the son of Nun.

18 And you shall take one ruler from *each* tribe to divide the land to you by lot.

19 And these *are* the names of the men: of the tribe of Judah, Caleb the son of Jephunneh.

20 Of the tribe of Simeon, Shemuel the son of Ammihud.

21 Of the tribe of Benjamin, Elidad the son of Chislon.

²² Of the tribe of Dan the prince *was* Bukki the son of Jogli.

²³ Of the sons of Joseph of the tribe of the sons of Mannasseh, the prince was Hanniel the son of Suphi.

²⁴ Of the tribe of the sons of Ephraim, the prince was Kemuel the son of Shiphtan.

²⁵ Of the tribe of Zebulun, the prince was Eliazaphan the son of Parnach.

²⁶ Of the tribe of the sons of Issachar, the prince was Paltiel the son of Azzan.

²⁷ Of the tribe of the children of Asher, the prince was Ahihud the son of Shelomi.

²⁸ Of the tribe of Naphtali, the prince was Pedahel the son of Ammihud."

²⁹ These did the Lord command to distribute *the inheritances* to the children of Israel in the land of Canaan.

NUMBERS CHAPTER 35

Cities for the Levites

¹ And the Lord spoke to Moses to the west of Moab by the Jordan near Jericho, saying,

² "Give orders to the children of Israel, and they shall give to the Levites cities to dwell in from the lot of their possession, and they shall give to the Levites the suburbs of the cities round about them.

³ And the cities shall be for them to dwell in, and their enclosures shall be for their cattle and all their beasts.

⁴ And the suburbs of the cities which you shall give to the Levites, shall be from the wall of the city and outwards two thousand cubits round about.

⁵ And you shall measure outside the city on the east side two thousand cubits, and on the south side two thousand cubits, and on the west side two thousand cubits, and on the north side two thousand cubits; and your city shall be in the midst of this, and the suburbs of the cities *as described*.

⁶ And you shall give the cities to the Levites, the six cities of refuge which you shall give for the manslayer to flee there, and in addition to these, forty-two cities.

⁷ You shall give to the Levites in all forty-eight cities, them and their suburbs.

⁸ And as for the cities which you shall give out of the possession of the children of Israel, from those *that have much you shall give* much, and from those that have less you shall give less: they shall give of their cities to the Levites each one according to his inheritance which they shall inherit."

Cities of Refuge

⁹ And the Lord spoke to Moses, saying,

¹⁰ "Speak to the children of Israel, and you shall say to them, 'You are to cross over the Jordan into the land of Canaan.

¹¹ And you shall appoint to yourselves cities: they shall be to you cities of refuge for the manslayer to flee to, everyone who has killed another unintentionally.

¹² And the cities shall be to you places of refuge from the avenger of blood, and the manslayer shall not die until he stands before the congregation for judgment.

¹³ And the cities which you shall assign, *even* the six cities, shall be places of refuge for you.

¹⁴ You shall assign three cities on the other side of the Jordan, and you shall assign three cities in the land of Canaan.

¹⁵ It shall be a place of refuge for the children of Israel, and for the stranger, and for him that sojourns among you; these cities shall be for a place of refuge, for everyone to flee there who has killed a man unintentionally.

¹⁶ 'And if he should strike him with an iron instrument, and the man should die, he is a murderer; let the murderer by all means be put to death.

¹⁷ And if he should strike him with a stone *thrown* from his hand, whereby a man may die, and he *thus* dies, he is a murderer; let the murderer by all means be put to death.

¹⁸ And if he should stike him with an instrument of wood from his hand, whereby he may die, and he *thus* dies, he is a murderer; let the murderer by all means be put to death.

¹⁹ The avenger of blood himself shall slay the murderer: whenever he shall meet him, he shall put him to death.

²⁰ And if he should thrust him, out of hatred, or cast anything upon him from an ambush, and the man should die,

²¹ or if he has stricken him with his hand through anger, and the man should die, let the man that struck him be put to death by all means, he is a murderer: let the murderer by all means be put to death; the avenger of blood shall slay the murderer when he meets him.

²² But if he should thrust him suddenly, not through enmity, or cast anything upon him, not from an ambush,

²³ or *strike him* with any stone, whereby a man may die, unawares, and it should fall upon him, and he should die, but he was not his enemy, nor sought to hurt him;

²⁴ then the assembly shall judge between the smiter and the avenger of blood, according to these judgments.

²⁵ And the congregation shall rescue the manslayer from the avenger of blood, and the congregation shall restore him to his city of refuge, where he fled for refuge; and he shall dwell there till the death of the high priest, whom they anointed with the holy oil.

²⁶ But if the manslayer should in any way go out beyond the bounds of the city where he fled for refuge,

²⁷ and the avenger of blood should find him outside the bounds of the city of his refuge, and the avenger of blood should kill the manslayer, he is not guilty.

²⁸ For he ought to have remained in the city of refuge till the high priest died; and after the death of the high priest the manslayer shall return to the land of his possession.

²⁹ 'And these things shall be to you for an ordinance of judgment throughout your generations in all your dwellings.

30 Whoever kills a man, you shall slay the murderer on the testimony of witnesses; and one witness shall not testify against a soul that he should die.

31 And you shall not accept ransoms for life from a murderer who is worthy of death, for he shall be surely put to death.

32 You shall not accept a ransom *to excuse* his fleeing to the city of refuge, so that he should again dwell in the land, until the death of the high priest.

33 So shall you not pollute with murder the land in which you dwell; for this blood pollutes the land, and the land shall not be purged from the blood shed upon it, but by the blood of him that shed it.

34 And you shall not defile the land on which you dwell, on which I dwell in the midst of you; for I am the Lord dwelling in the midst of the children of Israel.'"

NUMBERS CHAPTER 36

Marriage of Female Heirs

1 And the heads of the tribe of the sons of Gilead the son of Machir the son of Mannasseh, of the tribe of the sons of Joseph, drew near, and spoke before Moses, and before Eleazar the priest, and before the heads of the houses of the families of the children of Israel.

2 And they said, "The Lord commanded our lord *Moses* to render the land of inheritance by lot to the children of Israel; and the Lord appointed our lord to give the inheritance of Zelophehad our brother to his daughters.

3 And they will become wives in one of the tribes of the children of Israel. So their inheritance shall be taken away from the possession of our fathers, and shall be added to the inheritance of the tribe into which the women shall marry, and shall be taken away from the portion of our inheritance.

4 And if there shall be a release of the children of Israel, then shall their inheritance be added to the inheritance of the tribe into which the women marry, and their inheritance shall be taken away from the inheritance of our family's tribe."

5 And Moses charged the children of Israel by the commandment of the Lord, saying, "Thus says the tribe of the children of Joseph.

6 This *is* the thing which the Lord has appointed the daughters of Zelophehad, saying, 'Let them marry where they please, only let them marry *men* of their father's tribe.

7 So shall not the inheritance of the children of Israel go about from tribe to tribe, for the children of Israel shall steadfastly continue each in the inheritance of his family's tribe.

8 And whatever daughter is heiress to a property of the tribes of the children of Israel, *such* women shall be married each to one of her father's tribe, that the sons of Israel may each inherit the property of his father's tribe.

9 And the inheritance shall not go about from one tribe to another, but the children of Israel shall steadfastly continue each in his own inheritance.'"

10 As the Lord commanded Moses, so did they to the daughters of Zelophehad.

11 So Mahlah, Tirzah, Hoglah, Milcah, and Noah, the daughters of Zelophehad, married their cousins;

12 they were married *to men* of the tribe of Mannasseh of the sons of Joseph; and their inheritance was attached to the tribe of their father's family.

13 These *are* the commandments, and the ordinances, and the judgments, which the Lord commanded by the hand of Moses, at the west of Moab, at the Jordan by Jericho.

THE BOOK OF DEUTERONOMY

The Events at Horeb Recalled

1 These *are* the words which Moses spoke to all Israel on this side of the Jordan in the desert towards the west near the Red Sea, between Paran, Tophel, Laban, and Aulon, and the gold works.

2 *It is* a journey of eleven days from Horeb to Mount Seir as far as Kadesh Barnea.

3 And it came to pass in the fortieth year, in the eleventh month, on the first *day* of the month, *that* Moses spoke to all the children of Israel, according to all things which the Lord commanded him for them;

4 after he had killed Sihon king of the Amorites who dwelt in Heshbon, and Og the king of Bashan who dwelt in Ashtaroth and in Edrei.

5 Beyond the Jordan in the land of Moab, Moses began to declare this law, saying,

6 "The Lord your God spoke to us in Horeb, saying, 'You have dwelt *long* enough in this mountain.

7 Turn and depart, and enter into the mountain of the Amorites, and *go* to all that dwell near *the* Arabah, to the mountain and the plain and to the south, and the land of the Canaanites near the sea, and to Lebanon, as far as the great river, the River Euphrates.

8 Behold, *I* have delivered the land unto you; go in and inherit the land, which I swore to your fathers, Abraham, Isaac, and Jacob; to give it to them and to their descendants after them.'

Appointment of Tribal Leaders

9 "And I spoke to you at that time, saying, 'I shall not be able by myself to bear you.

10 The Lord your God has multiplied you, and behold, you are today as the stars of heaven in multitude.

11 *May* the Lord God of your fathers add to you a thousand times more numerous than you *already* are, and bless you, as He has spoken to you.

12 How shall I alone be able to bear your labor, and your burden, and your complaints?

¹³ Take to yourselves wise and understanding and prudent men for your tribes, and I will set your leaders over you.

¹⁴ And you answered me and said, 'The thing which you have told us *is* good.'

¹⁵ So I took wise and understanding and prudent men from among you, and I set them to rule over you as rulers of thousands, rulers of hundreds, rulers of fifties, rulers of tens, and officers to your judges.

¹⁶ And I instructed your judges at that time, saying, 'Hear *the cases* between your brothers, and judge rightly between a man and *his* brother, and the stranger that is with him.

¹⁷ You shall not have respect to persons in judgment, you shall judge small and great equally; you shall not shrink from before the person of a man, for the judgment is God's; and whatsoever matter shall be too hard for you, you shall bring it to me, and I will hear it.'

¹⁸ And I gave to you at that time all the commandments which you shall perform.

Israel's Refusal to Enter the Land

¹⁹ "So we departed from Horeb, and went through all that great and terrible wilderness, which you saw, by the way of the mountain of the Amorite, as the Lord our God charged us, and we came as far as Kadesh Barnea.

²⁰ And I said to you, 'You have come as far as the mountain of the Amorite, which the Lord our God gives to you.

²¹ Behold, the Lord your God has delivered to us the land before you; go up and inherit it as the Lord God of your fathers said to you; fear not, neither be afraid.'

²² And you all came to me, and said, 'Let us send men before us, and let them go up to the land for us; and let them bring back to us a report of the way by which we shall go up, and of the cities into which we shall enter.'

²³ And the saying pleased me: and I took of you twelve men; one man from each tribe.

²⁴ And they turned, and went up to the mountain, and they came as far as the Valley of the Cluster, and surveyed it.

²⁵ And they took in their hands of the fruit of the land, and brought it to you, and said, 'The land is good which the Lord our God gives us.'

²⁶ Yet you would not go up, but rebelled against the words of the Lord our God.

²⁷ And you murmured in your tents, and said, 'Because the Lord hated us, He has brought us out of the land of Egypt to deliver us into the hands of the Amorites, to destroy us.

²⁸ Where can we go up?' And your brothers drew away your heart, saying, '*It is a* great nation and populous, and mightier than we; and *there are* cities great and walled up to heaven. Moreover we saw the sons of the giants there.'

²⁹ And I said to you, 'Do not fear, neither be afraid of them;

³⁰ the Lord your God, who goes before your face, He shall fight against them together with you effectually, according to all that He did for you in the land of Egypt;

³¹ and in this wilderness which you saw, by the way of the mountain of the Amorite; how the Lord your God will bear you like a son, as if any man should carry his son, through all the way which you have gone, until you came to this place.'

³² And concerning this matter you did not believe the Lord our God,

³³ who goes before you in the way to choose you a place, guiding you in the fire by night, showing you the way by which you should go, and a cloud by day.

The Penalty for Israel's Rebellion

³⁴ 'And the Lord heard the voice of your words, and being greatly provoked, He swore an oath, saying,

³⁵ 'Not one of these men shall see this good land, which I swore to their fathers,

³⁶ except Caleb the son of Jephunneh, he shall see it; and to him I will give the land on which he went up, and to his sons, because he attended to the things of the Lord.'

³⁷ And the Lord was angry with me for your sake, saying, 'Neither shall you by any means enter therein.

³⁸ Joshua the son of Nun, who stands by you, he shall enter in there; strengthen him, for he shall cause Israel to inherit it.

³⁹ And every young child who this day knows not good or evil, they shall enter therein, and to them I will give it, and they shall inherit it.'

⁴⁰ And you turned and marched into the wilderness, in the way by the Red Sea.

⁴¹ 'And you answered and said, 'We have sinned before the Lord our God; we will go up and fight according to all that the Lord our God has commanded us.' And everyone, having taken up their weapons of war, and being gathered together, went up to the mountain.

⁴² And the Lord said to me, 'Tell them, "You shall not go up, neither shall you fight, for I am not with you; lest you be destroyed before your enemies."'

⁴³ "And I spoke to you, and you did not listen to me; and you transgressed the commandment of the Lord; and you forced your way and went up into the mountain.

⁴⁴ And the Amorite who dwelt in that mountain came out to meet you, and pursued you as bees do, and wounded you from Seir to Hormah.

⁴⁵ And you sat down and wept before the Lord our God, and the Lord would not listen to your voice, neither did He take heed to you.

⁴⁶ And you dwelt in Kadesh many days, as many days as you dwelt *there*.

DEUTERONOMY CHAPTER 2

The Desert Years

¹ 'Then we turned and departed into the wilderness, by the way of the Red Sea, as the Lord spoke to me, and we circled around Mount Seir for many days.

² And the Lord said to me,

³ 'You have circled around this mountain for long enough; turn therefore toward the north.

4 And command the people, saying, "You are going through the territory of your brothers the children of Esau, who dwell in Seir; and they shall fear you, and dread you greatly.

5 Do not engage in war against them, for I will not give you of their land, *not* even enough to set your foot upon, for I have given Mount Seir to the children of Esau as an inheritance.

6 Buy food from them for money, and eat, and you shall receive water from them by measure for money, and drink.

7 For the Lord our God has blessed you in every work of your hands. Consider how you went through that great and terrible wilderness—behold, the Lord your God *has been* with you for forty years; you did not lack anything.'"

8 'And we passed by our brothers the children of Esau, who dwelt in Seir, by the way of *the* Arabah from Elath and from Ezion Geber; and we turned and passed by the way of the desert of Moab.

9 And the Lord said to me, "Do not quarrel with the Moabites, and do not engage in war with them; for I will not give you of their land for an inheritance, for I have given Ar to the children of Lot, to inherit."

10 Formerly the Emim dwelt in it, a great and numerous nation and powerful, like the Anakim.

11 These also shall be accounted as Rephaim, like the Anakim; and the Moabites call them Emim.

12 And the Horites dwelt in Seir before, and the sons of Esau destroyed them, and utterly consumed them from before them; and they dwelt in their place, as Israel did to the land of his inheritance, which the Lord gave to them.

13 "Now then, arise and depart, and cross over the Valley of Zered."

14 'And the days in which we traveled from Kadesh Barnea, till we crossed over the Valley of Zered, *were* thirty-eight years, until the whole generation of the men of war had failed, dying out of the camp, as the Lord God had sworn to them.

15 And the hand of the Lord was upon them, to destroy them out of the midst of the camp, until they were consumed.

16 'And it came to pass when all the men of war dying out of the midst of the people had fallen,

17 that the Lord spoke to me, saying,

18 "You shall pass over this day the borders of Moab, to Ar;

19 and you shall draw near to the children of Ammon: do not quarrel with them, nor wage war with them; for I will not give you of the land of the children of Ammon for an inheritance, because I have given it to the children of Lot for an inheritance."

20 (It shall be accounted a land for the Rephaim, for the Rephaim dwelt there before, and the Ammonites call them Zamzummim.

21 A great nation and populous, and mightier than you, as also the Anakim; yet the Lord destroyed them from before them, and they inherited *their land*, and they dwelt *there* instead of them until this day.

22 As they did to the children of Esau that dwell in Seir, even as they destroyed the Horite from before them, and inherited their country, and dwelt *therein* instead of them until this day.

23 And the Avim who dwell in Asedoth to Gaza, and the Cappadocians who came out of Cappadocia, destroyed them, and dwelt in their place.)

24 "Now then arise and depart, and pass over the valley of Ar; behold, I have delivered into your hands Sihon the king of Heshbon the Amorite, and his land. Begin to inherit *it*; engage in war with him this day.

25 Begin to put your terror and your fear on the face of all the nations under heaven, who shall be troubled when they have heard your name, and shall be in anguish before you."

Defeat of King Sihon

26 'And I sent ambassadors from the Wilderness of Kedemoth to Sihon king of Heshbon with peaceable words, saying,

27 'I will pass through your land; I will go by the road, I will not turn aside to the right hand or to the left.

28 You shall give me food for money, and I will eat; and you shall give me water for money, and I will drink; I will only go through on my feet:

29 as the sons of Esau did to me, who dwelt in Seir, and the Moabites who dwelt in Ar, until I have passed the Jordan, into the land which the Lord our God gives us.'

30 And Sihon king of Heshbon would not allow us to pass by him, because the Lord our God hardened his spirit, and made his heart stubborn, that he might be delivered into your hands, as it is this day.

31 And the Lord said to me, 'Behold, I have begun to deliver before you Sihon the king of Heshbon the Amorite, and his land: begin to inherit his land.'

32 And Sihon the king of Heshbon came forth to meet us, he and all his people to war at Jahaz.

33 And the Lord our God delivered him before our face, and we struck him, and his sons, and all his people.

34 And we took possession of all his cities at that time, and we utterly destroyed every city in succession, and their wives, and their children; we left no living prey.

35 Only we took the livestock captive, and took the spoil of the cities.

36 From Ar, which is by the brink of the brook of Arnon, and the city which is in the valley, and as far as the mount of Gilead; there was not a city which escaped us: the Lord our God delivered all of them into our hands.

37 Only we did not draw near to the children of Ammon, even all the parts bordering on the brook Jabbok, and the cities in the mountain country, as the Lord our God commanded us.

DEUTERONOMY CHAPTER 3

Defeat of King Og

[1] 'And we turned and went by the way leading to Bashan. And Og the king of Bashan came out to meet us, he and all his people, to battle at Edrei.

[2] And the Lord said to me, 'Do not fear him, for I have delivered him and all his people, and all his land, into your hands; and you shall do to him as you did to Sihon king of the Amorites who dwelt in Heshbon.'

[3] And the Lord our God delivered him into our hands, even Og the king of Bashan, and all his people; and we struck him until we left none of his descendants.

[4] And we mastered all his cities at that time; there was not a city which we did not take from them; sixty cities, all the country round about Argob, belonging to King Og in Bashan;

[5] all strong cities, lofty walls, gates and bars, besides the very many cities of the Perizzites.

[6] We utterly destroyed *them* as we dealt with Sihon the king of Heshbon, so we utterly destroyed every city in order, and the women and children,

[7] and all the cattle; and we took for a prey to ourselves the spoil of the cities.

[8] And we took at that time the land out of the hands of the two kings of the Amorites, who were beyond the Jordan, *extending* from the brook of Arnon even unto Hermon.

[9] (The Phoenicians call Hermon Sirion, but the Amorite calls it Senir).

[10] All the cities of Misor, and all Gilead, and all Bashan as far as Salcha and Edrei, cities of the kingdom of Og in Bashan.

[11] For only Og the king of Bashan was left of the Rephaim. Behold, his bed *was* a bed of iron; behold, *it is* in the chief city of the children of Ammon; the length of it *is* nine cubits, and the breadth of it four cubits, according to the cubit of a man.

[12] 'And we inherited that land at that time from Ar, which is by the border of the River Arnon, and half the mount of Gilead; and I gave his cities to Reuben and to Gad.

[13] And the rest of Gilead, and all Bashan the kingdom of Og I gave to the half-tribe of Manasseh, and all the country round about Argob, all that Bashan; it shall be accounted the land of Rephaim.

[14] And Jair the son of Manasseh took all the country round about Argob as far as the borders of Gargasi and Machathi: he called them by his name Bashan Thavoth Jair, until this day.

[15] And to Machir I gave Gilead.

[16] And to Reuben and to Gad I gave *the land* under Gilead as far as the brook of Arnon, the border between the brook and as far as Jabbok; the brook *is* the border to the children of Ammon.

[17] And the Arabah and the Jordan *are* the boundaries of Chinnereth, even to the Sea of the Arabah, the Salt Sea under Asedoth Pisga eastward.

[18] 'And I commanded you at that time, saying, 'The Lord your God has given you this land by lot: arm yourselves, everyone *that is* powerful, and go before your brothers the children of Israel.

[19] Only your wives and your children and your livestock (I know that you have much livestock), let them dwell in your cities which I have given you;

[20] until the Lord your God give your brothers rest, as also He has given to you, and they also shall inherit the land, which the Lord our God gives them on the other side of the Jordan; then you shall return, each one to his inheritance which I have given you.'

[21] And I commanded Joshua at that time, saying, 'Your eyes have seen all things which the Lord our God did to these two kings; so shall the Lord our God do to all the kingdoms against which you shall cross over.

[22] You shall not be afraid of them, because the Lord our God Himself shall fight for you.'

Moses Views Canaan from Pisgah

[23] 'And I pleaded with the Lord at that time, saying,

[24] 'Lord God, You have begun to show to Your servant Your strength and Your power, and Your mighty hand and Your outstretched arm: for what god is there in heaven or on earth who will do as You have done, and according to Your might?

[25] I will therefore go over and see this good land that is beyond the Jordan, this good mountain, and Lebanon.'

[26] But the Lord showed me no regard because of you, and He would not listen to me; and the Lord said to me, 'Enough already, do not speak of this matter to Me anymore!

[27] Go up to the top of the quarried rock, and look with your eyes towards the west, the north, the south, and the east, and behold *it* with your eyes, for you shall not cross over this Jordan.

[28] And command Joshua, and strengthen him, and encourage him; for he shall go before the face of this people, and he shall give them the inheritance of all the land which you have seen.' [29] And we stayed in the valley near Beth Peor.

DEUTERONOMY CHAPTER 4

Moses Commands Obedience

[1] 'And now, O Israel, hear the statutes and judgments, *hear* all that I teach you this day to do, that you may live, and be multiplied, and that you may go in and inherit the land, which the Lord God of your fathers gives to you.

[2] You shall not add to the word which I command you, and you shall not take from it: keep the commandments of the Lord our God, all that I command you this day.

[3] Your eyes have seen all that the Lord our God did in Baal Peor; for every man that went after Baal of Peor, the Lord your God has utterly destroyed him from among you.

4 But you that kept close to the Lord your God are all alive this day.

5 Behold, I have shown you the statutes and judgments as the Lord has commanded me, that you should do so in the land into which you go, to inherit it.

6 And you shall keep and do them: for this is your wisdom and understanding before all nations, as many as shall hear all these ordinances; and they shall say, 'Behold, this great nation *is* a wise and understanding people.

7 For what manner of nation *is so* great, which has God so near to them as the Lord our God *is* in all things in whatsoever we may call upon Him?

8 And what manner of nation *is so* great, which has righteous statutes and judgments according to all this law, which I set before you this day?'

9 'Take heed to yourself, and guard your heart diligently: forget not any of the things, which your eyes have seen, and let them not depart from your heart all the days of your life; and you shall teach your sons and your sons' sons,

10 *even the things that happened in* the day in which you stood before the Lord our God in Horeb in the day of the assembly; for the Lord said to me, 'Gather the people to Me, and let them hear My words, that they may learn to fear Me all the days which they live upon the earth, and they shall teach their sons.'

11 And you drew near and stood under the mountain; and the mountain burned with fire up to heaven: *there was* darkness, blackness, *and a* tempest.

12 And the Lord spoke to you out of the midst of the fire a voice of words, which you heard: and you saw no likeness, only *you heard* a voice.

13 And He declared to you His covenant, which He commanded you to keep, even the Ten Commandments; and He wrote them on two tablets of stone.

14 And the Lord commanded me at that time, to teach you statutes and judgments, that you should do them on the land, into which you go to inherit it.

15 'And take careful heed to your hearts, for you saw no form in the day in which the Lord spoke to you in Horeb in the mountain, out of the midst of the fire;

16 lest you transgress, and make to yourselves a carved image, any kind of figure, the likeness of male or female,

17 the likeness of any beast of those that are on the earth, the likeness of any winged bird which flies under heaven,

18 the likeness of any reptile which creeps on the earth, the likeness of any fish of those which are in the waters under the earth;

19 and lest having looked up to the sky, and having seen the sun and the moon and the stars, and all the heavenly bodies, you should go astray and worship them, and serve them, which the Lord your God has distributed to all the nations under heaven.

20 But God took you, and led you forth out of the land of Egypt, out of the iron furnace, out of Egypt, to be to Him a people of inheritance, as it is this day.

21 And the Lord God was angry with me for the things which you said, and swore that I would not go over this Jordan, and that I would not enter into the land, which the Lord your God has given to you for an inheritance.

22 For I am to die in this land, and shall not pass over this Jordan; but you are to pass over, and shall inherit this good land.

23 Take heed to yourselves, lest you forget the covenant of the Lord our God, which He made with you, and you transgress, and make to yourselves a graven image of any of the things concerning which the Lord your God has commanded you.

24 For the Lord your God is a consuming fire, a jealous God.

25 And when you have begotten sons and grandsons, and you have dwelt a long time on the land, and have transgressed, and made a graven image of any kind, and have done wickedly before the Lord your God to provoke Him;

26 I call heaven and earth this day to witness against you, that you shall surely perish from off the land, into which you go across the Jordan to inherit it; you shall not prolong your days upon it, but shall be utterly cut off.

27 And the Lord shall scatter you among all nations, and you shall be left few in number among all the nations, among which the Lord shall bring you.

28 And there you shall serve other gods, the works of the hands of men, *of* wood and stone, which cannot see, nor can they hear, nor eat, nor smell.

29 And there you shall seek the Lord your God, and you shall find Him whenever you shall seek Him with all your heart, and with all your soul in your affliction.

30 And all these things shall come upon you in the last days, and you shall turn to the Lord your God, and shall hearken to His voice.

31 Because the Lord your God *is* a merciful God; He will not forsake you, nor destroy you; He will not forget the covenant of your fathers, which the Lord has sworn to them.

32 'Ask of the former days which were before you, from the day when God created man upon the earth; from one end of heaven to the other, if such a great event as this has ever transpired; if such a thing has ever been heard;

33 if a nation has heard the voice of the living God speaking out of the midst of the fire, as you have heard, and have lived! 34 Or did God *ever* try to go and take for Himself a nation out of the midst of *another* nation by trials, by signs, by wonders, by war, by a mighty hand and an outstretched arm, and by great sights, according to all the things which the Lord our God did in Egypt in your sight?

35 So that you should know that the Lord your God, He is God, and there is none beside Him.

36 His voice was made audible from heaven to instruct you, and He showed you His great fire upon the earth, and you heard His words out of the midst of the fire.

37 Because He loved your fathers, He also has chosen you, their descendants after them, and He Himself brought you out of Egypt by His great strength,

38 to destroy nations greater and stronger than you before your face, to bring you in, to give you their land to inherit, as you have this day.

39 And you shall know this day, and shall consider in your heart, that the Lord your God, He *is* God in heaven above, and on earth below, and there is no one else besides Him.

40 *Therefore* you shall keep His commandments and His statutes, all that I command you this day; that it may be well with you, and with your sons after you, that you may live long upon the earth, which the Lord your God is giving you forever.'

Cities of Refuge East of the Jordan

41 Then Moses separated three cities beyond the Jordan on the east,

42 that the manslayer might flee there, *one* who has killed his neighbor unintentionally, and should not have hated him in times past, and he shall flee to one of these cities and live:

43 Bezer in the wilderness, in the plain country of Reuben, and Ramoth in Gilead *belonging to* Gad, and Golan in Bashan *belonging to* Manasseh.

Transition to the Second Address

44 This *is* the law which Moses set before the children of Israel.

45 These *are* the testimonies, and the statutes, and the judgments which Moses spoke to the sons of Israel, when they came out of the land of Egypt,

46 on the other side of the Jordan, in the valley near Beth Peor, in the land of Sihon king of the Amorites, who dwelt in Heshbon, whom Moses and the sons of Israel killed when they came out of the land of Egypt.

47 And they inherited his land, and the land of Og king of Bashan, two kings of the Amorites, who were beyond the Jordan towards the east,

48 from Ar, which is on the border of the brook Arnon, even to Mount Zion, which is Hermon.

49 All the Arabah beyond the Jordan eastward under Asedoth hewn in the rock.

DEUTERONOMY CHAPTER 5

The Ten Commandments

1 And Moses called all Israel, and said to them, "Hear, O Israel, the ordinances and statutes, all that I speak in your ears this day, and you shall learn them, and observe to do them.

2 The Lord your God made a covenant with you in Horeb.

3 The Lord did not make this covenant with your fathers, but with you: you are all here alive this day.

4 The Lord spoke to you face to face in the mountain out of the midst of the fire.

5 And I stood between the Lord and you at that time to report to you the words of the Lord, for you were afraid because of the fire, and you did not go up to the mountain. *He said,*

6 'I am the Lord your God, who brought you out of the land of Egypt, out of the house of bondage.

7 'You shall have no other gods before Me.

8 'You shall not make for yourself an image, nor likeness of anything, whatever things that are in heaven above, or that is in the earth below, or that are in the waters beneath the earth.

9 You shall not bow down to them, nor shall you serve them; for I am the Lord your God, a jealous God, visiting the sins of the fathers upon the children to the third and fourth generation to them that hate Me, 10 and showing mercy to thousands of them that love Me, and that keep My commandments.

11 'You shall not take the name of the Lord your God in vain, for the Lord your God will certainly not acquit him that takes His name in vain.

12 'Observe the Sabbath day—set it apart, as the Lord your God has commanded you.

13 Six days you shall work, and you shall do all of your works;

14 but on the seventh day *is* the Sabbath of the Lord your God: you shall do no work on *that day*, neither you, your son, your daughter, your male servant, your female servant, your ox, your donkey, your livestock, nor the stranger that sojourns in the midst of you; that your male servant may rest, and your maid and your ox, as well as you.

15 And you shall remember that you were a slave in the land of Egypt, and the Lord your God brought you out from there with a mighty hand, and an outstretched arm; therefore the Lord has commanded you to observe the Sabbath day, and to set it apart.

16 'Honor your father and your mother, as the Lord your God has commanded you; that it may be well with you, and that you may live long upon the land, which the Lord your God gives to you.

17 'You shall not commit murder.

18 'You shall not commit adultery.

19 'You shall not steal.

20 'You shall not bear false witness against your neighbor.

21 'You shall not covet your neighbor's wife; you shall not covet your neighbor's house, nor his field, nor his male servant, nor his maid, nor his ox, nor his donkey, nor any beast of his, nor anything that belongs to your neighbor.'

22 "These words the Lord spoke to all the assembly of you in the mountain out of the midst of the fire—there *was* darkness, blackness, a storm, *and* a loud voice—and He added nothing else, and He wrote them on two tablets of stone, and He gave them to me.

Moses the Mediator of God's Will

23 "And it came to pass when you heard the voice out of the midst of the fire, (for the mountain burned with fire) that you came to me, even all the heads of your tribes, and your elders,

24 and you said, 'Behold, the Lord our God has shown us His glory, and we have heard His voice out of the midst of the fire: this day we have seen that God shall speak to man, and he shall live.

25 And now do not let us die, for this great fire will consume us, if we shall hear the voice of the Lord our God anymore, and we shall die.

26 For what man *is there,* who has heard the voice of the living God, speaking out of the midst of the fire, as we *have heard,* and shall live?

27 But draw near, and hear all that the Lord our God shall say, and you shall speak to us all things whatsoever the Lord our God shall speak to you, and we will hear, and do.'

28 And the Lord heard the voice of your words as you spoke to me; and the Lord said to me, 'I have heard the voice of the words of this people, even all things that they have said to you. *They have* well *said* all that they have spoken.

29 O that there were such a heart in them, that they would fear Me, and keep My commandments at all times, that it might be well with them, and with their sons forever!

30 Go, say to them, 'Return to your houses,'

31 but you stand here with Me, and I will tell you all the commands and the statutes and the judgments which you shall teach them, and let them do so in the land which I give them for an inheritance.

32 And you shall take heed to do as the Lord your God has commanded you; you shall not turn aside to the right or to the left,

33 according to all the way which the Lord your God commanded you to walk in it, that He may give you rest; and that it may be well with you, and you may prolong your days on the land which you shall inherit.

DEUTERONOMY CHAPTER 6

The Great Commandment

1 "And these *are* the commands, and the statutes, and the judgments, as many as the Lord our God gave commandment, to teach you to do so in the land on which you enter to inherit it.

2 That you may fear the Lord your God, and keep all His statutes, and His commandments, which I command you today, you, your sons, and your grandsons, all the days of your life, that you may live many days.

3 Therefore hear, O Israel, and observe to do them, that it may be well with you, and that you may be greatly multiplied, as the Lord God of your fathers said that He would give you a land flowing with milk and honey. And these *are* the statutes and the judgments, which the Lord

commanded the children of Israel in the wilderness, when they had gone forth from the land of Egypt.

4 "Hear, O Israel, the Lord our God is one Lord.

5 And you shall love the Lord your God with all your mind, and with all your soul, and with all your strength.

6 "And these words, all that I command you this day, shall be in your heart and in your soul.

7 And you shall teach them to your children, and you shall speak of them sitting in the house, and walking on the road, and lying down, and rising up.

8 And you shall fasten them for a sign upon your hand, and it shall be immovable before your eyes.

9 And you shall write them on the lintels of your houses and of your gates.

Caution Against Disobedience

10 "And it shall come to pass, when the Lord your God has brought you into the land which He swore to your fathers, to Abraham, and to Isaac, and to Jacob, to give you great and beautiful cities which you did not build,

11 houses full of all good things which you did not fill, wells dug in the rock which you did not dig, vineyards and olive trees which you did not plant, then having eaten and been filled,

12 beware lest you forget the Lord your God that brought you forth out of the land of Egypt, out of the house of bondage.

13 You shall fear the Lord your God, and Him only shall you serve; and you shall cleave to Him, and by His name you shall swear.

14 Do not go after other gods, of the gods of the nations that are around you,

15 for the Lord your God in the midst of you *is* a jealous God, lest the Lord your God be very angry with you, and destroy you from off the face of the earth.

16 "You shall not tempt the Lord your God, as you tempted Him in the temptation.

17 You shall by all means keep the commandments of the Lord your God, the testimonies, and the statutes, which He has commanded you.

18 And you shall do that which is pleasing and good before the Lord your God, that it may be well with you, and that you may go in and inherit the good land, which the Lord swore to your fathers,

19 to chase all your enemies from before your face, as the Lord has spoken.

20 "And it shall come to pass, when your son shall ask you at a future time, saying, 'What are the testimonies, and the statutes, and the judgments, which the Lord our God has commanded us?'

21 Then shall you say to your son, 'We were slaves to Pharaoh in the land of Egypt, and the Lord brought us forth from there with a mighty hand, and with an outstretched arm.

²² And the Lord did great signs and wonders in Egypt, on Pharaoh and on his house before us.

²³ And He brought us out from there to give us this land, which He swore to give to our fathers.

²⁴ And the Lord commanded us to observe all these ordinances; to fear the Lord our God, that it may be well with us forever, that we may live, as it is this day.

²⁵ And there shall be mercy to us, if we take heed to keep all these commandments before the Lord our God, as He has commanded us.'

DEUTERONOMY CHAPTER 7

A Chosen People

¹ "And when the Lord your God shall bring you into the land into which you go, to possess it, and shall remove great nations from before you, the Hittite, the Girgashite, the Amorite, the Canaanite, the Perizzite, the Hivite, and the Jebusite, seven nations *more* numerous and stronger than you,

² and the Lord your God shall deliver them into your hands, then you shall strike them; you shall utterly destroy them: 'you shall not make a covenant with them, neither shall you pity them;

³ neither shall you contract marriages with them; you shall not give your daughter to his son, and you shall not take his daughter to your son.

⁴ For he will draw away your son from Me, and he will serve other gods; and the Lord will be very angry with you, and will soon utterly destroy you.

⁵ But thus shall you do to them: you shall destroy their altars, and break down their pillars, and cut down their groves, and you shall burn with fire the graven images of their gods.

⁶ "For you are a holy people to the Lord your God; and the Lord your God chose you to be to Him a peculiar people beyond all nations that *are* upon the face of the earth.

⁷ It is not because you are more numerous than all *other* nations that the Lord has preferred you, and the Lord has chosen you: for you are fewer in number than all *other* nations. ⁸ But because the Lord has loved you, and He is keeping the oath which He swore to your fathers; the Lord has brought you out with a strong hand, and the Lord has redeemed you from the house of bondage, out of the hand of Pharaoh king of Egypt.

⁹ You shall know therefore, that the Lord your God, He *is* God, a faithful God, who keeps *His* covenant and mercy for them that love Him, and for those that keep His commandments to a thousand generations,

¹⁰ and who repays those that hate Him to their face, to utterly destroy them; and will not be slack with them that hate Him; He will repay them to their face.

¹¹ Therefore you shall keep the commands and the statutes and these judgments, which I command you this day to do.

Blessings for Obedience

¹² "And it shall come to pass when you shall have heard these statutes, and have kept and done them, that the Lord your God shall keep for you the covenant and the mercy, which He swore to your fathers.

¹³ And He will love you and bless you and multiply you; and He will bless the offspring of your body, and the fruit of your land, your grain, your wine, your oil, your herds of oxen, and the flocks of your sheep, on the land which the Lord swore to your fathers, to give to you.

¹⁴ You shall be blessed beyond all *other* nations; there shall not be among you an impotent or barren one, or among your livestock.

¹⁵ And the Lord your God shall remove all sickness from you; and none of the evil diseases of Egypt, which you have seen, and all that you have known, will He lay upon you; but He will lay them upon all those that hate you.

¹⁶ And you shall eat all the spoils of the nations which the Lord your God gives to you; your eye shall not spare them, and you shall not serve their gods; for this is an offense to you.

¹⁷ "But if you should say in your heart, 'This nation *is* greater than I, how shall I be able to destroy them utterly?'

¹⁸ You shall not fear them; you shall surely remember all that the Lord your God did to Pharaoh and to all the Egyptians;

¹⁹ the great trials which your eyes have seen, those signs and great wonders, the strong hand and the outstretched arm; how the Lord your God brought you forth: so the Lord your God will do to all the nations, whom you fear in their presence.

²⁰ And the Lord your God shall send against them the hornets, until those that are left and those that are hidden from you are utterly destroyed.

²¹ You shall not be wounded before them, because the Lord your God in the midst of you *is* a great and powerful God.

²² And the Lord your God shall consume these nations before you by little and little: you shall not be able to consume them speedily, lest the land become desert, and the wild beasts of the field be multiplied against you.

²³ And the Lord your God shall deliver them into your hands, and you shall destroy them with a great destruction, until you have utterly destroyed them.

²⁴ And He shall deliver their kings into your hands, and you shall destroy their name from that place; none shall stand up in opposition before you, until you have utterly destroyed them.

²⁵ You shall burn with fire the graven images of their gods: you shall not covet *their* silver, neither shall you take to yourself gold from them, lest you be snared by it, for it is an abomination to the Lord your God.

²⁶ And you shall not bring an abomination into your house, so should you be an accursed thing like it; you shall utterly detest it, and altogether abominate it, because it is an accursed thing.

DEUTERONOMY CHAPTER 8

A Warning Not to Forget God in Prosperity

[1] "You shall observe to do all the commands which I charge you today, that you may live and be multiplied, and enter in and inherit the land, which the Lord your God swore to your fathers.

[2] And you shall remember all the way which the Lord your God has led you in the wilderness, that He might afflict you, and try you, and that the things in your heart might be made manifest, whether you would keep His commandments or not.

[3] And He afflicted you and let you hunger, and fed you with manna, which your fathers knew not; that He might teach you that man shall not live by bread alone, but by every word that proceeds out of the mouth of God shall man live.

[4] Your garments did not grow old from off you, your shoes were not worn from off you, your feet were not *painfully* hardened, behold, for these forty years!

[5] And you shall know in your heart, that as if any man should chasten his son, so the Lord your God will chasten you.

[6] And you shall keep the commands of the Lord your God, to walk in His ways, and to fear Him.

[7] For the Lord your God will bring you into a good and extensive land, where there are torrents of waters, and fountains of deep places issuing through the plains and through the mountains;

[8] a land of wheat and barley, *with* vines, figs, and pomegranates; a land of olive oil and honey;

[9] a land on which you shall not eat your bread with poverty, and you shall not need anything upon it; a land whose stones are iron, and out of its mountains you shall dig copper.

[10] And you shall eat and be filled, and shall bless the Lord your God on the good land, which He has given you.

[11] "Take heed to yourself that you do not forget the Lord your God, so as not to keep His commands, and His judgments, and His statutes, which I command you this day,

[12] lest when you have eaten and are full, and have built nice houses, and dwelt in them;

[13] and your oxen and your sheep are multiplied to you, and your silver and your gold are multiplied to you, and all your possessions are multiplied to you,

[14] *that* you should be exalted in your heart, and forget the Lord your God, who brought you out of the land of Egypt, out of the house of bondage;

[15] who brought you through that great and terrible wilderness, where the biting serpent *is*, and the scorpion, and drought, where there was no water; who brought you a fountain of water out of the flinty rock;

[16] who fed you with manna in the wilderness, which you did not know, and your fathers did not know; that He might afflict you, and thoroughly test you, and do you good in your latter days.

[17] Lest you should say in your heart, 'My strength, and the power of my *own* hand have worked for me this great wealth!'

[18] But you shall remember the Lord your God, that He gives you strength to get wealth; even that He may establish His covenant, which the Lord swore to your fathers, as it is this day.

[19] And it shall come to pass, *that* if you do at all forget the Lord your God, and should go after other gods, and serve them, and worship them, I call heaven and earth to witness against you this day, that you shall surely perish!

[20] As also the other nations which the Lord God destroys before your face, so shall you perish, because you would not heed the voice of the Lord your God.

DEUTERONOMY CHAPTER 9

The Consequences of Rebelling Against God

[1] "Hear, O Israel: You go this day across the Jordan to inherit nations greater and stronger than yourselves, cities great and walled up to heaven;

[2] a people great and many and tall, the sons of Anak, whom you know, and concerning whom you have heard *it said*, 'Who can stand before the children of Anak?'

[3] And you shall know today, that the Lord your God, He shall go before your face; He is a consuming fire; He shall destroy them, and He shall turn them back before you, and shall destroy them quickly, as the Lord had said to you.

[4] Do not say in your heart, when the Lord your God has destroyed these nations before your face, *that* 'For my righteousness the Lord brought me in to inherit this good land.'

[5] Not for your righteousness, nor for the holiness of your heart, do you go in to inherit their land, but because of the wickedness of these nations, the Lord shall destroy them from before you, and that He may establish the covenant, which the Lord swore to our fathers, to Abraham, Isaac, and Jacob.

[6] And you shall know this day, that *it is* not for your righteousnesses that the Lord your God gives to you this good land to inherit, for you are a stiff-necked people.

[7] "Remember, *and* do not forget, how much you provoked the Lord your God in the wilderness; from the day that you came forth out of Egypt, even till you came into this place, you continued to be disobedient toward the Lord.

[8] Also in Horeb you provoked the Lord, and the Lord was angry with you, to destroy you;

[9] when I went up into the mountain to receive the tablets of stone, the tablets of the covenant, which the Lord made with you, and I was in the mountain forty days and forty nights, I ate no bread and drank no water.

[10] And the Lord gave me the two tablets of stone written with the finger of God, and on them there had been written

all the words which the Lord spoke to you in the mountain, in the day of the assembly.

[11] And it came to pass after forty days and forty nights, *that* the Lord gave me the two tablets of stone, the tablets of the covenant.

[12] And the Lord said to me, 'Arise, go down quickly from here, for your people whom you brought out of the land of Egypt have transgressed; they have gone aside quickly out of the way which I commanded them, and have made themselves a molten image.'

[13] "And the Lord spoke to me, saying, 'I have spoken to you once and again, saying, "I have seen this people, and behold, they are a stiff-necked people."

[14] And now I shall utterly destroy them, and I will blot out their name from under heaven, and will make of you a nation great and strong, and more numerous than this.'

[15] And I turned and went down from the mountain; and the mountain burned with fire to heaven; and the two tablets of the testimonies *were* in my two hands.

[16] And when I saw that you had sinned against the Lord your God, and had made for yourselves a molten image, and had gone astray out of the way, which the Lord commanded you to keep;

[17] then I took hold of the two tablets, and cast them out of my hands, and broke them before you.

[18] And I made my petition before the Lord as also at the first forty days and forty nights: I ate no bread and drank no water, on account of all your sins which you sinned in doing evil before the Lord God, to provoke Him.

[19] And I was greatly terrified because of the wrath and anger, because the Lord was provoked with you utterly, to destroy you; yet the Lord hearkened to me at this time also.

[20] And He was angry with Aaron to destroy him utterly, and I prayed for Aaron also at that time.

[21] And your sin which you had made, the calf, I took *it*, and I burned it with fire, and pounded it and ground it down till it became fine; and it became like dust, and I cast the dust into the brook that descended from the mountain.

[22] "Also in the burning, and in the temptation, and at the Graves of Lust, you provoked the Lord.

[23] And when the Lord sent you forth from Kadesh Barnea, saying, 'Go up and inherit the land which I give to you,' then you disobeyed the word of the Lord your God, and did not believe Him, and you did not listen to His voice.

[24] You were disobedient in the things relating to the Lord from the day in which He became known to you.

[25] And I prayed before the Lord forty days and forty nights, the number that I prayed *before*, for the Lord said that He would utterly destroy you.

[26] "And I prayed to God, and said, 'O Lord, great God, do not destroy Your people and Your inheritance, whom You redeemed, whom You brought out of the land of Egypt with Your great power, and with Your strong hand, and with Your outstretched arm.

[27] Remember Abraham, Isaac, and Jacob Your servants, to whom You swore by Yourself: look not upon the hardness of heart of this people, and their wickedness, and their sins,

[28] lest the inhabitants of the land from which You brought us out speak, saying, 'Because the Lord could not bring them into the land of which He spoke to them, and because He hated them, has He brought them forth to slay them in the wilderness.'

[29] And these *are* Your people and Your portion, whom You brought out of the land of Egypt with Your great strength, and with Your mighty hand, and with Your outstretched arm.

DEUTERONOMY CHAPTER 10

The Second Pair of Tablets

[1] "At that time the Lord said to me, 'Hew for yourself two stone tablets like the first, and come up to Me into the mountain, and you shall make for yourself an ark of wood.

[2] And I shall write upon the tablets the words which were on the first tablets which you broke, and you shall put them into the ark.'

[3] So I made an ark of boards of incorruptible wood, and I hewed tablets of stone like the first, and I went up to the mountain, and the two tablets were in my hand.

[4] And He wrote upon the tablets according to the first writing, the Ten Commandments, which the Lord spoke to you in the mountain out of the midst of the fire, and the Lord gave them to me.

[5] And I turned and came down from the mountain, and I put the tablets into the ark which I had made; and there they were, as the Lord commanded me."

[6] And the children of Israel departed from Beeroth of the sons of Jakim *to* Moserah; where Aaron died, and there he was buried, and Eleazar his son was priest in his place·

[7] From there they departed to Gudgodah; and from Gudgodah to Jotbathah, a land of torrents of water.

[8] At that time the Lord separated the tribe of Levi, to bear the ark of the covenant of the Lord, to stand near before the Lord, to minister and bless in His name, to this day.

[9] Therefore the Levites have no part nor inheritance among their brothers; the Lord Himself *is* their inheritance, as He said to them.

[10] And I remained in the mountain for forty days and forty nights. And the Lord heard me at that time also, and the Lord would not destroy you.

[11] And the Lord said to me, 'Go, set out before this people, and let them go in and inherit the land, which I swore to their fathers to give to them.'

The Essence of the Law

[12] "And now, O Israel, what does the Lord your God require of you, but to fear the Lord your God, and to walk in all His ways, and to love Him, and to serve the Lord your God with all your heart, and with all your soul;

13 to keep the commandments of the Lord your God, and His statutes, all that I command you this day, that it may be well with you?

14 Behold, the heaven and the heaven of heavens belong to the Lord your God, the earth and all things that are in it.

15 Only the Lord chose your fathers, to love them, and He chose out their descendants after them, *even* you, beyond all nations, as it is this day.

16 Therefore you shall circumcise the hardness of your heart, and you shall not stiffen your neck.

17 For the Lord your God, He *is the* God of gods and the Lord of lords, the great and mighty; the awesome God, who is no respector of persons, nor will He by any means accept a bribe;

18 executing judgment for the stranger and orphan and widow, and He loves the stranger, to give him food and clothing.

19 And you shall love the stranger; for you *also* were strangers in the land of Egypt.

20 You shall fear the Lord your God, and serve Him, and you shall cleave to Him, and shall swear by His name.

21 He *is* your boast, and He *is* your God, who has done in the midst of you all these great and glorious things, which your eyes have seen.

22 With seventy souls your fathers went down into Egypt; but the Lord your God has made you as the stars of heaven in multitude.

DEUTERONOMY CHAPTER 11

Rewards for Obedience

1 "Therefore you shall love the Lord your God, and shall observe His appointments, and His statutes, and His commandments, and His judgments, at all times.

2 And you shall know this day; for *I speak* not to your children, who know not and have not seen the discipline of the Lord your God, and His wonderful works, and His strong hand, and His outstretched arm,

3 and His miracles, and His wonders, which He did in the midst of Egypt on Pharaoh king of Egypt, and all his land;

4 and what He did to the army of the Egyptians, and to their chariots, and their cavalry, and their army; how He made the water of the Red Sea to overwhelm the face of them as they pursued after you, and the Lord destroyed them until this day; 5 and all the things which He did to you in the wilderness until you came into this place;

6 and all the things that He did to Dathan and Abiram the sons of Eliab the son of Reuben, whom the earth, opening her mouth, swallowed up, and their houses, and their tents, and all their substance that was with them, in the midst of all Israel;

7 for your eyes have seen all the mighty works of the Lord, which He did among you to this day.

8 "And you shall keep all His commandments, as many as I command you this day, that you may live and be multiplied;

and that you may go in and inherit the land, into which you go across the Jordan, to inherit it;

9 that you may live long upon the land, which the Lord swore to your fathers to give to them, and to their descendants after them, a land flowing with milk and honey.

10 For the land into which you go to inherit it is not as the land of Egypt, from which you came out of, where they sowed the seed, and watered it with their feet, as a garden of herbs;

11 but the land into which you go to inherit it is a land of mountains and plains; it shall drink the water of the rain of heaven.

12 A land which the Lord your God surveys continually, the eyes of the Lord your God are upon it from the beginning of the year to the end of the year.

13 "Now if you will indeed hearken to all the commandments which I charge you this day, to love the Lord your God, and to serve Him with all your heart, and with all your soul,

14 then He shall give to your land the early and latter rain in its season, and you shall bring in your grain, your wine, and your oil.

15 And He shall give food in your fields to your livestock; and when you have eaten and are full,

16 take heed to yourself that your heart be not puffed up, and you transgress, and serve other gods, and worship them;

17 and the Lord be angry with you, and restrain the heavens; and there shall not be rain, and the earth shall not yield its fruit, and you shall perish quickly from off the good land, which the Lord has given you.

18 "And you shall store these words in your heart and in your soul, and you shall bind them as a sign on your hand, and it shall be fixed before your eyes.

19 And you shall teach them to your children, so as to speak about them when you sit in the house, and when you walk by the way, and when you sleep, and when you rise up.

20 And you shall write them on the doorposts of your houses, and on your gates;

21 that your days may be long, and the days of your children, upon the land which the Lord swore to your fathers to give to them, as the days of heaven upon the earth.

22 "And it shall come to pass that if you will indeed hearken to all these commandments which I charge you to observe this day, to love the Lord our God, and to walk in all His ways, and to cleave close to Him;

23 then the Lord shall cast out all these nations before you, and you shall inherit great nations stronger than yourselves.

24 Every place on which the sole of your foot shall tread shall be yours; from the wilderness and Lebanon, and from the great river, the River Euphrates, even as far as the Western Sea shall be your coasts.

25 No one shall stand before you; and the Lord your God will put the fear of you and the dread of you on the face of all the land, on which you shall tread, as He told you.

26 "Behold, I set before you this day a blessing and a curse:

27 a blessing, if you hearken to the commands of the Lord your God, all that I command you this day;

28 and a curse, if you do not hearken to the commands of the Lord our God, as many as I command you this day, and you wander from the way which I have commanded you, having gone to serve other gods, which you do not know.

29 And it shall come to pass when the Lord your God shall have brought you into the land into which you go over to inherit it, then you shall put blessing on Mount Gerizim, and the curse upon Mount Ebal.

30 Behold, are not these beyond the Jordan, behind, westward in the land of Canaan, which lies westward near Gilgal, beside the terebinth trees of Moreh?

31 For you are passing over the Jordan, to go in and inherit the land, which the Lord our God gives you to inherit always, and you shall dwell in it.

32 And you shall take heed to observe all His statutes, and these judgments, as many as I set before you this day.

DEUTERONOMY CHAPTER 12

Pagan Shrines to be Destroyed

1 "And these *are* the ordinances and the judgments, which you shall observe to do in the land, which the Lord God of your fathers gives you for an inheritance, all the days which you live upon the land.

2 You shall utterly destroy all the places in which they served their gods, whose *land* you inherit, on the high mountains and on the hills, and under the thick tree.

3 And you shall destroy their altars, and break in pieces their pillars, and you shall cut down their groves, and you shall burn with fire the graven images of their gods, and you shall abolish their name out of that place.

4 You shall not do so to the Lord your God.

5 But in the place which the Lord your God shall choose in one of your cities to name His name there, and to be called upon, you shall even seek *Him* out and go there.

6 And you shall carry there your burnt offerings, and your sacrifices, and your firstfruits, and your vowed offerings, and your freewill offerings, and your offerings of thanksgiving, the firstborn of your herds, and of your flocks.

7 And you shall eat there before the Lord your God, and you shall rejoice in all the things on which you shall lay your hand, you and your houses, as the Lord your God has blessed you.

8 You shall not do altogether as we do here this day, every man that which is pleasing in his own sight.

9 For as yet you have not arrived at the rest and the inheritance, which the Lord our God gives you.

10 And you shall cross over the Jordan, and shall dwell in the land, which the Lord our God takes as an inheritance for you; and He shall give you rest from all your enemies round about, and you shall dwell safely.

11 And there shall be a place which the Lord your God shall choose for His name to be called there, from which shall you bring all things that I order you this day; your burnt offerings, and your sacrifices, and your tithes, and the firstfruits of your hands, and every choice gift of yours, whatsoever you shall vow to the Lord your God.

12 And you shall rejoice before the Lord your God, you and your sons, and your daughters, and your male servants and your female servants, and the Levite that is at your gates; because he has no portion or inheritance with you.

13 Take heed to yourself that you offer not your burnt offerings in any place which you shall see;

14 except in the place which the Lord your God shall choose, in one of your tribes, there shall you offer your burnt offerings, and there shall you do all things whatsoever I charge you this day.

15 "But you shall kill according to all your desire, and shall eat flesh according to the blessing of the Lord your God, which He has given you in every city; the unclean that is within you and the clean shall eat it on equal terms, as the doe or the stag.

16 Only you shall not eat the blood; you shall pour it out on the ground as water.

17 You shall not be able to eat in your cities the tithe of your grain, and of your wine, and of your oil, the firstborn of your herd and of your flock, and all *your* vows, as many as you have vowed, and your thank offerings, and the firstfruits of your hands.

18 But before the Lord your God you shall eat it, in the place which the Lord your God shall choose for Himself; you, your son, your daughter, your male servant, your female servant, and the stranger that is within your gates; and you shall rejoice before the Lord your God, on whatsoever you shall lay your hand.

19 Take heed to yourself that you do not forsake the Levite all the time that you live upon the earth.

20 "And if the Lord your God shall enlarge your borders, as He said to you, and you shall say, 'I will eat flesh'; if your soul should desire to eat flesh, you shall eat flesh according to all the desire of your soul.

21 And if the place is far from you, which the Lord your God shall choose for Himself, that His name be called upon it, then you shall kill of your herd and of your flock which God shall have given you, even as I commanded you, and you shall eat in your cities according to the desire of your soul.

22 As the doe and the stag are eaten, so shall you eat it; the unclean in you and the clean shall eat it in like manner.

23 Take diligent heed that you eat no blood, for blood *is* the life of it; the life shall not be eaten with the flesh.

24 You shall not eat *it*; you shall pour it out on the ground as water.

25 You shall not eat it, that it may be well with you and with your sons after you, if you shall do that which is good and pleasing before the Lord your God.

26 But you shall take your holy things, if you have any, and your vowed offerings, and come to the place which the Lord your God shall choose to have His name named upon it.

[27] And you shall sacrifice your burnt offerings, you shall offer the flesh upon the altar of the Lord your God; but the blood of your sacrifices you shall pour out at the foot of the altar of the Lord your God, but the flesh you shall eat.

[28] Beware and hearken, and you shall do all the commands which I charge you, that it may be well with you and with your sons forever, if you shall do that which is pleasing and good before the Lord your God.

Warning Against Idolatry

[29] "And if the Lord your God shall utterly destroy the nations from before you, to which you go to possess, to inherit their land, and you shall inherit it, and dwell in their land;

[30] take heed to yourself that you do not desire to follow after those that have been destroyed from before you, saying, 'How do these nations act towards their gods? I will do likewise.'

[31] You shall not do so to your God; for they have sacrificed to their gods the abominations of the Lord which He hates, for they burn their sons and their daughters in *the* fire, to *sacrifice to* their gods.

[32] Every word that I command you this day, you shall observe to do: you shall not add to it, neither shall you take away from it.

DEUTERONOMY CHAPTER 13

[1] "And if there should arise within you a prophet, or one who dreams a dream, and he gives you a sign or a wonder,

[2] and the sign or the wonder come to pass which he spoke to you, saying, 'Let us go and serve other gods, which you know not';

[3] you shall not hearken to the words of that prophet, or the dreamer of that dream, because the Lord your God is testing you, to see whether you love your God with all your heart and with all your soul.

[4] You shall follow the Lord your God, and fear Him, and you shall hear His voice, and attach yourselves to Him.

[5] And that prophet or that dreamer of a dream shall die; for he has spoken to make you err from the Lord your God who brought you out of the land of Egypt, who redeemed you from bondage, to thrust you out of the way which the Lord your God commanded you to walk in. So shall you abolish the evil from among you.

[6] "And if your brother by your father or mother, or your son, or daughter, or your wife in your bosom, or friend who is equal to your own soul, should entice you secretly, saying, 'Let us go and serve other gods,' which neither you nor your fathers have known,

[7] of the gods of the nations that are round about you, who are near you or at a distance from you, from one end of the earth to the other;

[8] you shall not consent to him, neither shall you hearken to him; and your eye shall not spare him, you shall feel no regret for him, neither shall you at all protect him:

[9] you shall surely report concerning him, and your hands shall be upon him among the first to slay him, and the hands of all the people at the last.

[10] And they shall stone him with stones, and he shall die, because he sought to draw you away from the Lord your God who brought you out of the land of Egypt, out of the house of bondage.

[11] And all Israel shall hear, and fear, and shall not again do according to this evil thing among you.

[12] And if in one of your cities which the Lord God gives you to dwell in, you shall hear men saying,

[13] 'Evil men have gone out from you, and have caused all the inhabitants of their land to fall away, saying, 'Let us go and worship other gods', whom you knew not,'

[14] then you shall inquire and ask, and search diligently, and behold, *if* the thing is clearly true, and this abomination has taken place among you,

[15] you shall utterly destroy all the inhabitants of that land with the edge of the sword; you shall solemnly curse it, and all the things that are in it.

[16] And all its spoils you shall gather into its public ways, and you shall burn the city with fire, along with all its spoils publicly before the Lord your God; and it shall be uninhabited forever, it shall not be built again.'

[17] And none of the cursed things shall cleave to your hand, that the Lord may turn from His fierce anger, and show you mercy, and pity you, and multiply you, as He swore to your fathers;

[18] if you will hear the voice of the Lord your God, to keep His commandments, all that I charge you this day, to do that which is good and pleasing before the Lord your God.

DEUTERONOMY CHAPTER 14

Pagan Practices Forbidden

[1] "You are the children of the Lord your God: you shall not make any baldness between you eyes for the dead.

[2] For you are a holy people to the Lord your God, and the Lord your God has chosen you to be a peculiar people to Himself of all the nations on the face of the earth.

Clean and Unclean Meat

[3] You shall not eat any abominable thing.

[4] These *are* the beasts which you shall eat: the calf of the herd, and lamb of the sheep, and kid of the goats;

[5] the deer, the gazelle, the roe deer, the wild goat, and the mountain goat.

[6] Every beast that divides the hoofs, and makes claws of two divisions, and that chews the cud among beasts, these you shall eat.

[7] And these you shall not eat: of them that chew the cud, and of those that divide the hoofs, and make distinct claws; the camel, and the hare, and the rabbit; because they chew the cud, and do not divide the hoof, these are unclean to you.

8 And as for the swine, because he divides the hoof, and makes claws of the hoof, yet he does not chew the cud, he is unclean to you; you shall not eat of their flesh, you shall not touch their dead bodies.

9 "And these you shall eat of all that are in the water, you shall eat all that have fins and scales.

10 And all that do not have fins and scales you shall not eat, they are unclean to you.

11 You shall eat every clean bird.

12 And these among them you shall not eat: the eagle, the ossifrage, the sea-eagle,

13 the vulture, the kite and the like to it,

14 (This verse omitted in LXX)

15 the sparrow, the owl, the seagull,

16 the heron, the swan, the stork,

17 the cormorant, the hawk and its like, the hoopoe, the raven,

18 the pelican, and the diver and the like to it, and the redbill and the bat.

19 All winged animals that creep are unclean to you; you shall not eat of them.

20 You shall eat every clean bird.

21 "You shall eat nothing that dies of itself; it shall be given to the sojourner in your cities and he shall eat it, or you shall sell it to a stranger, because you are a holy people unto the Lord your God. You shall not boil a lamb in his mother's milk.

Tithing Principles

22 "You shall tithe a tenth of all the produce of your seed, the fruit of your field, year by year.

23 And you shall eat it in the place which the Lord your God shall choose to have His name called there; you shall bring the tithe of your grain and of your wine, and of your oil, the firstborn of your herd and of your flock, that you may learn to fear the Lord your God at all times.

24 And if the journey is too far for you, and you are not able to bring them, because the place *is* far from you which the Lord your God shall choose to have His name called there, because the Lord your God will bless you;

25 then you shall sell them for money, and you shall take the money in your hands, and you shall go to the place which the Lord your God shall choose.

26 And you shall give the money for whatsoever your soul shall desire, for oxen or for sheep, or for wine, or *you shall lay it out* on strong drink, or on whatsoever your soul may desire, and you shall eat there before the Lord your God, and you shall rejoice and your house,

27 and the Levite that is in your cities, because he has not a portion or inheritance with you.

28 "After three years you shall bring out all the tithes of your fruits, in that year you shall lay it up in your cities.

29 And the Levite shall come, because he has no part or lot with you, and the stranger, and the orphan, and the widow which is in your cities, and they shall eat and be filled, that the Lord your God may bless you in all the works which you shall do.

DEUTERONOMY CHAPTER 15

Laws Concerning the Sabbatical Year

1 "Every seven years you shall make a release.

2 And this *is* the ordinance of the release: you shall release every private debt which your neighbor owes you, and you shall not ask payment of it from your brother; for it has been called a release to the Lord your God.

3 Of a stranger you shall ask again whatsoever he has of yours, but to your brother you shall release his debt to you.

4 For *thus* there shall not be a poor person in the midst of you, for the Lord your God will surely bless you in the land which the Lord your God gives you by inheritance, that you should inherit it.

5 And if you shall indeed hearken to the voice of the Lord your God, to keep and do all these commandments, as many as I charge you this day,

6 (for the Lord your God has blessed you in the way of which He spoke to you) then you shall lend to many nations, but you shall not borrow; and you shall rule over many nations, but they shall not rule over you.

7 "And if there shall be in the midst of you a poor *man* from among your brothers, in one of your cities in the land, which the Lord your God gives you, you shall not harden your heart, neither shall you by any means close up your hand from your brother who is in need.

8 You shall surely open your hands to him, and shall lend to him as much as he wants according to his need.

9 Take heed to yourself that there be not a secret thing in your heart—an iniquity, saying, 'The seventh year, the year of release, is approaching.' And your eye shall be evil to your brother that is in need, and you shall not give to him, and he shall cry against you to the Lord, and there shall be great sin in you.

10 You shall surely give to him, and you shall lend to him as much as he wants, according as he is in need. And you shall not grudge in your heart as you give to him, because on this account the Lord your God will bless you in all your works, and in all things on which you shall lay your hand.

11 For the poor shall not fail off your land, therefore I charge you to do this thing, saying, 'You shall surely open your hands to your poor brother, and to him that is distressed upon your land.'

12 "And if your brother *or sister*, a Hebrew man or a Hebrew woman, are sold to you, he shall serve you six years, and in the seventh year you shall send him out free from you.

13 And when you shall send him out free from you, you shall not send him out empty.

14 You shall give him provision for the way from your flock, and from your grain, and from your wine; as the Lord your God has blessed you, *so* you shall give to him.

¹⁵ And you shall remember that you *also* were a slave in the land of Egypt, and the Lord your God redeemed you from there; therefore I charge you to do this thing.

¹⁶ And if he should say to you, 'I will not go out from you,' because he continues to love you and your house, because he is well with you;

¹⁷ then you shall take an awl, and bore his ear through to the door, and he shall be your servant forever; and in like manner shall you do to your male servant.

¹⁸ It shall not seem hard to you when they are sent out free from you, because *your servant* has served you six years according to the annual hire of a hireling; so the Lord your God shall bless you in all things whatsoever you may do.

The Firstborn of Livestock

¹⁹ "Every firstborn that shall be born among your cows and your sheep, you shall sanctify the males to the Lord your God; you shall not work with your firstborn calf, and you shall not shear the firstborn of your sheep.

²⁰ You shall eat it before the Lord year by year in the place which the Lord your God shall choose, you and your house.

²¹ And if there be in it a blemish, if it is lame or blind, (an evil blemish) you shall not sacrifice it to the Lord your God.

²² You shall eat it in your cities; the unclean in you and the clean shall eat it in like manner, as the doe or the deer.

²³ Only you shall not eat the blood; you shall pour it out on the earth as water.

DEUTERONOMY CHAPTER 16

The Passover Reviewed

¹ "Observe the month of new *grain*, and you shall sacrifice the Passover to the Lord your God; because in the month of new grain you came out of Egypt by night.

² And you shall sacrifice the Passover to the Lord your God, sheep and oxen in the place which the Lord your God shall choose to have His name called upon it.

³ You shall not eat leaven with it; seven days shall you eat unleavened *bread* with it, *the* bread of affliction, because you came forth out of Egypt in haste; that you may remember the day of your coming forth out of the land of Egypt all the days of your life.

⁴ Leaven shall not be seen with you in all your borders for seven days, and there shall not be left of the flesh which you shall sacrifice at even on the first day until the morning.

⁵ You shall not have power to sacrifice the Passover in any of the cities, which the Lord your God gives you.

⁶ But in the place which the Lord your God shall choose, to have His name called there, you shall sacrifice the Passover at sunset, at the time when you came out of Egypt.

⁷ And you shall boil and roast and eat it in the place, which the Lord your God shall choose; and you shall return in the morning, and go to your house.

⁸ Six days shall you eat unleavened bread, and on the seventh day is a holiday, a feast to the Lord your God: you shall not do in it any work, except what must be done by anyone.

The Feast of Weeks Reviewed

⁹ "Seven weeks shall you number to yourself; when you have begun *to put* the sickle to the grain, you shall begin to number seven weeks.

¹⁰ And you shall keep the Feast of Weeks to the Lord your God, accordingly as your hand has power, in as many things as the Lord your God shall give you.

¹¹ And you shall rejoice before the Lord your God, you and your son, and your daughter, your male servant and your female servant, and the Levite, and the stranger, and the orphan, and the widow which dwells among you, in whatsoever place the Lord your God shall choose, that His name should be called there.

¹² And you shall remember that you were a servant in the land of Egypt, and you shall observe and do these commands.

The Feast of Tabernacles Reviewed

¹³ "You shall keep for yourself the Feast of Tabernacles seven days, when you gather in *your produce* from your threshing floor and your winepress.

¹⁴ And you shall rejoice in your feast, you, your son, your daughter, your male servant, your female servant, along *with* the Levite, the stranger, the orphan, and the widow that is in your cities.

¹⁵ Seven days shall you keep a feast to the Lord your God in the place which the Lord your God shall choose for Himself; and if the Lord your God shall bless you in all your fruits, and in every work of your hands, then you shall rejoice.

¹⁶ Three times in the year shall all your males appear before the Lord your God in the place which the Lord shall choose in the Feast of Unleavened Bread, and in the Feast of Weeks, and in the Feast of Tabernacles: you shall not appear before the Lord your God empty.

¹⁷ Each one according to his ability, according to the blessing of the Lord your God, which He has given you.

Municipal Judges and Officers

¹⁸ "You shall make for yourself judges and officers in your cities, which the Lord your God gives you in *your* tribes, and they shall judge the people with righteous judgment;

¹⁹ they shall not pervert judgment, nor favor persons, nor receive a gift; for gifts blind the eyes of the wise, and pervert the words of the righteous.

²⁰ You shall justly pursue justice, that you may live, and go in and inherit the land which the Lord your God gives you.

Forbidden Forms of Worship

²¹ "You shall not plant for yourself a grove; you shall not plant for yourself any tree near the altar of your God.

22 You shall not set up for yourself a pillar, which the Lord your God hates.

DEUTERONOMY CHAPTER 17

1 "You shall not sacrifice to the Lord your God a calf or a sheep, in which there is a blemish, *or* any evil thing; for it is an abomination to the Lord your God.

2 "And if there should be found in any of your cities which the Lord your God gives you, a man or a woman who shall do that which is evil before the Lord your God, so as to transgress His covenant,

3 and they should go and serve other gods, and worship them, the sun, or the moon, or any of the host of heaven, which He commanded you not to do,

4 and it be told you, and you shall have inquired diligently, and behold, the thing really did take place, and this abomination really has been done in Israel;

5 then shall you bring out that man, or that woman, and you shall stone them with stones, and they shall die.

6 He shall die on the testimony of two or three witnesses; a man who is put to death shall not be put to death for one witness.

7 And the hand of the witnesses shall be upon him among the first to put him to death, and the hand of the people at the last; so shall you remove the evil one from among yourselves.

Legal Decisions by Priests and Judges

8 "And if a matter shall be too hard for you in judgment, between blood and blood, and between cause and cause, and between stroke and stroke, and between contradiction and contradiction, matters of judgment in your cities;

9 then you shall arise and go up to the place which the Lord your God shall choose, and you shall come to the priests the Levites, and to the judge who shall be in those days, and they shall search out *the matter* and report the judgment to you.

10 And you shall do according to the sentence which they shall report to you out of the place in which the Lord your God shall choose, and you shall observe to do all things having been appointed to you by the law.

11 You shall do according to the law and to the judgment which they shall declare to you: you shall not swerve to the right hand or to the left from any sentence which they shall report to you.

12 And any man that shall act in arrogance, so as not to adhere to the priest who stands to minister in the name of the Lord your God, or the judge who shall preside in those days, that man shall die, and you shall remove the evil one out of Israel.

13 And all the people shall hear and fear, and shall no longer act presumptuously.

Limitations of Royal Authority

14 "And when you shall enter into the land which the Lord your God gives you, and shall inherit it and dwell in it, and shall say, 'I will set a ruler over me, as also the other nations round about me';

15 you shall surely set over you the ruler whom the Lord God shall choose: of your brothers you shall set over you a ruler; you shall not have power to set over you a stranger, because he is not your brother.

16 For he shall not multiply to himself horses, and he shall by no means turn the people back to Egypt, lest he should multiply to himself horses; for the Lord said, 'You shall not return that way again.'

17 And he shall not multiply to himself wives, lest his heart turn away; and he shall not greatly multiply to himself silver and gold.

18 "And when he shall be established in his government, then shall he write for himself this repetition of the law into a book by the hands of the priests the Levites;

19 and it shall be with him, and he shall read in it all the days of his life, that he may learn to fear the Lord your God, and to keep all these commandments, and to observe these ordinances;

20 that his heart be not lifted up above his brothers, that he depart not from the commandments on the right hand or on the left; that he and his sons may reign long in his dominion among the children of Israel.

DEUTERONOMY CHAPTER 18

Privileges of Priests and Levites

1 "The priests, the Levites, even the whole tribe of Levi, shall have no part nor inheritance with Israel; the burnt offerings of the Lord *are* their inheritance, they shall eat them.

2 And they shall have no inheritance among their brothers; the Lord Himself *is* his portion, as He said to him.

3 "And this *is* the due of the priests in the things coming from the people from those who offer sacrifices, whether it be a calf or a sheep; and you shall give the shoulder to the priest, and the cheeks, and the stomach;

4 and the firstfruits of your grain, and of your wine, and of your oil; and you shall give to him the firstfruits of the fleeces of your sheep:

5 because the Lord has chosen him out of all your tribes, to stand before the Lord your God, to minister and bless in His name, himself and his sons among the children of Israel.

6 "And if a Levite should come from one of the cities of all the children of Israel, where he himself dwells, accordingly as his mind desires, to the place which he shall have chosen,

7 he shall minister to the name of the Lord his God, as all his brothers the Levites, who stand there before the Lord your God.

8 He shall eat an allotted portion, besides the sale of his inheritance.

Avoid Wicked Customs

⁹ "And when you shall have entered into the land which the Lord your God gives you, you shall not learn to do according to the abominations of those nations.

¹⁰ There shall not be found in you one who purges his son or his daughter with fire, or one who uses divination, or *one* who deals with omens, or a sorcerer

¹¹ employing an incantation, or one who has in him a divining spirit, or an observer of signs who questions the dead.

¹² For everyone that does these things is an abomination to the Lord your God; for because of these abominations the Lord shall destroy them from before your face.

¹³ You shall be perfect before the Lord your God.

¹⁴ For all these nations whose *land* you shall inherit, they will listen to omens and divinations; but the Lord your God has not permitted you *to do* so.

A New Prophet Like Moses

¹⁵ "The Lord your God shall raise up to you a Prophet from among your brothers, like me; Him shall you hear,

¹⁶ according to all the things which you desired from the Lord your God in Horeb in the day of the assembly, saying, 'We will not again hear the voice of the Lord your God,' and 'we will not anymore see this great fire, lest we die.'

¹⁷ And the Lord said to me, 'They have spoken rightly, all that they have said to you.

¹⁸ I will raise up to them a Prophet from among their brothers, like you; and I will put My words in His mouth, and He shall speak to them as I shall command Him.

¹⁹ And whoever shall not hearken to all the words that *the* Prophet shall speak in My name, I will take vengeance on him.

²⁰ But whichever prophet that shall impiously speak in My name a word which I have not commanded him to speak, and whosoever shall speak in the name of other gods, that prophet shall die.

²¹ But if you shall say in your heart, 'How shall we know the word which the Lord has not spoken?'

²² Whatever words that prophet shall speak in the name of the Lord, and they shall not come true, and not come to pass, this *is* the thing which the Lord has not spoken; that prophet has spoken wickedly: you shall not spare him.'

DEUTERONOMY CHAPTER 19

Laws Concerning the Cities of Refuge

¹ "And when the Lord your God has destroyed the nations, whose land God gives to you, and you shall inherit them, and dwell in their cities, and in their houses,

² you shall separate for yourself three cities in the midst of your land, which the Lord your God gives to you.

³ Take a survey of your way, and you shall divide the coasts of your land, which the Lord your God apportions to you, into three parts, and there shall be there a refuge for every manslayer.

⁴ "And this shall be the ordinance of the manslayer who shall flee there, and shall live: whosoever has killed his neighbor ignorantly, seeing that he did not hate him in times past.

⁵ And whoever shall enter with his neighbor into the thicket, to gather wood, if the hand of him that cuts wood with the ax should be violently shaken, and the ax head should fall off from the handle and strike his neighbor, and he should die, then he shall flee to one of these cities, and live;

⁶ lest the avenger of blood pursue after the manslayer, because his heart is hot, and overtake him, if the way be too long, and kill him, though there is to this man no sentence of death, because he did not hate him in times past.

⁷ Therefore I command you, saying, 'You shall separate for yourself three cities.'

⁸ And if the Lord shall enlarge your borders, as He swore to your fathers, and the Lord shall give to you all the land which He said he would give to your fathers;

⁹ if you shall hearken to do all these commands which I charge you this day, to love the Lord your God, to walk in all His ways continually, you shall add for yourself yet three cities to these three.

¹⁰ So innocent blood shall not be spilled in the land which the Lord your God gives you to inherit, and there shall not be in you one guilty of blood.

¹¹ "But if there should be in you a man hating his neighbor, and he should lie in wait for him, and rise up against him, and strike him, that he should die, and he should flee to one of these cities,

¹² then shall the elders of his city send, and take him from there, and they shall deliver him into the hands of the avengers of blood, and he shall die.

¹³ Your eye shall not spare him; so shall you purge innocent blood from Israel, and it shall be well with you.

Property Boundaries

¹⁴ "You shall not move the landmarks of your neighbor, which your fathers set in the inheritance, in which you have obtained a share in the land, which the Lord your God gives you to inherit.

Laws Concerning Witnesses

¹⁵ "One witness shall not stand to testify against a man for any iniquity, or for any fault, or for any sin which he may commit; by the mouth of two witnesses, or by the mouth of three witnesses, shall every word be established.

¹⁶ And if an unjust witness should rise up against a man, alleging iniquity against him,

¹⁷ then shall the two men between whom the controversy is, stand before the Lord, and before the priests, and before the judges, who may be in those days.

[18] And the judges shall make diligent inquiry; and behold, *if* an unjust witness has given unjust testimony, *and* has stood up against his brother,

[19] then shall you do to him as he wickedly devised to do against his brother, and you shall remove the evil from yourselves.

[20] And the rest shall hear and fear, and do no more according to this evil thing in the midst of you.

[21] Your eye shall not spare him; *you shall exact* life for life, eye for eye, tooth for tooth, hand for hand, and foot for foot.

DEUTERONOMY CHAPTER 20

Rules of Warfare

[1] "And if you should go forth to war against your enemies, and should see a horse and rider, and a people more numerous than yourself; you shall not be afraid of them, for the Lord your God *is* with you, who brought you up out of the land of Egypt.

[2] And it shall come to pass whenever you shall draw near to battle, that the priest shall draw near and speak to the people, and shall say to them,

[3] 'Hear, O Israel; you are going this day to battle against your enemies: let not your heart faint; fear not, neither be confounded, neither turn aside from their face.

[4] For *it is* the Lord your God who advances with you, to fight with you against your enemies, *and* to save you.'

[5] And the scribes shall speak to the people, saying, 'What man *is there* that has built a new house, and has not dedicated it? Let him go and return to his house, lest he die in the war, and another man dedicate it.

[6] And what man *is there* that has planted a vineyard, and not been made merry with it? Let him go and return to his house, lest he die in the battle, and another man be made merry with it.

[7] And what man *is there* that has betrothed a wife, and has not taken her? Let him go and return to his house, lest he die in the battle, and another man take her.'

[8] And the scribes shall speak further to the people, and say, 'What man *is there* that fears, and is cowardly in his heart? Let him go and return to his house, lest he make the heart of his brother fail, as his own.'

[9] And it shall come to pass when the scribes shall have ceased speaking to the people, that they shall appoint generals of the army to be leaders of the people.

[10] "And if you shall draw near to a city to overcome them by war, then call them out peaceably.

[11] If then they should answer peaceably to you, and open to you, it shall be that all the people found in it shall be tributary and subject to you.

[12] But if they will not hearken to you, but wage war against you, you shall besiege it;

[13] until the Lord your God shall deliver it into your hands, and you shall strike every male in it with the edge of the sword;

[14] except the women and the little ones; and all the livestock, and whatsoever shall be in the city, and all the plunder you shall take as spoil for yourself, and shall eat all the plunder of your enemies whom the Lord your God gives you.

[15] Thus shall you do to all the cities that are very far off from you, not *being* of the cities of these nations which the Lord your God gives you to inherit their land.

[16] *Of these* you shall not take anything alive;

[17] but you shall surely curse them, the Hittite, the Amorite, the Canaanite, the Perizzite, the Hivite, the Jebusite, and the Girgashite; as the Lord your God commanded you:

[18] that they may not teach you to do all their abominations, which they did to their gods, and *so* you should sin before the Lord your God.

[19] "And if you should besiege a city many days to prevail against it by war to take it, you shall not destroy its trees, by applying an iron tool to them, but you shall eat of it, and shall not cut it down. Is the tree that is in the field a man, to enter before you into the work of the siege?

[20] But the tree which you know to be not fruit-bearing, this you shall destroy and cut down; and you shall construct a mound against the city, which makes war against you, until it is delivered up.

DEUTERONOMY CHAPTER 21

The Law Concerning Unsolved Murder

[1] "And if one should be found slain with the sword in the land, which the Lord your God gives you to inherit, having fallen in the field, and they do not know who has killed *him*,

[2] then your elders and your judges shall come forth, and shall measure the distances of the cities round about the slain man.

[3] And it shall be that the city which is nearest to the slain man, the elders of that city shall take a heifer of the herd, which has not labored, and which has not pulled with a yoke.

[4] And the elders of that city shall bring down the heifer into a rough valley, which has not been tilled and is not sown, and they shall slay the heifer in the valley.

[5] And the priests, the Levites, shall come near, because the Lord God has chosen them to stand by Him, and to bless in His name, and by their word shall every controversy and every assault be *decided*.

[6] And all the elders of that city who draw near to the slain man shall wash their hands over the head of the heifer which was slain in the valley;

[7] and they shall answer and say, 'Our hands have not shed this blood, and our eyes have not seen *it*.

[8] Be merciful to Your people Israel, O Lord, whom You have redeemed, that innocent blood may not be charged on Your people Israel'; and atonement shall be provided on their behalf for the blood.

9 And you shall take away innocent blood from among you, if you should do that which is good and pleasing before the Lord your God.

Female Captives

10 "And if when you go out to war against your enemies, the Lord your God should deliver them into your hands, and you should take their spoil,

11 and *if* you should see among the spoil a woman beautiful in countenance, and should desire her, and take her to yourself for a wife,

12 and should bring her within your house; then shall you shave her head, and trim her nails,

13 and shall take away her garments of captivity from off her, and she shall abide in your house, and shall mourn her father and mother for a full month; and afterwards you shall go in to her and dwell with her, and she shall be your wife.

14 And it shall be if you do not delight in her, you shall send her out free; and she shall not by any means be sold for money, you shall not treat her contemptuously, because you have humbled her.

The Right of the Firstborn

15 "And if a man has two wives, the one loved and the other hated, and both the loved and the hated should have born him *children*, and the son of the hated should be firstborn;

16 then it shall be that whenever he shall divide by inheritance his goods to his sons, he shall not be able to give the right of the firstborn to the son of the loved one, having overlooked the son of the hated, which is the firstborn.

17 But he shall acknowledge the firstborn of the hated one, to give to him double of all things which shall be found by him, because he is the first of his children, and to him belongs the birthright.

The Rebellious Son

18 "And if any man has a disobedient and contentious son, who will not listen to the voice of his father and the voice of his mother, and they should correct him, and he should not listen to them,

19 then shall his father and his mother take hold of him, and bring him forth to the elders of his city, and to the gate of the place;

20 and they shall say to the men of their city, 'This our son is disobedient and contentious, *and* he will not listen to our voice, he is a reveler and a drunkard.'

21 And the men of his city shall stone him with stones, and he shall die; and you shall remove the evil one from yourselves, and the rest shall hear and fear.

Miscellaneous Laws

22 "And if there be sin in anyone, *and* the judgment of death *be upon him*, and he be put to death, and you hang him on a tree;

23 his body shall not remain all night upon the tree, but you shall by all means bury it in that day; for everyone that is hanged on a tree is cursed of God; and you shall by no means defile the land which the Lord your God gives you for an inheritance.

DEUTERONOMY CHAPTER 22

1 "When you see the calf of your brother or his sheep wandering in the way, you shall not overlook them; you shall by all means turn them back to your brother, and you shall restore them to him.

2 And if your brother is not near you, or if you do not know him, you shall bring it into your own house; and it shall be with you until your brother shall seek them, and you shall restore them to him.

3 Thus shall you do to his donkey, and thus shall you do to his garment, and thus shall you do to everything that your brother has lost; whatsoever things have been lost by him, and you have found, you shall not have power to overlook.

4 "You shall not see the donkey of your brother, or his calf, fallen in the way; you shall not overlook them, you shall surely help him to raise them up.

5 The clothing of a man shall not be on a woman, neither shall a man put on a woman's dress; for everyone that does these things is an abomination to the Lord your God.

6 "And if you should come upon a brood of birds before your face in the way or upon any tree, or upon the earth, young or eggs, and the mother is brooding on the young or the eggs, you shall not take the mother with the young ones.

7 You shall by all means let the mother go, but you shall take the young to yourself; that it may be well with you, and that you may live long.

8 If you should build a new house, then shall you make a parapet to your house; so you shall not bring blood-guiltiness upon your house, if one should in any way fall from it.

9 "You shall not sow your vineyard with different kinds of seed, lest the fruit be defiled, and whatsoever seed you may sow, with the fruit of your vineyard.

10 "You shall not plow with an ox and a donkey together.

11 "You shall not wear a mingled *garment*, woolen and linen together.

12 "You shall make fringes on the four borders of your garments, with whatever you may be clothed with.

Laws of Sexual Morality

13 "And if anyone should take a wife, and dwell with her, and hate her,

14 and attach to her reproachful words, and bring against her an evil name, and say, 'I took this woman, and when I came to her I found out that she was not a virgin';

15 then the father and the mother of the young woman shall take and bring out the evidence of the young woman's virginity to the elders of the city to the gate.

16 And the father of the young woman shall say to the elders, 'I gave this my daughter to this man for a wife;

17 and now he has hated her, and attaches reproachful words to her, saying, "I have not found tokens of virginity with your daughter"; and these *are* the evidences of my daughter's virginity.' And they shall unfold the garment before the elders of the city.

18 And the elders of that city shall take that man, and shall chastise him,

19 and shall fine him a hundred shekels, and shall give *them* to the father of the young woman, because he has brought forth an evil name against a virgin of Israel; and she shall be his wife: he shall never be able to put her away.

20 But if this report should be true, and the evidences of virginity are not found for the young woman;

21 then shall they bring out the young woman to the doors of her father's house, and they shall stone her with stones, and she shall die; because she has done a disgraceful thing among the children of Israel, to defile the house of her father by harlotry: so you shall remove the evil one from among you.

22 "And if a man should be found lying with a woman married to a man, you shall kill them both, the man that lay with the woman, and the woman; so shall you remove the wicked one out of Israel.

23 "And if there should be a young woman espoused to a man, and a man should have found her in the city and have lain with her;

24 you shall bring them both out to the gate of their city, and they shall be stoned with stones, and they shall die; the young woman, because she did not cry out in the city; and the man, because he humbled his neighbor's spouse: so shall you remove the evil one from yourselves.

25 "But if a man should find in the field a young woman that is betrothed, and he should force her and lie with her, you shall slay the man that lay with her only.

26 And the young woman has not *committed* a sin worthy of death; as if a man should rise up against his neighbor, and slay him, so *is* this thing;

27 because he found her in the field; the betrothed young woman cried, and there was none to help her.

28 "And if anyone should find a young virgin who has not been betrothed, and should force *her* and lie with her, and *the matter* should be found out,

29 *then* the man who lay with her shall give to the father of the damsel fifty silver shekels, and she shall be his wife, because he has humbled her; he shall never be able to put her away.

30 "A man shall not take his father's wife, and shall not uncover his father's bed.

DEUTERONOMY CHAPTER 23

Those Excluded from the Assembly

1 "He that is fractured or mutilated in his private parts shall not enter into the assembly of the Lord.

2 *One born* of a harlot shall not enter into the assembly of the Lord.

3 "The Ammonite and Moabite shall not enter into the assembly of the Lord, even until the tenth generation he shall not enter into the assembly of the Lord, even forever;

4 because they did not meet you with bread and water by the way, when you went out of Egypt; and because they hired against you Balaam the son of Beor of Mesopotamia to curse you.

5 But the Lord your God would not hearken to Balaam; and the Lord your God changed the curses into blessings, because the Lord your God loved you.

6 You shall not speak peaceably or profitably to them all your days forever.

7 "You shall not abhor an Edomite, because he is your brother; you shall not abhor an Egyptian, because you were a stranger in his land.

8 If sons should be born to them, in the third generation they shall enter into the assembly of the Lord.

Cleanliness of the Camp Site

9 "And if you should go forth to engage with your enemies, then you shall keep yourself from every wicked thing.

10 If there should be in you a man who is not clean by reason of his issue by night, then he shall go forth out of the camp, and he shall not enter into the camp.

11 And it shall come to pass toward evening he shall wash his body with water, and when the sun has gone down, he shall go into the camp.

12 And you shall have a place outside of the camp, and you shall go out there,

13 and you shall have an implement among your equipment; and it shall come to pass that when you relieve yourself outside *the camp*, that you shall dig with it, and you shall cover your refuse.

14 Because the Lord your God walks in your camp to deliver you, and to give up your enemy from before your face; and your camp shall be holy, and there shall not appear in you a disgraceful thing, so that He should turn away from you.

Miscellaneous Laws

15 "You shall not deliver a servant to his master, who *coming* from his master attaches himself to you.

16 He shall dwell with you, he shall dwell among you where he shall please; you shall not afflict him.

17 "There shall not be a harlot of the daughters of Israel, and there shall not be a fornicator of the sons of Israel; there shall not be a cult prostitute among the daughters of Israel, and there shall not be a cult prostitute among the sons of Israel.

18 You shall not bring the hire of a harlot, nor the price of a dog into the house of the Lord your God, for any vow, because both are an abomination to the Lord your God.

19 "You shall not lend with interest to your brother—interest on money or food or anything which you may lend.

20 You may lend with interest to a stranger, but to your brother you shall not lend with interest; that the Lord your God may bless you in all your works upon the land, into which you are entering to inherit it.

21 "And if you will vow a vow to the Lord your God, you shall not delay to pay it; for the Lord your God will surely require it of you, and *otherwise* it shall be sin to you.

22 But if you should be unwilling to vow, it is not sin to you.

23 You shall observe the words that proceed from between your lips; and as you have vowed a gift to the Lord God, *so* shall you do that which you have spoken with your mouth.

24 "And if you should go into the vineyard of your neighbor, you shall eat grapes sufficient to satisfy your desire; but you may not put them into a vessel.

25 And if you should go into the grainfield of your neighbor, then you may gather the heads with your hands; but you shall not put the sickle to your neighbor's grain.

DEUTERONOMY CHAPTER 24

Laws Concerning Marriage and Divorce

1 "And if anyone should take a wife, and should dwell with her, then it shall come to pass if she should not have found favor before him, because he has found some unbecoming thing in her, that he shall write for her a certificate of divorce, and give it into her hands, and he shall send her away out of his house. 2 And *if* she should go away and be married to another man;

3 and the last husband should hate her, and write for her a certificate of divorce, and should give it into her hands, and send her away out of his house, and the last husband should die, who took her to himself for a wife;

4 the former husband who sent her away shall not be able to return and take her to himself for a wife, after she has been defiled; because it is an abomination before the Lord your God, and you shall not defile the land which the Lord your God gives you to inherit.

Miscellaneous Laws

5 "And if anyone should have recently taken a wife, he shall not go out to war, neither shall anything be laid upon him; he shall be free in his house; for one year he shall cheer his wife whom he has taken.

6 "You shall not take for a pledge the lower millstone, nor the upper millstone; for he who does so takes *one's* living for a pledge.

7 "And if a man should be caught stealing one of his brothers of the children of Israel, and having overcome him he should sell him, that thief shall die; so shall you remove that evil one from yourselves.

8 "Take heed to yourself *regarding* the plague of leprosy: you shall take great heed to do according to all the law, which the priests, the Levites, shall report to you; take heed to do, as I have commanded you.

9 Remember all that the Lord your God did to Miriam in the way, when you were going out of Egypt.

10 "If your neighbor owes you a debt, any debt whatsoever, you shall not go into his house to take his pledge:

11 you shall stand outside, and the man who is in your debt shall bring the pledge out to you.

12 And if the man is poor, you shall not keep his pledge overnight.

13 You shall surely restore his pledge at sunset, and he shall sleep in his *own* cloak, and he shall bless you; and it shall be mercy to you before the Lord your God.

14 You shall not unjustly withhold the wages of the poor and needy of your brothers, or of the strangers who are in your cities.

15 You shall pay him his wages the same day, the sun shall not go down upon it, because he is poor and he trusts in it; and he shall cry against you to the Lord, and it shall be sin to you.

16 "The fathers shall not be put to death for the children, and the sons shall not be put to death for the fathers; everyone shall be put to death for his own sin.

17 You shall not pervert the judgment of the stranger and the fatherless, and the widow; you shall not take the widow's garment for a pledge.

18 And you shall remember that you were a slave in the land of Egypt, and the Lord your God redeemed you from there; therefore I command you to do this thing.

19 "And when you have reaped the grain in your field, and have forgotten a sheaf in your field, you shall not return to take it; it shall be for the stranger and the orphan and the widow, that the Lord your God may bless you in all the works of your hands.

20 And if you should gather your olives, you shall not return to collect the remainder; it shall be for the stranger, and the fatherless, and the widow, and you shall remember that you were a slave in the land of Egypt; therefore I command you to do this thing.

21 And whenever you shall gather the grapes of your vineyard, you shall not glean what you have left; it shall be for the stranger, and the orphan, and the widow;

22 and you shall remember that you were a slave in the land of Egypt; therefore I command you to do this thing.

DEUTERONOMY CHAPTER 25

1 "And if there should be a dispute between men, and they should come forward to judgment, and *the judges* judge, and acquit the righteous, and condemn the wicked;

2 then it shall come to pass, if the unrighteous should be worthy of stripes, you shall lay him down before the judges, and they shall scourge him before them according to his iniquity.

3 And they shall scourge him with forty stripes in number, they shall not inflict more; for if you should scourge him *with* more stripes beyond these stripes, your brother will be disgraced before you.

4 "You shall not muzzle the ox that treads out the grain.

Marriage Duty of the Surviving Brother

5 "And if brothers should live together, and one of them should die, and should not have descendants, the wife of the deceased shall not marry out *of the family* to a man not related: her husband's brother shall go in to her, and shall take her to himself for a wife, and shall dwell with her.

6 And it shall come to pass that the child which she shall bear, shall be named by the name of the deceased, and his name shall not be blotted out of Israel.

7 And if the man should not be willing to take his brother's wife, then shall the woman go up to the gate to the elders, and she shall say, 'My husband's brother will not raise up the name of his brother in Israel, my husband's brother has refused.'

8 And the elders of his city shall call him, and speak to him; and if he stand and say, 'I will not take her,'

9 then his brother's wife shall come forward before the elders, and shall loose one shoe from off his foot, and shall spit in his face, and shall answer and say, 'Thus shall they do to the man who will not build his brother's house in Israel.'

10 And his name shall be called in Israel, 'The house of him that has had his shoe loosed.'

Miscellaneous Laws

11 "And if men should fight together, a man with his brother, and the wife of one of them should advance to rescue her husband out of the hand of him that strikes him, and she should stretch forth her hand, and take hold of his private parts;

12 you shall cut off her hand; your eye shall not spare her.

13 "You shall not have in your bag differing weights, a heavy and a light.

14 You shall not have in your house differing measures, a large and a small.

15 You shall have a true and just weight, and a true and just measure, that you may live long upon the land which the Lord your God gives you for an inheritance.

16 For everyone that does this *is* an abomination to the Lord your God, even everyone that does injustice.

Destroy the Amalekites

17 "Remember what things Amalek did to you by the way, when you went forth out of the land of Egypt,

18 how he withstood you in the way, and harassed your rear, *even* those that were weary behind you, and you hungered and were weary; and he did not fear God.

19 And it shall come to pass whenever the Lord your God shall have given you rest from all your enemies round about you, in the land which the Lord your God gives you to inherit, you shall blot out the name of Amalek from under heaven, and shall not forget *to do it*.

First Fruits and Tithes

1 "And it shall be, when you have entered into the land which the Lord your God gives you to inherit, and you have inherited it, and you have dwelt upon it,

2 that you shall take of the first of the fruits of your land, which the Lord your God gives you, and you shall put them into a basket, and you shall go to the place which the Lord your God shall choose to have His name called there.

3 And you shall come to the priest who shall be in those days, and you shall say to him, 'I testify this day to the Lord my God, that I have come into the land which the Lord swore to our fathers to give to us.'

4 And the priest shall take the basket out of your hands, and shall set it before the altar of the Lord your God.

5 "And he shall answer and say before the Lord your God, 'My father abandoned Syria, and went down into Egypt, and sojourned there with a small number, and became there a mighty nation and a great multitude.

6 And the Egyptians afflicted us, and humbled us, and imposed hard tasks on us,

7 and we cried to the Lord our God, and the Lord heard our voice, and saw our humiliation, and our labor, and our affliction.

8 And the Lord brought us out of Egypt Himself with His great strength, and His mighty hand, and His outstretched arm, and with great visions, and with signs, and with wonders.

9 And He brought us into this place, and gave us this land, a land flowing with milk and honey.

10 And now behold, I have brought the firstfruits of the land, which you gave me, O Lord, a land flowing with milk and honey'; and you shall leave it before the Lord your God, and you shall worship before the Lord your God;

11 and you shall rejoice in all the good *things* which the Lord your God has given you, *you* and your family, and the Levite, and the stranger that is within you.

12 "And when you have completed all the tithing of your fruits in the third year, you shall give the second tenth to the Levite, the stranger, the fatherless, and the widow; and they shall eat it in your cities, and be merry.

13 And you shall say before the Lord your God, 'I have fully collected the holy things out of my house, and I have given them to the Levite, the stranger, the orphan, and the widow, according to all commands which You have commanded me: I did not transgress Your command, and I did not forget it.

14 And in my distress I did not eat of them, I have not gathered of them for an unclean purpose, I have not given of

them to the dead; I have hearkened to the voice of the Lord our God, I have done as You have commanded me.

[15] Look down from Your holy house, from heaven, and bless Your people Israel, and the land which You have given them, as You swore to our fathers, to give to us a land flowing with milk and honey.'

Concluding Exhortation

[16] "On this day the Lord your God charged you to keep all the statutes and judgments; and you shall observe and do them, with all your heart, and with all your soul.

[17] You have chosen God this day to be your God, and to walk in all His ways, and to observe His statutes and judgments, and to hearken to His voice.

[18] And the Lord has chosen you this day, that you should be to Him a peculiar people, as He said, to keep His commands;

[19] and that you should be above all nations, as He has made you renowned, and a boast, and glorious, that you should be a holy people to the Lord your God, as He has spoken."

DEUTERONOMY CHAPTER 27

The Law Inscribed on Stones

[1] And Moses and the elders of Israel commanded *the people*, saying, "Keep all these commands, all that I command you this day.

[2] And it shall come to pass in the day when you shall cross over the Jordan into the land which the Lord your God gives you, that you shall set up for yourself great stones, and shall plaster them with plaster.

[3] And you shall write on these stones all the words of this law, as soon as you have crossed the Jordan, when you have entered into the land, which the Lord God of your fathers gives you, a land flowing with milk and honey, according as the Lord God of your fathers said to you.

[4] And it shall be as soon as you have gone over the Jordan, you shall set up these stones, which I command you this day, on Mount Ebal, and you shall plaster them with plaster.

[5] And you shall build there an altar to the Lord your God, an altar of stones; you shall not lift up iron upon it.

[6] Of whole stones shall you build an altar to the Lord your God, and you shall offer upon it burnt offerings to the Lord your God.

[7] And you shall there offer a peace offering; and you shall eat and be filled, and rejoice before the Lord your God.

[8] And you shall write upon the stones all this law very plainly."

[9] Then Moses and the priests, the Levites, spoke to all Israel, saying, "Be silent and hear, O Israel; this day you have become a people to the Lord your God.

[10] And you shall obey the voice of the Lord your God, and you shall keep all His commandments and His statutes, as many as I command you this day."

Cursings Pronounced from Mount Ebal

[11] And Moses charged the people on that day, saying,

[12] "These shall stand to bless the people on Mount Gerizim, having gone over the Jordan: Simeon, Levi, Judah, Issachar, Joseph, and Benjamin.

[13] And these shall stand for cursing on Mount Ebal: Reuben, Gad, Asher, Zebulun, Dan, and Nephthali.

[14] And the Levites shall answer and say to all Israel with a loud voice,

[15] "'Cursed *is* the man who shall make a graven or molten image, an abomination to the Lord, the work of the hands of craftsmen, and shall put it in a secret place.' And all the people shall answer and say, 'Amen.'

[16] "'Cursed is the man that dishonors his father or his mother.' And all the people shall say, 'Amen.'

[17] "'Cursed is the man that removes his neighbor's landmarks.' And all the people shall say, 'Amen.'

[18] "'Cursed is the man who misleads a blind man down the road.' And all the people shall say, 'Amen.'

[19] "'Cursed is everyone that shall pervert the judgment of the stranger, and orphan, and widow.' And all the people shall say, 'Amen.'

[20] "'Cursed is the man that lies with his father's wife, because he has uncovered his father's nakedness.' And all the people shall say, 'Amen.'

[21] "'Cursed is the man that lies with any beast.' And all the people shall say, 'Amen.'

[22] "'Cursed is the man that lies with his sister by his father or his mother.' And all the people shall say, 'Amen.'

[23] "'Cursed is the man that lies with his daughter-in-law.' And all the people shall say, 'Amen.'

[23a] "'Cursed is the man that lies with his wife's sister.' And all the people shall say, 'Amen.'

[24] "'Cursed is the man that attacks his neighbor secretly.' And all the people shall say, 'Amen.'

[25] "'Cursed is the man that shall take a bribe to slay an innocent man.' And all the people shall say, Amen.'

[26] "'Cursed is every man that shall not continue in all the words of this law, to do them.' And all the people shall say, 'Amen.'

DEUTERONOMY CHAPTER 28

Blessings for Obedience

[1] "And it shall come to pass, *that* if you will indeed hear the voice of the Lord your God, to observe and do all these commandments which I charge you this day, that the Lord your God shall set you on high above all the nations of the earth;

[2] and all these blessings shall come upon you, and shall find you. If you will indeed hear the voice of the Lord your God,

[3] blessed *shall* you *be* in the city, and blessed shall you be in the field.

[4] Blessed shall be the offspring of your body, and the fruits of your land, and the herds of your oxen, and the flocks of your sheep.

[5] Blessed shall be your barns, and your stores.

[6] Blessed shall you be in your coming in, and blessed shall you be in your going out.

[7] "The Lord shall cause your enemies that rise against you to be utterly broken before your face—they shall come out against you one way, and they shall flee seven ways from before you.

[8] The Lord shall send upon you His blessing in your barns, and on all on which you shall put your hand, in the land which the Lord your God gives you.

[9] The Lord shall raise you up as a holy people unto Himself, as He swore to your fathers; if you will hear the voice of the Lord your God, and walk in all His ways.

[10] And all the nations of the earth shall see you, that the name of the Lord is called upon you, and they shall stand in awe of you.

[11] And the Lord your God shall multiply you for good in the offspring of your body, and in the offspring of your livestock, and in the fruits of your land, on your land which the Lord swore to your fathers to give to you.

[12] May the Lord open to you His good treasure *from out of* the heavens, to give rain to your land in season; may He bless all the works of your hands. So shall you lend to many nations, but you shall not borrow; and you shall rule over many nations, but they shall not rule over you.

[13] The Lord your God shall make you the head, and not the tail; and you shall then be above and you shall not be below, if you will obey the voice of the Lord your God, in all things that I command you this day to observe.

[14] You shall not turn aside from any of the commandments, which I command you this day, to the right hand or to the left, to go after other gods, to serve them.

Cursings for Disobedience

[15] "But it shall come to pass, if you will not obey the voice of the Lord your God, to observe all His commandments, as many as I command you this day, then all these curses shall come on you, and overtake you.

[16] Cursed *shall* you *be* in the city, and cursed shall you be in the field.

[17] Cursed shall be your barns and your stores.

[18] Cursed shall be the offspring of your body, and the fruits of your land, the herds of your oxen, and the flocks of your sheep.

[19] Cursed shall you be in your coming in, and cursed shall you be in your going out.

[20] "The Lord shall send upon you *various* needs, and famine, and consumption of all things on which you shall put your hand, until He has utterly destroyed you, and until He has consumed you quickly because of your evil deeds, because you have forsaken Him.

[21] The Lord shall cause the pestilence to cleave to you, until He has consumed you off the land into which you go to inherit it.

[22] The Lord will strike you with distress, and fever, and cold, and inflammation, and blighting, and paleness, and they shall pursue you until they have destroyed you.

[23] And you shall have over your head a sky of brass, and the earth under you shall be iron.

[24] The Lord your God shall make the rain of your land dust; and dust shall come down from heaven, until it has destroyed you, and until it has quickly consumed you.

[25] The Lord shall give you up for slaughter before your enemies; you shall go out against them one way, and flee from their face seven ways; and you shall be a dispersion in all the kingdoms of the earth.

[26] And your dead men shall be food to the birds of the sky, and to the beasts of the earth; and there shall be none to scare them away.

[27] The Lord shall strike you with the botch of Egypt in the seat, and with a malignant scab, and itch, so that you can not be healed.

[28] The Lord shall strike you with insanity, and blindness, and astonishment of mind.

[29] And you shall grope at midday, as a blind man gropes in the darkness, and you shall not prosper in your ways; and then you shall be unjustly treated, and plundered continually, and there shall be no helper.

[30] You shall take a wife, and another man shall have her; you shall build a house, and you shall not dwell in it; you shall plant a vineyard, and shall not gather the grapes of it.

[31] Your calf *shall be* slain before you, and you shall not eat of it; your donkey shall be violently taken away from you, and shall not be restored to you: your sheep shall be given to your enemies, and you shall have no helper.

[32] Your sons and your daughters shall be given to another nation, and your eyes, wasting away, shall look for them; your hand shall have no strength.

[33] A nation which you know not shall eat the produce of your land, and all your labors; and you shall be perpetually injured and crushed.

[34] And you shall be distracted, because of the sights of your eyes which you shall see.

[35] The Lord shall strike you with an evil sore, on the knees and the legs, so that you shall not be able to be healed from the sole of your foot to the crown of your head.

[36] The Lord shall carry away you and your princes, whom you shall set over you, to a nation which neither you nor your fathers know; and there shall you serve other gods, *of* wood and stone.

[37] And there shall you be a wonder and a parable, and a tale, among all the nations, to which the Lord your God shall carry you away.

[38] You shall carry forth much seed into the field, and you shall bring in little, because the locust shall devour it.

39 You shall plant a vineyard, and dress it, and shall not drink the wine, neither shall you delight yourself with it, because the worm shall devour it.

40 You shall have olive trees in all your borders, and you shall not anoint yourself with oil, because your olive shall utterly cast *its fruit*.

41 You shall beget sons and daughters, and they shall not be *yours*, for they shall depart into captivity.

42 All your trees and the fruits of your land shall the blight consume.

43 The stranger that is within you shall be lifted up, and you shall be brought down very low.

44 He shall lend to you, and you shall not lend to him; he shall be the head, and you shall be the tail.

45 "And all these curses shall come upon you, and shall pursue you, and shall overtake you, until He has consumed you, and until He has destroyed you, because you did not listen to the voice of the Lord your God, to keep His commandments and His statutes which He has commanded you.

46 And *these things* shall be signs for you, and wonders among your descendants forever;

47 because you did not serve the Lord your God with gladness and a good heart, because of the abundance of all things.

48 And you shall serve your enemies, which the Lord will send forth against you, in hunger, and in thirst, and in nakedness, and in the desire of all things; and you shall wear upon your neck a yoke of iron until He has destroyed you.

49 The Lord shall bring upon you a nation from the extremity of the earth, like the swift flying of an eagle, a nation whose voice you shall not understand;

50 a nation bold in countenance, which shall not respect the person of the aged and shall not pity the young.

51 And it shall eat up the young of your livestock, and the fruits of your land, so as not to leave to you grain, wine, oil, the herds of your oxen, and the flocks of your sheep, until it has destroyed you;

52 and has utterly crushed you in your cities, until the high and strong walls be destroyed in which you trusted, in all your land; and it shall afflict you in your cities, which He has given to you.

53 And you shall eat the fruit of your body, the flesh of your sons and of your daughters, all that He has given you, in your desperate straits and your affliction, with which your enemy shall afflict you.

54 He that is tender and very delicate within you shall look with an evil eye upon his brother, and the wife in his bosom, and the children that are left, which may have been left to him;

55 so as *not* to give to one of them of the flesh of his children, whom he shall eat, because of his having nothing left him in your desperate straits, and in your affliction, with which your enemies shall afflict you in all your cities.

56 And she that is tender and delicate among you, whose foot has not ventured to go upon the earth for delicacy and tenderness, shall look with an evil eye on her husband in her bosom, and her son and her daughter,

57 and her offspring that comes out between her feet, and the child which she shall bear; for she shall eat them because of the needs of all things, secretly in your desperate straits, and in your affliction, with which your enemy shall afflict you in your cities.

58 "If you are not careful to keep all the words of this law, which have been written in this book, to fear this glorious and wonderful name, THE LORD YOUR GOD;

59 then shall the Lord magnify your plagues, and the plagues of your descendants, great and wonderful plagues, and evil and abiding diseases.

60 And He shall bring upon you all the evil pain of Egypt, of which you were afraid, and they shall cleave to you.

61 And the Lord shall bring upon you every sickness, and every plague that is not written, and everyone that is written in the book of this law, until He has destroyed you.

62 And you shall be left few in number, whereas you were as the stars of the sky in multitude; because you did not obey the voice of the Lord your God.

63 And it shall come to pass that as the Lord rejoiced over you to do you good, and to multiply you, so the Lord will rejoice over you to destroy you; and you shall be quickly removed from the land, into which you go to inherit it.

64 "And the Lord your God shall scatter you among all nations, from one end of the earth to the other; and there you shall serve other gods *of* wood and stone, which neither you nor your fathers have known.

65 Moreover among those nations He will not give you quiet, neither by any means shall the sole of your foot have rest; and the Lord shall give you there another and a misgiving heart, and failing eyes, and a wasting soul.

66 And your life shall be in suspense before your eyes, and you shall be afraid by day and by night, and you shall have no assurance of your life.

67 In the morning you shall say, 'If only it were evening!' And in the evening you shall say, 'If only it were morning!' For the fear of your heart with which you shall fear, and for the sights of your eyes which you shall see.

68 And the Lord shall bring you back to Egypt in ships, by the way of which I said, 'You shall not see it again'; and you shall be sold there to your enemies as male and female slaves, and no one shall buy you."

DEUTERONOMY CHAPTER 29

The Covenant Renewed in Moab

1 These *are* the words of the covenant, which the Lord commanded Moses to make with the children of Israel in the land of Moab, besides the covenant which He made with them in Horeb.

2 And Moses called all the sons of Israel and said to them, "You have seen all the things that the Lord did to Pharaoh in the land of Egypt and *to* his servants, and all his land;

3 the great temptations which your eyes have seen, the signs, and those great wonders.

4 Yet the Lord God has not given you a heart to know, and eyes to see, and ears to hear, until this day.

5 And He led you forty years in the wilderness; your garments did not grow old, and your sandals were not worn away from off of your feet.

6 You did not eat bread, you did not drink wine or strong drink, that you might know that I *am* the Lord your God.

7 And you came as far as this place; and there came forth Sihon king of Heshbon, and Og king of Bashan, to meet us in war.

8 And we struck them and took their land, and I gave it for an inheritance to Reuben and Gad, and to the half-tribe of Manasseh.

9 And you shall take heed to do all the words of this covenant, that you may understand all things that you shall do.

10 "You all stand today before the Lord your God, the heads of your tribes, and your elders, and your judges, and your officers, every man of Israel,

11 your wives, and your children, and the stranger who is in the midst of your camp, from your woodcutters, even to those who draw water,

12 that you should enter into the covenant of the Lord your God and into His oaths, as many as the Lord your God appoints you this day;

13 that He may appoint you to Himself for a people, and He shall be your God, as He has said to you, and as He swore to your fathers, Abraham, Isaac, and Jacob.

14 "And I do not appoint to you alone this covenant and this oath;

15 but to those also who are here with you today before the Lord your God, and to those who are not here with you today. 16 For you know how we dwelt in the land of Egypt, how we came through the midst of the nations through whom you came.

17 And you beheld their abominations, and their idols, wood and stone, silver and gold, which are among them.

18 Lest there be among you man, or woman, or family, or tribe, whose heart has turned aside from the Lord your God, having gone to serve the gods of these nations; lest there be in you a root springing up with gall and bitterness.

19 And it shall be if one shall hear the words of this curse, and shall flatter himself in his heart, saying, 'Let good happen to me, for I will walk in the error of my heart,' lest the sinner destroy the guiltless with *him*:

20 God shall by no means be willing to pardon him, but rather the wrath of the Lord and His jealousy shall flame out against that man; and all the curses of this covenant shall attach themselves to him, which are written in this book, and the Lord shall blot out his name from under heaven.

21 And the Lord shall separate that man for evil among all the children of Israel, according to all the curses of the covenant that are written in the book of this law.

22 And another generation shall say—even your sons who shall rise up after you, and the stranger who shall come from a land afar off, and shall see the plagues of that land and their diseases, which the Lord has sent upon it,

23 brimstone and burning salt, (the whole land shall not be sown, neither shall any green thing spring up, nor rise upon it, as Sodom and Gomorrah were overthrown, Admah and Zeboiim, which the Lord overthrew in His wrath and anger)—

24 and all the nations shall say, 'Why has the Lord done thus to this land? What *is* this great fierceness of anger?'

25 And *men* shall say, 'Because they forsook the covenant of the Lord God of their fathers, the things which He appointed to their fathers, when He brought them out of the land of Egypt,

26 and they went and served other gods which they did not know, neither did He assign *them* to them.'

27 And the Lord was exceedingly angry with that land to bring upon it according to all the curses which are written in the book of this law.

28 And the Lord removed them from their land in anger, and wrath, and very great indignation, and cast them out into another land as *it is* this day.

29 The secret things *belong* to the Lord our God, but the things that are revealed *belong* to us and to our children forever, to do all the words of this law.

DEUTERONOMY CHAPTER 30

The Blessings of Returning to God

1 "And it shall come to pass when all these things shall have come upon you, the blessing and the curse, which I have set before your face, and you shall call *them* to mind among all the nations in which the Lord has scattered you,

2 and shall return to the Lord your God, and shall listen to His voice, according to all the things which I command you this day, with all your heart, and with all your soul;

3 then the Lord shall heal your iniquities, and shall pity you, and shall again gather you out from all the nations, among which the Lord has scattered you.

4 If your dispersion be from one end of heaven to the other, from there the Lord your God shall gather you, and from there the Lord your God shall take you.

5 And the Lord your God shall bring you in from there into the land which your fathers have inherited, and you shall inherit it; and He will do you good, and multiply you above your fathers.

6 And the Lord shall purge your heart, and the heart of your offspring, to love the Lord your God with all your heart, and with all your soul, that you may live.

⁷ And the Lord your God will put these curses upon your enemies, and upon those that hate you, who have persecuted you.

⁸ And you shall return and obey the voice of the Lord your God, and shall keep His commandments, all that I charge you this day.

⁹ And the Lord your God shall bless you in every work of your hands, in the offspring of your body, and in the offspring of your cattle, and in the fruits of your land, because the Lord your God will again rejoice over you for good, as He rejoiced over your fathers,

¹⁰ if you will obey the voice of the Lord your God, to keep His commandments, and His statutes, and His judgments written in the book of this law, if you turn to the Lord your God with all your heart, and with all your soul.

Exhortation to Choose Life

¹¹ "For this command which I give you this day is not grievous, neither is it far from you.

¹² It is not in heaven above, *as if there were one* saying, 'Who shall go up for us into heaven, and shall take it for us, and we will hear and do it?'

¹³ Neither is it beyond the sea, saying, 'Who will go over for us to the other side of the sea, and take it for us, and make it audible to us, and we will do it?'

¹⁴ The word is very near you, in your mouth, and in your heart, and in your hands, to do it.

¹⁵ "Behold, I have set before you this day life and death, good and evil.

¹⁶ If you will obey the commandments of the Lord your God which I command you this day, to love the Lord your God, to walk in all His ways, and to keep His statutes, and His judgments; then you shall live, and shall be many in number, and the Lord your God shall bless you in all the land into which you go to inherit it.

¹⁷ But if your heart should change, and you will not obey, and you shall go astray and worship other gods, and serve them,

¹⁸ I declare to you this day, that you shall utterly perish, and you shall by no means live long upon the land into which you go over the Jordan to inherit it.

¹⁹ I call both heaven and earth to witness this day against you, I have set before you life and death, blessing and curse: choose life, that you and your offspring may live;

²⁰ to love the Lord your God, to listen to His voice, and cleave to Him; for this *is* your life, and the length of your days, that you should dwell upon the land, which the Lord swore to your fathers, Abraham, Isaac, and Jacob, to give to them.

DEUTERONOMY CHAPTER 31

Joshua Becomes Moses' Successor

¹ And Moses finished speaking all these words to all the children of Israel,

² and said to them, "I am this day a hundred and twenty years *old*; I shall not be able any longer to come in or go out; and the Lord said to me, 'You shall not go over this Jordan.'

³ The Lord your God who goes before you, He shall destroy these nations before you, and you shall inherit them: and *it shall be* that Joshua shall go before your face, as the Lord has spoken.

⁴ And the Lord your God shall do to them as He did to Sihon and Og, the two kings of the Amorites, who were beyond the Jordan, and to their land, as He destroyed them.

⁵ And the Lord has delivered them to you; and you shall do to them, as I commanded you.

⁶ Be courageous and strong; fear not, neither be cowardly nor afraid before them; for *it is* the Lord your God that advances with you in the midst of you, neither will He by any means forsake you, nor desert you.

⁷ "And Moses called Joshua, and said to him before all Israel, 'Be courageous and strong; for you shall go in before this people into the land which the Lord swore to your fathers to give to them, and you shall give it to them for an inheritance.'

⁸ And the Lord that goes with you shall not forsake you nor abandon you; fear not, neither be afraid."

The Law to be Read Every Seventh Year

⁹ And Moses wrote the words of this law in a book, and gave it to the priests, the sons of Levi, who bear the ark of the covenant of the Lord, and to the elders of the sons of Israel.

¹⁰ And Moses charged them in that day, saying, "After seven years, in the time of the year of release, in the Feast of Tabernacles,

¹¹ when all Israel comes together to appear before the Lord your God, in the place which the Lord shall choose, you shall read this law before all Israel in their ears,

¹² having assembled the people, the men, and the women, and the children, and the stranger that is in your cities, that they may hear, and that they may learn to fear the Lord your God; and they shall hear and learn to do all the words of this law.

¹³ And their sons who have not known shall hear, and shall learn to fear the Lord your God all the days that they live upon the land, into which you go over the Jordan to inherit it."

Moses and Joshua Receive God's Charge

¹⁴ And the Lord said to Moses, "Behold, the days of your death are at hand; call Joshua, and stand by the doors of the tabernacle of testimony, and I will give him a command." And Moses and Joshua went to the tabernacle of testimony, and stood by the doors of the tabernacle of testimony.

¹⁵ And the Lord descended in a cloud, and stood by the doors of the tabernacle of testimony; and the pillar of the cloud stood by the doors of the tabernacle of testimony.

16 And the Lord said to Moses, "Behold, you shall sleep with your fathers, and this people shall arise and whore after the strange gods of the land, into which they are entering: and they will forsake Me, and break My covenant, which I made with them.

17 And I will be very angry with them in that day, and I will leave them and turn My face away from them, and they shall be devoured. And many evils and afflictions shall come upon them, and they shall say in that day, 'Because the Lord my God is not with me, these evils have come upon me.'

18 And I will surely turn away My face from them in that day, because of all their evil doings which they have done, because they turned aside after strange gods.

19 And now write the words of this song, and teach it to the children of Israel, and you shall put it into their mouth, that this song may witness for Me among the children of Israel to their face.

20 For I will bring them into the good land, which I swore to their fathers, to give to them a land flowing with milk and honey, and they shall eat and be filled and satisfy *themselves*. Then they shall turn aside after other gods, and serve them, and they shall provoke Me, and break My covenant.

21 And this song shall stand up to witness against them; for they shall not forget it out of their mouth, or out of the mouth of their offspring; for I know their wickedness, what they are doing here this day, before I have brought them into the good land, which I swore to their fathers."

22 And Moses wrote this song in that day, and taught it to the children of Israel.

23 And he charged Joshua, and said, "Be courageous and strong, for you shall bring the sons of Israel into the land, which the Lord swore to them, and He shall be with you."

24 And when Moses finished writing all the words of this law in a book, even to the end,

25 then he charged the Levites who bear the ark of the covenant of the Lord, saying,

26 "Take the book of this law, and you shall put it inside the ark of the covenant of the Lord your God; and it shall be there among you for a testimony.

27 For I know your provocation, and your stiff neck; for yet during my life with you at this day, you have been provoking in your conduct toward God: how shall you not also be so after my death?

28 Gather together to me the heads of your tribes, and your elders, and your judges, and your officers, that I may speak in their ears all these words; and I call both heaven and earth to witness against them.

29 For I know that after my death you will utterly transgress, and turn aside out of the way which I have commanded you; and evils shall come upon you in the latter days, because you will do evil before the Lord, to provoke Him to anger by the works of your hands."

30 And Moses spoke all the words of this song even to the end, in the ears of the whole assembly.

DEUTERONOMY CHAPTER 32

The Song of Moses

1 "Attend, O heaven, and I will speak; and let the earth hear the words out of my mouth.

2 Let my speech be looked for as the rain, and my words come down as dew, as the showers upon the herb, and as snow upon the grass.

3 For I have called on the name of the Lord; ascribe greatness to our God.

4 *As for God*, His works *are* true, and all His ways *are* justice. God *is* faithful, and there is no unrighteousness *in Him*; just and holy *is* the Lord.

5 They have sinned, not *pleasing* Him; spotted children, a crooked and perverse generation.

6 Do you thus recompense the Lord? O foolish and unwise people. Did not He Himself, your Father, purchase you, and make you, and form you?

7 Remember the days of old, consider the years for past ages; ask your father, and he shall relate to you, *ask* your elders, and they shall tell you.

8 When the Most High divided the nations, when He separated the sons of Adam, He set the bounds of the nations according to the number of the angels of God.

9 And His people Jacob became the portion of the Lord, Israel was the line of His inheritance.

10 He maintained him in the wilderness, in burning thirst and a dry land: He led him about and instructed him, and kept him as the apple of *His* eye.

11 As an eagle would watch over his brood, and yearns over his young, he receives them, having spread his wings, and takes them up on his back.

12 The Lord alone has led them, there was no strange god with them.

13 He brought them up on the strength of the land; He fed them with the fruits of the fields; they sucked honey out of the rock, and oil out of the solid rock.

14 Butter of cows, and milk of sheep, with the fat of lambs and rams, of calves and kids, with fat of kidneys of wheat; and he drank wine, the blood of the grape.

15 "So Jacob ate and was filled, and the beloved one kicked; he grew fat, he became thick and broad: then he forsook the God that made him, and departed from God his Savior."

16 "They provoked Me to anger with strange gods; with their abominations they bitterly angered Me."

17 "They sacrificed to demons, and not to God; to gods whom they did not know: new and fresh *gods* came in, whom their fathers did not know.

18 You have forsaken the God that fathered you, and forgotten the God who feeds you.

19 And the Lord saw, and was jealous; and He was provoked by the anger of His sons and daughters,

20 and said, 'I will turn away My face from them, and will show what shall happen to them in the last days; for it is a perverse generation, sons in whom is no faith.

21 They have provoked Me to jealousy by *that which is* not God, they have exasperated Me with their idols; and I will provoke them to jealousy with them that are not a nation, I will anger them with a nation void of understanding.

22 For a fire has been kindled out of My wrath, it shall burn to hell below; it shall devour the land, and the fruits of it; it shall set on fire the foundations of the mountains.

23 'I will gather evils upon them, and will fight with My weapons against them.

24 *They shall be* consumed with hunger and the devouring of birds, and there shall be irremediable destruction: I will send forth against them the teeth of wild beasts, with the rage of *serpents* creeping on the ground.

25 Outside, the sword shall bereave them of children, and terror *shall issue* out of the secret chambers; the young man shall perish with the virgin, the suckling with him who has grown old.

26 I said, I will scatter them, and I will cause their memorial to cease from among men.

27 Were it not for the wrath of the enemy, lest they should live long, lest their enemies should combine against them; lest they should say, Our own outstretched arm, and not the Lord's, has done all these things.'

28 It is a nation that has lost counsel, neither is there understanding in them.

29 They had not sense to understand; let them reserve these things against the time to come.

30 How should one pursue a thousand, and two put tens of thousands to flight, if God had not sold them, and the Lord had not delivered them up?

31 For their gods are not as our God, but our enemies *are* void of understanding.

32 For their vine *is* of the vine of Sodom, and their vinebranch of Gomorrah: their grape *is* a grape of gall, their cluster *is* one of bitterness.

33 Their wine *is* the rage of serpents, and the incurable rage of asps.

34 "'Lo! Are not these things stored up by Me, and sealed among My treasures?

35 In the day of vengeance I will recompense, whenever their foot shall be tripped up; for the day of their destruction *is* near to them, and the judgments at hand are close upon you.'

36 For the Lord shall judge His people, and shall be comforted over His servants; for He saw that they were utterly weakened, and failed in the hostile invasion, and have become feeble.

37 And the Lord said, 'Where are their gods on whom they trusted?

38 The fat of whose sacrifices you ate, and you drank the wine of their drink offerings? Let them arise and help you, and be your protectors.

39 Behold I, even I, am *He*, and there is no God beside Me: I kill, and I will make alive: I will strike, and I will heal; and there is none who shall deliver out of My hands.

40 For I will lift up My hand to heaven, and swear by My right hand, and I will say, "I live forever."

41 For I will sharpen My sword like lightning, and My hand shall take hold of judgment; and I will render judgment to My enemies, and will recompense them that hate Me.

42 I will make My weapons drunk with blood, and My sword shall devour flesh, *it shall gorge itself* with the blood of the wounded, and from the captivity of the heads of *their* enemies that rule over them.'

43 Rejoice, you heavens, with Him, and let all the angels of God worship Him; rejoice you Gentiles, with His people, and let all the sons of God strengthen themselves in Him; for He shall avenge the blood of His sons, and He shall render vengeance, and recompense justice to His enemies, and He will repay them that hate Him; and the Lord shall purge the land of His people."

44 And Moses wrote this song in that day, and taught it to the children of Israel; and Moses went in and spoke all the words of this law in the ears of the people, he and Joshua the *son* of Nun.

45 And Moses finished speaking to all Israel.

46 And he said to them, "Take heed with your heart to all these words, which I testify to you this day, which you shall command your sons, to observe and do all the words of this law.

47 For this *is* no vain word to you; for it *is* your life, and because of this word you shall live long upon the land, into which you go over the Jordan to inherit it."

48 And the Lord spoke to Moses in this day, saying,

49 "Go up this mountain of Abarim, this Mount Nebo which is in the land of Moab over against Jericho, and behold the land of Canaan, which I give to the sons of Israel:

50 and *you shall* die on the mountain which you ascend, and be gathered to your people; as Aaron your brother died on Mount Hor, and was gathered to his people.

51 Because you disobeyed My word among the children of Israel, at the Waters of Strife, of Kadesh, in the Wilderness of Zin; because you did not hallow Me among the sons of Israel.

52 You shall see the land before *you*, but you shall not enter into it."

DEUTERONOMY CHAPTER 33

Moses' Final Blessing on Israel

1 And this *is* the blessing with which Moses the man of God blessed the children of Israel before his death.

2 And he said, "The Lord has come from Sinai, and has appeared from Seir to us, and has shone forth from Mount Paran, with the ten thousands of Kadesh; on His right hand *were* His angels with Him.

³ And He spared His people, and all His saints *are* in Your hand; and they are under You. And he received of His words ⁴ the law which Moses commanded us, an inheritance to the assemblies of Jacob.

⁵ And he shall be prince with the beloved one, when the princes of the people are gathered together with the tribes of Israel.

⁶ "Let Reuben live, and not die; and let him be many in number."

⁷ And this *is the blessing* of Judah: "Hear, Lord, the voice of Judah, and visit his people: his hands shall contend for him, and You shall be a help from his enemies."

⁸ And to Levi he said, "*Let* Levi give his manifestations and his truth to the holy One, whom they tempted in the temptation; they reviled Him at the Water of Strife.

⁹ Who says to his father and mother, 'I have not seen you'; and he disowned his brothers, and he refused to know his children; he kept Your oracles, and observed Your covenant. ¹⁰ They shall declare Your ordinances to Jacob, and Your law to Israel; they shall place incense in *the time of* Your wrath continually upon Your altar.

¹¹ Bless his substance, O Lord, and accept the works of his hands; break the loins of his enemies that have risen up against him, and let not them that hate him rise up."

¹² And to Benjamin he said, "The beloved of the Lord shall dwell in confidence, and God overshadows him always, and he rested between His shoulders.

¹³ And to Joseph he said, "His land *is* of the blessing of the Lord, of the seasons of sky and dew, and of the deeps of wells below,

¹⁴ and of the fruits of the changes of the sun in season, and of the produce of the months,

¹⁵ from the top of the ancient mountains, and from the top of the everlasting hills,

¹⁶ and of the fullness of the land in season; and let the things pleasing to him that dwelt in the bush come on the head of Joseph, and on the crown *of him who was* glorified above his brothers.

¹⁷ His beauty *is as* the firstborn bull, his horns *are* the horns of a unicorn; with them he shall thrust the nations at once, even from the end of the earth: these *are* the ten thousands of Ephraim, and these *are* the thousands of Manasseh."

¹⁸ And to Zebulun he said, "Rejoice, Zebulun, in your going out, and Issachar in his tents.

¹⁹ They shall utterly destroy the nations, and you shall call *men* there, and there offer the sacrifice of righteousness; for the wealth of the sea shall suckle you, and so shall the emporiums of them that dwell by the sea coast."

²⁰ And to Gad he said, "Blessed *be* the one that enlarges Gad: as a lion he rested, having broken the arm and the ruler.

²¹ And he saw his firstfruits, that there the land of the princes gathered with the chiefs of the people was divided; the Lord wrought righteousness, and His judgment with Israel."

²² And to Dan he said, "Dan *is* a lion's whelp, and shall leap out of Bashan."

²³ And to Naphthali he said, "Naphthali *has* the fullness of good things; and let him be filled with blessing from the Lord: he shall inherit the west and the south."

²⁴ And to Asher he said, "Asher *is* blessed with children; and he shall be acceptable to his brothers: he shall dip his food in oil.

²⁵ His sandal shall be iron and brass; as your days *be*, so *shall be* your strength.

²⁶ There is not *any such* as the God of the beloved; He who rides upon the heaven *is* your helper, and the Magnificent One of the firmament.

²⁷ And the rule of God shall protect you, and *that* under the strength of the everlasting arms; and He shall cast forth the enemy from before your face, saying, 'Perish.'

²⁸ And Israel shall dwell in confidence alone on the land of Jacob, with grain and wine; and the sky *shall be* misty with dew upon you.

²⁹ Blessed *are* you, O Israel; who *is* like you, O people saved by the Lord? Your helper shall hold His shield over you, and *His* sword *is* your boast; and your enemies shall speak falsely to you, and you shall tread upon their neck."

DEUTERONOMY CHAPTER 34

The Death of Moses

¹ And Moses went up from the plains of Moab, to Mount Nebo, to the top of Pisgah, which is before Jericho; and the Lord showed him all the land of Gilead, to Dan, and all the land of Nephthali,

² and all the land of Ephraim and Manasseh, and all the land of Judah to the farthest sea;

³ and the wilderness, and the country round about Jericho, the city of palm trees, to Zoar.

⁴ And the Lord said to Moses, "This *is* the land of which I swore to Abraham, Isaac, and Jacob, saying, 'To your descendants will I give it': and I have showed it to your eyes, but you shall not go in to it."

⁵ So Moses the servant of the Lord died in the land of Moab, by the word of the Lord.

⁶ And they buried him in Gai near Beth Peor; and no one has seen his tomb to this day.

⁷ And Moses was a hundred and twenty years old at his death; his eyes were not dimmed, nor were his natural powers destroyed.

⁸ And the children of Israel wept for Moses in Araboth of Moab at the Jordan near Jericho for thirty days; and the days of weeping and mourning for Moses were completed.

⁹ And Joshua the son of Nun was filled with the spirit of knowledge, for Moses had laid his hands upon him; and the children of Israel hearkened to him; and they did as the Lord commanded Moses.

¹⁰ And there rose up no more a prophet in Israel like Moses, whom the Lord knew face to face,

[11] in all the signs and wonders, which the Lord sent him to work in Egypt on Pharaoh, and his servants, and all his land;
[12] the great wonders, and the mighty hand which Moses displayed before all Israel.

THE BOOK OF JOSHUA

God's Commission to Joshua

[1] And it came to pass after the death of Moses, that the Lord spoke to Joshua the son of Nun, the minister of Moses, saying,
[2] "Moses My servant is dead; now then arise, go over the Jordan, you and all this people, into the land which I give them.
[3] Every spot on which you shall tread I will give it to you, as I said to Moses.
[4] The wilderness and Lebanon, as far as the great river, the River Euphrates, and as far as the extremity of the sea; your coasts shall be from the setting of the sun.
[5] Not a man shall stand against you all the days of your life; and as I was with Moses, so will I also be with you, and I will not fail you, or neglect you.
[6] Be strong and of good courage, for you shall divide the land to this people, which I swore to give to your fathers.
[7] Be strong, therefore, and very courageous, to observe and do as Moses My servant commanded you; and you shall not turn from there to the right hand or to the left, that you may be wise in whatsoever you may do.
[8] And the Book of this Law shall not depart from your mouth, and you shall meditate on it day and night, that you may know how to do all the things that are written *in it*; then shall you prosper, and make your ways prosperous, and then shall you be wise.
[9] Behold, I have commanded you; be strong and courageous, be not cowardly nor fearful, for the Lord your God is with you in all places in which you go."

Preparations for the Invasion

[10] And Joshua commanded the scribes of the people, saying, [11] "Go into the midst of the camp of the people, and command the people, saying, 'Prepare provisions; for yet three days and you shall go over this Jordan, entering in to take possession of the land, which the Lord God of your fathers gives to you.'"
[12] And to Reuben, and to Gad, and to the half tribe of Manasseh, Joshua said,
[13] "Remember the word which Moses the servant of the Lord commanded you, saying, 'The Lord your God has caused you to rest, and has given you this land.'
[14] Let your wives and your children and your cattle dwell in the land, which He has given you; and you shall go over well armed before your brothers, everyone of you who is strong; and you shall fight on their side;
[15] until the Lord your God shall have given your brothers rest, as also to you, and they also shall have inherited the land, which the Lord your God gives them; then you shall depart each one to his inheritance, which Moses gave you beyond the Jordan, eastward."
[16] And they answered Joshua and said, "We will do all things which you commanded us, and we will go to every place that you shall send us.
[17] Just as we obeyed Moses, we will obey you; only let the Lord our God be with you, as He was with Moses.
[18] And whoever shall disobey you, and whoever shall not obey your words as you shall command him, let him die; but be strong and courageous."

JOSHUA CHAPTER 2

Spies Sent to Jericho

[1] And Joshua the son of Nun sent out of Shittim two young men to spy *the land*, saying, "Go up and view the land; especially Jericho." And the two young men went and entered into Jericho. And they entered into the house of a harlot, whose name *was* Rahab, and lodged there.
[2] And it was reported to the king of Jericho, saying, "Men of the sons of Israel have come in here to spy out the land."
[3] And the king of Jericho sent and spoke to Rahab, saying, "Bring out the men that entered into your house this night; for they have come to spy out the land."
[4] And the woman took the two men and hid them; and she spoke to the messengers, saying, "The men came in to me,
[5] but when the gate was shut in the evening, the men went out; I do not know where they have gone; follow after them, *perhaps* you may overtake them."
[6] But she *had* brought them up upon the house, and hid them in the flax stalks that were spread by her on the house.
[7] And the men followed after them on the way to the Jordan, and the gate was shut.
[8] And it came to pass when the men who pursued after them had gone forth, and before the spies had laid down to sleep, that she came up to them on the top of the house;
[9] and she said to them, "I know that the Lord has given you the land, for the fear of you has fallen upon us.
[10] For we have heard that the Lord God dried up the Red Sea before you, when you came out of the land of Egypt, and all that He did to the two kings of the Amorites, who were beyond the Jordan, to Sihon and Og, whom you utterly destroyed.
[11] And when we heard it we were amazed in our heart, and there was no longer any spirit in any of us because of you, for the Lord your God *is* God in heaven above, and on the earth below.
[12] And now swear to me by the Lord God; since I have dealt mercifully with you, so shall you also deal mercifully with the house of my father,
[13] and save alive the house of my father, my mother, and my brothers, and all my house, and all that they have, and you shall rescue my soul from death."

14 And the men said to her, "Our life for yours, *even* unto death." And she said, "When the Lord has delivered the city to you, you shall deal mercifully and truly with me."

15 And she let them down by the window,

16 and she said to them, "Depart into the hill country, lest the pursuers meet you, and you shall be hidden there three days until your pursuers return from after you, and afterwards you shall depart on your way."

17 And the men said to her, "We are clear of this your oath.

18 Behold, we shall enter into a part of the city, and you shall set a sign; you shall bind this scarlet cord in the window, by which you have let us down, and you shall bring in to yourself, into your house, your father, and your mother, and your brothers, and all the family of your father.

19 And it shall come to pass that whoever shall go outside the door of your house, his guilt shall be upon him, and we shall be freed of this your oath; and we will be responsible for all that shall be found with you in your house.

20 But if anyone should injure us, or betray *us* regarding this, *then* we shall be freed of this your oath."

21 And she said to them, "Let it be according to your word." And she sent them out, and they departed.

22 And they came to the hill country, and remained there three days; and the pursuers searched all the roads, and did not find them.

23 And the two young men returned, and came down out of the mountain; and they went over to Joshua the son of Nun, and told him all the things that had happened to them.

24 And they said to Joshua, "The Lord has delivered all the land into our power, and all the inhabitants of that land tremble because of us."

JOSHUA CHAPTER 3

Israel Crosses the Jordan

1 And Joshua rose up early in the morning, and departed from Shittim; and they came as far as the Jordan, and lodged there before they crossed over.

2 And it came to pass after three days, *that* the scribes went through the camp;

3 and they commanded the people, saying, "When you shall see the ark of the covenant of the Lord our God, and our priests and the Levites bearing it, you shall depart from your places, and you shall go after it.

4 But let there be a distance between you and it; you shall stand as much as two thousand cubits *from it*. Do not draw near to it, that you may know the way which you are to go; for you have not gone the way before."

5 And Joshua said to the people, "Consecrate yourselves, for tomorrow the Lord shall do wonders among you."

6 And Joshua said to the priests, "Take up the ark of the covenant of the Lord, and go before the people." And the priests took up the ark of the covenant of the Lord, and went before the people.

7 And the Lord said to Joshua, "This day do I begin to exalt you before all the children of Israel, that they may know that as I was with Moses, so will I also be with you.

8 And now charge the priests that bear the ark of the covenant, saying, 'As soon as you shall enter on a part of the water of the Jordan, then you shall stand in the Jordan.'"

9 And Joshua said to the children of Israel, "Come here, and listen to the word of the Lord our God.

10 Hereby you shall know that the living God *is* among you, and will utterly destroy from before our face the Canaanite, the Hittite, the Perizzite, the Hivite, the Amorite, the Girgashite, and the Jebusite.

11 Behold, the ark of the covenant of the Lord of all the earth passes over the Jordan.

12 Choose for yourselves twelve men of the sons of Israel, one from each tribe.

13 And it shall come to pass, when the feet of the priests that bear the ark of the covenant of the Lord of the whole earth shall rest in the water of the Jordan, the water of the Jordan *below* shall fail, and the water coming down from above shall stop."

14 So the people set out from their tents to cross over the Jordan, and the priests bore the ark of the covenant of the Lord before the people.

15 And when the priests that bore the ark of the covenant of the Lord entered the Jordan, and the feet of the priests that bore the ark of the covenant of the Lord were dipped in part of the water of the Jordan (now the Jordan overflowed all its banks about the time of wheat harvest),

16 then the waters that came down from above stopped; there stood one solid heap very far off, as far as the region of Zaretan, and the lower part came down to the sea of the Arabah, the Salt Sea, till it completely failed; and the people stood opposite Jericho.

17 And the priests that bore the ark of the covenant of the Lord stood on dry land in the midst of the Jordan; and all the children of Israel went through on dry land, until all the people had completely crossed over the Jordan.

JOSHUA CHAPTER 4

The Memorial Stones

1 And when the people had completely passed over the Jordan, the Lord spoke to Joshua, saying,

2 "Take men from among the people, one from each tribe,

3 and command them; and you shall take out of the midst of the Jordan twelve fit stones, and having carried them across together with yourselves, place them in your camp, where you shall encamp for the night."

4 And Joshua, having called twelve men of distinction among the children of Israel, one of each tribe,

5 said to them, "Advance before me in the presence of the Lord into the midst of the Jordan, and each having taken up a stone from there, let him carry it on his shoulders, according to the number of the twelve tribes of Israel,

⁶ that these may be to you continually for an appointed sign, that when your son asks you in the future, saying, 'What are these stones to us?'

⁷ then you may explain to your son, saying, 'The River Jordan was dried up from before the ark of the covenant of the Lord of the whole earth, when it crossed over'; and these stones shall be for a memorial for you for the children of Israel forever."

⁸ And the children of Israel did so, as the Lord commanded Joshua; and they took up twelve stones out of the midst of the Jordan, (as the Lord commanded Joshua, when the children of Israel had completely passed over) and carried these stones with them into the camp, and laid them down there.

⁹ And Joshua also set twelve other stones in the Jordan itself, in the place that was under the feet of the priests that bore the ark of the covenant of the Lord; and they are there to this day.

¹⁰ And the priests that bore the ark of the covenant stood in the Jordan, until Joshua *had* finished all that the Lord commanded him to report to the people; and the people hurried and passed over.

¹¹ And it came to pass when all the people had passed over, that the ark of the covenant of the Lord passed over, and the stones before them.

¹² And the sons of Reuben, and the sons of Gad, and the half tribe of Manasseh passed over armed before the children of Israel, as Moses commanded them.

¹³ Forty thousand armed for battle went over before the Lord to war, to the city of Jericho.

¹⁴ In that day the Lord magnified Joshua before all the people of Israel; and they feared him, as *they did* Moses, as long as he lived.

¹⁵ And the Lord spoke to Joshua, saying,

¹⁶ "Command the priests that bear the ark of the covenant of the testimony of the Lord, to go up out of the Jordan."

¹⁷ And Joshua commanded the priests, saying, "Come up from the Jordan."

¹⁸ And it came to pass when the priests who bore the ark of the covenant of the Lord had come up from the midst of the Jordan, and set their feet upon the land, *that* the water of the Jordan rushed back to its place, and went as before over all of its banks.

¹⁹ And the people went up out of the Jordan on the tenth day of the first month; and the children of Israel encamped in Gilgal, to the east of Jericho.

²⁰ And Joshua set these twelve stones which he took out of the Jordan, in Gilgal,

²¹ saying, "When your sons ask you, saying, 'What are these stones?'

²² Tell your sons, that Israel went over this Jordan on dry land, ²³ when the Lord our God had dried up the water of the Jordan from before them, until they had passed over; as the Lord our God did to the Red Sea, which the Lord our God dried up from before us, until we passed over.

²⁴ That all the nations of the earth might know, that the power of the Lord is mighty, and that you might worship the Lord our God in every work."

JOSHUA CHAPTER 5

The New Generation Circumcised

¹ And it came to pass when the kings of the Amorites who were beyond the Jordan heard, and the kings of Phoenicia by the sea, that the Lord God had dried up the River Jordan from before the children of Israel when they passed over, that their hearts failed, and they were terror stricken, and there was no sense in them because of the children of Israel.

² And about this time the Lord said to Joshua, "Make for yourself stone knives of sharp stone, and sit down and circumcise the children of Israel the second time."

³ And Joshua made sharp knives of stone, and circumcised the children of Israel at the place called the Hill of Foreskins.

⁴ And *this is* the way in which Joshua purified the children of Israel: as many as were born in the way, and as many as were uncircumcised of them that came out of Egypt,

⁵ all these Joshua circumcised; for forty-two years Israel wandered in the Wilderness of Mabdaris—

⁶ Therefore most of the fighting men that came out of the land of Egypt were uncircumcised, who disobeyed the commandments of God; concerning whom also He determined that they should not see the land, which the Lord swore to give to their fathers, a land flowing with milk and honey.

⁷ And in their place He raised up their sons, whom Joshua circumcised, because they were uncircumcised, having been born by the way.

⁸ And when they had been circumcised, they rested there in the camp until they were healed.

⁹ And the Lord said to Joshua the son of Nun, "On this day have I removed the reproach of Egypt from you." And he called the name of that place Gilgal.

The Passover at Gilgal

¹⁰ And the children of Israel kept the Passover on the fourteenth day of the month, at evening, to the west of Jericho on the opposite side of the Jordan in the plain.

¹¹ And they ate of the unleavened grain of the earth, and the new *grain*.

¹² In this day the manna failed, after they had eaten of the grain of the land, and the children of Israel no longer had manna: and they took the fruits of the land of the Phoenicians in that year.

Joshua's Vision

¹³ And it came to pass when Joshua was in Jericho, that he looked up with his eyes and saw a Man standing before him, and *there was* a drawn sword in His hand. And Joshua drew near and said to Him, "Are You for us, or for our enemies?"

14 And He said to him, "I have now come, the Commander of the army of the Lord." And Joshua fell on his face upon the earth, and said to Him, "O Lord, what do You command Your servant?"

15 And the Commander of the Lord's army said to Joshua, "Loose your shoe from off your feet, for the place where you now stand is holy."

JOSHUA CHAPTER 6

The Destruction of Jericho

1 Now Jericho was closely shut up and besieged, and none went out of it, and none came in.

2 And the Lord said to Joshua, "Behold, I deliver Jericho into your power, and its king, *and its* mighty men.

3 And set the men of war round about it.

4 And it shall be *that* when you shall sound with the trumpet, all the people shall shout together.

5 And when they have shouted, the walls of the city shall fall by themselves; and all the people shall enter, each one rushing directly into the city."

6 And Joshua the *son* of Nun went in to the priests, and spoke to them, saying, "Let seven priests having seven sacred trumpets proceed thus before the Lord, and let them sound loudly; and let the ark of the covenant of the Lord follow.

7 Command the people to go around, and encompass the city; and let your men of war pass on, armed before the Lord.

8 (This verse omitted in LXX)

9 "And let the men of war proceed before, and the priests bringing up the rear behind the ark of the covenant of the Lord *proceed* the sounding the trumpets."

10 And Joshua commanded the people, saying, "Do not cry out, nor let anyone hear your voice, until He Himself declares to you the time to cry out, and then you shall cry out."

11 And the ark of the covenant of God, having gone round immediately, returned into the camp, and lodged there.

12 And on the second day Joshua rose up in the morning, and the priests took up the ark of the covenant of the Lord.

13 And the seven priests bearing the seven trumpets went on before the Lord; and afterwards the men of war went on, and the remainder of the multitude went after the ark of the covenant of the Lord, and the priests sounded with the trumpets.

14 And all the rest of the multitude compassed the city six times from within a short distance, and went back again into the camp; this they did for six days.

15 And on the seventh day they rose up early, and compassed the city on that day seven times.

16 And it came to pass at the seventh circuit the priests blew the trumpets, and Joshua said to the children of Israel, "Shout, for the Lord has given you the city.

17 And the city shall be devoted, it and all things that are in it, to the Lord of hosts: only save Rahab the harlot, and everything in her house.

18 But keep yourselves strictly from the accursed thing, lest you set your mind upon and take of the accursed thing, and you make the camp of the children of Israel an accursed thing, and destroy us.

19 And all the silver, or gold, or brass, or iron, shall be holy to the Lord; it shall be carried into the treasury of the Lord."

20 And the priests sounded with the trumpets. And when the people heard the trumpets, all the people shouted at once with a loud and strong shout, and all the wall fell round about, and all the people went up into the city.

21 And Joshua devoted it to destruction, and all things that were in the city, man and woman, young man and old, calf and donkey, with the edge of the sword.

22 And Joshua said to the two young men who had acted as spies, "Go into the house of the woman, and bring her out from there, and all that she has."

23 And the two young men who had spied out the city entered into the house of the woman, and brought out Rahab the harlot, and her father, and her mother, and her brothers, and her kindred, and all that she had; and they set her outside the camp of Israel.

24 And the city was burned with fire, with all the things that were in it: only of the silver, gold, brass, and iron, they gave to be brought into the treasury of the Lord.

25 And Joshua spared Rahab the harlot, and all the house of her father, and caused her to dwell in Israel until this day, because she hid the spies which Joshua sent to spy out Jericho.

26 And Joshua adjured *them* on that day before the Lord, saying, "Cursed *be* the man who shall build that city—he shall lay the foundation of it in his firstborn, and he shall set up the gates of it in his youngest son." And so did Hozan of Bethel; he laid the foundation in Abiron his firstborn, and set up the gates of it in his youngest surviving son.

27 And the Lord was with Joshua, and his name was in all the land.

JOSHUA CHAPTER 7

The Sin of Achan and Its Punishment

1 But the children of Israel committed a great trespass, and kept back *part* of the accursed thing; and Achan the son of Carmi, the son of Zambri, the son of Zabdi, of the tribe of Judah, took of the accursed thing; and the Lord was very angry with the children of Israel.

2 And Joshua sent men to Ai, which is by Beth Aven, saying, "Spy out Ai." And the men went up and spied out Ai.

3 And they returned to Joshua, and said to him, "Let not all the people go up, but let about two or three thousand men go up and besiege the city, for *they* are few."

4 And there went up about three thousand men, and they fled from before the men of Ai.

5 And the men of Ai struck down about thirty-six men, and they pursued them from the gate, and destroyed them from the steep hill; and the heart of the people was alarmed and became as water.

6 And Joshua tore his clothes. And Joshua fell to the ground on his face before the Lord until evening, he and the elders of Israel; and they cast dust on their heads.

7 And Joshua said, "I pray, O Lord, why has Your servant brought this people over the Jordan to deliver them to the Amorite to destroy us? If only we would had remained, and settled ourselves beyond the Jordan!

8 And what shall I say since Israel has turned his back before his enemy?

9 And when the Canaanites and all the inhabitants of the land hear it, they shall compass us round about and destroy us from off the land: and what will You do *for* Your great name?"

10 And the Lord said to Joshua, "Rise up; why have you fallen upon your face?

11 The people have sinned, and transgressed the covenant which I made with them; they have stolen from the accursed thing, and put it into their store.

12 And the children of Israel will not be able to stand before their enemies; they will turn their back before their enemies, for they have become an accursed thing: I will no longer be with you, unless you remove the accursed thing from yourselves.

13 Rise up, sanctify the people, and tell them to sanctify themselves for tomorrow. Thus says the Lord God of Israel: The accursed thing is among you; you shall not be able to stand before your enemies, until you have removed the accursed thing from among you.

14 And you shall all be gathered together by your tribes in the morning, and it shall come to pass that the tribe which the Lord shall show, you shall bring by families; and the family which the Lord shall show, you shall bring by households; and the household which the Lord shall show you shall bring, man by man.

15 And the man who shall be pointed out shall be burned with fire, and all that he has; because he has transgressed the covenant of the Lord, and has done wickedness in Israel."

16 And Joshua rose up early, and brought the people by their tribes; and the tribe of Judah was pointed out.

17 And *Judah* was brought by its families, and the family of the Zarhites was pointed out.

18 And it was brought man by man, and Achan the son of Zabdi the son of Zerah was pointed out.

19 And Joshua said to Achan, "Give glory this day to the Lord God of Israel, and make confession; and tell me what you have done, and do not hide it from me."

20 And Achan answered Joshua and said, "Indeed I have sinned against the Lord God of Israel; thus and thus have I done.

21 I saw in the spoil an embroidered mantle, and two hundred shekels of silver, and one golden wedge of fifty shekels, and I desired them and took them; and behold, they are hid in my tent, and the silver is hid under them."

22 And Joshua sent messengers, and they ran to the tent into the camp; and these things were hidden in his tent, and the silver under them.

23 And they brought them out of the tent, and brought them to Joshua and the elders of Israel, and they laid them before the Lord.

24 And Joshua took Achan the son of Zerah, and brought him to the valley of Achor, and his sons, his daughters, his calves, his donkeys, his sheep, his tent, and all his property, and all the people with him; and he brought them to the valley of Achor.

25 And Joshua said to Achan, "Why have you destroyed us? The Lord destroy you this day!" And all Israel stoned him with stones.

26 And they set up over him a great heap of stones; and the Lord ceased from His fierce anger. Therefore he called the place the Valley of Achor to this day.

JOSHUA CHAPTER 8

The Fall of Ai

1 And the Lord said to Joshua, "Do not fear, nor be dismayed. Take with you all the men of war, and arise, go up to Ai. Behold, I have given into your hands the king of Ai, and his land.

2 And you shall do to Ai as you did to Jericho and its king; and you shall take to yourself the spoil of its livestock; set now for yourself an ambush for the city behind."

3 And Joshua and all the men of war rose to go up to Ai; and Joshua chose out thirty thousand mighty men, and he sent them away by night.

4 And he commanded them, saying, "Go, and lie in ambush behind the city: do not go far from the city, and you shall all be ready.

5 Then I and all the people *who are* with me shall draw near to the city. And it shall come to pass when the inhabitants of Ai shall come forth to meet us as before, that we will flee from before them.

6 And when they shall come out after us, we will draw them away from the city; and they will say, 'These men flee from before us, just like before.'

7 And you shall rise up out of the ambush, and go into the city.

8 You shall do according to this word. Behold, I have commanded you."

9 And Joshua sent them, and they went to lie in ambush; and they lay between Bethel and Ai, west of Ai.

10 And Joshua rose up early in the morning and numbered the people. And he went up, he and the elders before the people, to Ai.

¹¹ And all the men of war went up with him, and they went forward and came over against the city eastward.

¹² And the ambush *was* on the west side of the city.

¹³ (This verse omitted in LXX)

¹⁴ And it came to pass when the king of Ai saw *it*, he hastened and went out to meet them direct to the battle, he and all the people *that were* with him. And he did not know that there was an ambush *formed* against him behind the city.

¹⁵ And Joshua and Israel saw, and retreated from before them.

¹⁶ And they pursued after the children of Israel, and they themselves went to a distance from the city.

¹⁷ There was no one left in Ai who did not pursue after Israel; and they left the city open, and pursued after Israel.

¹⁸ And the Lord said to Joshua, "Stretch forth your hand with the spear that is in your hand toward the city, for I have delivered it into your hands; and those lying in wait shall rise up quickly out of their place."

¹⁹ And Joshua stretched out his hand *and* his spear toward the city, and the ambush rose up quickly out of their place. And they came forth when he stretched out his hand, and they entered into the city, and took it; and they hastened and burned the city with fire.

²⁰ And when the inhabitants of Ai looked behind them, they saw then the smoke going up out of the city, *rising* up to heaven, and they were no longer able to flee this way or that way.

²¹ And Joshua and all Israel saw that the ambush had taken the city, and that the smoke of the city went up to heaven; and they turned and struck down the men of Ai.

²² And these came forth out of the city to meet them; and they were in the midst of the army, some on this side, and some on that; and they struck them until there was not one of them left who survived and escaped.

²³ And they took the king of Ai alive, and brought him to Joshua.

²⁴ And when the children of Israel had ceased slaying all that were in Ai, and in the fields, and in the mountain on the descent, from where they pursued them, *even* to the end, then Joshua returned to Ai, and attacked it with the edge of the sword.

²⁵ And those that fell in that day, men and women, were twelve thousand: *they killed* all the inhabitants of Ai.

²⁶ (This verse omitted in LXX)

²⁷ Beside the spoils that were in the city, all things which the children of Israel took as spoil for themselves according to the command of the Lord, as the Lord commanded Joshua.

²⁸ And Joshua burned the city with fire: he made it an uninhabited heap forever, *even* to this day.

²⁹ And he hanged the king of Ai on the gallows, and he remained on the tree till evening. And when the sun went down, Joshua commanded, and they took down his body from the tree, and cast it into a pit, and they set over him a heap of stones to this day.

Joshua Renews the Covenant

³⁰ Then Joshua built an altar to the Lord God of Israel on Mount Ebal,

³¹ as Moses the servant of the Lord commanded the children of Israel, as it is written in the law of Moses, an altar of unhewn stones, on which iron had not been lifted up; and he offered there burnt offerings to the Lord, and a peace offering.

³² And Joshua wrote upon the stones a copy of the law, the law of Moses, before the children of Israel.

³³ And all Israel, and their elders, and their judges, and their scribes, passed on one side and on the other before the ark; and the priests and the Levites took up the ark of the covenant of the Lord; and the stranger and the native *were there*, who were half of them near Mount Gerizim, and half near Mount Ebal, as Moses the servant of the Lord commanded at first, to bless the people.

³⁴ And afterwards Joshua read all the words of the law, the blessings and the curses, according to all the things written in the law of Moses.

³⁵ There was not a word of all that Moses commanded Joshua which Joshua did not read in the ears of all the assembly of the children of Israel, *before* the men, the women, the children, and the strangers that joined themselves to Israel.

JOSHUA CHAPTER 9

The Treaty with the Gibeonites

¹ And when the kings of the Amorites on the other side of the Jordan, who were in the mountain country, and in the plain, and in all the coast of the great sea, and those who were near Lebanon, and the Hittites, the Canaanites, the Perizzites, the Hivites, the Amorites, the Girgashites, and the Jebusites, heard *of it*,

² they all came together at the same time to make war against Joshua and Israel.

³ And the inhabitants of Gibeon heard of all that the Lord did to Jericho and Ai.

⁴ And they also worked craftily, and they went and made provisions and prepared themselves; and having taken old sacks on their shoulders, and old and torn wineskins,

⁵ and the upper part of their shoes and their sandals *appeared* old and clouted on their feet, and their garments laid upon them, and their provisions were dry and moldy and corrupt.

⁶ And they came to Joshua into the camp of Israel, to Gilgal, and said to Joshua and Israel, "We have come from a far land. Now then, make a covenant with us."

⁷ And the children of Israel said to the Hivites, "Perhaps you dwell amongst us; how should I make a covenant with you?"

⁸ And they said to Joshua, "We are your servants." And Joshua said to them, "Who are you, and where do you come from?"

9 And they said, "Your servants have come from a very far country in the name of the Lord your God: for we have heard His name, and all that He did in Egypt,

10 and all that He did to the kings of the Amorites, who were beyond the Jordan, to Sihon king of the Amorites, and Og king of Bashan, who dwelt in Ashtaroth.

11 And our elders, and all that inhabit our land, when they heard, *they* spoke to us, saying, 'Take to yourselves provisions for the way, and go to meet them; and you shall say to them, "We are your servants, and now make a covenant with us."'

12 These *are* the loaves—we took them hot for our journey on the day in which we came out to come to you. And now they have dried up, and have become moldy.

13 And these *are* the skins of wine which we filled when they were new, and now they are torn; and our garments and our shoes are worn out because of the very long journey."

14 And the chiefs took of their provisions, but they did not ask *counsel from* the Lord.

15 And Joshua made peace with them, and they made a covenant with them to preserve them; and the princes of the congregation swore to them.

16 And it came to pass, three days after they had made a covenant with them, *that* they heard that they were close neighbors *of theirs*, and that they dwelt among them.

17 And the children of Israel departed and came to their cities; and their cities *were* Gibeon, Chephirah, Beeroth, and the cities of Jearim.

18 But the children of Israel did not fight with them, because all the princes swore to them by the Lord God of Israel; and all the congregation murmured at the princes.

19 And the princes said to all the congregation, "We have sworn to them by the Lord God of Israel, and now we shall not be able to touch them.

20 This we will do: take them alive, and we will preserve them: so there shall not be wrath against us by reason of the oath which we swore to them.

21 They shall live, and shall be woodcutters and water carriers to all the congregation, as the princes said to them."

22 And Joshua called them together and said to them, "Why have you deceived me, saying, 'We live very far from you'; whereas you are fellow countrymen of those who dwell among us?

23 And now you are cursed. There shall not fail of you a slave, or a woodcutter, or a water carrier to me and my God."

24 And they answered Joshua, saying, "It was reported to us what the Lord your God commanded His servant Moses, to give you this land, and to destroy us and all that dwelt on it from before you, and we feared very much for our lives because of you, and *therefore* we did this thing.

25 And now, behold, we *are* in your power; do to us as it is pleasing to you, and as it seems *good* to you."

26 And they did so to them. And Joshua rescued them in that day out of the hands of the children of Israel, and they did not kill them.

27 And in that day, Joshua made them woodcutters and water carriers to the whole congregation, and for the altar of God. Therefore the inhabitants of Gibeon became woodcutters and water carriers for the altar of God to this day, even for the place which the Lord should choose.

JOSHUA CHAPTER 10

The Sun Stands Still

1 And when Adoni-Zedek king of Jerusalem heard that Joshua had taken Ai, and had destroyed it, as he did to Jericho and its king, even so they did to Ai and its king, and that the inhabitants of Gibeon had gone over to Joshua and Israel;

2 then they were greatly terrified by them, for *the king* knew that Gibeon *was* a great city, as one of the chief cities, and all its men *were* mighty.

3 So Adoni-Zedek king of Jerusalem sent to Hoham king of Hebron, and to Piram king of Jarmuth, and to Japhia king of Lachish, and to Debir king of Eglon, saying,

4 "Come up here to me, and help me, and let us take Gibeon; for the Gibeonites have gone over to Joshua and to the children of Israel."

5 And the five kings of the Jebusites went up, the king of Jerusalem, the king of Hebron, the king of Jarmuth, the king of Lachish, and the king of Eglon, they and all their people; and encamped around Gibeon, and besieged it.

6 And the inhabitants of Gibeon sent to Joshua into the camp to Gilgal, saying, "Do not relax your hands from your servants: come up quickly to us, and help us, and rescue us; for all the kings of the Amorites who dwell in the hill country are gathered together against us."

7 And Joshua went up from Gilgal, he and all the people of war with him, everyone mighty in strength.

8 And the Lord said to Joshua, "Do not fear them, for I have delivered them into your hands; there shall not be one of them left from before you."

9 And when Joshua came suddenly upon them, he *had* advanced all the night out of Gilgal.

10 And the Lord struck them with terror before the children of Israel; and the Lord destroyed them with a great slaughter at Gibeon; and they pursued them along the way that goes up to Beth Horon, and they struck them as far as Azekah and to Makkedah.

11 And when they fled from the face of the children of Israel at the descent of Beth Horon, then the Lord cast upon them hailstones from heaven to Azekah; and there were more that died by the hailstones than those whom the children of Israel slew with the sword in the battle.

12 Then Joshua spoke to the Lord, in the day in which the Lord delivered the Amorite into the power of Israel, when He destroyed them in Gibeon, and they were destroyed from

before the children of Israel. And Joshua said, "Let the sun stand still against Gibeon, and the moon against the Valley of Aijalon."

¹³ And the sun and the moon stood still, until God executed vengeance on their enemies. And the sun stood still in the sky; it did not proceed to set till the end of one day.

¹⁴ And there was not such a day either before or after, so that God should hearken to a man, because the Lord fought on the side of Israel.

¹⁵ (This verse omitted in LXX)

Five Kings Defeated

¹⁶ And these five kings fled, and hid themselves in a cave that is in Makkedah.

¹⁷ And it was told Joshua, saying, "The five kings have been found hid in the cave that is in Makkedah."

¹⁸ And Joshua said, "Roll stones to the mouth of the cave, and set men to watch over them.

¹⁹ But do not stand there yourselves, but pursue after your enemies, and attack the rear of them, and do not allow them to enter into their cities; for the Lord our God has delivered them into our hands."

²⁰ And it came to pass when Joshua and all Israel ceased destroying them utterly with a very great slaughter, that those who escaped took refuge in the strong cities.

²¹ And all the people returned safe to Joshua to Makkedah; and none of the children of Israel murmured with his tongue.

²² And Joshua said, "Open the cave, and bring out these five kings out of the cave."

²³ And they brought out the five kings out of the cave, the king of Jerusalem, and the king of Hebron, and the king of Jarmuth, and the king of Lachish, and the king of Eglon.

²⁴ And when they brought them out to Joshua, then Joshua called together all Israel, and the chiefs of the army that went with him, saying to them, "Come forward and set your feet on their necks." So they came and set their feet on their necks.

²⁵ And Joshua said to them, "Do not fear them, neither be cowardly; *but* be courageous and strong, for thus the Lord will do to all your enemies against whom you fight."

²⁶ And Joshua killed them, and hanged them on five trees; and they hung upon the trees until the evening.

²⁷ And it came to pass toward the setting of the sun, *that* Joshua commanded, and they took them down from the trees, and cast them into the cave into which they *had* fled for refuge, and rolled stones to the cave, *which remain* to this day.

²⁸ And they took Makkedah on that day, and killed the inhabitants with the edge of the sword, and they utterly destroyed every living thing that was in it. And there was none left in it that was preserved and had escaped; and they did to the king of Makkedah, as they did to the king of Jericho.

²⁹ And Joshua and all Israel with him departed out of Makkedah to Libnah, and besieged Libnah.

³⁰ And the Lord delivered it into the hands of Israel. And they took it, and its king, and killed the inhabitants with the edge of the sword, and everything breathing in it; and there was not left in it any that survived and escaped; and they did to its king, as they did to the king of Jericho.

³¹ And Joshua and all Israel with him departed from Libnah to Lachish, and he encamped about it, and besieged it.

³² And the Lord delivered Lachish into the hands of Israel; and they took it on the second day, and they put the inhabitants to death with the edge of the sword, and utterly destroyed it, as they had done to Libnah.

³³ Then Horam the king of Gezer went up to help Lachish; and Joshua struck him and his people with the edge of the sword, until there was not left to him one that was preserved and escaped.

³⁴ And Joshua and all Israel with him departed from Lachish to Eglon, and he besieged it and took it.

³⁵ And the Lord delivered it into the hand of Israel; and he took it on that day, and killed the inhabitants with the edge of the sword, and killed everything breathing in it, as they did to Lachish.

³⁶ And Joshua and all Israel with him departed to Hebron, and encamped about it.

³⁷ And he struck it with the edge of the sword, and all the living creatures that were in it; there was no one preserved. They destroyed it and all things in it, as they did to Eglon.

³⁸ And Joshua and all Israel returned to Debir; and they encamped about it;

³⁹ and they took it, and its king, and its villages. And he struck it with the edge of the sword, and they destroyed it, and everything breathing in it; and they did not leave in it anyone that was preserved: as they did to Hebron and her king, so they did to Debir and her king.

⁴⁰ And Joshua conquered all the land of the hill country, and the Negev and the plain country, and Ashedoth, and her kings. They did not leave of them one that was saved: and they utterly destroyed everything that had the breath of life, as the Lord God of Israel had commanded,

⁴¹ from Kadesh Barnea to Gaza, all Goshen, as far as Gibeon.

⁴² And Joshua struck, once for all, all their kings, and their land, because the Lord God of Israel fought on the side of Israel.

JOSHUA CHAPTER 11

The Northern Conquest

¹ And when Jabin the king of Hazor heard *these things*, he sent to Jobab king of Madon, and to the king of Shimron, and to the king of Achshaph,

² and to the kings who were by the great Sidon, to the hill country and to Arabah opposite Chinneroth, and to the plain, and to Dor,

³ and to the Canaanites on the coast eastward, and to the Amorites on the coast, and the Hittites, and the Perizzites,

and the Jebusites in the mountains, and the Hivites, and those dwelling below Hermon in the land of Mizpah.

⁴ And they and their kings with them went forth, as the sand of the sea in multitude, and horses, and very many chariots.

⁵ And all the kings assembled in person, and came to the same place, and encamped at the waters of Merom to fight against Israel.

⁶ And the Lord said to Joshua, "Be not afraid of them, for tomorrow *at* this time I will put them to flight before Israel: you shall hamstring their horses, and burn their chariots with fire."

⁷ And Joshua and all the men of war came upon them at the water of Merom suddenly; and they attacked them in the hill country.

⁸ And the Lord delivered them into the power of Israel; and they struck them and pursued them to Great Sidon, and to Misrephoth, and to the plains of Mizpah eastward; and they destroyed them till there was not one of them left that survived.

⁹ And Joshua did to them as the Lord commanded him: he hamstrung their horses, and burned their chariots with fire.

¹⁰ And Joshua returned at that time, and took Hazor and its king; now Hazor in former times was the chief of these kingdoms.

¹¹ And they killed with the sword all that breathed in it, and utterly destroyed them all, and there was no living thing left in it; and they burned Hazor with fire.

¹² And Joshua took all the cities of the kingdoms, and their kings, and killed them with the edge of the sword; and utterly destroyed them, as Moses the servant of the Lord had commanded.

¹³ But all the walled cities Israel did not burn; but Israel burned Hazor only.

¹⁴ And the children of Israel took all its spoils to themselves; and they killed all the men with the edge of the sword, and they destroyed them; they left not one of them breathing.

¹⁵ As the Lord commanded His servant Moses, even so Moses commanded Joshua; and so Joshua did, he transgressed no precept of all that Moses commanded him.

Summary of Joshua's Conquests

¹⁶ And Joshua took all the hill country, and all the land of the Negev, and all the land of Goshen, and the plain country, and that toward the west, and the mountain of Israel and the low country by the mountain;

¹⁷ from the mountain of Halak, and that which goes up to Seir, and as far as Baal Gad, and the plains of Lebanon, below Mount Hermon. And he took all their kings, and killed them.

¹⁸ And for many days Joshua waged war with these kings.

¹⁹ And there was no city which Israel did not take; they took them all in war.

²⁰ For it was of the Lord to harden their hearts to go forth to war against Israel, that they might be utterly destroyed, that

mercy should not be granted to them, but that they should be utterly destroyed, as the Lord said to Moses.

²¹ And Joshua came at that time, and utterly destroyed the Anakim out of the hill country, from Hebron and from Debir, and from Anab, and from all the race of Israel, and from all the mountain of Judah with their cities; and Joshua utterly destroyed them.

²² There was not *anyone* left of the Anakim by the children of Israel, only there was left of them in Gaza, and in Gath, and in Ashdod.

²³ And Joshua took all the land, as the Lord commanded Moses; and Joshua gave them for an inheritance to Israel by division according to their tribes; and the land ceased from war.

JOSHUA CHAPTER 12

The Kings Conquered by Moses

¹ And these *are* the kings of the land, whom the children of Israel killed, and inherited their land beyond the Jordan from the east, from the valley of Arnon, to Mount Hermon, and all the land of the Arabah on the east.

² Sihon king of the Amorites, who dwelt in Heshbon, ruling from Arnon, which is in the valley, on the side of the valley, and half of Gilead as far as Jabbok, the borders of the children of Ammon.

³ And the Arabah as far as the Sea of Chinneroth to the east, and as far as the Sea of the Arabah; the Salt Sea eastward *by* the way to Beth Jeshimoth, from Taman below the slopes of Pisgah.

⁴ And Og king of Bashan, who dwelt in Ashtaroth and in Edrei, was left of the giants

⁵ ruling from Mount Hermon and from Salcah, and *over* all the land of Bashan to the borders of the Geshurites and the Maachathites, and the half of Gilead of the borders of Sihon king of Heshbon.

⁶ Moses the servant of the Lord and the children of Israel struck them; and Moses gave them by way of inheritance to Reuben and Gad, and to the half tribe of Manasseh.

The Kings Conquered by Joshua

⁷ And these *are* the kings of the Amorites, whom Joshua and the children of Israel killed beyond the Jordan by the sea of Balagad in the plain of Lebanon, and as far as the mountain of Halak, as men go up to Seir. And Joshua gave it to the tribes of Israel to inherit according to their portion.

⁸ In the mountain, and in the plain, and in the Arabah, and in Ashedoth, and in the wilderness, and the Negev—the Hittite, the Amorite, the Canaanite, the Perizzite, the Hivite, and the Jebusite:

⁹ the king of Jericho, one; and the king of Ai, which is near Bethel, one;

¹⁰ the king of Jerusalem, one; the king of Hebron, one;

¹¹ the king of Jarmuth, one; the king of Lachish, one;

¹² the king of Eglon, one; the king of Gezer, one;

¹³ the king of Debir, one; the king of Geder, one;

¹⁴ the king of Hormah, one; the king of Arad, one;

¹⁵ the king of Libnah, one; the king of Adullam, one;

¹⁶ the king of Elath, one;

¹⁷ the king of Tappuah, one; the king of Hepher, one;

¹⁸ the king of Aphek; the king of Lasharon;

¹⁹ the king of Madon, one;

²⁰ the king of Shimron Meron, one; the king of Achshaph, one;

²¹ the king of Kadesh, one; the king of Taanach, one;

²² the king of Maredoth, one; the king of Jokneam of Carmel, one;

²³ the king of Adullam *of* Dor, one; the king of Gilgal of Galilee, one;

²⁴ the king of Tirzah, one—all these *were* twenty-nine kings.

JOSHUA CHAPTER 13

The Parts of Canaan Still Unconquered

¹ And Joshua *was* old and very advanced in years; and the Lord said to Joshua, "You are advanced in years, and there is much land left to inherit.

² And this *is* the land that is left: the borders of the Philistines, the Geshurites, and the Canaanites,

³ from the wilderness before Egypt, as far as the borders of Ekron on the left of the Canaanites; *the land* is reckoned to the five principalities of the Philistines, to the inhabitants of Gaza, and of Ashdod, and of Ashkelon, and of Gath, and of Ekron, and to the Hivite;

⁴ from Taman even to all the land of Canaan before Gaza, and the Sidonians as far as Aphek, as far as the borders of the Amorites.

⁵ And all the land of Gebalites of the Philistines, and all Lebanon eastward from Gilgal, under Mount Hermon as far as the entering in of Hamath;

⁶ everyone that inhabits the hill country from Lebanon as far as the Brook Misrephoth. All the Sidonians, I will destroy them from before Israel; but give them by inheritance to Israel, as I commanded you.

⁷ And now divide this land by lot to the nine tribes, and to the half-tribe of Manasseh.

Dividing the Land

⁸ "From the Jordan to the Great Sea westward you shall divide it to *them*. The Great Sea shall be the boundary." *But* to the two tribes and to the half-tribe of Manasseh, to Reuben and to Gad, Moses gave *an inheritance* beyond the Jordan: Moses the servant of the Lord gave *it* to them eastward,

⁹ from Aroer, which is on the bank of the Brook of Arnon, and the city in the midst of the valley, and all the plain of Medeba as far as Dibon.

¹⁰ All the cities of Sihon king of the Amorites, who reigned from Heshbon to the coasts of the children of Ammon;

¹¹ and the region of Gilead, and the borders of the Geshirites and the Maachathites, and all Mount Hermon, and all the land of Bashan to Salcah.

¹² All the kingdom of Og in the region of Bashan, who reigned in Ashtaroth and in Edrei—he was left of the giants; and Moses struck him, and destroyed him.

¹³ But the children of Israel did not destroy the Geshurite and the Maachathite and the Canaanite; and the king of the Geshurites and the Maachathites dwelt among the children of Israel to this day.

¹⁴ Only no inheritance was given to the tribe of Levi: the Lord God of Israel, He *is* their inheritance, as the Lord said to them; and this *is* the division which Moses made to the children of Israel in Araboth Moab, on the other side of the Jordan, by Jericho.

The Land of Reuben

¹⁵ And Moses gave the land to the tribe of Reuben according to their families.

¹⁶ And their borders were from Aroer, which is opposite the Brook of Arnon, and *theirs is* the city that is in the valley of Arnon; and all Misor,

¹⁷ to Heshbon, and all the cities in Misor, Dibon, Bamoth Baal, Beth Baal Meon,

¹⁸ Bashan, Kedamoth, Mephaath,

¹⁹ Kirjathaim, Sibmah, Zereth, Shahar in Mount Enab,

²⁰ Beth Peor, the slopes of Pisgah, Beth Jeshimoth—

²¹ and all the cities of Misor, and all the kingdom of Sihon king of the Amorites, whom Moses struck, even him and the princes of Midian: Evi, Rekem, Zur, Hur, and Reba, prince of the spoils of Sihon, dwelling in the country.

²² And Balaam the son of Beor the prophet they killed in the battle.

²³ And the borders of Reuben were the banks of the Jordan. This *is* the inheritance of the children of Reuben according to their families, the cities and their villages.

The Land of Gad

²⁴ And Moses gave an inheritance to the sons of Gad according to their families.

²⁵ And their borders were Jazer, all the cities of Gilead, and half the land of the children of Ammon to the Arabah, which is before Arad.

²⁶ And from Heshbon to Ramath by Mizpah, and Betonim, and from Mahanaim to the borders of Debir,

²⁷ and in the valley of Beth Haram, Beth Nimrah, Succoth, and Zaphon, and the rest of the kingdom of Sihon king of Heshbon; and the Jordan shall be the boundary as far as part of the Sea of Chinnereth beyond the Jordan eastward.

²⁸ This *is* the inheritance of the children of Gad according to their families and according to their cities; according to their families they will turn their backs before their enemies, because their cities and their villages were according to their families.

Half the Tribe of Manasseh

²⁹ And Moses gave to half the tribe of Manasseh according to their families.

³⁰ And their borders were from Mahanaim, and all the kingdom of Bashan, and all the kingdom of Og king of Bashan, and all the villages of Jair, which are in the region of Bashan, sixty cities;

³¹ half of Gilead, and in Ashtaroth, and in Edrei, royal cities of Og in the land of Bashan, *Moses gave* to the sons of Machir the sons of Manasseh, even to the half-tribe sons of Machir the sons of Manasseh, according to their families.

³² These *are* they whom Moses caused to inherit beyond the Jordan in Araboth Moab, beyond the Jordan by Jericho, eastward.

JOSHUA CHAPTER 14

¹ And these *are* those of the children of Israel that received their inheritance in the land of Canaan, to whom Eleazar the priest, and Joshua the *son* of Nun, and the heads of the families of the tribes of the children of Israel, gave inheritance.

² They inherited according to their lots, as the Lord commanded by the hand of Joshua to the nine tribes and the half tribe, on the other side of the Jordan.

³ But to the Levites he gave no inheritance among them.

⁴ For the sons of Joseph were two tribes, Manasseh and Ephraim; and there was no inheritance in the land given to the Levites, only cities to dwell in, and their suburbs separated for the livestock, and their cattle.

⁵ As the Lord commanded Moses, so did the children of Israel; and they divided the land.

Caleb Inherits Hebron

⁶ And the children of Judah came to Joshua in Gilgal, and Caleb the *son* of Jephunneh the Kenizzite said to him, "You know the word that the Lord spoke to Moses the man of God concerning me and you in Kadesh Barnea.

⁷ For I was forty years old when Moses the servant of God sent me out of Kadesh Barnea to spy out the land; and I returned him an answer according to his mind.

⁸ My brothers who went up with me turned away the heart of the people, but I applied myself to follow the Lord my God.

⁹ And Moses swore on that day, saying, 'The land on which your foot has trodden, it shall be your inheritance and your children's forever, because you have applied yourself to follow the Lord our God.'

¹⁰ And now the Lord has kept me alive as He said: this *is* the forty-fifth year since the Lord spoke that word to Moses; and Israel journeyed in the wilderness; and now, behold, I *am* this day eighty-five years old.

¹¹ I am still strong this day, as when the Lord sent me: just so strong am I now to go out and to come in for war.

¹² And now I ask of you this mountain, as the Lord said in that day; for you heard this word on that day. And now the Anakim are there, cities great and strong. If then the Lord should be with me, I will utterly destroy them, as the Lord said to me."

¹³ And Joshua blessed him, and gave Hebron to Caleb the son of Jephunneh the son of Keniz for an inheritance.

¹⁴ Therefore Hebron became the inheritance of Caleb the *son* of Jephunneh the Kenizzite until this day, because he followed the commandment of the Lord God of Israel.

¹⁵ And the name of Hebron before formerly was Kirjath Arba, it *is* the metropolis of the Anakim. And the land rested from war.

JOSHUA CHAPTER 15

The Land of Judah

¹ And the borders of the tribe of Judah according to their families were from the borders of Edom from the Wilderness of Zin, as far as Kadesh to the south.

² And their borders were from the south as far as a part of the Salt Sea from the high country that extends southward.

³ And they proceed before the Ascent of Akrabbim, and go out around Zin, and go up from the south to Kadesh Barnea; and go out to Hezron, and proceed up to Adar, and go out by the way that is west of Karkaa.

⁴ And *from there* they go out to Azmon, and issue at the valley of Egypt; and the termination of its boundaries shall be at the sea. These are their boundaries southward.

⁵ And their boundaries eastward *are* all the Salt Sea as far as the Jordan; and their borders from the north, and from the border of the sea, and from part of the Jordan—

⁶ the borders go up to Beth Hoglah, and they go along from the north to Beth Arabah, and the borders go on up to the stone of Bohan the son of Reuben.

⁷ And the borders continue on to the fourth part of the Valley of Achor, and go down to Gilgal, which is before the Ascent of Adummim, which is southward in the valley, and terminate at the water of the Fountain of the Sun. And their going forth shall be the Fountain of Rogel.

⁸ And the borders go up to the Valley of Hinnom, behind Jebus southward; this is Jerusalem: and the borders terminate at the top of the mountain, which is before the Valley of Hinnom toward the sea, which is by the side of the land of Rephaim northward.

⁹ And the border *going forth* from the top of the mountain terminates at the fountain of the water of Nephtoah, and terminates at Mount Ephron; and the border will lead to Baalah; this is the city of Jearim.

¹⁰ And the border will go round from Baalah to the sea, and will go on to the mount of Assar behind the city of Jearim northwards; this is Chesalon: and it will come down to the City of Sun, and will go on to the south.

¹¹ And the border terminates behind Ekron northward, and the borders will terminate at Succhoth, and the borders will go on to the south, and will terminate at Libnah, and the issue of the borders will be at the sea; and their borders

shall be toward the sea, the Great Sea shall be the boundary.

¹² These *are* the borders of the children of Judah round about according to their families.

Caleb Occupies Hebron and Debir

¹³ And to Caleb the son of Jephunneh he gave a portion in the midst of the children of Judah by the command of God; and Joshua gave him the city of Arba the metropolis of Anak; this is Hebron.

¹⁴ And Caleb the son of Jephunneh destroyed from there the three sons of Anak: Sheshai, Talmai, and Ahiman.

¹⁵ And Caleb went up from there to the inhabitants of Debir; and the name of Debir before was the City of Letters.

¹⁶ And Caleb said, "Whosoever shall take and destroy the City of Letters, and master it, to him will I give my daughter Achsah for a wife."

¹⁷ And Othniel the son of Kenaz the brother of Caleb took it; and he gave him Achsah his daughter for a wife.

¹⁸ And it came to pass as she went out that she counseled him, saying, "I will ask of my father a field." And she cried from off her donkey. And Caleb said to her, "What is it?"

¹⁹ And she said to him, "Give me a blessing, for you have set me in the land of the Negev. Give me Botthanis." So he gave her Gonaethla the upper, and Gonaethla the lower.

The Cities of Judah

²⁰ This *is* the inheritance of the tribe of the children of Judah.

²¹ And their cities were cities belonging to the tribe of the children of Judah on the borders of Edom by the wilderness, and Kabzeel, Eder, Jagur,

²² Kinah, Dimonah, Adadah,

²³ Kadesh, Hazor, Ithnan,

²⁴ and Balmaenan, and their villages,

²⁵ and the cities of Hezron, which *is* Hazor,

²⁶ Amam, Shema, Moladah,

²⁷ Seri, Beth Pelet,

²⁸ Hazar Shual, Beersheba; and their villages, and their hamlets,

²⁹ Balah Bacoc, Asom,

³⁰ Eltolad, Bethel, Hormah,

³¹ Ziklag, Madmannah, Sansannah,

³² Lebaoth, Shilhim, Ain; twenty-nine cities, and their villages.

³³ In the plain country: Eshtaol, Zorah, Ashtah,

³⁴ Zanoah, Tano, Iluthoth, Maeani,

³⁵ Jarmuth, Adullam, Membra, Socoh, Azekah,

³⁶ Sharaim, Gederah, and its villages; fourteen cities, and their villages;

³⁷ Zenan, Hadashah, Migdal,

³⁸ Dilean, Mizpah, Joktheel,

³⁹ Bozkath, Eglon,

⁴⁰ Cabbon, Lahmas, Machos,

⁴¹ Gederoth, Beth Dagon, Naamah, Makkedah: sixteen cities, and their villages;

⁴² Libnah, Ether, Ashan,

⁴³ Jiphtah, Nezib,

⁴⁴ Keilah, Akiezi, Achzib, Mereshah, and Elom: ten cities, and their villages;

⁴⁵ Ekron and her villages, and their hamlets:

⁴⁶ from Ekron: Gemna, and all the cities that are near Ashdod, and their villages.

⁴⁷ Ashdod, and her villages, and her hamlets: Gaza, and its villages and its hamlets as far as the river of Egypt, and the Great Sea is the boundary.

⁴⁸ And in the hill country: Shamir, Jattir, Sochah,

⁴⁹ Danna and the City of Letters, this *is* Debir;

⁵⁰ Anab, Eshtemoth, Anim,

⁵¹ Goshen, Holon, and Hanna, and Giloh: eleven cities, and their villages;

⁵² Arab, Dumah, Eshean,

⁵³ Janum, Beth Tappuah, Aphekah,

⁵⁴ Humtah, the city Arba, this is Hebron, and Zior: nine cities and their villages;

⁵⁵ Maon, Carmel, Ziph, Juttah,

⁵⁶ Jezreel, Jokdeam, Zanoah,

⁵⁷ Gibeah, Timnah; nine cities, and their villages;

⁵⁸ Halhul, Beth Zur, Gedor,

⁵⁹ Maarath, Beth Anoth, Eltekon; six cities, and their villages; Theco, and Ephratha, this is Bethlehem, and Pagor, Etan, Culon, Tatam, Thobes, Carem, Galem, Thether, and Manocho: eleven cities, and their villages;

⁶⁰ Kirjath Baal, this *is* the city of Jearim, and Sotheba: two cities, and their villages:

⁶¹ in the wilderness: Beth Arabah, Middin, Secacah;

⁶² Aeochioza, Naphlazon, the cities of Sadon, and En Gedi; seven cities, and their villages.

⁶³ And the Jebusite dwelt in Jerusalem, and the children of Judah could not destroy them; and the Jebusites dwelt in Jerusalem to this day.

JOSHUA CHAPTER 16

The Land of Ephraim

¹ And the borders of the children of Joseph were from the Jordan by Jericho towards the east; and they will go up from Jericho to the hill country, to the wilderness, to Bethel Luz.

² And they will go out to Bethel, and will proceed to the borders of Ataroth.

³ And they will go across to the sea to the borders of Aptalim, as far as the borders of Beth Horon the lower, and the going forth of them shall be to the sea.

⁴ And the sons of Joseph, Ephraim and Manasseh, took their inheritance.

⁵ And the borders of the children of Ephraim were according to their families, and the borders of their inheritance were eastward to Ataroth, and Eroc as far as Beth Horon the upper, and Gaza.

6 And the borders will proceed to the sea to Michmethath north of Therma; they will go round eastward to Thenasa, and Selles, and will pass on eastward to Janohah,

7 and to Macho, and Ataroth, and *these are* their villages; and they will come to Jericho, and will issue at the Jordan.

8 And the borders will proceed from Tappuah, to the sea, *and* to Kanah; and their termination will be at the sea; this *is* the inheritance of the tribe of Ephraim according to their families.

9 And the cities separated to the sons of Ephraim *were* in the midst of the inheritance of the sons of Manasseh, all the cities and their villages.

10 And Ephraim did not destroy the Canaanite who dwelt in Gezer; and the Canaanite dwelt in Ephraim to this day, until Pharaoh the king of Egypt went up and took it, and burned it with fire. And the Canaanites, and Perizzites, and the inhabitants in Gaza they destroyed, and Pharaoh gave them for a dowry to his daughter.

JOSHUA CHAPTER 17

The Other Half-Tribe of Manasseh

1 And the borders of the tribe of the children of Manasseh, (for he *was* the firstborn of Joseph,) *assigned* to Machir the firstborn of Manasseh the father of Gilead, for he was a warrior, *were* in the land of Gilead and of Bashan.

2 And there was *land* assigned to the other sons of Manasseh according to their families: to the sons of Jezi, and to the sons of Kelez, and to the sons of Jeziel, and to the sons of Shechem, and to the sons of Symarim, and to the sons of Opher: these *are* the males according to their families.

3 And Zelophehad the son of Hepher had no sons but daughters: and these *are* the names of the daughters of Zelophehad: Mahlah, Noah, Hoglah, Milcah, and Tirzah.

4 And they stood before Eleazar the priest, and before Joshua, and before the rulers, saying, "God commanded by the hand of Moses to give us an inheritance in the midst of our brothers." So there was given to them by the command of the Lord an inheritance among the brothers of their father.

5 And their lot fell *to them* from Manasseh, and *to the* plain of Labec of the land of Gilead, which is beyond the Jordan.

6 For the daughters of the sons of Manasseh inherited a portion in the midst of their brothers, and the land of Gilead was assigned to the remainder of the sons of Manasseh.

7 And the borders of the sons of Manasseh were Delanath, which is before the sons of Anath, and it proceeds to the borders to Jamin and Jassib to the fountain of En Tappuah.

8 It shall belong to Manasseh, and Tappuah on the borders of Manasseh *shall belong* to the sons of Ephraim.

9 And the borders shall go down to the valley of Carana southward by the valley of Jariel, (*there is* a terebinth tree *belonging* to Ephraim between *that and* the city of Manasseh) and the borders of Manasseh *are* northward to the brook; and the sea shall be its termination.

10 Southward *the land belongs* to Ephraim, and northward to Manasseh; and the sea shall be their cost; and northward they shall border upon Aseb, and eastward upon Issachar.

11 And Manasseh shall have in *the portion of* Issachar and Beth Shean and their villages, and the inhabitants of Dor, and its villages, and the inhabitants of Megiddo, and its villages, and the third part of Mapheta, and its villages.

12 And the sons of Manasseh were not able to destroy these cities; and the Canaanite began to dwell in that land.

13 And it came to pass that when the children of Israel were strong, they made the Canaanites subject *to them*, but they did not utterly destroy them.

The Sons of Joseph Protest

14 And the sons of Joseph answered Joshua, saying, "Why have you caused us to inherit one inheritance, and *only* one lot, seeing we are a great people, and God has blessed us?"

15 And Joshua said to them, "If you are a great people, go up to the forest, and clear *the land* for yourself, if Mount Ephraim is too small for you."

16 And they said, "Mount Ephraim does not please us, and the Canaanite dwelling in it in Beth Shean, and in its villages, *and* in the valley of Jezreel, has choice cavalry and iron."

17 And Joshua said to the sons of Joseph, "If you are a great people, and have great strength, you shall not have *only* one inheritance.

18 For you shall have the wood, for there is a wood, and you shall clear it, and *the land* shall be yours; even when you shall have utterly destroyed the Canaanite, for he has chosen cavalry; yet you are stronger than he."

JOSHUA CHAPTER 18

The Remainder of the Land Divided

1 And all the congregation of the children of Israel were assembled at Shiloh, and there they pitched the tabernacle of witness. And the land was subdued by them.

2 And the sons of Israel remained, *even* those who had not received their inheritance, seven tribes.

3 And Joshua said to the sons of Israel, "How long will you be slack to inherit the land, which the Lord our God has given you?

4 Appoint of yourselves three men of each tribe, and let them rise up and go through the land, and let them describe it before me, as it will be proper to divide it."

5 And they came to him. And he divided to them seven portions, *saying*, "Judah shall stand to them a border southward, and the sons of Joseph shall stand to them northward.

6 And divide the land into seven parts, and bring its description here to me, and I will give you a lot before the Lord our God.

7 For the sons of Levi have no part among you; for the priesthood of the Lord *is* his portion; and Gad, and Reuben,

and the half-tribe of Manasseh have received their inheritance beyond the Jordan eastward, which Moses the servant of the Lord gave to them."

[8] And the men rose up and went; and Joshua commanded the men who went to explore the land, saying, "Go and explore the land, and come to me, and I will bring you forth a lot here before the Lord in Shiloh."

[9] And they went, and explored the land. And they viewed it, and described it according to the cities, seven parts in a book, and brought *the book* to Joshua.

[10] And Joshua cast the lot for them in Shiloh before the Lord.

The Land of Benjamin

[11] And the lot of the tribe of Benjamin came forth first according to their families. And the borders of their lot came forth between the children of Judah and the children of Joseph.

[12] And their borders were northward: the borders shall go up from the Jordan behind Jericho northward, and shall go up to the mountain westward, and the issue of it shall be the Wilderness of Beth Aven.

[13] And the borders will go forth from there to Luz, behind Luz, from the south of it; this is Bethel. And the borders shall go down to Ataroth Adar, to the hill country, which is southward of Beth Horon.

[14] And the borders shall pass through and proceed to the part that looks toward the sea, on the south, from the mountain in front of Beth Horon southward, and its termination shall be at Kirjath Baal, which is Kirjath Jearim, a city of the children of Judah; this is the part toward the west.

[15] And the south side on the part of Kirjath Baal; and the borders shall go across to Gasin, to the fountain of the water of Nephtoah.

[16] And the borders shall extend down on one side, this is in front of the Valley of the Son of Hinnom, which is on the side of Rephaim northward, and it shall come down to Gehenna behind Jebus southward: it shall come down to En Rogel.

[17] And *the borders* shall go across to En Shemesh,

[18] and shall proceed to Galiloth, which is in front by the going up of Ethamin; and they shall come down to the stone of Beon of the sons of Reuben, and shall pass over behind Beth Arabah northward, and shall go down to the borders behind the sea northward.

[19] And the termination of the borders shall be at the creek of the Salt Sea northward to the side of the Jordan southward: these are their southern borders.

[20] And the Jordan shall be their boundary on the east: this *is* the inheritance of the children of Benjamin, these *are* their borders round about according to their families.

[21] And the cities of the children of Benjamin according to their families were: Jericho, Beth Haglah, Emek,

[22] Beth Arabah, Sara, Besana,

[23] Avim, Parah, Ephratha,

[24] Carapha, Cephira, Moni, Gabaa, twelve cities and their villages;

[25] Gibeon, Ramah, Beeroth,

[26] Mizpah, Miron, Mozah;

[27] Phira, Caphan, Nacan, Selecan, Taralah,

[28] Jebus (this is Jerusalem), Gibeath, *and* Jearim; thirteen cities, and their villages. This *is* the inheritance of the sons of Benjamin according to their families.

JOSHUA CHAPTER 19

The Land of Simeon

[1] And the second lot came out for the children of Simeon; and their inheritance was in the midst of the lots of the children of Judah.

[2] And their lot was Beersheba, Sheba, Moladah,

[3] Hazar Shual, Balah, Jason,

[4] Erthula, Bula, and Hormah,

[5] Ziklag, Beth Marcaboth, Hazar Susah,

[6] Beth Lebaoth, and their fields, thirteen cities, and their villages.

[7] Rimmon, Thalcha, Ether, Ashan; four cities and their villages,

[8] round about their cities as far as Balec as *men* go to Bameth southward: this *is* the inheritance of the tribe of the children of Simeon according to their families.

[9] The inheritance of the tribe of the children of Simeon *was a part* of the lot of Judah, for the portion of the children of Judah was greater than theirs; and the children of Simeon inherited in the midst of their lot.

The Land of Zebulun

[10] And the third lot came out to Zebulun according to their families; the bounds of their inheritance shall be— Esedekgola shall be their border,

[11] the sea and Maralah, and it shall reach to Beth Arabah in the valley, which is opposite Jokneam.

[12] And the border returned from Sarid in an opposite direction eastward, to the borders of Chisloth Tabor, and shall pass on to Daberath, and shall proceed upward to Japhia.

[13] And from there it shall come round in the opposite direction eastward to Gath Hepher to Eth Kazin, and shall go on to Rimmon.

[14] And the borders shall come round northward to Hannathon, and their going out shall be at Jiphthah El.

[15] Included were Kattath, Nahallal, Shimron, Jericho, and Bethlehem.

[16] This *is* the inheritance of the tribe of the sons of Zebulun according to their families, *these* cities and their villages.

The Land of Issachar

[17] And the fourth lot came out to Issachar.

[18] And their borders were Jezreel, Chesulloth, Shunem,

[19] Haphraim, Shion, Anaharath,

20 Anachereth, Dabiron, Kishion, Abez,

21 Remeth, En Gannim, En Haddah, Emarek, and Beth Pazzez.

22 And the boundaries shall border upon Tabor, and upon Shahazimah westward, and Beth Shemesh; and the extremity of his bounds shall be the Jordan.

23 This *is* the inheritance of the tribe of the children of Issachar according to their families, the cities and their villages.

The Land of Asher

24 And the fifth lot came out to Asher according to their families.

25 And their borders were Helkath, Aleph, Baethok, Achshaph, 26 Alammelech, Amad, Mishal, and the lot will border on Carmel westward, along *the Brook* Shihor Libnah.

27 And it will return westward from Beth Dagon, and will join Zebulun and Ekgai, and Jiphthah El northwards, and the borders will come to Beth Emk and Neiel, and will go on to Cabul,

28 Ebron, Rehob, Hammon, and Kanah, to Great Sidon.

29 And the borders shall turn back to Ramah, and to the fountain of Masphassat, and the Tyrians; and the borders shall return to Jasiph, and their going forth shall be the sea, and Apoleb, and Achzib.

30 Also Archob, Aphek, and Rehob.

31 This *is* the inheritance of the tribe of the sons of Asher according to their families, the cities and their villages.

The Land of Naphtali

32 And the sixth lot came out to Nephthali.

33 And their borders were Moolam, Mola, Besemiin, Arme, Naboc, and Jephthamai, as far as Dodam; and their goings out were the Jordan.

34 And the coasts will return westward by Athabor, and will go out from there to Jacanah, and will border on Zebulun southward, and Asher will join *it* westward, and the Jordan eastward.

35 And the walled cities of the Tyrians *are*: Tyre, Omathadaketh, Kenereth,

36 Adamah, Ramah, Hazor,

37 Kadesh, Edrei, En Hazor,

38 Yiron, Migdal El, Horem, and Beth Shemesh.

39 This *is* the inheritance of the tribe of the children of Nephthali.

The Land of Dan

40 And the seventh lot came out to Dan.

41 And their borders were Sarath, Asa, the cities of Sammaus,

42 Shaalabbin, Aijalon, Silatha,

43 Elon, Timnah, Ekron,

44 Eltekeh, Gibbethon, Baalath,

45 Jehud, Bene Berak, and Gath Rimmon.

46 And westward of Hieracon the border *was* near to Joppa.

47 And the sons of Dan went and fought against Lachish, and took it, and struck it with the edge of the sword. And they dwelt in it, and called the name of it Leshem. And the Amorite continued to dwell in Edom and in Salamin; and the hand of Ephraim prevailed against them, and they became tributaries to them.

48 This *is* the inheritance of the tribe of the children of Dan, according to their families, these *are* their cities and their villages. And the children of Dan did not drive out the Amorite who afflicted them in the mountain; and the Amorite would not allow them to come down into the valley, but they forcibly took from them the border of their portion.

Joshua's Inheritance

49 And they proceeded to take possession of the land according to their borders, and the children of Israel gave an inheritance to Joshua the son of Nun among them,

50 by the command of God, and they gave him the city which he asked for, Timnah Serah, which is in the mount of Ephraim. And he built the city, and dwelt in it.

51 These *are* the divisions which Eleazar the priest divided by lot, and Joshua the *son* of Nun, and the heads of families among the tribes of Israel, according to the lots, in Shiloh before the Lord by the doors of the tabernacle of testimony, and they went to take possession of the land.

JOSHUA CHAPTER 20

The Cities of Refuge

1 And the Lord spoke to Joshua, saying,

2 "Speak to the children of Israel, saying, 'Assign the cities of refuge, *of* which I spoke to you by Moses.

3 *Even* a refuge to the manslayer who has killed a man unintentionally; and the cities shall be to you a refuge, and the manslayer shall not be put to death by the avenger of blood, until he has stood before the congregation for judgment.'"

4 (This verse omitted in LXX)

5 (This verse omitted in LXX)

6 (This verse omitted in LXX)

7 And Joshua separated Kadesh in Galilee in the mountains of Nephthali, and Shechem in the mountains of Ephraim, and the city of Arba; this is Hebron, in the mountains of Judah.

8 And beyond the Jordan he appointed Bezer in the wilderness in the plain out of the tribe of Reuben, and Ramoth in Gilead out of the tribe of Gad, and Golan in the country of Bashan out of the tribe of Manasseh.

9 These *were* the cities selected for the sons of Israel, and for the stranger abiding among them, that everyone who kills a man unintentionally should flee to there, that he should not die by the hand of the avenger of blood, until he should stand before the congregation for judgment.

JOSHUA CHAPTER 21

The Cities of the Levites

[1] And the heads of the families of the sons of Levi drew near to Eleazar the priest, and to Joshua the *son* of Nun, and to the heads of families of the tribes of Israel.

[2] And they spoke to them in Shiloh in the land of Canaan, saying, "The Lord gave commandment by Moses to give us cities to dwell in, and the country round about for our livestock."

[3] So the children of Israel gave to the Levites in their inheritance by the command of the Lord the cities and the country round.

[4] And the lot came out for the children of Caath; and the sons of Aaron, the priests the Levites, had by lot thirteen cities out of the tribe of Judah, and out of the tribe of Simeon, and out of the tribe of Benjamin.

[5] And to the sons of Caath that were left were *given* ten cities *by* lot, out of the tribe of Ephraim, and out of the tribe of Dan, and out of the half-tribe of Manasseh.

[6] And the sons of Gershon had thirteen cities, out of the tribe of Issachar, and out of the tribe of Asher, and out of the tribe of Nephthali, and out of the half-tribe of Manasseh in Bashan. [7] And the sons of Merari according to their families had by lot twelve cities, out of the tribe of Reuben, and out of the tribe of Gad, and out of the tribe of Zebulun.

[8] And the children of Israel gave to the Levites the cities and their suburbs, as the Lord commanded Moses, by lot.

[9] And the tribe of the children of Judah, and the tribe of the children of Simeon, and *part* of the tribe of the children of Benjamin gave these cities, and they were assigned

[10] to the sons of Aaron of the family of Caath of the sons of Levi, for the lot fell to these.

[11] And they gave to them Kirjath Arba the metropolis of the sons of Anak; this is Hebron in the mountains of Judah, and the suburbs surrounding it.

[12] But the lands of the city, and its villages Joshua gave to the sons of Caleb the son of Jephunneh for a possession.

[13] And to the sons of Aaron he gave the city of Hebron for a refuge for the manslayer, and the suburbs belonging to it; and Limnah and the suburbs belonging to it;

[14] and Elom and its suburbs; and Tema and its suburbs;

[15] and Gella and its suburbs; and Dabir and its suburbs;

[16] and Asa and its suburbs; and Tany and its suburbs; and Beth Shemesh and its suburbs: nine cities from these two tribes.

[17] And from the tribe of Benjamin, Gibeon and its suburbs; and Geba and its suburbs;

[18] and Anathoth and its suburbs; and Gamala and its suburbs; four cities.

[19] All the cities of the sons of Aaron the priests *were* thirteen.

[20] And to the families, *even* the sons of Caath the Levites, that were left of the sons of Caath, there was *given* their priests' city,

[21] out of the tribe of Ephraim; and they gave them the manslayer's city of refuge, Shechem and its suburbs, Gaza and its appendages, and its suburbs;

[22] and Beth Horon and its suburbs, four cities;

[23] and the tribe of Dan, Eltekeh and its suburbs; and Gibbethon and its suburbs;

[24] and Aijalon and its suburbs; and Garh Rimmon and its suburbs, four cities.

[25] And out of the half-tribe of Manasseh, Tanach and its suburbs; and Jebatha and its suburbs; two cities.

[26] In all *were given* ten cities, and the suburbs of each belonging to them, to the families of the sons of Caath that remained.

[27] And *Joshua gave* to the sons of Gershon the Levites out of the other half-tribe of Manasseh cities set apart for the manslayers, Golan in the country of Bashan, and its suburbs; and Bosora and its suburbs; two cities.

[28] And out of the tribe of Issachar, Kishion and its suburbs; and Daberath and its suburbs;

[29] and Jarmuth and its suburbs; and the Well of Letters and its suburbs; four cities.

[30] And out of the tribe of Asher, Basella and its suburbs; and Dabbon and its suburbs;

[31] and Helkath and its suburbs; and Rehob and its suburbs; four cities.

[32] And of the tribe of Nephthali, the city set apart for the manslayer, Kadesh in Galilee, and its suburbs; and Nemmath and its suburbs; and Themmon and its suburbs; three cities.

[33] All the cities of Gershon according to their families *were* thirteen cities.

[34] And to the family of the sons of Merari the Levites that remained, *he gave* out of the tribe of Zebulun, Maan and its suburbs; and Kartah and its suburbs,

[35] and Sella and its suburbs, three cities.

[36] And beyond the Jordan over against Jericho, out of the tribe of Reuben, the city of refuge for the manslayer, Bezer in the wilderness; Miso and its suburbs;

[37] and Jazer and its suburbs; and Decmon and its suburbs; and Mapha and its suburbs, four cities.

[38] And out of the tribe of Gad the city of refuge for the manslayer, both Ramoth in Gilead, and its suburbs; Camin and its suburbs;

[39] and Heshbon and its suburbs; and Jazer and its suburbs: the cities *were* four in all.

[40] All *these* cities *were given* to the sons of Merari according to the families of them that were left out of the tribe of Levi; and their limits were the twelve cities.

[41] All the cities of the Levites in the midst of the possession of the children of Israel *were* forty-eight cities, and their suburbs round about these cities:

[42] a city and the suburbs round about the city to all these cities: and Joshua ceased dividing the land by their borders. And the children of Israel gave a portion to Joshua because of the commandment of the Lord: they gave him the city

which he asked. They gave him Thamnasachar in Mount Ephraim; and Joshua built the city, and dwelt in it. And Joshua took the knives of stone in which he circumcised the children of Israel that were born in the desert by the way, and put them in Thamnasachar.

The Promise Fulfilled

[43] So the Lord gave to Israel all the land which He swore to give to their fathers: and they inherited it, and dwelt in it.

[44] And the Lord gave them rest round about, as He swore to their fathers; not one of all their enemies maintained his ground against them; the Lord delivered all their enemies into their hands.

[45] There failed not one of the good things which the Lord spoke to the children of Israel; all came to pass.

JOSHUA CHAPTER 22

Eastern Tribes Return to Their Land

[1] Then Joshua called together the sons of Reuben, and the sons of Gad, and the half-tribe of Manasseh,

[2] and said to them, "You have heard all that Moses the servant of the Lord commanded you, and you have obeyed my voice in all that he commanded you.

[3] You have not deserted your brothers these many days. Until this day you have kept the commandment of the Lord your God.

[4] And now the Lord our God has given our brothers rest, as He told them. Now then, return and depart to your homes, and to the land of your possession, which Moses gave you on the other side of the Jordan.

[5] But take great heed to do the commands and the law which Moses the servant of the Lord commanded you to do; to love the Lord our God, to walk in all His ways, to keep His commands, and to cleave to Him, and serve Him with all your mind, and with all your soul."

[6] And Joshua blessed them, and dismissed them; and they went to their homes.

[7] And to *one* half the tribe of Manasseh Moses gave a portion in the land of Bashan, and to *the other* half Joshua gave a portion with his brothers on the other side of the Jordan westward: and when Joshua sent them away to their homes, then he blessed them.

[8] And they departed with much wealth to their houses, and they divided the spoil of their enemies with their brothers; very much livestock, and silver, and gold, and iron, and much clothing.

[9] So the sons of Reuben, and the sons of Gad, and the half-tribe of Manasseh, departed from the children of Israel in Shiloh in the land of Canaan, to go away into Gilead, into the land of their possession, which they inherited by the command of the Lord, by the hand of Moses.

An Altar by the Jordan

[10] And they came to Gilead of the Jordan, which is in the land of Canaan. And the children of Reuben, and the children of Gad, and the half-tribe of Manasseh built there an alter by the Jordan, a great altar to look at.

[11] And the children of Israel heard *someone* say, "Behold, the sons of Reuben, and the sons of Gad, and the half-tribe of Manasseh have built an alter at the borders of the land of Canaan at Gilead of the Jordan, on the opposite side to the children of Israel."

[12] And all the children of Israel gathered together to Shiloh, so as to go up and fight against them.

[13] And the children of Israel sent to the sons of Reuben, and the sons of Gad, and to the sons of the half-tribe of Manasseh into the land of Gilead, both Phinehas the son of Eleazar the son of Aaron the priest,

[14] and ten of the chiefs with him; *there was* one chief of every household out of all the tribes of Israel (the heads of families are the captains of thousands in Israel).

[15] And they came to the sons of Reuben, and to the sons of Gad, and to the half-tribe of Manasseh into the land of Gilead; and they spoke to them, saying,

[16] "Thus says the whole congregation of the Lord: What *is* this transgression that you have transgressed before the God of Israel, to turn away today from the Lord, in that you have built for yourselves an altar, so that you should be apostates from the Lord?

[17] Is the sin of Peor too little for you, whereas we have not been cleansed from it until this day, though there was a plague among the congregation of the Lord?

[18] And you have revolted this day from the Lord; and it shall come to pass if you revolt this day from the Lord, that tomorrow there shall be wrath upon all Israel.

[19] And now if the land of your possession *is too* little, cross over to the land of the possession of the Lord, where the tabernacle of the Lord dwells, and receive an inheritance among us; and do not become apostates from God, neither do you apostatize from the Lord, because of your having built an altar apart from the altar of the Lord our God.

[20] Behold, did not Achan the *son* of Zerah commit a trespass, *taking* of the accursed thing, and there was wrath on the whole congregation of Israel? And he himself died alone in his own sin."

[21] And the sons of Reuben, and the sons of Gad, and the half-tribe of Manasseh answered, and spoke to the captains of the thousands of Israel, saying,

[22] "God, *even* God is the Lord, and *even* God Himself knows, and Israel shall know; if we have transgressed before the Lord by apostasy, let Him not deliver us this day.

[23] And if we have built to ourselves an altar, so as to apostatize from the Lord our God, so as to offer upon it a sacrifice of burnt offerings, so as to offer upon it a sacrifice of peace offering, the Lord shall require it.

[24] But we have done this for the sake of precaution *concerning this* thing, saying, 'Lest hereafter your sons

should say to our sons, "What have you to do with the Lord God of Israel?"

²⁵ Whereas the Lord has set boundaries between us and you, even the Jordan, and you have no portion in the Lord: so your sons shall alienate our sons, that they should not worship the Lord.

²⁶ And we gave orders to do thus, to build this altar, not for burnt offerings, nor for meat offerings;

²⁷ but that this may be a witness between you and us, and between our generations after us, that we may do service to the Lord before Him, with our burnt offerings and our meat offerings and our peace offerings: so your sons shall not say to our sons, hereafter, "You have no portion in the Lord."

²⁸ And we said, "If ever it should come to pass that they should speak *so* to us, or to our posterity hereafter; then shall they say, 'Behold the likeness of the altar of the Lord, which our fathers made, not for the sake of burnt offerings, nor for the sake of meat offerings, but it is a witness between you and us, and between our sons."

²⁹ Far be it from us therefore that we should turn away from the Lord this day, so as to apostatize from the Lord, that we should build an altar for burnt offerings, and for peace offerings, besides the altar of the Lord which is before His tabernacle."

³⁰ And Phinehas the priest and all the chiefs of the congregation of Israel who were with him heard the words which the children of Reuben, and the children of Gad, and the half-tribe of Manasseh spoke, and it pleased them.

³¹ And Phinehas the priest said to the sons of Reuben, and to the sons of Gad, and to the half of the tribe of Manasseh, "Today we know that the Lord *is* with us, because you have not trespassed grievously against the Lord, and because you have delivered the children of Israel out of the hand of the Lord."

³² So Phinehas the priest and the princes departed from the children of Reuben, and from the children of Gad, and from the half-tribe of Manasseh out of Gilead into the land of Canaan to the children of Israel; and reported the words to them.

³³ And it pleased the children of Israel; and they spoke to the children of Israel, and blessed the God of the children of Israel, and told them to go up no more to war against the others to destroy the land of the children of Reuben, and the children of Gad, and the half-tribe of Manasseh. So they dwelt upon it.

³⁴ And Joshua gave a name to the altar of the children of Reuben, and the children of Gad, and the half-tribe of Manasseh; and said, "It is a testimony in the midst of them, that the Lord is their God."

JOSHUA CHAPTER 23

Joshua's Farewell Address

¹ And it came to pass after many days after the Lord had given Israel rest from all his enemies round about, that Joshua was old and advanced in years.

² And Joshua called together all the children of Israel, and their elders, and their chiefs, and their judges, and their officers, and said to them, "I am old and advanced in years.

³ And you have seen all that the Lord our God has done to all these nations before us; *for it* is the Lord your God who has fought for you.

⁴ See, that I have given to you these nations that are left to you by lots to your tribes, all the nations beginning at the Jordan; and *some* I have destroyed; and the boundaries shall be at the Great Sea westward.

⁵ And the Lord our God, He shall destroy them before us, until they utterly perish; and He shall send against them the wild beasts, until He has utterly destroyed them and their kings from before you; and you shall inherit their land, as the Lord our God said to you.

⁶ Therefore strive diligently to observe and do all things written in the Book of the Law of Moses, that you do not turn to the right hand or to the left;

⁷ that you do not mix with these nations that are left; and the names of their gods shall not be named among you, neither shall you serve them, neither shall you bow down to them.

⁸ But you shall cleave to the Lord our God, as you have done until this day.

⁹ And the Lord shall destroy them before you, *even* great and strong nations; and no one has stood before us until this day. ¹⁰ One of you has chased a thousand, for the Lord our God, He fought for you, as He said to us.

¹¹ And take great heed to love the Lord our God.

¹² For if you shall turn aside and attach yourselves to these nations that are left with you, and make marriages with them, and become mingled with them and they with you,

¹³ know that the Lord will no more destroy these nations from before you; and they will be to you snares and stumbling blocks, and nails in your heels, and darts in your eyes, until you are destroyed from off this good land, which the Lord your God has given you.

¹⁴ "But I hasten to go the way of *death*, as all that are upon the earth also *do*. And you know in your heart and in your soul, that not one word has fallen *to the ground* of all the words which the Lord our God has spoken respecting all that concerns us; there has not one of them failed.

¹⁵ And it shall come to pass, that as all the good things have come upon us which the Lord God *promised you, so shall* He bring upon you all the evil things, until He has destroyed you from off this good land, which the Lord has given you,

¹⁶ when you transgress the covenant of the Lord our God, which He has commanded us, and go and serve other gods, and bow down to them."

JOSHUA CHAPTER 24

The Tribes Renew the Covenant

¹ And Joshua gathered all the tribe of Israel to Shiloh, and called their elders, and their officers, and their judges, and set them before God.

[2] And Joshua said to all the people, "Thus says the Lord God of Israel: 'Your fathers at first sojourned beyond the river, *even* Terah, the father of Abraham and the father of Nahor; and they served other gods.

[3] And I took your father Abraham from the other side of the river, and I guided him through all the land, and I multiplied his descendants;

[4] and I gave to him Isaac, and to Isaac Jacob and Esau: and I gave to Esau Mount Seir for him to inherit. And Jacob and his sons went down to Egypt, and became there a great and populous and mighty nation, and the Egyptians afflicted them.

[5] And I struck Egypt with the wonders that I wrought among them.'

[6] And afterwards *God* brought out our fathers from Egypt, and you entered into the Red Sea; and the Egyptians pursued after our fathers with chariots and horses into the Red Sea.

[7] And we cried aloud to the Lord, and He put a cloud and darkness between us an the Egyptians, and He brought the sea upon them, and covered them; and your eyes have seen all that the Lord did in the land of Egypt; and you were in the wilderness many days.

[8] And He brought us into the land of the Amorites that dwelt beyond the Jordan, and the Lord delivered them into our hands; and you inherited their land, and utterly destroyed them from before you.

[9] And Balak, king of Moab, son of Siphor, rose up, and made war against Israel, and sent and called Balaam to curse us.

[10] But the Lord your God would not destroy you; and He greatly blessed us, and rescued us out of their hands, and delivered them *to us*.

[11] And you crossed over the Jordan, and came to Jericho; and the inhabitants of Jericho fought against us, the Amorite, the Canaanite, the Perizzite, the Hivite, the Jebusite, the Hittite, and the Girgashite, and the Lord delivered them into our hands.

[12] And He sent forth the hornet before you; and He drove them out from before you, *even* twelve kings of the Amorites, not with your sword, nor with your bow.

[13] And He gave you a land on which you did not labor, and cities which you did not build, and you were settled in them; and you eat *of* vineyards and olive yards which you did not plant.

[14] "And now fear the Lord, and serve Him in righteousness and justice; and remove the strange gods, which our fathers served beyond the river, and in Egypt; and serve the Lord.

[15] But if it does not seem good to you to serve the Lord, choose for yourselves this day whom you will serve, whether the gods of your fathers that were on the other side of the river, or the gods of the Amorites, among whom you dwell upon their land. But as for me and my house, we will serve the Lord, for He is holy."

[16] And the people answered and said, "Far be it from us to forsake the Lord, so as to serve other gods.

[17] The Lord our God, He is God; He brought up us and our fathers from Egypt, and kept us in all the way in which we walked, and among all the nations through whom we passed.

[18] And the Lord cast out the Amorite, and all the nations that inhabited the land from before us: indeed, we will serve the Lord, for He is our God."

[19] And Joshua said to the people, "Indeed you will not be able to serve the Lord, for God is holy; and He being jealous will not forgive your sins and your transgressions.

[20] Whenever you shall forsake the Lord and serve other gods, then He shall come upon you and afflict you, and consume you, because He has done you good."

[21] And the people said to Joshua, "No, but we will serve the Lord!"

[22] And Joshua said to the people, "You *are* witnesses against yourselves, that you have chosen the Lord, to serve Him.

[23] And now take away the strange gods that are among you, and set your heart right toward the Lord God of Israel."

[24] And the people said to Joshua, "We will serve the Lord, and we will listen to His voice."

[25] So Joshua made a covenant with the people on that day, and gave them a law and an ordinance in Shiloh before the tabernacle of the God of Israel.

[26] And he wrote these words in the Book of the Laws of God. And Joshua took a great stone, and set it up under the oak before the Lord.

[27] And Joshua said to the people, "Behold, this stone shall be among you for a witness, for it has heard all the words that have been spoken to it by the Lord; for He has spoken to you this day; and this *stone* shall be among you for a witness in the last days, whenever you shall deal falsely with the Lord my God."

[28] And Joshua dismissed the people, and they went every man to his place.

The Death of Joshua

[29] And it came to pass after these things that Joshua the son of Nun the servant of the Lord died, *at the age* of a hundred and ten years.

[30] And they buried him by the borders of his inheritance in Timnath Serah in the mount of Ephraim, northward of the mount of Gilead. There they put with him into the tomb in which they buried him, the knives of stone with which he circumcised the children of Israel in Gilgal, when he brought them out of Egypt, as the Lord appointed them; and there they are to this day.

[31] And Israel served the Lord all the days of Joshua, and all the days of the elders that lived as long as Joshua, and all that knew all the works of the Lord which He had done for Israel.

32 And the children of Israel brought up the bones of Joseph out of Egypt, and buried *them* in Shechem, in the portion of the land which Jacob bought of the Amorites who dwelt in Shechem for a hundred ewe lambs; and he gave it to Joseph for a portion.

33 And it came to pass afterwards that Eleazar the high priest the son of Aaron died, and was buried in Gibeah of Phinehas his son, which he gave him in Mount Ephraim. In that day the children of Israel took the ark of God, and carried it about among them. And Phinehas exercised the priest's office in the place of Eleazar his father till he died, and he was buried in his own place Gibeah. But the children of Israel departed everyone to their place, and to their own city: and the children of Israel worshipped Astarte, and Astaroth, and the gods of the nations round about them; and the Lord delivered them into the hands of Eglom king of Moab, and he ruled over them eighteen years.

THE BOOK OF JUDGES

Israel's Failure to Complete the Conquest of Canaan

1 And it came to pass after the death of Joshua, that the children of Israel inquired of the Lord, saying, "Who shall go up for us first against the Canaanites, to fight against them?"

2 And the Lord said, "Judah shall go up: behold, I have delivered the land into his hand."

3 And Judah said to his brother Simeon, "Come up with me into my lot, and let us array ourselves against the Canaanites, and I also will go with you into your lot." And Simeon went with him.

4 And Judah went up; and the Lord delivered the Canaanite and the Perizzite into their hands, and they attacked them in Bezek to *the number of* ten thousand men.

5 And they overtook Adoni-Bezek in Bezek, and fought against him; and they attacked the Canaananite and the Perizzite.

6 And Adoni-Bezek fled, and they pursued after him, and took him, and cut off his thumbs and his big toes.

7 And Adoni-Bezek said, "Seventy kings, having their thumbs and their big toes cut off, gathered their food under my table: as I therefore have done, so God has recompensed me." So they brought him to Jerusalem, and he died there.

8 And the children of Judah fought against Jerusalem, and took it, and struck them with the edge of the sword, and they burned the city with fire.

9 And afterwards the children of Judah went down to fight with the Canaanite dwelling in the hill country, and the south, and the plain country.

10 And Judah went to the Canaanite who dwelt in Hebron; and Hebron came out against him (and the name of Hebron before was Kirjath Arba) and they killed Sheshai, Ahiman, and Talmai, children of Enac.

11 And they went up from there to the inhabitants of Debir; and the name of Debir before was Kirjath Serpher, the City of Letters.

12 And Caleb said, "Whosoever shall attack the City of Letters, and shall first take it, I will give to him Achsah my daughter for a wife."

13 And Othniel the younger son of Kenaz the brother of Caleb took it; and Caleb gave him his daughter Achsah for a wife.

14 And it came to pass as she went in, that Othniel urged her to ask a field of her father; and she murmured and cried from off her donkey *and said*, "You have sent me forth into a south land." And Caleb said to her, "What do you wish?"

15 And Achsah said to him, "Give me, I pray, a blessing, for you have sent me forth into a south land, and you shall give me the ransom of water." And Caleb gave her according to her heart the ransom of the upper *springs* and the ransom of the lower *springs*.

16 And the children of Jethro the Kenite, the father-in-law of Moses, went up from the City of Palm Trees with the children of Judah, to the wilderness that is in the south of Judah, which is at the descent of Arad, and they dwelt with the people.

17 And Judah went with Simeon his brother, and attacked the Canaanite that inhabited Zephath, and they utterly destroyed them; and they called the name of the city Anathema.

18 But Judah did not inherit Gaza nor her coasts, nor Ashkelon or her coasts, nor Ekron or her coasts, nor Ashdod or the lands around it.

19 And the Lord was with Judah, and he inherited the mountain; for they were not able to destroy the inhabitants of the valley, for Rechab prevented them.

20 And they gave Hebron to Caleb, as Moses said; and then he inherited the three cities of the children of Anak.

21 But the children of Benjamin did not take the inheritance of the Jebusite who dwelt in Jerusalem; and the Jebusite dwelt with the children of Benjamin in Jerusalem until this day.

22 And the sons of Joseph, they also went up to Bethel; and the Lord was with them.

23 And they encamped and surveyed Bethel: and the name of the city before was Luz.

24 And the spies looked, and behold, a man went out of the city, and they took him; and they said to him, "Show us the way into the city, and we will deal mercifully with you."

25 And he showed them the way into the city; and they struck the city with the edge of the sword; but they let go the man and his family.

26 And the man went into the land of the Hittites, and built there a city, and called the name of it Luz; which is its name to this day.

27 And Manasseh did not drive out *the inhabitants* of Beth-Shean, which is a city of Scythians, nor her towns, nor her suburbs; nor Taanach, nor her towns; nor the inhabitants of

Dor, nor her suburbs, nor her towns; nor the inhabitant of Balac, nor her suburbs, nor her towns; nor the inhabitants of Megiddo, nor her suburbs, nor her towns; nor the inhabitants of Jeblaam, nor her suburbs, nor her towns; and the Canaanite began to dwell in this land.

28 And it came to pass when Israel was strong, that he put the Canaanite under forced labor, but did not utterly drive them out.

29 And Ephraim did not drive out the Canaanite that dwelt in Gezer; and the Canaanite dwelt in the midst of him in Gezer, and became forced labor.

30 And Zebulun did not drive out the inhabitants of Kedron, nor the inhabitants of Domana: and the Canaanite dwelt in the midst of them, and became forced labor to them.

31 And Asher did not drive out the inhabitants of Accho, and those people became tributary to him, nor did he drive out the inhabitants of Dor, nor the inhabitants of Sidon, nor the inhabitants of Ahlab, nor Achzib, nor Helbah, nor Aphik, nor Rehob.

32 And Asher dwelt in the midst of the Canaanite who inhabited the land, for he could not drive him out.

33 And Nephthali did not drive out the inhabitants of Beth Shemeth, nor the inhabitants of Beth Anath; and Nephthali dwelt in the midst of the Canaanite who inhabited the land; but the inhabitants of Beth Shemeth and of Beth Anath became forced labor to them.

34 And the Amorite drove out the children of Dan into the mountains, for they did not allow them to come down into the valley.

35 And the Amorite began to dwell in the mountain of shells, in which are bears, and foxes, in Myrsinon, and in Shaalabbin; and the hand of the house of Joseph was heavy upon the Amorite, and he became forced labor to them.

36 And the border of the Amorite was from the Ascent of Akrabbin, from the rock and upwards.

JUDGES CHAPTER 2

Israel's Disobedience

1 And an angel of the Lord went up from Gilgal to the *place of* weeping, and to Bethel, and to the house of Israel, and said to them, "Thus says the Lord: 'I brought you up out of Egypt, and I brought you into the land which I swore to your fathers; and I said, I will never break My covenant that I have made with you.

2 And you shall make no covenant with them that dwell in this land, neither shall you worship their gods; but you shall destroy their graven images, you shall pull down their altars: but you did not listen to My voice, for you did these things.

3 And I said, I will not drive them out from before you, but they shall be for a distress to you, and their gods shall be to you for an offense.'"

4 And it came to pass when the angel of the Lord spoke these words to all the children of Israel, that the people lifted up their voice and wept.

5 And they named the name of that place Weepings; and they sacrificed there to the Lord.

6 And Joshua dismissed the people, and they went every man to his inheritance, to inherit the land.

The Death of Joshua

7 And the people served the Lord all the days of Joshua, and all the days of the elders that lived many days with Joshua, as many as knew all the great work of the Lord, what things He had done in Israel.

8 And Joshua the son of Nun, the servant of the Lord, died, *being* one hundred and ten years old.

9 And they buried him in the border of his inheritance, in Timnath Heres, in Mount Ephraim, on the north of the mountain of Gaash.

10 And all that generation were gathered to their fathers: and another generation rose up after them, who did not know the Lord, nor yet the work which He wrought in Israel.

Israel's Unfaithfulness

11 And the children of Israel did evil before the Lord, and served Baalam.

12 And they forsook the Lord God of their fathers, who brought them out of the land of Egypt, and walked after other gods, of the gods of the nations round about them; and they worshipped them.

13 And they provoked the Lord, and forsook Him, and served Baal and the Ashtoreths.

14 And the Lord was very angry with Israel; and He gave them into the hands of the plunderers, and they plundered them; and He sold them into the hands of their enemies round about, and they could not any longer resist their enemies,

15 among whomsoever they went; and the hand of the Lord was against them for evil, as the Lord spoke, and as the Lord swore to them; and He greatly afflicted them.

16 And the Lord raised up judges, and the Lord saved them out of the hands of those that spoiled them: and yet they would not listen to the judges,

17 for they went whoring after other gods, and worshipped them; and they turned quickly out of the way in which their fathers walked, in obeying the words of the Lord; *and* they did not do so.

18 And because the Lord raised up judges for them, so the Lord was with the judge, and saved them out of the hand of their enemies all the days of the judge; for the Lord was moved at their groaning by reason of them that besieged them and afflicted them.

19 And it came to pass when the judge died, that they went back, and again corrupted *themselves* worse than their fathers to go after other gods, to serve them and to worship them: they did not abandon their own doings, nor their stubborn ways.

20 And the Lord was very angry with Israel, and said, "Because this nation has forsaken My covenant which I commanded their fathers, and has not listened to My voice,

21 therefore I will no longer drive out a man of the nations before their face, which Joshua the son of Nun left in the land." And *the Lord* left *them,*

22 to test Israel with them, whether they would keep the way of the Lord, to walk in it, as their fathers kept it, or not.

23 So the Lord will leave these nations, so as not to cast them out suddenly; nor did He deliver them into the hand of Joshua.

JUDGES CHAPTER 3

The Nations Remaining in the Land

1 And these are the nations which the Lord left, that He might test Israel by them, *that is,* all that had not known the wars of Canaan.

2 Only for the sake of the generations of Israel, to teach them war, only the men before them did not know them.

3 *These are the nations:* the five lordships of the Philistines, and every Canaanite, and the Sidonian, and the Hivite who dwelt in Lebanon from the mount of Hermon to Hamath.

4 And *this* was done in order to test Israel by them, to know whether they would obey the commands of the Lord, which He charged their fathers by the hand of Moses.

5 And the children of Israel dwelt in the midst of the Canaanite, and the Hittite, and the Amorite, and the Perizzite, and the Hivite, and the Jebusite.

6 And they took their daughters for wives to themselves, and they gave their daughters to their sons, and served their gods.

Othniel

7 And the children of Israel did evil in the sight of the Lord, and forgot the Lord their God, and served Baalam and the groves.

8 And the Lord was very angry with Israel, and sold them into the hand of Cushan-Rishathaim king of Syria of the rivers: and the children of Israel served Cushan-Rishathaim eight years.

9 And the children of Israel cried to the Lord. And the Lord raised up a deliverer to Israel, and he delivered them, Othniel the son of Kenaz, Caleb's younger brother.

10 And the Spirit of the Lord came upon him, and he judged Israel; and he went out to war against Cushan-Rishathaim. And the Lord delivered into his hand Cushan-Rishathaim king of Syria of the rivers, and his hand prevailed against Cushan-Rishathaim.

11 And the land was quiet forty years; and Othniel the son of Kenaz died.

Ehud

12 And the children of Israel continued to do evil before the Lord. And the Lord strengthened Eglon king of Moab against Israel, because they had done evil before the Lord.

13 And he gathered to himself all the children of Ammon and Amalek, and went and struck Israel, and took possession of the City of Palm Trees.

14 And the children of Israel served Eglon the king of Moab eighteen years.

15 And the children of Israel cried to the Lord; and He raised up to them a deliverer, Ehud the son of Gera, a Benjamite, a man who used both hands alike: and the children of Israel sent gifts by his hand to Eglon king of Moab.

16 And Ehud made himself a two-edged dagger of a span long, and he secured it under his cloak upon his right thigh.

17 And he went, and brought the presents to Eglon king of Moab. And Eglon *was* a very handsome man.

18 And it came to pass when Ehud *had* made an end of offering his gifts, that he dismissed those that brought the gifts.

19 And he himself returned from the quarries that are by Gilgal. And Ehud said, "I have a secret message for you, O king!" And Eglon said to him, "Be silent." And he sent away from his presence all who waited upon him.

20 And Ehud went in to him; and he sat alone in his own upper summer chamber. And Ehud said, "I have a message from God for you, O king." And Eglon rose up from his throne near to him.

21 And it came to pass as he arose, that Ehud stretched forth his left hand, and took the dagger off his right thigh, and plunged it into his belly;

22 and drove in also the handle after the blade, and the fat closed in upon the blade, for he did not draw the dagger out of his belly.

23 And Ehud went out to the porch, and shut the doors of the chamber behind him, and locked *them,* and passed on by the appointed *guards.*

24 And he went out. And Eglon's servants came, and saw, and behold, the doors of the upper chamber were locked. And they said, "Does he not uncover his feet in the summer-chamber?"

25 And they waited till they were ashamed, and behold, there was no one that opened the doors of the upper chamber; and they took the key, and opened them. And behold, their master was fallen down dead upon the ground.

26 And Ehud escaped while they were in a tumult, and no one paid attention to him; and he passed by the quarries, and escaped to Seirah.

27 And it came to pass when Ehud came into the land of Israel, that he blew the horn in Mount Ephraim, and the children of Israel came down with him from the mountain, and he was before them.

28 And he said to them, "Come down after me, for the Lord God has delivered our enemies, even Moab, into our hand." So they went down after him, and seized on the fords of the

Jordan before Moab, and he did not allow a man to pass over. [29] And they struck Moab on that day, *and killed* about ten thousand men, every lusty *person* and every mighty man; and not a man escaped.

[30] So Moab was humbled in that day under the hand of Israel, and the land had rest eighty years; and Ehud judged them till he died.

Shamgar

[31] And after him rose up Shamgar the son of Anath, and he struck the Philistines to the number of six hundred men with a plow share of an ox; and he too delivered Israel.

JUDGES CHAPTER 4

Deborah

[1] And the children of Israel continued to do evil against the Lord; and Ehud was dead.

[2] And the Lord sold the children of Israel into the hand of Jabin king of Canaan, who ruled in Hazor; and the chief of his army was Sisera, and he dwelt in Harosheth of the Gentiles.

[3] And the children of Israel cried to the Lord, because he had nine hundred chariots of iron; and he mightily oppressed Israel twenty years.

[4] And Deborah, a prophetess, the wife of Lapidoth, she judged Israel at that time.

[5] And she sat under the palm tree of Deborah between Ramah and Bethel in Mount Ephraim; and the children of Israel went up to her for judgment.

[6] And Deborah sent and called Barak the son of Abinoam out of Kedesh Nephtali, and she said to him, "Has not the Lord God of Israel commanded you? And you shall depart to Mount Tabor, and shall take with yourself ten thousand men of the sons of Nephtali and of the sons of Zebulun.

[7] And I will bring to you to the torrent of Kison Sisera the captain of the host of Jabin, and his chariots, and his multitude, and I will deliver them into your hands."

[8] And Barak said to her, "If you will go with me, I will go; and if you will not go, I will not go; for I know not the day on which the Lord prospers His messenger with me."

[9] And she said, "I will surely go with you; but know that your honor shall not attend on the expedition on which you go, for the Lord shall sell Sisera into the hands of a woman." And Deborah arose, and went with Barak out of Kedesh.

[10] And Barak called out Zebulun and Nephtali out of Kedesh, and ten thousand men went up at his heels, and Deborah went up with him.

[11] And Heber the Kenite had removed from Caina, from the sons of Jethro, the father-in-law of Moses, and pitched his tent by the oak of the covetous ones, which is near Kedesh.

[12] And it was told Sisera that Barak the son of Abinoam had gone up to Mount Tabor.

[13] And Sisera summoned all his chariots, nine hundred chariots of iron and all the people with him, from Harosheth of the Gentiles to the brook of Kishon.

[14] And Deborah said to Barak, "Rise up, for this is the day on which the Lord has delivered Sisera into your hand, for the Lord shall go forth before you." And Barak went down from Mount Tabor, and ten thousand men after him.

[15] And the Lord routed Sisera, and all his chariots, and all his army, with the edge of the sword before Barak; and Sisera descended from off his chariot, and fled on his feet.

[16] And Barak pursued after the chariots and after the army, into Harosheth of the Gentiles; and the whole army of Sisera fell by the edge of the sword, there was none left.

[17] And Sisera fled on his feet to the tent of Jael the wife of Heber, his friend the Kenite; for there was peace between Jabin king of Hazor and the house of Heber the Kenite.

[18] And Jael went out to meet Sisera, and said to him, "Turn aside, my lord, turn aside to me, fear not." So he turned aside to her into the tent; and she covered him with a rug.

[19] And Sisera said to her, "Give me a little water to drink, for I am thirsty." So she opened a bottle of milk, and gave him to drink, and covered him.

[20] And Sisera said to her, "Stand now by the door of the tent, and it shall come to pass if any man come to you, and ask of you, and say, 'Is there *any* man here?' Then you shall say, 'There is not.'"

[21] And Jael the wife of Heber took a tent peg, and took a hammer in her hand, and went secretly to him, and fastened the peg in his temple, and it went through to the ground, and he fainted away, and darkness fell upon him and he died.

[22] And behold, Barak was pursuing Sisera. And Jael went out to meet him, and she said to him, "Come, and I will show you the man whom you seek." And he went in to her, and behold, Sisera had fallen down dead, and the peg was in his temple.

[23] So God routed Jabin king of Canaan in that day before the children of Israel.

[24] And the hand of the children of Israel prevailed more and more against Jabin king of Canaan, until they utterly destroyed Jabin king of Canaan.

JUDGES CHAPTER 5

The Song of Deborah

[1] And Deborah and Barak son of Abinoam sang in that day, saying,

[2] "A revelation was made in Israel when the people were made willing: Bless the Lord!

[3] Hear, O kings, and give ear, O you rulers: I will sing, it is I *who will sing* to the Lord, it is I, I will sing a psalm to the Lord God of Israel.

[4] O Lord, in Your going forth on Seir, when You went forth out of the land of Edom, the earth quaked and the heaven dropped the dew, and the clouds dropped water.

5 The mountains were shaken before the face of the Lord Eloi, this Sinai, before the face of the Lord God of Israel.

6 In the days of Shamgar son of Anath, in the days of Jael, they deserted the *right* ways, and went in *through the* byways; they went in crooked paths.

7 The mighty men in Israel failed, they failed until *I*, Deborah arose, until *there* arose a mother in Israel.

8 They chose new gods; then the cities of rulers fought; there was not a shield or spear seen among forty thousand in Israel.

9 My heart inclines to the orders given in Israel; you that are willing among the people, bless the Lord.

10 You that mount a donkey at noonday, you that sit on the judgment seat, and walk by the roads of them that sit in judgment by the way. Declare,

11 *you that are delivered* from the noise of disturbers among those that draw water; there shall they relate righteous acts: O Lord, increase righteous acts in Israel. Then the people of the Lord went down to the cities.

12 Awake, awake, Deborah; awake, awake, utter a song. Arise, Barak, and lead your captivity captive, O son of Abinoam.

13 Then the remnant went down to the strong, the people of the Lord went down for him among the mighty ones from me. 14 Ephraim rooted them out in Amalek, behind you was Benjamin among your people: the inhabitants of Machir came down with me searching out the enemy, and from Zebulun came those that draw with the scribe's pen of record.

15 And princes in Issachar were with Deborah and Barak, thus she sent Barak on his feet in the valleys into the portions of Reuben; great *pangs* reached to the heart.

16 Why did they sit between the sheep folds to hear the bleating of flocks for the divisions of Reuben? *There were* great searchings of heart.

17 Gilead is on the other side of the Jordan where he pitched his tents; and why does Dan remain in ships? Asher sat down on the sea coasts, and he will dwell at his ports.

18 Zebulun risked their lives to the death, and Nephtali came to the high places of their land.

19 Kings set themselves in array, then the kings of Canaan fought in Taanach at the water of Megiddo; they took no gift of money.

20 The stars from heaven set themselves in array, they set themselves *to fight* with Sisera out of their paths.

21 The brook of Kishon swept them away, the ancient brook, the brook Kishon: my mighty soul will trample him down.

22 When the hoofs of the horse were entangled, his mighty ones earnestly hastened

23 to curse Meroz: 'Curse *it*,' said the angel of the Lord; cursed *is* everyone that dwells in it, because they came not to the help of the Lord, to His help among the mighty.

24 Blessed among women is Jael wife of Heber the Kenite; let her be blessed above women in tents.

25 He asked for water, she gave him milk in a dish; she brought the butter of princes.

26 She stretched forth her left hand to the nail, and her right hand to the workman's hammer, and she struck Sisera with it, she nailed through his head and killed him; she nailed through his temples.

27 He rolled down between her feet; he fell and lay between her feet; he bowed and fell: where he bowed, there he fell dead.

28 The mother of Sisera looked down through the window out of the loophole, saying, 'Why was his chariot ashamed? Why did the wheels of his chariots tarry?'

29 Her wise ladies answered her, and she returned answers to herself, *saying,*

30 'Will they not find him dividing the spoil? He will surely be gracious to every man." *There are* spoils of dyed garments for Sisera, spoils of various dyed garments, dyed embroidered garments, they are the spoils for his neck.

31 Thus let all Your enemies perish, O Lord: and they that love Him shall be as the going forth of the sun in his strength." And the land had rest forty years.

JUDGES CHAPTER 6

The Midianite Oppression

1 And the children of Israel did evil in the sight of the Lord, and the Lord gave them into the hand of Midian for seven years.

2 And the hand of Midian prevailed against Israel. And the children of Israel made for themselves caves in the mountains, and the dens, and the holes in the rocks, because of Midian.

3 And it came to pass when the children of Israel sowed, that Midian and Amalek went up, and the children of the east went up together with them.

4 And they encamped against them, and destroyed their fruits until they came to Gaza; and they left no sustenance in the land of Israel, not even ox or donkey among the herds.

5 For they and their stock came up, and their tents were with them, as the locust in multitude, and there was no number to them and their camels; and they came to the land of Israel, and laid it waste.

6 And Israel was greatly impoverished because of Midian.

7 And the children of Israel cried to the Lord because of Midian.

8 And the Lord sent a prophet to the children of Israel; and he said to them, "Thus says the Lord God of Israel: I am He that brought you up out of the land of Egypt, and I brought you up out of the house of your bondage.

9 And I delivered you out of the hand of Egypt, and out of the hand of all that afflicted you, and I cast them out before you; and I gave you their land.

10 And I said to you, I am the Lord your God: you shall not fear the gods of the Amorites, in whose land you dwell; but you did not listen to My voice."

Gideon

[11] And an angel of the Lord came, and sat down under the fir tree, which was in Ephratha in the land of Joash father of Esdri. And Gideon his son was threshing wheat in a wine press in order to escape from the face of Midian.

[12] And the Angel of the Lord appeared to him and said to him, "The Lord is with you, you *who are* mighty in strength!"

[13] And Gideon said to him, "Be gracious with me, my Lord: but if the Lord is with us, why have these evils found us? And where are all His miracles, which our fathers have related to us, saying, 'Did not the Lord bring us up out of Egypt?' And now He has cast us out, and given us into the hand of Midian."

[14] And the Angel of the Lord turned to him and said, "Go in this your strength, and you shall save Israel out of the hand of Midian: behold, I have sent you."

[15] And Gideon said to him, "*Be gracious* with me, my Lord: how shall I save Israel? Behold, my thousand is weakened in Manasseh, and I am the least in my father's house."

[16] And the Angel of the Lord said to him, "The Lord shall be with you, and you shall strike Midian as one man."

[17] And Gideon said to him, "If now I have found mercy in Your eyes, and You will do this day for me all that You have spoken of with me,

[18] do not depart from here until I come to You, and I will bring forth an offering and offer it before You." And He said, "I will remain until you return."

[19] And Gideon went in, and prepared a young goat, and unleavened bread from an ephah of fine flour; and he put the flesh in the basket, and poured the broth into the pot, and brought them forth to Him under the terebinth tree, and drew near.

[20] And the Angel of God said to him, "Take the flesh and the unleavened cakes, and put them on that rock, and pour out the broth close by"; and he did so.

[21] And the Angel of the Lord stretched out the end of the rod that was in His hand, and touched the flesh and the unleavened bread; and fire came up out of the rock, and consumed the flesh and the unleavened bread, and the Angel of the Lord vanished from his sight.

[22] And Gideon saw that He was the Angel of the Lord; and Gideon said, "Ah, O Lord my God! For I have seen the Angel of the Lord face to face."

[23] And the Lord said to him, "Peace be with you, fear not, you shall not die."

[24] And Gideon built there an altar to the Lord, and called it The Peace of the Lord, until this day, as it is still in Ephratha of the father of Esdri.

[25] And it came to pass in that night, that the Lord said to him, "Take the young bull which your father has, even the second bull of seven years old, and you shall destroy the altar of Baal which your father has, and the grove which is by it you shall destroy.

[26] And you shall build an altar to the Lord your God on the top of this rock in the proper arrangement, and you shall take the second bull, and shall offer up burnt offerings with the wood of the grove, which you shall destroy."

[27] And Gideon took ten men of his servants, and did as the Lord spoke to him. And it came to pass, as he feared the house of his father and the men of the city if he should do it by day, that he did it by night.

Gideon Destroys the Altar of Baal

[28] And the men of the city rose up early in the morning. And behold, the altar of Baal had been demolished, and the grove by it had been destroyed; and they saw the second bull, which Gideon offered on the altar that had been built.

[29] And a man said to his neighbor, "Who has done this thing?" And they inquired and searched, and learned that Gideon the son of Joash had done this thing.

[30] And the men of the city said to Joash, "Bring out your son, and let him die, because he has destroyed the altar of Baal, and because he has destroyed the grove that is by it."

[31] And Gideon the son of Joash said to all the men who rose up against him, "Do you now plead for Baal, or will you save him? Whoever will plead for him, let him be slain this morning: if he be a god let him plead for himself, because *one* has thrown down his altar."

[32] And he called it in that day Jerubbaal, saying, "Let Baal plead against him," because his altar has been thrown down.

[33] And all Midian, and Amalek, and the sons of the east gathered themselves together, and encamped in the Valley of Jezreel.

[34] And the Spirit of the Lord came upon Gideon, and he sounded his trumpet, and Abiezer came to help after him.

[35] And *Gideon* sent messengers into all Manasseh, and into Asher, and into Zebulun, and into Nephtali; and he went up to meet them.

The Sign of the Fleece

[36] And Gideon said to God, "If you will save Israel by my hand, as You have said,

[37] behold, I put the fleece of wool in the threshing floor: if there be dew on the fleece only, and drought on all the ground, I shall know that You will save Israel by my hand, as You have said."

[38] And it was so. And he rose up early in the morning, and wrung the fleece, and dew dropped from the fleece, a bowl full of water.

[39] And Gideon said to God, "Let not Your anger be kindled with me, and I will speak yet once; I will even yet make one trial more with the fleece: let now the drought be upon the fleece only, and let there be dew on all the ground."

[40] And God did so in that night; and there was drought on the fleece only, and on all the ground there was dew.

JUDGES CHAPTER 7

Gideon Surprises and Routs the Midianites

[1] And Jerubbaal (that is, Gideon) rose early, and all the people with him, and encamped at the fountain of Harod. And the camp of Midian was to the north of him, *reaching* from the hill of Moreh, in the valley.

[2] And the Lord said to Gideon, "The people that are with you *are too* many, so that I may not deliver Midian into their hand, lest at any time Israel boast against Me, saying, 'My hand has saved me.'

[3] And now speak in the ears of the people, saying, 'Who is afraid and fearful? Let him turn and depart from Mount Gilead.'" And there returned of the people twenty-two thousand, and ten thousand were left.

[4] And the Lord said to Gideon, "The people are still too numerous; bring them down to the water, and I will purge them there for you; and it shall come to pass that of whom I shall say to you, This one shall go with you, even he shall go with you; and of whomever I shall say to you, This one shall not go with you, *even* he shall not go with you."

[5] And he brought the people down to the water; and the Lord said to Gideon, "Whoever shall lap of the water with his tongue as if a dog should lap, you shall set him apart; likewise whoever shall bow down upon his knees to drink."

[6] And the number of those that lapped with their hand to their mouth was three hundred men; and all the rest of the people bowed upon their knees to drink water.

[7] And the Lord said to Gideon, "I will save you by the three hundred men that lapped, and I will give Midian into your hand; and all the *rest of the* people shall go everyone to his place."

[8] And they took the provision of the people in their hand, and their horns; and he sent away every man of Israel, each to his tent, and he strengthened the three hundred. And the army of Midian was beneath him in the valley.

[9] And it came to pass in that night that the Lord said to him, "Arise, go down into the camp, for I have delivered them into your hand.

[10] And if you are afraid to go down, go down to the camp with Purah your servant.

[11] And you shall hear what they shall say, and afterwards your hands shall be strong, and you shall go down into the camp." And he went down with Purah his servant to the extremity of the *companies of* fifty, which were in the camp.

[12] And Midian and Amalek and all the children of the east *were* scattered in the valley, as numerous as locusts; and there was no number to their camels, but they were as the sand on the seashore in multitude.

[13] And Gideon came, and behold, a man *was* relating a dream to his neighbor, and he said, "Behold, I have dreamed a dream, and behold, a cake of barley bread rolling into the camp of Midian, and it came as far as a tent, and struck it, and it fell, and it turned it up, and the tent fell."

[14] And his neighbor answered and said, "This is none other than the sword of Gideon, son of Joash a man of Israel: God has delivered Midian and all the host into his hand."

[15] And it came to pass when Gideon heard the account of the dream and the interpretation of it, that he worshipped the Lord, and returned to the camp of Israel, and said, "Rise up, for the Lord has delivered the camp of Midian into our hand."

[16] And he divided the three hundred men into three companies, and put horns in the hands of all, and empty pitchers, and torches in the pitchers.

[17] And he said to them, "You shall look at me, and so shall you do; and behold, I will go to the beginning of the camp, and it shall come to pass *that* as I do, so shall you do.

[18] And I will blow the trumpet, and all you with me shall blow *your* trumpets round about the whole camp, and you shall say, 'For the Lord and Gideon.'"

[19] And Gideon and the hundred men that were with him came to the extremity of the army in the beginning of the middle watch; and they completely roused the guards, and blew the trumpets, and they smashed the pitchers that were in their hands,

[20] and the three companies blew their trumpets, and smashed their pitchers, and held the torches in their left hands, and in their right hands their horns to sound with; and they cried out, "A sword for the Lord and for Gideon."

[21] And *every* man stood in his place round about the camp; and all the army ran, and sounded *an alarm*, and fled.

[22] And they sounded with the three hundred horns; and the Lord set *every* man's sword in all the camp against his neighbor.

[23] And the army fled as far as Bethseed Tagaragatha Abelmeula to Tabath. And the men of Israel from Nephtali, and from Asher, and from all Manasseh, came to help, and followed after Midian.

[24] And Gideon sent messengers into all of Mount Ephraim, saying, "Come down to meet Midian, and take to yourselves the water as far as Beth Barah and the Jordan." And every man of Ephraim cried out, and they took the water before hand unto Beth Barah and the Jordan.

[25] And they took the princess of Midian, even Oreb and Zeeb; and they slew Oreb at the rock of Oreb, and they slew Zeeb at the winepress of Zeeb. And they pursued Midian, and brought the heads of Oreb and Zeeb to Gideon from beyond the Jordan.

JUDGES CHAPTER 8

Gideon's Triumph and Vengeance

[1] And the men of Ephraim said to Gideon, "What *is* this *that* you have done to us, in that you did not call us when you went to fight with Midian?" And they contended with him sharply.

[2] And he said to them, "What have I now done in comparison of you? *Is* not the gleaning of Ephraim better than the vintage of Abiezer?

3 The Lord has delivered into your hand the princes of Midian, Oreb and Zeeb; and what could I do in comparison of you?" Then was their spirit calmed toward him, when he spoke this word.

4 And Gideon came to the Jordan, and crossed over, himself and the three hundred with him, hungry yet still pursuing.

5 And he said to the men of Soccoth, "Give some bread to feed this people that follow me; because they are faint, and behold, I am following after Zebah and Zalmunna, kings of Midian."

6 And the princes of Soccoth said, "Are the hands of Zebah and Zalmunna now in your hand, that we should give bread to your army?"

7 And Gideon said, "Therefore when the Lord gives Zebah and Zalmunna into my hand, then will I tear your flesh with the thorns of the wilderness, and the Barkenim."

8 Then he went up to Penuel, and spoke to them likewise. And the men of Penuel answered him as the men of Soccoth *had* answered him.

9 And Gideon said to the men of Penuel, "When I return in peace, I will break down this tower."

10 And Zebah and Zalmunna *were* in Karkor, and their armies *were* with them, about fifteen thousand, all that were left of the whole army of the aliens; and those that fell *were* a hundred and twenty thousand men that drew the sword.

11 And Gideon went up by the way of them that dwelt in tents, eastward of Nobah and Jogbehah; and he attacked the army, while the camp was secure.

12 And Zebah and Zalmunna fled; and he pursued after them, and took the two kings of Midian, Zebah and Zalmunna, and routed all the army.

13 And Gideon the son of Joash returned from the battle, down from the battle of Heres.

14 And he took prisoner a young lad of the men of Soccoth, and questioned him. And he wrote to him the names of the princes of Soccoth and of their elders, seventy-seven men.

15 And Gideon came to the princes of Soccoth, and said, "Behold Zebah and Zalmunna, about whom you reproached me, saying, 'Are the hands of Zebah and Zalmunna now in your hand, that we should give bread to your men that are faint?'"

16 And he took the elders of the city, with the thorns and briers of the wilderness, and with them he threshed the men of the city.

17 And he overthrew the tower of Penuel, and killed the men of the city.

18 And he said to Zebah and Zalmunna, "Where are the men whom you killed in Tabor?" And they said, "As you *are*, so *were* they, according to the likeness of the son of a king."

19 And Gideon said, "They were my brothers and the sons of my mother: as the Lord lives, if you had preserved them alive, I would not have slain you."

20 And he said to Jether his firstborn, "Rise up and kill them." But the lad did not draw his sword, for he was afraid, and he was still very young.

21 And Zebah and Zalmunna said, "Rise up, and fall on us, for your power is as that of a man." And Gideon arose, and killed Zebah and Zalmunna: and he took the round ornaments that were on the necks of their camels.

Gideon's Idolatry

22 And the men of Israel said to Gideon, "Rule over us, my lord, you and your son, and your grandson also, for you have saved us out of the hand of Midian."

23 And Gideon said to them, "I will not rule, and my son shall not rule among you; *but* the Lord shall rule over you."

24 And Gideon said to them, "I will make a request of you: give me every man an earring out of his spoils." (for they had golden earrings, for they were Ishmaelites).

25 And they said, "We will certainly give them." And he opened his garment, and each man cast in an earring out of his spoils.

26 And the weight of the golden earrings which he asked was one thousand seven hundred pieces of gold, besides the crescents, and the chains, and the garments, and the purple cloths that were on the kings of Midian, and besides the chains that were on the necks of their camels.

27 And Gideon made an ephod of it, an set it in his city in Ephratha; and all Israel went whoring after it, and it became a stumbling block to Gideon and his house.

28 Thus Midian was subdued before the children of Israel, and they did not lift up their head any longer. And the land had rest forty years in the days of Gideon.

The Death of Gideon

29 And Jerubbaal the son of Joash went and dwelt in his house.

30 Now Gideon had seventy sons begotten from his own body, for he had many wives.

31 And his concubine was in Shechem, and she also bore him a son, and gave him the name Abimelech.

32 And Gideon son of Joash died in his city, and he was buried in the tomb of Joash his father in Ephratha of Abi-Esdri.

33 And it came to pass when Gideon was dead, that the children of Israel turned, and went a whoring after the Baals, and made for themselves a covenant with Baal, that he should be their god.

34 And the children of Israel forgot the Lord their God who had delivered them out of the hand of all that afflicted them.

35 And they did not deal mercifully with the house of Jerubbaal, (that is, Gideon) according to all the good which he did to Israel.

JUDGES CHAPTER 9

Abimelech's Treachery

¹ And Abimelech son of Jerubbaal went to Shechem, to his mother's brothers; and he spoke to them and to all the family of the house of his mother's father, saying,

² "Speak in the ears of all the men of Shechem, saying, 'Which is better for you, that seventy men, even all the sons of Jerubbaal, should reign over you, or that one man should reign over you?' And remember that I am your own flesh and bone."

³ And his mother's brothers spoke all these words concerning him in the ears of all the men of Shechem, and their heart turned after Abimelech, for they said, "He is our brother."

⁴ And they gave him seventy *pieces* of silver out of the house of Baal-Berith; and Abimelech hired for himself worthless and cowardly men, and they went after him.

⁵ And he went to the house of his father to Ephratha, and killed his brothers, the sons of Jerubbaal, seventy men upon one stone; but Jotham the youngest son of Jerubbaal was left, for he hid himself.

⁶ And all the men of Shechem, and all the house of Beth Millo were gathered together, and they went and made Abimelech king by the Oak of Sedition, which was at Shechem.

The Parable of the Trees

⁷ And it was reported to Jotham, and he went and stood on the top of Mount Gerizim, and lifted up his voice, and wept, and said to them, "Hear me, you men of Sicima, and God shall hear you.

⁸ The trees once went forth to anoint a king over them; and they said to the olive, 'Reign over us.'

⁹ But the olives said to them, 'Shall I leave my fatness, with which men shall glorify God, and go to be promoted over the trees?'

¹⁰ And the trees said to the fig tree, 'Come, reign over us.'

¹¹ But the fig tree said to them, 'Shall I leave my sweetness and my good fruits, and go to be promoted over the trees?'

¹² And the trees said to the vine, 'Come, reign over us.'

¹³ And the vine said to them, 'Shall I leave my wine that cheers God and men, and go to be promoted over the trees?'

¹⁴ Then all the trees said to the bramble, 'Come, and reign over us.'

¹⁵ And the bramble said to the trees, 'If in truth you anoint me to reign over you, come, stand under my shadow; and if not, let fire come out from me and devour the cedars of Lebanon.'

¹⁶ "And now, if you have done it in truth and integrity, and have made Abimelech king, and if you have dealt well with Jerubbaal, and with his house, and if you have done to him according to the reward of his hand,

¹⁷ as my father fought for you, and put his life in jeopardy, and delivered you out of the hand of Midian;

¹⁸ and you have risen up this day against the house of my father, and have slain his sons, seventy men, upon one stone, and have made Abimelech the son of his bondwoman king over the men of Shechem, because he is your brother:

¹⁹ if then you have done truly and faithfully with Jerubbaal, and with his house this day, *then* rejoice in Abimelech, and let him also rejoice over you.

²⁰ But if not, let fire come out from Abimelech, and devour the men of Shechem, and the house of Beth Millo; and let fire come out from the men of Shechem and from the house of Beth Millo, and devour Abimelech."

²¹ And Jotham fled and ran away, and went as far as Beer, and dwelt there out of the way of his brother Abimelech.

The Downfall of Abimelech

²² And Abimelech reigned over Israel three years.

²³ And God sent an evil spirit between Abimelech and the men of Shechem; and the men of Shecem dealt treacherously with the house of Abimelech,

²⁴ to bring the injury done to the seventy sons of Jerubbaal, and to lay their blood upon their brother Abimelech, who killed them, and upon the men of Shechem, because they strengthened his hands to slay his brothers.

²⁵ And the men of Shechem set men in ambush against him on the top of the mountains, and robbed everyone who passed by them on the road. And it was reported to Abimelech the king.

²⁶ And Gaal son of Ebed came, and his brothers, and passed by Shechem, and the men of Shechem trusted in him.

²⁷ And they went out into the field, and gathered their grapes, and trod them, and made merry; and they brought *the grapes* into the house of their god, and ate and drank, and cursed Abimelech.

²⁸ And Gaal the son of Jobel said, "Who is Abimelech, and who is the son of Shechem, that we should serve him? Is he not the son of Jerubbaal, and is not Zebul his manager, his servant with the son of Hamor the father of Shechem? And why should we serve him?

²⁹ If only this people were under my hand! Then would I remove Abimelech, and I would say to him, 'Multiply your host, and come out.'"

³⁰ And Zebul the ruler of the city heard the words of Gaal the son of Ebed, and he was very angry.

³¹ And he sent messengers to Abimelech secretly, saying, "Behold, Gaal the son of Ebed and his brothers have come to Shechem; and behold, they have besieged the city against you.

³² And now rise up by night, you and the people with you, and lay wait in the field.

³³ And it shall come to pass in the morning at sunrise, *that* you shall rise up early and draw toward the city; and behold,

he and the people with him will come forth against you, and you shall do to him according to your power."

³⁴ And Abimelech and all the people with him rose up by night, and formed an ambush against Shechem in four companies.

³⁵ And Gaal the son of Ebed went forth, and stood by the door of the gate of the city. And Abimelech and the people with him rose up from the ambush.

³⁶ And Gaal the son of Ebed saw the people, and said to Zebul, "Behold, a people comes down from the top of the mountains." And Zebul said to him, "You see the shadow of the mountains as men."

³⁷ And Gaal continued to speak and said, "Behold, a people comes down westward from the part bordering on the middle of the land, and another company comes by the way of Diviners' Terebinth Tree."

³⁸ And Zebul said to him, "And where is your mouth as you spoke, Who is Abimelech that we should serve him? Is not this the people whom you despised? Go forth now, and set the battle in array against him."

³⁹ And Gaal went forth before the men of Shechem, and set the battle in array against Abimelech.

⁴⁰ And Abimelech pursued him, and he fled from before him; and many fell down slain as far as the door of the gate.

⁴¹ And Abimelech entered into Aruma, and Zebul cast out Gaal and his brothers, so that they should not dwell in Shechem.

⁴² And it came to pass on the second day that the people went out into the field, and one brought word to Abimelech.

⁴³ And he took the people, and divided them into three companies, and formed an ambush in the field. And he looked, and behold, the people went forth out of the city, and he rose up against them, and struck them.

⁴⁴ And Abimelech and the chiefs of companies that were with him rushed forward, and stood by the door of the gate of the city; and the two *other* companies rushed forward upon all that were in the field, and struck them.

⁴⁵ And Abimelech fought against the city all that day, and took the city, and killed the people that were in it, and destroyed the city, and sowed it with salt.

⁴⁶ And all the men of the tower of Shechem heard, and came to the gathering of Bethel-Berith.

⁴⁷ And it was reported to Abimelech, that all the men of the tower of Shechem were gathered together.

⁴⁸ And Abimelech went up to the mount of Zalmon, and all the people that were with him; and Abimelech took an axe in his hand, and cut down a branch of a tree, and took it, and laid it on his shoulders; and said to the people that were with him, "What you see me doing, do quickly as I do."

⁴⁹ And every man likewise cut down a branch, and went after Abimelech, and laid them against the place of gathering, and burned the place of gathering over them with fire. And they died, even all the men of the tower of Sicima, about a thousand men and women.

⁵⁰ And Abimelech went out of Bethel-Berith, and encamped against Thebes, and took it.

⁵¹ And there was a strong tower in the midst of the city; and all the men and the women of the city fled there, and shut *the door* behind them, and went up on the roof of the tower.

⁵² And Abimelech drew near to the tower, and they besieged it; and Abimelech drew near to the door of the tower to burn it with fire.

⁵³ And a woman cast a piece of a millstone upon the head of Abimelech, and broke his skull.

⁵⁴ And he cried out quickly to the young man his armor bearer, and said to him, "Draw your sword, and kill me, lest at any time they should say, 'A woman killed him.'" And his young man thrust him through and he died.

⁵⁵ And the men of Israel saw that Abimelech was dead, and they went each to his place.

⁵⁶ So God repaid the wickedness of Abimelech, which he did against his father, in slaying his seventy brothers.

⁵⁷ And all the wickedness of the men of Shechem God repaid upon their heads; and the curse of Jotham the son of Jerubbaal came upon them.

JUDGES CHAPTER 10

Tola

¹ And after Abimelech, Tola the son of Puah rose up to save Israel, *being* the son of his father's brother, a man of Issachar; and he dwelt in Shamir in Mount Ephraim.

² And he judged Israel twenty-three years, and died, and was buried in Shamir.

Jair

³ And after him arose Jair of Gilead, and he judged Israel twenty-two years.

⁴ And he had thirty-two sons riding on thirty-two colts, and they had thirty-two cities; and they called them Jair's towns until this day in the land of Gilead.

⁵ And Jair died, and was buried in Camon.

Oppression by the Ammonites

⁶ And the children of Israel did evil again in the sight of the Lord, and served the Baals and Ashtoreth, and the gods of Aram, and the gods of Sidon, and the gods of Moab, and the gods of the children of Ammon, and the gods of the Philistines; and they forsook the Lord, and did not serve Him.

⁷ And the Lord was very angry with Israel, and sold them into the hands of the Philistines, and into the hand of the children of Ammon.

⁸ And they afflicted and bruised the children of Israel at that time eighteen years, all the children of Israel beyond the Jordan in the land of the Amorite in Gilead.

⁹ And the children of Ammon went over the Jordan to fight with Judah, and Benjamin, and with Ephraim; and the children of Israel were greatly afflicted.

[10] And the children of Israel cried to the Lord, saying, "We have sinned against You, because we have forsaken God, and served the Baals."

[11] And the Lord said to the children of Israel, "Did I not save you from Egypt and from the Amorite, and from the children of Ammon, and from the Philistines,

[12] and from the Sidonians, and Amalek, and Midian, who afflicted you? And you cried to Me, and I saved you out of their hand?

[13] Yet you forsook Me and served other gods; therefore I will not save you anymore.

[14] Go, and cry to the gods whom you have chosen for yourselves, and let them save you in the time of your affliction."

[15] And the children of Israel said to the Lord, "We have sinned: do unto us according to all that is good in Your eyes; only deliver us this day."

[16] And they put away the strange gods from the midst of them, and served the Lord only, and His soul was pained for the trouble of Israel.

[17] And the children of Ammon went up, and encamped in Gilead; and the children of Israel were gathered together and encamped on the hill.

[18] And the people, the princes of Gilead, said, every man to his neighbor, "Who is he that shall begin to fight against the children of Ammon? He shall even be head over all that dwell in Gilead."

JUDGES CHAPTER 11

Jephthah

[1] And Jephthah the Gileadite *was* a mighty man; and he *was* the son of a harlot, who bore Jephthah to Gilead.

[2] And the wife of Gilead bore him sons; and the sons of his wife grew up, and they cast out Jephthah, and said to him, "You shall not inherit in the house of our father, for you are the son of a concubine."

[3] And Jephthah fled from the face of his brothers, and dwelt in the land of Tob; and worthless men gathered to Jephthah, and went out with him.

[4] And it came to pass when the children of Ammon prepared to fight with Israel,

[5] that the elders of Gilead went to fetch Jephthah from the land of Tob.

[6] And they said to Jephthah, "Come and be our leader, and we will fight with the sons of Ammon."

[7] And Jephthah said to the elders of Gilead, "Did you not hate me, and cast me out of my father's house, and banish me from you? And why have you come to me now, when you need me?"

[8] And the elders of Gilead said to Jephthah, "Therefore have we now turned to you, that you should go with us, and fight against the sons of Ammon, and be our leader over all the inhabitants of Gilead."

[9] And Jephthah said to the elders of Gilead, "If you turn me back to fight with the children of Ammon, and the Lord should deliver them before me, then will I be your leader."

[10] And the elders of Gilead said to Jephthah, "The Lord be witness between us, if we shall not do according to your word."

[11] And Jephthah went with the elders of Gilead, and the people made him head and ruler over them. And Jephthah spoke all his words before the Lord in Mizpah.

[12] And Jephthah sent messengers to the king of the children of Ammon, saying, "What have I to do with you, that you have come against me to fight in my land?"

[13] And the king of the children of Ammon said to the messengers of Jephthah, "Because Israel took my land when he went up out of Egypt, from Arnon to Jabbok, and to the Jordan: now then return them peaceably and I will depart."

[14] And Jephthah again sent messengers to the king of the children of Ammon,

[15] and said to him, "Thus says Jephthah: Israel did not take the land of Moab, nor the land of the children of Ammon;

[16] for in their going up out of Egypt Israel went in the wilderness as far as the Red Sea, and came to Kadesh.

[17] And Israel sent messengers to the king of Edom, saying, 'I will pass, if it please you, by your land'; and the king of Edom would not consent. And *Israel* also sent to the king of Moab, and he did not consent; and Israel sojourned in Kadesh.

[18] And *they* journeyed in the wilderness, and bypassed the land of Edom and the land of Moab. And they came by the east of the land of Moab, and encamped in the country beyond Arnon, and did not enter the borders of Moab, for Arnon is the border of Moab.

[19] And Israel sent messengers to Sihon king of the Amorite, king of Hesbron, and Israel said to him, 'Let us pass through your land to our place.'

[20] And Sihon did not trust Israel to pass through his territory; and Sihon gathered all his people, and they encamped at Jahaz; and he set the battle in array against Israel.

[21] And the Lord God of Israel delivered Sihon and all his people into the hand of Israel, and they struck him; and Israel inherited all the land of the Amorite who dwelt in that land,

[22] from Arnon and to Jabbok, and from the wilderness to the Jordan.

[23] And now the Lord God of Israel has removed the Amorite from before His people Israel, and shall you inherit his *land*?

[24] Will you not inherit those possessions which Chemosh your god shall cause you to inherit; and shall not we inherit the *land of* all those whom the Lord our God has removed from before you?

[25] And now are you any better than Balak son of Zippor, king of Moab? Did he indeed fight with Israel, or indeed make war with him,

26 when Israel dwelt in Hesbron and in its coasts, and in the land of Aroer and in its coasts, and in all the cities by the Jordan, three hundred years? And why did you not recover them in that time?

27 And now I have not sinned against you, but you wronged me in preparing war against me: may the Lord, the Judge, render judgment this day between the children of Israel and the children of Ammon."

28 But the king of the children of Ammon did not heed the words of Jephthah, which he sent to him.

Jephthah's Vow

29 And the Spirit of the Lord came upon Jephthah, and he passed over Gilead, and Manasseh, and passed by the watchtower of Gilead to the other side of the children of Ammon.

30 And Jephthah vowed a vow to the Lord, and said, "If You will indeed deliver the children of Ammon into my hand,

31 then it shall come to pass that whosoever shall first come out of the door of my house to meet me when I return in peace from the children of Ammon, he shall be the Lord's: I will offer him up for a burnt offering."

32 And Jephthah advanced to meet the sons of Ammon to fight against them; and the Lord delivered them into his hand.

33 And he struck them from Aroer till *one* comes to Arnon, twenty cities in number, and as far as Abel-Keramim, with a very great destruction. And the children of Ammon were subdued before the children of Israel.

Jephthah's Daughter

34 And Jephthah came to Mizpah, to his house; and behold, his daughter came forth to meet him with timbrels and dances; and she was his only child, *for* he had no other son or daughter.

35 And it came to pass when he saw her, that he tore his clothes, and said, "Alas, my daughter, you have indeed troubled me, and you are the cause of my trouble; and I have opened my mouth against you to the Lord, and I shall not be able to return from it."

36 And she said to him, "Father, have you opened your mouth to the Lord? Do to me accordingly as *the word* went out of your mouth, in that the Lord has worked vengeance for you on your enemies of the children of Ammon."

37 And she said to her father, "Let my father now do this thing: let me alone for two months, and I will go up and down on the mountains, and I will lament my virginity, I and my companions."

38 And he said, "Go." And he sent her away for two months. And she went, and her companions, and she lamented her virginity on the mountains.

39 And it came to pass at the end of the two months that she returned to her father; and he performed upon her his vow which he vowed; and she knew no man.

40 And it was an ordinance in Israel, *that* the daughters of Israel went year by year to lament the daughter of Jephthah the Gileadite for four days in the year.

JUDGES CHAPTER 12

Jephthah's Conflict with Ephraim

1 And the men of Ephraim assembled *themselves*, and passed on to the north, and said to Jephthah, "Why did you go over to fight with the children of Ammon, and did not call us to go with you? We will burn your house over you with fire."

2 And Jephthah said to them, "I and my people and the children of Ammon were very much engaged in war; and I called for you, and you did not save me out of their hand.

3 And I saw that you were no helper, and I put my life in my hand, and passed on to the sons of Ammon; and the Lord delivered them into my hand: and why then have you come up against me this day to fight with me?"

4 And Jephthah gathered all the men of Gilead, and fought with Ephraim; and the men of Gilead struck Ephraim, because they that had escaped of Ephraim said, "You *are* of Gilead in the midst of Ephraim and in the midst of Manasseh."

5 And Gilead took the fords of the Jordan before Ephraim; and they that escaped of Ephraim said to them, "Let us go over." And the men of Gilead said, "Are you an Ephraimite?" And he said, "No."

6 Then they said to him, "Say now Stachys." And he did not correctly pronounce it. So they took him, and killed him at the fords of the Jordan; and there fell at that time of Ephraim forty-two thousand.

7 And Jephthah judged Israel six years; and Jephthah the Gileadite died, and was buried in his city, *which was* Gilead.

Ibzan, Elon, and Abdon

8 And after him Ibzan of Bethlehem judged Israel.

9 And he had thirty sons and thirty daughters, whom he sent forth; and he brought in thirty daughters for his sons from outside; and he judged Israel seven years.

10 And Ibzan died, and was buried in Bethlehem.

11 And after him Elon of Zebulun judged Israel ten years.

12 And Elon of Zebulun died, and was buried in Aijalon in the land of Zebulun.

13 And after him Abdon the son of Hillel, the Pirathonite, judged Israel.

14 And he had forty sons, and thirty grandsons, that rode upon seventy colts: and he judged Israel eight years.

15 And Abdon the son of Hillel, the Pirathonite, died, and was buried in Pirathon in the land of Ephraim in the mount of Amalek.

JUDGES CHAPTER 13

The Birth of Samson

1 And the children of Israel yet again committed iniquity before the Lord; and the Lord delivered them into the hand of the Philistines for forty years.

2 And there was a man of Zorah, of the family of the kindred of Dan, and his name was Manoah, and his wife was barren, and bore no children.

3 And the Angel of the Lord appeared to the woman, and said to her, "Behold, you are barren and have not given birth; yet you shall conceive a son.

4 And now be very cautious, and drink no wine nor strong drink, and eat no unclean thing;

5 for behold, you are with child, and shall bring forth a son; and there shall come no razor upon his head, for the child shall be a Nazarite to God from the womb; and he shall begin to save Israel from the hand of the Philistines."

6 And the woman went in, and spoke to her husband, saying, "A Man of God came to me, and His appearance *was as* of an angel of God, very fearful. And I did not ask Him where He was *from*, and He did not tell me His name.

7 And He said to me, 'Behold, you are with child, and shall bring forth a son; and now drink no wine nor strong drink, and eat no unclean thing; for the child shall be holy to God from the womb until the day of his death.'"

8 And Manoah prayed to the Lord and said, "I pray to You, O Lord my Lord, *concerning* the Man of God whom You sent; let Him now come to us once more, and teach us what we shall do with the child about to be born."

9 And the Lord heard the voice of Manoah, and the Angel of God came yet again to the woman. And she sat in the field, and Manoah her husband was not with her.

10 And the woman made haste and ran, and brought word to her husband, and said to him, "Behold the Man who came in *the other* day to me has appeared to me."

11 And Manoah arose and followed his wife, and came to the Man, and said to Him, "Are you the Man that spoke to the woman?" And the Angel said, "I *am*."

12 And Manoah said, "Now shall *Your* word come to pass: what shall be the ordering of the child, and our dealings with him?" 13 And the Angel of the Lord said to Manoah, "Of all things concerning which I spoke to the woman, she shall beware.

14 She shall eat of nothing that comes of the vine yielding wine, and let her not drink wine or strong liquor, and let her not eat anything unclean: all things that I have commanded her she shall observe."

15 And Manoah said to the Angel of the Lord, "Let us detain You here, and prepare before You a young goat."

16 And the Angel of the Lord said to Manoah, "If you should detain Me, I will not eat of your bread; and if you would offer a burnt offering, you shall offer it to the Lord: for Manoah did not know that He was the Angel of the Lord.

17 And Manoah said to the Angel of the Lord, "What is Your name, that *when* Your word shall come to pass, we may glorify You?"

18 And the Angel of the Lord said to him, "Why do you thus ask after My name; seeing it is Wonderful?"

19 And Manoah took a young goat, and its grain offering, and offered it on the rock to the Lord; and *the Angel* wrought a distinct work, and Manoah and his wife were looking on.

20 And it came to pass when the flame went up above the altar toward heaven, that the Angel of the Lord went up in the flame; and Manoah and his wife were looking, and they fell upon their face to the earth.

21 And the Angel appeared no more to Manoah and to his wife. Then Manoah knew that this *was* the Angel of the Lord.

22 And Manoah said to his wife, "We shall surely die, because we have seen God."

23 But his wife said to him, "If the Lord were pleased to slay us, He would not have received of our hand a burnt offering and a grain offering; and He would not have shown us all these things, neither would He have caused us to hear all these things as *He did* at this time."

24 And the woman brought forth a son, and she called his name Sampson; and the child grew, and the Lord blessed him.

25 And the Spirit of the Lord began to go out with him in the camp of Dan, and between Zorah and Esthaol.

JUDGES CHAPTER 14

Samson's Marriage

1 And Sampson went down to Timnah, and saw a woman in Timnah of the daughters of the Philistines.

2 And he went up and told his father and his mother, and said, "I have seen a woman in Timnah of the daughters of the Philistines; and now take her to me for a wife."

3 And his father and his mother said to him, "Are there no daughters among your brothers, and *is there not* a woman of all my people, that you *would* go to take a wife of the uncircumcised Philistines?" And Sampson said to his father, "Take her for me, for she is right in my eyes."

4 And his father and his mother did not know that it was of the Lord, that He sought to be revenged on the Philistines. And at that time the Philistines lorded it over Israel.

5 And Sampson and his father and his mother went down to Timnah, and he came to the vineyard of Timnah. And behold, a young lion roared in meeting him.

6 And the Spirit of the Lord came powerfully upon him, and he crushed *the lion* as he would have crushed a young goat, and there was nothing in his hands. And he did not tell his father or his mother what he had done.

7 And they went down and spoke to the woman, and she was pleasing in the eyes of Sampson.

8 And after some time he returned to take her, and he turned aside to see the carcass of the lion. And behold, a swarm of bees and honey *were* in the mouth of the lion.

⁹ And he took it into his hands, and went on eating, and he went to his father and his mother, and gave to them, and they did eat; but he did not tell them that he took the honey out of the mouth of the lion.

¹⁰ And his father went down to the woman, and Sampson made there a banquet for seven days, for so the young men are used to doing.

¹¹ And it came to pass when they saw him, that they took thirty guests, and they were with him.

¹² And Sampson said to them, "I put to you a riddle: if you will indeed tell it to me, and discover it within the seven days of the feast, I will you give thirty sheets and thirty changes of clothing.

¹³ And if you cannot tell it me, you shall give me thirty linen garments and thirty changes of clothing." And they said to him, "Put forth your riddle, and we will hear it."

¹⁴ And he said to them, "Out of the eater came something to eat, and out of the strong came something sweet." And they could not explain the riddle for three days.

¹⁵ And it came to pass on the fourth day, that they said to the wife of Sampson, "Deceive now your husband, and let him tell you the riddle, lest we burn you and your father's house with fire: did you invite us to do us violence?"

¹⁶ And Sampson's wife wept before him, and said, "You just hate me! You don't love me! For the riddle which you have put to my people you have not told me." And Sampson said to her, "If I have not told it to my father and my mother, shall I tell it to you?"

¹⁷ And she wept before him the *entire* seven days in which the banquet lasted. And it came to pass on the seventh day, that he told her, because she troubled him; and she told it to her people.

¹⁸ And the men of the city said to him on the seventh day, before sunrise, "What is sweeter than honey? And what is stronger than a lion?" And Sampson said to them, "If you had not plowed with my heifer, you would not have known my riddle."

¹⁹ And the Spirit of the Lord came upon him powerfully, and he went down to Ashkelon, and destroyed thirty men among the inhabitants, and took their garments, and gave the changes of clothing to them that told the riddle. And Sampson was very angry, and went up to the house of his father.

²⁰ And the wife of Sampson was *given* to one of his friends, with whom he was on terms of friendship.

JUDGES CHAPTER 15

Samson Defeats the Philistines

¹ And it came to pass after a time, in the days of wheat harvest, that Sampson visited his wife with a young goat, and said, "I will go in to my wife even into the chamber." But her father did not allow him to go in.

² And her father spoke, saying, "I said that you surely did hate her, and I gave her to one of your friends: is not her younger sister better than she? Let her be to you instead of her."

³ And Sampson said to them, "Even for once am I guiltless with regard to the Philistines, in that I do mischief among them."

⁴ And Sampson went and caught three hundred foxes, and took torches, and turned *the foxes* tail to tail, and put a torch between two tails, and fastened it.

⁵ And he set fire to the torches, and sent *the foxes* into the grain of the Philistines; and everything was burnt from the threshing floor to the standing grain, and even to the vineyard and olives.

⁶ And the Philistines said, "Who *has done* these things?" And they said, "Sampson the son in law of the Timnite, because he has taken his wife, and given her to one of his friends." And the Philistines went up, and burned her and her father's house with fire.

⁷ And Sampson said to them, "Though you may have dealt thus with her, verily I will be avenged of you, and afterwards I will cease."

⁸ And he struck them, leg on thigh, *with* a great overthrow; and went down and dwelt in a cave of the rock of Etam.

⁹ And the Philistines went up, and encamped in Judah, and spread themselves abroad in Lehi.

¹⁰ And the men of Judah said, "Why have you come up against us?" And the Philistines said, "We have come up to bind Sampson, and to do to him as he has done to us."

¹¹ And the three thousand men of Judah went down to the hole of the rock Etam, and they said to Sampson, "Don't you know that the Philistines rule over us? And what *is* this *that* you have done to us?" And Sampson said to them, "As they did to me, so have I done to them."

¹² And they said to him, "We have come down to bind you, to deliver you into the hand of the Philistines." And Sampson said to them, "Swear to me that you will not fall upon me yourselves."

¹³ And they spoke to him, saying, "No, but we will only bind you securely, and deliver you into their hand, and will by no means kill you." And they bound him with two new ropes, and brought him from that rock.

¹⁴ And they came to Lehi. And the Philistines shouted, and ran to meet him. And the Spirit of the Lord came mightily upon him, and the ropes that were upon his arms became as flax which is burned with fire; and his bonds were consumed from off his hands.

¹⁵ And he found the jawbone of a donkey that had been cast away, and he put forth his hand and took it, and he struck down a thousand men with it.

¹⁶ And Sampson said, "With the jawbone of a donkey I have utterly destroyed them, for with the jawbone of a donkey I have struck down a thousand men."

¹⁷ And it came to pass when he ceased speaking, that he cast the jawbone out of his hand; and he called that place the Lifting of the Jawbone.

18 And he was very thirsty, and wept before the Lord, and said, "You have been well pleased to grant this great deliverance by the hand of Your servant, and now shall I die of thirst, and fall into the hand of the uncircumcised?"

19 And God broke open a hollow place in the jaw, and there came out water, and he drank; and his spirit returned and he revived. Therefore the name of the fountain was called The Well of the Invoker, which is in Lehi, to this day.

20 And he judged Israel in the days of the Philistines twenty years.

JUDGES CHAPTER 16

Samson and Delilah

1 And Sampson went to Gaza, and he saw a harlot there, and went in to her.

2 And it was reported to the Gazites, saying, "Sampson has come here." And they surrounded him and laid wait for him all night in the gate of the city, and they were quiet all the night, saying, "Let us wait until the sun rises, and *then* we will kill him."

3 And Sampson slept till midnight, and rose up at midnight, and took hold of the doors of the gate of the city with the two posts, and lifted them up with the bar, and laid them on his shoulders, and he went up to the top of the mountain that is before Hebron, and laid them there.

4 And it came to pass after this that he loved a woman in Sorek, and her name was Delilah.

5 And the princes of the Philistines came up to her, and said to her, "Deceive him, and see where his great strength is, and by what means we may prevail against him, and bind him to humble him; and we will give you each eleven hundred pieces of silver."

6 And Delilah said to Sampson, "Tell me, wherein lies your great strength, and with what may you be bound, so that you may be humbled."

7 And Sampson said to her, "If they bind me with seven moist cords that have not been spoiled, then shall I be weak, and be as one of the ordinary men."

8 And the princes of the Philistines brought to her seven moist cords that had not been spoiled, and she bound him with them.

9 And the *men* lying in wait remained with her in the chamber; and she said to him, "The Philistines are upon you, Sampson." And he broke the cords as if anyone should break a strand of yarn when it has touched the fire, and *the secret of* his strength was not known.

10 And Delilah said to Sampson, "Behold, you have mocked me, and told me lies; now then, tell me *with* what shall you be bound."

11 And he said to her, "If they should bind me securely with new ropes with which work has not been done, then shall I be weak, and shall be as another man."

12 And Delilah took new ropes, and bound him with them, and the *men* lying in wait came out of the chamber, and she said, "The Philistines are upon you, Sampson." And he broke them off his arms like a thread.

13 And Delilah said to Sampson, "Behold, you have deceived me, and told me lies; tell me, I intreat you, *with* what may you be bound." And he said to her, "If you should weave the seven locks of my head with the web, and should fasten them with the pin into the wall, then shall I be weak as another man."

14 And it came to pass when he was asleep, that Delilah took the seven locks of his head, and wove them with the web, and fastened them with the pin into the wall. Then she said, "The Philistines are upon you, Sampson." And he awoke out of his sleep, and carried away the pin of the web out of the wall.

15 And Delilah said to Sampson, "How can you say 'I love you,' when your heart is not with me? This *is the* third time you have deceived me, and have not told me where your great strength *lies*."

16 And it came to pass as she pressed him sore with her words continually, and pestered him, that his spirit failed, to the point of death.

17 Then he told her all his heart, and said to her, "A razor has not come upon my head, because I have been holy to God from my mother's womb; if then I should be shaven, my strength will depart from me, and I shall be weak, and I shall be as all other men."

18 And Delilah saw that he told her all his heart, and she sent and called the princes of the Philistines, saying, "Come up yet this once; for he has told me all his heart." And the chiefs of the Philistines went up to her, and brought the money in their hands.

19 And Delilah made Sampson sleep upon her knees. And she called a man, and he shaved the seven locks of his head, and she began to humble him, and his strength departed from him.

20 And Delilah said, "The Philistines are upon you, Sampson." And he awoke out of his sleep and said, "I will go out as at former times, and shake myself"; and he did not know that the Lord had departed from him.

21 And the Philistines took him, and put out his eyes, and brought him down to Gaza, and bound him with fetters of brass; and he became a grinder in the prison house.

22 And the hair of his head began to grow as before it was shaven.

The Death of Samson

23 And the chiefs of the Philistines met to offer a great sacrifice to their god Dagon, and to make merry. And they said, "*Our* god has given into our hand our enemy Sampson."

24 And the people saw him, and sang praises to their god; "For our god," *they said*, "has delivered our enemy into our hand, who wasted our land, and who multiplied our slain."

25 And when their heart was merry, then they said, "Call Sampson out of the prison house, and let him play before

us." And they called Sampson out of the prison house, and he played before them; and they struck him with the palms of their hands, and set him between the pillars.

26 And Sampson said to the young man that held his hand, "Allow me to feel the pillars on which the house *rests*, and I will lean myself upon them."

27 And the house *was* full of men and women, and there *were* all the chiefs of the Philistines, and on the roof were about three thousand men and women looking at the sports of Sampson.

28 And Sampson wept before the Lord, and said, "O Lord, my Lord, remember me, I pray, and strengthen me, O God, just this once, and I will be avenged of the Philistines for my two eyes."

29 And Sampson took hold of the two pillars on which the house stood, and leaned on them, and laid hold of one with his right hand, and the other with his left.

30 And Sampson said, "Let my wife perish with the Philistines." And he bowed himself mightily; and the house fell upon the princes, and upon all the people that were in it. And the dead whom Sampson slew in his death were more than those whom he slew in his life.

31 And his brothers and his father's house went down, and they took him; and they went up and buried him between Zorah and Eshtaol in the tomb of his father Manoah; and he judged Israel twenty years.

JUDGES CHAPTER 17

Michah's Idolatry

1 And there was a man of Mount Ephraim, and his name was Micah.

2 And he said to his mother, "The eleven hundred pieces of silver which you took of yourself, and *about which* you cursed me, and spoke in my ears, *saying*, 'Behold, the silver is with me'; I took it." And his mother said, "Blessed be my son of the Lord."

3 And he restored the eleven hundred pieces of silver to his mother. And his mother said, "I had wholly consecrated the money to the Lord out of my hand for my son, to make a graven and a molten *image*, and now I will restore it to you."

4 But he returned the silver to his mother, and his mother took two hundred pieces of silver, and gave them to a silversmith, and he made it a graven and a molten image; and it was in the house of Micah.

5 And the house of Micah *was* to him the house of God, and he made an ephod and teraphim, and he consecrated one of his sons, and he became to him a priest.

6 And in those days there was no king in Israel; every man did that which was right in his own eyes.

7 And there was a young man in Bethlehem of the tribe of Judah, and he *was* a Levite, and he was sojourning there.

8 And the man departed from Bethlehem the city of Judah to sojourn in whatever place he might find. And he came as far as Mount Ephraim, and to the house of Micah to accomplish his journey.

9 And Micah said to him, "Where do you come from?" And he said to him, "I am a Levite of Bethlehem in Judah, and I go to sojourn in any place I may find."

10 And Micah said to him, "Dwell with me, and be to me a father and a priest; and I will give you ten pieces of silver every year, and a change of clothing, and your living."

11 And the Levite went and began to dwell with the man; and the young man was to him as one of his sons.

12 And Micah consecrated the Levite, and he became to him a priest, and he was in the house of Micah.

13 And Micah said, "Now I know that the Lord will do me good, because a Levite has become my priest."

JUDGES CHAPTER 18

The Migration of Dan

1 In those days there was no king in Israel; and in those days the tribe of Dan sought for itself an inheritance to inhabit, because no inheritance had fallen to it until that day in the midst of the tribes of the children of Israel.

2 And the sons of Dan sent from their families five men of valor, from Zorah and from Eshtaol, to spy out the land and to search it. And they said to them, "Go and search out the land." And they came as far as the mount of Ephraim to the house of Micah, and they lodged there

3 in the house of Micah, and they recognized the voice of the young man the Levite, and turned in there. And they said to him, "Who brought you in here? And what are you doing in this place? And what do you have here?"

4 And he said to them, "Thus and thus did Micah to me, and he hired me, and I became his priest."

5 And they said to him, "Inquire now of God, and we shall know whether our way will prosper, on which we are going."

6 And the priest said to them, "Go in peace; your way in which you go is before the Lord."

7 And the five men went on, and came to Laish; and they saw the people in the midst of it dwelling securely, at ease as is the manner of the Sidonians, and there is no one perverting or shaming a matter in the land, nor an heir extorting treasures; and they are far from the Sidonians, and they have no ties with anyone.

8 And the five men came to their brothers at Zorah and Eshtaol, and said to their brothers, "Why do you sit here idle?"

9 And they said, "Arise, and let us go up against them, for we have seen the land, and behold, it is very good, yet you are still: do not delay to go, and to enter in to possess the land.

10 And whenever you shall go, you shall come in upon a secure people, and the land is extensive, for God has given it into your hand; a place where there is no lack of anything that the earth affords."

¹¹ And there departed six hundred men of the families of Dan, from Zorah and from Eshtaol, girded with weapons of war.

¹² And they went up, and encamped in Kirjath Jearim in Judah; therefore it was called in that place the Camp of Dan, until this day: behold, it is behind Kirjath Jearim.

¹³ And they went on from there to the mount of Ephraim, and came to the house of Micah.

¹⁴ And the five men who went to spy out the land of Laish answered and said to their brothers, "You know that there is in this place an ephod, and teraphim, and a graven and a molten image; and now consider what you shall do."

¹⁵ And they turned aside there, and went into the house of the young man, the Levite, even into the house of Micah, and asked him how he was.

¹⁶ And the six hundred men of the sons of Dan who were girded with their weapons of war stood by the door of the gate.

¹⁷ And the five men who went to spy out the land went up, and entered into the house of Micah, and the priest stood.

¹⁸ And they took the graven image, and the ephod, and the teraphim, and the molten image; and the priest said to them, "What are you doing?"

¹⁹ And they said to him, "Be silent, lay your hand upon your mouth, and come with us, and be to us a father and a priest: is it better for you to be the priest of the house of one man, or to be the priest of a tribe and house for a family of Israel?"

²⁰ And the heart of the priest was glad, and he took the ephod, and the teraphim, and the graven image, and the molten image, and went in the midst of the people.

²¹ So they turned and departed, and put their children and their property and their baggage before them.

²² They went some distance from the house of Micah, and behold, Micah and the men in the houses near Micah's house cried out, and overtook the children of Dan.

²³ And the children of Dan turned their face, and said to Micah, "What is the matter with you that you have cried out?"

²⁴ And Micah said, "Because you have taken my graven image which I made, and my priest, and have gone; and what have I remaining? And what is this that you say to me, 'Why do you cry?'"

²⁵ And the children of Dan said to him, "Let not your voice be heard with us, lest angry men run upon you, and take away your life, and the lives of your house."

²⁶ And the children of Dan went their way; and Micah saw that they were stronger than himself, and he returned to his house.

The Danites Settle in Laish

²⁷ And the children of Dan took what Micah had made, and the priest that he had, and they came to Laish, to a people quiet and secure; and they struck them with the edge of the sword, and burned the city with fire.

²⁸ And there was no deliverer, because the city is far from the Sidonians, and they have no ties with anyone, and it is in the valley of the house of Raab; and they built the city, and dwelt in it.

²⁹ And they called the name of the city Dan, after the name of Dan their father, who was born to Israel; and the name of the city was Laish before.

³⁰ And the children of Dan set up the graven image for themselves; and Jonathan son of Gershom son of Manasseh, he and his sons were priests to the tribe of Dan till the time of the carrying away of the nation.

³¹ And they set up for themselves the graven image which Micah had made, all the days that the house of God was in Shiloh; and it was so in those days that there was no king in Israel.

JUDGES CHAPTER 19

The Levite's Concubine

¹ And there was a Levite sojourning in the sides of Mount Ephraim, and he took to himself a concubine from Bethlehem Judah.

² And his concubine departed from him, and went away from him to the house of her father to Bethlehem Judah, and she was there four months.

³ And her husband rose up, and went after her to speak kindly to her, to recover her to himself. And he had his young man with him, and a pair of donkeys; and she brought him into the house of her father. And the father of the young woman saw him, and was well pleased to meet him.

⁴ And his father-in-law, the father of the young woman, constrained him, and he stayed with him for three days; and they ate and drank, and lodged there.

⁵ And it came to pass on the fourth day that they rose early, and he stood up to depart. And the father of the young woman said to his son-in-law, "Strengthen your heart with a morsel of bread, and afterwards you shall go."

⁶ So they two sat down together and ate and drank. And the father of the young woman said to her husband, "Now stay the night, and let your heart be merry."

⁷ And the man rose up to depart; but his father-in-law constrained him, and he stayed and lodged there.

⁸ And he rose early in the morning on the fifth day to depart; and the father of the young woman said, "Now strengthen your heart, and do not be a soldier until the day declines"; and the two ate.

⁹ And the man rose up to depart, he and his concubine, and his young man. But his father in law, the father of the young woman said to him, "Behold now, the day has declined toward evening; lodge here, and let your heart rejoice; and you shall rise early tomorrow for your journey, and you shall go to your home."

¹⁰ However the man would not lodge there, but he arose and departed, and came to the part opposite Jebus, (this is

Jerusalem) and *there was* with him a pair of donkeys, saddled, and his concubine was with him.

¹¹ And they came as far as Jebus. And the day had far advanced, and the young man said to his master, "Come, and let us turn aside to this city of the Jebusites, and let us lodge in it."

¹² And his master said to him, "We will not turn aside to a strange city, where there is none of the children of Israel, but we will pass on as far as Gibeah."

¹³ And he said to his young man, "Come, and let us draw near to one of the places, and we will lodge in Gibeah or in Ramah."

¹⁴ And they passed by and went on, and the sun went down upon them near to Gibeah, which is in Benjamin.

¹⁵ And they turned aside there to go in to lodge in Gibeah. And they went in, and sat down in the street of the city, and there was no one would take them into *his* house to spend the night.

¹⁶ And behold, an old man came out of the field from his work in the evening; and the man was of Mount Ephraim, and he sojourned in Gibeah, and the men of the place were sons of Benjamin.

¹⁷ And he lifted up his eyes, and saw a traveler in the street of the city; and the old man said to him, "Where are you going, and where do you come from?"

¹⁸ And he said to him, "We are passing by from Bethlehem Judah to the sides of Mount Ephraim; I am from there, and I went as far as Bethlehem Judah, and I am going home, and there is no man to take me into his house.

¹⁹ Although we have both straw and food for our donkeys, and bread and wine for me and my maid and the young man with your servants; there is no lack of anything."

²⁰ And the old man said, "Peace be unto you; however *let* all your needs be upon me, and by no means lodge in the street." ²¹ And he brought him into his house, and made room for his donkeys; and they washed their feet, and ate and drank.

Gibeah's Crime

²² And they *were* enjoying themselves, when behold, the men of the city, sons of transgressors, surrounded the house, knocking at the door. And they spoke to the old man, the owner of the house, saying, "Bring out the man who came into your house, that we may know him."

²³ And the master of the house came out to them, and said, "No, brothers, I beg you, do not act so wickedly, seeing this man has come into my house; do not commit this outrage.

²⁴ Behold my daughter *is* a virgin, and the man's concubine *is here as well*: I will bring them out. Humble them, and do to them as you please; but to this man do not do such a vile thing!"

²⁵ But the men would not consent to hear him. So the man laid hold of his concubine, and brought her out to them; and they knew her, and abused her all night till the morning, and let her go when the morning dawned.

²⁶ And the woman came toward morning, and fell down at the door of the house where her husband was, until it was light.

²⁷ And her husband rose up in the morning, and opened the doors of the house, and went forth to go on his journey; and behold, the woman his concubine had fallen down by the doors of the house, and her hands were on the threshold.

²⁸ And he said to her, "Get up, and let us go"; but she did not answer, for she was dead. And he took her upon his donkey, and went to his place.

²⁹ And he took his sword, and laid hold of his concubine, and divided her into twelve parts, and sent them to every coast of Israel.

³⁰ And it was so, that everyone who saw it said, "*Such a day* as this has not happened nor has been seen from the day of the going up of the children of Israel out of the land of Egypt until this day: take counsel concerning it, and speak."

JUDGES CHAPTER 20

Israel's War with the Benjamites

¹ And all the children of Israel went out, and all the congregation was gathered as one man, from Dan even to Beersheba, and in the land of Gilead, to the Lord at Mizpah.

² And all the tribes of Israel stood before the Lord in the assembly of the people of God, four hundred thousand footmen that drew *the* sword.

³ And the children of Benjamin heard that the children of Israel had gone up to Mizpah: and the children of Israel came and said, "Tell us, where did this wickedness take place?"

⁴ And the Levite, the husband of the woman that was slain, answered and said, "I and my concubine went to Gibeah of Benjamin to lodge.

⁵ And the men of Gibeah rose up against me, and surrounded the house by night against me; they wanted to kill me, and they have humbled my concubine, and she is dead.

⁶ And I laid hold of my concubine, and divided her in pieces, and sent *the parts* into every coast of the inheritance of the children of Israel; for they have committed lewdness and an abomination in Israel.

⁷ Behold, all you are children of Israel; and consider and take counsel here among yourselves."

⁸ And all the people rose up as one man, saying, "None of us shall return to his tent, and none of us shall return to his house.

⁹ And now this is the thing which shall be done in Gibeah: we will go up against it by lot.

¹⁰ Moreover we will take ten men for a hundred for all the tribes of Israel, and a hundred for a thousand, and a thousand for ten thousand, to take provision, to cause them to come to Gibeah of Benjamin, to do to it according to all the abomination which they have done in Israel."

[11] And all the men of Israel were gathered to the city as one man.

[12] And the tribes of Israel sent men through the whole tribe of Benjamin, saying, "What is this wickedness that has been done among you?

[13] Now then give up the men, the sons of transgressors that are in Gibeah, and we will put them to death, and purge out *the* wickedness from Israel." But the children of Benjamin did not consent to obey the voice of their brothers the children of Israel.

[14] And the children of Benjamin were gathered from their cities to Gibeah, to go forth to fight with the children of Israel.

[15] And the children of Benjamin from their cities were numbered in that day, twenty-three thousand, *every* man drawing a sword, besides the inhabitants of Gibeah, who were numbered seven hundred chosen men of all the people, able to use both hands alike.

[16] All these could sling with stones at a hair, and not miss.

[17] And the men of Israel, exclusive of Benjamin, were numbered four hundred thousand men that drew *the* sword; all these were men of war.

[18] And they arose and went up to Bethel, and inquired of God. And the children of Israel said, "Who shall go up for us first to fight with the children of Benjamin?" And the Lord said, "Judah shall go up first as leader."

[19] And the children of Israel rose up in the morning, and encamped against Gibeah.

[20] And they went out, all the men of Israel, to fight with Benjamin, and engaged with them at Gibeah.

[21] And the sons of Benjamin went forth from Gibeah, and they destroyed in Israel on that day twenty-two thousand men down to the ground.

[22] And the men of Israel strengthened themselves, and again engaged in battle in the place where they had engaged on the first day.

[23] And the children of Israel went up, and wept before the Lord till evening, and inquired of the Lord, saying, "Shall we again draw near to battle with our brothers the children of Benjamin?" And the Lord said, "Go up against them."

[24] And the children of Israel advanced against the children of Benjamin on the second day.

[25] And the children of Benjamin went forth to meet them from Gibeah on the second day, and destroyed of the children of Israel yet eighteen thousand more men down to the ground: all these drew *the* sword.

[26] And the children of Israel and all the people went up, and came to Bethel. And they wept, and sat there before the Lord; and they fasted on that day until evening, and offered burnt offerings and perfect sacrifices before the Lord,

[27] for the ark of the Lord God was there in those days,

[28] and Phineas the son of Eleazar the son of Aaron stood before it in those days; and the children of Israel inquired of the Lord, saying, "Shall we yet again go forth to fight with our brothers the sons of Benjamin?" And the Lord said, "Go up, for tomorrow I will give them into your hands."

[29] And the children of Israel set an ambush against Gibeah round about it.

[30] And the children of Israel went up against the children of Benjamin on the third day, and arrayed themselves against Gibeah as before.

[31] And the children of Benjamin went out to meet the people, and were all drawn out of the city, and began to strike and kill the people as before in the roads, one of which goes up to Bethel, and one to Gibeah in the field, about thirty men of Israel.

[32] And the children of Benjamin said, "They fall before us as at the first." But the children of Israel said, "Let us flee, and draw them out from the city into the roads"; and they did so.

[33] And all the men rose up out of their places, and engaged in Baal Tamar. Then Israel's men in ambush advanced from their place from Maraagabe.

[34] And there came over against Gibeah ten thousand chosen men out of all Israel; and the fight was severe; and they did not know that evil was coming upon them.

[35] And the Lord struck Benjamin before the children of Israel; and the children of Israel destroyed of Benjamin in that day a hundred and twenty-five thousand men: all these drew *the* sword.

[36] And the children of Benjamin saw that they were smitten; and the men of Israel gave place to Benjamin, because they trusted in the men in ambush which they had prepared against Gibeah.

[37] And when they retreated, then those in ambush rose up, and they moved toward Gibeah, and the whole ambush came forth, and they struck the city with the edge of the sword.

[38] And the children of Israel had a signal of battle with those *waiting* in ambush, that they should send up a signal of smoke from the city.

[39] And the children of Israel saw that those in ambush had seized Gibeah, and they stood in line of battle; and Benjamin began to strike down wounded ones among the men of Israel, about thirty men; for they said, "Surely they fall again before us, as in the first battle."

[40] And the signal went up increasingly over the city as a pillar of smoke. And Benjamin looked behind him, and behold the destruction of the city went up to heaven.

[41] And the men of Israel turned back, and the men of Benjamin panicked, because they saw that evil had come upon them.

[42] And they turned to the way of the wilderness from before the children of Israel, and fled: but the battle overtook them, and those from the cities destroyed them in the midst of them.

[43] And they cut down Benjamin, and pursued him from Nua closely till they came opposite Gibeah on the east.

[44] And there fell of Benjamin eighteen thousand men: all these *were* men of might.

45 And the rest turned, and fled to the wilderness to the rock of Rimmon; and the children of Israel picked off of them five thousand men; and the children of Israel went down after them as far as Gidom, and they killed two thousand of them.

46 And all that fell of Benjamin were twenty-five thousand men that drew *the* sword in that day: all these were men of might.

47 And the rest turned, and fled to the wilderness to the rock of Rimmon, even six hundred men; and they sojourned four months in the rock of Rimmon.

48 And the children of Israel returned to the children of Benjamin, and struck them with the edge of the sword from the city of Methla, even to the cattle, and everything that was found in all the cities: and they burned with fire the cities they found.

JUDGES CHAPTER 21

Wives Provided for the Benjamites

1 Now the children of Israel swore in Mizpah, saying, "No man of us shall give his daughter to Benjamin for a wife."

2 And the people came to Bethel, and sat there until evening before God. And they lifted up their voice and wept with a great weeping;

3 and said, "Why, O Lord God of Israel, has this come to pass, that today one tribe should be counted *as missing* from Israel?"

4 And it came to pass on the next day that the people rose up early, and built an altar there, and offered up burnt offerings and peace offerings.

5 And the children of Israel said, "Who of all the tribes of Israel, did not go up among the congregation, to the Lord?" For there was a great oath concerning those who did not go up to the Lord to Mizpah, saying, "He shall surely be put to death."

6 And the children of Israel relented toward Benjamin their brother, and said, "Today one tribe is cut off from Israel.

7 What shall we do for wives for the rest that remain? Whereas we have sworn by the Lord, not to give them of our daughters for wives."

8 And they said, "What one man is there of the tribes of Israel, who did not go up to the Lord to Mizpah?" And behold, no man came to the camp from Jabesh Gilead to the assembly.

9 And the people were numbered, and there was not there a man from the inhabitants of Jabesh Gilead.

10 And the congregation sent there twelve thousand men of the strongest, and they commanded them, saying, "Go and strike the inhabitants of Jabesh Gilead with the edge of the sword.

11 And this shall you do: every male and every woman that has known the lying with a man you shall devote to *destruction*, but the virgins you shall save alive." And they did so.

12 And they found among the inhabitants of Jabesh Gilead four hundred young virgins, who had not known a man by lying with him; and they brought them to Shiloh in the land of Canaan.

13 And all the congregation sent and spoke to the children of Benjamin at the rock of Rimmon, and invited them to *make* peace.

14 And Benjamin returned to the children of Israel at that time, and the children of Israel gave them the women whom they had saved alive of the daughters of Jabesh Gilead; and they were content.

15 And the people grieved for Benjamin, because the Lord had made a void in the tribes of Israel.

16 And the elders of the congregation said, "What shall we do for wives for them that remain?" For the women have been destroyed out of Benjamin.

17 And they said, "*There must be* an inheritance of those that have escaped of Benjamin; and so a tribe shall not be destroyed out of Israel.

18 For we shall not be able to give them wives of our daughters, because we swore among the children of Israel, saying, 'Cursed is he that gives a wife to Benjamin.'"

19 And they said, "Lo! Now *there is* a feast of the Lord from year to year in Shiloh, which is on the north of Bethel, eastward on the way that goes up from Bethel to Shechem, and from the south of Lebonah.

20 And they commanded the children of Benjamin, saying, "Go and lie in wait in the vineyards;

21 and you shall see; and lo! If there come out the daughters of the inhabitants of Shiloh to perform their dances, then shall you go out of the vineyards and seize for yourselves every man a wife of the daughters of Shiloh, and go into the land of Benjamin.

22 And it shall come to pass, when their fathers or their brothers come to dispute with us, that we will say to them, 'Grant them freely to us, for we have not taken every man his wife in the battle: because you did not give to them according to the occasion, you transgressed.'"

23 And the children of Benjamin did so; and they took wives according to their number from the dancers whom they seized. And they went and returned to their inheritance, and built the cities, and dwelt in them.

24 And the children of Israel departed from there at that time, every man to his tribe and his family; they went out from there, every man to his inheritance.

25 And in those days there was no king in Israel; every man did that which was right in his own sight.

THE BOOK OF RUTH

Elimelech's Family Goes to Moab

1 And it came to pass *in the days* when the judges ruled, that there was a famine in the land. And a man went from Bethlehem, Judah to sojourn in the land of Moab—he, his wife, and his two sons.

2 And the man's name *was* Elimelech, and his wife's name *was* Naomi, and the names of his two sons *were* Mahlon and Chilion—Ephrathites of Bethlehem, Judah. And they came to the land of Moab, and remained there.

3 And Elimelech, Naomi's husband died; and she was left, and her two sons.

4 And they took to themselves wives, women of Moab; the name of the one *was* Orpah, and the name of the second *was* Ruth; and they dwelt there about ten years.

5 And both Mahlon and Chilion died also; and the woman survived her husband and her two sons.

Naomi and Her Moabite Daughters-In-Law

6 And she rose up, and her two daughters-in-law, and they returned out of the country of Moab, for she heard in the country of Moab that the Lord *had* visited His people to give them bread.

7 And she went forth out of the place where she was, and her two daughters-in-law with her; and they went by the way to return to the land of Judah.

8 And Naomi said to her daughters-in-law, "Go now, and each of you return to the house of her mother. The Lord deal mercifully with you, as you have dealt with the dead, and with me.

9 The Lord grant you that you may find rest, each of you in the house of her husband." And she kissed them, and they lifted up their voice, and wept.

10 And they said to her, "We will return with you to your people."

11 And Naomi said, "Return now, my daughters; and why do you go with me? Have I yet sons in my womb to be your husbands?

12 Turn now, my daughters, for I am too old to be married: for I said, Suppose I were married, and should bear sons;

13 would you wait for them till they should be grown? Or would you refrain from being married for their sakes? Not so, my daughters, for I am grieved for you, that the hand of the Lord has gone forth against me."

14 And they lifted up their voice, and wept again; and Orpah kissed her mother-in-law and returned to her people; but Ruth followed her.

15 And Naomi said to Ruth, "Behold, your sister-in-law has returned to her people and to her gods; turn now also after your sister-in-law."

16 And Ruth said, "Do not urge me to leave you, or to return from following you; for wherever you go, I will go, and wherever you lodge, I will lodge; your people *shall be* my people, and your God my God.

17 And wherever you die, I will die, and there will I be buried: the Lord do so to me, and more also, *if I leave you*, for death *only* shall divide between me and you."

18 And Naomi, seeing that she was determined to go with her, ceased to speak to her anymore.

19 Now they both went until they came to Bethlehem. And it came to pass, when they arrived at Bethlehem, that all the city was excited because of them, and they said, "Is this Naomi?"

20 And she said to them, "No, do not call me Naomi; call me 'Bitter,' for the Mighty One has dealt very bitterly with me.

21 I went out full, and the Lord has brought me back empty. And why do you call me Naomi, seeing the Lord has humbled me and the Mighty One has afflicted me?"

22 So Naomi and Ruth the Moabitess, her daughter-in-law, returned from the country of Moab; and they came to Bethlehem at the beginning of barley harvest.

RUTH CHAPTER 2

Ruth Meets Boaz

1 And Naomi had *a friend*, an acquaintance of her husband, and the man *was* a mighty man of the kindred of Elimelech, and his name *was* Boaz.

2 And Ruth the Moabitess said to Naomi, "Let me go now to the field, and I will glean among the ears behind the man with whomsoever I shall find favor." And she said to her, "Go, daughter."

3 And she went; and came and gleaned in the field behind the reapers; and she happened by chance to come on a portion of the land of Boaz, of the kindred of Elimelech.

4 And behold, Boaz came from Bethlehem, and said to the reapers, "The Lord *be* with you." And they said to him, "The Lord bless you."

5 And Boaz said to his servant who was set over the reapers, "Whose young woman *is* this?"

6 And his servant who was set over the reapers answered and said, "It is the young Moabite woman who returned with Naomi out of the land of Moab.

7 And she said, 'I beseech you, let me glean and gather among the sheaves after the reapers.' And she came and stood from morning till evening, and did not rest, *even a little*, in the field."

8 And Boaz said to Ruth, "Have you not heard, *my* daughter? Do not depart to glean in another field; do not depart from here, *but* join yourself here with my young women.

9 *Let* your eyes *be* on the field where *my men* reap, and you shall go after them. Behold, I have charged the young men not to touch you, and when you shall thirst, then you shall go to the vessels, and drink of that which the young men have drawn."

10 And she fell upon her face, and bowed down to the ground, and said to him, "How is it that I have found grace in your eyes, that you should take notice of me, seeing that I am a stranger?"

11 And Boaz answered and said to her, "It has been fully reported to me how you have dealt with your mother-in-law after the death of your husband, and how you left your father and your mother, and the land of your birth, and came to a people whom you did not know before.

[12] The Lord recompense your work; may a full reward be given to you from the Lord God of Israel, to whom you have come to trust under His wings."

[13] And she said, "Let me find grace in your sight, my lord, because you have have comforted me, and because you have spoken kindly to your maidservant, and behold, I shall be as one of your servants."

[14] And Boaz said to her, "Now *it is* time to eat; come here, and you shall eat of the bread, and you shall dip your piece of bread in the vinegar." So Ruth sat by the side of the reapers; and Boaz handed her parched grain, and she ate, and was satisfied, and left.

[15] And she rose up to glean; and Boaz commanded his young men, saying, "Let her even glean among the sheaves, and do not reproach her.

[16] And by all means carry it for her, and you shall surely let fall for her some of that which is heaped up; and let her eat, and glean, and do not rebuke her."

[17] So she gleaned in the field till evening, and beat out that she had gleaned, and it was about an ephah of barley.

[18] And she took *it* up, and went into the city. And her mother-in-law saw what she had gleaned, and Ruth brought forth and gave to her the food which she had left from what she had been satisfied with.

[19] And her mother-in-law said to her, "Where have you gleaned today, and where have you worked? Blessed be the man that took notice of you." And Ruth told her mother-in-law where she *had* worked, and said, "The name of the man with whom I worked today *is* Boaz."

[20] And Naomi said to her daughter-in-law, "Blessed is he of the Lord, because He has not failed in His mercy with the living and the dead." And Naomi said to her, "This man is our relative, and is one of our relations."

[21] And Ruth said to her mother-in-law, "Yes, he also said to me, 'Keep close to my young women, until the men shall have finished all my reaping.'"

[22] And Naomi said to Ruth her daughter-in-law, "*It is* well, daughter, that you went out with his young women; thus they shall not meet you in another field."

[23] And Ruth joined herself to the young women of Boaz, to glean until they had finished the barley harvest and the wheat harvest.

RUTH CHAPTER 3

Ruth and Boaz at the Threshing Floor

[1] And she lodged with her mother-in-law. And Naomi her mother-in-law said to her, "My daughter, shall I not seek rest for you, that it may be well with you?

[2] And now *is* not Boaz our kinsman, with whose young women you were with? Behold, he winnows barley this night in the floor.

[3] But wash, and anoint yourself, and put your best clothing on, and go up to the threshing floor—do not make yourself known to the man until he has done eating and drinking.

[4] And it shall come to pass when he lies down, that you shall mark the place where he lies down, and shall come and lift up the covering of his feet, and shall lie down; and he shall tell you what you shall do."

[5] And Ruth said to her, "All that you say, I will do."

[6] And she went down to the threshing floor, and did according to all that her mother-in-law instructed her.

[7] And Boaz ate and drank, and his heart was glad, and he came to lie down by the side of the heap of grain; and she came secretly, and lifted up the covering of his feet.

[8] And it came to pass at midnight that the man was amazed, and troubled, and behold, a woman lay at his feet.

[9] And he said, "Who are you?" And she said, "I am your maidservant Ruth; spread your skirt over your maidservant, for you are a close relative."

[10] And Boaz said, "Blessed *are* you of the Lord God, *my* daughter, for you have made your latter kindness greater than the former, in that you did not follow after the young men, whether *any be* poor or rich.

[11] And now fear not, my daughter, whatever you shall say I will do for you; for all the tribe of my people knows that you are a virtuous woman.

[12] And now I am truly a relative to you; nevertheless there is a relative closer than I.

[13] Lodge *here* for the night, and it shall be in the morning, if he will perform the duty of a close relative for you—good, let him do it. But if he will not perform the duty of a close relative for you, then I will perform the relative's duty for you, *as* the Lord lives; lie down till the morning."

[14] And she laid at his feet until the morning; and she rose up before a man could recognize his neighbor; and Boaz said, "Let it not be known that a woman came into the threshing floor."

[15] And he said to her, "Bring the apron that is upon you." And she held it, and he measured six measures of barley, and put them upon her, and she went into the city.

[16] And Ruth went in to her mother-in-law, and she said to her, "*My* daughter!" And *Ruth* told her all that the man had done for her.

[17] And she said to her, "He gave me these six measures of barley, for he said to me, 'do not go empty to your mother-in-law.'"

[18] And she said, "Sit still, *my* daughter, until you shall know how the matter will fall out; for the man will not rest until the matter is resolved this day."

RUTH CHAPTER 4

Boaz Redeems Ruth

[1] And Boaz went up to the gate, and sat there. And behold, the relative passed by, of whom Boaz spoke. And Boaz said to him, "Turn aside, *and* sit down here." And he turned aside and sat down.

[2] And Boaz took ten men of the elders of the city, and said, "Sit here"; and they sat down.

³ And Boaz said to the relative, "*The matter regards* the portion of the field which was our brother Elimelech's which was given to Naomi, who has now returned out of the land of Moab.

⁴ And I said, 'I will inform you, saying, Buy it before those that sit, and before the elders of my people: if you will redeem it, redeem it, but if you will not redeem it, *then* tell me, and I shall know; for there is no one beside you to redeem *it*, and I am after you.'" And he said, "I am *here*, I will redeem it."

⁵ And Boaz said, "On the day you buy the field from the hand of Naomi and of Ruth the Moabitess, the wife of the deceased, you must also buy her, so as to raise up the name of the dead upon his inheritance."

⁶ And the kinsman said, I shall not be able to redeem it for myself, lest I ruin my own inheritance; you redeem my right for yourself, for I shall not be able to redeem *it*."

⁷ And this *was* the ordinance in former times in Israel for redemption, and for a bargain, to confirm every word: A man loosed his shoe, and gave it to his neighbor that redeemed his right; and this was *for* a testimony in Israel.

⁸ And the kinsman said to Boaz, "Buy my right for yourself." And he took off his shoe and gave it to him.

⁹ And Boaz said to the elders and to all the people, "You *are* witnesses this day, that I have bought all that was Elimelech's, and all that belonged to Chilion and Mahlon, from the hand of Naomi.

¹⁰ Moreover I have bought for myself for a wife Ruth the Moabitess, the wife of Mahlon, to raise up the name of the dead upon his inheritance; so the name of the dead shall not be destroyed from among his brothers, and from the tribe of his people: you *are* witnesses this day."

¹¹ And all the people who were in the gate said, "*We are* witnesses"; and the elders said, "The Lord make your wife who goes into your house, as Rachel and as Leah, who both *together* built the house of Israel, and wrought mightily in Ephratha, and there shall be a name *to you* in Bethlehem.

¹² And let your house be as the house of Perez, whom Tamar bore to Judah, of the descendants which the Lord shall give you of this maidservant."

Descendants of Boaz and Ruth

¹³ And Boaz took Ruth, and she became his wife, and he went in to her; and the Lord gave her conception, and she bore a son.

¹⁴ And the woman said to Naomi, "Blessed *is* the Lord, who has not allowed a redeemer to fail you this day, even to make your name famous in Israel.

¹⁵ And he shall be to you a restorer of your soul, and one to cherish *in* your old age; for your daughter-in-law who has loved you, who is better to you than seven sons, has born him."

¹⁶ And Naomi took the child and laid it in her bosom, and became a nurse to it.

¹⁷ And the neighbors gave him a name, saying, "A son has been born to Naomi"; and they called his name Obed; this *is* the father of Jesse, the father of David.

¹⁸ And these *are* the generations of Perez: Perez fathered Hezron;

¹⁹ Hezron fathered Ram; and Ram fathered Amminadab.

²⁰ And Aminadab fathered Nahshon; and Nahshon fathered Salmon.

²¹ And Salmon fathered Boaz; and Boaz fathered Obed.

²² And Obed fathered Jesse; and Jesse fathered David.

THE FIRST BOOK OF SAMUEL

The Family of Elkanah

¹ There was a man of Ramathaim Zophim, of Mount Ephraim, and his name *was* Elkanah, a son of Jeroham, the son of Elias, the son of Tohu, in Nasib Ephraim.

² And he had two wives; the name of the one was Anna, and the name of the second *was* Peninnah. And Peninnah had children, but Anna had no child.

³ And the man went up from year to year from his city, from Ramathaim, to worship and sacrifice to the Lord God of Sabaoth at Shiloh. And *there were* Eli and his two sons, Hophni and Phineas, the priests of the Lord.

⁴ And the day came, and Elkanah sacrificed, and gave portions to his wife Peninnah and her children.

⁵ And to Anna he gave a prime portion, because she had no child, only Elkanah loved Anna more than the other; but the Lord had closed her womb.

⁶ For the Lord gave her no child in her affliction, and according to the despondency of her affliction; and she was dispirited on this account, that the Lord had shut up her womb so as not to give her a child.

⁷ So she did year by year, in going up to the house of the Lord; and she was dispirited, and wept, and did not eat.

Hannah's Vow

⁸ And Elkanah her husband called to her, "Anna." And she said to him, "Here am I, my lord." And he said to her, "Why do you weep? And why do you not eat? And why does your heart grieve you? Am I not better to you than ten children?"

⁹ And Anna rose up after they had eaten in Shiloh, and stood before the Lord. And Eli the priest was on a seat by the threshold of the temple of the Lord.

¹⁰ And she was very much grieved in *her* spirit, and prayed to the Lord, and wept abundantly.

¹¹ And she vowed a vow to the Lord, saying, "O Lord God of Sabaoth, if You will indeed look upon the humiliation of Your maidservant and remember me, and give to Your maidservant a male child, then will I indeed dedicate him to You till the day of his death; and he shall drink no wine nor strong drink, and no razor shall come upon his head."

¹² And it came to pass, while she was praying a long *time* before the Lord, that Eli the priest watched her mouth.

¹³ And she was speaking in her heart, and her lips moved, but her voice was not heard. And Eli accounted her a drunken woman.

¹⁴ And the servant of Eli said to her, "How long will you be drunken? Put away your wine from you, and go out from the presence of the Lord."

¹⁵ And Anna answered and said, "No my lord, *I live* in a hard day, and I have not drunk wine or strong drink, and I pour out my soul before the Lord.

¹⁶ Count not your maidservant for a wicked woman, for by reason of the abundance of my complaint I have continued *my prayer* until now."

¹⁷ And Eli answered and said to her, "Go in peace, *and may* the God of Israel give you all your petition, which you have asked of Him."

¹⁸ And she said, "Your maidservant has found favor in your eyes." And the woman went her way, and entered into her lodging, and ate and drank with her husband, and her countenance was sad no longer.

The Birth of Samuel

¹⁹ And they rose early in the morning, and worshipped the Lord, and they went their way. And Elkanah went into his house at Ramathaim, and had relations with his wife Anna; and the Lord remembered her, and she conceived.

²⁰ And it came to pass when the time had come, that she brought forth a son, and called his name Samuel, and said, "Because I asked him of the Lord God of Sabaoth."

²¹ And the man Elkanah and all his house went up to offer in Shiloh the yearly sacrifice, and his vows, and all the tithes of his land.

²² But Anna did not go up with him, for she said to her husband, "*I will not go up* until the child goes up, when I have weaned him, and he shall be presented before the Lord, and he shall abide there continually."

²³ And Elkanah her husband said to her, "Do that which is good in your eyes, abide still until you have weaned him; and may the Lord establish that which comes out of your mouth." And the woman waited, and suckled her son until she had weaned him.

²⁴ And she went up with him to Shiloh with a calf of three years old, and loaves, and an ephah of fine flour, and a skin of wine. And she entered into the house of the Lord in Shiloh, and the child with them.

²⁵ And they brought him before the Lord; and his father slaughtered his offering which he offered from year to year to the Lord; and he brought the child near, and slaughtered the calf; and Anna the mother of the child brought him to Eli.

²⁶ And she said, "I pray, my lord, as your soul lives, I am the woman that stood in your presence with you while praying to the Lord.

²⁷ For I have prayed for this child; and the Lord has given me my request that I asked of Him.

²⁸ And I lend him to the Lord all his days that he lives, a loan to the Lord."

1 SAMUEL CHAPTER 2

Hannah's Prayer

¹ And she said, "My heart is established in the Lord, my horn is exalted in my God; my mouth is enlarged over my enemies, I have rejoiced in Your salvation.

² For there is none holy like the Lord, and there is none righteous as our God; there is none holy besides You.

³ Boast not, and utter not high things; let not high sounding words come out of your mouth, for the Lord is a God of knowledge, and God prepares His own designs.

⁴ The bow of the mighty has grown feeble, and the weak have girded themselves with strength.

⁵ They that were full of bread have been brought low; and the hungry have forsaken the land; for the barren has born seven, and she that abounded in children has grown feeble.

⁶ The Lord kills and makes alive; He brings down to the grave, and brings up.

⁷ The Lord makes poor, and makes rich; He brings low, and lifts up.

⁸ He lifts up the poor from the earth, and raises the needy from the dunghill; to seat him with the princes of the people, and causing them to inherit the throne of glory;

⁹ granting his petition to him that prays; and He blesses the years of the righteous, for by strength cannot man prevail.

¹⁰ The Lord will weaken His adversary; the Lord is holy. Let not the wise man boast in his wisdom, nor let the mighty man boast in his strength, and let not the rich man boast in his wealth; but let him that boasts boast in this: to understand and know the Lord, and to execute judgment and justice in the midst of the earth. The Lord has gone up to the heavens, and has thundered: He will judge the extremities of the earth, and He gives strength to our kings, and will exalt the horn of His Christ."

¹¹ And she left him there before the Lord and departed to Ramathaim. And the child ministered in the presence of the Lord before Eli the priest.

Eli's Evil Sons

¹² And the sons of Eli the priest *were* evil sons, not knowing the Lord.

¹³ And the priest's claim from everyone of the people that sacrificed was this: the servant of the priest came when the flesh was in seething, and a flesh-hook of three teeth was in his hand.

¹⁴ And he struck it into the great caldron, or into the bronze vessel, or into the pot, and whatever came up with the flesh-hook, the priest took for himself. So they did to all Israel that came to sacrifice to the Lord in Shiloh.

¹⁵ And before the fat was burnt for a sweet savor, the servant of the priest would come, and say to the man that sacrificed, "Give some flesh to roast for the priest, and I will by no means take from you boiled flesh out of the caldron."

16 And if the man that sacrificed said, "First let the fat be burned, as it is fit, and take for yourself of all things which your soul desires," then he would say, "No, but you shall give it to me now; and if not I will take it by force."

17 So the sin of the young men was very great before the Lord, for they despised the offering of the Lord.

The Child Samuel at Shiloh

18 And Samuel ministered before the Lord, a child wearing a linen ephod.

19 And his mother made him a little robe, and brought it to him from year to year, in her going up in company with her husband to offer the yearly sacrifice.

20 And Eli blessed Elkanah and his wife, saying, "The Lord recompense to you descendants from this woman, in return for the loan which you have lent to the Lord." And the man returned to his place.

21 And the Lord visited Anna, and she bore yet three sons, and two daughters. And the child Samuel grew before the Lord.

Prophecy Against Eli's Household

22 And Eli was very old, and he heard what his sons did to the children of Israel.

23 And he said to them, "Why do you do such things, which I hear from the mouth of all the people of the Lord?

24 No my sons! For the report which I hear is not good. Do not *do* so, for the reports which I hear are not good, so that the people do not serve God.

25 If a man should at all sin against another, then shall they pray for him to the Lord; but if a man sin against the Lord, who shall intercede for him?" But they would not listen to the voice of their father, because the Lord desired to destroy them.

26 And the child Samuel grew, and was in favor with God and with men.

27 And a man of God came to Eli, and said, "Thus says the Lord, I plainly revealed Myself to the house of your father, when they were servants in Egypt to the house of Pharaoh.

28 And I chose the house of your father out of all the tribes of Israel to minister to Me in the priest's office, to go up to My altar, and to burn incense, and to wear an ephod. And I gave to the house of your father all the offerings by fire of the children of Israel for food.

29 Therefore why have you looked upon My incense offering and My grain offering with a shameless eye, and have honored your sons above Me, so that they should bless themselves with the firstfruits of every sacrifice of Israel before Me?

30 Therefore thus says the Lord God of Israel: I said, Your house and the house of your father shall pass before Me forever: but now the Lord says, 'Far be it from Me; for I will only honor them that honor Me, and he that despises Me shall be despised.

31 Behold, the days are coming when I will destroy your descendants, and the descendants of your father's house.

32 And you shall not have an old man in My house forever.

33 And if I do not destroy a man of yours from My altar, *it shall be* that his eyes may fail and his soul may perish; and everyone that remains in your house shall fall by the sword of men.

34 And this which shall come upon your two sons Hophni and Phineas shall be a sign to you: in one day they shall both die.

35 And I will raise up to Myself a faithful priest, who shall do all that is in My heart and in My soul; and I will build him a sure house, and he shall walk before My Christ forever.

36 And it shall come to pass that he that survives in your house will come and bow down before him for a little piece of silver, saying, "Put me into one of your priest's offices to eat bread."'"

1 SAMUEL CHAPTER 3

Samuel's Calling

1 And the child Samuel ministered to the Lord before Eli the priest. And the word of the Lord was precious in those days, *for* there was no distinct vision.

2 And it came to pass at that time that Eli was sleeping in his place; and his eyes began to fail, and could not see.

3 And the lamp of God *was burning* before it was trimmed, and Samuel slept in the temple, where the ark of God was.

4 And the Lord called, "Samuel, Samuel." And he said, "Behold, *here* I *am*."

5 And he ran to Eli and said, "*Here* I *am*, for you called me." And he said, "I did not call you; return, go to sleep." And he returned and went to sleep.

6 And the Lord called again, "Samuel, Samuel." And he went to Eli the second time, and said, "Behold *here* I *am*, for you called me." And he said, "I did not call you; return, go to sleep."

7 And *this was* before Samuel knew the Lord, and *before* the word of the Lord was revealed to him.

8 And the Lord called Samuel again for the third time; and he arose and went to Eli, and said, "Behold, I *am here*, for you called me." And Eli perceived that the Lord had called the child.

9 And he said, "Return, child, go to sleep; and it shall come to pass if He shall call you, that you shall say, 'Speak, for Your servant hears.'" So Samuel went and lay down in his place.

10 And the Lord came, and stood, and called him as before. And Samuel said, "Speak, for Your servant hears."

11 And the Lord said to Samuel, "Behold, I execute My words in Israel; whoever hears them, both his ears shall tingle.

12 In that day I will raise up against Eli all things that I have said against his house; I will begin, and I will make an end.

¹³ And I have told him that I will be avenged on his house perpetually for the iniquities of his sons, because his sons spoke evil against God, and he did not admonish them.

¹⁴ And *it shall* not *go on* so; I have sworn to the house of Eli, the iniquity of the house of Eli shall not be atoned for with incense or sacrifices forever."

¹⁵ And Samuel slept till morning, and rose early in the morning, and opened the doors of the house of the Lord; and Samuel feared to tell *Eli* the vision.

¹⁶ And Eli said to Samuel, "Samuel, *my* son." And he said, "Behold, *here* I *am*."

¹⁷ And he said, "What was the word that was spoken to you? I pray you do not hide it from me: may God do these things to you, and more also, if you hide from me anything of all the words that were spoken to you in your ears."

¹⁸ And Samuel reported all the words, and did not hide them from him. And Eli said, "He is the Lord, He shall do that which is good in His sight."

¹⁹ And Samuel grew, and the Lord was with him, and there did not fall one of his words to the ground.

²⁰ And all Israel knew, from Dan even to Beersheba, that Samuel was faithful as a prophet to the Lord.

²¹ And the Lord manifested Himself again in Shiloh, for the Lord revealed Himself to Samuel. And Samuel was believed by all Israel, from one end of the land to the other, to be a prophet *of* the Lord. And Eli *was* very old, and his sons kept advancing *in wickedness*, and their way *was* evil before the Lord.

1 SAMUEL CHAPTER 4

The Ark of God Captured

¹ And it came to pass in those days that the Philistines gathered themselves together against Israel to war; and Israel went out to meet them and encamped at Ebenezer, and the Philistines encamped in Aphek.

² And the Philistines prepared to fight with Israel, and the battle was turned against them. And the men of Israel fell before the Philistines, and four thousand men were killed in the battle in the field.

³ And the people came to the camp, and the elders of Israel said, "Why has the Lord caused us to fall this day before the Philistines? Let us take the ark of our God out of Shiloh, and let it proceed from the midst of us, and it shall save us from the hand of our enemies."

⁴ And the people sent to Shiloh, and they took from there the ark of the Lord who dwells between the cherubim. And both the sons of Eli, Hophni and Phineas, were with the ark.

⁵ And it came to pass when the ark of the Lord entered into the camp, that all Israel cried out with a loud voice, and the earth resounded.

⁶ And the Philistines heard the cry, and the Philistines said, "What is this great cry in the camp of the Hebrews?" And they understood that the ark of the Lord had come into the camp.

⁷ And the Philistines feared, and said, "These are the gods that have come with them into the camp.

⁸ Woe to us, O lord, deliver us today, for such a thing has not happened before. Woe to us; who shall deliver us out of the hand of these mighty gods? These are the gods that struck Egypt with every plague, and in the wilderness.

⁹ Strengthen yourselves and behave yourselves like men, O you Philistines, that you may not serve the Hebrews as they have served us, but be men, and fight with them!"

¹⁰ And they fought with them; and the men of Israel fell, and they fled, every man to his tent. And there was a very great slaughter; and there fell of Israel thirty thousand fighting men.

¹¹ And the ark of God was taken, and both the sons of Eli, Hophni and Phineas, died.

The Death of Eli

¹² And there ran a man of Benjamin out of the battle, and he came to Shiloh on that day. And his clothes were torn, and dust was upon his head.

¹³ And he came, and behold, Eli was upon the seat by the gate, watching the road, for his heart was greatly alarmed for the ark of God. And the man entered into the city to bring news, and the city cried out.

¹⁴ And Eli heard the sound of the cry, and said, "What is the voice of this cry?" And the men hastened and went in, and reported to Eli.

¹⁵ Now Eli was ninety years old, and his eyes were so dim that he could not see.

¹⁶ And Eli said to them that stood round about him, "What is the voice of this sound?" And the man hastened and advanced to Eli, and said to him, "I am he that has come out of the camp, and I have fled from the battle today." And Eli said, "What has happened, my son?"

¹⁷ And the young man answered and said, "The men of Israel fled from the face of the Philistines, and there was a great slaughter among the people, and both your sons are dead, and the ark of God has been taken."

¹⁸ And it came to pass, when he mentioned the ark of God, that he fell from the seat backward near the gate, and his back was broken, and he died, for he was an old man and heavy. And he judged Israel twenty years.

Ichabod

¹⁹ And his daughter-in-law, the wife of Phineas, was pregnant, *and* she *was* about to give birth. And she heard the news that the ark of God had been taken, and that her father-in-law and her husband were dead. And she wept and gave birth, for her pains came upon her.

²⁰ And in her time she was at the point of death; and the women that stood by her said to her, "Do not fear, for you have born a son." But she did not answer, and she did not understand in her heart.

21 And she called the child [1]Ichabod, because of the ark of God, and because of her father-in-law, and because of her husband.

22 And they said, "The glory of Israel has departed, for the ark of the Lord has been taken."

1 SAMUEL CHAPTER 5

The Philistines and the Ark

1 And the Philistines took the ark of God, and brought it from Ebenezer to Ashdod.

2 And the Philistines took the ark of the Lord, and brought it into the house of Dagon, and set it by Dagon.

3 And the people of Ashdod rose early, and entered into the house of Dagon; and looked, and behold, Dagon had fallen on his face before the ark of the Lord. So they lifted up Dagon, and set him in his place. And the hand of the Lord was heavy upon the Ashdodians, and He plagued them, and He struck them in their secret parts, *both in* Ashdod and her coasts.

4 And it came to pass when they rose early in the morning, behold, Dagon had fallen on his face before the ark of the covenant of the Lord; and the head of Dagon and both the palms of his hands were cut off each before the threshold, and both the wrists of his hands had fallen on the floor of the porch; only the stump of Dagon was left.

5 Therefore the priests of Dagon, and everyone that enters into the house of Dagon, do not tread upon the threshold of the house of Dagon in Ashdod to this day, for they step over *it.*

6 And the hand of the Lord was heavy upon Ashdod, and He brought evil upon them, and it burst out upon them into the ships, and rats sprang up in the midst of their country, and there was a great tumult of death in the city.

7 And the men of Ashdod saw that it was so, and they said, "The ark of the God of Israel shall not abide with us, for His hand is heavy upon us, and upon Dagon our god."

8 Therefore they sent and gathered the lords of the Philistines to them, and said, "What shall we do with the ark of the God of Israel?" And they said, "Let the ark of God come over to us." And the ark of the God of Israel came to Gath.

9 And it came to pass after it went about to Gath, that the hand of the Lord came upon the city, and *there was* very great confusion. And He struck the men of the city, *both* small and great, and struck them in their buttocks. And the Gittites made for themselves images of tumors.

10 And they sent away the ark of God to Ekron. And it came to pass when the ark of God went into Ekron, that the men of Ekron cried out, saying, "Why have you brought back the ark of the God of Israel to us, to kill us and our people?"

11 So they sent and gathered the lords of the Philistines, and they said, "Send away the ark of the God of Israel, and let it lodge in its place; and let it not slay us and our people."

12 (For there was a very great confusion in all the city, when the ark of the God of Israel entered there; and those who lived and died not were struck with tumors; and the cry of the city went up to heaven).

1 SAMUEL CHAPTER 6

The Ark Returned to Israel

1 And the ark was in the country of the Philistines for seven months, and their land brought forth swarms of rats.

2 And the Philistines called their priests, and their prophets, and their enchanters, and said, "What shall we do to the ark of the Lord? Teach us how we shall send it away to its *proper* place."

3 And they said, "If you send away the ark of the covenant of the Lord God of Israel, do not on any account send it away empty, but by all means render to it an offering for the plague; and then shall you be healed, and an atonement shall be made for you. Should not His hand be thus stayed from off you?"

4 And they said, "What is the offering for the plague which we shall return to it?" And they said,

5 "According to the number of the lords of the Philistines, five golden tumors, for the plague was on you, and on your rulers, and on the people; and golden rats, the likeness of the rats that destroyed your land. And you shall give glory to the Lord, that He may lighten His hand from off you, and from off your gods, and from off your land.

6 And why do you harden your hearts, as Egypt and Pharaoh hardened their hearts? Was it not so when He mocked them, that they let the people go, and they departed?

7 And now take wood and make a new wagon, and take two cows, that have calved for the first time, without their calves; and yoke the cows to the wagon, and lead the calves away from them, and take them home.

8 And you shall take the ark and put it on the wagon. And you shall restore to it the golden articles for the trespass offering in a coffer by the side of it; and you shall let it go, and sent it away, and you shall depart.

9 And you shall see, if it shall go the way of its coasts along by Beth Shemesh, He has brought upon us this great affliction; and if not, then shall we know that His hand has not touched us, and this has happened to us by chance."

10 And the Philistines did so. And they took two cows that had calved for the first time, and yoked them to the wagon, and shut up their calves at home.

11 And they set the ark of the Lord, and the coffer, and the golden rats on the wagon.

12 And the cows went straight on the way to the way of Beth Shemesh, they went along one track and labored, and did not turn aside to the right hand or to the left, and the lords of

---

1 Lit. *no glory*

the Philistines went after it as far as the coasts of Beth Shemesh. ¹³ And the men of Beth Shemesh were reaping the wheat harvest in the valley; and they lifted up their eyes, and saw the ark of the Lord, and rejoiced to meet it.

¹⁴ And the wagon entered into the field of Joshua, which was in Beth Shemesh, and they set there by it a great stone; and they split the wood of the wagon, and offered up the cows for a burnt offering to the Lord.

¹⁵ And the Levites brought up the ark of the Lord, and the coffer with it, and the golden articles upon it, and placed them on the great stone, and the men of Beth Shemesh offered burnt offerings and grain offerings on that day to the Lord.

¹⁶ And the five lords of the Philistines saw, and returned to Ekron in that day.

¹⁷ And these are the golden tumors which the lords of the Philistines gave as a trespass offering to the Lord: for Ashdod one, for Gaza one, for Ashkelon one, for Gath one, and for Ekron one.

¹⁸ And the golden rats according to the number of all the cities of the Philistines, belonging to the five lords, from the fenced city to the village of the Perizzite, and to the great stone, on which they placed the ark of the covenant of the Lord, that was in the field of Joshua of Beth Shemesh.

¹⁹ And the sons of Jeconiah were not pleased with the men of Beth Shemesh, because they looked into the ark of the Lord; and the Lord struck fifty thousand and seventy men among them. And the people mourned, because the Lord had inflicted on the people a very great plague.

The Ark at Kirjath Jearim

²⁰ And the men of Beth Shemesh said, "Who shall be able to pass before this holy Lord God? And to whom shall the ark of the Lord go up from us?"

²¹ And they send messengers to the inhabitants of Kirjath Jearim, saying, "The Philistines have brought back the ark of the Lord; go down and take it home to yourselves."

1 SAMUEL CHAPTER 7

¹ And the men of Kirjath Jearim came, and brought up the ark of the covenant of the Lord. And they brought it into the house of Aminadab on the hill; and they consecrated Eleazar his son to keep the ark of the covenant of the Lord.

Samuel Judges Israel

² And it came to pass from the time that the ark was in Kirjath Jearim, the days were multiplied, and *the time* was twenty years; and all the house of Israel looked after the Lord.

³ And Samuel spoke to all the house of Israel, saying, "If you return to the Lord with all your heart, *then* take away the strange gods from your midst, and the groves, and prepare your hearts to serve the Lord, and serve Him only; and He shall deliver you from the hand of the Philistines."

⁴ And the children of Israel took away Baalim and the groves of Astaroth, and served the Lord only.

⁵ And Samuel said, "Gather all Israel to Mizpah, and I will pray for you to the Lord."

⁶ And they were gathered together to Mizpah, and they drew water, and poured it out upon the earth before the Lord. And they fasted on that day, and said, "We have sinned before the Lord." And Samuel judged the children of Israel in Mizpah.

⁷ And the Philistines heard that all the children of Israel were gathered together to Mizpah. And the lords of the Philistines went up against Israel, and the children of Israel heard, and they feared before the Philistines.

⁸ And the children of Israel said to Samuel, "Do not cease to cry to the Lord your God for us, and He shall save us out of the hand of the Philistines."

⁹ And Samuel took a suckling lamb, and offered it up as a burnt offering with all the people to the Lord. And Samuel cried to the Lord for Israel, and the Lord heard him.

¹⁰ And Samuel was offering the burnt offering; and the Philistines drew near to battle against Israel; and the Lord thundered with a mighty sound in that day upon the Philistines, and they were confounded and overthrown before Israel.

¹¹ And the men of Israel went forth out of Mizpah, and pursued the Philistines, and struck them as far as Beth Car.

¹² And Samuel took a stone, and set it up between Mizpah and the old *city*; and he called the name of it Ebenezer, signifying, Stone of the Helper; and he said, Thus far has the Lord helped us."

¹³ So the Lord humbled the Philistines, and they no longer came into the border of Israel; and the hand of the Lord was against the Philistines all the days of Samuel.

¹⁴ And the cities which the Philistines took from the children of Israel were restored; and they restored them to Israel from Ekron to Gath. And they took the coast of Israel out of the hand of the Philistines; and there was peace between Israel and the Amorite.

¹⁵ And Samuel judged Israel all the days of his life.

¹⁶ And he went from year by year on a circuit to Bethel, Gilgal, and Mizpah; and he judged Israel in all these consecrated places.

¹⁷ And he *always* returned to Ramah, because his house was there; and there he judged Israel, and there he built an altar to the Lord.

1 SAMUEL CHAPTER 8

Israel Demands a King

¹ And it came to pass when Samuel was old, that he made his sons judges over Israel.

² And these are the names of his sons: Joel the firstborn, and the name of the second Abijah; *they were* judges in Beersheba.

3 And his sons did not walk in his ways, and they turned aside after gain, and took gifts, and perverted judgments.

4 And the men of Israel gathered themselves together, and came to Samuel at Ramah,

5 and they said to him, "Behold, you have grown old, and your sons do not walk in your ways. And now set over us a king to judge us, as also the other nations have."

6 And the thing was evil in the eyes of Samuel, when they said, "Give us a king to judge us"; and Samuel prayed to the Lord.

7 And the Lord said to Samuel, "Hear the voice of the people, in whatever they shall say to you; for they have not rejected you, but they have rejected Me from reigning over them.

8 According to all their doings which they have done to Me, from the day that I brought them out of Egypt until this day, even as they have deserted Me, and served other gods, so they also do to you.

9 And now heed their voice; only you shall solemnly testify to them, and you shall describe to them the manner of the king who shall reign over them."

10 And Samuel spoke every word of the Lord to the people who asked of him a king.

11 And he said, "This shall be the manner of the king that shall rule over you: he shall take your sons, and put them in his chariots, and among his horsemen, and running before his chariots,

12 and *his manner shall be* to make them to himself captains of hundreds and captains of thousands; and to reap his harvest, and gather his vintage, and prepare his instruments of war, and the implements of his chariots.

13 And he will take your daughters to be perfumers, and cooks, and bakers.

14 And he will take your fields, your vineyards, and your good olive groves, and give them to his servants.

15 And he will take the tithe of your seeds and your vineyards, and give it to his eunuchs, and to his servants.

16 And he will take your servants, and your handmaids, and your good herds and your donkeys, and he will take a tenth of them for his works.

17 And he will take a tenth of your flocks; and you shall be his servants.

18 And you shall cry out in that day because of your king whom you have chosen for yourselves, and the Lord shall not hear you in those days, because you have chosen for yourselves a king."

19 But the people would not listen to Samuel; and they said to him, "No, but there shall be a king over us.

20 And we also will be like all the nations; and our king shall judge us, and shall go out before us, and fight our battles."

21 And Samuel heard all the words of the people, and spoke them in the ears of the Lord.

22 And the Lord said to Samuel, "Heed their voice, and appoint them a king." And Samuel said to the men of Israel, "Let each man depart to his city."

1 SAMUEL CHAPTER 9

Saul Chosen to be King

1 And *there was* a man of the sons of Benjamin, and his name was Kish, the son of Abiel, the son of Jared, the son of Bechorath, the son of Aphiah, the son of a Benjamite, a man of might.

2 And this man had a son, and his name was Saul, of great stature, a handsome man. And there was not a more handsome man among the sons of Israel than he, high above all the people, from his shoulders and upward.

3 Now the donkeys of Kish, Saul's father, were lost. And Kish said to Saul his son, "Take with you one of the young men, and arise, go and look for the donkeys."

4 And they went through Mount Ephraim, and they went through the land of Shalisha, and did not find them. And they passed through the land of Shaalim, and they were not there. Then they passed through the land of the Benjamites, and did not find them.

5 And when they came to Zuph, Saul said to his young man that was with him, "Come and let us return, lest my father leave the donkeys, and become worried about us."

6 And the young man said to him, "Behold, there is a man of God in this city, and the man is of high repute; all that he shall speak will surely come to pass. Now then let us go, that he may tell us our way on which we have set out."

7 And Saul said to his young man that was with him, "But look, if we should go, what shall we bring the man of God? For we have ran out of bread, and we have nothing else to bring to the man of God."

8 And the young man answered Saul again and said, "Behold, I have here in my hand a fourth part of a shekel of silver, and you shall give it to the man of God, and he shall tell us our way."

9 Now formerly in Israel, everyone who went to inquire of God said, "Come and let us go to the seer"; for the people formerly called the prophet, the seer.

10 And Saul said to his servant, "Well said; come, let us go." So they went to the city where the man of God was.

11 As they went up the ascent to the city, they found some young women coming out to draw water, and they said to them, "Is the seer here?"

12 And the virgins answered them and said, "He is *here*: behold, *he is* before you. Now he is coming to the city, because of the day, for today *there is* a sacrifice for the people on the high place.

13 As soon as you shall enter into the city, so shall you find him in the city, before he goes up to the high place to eat; for the people will not eat until he comes in, for he blesses the sacrifice, and afterwards the guests eat. Now then go up, for you shall find him because of the holiday."

14 And they went up to the city. And as they were entering into the midst of the city, behold, Samuel came out to meet them, to go up to the high place.

¹⁵ And the Lord uncovered the ear of Samuel one day before Saul came to him, saying,

¹⁶ "At this time tomorrow I will send to you a man out of the land of Benjamin, and you shall anoint him to be ruler over My people Israel, and he shall save My people out of the hand of the Philistines, for I have looked upon the humiliation of My people, for their cry has come unto Me."

¹⁷ And Samuel looked upon Saul, and the Lord said to him, "Behold, the man of whom I spoke to you; this one shall rule over My people."

¹⁸ And Saul drew near to Samuel into the midst of the city, and said, "Tell me, now which is the house of the seer?"

¹⁹ And Samuel answered Saul and said, "I am he: go up before me to the high place, and eat with me today, and I will send you away in the morning, and I will tell you all that is in your heart.

²⁰ And concerning your donkeys that have been lost now these three days, do not worry about them, for they have been found. And to whom does the excellency of Israel belong? Does it not *belong* to you, and to your father's house?"

²¹ And Saul answered and said, "Am I not the son of a Benjamite, the least tribe of the people of Israel? And of the least family of the whole tribe of Benjamin? And why have you spoken to me according to this word?"

²² And Samuel took Saul and his servant, and brought them to the inn, and set *for* them there a place among the chief of those that were called, about seventy men.

²³ And Samuel said to the cook, "Give me the portion which I gave to you, which I told you to set aside."

²⁴ Now the cook had boiled the shoulder, and he set it before Saul. And Samuel said to Saul, "Behold that which is left, set before you, and eat; for it is set there for a testimony in preference to the others; take of it." So Saul ate with Samuel on that day.

²⁵ And he went down from the high place into the city, and they prepared a lodging for Saul on the roof, and he lay down.

²⁶ And it came to pass when the morning dawned, that Samuel called Saul on the roof, saying, "Rise up, and I will dismiss you." And Saul arose, and he and Samuel went out.

Samuel Anoints Saul

²⁷ As they went down to a part of the city, Samuel said to Saul, "Speak to the young man, and let him pass on before us. But you stand here now, and listen to the word of God."

1 SAMUEL CHAPTER 10

¹ And Samuel took a flask of oil, and poured it on his head, and kissed him, and said to him, "Has not the Lord anointed you for a ruler over His people, over Israel? And you shall rule among the people of the Lord, and you shall save them out of the hand of their enemies; and this *shall be* the sign to you that the Lord has anointed you to be ruler over His inheritance:

² As soon as you have departed from me this day, you shall find two men by the burial place of Rachel on the mount of Benjamin, rejoicing greatly. And they shall say to you, "The donkeys which you went to look for have been found; and behold, your father has given up the matter of the donkeys, and he is anxious for you, saying, 'What shall I do for my son?'

³ And you shall depart from there, and shall go beyond that as far as the Oak of Tabor, and you shall find there three men going up to God, to Bethel, one bearing three young goats, and another bearing three vessels of bread, and another bearing a skin of wine.

⁴ And they shall ask you how you are doing, and shall give you two *loaves* of bread, and you shall receive them from their hand.

⁵ And afterward you shall go to the hill of God, where the encampment of the Philistines is. Nasib the Philistine is there. And it shall come to pass when you have entered into the city, that you shall meet a band of prophets coming down from the high place; and before them will be lutes, a drum, a pipe, and a harp, and they shall prophesy.

⁶ And the Spirit of the Lord shall come upon you, and you shall prophesy with them, and you shall turn into another man.

⁷ And it shall come to pass when these signs come upon you—*then* do whatsoever your hand shall find, because God is with you.

⁸ And you shall go down in front of Gilgal, and behold, I will come down to you to offer a burnt offering, and peace offerings. You shall wait seven days until I come to you, and I will make known to you what you shall do."

⁹ And it came to pass when he turned his back to depart from Samuel, God gave him another heart; and all these signs came to pass in that day.

¹⁰ And he came there to the hill, and behold, a band of prophets was opposite him. And the Spirit of God came upon him, and he prophesied in the midst of them.

¹¹ And all that had known him before came, and saw, and behold, he was in the midst of the prophets. And the people said, everyone to his neighbor, "What is this that has happened to the son of Kish? Is Saul also among the prophets?"

¹² And one of them answered and said, "And who is his father?" And therefore it became a proverb, "Is Saul also among the prophets?"

¹³ And he ceased prophesying, and came to the hill.

¹⁴ And his uncle said to him and to his servant, "Where did you go?" And they said, "To look for the donkeys; and we saw that they were lost, and we went in to Samuel."

¹⁵ And his uncle said to Saul, "Tell me, I pray, what did Samuel say to you?"

16 And Saul said to his uncle, "He told me plainly that the donkeys were found." But regarding the kingdom, he did not tell.

Saul Proclaimed King

17 And Samuel summoned all the people before the Lord to Mizpah.

18 And he said to the children of Israel, "Thus has the Lord God of Israel spoken, saying, 'I brought up the children of Israel out of Egypt, and I rescued you out of the hand of Pharaoh king of Egypt, and out of all the kingdoms that afflicted you.

19 And you have this day rejected God, who is Himself your deliverer out of all your evils and afflictions. And you said, "No, but you shall set a king over us." And now stand before the Lord according to your tribes, and according to your families.'"

20 And Samuel brought near all the tribes of Israel, and the tribe of Benjamin was chosen by lot.

21 And he brought near the tribe of Benjamin by families, and the family of Matri was chosen by lot. And they brought near the family of Matri, man by man, and Saul the son of Kish was chosen. And he sought him, but he was not found.

22 And Samuel asked yet again of the Lord, "Will the man come here?" And the Lord said, "Behold, he is hid among the equipment."

23 And he ran and took him from there, and he set him in the midst of the people. And he was taller than all the people from his shoulders and upwards.

24 And Samuel said to all the people, "Have you seen whom the Lord has chosen to Himself, that there is no one like him among you all?" And all the people took notice, and said, "Long live the king!"

25 And Samuel told the people the manner of the king, and wrote it in a book, and set it before the Lord. And Samuel sent away all the people, and each went to his place.

26 And Saul departed to his house in Gibeah. And there went with Saul mighty men whose hearts God had touched.

27 But evil men said, "Who *is* this man *that* shall save us?" And they despised him, and brought him no gifts. ·

1 SAMUEL CHAPTER 11

Saul Defeats the Ammonites

1 And it came to pass about a month after this, that Nahash the Ammonite went up, and encamped against Jabesh Gilead. And all the men of Jabesh said to Nahash the Ammonite, "Make a covenant with us, and we will serve you."

2 And Nahash the Ammonite said to them, "On these terms will I make a covenant with you, that I will put out all of your right eyes, and I will lay a reproach upon Israel."

3 And the men of Jabesh said to him, "Give us seven days, and we will send messengers into all the coasts of Israel. If there should be no one to deliver us, we will come out to you."

4 And the messengers came to Saul at Gibeah, and they spoke the words into the ears of the people; and all the people lifted up their voice, and wept.

5 And behold, Saul came out of the field after the early morning. And Saul said, "Why do the people weep?" And they told him the words of the men of Jabesh.

6 And the Spirit of the Lord came upon Saul when he heard these words, and his anger was greatly kindled against them.

7 And he took two cows, and cut them in pieces, and sent them into all the coasts of Israel by the hand of messengers, saying, "Whosoever does not come forth after Saul and after Samuel, so shall they do to his oxen." And a transport from the Lord came upon the people of Israel, and they came out to battle as one man.

8 And he reviewed them at Bezek in Bama, every man of Israel six hundred thousand, and the men of Judah seventy thousand.

9 And he said to the messengers that came, "Thus shall you say to the men of Jabesh: 'Tomorrow you shall have deliverance when the sun is hot.'" And the messengers came to the city, and told the men of Jabesh, and they rejoiced.

10 And the men of Jabesh said to Nahash the Ammonite, "Tomorrow we will come forth to you, and you shall do to us what seems good in your sight."

11 So it was, on the next day, that Saul divided the people into three companies, and they went into the midst of the camp in the morning watch, and they killed the children of Ammon until the heat of the day. And it came to pass that those who were left were scattered, and there was not left two together among them.

12 And the people said to Samuel, "Who has said that Saul shall not reign over us? Give up the men, and we will put them to death."

13 And Saul said, "No man shall die this day, for today the Lord has brought about deliverance in Israel."

14 And Samuel spoke to the people, saying, "Let us go to Gilgal, and renew the kingdom there."

15 And all the people went to Gilgal, and Samuel anointed Saul there to be king before the Lord in Gilgal, and there he offered grain offerings and peace offerings before the Lord. And Samuel and all Israel rejoiced exceedingly.

1 SAMUEL CHAPTER 12

Samuel's Farewell Address

1 And Samuel said to all Israel, "Behold, I have listened to your voice in all things that you have said to me, and I have set a king over you.

2 And now behold, the king goes before you; and I have grown old and shall rest. And look, my sons are among you; I have gone about before you from my youth to this day.

3 Behold, *here I am*, answer against me before the Lord and before His anointed. Whose calf have I taken? Or whose donkey have I taken? Or who among you have I oppressed? Or from whose hand have I taken a bribe, even as *much as a* sandal? Bear witness against me, and I will make restitution to you."

4 And they said to Samuel, "You have not injured us, and you have not oppressed us; and you have not afflicted us, and you have not taken anything from anyone's hand."

5 And Samuel said to the people, "The Lord is witness among you, and His anointed is witness this day, that you have not found anything in my hand." And they said, *He is* witness.

6 And Samuel spoke to the people, saying, "The Lord who appointed Moses and Aaron is witness, who brought our fathers up out of Egypt.

7 And now stand still, and I will judge you before the Lord; and I will relate to you all the righteousness of the Lord, the things which He has done among you and your fathers.

8 When Jacob and his sons went into Egypt, and Egypt humbled them, then our fathers cried to the Lord, and the Lord sent Moses and Aaron. And they brought our fathers out of Egypt, and He made them to dwell in this place.

9 And they forgot the Lord their God, and He sold them into the hands of Sisera, commander of the army of Jabis, king of Hazor, and into the hands of the Philistines, and into the hands of the king of Moab. And He fought with them.

10 And they cried to the Lord, and said, 'We have sinned, for we have forsaken the Lord, and have served the Baals and the Ashtoreths; and now deliver us out of the hand of our enemies, and we will serve You.'

11 And He sent Jerubbaal, Barak, Jephthah, and Samuel, and rescued us out of the hand of our enemies round about, and you dwelt in security.

12 And you saw that Nahash king of the children of Ammon came against you, and you said, 'No, none but a king shall reign over us'; when the Lord our God is our king.

13 And now, behold the king whom you have chosen; and behold, the Lord has set a king over you.

14 If you should fear the Lord, and serve Him, and listen to His voice, and not resist the mouth of the Lord, and you and your king that reigns over you should follow the Lord, *then well.*

15 But if you should not listen to the voice of the Lord, and you should resist the mouth of the Lord, then shall the hand of the Lord be upon you and upon your king.

16 "And now stand still, and see this great thing, which the Lord will do before your eyes.

17 *Is it* not wheat harvest today? I will call upon the Lord, and He shall send thunder and rain. And know and see, that your wickedness is great which you have done before the Lord, having asked for yourselves a king."

18 And Samuel called upon the Lord, and the Lord sent thunder and rain in that day. And all the people greatly feared the Lord and Samuel.

19 And all the people said to Samuel, "Pray for your servants to the Lord your God, and let us not die; for we have added to all our sins this iniquity, in asking a king for ourselves."

20 And Samuel said to the people, "Do not fear: you have *indeed* done all this wickedness; only do not turn from following the Lord, and serve the Lord with all your heart.

21 And do not turn aside after *the gods* that are nothing, who will do nothing, and will not deliver you, because they are nothing.

22 For the Lord will not cast off His people for His great name's sake, because the Lord graciously took you to Himself for a people.

23 And far be it from me to sin against the Lord in ceasing to pray for you; but I will serve the Lord, and show you the good and the right way.

24 Only fear the Lord, and serve Him in truth and with all of your heart, for you see what great things He has done for you.

25 But if you continue to do evil, then shall you and your king be consumed."

1 SAMUEL CHAPTER 13

Saul's Unlawful Sacrifice

1 (This verse omitted in LXX)

2 And Saul chose for himself three thousand men of the men of Israel. And there were with Saul two thousand who were in Michmash, and in Mount Bethel, and a thousand were with Jonathan in Gibeah of Benjamin. And he sent the rest of the people *away*, every man to his tent.

3 And Jonathan attacked Nasib the Philistine that dwelt in the hill; and the Philistines heard of it, and Saul sounded the trumpet throughout all the land, saying, "The servants have despised us."

4 And all Israel heard it said, "Saul has attacked Nasib the Philistine." Now Israel had been put to shame before the Philistines, and the children of Israel went up after Saul in Gilgal.

5 And the Philistines gathered together to war with Israel; and they came up against Israel with thirty thousand chariots, six thousand horsemen, and people as numerous as the sand on the seashore. And they came up, and encamped in Michmash, opposite Beth Aven towards the south.

6 And the men of Israel saw that they were in a strait so that they could not draw near, and the people hid themselves in caves, sheepfolds, rocks, ditches, and pits.

7 And those that went over crossed the Jordan to the land of Gad and Gilead. And Saul was still in Gilgal, and all the people followed after him in amazement.

8 And he continued seven days for the appointed testimony, as Samuel told him. But Samuel did not come to Gilgal, and his people were dispersed from him.

9 And Saul said, "Bring *some* victims here, that I may offer burnt offerings and peace offerings." And he offered the burnt offering.

10 And it came to pass when he had finished offering the burnt offering, that Samuel arrived, and Saul went out to meet him, and to bless him.

11 And Samuel said, "What have you done?" And Saul said, "Because I saw how the people were scattered from me, and that you were not present as you had purposed according to the set time of the days, and the Philistines were gathered to Michmash.

12 Then I said, 'Now will the Philistines come down to me to Gilgal, and I have not sought the face of the Lord.' So I forced myself and offered the burnt offering."

13 And Samuel said to Saul, "You have done foolishly, for you have not kept my command, which the Lord commanded you, as now the Lord would have confirmed your kingdom over Israel forever.

14 But now your kingdom shall not stand, and the Lord shall seek for Himself a man after His own heart; and the Lord shall appoint him to be a ruler over His people, because you have not kept all that the Lord has commanded you."

15 And Samuel arose and departed from Gilgal, and the remnant of the people went after Saul to meet *him* after the men of war, when they had come out of Gilgal to Gibeah of Benjamin. And Saul numbered the people that were found with him, about six hundred men.

Preparations for Battle

16 And Saul and Jonathan his son, and the people that were found with them, halted in Gibeah of Benjamin, and they wept. And the Philistines had encamped in Michmash.

17 And men came forth in three companies to destroy out of the land of the Philistines; one company turning by the way of Ophrah toward the land of Shual,

18 and another company turning the way of Beth Horon, and another company turning to the road of the border that overlooks the Valley of Zeboim toward the wilderness.

19 And there was not found a blacksmith in all the land of Israel, for the Philistines said, "Lest the Hebrews make themselves swords or spears."

20 And all Israel went down to the land of the Philistines to forge everyone his reaping hook and his tool, and everyone his ax and his sickle.

21 And it was near the time of vintage. And their tools were *valued at* three shekels for a plow share, and there was the same rate for the ax and the sickle.

22 And it came to pass in the days of the war of Michmash, that there was not a sword or spear found in the hand of all the people that were with Saul and Jonathan; but they were found with Saul and Jonathan his son.

23 And there went out some from the camp of the Philistines to the place beyond Micmash.

1 SAMUEL CHAPTER 14

Jonathan Surprises and Routs the Philistines

1 And when a certain day arrived, Jonathan the son of Saul said to the young man that bore his armor, "Come, and let us go over to the garrison of the Philistines that is on the other side"; but he didn't tell his father.

2 And Saul sat on the top of the hill under the pomegranate tree that is in Migron, and there were with him about six hundred men.

3 And Ahijah son of Ahitub, Ichabod's brother, the son of Phinehas, the son of Eli, God's priest in Shiloh, was wearing an ephod. And the people did not know that Jonathan was gone.

4 And at the place in which Jonathan sought to pass over to the the Philistines' camp, there was a sharp rock on both sides of the passage. The name of the one *rock* was Bozez, and the name of the other *was* Seneh.

5 The one way was northward to one coming to Michmash, and the other way was southward to one coming to Gibeah.

6 And Jonathan said to the young man that bore his armor, "Come, let us go over to the garrison of these uncircumcised; *perhaps* the Lord may do something for us, for nothing restrains the Lord from saving by many or by few."

7 And his armorbearer said to him, "Do all that is in your heart: behold, I am with you, my heart is as your heart."

8 And Jonathan said, "Behold, we will go over to the men, and will come down suddenly upon them.

9 If they should say thus to us, 'Wait until we send you word'; then we will stand still by ourselves, and will not go up against them.

10 *But* if they should say thus to us, 'Come up to us'; then will we go up, for the Lord has delivered them into our hands. This *shall be* a sign to us."

11 And they both went in to the garrison of the Philistines. And the Philistines said, "Behold, the Hebrews come forth out of their caves, where they had hidden themselves."

12 And the men of the garrison answered Jonathan and his armorbearer, and said, "Come up to us, and we will show you something." And Jonathan said to his armorbearer, "Come up after me, for the Lord has delivered them into the hands of Israel."

13 And Jonathan went up on his hands and feet, and his armorbearer with him; and they looked on the face of Jonathan, and he struck them, and his armorbearer then killed *them* after him.

14 And the first slaughter which Jonathan and his armorbearer effected was twenty men, with darts and slings, and pebbles of the field.

15 And there was dismay in the camp, and in the field; and all the people in the garrison, and the spoilers were amazed; and they would not act, and the land was terrorstruck, and there was dismay from the Lord.

16 And the watchmen of Saul beheld in Gibeah of Benjamin, and behold, the army was thrown into confusion on every

side. [17] And Saul said to the people with him, Number yourselves now, and see who has gone out from you: and they numbered themselves, and behold, Jonathan and his armorbearer were not found.

[18] And Saul said to Ahijah, "Bring the ephod"; for he wore the ephod in that day before Israel.

[19] And it came to pass while Saul was speaking to the priest, that the sound in the camp of the Philistines continued to increase greatly; and Saul said to the priest, "Withdraw your hands."

[20] And Saul went up and all the people that were with him, and they came to the battle. And behold, every man's sword was against his neighbor, a very great confusion.

[21] And the servants who had been before with the Philistines, who had gone up to the army, turned themselves also to be with the Israelites who were with Saul and Jonathan.

[22] And all the Israelites who were hidden in Mount Ephraim heard also that the Philistines fled; and they also gathered themselves after them to battle. And the Lord saved Israel in that day. And the war passed through Bamoth; and all the people with Saul were about ten thousand men.

[23] And the battle extended itself to every city in the mount of Ephraim.

Saul's Rash Oath

[24] And Saul committed a great trespass of ignorance in that day, and he placed a curse on the people, saying, "Cursed is the man who shall eat bread before the evening; so I will avenge myself on my enemy." And none of the people tasted bread, though all the land was dining.

[25] Now all *the people* of the land came to a forest; and there was honey on the ground.

[26] And the people went into the place of the bees, and behold, they continued speaking; but there was none that put his hand to his mouth, for the people feared the oath *that Saul had made* unto the Lord.

[27] And Jonathan had not heard when his father adjured the people; and he reached forth the end of the staff that was in his hand, and dipped it into the honeycomb, and returned his hand to his mouth, and his countenance was brightened.

[28] And one of the people answered and said, "Your father solemnly adjured the people, saying, 'Cursed is the man who shall eat bread today.'" And the people were very faint,

[29] and Jonathan knew it, and said, "My father has destroyed the land: see how my countenance has brightened *now* that I have tasted a little of this honey.

[30] Surely if the people had this day eaten freely of the spoils of their enemies which they found, the slaughter among the Philistines would have been greater."

[31] And on that day he struck some of the Philistines in Michmash; and the people were very weary.

[32] And the people turned to the spoil; and the people took flocks, and herds, and calves, and killed them on the ground, and the people ate with the blood.

[33] And it was reported to Saul, saying, "The people have sinned against the Lord, eating with the blood." And Saul said, "Roll a large stone to me here."

[34] And Saul said, "Disperse yourselves among the people, and tell them to bring here everyone his calf, and everyone his sheep; and let them kill it on this stone and sin not against the Lord in eating with the blood." And the people brought each one that which was in his hand, and they killed them there.

[35] And Saul built an altar there to the Lord (this was the first altar that Saul built to the Lord).

[36] And Saul said, "Let us go down after the Philistines this night, and let us plunder among them till daybreak, and let us not leave a man among them." And they said, "Do all that is good in your sight." And the priest said, "Let us draw near to God here."

[37] And Saul inquired of God, "If I go down after the Philistines, will You deliver them into the hands of Israel?" And He did not answer him in that day.

[38] And Saul said, "Bring here all the chiefs of Israel, and know and see by whom this sin has been committed this day.

[39] For as the Lord lives who has saved Israel, if *the* answer should be against my son Jonathan, he shall surely die." And there was no one that answered out of all the people.

[40] And he said to all the men of Israel, "You shall be under subjection, and I and Jonathan my son will be under subjection." And the people said to Saul, "Do that which is good in your sight."

[41] And Saul said, "O Lord God of Israel, why have You not answered Your servant this day? Is the iniquity in me, or in Jonathan my son? Lord God of Israel, give clear *manifestations*, and if *the* lot should declare this, give holiness, I pray, to Your people of Israel." And Jonathan and Saul were taken, and the people escaped.

[42] And Saul said, "Cast *lots* between me and my son Jonathan: whomever the Lord shall cause to be taken by lot, let him die." And the people said to Saul, "This thing is not *to be done*." And Saul prevailed against the people, and they cast lots between him and Jonathan his son, and Jonathan was taken by lot.

[43] And Saul said to Jonathan, "Tell me what you have done." And Jonathan told him, and said, "I did indeed taste a little honey, with the end of my staff that was in my hand; and behold, I am to die!"

[44] And Saul said to him, "God do so to me, and more also, you shall surely die today."

[45] And the people said to Saul, "Shall he that has accomplished this great salvation in Israel be put to death this day? *As* the Lord lives, there shall not fall to the ground one of the hairs of his head; for the people of God have done good this day." And the people prayed for Jonathan in that day, and he did not die.

[46] And Saul went up from following the Philistines; and the Philistines departed to their place.

Saul's Continuing Wars

⁴⁷ So Saul received the kingdom. By lot he inherited the office *of ruling* over Israel. And he fought against all his enemies round about, against Moab, against the children of Ammon, against the children of Edom, against Beth Hor, against the king of Zobah, and against the Philistines. Wherever he turned, he was victorious.

⁴⁸ And he did valiantly, and struck Amalek, and rescued Israel out of the hand of them that trampled on him.

⁴⁹ And the sons of Saul were Jonathan, Jishui, and Malchishua. And *these were* the names of his two daughters: the name of the firstborn Merab, and the name of the second Michal.

⁵⁰ And the name of his wife was Ahinoam, the daughter of Ahimaaz. And the name of his captain of the army was Abner, the son of Ner, Saul's uncle.

⁵¹ And Kish was the father of Saul, and Ner the father of Abner was the son of Jamin, son of Abiel.

⁵² And the war was fierce against the Philistines all the days of Saul. And when Saul saw any mighty man, and any valiant man, then he took them to himself.

1 SAMUEL CHAPTER 15

Saul Spares Agag, King of Amalek

¹ And Samuel said to Saul, "The Lord sent me to anoint you king over Israel. And now hear the voice of the Lord.

² Thus said the Lord of hosts, 'Now will I take vengeance for what Amalek did to Israel, when he met him in the way as he came up out of Egypt.

³ And now go, and you shall strike Amalek and Hierim and all that belongs to him, and you shall not save anything of his alive, but you shall utterly destroy him. And you shall devote him and all his possessions *to destruction*, and you shall spare nothing belonging to him; and you shall slay both man and woman, infant and suckling, calf and sheep, camel and donkey.'"

⁴ And Saul summoned the people, and he numbered them in Gilgal, four hundred thousand troops, and Judah thirty thousand troops.

⁵ And Saul came to the cities of Amalek, and laid wait in the valley.

⁶ And Saul said to the Kenite, "Go, and depart out of the midst of the Amalekites, lest I put you with them; for you dealt mercifully with the children of Israel when they went up out of Egypt." So the Kenite departed from the midst of Amalek.

⁷ And Saul struck Amalek from Havilah to Shur, fronting Egypt.

⁸ And he took Agag the king of Amalek alive, and he killed all the people and Hierim with the edge of the sword.

⁹ And Saul and all the people saved Agag alive, and the best of the flocks, and of the herds, and of the fruits, of the vineyards, and of all the good things; and they would not destroy them. But every worthless and despised thing they destroyed.

Saul Rejected as King

¹⁰ And the word of the Lord came to Samuel, saying,

¹¹ "I greatly regret that I have made Saul to be king; for he has turned back from following Me, and has not kept My word." And Samuel was grieved, and cried to the Lord all night.

¹² And Samuel rose early and went to meet Israel in the morning. And it was told Saul, saying, "Samuel has come to Carmel, and he has raised up help for himself." And he turned his chariot, and came down to Gilgal to Saul. And behold, he was offering up a burnt offering to the Lord, the chief of the spoils which he brought out of Amalek.

¹³ And Samuel came to Saul. And Saul said to him, "Blessed are you of the Lord; I have performed all that the Lord has said."

¹⁴ And Samuel said, "What then is this bleating of sheep in my ears, and the sound of the oxen which I hear?"

¹⁵ And Saul said, "I have brought them out of Amalek, that which the people preserved, even the best of the sheep, and of the cattle, that it might be sacrificed to the Lord your God, and the rest I have utterly destroyed."

¹⁶ And Samuel said to Saul, "Stay, and I will tell you what the Lord has said to me this night." And he said to him, "Speak on."

¹⁷ And Samuel said to Saul, "Are you not little in His eyes, *though* a leader of one of the tribes of Israel? And *yet* the Lord anointed you to be king over Israel.

¹⁸ And the Lord sent you on a journey, and said to you, 'Go, and utterly destroy: you shall slay the sinners against Me, even the Amalekites; and you shall war against them until you have consumed them.'

¹⁹ And why did you not listen to the voice of the Lord, but instead swoop down upon the spoils, and do that which was evil in the sight of the Lord?"

²⁰ And Saul said to Samuel, "Because I listened to the voice of the people. Yet I went the way by which the Lord sent me, and I brought Agag the king of Amalek, and I destroyed Amalek.

²¹ But the people took of the spoils, the best flocks and herds out of that which was destroyed, to sacrifice before the Lord our God in Gilgal."

²² And Samuel said, "Does the Lord take *as great a* pleasure in burnt offerings and sacrifices, as *He does* in hearing the words of the Lord? Behold, to obey is better than a good sacrifice, and to heed than the fat of rams.

²³ For sin is as divination; idols bring on pain and grief. Because you have rejected the word of the Lord, the Lord also shall reject you from being king over Israel."

²⁴ And Saul said to Samuel, "I have sinned, in that I have transgressed the word of the Lord and the words you have spoken; for I feared the people, and I listened to their voice.

25 And now remove my sin, I pray, and turn back with me, and I will worship the Lord your God."

26 And Samuel said to Saul, "I will not turn back with you, for you have rejected the word of the Lord, and the Lord will reject you from being king over Israel."

27 And Samuel turned his face to depart, and Saul caught hold of the edge of his robe, and tore it.

28 And Samuel said to him, "The Lord has torn the kingdom of Israel from out of your hand this day, and will give it to your neighbor, who is better than you.

29 And Israel shall be divided in two: and *God* will not turn nor repent, for He is not as a man to repent."

30 And Saul said, "I have sinned; yet honor me, I pray, before the elders of Israel, and before my people; and turn back with me, and I will worship the Lord your God."

31 So Samuel turned back after Saul, and he worshipped the Lord.

32 And Samuel said, "Bring me Agag the king of Amalek." And Agag came to him trembling; and Agag said, "Is death thus bitter?"

33 And Samuel said to Agag, "As your sword has bereaved women of their children, so shall your mother be made childless among women." And Samuel hacked Agag *to pieces* before the Lord in Gilgal.

34 And Samuel departed to Ramah, and Saul went up to his house at Gibeah.

35 And Samuel did not see Saul again till the day of his death, for Samuel mourned after Saul, and the Lord regretted that He had made Saul king over Israel.

1 SAMUEL CHAPTER 16

David Anointed King

1 And the Lord said to Samuel, "How long will you mourn for Saul, seeing I have rejected him from reigning over Israel? Fill your horn with oil, and go; I will send you to Jesse, to Bethlehem; for I have seen among his sons a king for Me."

2 And Samuel said, "How can I go? If Saul hears of it, he will kill me." And the Lord said, Take a heifer in your hand, and you shall say, 'I have come to sacrifice to the Lord.'

3 And you shall call Jesse to the sacrifice, and I will make known to you what you shall do; and you shall anoint him whom I shall name to you."

4 And Samuel did all that the Lord told him; and he came to Bethlehem. And the elders of the city were trembling at meeting him, and said, "Do you come peaceably, O Seer?"

5 And he said, "Peaceably: I have come to sacrifice to the Lord. Sanctify yourselves, and rejoice with me this day." And he sanctified Jesse and his sons, and he called them to the sacrifice.

6 And it came to pass when they came in, that he saw Eliab, and said, "Surely the Lord's anointed is before Him."

7 But the Lord said to Samuel, "Look not on his appearance, nor on his stature, for I have rejected him; for God sees not as man sees; for man looks at the outward appearance, but God looks at the heart."

8 And Jesse called Abinadab, and he passed before Samuel. And he said, "Neither has God chosen this one."

9 And Jesse caused Shammah to pass by. And he said, "Neither has God chosen this one."

10 And Jesse caused his seven sons to pass before Samuel. And Samuel said, "The Lord has not chosen these."

11 And Samuel said to Jesse, "Have you no more sons?" And Jesse said, "*There is* yet a little one; behold, he tends the flock." And Samuel said to Jesse, "Send and fetch him, for we may not sit down till he comes."

12 And he sent and fetched him. And he was ruddy, with beautiful eyes, and very good looking. And the Lord said to Samuel, "Arise, and anoint David, for he is good."

13 And Samuel took the horn of oil, and anointed him in the midst of his brothers. And the Spirit of the Lord came upon David from that day forward. And Samuel arose, and departed to Ramah.

A Distressing Spirit Torments Saul

14 And the Spirit of the Lord departed from Saul, and an evil spirit from the Lord tormented him.

15 And Saul's servants said to him, "Behold now, and evil spirit from the Lord torments you.

16 Let now your servants speak before you, and let them seek for our lord a man skilled to play on the harp; and it shall come to pass when an evil spirit comes upon you, and he shall play on his harp, that you shall be well, and he shall refresh you."

17 And Saul said to his servants, "Now look for me a skillful player, and bring him to me."

18 And one of his servants answered and said, "Behold, I have seen a son of Jesse the Bethlehemite, and he understands playing *on the harp*, and the man is prudent, and a warrior, and wise in speech, and the man is handsome, and the Lord is with him."

19 And Saul sent messengers to Jesse, saying, "Send to me your son David who is with your flock."

20 And Jesse took a homer of bread, and a skin of wine, and one kid of the goats, and sent them by the hand of his son David to Saul.

21 And David went in to Saul, and stood before him. And he loved him greatly, and he became his armorbearer.

22 And Saul sent to Jesse, saying, "Let David stand before me, for he has found favor in my eyes."

23 And it came to pass when the evil spirit was upon Saul, that David took his harp, and played with his hand. And Saul was refreshed, and it was well with him, and the evil spirit departed from him.

1 SAMUEL CHAPTER 17

David and Goliath

¹ And the Philistines gathered their armies to battle, and gathered themselves to Sochoh of Judah, and encamped between Sochoh and Azekah in Ephes Dammin.

² And Saul and the men of Israel gathered together, and they encamped in the valley, and set the battle in array against the Philistines.

³ And the Philistines stood on the mountain on one side, and Israel stood on the mountain on the other side, and the valley was between them.

⁴ And there went forth a mighty man out of the army of the Philistines named Goliath, from Gath, whose height *was* ¹four cubits and a span.

⁵ And *he had* a helmet upon his head, and he wore a breastplate of chain armor; and the weight of his breastplate was five thousand shekels of brass and iron.

⁶ And *he had* bronze armor on his legs, and a bronze shield was between his shoulders.

⁷ And the staff of his spear was like a weaver's beam, and the spear's head *was formed* of six hundred shekels of iron; and his armorbearer went before him.

⁸ And he stood and cried to the army of Israel, and said to them, "Why have you come forth to set yourselves in battle array against us? Am I not a Philistine, and you Hebrews of Saul? Choose for yourselves a man, and let him come down to me.

⁹ And if he shall be able to fight against me, and kill me, then we will be your servants. But if I should prevail and kill him, then you shall be our servants, and serve us."

¹⁰ And the Philistine said, "Behold, I have defied the armies of Israel this very day: give me a man, and we will both of us fight in single combat."

¹¹ And Saul and all Israel heard these words of the Philistine, and they were dismayed, and greatly terrified.

¹² (This verse omitted in LXX)

¹³ (This verse omitted in LXX)

¹⁴ (This verse omitted in LXX)

¹⁵ (This verse omitted in LXX)

¹⁶ (This verse omitted in LXX)

¹⁷ (This verse omitted in LXX)

¹⁸ (This verse omitted in LXX)

¹⁹ (This verse omitted in LXX)

²⁰ (This verse omitted in LXX)

²¹ (This verse omitted in LXX)

²² (This verse omitted in LXX)

²³ (This verse omitted in LXX)

²⁴ (This verse omitted in LXX)

²⁵ (This verse omitted in LXX)

²⁶ (This verse omitted in LXX)

²⁷ (This verse omitted in LXX)

²⁸ (This verse omitted in LXX)

²⁹ (This verse omitted in LXX)

³⁰ (This verse omitted in LXX)

³¹ (This verse omitted in LXX)

³² And David said to Saul, "Let not the heart of my lord be dejected within him: your servant will go, and fight with this Philistine."

³³ And Saul said to David, "You will not in any way be able to go against this Philistine to fight with him, for you are just a youth, and he *is* a man of war from his youth."

³⁴ And David said to Saul, "Your servant was tending the flock for his father, and when a lion came and a bear, and took a lamb out of the flock,

³⁵ that I went forth after him, and killed him, and drew the spoil out of his mouth. And as he rose up against me, then I caught hold of his throat, and struck him, and killed him.

³⁶ Your servant has killed both the lion and the bear, and the uncircumcised Philistine shall be as one of them! Shall I not go and kill him, and remove this day *this* reproach from Israel? For who is this uncircumcised one, who has defied the army of the living God?

³⁷ The Lord who delivered me out of the paw of the lion and out the paw of the bear, He will deliver me out of the hand of this uncircumcised Philistine!" And Saul said to David, "Go, and the Lord shall be with you."

³⁸ And Saul clothed David with his armor, and put his bronze helmet on his head.

³⁹ And he fastened his sword over David's coat. And he tried walking with them once and again, and David said to Saul, "I shall not be able to go with these, for I have not tested them." So they removed them from him.

⁴⁰ And he took his staff in his hand, and he chose for himself five smooth stones out of the brook, and put them in a shepherd's bag, in a pouch which he had, and his sling was in his hand. And he approached the Philistine.

⁴¹ (This verse omitted in LXX)

⁴² And Goliath saw David, and despised him; for he was a lad, and ruddy, with a fair countenance.

⁴³ And the Philistine said to David, "Am I as a dog, that you come against me with a staff and stones?" And David said, "No, but worse than a dog." And the Philistine cursed David by his gods.

⁴⁴ And the Philistine said to David, "Come to me, and I will give your flesh to the birds of the air, and to the beasts of the earth."

⁴⁵ And David said to the Philistine, "You come to me with a sword, and with a spear, and with a shield; but I come to you in the name of the Lord God of hosts, of the army of Israel, which you have defied this day.

⁴⁶ And the Lord shall deliver you this day into my hand, and I will kill you, and take away your head from off of you, and I will give your limbs and the limbs of the army of the Philistines this day to the birds of the sky, and to the wild beasts of the earth; and all the earth shall know that there is a God in Israel.

---

¹ Masoretic text: *4 cubits*. Goliath is 3 feet shorter in LXX.

⁴⁷ And all this assembly shall know that the Lord delivers not by sword or spear, for the battle is the Lord's, and the Lord will deliver you into our hands."

⁴⁸ And the Philistine arose and went to meet David.

⁴⁹ And David stretched out his hand into his bag, and took out a stone, and slung it, and struck the Philistine on his forehead, and the stone penetrated through the helmet into his forehead, and he fell upon his face to the ground.

⁵⁰ (This verse omitted in LXX)

⁵¹ And David ran, and stood upon him, and took his sword, and killed him, and cut off his head. And the Philistines saw that their champion was dead, and they fled.

⁵² And the men of Israel and Judah arose, and shouted and pursued them as far as the entrance to Gath, and as far as the gate of Ashkelon. And the slain men of the Philistines fell in the way of the gates, both to Gath, and to Ekron.

⁵³ And the men of Israel returned from pursuing after the Philistines, and they destroyed their camp.

⁵⁴ And David took the head of the Philistine, and brought it to Jerusalem; but he put his armor in his tent.

⁵⁵ (This verse omitted in LXX)

⁵⁶ (This verse omitted in LXX)

⁵⁷ (This verse omitted in LXX)

⁵⁸ (This verse omitted in LXX)

1 SAMUEL CHAPTER 18

¹ (This verse omitted in LXX)

² (This verse omitted in LXX)

³ (This verse omitted in LXX)

⁴ (This verse omitted in LXX)

⁵ (This verse omitted in LXX)

Saul's Jealousy of David

⁶ And women came out to meet David from all the cities of Israel, singing and dancing, with timbrels, and with rejoicing, and with cymbals.

⁷ And the women began *this song*, and said, "Saul has slain his thousands, and David his ten thousands."

⁸ And it seemed evil in the eyes of Saul concerning this matter, and he said, "To David they have given ten thousands, and to me they have given thousands?"

⁹ (This verse omitted in LXX)

¹⁰ (This verse omitted in LXX)

¹¹ (This verse omitted in LXX)

¹² Now Saul was afraid on account of David.

¹³ And he removed *David* from *before* him, and made him a captain of a thousand for himself; and he went out and came in before the people.

¹⁴ And David was prudent in all his ways, and the Lord was with him.

¹⁵ And Saul saw that he was very wise, and he was afraid of him.

¹⁶ And all Israel and Judah loved David, because he came in and went out before the people.

¹⁷ (This verse omitted in LXX)

¹⁸ (This verse omitted in LXX)

¹⁹ (This verse omitted in LXX)

David Marries Michal

²⁰ And Michal, Saul's daughter, loved David. And it was told Saul, and the thing was pleasing in his eyes.

²¹ And Saul said, "I will give her to him, and she shall be a stumbling block to him." Now the hand of the Philistines was against Saul.

²² And Saul charged his servants, saying, "Speak privately to David, saying, 'Behold, the king delights in you, and all his servants love you. Now therefore, become the king's son-in-law.'"

²³ And the servants of Saul spoke these words in the ears of David. And David said, "*Is it* a light thing in your eyes to become son-in-law to the king? Seeing I am a humble man, and not honorable?"

²⁴ And Saul's servants reported to him according to these words which David spoke.

²⁵ And Saul said, "Thus shall you speak to David: 'The king wants no gift but one hundred foreskins of the Philistines, to avenge himself on the kings enemies.'" Now Saul thought to cast him into the hands of the Philistines.

²⁶ And Saul's servants reported these words to David, and David was well pleased to become the son-in-law to the king.

²⁷ And David arose, and went, he and his men, and killed among the Philistines ¹one hundred men. And he brought their foreskins, and he became the king's son-in-law, and *Saul* gave him Michal his daughter as a wife.

²⁸ And Saul saw that the Lord was with David, and that all Israel loved him.

²⁹ And he was yet more afraid of David.

³⁰ (This verse omitted in LXX)

1 SAMUEL CHAPTER 19

Jonathan Intercedes for David

¹ And Saul spoke to Jonathan his son, and to all his servants, that they should kill David.

² And Jonathan, Saul's son, delighted greatly in David. And Jonathan told David, saying, "Saul seeks to kill you; take heed to yourself therefore tomorrow morning, and hide yourself, and dwell in secret.

³ And I will go forth, and stand near my father in the field where you shall be, and I will speak concerning you to my father; and I will see what his answer may be, and I will tell you."

⁴ And Jonathan spoke favorably concerning David to Saul his father, and said to him, "Let not the king sin against your

---

¹ Masoretic text has *two hundred*

servant David, for he has not sinned against you, and his deeds are very good.

5 And he put his life in his hand, and killed the Philistine, and the Lord brought about a great deliverance. And all Israel saw, and rejoiced. Why then do you sin against innocent blood, to kill David without a cause?"

6 And Saul heeded the voice of Jonathan; and Saul swore, saying, "*As* the Lord lives, he shall not die."

7 And Jonathan called David, and told him all these words; and Jonathan brought David in to Saul, and he was before him as in former times.

8 And there was war again against Saul; and David did valiantly, and fought against the Philistines, and struck them with a very great slaughter, and they fled from before him.

9 And an evil spirit from God was upon Saul, and he was resting in his house, and a spear was in his hand, and David was playing on the harp with his hands.

10 And Saul sought to kill David with the spear; and David withdrew suddenly from the presence of Saul; and he drove the spear into the wall; and David retreated and escaped.

11 And it came to pass in that night, that Saul sent messengers to the house of David to watch him, in order to kill him in the morning. And Michal, David's wife, told him, saying, "Unless you save your life this night, tomorrow you shall be slain."

12 So Michal let David down by the window, and he departed, and fled, and escaped.

13 And Michal took statues, and laid them on the bed, and she put the liver of a goat by his head, and covered them with clothes.

14 And when Saul sent messengers to take David, they said that he was sick.

15 And he sent for David, saying, "Bring him to me on the bed, that I may kill him."

16 And the messengers came, and behold, the statues were on the bed, and the goat's liver was at his head.

17 And Saul said to Michal, "Why have you deceived me like this, and allowed my enemy to depart, and he has escaped?" And Michal said to Saul, "He said, 'Let me go, and if not, I will kill you.'"

18 So David fled, and escaped, and he came to Samuel to Ramah, and told him all that Saul had done to him. And Samuel and David went, and stayed at Naioth in Ramah.

19 And it was told Saul, saying, "Behold, David is at Naioth in Ramah."

20 And Saul sent messengers to take David, and they saw the assembly of the prophets, and Samuel stood as appointed over them; and the Spirit of God came upon the messengers of Saul, and they prophesied.

21 And it was told Saul, and he sent other messengers, and they also prophesied. And Saul sent again a third set of messengers, and they also prophesied.

22 And Saul was very angry, and went himself also to Ramah, and he came as far as the well of the threshing floor that is in Sechu. And he asked and said, "Where are Samuel and David?" And they said, "Behold, at Naioth in Ramah."

23 And he went from there to Naioth in Ramah. Then the Spirit of God came upon him also, and he went on prophesying till he came to Naioth in Ramah.

24 And he took off his clothes, and prophesied before them; and lay down naked all that day and all that night. Therefore they said, "Is Saul also among the prophets?"

1 Samuel Chapter 20

The Friendship of David and Jonathan

1 And David fled from Naioth in Ramah, and came into the presence of Jonathan; and he said, "What have I done, and what is my fault, and how have I sinned before your father, that he seeks my life?"

2 And Jonathan said to him, "Far be it from you! You shall not die! Behold, my father will not do anything great or small without first telling it to me. And why should my father hide this matter from me? This thing is not so."

3 And David answered Jonathan and said, "Your father surely knows that I have found favor in your sight, and he said, 'Do not let Jonathan know this, lest he refuse his consent.' But as the Lord lives, and your soul lives, as I said, there is but *a step* between me and death."

4 And Jonathan said to David, "What does your soul desire, and what shall I do for you?"

5 And David said to Jonathan, "Behold, tomorrow is the new moon, and I shall not on any account sit down to eat, but you shall let me go, and I will hide in the plain till the evening.

6 And if your father in any way inquires about me, then shall you say, 'David earnestly asked leave of me to run to Bethlehem his city, for there is a yearly sacrifice there for all his family.'

7 If he should say, "Fine,"—then all is safe for your servant: but if he should answer harshly to you, know that evil is determined by him.

8 And you shall deal mercifully with your servant; for you have brought your servant into a covenant of the Lord with yourself. And if there is iniquity in your servant, then kill me yourself, for why should you bring me to your father?"

9 And Jonathan said, "Far be it from you! For if I surely know that evil is determined by my father to come upon you, although it should not be against your cities, I will tell you."

10 And David said to Jonathan, "Who can tell me if your father should answer roughly?"

11 And Jonathan said to David, "Go, and stay in the field." And they went out both into the field.

12 And Jonathan said to David, "The Lord God of Israel knows that I will search out my father as I have an opportunity, three times, and behold, *if good* should be determined concerning David, and I do not send to you in the field,

¹³ may God do so to Jonathan and more, also! As I shall also report the evil to you, and make it known to you, and I will let you go; and you shall depart in peace, and the Lord shall be with you, as he was with my father.

¹⁴ And if indeed I continue to live, then shall you deal mercifully with me; and if I indeed die,

¹⁵ you shall not withdraw your mercy from my house forever, And if you do not, when the Lord cuts off the enemies of David, each from the face of the earth,

¹⁶ *should it happen* that the name of Jonathan be discovered by the house of David, then let the Lord seek out the enemies of David."

¹⁷ And Jonathan swore yet again to David, because he loved the soul of him that loved him.

¹⁸ And Jonathan said, "Tomorrow is the new moon, and you will be inquired about, because your seat will be observed as vacant.

¹⁹ And you shall stay three days, and watch an opportunity, and shall come to your place where you may hide yourself in the day of your business, and you shall wait by the stone Ezel.

²⁰ And I will shoot three arrows, aiming them at a mark.

²¹ And behold, I will send a lad, saying, 'Go find me the arrow.'

²² If I should expressly say to the lad, 'The arrow is here, and on this side of you, take it'; then come, for it is well with you, and there is no reason *for fear, as* the Lord lives. But if I should say thus to the young man, 'The arrow is on that side of you, and beyond'; go, for the Lord has sent you away.

²³ And as for the word which you and I have spoken, behold, the Lord is witness between me and you forever."

²⁴ So David hid himself in the field. And the new month arrived, and the king came to the table to eat.

²⁵ And he sat upon his seat as in former times, even on his seat by the wall, and he went before Jonathan. And Abner sat on one side of Saul, but David's place was empty.

²⁶ And Saul said nothing on that day, for he said, "Something has happened to him, and he is not clean, because he has not purified himself."

²⁷ And it came to pass on the next day, on the second day of the month, that David's place was empty; and Saul said to Jonathan his son, "Why has not the son of Jesse attended both yesterday and today at the table?"

²⁸ And Jonathan answered Saul and said to him, "David asked my permission to go to Bethlehem, his city.

²⁹ And he said, Let me go, I pray, for we have a family sacrifice in the city, and my brothers have sent for me. And now, if I have found favor in your eyes, I will go and see my brothers. Therefore he is not present at the table of the king."

³⁰ And Saul was exceedingly angry with Jonathan, and said to him, "You son of a traitorous woman! For do I not know that you are an accomplice with the son of Jesse to yourself, and to the shame of your mother's nakedness?

³¹ For as long as the son of Jesse lives upon the earth, your kingdom shall not be established: now then send and take the young man, for he shall surely die!"

³² And Jonathan answered Saul, "Why is he to die? What has he done?"

³³ And Saul lifted up his spear against Jonathan to kill him, so Jonathan knew that this evil was determined on by his father to kill David.

³⁴ And Jonathan sprang up from the table in great anger, and did not eat bread on the second day of the month, for he grieved bitterly for David, because his father determined *to do evil* against him.

³⁵ And morning came, and Jonathan went out to the field, as he appointed to do for a signal to David, and a little boy *was* with him.

³⁶ And he said to the lad, "Run, find me the arrows which I shoot." And the lad ran, and *Jonathan* shot an arrow, and sent it beyond him.

³⁷ And the lad came to the place where the arrow was which Jonathan shot; and Jonathan cried out after the lad and said, "The arrow is on that side of you, and beyond you."

³⁸ And Jonathan cried out after the lad, saying, "Make haste, and do not delay." And Jonathan's lad gathered up the arrows, and brought the arrows to his master.

³⁹ And the lad knew nothing; only Jonathan and David knew.

⁴⁰ And Jonathan gave his weapons to his lad, and said to his lad, "Go, enter into the city."

⁴¹ And when the lad went in, then David arose from the stone Ezel, and fell upon his face, and bowed down to him three times, and they kissed each other, and wept for each other, for a great while.

⁴² And Jonathan said to David, "Go in peace, and as we have both sworn in the name of the Lord, saying, 'The Lord shall be witness between me and you, and between my descendants and your descendants forever'—*even so let it be.*" And David arose and departed, and Jonathan went into the city.

1 SAMUEL CHAPTER 21

David in Nob

¹ And David came to Nob, to Abimelech the priest. And Abimelech was amazed at meeting him, and said to him, "Why are you alone, and no one is with you?"

² And David said to the priest, "The king gave me a command today, and said to me, 'Let no one know the matter on which I send you, and concerning which I have charged you'; and I have charged my servants to be in the place that is called, 'The Faithfulness of God, Phellani Maemoni.'

³ And now, if you have five loaves, give into my hand what is ready."

4 And the priest answered David and said, "There are no common loaves under my hand, for I have none but holy loaves: if the young men have been kept at least from women, then they shall eat them."

5 And David answered the priest and said to him, "Yes, we have been kept from women for three days: when I came forth for the journey all the young men were purified; but this journey is profane, for it shall be sanctified today on account of my weapons."

6 So Abimelech the priest gave him the showbread; for there were no loaves there, but only the presence loaves which had been removed from the presence of the Lord, in order that hot bread should be set on, on the day on which he took them.

7 And one of Saul's servants was there on that day, detained before the Lord, and his name was Doeg the Syrian, tending the mules of Saul.

8 And David said to Abimelech, "See if you have a spear or a sword here, for I have not brought my sword or my weapons, for the word of the king was urgent."

9 And the priest said, "Behold the sword of Goliath the Philistine, whom you killed in the valley of Elah; and it is wrapped in a cloth. If you will take it, take it for yourself, for there is no other *weapon* except that here." And David said, "Behold, there is none like it; give it to me."

David Flees to Gath

10 And he gave it to him. And David arose, and fled in that day from the presence of Saul. And David came to Achish king of Gath.

11 And the servants of Achish said to him, "Is this not David, the king of the land? Did not the dancing women begin the song to him, saying, 'Saul has killed his thousands, and David his ten thousands?'"

12 And David laid up the words in his heart, and was greatly afraid of Achish king of Gath.

13 And he changed his appearance in that day before *the king*, and pretended to be somebody else; and he pounded on the doors of the city, and used extravagant gestures with his hands, and fell against the doors of the gate, and his saliva ran down upon his beard.

14 And Achish said to his servants, "Behold, you see the man is mad; why have you brought him in to me?

15 Am I in need of madmen, that you have brought him in to me to play the madman? He shall not come into the house!"

1 SAMUEL CHAPTER 22

David and His Followers at Adullam

1 And David departed from there, and escaped. And he came to the cave of Adullam. And his brothers heard, and the house of his father, and they went down to him there.

2 And everyone that was in distress, and everyone that was in debt, and everyone that was troubled in mind gathered to him there, and he was a leader over them, and there were with him about four hundred men.

3 And David departed from there to Mizpah of Moab, and said to the king of Moab, "Let my father and my mother be with you here, until I know what God will do to me."

4 And he persuaded the King of Moab, and they dwelt with him continually, while David was in the stronghold.

5 And Gad the prophet said to David, "Do not dwell in the stronghold: go, and you shall enter the land of Judah." So David went, and came and dwelt in the city of Hereth.

Saul Murders the Priests at Nob

6 And Saul heard that David was discovered, and his men with him. Now Saul dwelt in the hill below the field that is in Ramah, and his spear was in his hand, and all his servants stood near him.

7 And Saul said to his servants that stood by him, "Hear now, you sons of Benjamin, will the son of Jesse indeed give all of you fields and vineyards, and will he make you all captains of hundreds and captains of thousands?

8 For you *are* all conspiring against me, and there is no one that informs me, whereas my son has made a covenant with the son of Jesse, and there is none of you that is sorry for me, or informs me, that my son has stirred up my servant against me for an enemy, as it is this day?"

9 And Doeg the Syrian who was over the mules of Saul answered and said, "I saw the son of Jesse as he came to Nob, to Abimelech son of Ahitub the priest.

10 And the priest inquired of God for him, and gave him provisions, and gave him the sword of Goliath the Philistine."

11 And the king sent to call Abimelech son of Ahitub and all his father's sons, the priests that were in Nob; and they all came to the king.

12 And Saul said, "Hear now, you son of Ahitub." And he said, "Behold, I am here, speak, my lord."

13 And Saul said to him, "Why have you and the son of Jesse conspired against me, that you should give him bread and a sword, and should inquire of God for him, to raise him up against me as an enemy, as he is this day?"

14 And he answered the king and said, "And who is there among all your servants as faithful as David, and he is a son-in-law of the king, and he is executor of all your commands, and is honorable in your house?

15 Have I begun today to inquire of God for him? By no means: let not the king bring a charge against his servant, and against any of my father's house, for your servant knew nothing about these matters, great or small."

16 And King Saul said, "You shall surely die, Abimelech; you and all your father's house."

17 And the king said to the bodyguards that attended on him, "Come here and kill the priests of the Lord, because their hand is with David, and because they knew that he fled, and they did not inform me." But the servants of the king would not lift their hands to fall upon the priest of the Lord.

18 And the king said to Doeg, "Turn, and fall upon the priests." So Doeg the Syrian turned, and killed the priests of the Lord in that day, three hundred and five men, all wearing an ephod.

19 And he struck Nob, the city of the priest, with the edge of the sword, both man and woman, infant and suckling, calf and ox, and also sheep.

20 And one son of Abimelech son of Ahitub escaped, and his name was Abiathar, and he fled after David.

21 And Abiathar told David that Saul had slain all the priests of the Lord.

22 And David said to Abiathar, "I knew it in that day, that Doeg the Syrian would surely tell Saul: I am guilty of the death of the house of your father.

23 Dwell with me; fear not, for wherever I shall seek a place of safety for my life, I will also seek a place for your life, for you are safely guarded while *you are* with me."

1 SAMUEL CHAPTER 23

David Saves the City of Keilah

1 And it was told David, saying, "Behold, the Philistines war in Keilah, and they rob, and they trample on the threshing floors."

2 And David inquired of the Lord, saying, "Shall I go and strike these Philistines?" And the Lord said, "Go, and you shall strike these Philistines, and shall save Keilah."

3 And the men of David said to him, "Behold, we are afraid here in Judea; and how shall it be if we go to Keilah? Shall we go after the spoils of the Philistines?"

4 And David inquired yet again of the Lord; and the Lord answered him, and said to him, "Arise and go down to Keilah, for I will deliver the Philistines into your hands."

5 So David and his men with him went to Keilah, and fought with the Philistines; and they fled from before him, and he carried off their cattle, and struck them with a great slaughter, and David rescued the inhabitants of Keilah.

6 And it came to pass when Abiathar the son of Abimelech fled to David, that he went down with David to Keilah, having an ephod in his hand.

7 And it was told Saul that David had come to Keilah. And Saul said, "God has sold him into my hands, for he is shut up, having entered into a city that has gates and bars."

8 And Saul charged all the people to go down to war to Keilah, to besiege David and his men.

9 And David knew that Saul spoke openly of mischief against him. So David said to Abiathar the priest, "Bring the ephod of the Lord."

10 And David said, "O Lord God of Israel, Your servant has indeed heard, that Saul seeks to come against Keilah to destroy the city on my account.

11 Will *the place* be shut up? And now will Saul come down, as Your servant has heard? Lord God of Israel, tell Your servant." And the Lord said, "It will be shut up."

12 (This verse omitted in LXX)

13 And David arose, and the men with him, in number about four hundred, and they went forth from Keilah, and went wherever they could go. And it was told Saul that David had escaped from Keilah, so he halted the expedition.

David Eludes Saul in the Wilderness

14 And he dwelt in Maserim in the wilderness, in the narrow passes; and dwelt in the wilderness in Mount Ziph, in the dry country. And Saul sought him continually, but the Lord did not deliver him into his hands.

15 And David perceived that Saul went forth to seek him. And David was in the dry mountain in the New Ziph.

16 And Jonathan son of Saul arose, and went to David to New *Ziph*, and strengthened his hands in the Lord.

17 And he said to him, "Do not fear, for the hand of Saul my father shall not find you; and you shall be king over Israel, and I shall be second to you; and Saul my father knows it."

18 So they both made a covenant before the Lord; and David dwelt in New *Ziph*, and Jonathan went to his home.

19 And the Ziphites came up out of the dry country to Saul to the hill, saying, "Behold, is not David hidden with us in Messara, in the narrows in New *Ziph* in the hill of Echela, which is on the right of Jeshimon?

20 And now *according to* all the king's desire to come down, let him come down to us; they have shut him up into the hands of the king."

21 And Saul said to them, "Blessed are you of the Lord, for you have been grieved on my account.

22 Go, I pray, and yet make preparations, and notice his place where his foot shall be, quickly, in that place which you spoke of, lest by any means he should deal craftily.

23 Take notice, then, and learn, and I will go with you. And it shall come to pass that if he is in the land, I will search him out among all the thousands of Judah."

24 And the Ziphites arose, and went before Saul. And David and his men were in the Wilderness of Maon, towards the west, to the right of Jeshimon.

25 And Saul and his men went to seek him. And they brought word to David, and he went down to the rock that was in the Wilderness of Maon. And Saul heard, and followed after David to the wilderness of Maon.

26 And Saul and his men went on one side of the mountain, and David and his men on the other side of the mountain. And David was hiding himself to escape from Saul; and Saul and his men encamped against David and his men, in order to take them.

27 And a messenger came to Saul, saying, "Make haste and come here, for the Philistines have invaded the land!"

28 So Saul returned from following after David, and went to meet the Philistines. Therefore that place was called The Divided Rock.

29 Then David rose up from there, and dwelt in the narrow passes of En Gedi.

1 SAMUEL CHAPTER 24

David Spares Saul

[1] And it came to pass when Saul returned from pursuing after the Philistines, that it was reported to him, saying, "David is in the Wilderness of En Gedi."

[2] And he took with him three thousand men, chosen out of all Israel, and went to seek David and his men in front of Sadiem. [3] And he came to the flocks of sheep that were by the way, and there was a cave there. And Saul went in to make preparation, and David and his men were sitting in the inner part of the cave.

[4] And the men of David said to him, "Behold, this is the day of which the Lord spoke to you, that He would deliver your enemy into your hands; and you shall do to him as it is good in your sight." So David arose and cut off the border of Saul's garment secretly.

[5] And it came to pass after this that David's heart troubled him because he had cut off the border of his garment.

[6] And David said to his men, "The Lord forbid that I should do this thing to my master, the Lord's anointed, to lift my hand against him; for he is the anointed of the Lord."

[7] So David persuaded his men by his words, and did not allow them to rise up and kill Saul. And Saul arose and went his way.

[8] And David rose up and went after him out of the cave. And David cried after Saul, saying, "My lord, O king!" And Saul looked behind him, and David stooped with his face to the ground, and bowed down to him.

[9] And David said to Saul, "Why do you listen to the words of the people, saying, 'Behold, David seeks you life?'

[10] Behold, your eyes have seen this day how that the Lord has delivered you into my hands in the cave. And I would not kill you, but I spared you, and said, 'I will not lift up my hand against my master, for he is the Lord's anointed.'

[11] And behold, the border of your garment is in my hand, I cut off the border, and did not kill you. Know then and see this day, there is no evil in my hand, nor impiety, nor rebellion; and I have not sinned against you, yet you lay snares for my life, to take it.

[12] The Lord judge between me and you, and the Lord vindicate you on yourself. But my hand shall not be upon you.

[13] As the old proverb says, 'Transgression will proceed from the wicked ones'; but my hand shall not be upon you.

[14] And now after whom do you come forth, O king of Israel? After whom do you pursue? After a dead dog, and after a flea? [15] The Lord be judge and umpire between me and you, the Lord look upon and judge my cause, and rescue me out of your hand."

[16] And it came to pass when David had finished speaking these words to Saul, that Saul said, "Is this your voice, *my* son David?" And Saul lifted up his voice, and wept.

[17] And Saul said to David, "You are more righteous than I, for you have recompensed me with good, but I have recompensed you with evil.

[18] And you have told me today what good you have done to me, how the Lord locked me up into your hands today, and you did not kill me.

[19] And if anyone should find his enemy in distress, and should send him forth in a good way, then the Lord will reward him with good, as you have done this day.

[20] And now, behold, I know that you shall surely reign, and the kingdom of Israel shall be established in your hand.

[21] Now then swear to me by the Lord, that you will not destroy my descendants after me, that you will not blot out my name from the house of my father."

[22] So David swore to Saul. And Saul departed to his place, and David and his men went up to the stronghold of Messara.

1 SAMUEL CHAPTER 25

The Death of Samuel

[1] And Samuel died, and all Israel assembled, and lamented him, and they buried him in his house in Ramah. And David arose, and went down to the Wilderness of Maon.

David and Abigail

[2] And there was a man in Maon, and his flocks were in Carmel, and *he was* a very great man; and he had three thousand sheep, and a thousand female goats. And he happened to be shearing his flock in Carmel.

[3] And the man's name *was* Nabal, and his wife's name was Abigail. And his wife *was* of good understanding and very beautiful in appearance. But the man was harsh, and evil in his doings, and the man was foolish.

[4] And David heard in the wilderness that Nabal the Carmelite was shearing his sheep.

[5] And David sent ten young men, and he said to the young men, "Go up to Carmel, and go to Nabal, and ask him in my name how he is.

[6] And thus you shall say, 'May you and your house prosper, and all yours be in prosperity.

[7] And now, behold, I have heard that your shepherds who were with us in the wilderness are shearing your sheep, and we did not hinder them, neither did we demand anything from them all the time they were in Carmel.

[8] Ask your servants, and they will tell you. Let then your servants find grace in your eyes, for we have come on a good day; please give whatsoever your hand may find, to your son David.'"

[9] So the servants came and spoke these words to Nabal, according to all these words in the name of David.

[10] And Nabal sprang up, and answered the servants of David, and said, "Who is David? And who is the son of Jesse? Nowadays there are many servants who depart from *their* masters.

[11] So shall I take my bread, and my wine, and my beasts that I have slain for my shearers, and shall I give them to men of whom I know not who they are?"

[12] So the servants of David turned back and returned, and came and reported to David according to these words.

[13] And David said to his men, "Gird on every man his sword." And they went up after David, about four hundred men. And two hundred stayed with the supplies.

[14] And one of the servants reported to Abigail, Nabal's wife, saying, "Behold, David sent messengers out of the wilderness to greet our master; but he turned away from them.

[15] And the men were very good to us; they did not hinder us, neither did they demand from us anything all the days that we were with them.

[16] And when we were in the field, they were like a wall surrounding us, both night and day, all the days that we were with them feeding the flock.

[17] And now consider what you will do; for mischief is determined against our master and against his house; for he is a son of Belial, and no one can speak to him."

[18] And Abigail made haste, and took two hundred loaves, and two vessels of wine, and five sheep readily dressed, and five ephahs of fine flour, and one homer of dried grapes, and two hundred cakes of figs, and put them upon donkeys.

[19] And she said to her servants, "Go on before me, and I shall come after you." But she did not tell her husband.

[20] And it came to pass when she had mounted her donkey and was going down by the covert of the mountain, that behold, David and his men came down to meet her, and she met them.

[21] And David said, "Perhaps I have kept all his possessions in the wilderness that he should wrong me, and we did not order the taking of anything, of all his goods; yet he has rewarded me evil for good.

[22] So God do to David and more also, if I leave one male of all that belongs to Nabal until the morning."

[23] And Abigail saw David, and she dismounted quickly from her donkey; and she fell before David on her face, and bowed down to him, bowing to the ground,

[24] even to his feet, and said, "On me, my lord, be my wrong. Let your servant speak in your ears, and hear the words of your servant.

[25] Let not my lord take to heart this pestilent man, for according to his name, so is he—Nabal is his name, and folly is with him! But I, your maidservant, did not see the servants of my lord whom you sent.

[26] And now my lord, as the Lord lives, and as your soul lives, as the Lord has kept you from coming against innocent blood and from executing vengeance for yourself, now therefore let your enemies, and those that seek evil against my lord, become as Nabal.

[27] And now accept this token of goodwill, which your servant has brought to my lord, and you shall give it to the servants that wait on my lord.

[28] Remove the trespass of your servant, I pray; for the Lord will surely make for my lord a sure house, for the Lord fights the battles of my lord, and no evil shall ever be found in you.

[29] And if a man shall rise up persecuting you and seeking your life, yet shall the life of my lord be bound up in the bundle of life with the Lord God, and you shall whirl the life of your enemies as in the midst of a sling.

[30] And it shall be when the Lord has brought to pass for my lord all the good things He has spoken concerning you, and shall appoint you to be ruler over Israel,

[31] then this shall not be an abomination and offense to my lord, to have shed innocent blood without cause, and for my lord to have avenged himself. And so may the Lord do good to my lord, and you shall remember your maidservant, to do her good."

[32] And David said to Abigail, "Blessed be the Lord God of Israel, who has sent you this very day to meet me.

[33] And blessed be your conduct, and blessed are you, who has hindered me this very day from coming to shed blood, and from avenging myself.

[34] But surely as the Lord God of Israel lives, who hindered me this day from doing you harm, if you had not hastened and come to meet me, then I said, 'Surely there shall not be one male left to Nabal till the morning.'"

[35] And David took of her hand all that she brought to him, and said to her, "Go in peace to your house: see, I have heeded your voice, and accepted your petition."

[36] And Abigail came to Nabal. And behold, he had a banquet in his house, as the banquet of a king, and the heart of Nabal was merry within him, and he was very drunk. And she told him nothing great or small till the morning light.

[37] And it came to pass in the morning, when Nabal recovered from his wine, that his wife told him these words. And his heart died within him, and he became as a stone.

[38] And it came to pass after about ten days, that the Lord struck Nabal, and he died.

[39] And David heard it and said, "Blessed be the Lord, who has judged the cause of my reproach at the hand of Nabal, and has delivered His servant from the power of evil; and the Lord has returned the mischief of Nabal upon his own head." And David sent and spoke concerning Abigail, to take her to himself for a wife.

[40] So the servants of David came to Abigail to Carmel, and spoke to her, saying, "David has sent us to you, to take you to himself for a wife."

[41] And she arose, and bowed down with her face to the earth, and said, "Behold, your servant is for a maid, to wash the feet of your servants."

[42] And Abigail arose and mounted her donkey, and five maidens followed her. And she went after the servants of David, and became his wife.

[43] And David took Ahinoam out of Jezreel, and they were both his wives.

[44] And Saul gave Michal his daughter, David's wife, to Palti the son of Laish who was of Gallim.

1 SAMUEL CHAPTER 26

David Spares Saul a Second Time

[1] And the Ziphites came out of the dry country to Saul to the hill, saying, "Behold, David hides himself with us in the hill Hachilah, opposite Jeshimon."

[2] And Saul arose, and went down to the Wilderness of Ziph, and with him went three thousand men chosen out of Israel, to seek David in the Wilderness of Ziph.

[3] And Saul encamped in the hill of Hachilah in front of Jeshimon, by the way, and David dwelt in the wilderness. And David saw that Saul came after him into the wilderness.

[4] And David sent spies, and ascertained that Saul had come prepared out of Keila.

[5] And David arose secretly, and went into the place where Saul was sleeping. And Abner the son of Ner was there, the captain of his army. And Saul was sleeping in a chariot, and the people had encamped along around him.

[6] And David answered and spoke to Abimelech the Hittite, and to Abishai the son of Zeruiah, the brother of Joab, saying, "Who will go in with me to Saul into the camp?" And Abishai said, "I will go in with you."

[7] So David and Abishai went in among the people by night. And behold, Saul was fast asleep in the chariot, and his spear was stuck in the ground near his head, and Abner and his people slept round about him.

[8] And Abishai said to David, "The Lord has delivered your enemy into your hands this day, and now I will strike him to the earth with this spear, once *for all*, and I will not have to strike him again."

[9] And David said to Abishai, "Do not kill him, for who shall lift up his hand against the Lord's anointed and be guiltless?"

[10] And David said, "As the Lord lives, the Lord shall strike him, or his day shall come and he die, or he shall go down to battle and be added *to his fathers*.

[11] The Lord forbid that I should lift up my hand against the Lord's anointed. And now take the spear from before his head, and the pitcher of water, and let us return home."

[12] So David took the spear, and the pitcher of water, and they went home. And there was no one that saw, and no one that knew, and there was no one that awoke, they were all asleep, for a stupor from the Lord had fallen upon them.

[13] So David went over to the other side, and stood on the top of a hill afar off, and there was a good distance between them. [14] And David called to the people and spoke to Abner, saying, "Will you not answer, Abner?" And Abner answered and said, "Who are you that calls?"

[15] And David said to Abner, "*Are* you not a man? And who is like you in Israel? Why then do you not guard your lord the king? For one out of the people went in to destroy your lord the king.

[16] And this thing is not good which you have done. As the Lord lives, you are worthy of death, you who guard your lord the king, the Lord's anointed. And now behold, the spear of the king, and the jug of water—where are the articles that should be at his head?"

[17] And Saul recognized the voice of David, and said, "Is this your voice, *my* son David?" And David said, "I am your servant, my lord, O king."

[18] And he said, "Why does my lord thus pursue after his servant? For in what *manner* have I sinned? And what unrighteousness has been found in me?

[19] And now, let my lord the king hear the word of his servant: if God stirs you up against me, let your offering be acceptable; but if *it is* the children of men, *may* they be cursed before the Lord, for they have cast me out this day, that I should not be established in the inheritance of the Lord, saying, 'Go, serve other gods.'

[20] And now let not my blood fall to the ground before the Lord, for the king of Israel has come forth to seek your life, as the night hawk pursues its *prey* in the mountains."

[21] And Saul said, "I have sinned: turn, *my* son David, for I will not hurt you, because my life was precious in your eyes; and today I have been foolish and I have erred exceedingly."

[22] And David answered and said, "Behold, the spear of the king. Let one of the servants come over and take it.

[23] And the Lord shall recompense each according to his righteousness and his truth, since the Lord delivered you this day into my hands, and I would not lift my hand against the Lord's anointed.

[24] And behold, as your life has been precious this very day in my eyes, so let my life be precious before the Lord, and may He protect me, and deliver me out of all affliction."

[25] And Saul said to David, "Blessed are you, my son; and you shall surely do valiantly, and *shall* surely prevail." And David went on his way, and Saul returned to his place.

1 SAMUEL CHAPTER 27

David Serves King Achish of Gath

[1] And David said in his heart, "Now shall I be one day delivered *for death* into the hands of Saul; and there is nothing better for me unless I should escape into the land of the Philistines, and Saul should cease from seeking me through every coast of Israel. So I shall escape out of his hand."

[2] So David arose, and the six hundred men that were with him, and he went to Achish, son of Maoch, king of Gath.

[3] And David dwelt with Achish, he and his men, each with his family; and David and both his wives, Ahinoam the Jezreelitess, and Abigail the wife of Nabal the Carmelite.

[4] And it was told Saul that David had fled to Gath. And he no longer sought after him.

[5] And David said to Achish, "If now your servant has found favor in your sight, let them give me a place in one of the cities in the country, and I will dwell there; for why does your servant dwell with you in a royal city?"

[6] And he gave him Ziklag in that day. Therefore Ziklag has belonged to the king of Judea to this day.

[7] And the number of the days that David dwelt in the country of the Philistines was four months.

[8] And David and his men went up, and made an attack on all the Geshurites and on the Amalekites. And behold, the land was inhabited, (even the land from Shur) by those who come from the fortified cities, even to the land of Egypt.

[9] And he attacked the land, and saved neither man nor woman alive; and they took flocks, herds, donkeys, camels, and clothing; and they returned and came to Achish.

[10] And Achish said to David, "On whom have you made an attack today?" And David said to Achish, "On the south of Judea, and on the south of Jerahmeel, and on the south of the Kenite."

[11] And David saved neither man nor woman alive, to bring them to Gath, saying, "Lest they carry a report to Gath, saying, 'These things David does.'" And this was his manner all the days that David dwelt in the country of the Philistines.

[12] So David had the full confidence of Achish, who said, "He is thoroughly disgraced among his people in Israel and he shall be my servant forever."

1 SAMUEL CHAPTER 28

[1] And it came to pass in those days that the Philistines gathered themselves together with their armies to go out to fight with Israel. And Achish said to David, "Know surely that you shall go forth to battle with me—you, and your men."

[2] And David said to Achish, "Thus now you shall know what your servant will do." And Achish said to David, "So will I make you captain of my bodyguard continually."

Saul Consults a Medium

[3] And Samuel had died, and all Israel lamented for him, and they buried him in his city, in Ramah. And Saul had removed out of the land those who had in them divining spirits, and the wizards.

[4] And the Philistines assembled themselves, and came and encamped in Shunem. And Saul gathered all the men of Israel, and they encamped in Gilboa.

[5] And Saul saw the camp of the Philistines, and he was alarmed, and his heart was greatly dismayed.

[6] So Saul inquired of the Lord, and the Lord answered him neither by dreams, nor by manifestations, nor by prophets.

[7] Then Saul said to his servants, "Seek for me a woman who has in her a divining spirit, and I will go to her, and inquire of her." And his servants said to him, "Behold, *there is* a woman who has in her a divining spirit at Endor."

[8] So Saul disguised himself, and put on different clothing, and he went, and two men with him, and they came to the woman by night. Then he said to her, "Divine to me by the divining spirit within you, and bring up to me him whom I shall name to you."

[9] And the woman said to him, "Behold, you know what Saul has done, how he has cut off those who had divining spirits in them, and the wizards from the land; and why do you spread a snare for my life to destroy it?"

[10] And Saul swore to her, and said, "As the Lord lives, no injury shall come upon you on this account."

[11] And the woman said, "Whom shall I bring up to you?" And he said, "Bring up to me Samuel."

[12] And the woman saw Samuel, and cried out with a loud voice. And the woman said to Saul, "Why have you deceived me? For you are Saul!"

[13] And the king said to her, "Do not fear; tell me, what did you see?" And the woman said to him, "I saw [1]gods ascending out of the earth."

[14] And he said to her, "What did you perceive *it to be?*" And she said to him, "*I see* an upright man ascending out of the earth, and he is clothed with a mantle." And Saul knew that this was Samuel, and he stooped with his face to the earth, and bowed down to him.

[15] And Samuel said, "Why have you troubled me, *to cause* me to ascend?" And Saul said, "I am greatly distressed, and the Philistines war against me, and God has departed from me, and He no longer hearkens to me, either by the hand of the prophets, or by dreams. And now I have called *on* you, to tell me what I shall do."

[16] And Samuel said, "Why do you ask me, seeing the Lord has departed from you, and taken part with your neighbor?

[17] And the Lord has done to you as the Lord has spoken by me; and the Lord will tear the kingdom out of your hand, and will give it to your neighbor David.

[18] Because you did not obey the voice of the Lord, and did not execute His fierce anger upon Amalek, therefore the Lord has done this thing to you this day.

[19] And the Lord shall deliver up Israel with you into the hands of the Philistines, and tomorrow you and your sons with you shall fall, and the Lord shall deliver the army of Israel into the hands of the Philistines."

[20] And Saul instantly fell to the ground, and was greatly afraid because of the words of Samuel; and there was no longer any strength in him, for he had eaten no bread all that day, and all that night.

[21] And the woman went in to Saul, and saw that he was greatly disquieted, and said to him, "Behold now, your maidservant has obeyed your voice, and I have put my life in my hand, and have heard the words which you have spoken to me.

[22] And now hear the voice of your maidservant, and I will set before you a piece of bread, and eat, and you shall be strengthened, for you will be going on your way."

[23] But he would not eat. So his servants and the woman constrained him, and he listened to their voice, and rose up from the earth, and sat upon a bench.

---

[1] Elohim was the original Hebrew word here translated "gods." (Θεους) This could mean magistrates, or spirits.

²⁴ And the woman had a fatted calf in the house; and she hastened and killed it. And she took meal and kneaded it, and baked unleavened cakes.

²⁵ And she brought *the meat* before Saul, and before his servants; and they ate, and rose up, and departed that night.

1 SAMUEL CHAPTER 29

The Philistines Reject David

¹ And the Philistines gathered all their armies to Aphek, and Israel encamped in Endor, which is in Jezreel.

² And the lords of the Philistines came by *the* hundreds and thousands, and David and his men went on in the rear with Achish.

³ And the lords of the Philistines said, "Who *are* these that pass by?" And Achish said to the captains of the Philistines, "*Is* not this David the servant of Saul king of Israel? He has been with us for some time, even this second year, and I have not found any fault in him from the day that he attached himself to me, even until this day."

⁴ And the captains of the Philistines were displeased at him, and they said to him, "Send the man away, and let him return to his place, which you have appointed for him; and let him not come with us to the war, and let him not be a traitor in the camp. And with what will he be reconciled to his master? Will it not be with the heads of those men?

⁵ *Is* not this David whom they celebrated in dances, saying, 'Saul has killed his thousands, and David his ten thousands?'"

⁶ And Achish called David and said to him, "*As* the Lord lives, you *are* right and approved in my eyes, and so is your going out and your coming in with me in the army, and I have not found any evil to charge against you, from the day that you came to me until this day. But you are not approved in the eyes of the lords.

⁷ Now then return and go in peace, thus you shall not do evil in the sight of the lords of the Philistines."

⁸ And David said to Achish, "What have I done to you? And what have you found in your servant from the *first* day that I was before you, even until this day, that I should not come and war against the enemies of the lord my king?"

⁹ And Achish answered David, "I know that you *are* good in my eyes, but the lords of the Philistines have said, "He shall not come with us to the war.

¹⁰ Now then rise up early in the morning, you and the servants of your lord that have come with you, and go to the place that I have appointed for you, and entertain no evil thought in your heart, for you are good in my sight. And rise early for your journey when it is light, and depart."

¹¹ So David arose early, he and his men, to depart and guard the land of the Philistines. And the Philistines went up to Jezreel to battle.

1 SAMUEL CHAPTER 30

David Avenges the Destruction of Ziklag

¹ And it came to pass when David and his men had entered Ziklag on the third day, that Amalek had made an attack upon the south, and upon Ziklag, and besieged Ziklag, and burned it with fire.

² And as to the women and all things that were in it, great and small, they killed neither man nor woman, but carried them away captive, and went on their way.

³ And David and his men came into the city, and behold, it was burned with fire; and their wives, and their sons, and their daughters were carried away captive.

⁴ And David and his men lifted up their voice, and wept till there was no longer any power within them to weep.

⁵ And both of David's wives were carried away captive, Ahinoam, the Jezreelitess, and Abigail the wife of Nabal the Carmelite.

⁶ And David was greatly distressed, because the people spoke of stoning him, because the souls of all the people were grieved, each for his sons and his daughters. But David strengthened himself in the Lord his God.

⁷ And David said to Abiathar the priest the son of Ahimelech, "Bring the ephod here to me."

⁸ And David inquired of the Lord, saying, "Shall I pursue after this troop? Shall I overtake them?" And He said to him, "Pursue, for you shall surely overtake them, and you shall surely rescue the *captives.*"

⁹ So David went, he and the six hundred men with him, and they came as far as the brook Besor, and the extra *men* stopped .

¹⁰ And he pursued them with four hundred men; and two hundred men remained behind, who tarried on the other side of the brook Besor.

¹¹ And they found an Egyptian in the field, and they took him, and brought him to David. And they gave him bread and he ate, and they caused him to drink water.

¹² And they gave him a piece of a cake of figs, and he ate, and his spirit was restored in him; for he had not eaten bread, and had not drunk water three days and three nights.

¹³ And David said to him, "To whom do you *belong*? And where are you from?" And the young man the Egyptian said, "I am the servant of an Amalekite; and my master left me, because I was taken ill three days ago.

¹⁴ And we made an attack on the south of the Cherethites, and on the parts of Judea, and on the south of Caleb, and we burned Ziklag with fire."

¹⁵ And David said to him, "Will you bring me down to this troop?" And he said, "Swear now to me by God, that you will not kill me, and that you will not deliver me into the hands of my master, and I will bring you down upon this troop."

¹⁶ So he brought him down there, and behold, they were scattered abroad upon the surface of the whole land, eating and drinking, and feasting by reason of all the great spoils which they had taken out of the land of the Philistines, and out of the land of Judah.

¹⁷ And David came upon them, and attacked them from the morning till the evening, and on the next day; and not one of them escaped, except four hundred young men, who were mounted on camels, and fled.

¹⁸ And David recovered all that the Amalekites had taken, and he rescued both of his wives.

¹⁹ And nothing was lacking to them, great or small; either of the spoils, or the sons and daughters, or anything that they had taken of theirs. And David recovered all.

²⁰ And he took all the flocks, and the herds, and led them away before the spoils. And it was said of these spoils, "These are the spoils of David."

²¹ And David came to the two hundred men who were left behind, that they should not follow after David, and he had caused them to remain by the brook of Besor. And they came forth to meet David, and to meet his people with him. And David drew near to the people, and they asked him how he did *it*.

²² Then every ill-disposed and bad man of the soldiers who had gone with David, answered and said, "Because they did not pursue together with us, we will not give them of the spoils which we have recovered, only let each one lead away with him his wife and his children, and let them return."

²³ And David said, "You shall not do so, after the Lord has delivered *the enemy* to us, and guarded us, and the Lord has delivered into our hands the troop that came against you.

²⁴ And who will hearken to these your words? For they are not inferior to us; for according to the portion of him that went down to the battle, so shall be the portion of him that abides with the baggage; they shall share alike."

²⁵ And it came to pass from that day forward, that it became an ordinance and a custom in Israel until this day.

²⁶ And David came to Ziklag, and sent of the spoils to the elders of Judah, and to his friends, saying, "Behold, *some* of the spoils of the enemies of the Lord";

²⁷ to those in Bethel, and to those in Ramoth of the south, and to those in Jattir.

²⁸ And to those in Aroer, and to those in Siphmoth, and to those in Saphi, and to those in Eshtemoa, and to those in Gath, and to those in Cimath, and to those in Saphec, and to those in Thimath,

²⁹ and to those in Carmel, and to those in the cities of Jeremeel, and to those in the cities of the Kenite;

³⁰ and to those in Jerimuth, and to those in Beersheba, and to those in Nombe,

³¹ and to those in Hebron, and to all the places which David and his men had passed through.

1 SAMUEL CHAPTER 31

The Death of Saul and His Sons

¹ And the Philistines fought with Israel. And the men of Israel fled from before the Philistines, and they fell down wounded in the mountain in Gilboa.

² And the Philistines pressed closely on Saul and his sons, and the Philistines killed Jonathan, Abinadab, and Malchishua, Saul's sons.

³ And the battle prevailed against Saul, and the archers found him, and wounded him below his ribs.

⁴ And Saul said to his armorbearer, "Draw your sword and pierce me through with it; lest these uncircumcised come and pierce me through, and mock me." But his armorbearer would not, for he feared greatly. So Saul took his sword and fell upon it.

⁵ And his armorbearer saw that Saul was dead, and he also fell upon his sword, and died with him.

⁶ So Saul died, and his three sons, and his armorbearer, together in that same day.

⁷ And the men of Israel who were on the other side of the valley, and those beyond the Jordan, saw that the men of Israel fled, and that Saul and his sons were dead; and they forsook their cities and fled. And the Philistines came and dwelt in them.

⁸ And it came to pass on the next day that the Philistines came to strip the dead, and they found Saul and his three sons fallen on the mountains of Gilboa.

⁹ And they turned him over, and stripped off his armor, and sent it into the land of the Philistines, *and* sending the good news to their idols and to the people.

¹⁰ And they set up his armor at the temple of Ashtoreth, and they fastened his body on the wall of Beth Shan.

¹¹ And the inhabitants of Jabesh Gilead heard what the Philistines had done to Saul.

¹² And they rose up, every man of might, and marched all night, and took the body of Saul and the body of Jonathan his son from the wall of Beth Shan; and they brought them to Jabesh, and burned them there.

¹³ And they took their bones, and buried them in the field that is in Jabesh, and fasted seven days.

THE SECOND BOOK OF SAMUEL

The Report of Saul's Death

¹ And it came to pass after Saul was dead, that David returned from attacking Amelek, and he stayed two days in Ziklag.

² And it came to pass on the third day, that behold, a man came from the camp, from the people of Saul, and his clothes were torn, and dust *was* upon his head. And it came to pass when he went in to David, that he fell upon the earth, and bowed down to him.

³ And David said to him, "Where have you come from?" And he said to him, "I have escaped out of the camp of Israel."

⁴ And David said to him, "What *is* the matter? Tell me." And he said, "The people fled out of the battle, and many of the people have fallen and are dead, and Saul and Jonathan his son are dead."

5 And David said to the young man who brought him the news, "How do you know that Saul and Jonathan his son are dead?"

6 And the young man that brought the news said to him, "By chance I happened to be upon Mount Gilboa; and Saul was leaning upon his spear; and behold, the chariots and the commanders of the cavalry pressed hard upon him.

7 And he looked behind him, and saw me, and called me. So I said, 'Behold, *here* I *am.*'

8 And he said to me, 'Who are you?' And I said, 'I am an Amalekite.'

9 And he said to me, 'Stand over me and kill me, for a dreadful darkness has come upon me, for all my life *is* in me.'

10 So I stood over him and killed him, because I knew he would not live after he had fallen; and I took the crown that was upon his head, and the bracelet that was upon his arm, and I have brought them here to my lord."

11 And David laid hold of his clothes, and tore them; and all the men who were with him tore their clothes.

12 And they lamented and wept, and fasted till evening for Saul, and for Jonathan his son, and for the people of Judah, and for the house of Israel, because they had fallen by the sword.

13 And David said to the young man who brought the news to him, "Where are you from?" And he said, "I am the son of an Amalekite sojourner."

14 And David said to him, "How was it that you were not afraid to lift up your hand to destroy the Lord's anointed?"

15 And David called one of his young men, and said, "Go and fall upon him." And he struck him, and he died.

16 And David said to him, "Your blood *be* upon your own head; for your mouth has testified against you, saying, 'I have slain the anointed of the Lord.'"

17 And David lamented with this lamentation over Saul and over Jonathan his son.

18 And he gave orders to teach it to the sons of Judah: behold, it is written in the Book of the Upright:

19 "Set up a pillar, O Israel, for the slain that have died upon your high places; how the mighty have fallen!

20 Tell it not in Gath, and tell it not as glad tidings in the streets of Ashkelon, lest the daughters of the Philistines rejoice, lest the daughters of the uncircumcised triumph.

21 You mountains of Gilboa, let neither dew nor rain descend upon you, nor fields of firstfruits *be upon you,* for there the shield of the mighty ones has been grievously assailed; the shield of Saul was not anointed with oil.

22 From the blood of the slain, and from the fat of the mighty, the bow of Jonathan did not return empty; and the sword of Saul did not turn back empty.

23 Saul and Jonathan, the beloved and the beautiful, were not divided: comely *were they* in their life, and in their death they were not divided. *They were* swifter than eagles, and they were stronger than lions.

24 Daughters of Israel, weep for Saul, who clothed you with scarlet together with your adorning, who added golden ornaments to your apparel.

25 How the mighty have fallen in the midst of the battle! O Jonathan, even the slain ones upon your high places!

26 I am grieved for you, my brother Jonathan; you were very lovely to me; your love to me was wonderful beyond the love of women.

27 How the mighty have fallen, and the weapons of war perished!"

2 SAMUEL CHAPTER 2

David Anointed King of Judah

1 And it came to pass after this that David inquired of the Lord, saying, "Shall I go up into one of the cities of Judah?" And the Lord said to him, "Go up." And David said, "Where shall I go up?" And He said, "To Hebron."

2 And David went up there to Hebron, *he* and both his wives, Ahinoam the Jezreelitess, and Abigail the wife of Nabal the Carmelite,

3 and the men that were with him, everyone and his family; and they dwelt in the cities of Hebron.

4 And the men of Judah came, and there they anointed David to reign over the house of Judah; and they reported to David, saying, "The men of Jabesh of the country of Gilead have buried Saul."

5 And David sent messengers to the rulers of Jabesh of the country of Gilead, and David said to them, "Blessed are you of the Lord, because you have shown this mercy toward your lord, even toward Saul the anointed of the Lord, and you have buried him and Jonathan his son.

6 And now may the Lord deal in mercy and truth towards you: and I also will repay towards you this good deed, because you have done this.

7 And now let your hands be made strong, and be valiant; for your master Saul is dead, and moreover the house of Judah has anointed me to be king over them."

8 But Abner, the son of Ner, the commander of Saul's army, took Ishbosheth the son of Saul, and brought him up from the camp to Mahanaim;

9 and made him king over the land of Gilead, and over Thasiri, and over Jezreel, and over Ephraim, and over Benjamin, and over all Israel.

10 Ishbosheth, Saul's son *was* forty years old when he reigned over Israel; and he reigned two years, but not over the house of Judah, who followed David.

11 And the days which David reigned in Hebron over the house of Judah were seven years and six months.

The Battle of Gibeon

[12] And Abner the son of Ner went forth, and the servants of Ishbosheth the son of Saul, from Manahaim to Gibeon.

[13] And Joab the son of Zeruiah, and the servants of David, went forth from Hebron, and met them at the Fountain of Gibeon, at the same place: and these sat down by the fountain on this side, and those by the fountain on that side.

[14] And Abner said to Joab, "Let now the young men arise, and compete before us." And Joab said, "Let them arise."

[15] And there arose and passed over by number twelve of the children of Benjamin, belonging to Ishbosheth the son of Saul, and twelve of the servants of David.

[16] And each one grasped the head of his neighbor with his hand, and his sword *was thrust* into the side of his neighbor, and they fell down together: and the name of that place was called The Portion of the Treacherous Ones, which is in Gibeon.

[17] And the battle was very severe in that day; and Abner and the men of Israel were beaten before the servants of David.

[18] Now the three sons of Zeruiah were there, Joab, Abishai, and Asahel: and Asahel was swift in his feet as a wild gazelle in the field.

[19] And Asahel followed after Abner, and turned not to go to the right hand or to the left from following Abner.

[20] And Abner looked behind him, and said, "Are you Asahel?" And he said, "I am."

[21] And Abner said to him, "Turn to the right or to the left, and lay hold for yourself on one of the young men, and take to yourself his armor." But Asahel would not turn back from following him.

[22] And Abner said yet again to Asahel, "Stand away from me, lest I strike you to the ground! And how could I show my face to Joab?

[23] And what is this? Return to Joab your brother!" But he would not stand away; and Abner struck him with the blunt end of the spear on his loins, and the spear went out behind him, and he fell down there and died on the spot. And it came to pass that everyone that came to the place where Asahel fell and died, stood still.

[24] And Joab and Abishai pursued after Abner, and the sun went down. And they went as far as the hill of Ammah, which is in the front of Giah, by the desert way of Gibeon.

[25] And the children of Benjamin who followed Abner gathered themselves together, and they formed themselves into one body, and stood on the top of a hill.

[26] And Abner called Joab and said, "Shall the sword devour perpetually? Do you not know that it will be bitter in the end? How long then will you refuse to tell the people to turn from following our brothers?"

[27] And Joab said, "As the Lord lives, if you had not spoken, surely by morning the people would have given up from following his brother."

[28] And Joab sounded the trumpet, and all the people departed, and did not pursue after Israel, and did not fight any longer.

[29] And Abner and his men departed at evening, *and went* all that night, and crossed over the Jordan, and went along the whole adjacent *country*, and they came to the camp.

[30] And Joab returned from following Abner, and he assembled all the people, and there were missing of the people of David, nineteen men, and Asahel.

[31] And the servants of David struck of the children of Benjamin, of the men of Abner, three hundred and sixty men belonging to him.

[32] And they took up Asahel, and buried him in the tomb of his father in Bethlehem. And Joab and the men with him went all the night, and the morning rose upon them in Hebron.

2 SAMUEL CHAPTER 3

Abner Defects to David

[1] And there was war for a long time between the house of Saul and the house of David; and the house of David grew continually stronger; but the house of Saul grew continually weaker.

[2] And sons were born to David in Hebron: and his firstborn was Ammon the son of Ahinoam the Jezreelitess.

[3] And his second son *was* Daluia, the son of Abigail the Carmelitess; and the third, Absalom the son of Maacah the daughter of Talmai the king of Geshur.

[4] And the fourth *was* Adonijah, the son of Haggith, and the fifth *was* Shephatiah, the son of Abital.

[5] And the sixth *was* Ithream, the son of David's wife Eglah. These were born to David in Hebron.

[6] And it came to pass while there was war between the house of Saul and the house of David, that Abner was governing the house of Saul.

[7] And Saul had a concubine *named* Rizpah, the daughter of Jol; and Ishbosheth the son of Saul said to Abner, "Why have you gone in to my father's concubine?"

[8] And Abner was very angry with Ishbosheth for this saying; and Abner said to him, "Am I a dog's head? I have this day showed kindness with the house of Saul your father, and with his brothers and friends, and have not gone over to the house of David, and do you this day seek a charge against me concerning injury to a woman?

[9] God do thus and more also to Abner, if as the Lord swore to David, so do I not to him this day;

[10] to take away the kingdom from the house of Saul, and to raise up the throne of David over Israel and over Judah from Dan to Beersheba."

[11] And Ishbosheth could not any longer answer Abner a word, because he feared him.

[12] And Abner immediately sent messengers to David, at Thailam where he was, saying, "Make your covenant with

242

me, and behold, my hand *is* with you to bring back to you all the house of Israel."

[13] And David said, "With a good will I will make a covenant with you; only I demand one condition of you: you shall not see my face, unless you bring Michal the daughter of Saul, when you come to see my face."

[14] And David sent messengers to Ishbosheth the son of Saul, saying, "Restore me my wife Michal, whom I took for a hundred foreskins of the Philistines."

[15] And Ishbosheth sent, and took her from her husband, from Paltiel the son of Laish.

[16] And her husband went with her weeping behind her as far as Bahurim. And Abner said to him, "Go, return"; and he returned.

[17] And Abner spoke to the elders of Israel, saying, "In former days you sought David to reign over you;

[18] and now perform *it*; for the Lord has spoken concerning David, saying, 'By the hand of My servant David I will save Israel out of the hand of all their enemies.'"

[19] And Abner spoke in the ears of Benjamin. And Abner went to speak in the ears of David at Hebron, all that seemed good in the eyes of Israel and in the eyes of the house of Benjamin.

[20] And Abner came to David at Hebron, and twenty men with him. And David made a banquet of wine for Abner and his men with him.

[21] Then Abner said to David, "I will arise now and go, and gather to my lord the king all of Israel; and I will make a covenant with him, and you shall reign over all whom your soul desires." And David sent Abner away, and he departed in peace.

Abner is Killed by Joab

[22] And behold, the servants of David and Joab arrived from their expedition, and they brought much spoil with them. And Abner was not with David in Hebron, because he had sent him away, and he had departed in peace.

[23] Now Joab and all his army came, and it was reported to Joab, saying, "Abner the son of Ner has come to David, and David has let him go, and he has departed in peace."

[24] And Joab went in to the king, and said, "What *is* this you have done? Behold, Abner came to you; and why have you let him go, and he has departed in peace?

[25] Surely you know the mischief of Abner the son of Ner, that he came to deceive you, and to know your going out and your coming in, and to know all things that you are doing?"

[26] And Joab returned from David, and sent messengers to Abner after *him*; and they brought him back from the Well of Sirah, but David was unaware.

[27] And he brought back Abner to Hebron, and Joab caused him to turn aside from the gate to speak to him, laying wait for him; and he stabbed him there in the stomach, and he died for the blood of Asahel the brother of Joab.

[28] And David heard *of it* afterwards, and said, "I and my kingdom are guiltless before the Lord, even forever, of the blood of Abner the son of Ner.

[29] Let it fall upon the head of Joab, and upon all the house of his father; and let there not be wanting of the house of Joab one that has an issue, or a leper, or that leans on a staff, or that falls by the sword, or that is in need of bread."

[30] For Joab and Abishai his brother laid wait continually for Abner, because he slew Asahel their brother at Gibeon in the battle.

[31] And David said to Joab and to all the people with him, "Tear your clothes, and put on sackcloth, and lament over Abner." And King David followed the coffin.

[32] And they buried Abner in Hebron. And the king lifted up his voice, and wept at his tomb, and all the people wept for Abner.

[33] And the king mourned over Abner, and said, "Shall Abner die according to the death of Nabal?

[34] Your hands were not bound, and your feet *were* not *put* in fetters; *one* brought *you* not near as Nabal; you have fallen before children of iniquity."

[35] And all the people assembled to weep for him. And all the people came to cause David to eat bread while it was yet day. And David swore, saying, "God do so to me, and more also, if I eat bread or anything else before the sun goes down."

[36] And all the people took notice, and all things that the king did before the people were pleasing in their sight.

[37] So all the people and all Israel perceived in that day, that it was not of the king to slay Abner the son of Ner.

[38] And the king said to his servants, "Do you not know that a great prince has fallen this day in Israel?

[39] And that I am this day a *mere* kinsman *of his*, and *as it were* a subject; but these men the sons of Zeruiah are too harsh for me: the Lord reward the evildoer according to his wickedness."

2 SAMUEL CHAPTER 4

Ishbosheth Assassinated

[1] And Ishbosheth the son of Saul heard that Abner the son of Ner had died in Hebron; and his hands were paralyzed, and all the men of Israel grew faint.

[2] And Ishbosheth the son of Saul had two men that were captains of bands: the name of the one *was* Baanah, and the name of the other *was* Rechab, sons of Rimmon the Berothite of the children of Benjamin; for Beeroth was reckoned to the children of Benjamin.

[3] And the Berothites ran away to Gittaim, and were sojourners there until this day.

[4] And Jonathan, Saul's son, *had* a son lame of his feet, five years old, and he was *in the way* when the news of Saul and Jonathan his son came from Jezreel, and his nurse took him up, and fled. And it came to pass as he made haste and

retreated, that he fell, and was crippled. And his name *was* Mephibosheth.

5 And Rechab and Baanah, the sons of Rimmon the Berothite set out, and they came in the heat of the day into the house of Ishbosheth; and he was sleeping on a bed at noon.

6 And behold, the porter of the house winnowed wheat, and he slumbered and slept. And the brothers Rechab and Baanah went secretly into the house.

7 And Ishbosheth was sleeping on his bed in his chamber. And they struck him, and killed him, and took off his head. And they took his head, and traveled all night by the western road.

8 And they brought the head of Ishbosheth to David at Hebron, and they said to the king, "Behold the head of Ishbosheth the son of Saul your enemy, who sought your life; and the Lord has executed vengeance on His enemies for my lord the king, as *it is* this day: even on Saul your enemy, and on his descendants."

9 And David answered Rechab and Baanah his brother, the sons of Rimmon the Berothite, and said to them, "*As* the Lord lives, who has redeemed my soul out of all affliction;

10 he that reported to me that Saul was dead, even he was as one bringing good news before me. But I seized him and killed him in Ziklag, to whom I ought, *as he thought,* to have given a reward for his news.

11 And now evil men have slain a righteous man in his house, *and* upon his bed. Now then, I will require his blood from your hand, and I will destroy you from off the earth."

12 And David commanded his young men, and they killed them, and cut off their hands and their feet; and they hung them up at the fountain in Hebron. And they buried the head of Ishbosheth in the tomb of Abner the son of Ner.

2 SAMUEL CHAPTER 5

David Anointed King of All Israel

1 And all the tribes of Israel came to David to Hebron, and they said to him, "Behold, we *are* your bone and your flesh.

2 And before, when Saul was king over us, you were the one who led Israel out and brought them in; and the Lord said to you, 'You shall feed My people Israel, and you shall be for a leader to My people Israel.'"

3 And all the elders of Israel come to the king at Hebron. And King David made a covenant with them at Hebron before the Lord; and they anointed David king over all Israel.

4 David *was* thirty years old when he began to reign, and he reigned forty years.

5 Seven years and six months he reigned in Hebron over Judah, and thirty-three years he reigned over all Israel and Judah in Jerusalem.

6 And David and his men departed to Jerusalem, to the Jebusites that inhabited the land. And it was said to David,

"You shall not come in here (for the blind and the lame withstood him, saying, 'David shall not come in here).'"

7 And David first took hold of Zion (that *is*, the City of David).

8 And David said on that day, "Everyone that attacks the Jebusites, let him attack with the dagger both the lame and the blind, and those that hate the soul of David." Therefore they said, "The lame and the blind shall not enter into the house of the Lord."

9 And David dwelt in the stronghold, and it was called the City of David, and he built the city itself round about from the citadel, and *he built* his own house.

10 And David advanced and became great, and the Lord Almighty *was* with him.

11 And Hiram king of Tyre sent messengers to David, and cedar wood, and carpenters, and stone masons; and they built a house for David.

12 And David knew that the Lord had prepared him to be king over Israel, and that his kingdom was exalted for the sake of His people Israel.

13 And David took again wives and concubines out of Jerusalem, after he came from Hebron: and David had still more sons and daughters born to him.

14 And these *are* the names of those that were born to him in Jerusalem: Shammua, Shobab, Nathan, Solomon,

15 Ibhar, Elishua, Nepheg, Japhia,

16 Elishama, Eliada, and Eliphelet.

Philistine Attack Repulsed

17 And the Philistines heard that David was anointed king over Israel; and all the Philistines went up to seek David. And David heard of it, and went down to the stronghold.

18 And the Philistines came, and assembled in the Valley of Giants.

19 And David inquired of the Lord, saying, "Shall I go up against the Philistines? And will You deliver them into my hands?" And the Lord said to David, "Go up, for I will surely deliver the Philistines into your hands."

20 And David came from the Upper Breaches, and attacked the Philistines there. And David said, "The Lord has destroyed the hostile Philistines from before me, as water is dispersed." Therefore the name of that place was called Over Breaches. 21 And they left their gods there, and David and his men took them.

22 And the Philistines came up yet again, and assembled in the Valley of Giants.

23 And David inquired of the Lord. And the Lord said, "You shall not go up to meet them: turn from them, and you shall meet them near the Place of Weeping."

24 And it shall come to pass when you hear the sound of a clashing together from the Grove of Weeping, then you shall go down to them, for then the Lord shall go forth before you to create havoc in the battle with the Philistines."

25 And David did as the Lord commanded him, and struck the Philistines from Gibeon as far as the land of Gezer.

2 SAMUEL CHAPTER 6

The Ark Brought to Jerusalem

¹ And David again gathered all the young men of Israel, about seventy thousand.

² And David arose and went, he and all the people that were with him, and some of the rulers of Judah, on an expedition *to a distant place*, to bring back from there the ark of God, upon which is called the name of the Lord of hosts who dwells between the cherubim.

³ And they put the ark of the Lord on a new cart, and took it out of the house of Abinadab who lived on the hill, and Uzzah and his brothers, the sons of Abinadab drove the cart with the ark.

⁴ And his brothers went before the ark.

⁵ And David and the children of Israel *were* playing before the Lord on well-tuned instruments mightily, and with songs, and with harps, and with lutes, and with drums, and with cymbals, and with pipes.

⁶ And they came as far as the threshing floor of Nachon. And Uzzah reached forth his hand to the ark of God to keep it steady, and took hold of it; for the ox shook it out of its place.

⁷ And the Lord was very angry with Uzzah, and God struck him there; and he died there by the ark of the Lord before God.

⁸ And David was dispirited because the Lord made a breach upon Uzzah; and that place was called the Breach of Uzzah until this day.

⁹ And David feared the Lord in that day, saying, "How shall the ark of the Lord come in to me?"

¹⁰ And David would not bring in the ark of the covenant of the Lord to himself into the City of David; and David turned it aside into the house of Obed-Edom the Gittite.

¹¹ And the ark of the Lord lodged in the house of Obed-Edom the Gittite for three months, and the Lord blessed all the house of Obed-Edom, and all his possessions.

¹² And it was reported to King David, saying, "The Lord has blessed the house of Obed-Edom, and all that he has, because of the ark of the Lord." And David went, and brought up the ark of the Lord from the house of Obed-Edom to the City of David with gladness.

¹³ And seven bands were with him bearing the ark, and for a sacrifice *there was* a calf, and lambs.

¹⁴ And David sounded with well-tuned instruments before the Lord, and David *was* clothed with a fine long robe.

¹⁵ And David and all the house of Israel brought up the ark of the Lord with shouting, and with the sound of a trumpet.

¹⁶ And it came to pass as the ark arrived at the City of David, that Michal the daughter of Saul looked through the window, and saw King David dancing and playing before the Lord; and she despised him in her heart.

¹⁷ And they brought the ark of the Lord, and set it in its place in the midst of the tabernacle which David pitched for it. And David offered burnt offerings before the Lord, *and* peace offerings.

¹⁸ And David made an end of offering the burnt offerings and peace offerings, and blessed the people in the name of the Lord of hosts.

¹⁹ And he distributed to all the people, even to all the host of Israel, from Dan to Beersheba, both men and women, to everyone a cake of bread, and a piece of meat, and a cake from the frying pan. And all the people departed, everyone to his home.

²⁰ And David returned to bless his house. And Michal the daughter of Saul came out to meet David and greeted him, and said, "How was the king of Israel glorified today, who was today uncovered in the eyes of the handmaids of his servants, as one of the dancers wantonly uncovers himself!"

²¹ And David said to Michal, "I will dance before the Lord. Blessed *be* the Lord who chose me before your father, and before all his house, to make me head over His people, even over Israel. Therefore I will play and dance before the Lord.

²² And I will again uncover myself thus, and I will be vile in your eyes, and with the maid servants by whom you said that I was not held in honor."

²³ And Michal the daughter of Saul had no child till the day of her death.

2 SAMUEL CHAPTER 7

God's Covenant with David

¹ And it came to pass when the king sat in his house, and the Lord had given him an inheritance on every side *free* from all his enemies round about him;

² that the king said to Nathan the prophet, "Behold now, I live in a house of cedar, and the ark of the Lord dwells in the midst of a tent."

³ And Nathan said to the king, "Go and do all that *is* in your heart, for the Lord *is* with you."

⁴ And it came to pass in that night, that the word of the Lord came to Nathan, saying,

⁵ "Go, and say to My servant David, 'Thus says the Lord: "You shall not build Me a house to dwell in.

⁶ For I have not dwelt in a house from the day that I brought up the children of Israel out of Egypt to this day, but I have been walking about in a lodging and in a tent,

⁷ wheresoever I went with all Israel. Have I ever spoken to any of the tribes of Israel, which I commanded to tend My people Israel, saying, 'Why have you not built Me a house of Cedar?'

⁸ And now thus shall you say to My servant David: 'Thus says the Lord Almighty: "I took you from the sheepfold, that you should be a prince over My people, over Israel.

⁹ And I was with you wherever you went, and I destroyed all your enemies before you, and I made you renowned according to the renown of the great ones on the earth.

¹⁰ And I will appoint a place for My people Israel, and I will plant them, and they shall dwell by themselves, and shall be distressed no longer; and the son of iniquity shall afflict them no longer, as he *has done* from the beginning,

¹¹ from the days when I appointed judges over My people Israel: and I will give you rest from all your enemies, and the Lord declares to you, that He shall build you a house.

¹² And it shall come to pass when your days have been fulfilled, and you sleep with your fathers, that I will raise up your descendants after you, even from your own body, and I will establish his kingdom.

¹³ He shall build for Me a house for My name, and I will set up his throne, even forever.

¹⁴ I will be to him a father, and he shall be to Me a son. And when he happens to transgress, then will I chasten him with the rod of men, and with the stripes of the sons of men.

¹⁵ But My mercy I will not take from him, as I took it from those whom I removed from My presence.

¹⁶ And his house shall be made sure, and his kingdom forever before Me, and his throne shall be established forever.""

¹⁷ According to all these words, and according to all this vision, so Nathan spoke to David.

David's Thanksgiving to God

¹⁸ Then King David came in, and sat before the Lord, and said, "Who am I, O Lord, my Lord, and what *is* my house, that You have loved me *like* this?

¹⁹ Whereas I was very little before You, O Lord, my Lord, yet You spoke concerning the house of Your servant for a long time *to come*. And *is* this the law of man, O Lord, my Lord?

²⁰ And what shall David yet say to You? And now You know Your servant, O Lord, my Lord.

²¹ And You have wrought for Your servant's sake, and according to Your heart You have brought about all this greatness, to make it known to Your servant,

²² that he may magnify You, O my Lord; for there is none like You, and there is no God but You among all of whom we have heard with our ears.

²³ And what other nation in the earth *is* like Your people Israel? Whereas God was his guide, to redeem for Himself a people, to make for Himself a name, to do mightily and nobly, so that You should cast out nations and *their* tabernacles from the presence of Your people, whom You redeemed for Yourself out of Egypt?

²⁴ And You have prepared for Yourself Your people Israel, to be a people forever, and You, O Lord, have become their God.

²⁵ And now, O my Lord, the Almighty Lord God of Israel, confirm the word forever which You have spoken concerning Your servant and his house: and now as You have said,

²⁶ Let Your name be magnified forever.

²⁷ Almighty Lord God of Israel, You have uncovered the ear of Your servant, saying, 'I will build you a house': therefore Your servant has found *in* his heart to pray this prayer to You.

²⁸ And now, O Lord my Lord, You are God; and Your words will be true, and You have spoken these good things concerning Your servant.

²⁹ And now begin and bless the house of Your servant, that it may continue forever before You; for You, O Lord, my Lord, have spoken, and the house of Your servant shall be blessed with Your blessing, so as to continue forever."

2 SAMUEL CHAPTER 8

David's Wars

¹ And it came to pass after this, that David attacked the Philistines, and put them to flight, and David took the tribute from out of the hand of the Philistines.

² Then David attacked Moab, and measured them out with lines, having laid them down on the ground. And there were two lines for slaying, and two lines he kept alive. And Moab became servants to David, yielding tribute.

³ Then David attacked Hadadezer the son of Rehob king of Zobah, as he went to extend his power to the River Euphrates.

⁴ And David took a thousand of his chariots, and seven thousand horsemen, and twenty thousand footmen: and David hamstrung all his chariot *horses*, but he reserved for himself a hundred chariots.

⁵ And Syria of Damascus came to help Hadadezer king of Zobah, and David struck down twenty-two thousand of the Syrians.

⁶ And David placed a garrison in Syria near Damascus, and the Syrians became servants and tributaries to David. And the Lord preserved David wherever he went.

⁷ And David took the golden bracelets which were on the servants of Hadadezer king of Zobah, and brought them to Jerusalem. And Susakim king of Egypt took them, when he went up to Jerusalem in the days of Rehoboam son of Solomon.

⁸ And King David took from Masbak, and from the choice cities of Hadadezer, very much brass; with that Solomon made the bronze sea, and the pillars, and the lavers, and all the furniture.

⁹ And Toi the king of Hemath heard that David had defeated all the armies of Hadadezer.

¹⁰ And Toi sent Joram his son to King David, to ask about his health, and to congratulate him on his fighting against Hadadezer and for attacking him, for he was an enemy to Hadadezer: and in his hands were vessels of silver, and vessels of gold, and vessels of brass.

¹¹ And these King David consecrated to the Lord, with the silver and the gold with which he consecrated out of all the cities which he conquered,

¹² out of Edom and out of Moab, and from the children of Ammon, and from the Philistines, and from Amelek, and from the spoils of Hadadezer son of Rehob king of Zobah.

¹³ And David made *himself* a name. And when he returned he struck Edom in Gebelem to *the number of* eighteen thousand.

¹⁴ And he set garrisons in Edom, even in all Edom: and all the Edomites were servants to the king. And the Lord preserved David wherever he went.

David's Administration

¹⁵ And David reigned over all of Israel: and David brought about judgment and justice over all his people.

¹⁶ And Joab the son of Zeruiah *was* over the army; and Jehoshaphat the son of Ahilud *was keeper* of the records.

¹⁷ And Zadok the son of Ahitub, and Ahimelech son of Abiathar, *were* priests; and Seraiah *was* the scribe,

¹⁸ and Benaiah son of Jehoida *was* counselor, and the Cherethite and the Pelethite and the sons of David were princes of the court.

2 SAMUEL CHAPTER 9

David's Kindness to Mephibosheth

¹ And David said, "Is there yet anyone left from the house of Saul, that I may deal kindly with him for Jonathan's sake?"

² And there was a servant of the house of Saul, and his name was Ziba. And they brought him to David. And the king said to him, "Are you Ziba?" And he said, "I *am* your servant."

³ And the king said, "Is there yet a man left of the house of Saul, that I may act towards him with the mercy of God?" And Ziba said to the king, "There is yet a son of Jonathan, lame *in* his feet."

⁴ And the king said, "Where *is* he?" And Ziba said to the king, "Behold, *he is* in the house of Machir the son of Ammiel of Lo Debar."

⁵ And King David went, and took him out of the house of Machir the son of Ammiel of Lo Debar.

⁶ And Mephibosheth the son of Jonathan the son of Saul came to King David, and he fell upon his face and bowed down before him. And David said to him, "Mephibosheth"; and he said, "Behold your servant."

⁷ And David said to him, "Do not fear, for I will surely deal mercifully with you for the sake of Jonathan your father, and I will restore to you all the land of Saul your grandfather; and you shall eat bread at my table continually."

⁸ And Mephibosheth bowed down and said, "Who is your servant, that you have looked upon a dead dog such as me?"

⁹ And the king called Ziba the servant of Saul, and said to him, "All that belonged to Saul and to all his house have I given to the son of your lord.

¹⁰ And you, your sons, and your servants shall till the land for him; and you shall bring in bread to the son of your lord, and he shall eat bread; and Mephibosheth the son of your lord shall eat bread continually at my table." Now Ziba had fifteen sons and twenty servants.

¹¹ And Ziba said to the king, "According to all that my lord the king has commanded his servant, so will your servant do." So Mephibosheth ate at the table of David, as one of the sons of the king.

¹² And Mephibosheth had a little son, and his name *was* Micha: and all the household of Ziba *were* servants to Mephibosheth.

¹³ And Mephibosheth dwelt in Jerusalem, for he continually ate at the table of the king; and he was lame in both of his feet.

2 SAMUEL CHAPTER 10

The Ammonites and Syrians Defeated

¹ And it came to pass after this that the king of the children of Ammon died, and Hanun his son reigned in his place.

² And David said, "I will show mercy to Hanun the son of Nahash, as his father dealt mercifully with me." And David sent to comfort him concerning his father by the hand of his servants; and the servants of David came into the land of the children of Ammon.

³ And the princes of the children of Ammon said to Hanun their lord, "*Is it* to honor your father before you that David has sent comforters to you? Has not David rather sent his servants to you, that they should search the city, and spy it out and examine it?"

⁴ And Hanun took the servants of David, and shaved their beards, and cut off their garments in the middle, and sent them away.

⁵ And they brought David word concerning the men; and he sent to meet them, for the men were greatly dishonored. And the king said, "Remain in Jericho till your beards have grown, and *then* you shall return."

⁶ And the children of Ammon saw that the people of David were ashamed; and the children of Ammon sent and hired the Syrians of Beth Rehob, and the Syrians of Zoba, and Rehob, twenty thousand footmen, and the king of Amelek with a thousand men, and Ish-Tob with twelve thousand men.

⁷ And David heard, and sent Joab and all of his army, *even* the mighty men.

⁸ And the children of Ammon went forth, and set the battle in array by the door of the gate. *Those* of Syria—Zobah, Rehob, Ish-Tob, and Amelek, being by themselves in the field.

⁹ And Joab saw that the battle was against him, both in front and from behind, and he chose out *some* of all the young men of Israel, and they set themselves in array against Syria.

¹⁰ And the rest of the people he gave into the hand of Abishai his brother, and they set the battle in array opposite to the children of Ammon.

¹¹ And he said, "If Syria is too strong for me, then shall you help me: and if the children of Ammon are too strong for you, then will we be ready to help you.

¹² Be courageous, and let us be strong for our people, and for the sake of the cities of our God, and the Lord shall do that which is good in His eyes."

¹³ And Joab and his people with him advanced to battle against Syria, and they fled from before him.

¹⁴ And the children of Ammon saw that the Syrians had fled, and they fled from before Abishai, and entered into the city. And Joab returned from the children of Ammon, and came to Jerusalem.

¹⁵ And the Syrians saw that they were defeated before Israel, and they gathered themselves together.

¹⁶ And Hadadezer sent and gathered the Syrians from the other side of the River Halamak, and they came to Helam; and Shobach the captain of the army of Hadadezer *was* at their head.

¹⁷ And it was reported to David, and he gathered all Israel and went over the Jordan, and came to Helam; and the Syrians set the battle in array against David, and fought with him.

¹⁸ And Syria fled from before Israel, and David destroyed of the Syrians seven hundred chariots, and forty thousand horsemen, and he struck Shobach the captain of his army, and he died there.

¹⁹ And all the kings *who were* servants of Hadadezer saw that they were defeated before Israel, and they went over to Israel, and served them: and Syria was afraid to help the children of Ammon anymore.

2 SAMUEL CHAPTER 11

David Commits Adultery with Bathsheba

¹ And it came to pass, when the time of year had come for kings to go out *to battle*, that David sent Joab, and his servants with him, and all Israel; and they destroyed the children of Ammon, and besieged Rabbath; but David remained at Jerusalem.

² And it came to pass toward evening, that David arose from his couch, and walked on the roof of the king's house, and saw from the roof a woman bathing; and the woman was very beautiful to look upon.

³ And David sent and inquired about the woman. And *one* said, "*Is* not this Bathsheba the daughter of Eliab, the wife of Uriah the Hittite?"

⁴ And David sent messengers, and took her, and went in to her, and he lay with her. And she was purified from her uncleanness, and returned to her house.

⁵ And the woman conceived; and she sent and told David, and said, "I am pregnant."

⁶ And David sent to Joab, saying, "Send me Uriah the Hittite." And Joab sent Uriah to David.

⁷ And Uriah arrived and went in to him, and David asked him how Joab was, and how the people were, and how the war was going.

⁸ And David said to Uriah, "Go to your house, and wash your feet." And Uriah departed from the house of the king, and a portion *of meat* from the king followed him.

⁹ And Uriah slept at the door of the king with the servants of his lord, and did not go down to his house.

¹⁰ And they brought David word, saying, "Uriah has not gone down to his house." And David said to Uriah, "Have you not come from a *long* journey? Why have you not gone down to your house?"

¹¹ And Uriah said to David, "The ark and Israel and Judah dwell in tents; and my lord Joab, and the servants of my lord are encamped in the open fields; and shall I go into my house to eat and drink, and lie with my wife? How *should I do this?* As your soul lives, I will not do this thing."

¹² And David said to Uriah, "Remain here today also, and tomorrow I will let you go." So Uriah remained in Jerusalem that day and the day following.

¹³ And David called him, and he ate before him and drank, and made him drunk. And he went out in the evening to lie upon his bed with the servants of his lord, and did not go down to his house.

¹⁴ And the morning came, and David wrote a letter to Joab, and sent it by the hand of Uriah.

¹⁵ And he wrote in the letter, saying, "Station Uriah in front of the *most* severe *part* of the fight, and retreat from behind him, that he may be wounded and die."

¹⁶ And it came to pass while Joab was watching against the city, that he set Uriah in a place where he knew that valiant men were.

¹⁷ And the men of the city went out, and fought with Joab. And some of the people of the servants of David fell, and Uriah the Hittite died also.

¹⁸ And Joab sent, and reported to David all the events of the war, so as to tell them to the king.

¹⁹ And he commanded the messenger, saying, "When you have finished reporting all the events of the war to the king,

²⁰ then it shall come to pass if the anger of the king shall arise, and he shall say to you, 'Why did you draw near to the city to fight? Did you not know that they would shoot from off the wall?

²¹ Who struck Abimelech the son of Jerubbaal, son of Ner? Did not a woman cast a piece of a millstone upon him from above the wall, and he died in Thebez? Why did you draw near to the wall?' Then you shall say, 'Your servant Uriah the Hittite is also dead.'"

²² So the messenger of Joab went to the king, to Jerusalem, and he came and reported to David all that Joab had told him, all the affairs of the war. And David was very angry with Joab, and said to the messenger, "Why did you draw near to the wall to fight? Did you not know that you would be

wounded from off the wall? Who struck Abimelech the son of Jerubbaal? Did not a woman cast upon him a piece of millstone from the wall, and he died in Thebez? Why did you draw near to the wall?"

²³ And the messenger said to David, "The men prevailed against us, and they came out against us into the field, and we came upon them, even to the door of the gate.

²⁴ And the archers shot at your servants from off the wall, and some of the king's servants died, and your servant Uriah the Hittite is dead as well."

²⁵ And David said to the messenger, "Thus shall you say to Joab: 'Let not the matter be grievous in your eyes, for the sword devours one way at one time and another way at another: strengthen your array against the city, and destroy it, and strengthen him.'"

²⁶ And the wife of Uriah heard that Uriah her husband was dead, and she mourned for her husband.

²⁷ And the time of mourning expired, and David sent and took her into his house, and she became his wife, and bore him a son: but the thing which David did was evil in the eyes of the Lord.

2 SAMUEL CHAPTER 12

Nathan's Parable and David's Confession

¹ And the Lord sent Nathan the prophet to David; and he went in to him, and said to him, "There were two men in one city, one rich and the other poor.

² And the rich *man* had very many flocks and herds.

³ But the poor *man had* only one little ewe lamb, which he had purchased, and preserved, and reared; and it grew up with himself and his children in common; it ate of his bread and drank of his cup, and slept in his bosom, and was to him as a daughter.

⁴ And a traveler came to the rich man, and he refused to take of his flocks and of his herds, to prepare for the traveler that came to him; and he took the poor man's lamb, and prepared it for the man that came to him."

⁵ And David was greatly moved with anger against the man; and David said to Nathan, "*As* the Lord lives, the man that did this thing shall surely die.

⁶ And he shall restore the lamb seven-fold, because he has not spared."

⁷ And Nathan said to David, "You are the man that has done this! Thus says the Lord God of Israel: 'I anointed you to be king over Israel, and I rescued you out the hand of Saul;

⁸ and I gave you the house of your master, and the wives of your master into your bosom, and I gave to you the house of Israel and Judah; and if that had been *too* little, I would have given you even more.

⁹ Why have you despised the word of the Lord, to do that which is evil in His eyes? You have slain Uriah the Hittite with the sword, and you have taken his wife to be your wife,

and you have slain him with the sword of the children of Ammon.

¹⁰ Now therefore the sword shall never depart from your house, because you have despised Me, and you have taken the wife of Uriah the Hittite, to be your wife.

¹¹ Thus says the Lord: Behold, I will raise up evil against you out of your *own* house, and I will take your wives from before your eyes, and will give them to your neighbor, and he shall lie with your wives in broad daylight.

¹² For you did it in secret, but I will do this thing in the sight of all Israel, and in broad daylight.'"

¹³ And David said to Nathan, "I have sinned against the Lord." And Nathan said to David, "The Lord has put away your sin; you shall not die.

¹⁴ Only because you have given great occasion of provocation to the enemies of the Lord by this thing, your son also that is born to you shall surely die."

¹⁵ And Nathan departed to his house.

David's Son Dies

And the Lord struck the child, which the wife of Uriah the Hittite bore to David, and it was ill.

¹⁶ And David inquired of God concerning the child, and David fasted, and went in and lay all night upon the ground.

¹⁷ And the elders of his house arose *and went* to him to raise him up from the ground, but he would not *rise*, nor did he eat bread with them.

¹⁸ And it came to pass on the seventh day that the child died. And the servants of David were afraid to tell him that the child was dead; for they said, "Behold, while the child was yet alive we spoke to him, and he would not listen to our voice; and should we tell him *now* that the child is dead?—for he would do *himself* harm."

¹⁹ And David knew that his servants were whispering, and David perceived that the child was dead. And David said to his servants, "Is the child dead?" And they said, "He is dead."

²⁰ Then David rose up from the ground, and he washed and anointed himself, and changed his clothes, and went into the house of God, and worshipped Him. And he went into his own house, and called for bread to eat, and they set bread before him and he ate.

²¹ And his servants said to him, "What *is* this thing that you have done concerning the child? While the child was yet living you fasted and wept, and kept watch; but when the child was dead you rose up and ate bread, and drank."

²² And David said, "While the child yet lived, I fasted and wept; for I said, 'Who knows if the Lord will pity me, and the child should live?'

²³ But now the child is dead, why should I fast thus? Shall I be able to bring him back again? I shall go to him, but he shall not return to me."

The Birth of Solomon

²⁴ And David comforted Bathsheba his wife, and he went in to her, and lay with her; and she conceived and bore a son, and he called his named Solomon, and the Lord loved him.

²⁵ And he sent by the hand of Nathan the prophet, and called his name Jedidiah, for the Lord's sake.

Rabbah is Captured

²⁶ And Joab fought against Rabbah of the children of Ammon, and took the royal city.

²⁷ And Joab sent messengers to David, and said, "I have fought against Rabbah, and taken the City of Waters.

²⁸ And now gather the rest of the people, and encamp against the city, and take it beforehand; lest I take the city first, and it be called by my name."

²⁹ And David gathered all the people, and went to Rabbah, and fought against it, and took it.

³⁰ And he took the crown of Molchom their king from off his head, and the weight of it was a talent of gold, with precious stones, and it was upon the head of David; and he carried forth very much spoil of the city.

³¹ And he brought forth the people that were in it, and put them under the saw, and under iron harrows, and axes of iron, and made them pass through the brick kiln: and thus he did to all the cities of the children of Ammon. And David and all the people returned to Jerusalem.

2 SAMUEL CHAPTER 13

Amnon and Tamar

¹ And it happened after this that Absalom the son of David had a very beautiful sister, and her name *was* Tamar; and Amnon the son of David loved her.

² And Amnon was distressed even to sickness, because of Tamar his sister; for she was a virgin, and it seemed impossible for Amnon to do anything to her.

³ Now Amnon had a friend, and his name *was* Jonadab, the son of Shimeah the brother of David: and Jonadab *was* a very cunning man.

⁴ And he said to him, "What ails you, that you are weak like this? O son of the king, morning by morning? Will you not tell me?" And Amnon said, "I love Tamar the sister of my brother Absalom."

⁵ And Jonadab said to him, "Lie upon your bed, and make yourself sick, and your father shall come in to see you; and you shall say to him, 'Let Tamar my sister come, and feed me with morsels, and let her prepare food before my eyes, that I may see and eat at her hands.'"

⁶ So Ammon laid down and made himself sick; and the king came in to see him. And Amnon said to the king, "Let my sister Tamar come to me, and make a couple of cakes in my sight, and I will eat them at her hand."

⁷ And David sent home to Tamar, saying, "Go now to your brother's house, and prepare food for him."

⁸ And Tamar went to the house of her brother Amnon, and he *was* lying down: and she took the dough and kneaded it, and made cakes in his sight, and baked the cakes.

⁹ And she took the frying pan and poured them out before him, but he would not eat. And Amnon said, "Send out every man from about me." And they removed every man from about him.

¹⁰ And Amnon said to Tamar, "Bring in the food into the closet, and I will eat of your hand." And Tamar took the cakes which she had made, and brought them to her brother Amnon into the chamber.

¹¹ And she brought *them* to him to eat, and he caught hold of her, and said to her, "Come, lie with me, my sister."

¹² And she said to him, "No, my brother, do not humble me, for it ought not to be so done in Israel; do not do this disgraceful thing!

¹³ And I, where shall I remove my reproach? And you shall be as one of the fools in Israel. And now, speak to the king, for surely he will not keep me from you."

¹⁴ But Amnon would not listen to her voice; and he prevailed against her, and humbled her, and lay with her.

¹⁵ Then Amnon hated her with very great hatred; for the hatred with which he hated her was greater than the love with which he had loved her, for the last wickedness was greater than the first. And Amnon said to her, "Get up, and get out!"

¹⁶ And Tamar spoke to him concerning this great mischief, *saying*, "This is greater than the other that you did to me, to send me away." But Amnon would not listen to her voice.

¹⁷ And he called his servant who had charge of the house, and said to him, "Put this *woman* out from me, and shut the door behind her."

¹⁸ And she had on herself a multi-colored robe, for so were the king's daughters that were virgins attired in their apparel. And his servant led her forth, and shut the door behind her.

¹⁹ And Tamar took ashes, and put them on her head. And she tore the robe that was on her, and she laid her hands on her head, and went crying continually.

²⁰ And Absalom her brother said to her, "Has your brother Amnon been with you? Now then, my sister, be silent, for he is your brother: be not careful to mention this matter." So Tamar dwelt as a widow in the house of her brother Absalom.

²¹ And King David heard of all these things, and was very angry; but he did not grieve the spirit of his son Amnon, because he loved him, for he was his firstborn.

²² And Absalom spoke to Amnon neither good nor bad, because Absalom hated Amnon, on account of his humbling of his sister Tamar.

Absalom Murders Amnon

²³ And it came to pass at the end of two whole years, that they were shearing *sheep* for Absalom in Baal Hazor, near Ephraim. And Absalom invited all the king's sons.

24 And Absalom came to the king and said, "Behold, your servant has a sheep-shearing; let now the king and his servants go with your servant."

25 And the king said to Absalom, "No, my son, let us not all go, and let us not be burdensome to you." And he pressed him; but he would not go, but blessed him.

26 And Absalom said to him, "And if not, let my brother Amnon go with us." And the king said to him, "Why should he go with you?"

27 And Absalom pressed him, and he sent with him Amnon and all the king's sons; and Absalom made a banquet like the banquet of the king.

28 And Absalom commanded his servants, saying, "Take notice when the heart of Amnon shall be merry with wine, and I shall say to you, 'Strike Amnon, and kill him.' Do not fear, for is it not I that command you? Be courageous, and be valiant."

29 And the servants of Absalom did to Amnon as Absalom commanded them. And all the sons of the king rose up, and they mounted every man his mule, and fled.

30 And it came to pass, when they were on the way, that a report came to David, saying, "Absalom has slain all the king's sons, and there is not one of them left."

31 Then the king arose, and tore his clothes, and lay upon the ground. And all his servants that were standing round him tore their clothes.

32 And Jonadab the son of Shimeah, David's brother, answered and said, "Let not my Lord the king say that he has slain all the young men the sons of the king, for Amnon alone is dead; for he was appointed *to death* by the mouth of Absalom from the day that he humbled his sister Tamar.

33 And now let not my lord the king take the matter to heart, saying, 'All the king's sons are dead': for Amnon alone is dead."

34 And Absalom escaped. And the watchman lifted up his eyes and looked; and behold, many people went in the road behind him from the side of the mountain in the descent. And the watchman came and told the king, and said, "I have seen men by the road of Horonaim, by the side of the mountain."

35 And Jonadab said to the king, "Behold, the king' sons are present: according to the word of your servant, so has it happened."

36 And it came to pass when he had finished speaking, that behold, the king's sons came, and lifted up their voices and wept; and the king also and all his servants wept with a very great weeping.

37 But Absalom fled, and went to Talmai son of Ammihud the king of Geshur, to the land of Hamaachad. And King David mourned for his son continually.

38 So Absalom fled, and departed to Geshur, and was there three years.

39 And King David ceased to go out after Absalom, for he was comforted concerning Amnon, regarding his death.

Absalom Returns to Jerusalem

1 Now Joab the son of Zeruiah knew that the heart of the king was toward Absalom.

2 And Joab sent to Tekoa, and took from there a cunning woman, and said to her, "Mourn, and put on mourning apparel, and do not anoint yourself with oil, and you shall be as a woman mourning for one that is dead thus for many days.

3 And you shall go to the king, and speak to him according to this word." And Joab put the words in her mouth.

4 So the woman of Tekoa went in to the king and fell upon her face to the earth, and bowed down before him, and said, "Help, O king, help."

5 And the king said to her, "What is the matter with you?" And she said, "I am indeed a widow woman, and my husband is dead.

6 And moreover your maid had two sons, and they fought together in the field, and there was no one to separate them; and the one struck down the other, his brother, and killed him.

7 And behold, the whole family rose up against your maid, and they said, 'Give up the one that struck down his brother, and we will put him to death for the life of his brother, whom he killed, and we will take away your heir.' So they will extinguish my remaining coal, so as not to leave my husband a remnant or name upon the face of the earth."

8 And the king said to the woman, "Go in peace to your house, and I will give orders concerning you."

9 And the woman of Tekoa said to the king, "On me, my lord, O king, and on my father's house *be* the iniquity, and the king and his throne *be* guiltless."

10 And the king said, "Who was it that spoke to you? You shall bring him to me, and *one* shall not touch him anymore."

11 And she said, "Let now the king remember concerning his Lord God in that the avenger of blood is multiplied to destroy, and let them not take away my son." And he said, "*As* the lord lives, not a hair on your son's *head* shall fall to the ground."

12 And the woman said, "Let now your servant speak a word to my lord the king." And he said, "Speak on."

13 And the woman said, "Why have you devised this thing against the people of God? Or *is* this word out of the king's mouth as a transgression, so that the king should not bring back his *own* banished *son*?

14 For we shall surely die, and be as water poured upon the earth, which shall not be gathered up, and God shall take the life, even as He devises to thrust forth from Him His outcast.

15 And now whereas I came to speak this word to my lord the king, *the reason is* that the people will see me, and your maid will say, 'Let one now speak to my lord the king,' if perhaps the king will perform the request of his maid;

[16] for the king will hear. Let him rescue his maid out of the hand of the man that seeks to cast out me and my son from the inheritance of God."

[17] And the woman said, "If now the word of my lord the king be gracious,—*well*: for as an angel of God, so *is* my lord the king, to hear good and evil; and the Lord your God shall be with you."

[18] And the king answered and said to the woman, "Do not hide from me, I pray, the matter which I ask you." And the woman said, "Let my lord the king by all means speak."

[19] And the king said, "*Is* not the hand of Joab in all this matter with you?" And the woman said to the king, "*As* your soul lives, my lord, O king, there is no turning to the right hand or to the left from all that my lord the king has spoken; for your servant Joab himself charged me, and he put all these words in the mouth of your maid.

[20] In order that this form of speech might come about *it was* that your servant Joab has arranged this matter; and my lord is wise as *is* the wisdom of an angel of God, to know all things that are in the earth."

[21] And the king said to Joab, "Behold now, I have done to you according to this your word: go, bring back the young man Absalom."

[22] And Joab fell on his face to the ground, and bowed down, and blessed the king. And Joab said, "Today your servant knows that I have found grace in your sight, my lord, O king, for my lord the king has performed the request of his servant."

[23] And Joab arose, and went to Geshur, and brought Absalom to Jerusalem.

[24] And the king said, "Let him return to his house, and not see my face." And Absalom returned to his house, and did not see the king's face.

David Forgives Absalom

[25] And there was not a man in Israel as handsome as Absalom. From the sole of his foot even to the crown of his head there was no blemish in him.

[26] And when he cut his hair, (and it was at the beginning of every year that he cut it, because it grew heavy upon him) even when he cut it, he weighed the hair of his head, *and it weighed* two hundred shekels according to the royal shekel.

[27] And there were born to Absalom three sons and one daughter, and her name was Tamar. She was a very beautiful woman, and she became the wife of Rehoboam son of Solomon, and she bore to him Abia.

[28] And Absalom remained in Jerusalem two full years, and he did not see the king's face.

[29] And Absalom sent to Joab to bring him in to the king, and he would not come to him. And he sent to him the second time, and he would not come.

[30] And Absalom said to his servants, "Behold, Joab's portion in the field *is* next to mine, and he has barley in it; go and set it on fire." And the servants of Absalom set the field on fire. And the servants of Joab come to him with their clothes torn, and they said to him, "The servants of Absalom have set *your* field on fire."

[31] And Joab arose, and came to Absalom into the house, and said to him, "Why have your servants set my field on fire?"

[32] And Absalom said to Joab, "Behold, I sent to you, saying, 'Come here, and I will send you to the king, saying, "Why did I come out of Geshur? It would have been better for me to have remained there.'" And now, behold, I have not seen the face of the king; but if there is iniquity in me, then put me to death."

[33] And Joab went in to the king, and brought him word. And he called Absalom, and he went in to the king, and bowed down before him, and fell upon his face to the ground, even in the presence of the king; and the king kissed Absalom.

2 SAMUEL CHAPTER 15

Absalom's Treason

[1] And it came to pass after this that Absalom prepared for himself chariots and horses, and fifty men to run before him.

[2] And Absalom rose early, and stood beside the way of the gate. And it came to pass that every man who had a cause came to the king for judgment. And Absalom cried to him, and said to him, "Of what city are you?" And he said, "Your servant *is* of one of the tribes of Israel."

[3] And Absalom said to him, "See, your affairs *are* right and clear, yet you have no one *appointed* by the king to hear you."

[4] And Absalom said, "O that one would make me a judge in the land; then every man who had a dispute or a cause would come to me, and I would judge him!"

[5] And it came to pass that when a man came near to bow down to him, that he stretched out his hand, and took hold of him, and kissed him.

[6] And thus Absalom did to all Israel that came to the king for judgment; and Absalom gained the hearts of the men of Israel.

[7] And it came to pass after forty years, that Absalom said to his father, "I will go now, and pay my vows which I vowed to the Lord in Hebron,

[8] for your servant vowed a vow when I dwelt at Geshur in Syria, saying, 'If the Lord should indeed restore me to Jerusalem, then will I serve the Lord.'"

[9] And the king said to him, "Go in peace." And he arose and went to Hebron.

[10] And Absalom sent spies throughout all the tribes of Israel, saying, "When you hear the sound of the trumpet, then shall you say, 'Absalom has become king in Hebron.'"

[11] And there went with Absalom two hundred chosen men from Jerusalem; and they went in their innocence, and knew nothing.

[12] And Absalom sent to Ahithophel the Gilonite, David's counselor, from his city, from Giloh, where he was

sacrificing. And there was a strong conspiracy; and the people with Absalom were increasingly numerous.

David Escapes from Jerusalem

¹³ And there came a messenger to David, saying, "The heart of the men of Israel has gone after Absalom."

¹⁴ And David said to all his servants who were with him in Jerusalem, "Rise up, and let us flee, for we have no refuge from Absalom. Make haste and go, lest he overtake us speedily, and bring evil upon us, and strike the city with the edge of the sword."

¹⁵ And the king's servants said to the king, "In all things which our lord the king chooses, behold, *we are* your servants."

¹⁶ And the king and all his house went out on foot. And the king left ten women from among his concubines to keep the house.

¹⁷ And the king and all his servants went out on foot; and they stayed in a house far *away*.

¹⁸ And all his servants passed on by his side, and every Cherethite, and every Pelethite, and they stood by the olive tree in the wilderness. And all the people marched near him, and all his court, and all the men of might, and all the men of war, six hundred; and they were present at his side. And every Cherethite, and every Pelethite, and all the six hundred Gittites that came on foot out from Gath, and they went on before the king.

¹⁹ And the king said to Ittai the Gittite, "Why do you also go with us? Return, and dwell with the king, for you are a stranger, and you have come forth as a sojourner out of your place.

²⁰ Whereas you came yesterday, shall I today cause you to travel with us, and shall you *thus* change your place? You came forth yesterday, and today shall I set you in motion to go along with us? I indeed will go wherever I may go: return then, and cause your brothers to return with you, and may the Lord deal mercifully and truly with you."

²¹ And Ittai answered the king and said, "*As* the Lord lives and as my lord the king lives, in the place wheresoever my lord shall be, whether it be for death or life, there shall your servant be."

²² And the king said to Ittai, "Come and pass over with me." So Ittai the Gittite and the king passed over, and all his servants, and all the multitude with him.

²³ And all the country wept with a loud voice. And all the people passed by over the Brook of Kidron; and the king crossed the Brook Kidron. And all the people and the king passed on toward the way of the wilderness.

²⁴ And behold, Zadok and all the Levites were also with him, bearing the ark of the covenant of the Lord. And they set down the ark of God; and Abiathar went up, until all the people had passed out of the city.

²⁵ And the king said to Zadok, "Carry back the ark of God into the city: if I should find favor in the eyes of the Lord,

then will He bring me back, and He will show me *both the ark* and its beauty.

²⁶ But if He should say thus, 'I have no pleasure in you'; behold, *here* I am, let Him do to me according to that which is good in His sight."

²⁷ And the king said to Zadok the priest, "Behold, you shall return to the city in peace, and Ahimaaz your son, and Jonathan the son of Abiathar, your two sons with you.

²⁸ Behold, I continue in arms in Araboth of the desert, until there should come news from you to report to me."

²⁹ So Zadok and Abiathar brought back the ark of the Lord to Jerusalem, and it remained there.

³⁰ And David went up by the ascent of *the Mount of* Olives, ascending and weeping, and had his head covered, and went barefoot. And all the people that were with him, *every man,* covered his head; and they went up, ascending and weeping.

³¹ And it was reported to David, saying, "Ahithophel also *is* among the conspirators with Absalom." And David said, "O Lord my God, negate the counsel of Ahithophel."

³² And David came as far as Ros, where he worshipped God. And behold, Hushai the chief friend of David came out to meet him, having torn his clothes, and dust *was* upon his head.

³³ And David said to him, "If you should go over with me, then will you be a burden to me;

³⁴ but if you shall return to the city, and shall say to Absalom, 'Your brothers have passed over, and the king your father has passed over after me: and now I am your servant, O king, permit me to live. At one time, even of late, I was the servant of your father, and now I *am* your humble servant'—so shall you negate for me the counsel of Ahithophel.

³⁵ And behold, Zadok and Abiathar the priests are with you; and it shall be that every word that you shall hear from the king's house you shall report it to Zadok and Abiathar the priests.

³⁶ Behold, their two sons are with them, Ahimaaz the son of Zadok, and Jonathan the son of Abiathar; and by them you shall report to me every word which you shall hear."

³⁷ So Hushai the friend of David went into the city, and Absalom came into Jerusalem.

2 SAMUEL CHAPTER 16

David's Adversaries

¹ And David passed on a little further from Ros; and behold, Ziba the servant of Memphibosheth *came* to meet him; and he had a couple of donkeys saddled, and upon them two hundred loaves, and a hundred *cakes of* raisins, and a hundred *cakes of* dates, and a skin of wine.

² And the king said to Ziba, "What do you mean to do with these?" And Ziba said, "The donkeys *are* for the household of the king to sit on, and the loaves and the dates *are* for the

young men to eat, and the wine *is* for them that are faint in the wilderness to drink."

³ And the king said, "And where *is* the son of your master?" And Ziba said to the king, "Behold, he remains in Jerusalem; for he said, 'Today shall the house of Israel restore to me the kingdom of my father.'"

⁴ And the king said to Ziba, "Behold, all Memphibosheth's property *is* yours." And Ziba bowed down and said, "My lord, O king, let me find favor in your eyes."

Shimei Curses David

⁵ And King David came to Bahurim; and behold, there came out from there a man of the family of the house of Saul, and his name *was* Shimei, the son of Gera. He came forth and cursed as he went,

⁶ and cast stones at David, and at all the servants of King David. And all the people and all the mighty men were on the right and left hand of the king.

⁷ And thus Shimei said when he cursed him, "Go out, go out, you bloody man, and you man of sin!

⁸ The Lord has returned upon you all the blood of the house of Saul, because you have reigned in his place; and the Lord has given the kingdom into the hand of Absalom your son; and behold, you *are taken* in your mischief, because you *are* a bloody man!"

⁹ Then Abishai the son of Zeruiah said to the king, "Why does this dead dog curse my lord the king? Let me go over now and take off his head!"

¹⁰ And the king said, "What have I to do with you, you sons of Zeruiah? Let him alone, and so let him curse, for the Lord has told him to curse David: and who shall say, 'Why have you done thus?'"

¹¹ And David said to Abishai and to all his servants, "Behold, my son who came forth out of my *own* loins seeks my life; and how much more *this* Benjamite! Let him curse, because the Lord has told him.

¹² If by any means the Lord may look upon my affliction, thus shall He return me good for his cursing this day."

¹³ And David and all the men with him went along the road, and Shimei went by the side of the hill next to him, cursing as he went, and casting stones at him, and sprinkling him with dirt.

¹⁴ And the king, and all the people with him, came away and refreshed themselves there.

The Advice of Ahithophel

¹⁵ And Absalom and all the men of Israel went into Jerusalem, and Ahithophel with him.

¹⁶ And it came to pass when Hushai the chief friend of David came to Absalom, that Hushai said to Absalom, "Long live the king!"

¹⁷ And Absalom said to Hushai, "*Is* this your kindness to your friend? Why did you not go forth with your friend?"

¹⁸ And Hushai said to Absalom, "No, but I follow whom the Lord, and this people, and all Israel have chosen—to him I will be, and with him I will sit.

¹⁹ And again, whom shall I serve? Should I not *serve* in the presence of his son? As I served in the sight of your father, so will I be in your presence."

²⁰ And Absalom said to Ahithophel, "Deliberate among yourselves concerning what we should do."

²¹ And Ahithophel said to Absalom, "Go in to your father's concubines, whom he left to keep his house; and all Israel shall hear that you have dishonored your father; and the hands of all that are with you shall be strengthened."

²² And they pitched a tent for Absalom on the roof, and Absalom went in to his father's concubines in the sight of all Israel.

²³ And the counsel of Ahithophel, which he counseled in former days, *was* as if one should inquire of the word of God: so *was* all the counsel of Ahithophel both to David and also to Absalom.

2 SAMUEL CHAPTER 17

¹ And Ahithophel said to Absalom, "Let me now choose out for myself twelve thousand men, and I will arise and follow after David this night.

² And I will come upon him when he *is* weary and weak-handed, and I will strike him with terror; and all the people with him shall flee, and I will strike only the king.

³ And I will bring back all the people to you, as a bride returns to her husband: only you seek the life of one man, and all the people shall have peace."

⁴ And the word *seemed* good in the eyes of Absalom, and in the eyes of all the elders of Israel.

The Advice of Hushai

⁵ And Absalom said, "Call now also Hushai the Archite, and let us hear what *is* in his mouth as well."

⁶ And Hushai went in to Absalom, and Absalom spoke to him, saying, "According to these words has Ahithophel spoken: shall we do according to his word? But if not, speak up."

⁷ And Hushai said to Absalom, "This counsel which Ahithophel has counseled this one time *is* not good."

⁸ And Hushai said, "You know your father and his men, that they are very mighty, and bitter in their spirit, as a bereaved bear in the field, *and as a wild boar in the plain*; and your father *is* a man of war, and will not give the people rest.

⁹ For behold, he is now hidden in one of the hills or in some *other* place; and it shall come to pass when he falls upon them at the beginning, that *someone* will certainly hear, and say, 'There has been a slaughter among the people that follow after Absalom.'

¹⁰ Then even he *that is* strong, whose heart is as the heart of a lion, it shall utterly melt: for all Israel knows that your

father *is* mighty, and that those who are with him *are* mighty men.

11 For thus I have surely given counsel, that all Israel shall be gathered to you, from Dan even to Beersheba, as the sand that is upon the seashore for multitude; and that your presence should go in the midst of them.

12 And we will come upon him in one of the places where we shall find him, and we will encamp against him, as the dew falls upon the earth; and we will not leave of him and of his men so much as one.

13 And if he shall have taken refuge with his army in a city, then shall all Israel take ropes to that city, and we will draw it even into the river, that there may not be left there even a stone."

14 And Absalom, and all the men of Israel said, "The counsel of Hushai the Archite *is* better than the counsel of Ahithophel." (For the Lord has purposed to defeat the good counsel of Ahithophel, that the Lord might bring all evil upon Absalom).

Hushai Warns David to Escape
15 And Hushai the Archite said to Zadok and Abiathar the priests, "Thus and thus has Ahithophel counseled Absalom and the elders of Israel; and thus and thus have I counseled.

16 And now send quickly and report to David, saying, 'Do not stay this night in Araboth of the wilderness: but go and make haste, lest *one* swallow up the king, and all the people with him."

17 And Jonathan and Ahimaaz stood by the Well of Rogel, and a maidservant went and reported to them, and they went to tell King David, so that they might not be seen entering into the city.

18 But a young man saw them and told Absalom, and the two went quickly, and entered into the house of a man in Bahurim; and he had a well in his court, and they went down into it.

19 And a woman took a covering, and spread it over the mouth of the well, and spread out ground grain upon it to dry, and the thing was not known.

20 And the servants of Absalom came to the woman into the house and said, "Where *are* Ahimaaz and Jonathan?" And the woman said to them, "'They have gone a little way beyond the water." And they sought after them, but did not find them; and they returned to Jerusalem.

21 And it came to pass after they were gone, that they came up out of the pit, and went on their way; and reported to King David, and said to David, "Arise, and go quickly over the water, for thus has Ahithophel counseled concerning you."

22 And David rose up and all the people with him, and they passed over the Jordan till the morning light; there was not one missing who did not pass over the Jordan.

23 And Ahithophel saw that his counsel was not followed, and he saddled his donkey, and rose and departed to his house into his city; and he gave orders to his household,

and hanged himself, and died, and was buried in the tomb of his father.

24 And David passed over to Mahanaim. And Absalom crossed over the Jordan, he and all the men of Israel with him.

25 And Absalom appointed Amasa over the army, in the place of Joab. And Amasa was the son of a man whose name was Jether of Jezreel: he went in to Abigail the daughter of Nahash, the sister of Zeruiah the mother of Joab.

26 And all Israel and Absalom encamped in the land of Gilead.

27 And it came to pass when David came to Manahaim, that Shobi the son of Nahash of Rabbah of the sons of Ammon, and Machir son of Ammiel of Lo Debar, and Barzillai the Gileadite of Rogelim,

28 brought ten embroidered beds (with double coverings) and ten caldrons, earthenware and wheat, barley and flour, meal and beans, and parched *seeds*,

29 honey and butter, sheep and cheese of the herd. And they brought them to David and to his people with him to eat; for *one* said, "The people *are* faint and hungry and thirsty in the wilderness."

2 SAMUEL CHAPTER 18

Absalom's Defeat and Death
1 And David numbered the people with him, and set over them captains of thousands and captains of hundreds.

2 And David sent the people away, a third part under the hand of Joab, a third part under the hand of Abishai the son of Zeruiah, the brother of Joab, and a third part under the hand of Ittai the Gittite. And David said to the people, "I also will surely go out with you."

3 And they said, "You shall not go out; for if we should indeed flee, they will not care for us; and if half of us should die, they will not mind us; for you *are* as ten thousand of us; and now *it is* well that you shall be to us an aid to help us in the city."

4 And the king said to them, "Whatever seems good in your eyes I will do." And the king stood by the side of the gate, and all the people went out by hundreds and by thousands.

5 And the king commanded Joab and Abishai and Ittai, saying, "Spare the young man Absalom for my sake." And all the people heard the king charging all the commanders concerning Absalom.

6 And all the people went out into the woods against Israel; and the battle was in the woods of Ephraim.

7 And the people of Israel fell down there before the servants of David, and there was a great slaughter in that day, *even* twenty thousand men.

8 And the battle there was scattered over the face of all the land. And the woods consumed more of the people than the sword consumed in that day.

9 And Absalom went to meet the servants of David. And Absalom was mounted on his mule, and the mule came under the thick boughs of a great oak; and his head was entangled in the oak, and he was suspended in the air; and the mule passed on from under him.

10 And a man saw it, and reported to Joab, and said, "Behold, I saw Absalom hanging in an oak."

11 And Joab said to the man who reported it to him, "Behold, did you indeed see him? Why then did you not strike him there to the ground? And I would have given you ten *pieces* of silver, and a belt."

12 And the man said to Joab, "Were I even to receive a thousand shekels of silver, I would not lift my hand against the king's son; for in our ears the king charged you and Abishai and Ittai, saying, 'Take care of the young man Absalom for me,'

13 so as to do no harm to his life: and nothing of the matter will be concealed from the king, and you will set yourself against me."

14 And Joab said, "I will begin this; I will not thus remain with you." And Joab took three spears in his hand, and thrust them into the heart of Absalom, while he was yet alive in the heart of the oak.

15 And ten young men that bore Joab's armor surrounded Absalom, and struck him, and killed him.

16 And Joab blew the trumpet, and the people returned from pursuing Israel, for Joab spared the people.

17 And he took Absalom, and cast him into a great cavern in the woods, into a deep pit, and set up over him a very great heap of stones: and all Israel fled, every man to his tent.

18 Now Absalom, while he was yet alive, had taken and set up for himself the pillar near which he was taken, and set it up so as to have the pillar in the king's valley; for he said he had no son to keep his name in remembrance: and he called the pillar Absalom's Hand, until this day.

David Hears of Absalom's Death

19 And Ahimaaz the son of Zadok said, "Let me run now and carry the good news to the king, for the Lord has delivered him from the hand of his enemies."

20 And Joab said to him, "You *shall* not *be* a messenger of good news this day; you shall bear them another day; but on this day you shall bear no news, because the king's son is dead."

21 And Joab said to Hushai, "Go, report to the king all that you have seen." And Hushai bowed down before Joab and went out.

22 And Ahimaaz the son of Zadok said again to Joab, "No, let me also run after Hushai." And Joab said, "Why would you thus run, my son? Come, you have no news for profit if you go."

23 And he said, "Why should I not run?" And Joab said to him, "Run." And Ahimaaz ran along the way of Kechar, and outran Hushai.

24 And David was sitting between the two gates. And the watchman went up on the top of the gate of the wall, and lifted up his eyes and looked, and behold, a man was running alone before him.

25 And the watchman cried out, and reported to the king. And the king said, "If he is alone, *he has* good news in his mouth." And the man came and drew near.

26 And the watchman saw another man running. And the watchman cried at the gate, and said, "Behold, another man is running alone." And the king said, "He also brings good news."

27 And the watchman said, "I see the running of the first as the running of Ahimaaz the son of Zadok." And the king said, "He *is* a good man, and will come to *report* good news."

28 And Ahimaaz cried out and said to the king, "Peace." And he bowed down to the king with his face to the ground, and said, "Blessed *be* the Lord your God, who has delivered up the men that lifted up their hands against my lord the king."

29 And the king said, "*Is* the young man Absalom safe?" And Ahimaaz said, "I saw a great multitude *at the time* of Joab's sending the king's servant and your servant, and I did not know what was there."

30 And the king said, "Turn aside, stand still here." And he turned aside, and stood.

31 And behold, Hushai came up, and said to the king, "Let my lord the king hear the good news, for the Lord has avenged you this day upon all them that rose up against you."

32 And the king said to Hushai, "Is it well with the young man Absalom?" And Hushai said, "Let the enemies of my lord the king, and all whosoever have risen up against him for evil, be as that young man."

David Mourns for Absalom

33 And the king was troubled, and went to the chamber over the gate, and wept. And thus he said as he went, "My son Absalom, my son, my son Absalom! I *pray* God I had died for you, *even* I *had died* for you, Absalom, my son, my son!"

2 Samuel Chapter 19

1 And they brought word to Joab, saying, "Behold, the king weeps and mourns for Absalom."

2 And the victory was turned that day into mourning for all the people, for the people heard it said that day, "The king grieves after his son."

3 And the people stole away that day to go into the city, as people steal away when they are ashamed as they flee in the battle.

4 And the king hid his face. And the king cried with a loud voice, "My son Absalom! Absalom my son!"

5 And Joab went in to the king, into the house, and said, "You have this day shamed the faces of all your servants that have delivered you this day, and *have saved* the lives of

your sons and of your daughters, and the lives of your wives, and of your concubines,

[6] forasmuch as you love them that hate you, and hate them that love you; and you have this day declared, that your princes and your servants are nothing *in your sight*; for I know this day, that if Absalom were alive, *and* all of us were dead today, then it would have been right in your sight.

[7] And now arise and go forth, and speak comfortably to your servants; for I have sworn by the Lord, that unless you will go forth this day, there shall not a man remain with you this night. And know for yourself, this thing *will* indeed *be* evil to you beyond all the evil that has come upon you from your youth until now."

[8] Then the king arose, and sat in the gate. And all the people reported, saying, "Behold, the king sits in the gate." And all the people went in before the king to the gate (for Israel had fled every man to his tent).

[9] And all the people disputed among all the tribes of Israel, saying, "King David delivered us from all our enemies, and he rescued us from the hand of the Philistines; and now he has fled from the land, and from his kingdom, and from Absalom.

[10] And Absalom, whom we anointed over us, is dead in battle. And now, why are you silent about bringing back the king? And the word of all Israel came to the king."

[11] And King David sent to Zadok and Abiathar the priests, saying, "Speak to the elders of Israel, saying, 'Why are you the last to bring back the king to his house, since the word of all Israel have come to the king, to this *very* house?

[12] You *are* my brothers, you *are* my bones and my flesh: why are you the last to bring back the king to his house?'

[13] And you shall say to Amasa, '*Are* you not my bone and my flesh? And now God do so to me and more also, if you shall not be commander of the army before me continually in the place of Joab.'"

[14] And he bowed the heart of all the men of Judah as that of one man; and they sent to the king, saying, "Return, you and all your servants."

[15] And the king returned, and came as far as the Jordan. And the men of Judah came to Gilgal on their way to meet the king, to cause the king to pass over the Jordan.

[16] And Shimei the son of Gera, the Benjamite, of Bahurim, made haste and went down with the men of Judah to meet King David.

[17] And a thousand men of Benjamin *were* with him, and Ziba the servant of the house of Saul, and his fifteen sons with him, and his twenty servants with him. And they went directly down to the Jordan before the king,

[18] and they performed the service of bringing the king over; and a ferryboat went across to move the household of the king, and to do that which was right in his eyes. And Shimei the son of Gera fell on his face before the king, as he went over the Jordan,

[19] and said to the king, "Let not my lord now impute iniquity, and remember not all the iniquity of your servant in the day in which my lord went out from Jerusalem, so that the king should mind it.

[20] For your servant knows that I have sinned; and behold, I have come this day before all Israel and the house of Joseph, to go down and meet my lord the king."

[21] But Abishai the son of Zeruiah answered and said, "Shall not Shimei be put to death for this, because he cursed the Lord's anointed?"

[22] And David said, "What have I to do with you, you sons of Zeruiah, that you lie in wait against me this day? Today no man in Israel shall be put to death, for I know not this day if I reign over Israel."

[23] And the king said to Shimei, "You shall not die"; and the king swore to him.

[24] And Memphibosheth the son of Saul's son went down to meet the king, and had not dressed his feet, nor trimmed his nails, nor shaved himself, neither had he washed his garments, from the day that the king departed, until the day that he arrived in peace.

[25] And it came to pass when he went into Jerusalem to meet the king, that the king said to him, "Why did you not go with me, Memphibosheth?"

[26] And Memphibosheth said to him, "My lord, O king, my servant deceived me; for your servant said to him, 'Saddle me the donkey, and I will ride upon it, and go with the king'; for your servant *is* lame.

[27] And he has dealt deceitfully with your servant to my lord the king. But my lord the king *is* like an angel of God; do that which is good in your eyes.

[28] For all of my father's house were as dead men before my lord the king; yet you have set your servant among them that eat at your table; and what right have I any longer even to cry to the king?"

[29] And the king said to him, "Why speak any longer of these matters? I have said, 'You and Ziba shall divide the land.'"

[30] And Memphibosheth said to the king, "Rather, let him take it all, since my lord the king has come in peace to his house."

[31] And Barzillai the Gileadite came down from Rogelim, and crossed over the Jordan with the king, that he might escort the king over the Jordan.

[32] And Barzillai was a very old man, eighty years old; and he had provided for the king when he dwelt in Mahanaim; for he was a very great man.

[33] And the king said to Barzillai, "You shall go over with me, and I will nourish your old age with me in Jerusalem."

[34] And Barzillai said to the king, "How many *are* the days of the years of my life, that I should go up with the king to Jerusalem?

[35] I am this day eighty years old: can I then distinguish between good and evil? Can your servant taste any longer what I eat or drink? Can I hear the voice of singing men or singing women any longer? And why shall your servant be a burden to my lord the king any longer?

³⁶ Your servant will go a little way over the Jordan with the king. And why does the king return me this recompense?

³⁷ Let your servant remain, I pray, and I will die in my city, by the tomb of my father and of my mother. And behold, your servant Chimham shall go over with my lord the king; and do to him as it seems good in your eyes."

³⁸ And the king said, "Let Chimham go over with me, and I will do to him what is good in my sight; and whatsoever you shall choose at my hand, I will do for you."

³⁹ And all the people crossed over the Jordan, and the king crossed over. And the king kissed Barzillai, and blessed him; and he returned to his place.

The Quarrel About the King

⁴⁰ And the king went over to Gilgal and Chimham went over with him. And all the men of Judah crossed over with the king, and also half the people of Israel.

⁴¹ And behold, all the men of Israel came to the king, and said to the king, "Why have our brothers the men of Judah stolen you away, and caused the king and all his house to pass over the Jordan, and all the men of David with him?"

⁴² And all the men of Judah answered the men of Israel and said, "Because the king is our relative: and why were you thus angry concerning this matter? Have we indeed eaten of the king's food? Or has he given us a gift, or has he sent us a portion?"

⁴³ And the men of Israel answered the men of Judah and said, "We have ten portions in the king, and we are older than you, we have also an interest in David above you: and why have you thus insulted us, and why was not our advice taken before that of Judah, to bring back our king?" And the speech of the men of Judah was sharper than the speech of the men of Israel.

2 Samuel Chapter 20

The Rebellion of Sheba

¹ And there was a transgressor there, and his name was Sheba, a Benjamite, the son of Bichri: and he blew the trumpet, and said, "We have no portion in David, neither have we *any* inheritance in the son of Jesse: to your tents, O Israel!"

² And all the men of Israel went up from following David after Sheba the son of Bichri; but the men of Judah remained loyal to their king, from Jordan even to Jerusalem.

³ And David went into his house at Jerusalem. And the king took the ten women, his concubines, whom he had left to keep the house, and he put them in a place of custody, and maintained them, and he did not go into them; and they were kept living as widows, till the day of their death.

⁴ And the king said to Amasa, "Call to me the men of Judah for three days, and be present here yourself."

⁵ And Amasa went to call Judah, and delayed beyond the time which David appointed him.

⁶ And David said to Amasa, "Now shall Sheba the son of Bichri do us more harm than Absalom: now then take with you the servants of your lord, and follow after him, lest he find for himself strong cities, so will he blind our eyes."

⁷ So there went out after him Amasa and the men of Joab, and the Cherethites and the Pelethites, and all the mighty men; and they went out from Jerusalem to pursue after Sheba the son of Bichri.

⁸ And they *were* by the great stone that is in Gibeon. And Amasa went in before them. And Joab had upon him a military cloak over his apparel, and over it he was girded with a dagger fastened upon his loins in its sheath; and the dagger came out, and fell *to the ground*.

⁹ And Joab said to Amasa, "Are you in health, *my* brother?" And the right hand of Joab took hold of the beard of Amasa to kiss him.

¹⁰ And Amasa did not see the dagger that was in the hand of Joab. And Joab struck him with it in his stomach, and his bowels were shed out upon the ground, and he did not repeat the blow, and he died. And Joab and Abishai his brother pursued after Sheba the son of Bichri.

¹¹ And there stood over him one of the servants of Joab, and said, "Who *is* he that is for Joab, and who *is* on the side of David following Joab?"

¹² And Amasa *was* wallowing in blood in the midst of the road. And a man saw that all the people stood still; and he removed Amasa out of the road into a field, and he threw a garment over him, because he saw everyone that came to him standing still.

¹³ And when he was quickly removed from the road, every man of Israel passed after Joab to pursue after Sheba the son of Bichri.

¹⁴ And he went through all the tribes of Israel to Abel, and to Beth Maachah; and all in Charri also were assembled, and followed after him.

¹⁵ And they came and besieged him in Abel and Beth Maachah: and they raised a siege mound against the city and it stood close to the wall; and all the people with Joab purposed to throw down the wall.

¹⁶ And a wise woman cried from the wall and said, "Hear, hear; say to Joab, 'Draw close, and I will speak to him.'"

¹⁷ And he drew close to her. And the woman said to him, "Are you Joab?" And he said, "I *am*." And she said to him, "Hear the words of your maid"; and Joab said, "I do hear."

¹⁸ And she spoke, saying, "In former times they said, 'Surely one was asked in Abel and Dan, whether the faithful in Israel failed in what they purposed'; they will surely ask in Abel, even in like manner, whether they have failed.

¹⁹ I am a peaceable one of the strong ones in Israel; but you seek to destroy a city and a mother city in Israel: why do you seek to ruin the inheritance of the Lord?"

²⁰ And Joab answered and said, "Far be it, far be it from me, that I should ruin or destroy.

²¹ Is not this the case, that a man of Mount Ephraim, Sheba, son of Bichri by name, has even lifted up his hand against

King David? Give him only to me, and I will depart from the city." And the woman said to Joab, "Behold, his head shall be thrown to you over the wall."

22 And the woman went in to all the people, and she spoke to all the city in her wisdom; and they took off the head of Sheba the son of Bichri; and took it away and threw it to Joab. And he blew the trumpet, and the people separated from the city away from him, every man to his tent. And Joab returned to Jerusalem to the king.

23 And Joab *was* over all the forces of Israel, and Benaiah the son of Jehoiada *was* over the Cherethites and over the Pelethites.

24 And Adoram *was* over the tribute; and Jehoshaphat the son of Ahilud *was* recorder.

25 And Sheva *was* scribe; and Zadok and Abiathar *were* the priests.

26 Moreover Ira the Jairite was priest to David.

2 SAMUEL CHAPTER 21

David Avenges the Gibeonites

1 And there was a famine in the days of David for three years, year after year; and David sought the face of the Lord. And the Lord said, "*There is* guilt upon Saul and his house because of his bloody murder, whereby he slew the Gibeonites."

2 So King David called the Gibeonites, and said to them (now the Gibeonites are not the children of Israel, but *are* of the remnant of the Amorites, and the children of Israel had sworn to them; but Saul sought to kill them in his zeal for the children of Israel and Judah),

3 "What shall I do for you? And with what shall I make atonement, that you may bless the inheritance of the Lord?"

4 And the Gibeonites said to him, "We have no *question about* silver or gold with Saul and with his house; and there is no man for us to put to death in Israel."

5 And he said, "What do you ask? Speak, and I will do it for you." And they said to the king, "The man who would have made an end of us, and persecuted us, who plotted against us to destroy us, let us utterly destroy him, so that he shall have no standing in all the coasts of Israel.

6 Let one give us seven men of his sons, and let us hang them up in the sun to the Lord in Gibeah of Saul, as chosen out for the Lord." And the king said, "I will give *them*."

7 But the king spared Memphibosheth son of Jonathan the son of Saul, because of the oath of the Lord that was between them, even between David and Jonathan the son of Saul.

8 And the king took the two sons of Rizpah the daughter of Aiah, whom she bore to Saul, Armoni and Memphibosheth, and the five sons of Michal daughter of Saul, whom she bore to Adriel son of Barzillai the Meholathite.

9 And he gave them into the hand of the Gibeonites, and they hanged them in the sun on the hill before the lord. And all seven of them fell together. Moreover they were put to death at the beginning of the days of harvest; *that* is, the barley harvest.

10 And Rizpah the daughter of Aiah took sackcloth, and fixed it for herself on the rock in the beginning of the barley harvest, until water dropped upon them out of heaven. And she did not allow the birds of the air to rest upon them by day, nor the beasts of the field by night.

11 And it was told David what Rizpah the daughter of Aiah the concubine of Saul had done (and they were faint, and Dan, the son of Joa of the offspring of the giants overtook them).

12 And David went and took the bones of Saul, and the bones of Jonathan his son, from the men of the sons of Jabesh Gilead, who stole them from the street of Beth Shan; for the Philistines set them there in the day in which the Philistines killed Saul in Gilboa.

13 And he carried up from there the bones of Saul and the bones of Jonathan his son, and gathered the bones of them that had been hanged.

14 And they buried the bones of Saul and the bones of Jonathan his son, and the bones of them that had been hanged, in the land of Benjamin in the hill, in the tomb of Kish his father; and they did all things that the king commanded. And after this God hearkened to *the prayers of* the land.

Philistine Giants Destroyed

15 And there was yet war between the Philistines and Israel. And David went down and his servants with him, and they fought with the Philistines, and David went.

16 And Ishbi-Benob, who was of the sons of Rapha, and the head of whose spear *was* three hundred shekels of brass in weight, who also was dressed with a club, even he thought to kill David.

17 But Abishai the son of Zeruiah helped him and struck the Philistine, and killed him. Then the men of David swore, saying, "You shall no longer go out with us to battle, and you shall not quench the lamp of Israel."

18 And after this there was a battle again with the Philistines in Gath. Then Sibbechai the Hushathite slew Saph of the sons of Rapha.

19 And there was a battle in Gob with the Philistines; and Elhanan son of Jaare-Oregim the Bethlehemite slew *the brother of* Goliath the Gittite; and the staff of his spear *was* as a weaver's beam.

20 And there was yet a battle in Gath. And there was a man of stature, and the fingers of his hands and the toes of his feet *were* six on each, twenty-four in number: and he also was born to Rapha.

21 And he defied Israel, and Jonathan son of Shimei brother of David, killed him.

22 These four were born descendants of the giants in Gath, the family of Rapha; and they fell by the hand of David, and by the hand of his servants.

2 SAMUEL CHAPTER 22

Praise for God's Deliverance

[1] And David spoke to the Lord the words of this song, in the day in which the Lord rescued him out of the hand of all his enemies, and out of the hand of Saul.

[2] And the song was thus: "O Lord, my rock, and my fortress, and my deliverer,

[3] my God; He shall be to me my guard, I will trust in Him: *He is* my protector, and the horn of my salvation, my helper, and my sure refuge; You shall save me from the unjust man.

[4] I will call upon the Lord, who is worthy to be praised, and I shall be saved from my enemies.

[5] For the troubles of death surrounded me, the floods of iniquity amazed me;

[6] the pangs of death surrounded me, the agonies of death prevented me.

[7] When I am afflicted I will call upon the Lord, and will cry to my God, and He shall hear my voice out of His temple, and my cry shall come into His ears.

[8] And the earth was troubled and trembled, and the foundations of heaven were confounded and shaken, because the Lord was angry with them.

[9] There went up a smoke in His wrath, and devouring fire proceeded out of His mouth; coals were kindled at it.

[10] And He bowed the heavens, and came down, and *there was* darkness under His feet.

[11] And He rode upon the cherubim and flew, and was seen upon the wings of the wind.

[12] And He made darkness His hiding place; His tabernacle round about Him was the darkness of waters, He condensed it with the clouds of the air.

[13] At the brightness before Him coals of fire were kindled.

[14] The Lord thundered out of heaven, and the Most High uttered His voice.

[15] And He sent forth arrows, and scattered them, and He flashed lightning, and dismayed them.

[16] And the channels of the sea were seen, and the foundations of the world were discovered, at the rebuke of the Lord, at the blast of the breath of His anger.

[17] He sent from above and took me; He drew me out of many waters.

[18] He delivered me from my strong enemies, from them that hated me, for they were stronger than I.

[19] The days of my affliction prevented me; but the Lord was my stay.

[20] And He brought me into a wide place, and rescued me, because He delighted in me.

[21] And the Lord recompensed me according to my righteousness; even according to the purity of my hands did He recompense me.

[22] Because, I kept the ways of the Lord, and did not wickedly depart from my God.

[23] For all His judgments and His ordinances *were* before me: I did not depart from them.

[24] And I shall be blameless before Him, and I will keep myself from my iniquity.

[25] And the Lord will recompense me according to my righteousness, and according to the purity of my hands in His sight.

[26] With the holy You will be holy, and with the blameless man You will be blameless,

[27] and with the excellent You will be excellent, and with the devious You will show Yourself shrewd.

[28] And You will save the poor people, and will bring down the eyes of the haughty.

[29] For You, O Lord, *are* my lamp, and the Lord shall shine forth to me in my darkness.

[30] For by You shall I run *as* a girded man, and by my God shall I leap over a wall.

[31] As for the Mighty One, His way *is* blameless: the word of the Lord *is* strong *and* tried in the fire; He is a protector to all that put their trust in Him.

[32] Who *is* strong, but the Lord? And who will be a Creator except our God?

[33] *It is* the Mighty One who strengthens me with might, and has prepared my way without fault.

[34] He makes my feet like the feet of deer, and sets me upon the high places.

[35] He teaches my hands to war, and has broken the bronze bow by my arm.

[36] And You have given me the shield of my salvation, and Your propitious dealing has increased me,

[37] so as to make room under me for my going, and my legs did not totter.

[38] I will pursue my enemies, and will utterly destroy them; and I will not turn again till I have consumed them.

[39] And I will crush them, and they shall not rise; and they shall fall under my feet.

[40] And You shall strengthen me with power for the war; You shall cause them that rise up against me to bow down under me.

[41] And You have caused my enemies to flee before me, even them that hated me, and You have slain them.

[42] They shall cry, and there shall be no helper; *they shall cry* to the Lord, but He does not listen to them.

[43] And I ground them as the dust of the earth, I beat them small as the mire of the streets.

[44] And You shall deliver me from the striving of the peoples, You shall keep me *to be* the head of the Gentiles; a people which I did not know served me.

[45] The foreigners submitted to me; they obeyed me as soon as they heard.

[46] The foreigners shall be cast away, and shall be overthrown out of their hiding places.

[47] The Lord lives, and blessed *be* my guardian, and my God, my strong keeper, *and He* shall be exalted.

48 The Lord who avenges me *is* strong, chastening the nations under me,

49 and bringing me out from my enemies; and You shall set me on high from among those that rise up against me; You shall deliver me from the violent man.

50 Therefore will I confess to You, O Lord, among the Gentiles, and sing to Your name.

51 He magnifies the salvation of His king, and works mercy for His anointed, even for David and for his descendants forever."

2 SAMUEL CHAPTER 23

David's Last Words

1 And these *are* the last words of David. Faithful *is* David the son of Jesse, and faithful *is* the man whom the Lord has raised up to be the anointed of the God of Jacob, and beautiful *are* the psalms of Israel.

2 The Spirit of the Lord spoke by me, and His word *was* on my tongue.

3 The God of Israel says, "The watchman out of Israel spoke to me a parable: I said among men, 'How will you strengthen the fear of the anointed?'

4 And in the morning light of God, let the sun arise in the morning, from the light of which the Lord passed on, and as it were from the rain of the tender grass upon the earth.

5 For my house *is* not so with the Mighty One; for He has made an everlasting covenant with me, ready, guarded at every time; for all my salvation and all my desire *is*, that the wicked should not flourish.

6 All these *are* as a thorn thrust forth, for they shall not be taken with the hand,

7 and a man shall not labor among them; and *one shall have* that which is fully armed with iron, and the staff of a spear, and he shall burn them with fire, and they shall be burnt in their shame."

David's Mighty Men

8 These *are* the names of the mighty men of David: Josheb-Basshebeth the Canaanite is a captain of the third *part;* Adino the Eznite, he drew his sword against eight hundred soldiers at once.

9 And after him Eleazer the son of his uncle, son of Dodai who was among the three mighty men with David; and when he defied the Philistines they were gathered there to war, and the men of Israel went up.

10 He arose and attacked the Philistines, until his hand was weary, and his hand stuck to the sword: and the Lord brought about a great salvation in that day, and the people rested behind him only to plunder *the slain.*

11 And after him Shammah the son of Agee the Hararite. And the Philistines were gathered to Theria; and there was there a portion of ground full of lentils; and the people fled before the Philistines.

12 And he stood firm in the midst of the portion, and rescued it, and attacked the Philistines; and the Lord brought about a great deliverance.

13 And three out of the thirty went down, and came to Cason to David, to the cave of Adullam; and *there was* an army of the Philistines, and they encamped in the valley of Rephaim.

14 And David *was* then in the stronghold, and the garrison of the Philistines *was* then in Bethlehem.

15 And David longed, and said, "Who will give me water to drink out of the well that is in Bethlehem by the gate?" Now the band of the Philistines *was* then in Bethlehem.

16 And the three mighty men broke through the army of the Philistines, and drew water out of the well that was in Bethlehem in the gate; and they took it, and brought it to David, and he would not drink it, but poured it out before the Lord.

17 And he said, "O Lord, *God* forbid that I should do this, that I should drink of the blood of the men who went at *the risk of* their lives." And he would not drink it. These things did these three mighty men.

18 And Abishai the brother of Joab the son of Zeruiah, *was* chief among the three, and he lifted up his spear against three hundred whom he killed; and he had a name among *these* three.

19 Of those three *he was* most honorable, and he became a chief over them, but he did not attain to the *first* three.

20 And Benaiah the son of Jehoiada, he was abundant in *mighty* deeds, from Kabzeel, and he killed the two sons of Ariel of Moab: and he went down and killed a lion in the midst of a pit on a snowy day.

21 He killed an Egyptian, a spectacular man, and in the hand of the Egyptian *was* a spear as the side of a ladder; and he went down to him with a staff, and snatched the spear from the Egyptian's hand, and killed him with his own spear.

22 These things did Benaiah the son of Jehoiada, and he had a name among the three mighty men.

23 He was honorable among the *second* three, but he did not attain to the *first* three: and David made him his reporter. And these *are* the names of King David's mighty men.

24 Asahel Joab's brother; he *was* among the thirty. Elhanan son of Dodai his uncle in Bethlehem.

25 Shammah the Harodite;

26 Helez the Paltite; Ira the son of Ikkesh the Tekoite;

27 Abiezer the Anathothite, of the sons of the Anathothites;

28 Zalmon the Ahohite; Maharai the Netophathite;

29 Ittai the son of Ribai of Gibeah, son of Benjamin the Ephrathite; Asmoth the Bardiamite; Emasu the Salabonite;

30 Adroi of the brooks;

31 Gadabiel son of the Arbathite;

32 the sons of Asan, Jonathan;

33 Shammah the Hararite; Ahiam the son of Sharar the Hararite;

34 Eliphelet the son of Ahasbai, the son of the Maachathite; Eliam the son of Ahithophel the Gilonite;

35 Hezrai the Carmelite, the son of Uraeoerchi;

36 Igal the son of Nathan; the son of much valor, *the son of* Galaddi; Elie the Ammonite;

37 Gelore the Bethorite, armorbearer to Joab, son of Zeruiah.

38 Ira the Ithrite; Gareb the Ithrite;

39 *and* Uriah the Hittite: thirty-seven in all.

2 SAMUEL CHAPTER 24

David's Census of Israel and Judah

1 And the Lord caused His anger to burn forth again in Israel, and He stirred up David against them, saying, "Go, number Israel and Judah."

2 And the king said to Joab commander of the army, who was with him, "Go now through all the tribes of Israel and Judah, from Dan even to Beersheba, and number the people, and I will know the number of the people."

3 And Joab said to the king, "Now may the Lord add to the people a hundredfold as many as they are, and *may* the eyes of my lord the king see it: but why does my lord the king desire this thing?"

4 Nevertheless the word of the king prevailed against Joab and the captains of the army. Therefore Joab and the captains of the army went out before the king to number the people of Israel.

5 And they went over the Jordan, and encamped in Aroer, on the right of the city which is in the midst of the valley of Gad and Jazer.

6 And they came to Gilead, and into the land of Tahtim Hodshi, which is Adasai, and they came to Danidan and Udan, and compassed Sidon.

7 And they came to Mapsar of Tyre, and to all the cities of the Hivite and the Canaanite; and they came by the South of Judah to Beersheba.

8 And they compassed the whole land; and they arrived at Jerusalem at the end of nine months and twenty days.

9 And Joab gave in the number of the census of the people to the king. And Israel consisted of eight hundred thousand men of might that drew the sword; and the men of Judah *were* five hundred thousand fighting men.

The Judgment on David's Sin

10 And the heart of David convicted him after he had numbered the people; and David said to the Lord, "I have sinned grievously, O Lord, *in* what I have now done: remove the iniquity of Your servant, I pray, for I have been exceedingly foolish."

11 And David rose early in the morning, and the word of the Lord came to the prophet Gad, the seer, saying, "Go, and speak to David, saying,

12 'Thus says the Lord: "I *shall* bring *one of* three things upon you: now choose one of them, and I will do *it* to you."'"

13 And Gad went in to David and told him, and said to him, "Choose *one of these things* to befall you, whether there shall come upon you *for* three years famine in your land; or that you should flee three months before your enemies, and they should pursue you; or that there should be three days of death in your land. Now then decide, and see what answer I shall return to Him that sent me."

14 And David said to Gad, "On every side I am in great distress: let me fall now into the hands of the Lord, for His compassions *are* great; and let me not fall into the hands of man."

15 So David chose for himself *the plague of* death: and *they were* the days of wheat harvest; and the Lord sent a pestilence upon Israel from morning till noon, and the plague began among the people; and there died of the people from Dan even to Beersheba seventy thousand men.

16 And the angel of the Lord stretched out His hand against Jerusalem to destroy it, and the Lord relented of the evil, and said to the angel that destroyed the people, "*It is* enough now, withhold your hand." And the angel of the Lord was by the threshing floor of Araunah the Jebusite.

17 And David spoke to the Lord when he saw the angel striking the people, and he said, "Behold, it is I that has done wrong, but these sheep, what have they done? Let Your hand be upon me, I pray, and upon my father's house."

David's Altar on the Threshing Floor

18 And Gad came to David in that day, and said to him, "Go up, and set up to the Lord and altar on the threshing floor of Araunah the Jebusite."

19 And David went up according to the word of Gad, as the Lord commanded him.

20 And Araunah looked out, and saw the king and his servants coming on before him. And Araunah went forth, and bowed down before the king with his face to the earth.

21 And Araunah said, "Why has my lord the king come to his servant?" And David said, "To buy from you the threshing floor, in order to build an altar to the Lord, that the plague may be restrained from off the people."

22 And Araunah said to David, "Let my lord the king take and offer to the Lord that which is good in his eyes: behold, *here are* oxen for a burnt offering, and the wheels and furniture of the oxen for wood."

23 *And* Araunah gave all to the king. And Araunah said to the king, "The Lord your God bless you."

24 And the king said to Araunah, "No, but I will surely buy it from you at a fair price, and I will not offer to the Lord my God a burnt offering for nothing." So David purchased the threshing floor and the oxen for fifty shekels of silver.

25 And David built there an altar to the Lord, and offered up burnt offerings and peace offerings; and Solomon made an addition to the altar afterwards, for it was little at first. And the Lord hearkened to the land, and the plague was withdrawn from Israel.

THE FIRST BOOK OF KINGS

Adonijah Presumes to be King

1 And King David *was* old and advanced in days, and they covered him with clothes, and he was not warmed.

2 And his servants said, "Let them seek for the king a young virgin, and she shall wait on the king, and cherish him, and lie with him, and my lord the king shall be warmed."

3 So they sought out a lovely young woman out of all the coasts of Israel; and they found Abishag the Shunammite, and they brought her to the king.

4 And the young woman was extremely beautiful, and she cherished the king, and ministered to him, but the king did not know her.

5 And Adonijah the son of Haggith exalted himself, saying, "I will be king"; and he prepared for himself chariots and horses, and fifty men to run before him.

6 And his father never at any time checked him, saying, "Why have you done *thus*?" And he was also very handsome in appearance, and his mother bore him after Absalom.

7 And he conferred with Joab the son of Zeruiah, and with Abiathar the priest, and they followed after Adonijah.

8 But Zadok the priest, and Benaiah the son of Jehoiada, and Nathan the prophet, and Shimei, and Rei, and the mighty men of David, did not follow Adonijah.

9 And Adonijah sacrificed sheep and calves and lambs by the stone of Zoheleth, which was near En Rogel. And he called all his brothers, and all the adult *men* of Judah, servants of the king.

10 But Nathan the prophet, and Benaiah, and the mighty *men*, and Solomon his brother, he did not call.

11 And Nathan spoke to Bathsheba the mother of Solomon, saying, "Have you not heard that Adonijah the son of Haggith reigns, and our lord David does not know it?

12 And now come, let me give you counsel, and you shall rescue your life, and the life of your son Solomon.

13 Make haste, and go in to King David, and you shall speak to him, saying, 'Has not you, my lord, O king, sworn to your maid, saying, "Your son Solomon shall reign after me, and he shall sit upon my throne?" Why then does Adonijah reign?'

14 And behold, while you are still speaking there with the king, I also will come in after you, and will confirm your words."

15 So Bathsheba went in to the king into the chamber. And the king was very old, and Abishag the Shunammite was ministering to the king.

16 And Bathsheba bowed down before the king; and the king said, "What is your request?"

17 And she said, "My lord, you swore by the Lord your God to your maid, saying, 'Your son Solomon shall reign after me, and shall sit upon my throne.'

18 And now, behold, Adonijah reigns, and you, my lord, O king, are unaware of it.

19 And he has sacrificed calves and lambs and sheep in abundance, and has called all the king's sons, and Abiathar the priest and Joab the commander-in-chief of the army; but Solomon your servant he has not called.

20 And you, my lord, O king, the eyes of all Israel *are* upon you, to tell them who shall sit upon the throne of my lord the king after him.

21 And it shall come to pass, when my lord the king shall sleep with his fathers, that I and Solomon my son shall be offenders."

22 And behold, while she was yet talking with the king, Nathan the prophet came. And it was reported to the king,

23 "Behold, Nathan the prophet *is here*." And he came in to the king's presence, and bowed down to the king with his face to the ground.

24 And Nathan said, "My lord, O king, did you say, Adonijah shall reign after me, and he shall sit upon my throne?

25 For he has gone down today, and has sacrificed calves and lambs and sheep in abundance, and has called all the king's sons, and the chiefs of the army, and Abiathar the priest; and behold, they are eating and drinking before him, and they said, '*Long* live King Adonijah.'

26 But he has not invited me your servant, nor Zadok the priest, nor Benaiah the son of Jehoiada, nor Solomon your servant.

27 Has this matter happened by the authority of my lord the king, and have you not made known to your servant who shall sit upon the throne of my lord the king after him?"

David Proclaims Solomon King

28 And King David answered and said, "Call Bathsheba to me." So she came in before the king, and stood before him.

29 And the king swore, and said, "*As* the Lord lives who redeemed my soul out of all affliction,

30 as I swore to you by the Lord God of Israel, saying, 'Solomon your son shall reign after me, and he shall sit upon my throne in my place,' so will I do this day."

31 And Bathsheba bowed with her face to the ground, and paid homage to the king, and said, "Let my lord King David live forever."

32 And King David said, "Call me Zadok the priest, and Nathan the prophet, and Benaiah the son of Jehoiada." And they came in before the king.

33 And the king said to them, "Take the servants of your lord with you, and mount my son Solomon upon my own mule, and bring him down to Gihon.

34 And there let Zadok the priest and Nathan the prophet anoint him to be king over Israel, and sound the trumpet, and you shall say, '*Long* live King Solomon!'

35 And he shall sit upon my throne, and reign in my place; and I have commanded that he should be ruler over Israel and Judah."

[36] And Benaiah the son of Jehoiada answered the king and said, "So let it be: may the Lord God of my lord the king confirm *it.*

[37] As the Lord was with my lord the king, so let Him be with Solomon, and let Him exalt his throne beyond the throne of my lord King David."

[38] And Zadok the priest went down, and Nathan the prophet, and Benaiah son of Jehoiada, and the Cherethites, and the Pelethites, and they mounted Solomon upon the mule of King David, and led him away to Gihon.

[39] And Zadok the priest took the horn of oil out of the tabernacle, and anointed Solomon, and blew the trumpet; and all the people said, "*Long* live King Solomon!"

[40] And all the people went up after him, and they danced in choirs, and rejoiced with great joy, and the earth quaked with their voice.

[41] And Adonijah and all his guests heard, and they had *just* left off eating. And Joab heard the sound of the trumpet, and said, "Why is the voice of the city in an uproar?"

[42] While he was yet speaking, behold, Jonathan the son of Abiathar the priest came in. And Adonijah said, "Come in, for you are a mighty man, and *you come* to bring good news."

[43] And Jonathan answered and said, "Verily our lord King David has made Solomon king;

[44] and the king has sent with him Zadok the priest, and Nathan the prophet, and Benaiah the son of Jehoiada, and the Cherethites, and the Pelethites, and they have mounted him on the king's mule;

[45] and Zadok the priest and Nathan the prophet have anointed him in Gihon, and have gone up from there rejoicing, and the city has resounded: this *is* the sound which you have heard.

[46] And Solomon is seated upon the throne of the kingdom.

[47] And the servants of the king have gone in to bless our lord King David, saying, 'God make the name of Solomon better than your name, and make his throne greater than your throne'; and the king worshipped upon his bed.

[48] Moreover thus said the king, 'Blessed *be* the Lord God of Israel, who has this day appointed one of my descendants sitting on my throne, and my eyes have seen it.'"

[49] And all the guests of Adonijah were dismayed, and every man went his way.

[50] And Adonijah feared because of Solomon, and arose, and departed, and laid hold on the horns of the altar.

[51] And it was reported to Solomon, saying, "Behold, Adonijah fears King Solomon, and holds the horns of the altar, saying, 'Let Solomon swear to me this day, that he will not slay his servant with the sword.'"

[52] And Solomon said, "If he should be a valiant man, there shall not a hair of his head fall to the ground; but if evil be found in him, he shall die."

[53] And King Solomon sent, and they brought him away from the altar; and he went in and bowed down to King Solomon. And Solomon said to him, "Go to your house."

1 KINGS CHAPTER 2

David's Instructions to Solomon

[1] And the days of David drew near that he should die. And he addressed his son Solomon, saying, "I go the way of all the earth;

[2] but be strong, and show yourself a man;

[3] and keep the charge of the Lord your God, to walk in His ways, to keep the commandments and the ordinances and the judgments which are written in the Law of Moses; that you may understand what you shall do in all things that I command you:

[4] that the Lord may confirm His word which He spoke, saying, 'If your children shall take heed to their way to walk before Me in truth with all their heart,' *I promise you*, saying, 'there shall not fail you a man on the throne of Israel.'

[5] Moreover you know all that Joab the son of Zeruiah did to me, what he did to the two captains of the forces of Israel, to Abner the son of Ner, and to Amasa the son of Jether, that he killed them, and shed the blood of war in peace *time*, and put innocent blood on his belt that was around his waist, and on his sandal that was on his foot.

[6] Therefore you shall deal *with him* according to your wisdom, and you shall not bring down his grey hairs in peace to the grave.

[7] But you shall deal kindly with the sons of Barzillai the Gileadite, and they shall be among those that eat at your table; for thus they drew near to me when I fled from the face of your brother Absalom.

[8] And behold, *there is* with you Shimei the son of Gera, a Benjamite of Bahurim: and he cursed me with a grievous curse in the day when I went into the camp; and he came down to the Jordan to meet me, and I swore to him by the Lord, saying, 'I will not put you to death with the sword.'

[9] But you shall by no means hold him guiltless, for you are a wise man, and will know what you shall do to him, and shall bring down his grey hairs with blood to the grave."

The Death of David

[10] And David slept with his fathers, and was buried in the City of David.

[11] And the days in which David reigned over Israel *were* forty years; he reigned seven years in Hebron, and thirty-three years in Jerusalem.

[12] And Solomon sat on the throne of his father David, and his kingdom was established greatly.

Solomon Executes Adonijah

[13] And Adonijah the son of Haggith came to Bathsheba the mother of Solomon, and bowed down to her. And she said, "Do you enter peaceably?" And he said, "Peaceably."

[14] *He said,* "I have business with you." And she said to him, "Speak on."

¹⁵ And he said to her, "You know that the kingdom was mine, and all Israel turned their face toward me for a king; but the kingdom was turned *from me* and became my brother's; for it was *appointed* to him from the Lord.

¹⁶ And now I make one request of you, do not turn away your face." And Bathsheba said to him, "Speak *on*."

¹⁷ And he said to her, "Speak to King Solomon, for he will not turn away his face from you, and let him give me Abishag the Shunammite for a wife."

¹⁸ And Bathsheba said, "Very well; I will speak to the king for you."

¹⁹ And Bathsheba went in to King Solomon to speak to him concerning Adonijah. And the king rose up to meet her, and kissed her, and sat on the throne, and a throne was set for the mother of the king, and she sat on his right hand.

²⁰ And she said to him, "I ask of you one little request; do not turn away my face from you." And the king said to her, "Ask, my mother, and I will not reject you."

²¹ And she said, "Let Abishag the Shunammite be given to Adonijah your brother for a wife."

²² And King Solomon answered and said to his mother, "And why have you asked *for* Abishag for Adonijah? Ask for him the kingdom also; for he *is* my older brother, and he has for his companion Abiathar the priest, and Joab the son of Zeruiah the commander-in-chief."

²³ And King Solomon swore by the Lord, saying, "God do so to me, and more also, *if it be not* that Adonijah has spoken this word against his own life.

²⁴ And now *as* the Lord lives who has established me, and set me on the throne of my father David, and He has made me a house, as the Lord spoke, this day shall Adonijah be put to death."

²⁵ So King Solomon sent by the hand of Benaiah the son of Jehoiada, and he killed him, and Adonijah died in that day.

Abiathar Exiled, Joab Executed

²⁶ And the king said to Abiathar the priest, "Depart quickly to Anathoth, to your farm, for you are worthy of death this day; but I will not slay you, because you have borne the ark of the covenant of the Lord before my father, and because you were afflicted in all things in which my father was afflicted."

²⁷ And Solomon removed Abiathar from being a priest of the Lord, that the word of the Lord might be fulfilled, which he spoke concerning the house of Eli in Shiloh.

²⁸ And the report came to Joab son of Zeruiah; for Joab had turned after Adonijah, and did not follow after Solomon. And Joab fled to the tabernacle of the Lord, and caught hold of the horns of the altar.

²⁹ And it was told Solomon, saying, "Joab has fled to the tabernacle of the Lord, and behold, he has taken hold of the horns of the altar." And King Solomon sent to Joab, saying, "What ails you, that you have fled to the altar?" And Joab said, "Because I was afraid of you, and fled for refuge to the Lord." And Solomon sent Benaiah son of Jehoiada, saying, "Go and slay him, and bury him."

³⁰ And Benaiah son of Jehoiada came to Joab to the tabernacle of the Lord, and said to him, "Thus says the king: 'Come forth.'" And Joab said, "I will not come forth, for I will die here." And Benaiah son of Jehoiada returned and spoke to the king, saying, "Thus has Joab spoken, and thus has he answered me."

³¹ And the king said to him, "Go, and do to him as he has spoken, and kill him. And you shall bury him, and you shall remove this day the blood which he shed without cause, from me and from the house of my father.

³² And the Lord has returned upon his own head the blood of his unrighteousness, inasmuch as he attacked two men more righteous and better than himself, and killed them with the sword, and my father David knew not of their blood, *even* Abner the son of Ner the commander-in-chief of Israel, and Amasa the son of Jether the commander-in-chief of Judah.

³³ And their blood is returned upon his head, and upon the head of his descendants forever; but to David, and his descendants, and his house, and his throne, may there be peace forever from the Lord."

³⁴ So Benaiah son of Jehoiada went up, and attacked him, and killed him, and buried him in his house in the wilderness.

³⁵ And the king appointed Benaiah son of Jehoiada in his place over the army; and the kingdom was established in Jerusalem. And *as for* Zadok the priest, the king appointed him to be high priest in place of Abiathar. And Solomon son of David reigned over Israel and Judah in Jerusalem. And the Lord gave understanding to Solomon, and very much wisdom, and largeness of heart, as the sand by the seashore.

Shimei Executed

³⁶ And the king called Shimei, and said to him, "Build yourself a house in Jerusalem, and dwell there, and you shall not go out from there anywhere.

³⁷ And it shall come to pass in the day that you shall go forth and cross over the Brook Kidron, know assuredly that you shall certainly die: your blood shall be upon your head." And the king caused him to swear in that day.

³⁸ And Shimei said to the king, "Good *is* the word that you have spoken, my lord O king: thus will your servant do." And Shimei dwelt in Jerusalem three years.

³⁹ And it came to pass after the three years, that two servants of Shimei ran away to Achish son of Maachah king of Gath. And it was told Shimei, saying, "Behold, your servants *are* in Gath."

⁴⁰ And Shimei rose up, and saddled his donkey, and went to Gath, to Achish, to seek out his servants. And Shimei went, and brought his servants out of Gath.

⁴¹ And it was told Solomon, saying, "Shimei has gone out of Jerusalem to Gath, and has brought back his servants."

⁴² And the king sent and called Shimei, and said to him, "Did I not adjure you by the Lord, and testify to you, saying,

'In whatsoever day you shall go out of Jerusalem, and go to the right or left, know certainly that you shall surely die?'

⁴³ And why have you not kept the oath of the Lord, and the commandment which I commanded you?"

⁴⁴ And the king said to Shimei, "You know all your mischief which your heart knows, which you did to David my father; and the Lord has recompensed your mischief on your *own* head.

⁴⁵ But King Solomon *shall be* blessed, and the throne of David shall be established before the Lord forever."

⁴⁶ And Solomon commanded Benaiah the son of Jehoiada, and he went forth and killed him.

And King Solomon was very prudent and wise. And Judah and Israel *were* very many, as the sand which is by the sea in multitude, eating and drinking, and rejoicing. And Solomon was chief in all the kingdoms, and they brought gifts, and served Solomon all the days of his life. And Solomon began to open the domains of Lebanon, and he built Terman in the wilderness.

And this was the daily provision of Solomon: thirty measures of fine flour, and sixty measures of ground meal, ten choice calves, and twenty oxen from the pastures, and a hundred sheep, besides stags, and does, and choice fed birds. For he ruled in all the country on this side of the river, from Raphi unto Gaza, over all the kings on this side of the river. And he was at peace on all sides round about; and Judah and Israel dwelt safely, everyone under his vine and under his fig tree, eating and drinking and feasting, from Dan even to Beersheba, all the days of Solomon.

And these *were* the princes of Solomon: Azariu son of Zadok the priest, and Orniu son of Nathan chief of the officers, and he went to his house; and Suba the scribe, and Basa son of Achithalam the recorder, and Abi son of Joab commander-in-chief, and Achire son of Edrai *was* over the levites, and Benaiah son of Jehoiada over the household and over the brickwork, and Cachur the son of Nathan *was* counselor.

1 KINGS CHAPTER 3

Solomon's Prayer for Wisdom

¹ And Solomon had forty thousand brood mares for his chariots, and twelve thousand horses. And he reigned over all the kings from the river and to the land of the Philistines, and to the borders of Egypt: so Solomon the son of David reigned over Israel and Judah in Jerusalem.

² Nevertheless the people burnt incense on the high places, because a house had not yet been built to the Lord.

³ And Solomon loved the Lord, and he walked in the ordinances of David his father; except that he sacrificed and burnt incense on the high places.

⁴ And he arose and went to Gibeon to sacrifice there, for that *was the* highest place, and great. Solomon offered a burnt offering of a thousand *victims* on the altar in Gibeon.

⁵ And the Lord appeared to Solomon in a dream by night, and the Lord said to Solomon, "Ask some petition for yourself."

⁶ And Solomon said, "You have dealt very mercifully with Your servant David my father according as he walked before You in truth, and in righteousness, and in uprightness of heart with You, and You have kept for him this great mercy, to set his son upon his throne, as *it is* this day.

⁷ And now, O Lord my God, You have appointed Your servant in the place of David my father; and I am a little child, and know not my going out and my coming in.

⁸ But Your servant *is* in the midst of Your people whom You have chosen, a great people, which cannot be numbered.

⁹ Give therefore to Your servant a heart to hear and to judge Your people justly, and to discern between good and evil: for who will be able to judge this Your great people?"

¹⁰ And it was pleasing before the Lord, that Solomon asked this thing.

¹¹ And the Lord said to him, "Because you have asked this thing of Me, and have not asked for yourself long life, and have not asked for wealth, nor have you asked for the lives of your enemies, but *rather* have asked for yourself understanding to hear judgment;

¹² behold, I have done according to your word: behold, I have given you an understanding and wise heart: there has not been *anyone* like you before you, and after you there shall not arise one like you.

¹³ And I have *also* given to you what you have not asked—wealth and glory, so that there has not been anyone like you among kings.

¹⁴ And if you will walk in My ways, to keep My commandments and My ordinances, as David your father walked, then will I multiply your days."

¹⁵ And Solomon awoke, and behold, *it was* a dream. And he arose and came to Jerusalem, and stood before the altar that was in front of the ark of the covenant of the Lord in Zion. And he offered burnt offerings, and sacrificed peace offerings, and made a great banquet for himself and all his servants.

Solomon's Wise Judgment

¹⁶ Then two harlots appeared before the king, and they stood before him.

¹⁷ And the one woman said, "Hear me, *my* lord: I and this woman dwelt in one house, and we *both* delivered *a child* in the house.

¹⁸ And it came to pass on the third day after I was delivered, this woman also was delivered. And we *were* together; and there was no one with us besides our two selves in the house.

¹⁹ And this woman's child died in the night because she laid on him.

²⁰ And she arose in the middle of the night, and took my son from my arms, and laid him in her bosom, and laid her dead son in my bosom.

21 And I arose in the morning to suckle my son, and he was dead. And behold, I looked at him in the morning, and behold, it was not my son whom I bore."

22 And the other woman said, "No, but the living *one is* my son, and the dead *one is* your son." So they spoke before the king.

23 And the king said to them, "You say, 'This *is* my son, the living *one*, and this woman's son *is* the dead one.' And you say, 'No, but the living *one is* my son, and the dead *one is* your son.'"

24 And the king said, "Bring me a sword." And they brought a sword before the king.

25 And the king said, "Divide the live child, *this* infant, in two; and give half to one, and half to the other."

26 And the woman whose the living child was answered and said to the king (for her heart yearned over her son), "I beseech you, *my* lord, give her the child, and by no means kill him." But the other said, "Let him be neither mine nor hers; *but* divide *him*."

27 Then the king answered and said, "Give the child to her that said, 'Give it to her, and by no means kill him': she *is his* mother."

28 And all Israel heard this judgment which the king had rendered, and they feared before the king; because they saw that the wisdom of God *was* in him, to execute judgment.

1 KINGS CHAPTER 4

Solomon's Administration

1 And King Solomon reigned over Israel.

2 And these *are* the princes which he had: Azariah son of Zadok.

3 Eliaph and Ahijah son of Shisha, scribes; and Jehoshaphat son of Ahilud, recorder.

4 And Benaiah son of Jehoiada over the army; and Zadok and Abiathar *were* priests.

5 And Azariah the son of Nathan *was* over the officers; and Zabud son of Nathan *was* the king's friend.

6 And Ahhisar was manager, and Eliac the *chief* manager; and Eliab the son of Saph *was* over the family: and Adoniram the son of Abda over the tribute.

7 And Solomon had twelve officers over all Israel, to provide for the king and his household; each one's turn came to supply for a month in the year.

8 And these *were* their names: Ben Hur in the mount of Ephraim, one.

9 The son of Dekar, in Makaz, and in Shaalbim, and Beth Shamesh, and Elon as far as Bethana, one.

10 The son of Esdi in Araboth; his *was* Sochoh, and all the land of Hepher.

11 All Nephthador *belonged to* the son of Aminadab, Tephath daughter of Solomon was his wife, one.

12 Baana son of Ahilud *had* Taanach and Megiddo, and *his was* the whole house of Shean which was by Sesathan below Esrae, and from Beth Shean as far as Abel Meholah, as far as Maeber Lucam, one.

13 The son of Naber in Ramoth Gilead, to him fell *the* lot of Argob in Bashan, sixty great cities with walls, and bronze bars, one.

14 Ahinadab son of Iddo, *had* Mahanaim.

15 Ahimaaz *was* in Naphtali, and he took Basemath daughter of Solomon as wife, one.

16 Baanah son of Hushai, in Asher and in Aloth, one.

17 Jehoshaphat son of Paruah *was* in Issachar.

18 Shimei son of Elah, in Benjamin.

19 Geber son of Uri in the land of Gad, *the land* of Sihon king of Heshbon, and of Og king of Bashan, and one officer in the land of Judah.

20 (This verse omitted in LXX)

21 (This verse omitted in LXX)

Magnificence of Solomon's Rule

22 And these *were* the provisions for Solomon: in one day thirty measures of fine flour, and sixty measures of fine pounded meal,

23 and ten choice calves, and twenty pastured oxen, and a hundred sheep, besides stags, and choice fatted does.

24 For he had dominion on this side of the river, and he was at peace on all sides round about.

25 (This verse omitted in LXX)

26 (This verse omitted in LXX)

27 And thus the officers provided for King Solomon. And everyone in his *appointed* month *followed* all the orders for the table of the king; they omitted nothing.

28 And they carried the barley and the straw for the horses and the chariots to the place where the king might be, each according to his charge.

29 And the Lord gave understanding to Solomon, and very much wisdom, and enlargement of heart, as the sand on the seashore.

30 And Solomon abounded greatly beyond the wisdom of all the ancients, and beyond all the wise men of Egypt.

31 And he was wiser than all *other* men; and he was wiser than Ethan the Ezrahrite, and *than* Heman, and *than* Chalcol and Darda the son of Mahol.

32 And Solomon spoke three thousand proverbs, and his songs were five thousand.

33 And he spoke of trees, from the cedar in Lebanon even to the hyssop which comes out through the wall: he spoke also of cattle, and of birds, and of reptiles, and of fish.

34 And all the nations came to hear the wisdom of Solomon, and *ambassadors* from all the kings of the earth, as many as heard of his wisdom. And Solomon took to himself the daughter of Pharaoh as wife, and brought her into the City of David until he had finished the house of the Lord, and his own house, and the wall of Jerusalem. Then he went up to Pharaoh the king of Egypt, and took Gazer, and burnt it and

the Canaanite dwelling in Mergab; and Pharaoh gave them as a dowry to his daughter the wife of Solomon; and Solomon rebuilt Gazer.

1 KINGS CHAPTER 5

Solomon Prepares to Build the Temple

¹ And Hiram king of Tyre sent his servants to anoint Solomon in the place of David his father, because Hiram always loved David.

² And Solomon sent to Hiram, saying,

³ "You knew my father David, that he could not build a house to the name of the Lord my God because of the wars that compassed him about, until the Lord put them under the soles of his feet.

⁴ And now the Lord my God has given me rest round about; there is no one plotting against *me*, and there is no evil trespass *against me*.

⁵ And behold, I intend to build a house to the name of the Lord my God, as the Lord God spoke to my father David, saying, 'Your son whom I will set on your throne in your place, he shall build a house for My name.'

⁶ And now command, and let *men* cut wood for me out of Lebanon. And behold, my servants *shall be* with your servants, and I will give you the wages of your service, according to all that you shall say, because you know that we have no one skilled in cutting timber like the Sidonians."

⁷ And it came to pass, as soon as Hiram heard the words of Solomon, that he rejoiced greatly, and said, "Blessed *be* God this day, who has given to David a wise son over this numerous people."

⁸ And he sent to Solomon, saying, "I have listened concerning all that you have sent to me, for I will do all your will: *as for* timber of cedar and fir,

⁹ my servants shall bring them down from Lebanon to the sea: I will form them *into* rafts, *and bring them* to the place which you shall send to me *about*; and I will land them there, and you shall take *them* up; and you shall do my will, in giving bread to my household.

¹⁰ So Hiram gave to Solomon cedars, and fir trees, and all his desire.

¹¹ And Solomon gave to Hiram twenty thousand measures of wheat as food for his house, and twenty thousand baths of beaten oil; thus Solomon gave to Hiram yearly.

¹² And the Lord gave wisdom to Solomon as He promised him; and there was peace between Hiram and Solomon, and they made a covenant between them.

¹³ And the king raised a levy out of all Israel, and the levy was thirty thousand men.

¹⁴ And he sent them to Lebanon, ten thousand taking turn every month; they were a month in Lebanon and two months at home; and Adoniram *was* over the levy.

¹⁵ And Solomon had seventy thousand bearers of burdens, and eighty thousand hewers of stone in the mountain;

¹⁶ besides the rulers that were appointed over the works of Solomon, *there were* three thousand six hundred masters who wrought in the works.

¹⁷ (This verse omitted in LXX)

¹⁸ And they prepared the stones and the timber *during* three years.

1 KINGS CHAPTER 6

Solomon Builds the Temple

¹ And it came to pass in the four hundred and fortieth year after the departure of the children of Israel out of Egypt, in the fourth year and second month of the reign of King Solomon over Israel, that the king commanded that they should take great *and* costly stones for the foundation of the house, and hewn stones. And the men of Solomon, and the men of Hiram hewed *the stones*, and laid them *for a foundation*. In the fourth year he laid the foundation of the house of the Lord, in the month of Ziv, in the second month. In the eleventh year, in the eighth month, the house was completed according to all its plan, and according to all its arrangement.

² And the house which the king built to the Lord *was* forty cubits in length, and twenty cubits in breadth, and its height *was* twenty-five cubits.

³ And the porch in front of the temple *was* twenty cubits in length according to the breadth of the house in front of the house. And he built the house, and finished it.

⁴ And he made secret windows for the house inclining inward.

⁵ And against the wall of the house he set chambers round about the temple and the ark.

⁶ The under side *was* five cubits broad, and the middle *part* six, and the third *was* seven cubits broad; for he formed an interval to the house round about without the house, that they might not touch the walls of the house.

⁷ And the house was built in the construction of it with rough hewn stones; and there was not heard in the house in the building of it *neither* hammer or ax, or any iron tool.

⁸ And the porch of the under side *was* below the right wing of the house, and *there was* a winding ascent into the middle *chamber*, and from the middle to the third story.

⁹ So he built the house and finished it; and he made the ceiling of the house with cedars.

¹⁰ And he made the partitions through all the house, each five cubits high, and enclosed each partition with cedar boards.

¹¹ (This verse omitted in LXX)

¹² (This verse omitted in LXX)

¹³ (This verse omitted in LXX)

¹⁴ (This verse omitted in LXX)

¹⁵ And he framed the walls of the house inside with cedar boards, from the floor of the house and on to the inner walls and to the beams; he lined the parts enclosed with boards

inside, and compassed the inward parts of the house with planks of fir.

16 And he built the twenty cubits from the top of the wall, one side from the floor to the beams, and he made it from the oracle to the Most Holy Place.

17 And the temple was forty cubits *long,*

18 (This verse omitted in LXX)

19 in front of the oracle in the midst of the house inside, *in order* to put there the ark of the covenant of the Lord.

20 The length *was* twenty cubits, and the breadth *was* twenty cubits, and the height of it was twenty cubits. And he covered it with perfect gold, and he made an altar in front of the oracle, and covered it with gold.

21 And he covered the whole house with gold, till he had finished *gilding* the whole house.

22 (This verse omitted in LXX)

23 And he made in the oracle two cherubim of ten cubits high.

24 And the wing of one cherub was five cubits, and his other wing was five cubits; ten cubits from the tip of one wing to the tip of the other wing.

25 Thus it was with the other cherub, both were alike finished with one measure.

26 And the height of the one cherub *was* ten cubits, and so with the second cherub.

27 And both the cherubim *were* in the midst of the innermost part of the house; and they spread out their wings, and one wing touched the wall, and the wing of the other cherub touched the other wall; and their wings in the midst of the house touched each other.

28 And he covered the cherubim with gold.

29 He engraved all the walls of the house round about with the engraving of cherubim, and *he sculptured* palm trees within and without *the house.*

30 And he covered the floor of the house within and without with gold.

31 And for the doorway of the oracle he made doors of juniper wood; *there were* porches in a four-fold way.

32 (This verse omitted in LXX)

33 (This verse omitted in LXX)

34 In both the doors *were* planks of fir; the one door had two leaves and their hinges, and the other door had two leaves and turned *on hinges,*

35 being carved with cherubim, and *there were* palm trees and open flower leaves, and it *was* overlaid with gold gilded upon the engraving.

36 And he built the inner court, three rows of hewn stones, and a row of wrought cedar round about, and he made the curtain of the court of the porch of the house that was in front of the temple.

37 (This verse omitted in LXX)

38 (This verse omitted in LXX)

1 KINGS CHAPTER 7

Solomon's Other Buildings

1 And Solomon built a house for himself in thirteen years.

2 And he built the house with the wood of Lebanon; its length *was* a hundred cubits, and its breadth *was* fifty cubits, and its height *was* of thirty cubits, and *it was made* with three rows of cedar pillars, and the pillars had sidepieces of cedar.

3 And he formed the house with chambers above on the sides of the pillars, and the number of the pillars *was* forty-five,

4 and *there were* three chambers, and space against space in three rows.

5 And all the doors and spaces formed like chambers *were* square, and from door to door *was a correspondence* in three rows.

6 And *he made* the porch of the pillars, *they were* fifty *cubits* long and fifty broad, the porch joining them in front; and the *other* pillars and the thick beam *were* in front of the house by the porches.

7 And *there was* the Porch of Seats where he would judge, the Porch of Judgment.

8 And their house where he would dwell *had* one court communicating with these according to this work; and *he built* the house for the daughter of Pharaoh whom Solomon had taken, according to this porch.

9 All these *were* of costly stones, sculptured at intervals within even from the foundation even to the top, and outward to the great court,

10 founded with large costly stones, stones of ten cubits and eight cubits *long.*

11 And above with costly stones, according to the measure of hewn stones, and with cedars.

12 *There were* three rows of hewn *stones* round about the great hall, and a row of sculptured cedar: and Solomon finished all his house.

Hiram the Craftsman

13 And King Solomon sent, and took Hiram out of Tyre,

14 the son of a widow woman; and he *was* of the tribe of Naphtali, and his father *was* a Tyrian; a worker in brass, and accomplished in art and skill and knowledge to work every work in brass. And he was brought in to King Solomon, and he wrought all the works.

15 And he cast the two pillars for the porch of the house: eighteen cubits *was* the height of *each* pillar, and a circumference of fourteen cubits encompassed it, even the thickness of the pillar: the flutings *were* four fingers *wide,* and thus *was* the other pillar *formed.*

16 And he made two molded chapiters to put on the heads of the pillars: five cubits *was* the height of one chapiter, and five cubits *was* the height of the other chapiter.

17 And he made two ornaments of network to cover the chapiters of the pillars; a net for one chapiter, and a net for the other chapiter.

18 And hanging work, two rows of bronze pomegranates, formed with network, hanging work, row upon row: and thus he framed *the ornaments* for the second chapiter.

19 And on the heads of the pillars he made lilywork against the porch, of four cubits,

20 and a chamber over both the pillars, and above the sides an addition *equal to* the chamber in width.

21 And he set up the pillars of the porch of the temple; and he set up the one pillar, and called its name Jachin: and he set up the second pillar, and called its name Boaz.

22 (This verse omitted in LXX)

23 And he made the sea, ten cubits from one rim to the other, the same was completely circular round about: its height *was* five cubits, and its circumference thirty-three cubits.

24 And stays underneath its rim round about compassed it ten cubits round.

25 And *there were* twelve oxen under the sea: three looking to the north, and three looking to the west, and three looking to the south, and three looking to the east: and all their hind parts *were* inward, and the sea *was* above upon them.

26 And its rim *was* as the work of the rim of a cup, a lilyflower, and the thickness of it *was* a span.

27 And he made ten bronze bases: five cubits *was* the length of one base, and four cubits the breadth of it, and its height *was* six cubits.

28 And this work of the bases *was* formed with a border the them, and *there was* a border between the ledges.

29 And upon their borders between the projection *were* lions, and oxen, and cherubim; and on the projections, even so above, and also below *were* the places of lions and oxen, hanging work.

30 And *there were* four bronze wheels to one base; and *there were* bronze bases, and their four sides *answering to them*, side pieces under the bases.

31 And *there were* axles in the wheels under the base.

32 And the height of one wheel *was* a cubit and a half.

33 And the work of the wheels *was* as the work of chariot wheels: their axles, and their hubs, and *the rest of* their work, *were* all of cast bronze.

34 The four side pieces were at the four corners of each base; its shoulders *were formed* of the base.

35 And on the top of the base half a cubit *was* the size of it, *there was* a circle on the top of the base, and *there was* the top of its spaces and its borders: and it was open at the top of its spaces.

36 And its borders *were* cherubim, and lions, and palm trees, upright, each *was* joined in front *and* within and round about.

37 According to the same form he made all the ten bases, *even* one order and one measure to all.

38 And he made ten bronze lavers, each laver containing forty baths, *and* measuring four cubits, each laver *placed* on a several base throughout the ten bases.

39 And he put five bases on the right side of the house, and five on the left side of the house. And the sea was placed on the right side of the house eastward in the direction of the south.

Furnishings of the Temple

40 And Hiram made the caldrons, and the pans, and the bowls; and Hiram finished making all the works that he wrought for King Solomon in the house of the Lord;

41 two pillars and the wreathen works of the pillars on the heads of the two pillars; and the two networks to cover both the wreathen works of the flutings that were upon the pillars.

42 The four hundred pomegranates for both the networks, two rows of pomegranates for one network, to cover both the wreathen works of the bases belonging to both pillars.

43 And the ten bases, and the ten lavers upon the bases.

44 And one sea, and the twelve oxen under the sea.

45 And the caldrons, and pans, and bowls, and all the furniture, which Hiram made for King Solomon for the house of the Lord; and *there were* forty-eight pillars of the house of the king and of the house of the Lord; all the works of the king which Hiram made were entirely of brass.

46 In the country round about the Jordan did he cast them, in the clay land between Succoth and Zaretan.

47 There was no reckoning of the brass of which he made all these works, from the very great abundance, there was no end of the weight of the brass.

48 And King Solomon took the furniture which *Hiram* made for the house of the Lord, the golden altar, and the golden table of showbread.

49 And *he put* the five lamptands on the left, and five on the right in front of the oracle, *being* of pure gold, and the lampstands, and the lamps, and the snuffers of gold.

50 And *there* the porches *were made*, and the nails, and the bowls, and the spoons, and the golden censers, of pure gold: and the panels of the doors of the innermost part of the house, *even* the Holy of Holies, and the golden doors of the temple.

51 So the work of the house of the Lord which Solomon wrought was finished; and Solomon brought in the holy things of David his father, and all the holy things of Solomon. He put the silver, and the gold, and the furniture into the treasures of the house of the Lord.

1 KINGS CHAPTER 8

The Ark Brought into the Temple

1 And it came to pass when Solomon had finished building the house of the Lord and his own house after twenty years, that King Solomon assembled all the elders of Israel in Zion, to bring the ark of the covenant of the Lord out of the City of David (this is Zion),

2 in the month of Ethanim.

3 And the priests took up the ark,

⁴ and the tabernacle of testimony, and the holy furniture that was in the tabernacle of testimony.

⁵ And the king and all Israel *were occupied* before the ark, sacrificing sheep *and* oxen, without number.

⁶ And the priests bring in the ark into its place, into the oracle of the house, even into the Holy of Holies, under the wings of the cherubim.

⁷ For the cherubim spread out their wings over the place of the ark, and the cherubim covered the ark and its holy things above.

⁸ And the holy poles projected, and the ends of the holy poles appeared out of the holy places in front of the oracle, and were not seen outside.

⁹ There was nothing in the ark except the two tablets of stone, the tablets of the covenant which Moses put *there* in Horeb, which *tablets* the Lord made *as a covenant* with the children of Israel in their going forth from the land of Egypt.

¹⁰ And it came to pass when the priests departed out of the holy place, that the cloud filled the house.

¹¹ And the priests could not stand to minister because of the cloud, because the glory of the Lord filled the house.

¹² (This verse omitted in LXX)

¹³ (This verse omitted in LXX)

Solomon's Speech

¹⁴ And the king turned his face, and the king blessed all Israel, (and the whole assembly of Israel stood)

¹⁵ and he said, "Blessed *be* the Lord God of Israel today, who spoke by His mouth concerning David my father, and has fulfilled it with his hands, saying,

¹⁶ 'From the day that I brought out My people Israel out of Egypt, I have not chosen a city in *any* one tribe of Israel to build a house, so that My name should be there, but I chose Jerusalem that My name should be there, and I chose David to be over My people Israel.'

¹⁷ And it was in the heart of my father to build a house to the name of the Lord God of Israel.

¹⁸ And the Lord said to David my father, 'Forasmuch as it came into your heart to build a house for My name, you did well that it came upon your heart.

¹⁹ Nevertheless you shall not build the house, but your son that has proceeded out of your loins, he shall build the house for My name.'

²⁰ And the Lord has confirmed the word that He spoke, and I have risen up in the place of my father David, and I have sat down on the throne of Israel, as the Lord has spoken, and I have built the house to the name of the Lord God of Israel.

²¹ And I have set there a place for the ark, in which is the covenant of the Lord, which the Lord made with our fathers, when He brought them out of the land of Egypt."

Solomon's Prayer of Dedication

²² And Solomon stood up in front of the altar before all the congregation of Israel; and he spread out his hands toward heaven,

²³ and he said: "Lord God of Israel, there is no God like You in heaven above and on the earth below, keeping covenant and mercy with Your servant who walks before You with all his heart;

²⁴ which You have kept toward Your servant David my father; for You have spoken by Your mouth and You have fulfilled it with Your hands, as *it is* this day.

²⁵ And now, O Lord God of Israel, keep for Your servant David my father, *the promises* which You have spoken to him, saying, 'There shall not be taken from you a man sitting before Me on the throne of Israel, provided only your children shall take heed to their ways, to walk before Me as you has walked before Me.'

²⁶ And now, O Lord God of Israel, let Your word to David my father be confirmed, I pray.

²⁷ But will God indeed dwell with men upon the earth? If the heaven and heaven of heavens will not suffice You, how much less even this house which I have built for Your name?

²⁸ Yet, O Lord God of Israel, You shall look upon my petition, to hear the prayer which Your servant prays to You in Your presence this day,

²⁹ that Your eyes may be open toward this house day and night, even toward the place which You said, 'My name shall be there,' to hear the prayer which Your servant prays at this place day and night.

³⁰ And You shall hearken to the prayer of Your servant, and of Your people Israel, which they shall pray toward this place; and You shall hear in Your dwelling place in heaven, and You shall do and be gracious.

³¹ "Whatsoever trespasses anyone shall commit against his neighbor, and if he shall take upon him an oath so that he should swear, and he shall come and make confession before Your altar in this house,

³² then shall You hear from heaven, and do, and You shall judge Your people Israel, that the wicked should be condemned, to recompense his way upon his head; and to justify the righteous, to give to him according to his righteousness.

³³ "When Your people Israel falls before their enemies, because they shall sin against You, and they shall return and confess to Your name, and they shall pray and make petition in this house,

³⁴ then shall You hear from heaven, and be gracious to the sins of Your people Israel, and You shall restore them to the land which You gave to their fathers.

³⁵ "When the heavens are restrained, and there is no rain, because they shall sin against You, and they shall pray toward this place, and they shall make confession to Your name, and shall turn from their sins when You have humbled them,

[36] then You shall hear from heaven, and be merciful to the sins of Your servant and of Your people Israel; for You shall show them the good way, to walk in it, and You shall give rain upon the earth which You have given to Your people for an inheritance.

[37] "If there should be famine, if there should be death, because there should be blasting, locust, or if there be mildew, and if their enemy oppress them in one of their cities, *with regard to* every calamity, every trouble,

[38] every prayer, every supplication whatever shall be made by any man, as they shall know each the plague of his heart, and shall spread abroad his hands to this house,

[39] then shall You listen from heaven, out of Your established dwelling place, and shall be merciful, and shall do, and recompense to *every* man according to his ways, as You shall know his heart, for You alone know the heart of all the children of men;

[40] that they may fear You all the days that they live upon the land, which You has given to our fathers.

[41] "And for the stranger who is not of Your people,

[42] when they shall come and pray toward this place,

[43] then shall You hear *them* from heaven, out of Your established dwelling place, and You shall do according to all that the stranger shall call upon You for, that all the nations may know Your name, and fear You, as *do* Your people Israel, and may know that Your name has been called on this house which I have built.

[44] "If it be that Your people shall go forth to war against their enemies in the way by which You shall turn them, and pray in the name of the Lord toward the city which You have chosen, and the house which I have built for Your name,

[45] then shall You hear from heaven their supplication and their prayer, and shall execute judgment for them.

[46] "If it be that they shall sin against You, (for there is not a man who will not sin) and You shall bring them and deliver them up before their enemies, and they that take *them* captive shall carry *them* to a land far or near,

[47] and they shall turn their hearts in the land where they have been carried captives, and turn in the land of their sojourning, and petition You, saying, 'We have sinned, we have done unjustly, we have transgressed,'

[48] and they shall turn to You with all their heart, and with all their soul, in the land of their enemies where You have carried them captives, and shall pray to You toward their land which You have given to their fathers, and the city which You have chosen, and the house which I have built for Your name;

[49] then shall You hear from heaven, Your established dwelling place,

[50] and You shall be merciful to their unrighteousness in which they have trespassed against You, and according to all their transgressions that they have transgressed against You, and You shall cause them to be pitied before them that carried them captives, and they shall have compassion on them;

[51] for *they are* Your people and Your inheritance, whom You brought out of the land of Egypt, out of the midst of the iron furnace.

[52] And let Your eyes and Your ears be opened to the supplication of Your servant, and to the supplication of Your people Israel, to listen to them in all things for which they shall call upon You,

[53] because You have set them apart for an inheritance to Yourself out of all the nations of the earth, as You spoke by the hand of Your servant Moses, when You brought our fathers out of the land of Egypt, O Lord God."

Then Solomon spoke concerning the house, when he had finished building it; He manifested the sun in the heaven. The Lord said He would dwell in darkness; build my house, a beautiful house for yourself to dwell in anew. Behold, is not this written in the Book of the Song?

Solomon Blesses the Assembly

[54] And it came to pass when Solomon had finished praying to the Lord all this prayer and supplication, that he rose up from before the altar of the Lord, *after* having knelt upon his knees, and his hands *were* spread out towards heaven.

[55] And he stood, and blessed all the congregation of Israel with a loud voice, saying,

[56] "Blessed *be* the Lord this day, who has given rest to His people Israel, according to all that He said: there has not failed one word among all His good words which He spoke by the hand of His servant Moses.

[57] May the Lord our God be with us, as He was with our fathers; let Him not desert us nor turn from us,

[58] that He may turn our hearts toward Him to walk in all His ways, and to keep all His commandments and His ordinances, which He commanded our fathers.

[59] And let these words, which I have prayed before the Lord our God, *be* near to the Lord our God day and night, to maintain the cause of Your servant, and the cause of Your people Israel forever,

[60] that all the nations of the earth may know that the Lord God, He *is* God, and there is no other.

[61] And let our hearts be perfect toward the Lord our God, to walk circumspectly in all His ordinances, and to keep His commandments, as it is this day."

Solomon Dedicates the Temple

[62] And the king and all the children of Israel offered sacrifice before the Lord.

[63] And King Solomon offered for the sacrifices of peace offering which he sacrificed to the Lord, twenty-two thousand oxen, and a hundred and twenty thousand sheep. And the king and all the children of Israel dedicated the house of the Lord.

[64] In that day the king consecrated the middle of the court in the front of the house of the Lord; for there he offered the burnt offering, and the sacrifices, and the fat of the peace offerings, because the bronze altar which was before the

Lord *was too* small to bear the burnt offering and the sacrifices of peace offerings.

65 So Solomon kept the feast in that day, and all Israel with him, even a great assembly from the entering in of Hamath to the river of Egypt, before the Lord our God in the house which he built, eating and drinking, and rejoicing before the Lord our God for seven days.

66 And on the eighth day he sent the people away; and they blessed the king, and each departed to his tent rejoicing, and *their* hearts *were* glad because of the good things which the Lord had done for His servant David, and for Israel His people.

1 KINGS CHAPTER 9

God's Second Appearance to Solomon

1 And it came to pass when Solomon had finished building the house of the Lord, and the king's house, and all the work of Solomon, whatever he wished to perform,

2 that the Lord appeared to Solomon a second time, as He appeared in Gibeon.

3 And the Lord said to him, "I have heard the voice of your prayer, and your supplication which you have made before Me. I have done for you according to all your prayer; I have sanctified this house which you have built to put My name there forever, and My eyes and My heart shall be there always.

4 And if you will walk before Me as David your father walked, in holiness of heart and uprightness, and so as to do according to all that I commanded him, and shall keep My ordinances and My commandments,

5 then will I establish the throne of your kingdom in Israel forever, as I spoke to David your father, saying, 'There shall not fail you a man to rule in Israel.'

6 But if you or your children do in any way revolt from Me, and do not keep My commandments and My ordinances, which Moses set before you, and you go and serve other gods, and worship them,

7 then I will cut off Israel from the land which I have given them, and this house which I have consecrated to My name I will cast out of My sight; and Israel shall be a desolation and a byword to all nations.

8 And this house, which is high, shall be *so that* everyone that passes by it shall be amazed, and shall hiss; and they shall say, 'Why has the Lord done thus to this land, and to this house?'

9 And *men* shall say, 'Because they forsook the Lord their God, who brought out their fathers from Egypt, out of the house of bondage, and they attached themselves to strange gods, and worshipped them, and served them; therefore the Lord has brought this evil upon them.'"

Solomon and Hiram Exchange Gifts

10 *During* twenty years in which Solomon was building the two houses, the house of the Lord, and the house of the king,

11 Hiram king of Tyre helped Solomon with cedar wood, and fir wood, and with gold, and all that he wished for. Then the king gave Hiram twenty cities in the land of Galilee.

12 So Hiram departed from Tyre, and went into Galilee to see the cities which Solomon gave to him; and they did not please him. And he said,

13 "What *are* these cities which you have given me, *my* brother?" And he called them Boundary until this day.

14 And Hiram brought to Solomon a hundred and twenty talents of gold.

Solomon's Additional Achievements

15 This was the arrangement of the provision which King Solomon fetched to build the house of the Lord, and the house of the king, and the wall of Jerusalem, and the citadel; to fortify the City of David, and Assyria, and Migdol, and Gezer, and Beth Horon the upper, and Jethermath, and all the cities of the chariots, and all the cities of the horsemen, and the fortification of Solomon which he purposed to build in Jerusalem and in all the land,

16 (This verse omitted in LXX)

17 (This verse omitted in LXX)

18 (This verse omitted in LXX)

19 (This verse omitted in LXX)

20 so that none of the people should rule over him that was left of the Hittite and the Amorite, and the Perizzite and the Canaanite, and the Hivite and the Jebusite, and the Girgashite, who were not of the children of Israel, their descendants who had been left with him in the land, whom the children of Israel could not utterly destroy; and Solomon made them tributaries until this day.

21 (This verse omitted in LXX)

22 But of the children of Israel Solomon made nothing; for they were the warriors, and his servants and rulers, and captains of the third order, and the captains of his chariots, and his horsemen.

23 (This verse omitted in LXX)

24 Then Solomon brought up the daughter of Pharaoh out of the City of David into his house which he built for himself in those days,

25 (This verse omitted in LXX)

26 even that for which King Solomon built a ship in Ezion Geber near Elath on the shore of the extremity of the sea in the land of Edom.

27 And Hiram sent in the ship together with the servants of Solomon servants of his own, mariners to row, men acquainted with the sea.

28 And they came to Ophir, and took from there a hundred and twenty talents of gold, and brought them to King Solomon.

1 KINGS CHAPTER 10

The Queen of Sheba Visits

[1] Now the queen of Sheba heard of the name of Solomon, and the name of the Lord, and she came to test him with riddles.

[2] And she came to Jerusalem with a very great company. And *there came* camels bearing spices, and very much gold, and precious stones. And she came in to Solomon, and told him all that was in her heart.

[3] And Solomon answered all her questions. And there was not a question overlooked by the king which he did not answer her.

[4] And the queen of Sheba saw all the wisdom of Solomon, and the house which he built,

[5] and the provision of Solomon and the sitting of his attendants, and the standing of his servants, and his clothing, and his cup-bearers, and his burnt offering which he offered in the house of the Lord, and she was utterly amazed.

[6] And she said to King Solomon, "*It was* a true report which I heard in my land of your words and your wisdom.

[7] But I did not believe those that told it to me, until I came and my eyes saw: and behold, the words as they reported to me are not the half *of it*; you have exceeded in goodness all the report which I heard in my land.

[8] Blessed *are* your wives, blessed *are* these your servants who stand before you continually, who hear all your wisdom.

[9] Blessed be the Lord your God, who has taken pleasure in you, to set you upon the throne of Israel, because the Lord loved Israel to establish *him* forever; and He has made you king over them, to execute judgment with justice, and in their causes."

[10] And she gave to Solomon a hundred and twenty talents of gold, and very many spices, and precious stones; there had not come any other spices so abundant as those which the queen of Sheba gave to King Solomon.

[11] And the ships of Hiram which brought the gold from Ophir, brought very much hewn timber and precious stones.

[12] And the king made the hewn timber *into* buttresses of the house of the Lord and the king's house, and lyres and harps for the singers; such hewn timber had not come upon the earth, nor have been seen anywhere until this day.

[13] And King Solomon gave to the queen of Sheba all that she desired, whatsoever she asked, besides all that he had given her by the hand of King Solomon. And she returned, and came into her own land, she and her servants.

[14] And the weight of gold that came to Solomon in one year was six hundred and sixty-six talents of gold.

[15] Besides the tributes of them that were subjects, both merchants and all the kings of the *country* beyond *the river*, and of the princess of the land.

[16] And Solomon made three hundred spears of hammered gold: three hundred shekels of gold were upon one spear.

[17] And three hundred shields of hammered gold: and three pounds of gold were in one shield. And the king put them in the house of the forest of Lebanon.

[18] And the king made a great ivory throne, and gilded it with pure gold.

[19] The throne *had* six steps, and calves in bold relief to the throne behind it, and sidepieces on either hand of the place of the seat, and two lions standing by the sidepieces,

[20] and twelve lions standing there on the six steps on either side: it was not so done *like that* in any *other* kingdom.

[21] And all the vessels made by Solomon *were* of gold, and the lavers *were* golden, and all the vessels of the house of the forest of Lebanon were of pure gold; there was no silver, for it was not accounted of in the days of Solomon.

[22] For Solomon had a ship of Tarshish in the sea with the ships of Hiram; one ship came to the king every three years out of Tarshish, *laden with* gold and silver, and wrought stones, and hewn stones. This was the arrangement of the provision which King Solomon fetched to build the house of the Lord, and the house of the king, and the wall of Jerusalem, and the citadel; to fortify the City of David, and Assyria, and Migdol, and Gezer, and Beth Horon the upper, and Jethermath, and all the cities of the chariots, and all the cities of the horsemen, and the fortification of Solomon which he purposed to build in Jerusalem and in all the land, so that none of the people should rule over him that was left of the Hittite and the Amorite and the Perizzite and the Canaanite and the Hivite and the Jebusite and the Girgashite, who were not of the children of Israel, their descendants who had been left with him in the land, whom the children of Israel could not utterly destroy.

And Solomon made them tributaries until this day. But of the children of Israel Solomon made nothing, for they were the warriors, and his servants and rulers, and captains of the third order, and the captains of his chariots, and his horsemen.

[23] And Solomon increased beyond all the kings of the earth in wealth and wisdom.

[24] And all the kings of the earth sought the presence of Solomon, to hear his wisdom which the Lord *had* put into his heart.

[25] And everyone brought their own gifts—vessels of gold, articles of clothing, armor, spices, horses, and mules, a rate year by year.

[26] And Solomon had four thousand mares for his chariots, and twelve thousand horsemen; and he put them in the cities of his chariots, and with the king in Jerusalem. And he ruled over all the kings from the river to the land of the Philistines, and to the borders of Egypt.

[27] And the king made gold and silver in Jerusalem as stones, and he made cedars as the sycamores in the plain for multitude.

[28] And the goings forth of Solomon's horsemen *was* also out of Egypt, and the king's merchants *were* of Keveh; and they received them out of Keveh at a price.

29 And that which proceeded out of Egypt went up *thus,* *even* a chariot for a hundred *shekels* of silver, and a horse for fifty *shekels* of silver; and thus for all the kings of the Hittites, and the kings of Syria, they came out by sea.

1 KINGS CHAPTER 11

Solomon Turns from God

1 And King Solomon was a lover of women. And he took strange women, as well as the daughter of Pharaoh, Moabite and Ammonite women, Syrians and Edomites, Hittites and Amorites;

2 of the nations concerning whom the Lord forbade the children of Israel, *saying,* "You shall not go in to them, and they shall not come in to you, lest they turn away your hearts after their idols"; Solomon clung to these in love.

3 And he had seven hundred wives, princesses, and three hundred concubines. And the strange women turned away his heart after their gods.

4 And it came to pass in the time of Solomon's old age, that his heart was not perfect with the Lord his God, as *was* the heart of David his father.

5 For Solomon went after Ashtoreth, the abomination of the Sidonians.

6 And Solomon did that which was evil in the sight of the Lord: he did not seek after the Lord, as David his father.

7 Then Solomon built a high place to Chemosh the idol of Moab, and to their king the idol of the children of Ammon.

8 And thus he acted towards all his strange wives, who burnt incense and sacrificed to their idols.

9 And the Lord was angry with Solomon, because he turned away his heart from the Lord God of Israel, who had appeared twice to him,

10 and charged him concerning this matter, by no means to go after other gods, but to take heed to do what the Lord God commanded him; neither was his heart perfect with the Lord, according to the heart of David his father.

11 And the Lord said to Solomon, "Because it has been thus with you, and you has not kept My commandments and My ordinances which I commanded you, I will surely tear your kingdom out of your hand, and give it to your servant.

12 Only in your days I will not do it for the sake of David your father; *but* I will take it out of the hand of your son.

13 Only I will not take away the whole kingdom; I will give one tribe to your son for David My servant's sake, and for the sake of Jerusalem, the city which I have chosen."

God Raises Adversaries

14 And the Lord raised up an enemy to Solomon, Hadad the Edomite, and Esrom son of Eliadae who *dwelt* in Ramah, *and* Hadadezer, king of Zobah his master (and men gathered to him, and he was head of the conspiracy, and he seized on Damasec), and they were adversaries to Israel all the days of Solomon: and Hadad the Edomite *was* of the royal seed in Edom.

15 And it happened, that while David was utterly destroying Edom, while Joab captain of the army was going to bury the dead, when they slew every male in Edom;

16 (for Joab and all Israel abode there six months in Edom, until he utterly destroyed every male in Edom)

17 that Hadad ran away, he and all the Edomites of the servants of his father with him; and they went into Egypt; and Hadad *was then* a little child.

18 And there rose up men out of the city of Midian, and they came to Paran, and they took men with them, and came to Pharaoh king of Egypt. And Hadad went in to Pharaoh, and he gave him a house, and appointed him provisions.

19 And Hadad found great favor in the sight of Pharaoh, and he gave him his wife's sister in marriage, the elder sister of Tahpenes.

20 And the sister of Tahpenes bore to him (to Hadad) Genubath her son; and Tahpenes brought him up in the midst of the sons of Pharaoh, and Genubath was in the midst of the sons of Pharaoh.

21 And Hadad heard in Egypt that David slept with his fathers, and that Joab the captain of the army was dead; and Hadad said to Pharaoh, "Let me go, and I will return to my country."

22 And Pharaoh said to Hadad, "What do you lack here with me, that behold, you seek to depart to your country?" And Hadad said to him, "By all means let me go."

23 (This verse omitted in LXX)

24 (This verse omitted in LXX)

25 So Hadad returned to his country. This *is* the mischief which Hadad did, and he was a bitter enemy of Israel, and he reigned in the land of Edom.

26 And Jeroboam the son of Nebat, the Ephrathite of Zereda, the son of a widow, *was* a servant of Solomon.

27 And this was the occasion of his lifting up *his* hands against King Solomon. Now King Solomon built the citadel, and he completed the fortification of the City of David his father.

28 And the man Jeroboam was very strong; and Solomon saw the young man, that he was active, and he set him over the levies of the house of Joseph.

29 And it came to pass at that time, that Jeroboam went forth from Jerusalem, and Ahijah the Shilonite, the prophet, found him in the road, and caused him to turn aside out of the way. And Ahijah was clothed with a new garment, and those two *were* alone in the field.

30 And Ahijah laid hold of his new garment that was upon him, and tore it *into* twelve pieces.

31 And he said to Jeroboam, "Take to yourself ten pieces, for thus says the Lord God of Israel: 'Behold, I tear the kingdom out of the hand of Solomon, and will give you ten tribes.

32 Yet he shall have two tribes, for the sake of My servant David, and for the sake of Jerusalem, the city which I have chosen out of all the tribes of Israel.

33 Because he forsook Me, and sacrificed to Ashtoreth the abomination of the Sidonians, and to Chemosh, and to the idols of Moab, and to their king the abomination of the children of Ammon, and he walked not in My ways, to do that which was right before Me, as David his father *did*.

34 However, I will not take the whole kingdom out of his hand, (for I will certainly resist him all the days of his life), for the sake of My servant David, whom I have chosen.

35 But I will take the kingdom out of the hand of his son, and give you ten tribes.

36 But to his son I will give the two *remaining* tribes, that My servant David may have an establishment continually before Me in Jerusalem, the city which I have chosen for Myself, to put My name there.

37 And I will take you, and you shall reign as your soul desires, and you shall be king over Israel.

38 And it shall come to pass, if you will keep all the commandments that I shall give you, and will walk in My ways, and do that which is right before Me, to keep My ordinances and My commandments, as David My servant did, that I will be with you, and will build you a sure house, as I built to David.'"

39 (This verse omitted in LXX)

40 And Solomon sought to slay Jeroboam; but he arose and fled into Egypt, to Shishak king of Egypt, and he was in Egypt until Solomon died.

The Death of Solomon

41 And the rest of the history of Solomon, and all that he did, and all his wisdom, behold, are not these things written in the book of the life of Solomon?

42 And the days *during* which Solomon reigned in Jerusalem over all Israel *were* forty years.

43 And Solomon slept with his fathers, and they buried him in the City of David his father. And it came to pass when Jeroboam son of Nebat heard *of it*, even while he was yet in Egypt as he fled from the face of Solomon and dwelt in Egypt, he immediately came back into his own city, into the land of Sarira in the mount of Ephraim. And King Solomon slept with his fathers, and Rehoboam his son reigned in his place.

1 KINGS CHAPTER 12

King Rehoboam Acts Foolishly

1 And King Rehoboam went to Shechem;

2 for all Israel was coming to Shechem to make him king.

3 And the people spoke to King Rehoboam, saying, "Your father made our yoke heavy;

4 but lighten somewhat of the load, and of the heavy yoke which your father put upon us, and we will serve you."

5 And he said to them, "Depart for three days, and return to me." And they departed.

6 Then the king referred *the matter* to the elders, who stood before Solomon his father while he was yet living, saying, "How do you advise that I should answer this people?"

7 And they spoke to him, saying, "If you will this day be a servant to this people, and serve them, and speak to them good words, then will they be your servants continually."

8 But he forsook the counsel of the old men which they gave him, and consulted with the young men who were brought up with him, who stood in his presence.

9 And he said to them, "What counsel do you give? And what shall I answer to this people who speak to me, saying, 'Lighten somewhat of the yoke which your father has put upon us?'"

10 And the young men who had been brought up with him, who stood before his face, spoke to him, saying, "Thus shall you say to this people who have spoken to you, saying, 'Your father made our yoke heavy, and would you now lighten it from off us.' Thus shall say to them: 'My little *finger shall be* thicker than my father's loins.

11 And whereas my father put a heavy yoke on you, I also will add to your yoke: my father chastised you with whips, but I will chastise you with scorpions.'"

12 And all Israel came to King Rehoboam on the third day, as the king spoke to them, saying, "Return to me on the third day."

13 And the king answered the people harshly. And Rehoboam forsook the counsel of the old men which they counseled him.

14 And he spoke to them according to the counsel of the young men, saying, "My father made your yoke heavy, and I will add to your yoke; my father chastised you with whips, but I will chastise you with scorpions."

15 And the king did not listen to the people, for the turn *of events* was from the Lord, that He might establish His word which He spoke by Ahijah the Shilonite concerning Jeroboam the son of Nebat.

The Kingdom Divided

16 And all Israel saw that the king did not listen to them. And the people answered the king, saying, "What portion do we have in David? Neither have we any inheritance in the son of Jesse. Depart to your tents O Israel! Now see to your own house, O David!"

17 So Israel departed to his tents.

18 And the king sent Adoniram who was over the tribute; and they stoned him with stones, and he died. And King Rehoboam made haste to rise and flee to Jerusalem.

19 So Israel rebelled against the house of David until this day.

20 And it came to pass when all Israel heard that Jeroboam had returned out of Egypt, that they sent and called him to the assembly, and they made him king over Israel; and none

followed the house of David except the tribe of Judah and Benjamin only.

²¹ And Rehoboam went into Jerusalem, and he assembled the congregation of Judah, and the tribe of Benjamin, a hundred and twenty thousand young men, warriors, to fight against the house of Israel, to recover the kingdom to Rehoboam the son of Solomon.

²² And the word of the Lord came to Shemaiah the man of God, saying,

²³ "Speak to Rehoboam the son of Solomon, king of Judah, and to all the house of Judah and Benjamin, and to the remnant of the people, saying,

²⁴ Thus says the Lord: 'You shall not go up, neither shall you fight with your brothers the sons of Israel. Return each man to his own home, for this thing is from Me.'" And they obeyed the word of the Lord, and they ceased from going up, according to the word of the Lord.

So King Solomon slept with his fathers, and was buried with his fathers in the City of David; and Rehoboam his son reigned in his place in Jerusalem, being sixteen years old when he began to reign, and he reigned twelve years in Jerusalem. And his mother's name *was* Naanan, daughter of Ana son of Naas king of the children of Ammon. And he did that which was evil in the sight of the Lord, and he did not walk in the way of David his father.

And there was a man of Mount Ephraim, a servant to Solomon, and his name *was* Jeroboam; and the name of his mother *was* Sarira, a harlot; and Solomon made him head of the levies of the house of Joseph. And he built for Solomon Sarira in Mount Ephraim; and he had three hundred chariots of horses. He built the citadel with the levies of the house of Ephraim; he fortified the City of David, and aspired to the kingdom. And Solomon sought to kill him; and he was afraid, and escaped to Shishak king of Egypt, and was with him until Solomon died.

And Jeroboam heard in Egypt that Solomon was dead; and he spoke in the ears of Shishak king of Egypt, saying, "Let me go, and I will depart into my land." And Shishak said to him, "Ask any request, and I will grant it you." And Shishak gave to Jeroboam Ano the oldest sister of Tahpenes his wife, to be his wife. She was great among the daughters of the king, and she bore to Jeroboam Abia his son. And Jeroboam said to Shishak, "Let me indeed go, and I will depart."

And Jeroboam departed out of Egypt, and came into the land of Sarira that was in Mount Ephraim, and there the whole tribe of Ephraim assembled, and Jeroboam built a fortress there. And his young child was sick with a very severe sickness; and Jeroboam went to inquire concerning the child. And he said to Ano his wife, "Arise, go and inquire of God concerning the child, whether he shall recover from his sickness."

Now there was a man in Selom, and his name *was* Ahijah. And he was sixty years old, and the word of the Lord *was* with him. And Jeroboam said to his wife, "Arise, and take in your hand loaves for the man of God, and cakes for his children, and grapes and a pot of honey." And the woman arose, and took in her hand bread, and two cakes, and grapes, and a pot of honey, for Ahijah. And the man *was* old, and his eyes were dim, so that he could not see. And she arose up from Sarira and went. And it came to pass when she had come into the city of Ahijah the Shilonite, that Ahijah said to his servant, "Go out now to meet Ano the wife of Jeroboam, and you shall say to her, 'Come in, and do not stand *still*; for thus says the Lord: "I send grievous tidings to you."'" And Ano went in to the man of God; and Achia said to her, "Why have you brought me bread and grapes, and cakes, and a pot of honey? Thus says the Lord: 'Behold, you shall depart from Me, and it shall come to pass when you have entered into the city, into Sarira, that your maidens shall come out to meet you, and shall say to you, "The child is dead"; for thus says the Lord: "Behold, I will destroy every male of Jeroboam, and there shall be the dead of Jeroboam in the city, *them* the dogs shall eat, and him that has died in the field shall the birds of the air eat, and he shall lament for the child, *saying*, 'Woe is *me*, Lord!' For there has been found in him some good thing touching the Lord." And the woman departed, when she heard this.

And it came to pass as she entered into Sarira, that the child died; and there came forth a wailing to meet *her*.

And Jeroboam went to Shechem in Mount Ephraim, and assembled there the tribes of Israel; and Rehoboam the son of Solomon went up there.

And the word of the Lord came to Samaias son of Enlami, saying, "Take to yourself a new garment which has not gone into the water, and tear it *into* twelve pieces; and you shall give *some* to Jeroboam, and you shall say to him, Thus says the Lord: 'Take to yourself ten pieces to cover you.' And Jeroboam took *them*. And Samaias said, "Thus says the Lord concerning the ten tribes of Israel." And the people said to Rehoboam the son of Solomon, "Your father made his yoke heavy upon us, and made the meat of his table heavy; and now you shall lighten them upon us, and we will serve you." And Rehoboam said to the people, "Wait three days, and I will give you an answer." And Rehoboam said, "Bring in to me the elders, and I will take counsel with them what I shall answer to the people on the third day." So Rehoboam spoke in their ears, as the people sent to him to *say*; and the elders of the people said, "Thus the people have spoken to you." And Rehoboam rejected their counsel, and it did not please him. And he sent and brought in those who had been brought up with him; and he said to them, "Thus and thus has the people sent to me to say," And they that had been brought up with him said, "Thus shall you speak to the people, saying, 'My little *finger* shall be thicker than my father's loins; my father scourged you with whips, but I will rule you with scorpions.'" And the saying pleased Rehoboam, and he answered the people as the young men, they that were brought up with him, counseled him.

And all the people spoke as one man, everyone to his neighbor, and they cried out all together, saying, "We have no part in David, nor inheritance in the son of Jesse: to your tents, O Israel, all of you; for this man *is* not for a prince or a ruler over us." And all the people were dispersed from Shechem, and they departed everyone to his tent.

And Rehoboam strengthened himself and departed, and mounted his chariot, and entered into Jerusalem. And the whole tribe of Judah followed him, and the whole tribe of Benjamin.

And it came to pass at the beginning of the year, that Rehoboam gathered all the men of Judah and Benjamin, and went up to fight with Jeroboam at Shechem. And the word of the Lord came to Samaeas the man of God, saying, "Speak to Rehoboam king of Judah, and to all the house of Judah and Benjamin, and to the remnant of the people, saying, Thus says the Lord: 'You shall not go up, neither shall you fight with your brothers the sons of Israel; return every man to his house, for this thing is from Me.'" And they obeyed the word of the Lord, and ceased to go up, according to the word of the Lord.

25 And Jeroboam built Shechem in Mount Ephraim and dwelt in it, and went forth from there and built Penuel.

26 And Jeroboam said in his heart, "Behold, now the kingdom will return to the house of David.

27 If this people shall go up to offer sacrifice in the house of the Lord at Jerusalem, then the heart of the people will return to their lord, and to their master, to Rehoboam king of Judah, and they will kill me."

28 And the king took counsel, and went, and made two golden heifers, and said to the people, "It is too much for you to go up to Jerusalem: behold, *here are* your gods, O Israel, who brought you up out of the land of Egypt!"

29 And he put one in Bethel, and he put the other in Dan.

30 And this thing became a sin; and the people went before one as far as Dan, and left the house of the Lord.

31 And he made houses on the high places, and made priests of any part of the people, who were not of the sons of Levi.

32 And Jeroboam appointed a feast in the eighth month, on the fifteenth day of the month, according to the feast in the land of Judah;

33 and went up to the altar which he made in Bethel to sacrifice to the heifers which he made, and he placed in Bethel the priests of the high places which he had made. And he went up to the altar which he had made, on the fifteenth day in the eighth month, at the feast which he devised out of his own heart; and he made a feast to the children of Israel, and went up to the altar to sacrifice.

1 KINGS CHAPTER 13

Jeroboam Warned, Stricken

1 And behold, there came a man of God out of Judah by the word of the Lord to Bethel, and Jeroboam stood at the altar to sacrifice.

2 And he cried against the altar by the word of the Lord, and said, "O altar, altar, thus says the Lord: 'Behold, a son is *to be* born to the house of David, Josiah by name; and he shall offer upon you the priests of the high places, *even* of them that sacrifice upon you, and *he* shall burn men's bones upon you.

3 And in that day one shall give a sign, saying, "This *is* the word which the Lord has spoken, saying, 'Behold, the altar shall be split apart, and the fatness upon it shall be poured out.'"

4 And it came to pass when King Jeroboam heard the words of the man of God who called on the altar that was in Bethel, that the king stretched forth his hand from the altar, saying, "Take hold of him." And behold, his hand which he stretched forth against him withered, and he could not draw it back to himself.

5 And the altar was split apart, and the fatness was poured out from the altar, according to the sign which the man of God gave by the word of the Lord.

6 And King Jeroboam said to the man of God, "Entreat the Lord your God, and let my hand be restored to me." And the man of God entreated the Lord, and He restored the king's hand to him, and it became as before.

7 And the king said to the man of God, "Enter with me into the house, and dine, and I will give you a gift."

8 And the man of God said to the king, "If you should give me half of your house, I would not go in with you, neither will I eat bread, neither will I drink water in this place; for thus the Lord charged me by *His* word, saying,

9 'Eat no bread, and drink no water, and return not by the way in which you came.'"

10 So he departed by another way, and did not return by the way in which he came to Bethel.

The Disobedient Prophet

11 And there dwelt an old prophet in Bethel. And his sons came and told him all the works that the man of God did on that day in Bethel, and the words which he spoke to the king. And they turned the face of their father.

12 And their father spoke to them, saying, "Which way did he go?" And his sons showed him the way by which the man of God who came out of Judah went up.

13 And he said to his sons, "Saddle me the donkey." So they saddled his donkey, and he mounted it,

14 and went after the man of God, and found him sitting under an oak. And he said to him, "Are you the man of God that came out of Judah?" And he said to him, "I *am*."

15 And he said to him, "Come with me, and eat bread."

16 And he said, "I shall by no means be able to return with you, neither will I eat bread, neither will I drink water in this place.

17 For thus the Lord commanded me by *His* word, saying, 'You shall not eat bread there, nor shall you drink water, and do not return by the way in which you came.'"

18 And he said to him, "I also am a prophet as you *are*; and an angel spoke to me by the word of the Lord, saying, 'Bring him back with you into your house, and let him eat bread and drink water'"; but he lied to him.

19 And he brought him back, and he ate bread and drank water in his house.

20 And it came to pass while they were sitting at the table, that the word of the Lord came to the prophet that brought him back;

21 and he spoke to the man of God that came out of Judah, saying, "Thus says the Lord: 'Because you have resisted the word of the Lord, and have not kept the commandment which the Lord your God has commanded you,

22 but have returned, and eaten bread and drunk water in the place of which He spoke to you, saying, "You shall not eat bread, and shall not drink water," *therefore* your body shall by no means enter into the tomb of your fathers.'"

23 And it came to pass after he had eaten bread and drunk water, that he saddled the donkey for him, and he turned and departed.

24 And a lion found him on the road, and killed him; and his body was cast out in the road, and the donkey was standing by it, and the lion *also* was standing by the body.

25 And behold, men *were* passing by, and saw the corpse cast out in the road, and the lion was standing near the corpse. And they went in and spoke *of it* in the city where the old prophet dwelt.

26 And *the prophet* that turned him back out of the road heard, and said, "This is the man of God who rebelled against the word of the Lord."

27 (This verse omitted in LXX)

28 And he went and found the body cast in the road, and the donkey and the lion were standing by the body. And the lion had not devoured the body of the man of God, and had not torn the donkey.

29 And the prophet took up the body of the man of God, and laid it on his donkey. And the prophet brought him back to his city, to bury him in his own tomb,

30 and they mourned over him, *saying*, "Alas, brother."

31 And it came to pass after he had lamented him, that he spoke to his sons, saying, "Whenever I die, bury me in this tomb in which the man of God is buried; lay me by his bones, that my bones may be preserved with his bones.

32 For the word will surely come to pass which he spoke by the word of the Lord against the altar in Bethel, and against the high houses in Samaria."

33 And after this Jeroboam did not turn from his sin, but he turned and made some of the people priests of the *high places*. Whoever would, he consecrated him, and he became a priest for the high places.

34 And this thing became sin to the house of Jeroboam, even to its destruction and its removal from the face of the earth.

1 KINGS CHAPTER 14

1 (This verse omitted in LXX)
2 (This verse omitted in LXX)
3 (This verse omitted in LXX)
4 (This verse omitted in LXX)
5 (This verse omitted in LXX)
6 (This verse omitted in LXX)
7 (This verse omitted in LXX)
8 (This verse omitted in LXX)
9 (This verse omitted in LXX)
10 (This verse omitted in LXX)
11 (This verse omitted in LXX)
12 (This verse omitted in LXX)
13 (This verse omitted in LXX)
14 (This verse omitted in LXX)
15 (This verse omitted in LXX)
16 (This verse omitted in LXX)
17 (This verse omitted in LXX)
18 (This verse omitted in LXX)
19 (This verse omitted in LXX)
20 (This verse omitted in LXX)

Rehoboam Rules over Judah

21 And Rehoboam son of Solomon ruled over Judah. Rehoboam was forty-one years old when he began to reign, and he reigned seventeen years in the city of Jerusalem, which the Lord chose to put His name there out of all the tribes of Israel. And his mother's name *was* Naamah the Ammonitess.

22 And Rehoboam did evil in the sight of the Lord; and he provoked Him in all the things which their fathers did in their sins which they sinned.

23 And they built for themselves high places, and pillars, and *planted* groves on every high hill, and under every shady tree. 24 And there was a conspiracy in the land, and they did according to all the abominations of the nations which the Lord removed from before the children of Israel.

25 And it came to pass in the fifth year of the reign of Rehoboam, that Shishak king of Egypt came up against Jerusalem;

26 and took all the treasures of the house of the Lord, and the treasures of the king's house, and the golden spears which David took out of the hand of the sons of Adrazar king of Sheba, and brought them into Jerusalem, even all that he took, *and* the golden shields which Solomon had made, *and carried them away into Egypt.*

27 And King Rehoboam made bronze shields in place of them. And the chiefs of the body guard, who kept the gate of the house of the king, were placed in charge over them.

28 And it came to pass when the king went into the house of the Lord, that the body guard took them up, and fixed them in the chamber of the body guard.

29 And the rest of the history of Rehoboam, and all that he did, behold, are they not written in the book of the chronicles of the kings of Judah?

30 And there was war between Rehoboam and Jeroboam continually.

31 And Rehoboam slept with his fathers, and was buried with his fathers in the City of David, and Abijam his son reigned in his place.

1 KINGS CHAPTER 15

Abijam Reigns over Judah

1 And in the eighteenth year of the reign of Jeroboam son of Nebat, Abijam son of Rehoboam reigned over Judah.

2 And he reigned three years over Jerusalem; and his mother's name *was* Maachah, daughter of Absalom.

3 And he walked in the sins of his father which he wrought in his presence, and his heart was not perfect with the Lord his God, as *was* the heart of his father *David.*

4 Nevertheless for David's sake the Lord gave him a remnant, that He might establish his children after him, and might establish Jerusalem.

5 Forasmuch as David did that which was right in the sight of the Lord; he did not turn from anything that He commanded him all the days of his life.

6 (This verse omitted in LXX)

7 And the rest of the history of Abijam, and all that he did, behold, are not these written in the book of the chronicles of the kings of Judah? And there was war between Abijam and Jeroboam.

Asa Succeeds Abijam

8 And Abijam slept with his fathers in the twenty-fourth year of Jeroboam; and he is buried with his fathers in the City of David, and Asa his son reigned in his place.

9 In the twenty-fourth year of Jeroboam king of Israel, Asa began to reign over Judah.

10 And he reigned forty-one years in Jerusalem; and his mother's name *was* Ana, daughter of Absalom.

11 And Asa did that which was right in the sight of the Lord, as David his father.

12 And he removed the sodomites from out of the land, and abolished all the practices which his fathers had kept up.

13 And he removed Ana his mother from being queen, forasmuch as she gathered a meeting in her grove: and Asa cut down her retreats, and burnt them with fire in the Brook of Kidron.

14 But he did not remove the high places; nevertheless the heart of Asa was perfect with the Lord all of his days.

15 And he brought in the pillars of his father, he even brought in his gold and silver pillars into the house of the Lord, and *his* vessels.

16 And there was war between Asa and Baasha king of Israel all their days.

17 And Baasha king of Israel went up against Judah, and built Ramah, so that no one should go out or come in for Asa king of Judah.

18 And Asa took all the silver and the gold that was found in the treasures of the house of the Lord, and in the treasures of the king's house, and gave them into the hands of his servants; and King Asa sent them out to the son of Hadad, the son of Tabrimmon son of Hezion king of Syria, who dwelt in Damascus, saying,

19 "Make a covenant between me and you, and between my father and your father: Behold, I have sent forth to you gold and silver *for* gifts: come, break your treaty with Baasha king of Israel, that he may go up from me."

20 And the son of Hadad heeded King Asa, and sent the chiefs of his forces to the cities of Israel; and they struck Ijon, Dan, and Abel of the house of Maachah, and all Chinneroth, as far as the whole land of Naphtali.

21 And it came to pass when Baasha heard it, that he left off building Ramah, and returned to Tirzah.

22 And King Asa charged all Judah without exception. And they took up the stones of Ramah and its timbers *with* which Baasha was building; and King Asa built with them upon the whole hill of Benjamin, and the watchtower.

Jehoshaphat Succeeds Asa

23 And the rest of the history of Asa, and all his mighty deeds which he did, and the cities which he built, behold, are not these written in the book of the chronicles of the kings of Judah? Nevertheless in the time of his old age he was diseased in his feet.

24 And Asa slept with his fathers, and was buried with his fathers in the City of David his father, and Jehoshaphat his son reigned in his place.

Nadab, then Baasha, Rules over Israel

25 And Nadab son of Jeroboam reigned over Israel in the second year of Asa king of Judah, and he reigned two years in Israel.

26 And he did that which was evil in the sight of the Lord, and walked in the way of his father, and in his sins that he caused Israel to sin.

27 And Baasha son of Ahijah, *who was* over the house of Belaan son of Achia, conspired against him, and killed him in Gibbethon of the Philistines; for Nebat and all Israel were besieging Gibbethon.

28 And Baasha slew him in the third year of Asa king of Judah; and reigned in his place.

29 And it came to pass when he reigned, that he killed the whole house of Jeroboam, and left none that breathed of Jeroboam, until he had destroyed him utterly, according to the word of the Lord which he spoke by his servant Ahijah the Shilonite,

30 for the sins of Jeroboam, who led Israel into sin, even by his provocation wherewith he provoked the Lord God of Israel.

³¹ And the rest of the history of Nadab, and all that he did, behold, are not these written in the book of the chronicles of the kings of Israel?

³² (This verse omitted in LXX)

³³ And in the third year of Asa king of Judah, Baasha the son of Ahijah began to reign over Israel in Tirzah, twenty-four years.

³⁴ And he did that which was evil in the sight of the Lord, and walked in the way of Jeroboam the son of Nebat, and in his sins, as he caused Israel to sin.

1 KINGS CHAPTER 16

Prophecy against Baasha

¹ And the word of the Lord came to Jehu son of Hanani against Baasha, *saying,*

² "Forasmuch as I lifted you up from the earth, and made you ruler over My people Israel; and you have walked in the way of Jeroboam, and have caused My people Israel to sin, to provoke Me with their vanities;

³ Behold, I will raise up *enemies* after Baasha, and after his house; and I will make your house as the house of Jeroboam son of Nebat.

⁴ All that die who belong to Baasha in the city the dogs shall devour, and all that die in the field the birds of the sky shall devour."

⁵ Now the rest of the history of Baasha, and all that he did, and his mighty acts, behold, are not these written in the book of the chronicles of the kings of Israel?

⁶ And Baasha slept with his fathers, and they buried him in Tirzah; and Elah his son reigned in his place.

⁷ And the Lord spoke by Jehu the son of Hanani against Baasha, and against his house, *even* all the evil which he did before the Lord to provoke Him to anger by the works of his hands, in being like the house of Jeroboam; and because he killed him.

⁸ And Elah son of Baasha reigned over Israel two years in Tirzah.

⁹ And Zimri, captain of half his cavalry, conspired against him, while he was in Tirzah, drinking himself drunk in the house of Arza the manager at Tirzah.

¹⁰ And Zimri went in and struck him and killed him, and reigned in his place.

¹¹ And it came to pass when he reigned, when he sat upon his throne,

¹² that he killed all the house of Baasha, according to the word which the Lord spoke against the house of Baasha, and to Jehu the prophet,

¹³ for all the sins of Baasha and Elah his son, as he led Israel astray to sin, to provoke the Lord God of Israel with their vanities.

¹⁴ And the rest of the deeds of Elah which he did, behold, are not these written in the book of the chronicles of the kings of Israel?

¹⁵ And Zimri reigned in Tirzah *for* seven days. And the army of Israel *was* encamped against Gibbethon of the Philistines.

¹⁶ And the people heard in the army, saying, "Zimri has conspired and killed the king." And the people of Israel made Omri the captain of the army king in that day in the camp over Israel.

¹⁷ And Omri went up, and all Israel with him, out of Gibbethon; and they besieged Tirzah.

¹⁸ And it came to pass when Zimri saw that his city was taken, that he went into the inner chamber of the house of the king, and burned the king's house over him, and died,

¹⁹ because of his sins which he committed, doing that which was evil in the sight of the Lord, so as to walk in the way of Jeroboam the son of Nebat, and in his sins which he caused Israel to sin.

²⁰ And the rest of the history of Zimri, and his conspiracies wherein he conspired, behold, are not these written in the book of the chronicles of the kings of Israel?

²¹ Then the people of Israel divided: half the people went after Tibni the son of Ginath to make him king, and half the people went after Omri.

²² The people that followed Omri overpowered the people that followed Tibni son of Ginath; and Tibni died and Joram his brother at that time, and Omri reigned after Tibni.

²³ In the thirty-first year of King Asa, Omri began to reign over Israel *for* twelve years: he reigned six years in Tirzah.

²⁴ And Omri bought the mount of Samaria from Shemer the lord of the mountain for two talents of silver; and he built *upon* the mountain, and they called the name of the mountain *on* which he built, after the name of Shemer the lord of the mount, Samaria.

²⁵ And Omri did that which was evil in the sight of the Lord, and did wickedly beyond all that were before him.

²⁶ And he walked in all the way of Jeroboam the son of Nebat, and in his sins wherewith he caused Israel to sin, to provoke the Lord God of Israel by their vanities.

²⁷ And the rest of the acts of Omri, and all that he did, and all his might, behold, *are* not these things written in the book of the chronicles of the kings of Israel?

²⁸ And Omri slept with his fathers, and is buried in Samaria, and Ahab his son reigned in his place.

And in the eleventh year of Omri, Jehoshaphat the son of Asa reigned, *being* thirty-five years old in the beginning of his reign, and he reigned twenty-five years in Jerusalem. And his mother's name *was* Gazuba, daughter of Seli. And he walked in the way of Asa his father, and did not turn from it, *even* from doing right in the eyes of the Lord; only they did not remove *any* of the high places; they sacrificed and burnt incense on the high places. Now the engagements which Jehoshaphat made with the king of Israel, and all his mighty deeds which he performed, and the enemies whom he fought against, behold, *are* not these written in the book of the chronicles of the kings of Judah? And the remains of the prostitution which they practiced in the days of Asa his father, he removed out of the land. And there was no king in Syria, *but* a deputy. Then the king of Israel said to Jehoshaphat, "I will send forth your servants and my servants in the ship"; but Jehoshaphat would not.

And Jehoshaphat slept with his fathers, and is buried with his fathers in the City of David, and Joram his son reigned in his place.

²⁹ In the second year of Jehoshaphat king of Judah, Ahab son of Omri reigned over Israel in Samaria twenty-two years.

³⁰ And Ahab did that which was evil in the sight of the Lord, and did more wickedly than all that were before him.

³¹ And it was not enough for him to walk in the sins of Jeroboam the son of Nebat, but he took Jezebel the daughter of Ethebaal king of the Sidonians for a wife; and he went and served Baal, and worshipped him.

³² And he set up an alter to Baal, in the house of his abominations, which he built in Samaria.

³³ And Ahab made a grove; and Ahab did yet more abominably, to provoke the Lord God of Israel, and *to sin against* his own life so that he should be destroyed: he did evil above all the kings of Israel that were before him.

³⁴ And in his days Hiel of Bethel built Jericho: he laid the foundation of it with Abiram his firstborn, and he set up the doors of it with Segub his younger son, according to the word of the Lord which he spoke by Joshua the son of Nun.

1 KINGS CHAPTER 17

Elijah Predicts Drought

¹ And Elijah the prophet, the Tishbite, of the inhabitants of Gilead, said to Ahab, "As the Lord God of hosts, the God of Israel, lives, before whom I stand, there shall not be these years neither dew nor rain, except by the word of my mouth." ² And the word of the Lord came to Elijah, *saying*,

³ "Depart from here and go east, and hide yourself by the Brook of Cherith, that is before the Jordan.

⁴ And it shall be *that* you shall drink water from the brook, and I will command the ravens to feed you there."

⁵ And Elijah did according to the word of the Lord, and he sat by the Brook of Cherith before the Jordan.

⁶ And the ravens brought him loaves in the morning, and flesh in the evening, and he drank water out of the brook.

⁷ And it came to pass after some time, that the brook was dried up, because there had been no rain upon the earth.

⁸ And the word of the Lord came to Elijah, *saying*,

⁹ "Arise, and go to Zarephath of the Sidonians; behold, I have commanded a widow woman there to provide for you."

¹⁰ And he arose and went to Zarephath, and came to the gate of the city. And behold, a widow woman was there gathering sticks. And Elijah cried after her, and said to her, "Fetch me a little water in a vessel, that I may drink."

¹¹ And she went to fetch it; and Elijah cried after her and said, "Bring me the piece of bread that is in your hand."

¹² And the woman said, "*As* the Lord your God lives, I have not a cake, but only a handful of meal in this pitcher, and a little oil in a jar; and behold, I am going to gather two sticks, and I shall go in and dress it for myself and my children, and we shall eat it and die."

¹³ And Elijah said to her, "Be of good courage, go in and do according to your word; but make me a little cake from it first, and you shall bring *it* out to me, and you shall make *some* for yourself and your children last.

¹⁴ For thus says the Lord: 'The pitcher of meal shall not fail, and the jar of oil shall not diminish, until the day that the Lord gives rain upon the earth.'"

¹⁵ And the woman went and did *so*, and did eat, she, *Elijah*, and her children.

¹⁶ And the pitcher of meal did not fail, and the jar of oil was not diminished, according to the word of the Lord which He spoke by the hand of Elijah.

Elijah Raises the Widow's Son

¹⁷ And it came to pass afterward, that the son of the woman, the mistress of the house, was sick; and his sickness was very severe, until there was no breath left in him.

¹⁸ And she said to Elijah, "What have I to do with you, O man of God? Have you come in to me to bring my sins to remembrance, and to slay my son?"

¹⁹ And Elijah said to the woman, "Give me your son." And he took him out of her bosom, and took him up to the chamber in which he himself lodged, and laid him on the bed.

²⁰ And Elijah cried aloud and said, "Alas, O Lord, the witness of the widow with whom I sojourn, You have brought tragedy *for her* in slaying her son."

²¹ And he breathed on the child three times, and called on the Lord, and said, "O Lord my God, let the soul of this child return to him, I pray."

²² And it was so, and the child cried out,

²³ and he brought him down from the upper chamber into the house, and gave him to his mother." And Elijah said, "See, your son lives."

²⁴ And the woman said to Elijah, "Behold, I know that you *are* a man of God, and the word of the Lord in your mouth *is* true."

1 KINGS CHAPTER 18

Obadiah Meets Elijah

¹ And it came to pass after many days, that the word of the Lord came to Elijah in the third year, saying, "Go, and appear before Ahab, and I will bring rain upon the face of the earth."

² And Elijah went to appear before Ahab. And the famine was severe in Samaria.

³ And Ahab called Obadiah the steward. Now Obadiah feared the Lord greatly.

⁴ And it came to pass when Jezebel had killed the prophets of the Lord, that Obadiah took a hundred prophets, and hid them by fifties in a cave, and fed them with bread and water.

⁵ And Ahab said to Obadiah, "Come, and let us go through the land, and to the fountains of water, and to the brooks, if by any means we may find grass, and may save the horses and mules, and so they will not perish."

⁶ So they divided the land between them, to pass through it; Ahab went one way, and Obadiah went by another way alone.

⁷ And Obadiah was alone in the road; and Elijah came alone to meet him. And Obadiah made haste, and fell upon his face, and said, "My lord Elijah, is it you?"

⁸ And Elijah said to him, "*It is* I: go *and* say to your master, 'Behold, Elijah *is here*.'"

⁹ And Obadiah said, "What sin have I committed, that you give your servant into the hand of Ahab to slay me?

¹⁰ *As* the Lord your God lives, there is not a nation or kingdom where my lord has not sent to seek you; and if they said, 'He is not *here*,' then has he set fire to the kingdom and its territories, because he has not found you.

¹¹ And now you say, 'Go, tell your lord, Behold, Elijah *is here*.'

¹² And it shall come to pass when I shall have departed from you, that the Spirit of the Lord shall carry you to a land which I do not know, and I shall go in to tell the matter to Ahab, and he will not find you, and he will slay me; yet your servant fears the Lord from his youth.

¹³ Has it not been told to you my lord, what I did when Jezebel slew the prophets of the Lord, how that I hid a hundred men of the prophets of the Lord, by fifty in a cave, and fed them with bread and water?

¹⁴ And now you say to me, 'Go, say to your master, Behold, Elijah *is here*'; and he shall slay me."

¹⁵ And Elijah said, "*As* the Lord of hosts lives, before whom I stand, today I will appear before him."

¹⁶ And Obadiah went to meet Ahab, and told him. And Ahab made haste, and went to meet Elijah.

¹⁷ And it came to pass when Ahab saw Elijah, that Ahab said to Elijah, "Are you he that corrupts Israel?"

¹⁸ And Elijah said, "I do not corrupt Israel; but it is you and your father's house, in that you forsake the Lord your God, and you have gone after the Baals.

¹⁹ And now, send *and* gather to me all Israel to Mount Carmel, and the four hundred and fifty prophets of shame, and the four hundred prophets of the groves, that eat *at* Jezebel's table."

God or Baal on Mount Carmel

²⁰ And Ahab sent to all Israel, and gathered all the prophets to Mount Carmel.

²¹ And Elijah drew near to them all. And Elijah said to them, "How long will you *remain* lame on both feet? If the Lord is God, follow Him; but if Baal, follow him." And the people answered not a word.

²² And Elijah said to the people, "I alone am left, the prophet of the Lord; and the prophets of Baal *are* four hundred and fifty men, and the prophets of the groves *are* four hundred.

²³ Let them give us two bulls, and let them choose one for themselves, and cut it in pieces, and lay it on the wood, and put no fire *on* the wood: and I will dress the other bull, but put no fire on it.

²⁴ Then you call loudly on the name of your gods, and I will call on the name of the Lord my God, and it shall come to pass that the God who shall answer by fire, He *is* God." And all the people answered and said, "The word which you have spoken *is* good."

²⁵ And Elijah said to the prophets of shame, "Choose for yourselves one bull, and dress it first, for you *are* many; and call on the name of your god; but apply no fire."

²⁶ And they took the bull and dressed it, and called on the name of Baal from morning till noon, and said, "Hear us, O Baal, hear us." And there was no voice, neither was there hearing, and they ran up and down on the alter which they had made.

²⁷ And it was noon, and Elijah the Tishbite mocked them, and said, "Call with a loud voice, for he is a god; for he is meditating, or else perhaps he is engaged in business, or perhaps he is asleep, and needs to be awakened."

²⁸ And they cried with a loud voice, and cut themselves according to their custom with knives and lancets until the blood gushed out upon them.

²⁹ And they prophesied until the evening came. And it came to pass as it was the time of the offering of the sacrifice, that Elijah the Tishbite spoke to the prophets of the abominations, saying, "Stand aside for now, and I will offer my sacrifice." And they stood aside and departed.

³⁰ And Elijah said to the people, "Come near to me." And all the people came near to me.

³¹ And Elijah took twelve stones, according to the number of the tribes of Israel, as the Lord spoke to him, saying, "Israel shall be your name."

³² And he built up the stones in the name of the Lord, and repaired the altar that had been broken down; and he made a trench that would hold two measures of seed round about the altar.

³³ And he piled the cleft wood on the altar which he *had* made, and divided the burnt offering, and laid *it* on the wood, and laid *it* in order on the altar, and said, "Fetch me four pitchers of water, and pour *it* on the burnt offering, and on the wood." And they did so.

³⁴ And he said, "Do it a second time." And they did it a second time. And he said, "Do it a third time." And they did it a third time.

³⁵ And the water ran round about the altar, and they filled the trench with water.

Elijah's Prayer

³⁶ And Elijah cried aloud to the heavens, and said, "Lord God of Abraham, Isaac, and Israel, answer me, O Lord, answer me this day by fire, and let all this people know that You are the Lord, the God of Israel, and *that* I *am* Your servant, and for Your sake I have done these works.

³⁷ Hear me, O Lord, hear me, and let this people know that You are the Lord God, and *that* You have turned back the heart of this people."

³⁸ Then fire fell from the Lord out of heaven, and devoured the burnt offerings, and the wood and the water that was in the trench, and the fire licked up the stones and the earth.

³⁹ And all the people fell upon their faces and said, "Truly the Lord *is* God! He *is* God!"

⁴⁰ And Elijah said to the people, "Take the prophets of Baal; let not one of them escape." And they took them; and Elijah brought them down to the Brook Kishon, and he executed them there.

⁴¹ And Elijah said to Ahab, "Go up, and eat and drink, for *there is* a sound of the coming of rain."

⁴² And Ahab went up to eat and to drink; and Elijah went up to Carmel, and stooped to the ground, and put his face between his knees,

⁴³ and said to his servant, "Go up, and look toward the sea." And the servant looked, and said, "There is nothing." And Elijah said, "Go again, seven times."

⁴⁴ And the servant went again seven times. And it came to pass at the seventh time, that behold, a little cloud like the sole of a man's foot brought water; and he said, "Go up, and say to Ahab, "Make ready your chariot, and go down, lest the rain overtake you.'"

⁴⁵ And it came to pass in the meanwhile, that the heavens grew black with clouds and wind, and there was a great rain. And Ahab wept, and went to Jezreel.

⁴⁶ And the hand of the Lord *was* upon Elijah, and he girded up his loins, and ran before Ahab to Jezreel.

1 KINGS CHAPTER 19

Elijah Flees from Jezebel

¹ And Ahab told Jezebel his wife all that Elijah *had* done, and how he *had* slain the prophets with the sword.

² And Jezebel sent to Elijah, and said, "If you are Elijah and I am Jezebel, God do so to me and more also, if I do not make your life by this time tomorrow as the life of one of them!"

³ And Elijah feared, and rose, and departed for his life. And he came to Beersheba, *to* the land of Judah, and he left his servant there.

⁴ And he himself went a day's journey in the wilderness, and came and sat under a juniper tree; and asked concerning his life that he might die, and said, "Let it be enough now, O Lord, take my life from me, I pray, for I am no better than my fathers."

⁵ And he lay down and slept there under the tree. And behold, someone touched him, and said to him, "Arise and eat."

⁶ And Elijah looked, and behold, at his head there was a cake of bread and a jar of water. And he arose, and ate and drank, and returned and laid down.

⁷ And the Angel of the Lord returned again, and touched him, and said to him, "Arise and eat, for the journey *is* too great for you."

⁸ And he arose, and ate and drank, and went in the strength of that food for forty days and forty nights, to Mount Horeb.

Elijah at Horeb

⁹ And he entered there into a cave, and rested there. And behold, the word of the Lord *came* to him, and He said, "What are you *doing* here, Elijah?"

¹⁰ And Elijah said, "I have been very jealous for the Lord Almighty, because the children of Israel have forsaken You; they have dug down Your altars, and have slain Your prophets with the sword; and I alone am left, and they seek my life, to take it."

¹¹ And He said, "You shall go forth tomorrow, and shall stand before the Lord in the mount; and behold, the Lord will pass by." And a great *and* strong wind tore into the mountains, and crushed the rocks before the Lord; *but* the Lord *was* not in the wind. And after the wind *there was* an earthquake; *but* the Lord *was* not in the earthquake.

¹² And after the earthquake *there was* a fire; *but* the Lord *was* not in the fire. And after the fire *there was* the voice of a gentle breeze.

¹³ And it came to pass when Elijah heard, that he wrapped his face in his mantle, and went forth and stood in the cave. And behold, a voice *came* to him and said, "What are you *doing* here, Elijah?"

¹⁴ And Elijah said, "I have been very jealous for the Lord Almighty; for the children of Israel have forsaken Your covenant, and they have overthrown Your altars, and have slain Your prophets with the sword! And I alone am left, and they seek my life, to take it."

¹⁵ And the Lord said to him, "Go, return, and you shall come into the way of the Wilderness of Damascus; and you shall go and anoint Hazael to be king over Syria.

¹⁶ And Jehu the son of Nimshi shall you anoint to be king over Israel; and Elisha the son of Shaphat shall you anoint to be prophet in your place.

¹⁷ And it shall come to pass that whoever escapes from the sword of Hazael, Jehu shall slay; and whoever escapes from the sword of Jehu, Elisha shall slay.

¹⁸ And you shall leave in Israel seven thousand men, all the knees which had not bowed themselves to Baal, and every mouth which had not worshipped him."

¹⁹ And he departed from there, and found Elisha the son of Shaphat, and he was plowing with oxen; *there were* twelve yoke before him, and he was with the twelve, and he passed by to him, and cast his mantle upon him.

²⁰ And Elisha left the cattle, and ran after Elijah and said, "I will kiss my father, and follow after you." And Elijah said, "Go, return, for I have done it for you."

²¹ And he returned from following him, and took a yoke of oxen, and slaughtered them, and boiled them with the instruments of the oxen, and gave to the people, and they ate. And he arose, and went after Elijah, and ministered to him.

1 KINGS CHAPTER 20

War with Aram

¹ And the son of Hadad gathered all his forces, and went up and besieged Samaria, *he* and thirty-two kings with him, and all *his* horses and chariots; and they went up and besieged Samaria, and fought against it.

² And he sent into the city to Ahab king of Israel, and said to him, "Thus says the son of Hadad:

³ 'Your silver and your gold are mine, and your wives and your children are mine.'"

⁴ And the king of Israel answered and said, "As you have said, my lord, O king, I am yours, and all mine *as well*."

⁵ And the messengers came again, and said, "Thus says the son of Hadad: 'I sent to you, saying, "You shall give me your silver and your gold, and your wives and your children."

⁶ For at this time tomorrow, I will send my servants to you, and they shall search your house, and the houses of your servants, and it shall be that all the desirable objects of their eyes on which they shall lay their hands, they shall take *them*.'"

⁷ And the king of Israel called all the elders of the land, and said, "Take notice now and consider, that this man seeks mischief; for he has sent to me concerning my wives, and concerning my sons an concerning my daughters; I have not kept back from him my silver and my gold."

⁸ And the elders and all the people said to him, "Do not listen or consent."

⁹ And he said to the messengers of the son of Hadad, "Say to your master, 'All things that you have sent to your servant about at first I will do; but this thing I shall not be able to do.'" And the men departed, and carried back the answer to him.

¹⁰ And the son of Hadad sent to him, saying, "God do so to me and more also, if the dust of Samaria shall suffice for foxes to all the people, even my infantry."

¹¹ And the king of Israel answered and said, "Let it be sufficient; let not the humpbacked boast as he that is upright." ¹² And it came to pass when he returned him this answer, he and all the kings with him were drinking in tents. And he said to his servants, "Form a trench." And they made a trench against the city.

Ahab Victorious

¹³ And behold, a prophet came to Ahab king of Israel, and said, "Thus says the Lord: 'Have you seen this great multitude? Behold, I give it this day into your hands, and you shall know that I *am* the Lord.'"

¹⁴ And Ahab said, "By whom?" And he said, "Thus says the Lord: 'By the young men of the heads of the districts.'" And Ahab said, "Who shall begin the battle?" And he said, "You."

¹⁵ And Ahab numbered the young men, the heads of the districts, and they were two hundred and thirty. And afterwards he numbered the people, every man fit for war, seven thousand.

¹⁶ And he went forth at noon, and the son of Hadad was drinking *and* getting drunk in Succoth, he and the kings, thirty-two kings, *who were* his allies.

¹⁷ And the young men, the heads of the districts went forth first; and they sent and reported to the king of Syria, saying, "There are men that have come forth out of Samaria."

¹⁸ And he said to them, "If they come forth peaceably, take them alive; and if they come forth to war, take them alive;

¹⁹ and let not the young men, the heads of the districts go forth of the city." And the force that was behind them

²⁰ killed each one the man next to him; and each one a second time killed the man next to him. And Syria fled, and Israel pursued them; and the son of Hadad, the king of Syria, escaped on the horse of a horseman.

²¹ And the king of Israel went forth, and took all the horses and the chariots, and attacked *the enemy* with a great slaughter in Syria.

²² And the prophet came to the king of Israel and said, "Strengthen yourself, and observe, and see what you shall do; for in the spring of the year the son of Hadad king of Syria shall come up against you."

²³ And the servants of the king of Syria said, "The God of Israel *is* a God of mountains, and not a God of valleys; therefore has he prevailed against us; but if we should fight against them in the plain, assuredly we shall prevail against them.

²⁴ Therefore do this: Send away the kings, each one to his place, and set princes in their place.

²⁵ And we will give you *another* army according to the army that was destroyed, and cavalry according to the cavalry, and chariots according to the chariots, and we will fight against them in the plain, and we shall prevail against them." And he did according to their voice.

Another Aramean War

²⁶ And it came to pass at the return of the year, that the son of Hadad reviewed Syria, and went up to Aphek to war against Israel.

²⁷ And the children of Israel were numbered, and came to meet them. And Israel encamped before them as two little flocks of goats, but Syria filled the land.

²⁸ Then the man of God came, and said to the king of Israel, "Thus says the Lord: 'Because Syria has said, "The Lord God of Israel *is* a God of the hills, and He *is* not a God of the valleys," therefore will I give this great army into your hand, and you shall know that I *am* the Lord.'"

²⁹ And they encamped opposite each other for seven days. And it came to pass on the seventh day that the battle drew on, and Israel attacked Syria, *even* a hundred thousand footmen in one day.

³⁰ And the rest fled to Aphek, into the city; and the wall fell upon twenty-seven thousand men that were left. And the son of Hadad fled, and entered into an inner chamber, into a closet.

³¹ And he said to his servants, "I know that the kings of Israel are merciful kings: let us now put sackcloth upon our loins, and ropes upon our heads, and let us go forth to the king of Israel, if by any means he will save our souls alive."

³² So they put sackcloth upon their loins, and put ropes upon their heads, and said to the king of Israel, "Your servant the son of Hadad says, 'Let our souls live, I pray.'" And he said, "Does he yet live? He is my brother."

³³ And the men divined, and offered drink offerings; and they caught the word out of his mouth, and said, "Your brother the son of Hadad." And he said, "Go in and fetch him." And the son of Hadad went out to him, and they caused him to go up to him into the chariot.

³⁴ And he said to him, "The cities which my father took from your father I will restore to you; and you shall make streets for yourself in Damascus, as my father made streets in Samaria; and I will let you go with a covenant." And he made a covenant with him, and let him go.

³⁵ And a certain man of the sons of the prophets said to his neighbor by the word of the Lord, "Strike me." And the man would not strike him.

³⁶ And he said to him, "Because you have not heeded the voice of the Lord, therefore behold, as you depart from me, a lion shall kill you." And he departed from him, and a lion found him, and killed him.

³⁷ And he found another man, and said, "Strike me." And the man struck him, and wounded *him.*

³⁸ And the prophet went and stood before the king of Israel by the road, and bound his eyes with a bandage.

³⁹ And it came to pass as the king passed by, that he cried aloud to the king, and said, "Your servant went out to war, and behold, a man brought *another* man to me, and said to me, "Guard this man; and if he should by any means escape, then your life shall go for his life, or you shall pay a talent of silver. ⁴⁰ And it came to pass, that your servant looked round this way and that way, and the man was gone." And the king of Israel said to him, "Behold, you have also destroyed snares *set* for me."

⁴¹ And he hastened to take away the bandage from his eyes; and the king of Israel recognized him, that he was one of the prophets.

⁴² And he said to him, "Thus says the Lord: 'Because you have allowed this man appointed to destruction to escape out of your hand, therefore your life shall go for his life, and your people for his people.'"

⁴³ And the king of Israel departed, confounded and discouraged, and came to Samaria.

Ahab Covets Naboth's Vineyard

¹ And Naboth the Jezreelite had a vineyard, near the threshing floor of Ahab king of Samaria.

² And Ahab spoke to Naboth, saying, "Give me your vineyard, and I will have it for a garden of herbs, for it *is* near my house; and I will give you another vineyard better than *that* one; or if it please you, I will give you money, the price of this your vineyard, and I will have it for a garden of herbs."

³ And Naboth said to Ahab, "God forbid that I should give you the inheritance of my fathers."

⁴ And the spirit of Ahab was troubled, and he lay down upon his bed, and covered his face, and ate no bread.

⁵ And Jezebel his wife went in to him, and spoke to him, *saying,* "Why *is* your spirit troubled, and *why* do you eat no bread?"

⁶ And he said to her, "Because I spoke to Naboth the Jezreelite, saying, 'Give me your vineyard for money; or if you will, I will give you another vineyard for it'; and he said, 'I will not give you the inheritance of my fathers.'"

⁷ And Jezebel his wife said to him, "Do you now thus act *this way, being* king over Israel? Arise, and eat bread, and be your own *master,* and I will give you the vineyard of Naboth the Jezreelite."

⁸ And she wrote a letter in the name of Ahab, and sealed it with his seal, and sent the letter to the elders, and to the freemen who dwelt with Naboth.

⁹ And it was written in the letters, saying, "Proclaim a fast, and set Naboth in a chief place among the people.

¹⁰ And set two men, sons of transgressors, before him, and let them testify against him, saying, 'He blasphemed God and the king': and let them lead him forth, and stone him, and let him die."

Jezebel's Plot

¹¹ And the men of his city, the elders, and the nobles who dwelt in his city, did as Jezebel sent to them, and as it had been written in the letters which she sent to them.

¹² And they proclaimed a fast, and set Naboth in a chief place among the people.

¹³ And two men, sons of transgressors, came in, and sat opposite him, and bore witness against him, saying, "You have blasphemed God and the king." And they led him forth out of the city, and stoned him with stones, and he died.

¹⁴ And they sent to Jezebel, saying, "Naboth has been stoned, and is dead."

¹⁵ And it came to pass, when Jezebel heard *it,* that she said to Ahab, "Arise, take possession of the vineyard of Naboth the Jezreelite, who would not sell it to you; for Naboth is no longer alive, for he is dead."

¹⁶ And it came to pass, when Ahab heard that Naboth the Jezreelite was dead, that he tore his clothes, and put on

sackcloth. And it came to pass afterward, that Ahab arose and went down to the vineyard of Naboth the Jezreelite, to take possession of it.

¹⁷ And the Lord spoke to Elijah the Tishbite, saying,

¹⁸ "Arise, and go down to meet Ahab king of Israel, who is in Samaria, for he *is* in the vineyard of Naboth, for he has gone down there to take possession of it.

¹⁹ And you shall speak to him, saying, 'Thus says the Lord: "Forasmuch as you have slain and taken possession, therefore thus says the Lord, In every place where the swine and the dogs have licked the blood of Naboth, there shall the dogs lick your blood; and the harlots shall wash themselves in your blood."'"

²⁰ And Ahab said to Elijah, "Have you found me, O my enemy?" And he said, "I have found *you*; because you have wickedly sold yourself to work evil in the sight of the Lord, to provoke Him to anger:

²¹ behold, I bring evil upon you; and I will kindle a fire after you, and I will utterly destroy every male of Ahab, and him that is shut up and him that is left in Israel.

²² And I will make your house as the house of Jeroboam the son of Nebat, and as the house of Baasha son of Ahijah, because of the provocations in which you have provoked *Me*, and caused Israel to sin."

²³ And the Lord spoke of Jezebel, saying, "The dogs shall devour her within the walls of Jezreel.

²⁴ The one that dies of Ahab in the city shall the dogs eat, and the one that dies in the field of Ahab shall the birds of the sky eat."

²⁵ But Ahab *did* wickedly, in that he sold himself to do that which was evil in the sight of the Lord, as his wife Jezebel led him astray.

²⁶ And he did very abominably in following after the abominations, according to all that the Amorite did, whom the Lord utterly destroyed from before the children of Israel.

²⁷ And because of the word, Ahab was pierced with sorrow before the Lord, and he wept, and tore his clothes, and put sackcloth upon his body, and fasted; he put on sackcloth also in the day that he struck Naboth the Jezreelite, and went his way.

²⁸ And the word of the Lord came by the hand of his servant Elijah concerning Ahab, and the Lord said,

²⁹ "Have you seen how Ahab has been pricked *to the heart* before Me? I will not bring on the evil in his days, but in his son's days will I bring on the evil."

1 KINGS CHAPTER 22

Ahab's Third Campaign Against Aram

¹ And he rested three years, and there was no war between Syria and Israel.

² And it came to pass in the third year, that Jehoshaphat king of Judah went down to the king of Israel.

³ And the king of Israel said to his servants, "Do you know that Ramoth Gilead *is* ours, and we are slow to take it out of the hand of the king of Syria?"

⁴ And the king of Israel said to Jehoshaphat, "Will you go up with us to Ramoth Gilead to battle?"

⁵ And Jehoshaphat said, "As I *am*, so *are* you also; as my people, *so are* your people; as my horses, *so are* your horses." And Jehoshaphat king of Judah said to the king of Israel, "Please inquire of the Lord today."

⁶ And the king of Israel gathered all the prophets together, about four hundred men. And the king said to them, "Shall I go up to Ramoth Gilead to battle, or shall I refrain?" And they said, "Go up, for the Lord will surely give *it* into the hands of the king."

⁷ And Jehoshaphat said to the king of Israel, "Is there not *still* a prophet of the Lord here, that we may inquire of the Lord by him?"

⁸ And the king of Israel said to Jehoshaphat, "There is one man here *for us* to inquire of the Lord by; but I hate him, for he does not speak good of me, but only evil; Micaiah son of Imlah." And Jehoshaphat king of Judah said, "Let not the king say such things!"

⁹ And the king of Israel called a eunuch and said, "*Bring* Micaiah son of Imlah *here* quickly."

¹⁰ And the king of Israel and Jehoshaphat king of Judah sat, each on his throne, armed in the gates of Samaria; and all the prophets prophesied before them.

¹¹ And Zedekiah son of Chenaanah made for himself iron horns, and said, "Thus says the Lord: With these you shall push the Syrians, until they are consumed."

¹² And all the prophets prophesied in like manner, saying, "Go up to Ramoth Gilead, and *the thing* shall prosper, and the Lord shall deliver it and the king of Syria into your hands."

Micaiah Predicts Defeat

¹³ And the messenger that went to call Micaiah spoke to him, saying, "Behold now, all the prophets speak good *things* with one accord concerning the king; let now your words be like the words of one of them, and speak good things."

¹⁴ And Micaiah said, "*As* the Lord lives, whatsoever the Lord shall say to me, that will I speak."

¹⁵ And he came to the king. And the king said to him, "Micaiah, shall I go up to Ramoth Gilead to battle, or shall I refrain?" And he said, "Go up, for the Lord shall deliver it into the hand of the king."

¹⁶ And the king said to him, "How often must I adjure you, that you speak truth to me in the name of the Lord?"

¹⁷ And he said, "Not so. I saw all Israel scattered on the mountains as a flock without a shepherd. And the Lord said, '*Is* not God *the* Lord of these? Let each one return to his home in peace.'"

18 And the king of Israel said to Jehoshaphat king of Judah, "Did I not say to you that this man does not prophesy good to me, but *he speaks* nothing but evil?"

19 And Micaiah said, "Not so, *it is* not I: hear the word of the Lord: I saw the God of Israel sitting on His throne, and all the host of heaven stood about Him on His right hand and on His left.

20 And the Lord said, 'Who will deceive Ahab king of Israel, that he may go up and fall in Ramoth Gilead?' And one spoke one way, and another *spoke* another way.

21 And there came forth a spirit and stood before the Lord, and said, 'I will deceive him.'

22 And the Lord said to him, 'In what way?' And he said, 'I will go forth, and I will be a lying spirit in the mouth of all his prophets.' And he said, 'You shall deceive him; yes, and you shall prevail: go forth, and do so.'

23 And now, behold, the Lord has put a lying spirit in the mouth of all these your prophets, and the Lord has spoken evil against you."

24 And Zedekiah the son of Chenaanah came near and struck Micaiah on the cheek, and said, "What sort of a spirit of the Lord *has* spoken in you?"

25 And Micaiah said, "Behold, you shall see in that day, when you shall go into an innermost chamber to hide yourself there."

26 And the king of Israel said, "Take Micaiah, and take him away to Semer the keeper of the city;

27 and tell Joash the king's son to put this *fellow* in prison, and to feed him with bread of affliction and water of affliction, until I return in peace."

28 And Micaiah said, "If you ever return in peace, the Lord has not spoken by me."

Defeat and Death of Ahab

29 So the king of Israel went up, and Jehoshaphat king of Judah with him to Ramoth Gilead.

30 And the king of Israel said to Jehoshaphat king of Judah, "I will disguise myself, and enter into the battle, and you put on my robes." So the king of Israel disguised himself, and went into the battle.

31 And the king of Syria had charged the thirty-two captains of his chariots, saying, "Fight *against* neither small nor great, but *rather* against the king of Israel only."

32 And it came to pass, when the captains of the chariots saw Jehoshaphat king of Judah, that they said, "This seems *to be* the king of Israel." And they surrounded him, *and were* about to fight *against* him, but Jehoshaphat cried out.

33 And it came to pass, when the captains of the chariots saw that this was not the king of Israel, that they returned from him.

34 And one drew a bow with a good aim, and struck the king of Israel between the lungs and the breastplate. And he said to his charioteer, "Turn your hands, and carry me away out of the battle, for I am wounded."

35 And the war was turned in that day, and the king was standing on the chariot, against Syria from morning till evening; and he shed the blood out of his wound, into the bottom of the chariot, and died at evening, and the blood ran out of the wound into the bottom of the chariot.

36 And the herald of the army stood at sunset, saying, "Let every man go to his own city and his own land,

37 for the king is dead."
And they came to Samaria, and buried the king in Samaria.

38 And they washed the chariot at the fountain of Samaria; and the swine and the dogs licked up the blood, and the harlots washed themselves in the blood, according to the word of the Lord which He spoke.

39 And the rest of the acts of Ahab, and all that he did, and the ivory house which he built, and all the cities which he built, behold, *are* not these things written in the book of the chronicles of the kings of Israel?

40 And Ahab slept with his fathers, and Ahaziah his son reigned in his place.

41 And Jehoshaphat the son of Asa reigned over Judah. In the fourth year of Ahab king of Israel Jehoshaphat began to reign.

42 *He was* thirty-five years old when he began to reign, and he reigned twenty-five years in Jerusalem; and his mother's name *was* Azuba daughter of Shilhi.

43 And he walked in all the way of Asa his father: he did not turn from it, even from doing that which was right in the eyes of the Lord. Only he did not take away *any* of the high places; the people still sacrificed and burnt incense on the high places.

44 And Jehoshaphat was at peace with the king of Israel.

45 And the rest of the acts of Jehoshaphat, and his mighty deeds, whatever he did, behold, *are* not these things written in the book of the chronicles of the kings of Judah?

46 (This verse omitted in LXX)

47 (This verse omitted in LXX)

48 (This verse omitted in LXX)

49 (This verse omitted in LXX)

50 And Jehoshaphat slept with his fathers, and was buried by his fathers in the City of David his father, and Jehoram his son reigned in his place.

51 And Ahaziah son of Ahab reigned over Israel in Samaria: in the seventeenth year of Jehoshaphat king of Judah, Ahaziah son of Ahab reigned over Israel in Samaria two years.

52 And he did that which was evil in the sight of the Lord, and walked in the way of Ahab his father, and in the way of Jezebel his mother, and in the sins of the house of Jeroboam the son of Nebat, who caused Israel to sin.

53 And he served the Baals and worshipped them, and provoked the Lord God of Israel, according to all that had been done before him.

THE SECOND BOOK OF KINGS

Ahaziah's Messengers Meet Elijah

¹ And Moab rebelled against Israel after the death of Ahab.

² *Now* Ahaziah fell through the lattice that was in his upper chamber in Samaria, and was sick. And he sent messengers, and said to them, "Go and inquire of Baal-Zebub, the god of Ekron, whether I shall recover of this my sickness." And they went to inquire of him.

³ And an angel of the Lord called Elijah the Tishbite, saying, "Arise, and go to meet the messengers of Ahaziah king of Samaria, and you shall say to them, '*Is it* because there is no God in Israel, *that* you go to inquire of Baal-Zebub, the god of Ekron? But *it shall* not *be* so,

⁴ for thus says the Lord: "The bed on which you have gone up, you shall not come down from it, for you shall surely die."'" And Elijah went, and delivered to them *the message*.

⁵ And the messenger returned to him, and he said to them, "Why have you returned?"

⁶ And they said to him, "A man came up to meet us, and said to us, 'Go, return to the king that sent you, and say to him, "Thus says the Lord: *Is it* because there is no God in Israel, *that* you go to inquire of Baal-Zebub, the god of Ekron? *It shall* not *be* so: the bed on which you have gone up, you shall not come down from it, for you shall surely die.'"

⁷ So they returned and reported to the king as Elijah said. And he said to them, "What *was* the manner of the man who went up to meet you, and spoke to you these words?"

⁸ And they said to him, "*He was* a hairy man, and girded with a leather belt about his loins." And he said, This is Elijah the Tishbite.

⁹ And he sent to him a captain of fifty with his fifty *men*. And he went up to him; and behold, Elijah sat on the top of a mountain. And the captain of fifty spoke to him and said, "O man of God, the king has called you, come down."

¹⁰ And Elijah answered and said to the captain of fifty, "If I *am* a man of God, fire shall come down out of heaven, and devour you and your fifty *men*." And fire came down out of heaven, and devoured him and the fifty.

¹¹ And the king sent a second time to him another captain of fifty, and his fifty. And the captain of fifty spoke to him and said, "O man of God, thus says the king, 'Come down quickly.'"

¹² And Elijah answered and spoke to him and said, "If I *am* a man of God, fire shall come down out of heaven, and devour you and your fifty." And fire came down out of heaven, and devoured him and his fifty.

¹³ And the king sent yet again a captain and his fifty. And the third captain of fifty came, and knelt on his knees before Elijah, and entreated him, and spoke to him and said, "O man of God, let my life, and the life of these fifty your servants, be precious in your eyes.

¹⁴ Behold, fire came down from heaven, and devoured the two first captains of fifty; and now, I pray, let my life be precious in your eyes."

¹⁵ And the Angel of the Lord spoke to Elijah and said, "Go down with him, do not be afraid of them." And Elijah rose up, and went down with him to the king.

¹⁶ And Elijah spoke to him, and said, "Thus says the Lord: 'Why have you sent messengers to inquire of Baal-Zebub, the god of Ekron? *It shall* not *be* so; the bed on which you have gone up, you shall not come down from it, for you shall surely die.'"

Jehoram Reigns over Israel

¹⁷ So he died according to the word of the Lord which Elijah had spoken.

¹⁸ And the rest of the acts of Ahaziah which he did, behold, *are* they not written in the book of the chronicles of the kings of Israel? And Jehoram son of Ahab reiged over Israel in Samaria twelve years, *beginning* in the eighteenth year of Jehoshaphat king of Judah. And he did that which was evil in the sight of the Lord, only not as his brothers, nor as his mother; and he removed the pillars of Baal which his father had made, and broke them in pieces; only he was joined to the sins of the house of Jeroboam, who led Israel to sin; he did not depart from them. And the Lord was very angry with the house of Ahab.

2 KINGS CHAPTER 2

Elijah Taken to Heaven

¹ And it came to pass, when the Lord was about to take Elijah with a whirlwind into heaven, that Elijah and Elisha went out of Gilgal.

² And Elijah said to Elisha, "Stay here, please; for God has sent me to Bethel." And Elisha said, "*As* the Lord lives and your soul lives, I will not leave you." So they came to Bethel.

³ And the sons of the prophets who were in Bethel came to Elisha, and said to him, "Do you know that the Lord this day is going to take away your master from over you?" And he said, "Yes, I know *it*; be silent."

⁴ And Elijah said to Elisha, "Stay here, please; for the Lord has sent me to Jericho." And he said, "*As* the Lord lives and as your soul lives, I will not leave you." And they came to Jericho. ⁵ And the sons of the prophets who were in Jericho drew near to Elisha, and said to him, "Do you know that the Lord this day is going to take away your master from over you?" And he said, "Yes, I know *it*; hold your peace."

⁶ And Elijah said to him, "Stay here please, for the Lord has sent me to the Jordan." And Elisha said, "*As* the Lord lives and as your soul lives, I will not leave you." And they both went on.

⁷ And fifty men of the sons of the prophets *went also*, and they stood opposite *the Jordan*, afar off; and both stood on *the bank* of the Jordan.

⁸ And Elijah took his mantle, and wrapped it together, and struck the water, and the water was divided on this side and on that side, and they both went over on dry ground.

⁹ And it came to pass while they were crossing over, that Elijah said to Elisha, "Ask what I shall do for you before I am taken up from you." And Elisha said, "Let there be a double *portion* of your spirit upon me."

¹⁰ And Elijah said, "You have asked a hard thing: if you shall see me when I am taken up from you, then shall it be so to you; and if not, it shall not be *so*."

¹¹ And it came to pass as they were going, that they went on talking; and behold, a chariot of fire *appeared*, with horses of fire, and it separated the two of them; and Elijah was taken up in a whirlwind into heaven.

¹² And Elisha saw, and cried, "Father, father, the chariot of Israel, and his horseman!" And he saw him no more. And he took hold of his garments, and tore them into two pieces.

¹³ And he took up the mantle of Elijah, which fell from off him upon Elisha; and Elisha returned, and stood upon the brink of the Jordan.

¹⁴ And he took the mantle of Elijah, which fell from off him, and struck the water, and said, "Where is the Lord God of Elijah?" And he struck the waters, and they were divided this way and that; and Elisha went over.

Elisha Succeeds Elijah

¹⁵ And the sons of the prophets who were in Jericho on the opposite side saw him, and said, "The spirit of Elijah has rested upon Elisha." And they came to meet him, and bowed down before him to the ground.

¹⁶ And they said to him, "Behold now, *there are* with your servants fifty men of strength: let them go now, and seek your master: perhaps the Spirit of the Lord has taken him up, and cast him into the Jordan, or on one of the mountains, or on one of the hills." And Elisha said, "You shall not send *them*."

¹⁷ And they pressed him until he was ashamed; and he said, "Send *them*." And they sent fifty men, and sought *him for* three days, and did not find him.

¹⁸ And they returned to him, for he dwelt in Jericho. And Elisha said, "Did I not say to you, 'Do not go?'"

¹⁹ And the men of the city said to Elisha, "Behold, the situation of the city *is* good, as *our* lord sees; but the waters *are* bad, and the ground barren."

²⁰ And Elisha said, "Bring me a new pitcher, and put salt in it." And they took *one*, and brought *it* to him.

²¹ And Elisha went out to the spring of the waters, and cast in the salt there, and said, "Thus says the Lord: 'I have healed these waters; there shall be no more death there or barrenness.'"

²² And the waters were healed to this day, according to the word of Elisha which he spoke.

²³ And he went up there to Bethel. And as he was going up by the road, there came up also little children from the city, and mocked him, and said to him, "Go up, baldhead, go up!"

²⁴ And he turned after them, and saw them, and cursed them in the name of the Lord. And behold, there came out two bears out of the woods, and they mauled forty-two children among them.

²⁵ And he went from there to Mount Carmel, and returned from there to Samaria.

2 KINGS CHAPTER 3

Jehoram Meets Moab Rebellion

¹ Now Jehoram the son of Ahab began to reign in Israel in the eighteenth year of Jehoshaphat king of Judah, and he reigned twelve years.

² And he did that which was evil in the sight of the Lord, only not as his father, nor as his mother; and he removed the pillars of Baal which his father had made.

³ Only he adhered to the sin of Jeroboam the son of Nebat, who made Israel to sin; he did not depart from it.

⁴ And Mesha king of Moab was a sheepbreeder, and he rendered to the king of Israel in the beginning *of the year*, a hundred thousand lambs, and a hundred thousand rams, with the wool.

⁵ And it came to pass, after the death of Ahab, that the king of Moab rebelled against the king of Israel.

⁶ And King Jehoram went forth in that day out of Samaria, and numbered Israel.

⁷ And he went and sent to Jehoshaphat king of Judah, saying, "The king of Moab has rebelled against me: will you go with me against Moab to war?" And he said, "I will go up: you are as I *am*, *and* I am as you; as my people, so *are* your people, as my horses, so *are* your horses."

⁸ And he said, "What way shall I go up?" And he said, "The way of the Wilderness of Edom."

⁹ And the king of Israel went, and the king of Judah, and the king of Edom; and they marched on that roundabout route for seven days; and there was no water for the army, and for the cattle that went with them.

¹⁰ And the king of Israel said, "Alas! That the Lord should have called the three kings on their way, to give them into the hand of Moab."

¹¹ And Jehoshaphat said, "Is there not a prophet of the Lord here, that we may inquire of the Lord by him?" And one of the servants of the king of Israel answered and said, "Elisha son of Shaphat is here, who poured water on the hands of Elijah."

¹² And Jehoshaphat said, "He has the word of the Lord." And the king of Israel, and Jehoshaphat king of Judah, and the king of Edom went down to him.

¹³ And Elisha said to the king of Israel, "What have I to do with you? Go to the prophets of your father, and the prophets of your mother." And the king of Israel said to him, "Has the Lord called the three kings to deliver them into the hands of Moab?"

¹⁴ And Elisha said, "*As the Lord of hosts lives, before whom I stand, unless I regarded the presence of Jehoshaphat the king of Judah, I would not have looked on you, nor seen you.*

¹⁵ And now fetch me a harpist." And it came to pass, as the harpist played, that the hand of the Lord came upon him.

¹⁶ And he said, "Thus says the Lord: 'Make this valley full of trenches.

¹⁷ For thus says the Lord: You shall not see wind, neither shall you see rain, yet this valley shall be filled with water, and you and your flocks and your cattle shall drink.

¹⁸ And this *is* a light *thing* in the eyes of the Lord: I will also deliver Moab into your hand.

¹⁹ And you shall strike every strong city, and you shall cut down every good tree, and you shall stop all wells of water, and spoil every good piece *of land* with stones.'"

²⁰ And it came to pass in the morning, when the sacrifice was offered, that behold, waters came from the way of Edom, and the land was filled with water.

²¹ And all Moab heard that the three kings had come up to fight against them. And they cried out on every *side, even* all that were girded with a belt, and they said, "Lo!" And stood upon the border.

²² And they rose early in the morning, and the sun rose upon the waters, and the Moabites saw the water on the opposite side, red as blood.

²³ And they said, "This *is* the blood of the sword; and the kings have fought, and each man has killed his neighbor; now then to the spoils, O Moab!"

²⁴ And they entered into the camp of Israel; and Israel arose and attacked the Moabites, and they fled from before them; and they went on and attacked Moab as they went.

²⁵ And they razed the cities, and cast every man his stone on every good piece *of land* and filled it; and they stopped every well, and cut down every good tree, until they left *only* the stones of the wall cast down; and the slingers surrounded *the land*, and attacked it.

²⁶ And the king of Moab saw that the battle prevailed against him; and he took with him seven hundred men that drew the sword, to cut through to the king of Edom, and they could not.

²⁷ And he took his eldest son whom he had designed to reign in his place, and offered him up for a burnt offering on the walls. And there was a great indignation against Israel; and they departed from him, and returned to their land.

2 KINGS CHAPTER 4

The Widow's Oil

¹ And one of the wives of the sons of the prophets cried to Elisha, saying, "Your servant my husband is dead; and you know that your servant feared the Lord; and the creditor has come to take my two sons to be his servants."

² And Elisha said, "What shall I do for you? Tell me what you have in the house." And she said, "Your servant has nothing in the house, except oil that I anoint myself with."

³ And he said to her, "Go, borrow for yourself empty vessels from all of your neighbors; borrow not a few.

⁴ And you shall go in and shut the door upon you and upon your sons, and you shall pour forth into these vessels, and remove that which is filled."

⁵ And she departed from him, and shut the door upon herself and upon her sons. They brought the vessels near to her, and she poured in until the vessels were filled.

⁶ And she said to her sons, "Bring me another vessel." And they said to her, "There is no more vessels." And the oil ceased.

⁷ And she came and told the man of God. And Elisha said, "Go, sell the oil, and you shall pay your debts, and you and your sons shall live from the remaining oil."

The Shunammite Woman

⁸ Now it happened one day that Elisha passed over to Shunem, and *there was* a great lady there, and she constrained him to eat bread. And it came to pass as often as he went into *the city, that* he turned aside to eat there.

⁹ And the woman said to her husband, "See now, I know that this *is* a holy man of God who comes over continually to us.

¹⁰ Let us now make for him an upper chamber, a small place; and let us put a bed there for him, and a table, and a stool, and a lamp; and it shall come to pass that when he comes in to us, he shall turn in there."

¹¹ And it happened one day that he went in there, and turned aside into the upper chamber, and lay there.

¹² And he said to Gehazi his servant, "Call me this Shunammite." So he called her, and she stood before him.

¹³ And he said to him, "Say now to her, 'Behold, you have taken all this trouble for us; what should I do for you? Have you any request *to make* to the king, or to the captain of the army?'" And she said, "I dwell in the midst of my people."

¹⁴ And he said to Gehazi, "What must we do for her?" And Gehazi his servant said, "Indeed she has no son, and her husband *is* old."

¹⁵ And he called her, and she stood by the door.

¹⁶ And Elisha said to her, "At this time *next year*, as the season *is*, you *shall be* alive, and embrace a son." And she said, "No, my lord, do not lie to your servant."

¹⁷ And the woman conceived, and bore a son at the very time, as the season was, being alive, as Elisha said to her.

¹⁸ And the child grew. And it came to pass when he went out to his father to the reapers,

¹⁹ that he said to his father, "My head, my head." And *his father* said to a servant, "Carry him to his mother."

²⁰ And he carried him to his mother, and he lay upon her knees till noon, and died.

²¹ And she carried him up and laid him on the bed of the man of God; and she shut the door upon him, and went out.

²² And she called her husband, and said, "Send now for me one of the young men, and one of the donkeys, and I will ride quickly to the man of God, and return."

²³ And he said, "Why are you going to him today? It is neither new moon, nor the Sabbath." And she said, "*It is* well."

²⁴ And she saddled the donkey, and said to her servant, "Be quick, proceed: spare not on my account to ride, unless I shall tell you. Go, and you shall proceed, and come to the man of God, to Mount Carmel."

²⁵ And she rode and came to the man of God to the mountain.

And it came to pass when Elisha saw her coming, that he said to Gehazi his servant, "Behold, that Shunammite comes.

²⁶ Now run to meet her, and you shall say, '*Is it* well with you? *Is it* well with your husband? *Is it* well with the child?'" And she said, "*It is* well."

²⁷ And she came to Elisha to the mountain, and laid hold of his feet; and Gehazi drew near to thrust her away. And Elisha said, "Leave her alone, for her soul *is* very grieved inside of her, and the Lord has hidden *it* from me, and has not told *it* to me."

²⁸ And she said, "Did I ask a son of my lord? For did I not say, 'Do not deal deceitfully with me?'"

²⁹ And Elisha said to Gehazi, "Gird up your loins, and take my staff in your hand, and go: if you meet any man, you shall not greet him, and if a man greet you, you shall not answer him; and you shall lay my staff on the child's face."

³⁰ And the mother of the child said, "*As* the Lord lives and *as* your soul lives, I will not leave you." And Elisha arose, and went after her.

³¹ And Gehazi went on before her, and laid his staff on the child's face; but there was neither voice nor any hearing. So he returned to meet him, and told him, saying, "The child has not awakened."

³² And Elisha went into the house, and behold, the dead child was laid upon his bed.

³³ And Elisha went into the house, and shut the door upon themselves, the two, and prayed to the Lord.

³⁴ And he went up, and lay upon the child, and put his mouth upon his mouth, and his eyes upon his eyes, and his hands upon his hands, and bowed himself upon him, and the flesh of the child grew warm.

³⁵ And he returned, and walked up and down in the house. And he went up, and bowed himself on the child seven times, and the child opened his eyes.

³⁶ And Elisha cried out to Gehazi, and said, "Call this Shunammite." So he called her, and she came in to him. And Elisha said, "Take your son."

³⁷ And the woman went in, and fell at his feet, and bowed down to the ground; and she took her son, and went out.

The Poisonous Stew

³⁸ And Elisha returned to Gilgal. And a famine *was* in the land; and the sons of the prophets sat before him. And Elisha said to his servant, "Set on the great pot, and boil stew for the sons of the prophets."

³⁹ And he went out into the field to gather herbs, and found a vine in the field, and gathered wild gourds from it, and filled his garment; and he cast them into the caldron of stew, for they did not know what they were.

⁴⁰ And he poured it out for the men to eat. And it came to pass, when they were eating of the stew, that behold, they cried out, and said, "*There is* death in the pot, O man of God!" And they could not eat.

⁴¹ And he said, "Take meal, and cast it into the pot." And Elisha said to his servant Gehazi, "Pour out for the people, and let them eat." And there was no longer anything harmful in the pot.

⁴² And there came a man over from Baal Shalisha, and brought to the man of God twenty barley loaves and cakes of figs, of the firstfruits. And he said, "Give to the people, and let them eat."

⁴³ And his servant said, "Why should I set this before a hundred men?" And he said, "Give to the people, and let them eat; for thus says the Lord: 'They shall eat and *have some* left over.'"

⁴⁴ So they ate, and *had some* left over, according to the word of the Lord.

2 KINGS CHAPTER 5

Naaman is Healed

¹ Now Naaman, the captain of the army of Syria, was a great man before his master, and highly respected, because by him the Lord had given deliverance to Syria, and the man was mighty in strength, *but he was* a leper.

² And the Syrians went forth in small bands, and took captive out of the land of Israel a young girl; and she waited on Naaman's wife.

³ And she said to her mistress, "If only my master were before the prophet of God in Samaria; then he would heal him from his leprosy."

⁴ And she went in and told her master, and said, "Thus and thus spoke the girl from the land of Israel."

⁵ Then the king of Syria said to Naaman, "Go now, and I will send a letter to the king of Israel." And he went, and took in his hand ten talents of silver, and six thousand pieces of gold, and ten changes of clothing.

⁶ And he brought the letter to the king of Israel, saying, "Now then, as soon as this letter shall reach you, behold, I have sent to you my servant Naaman, and you shall heal him from his leprosy."

⁷ And it came to pass, when the king of Israel read the letter, *that* he tore his clothes, and said, "*Am I* God, *able* to kill and to make alive, that this *man* sends to me to heal a

man of his leprosy? Consider, however, and see that this *man* seeks an occasion against me."

8 And it came to pass, when Elisha heard that the king of Israel had tore his clothes, that he sent to the king of Israel, saying, "Why have you torn your clothes? Let Naaman come to me, and let him know that there is a prophet in Israel."

9 So Naaman came with horse and chariot, and stood at the door of the house of Elisha.

10 And Elisha sent a messenger to him, saying, "Go and wash seven times in the Jordan, and your flesh shall return to you, and you shall be cleansed."

11 But Naaman became furious, and went away and said, "Behold, I said to myself, 'He will by all means come out to me, and stand, and call on the name of his God, and lay his hand upon the place, and heal the leprosy.'

12 *Are* not the Abanah and Pharpar, rivers of Damascus, better than all the waters of Israel? May I not go and wash in them, and be cleansed?" And he turned and went away in a rage.

13 And his servants came near and said to him, "*Suppose* the prophet had spoken a great thing to you, would you not perform it? Yet he has but said to you, 'Wash, and be cleansed.'"

14 So Naaman went down, and dipped himself seven times in the Jordan, according to the word of Elisha; and his flesh returned to him as the flesh of a little child, and he was cleansed.

Gehazi's Greed

15 And he and all his company returned to Elisha, and he came and stood before him, and said, "Behold, I know that there is no God in all the earth, except in Israel; and now receive a blessing from your servant."

16 And Elisha said, "*As* the Lord lives, before whom I stand, I will not take *anything*." And he pressed him to take *something*; but he would not.

17 And Naaman said, "Well then, if not, let there be given to your servant the load *of a* yoke of mules; and you shall give me of the red earth; for your servant will no longer offer burnt offerings or sacrifice to other gods, but only to the Lord by *reason of* this thing.

18 And let the Lord be merciful to your servant when my master goes into the house of Rimmon to worship there, and he shall lean on my hand, and I shall bow down in the house of Rimmon, when he bows down in the house of Rimmon; even let the Lord be merciful to your servant in this matter."

19 And Elisha said to Naaman, "Go in peace." And he departed from him a little way.

20 And Gehazi the servant of Elisha said, "Behold, my Lord has spared this Syrian Naaman, so as not to take of his hand what he has brought; as the Lord lives, I will surely run after him, and take something from him."

21 So Gehazi followed after Naaman. And Naaman saw him running after him, and turned back from his chariot to meet him.

22 And *Gehazi* said, "All is well: my master has sent me, saying, 'Behold, now two young men of the sons of the prophets have come to me from Mount Ephraim; please give them a talent of silver, and two changes of clothes.'"

23 And *Naaman* said, "Take two talents of silver." And he took two talents of silver in two bags, and two changes of clothing, and put them upon two of his servants, and they bore them before him.

24 And he came to a secret place, and took them from their hands, and laid them up in the house, and dismissed the men.

25 And he went in himself and stood before his master. And Elisha said to him,

26 "From where *have you come*, Gehazi?" And Gehazi said, "Your servant has not been anywhere." And Elisha said to him, "Did not my heart go with you, when the man returned from his chariot to meet you? And now you have received silver, and now you have received clothing, olive groves and vineyards, sheep and oxen, menservants, and maidservants.

27 The leprosy also of Naaman shall cleave to you, and to your descendants forever." And he went out from his presence leprous, like snow.

2 KINGS CHAPTER 6

The Axe Head Recovered

1 And the sons of the prophets said to Elisha, "Behold now, the place where we dwell before you is too narrow for us.

2 Let us go to the Jordan, and take from there every man a beam, and make for ourselves a place to dwell there."

3 And he said, "Go." And one of them said gently, "Come with your servants." And he said, "I will go."

4 And he went with them, and they came to the Jordan, and began to cut down wood.

5 And behold, one was cutting down a beam, and the axe head fell into the water. And he cried out, "Alas, master"; and it was hidden.

6 And the man of God said, "Where did it fall?" And he showed him the place. And he broke off a stick, and threw it in there, and the iron came to the surface.

7 And he said, "Pick it up for yourself." And he stretched out his hand, and took it.

8 And the king of Syria was at war with Israel. And he consulted with his servants, saying, "I will encamp in such a place."

9 And Elisha sent to the king of Israel, saying, "Take heed that you do not pass by that place, for the Syrians are hidden there."

10 And the king of Israel sent to the place which Elisha mentioned to him, and he was watchful there, not just once or twice.

11 And the mind of the king of Syria was very much disturbed concerning this thing. And he called his servants,

and said to them, "Will you not tell me who betrays me to the king of Israel?"

[12] And one of his servants said, "None, my Lord, O king, but Elisha the prophet that is in Israel reports to the king of Israel all the words that you speak in your bedroom."

[13] And he said, "Go, see where this man *is*, and I will send and take him." And they sent word to him, saying, "Behold, *he is* in Dothan."

[14] And he sent horses there, and chariots, and a great army. And they came by night, and surrounded the city.

[15] And the servant of Elisha rose up early and went out; and behold, an army surrounded the city, and horses and chariots. And the servant said to him, "O master, what shall we do?"

[16] And Elisha said, "Do not fear, for they who are with us *are* more than they that are with them."

[17] And Elisha prayed, and said, "Lord, open the eyes of the servant, I pray, and let him see." And the Lord opened his eyes, and he saw. And behold, the mountain *was* full of horses, and there were chariots of fire round about Elisha.

[18] And they came down to him; and he prayed to the Lord, and said, "Strike this people, I pray, with blindness." And He struck them with blindness, according to the word of Elisha.

[19] And Elisha said to them, "This *is* not the city, and this *is* not the way: follow me, and I will bring you to the man whom you seek." And he led them away to Samaria.

[20] And it came to pass when they entered into Samaria, that Elisha said, "O Lord, open their eyes, and let them see." And the Lord opened their eyes, and they saw; and behold, they were in the midst of Samaria.

[21] And the king of Israel said to Elisha, when he saw them, "Shall I *not* kill them, *my* father?"

[22] And he said, "You shall not kill them, unless you would kill those whom you have taken captive with your sword and with your bow, *but* set bread and water before them, and let them eat and drink, and depart to their master."

[23] And he set before them a great feast, and they ate and drank. And he dismissed them, and they departed to their master. And the bands of Syria came no longer into the land of Israel.

The Siege of Samaria—Cannibalism

[24] And it came to pass after this, that the son of Hadad king of Syria gathered all his army, and went up, and besieged Samaria.

[25] And there was a great famine in Samaria. And behold, they besieged it, until a donkey's head was *sold* for fifty pieces of silver, and the fourth part of a cab of dove's dung at five pieces of silver.

[26] And the king of Israel was passing by on the wall, and a woman cried to him, saying, "Help, my lord, O king."

[27] And he said to her, "Unless the Lord help you, how shall I help you? From the threshing floor, or from the winepress?"

[28] And the king said to her, "What is *the matter* with you?" And the woman said to him, "This *woman* said to me, 'Give your son, and we will eat him today, and we will eat my son tomorrow.'

[29] So we boiled my son, and ate him. And I said to her on the next day, '*Now* give your son, and let us eat him'; but she has hidden her son."

[30] And it came to pass, when the king of Israel heard the words of the woman, *that* he tore his clothes; and he passed by on the wall, and the people saw sackcloth upon his flesh.

[31] And he said, "God do so to me and more also, if the head of Elisha shall remain on him today!"

[32] And Elisha was sitting in his house, and the elders were sitting with him; and *the king* sent a man before him. *But* before the messenger came to him, *Elisha* said to the elders, "Do you see that this son of a murderer has sent to take away my head? See, as soon as the messenger has come, shut the door, and forcibly detain him at the door: *is* not the sound of his master's feet behind him?"

[33] While he was yet speaking with them, behold, a messenger came to him. And he said, "Behold, this evil *is* of the Lord; why should I wait for the Lord any longer?"

2 KINGS CHAPTER 7

Elisha Promises Food

[1] Then Elisha said, "Hear the word of the Lord; Thus says the Lord: 'At this time tomorrow a measure of fine flour *shall be sold* for a shekel, and two measures of barley for a shekel, in the gates of Samaria.'"

[2] And the officer on whose hand the king rested answered Elisha and said, "Behold, *if* the Lord would make floodgates in heaven, might this thing be?" And Elisha said, "Behold, you shall see with your eyes, but shall not eat thereof."

[3] And there were four leprous men by the gate of the city; and one said to his neighbor, "Why do we sit here until we die?

[4] If we should say, 'Let us go into the city,' then *there is* famine in the city, and we shall die there; and if we sit here, then we shall die. Now then come, and let us fall upon the camp of the Syrians: if they should take us alive, then we shall live; and if they should put us to death, then we shall *only* die."

[5] And they rose up while it was yet night, to go into the camp of the Syrians; and they came into a part of the Syrian camp, and behold, there *was* no man there.

[6] For the Lord had made the Syrian army to hear a sound of chariots, and a sound of horses, *and* the sound of a great army. And *each* man said to his fellow, "Now has the king of Israel hired against us the kings of the Hittites, and the kings of Egypt, to come against us."

[7] And they arose and fled while it was yet dark, and left their tents, and their horses, and their donkeys in the camp, as they were, and fled for their lives.

[8] And these lepers entered a little way into the camp, and went into one tent, and ate and drank, and took silver and

gold and clothing from there. Then they came back and returned there, and entered into another tent, and took from there *also*, and went and hid *the spoils*.

⁹ And *one* man said to his neighbor, "We are not doing *right*; this day is a day of good news, and we hold our peace, and are waiting till the morning light, and *then we* shall find calamity; now them come, and let us go into *the city*, and report *these things* to the house of the king."

¹⁰ So they went and cried toward the gate of the city, and reported to them, saying, "We went into the camp of the Syrians, and behold, there is not there a man, nor voice of man, only horses tied up and donkeys, and their tents still standing."

¹¹ And the porters cried aloud, and reported to the house of the king inside.

¹² And the king rose up by night, and said to his servants, "I will now tell you what the Syrians have done to us. They know that we are hungry, and they have gone forth from the camp and hidden themselves in the field, saying, 'They will come out of the city, and we shall catch them alive, and go into the city.'"

¹³ And one of his servants answered and said, "Let them now take five of the horses that were left, which were left here; behold, they are the number left to all the multitude of Israel; and we will send there and see."

¹⁴ So they took two horsemen. And the king of Israel sent after the king of Syria, saying, "Go, and see."

¹⁵ And they went after them, even to the Jordan. And behold, all along the road was full of garments and vessels, which the Syrians had cast away in their panic. And the messengers returned, and brought word to the king.

¹⁶ And the people went out, and plundered the camp of the Syrians. And a measure of fine flour was sold for a shekel, according to the word of the Lord, and two measures of barley for a shekel.

¹⁷ And the king appointed the officer on whose hand the king leaned *to have charge* over the gate; and the people trampled on him in the gate, and he died, as the man of God *had* said, who spoke when the messenger came down to him.

¹⁸ So it came to pass as Elisha had spoken to the king, saying, "Two measures of barley *shall be sold* for a shekel, and a measure of fine flour for a shekel; and it shall be as at this time tomorrow in the gate of Samaria."

¹⁹ And the officer answered Elisha, and said, "Behold, *if the* Lord makes floodgates in heaven, shall this thing be?" And Elisha said, "Behold, you shall see *it* with your eyes, but you shall not eat thereof."

²⁰ And it was so; for the people trampled on him in the gate, and he died.

2 KINGS CHAPTER 8

Jehoram Restores the Shunammite's Land

¹ And Elisha spoke to the woman whose son he *had* restored to life, saying, "Arise and go, you and your household, and sojourn wherever you may sojourn; for the Lord has called for a famine upon the land; indeed it will come upon the land *for* seven years."

² And the woman arose, and did according to the word of Elisha, both she and her house; and they sojourned in the land of the Philistines seven years.

³ And it came to pass at the end of the seven years, that the woman returned out of the land of the Philistines to the city, and came to cry to the king for her house and for her land.

⁴ And the king spoke to Gehazi the servant of Elisha the man of God, saying, "Please tell me of all the great things that Elisha has done."

⁵ And it came to pass, as he was telling the king how he had restored to life the dead son, behold, the woman whose son Elisha restored to life *came* crying to the king for her house and for her land. And Gehazi said, "My lord, O king, this *is* the woman, and this *is* her son, whom Elisha restored to life."

⁶ And the king asked the woman, and she told him. And the king appointed her a eunuch, saying, "Restore all that was hers, and all the fruits of the field from the day that she left the land until now."

⁷ And Elisha came to Damascus; and the king of Syria the son of Hadad was ill, and they brought him word, saying, "The man of God has come here."

⁸ And the king said to Hazael, "Take in your hand a present, and go to meet the man of God, and inquire of the Lord by him, saying, 'Shall I recover of this my disease?'"

⁹ And Hazael went to meet him, and he took a present in his hand, of all the good things of Damascus, forty camel-loads, and came and stood before him, and said to Elisha, "Your son the son of Hadad, the king of Syria, has sent me to you to inquire, saying, 'Shall I recover of this my disease?'"

¹⁰ And Elisha said, "Go *and* say, 'You shall certainly live'; yet the Lord has showed me that he shall surely die."

¹¹ And he stood before him, and fixed *his countenance* till he was ashamed. And the man of God wept.

¹² And Hazael said, "Why does my lord weep?" And he said, "Because I know all the evil that you will do to the children of Israel: you will utterly destroy their strongholds with fire, and you will slay their choice men with the sword, and you will dash their infants *against the ground*, and their pregnant women you will rip up."

¹³ And Hazael said, "Who is your servant? A dead dog, that he should do this thing?" And Elisha said, "The Lord has shown me that you *shall* rule over Syria."

¹⁴ And he departed from Elisha, and went in to his master; and he said to him, "What did Elisha say to you?" And he said, "He said to me, 'You shall surely live.'"

¹⁵ And it came to pass on the next day that he took a thick cloth, and dipped it in water, and spread it over his face, and he died. And Hazael reigned in his place.

¹⁶ In the fifth year of Joram son of Ahab king of Israel, and while Jehoshaphat was king of Judah, Jehoram the son of Jehoshaphat king of Judah began to reign.

¹⁷ He was thirty-two years old when he began to reign, and he reigned eight years in Jerusalem.

¹⁸ And he walked in the way of the kings of Israel, as did the house of Ahab; for the daughter of Ahab was his wife. And he did that which was evil in the sight of the Lord.

¹⁹ But the Lord would not destroy Judah for David His servant's sake, as He said he would give a light to him and to his sons continually.

²⁰ In his days Edom revolted from under the hand of Judah, and they made a king over themselves.

²¹ And Jehoram went up to Zair, and all the chariots that were with him. And it came to pass after he had arisen, that he attacked Edom who compassed him about, and the captains of the chariots; and the people fled to their tents.

²² Yet Edom revolted from under the hand of Judah till this day. Then Libnah revolted at that time.

²³ And the rest of the acts of Joram, and all that he did, behold, are not these written in the book of the chronicles of the kings of Judah?

²⁴ So Joram slept with his fathers, and was buried with his fathers in the city of his father David; and Ahaziah his son reigned in his place.

²⁵ In the twelfth year of Joram son of Ahab king of Israel, Ahaziah son of Jehoram began to reign.

²⁶ Ahaziah was twenty-two years old when he began to reign, and he reigned one year in Jerusalem; and the name of his mother *was* Athaliah, daughter of Omri king of Israel.

²⁷ And he walked in the way of the house of Ahab, and did that which was evil in the sight of the Lord, as did the house of Ahab.

²⁸ And he went with Joram the son of Ahab to war against Hazael king of the Syrians in Ramoth Gilead; and the Syrians wounded Joram.

²⁹ Then King Joram returned to be healed in Jezreel of the wounds with which they wounded him in Ramoth, when he fought with Hazael king of Syria. And Ahaziah son of Jehoram went down to see Joram the son of Ahab in Jezreel, because he was sick.

2 KINGS CHAPTER 9

Jehu Anointed King of Israel

¹ And Elisha the prophet called one of the sons of the prophets, and said to him, "Gird up your loins, and take this flask of oil in your hand, and go to Ramoth Gilead.

² And you shall enter there, and there you shall see Jehu the son of Jehoshaphat son of Nimshi. And you shall go in and make him rise up from among his brothers, and you shall bring him into a secret chamber.

³ And you shall take the flask of oil, and pour *it* on his head, and say, 'Thus says the Lord: I have anointed you king over Israel.' And you shall open the door and flee, and do not delay."

⁴ And the young man the prophet went to Ramoth Gilead.

⁵ And he went in, and behold, the captains of the army were sitting; and he said, "I have a message for you, O captain." And Jehu said, "To which one of us?" And he said, "To you, O captain."

⁶ And he arose, and went into the house, and he poured the oil upon his head, and said to him, "Thus says the Lord God of Israel: 'I have anointed you to be king over the people of the Lord, even over Israel.

⁷ And you shall utterly destroy the house of Ahab your master from before Me, and shall avenge the blood of My servants the prophets, and the blood of all the servants of the Lord, at the hand of Jezebel,

⁸ and at the hand of the whole house of Ahab; and you shall utterly cut off from the house of Ahab every male, and him that is shut up and left in Israel.

⁹ And I will make the house of Ahab like the house of Jeroboam the son of Nebat, and as the house of Baasha the son of Ahijah.

¹⁰ And the dogs shall eat Jezebel in the portion of Jezreel, and there shall be none to bury her.'" And he opened the door, and fled.

¹¹ And Jehu went forth to the servants of his master, and they said to him, "*Is* all well? Why has this madman come to you?" And he said to them, "You know the man, and his babble."

¹² And they said, "Lie! Tell us now." And Jehu said to them, "Thus and thus he spoke to me, saying, 'Thus says the Lord: "I have anointed you to be king over Israel."'"

¹³ And when they heard it, they made haste, and every man took his garment, and put it under him on the top of the stairs, and blew the trumpet, and said, "Jehu is king."

Joram of Israel Killed

¹⁴ So Jehu the son of Jehoshaphat the son of Nimshi conspired against Joram, and Joram was defending Ramoth Gilead, he and all Israel, because of Hazael king of Syria.

¹⁵ And King Joram had returned to be healed in Jezreel of the wounds which the Syrians had given him, in his war with Hazael king of Syria. And Jehu said, "If your heart is with me, let there not go forth out of the city one fugitive to go and report to Jezreel."

¹⁶ And Jehu rode and advanced, and came down to Jezreel, for Joram king of Israel was getting healed in Jezreel of the arrow-wounds in which the Syrians *had* wounded him in Ramoth in the war with Hazael king of Syria; for he *was* strong, and a mighty man. And Ahaziah king of Judah had come down to see Joram.

¹⁷ And there went up a watchman upon the tower of Jezreel, and saw the dust *made by* Jehu as he approached. And he said, "I see dust." And Joram said, "Take a horseman, and send to meet them, and let him say, 'Peace.'"

¹⁸ And there went a horseman to meet them, and said, "Thus says the king: 'Peace.'" And Jehu said, "What have you to do with peace? Turn behind me." And the watchman reported, saying, "The messenger came up to them, but has not returned."

¹⁹ And he sent another horseman, and he came to him, and said, "Thus says the king: 'Peace.'" And Jehu said, "What have you to do with peace? Turn behind me."

²⁰ And the watchman reported, saying, "He came up to them, but has not returned; and the driver drives like Jehu the son of Nimshi, for it is with furious *haste.*"

²¹ And Joram said, "Make ready." And one made ready the chariot. And Joram the king of Israel went forth, and Ahaziah king of Judah, each in his chariot, and they went to meet Jehu, and found him on the property of Naboth the Jezreelite.

²² And it came to pass when Joram saw Jehu, that he said, "*Is it* peace, Jehu?" And Jehu said, "How *can it be* peace, as long as *there are* the harlotries of your mother Jezebel, and her abundant witchcrafts?"

²³ And Joram turned his hands and fled, and said to Ahaziah, "Treachery, Ahaziah!"

²⁴ And Jehu bent his bow with his full strength, and struck Joram between his arms, and his arrow went out at his heart, and he sank down upon his knees.

²⁵ And *Jehu* said to Bidkar his chief officer, "Cast him into the portion of ground of Naboth the Jezreelite, for you and I remember, *as we were* riding on chariots after Ahab his father, that the Lord took up this burden against him, *saying,*

²⁶ 'Surely, I have seen yesterday the blood of Naboth, and the blood of his sons,' says the Lord; 'and I will recompense him on this property,' says the Lord. Now then, I pray, take him up and cast him into the plot *of ground*, according to the word of the Lord."

Ahaziah of Judah Killed

²⁷ But when Ahaziah king of Judah saw *it*, he fled by the way of Beth Haggan. And Jehu pursued after him, and said, "*Shoot* him also." So one shot him in the chariot at the Ascent of Gur, which is by Ibleam. And he fled to Megiddo, and died there.

²⁸ And his servants put him on a chariot, and brought him to Jerusalem, and they buried him in his tomb in the City of David.

²⁹ And in the eleventh year of Joram king of Israel, Ahaziah began to reign over Judah.

Jezebel's Violent Death

³⁰ Now when Jehu came to Jezreel, Jezebel had heard *of it*, and colored her eyes, and adorned her head, and looked out through the window.

³¹ And Jehu entered into the city, and she said, "*Is it* peace, Zimri, murderer of your master?"

³² And he lifted up his face toward the window, and saw her, and said, "Who are you? Come down with me." And two eunuchs looked down towards him.

³³ And he said, "Throw her *down.*" And they threw her *down*, and some of her blood was sprinkled on the wall, and on the horses; and they trampled on her.

³⁴ And *Jehu* went in and ate and drank, and said, "Look after this accursed woman, and bury her, for she is a king's daughter."

³⁵ And they went to bury her; but they found no more of her but the skull and the feet and the palms of her hands.

³⁶ And they returned and told him. And he said, "*It is* the word of the Lord, which He spoke by the hand of Elijah the Tishbite, saying, 'In the portion of Jezreel shall the dogs eat the flesh of Jezebel.

³⁷ And the carcass of Jezebel shall be as dung on the face of the field in the portion of Jezreel, so that they shall not say, "*This is* Jezebel."'"

2 KINGS CHAPTER 10

Ahab's Seventy Sons Killed

¹ And Ahab *had* seventy sons in Samaria. And Jehu wrote a letter, and sent it into Samaria to the rulers of Samaria, and to the elders, and to the guardians of *the children of* Ahab, saying,

² "Now then, as soon as this letter shall have reached you, seeing *there are* with you the sons of your master, and with you chariots and horses, and strong cities, and arms,

³ choose the best and fittest among your master's sons, and set him on the throne of his father, and fight for the house of your master."

⁴ And they feared greatly, and said, "Behold, two kings did not stand before him, and how shall we stand?"

⁵ So those that were over the house, and those that were over the city, and the elders and the guardians sent to Jehu, saying, "We also *are* your servants, and whatsoever you shall say to us we will do; we will not make *any* man king; we will do that which is right in your eyes."

⁶ And Jehu wrote them a second letter, saying, "If you *are* for me, and obey my voice, take the heads of the men, your master's sons, and bring *them* to me at this time tomorrow in Jezreel." Now the sons of the king were seventy men; these great men of the city brought them up.

⁷ And it came to pass, when the letter came to them, that they took the king's sons and killed them, *all* seventy men, and put their heads in baskets, and sent them to him at Jezreel.

⁸ And a messenger came and told *him*, saying, "They have brought the heads of the king's sons." And he said, "Lay them *in* two heaps by the door of the gate until morning."

⁹ And morning came, and he went forth and stood, and said to all the people, "You are righteous: behold, I conspired against my master, and killed him, but who killed all these?

¹⁰ See now that there shall not fall to the ground anything of the word of the Lord, which the Lord spoke against the house of Ahab, for the Lord has performed all that He spoke of by the hand of His servant Elijah."

¹¹ So Jehu killed all that were left of the house of Ahab in Jezreel, and all his great men, and his acquaintances, and his priests, so as not to leave him *any* remnant.

Ahaziah's Forty-two Brothers Killed

¹² And he arose and went to Samaria, *and* he *was* in Beth Eked on the way.

¹³ And Jehu found the brothers of Ahaziah king of Judah, and said, "Who *are* you?" And they said, "We *are* the brothers of Ahaziah, and we have come down to greet the sons of the king, and the sons of the queen."

¹⁴ And he said, "Take them alive." And they killed them at Beth Eked, forty-two men: he left not a man of them.

The Rest of Ahab's Brothers Killed

¹⁵ And he went from there and found Jehonadab the son of Rechab *coming* to meet him. And he greeted him, and Jehu said to him, "Is your heart right with my heart, as my heart *is* with your heart?" And Jehonadab said, "It is." And Jehu said, "If it is then, give me your hand." And he gave him his hand, and he took him up with him into the chariot.

¹⁶ And he said to him, "Come with me, and see my zeal for the Lord." And he caused him to sit in his chariot.

¹⁷ And he entered into Samaria, and he killed all that were left of Ahab in Samaria, until he had utterly destroyed him, according to the word of the Lord, which He spoke to Elijah.

Worshippers of Baal Killed

¹⁸ And Jehu gathered all the people and said to them, "Ahab served Baal a little; Jehu shall serve him much.

¹⁹ Now then, call all the prophets of Baal, call all his servants and his priests to me; let not a man be wanting: for I have a great sacrifice *to offer* to Baal; everyone who shall be missing shall die." But Jehu acted deceptively, so that he might destroy the servants of Baal.

²⁰ And Jehu said, "Consecrate a solemn festival to Baal." So they made a proclamation.

²¹ And Jehu sent throughout all Israel, saying, "Now then, let all of *Baal's* servants, and all his priests, and all his prophets *come*, let none be lacking: for I am going to offer a great sacrifice. Whosoever shall be missing shall not live." So all the servants of Baal came, and all his priests, and all his prophets: there was not one left who did not come. And they entered into the house of Baal; and the house of Baal was filled from one end to the other.

²² And he said to the man who was over the house of the wardrobe, "Bring forth a robe for all the servants of Baal." And the keeper of the robes brought forth to them.

²³ And Jehu and Jehonadab the son of Rechab entered into the house of Baal, and said to the servants of Baal, "Search, and see whether there is among you any of the servants of the Lord, or only the servants of Baal, by themselves."

²⁴ And he went in to offer sacrifices and burnt offerings. And Jehu set for himself eighty men outside, and said, "Every man who shall escape of the men whom I bring into your hand, the life of him *that spares him* shall go for his life."

²⁵ And it came to pass, when he had finished offering the burnt offering, that Jehu said to the footmen and to the officers, "Go in and kill them; let not a man among them escape." So they struck them down with the edge of the sword, and the footmen and the officers cast *the bodies* forth, and went to the city of the house of Baal.

²⁶ And they brought out the pillar of Baal, and burned it.

²⁷ And they tore down the pillars of Baal, and made his house a refuse dump to this day.

²⁸ So Jehu abolished Baal out of Israel.

²⁹ Nevertheless Jehu did not depart from following the sins of Jeroboam the son of Nebat, who led Israel to sin: *these were* the golden heifers in Bethel and in Dan.

³⁰ And the Lord said to Jehu, "Because of all your deeds in which you have acted well in doing that which was right in My eyes, according to all things which you have done to the house of Ahab, *as they were* in My heart, your sons to the fourth generation shall sit upon the throne of Israel."

³¹ But Jehu was not careful to walk in the law of the Lord God of Israel with all his heart: he did not depart from following the sins of Jeroboam, who made Israel to sin.

Death of Jehu

³² In those days the Lord began to cut Israel short; and Hazael conquered them in every coast of Israel;

³³ from the Jordan eastward all the land of Gilead belonging to the Gadites, of Gad and that of Reuben, and of Manasseh, from Aroer, which is on the brink of the Brook of Arnon, and Gilead and Bashan.

³⁴ And the rest of the acts of Jehu, and all that he did, and all his might, and the wars which he engaged, *are* not these things written in the book of the chronicles of the kings of Israel?

³⁵ And Jehu slept with his fathers; and they buried him in Samaria. And Jehoahaz his son reigned in his place.

³⁶ And the days which Jehu reigned over Israel *were* twenty-eight years in Samaria.

2 Kings Chapter 11

Athaliah Reigns in Judah

¹ And Athaliah the mother of Ahaziah saw that her son was dead, and she destroyed all the royal heirs.

² And Jehosheba daughter of King Joram, sister of Ahaziah, took Joash the son of her brother, and stole him from among the king's sons that were put to death, and hid him and his nurse in the bedchamber from the face of Athaliah, and he was not slain.

³ And he remained with her, hid in the house of the Lord, *for* six years. And Athaliah reigned over the land.

Joash Crowned King of Judah

⁴ And in the seventh year Jehoiada sent and took the captains of hundreds–of the bodyguards and the escorts—and brought them to him into the house of the Lord, and made a covenant of the Lord with them, and adjured them, and Jehoiada showed them the king's son,

⁵ and charged them, saying, "This *is* the thing which you shall do.

⁶ Let a third part of you go in *on* the Sabbath day, and keep the watch of the king's house in the porch; and another third at the gate of Sur, and a third at the gate behind the footmen; and keep guard of the house.

⁷ And there *shall be* two parties among you, even everyone that goes out on the Sabbath, and they shall keep the guard of the Lord's house before the king.

⁸ And surround the king on all sides, every man with his weapon in his hand, and he that goes into the ranges shall die. And they shall be with the king in his going out and in his coming in."

⁹ And the captains of hundreds did all the things that the wise Jehoiada commanded; and they took each his men, both those that went in on the Sabbath day, and those that went out on the Sabbath day, and went in to Jehoiada the priest.

¹⁰ And the priest gave to the captains of hundreds the swords and spears of King David that were in the house of the Lord.

¹¹ And the footmen stood each with his weapon in his hand from the right corner of the house to the left corner of the house, *by* the altar and the house round about the king.

¹² And he brought forth the king's son, and put the crown on him and *gave him* the Testimony; and they made him king, and anointed him, and they clapped *their* hands and said, "Long live the king!"

Death of Athaliah

¹³ And Athaliah heard the sound of the people running, and she went in to the people to the house of the Lord.

¹⁴ And she looked, and behold, the king stood near a pillar according to custom; and the singers and the trumpeters were before the king and all the people of the land, rejoicing and sounding with trumpets. And Athaliah tore her clothes and cried, "Treason! Treason!"

¹⁵ And Jehoiada the priest commanded the captains of hundreds who were over the army, and said to them, "Take her outside under guard, *and* he that goes in after her shall

certainly die by the sword." (For the priest said, "Let her not, however, be slain in the house of the Lord.")

¹⁶ And they laid hands upon her, and went in by the way of the horses' entrance into the house of the Lord, and she was slain there.

¹⁷ And Jehoiada made a covenant between the Lord and the king and the people, that they should be the Lord's people; also between the king and the people.

¹⁸ And all the people of the land went into the house of Baal and tore it down, and completely broke in pieces his altars and his images, and they slew Mattan the priest of Baal before the altars. And the priest appointed overseers over the house of the Lord.

¹⁹ And he took the captains of the hundreds, and the bodyguards and the escorts, and all the people of the land, and brought down the king out of the house of the Lord; and they went in by the way of the gate of the footmen of the king's house, and seated him there on the throne of the kings.

²⁰ And all the people of the land rejoiced, and the city was at rest: and they slew Athaliah with the sword in the house of the king.

²¹ Joash *was* seven years old when he began to reign.

2 KINGS CHAPTER 12

Joash Repairs the Temple

¹ Joash began to reign in the seventh year of Jehu, and he reigned forty years in Jerusalem. And his mother's name *was* Zibiah of Beersheba.

² And Joash did that which was right in the sight of the Lord all the days that Jehoiada the priest instructed him.

³ Only there were not *any* of the high places removed, and the people still sacrificed there, and burned incense on the high places.

⁴ And Joash said to the priests, "*As for* all the money of the holy things that are brought into the house of the Lord, the money of valuation, *as* each man brings the money of valuation, all the money which any man may feel led to bring into the house of the Lord,

⁵ let the priests take it to themselves, every man from *the proceeds of* his sale: and they shall repair the breaches of the house in all *places* wheresoever a breach shall be found."

⁶ And it came to pass in the twenty-third year of King Joash, that the priests *had* not *yet* repaired the breaches of the house.

⁷ And King Joash called Jehoiada the priest, and the *other* priests, and said to them, "Why have you not repaired the breaches of the house? Now then receive no *more* money from your sales, for you shall give it to *repair the* breaches of the house."

⁸ And the priests consented to receive no more money from the people, and not to repair the breaches of the house.

⁹ And Jehoiada the priest took a chest, and bored a hole in its lid, and set it by the altar in the house of a man *belonging to* the house of the Lord, and the priests that kept the door put all the money *there* that was found in the house of the Lord.

¹⁰ And it came to pass, when they saw that *there was* much money in the chest, that the king's scribe and the high priest went up, and they tied up and counted the money that was found in the house of the Lord.

¹¹ And they gave the money that had been collected into the hands of those that did the works, the overseers of the house of the Lord; and they gave it out to the carpenters and to the builders that worked in the house of the Lord,

¹² and to the masons, and to the hewers of stone, to purchase timber and hewn stone to repair the breaches of the house of the Lord, for all that was spent on the house of the Lord, to repair *it*.

¹³ However there were not to be made for the house of the Lord silver plates, studs, bowls, or trumpets, any vessel of gold or vessel of silver, of the money that was brought into the house of the Lord,

¹⁴ for they were to give it to the workmen, and they repaired the house of the Lord with it.

¹⁵ Also they took no account of the men into whose hands they gave the money to give to the workmen, for they acted faithfully.

¹⁶ Money for a sin offering, and money for a trespass offering, whatever happened to be brought into the house of the Lord, went to the priests.

Hazael Threatens Jerusalem

¹⁷ Then went up Hazael king of Syria, and fought against Gath, and took it. And Hazael set his face to go against Jerusalem.

¹⁸ And Joash king of Judah took all the holy things which Jehoshaphat and Jehoram and Ahaziah, his fathers, and the kings of Judah *had* consecrated, and what he himself had dedicated, and all the gold that was found in the treasures of the Lord's house and the king's house, and he sent *them* to Hazael king of Syria; and he went up from Jerusalem.

Death of Joash

¹⁹ And the rest of the acts of Joash, and all that he did, behold, *are* not these things written in the book of the chronicles of the kings of Judah?

²⁰ And his servants rose up and formed a conspiracy, and killed Joash in the house of Millo that is in Silla.

²¹ And Jozachar the son of Shimeath, and Jehozabad the son of Shomer, his servants, struck him, and he died; and they buried him with his fathers in the City of David. And Amaziah his son reigned in his place.

2 KINGS CHAPTER 13

Jehoahaz Reigns in Jerusalem

¹ In the twenty-third year of Joash son of Ahaziah, king of Judah, Jehoahaz the son of Jehu began to reign in Samaria, *and he reigned* seventeen years.

² And he did that which was evil in the sight of the Lord, and walked after the sins of Jeroboam the son of Nebat, who led Israel to sin; he did not depart from them.

³ And the Lord was very angry with Israel, and delivered them into the hand of Hazael king of Syria, and into the hand of the son of Hadad son of Hazael, all their days.

⁴ And Jehoahaz pleaded with the Lord, and the Lord listened to him, for He saw the affliction of Israel, because the king of Syria afflicted them.

⁵ And the Lord gave deliverance to Israel, and they escaped from under the hand of Syria. And the children of Israel dwelt in their tents as before.

⁶ Only they did not depart from the sins of the house of Jeroboam, who led Israel to sin: they walked in them; moreover the grove also remained in Samaria.

⁷ Whereas there was not left any army to Jehoahaz, except fifty horsemen and ten chariots, and ten thousand infantry; for the king of Syria had destroyed them, and they made them as dust for trampling.

⁸ And the rest of the acts of Jehoahaz, and all that he did, and his mighty acts, *are* not these things written in the book of the chronicles of the kings of Israel?

⁹ And Jehoahaz slept with his fathers, and they buried him in Samaria. And Joash his son reigned in his place.

Jehoash Reigns in Israel

¹⁰ In the thirty-seventh year of Joash king of Judah, Jehoash the son of Jehoahaz began to reign over Israel in Samaria, *and reigned* sixteen years.

¹¹ And he did that which was evil in the sight of the Lord; he did not depart from all the sins of Jeroboam the son of Nebat, who led Israel to sin, *but* he walked in them.

¹² And the rest of the acts of Joash, and all that he did, and his mighty acts which he performed together with Amaziah king of Judah, *are* not these written in the book of the chronicles of the kings of Israel?

¹³ And Joash slept with his fathers, and Jeroboam sat upon his throne, and he was buried in Samaria with the kings of Israel.

Death of Elisha

¹⁴ Now Elisha was sick with the sickness of which he died *from*. And Joash king of Israel went down to him, and wept over his face, and said, "My father, *my* father, the chariots of Israel, and their horseman!"

¹⁵ And Elisha said to him, "Take a bow and some arrows." And he took to himself a bow and some arrows.

16 And he said to the king, "Put your hand on the bow." And Joash put his hand upon *it*. And Elisha put his hands upon the king's hands.

17 And he said, "Open the window eastward." And he opened it. And Elisha said, "Shoot." And he shot. And *Elisha* said, "The arrow of the Lord's deliverance, and the arrow of deliverance from Syria; and you shall strike the Syrians in Aphek until you have consumed them."

18 And Elisha said to him, "Take a bow and some arrows." And he took them. And *he* said to the king of Israel, "Strike the ground." And the king struck three times, and he stopped.

19 And the man of God was grieved at him, and said, "If you had struck five or six times, then you would have struck Syria till you had consumed them; but now you shall strike Syria *only* three times."

20 Then Elisha died, and they buried him. And the bands of the Moabites came into the land, at the beginning of the year.

21 And it came to pass as they were burying a man, that behold, they saw a band *of men*, and they cast the man into the grave of Elisha. And as soon as he touched the bones of Elisha, he revived and stood up on his feet.

22 And Hazael greatly afflicted Israel all the days of Jehoahaz.

23 And the Lord had mercy and compassion upon them, and had regarded them, because of His covenant with Abraham, Isaac, and Jacob; and the Lord would not destroy them, and did not cast them out from His presence.

24 And Hazael king of Syria died, and the son of Hadad his son reigned in his place.

25 And Jehoash the son of Jehoahaz returned, and took the cities out of the hand of the son of Hadad, the son of Hazael, which he had taken out of the hand of Jehoahaz his father in the war: three times did Joash defeat him, and he recovered the cities of Israel.

2 KINGS CHAPTER 14

Amaziah Reigns in Judah

1 In the second year of Joash the son of Jehoahaz king of Israel, Amaziah the son of Joash the king of Judah began to reign.

2 He was twenty-five years old when he began to reign, and he reigned twenty-nine years in Jerusalem. And his mother's name *was* Jehoaddan of Jerusalem.

3 And he did that which was right in the sight of the Lord, but not as David his father: he did according to all things that his father Joash did.

4 Only he did not remove the high places; as yet the people *still* sacrificed and burnt incense on the high places.

5 And it came to pass when the kingdom was established in his hand, that he killed his servants that had slain his father the king.

6 But he did not kill the sons of those that had slain him; according as it is written in the book of the Law of Moses, as the Lord gave commandment, saying, "The fathers shall not be put to death for the children, and the children shall not be put to death for the fathers; but everyone shall die for his own sins."

7 He killed ten thousand of the Edomites in the Valley of Salt, and took Sela in the war, and called its name Joktheel to this day.

8 Then Amaziah sent messengers to Joash son of Jehoahaz son of Jehu king of Israel, saying, "Come, let us look one another in the face."

9 And Joash the king of Israel sent to Amaziah king of Judah, saying, "The thistle that was in Lebanon sent to the cedar that was in Lebanon, saying, 'Give your daughter to my son for a wife'; and the wild beasts of the field that were in Lebanon passed by and trod down the thistle.

10 You have attacked and wounded Edom, and your heart has lifted you up: stay at home and glorify yourself; for why are you quarrelsome to your hurt? So *both* you and Judah with you will fall."

11 Nevertheless Amaziah did not listen. So Joash king of Israel went up, and he and Amaziah king of Judah looked one another in the face in Beth Shemesh of Judah.

12 And Judah was overthrown before Israel, and *every* man fled to his tent.

13 And Joash king of Israel took Amaziah the son of Johoash the son of Ahaziah, in Beth Shemesh; and he came to Jerusalem, and broke down the wall of Jerusalem, *beginning* at the gate of Ephraim as far as the Corner Gate, four hundred cubits.

14 And he took the gold and the silver, and all the vessels that were found in the house of the Lord, and in the treasures of the king's house, and the hostages, and returned to Samaria.

15 And the rest of the acts of Joash, *even* all that he did in his might, how he fought with Amaziah king of Judah, are not these things written in the book of the chronicles of the kings of Israel?

16 And Joash slept with his fathers, and was buried in Samaria with the kings of Israel; and Jeroboam his son reigned in his place.

17 And Amaziah the son of Joash king of Judah lived fifteen years after the death of Joash son of Jehoahaz king of Israel.

18 And the rest of the acts of Amaziah, and all that he did, *are* not these written in the book of the chronicles of the kings of Judah?

19 And they formed a conspiracy against him in Jerusalem, and he fled to Lachish; and they sent after him to Lachish, and killed him there.

20 And they brought him upon horses; and he was buried in Jerusalem with his fathers in the City of David.

²¹ And all the people of Judah took Azariah, and he was sixteen years old, and made him king instead of his father Amaziah.

²² He built Elath and restored it to Judah, after the king slept with his fathers.

²³ In the fifteenth year of Amaziah son of Joash king of Judah, Jeroboam son of Joash began to reign over Israel in Samaria, *and reigned* forty-one years.

²⁴ And he did that which was evil in the sight of the Lord. He did not depart from all the sins of Jeroboam the son of Nebat, who led Israel to sin.

²⁵ He recovered the coast of Israel from the entrance of Hamath to the Sea of the Arabah, according to the word of the Lord God of Israel, which He spoke by His servant Jonah the son of Amittai, the prophet of Gath Hepher.

²⁶ For the Lord saw *that* the affliction of Israel *was* very bitter, and that they were few in number, straitened and in need, and destitute, and Israel had no helper.

²⁷ And the Lord said that He would not blot out the descendants of Israel from under heaven; so He delivered them by the hand of Jeroboam the son of Joash.

²⁸ And the rest of the acts of Jeroboam and all that he did, and his mighty deeds, which he achieved in war, and how he recaptured for Israel, from Damascus and Hamath, *all that belonged* to Judah, *are* not these things written in the book of the chronicles of the kings of Israel?

²⁹ And Jeroboam slept with his fathers, even with the kings of Israel; and Zechariah his son reigned in his place.

2 KINGS CHAPTER 15

Azariah Reigns in Judah

¹ In the twenty-seventh year of Jeroboam king of Israel, Azariah the son of Amaziah king of Judah began to reign.

² He was sixteen years old when he began to reign, and he reigned fifty-two years in Jerusalem. And his mother's name was Jecholiah of Jerusalem.

³ And he did that which was right in the eyes of the Lord, according to all things that Amaziah his father did.

⁴ Only he did not take away *any* of the high places; for the people still sacrificed and burnt incense on the high places.

⁵ And the Lord plagued the king, and he was leprous till the day of his death; and he reigned in a separate house. And Jotham the king's son *was* over the household, judging the people of the land.

⁶ And the rest of the acts of Azariah, and all that he did, *are* not these written in the book of the chronicles of the kings of Judah?

⁷ And Azariah slept with his fathers, and they buried him with his fathers in the City of David. And Jotham his son reigned in his place.

Zechariah Reigns in Israel

⁸ In the thirty-eighth year of Azariah king of Judah, Zechariah the son of Jeroboam began to reign over Israel in Samaria, *and reigned* six months.

⁹ And he did that which was evil in the eyes of the Lord, as his fathers had done. He did not depart from all the sins of Jeroboam the son of Nebat, who made Israel to sin.

¹⁰ And Shallum the son of Jabesh, *and others* conspired against him, and they struck him *in* Keblam and killed him, and he reigned in his place.

¹¹ And the rest of the acts of Zechariah, behold, they are written in the book of the chronicles of the kings of Israel.

¹² *This was* the word of the Lord which He spoke to Jehu, saying, "Your sons of the fourth generation shall sit upon the throne of Israel." And it was so.

Shallum Reigns in Israel

¹³ And Shallum the son of Jabesh reigned. And in the thirty-ninth year of Azariah king of Judah, Shallum began to reign in Samaria. *He reigned* a full month.

¹⁴ And Menahem the son of Gadi went up out of Tirzah and came to Samaria, and struck Shallum the son of Jabesh in Samaria, and killed him.

¹⁵ And the rest of the acts of Shallum, and his conspiracy wherein he was engaged, behold, they are written in the book of the chronicles of the kings of Israel.

¹⁶ Then Menahem attacked both Tipsah and all that were in it, and its borders extending beyond Tipsah, because they did not open to him. And he attacked it, and ripped up the pregnant women.

Menahem Reigns in Israel

¹⁷ In the thirty-ninth year of Azariah king of Judah, Menahem the son of Gadi began to reign over Israel in Samaria, *and reigned* ten years.

¹⁸ And he did that which was evil in the sight of the Lord. He did not depart from all the sins of Jeroboam the son of Nebat, who led Israel to sin.

¹⁹ In his days Pul king of the Assyrians went up against the land: and Menahem gave to Pul a thousand talents of silver to aid him with his power.

²⁰ And Menahem raised the silver *by a tax* upon Israel, even on every mighty man in wealth, to give to the king of the Assyrians; fifty shekels *were levied* on each man; and the king of the Assyrians departed, and remained not there in the land.

²¹ And the rest of the acts of Menahem, and all that he did, behold, are not these written in the book of the chronicles of the kings of Israel?

²² And Menahem slept with his fathers, and Pekahiah his son reigned in his place.

Pekah Reigns Israel

²³ In the fiftieth year of Azariah king of Judah, Pekah the son of Menahem began to reign over Israel in Samaria, *and reigned* two years.

24 And he did that which was evil in the sight of the Lord. He did not depart from the sins of Jeroboam the son of Nebat, who made Israel to sin.

25 And Pekah the son of Remaliah, his officer, conspired against him, and struck him in Samaria, in the front of the king's house, with Argob and Arieh, and with him *there were* fifty men of the four hundred. And he killed him, and reigned in his place.

26 And the rest of the acts of Pekah, and all that he did, behold, they are written in the book of the chronicles of the kings of Israel.

27 In the fifty-second year of Azariah king of Judah, Pekah the son of Remaliah began to reign over Israel in Samaria, *and reigned* twenty years.

28 And he did that which was evil in the eyes of the Lord. He did not depart from all the sins of Jeroboam the son of Nebat, who led Israel to sin.

29 In the days of Pekah king of Israel, Tiglath-Pileser king of the Assyrians came, and took Ijon, Abel, Beth Maachah, Janoah, Kedesh, Hazor, Gilead, and Galilee, *even* all the land of Naphtali, and carried them away to the Assyrians.

30 And Hoshea son of Elah formed a conspiracy against Pekah the son of Remaliah, and struck him and killed him, and reigned in his place, in the twentieth year of Jotham the son of Azariah.

31 And the rest of the acts of Pekah, and all that he did, behold, these *are* written in the book of the chronicles of the kings of Israel.

Jotham Reigns in Judah

32 In the second year of Pekah son of Remaliah king of Israel, Jotham the son of Azariah king of Judah began to reign.

33 He was twenty-five years old when he began to reign, and he reigned sixteen years in Jerusalem. And his mother's name *was* Jerusha, daughter of Zadok.

34 And he did that which was right in the sight of the Lord, according to all things that his father Azariah did.

35 Nevertheless he did not take away the high places; for the people still sacrificed and burnt incense on the high places. He built the Upper Gate of the Lord's house.

36 And the rest of the acts of Jotham, and all that he did, *are* not these written in the book of the chronicles of the kings of Judah?

37 In those days the Lord began to send Rezin king of Syria, and Pekah son of Remaliah against Judah.

38 And Jotham slept with his fathers, and was buried with his fathers in the City of David his father. And Ahaz his son reigned in his place.

2 KINGS CHAPTER 16

Ahaz Reigns in Judah

1 In the seventeenth year of Pekah son of Remaliah, Ahaz the son of Jotham king of Judah began to reign.

2 Ahaz was twenty years old when he began to reign, and he reigned sixteen years in Jerusalem; and he did not do what was right in the eyes of the Lord his God faithfully, as David his father *had done*.

3 And he walked in the way of the kings of Israel; indeed, he made his son to pass through the fire, according to the abominations of the heathen whom the Lord cast out from before the children of Israel.

4 And he sacrificed and burnt incense on the high places, and upon the hills, and under every shady tree.

5 Then Rezin king of Syria and Pekah son of Remaliah king of Israel went up against Jerusalem to war, and besieged Ahaz, but could not prevail *against him*.

6 At that time Rezin king of Syria captured Elath for Syria, and drove out the Jews from Elath, and the Edomites came to Elath, and dwelt there to this day.

7 And Ahaz sent messengers to Tiglath-Pileser king of the Assyrians, saying, "I am your servant and your son: come up, deliver me out of the hand of the king of Syria, and out of the hand of the king of Israel, who are rising up against me."

8 And Ahaz took the silver and the gold that was found in the treasures of the house of the Lord, and of the king's house, and sent gifts to the king.

9 And the king of the Assyrians listened to him. And the king of the Assyrians went up to Damascus and took it, and removed the inhabitants, and killed King Rezin.

10 And King Ahaz went to Damascus to meet Tiglath-Pileser king of the Assyrians at Damascus. And he saw an altar at Damascus. And King Ahaz sent the pattern of the altar, and its proportions, and all its workmanship to Urijah the priest .

11 And Urijah the priest built the altar, according to all *the directions* which King Ahaz sent from Damascus.

12 And the king saw the altar, and went up to it,

13 and offered his burnt offering, and his meat offering, and his drink offering, and poured out the blood of his peace offerings on the bronze altar that was before the Lord.

14 And he brought forward *the one* before the house of the Lord from between the altar and the house of the Lord, and he set it openly by the side of the altar northward.

15 And King Ahaz charged Urijah the priest, saying, "Offer upon the great altar the burnt offering in the morning, and the meat offering in the evening, and the burnt offering of the king and his meat offering, and the burnt offering of all the people and their meat offering, and their drink offering; and you shall pour all the blood of the burnt offering, and all the blood of *any other* sacrifice upon it; and the bronze altar shall be for me in the morning."

16 And Urijah the priest did according to all that King Ahaz commanded him.

¹⁷ And King Ahaz cut off the borders of the bases, and removed the laver from off them, and took down the sea from the bronze oxen that were under it, and set it upon a base of stone.

¹⁸ And he made a base for the throne in the house of the Lord, and he turned the king's entrance outside in the house of the Lord because of the king of the Assyrians.

¹⁹ And the rest of the acts of Ahaz, even all that he did, *are* not these written in the book of the chronicles of the kings of Judah?

²⁰ And Ahaz slept with his fathers, and was buried in the City of David. And Hezekiah his son reigned in his place.

2 KINGS CHAPTER 17

Hoshea Reigns in Israel

¹ In the twelfth year of Ahaz king of Judah, Hoshea the son of Elah began to reign in Samaria, *and he reigned* nine years.

² And he did evil in the eyes of the Lord, only not as the kings of Israel that were before him.

³ Shalmaneser king of the Assyrians came up against him; and Hoshea became his servant, and paid him tribute.

⁴ And the king of the Assyrians found iniquity in Hoshea, in that he sent messengers to So, king of Egypt, and he did not bring a tribute to the king of the Assyrians in that year. And the king of the Assyrians besieged him, and bound him in the prison house.

Israel Carried Captive to Assyria

⁵ And the king of the Assyrians went up against all the land, and went up to Samaria, and besieged it *for* three years.

⁶ In the ninth year of Hoshea, the king of the Assyrians took Samaria, and carried Israel away to the Assyrians, and settled them in Halah and in Habor, *near* the River of Gozan, and *in* the mountains of the Medes.

⁷ For it came to pass that the children of Israel *had* transgressed against the Lord their God, who had brought them up out of the land of Egypt, from under the hand of Pharaoh king of Egypt, and they feared other gods,

⁸ and walked in the statutes of the nations which the Lord had cast out from before the face of the children of Israel, and of the kings of Israel, as many as did *such things,*

⁹ and *in those* of the children of Israel, as many as secretly practiced customs, not as *they should have done,* against the Lord their God;

¹⁰ and they built for themselves high places in all their cities, from the tower of the watchmen to the fortified city, and they made for themselves pillars and groves on every high hill, and under every shady tree.

¹¹ And they burned incense there on all the high places, as the nations *did* whom the Lord removed from before them, and dealt with familiar spirits, and they carved *images* to provoke the Lord to anger.

¹² And they served the idols, of which the Lord said to them, "You shall not do this thing *against* the Lord."

¹³ And the Lord testified against Israel and against Judah, even by the hand of all His prophets, *and* of every seer, saying, "Turn from your evil ways, and keep My commandments and My ordinances, and all the law which I commanded your fathers, *and* all that I sent to them by the hand of My servants the prophets."

¹⁴ But they did not obey, and *they* made their necks harder than the necks of their fathers.

¹⁵ And they did not keep any of His testimonies which He charged them; and they walked after vanities, and became vain, and after the nations round about them, concerning which the Lord had charged them not to do accordingly.

¹⁶ They forsook the commandments of the Lord their God, and made themselves graven images, *even* two heifers, and they made groves, and worshipped all the host of heaven, and served Baal.

¹⁷ And they caused their sons and their daughters to pass through the fire, and practiced divinations and soothsaying, and sold themselves to work wickedness in the sight of the Lord, to provoke Him.

¹⁸ And the Lord was very angry with Israel, and removed them out of His sight; and there was none left but the tribe of Judah alone.

¹⁹ Even Judah as well did not keep the commandments of the Lord their God, but they walked according to the customs of Israel which they practiced, and rejected the Lord.

²⁰ And the Lord was angry with the whole house of Israel, and troubled them, and gave them into the hand of them that spoiled them, until He cast them out of His presence.

²¹ Forasmuch as Israel revolted from the house of David, and they made Jeroboam the son of Nebat king; and Jeroboam drew Israel away from following the Lord, and led them to sin a great sin.

²² And the children of Israel walked in all the sins of Jeroboam which he committed; they did not depart from it,

²³ until the Lord removed Israel from His presence, as the Lord spoke by all His servants the prophets; and Israel was removed from off their land to the Assyrians to this day.

Assyria Resettles Samaria

²⁴ And the king of Assyria brought from Babylon the men of Cuthah, *and men* from Ava, and from Hamath and Sepharvaim, and they were settled in the cities of Samaria in the place of the children of Israel. And they inherited Samaria, and were settled in its cities.

²⁵ And it was so at the beginning of their establishment there, *that* they did not fear the Lord, and the Lord sent lions among them, which killed some of them.

²⁶ And they spoke to the king of the Assyrians, saying, "The nations whom you have removed and substituted in the cities of Samaria *for the Israelites,* do not know the manner of the God of the land; and He has sent the lions against

them, and behold, the *lions* are killing them, because they do not know the manner of the God of the land."

27 And the king of the Assyrians commanded, saying, "Bring some *Israelites* there, and let them go and dwell there, and they shall teach them the manner of the God of the land."

28 And they brought one of the priests whom they had removed from Samaria, and he settled in Bethel, and taught them how they should fear the Lord.

29 But the nations each made their own gods, and put them in the house of the high places which the Samaritans *had* made, each nation in the cities in which they dwelt.

30 And the men of Babylon made Soccoth Benoth, and the men of Cuth made Nergel, and the men of Hamath made Ashima,

31 and the Avites made Nibhaz and Tartak; and the *inhabitants* of Sepharvaim *did evil* when they burned their sons in the fire to Adrammelech and Anammelech, the gods of Sepharvaim.

32 And they feared the Lord, yet they established their abominations in the houses of the high places which they made in Samaria, each nation in the city in which they dwelt. And they feared the Lord, and they made for themselves priests of the high places, and sacrificed for themselves in the house of the high places.

33 And they feared the Lord, yet served their own gods, according to the rituals of the nations from among whom they were carried away.

34 Until this day they did according to their manner: they feared *the Lord*, and they did according to their customs, and according to their manner, and according to the law, and according to the commandment which the Lord commanded the sons of Jacob, whose name He made Israel.

35 And the Lord made a covenant with them, and commanded them, saying, "You shall not fear other gods, neither shall you worship them, nor serve them, nor sacrifice to them;

36 but only to the Lord, who brought you up out of the land of Egypt with great strength, and with an outstretched arm: Him shall you fear, and Him shall you worship; to Him shall you sacrifice.

37 You shall observe continually the ordinances and the judgments and the law and the commandments which He wrote for you to do; and you shall not fear other gods.

38 Neither shall you forget the covenant which He made with you; and you shall fear no other gods.

39 But you shall fear the Lord your God, and He shall deliver you from all your enemies.

40 Neither shall you comply with their practice, which they follow."

41 So these nations feared the Lord, and served their graven images: even their sons and their son's sons do to this day, even as their fathers did.

Hezekiah Reigns in Judah

1 And it came to pass in the third year of Hoshea son of Elah king of Israel, *that* Hezekiah son of Ahaz king of Judah began to reign.

2 He was twenty-five years old when he began to reign, and he reigned twenty-nine years in Jerusalem. And his mother's name *was* Abi, daughter of Zechariah.

3 And he did that which was right in the sight of the Lord, according to all that his father David had done.

4 He removed the high places, and broke in pieces the pillars, and utterly destroyed the groves, and the bronze serpent which Moses had made, because until those days the children of Israel burned incense to it; and he called it Nehushtan.

5 He trusted in the Lord God of Israel. And after him there was none like him among the kings of Judah, nor among those that were before him.

6 And he held fast to the Lord, he did not depart from following Him; and he kept His commandments, as many as He commanded Moses.

7 And the Lord was with him; and he was wise in all that he undertook. And he revolted from the king of the Assyrians, and did not serve him.

8 He struck the Philistines, *even* to Gaza, and to the border of it, from the tower of the watchmen even to the strong city.

9 And it came to pass in the fourth year of King Hezekiah (this is the seventh year of Hoshea son of Elah king of Israel), *that* Shalmaneser king of the Assyrians came up against Samaria, and besieged it.

10 And he took it at the end of three years, in the sixth year of Hezekiah, (this *is* the ninth year of Hoshea king of Israel, when Samaria was taken).

11 And the king of the Assyrians carried away the Samaritans to Assyria, and put them in Halah and in Habor, *by* the River Gozan, and *in* the mountains of the Medes;

12 because they did not heed the voice of the Lord their God, and transgressed His covenant, in all things that Moses the servant of the Lord commanded, and they would neither hear nor do *them*.

13 And in the fourteenth year of King Hezekiah, Sennacherib king of the Assyrians came up against the strong cities of Judah, and took them.

14 And Hezekiah king of Judah sent messengers to the king of the Assyrians to Lachish, saying, "I have offended; depart from me: whatsoever you shall lay upon me, I will bear." And the king of Assyria laid upon Hezekiah king of Judah *a tribute of* three hundred talents of silver, and thirty talents of gold.

15 And Hezekiah gave all the silver that was found in the house of the Lord, and in the treasures of the king's house.

16 At that time Hezekiah cut off *the gold from* the doors of the temple, and *from* the pillars which Hezekiah king of

Judah *had* overlaid with gold, and gave it to the king of the Assyrians.

Sennacherib Boasts Against the Lord

[17] And the king of the Assyrians sent Tartan and Rabsaris and Rabshakeh from Lachish to King Hezekiah with a strong force against Jerusalem. And they went up and came to Jerusalem, and stood by the aqueduct of the upper pool, which is by the way of the fuller's field.

[18] And they cried out to Hezekiah. And Eliakim the son of Hilkiah the manager, and Shebna the scribe, and Joah the son of Asaph the recorder, came out to them,

[19] and Rabshakeh said to them, "Say now to Hezekiah, Thus says the king, the great king of the Assyrians: 'What confidence *is* this in which you trust?

[20] You have said, (but *they are* mere words) "*I have* counsel and strength for war." Now then, in whom do you trust, that you have revolted from me?

[21] See now, are you trusting for yourself on this broken staff of reed, *even* upon Egypt? Whosoever shall lean upon it, it shall even go into his hand, and pierce it: so *is* Pharaoh king of Egypt to all that trust on him.

[22] And whereas you have said to me, "We trust on the Lord God," *is* not this He, whose high places and altars Hezekiah has removed, and has said to Judah and Jerusalem, "You shall worship before this altar in Jerusalem?"

[23] Now therefore, I urge you, make an agreement with my lord the king of the Assyrians, and I will give you two thousand horses, if you shall be able on your part to set riders upon them.

[24] How then will you turn away the face of one petty governor, from among the least of my master's servants, seeing that you trust on Egypt for chariots and horsemen for yourself.

[25] And now have we come up without the Lord against this place to destroy it? The Lord said to me, "Go up against this land, and destroy it."'"

[26] And Eliakim the son of Hilkiah, Shebna, and Joah said to Rabshakeh, "Speak now to your servants in the Syrian language, for we understand it; and do not speak to us in the Jewish language; and why do you speak in the ears of the people that are on the wall?"

[27] And Rabshakeh said to them, "Has my master sent me to your master, and to you, to speak these words? *Has he* not *sent me* to the men who sit on the wall, that they may eat their own dung, and drink their own waste together with you?"

[28] And Rabshakeh stood and cried with a loud voice in the Jewish language, and spoke, and said, "Hear the words of the great king of the Assyrians:

[29] thus says the king: 'Let not Hezekiah encourage you with words: for he shall not be able to deliver you out of his hand.

[30] And let not Hezekiah cause you to trust on the Lord, saying, "The Lord will certainly deliver us; this city shall not be delivered into the hand of the king of the Assyrians"; do not listen to Hezekiah.

[31] For thus says the king of the Assyrians: "Gain my favor, and come forth to me, and every man shall drink *of the wine* of his own vine, and every man shall eat of his own fig tree, and shall drink water out of his own cistern;

[32] until I come and remove you to a land like your own land, a land of grain and wine, and bread and vineyards, a land of olive oil and honey, and you shall live and not die; and do not listen to Hezekiah, for he deceives you, saying, "The Lord shall deliver you."

[33] Have the gods of the nations in any way delivered each their own land out of the hand of the king of the Assyrians?

[34] Where is the god of Hamath, and of Arpad? Where is the god of Sepharvaim and Hena and Ivah? Indeed, have they delivered Samaria out of my hand?

[35] Who *is there* among all the gods of the countries, who have delivered their countries out of my hand, that the Lord should deliver Jerusalem out of my hand?'"

[36] But *the men* were silent, and answered him not a word; for *there was* a commandment of the king, saying, "You shall not answer him."

[37] And Eliakim the son of Hilkiah, the manager, and Shebna the scribe, and Joah the son of Asaph the recorder came in to Hezekiah, having torn their clothes; and they reported to him the words of Rabshakeh.

2 KINGS CHAPTER 19

Isaiah Assures Deliverance

[1] And it came to pass when King Hezekiah heard it, that he tore his clothes, and put on sackcloth, and went into the house of the Lord.

[2] And he sent Eliakim the manager, and Shebna the scribe, and the elders of the priests, clothed with sackcloth, to Isaiah the prophet, the son of Amoz.

[3] And they said to him, "Thus says Hezekiah: 'This day *is* a day of tribulation and rebuke and provocation; for the children have come to the birth, but the mother has no strength.

[4] Perhaps the Lord your God will hear all the words of Rabshakeh, whom the king of Assyria his master has sent to reproach the living God, and to revile Him with the words which the Lord your God has heard; and you shall offer *your* prayer for the remnant that is found.'"

[5] So the servants of King Hezekiah came to Isaiah.

[6] And Isaiah said to them, "Thus shall you say to your master, Thus says the Lord: 'Be not afraid of the words which you have heard, in which the servants of the king of the Assyrians have blasphemed *Me*.

[7] Behold, I shall send a blast upon him, and he shall hear a report, and shall return to his own land; and I will overthrow him with the sword in his own land.'"

Sennacherib's Threat

8 So Rabshakeh returned, and found the king of Assyria warring against Libnah; for he heard that he *had* departed from Lachish.

9 And he heard concerning Tirhakah king of the Ethiopians, saying, "Behold, he has come forth to fight with you." And he returned, and sent messengers to Hezekiah, saying,

10 "Let not your God on whom you trust encourage you, saying, 'Jerusalem shall not be delivered into the hands of the king of the Assyrians.'

11 Behold, you have heard all that the kings of the Assyrians have done in all the lands, to waste them utterly—and shall you be delivered?

12 Have any of the gods of the *other* nations delivered them, whom my fathers destroyed: Gozan and Haran and Rezeph and the sons of Eden who were in Telassar?

13 Where is the king of Hamath, and the king of Arpad? And where is the king of the city of Sepharvaim, and of Hena, and Ivah?"

14 And Hezekiah took the letter from the hand of the messengers, and read it. And he went up to the house of the Lord, and Hezekiah spread it before the Lord,

15 and said, "O Lord God of Israel, that dwells over the cherubim, You are the only God in all the kingdoms of the earth; You have made heaven and earth.

16 Incline Your ear, O Lord, and hear: open Your eyes and see, O Lord; and hear the words of Sennacherib, which he has sent to reproach the living God.

17 For truly, Lord, the kings of Assyria have wasted the nations,

18 and have cast their gods into the fire: because they are not gods, but the works of men's hands, wood and stone; and they have destroyed them.

19 And now, O Lord our God, deliver us out of his hand, and all the kingdoms of the earth shall know that You alone *are* the Lord God."

The Word of the Lord Concerning Sennacherib

20 And Isaiah the son of Amoz sent to Hezekiah, saying, "Thus says the Lord God of hosts, the God of Israel: 'I have heard your prayer to Me concerning Sennacherib king of the Assyrians.

21 This *is* the word which the Lord has spoken against him: "The virgin daughter of Zion has made light of you, and mocked you; the daughter of Jerusalem has shaken her head at you.

22 "Whom have you reproached, and whom have you reviled? And against whom have you lifted up your voice, and raised your eyes on high? *Is it not* against the Holy One of Israel?

23 By your messengers you have reproached the Lord, and have said, 'I will go up with the multitude of my chariots, to the height of the mountains, to the sides of Lebanon, and I have cut down the height of his cedar, *and* his choice cypresses; and I have come into the midst of the forest and of Carmel.

24 I have refreshed *myself*, and have drunk strange waters, and I have dried up with the sole of my foot all the rivers of the fortified places.'

25 "I have brought about *the matter*, I have brought it to a conclusion; and it has come to the destruction of the bands of warlike prisoners, *even of* strong cities.

26 And they that dwelt in them were weak in hand, they quaked and were confounded, they became *as* grass of the field, or *as* the green herb, the grass *growing on* houses, and that which is trodden down by him that stands *upon it.*

27 "But I know your sitting down and your going forth, and your rage against Me.

28 Because you were angry against Me, and your fierceness has come up into My ears, therefore will I put My hooks in your nostrils, and My bridle in your lips, and I will turn you back by the way in which you came.

29 "And this shall be a sign to you: eat this year the things that grow of themselves, and in the second year the things which spring up. And in the third year *let there be* sowing and reaping, and planting of vineyards, and eat their fruits.

30 And he shall increase him that has escaped of the house of Judah, and the remnant *shall strike* the root beneath, and it shall produce fruit above.

31 For from Jerusalem shall go forth a remnant, and he that escapes from Mount Zion: the zeal of the Lord of hosts shall do this.

32 "*Is it* not so? Thus says the Lord concerning the king of the Assyrians: 'He shall not enter into this city, and he shall not shoot an arrow there, neither shall a shield come against it, neither shall he heap a mound against it.

33 In the way in which he comes, by *that same* way shall he return, and he shall not enter into this city,' says the Lord.

34 'And I will defend this city as with a shield, for My own sake, and for the sake of My servant David.'"

Sennacherib's Defeat and Death

35 And it came to pass at night that the Angel of the Lord went forth, and killed in the camp of the Assyrians a hundred and eighty-five thousand. And they rose early in the morning, and behold, *these were* all dead corpses.

36 And Sennacherib king of the Assyrians departed, and went and returned, and dwelt in Nineveh.

37 And it came to pass, while he was worshipping in the house of Nisrosh his god, that Adrammelech and Sharezer his sons killed him with the sword; and they escaped into the land of Ararat. And Esarhaddon his son reigned in his place.

2 KINGS CHAPTER 20

Hezekiah's Life Extended

1 In those days Hezekiah was sick, *even* unto death. And Isaiah the prophet, the son of Amoz, came in to him, and

said to him, "Thus says the Lord: 'Give charge to your household; *for* you shall die, and not live.'"

2 And Hezekiah turned to the wall, and prayed to the Lord, saying,

3 "O Lord, remember, I pray, how I have walked before You in truth and with a perfect heart, and have done that which is good in Your eyes." And Hezekiah wept with a great weeping.

4 And Isaiah was in the middle court, and the word of the Lord came to him, saying,

5 "Turn back, and you shall say to Hezekiah the ruler of My people, 'Thus says the Lord God of your father David: I have heard your prayer, I have seen your tears; behold, I will heal you; on the third day you shall go up to the house of the Lord.

6 And I will add to your days fifteen years; and I will deliver you and this city out of the hand of the king of the Assyrians, and I will defend this city for My own sake, and for the sake of My servant David.'"

7 And *Isaiah* said, "Let them take a cake of figs, and lay it upon the ulcer, and he shall be well."

8 And Hezekiah said to Isaiah, "What *is* the sign that the Lord will heal me, and I shall go up to the house of the Lord on the third day?"

9 And Isaiah said, "This *is* the sign from the Lord, that the Lord will perform the word which He has spoken: the shadow *of the dial* shall advance ten degrees; *or* if it should go back ten degrees *this would also be the sign*."

10 And Hezekiah said, "*It is* a light thing for the shadow to go down ten degrees; but let the shadow return ten degrees backward on the dial."

11 And Isaiah the prophet cried to the Lord, and the shadow returned back ten degrees on the dial.

Envoys from Babylon

12 At that time Merodoch Baladan, son of Baladan king of Babylon, sent letters and a present to Hezekiah, because he had heard that Hezekiah was sick.

13 And Hezekiah rejoiced at them, and showed all the house of his spices, the silver and the gold, the spices and the fine oil, and the armory, and all that was found in his treasures; there was nothing which Hezekiah did not show them in his house, and in all his dominion.

14 And Isaiah the prophet went in to King Hezekiah, and said to him, "What did these men say to you? And where did they come from?" And Hezekiah said, "They came to me from a distant land, from Babylon."

15 And he said, "What did they see in your house?" And he said, "They saw everything that *was* in my house: there was nothing in my house which I did not show them; moreover, all that was in my treasuries as well."

16 And Isaiah said to Hezekiah, "Hear the word of the Lord:

17 'Behold, the days are coming that all things that are in your house shall be taken, and all that your fathers have treasured up to this day *shall be carried* to Babylon; and there shall not fail a word which the Lord has spoken.

18 And as for your sons which shall come forth of you, which you shall beget, *the enemy* shall take them, and they shall be eunuchs in the house of the king of Babylon.'"

19 And Hezekiah said to Isaiah, "Good *is* the word of the Lord which He has spoken: *only* let there be peace in my days."

Death of Hezekiah

20 And the rest of the acts of Hezekiah, and all his might, and all that he made, the fountain and the aqueduct, and *how* he brought water into the city, *are* not these things written in the book of the chronicles of the kings of Judah?

21 And Hezekiah slept with his fathers: and Manasseh his son reigned in his place.

2 KINGS CHAPTER 21

Manasseh Reigns in Judah

1 Manasseh *was* twelve years old when he began to reign, and he reigned fifty-five years in Jerusalem; and his mother's name *was* Hephzibah.

2 And he did that which was evil in the eyes of the Lord, according to the abominations of the nations which the Lord cast out from before the children of Israel.

3 And he rebuilt the high places which Hezekiah his father *had* demolished, and set up an altar to Baal, and made groves as Ahab king of Israel *had made*; and worshipped the whole host of heaven, and served them.

4 And he built an altar in the house of the Lord, whereas *God* had said, "In Jerusalem I will place My name."

5 And he built an altar to the whole host of heaven in the two courts of the house of the Lord.

6 And he caused his sons to pass through the fire, and practiced witchcraft and soothsaying, and made groves, and multiplied wizards, so as to do that which was evil in the sight of the Lord, to provoke Him to anger.

7 And he set up the graven image of the grove in the house of which the Lord said to David, and to Solomon his son, "In this house and in Jerusalem which I have chosen out of all the tribes of Israel, will I place My name forever.

8 And I will not again remove the foot of Israel from the land which I gave to their fathers, *even of those* who shall keep all that I commanded, according to all the commandments which My servant Moses commanded them."

9 But they did not listen; and Manasseh led them astray to do evil in the sight of the Lord, beyond the nations whom the Lord utterly destroyed from before the children of Israel.

10 And the Lord spoke by His servants the prophets, saying,

11 "Forasmuch as Manasseh the king of Judah has done all these evil abominations, beyond all that the Amorites did who lived before *him*, and has led Judah also into sin by their idols,

¹² *it shall* not *be* so. Thus says the Lord God of Israel: Behold, I bring calamities upon Jerusalem and Judah, so that both the ears of everyone that hears shall tingle.

¹³ And I will stretch out over Jerusalem the measure of Samaria, and the plummet of the house of Ahab; and I will wipe Jerusalem as a jar is wiped, and turned upside down in the wiping.

¹⁴ And I will reject the remnant of My inheritance, and will deliver them into the hands of their enemies; and they shall be for a plunder and for a spoil to all their enemies;

¹⁵ forasmuch as they have done wickedly in My sight, and have provoked Me from the day that I brought out their fathers out of Egypt, even to this day."

¹⁶ Moreover Manasseh shed very much innocent blood, until he filled Jerusalem *with it* from one end to the other, beside his sins with which he caused Judah to sin, in doing evil in the eyes of the Lord.

¹⁷ And the rest of the acts of Manasseh, and all that he did, and his sin which he sinned, *are* not these things written in the book of the chronicles of the kings of Judah?

¹⁸ And Manasseh slept with his fathers, and was buried in the garden of his house, *even* in the garden of Uzza; and Amon his son reigned in his place.

Amon's Reign and Death

¹⁹ Amon was twenty-two years old when he began to reign, and he reigned two years in Jerusalem; and his mother's name *was* Meshullemeth, daughter of Haruz of Jotbah.

²⁰ And he did that which was evil in the sight of the Lord, as Manasseh his father had done.

²¹ And he walked in all the way in which his father had walked, and served the idols which his father served, and worshipped them.

²² And he forsook the Lord God of his fathers, and did not walk in the way of the Lord.

²³ And the servants of Amon conspired against him, and killed the king in his house.

²⁴ And the people of the land killed all that had conspired against King Amon; and the people of the land made Josiah king in his place.

²⁵ And the rest of the acts of Amon, *even* all that he did, behold, *are* not these written in the book of the chronicles of the kings of Judah?

²⁶ And they buried him in his tomb in the garden of Uzza; and Josiah his son reigned in his place.

2 KINGS CHAPTER 22

Josiah Reigns in Judah

¹ Josiah *was* eight years old when he began to reign, and he reigned thirty-one years in Jerusalem; and his mother's name *was* Jedidah, daughter of Adaiah of Bozkath.

² And he did that which was right in the sight of the Lord, and walked in all the ways of David his father; he did not turn aside to the right hand or to the left.

Hilkiah Finds the Book of the Law

³ And it came to pass in the eighteenth year of King Josiah, in the eighth month, that the king sent Shaphan the son of Azaliah the son of Meshullam the scribe, to the house of the Lord, saying,

⁴ "Go up to Hilkiah the high priest, and take account of the money that is brought into the house of the Lord, which they that keep the door have collected of the people.

⁵ And let them give it into the hand of the workmen that are appointed in the house of the Lord." And he gave it to the workmen in the house of the Lord, to repair the breaches of the house,

⁶ *even* to the carpenters, builders, and masons, *and* also to purchase timber and hewn stones, to repair the breaches of the house.

⁷ Only they did not call them to account for the money that was given to them, because they dealt faithfully.

⁸ And Hilkiah the high priest said to Shaphan the scribe, "I have found the Book of the Law in the house of the Lord." And Hilkiah gave the book to Shaphan, and he read it.

⁹ And he went from the house of the Lord to the king, and reported the matter to the king, and said, "Your servants have collected the money that was found in the house of the Lord, and have given it into the hand of the workmen that are appointed in the house of the Lord."

¹⁰ And Shaphan the scribe spoke to the king, saying, "Hilkiah the priest has given me a book." And Shaphan read it before the king.

¹¹ And it came to pass, when the king heard the words of the Book of the Law, that he tore his clothes.

¹² And the king commanded Hilkiah the priest, and Ahikam the son of Shaphan, and Achobor the son of Michaiah, and Shaphan the scribe, and Asaiah the king's servant, saying,

¹³ "Go, inquire of the Lord for me, and for all the people, and for all Judah, and concerning the words of this book that has been found; for the wrath of the Lord that has been kindled against us *is* great, because our fathers did not heed the words of this book, to do according to all the things written concerning us."

¹⁴ So Hilkiah the priest went, and Ahikam, Achobor, Shaphan, and Asaiah, to Huldah the prophetess, the mother of Shallum, son of Tikvah, son of Harhas, keeper of the wardrobe; and she dwelt in Jerusalem in Masena; and they spoke to her.

¹⁵ And she said to them, "Thus says the Lord God of Israel: 'Say to the man that sent you to Me,

¹⁶ "Thus says the Lord: 'Behold, I will bring evil upon this place, and upon them that dwell in it, *even* all the words of the book which the king of Judah has read,

¹⁷ because they have forsaken Me, and burnt incense to other gods, that they might provoke Me with the works of

their hands; therefore My wrath shall burn forth against this place, and shall not be quenched.

[18] And to the king of Judah that sent you to inquire of the Lord—thus shall you say to him; "Thus says the Lord God of Israel: '*As for* the words which you have heard;

[19] because your heart was tender, and you were humbled before *Me*, when you heard all that I spoke against this place, and against the inhabitants of it, that it should be utterly destroyed and accursed, and you tore your clothes, and wept before Me; I also have heard, says the Lord.

[20] It shall not be so. *Therefore*, behold, I *will* add you to your fathers, and you shall be gathered to your tomb in peace, and your eyes shall not see *any* among all the evils which I bring upon this place."''"

2 KINGS CHAPTER 23

Josiah's Reformation

[1] So they reported the word to the king. And the king sent and gathered all the elders of Judah and Jerusalem to himself.

[2] And the king went up to the house of the Lord, and every man of Judah, and all who dwelt in Jerusalem with him, and the priests, and the prophets, and all the people small and great; and he read in their ears all the words of the Book of the Covenant that was found in the house of the Lord.

[3] And the king stood by a pillar, and made a covenant before the Lord, to walk after the Lord, to keep His commandments and His testimonies and His ordinances with all *his* heart and with all *his* soul, to confirm the words of this covenant; *even all* the things written in this book. And all the people took a stand for the covenant.

[4] And the king commanded Hilkiah the high priest, and the priests of the second order, and those that kept the door, to bring out of the temple of the Lord all the vessels that were made for Baal, and for the grove, and all the host of heaven, and he burned them outside Jerusalem in the fields of Kidron, and took the ashes of them to Bethel.

[5] And he burned the idolatrous priests, whom the kings of Judah *had* appointed (and they burned incense in the high places and in the cities of Judah, and the places around about Jerusalem); and those that burned incense to Baal, and to the sun, and to the moon, and to Mazuroth, and to the whole host of heaven.

[6] And he carried out the grove from the house of the Lord to the Brook Kidron, and burned it at the Brook Kidron, and reduced it to powder, and cast its powder on the tombs of the sons of the people.

[7] And he pulled down the house of the sodomites that were by the house of the Lord, where the women wove tents for the grove.

[8] And he brought up all the priests from the cities of Judah, and defiled the high places where the priests burned incense, from Geba even to Beersheba; and he pulled down the house of the gates that was by the door of the gate of Joshua the ruler of the city, on a man's left hand at the gate of the city.

[9] Only the priests of the high places did not go up to the altar of the Lord in Jerusalem, for they only ate leavened bread in the midst of their brothers.

[10] And he defiled Topheth which is in the valley of the Son of Hinnom, *constructed* for a man to cause his son or his daughter to pass through fire to Molech.

[11] And he burned the horses which the king of Judah had given to the sun in the entrance of the house of the Lord, by the treasury of Nathan the king's eunuch, in the suburbs; and he burned the chariot of the sun with fire.

[12] And the altars that were on the roof of the upper chamber of Ahaz, which the kings of Judah had made, and the altars which Manasseh had made in the two courts of the house of the Lord, did the king pull down and forcibly remove from there, and cast their dust into the Brook of Kidron.

[13] And the king defiled the house that was before Jerusalem, on the right hand of the Mount of Mosthath, which Solomon king of Israel built to Ashtoreth the abomination of the Sidonians, and to Chemosh the abomination of the Moabites, and to Molech the abomination of the children of Ammon.

[14] And he broke in pieces the pillars, and utterly destroyed the groves, and filled their places with the bones of men.

[15] Also the high altar in Bethel, which Jeroboam the son of Nebat, who made Israel to sin, had made, even that high altar he tore down, and dismantled its stones, and reduced it to powder, and burnt the grove.

[16] And Josiah turned aside, and saw the tombs that were there in the city, and sent, and took the bones out of the tombs, and burned them on the altar, and defiled it, according to the word of the Lord which the man of God spoke, when Jeroboam stood by the altar at the feast; and he turned and raised his eyes to the tomb of the man of God that spoke these words.

[17] And he said, "What *is* that mound which I see?" And the men of the city said to him, "*It is the grave of* the man of God that came out of Judah, and uttered these things which you have done upon the altar of Bethel."

[18] And he said, "Leave him alone; let no one disturb his bones." So his bones were spared, together with the bones of the prophet that came out of Samaria.

[19] Moreover Josiah removed all the houses of the high places that were in the cities of Samaria, which the kings of Israel made to provoke the Lord, and did to them all that he did in Bethel.

[20] And he sacrificed all the priests of the high places that were there on the altars, and burned the bones of men upon them, and returned to Jerusalem.

[21] And the king commanded all the people, saying, "Keep the Passover to the Lord your God, as it is written in the Book of the Covenant."

²² Such a Passover as this had not been kept from the days of the judges who judged Israel, even all the days of the kings of Israel, and of the kings of Judah.

²³ But in the eighteenth year of King Josiah, was the Passover kept to the Lord in Jerusalem.

²⁴ Moreover Josiah removed the sorcerers and the wizards and the spiritists and the idols, and all the abominations that had been set up in the land of Judah and in Jerusalem, that he might keep the words of the law that were written in the book, which Hilkiah the priest had found in the house of the Lord.

²⁵ There was no king like him before him, who turned to the Lord with all his heart, and with all his soul, and with all his strength, according to all the Law of Moses; and after him there rose none like him.

Impending Judgment on Judah

²⁶ Nevertheless the Lord did not turn from the fierceness of His great anger, wherewith He was wroth in His anger against Judah, because of the provocations with which Manasseh provoked Him.

²⁷ And the Lord said, "I will also remove Judah from My presence, as I removed Israel, and I will reject this city which I have chosen, *even* Jerusalem, and the house *of* which I said, 'My name shall be there.'"

Josiah Dies in Battle

²⁸ And the rest of the acts of Josiah, and all that he did, *are* not these things written in the book of the chronicles of the kings of Judah?

²⁹ And in his days Pharaoh Necho king of Egypt went up against the king of the Assyrians, to the River Euphrates; and Josiah went out to meet him. And Necho killed him in Megiddo when he saw him.

³⁰ And his servants carried him dead from Megiddo, and brought him to Jerusalem, and buried him in his tomb. And the people of the land took Jehoahaz the son of Josiah, and anointed him, and made him king in the place of his father.

The Reign and Captivity of Jehoahaz

³¹ Jehoahaz was twenty-three years old when he began to reign, and he reigned three months in Jerusalem; and his mother's name *was* Hamutal, daughter of Jeremiah of Libnah. ³² And he did that which was evil in the sight of the Lord, according to all that his fathers had done.

³³ And Pharaoh Necho removed him to Riblah in the land of Hamath, so that he should not reign in Jerusalem; and he imposed a tribute on the land, a hundred talents of silver, and a hundred talents of gold.

³⁴ And Pharaoh Necho made Eliakim son of Josiah king of Judah over them, in the place of his father Josiah, and he changed his name *to* Jehoiakim, and he took Jehoahaz and brought him to Egypt, and he died there.

Jehoiakim Reigns in Judah

³⁵ And Jehoiakim gave the silver and the gold to Pharaoh; but he assessed the land to give the money at the command of Pharaoh: they gave the silver and the gold, *each* man according to his assessment, together with the people of the land to give to Pharaoh Necho.

³⁶ Jehoiakim was twenty-five years old when he began to reign, and he reigned eleven years in Jerusalem; and his mother's name *was* Zebudah, daughter of Pedaiah of Rummah.

³⁷ And he did that which was evil in the eyes of the Lord, according to all that his fathers had done.

2 KINGS CHAPTER 24

Judah Overrun by Enemies

¹ In his days Nebuchadnezzar king of Babylon came up, and Jehoiakim became his servant *for* three years. And *then* he turned and revolted against him.

² And the Lord sent *raiding* bands of Chaldeans against him, and bands of Syrians, and bands of Moabites, and bands of Ammonites, and sent them into the land of Judah to prevail *against it*, according to the word of the Lord which He spoke by His servants the prophets.

³ Moreover it was the purpose of the Lord concerning Judah, to remove them from His presence, because of the sins of Manasseh, according to all that he did.

⁴ Moreover he shed innocent blood, and filled Jerusalem with innocent blood, and the Lord would not pardon *it*.

⁵ And the rest of the acts of Jehoiakim, and all that he did, behold, *are* not these written in the book of the chronicles of the kings of Judah?

⁶ And Jehoiakim slept with his fathers; and Jehoiachin his son reigned in his place.

⁷ And the king of Egypt came no more out of his land, for the king of Babylon took away all that belonged to the king of Egypt, from the river of Egypt as far as the River Euphrates.

The Reign and Captivity of Jehoiachin

⁸ Jehoiachin *was* eighteen years old when he began to reign, and he reigned three months in Jerusalem; and his mother's name *was* Nehushta, daughter of Elnathan, of Jerusalem.

⁹ And he did that which was evil in the sight of the Lord, according to all that his father had done.

¹⁰ At that time Nebuchadnezzar king of Babylon went up to Jerusalem, and the city was besieged.

¹¹ And Nebuchadnezzar king of Babylon came against the city, and his servants besieged it.

¹² And Jehoiachin king of Judah came forth to the king of Babylon, he and his servants, and his mother, and his princes, and his eunuchs; and the king of Babylon took him in the eighth year of his reign.

The Captivity of Jerusalem

13 And he brought forth from there all the treasures of the house of the Lord, and the treasures of the king's house, and he cut up all the golden vessels which Solomon the king of Israel *had* made in the temple of the Lord, according to the word of the Lord.

14 And he carried away *the inhabitants of* Jerusalem, and all the captains, and the mighty men, taking captive ten thousand prisoners, and every craftsmen and smith; and only the poor of the land were left.

15 And he carried Jehoiachin away to Babylon, and the king's mother, and the king's wives, and his eunuchs; and he carried away the mighty men of the land into captivity from Jerusalem to Babylon.

16 And all the men of might, even seven thousand, and one thousand craftsmen and smiths; all *were* mighty *men* fit for war; and the king of Babylon carried them captive to Babylon.

Zedekiah Reigns in Judah

17 And the king of Babylon made Mattaniah his son king in his place, and called his name Zedekiah.

18 Zedekiah *was* twenty-one years old when he began to reign, and he reigned eleven years in Jerusalem; and his mother's name *was* Hamutal daughter of Jeremiah.

19 And he did that which was evil in the sight of the Lord, according to all that Jehoiachin had done.

20 For it was according to the Lord's anger against Jerusalem and on Judah, until He cast them out of His presence, that Zedekiah revolted against the king of Babylon.

2 KINGS CHAPTER 25

The Fall and Captivity of Judah

1 And it came to pass in the ninth year of his reign, in the tenth month, *that* Nebuchadnezzar king of Babylon, and all his army, came against Jerusalem; and he encamped against it, and built a mound against it.

2 And the city was besieged until the eleventh year of King Zedekiah, on the ninth day of the month.

3 And the famine prevailed in the city, and there was no bread for the people of the land.

4 And the city was broken up, and all the men of war went forth by night, by the way of the gate between the walls (this is *the gate* of the king's garden). And the Chaldeans *were set* against the city round about; and *the king* went by the way of the plain.

5 And the army of the Chaldeans pursued the king, and overtook him in the plains of Jericho; and all his army was dispersed from about him.

6 And they took the king, and brought him to the king of Babylon, to Riblah; and he pronounced judgment upon him.

7 And he killed the sons of Zedekiah before his eyes, and put out the eyes of Zedekiah, and bound him in fetters, and brought him to Babylon.

8 And in the fifth month, on the seventh day of the month (this *is* the nineteenth year of Nebuchadnezzar king of Babylon), Nebuzaradan, captain of the guard, who stood before the king of Babylon, came to Jerusalem.

9 And he burned the house of the Lord, and the king's house, and all the houses of Jerusalem, even every house did the captain of the guard burn.

10 And the army of the Chaldeans pulled down the wall of Jerusalem round about.

11 And Nebuzaradan the captain of the guard removed the rest of the people that were left in the city, and the men who had deserted to the king of Babylon, and the rest of the multitude.

12 But the captain of the guard left some of the poor of the land to be vinedressers and farmers.

13 And the Chaldeans broke to pieces the bronze pillars that were in the house of the Lord, and the bases, and the bronze sea that was in the house of the Lord, and carried its brass to Babylon.

14 And the caldrons, and the shovels, and the bowls, and the censers, and all the bronze vessels with which they ministered with, he took.

15 And the captain of the guard took the fire pans, and the gold and silver bowls.

16 Two pillars, and one sea, and the bases which Solomon had made for the house of the Lord; there was no weight of the brass of all the vessels.

17 The height of one pillar *was* eighteen cubits, and the chapiter upon it was of brass. And the height of the chapiter was three cubits: the border, and the pomegranates on the chapiter round about were all of brass; and so it was with the second pillar with its border.

18 And the captain of the guard took Seraiah the high priest, and Zephaniah the second in order, and the three doorkeepers.

19 And they took out of the city one eunuch who was commander of the men of war, and five men that saw the face of the king, that were found in the city, and the secretary of the commander-in-chief, who took account of the people of the land, and sixty men of the people of the land that were found in the city.

20 And Nebuzaradan the captain of the guard took them, and brought them to the king of Babylon, to Riblah.

21 And the king of Babylon struck them and killed them at Riblah in the land of Hamath. So Judah was carried away from his land.

Gedaliah Made Governor of Judah

22 And *as for* the people that were left in the land of Judah, whom Nebuchadnezzar king of Babylon left, over them he set Gedaliah son of Ahikam son of Shaphan.

²³ And all the captains of the army, they and their men, heard that the king of Babylon had *thus* appointed Gedaliah; and they came to Gedaliah, to Mizpah, both Ishmael the son of Nethaniah, and Johanan son of Careah, and Seraiah son of Tanhumeth the Netophathite, and Jaazaniah the son of a Maachathite, they and their men.

²⁴ And Gedaliah swore to them and their men, and said to them, "Do not fear the incursion of the Chaldeans; dwell in the land, and serve the king of Babylon, and it shall be well with you."

²⁵ And it came to pass in the seventh month *that* Ishmael, son of Nethaniah, son of Elishama, of the royal family came, and ten men with him, and he struck and killed Gedaliah, *him* and the Jews and the Chaldeans that were with him in Mizpah.

²⁶ And all the people, great and small rose up, *they* and the captains of the forces, and went into Egypt; because they were afraid of the Chaldeans.

Jehoiachin Released from Prison

²⁷ And it came to pass in the thirty-seventh year of the carrying away of Jehoiachin king of Judah, in the twelfth month, on the twenty-seventh day of the month, *that* Evil-Merodach king of Babylon, in the *first* year of his reign, lifted up the head of Jehoiachin king of Judah, and brought him out of his prison house.

²⁸ And he spoke kindly to him, and set his throne above the thrones of the kings that were with him in Babylon;

²⁹ and changed his prison garments; and he ate bread continually before him all the days of his life.

³⁰ And his portion, a continual portion, was given to him out of the house of the king, a daily rate for every day, all the days of his life.

THE FIRST BOOK OF CHRONICLES

The Family of Adam—Seth to Abraham

¹ Adam, Seth, Enosh,

² Cainan, Mahalalel, Jared,

³ Enoch, Methuselah, Lamech,

⁴ Noah. The sons of Noah: Shem, Ham, Japheth.

⁵ The sons of Japheth: Gomer, Magog, Madai, Javan, Helisa, Tubal, Meshech, and Tiras.

⁶ And the sons of Gomer: Ashkenaz, Diphath, and Togarmah.

⁷ And the sons of Javan: Elishah, Tarshishah, the Kittim, and the Rodanim.

⁸ And the sons of Ham: Cush, Mizraim, Put and Canaan.

⁹ And the sons of Cush: Seba, Havilah, Sabta, Raamah, Sabtecha. And the sons of Raamah: Sheba and Dedan.

¹⁰ And Cush fathered Nimrod: he began to be a mighty hunter on the earth.

¹¹ (This verse omitted in LXX)

¹² (This verse omitted in LXX)

¹³ (This verse omitted in LXX)

¹⁴ (This verse omitted in LXX)

¹⁵ (This verse omitted in LXX)

¹⁶ (This verse omitted in LXX)

¹⁷ The sons of Shem: Elam, Asshur,

¹⁸ (This verse omitted in LXX)

¹⁹ (This verse omitted in LXX)

²⁰ (This verse omitted in LXX)

²¹ (This verse omitted in LXX)

²² (This verse omitted in LXX)

²³ (This verse omitted in LXX)

²⁴ Arphaxad, Shelah,

²⁵ Eber, Peleg, Reu,

²⁶ Serug, Nahor, Terah,

²⁷ *and* Abraham.

²⁸ And the sons of Abraham: Isaac and Ishmael.

The Family of Ishmael

²⁹ And these *are* their generations: the firstborn of Ishmael *was* Nabajoth, then Kedar, Adbeel, Mibsam,

³⁰ Mishma, Dumah, Massa, Hadad, Tema,

³¹ Jetur, Naphish, Kedemah. These *were* the sons of Ishmael.

³² And the sons of Keturah, Abraham's concubine, *were* Zimram, Jokshan, Medan, Midian, Ishbak, and Shuah. And the sons of Jokshan *were* Dedan, and Sheba.

³³ And the sons of Midian *were* Ephah, Epher, Hanoch, Abida, and Eldaah; all these *were* the sons of Keturah.

The Family of Isaac

³⁴ And Abraham fathered Isaac. And the sons of Isaac *were* Jacob and Esau.

³⁵ The sons of Esau *were* Eliphaz, Reuel, Jeush, Jaalam, and Korah.

³⁶ The sons of Eliphaz *were* Teman, Omar, Zephi, Gatam, Kenaz, Timna, and Amalek.

³⁷ And the sons of Reuel *were* Nahath, Zerah, Shammah, and Mizzah.

³⁸ The sons of Seir *were* Lotan, Shobal, Zibeon, Anah, Dishon, Ezer, and Dishan.

³⁹ And the sons of Lotan *were* Hori and Homam; and the sister of Lotan *was* Timna.

⁴⁰ The sons of Shobal *were* Alian, Manahath, Ebal, Shephi, and Onam. And the sons of Zibeon *were* Ajah and Anah.

⁴¹ The son of Anah *was* Dishon. And the sons of Dishon *were* Hamran, Eshban, Ithran, and Cheran.

⁴² And the sons of Ezer *were* Bilhan, Zaavan, and Jaakan. The sons of Dishan *were* Uz and Aran.

The Kings of Edom

⁴³ And these *were* their kings: Balak the son of Beor; and the name of his city *was* Dinhabah.

⁴⁴ And Balak died, and Jobab the son of Zerah of Bozrah reigned in his place.

45 And Jobab died, and Husham of the land of the Temanites reigned in his place.

46 And Husham died, and Hadad the son of Bedad reigned in his place, who attacked Midian in the field of Moab. And the name of his city *was* Avith.

47 And Hadad died, and Samlah of Masrekah reigned in his place.

48 And Samlah died, and Saul of Rehoboth-by-the-River reigned in his place.

49 And Saul died, and Baal-Hanan son of Achbor reigned in his place.

50 And Baal-Hanan died, and Hadad son of Bedad reigned in his place; and the name of his city *was* Pai.

51 The princes of Edom *were* Prince Timnah, Prince Aliah, Prince Jetheth,

52 Prince Oholibamah, Prince Elah, Prince Pinon,

53 Prince Kenaz, Prince Teman, Prince Mibzar, Prince Magdiel,

54 and Prince Iram. These *were* the princes of Edom.

1 CHRONICLES CHAPTER 2

The Family of Israel

1 These *are* the names of the sons of Israel:

2 Reuben, Simeon, Levi, Judah, Issachar, Zebulun, Dan, Joseph, Benjamin, Naphtali, Gad, and Asher.

3 The sons of Judah *were* Er, Onan, and Shelah. *These* three were born to him of the daughter of Shua the Canaanite woman. And Er, the firstborn of Judah, *was* wicked before the Lord, and He killed him.

4 And Tamar his daughter-in-law bore to him Perez and Zerah. All the sons of Judah *were* five.

5 The sons of Perez *were* Hezron and Hamul.

6 And the sons of Zerah *were* Zimri, Ethan, Heman, Calcol, and Dara—five *in* all.

7 And the son of Carmi *was* Achar the troubler of Israel, who was disobedient in the accursed thing.

8 And the son of Ethan *was* Azariah.

9 Also the sons of Hezron who were born to him *were* Jerahmeel, Ram, and Chelubai.

10 And Ram fathered Amminadab, and Amminadab fathered Nahshon, chief of the house of Judah.

11 And Nahshon fathered Salma, and Salmon fathered Boaz,

12 and Boaz fathered Obed, and Obed fathered Jesse.

13 And Jesse fathered his firstborn Eliab, Abinadab *was* his second, Shimea the third,

14 Nethanel the fourth, Raddai the fifth,

15 Ozem the sixth, *and* David the seventh.

16 And their sisters *were* Zeruiah and Abigail. And the sons of Zeruiah *were* Abishai, Joab, and Asahel, three.

17 And Abigail bore Amasa; and the father of Amasa *was* Jether the Ishmaelite.

18 And Caleb the son of Hezron took Azubah to wife, by Jerioth. Now these *were* her sons: Jesher, Shobab, and Ardon.

19 And Azubah died; and Caleb took to himself Ephrath *as a wife*, and she bore to him Hur.

20 And Hur fathered Uri, and Uri fathered Bezalel.

21 And after this Hezron went in to the daughter of Machir the father of Gilead, and he took her when he was sixty-five years old; and she bore him Segub.

22 And Segub fathered Jair, and he had twenty-three cities in Gilead.

23 And he took Geshur and Aram, the towns of Jair from them; *with* Kenath and its towns, sixty cities. All these *belonged to* the sons of Machir the father of Gilead.

24 And after the death of Hezron, Caleb came to Ephrathah; and the wife of Hezron *was* Abijah; and she bore him Ashur the father of Tekoa.

25 And the sons of Jerahmeel the firstborn of Hezron *were* Ram, the firstborn, and Bunah, Oren, and Ozem his brother.

26 And Jerahmeel had another wife, and her name *was* Atarah. She is the mother of Onam.

27 And the sons of Ram the firstborn of Jerahmeel were Maaz, Jamin, and Eker.

28 And the sons of Onam were Shammai, and Jada. And the sons of Shammai *were* Nadab and Abishur.

29 And the name of the wife of Abishur *was* Abihail, and she bore him Ahban and Molid.

30 And the sons of Nadab *were* Seled and Appaim. And Seled died without children.

31 And the son of Appaim *was* Ishi; and the son of Ishi *was* Sheshan; and the son of Sheshan *was* Ahlai.

32 And the sons of Jada *were* Jether and Jonathan. And Jether died childless.

33 And the sons of Jonathan *were* Peleth and Zaza. These were the sons of Jerahmeel.

34 Now Sheshan had no sons, but daughters. And Sheshan had an Egyptian servant, and his name *was* Jarha.

35 And Sheshan gave his daughter to Jarha his servant as wife, and she bore him Attai.

36 And Attai fathered Nathan, and Nathan fathered Zabad,

37 and Zabad fathered Ephlal, and Ephlal fathered Obed;

38 and Obed fathered Jehu, and Jehu fathered Azariah;

39 and Azariah fathered Helez, and Helez fathered Eleasah,

40 and Eleasah fathered Sismai, and Sismai fathered Shallum,

41 and Shallum fathered Jekamiah, and Jekamiah fathered Elishama, and Elishama fathered Ishmael.

The Family of Caleb

42 And the sons of Caleb the brother of Jerahmeel *were* Mesha his firstborn, he *is* the father of Ziph; and the sons of Mareshah the father of Hebron.

43 And the sons of Hebron *were* Korah, Tappuah, Rekem, and Shema.

⁴⁴ And Shema fathered Raham the father of Jorkoam: and Jorkoam fathered Shammai.

⁴⁵ And his son *was* Maon; and Maon *is* the father of Beth Zur.

⁴⁶ And Ephah the concubine of Caleb bore Haran, Moza, and Gazez.

⁴⁷ And the sons of Jahdai *were* Regem, Jotham, Geshan, Pelet, Ephah, and Shaaph.

⁴⁸ And Caleb's concubine Maachah bore Sheber and Tirhanah.

⁴⁹ She also bore Shaaph the father of Madmannah, and Sheva the father of Machbenah, and the father of Gibea. And the daughter of Caleb *was* Achsah.

⁵⁰ These were the sons of Caleb: the sons of Hur the firstborn of Ephrathah *were* Shobal the father of Kirjath Jearim,

⁵¹ Salma the father of Bethlehem, and Hareph the father of Beth Gader.

⁵² And the descendants of Shobal the father of Kirjath Jearim were *the* Haroeh, and the Manuhoth,

⁵³ and the Shumathites, the Aethalim, the Miphithim, the Hesamathim, and the Hemasaraim; from these went forth the Zorathites and the Eshtaolites.

⁵⁴ The sons of Salma *were* Bethlehem, the Netophathites, Atroth Beth Joab, and half of the family of Malathi, Esari.

⁵⁵ The families of the scribes dwelling in Jabez *were* the Tirathites, the Shimeathites, and the Suchathites, these *were* the Kenites that came from Hammath, the father of the house of Rechab.

1 CHRONICLES CHAPTER 3

The Family of David

¹ Now these were the sons of David that were born to him in Hebron: the firstborn *was* Amnon, *born* of Ahinoam the Jezreelitess; the second Daniel, of Abigail the Carmelitess.

² The third, Absalom, the son of Maacah the daughter of Talmai king of Geshur; the fourth, Adonijah the son of Haggith.

³ The fifth, Shephatiah, *the son* of Abital; the sixth, Ithream, by Eglah his wife.

⁴ Six were born to him in Hebron; and he reigned there seven years and six months; and he reigned thirty-three years in Jerusalem.

⁵ And these were born to him in Jerusalem: Shimea, Shobab, Nathan, and Solomon—four by Bathshua the daughter of Ammiel.

⁶ Also *there* were Ibhar, Elishama, and Eliphelet,

⁷ Nogah, Nepheg, Japhia,

⁸ Elishama, Eliada, and Eliphelet, nine *in all*.

⁹ All *these* were the sons of David, besides the sons of the concubines, and *there was also* Tamar their sister.

The Family of Solomon

¹⁰ The sons of Solomon *were* Rehoboam, Abijah his son, Asa his son, Jehoshaphat his son,

¹¹ Joram his son, Ahaziah his son, Joash his son,

¹² Amaziah his son, Azariah his son, Jotham his son,

¹³ Ahaz his son, Hezekiah his son, Manasseh his son,

¹⁴ Amon his son, *and* Josiah his son.

¹⁵ And the sons of Josiah *were* Johanan the firstborn, the second Jehoiakim, the third Zedekiah, the fourth Shallum.

¹⁶ And the sons of Jehoiakim *were* Jeconiah his son, *and* Zedekiah his son.

The Family of Jeconiah

¹⁷ And the sons of Jeconiah *were* Assir, Shealtiel his son,

¹⁸ Malchiram, Pedaiah, Shenazzar, Jecamiah, Hoshama, and Nedabiah.

¹⁹ And the sons of Pedaiah *were* Zerubbabel and Shimei; and the sons of Zerubbabel *were* Meshullam, Hananiah, and Shelomith *was* their sister,

²⁰ and Hashubah, Ohel, Berechiah, Hasadiah, and Jushab-Hesed, five *in all*.

²¹ And the sons of Hananiah *were* Pelatiah and Jeshaiah his son, Rephaiah his son, Arnan his son, Obadiah his son, *and* Shechaniah his son.

²² And the son of Shechaniah *was* Shemaiah. And the sons of Shemaiah *were* Hattush, Joel, Bariah, Neariah, and Shaphat, six *in all*.

²³ And the sons of Neariah *were* Elioenai, Hezekiah, and Azrikam, three *in all*.

²⁴ And the sons of Elioenai *were* Hodaviah, Eliashib, Pelaiah, Akkub, Johanan, Delaiah, and Anani, seven *in all*.

1 CHRONICLES CHAPTER 4

The Family of Judah

¹ And the sons of Judah *were* Perez, Hezron, Carmi, Hur, and Shobal;

² and Reaiah his son. And Shoball fathered Jahath; and Jahath fathered Ahumai and Lahad. These *were* the generations of the Zorathites.

³ And these *were* the sons of Etam: Jezreel, Ishma, and Idbash. And their sister's name *was* Hazelelponi.

⁴ And Penuel *was* the father of Gedor, and Ezer the father of Hushah: these *are* the sons of Hur, the firstborn of Ephrathah, the father of Bethlehem.

⁵ And Ashur the father of Tekoa had two wives, Helah and Naarah.

⁶ And Naarah bore to him Ahuzzam, Hepher and Temeni, and Haahashtari: all these *were* the sons of Naarah.

⁷ And the sons of Helah *were* Zereth, Zohar, and Ethnan.

⁸ And Koz fathered Anub, Zobebah, and the families of the brother of Rechah, the son of Harum.

9 Now Jabez was more famous than his brothers; and his mother called his name Jabez, saying, "I have born *him* as a sorrowful one."

10 And Jabez called on the God of Israel, saying, "O that You would indeed bless me, and enlarge my coasts, and that Your hand might be with me, and that You would make me know that You will not grieve me!" And God granted him all that he asked.

11 And Chelub the father of Shuhah fathered Mehir; who *was* the father of Eshton.

12 And Eshton *fathered* Beth-Rapha, Paseah, and Tehinnah, the founder of the city of Nahash the brother of Eselom the Kenezite: these *were* the men of Rechah.

13 And the sons of Kenaz *were* Othniel and Seraiah. And the sons of Othniel *were* Hathath and Meonothai,

14 and Meonothai fathered Ophrah, and Seraiah fathered Joab, the father of Ge Harashim, for they were craftsmen.

15 And the sons of Caleb the son of Jephunneh *were* Iru, Elah, and Naam; and the son of Elah *was* Kenaz.

16 And the sons of Jehallelel *were* Ziph, Ziphah, Tiria, and Asarel.

17 And the sons of Ezrah *were* Jether, Mered, Epher, and Jalon; and *Mered's wife* fathered Miriam, Shammai, and Ishbah the father of Eshtemoa.

18 And his wife Jehudijah bore Jered the father of Gedor, and Heber the father of Sochoh, and Jekuthiel the father of Zanoah; and these *are* the sons of Bithiah the daughter of Pharaoh, whom Mered took.

19 And the sons of the wife of Hodiah, the sister of Naham the father of Keilah, *were* Garmi, and Eshtemoa the Maachathite.

20 And the sons of Shimon *were* Amnon, Rinnah, Ben-Hanan, and Tilon; and the sons of Ishi *were* Zoheth and Ben-Zoheth.

21 The sons of Shelah the son of Judah *were* Er the father of Lecah, Laadah the father of Mareshah, and the families of the house of the linen workers of the house of Ashbea.

22 And Jokim, and the men of Chozeba, and Joash; Saraph, who dwelt in Moab, and he changed their names to Abederin and Athukiim.

23 These *are* the potters who dwelt in Netaim and Gederah with the king; they grew strong in his kingdom, and dwelt there.

The Family of Simeon

24 The sons of Simeon *were* Nemuel, Jamin, Jarib, Zerah, and Shaul.

25 Shallum his son, Mibsam his son, Mishma his son,

26 Hamuel his son, Sabud his son, Zacchur his son, Shimei his son.

27 Shimei *had* sixteen sons, and six daughters; and his brothers had not many sons, neither did all their families multiply as the sons of Judah.

28 And they dwelt in Beersheba, Moladah, Hazar Shual,

29 Bilhah, Ezem, Tolad,

30 Bethuel, Hormah, Ziklag,

31 Beth Marcaboth, Hazar Susim, and Beth Biri; these *were* their cities until *the time of* King David.

32 And their villages *were* Etam, Ain, Rimmon Tochen, and Ashan—five cities.

33 And all their villages *were* round about these cities, as far as Baal: this *was* their possession, and their distribution:

34 Meshobab, Jamlech, and Joshah the son of Amaziah;

35 Joel, and Jehu the son of Joshibiah, the son of Seraiah, the son of Asiel;

36 Elioenai, Jaakobah, Jeshohaiah, Asaiah, Adiel, Jesimiel, and Benaiah;

37 Ziza the son of Shiphi, the son of Allon, the son of Jedaiah, the son of Shimri, the son of Shemaiah—

38 these went by the names of princes in their families, and they increased abundantly in their fathers' households.

39 And they went till they came to Gedor, to the east side of the valley, to seek pasture for their cattle.

40 And they found abundant and good pastures, and the land before them *was* wide, and *there was* peace and quietness; for *there were* some of the children of Ham who dwelt there before.

41 And these who are written by name came in the days of Hezekiah king of Judah, and they attacked the people's houses, and the Mineans whom they found there, and utterly destroyed them until this day. And they dwelt in their place, because *there was* pasture there for their cattle.

42 And some of them, *even* of the sons of Simeon, went to Mount Seir, *even* five hundred men; and Pelatiah, Neariah, Rephaiah, and Uzziel, sons of Ishi, *were* their rulers.

43 And they defeated the remnant that were left of Amalek, until this day.

1 CHRONICLES CHAPTER 5

The Family of Reuben

1 And the sons of Reuben the firstborn of Israel (for he *was* the firstborn; but because of his going up to his father's couch, *his father* gave his blessing to his son Joseph, *even* the son of Israel; and he was not reckoned as firstborn;

2 for Judah *was* very mighty even among his brothers, and one was to be a ruler out of him: but the blessing *was* Joseph's).

3 The sons of Reuben the firstborn of Israel *were* Hanoch, Pallu, Hezron, and Carmi.

4 The sons of Joel *were* Shemaiah, and Benaiah his son; and Gog his son, and Shimei his son.

5 His son *was* Micah, his son Reaiah, his son Joel,

6 his son Baal, whom Tiglath-Pileser king of Assyria carried away captive; he *is* the chief of the Reubenites.

7 And his brothers in his family, in their distribution according to their generations: the chief, Jeiel, and Zechariah.

8 And Bela the son of Azaz, the son of Shema, the son of Joel; he dwelt in Aroer, and even to Nebo, and Baal Meon.

9 And he dwelt eastward to the borders of the wilderness, from the River Euphrates; for they had much cattle in the land of Gilead.

10 And in the days of Saul they made war *with the Hagrites*; and they fell into their hands, all of them dwelling in their tents eastward of Gilead.

The Family of Gad

11 The sons of Gad dwelt over against them in the land of Bashan as far as Salcah.

12 Joel *was* the firstborn, and Shapham the second, and Jaanai the scribe in Bashan.

13 And their brothers according to the houses of their fathers *were*: Michael, Meshullam, Sheba, Jorai, Jachan, Zia, and Eber, seven *in all.*

14 These *were* the sons of Abihail the son of Huri, the son of Jaroah, the son of Gilead, the son of Michael, the son of Jeshishai, the son of Jahdo, the son of Buz,

15 who *was* the brother of the son of Abdiel, the son of Guni, *he was* chief of the house of their families.

16 They dwelt in Gilead, in Bashan, and in their villages, and *in* all the country round about Sharon to the border.

17 The numbering of *them* all took place in the days of Jotham king of Judah, and in the days of Jeroboam king of Israel.

18 The sons of Reuben and Gad, and the half-tribe of Manasseh, of mighty men, bearing shields and sword, and bending the bow, and skilled in war, *were* forty-four thousand seven hundred and sixty, going forth to battle.

19 And they made war with the Hagrites, Jetur, Naphish, and Nodab,

20 and they prevailed against them; and the Hagrites were given into their hands, *they* and all their tents, for they cried to God in the battle, and He listened to them, because they trusted on Him.

21 And they took captive their livestock: five thousand camels, two hundred and fifty thousand sheep, two thousand donkeys, and a hundred thousand men.

22 For many fell slain, because the war *was* of God. And they dwelt in their place until the captivity.

The Family of Manasseh (East)

23 And the half-tribe of Manasseh dwelt from Bashan to Baal, Hermon and Senir, and *to* Mount Hermon; and they increased in Lebanon.

24 And these were the heads of the houses of their families: Epher, Ishi, Eliel, Jeremiah, Hodaviah, and Jahdiel, mighty men of valor, men of renown, heads of the houses of their families.

25 But they rebelled against the God of their fathers, and went a-whoring after the gods of the nations of the land, whom God had cast out from before them.

26 And the God of Israel stirred up the spirit of Pul king of Assyria, and the spirit of Tiglath-Pileser king of Assyria, and carried away Reuben and Gad, and the half-tribe of Manasseh, and brought them to Halah, Habor, and to the river of Gozan, until this day.

1 CHRONICLES CHAPTER 6

The Family of Levi

1 The sons of Levi *were* Gershon, Kohath, and Merari.

2 And the sons of Kohath *were* Amram, Izhar, Hebron, and Uzziel.

3 And the children of Amram *were* Aaron, Moses, and Miriam. And the sons of Aaron *were* Nadab, Abihu, Eleazar, and Ithamar.

4 Eleazar fathered Phinehas, Phinehas fathered Abishua;

5 Abishua fathered Bukki, and Bukki fathered Uzzi;

6 Uzzi fathered Zerahiah, Zerahiah fathered Meraioth;

7 Meraioth fathered Amariah, and Amariah fathered Ahitub;

8 Ahitub fathered Zadok, and Zadok fathered Ahimaaz;

9 Ahimaaz fathered Azariah, and Azariah fathered Johanan;

10 Johanan fathered Azariah (he ministered as priest in the house which Solomon built in Jerusalem);

11 Azariah fathered Amariah, and Amariah fathered Ahitub;

12 Ahitub fathered Zadok, and Zadok fathered Shallum;

13 Shallum fathered Hilkiah, and Hilkiah fathered Azariah;

14 Azariah fathered Seraiah, and Seraiah fathered Jehozadak.

15 And Jehozadak went into captivity with Judah and Jerusalem under Nebuchadnezzar.

16 The sons of Levi *were* Gershon, Kohath, and Merari.

17 And these *are* the names of the sons of Gershon: Libni, and Shimei.

18 The sons of Kohath *were* Amram, Izhar, Hebron, and Uzziel. 19 The sons of Merari *were* Mahli and Mushi: and these *were* the families of Levi, according to their families.

20 Of Gershon were Libni his son, Jahath his son, Zimmah his son,

21 Joah his son, Iddo his son, Zerah his son, and Jeatherai his son.

22 The sons of Kohath *were* Amminadab his son, Korah his son, Assir his son,

23 Elkanah his son, Ebiasaph his son, Assir his son,

24 Tahath his son, Uriel his son, Uzziah his son, and Shaul his son.

25 And the sons of Elkanah *were* Amasai and Ahimoth.

26 *As for* Elkanah, his sons *were* Zophai, Nahath his son,

27 Eliab his son, Jeroham his son, and Elkanah his son.

28 The sons of Samuel *were* Joel the firstborn, and Abijah.

29 The sons of Merari *were* Mahli, Libni his son, Shimei his son, Uzzah his son;

30 Shimea his son, Haggiah his son, and Asaiah his son.

Musicians in the House of the Lord

[31] And these *were the men* whom David set over the service of the singers in the house of the Lord when the ark was at rest.

[32] And they ministered in front of the tabernacle of witness, *playing* on instruments, until Solomon built the house of the Lord in Jerusalem; and they stood according to their order for their services.

[33] And these *were the men* that stood, and their sons, of the sons of Kohath: Heman the psalm singer, son of Joel, the son of Samuel,

[34] the son of Elkanah, the son of Jeroham, the son of Eliel, the son of Toah,

[35] the son of Zuph, the son of Elkanah, the son of Mahath, the son of Amasai,

[36] the son of Elkanah, the son of Joel, the son of Azariah, the son of Zephaniah,

[37] the son of Tahath, the son of Assir, the son of Ebiasaph, the son of Korah,

[38] the son of Izhar, the son of Kohath, the son of Levi, the son of Israel.

[39] And his brother Asaph, who stood at his right hand; Asaph the son of Berachiah, the son of Shimea,

[40] the son of Michael, the son of Baaseiah, the son of Malchijah,

[41] the son of Ethni, the son of Zerah,

[42] the son of Adaiah, the son of Ethan, the son of Zimmah, the son of Shimei,

[43] the son of Jahath, the son of Gershon, the son of Levi.

[44] And the sons of Merari their brothers on the left hand *were* Ethan the son of Kishi, the son of Abdi, the son of Malluch,

[45] the son of Hashabiah,

[46] the son of Amzi, the son of Bani, the son of Shamer,

[47] the son of Mahli, the son of Mushi, the son of Merari, the son of Levi.

[48] And their brothers according to the houses of their fathers, *were* the Levites who were appointed to all the work of ministration of the tabernacle of the house of God.

The Family of Aaron

[49] And Aaron and his sons *were* to burn incense on the altar of burnt offerings, and on the altar of incense, for all the ministry *in* the Holy of Holies, and to make atonement for Israel, according to all things that Moses the servant of the Lord commanded.

[50] And these *were* the sons of Aaron: Eleazar his son, Phinehas his son, Abishua his son,

[51] Bukki his son, Uzzi his son, Zerahiah his son,

[52] Meraioth his son, Amarih his son, Ahitub his son,

[53] Zadok his son, and Ahimaaz his son.

[54] And these *are* their residences in their villages, in their coasts, to the sons of Aaron, to their family the Kohathites; for they had the lot.

[55] And they gave them Hebron in the land of Judah, and its suburbs round about it.

[56] But the fields of the city, and its villages, they gave to Caleb the son of Jephunneh.

[57] And to the sons of Aaron they gave the cities of refuge, *even* Hebron, and Libnah and her suburbs round about, Selna and her suburbs, Eshtemoa and her suburbs,

[58] Jethar and her suburbs, Debir and her suburbs,

[59] Ashan and her suburbs, and Beth Shemesh and her suburbs.

[60] And of the tribe of Benjamin: Geba and her suburbs, Alemeth and her suburbs, and Anathoth and her suburbs. All their cities *were* thirteen cities according to their families.

[61] And to the sons of Kohath that were left of their families, *there were given* out of the tribe, *namely*, out of the half-tribe of Manasseh, by lot, ten cities.

[62] And to the sons of Gershon according to their families *there were given* thirteen cities of the tribe of Issachar, of the tribe of Asher, of the tribe of Naphtali, and of the tribe of Manasseh in Bashan.

[63] And to the sons of Merari according to their families *there were given*, by lot, twelve cities of the tribe of Reuben, of the tribe of Gad, *and* of the tribe of Zebulun.

[64] So the children of Israel gave to the Levites the cities and their suburbs.

[65] And they gave by lot out of the tribe of the children of Judah, and out of the tribe of the children of Simeon, and out of the tribe of the children of Benjamin, these cities which they call by name.

[66] And *to the members* of the families of the sons of Kohath there were also given the cities of their borders out of the tribe of Ephraim.

[67] And they gave them the cities of refuge, Shechem and her suburbs in Mount Ephraim, Gezer and her suburbs,

[68] Jokmeam and her suburbs, Beth Horon and her suburbs,

[69] Aijalon and her suburbs, and Gath Rimmon and her suburbs.

[70] And of the half-tribe of Manasseh: Aner and her suburbs, and Bileam and her suburbs, to the sons of Kohath that were left, according to *each* family.

[71] To the sons of Gershon from the families of the half-tribe of Manasseh *they gave* Golan of Bashan and her suburbs, and Ashtaroth and her suburbs.

[72] And out of the tribe of Issachar: Kedesh and her suburbs, Daberath and her suburbs,

[73] Ramoth and Anem and their suburbs.

[74] And of the tribe of Asher: Mashal and her suburbs, Abdon and her suburbs,

[75] Hukok and her suburbs, and Rehob and her suburbs.

[76] And of the tribe of Naphtali: Kedesh in Galilee and her suburbs, Hammon and her suburbs, and Kirjathaim and her suburbs.

[77] To the sons of Merari that were left, *they gave* out of the tribe of Zebulun: Rimmon and her suburbs, and Tabor and her suburbs.

78 And beyond the Jordan, Jericho west of the Jordan, *they gave* out of the tribe of Reuben: Bezer in the wilderness and her suburbs, Jahzah and her suburbs,

79 Kedemoth and her suburbs, and Mephaath and her suburbs,

80 Out of the tribe of Gad: Ramoth Gilead and her suburbs, Mahanaim and her suburbs,

81 Heshbon and her suburbs, and Jazer and her suburbs.

1 CHRONICLES CHAPTER 7

The Family of Issachar

1 And *as* to the sons of Issachar, *they were* Tola, Puah, Jashub, and Shimron—four *in all*.

2 And the sons of Tola *were* Uzzi, Rephaiah, Jeriel, Jahmai, Jibsam, and Shemuel, chiefs of their fathers' houses *belonging to* Tola, men of might according to their generations; their number in the days of David *was* twenty-two thousand six hundred.

3 And the son of Uzzi *was* Izrahiah, and the sons of Izrahiah *were* Michael, Obadiah, Joel, and Ishiah, five *in all*, all rulers.

4 And with them, according to their generations, according to the houses of their families, *were men* mighty to set *armies* in array for war, thirty-six thousand, for they had multiplied *their* wives and children.

5 And their brothers among all the families of Issachar, also mighty men, *were* eighty-seven thousand—*this was* the number of them all.

The Family of Benjamin

6 The sons of Benjamin *were* Bela, Becher, and Jediael, three *in all*.

7 And the sons of Bela *were* Ezbon, Uzzi, Uzziel, Jerimoth, and Iri—five *in all*; heads of houses of families, mighty men; and their number *was* twenty-two thousand and thirty-four.

8 And the sons of Becher *were* Zemirah, Joash, Eliezer, Elioenai, Omri, Jerimoth, Abijah, Anathoth, and Alemeth. All these *were* the sons of Becher.

9 And their number according to their generations, (*they were* chiefs of their fathers' houses, men of might), *was* twenty thousand and two hundred.

10 And the son of Jediael *was* Bilhan, and the sons of Bilhan *were* Jeush, Benjamin, and Ehud, Chenaanah, Zethan, Tharshish, and Ahishahar.

11 All these *were* the sons of Jediael, chiefs of their families, men of might, seventeen thousand two hundred, going forth to war with might.

12 And Shuppim and Huppim *were* the sons of Ir, *and* Hushim *was* the son *was* Aher.

The Family of Naphtali

13 The sons of Naphtali *were* Jahziel, Guni, Jezer, and Shallum, the sons of Bilhah.

The Family of Manasseh (West)

14 The descendants of Manasseh: Asriel, whom his Syrian concubine bore; and she bore to him also Machir the father of Gilead.

15 And Machir took a wife for Huppim and Shuppim, and his sister's name was Maachah; and the name of the second *son* was Zelophehad; and to Zelophehad were born daughters.

16 And Maachah the wife of Machir bore a son, and called his name Peresh; and his brother's name *was* Sheresh; his sons *were* Ulam and Rakem.

17 And the son of Ulam *was* Bedan. These *were* the sons of Gilead, the son of Machir, the son of Manasseh.

18 And his sister Hammoleketh bore Ishhod, Abiezer, and Mahlah.

19 And the sons of Shemida were Ahian, Shechem, Likhi, and Aniam.

The Family of Ephraim

20 And the sons of Ephraim *were* Shuthelah, Bered his son, Tahath his son, Eladah his son, Tahath his son,

21 Zabad his son, Shuthelah his son, and Ezer and Elead. And the men of Gath who were born in the land killed them, because they went down to take their cattle.

22 And their father Ephraim mourned many days, and his brothers came to comfort him.

23 And he went in to his wife, and she conceived and bore a son, and he called his name Beriah, "Because," *he said*, "he was afflicted in my house."

24 And his daughter *was* Sheerah, and he was among them that were left, and he built Beth Horon the Upper and the Lower. And the descendants of Ozan *were* Sheerah,

25 Rephah his son, Resheph and Telah his sons, and Tahan his son,

26 Laadan his son, Ammihud his son, Elishama his son,

27 Nun *his* son, and Joshua his son.

28 And their possession and their dwelling *were* Bethel and her towns, to the east Naaran, to the west Gezer and her towns, and Shechem and her towns, as far as Gaza and her towns.

29 And as far as the borders of the sons of Manasseh, Beth Shean and her towns, Taanach and her towns, Megiddo and her towns, Dor and her towns. In this the children of Joseph the son of Israel dwelt.

The Family of Asher

30 The sons of Asher *were* Imnah, Ishvah, Ishvi, Beriah, and Serah their sister.

31 And the sons of Beriah *were* Heber and Malchiel; he *was* the father of Birzaith.

32 And Heber fathered Japhlet, Shomer, Hotham, and Shua their sister.

33 And the sons of Japhlet *were* Pasach, Bimhal, and Ashvath. These *were* the sons of Japhlet.

34 And the sons of Shomer *were* Ahi, Rohgah, Jehubbah, and Aram.

35 And the sons of Helem his brother *were* Zophah, Imna, Shelesh, and Amal.

36 The sons of Zophah *were* Suah, Harnepher, Shual, Beri, Imrah,

37 Bezer, Hod, Shamma, Shilshah, Jithran, and Beera.

38 And the sons of Jithran *were* Jephunneh, Pispah, and Ara.

39 And the sons of Ulla *were* Arah, Haniel, and Rizia.

40 All these *were* the sons of Asher, all heads of families, choice, mighty men, chief leaders. Their number for battle array *was* twenty-six thousand men.

1 Chronicles Chapter 8

Descendants of Benjamin

1 Now Benjamin fathered Bela his firstborn, Ashbel his second, Aharah the third, Nohah the fourth,

2 and Rapha the fifth.

3 And the sons of Bela were Addar, Gera, Abihud,

4 Abishua, Naaman, Ahoah,

5 Gera, Shephuphan, and Huram.

6 These *were* the sons of Ehud, who were the heads of families of them that dwell in Geba, and who forced them to move to Manahath:

7 Naaman, Ahijah, and Gera, who forced them to move. He fathered Uzza and Ahihud.

8 And Shaharaim fathered *children* in the plain of Moab, after that he had sent away Hushim and Baara his wives.

9 By Hodesh his wife he fathered Jobab, Zibia, Mesha, Malcam,

10 Jeuz, Sachiah, and Mirmah. These *were* heads of families.

11 And by Hushim he fathered Abitub and Elpaal.

12 And the sons of Elpaal *were* Eber, Misham, and Shemed; he built Ono and Lod, and its towns;

13 and Beriah and Shema, these *were* heads of families among the inhabitants of Aijalon, and they drove out the inhabitants of Gath.

14 And his brothers *were* Shashak, Jeremoth,

15 Zebadiah, Arad, Eder,

16 Michael, Ispah, and Joha, the sons of Beriah.

17 Zebadiah, Meshullam, Hizki, Heber,

18 Ishmerai, Jizliah, and Jobab *were* the sons of Elpaal.

19 Jakim, Zichri, Zabdi,

20 Elienai, Zillethai, Eliel,

21 Adaiah, Beraiah, and Shimrath *were* the sons of Shimei.

22 Ishpan, Eber, Eliel,

23 Abdon, Zichri, Hanan,

24 Hananiah, Ambri, Elam, Antothijah,

25 Jathin, Jephadias, and Penuel *were* the sons of Shashak.

26 Shamsherai, Shehariah, Athaliah,

27 Jaareshiah, Elijah, and Zichri *were* the sons of Jeroham.

28 These *were* heads of families, chiefs according to their generations; these dwelt in Jerusalem.

29 And the father of Gibeon dwelt in Gibeon; and his wife's name was Maacah.

30 And her firstborn son was Abdon, then Zur, Kish, Baal, Nadab, Ner,

31 Gedor and his brother, Zecher, and Mikloth.

32 And Mikloth fathered Shimeah; for these dwelt in Jerusalem in the presence of their brothers, with their brothers.

33 And Ner fathered Kish, and Kish fathered Saul, and Saul fathered Jonathan, Malchishua, Abinadab, and Esh-Baal.

34 And the son of Jonathan *was* Merib-Baal, and Merib-Baal fathered Micah.

35 And the sons of Micah *were* Pithon, Melech, Tarea, and Ahaz.

36 And Ahaz fathered Jehoaddah, and Jehoaddah fathered Alemeth, Azmaveth, and Zimri; and Zimri fathered Moza.

37 Moza fathered Binea: Raphah *was* his son, Eleasah his son, and Azel his son.

38 And Azel *had* six sons, and these *were* their names: Azrikam his firstborn, then Ishmael, Sheariah, Abdia, Hanan, and Asa: all these *were* the sons of Azel.

39 And the sons of Eshek his brother *were* Ulam his firstborn, then Jeush the second, and Eliphelet the third.

40 And the sons of Ulam were mighty men, bending the bow, and multiplying sons and grandsons, a hundred *and* fifty. All these *were* of the sons of Benjamin.

1 CHRONICLES CHAPTER 9

1 And *this is* all Israel, *even* their enrollment; and these *are* written down in the book of the kings of Israel and Judah, with the *names of them* that were carried away to Babylon for their transgressions.

2 And those that dwelt before in their possessions in the cities of Israel, the priests, the Levites, and the appointed ones.

Inhabitants of Jerusalem after the Exile

3 And there dwelt in Jerusalem some of the children of Judah, and of the children of Benjamin, and of the children of Ephraim, and Manasseh.

4 And Uthai the son of Ammihud, the son of Omri, the son of Imri, the son of Bani, son of the sons of Perez, the son of Judah.

5 And of the Shilonites: Asaiah the firstborn, and his sons.

6 Of the sons of Zerah: Jeuel, and their brothers, six hundred and ninety.

7 And of the sons of Benjamin: Sallu, son of Meshullam, son of Hodaviah, son of Hassenuah;

8 and Ibneiah son of Jeroham, and Elah: these *are* the sons of Uzzi, the son of Michri; Meshullam, son of Shephatiah, son of Reuel, son of Ibnijah;

⁹ and their brothers according to their generations, nine hundred and fifty-six; all the men *were* heads of families according to the houses of their fathers.

The Priests at Jerusalem

¹⁰ And of the priests: Jedaiah, Jehoiarib, and Jachin;

¹¹ Azaria the son of Hilkiah, the son of Meshullam, the son of Zadok, the son of Meraioth, the son of Ahitub, the officer over the house of God;

¹² and Adaiah son of Jeroham, son of Pashur, son of Malchijah, Maasai son of Adiel, son of Jahzerah, son of Meshullam, son of Meshillemith, son of Immer;

¹³ and their brothers, chiefs of their families, a thousand seven hundred and sixty, mighty *men* for the work of the ministration of the house of God.

The Levites at Jerusalem

¹⁴ And of the Levites: Shemaiah son of Hasshub, son of Azrikam, son of Hashabiah, of the sons of Merari;

¹⁵ Bakbakkar, Heresh, Galal, and Mattaniah son of Micah, son of Zichri, son of Asaph;

¹⁶ Obadiah, son of Shemaiah, son of Galal, son of Jeduthun, and Berechiah son of Asa, son of Elkanah, who dwelt in the villages of the Netophathites.

The Levite Gatekeepers

¹⁷ The gatekeepers *were* Shallum, Akkub, Talmon, Ahiman, and their brothers; Shallum *was* the chief.

¹⁸ And *he was stationed* there in the king's gate eastward; these *are* the gates of the companies of the sons of Levi.

¹⁹ And Shallum the son of Kore, the son of Ebiasaph, the son of Korah, and his brothers belonging to the house of his father, the Korahites *were* over the works of the service, keeping the watches of the tabernacle, and their fathers over the camp of the Lord, keeping the entrance.

²⁰ And Phinehas son of Eleazar was head over them before the Lord, and these *were* with him.

²¹ Zechariah the son of Meshelemiah *was* keeper of the door of the tabernacle of witness.

²² All the chosen porters in the gates *were* two hundred and twelve; these *were* in their courts, *this was* their distribution: these David and Samuel the seer established in their charge.

²³ And these and their sons *were* over the gates in the house of the Lord, and in the house of the tabernacle, to keep watch.

²⁴ The gates were toward the four winds, east, west, north, and south.

²⁵ And their brothers *were* in their courts, to enter in weekly from time to time with these.

²⁶ For four strong *men* have the charge of the gates; and the Levites were over the chambers, and they keep watch over the treasures of the house of God.

²⁷ For the charge *was* upon them, and these *were* charged with the keys to open the doors of the temple every morning.

²⁸ And *some* of them *were appointed* over the vessels of service, that they should carry them in by number, and carry them out by number.

²⁹ And *some* of them *were* appointed over the furniture, and over all the holy vessels, and over the fine flour, the wine, the oil, the frankincense, and the spices.

³⁰ And some of the priests were makers of the ointment, and *appointed to prepare* the spices.

³¹ And Mattithiah of the Levites, (he *was* the firstborn of Shallum the Korahite) *was set* in charge over the sacrifices of meat offerings of the pan belonging to the high priest.

³² And Banaiah the Kohathite *was set* over the showbread, from among his brothers, to prepare it every Sabbath.

³³ And these *were* the singers, heads of families of the Levites, *to whom were* established daily courses, for they were employed in the services day and night.

³⁴ These *were* the heads of the families of the Levites according to their generations; these chiefs dwelt in Jerusalem.

The Family of King Saul

³⁵ And Jeiel the father of Gibeon dwelt in Gibeon; and his wife's name *was* Maacah.

³⁶ And his firstborn son *was* Abdon, then Zur, Kish, Baal, Ner, Nadab,

³⁷ Gedor and *his* brother, Zecher, and Mikloth.

³⁸ And Mikloth fathered Shimeam. And these dwelt in the midst of their brothers in Jerusalem, *even* in the midst of their brothers.

³⁹ And Ner fathered Kish, and Kish fathered Saul, and Saul fathered Jonathan, Malchishua, Abinadab, and Esh-Baal.

⁴⁰ And the son of Jonathan *was* Merib-Baal, and Merib-Baal fathered Micah.

⁴¹ And the sons of Micah *were* Pithon, Melech, Tarea, and Ahaz

⁴² And Ahaz fathered Jarah; Jarah fathered Alemeth, Azmaveth, and Zimri; and Zimri fathered Moza.

⁴³ Moza fathered Binea, Rephaiah *was* his son, Eleasah his son, and Azel his son.

⁴⁴ And Azel had six sons, and these *were* their names: Azrikam his firstborn, then Ishmael, Sheariah, Obadiah, Hanan, and Asa: these *were* the sons of Azel.

1 CHRONICLES CHAPTER 10

Death of Saul and His Sons

¹ Now the Philistines warred against Israel; and they fled from before the Philistines, and fell down slain in Mount Gilboa.

² And the Philistines pursued after Saul, and after his sons; and the Philistines killed Jonathan, Abinadab, and Malchishua, Saul's sons.

³ And the battle prevailed against Saul, and the archers hit him with bows and arrows, and they were wounded by the

archers. ⁴ And Saul said to his armor-bearer, "Draw your sword, and pierce me through with it, lest these uncircumcised come and mock me." But his armor-bearer would not, for he was greatly afraid. So Saul took a sword, and fell upon it.

⁵ And his armor-bearer saw that Saul was dead, and he also fell upon his sword.

⁶ So Saul died, and his three sons on that day, and all his family died at the same time.

⁷ And all the men of Israel that were in the valley saw that Israel fled, and that Saul and his sons were dead, and they left their cities, and fled; and the Philistines came and dwelt in them.

⁸ And it came to pass on the next *day* that the Philistines came to strip the slain, and they found Saul and his sons fallen on Mount Gilboa.

⁹ And they stripped him, and took his head and his armor, and sent them into the land of the Philistines, to proclaim *this* good news to their idols, and to the people.

¹⁰ And they put his armor in the house of their god, and they put his head in the house of Dagon.

¹¹ And all the inhabitants of Gilead heard of all that the Philistines had done to Saul and to Israel.

¹² And all the mighty men rose up from Gilead, and they took the body of Saul, and the bodies of his sons, and they brought them to Jabesh, and buried their bones under the oak in Jabesh, and fasted seven days.

¹³ So Saul died for his transgressions in which he transgressed against God, against the word of the Lord, because he did not keep it, because Saul inquired of a wizard to seek *counse*l, and Samuel the prophet answered him;

¹⁴ and he did not seek the Lord. Therefore He killed him, and turned the kingdom to David the son of Jesse.

1 CHRONICLES CHAPTER 11

David Made King over All Israel

¹ And all Israel came to David in Hebron, saying, "Behold, we *are* your bones and your flesh.

² And in times past, when Saul was king, you were the one that led Israel in and out, and the Lord of Israel said to you, 'You shall feed My people Israel, and you shall be ruler over Israel.'"

³ And all the elders of Israel came to the king at Hebron; and King David made a covenant with them in Hebron before the Lord. And they anointed David to be king over Israel, according to the word of the Lord by Samuel.

The City of David

⁴ And the king and his men went to Jerusalem (this *is* Jebus); and there the Jebusites, the inhabitants of the land, said to David,

⁵ "You shall not enter in here." But he took the stronghold of Zion (this *is* the City of David).

⁶ And David said, "Whoever first shall strike the Jebusite, even he shall be chief and captain." And Joab the son of Zeruiah went up first, and became chief.

⁷ And David dwelt in the stronghold; therefore he called it the City of David.

⁸ And he fortified the city round about.

⁹ And David continued to increase, and the Lord Almighty *was* with him.

The Mighty Men of David

¹⁰ And these *are* the chiefs of the mighty men, whom David had, who strengthened *themselves* with him in his kingdom, with all Israel, to make him king, according to the word of the Lord concerning Israel.

¹¹ And this *is* the list of the mighty *men* of David: Jashobeam, son of a Hachmonite, first of the thirty; he drew his sword once against three hundred, whom he killed at one time.

¹² And after him Eleazar son of Dodo, the Ahohite; he was among the three mighty men.

¹³ He was with David in Pasdammim, and the Philistines were gathered there to battle, and *there was* a portion of the field full of barley; and the people fled before the Philistines.

¹⁴ And he stood in the midst of the portion, and rescued it, and attacked the Philistines; and the Lord wrought a great deliverance.

¹⁵ And three of the thirty chiefs went down to the rock to David, to the cave of Adullam, and the camp of the Philistines *was* in the giants' valley.

¹⁶ And David *was* then in the stronghold, and the garrison of the Philistines *was* then in Bethlehem.

¹⁷ And David longed, and said, "Who will give me water to drink from the well of Bethlehem, that is in the gate?"

¹⁸ And the three broke through the camp of the Philistines, and they drew water out of the well that was in Bethlehem, which was in the gate, and they took it, and came to David. But David would not drink it, and poured it out to the Lord, and said,

¹⁹ "God forbid that I should do this thing—shall I drink the blood of these men with their lives? For with *the peril of* their lives they brought it." So he would not drink it. These things were done by the three mighty *men*.

²⁰ And Abishai the brother of Joab, he was chief of *another* three; he drew his sword against three hundred *men* at one time and killed them; and he had a name among the *second* three.

²¹ He was more famous than the two *others* among the three, and he was chief *over* them; yet he did not reach to the *first* three.

²² And Benaiah the son of Jehoiada was the son of a valiant man; many *were* his acts for Kabzeel; he struck two lion-like men of Moab, and he went down and killed a lion in a pit on a snowy day.

23 And he killed an Egyptian, a great man five cubits *high*; and in the hand of the Egyptian *there was* a spear like a weavers' beam; and Benaiah went down to him with a staff, and took the spear out of the Egyptian's hand, and killed him with his own spear.

24 These things did Benaiah son of Jehoiada, and his name *was* among the three mighties.

25 He was distinguished beyond the thirty, yet he did not reach to the *first* three. And David set him over his family.

26 And the mighty *men* of the forces *were* Asahel the brother of Joab, Elhanan the son of Dodo of Bethlehem,

27 Shammoth the Harorite, Helez the Pelonite,

28 Ira the son of Ikkesh the Tekoite, Abiezer the Anathothite,

29 Sibbechai the Hushathite, Ilai the Ahohite,

30 Maharai the Netophathite, Heled the son of Baanah the Netophathite,

31 Ithai the son of Ribai of the hill of Benjamin, Benaiah the Pirathonite,

32 Hurai of Nachali Gaash, Abiel the Arabathite,

33 Azmaveth the Baharumite, Eliabah the Shaalbonite,

34 the sons of Hashem the Gizonite, Jonathan the son of Shageh the Hararite,

35 Ahiam the son of Sacar the Hararite, Eliphal the son of Ur,

36 *Hepher* the Mecherathrite, Ahijah the Pelonite,

37 Hezro the Carmelite, Naarai the son of Ezbai,

38 Joel the son of Nathan, Mibhar son of Hagri,

39 Zelek the Ammonite, Naharai the Berothite, armor-bearer to *Joab* the son of Zeruiah,

40 Ira the Ithrite, Gareb the Ithrite,

41 Uriah the Hittite, Zabad son of Ahlai,

42 Adina son of Shiza, a chief of the Reubenites, and thirty with him,

43 Hanan the son of Maachah, Joshaphat the Mithnite,

44 Uzzia the Ashterathite, Shama and Jeiel sons of Hotham the Aroerite,

45 Jediael the son of Shimri, and Joha his brother, the Tizite,

46 Eliel the Mahavite, Jeribai, Joshaviah his son, Elnaam, Ithmah the Moabite,

47 Eliel, Obed, and Jaasiel of Mezobaite.

1 CHRONICLES CHAPTER 12

David's Followers in the Wilderness

1 And these *are* those that came to Ziklag, when he yet kept himself close because of Saul the son of Kish; and these *were* among the mighty, aiding *him* in war,

2 and *using* the bow with the right hand and with the left, and slingers with stones, and *shooters* with bows. Of the brothers of Saul of Benjamin,

3 the chief *was* Ahiezer, then Joash son of Shemaah the Gibeathite; Jeziel and Pelet, sons of Azmaveth, Berachah, and Jehu of Anathoth;

4 Ishmaiah the Gibeonite, a mighty man among the thirty, and over the thirty; *and* Jeremiah, Jahaziel, Johanan, and Jozabad the Gederathite;

5 Eluzai, Jerimoth, Bealiah, Shemariah, and Shephatiah the Haruphite;

6 Elkanah, Jisshiah, Azarel, Joezer, and Jashobeam and the Korahites;

7 and Joelah and Zebadiah, the sons of Jeroham, and the *men* of Gedor.

8 And from Gad these separated themselves to David from the wilderness, strong mighty men of war, bearing shields and spears, and their faces *were as* the faces of lions, and they were as nimble as gazelles upon the mountains in speed;

9 Ezer the chief, Obadiah the second, Eliab the third,

10 Mishmannah the fourth, Jeremiah the fifth,

11 Attai the sixth, Eliel the seventh,

12 Johanan the eighth, Elzabad the ninth,

13 Jeremiah the tenth, Machbanai the eleventh.

14 These *were* chiefs of the army of the sons of Gad, the least one commander of a hundred, and the greatest one of a thousand.

15 These *are* the *men* that crossed over the Jordan in the first month, and it had overflowed all its banks; and they drove out all the inhabitants of the valleys, from the east to the west.

16 And there came *some* of the sons of Benjamin and Judah to the assistance of David.

17 And David went out to meet them, and said to them, "If you have come peaceably to me, let my heart be at peace with you; but if *you have come* to betray me to my enemies unfaithfully, *may* the God of your fathers look upon it, and bring judgment."

18 And the Spirit came upon Amasai, a captain of the thirty, and he said, "Go, David, son of Jesse, you and your people. Peace, peace be to you, and peace to your helpers, for your God has helped you." And David received them, and made them captains of the forces.

19 And *some* came to David from Manasseh, when the Philistines came against Saul to war. And he did not help them, because the captains of the Philistines took counsel, saying, "With the heads of those men will he return to his master Saul."

20 When David was going to Ziklag, those from Manasseh who defected to him were Adnah, Jozabath, Jediael, Michael, Jozabad, Elihu, and Zillethai.

21 And they fought on the side of David against a troop, for they *were* all men of might; and they were commanders in the army, *because* of *their* might.

22 For men came to David day by day, *till they amounted* to a great force, as the force of God.

23 And these *are* the names of the commanders of the army, who came to David to Hebron, to turn the kingdom of Saul to him according to the word of the Lord.

24 The sons of Judah, bearing shields and spears, six thousand eight hundred mighty in war.

25 Of the sons of Simeon mighty for battle, seven thousand one hundred.

26 Of the sons of Levi, four thousand six hundred.

27 And Jehoiada the chief *of the family* of Aaron, and with him three thousand seven hundred.

28 And Zadok, a young *man* mighty in strength, and *there were* twenty-two leaders of his father's house.

29 And of the sons of Benjamin, the brothers of Saul, three thousand; and still the greater part of them kept the guard of the house of Saul.

30 And of the sons of Ephraim, twenty thousand eight hundred mighty men, famous in the houses of their fathers.

31 And of the half-tribe of Manasseh, eighteen thousand, even *those* who were named by name, to make David king.

32 And of the sons of Issachar having wisdom with regard to the times, knowing what Israel should do, two hundred; and all their brothers with them.

33 And of Zebulun they that went out to battle, with all weapons of war, *were* fifty thousand to help David, not weak-handed.

34 And of Naphtali a thousand captains, and with them *men* with shields and spears, thirty-seven thousand.

35 And of the Danites, *men* ready for war, *were* twenty-eight thousand eight hundred.

36 And of Asher, they that went out to give aid in war, forty thousand.

37 And from the country beyond the Jordan, from Reuben, and the Gadites, and from the half-tribe of Manasseh, a hundred and twenty thousand, with all weapons of war.

38 All these *were* men of war, setting *the army* in battle array, with a peaceful mind *towards him*, and they came to Hebron to make David king over all Israel. And the rest of Israel *were of* one mind to make David king.

39 And they were there three days eating and drinking, for their brothers *had* made preparations.

40 And their neighbors, as far as Issachar and Zebulun and Naphtali, brought to them upon camels, donkeys, mules, and upon calves, victuals, meal, cakes of figs, raisins, wine, and oil, calves and sheep abundantly, for *there was* joy in Israel.

1 CHRONICLES CHAPTER 13

The Ark Brought from Jearim

1 And David took counsel with the captains of thousands and captains of hundreds, *and with* every commander.

2 And David said to the whole congregation of Israel, "If it *seems* good to you, and it should be prospered by the Lord our God, let us send to our brothers that are left in all the land of Israel, and let the priests, the Levites who are with them in the cities of their possession *come*, and let them be gathered to us.

3 And let us bring over to us the ark of our God; for men have not inquired *at* it since the days of Saul."

4 And all the congregation said that they would do thus; for the saying was right in the eyes of all the people.

5 So David assembled all Israel, from the borders of Egypt even to the entering in of Hamath, to bring in the ark of God from the city of Jearim.

6 And David brought it up. And all Israel went up to the City of David, which belonged to Judah, to bring up from there the ark of the Lord God who sits between the cherubim, where His name is proclaimed.

7 And they set the ark of God on a new wagon *brought* out of the house of Abinadab. And Uzza and his brothers drove the wagon.

8 And David and all Israel *were* playing before the Lord with all their might, and *that* together with singers, and with harps, and with lutes, with timbrels, and with cymbals, and with trumpets.

9 And they came as far as the threshing floor. And Uzza put forth his hand to hold the ark, because the bull had moved it from *its place.*

10 And the Lord was very angry with Uzza, and struck him there, because of his stretching forth his hand upon the ark. And he died there before God.

11 And David was dispirited, because the Lord *had* made a breach on Uzza. And he called that place the Breach of Uzza until this day.

12 And David feared God that day, saying, "How shall I bring the ark of God in to myself?"

13 So David did not bring the ark home to himself into the City of David, but he turned it aside into the house of Obed-Edom the Gittite.

14 And the ark of God abode in the house of Obed-Edom for three months; and God blessed Obed-Edom and all that he had.

1 CHRONICLES CHAPTER 14

David Established at Jerusalem

1 And Hiram king of Tyre sent messengers to David, and cedar timbers, and masons, and carpenters, to build a house for him.

2 And David knew that the Lord *had* established him to be king over Israel; because his kingdom was highly exalted, on account of His people Israel.

3 And David took more wives in Jerusalem. And there were born to David more sons and daughters.

4 And these *are* the names of those that were born, who were *born* to him in Jerusalem: Shammua, Shobab, Nathan, Solomon,

5 Ibhar, Elishua, Elpelet,

6 Nogah, Nepheg, Japhia,

7 Elishama, Beeliada, and Eliphelet.

The Philistines Defeated

8 And the Philistines heard that David was anointed king over all Israel. And all the Philistines went up to seek David. And David heard *it*, and went out to meet them.

9 And the Philistines came and assembled together in the giants' valley.

10 And David inquired of God, saying, "Shall I go up against the Philistines? And will You deliver them into my hand?" And the Lord said to him, "Go up, and I will deliver them into your hands."

11 And he went up to Baal Perazim, and David defeated them there. And David said, "God has broken through *my* enemies by my hand like a breach of water"; therefore he called the name of that place the Breach of Perazim.

12 And the Philistines left their gods there, and David gave orders to burn them with fire.

13 And the Philistines once more assembled themselves in the giants' valley.

14 And David inquired of God again. And God said to him, "You shall not go after them; turn away from them, and you shall come upon them near the pear trees.

15 And it shall be, when you shall hear the sound of their tumult in the tops of the pear trees, then you shall go into the battle; for God has gone out before you to strike the army of the Philistines."

16 And he did as God commanded him. And he drove back the army of the Philistines from Gibeon to Gezer.

17 And the name of David was *famous* in all the land; and the Lord put the terror of him on all the nations.

1 CHRONICLES CHAPTER 15

The Ark Brought to Jerusalem

1 And *David* made for himself houses in the City of David, and he prepared a place for the ark of God, and made a tent for it.

2 Then David said, "It is not *lawful for anyone* to bear the ark of God, but the Levites; for the Lord has chosen them to bear the ark of the Lord, and to minister to Him forever."

3 And David assembled all Israel at Jerusalem, to bring up the ark of the Lord to the place which he *had* prepared for it.

4 And David gathered together the sons of Aaron the Levites.

5 Of the sons of Kohath; *there was* Uriel the chief, and his brothers, a hundred and twenty.

6 Of the sons of Merari, Asaiah the chief, and his brothers, two hundred and twenty.

7 Of the sons of Gershom; Joel the chief, and his brothers, a hundred and thirty.

8 Of the sons of Elizaphan; Shemaiah the chief, and his brothers, two hundred.

9 Of the sons of Hebron; Eliel the chief, and his brothers eighty.

10 Of the sons of Uzziel; Amminadab the chief, and his brothers a hundred and twelve.

11 And David called Zadok and Abiathar the priests, and the Levites, Uriel, Asaiah, Joel, Shemaiah, Eliel, and Amminadab,

12 and said to them, "You *are* the heads of the families of the Levites: sanctify yourselves, you and your brothers, and you shall carry up the ark of the God of Israel, *to the place* which I have prepared for it.

13 For because you were not *ready* at the first, our God made a breach upon us, because we did not consult Him regarding the ordinance."

14 So the priests and the Levites sanctified themselves, to bring up the ark of the God of Israel.

15 And the sons of the Levites took the ark of God, (as Moses commanded by the word of God according to the Scripture) upon their shoulders with poles.

16 And David said to the chiefs of the Levites, "Set your brothers the singers with musical instruments, lutes, harps, and cymbals, to sound aloud with a voice of joy."

17 So the Levites appointed Heman the son of Joel; Asaph the son of Berechiah *was one* of his brothers; and Ethan the son of Kushaiah was of the sons of Merari their brothers;

18 and with them their brothers of the second rank *were* Zechariah, Jaaziel, Shemiramoth, Jehiel, Unni, Eliab, Benaiah, Maaseiah, Mattithiah, Elipheleh, Mikneiah, Obed-Edom, Jeiel, and Azaziah, the porters.

19 And the singers—Heman, Asaph, and Ethan, *were* to make *a sound* with bronze cymbals.

20 Zechariah, Aziel, Shemiramoth, Jehiel, Unni, Eliab, Maaseiah, and Benaiah, with lutes, according to Alamoth.

21 Mattithiah, Elipheleh, Mikneiah, Obed-Edom, Jeiel, and Azaziah, with harps of Sheminith, to make a loud noise.

22 And Chenaniah chief of the Levites *was* master of the bands, because he was skillful.

23 And Berechiah and Elkanah *were* doorkeepers for the ark.

24 Shebaniah, Joshaphat, Nethanel, Amasai, Zechariah, Benaiah, and Eliezer, the priests, were sounding with trumpets before the ark of God. And Obed-Edom and Jehiah *were* doorkeepers for the ark of God.

25 So David, and the elders of Israel, and the captains of thousands, went to bring up the ark of the covenant from the house of Obed-Edom with gladness.

26 And it came to pass when God strengthened the Levites bearing the ark of the covenant of the Lord, that they sacrificed seven calves and seven rams.

27 And David *was* clothed with a fine linen robe, and all the Levites *who were* bearing the ark of the covenant of the Lord, and the singers, and Chenaniah the master of the band of singers; also upon David *there was* a robe of fine linen.

28 And all Israel brought up the ark of the covenant of the Lord with shouting, and with the sound of a horn, and with

trumpets, and with cymbals, playing loudly on lutes and harps.

²⁹ And the ark of the covenant of the Lord arrived, and came to the City of David; and Michal the daughter of Saul looked down through the window, and saw King David dancing and playing, and she despised him in her heart.

1 CHRONICLES CHAPTER 16

The Ark Placed in the Tabernacle

¹ So they brought in the ark of God, and set it in the midst of the tabernacle which David pitched for it; and they offered burnt offerings and peace offerings before God.

² And David finished offering up burnt offerings and peace offerings, and blessed the people in the name of the Lord.

³ And he divided to every man of Israel (both men and women) one baker's loaf, and a cake.

⁴ And he appointed before the ark of the covenant of the Lord, Levites to minister *and* lift up the voice, and to give thanks and praise the Lord God of Israel.

⁵ Asaph *was* the chief, and next to him Zechariah, *then* Jeiel, Shemiramoth, Jehiel, Mattithiah, Eliab, Benaiah, and Obed-Edom; and Jeiel sounded with musical instruments, lutes *and* harps, and Asaph with cymbals.

⁶ And Benaiah and Jahaziel the priests *sounded* continually with trumpets before the ark of the covenant of God in that day.

David's Song of Thanksgiving

⁷ Then David first gave orders to praise the Lord *with this psalm* by the hand of Asaph and his brothers:

⁸ "Oh, give thanks to the Lord, call upon Him by His name, make known His designs among the people.

⁹ Sing *songs* to Him, and sing hymns to Him, relate to all *people* His wonderful deeds, which the Lord has wrought.

¹⁰ Praise His holy name, the heart that seeks His pleasure shall rejoice.

¹¹ Seek the Lord and be strong, seek His face at all times.

¹² Remember His wonderful works which He has done, His wonders, and the judgments of His mouth;

¹³ *you* seed of Israel His servants, *you* seed of Jacob His chosen ones!

¹⁴ "He *is* the Lord our God; His judgments *are* in all the earth.

¹⁵ Let us remember His covenant forever, His word which He commanded to a thousand generations,

¹⁶ which He covenanted with Abraham, and His oath *sworn* to Isaac.

¹⁷ He confirmed it to Jacob for an ordinance, to Israel *as an* everlasting covenant,

¹⁸ saying, 'To you will I give the land of Canaan, as the allotment of your inheritance,'

¹⁹ when they were few in number, when they were but little, and dwelt as strangers in it;

²⁰ and went from nation to nation, and from one kingdom to another people.

²¹ He did not permit a man to oppress them, and He reproved kings for their sakes,

²² saying, 'Touch not My anointed ones, and do not deal wrongfully with My prophets.'

²³ "Sing to the Lord, all the earth; proclaim His salvation from day to day.

²⁴ Declare among the nations His glory, His wondrous deeds among all peoples.

²⁵ For the Lord *is* great, and greatly to be praised: He *is* to be feared above all gods.

²⁶ For all the gods of the nations *are* idols; but our God made the heavens.

²⁷ Glory and praise *are* in His presence; strength and rejoicing *are* in His place.

²⁸ Give to the Lord, you families of the nations, give to the Lord glory and strength.

²⁹ Give to the Lord the glory *due* His name; take gifts and offer *them* before Him, and worship the Lord in His holy courts.

³⁰ Let the whole earth fear before Him; let the earth be established, and not be moved.

³¹ Let the heavens rejoice, and let the earth exalt; and let them say among the nations, 'The Lord reigns.'

³² The sea with its fullness shall resound and the tree of the field, and all things in it.

³³ Then shall the trees of the wood rejoice before the Lord, for He has come to judge the earth.

³⁴ Give thanks to the Lord, for *He is* good, and His mercy *endures* forever.

³⁵ And thus say, 'Save us, O God of our salvation, and gather us, and rescue us from among the heathen, that we may praise Your holy name, and glory in Your praises.'

³⁶ Blessed *be* the Lord God of Israel from everlasting to everlasting. And all the people shall say, Amen." So they praised the Lord.

³⁷ And they left there Asaph and his brothers before the ark of the covenant of the Lord, to minister before the ark continually, according to the service of each day; from day to day.

³⁸ And Obed-Edom and his brothers *were* sixty-eight *in number*, and Obed-Edom the son of Jeduthen, and Hosah, *were* to be gatekeepers.

³⁹ And *they appointed* Zadok the priest, and his brothers the priests, before the tabernacle of the Lord in the high place in Gibeon,

⁴⁰ to offer up burnt offerings continually morning and evening, and according to all things written in the law of the Lord, which He commanded the children of Israel by Moses the servant of God.

⁴¹ And with him *were* Heman and Jeduthun, and the rest chosen out by name to praise the Lord, for His mercy *endures* forever.

⁴² And with them *there were* trumpets and cymbals to sound aloud, and musical instruments for the songs of God; and the sons of Jeduthun *were* at the gate.

⁴³ And all the people departed, everyone to his own home. And David returned to bless his house.

1 CHRONICLES CHAPTER 17

God's Covenant with David

¹ And it came to pass as David dwelt in his house, that David said to Nathan the prophet, "Behold, I dwell in a house of cedar, but the ark of the covenant of the Lord *is* under *curtains* of skins."

² And Nathan said to David, "Do all that is in your heart; for God *is* with you."

³ And it came to pass in that night, that the word of the Lord came to Nathan, *saying,*

⁴ "Go and say to David My servant, 'Thus says the Lord: "You shall not build Me a house to dwell in.

⁵ For I have not dwelt in a house from the day that I brought up Israel until this day, but I have been in a tabernacle and a tent,

⁶ in all places through which I have gone with all Israel; did I ever speak to *any* one tribe of Israel whom I commanded to shepherd My people, saying, '*Why is it* that you have not built Me a house of cedar?'

⁷ And now thus shall you say to My servant David, Thus says the Lord Almighty: 'I took you from the sheepfold, from following the flocks, to be a ruler over My people Israel;

⁸ and I was with you in all places that you went, and I destroyed all your enemies from before you, and I made for you a name according to the name of the great ones that are upon the earth.

⁹ And I will appoint a place for My people Israel, and I will plant him, and he shall dwell by himself, and shall no longer be anxious; and the son of iniquity shall no longer afflict him, as at the beginning,

¹⁰ and from the days when I appointed judges over My people Israel. Also I have humbled all your enemies, and I will increase you, and the Lord shall build you a house.

¹¹ And it shall come to pass when your days shall be fulfilled, and you shall sleep with your fathers, that I will raise up your descendants after you, which shall be of your loins, and I will establish his kingdom.

¹² He shall build Me a house, and I will set up his throne forever.

¹³ I will be to him a Father, and he shall be to Me a son; and My mercy will I not withdraw from him, as I withdrew *it* from them that were before you.

¹⁴ And I will establish him in My house and in his kingdom forever; and his throne shall be set up forever.""'"

¹⁵ According to all these words, and according to all this vision, so spoke Nathan to David.

¹⁶ Then King David came and sat before the Lord, and said, "Who am I, O Lord God? And what *is* my house, that You have loved me forever?

¹⁷ And these things were little in Your sight, O God; You have also spoken concerning the house of Your servant for a long time to come, and You have looked upon me as a man looks upon his fellow, and have exalted me, O Lord God.

¹⁸ What shall David do more toward You to glorify *You*? And You know Your servant.

¹⁹ And You have wrought all this greatness according to Your heart.

²⁰ O Lord, there is none like You, and there is no God beside You, according to all things which we have heard with our ears.

²¹ Neither is there another nation upon the earth *such* as Your people Israel, whereas God led him in the way, to redeem a people for Himself, to make for Himself a great and glorious name, to cast out nations from before Your people, whom You have redeemed out of Egypt.

²² And You have appointed Your people Israel as a people to Yourself forever; and You, O Lord, became a God to them.

²³ "And now, O Lord, let the word which You have spoken to Your servant, and concerning his house, be confirmed forever, and do as You have spoken.

²⁴ And let Your name *be* established and magnified forever, *and let men* say, 'Lord, Lord, Almighty God of Israel'; and *let* the house of Your servant David *be* established before You.

²⁵ For You, O Lord my God, have revealed to the ear of Your servant that You will build him a house; therefore Your servant has found a willingness to pray before You.

²⁶ And now, O Lord, You Yourself are God, and You have spoken these good things concerning Your servant.

²⁷ And now You have begun to bless the house of Your servant, so that it should continue forever before You; for You, O Lord, have blessed *it*, and *may* You bless *it* forever."

1 CHRONICLES CHAPTER 18

David's Further Conquests

¹ And it came to pass afterwards, that David attacked the Philistines, and routed them, and took Gath and its villages out of the hand of the Philistines.

² And he defeated Moab; and the Moabites became servants to David, *and* tributaries.

³ And David defeated Hadadezer king of Zobah of Hamath, as he was going to establish power toward the River Euphrates.

⁴ And David took of them a thousand chariots, and seven thousand horsemen, and twenty thousand infantry *men*. And David hamstrung all the chariot *horses*, but he left a hundred chariots among them.

5 And the Syrians came from Damascus to help Hadadezer king of Zobah; and David killed of the Syrian *army* twenty-two thousand men.

6 And David put a garrison in Syria near Damascus; and they became tributary servants to David. And the Lord delivered David wherever he went.

7 And David took the golden shields that were on the servants of Hadadezer, and brought them to Jerusalem.

8 And David took very much bronze out of Tibhath and out of the chief cities of Chun; of this Solomon made the bronze sea, and the pillars, and the bronze vessels.

9 And Tou king of Hamath heard that David had defeated the whole force of Hadadezer king of Zobah.

10 And he sent Hadoram his son to King David to ask how he was, and to congratulate him because he had fought against Hadadezer, and had defeated him; for Tou was the enemy of Hadadezer.

11 And all the golden and silver and bronze vessels, even these King David consecrated to the Lord, with the silver and the gold which he took from all the nations; from Edom, Moab, and from the children of Ammon, and from the Philistines, and from Amalek.

12 And Abishai son of Zeruiah killed eighteen thousand of the Edomites in the Valley of Salt.

13 And he put garrisons in the valley; and all the Edomites became David's servants, and the Lord delivered David wherever he went.

14 So David reigned over all Israel, and he executed judgment and justice to all his people.

15 And Joab the son of Zeruiah *was* over the army, and Jehoshaphat the son of Ahilud *was* recorder.

16 And Zadok son of Ahitub, and Abimelech son of Abiathar *were* the priests; and Shavsha *was* the scribe;

17 and Benaiah the son of Jehoiada *was* over the Cherethites and the Pelethites, and the sons of David were the chief deputies of the king.

1 CHRONICLES CHAPTER 19

The Ammonites and Syrians Defeated

1 And it came to pass after this, *that* Nahash the king of the children of Ammon died, and his son reigned in his place.

2 And David said, "I will act kindly toward Hanun the son of Nahash, as his father acted kindly towards me." And David sent messengers to console with him over the death of his father. So the servants of David came into the land of the children of Ammon to Hanun, to comfort him.

3 And the chiefs of the children of Ammon said to Hanun, "Is it to honor your father before you, that David has sent comforters to you? Have not his servants come to you that they might search the city, and to spy out the land?"

4 And Hanun took the servants of David, and shaved them, and cut off half of their garments as far as their tunic, and sent them away.

5 And there came men to report to David concerning the men. And he sent to meet them, for they were greatly disgraced. And the king said, "Stay in Jericho until your beards have grown back, and then return."

6 And the children of Ammon saw that the people of David were ashamed, and Hanun and the children of Ammon sent a thousand talents of silver to hire for themselves chariots and horsemen out of Syria of Mesopotamia, and out of Syria Maacah, and from Zobah.

7 And they hired for themselves thirty-two thousand chariots, and the king of Maacah and his people; and they came and encamped before Medeba. And the children of Ammon assembled out of their cities, and came to fight.

8 And David heard, and sent Joab and all the army of the mighty men.

9 And the children of the Ammon came forth, and set themselves in battle array by the gate of the city; and the kings that had come forth encamped by themselves in the plain.

10 And Joab saw that they were surrounding *him*, to fight against him before and behind, and he chose *some* out of all the young men of Israel, and they set themselves in array against the Syrians.

11 And the rest of the people he gave into the hand of his brother Abishai, and they set themselves in array against the children of Ammon.

12 And he said, "If the Syrians should prevail against me, then shall you deliver me; and if the children of Ammon should prevail against you, then I will deliver you.

13 Be of good courage, and let us be strong, for our people, and for the cities of our God; and the Lord shall do what *is* good in His eyes."

14 So Joab and the people that were with him set themselves in battle array against the Syrians, and they fled from them.

15 And the children of Ammon saw that the Syrians fled, and they also fled from before Abishai, and from before Joab his brother, and they came to the city; and Joab came to Jerusalem.

16 And the Syrians saw that Israel had defeated them, and they sent messengers, and they brought out the Syrians from beyond the river; and Shophach the commander-in-chief of the forces of Hadadezer *was* before them.

17 And it was told David. And he gathered all Israel, and crossed over the Jordan, and came upon them, and set the battle in array against them. So David set *his army* in array to fight against the Syrians, and they fought against him.

18 And the Syrians fled from before Israel; and David slew of the Syrians seven thousand *riders in* chariots, and forty thousand infantry *men*, and he slew Shophach the commander-in-chief of the forces.

19 And the servants of Hadadezer saw that they were defeated before Israel, and they made peace with David and served him. And the Syrians would no longer help the children of Ammon.

1 CHRONICLES CHAPTER 20

Rabbah is Conquered

[1] And it came to pass at the return of the year, at the *time of the* going forth of kings *to war*, that Joab gathered the whole force of the army, and they ravaged the land of the children of Ammon; and he came and besieged Rabbah, but David stayed in Jerusalem. And Joab defeated Rabbah and destroyed it.

[2] And David took the crown of Molchom their king off his head, and the weight of it was found *to be* a talent of gold, and on it were precious stones. And it was *placed* on the head of David. And he brought out the spoils of the city, *which were* very great.

[3] And he brought out the people that were in it, and sawed them in half with saws, and *cut them* with iron axes, and with harrows. And thus David did to all the children of Ammon. And David and all his people returned to Jerusalem.

Philistine Giants Destroyed

[4] And it came to pass afterward that there was again war with the Philistines in Gezer. Then Sibbechai the Hushathite killed Sippai of the sons of the giants, and laid him low.

[5] And there *was* war again with the Philistines, and Elhanan the son of Jair killed Lahmi the brother of Goliath the Gittite, and the wood of his spear *was* as a weavers' beam.

[6] And there was again war in Gath, and there was a man of extraordinary size, and his fingers *and toes were* six on each hand and foot, twenty-four *total*. And he was descended from the giants.

[7] And he defied Israel, and Jonathan the son of Shimea the brother of David killed him.

[8] These were born to Rapha in Gath; all four were giants, and they fell by the hand of David, and by the hand of his servants.

1 CHRONICLES CHAPTER 21

The Census of Israel and Judah

[1] And the devil stood up against Israel, and moved David to number Israel.

[2] And King David said to Joab and to the captains of the forces, "Go, number Israel from Beersheba even to Dan, and bring me *the account*, and I shall know their number."

[3] And Joab said, "May the Lord add to His people a hundredfold as many as they *are* now, and *let* the eyes of my lord the king see *it*. All *are* the servants of my lord. Why does my lord seek this thing? *Do not* do this thing, lest it become a sin to Israel."

[4] Nevertheless the king's word prevailed against Joab, and Joab went out and passed through all Israel, and came to Jerusalem.

[5] And Joab gave the sum of the number of the people to David. And all Israel was one million one hundred thousand men that drew the sword. And the sons of Judah *were* four hundred and seventy thousand men that drew the sword.

[6] But he did not number Levi and Benjamin among them; for the word of the king was painful to Joab.

[7] And *there was* evil in the sight of the Lord respecting this thing; and He struck Israel.

[8] And David said to God, "I have sinned exceedingly, in that I have done this thing; and now, I pray, remove the sin of Your servant; for I have been exceedingly foolish."

[9] And the Lord spoke to Gad the seer, saying,

[10] "Go and speak to David, saying, 'Thus says the Lord: "Three things I offer you: choose one of them for yourself, and I will do it to you."'"

[11] And Gad came to David, and said to him, "Thus says the Lord, 'Choose for yourself,

[12] either three years of famine, or that you should flee three months from the face of your enemies, and the sword of your enemies *shall be employed* to destroy you, or that the sword of the Lord and pestilence *should be* three days in the land, and the angel of the Lord *shall* destroy among all the inheritance of Israel. And now consider what I shall answer to Him that sent the message.'"

[13] And David said to Gad, "They are very hard *choices* for me, even *all* three: let me fall now into the hands of the Lord, for His mercies *are* very abundant, and let me not fall by any means into the hands of man."

[14] So the Lord brought pestilence upon Israel, and there fell among Israel seventy thousand men.

[15] And God sent an angel to Jerusalem to destroy it. And as he was destroying, the Lord saw, and relented of the disaster, and said to the angel that was destroying, "That is enough; withhold your hand." And the angel of the Lord stood by the threshing floor of Ornan the Jebusite.

[16] And David lifted up his eyes, and saw the angel of the Lord, standing between earth and heaven, and his sword was drawn in his hand, stretched out over Jerusalem. And David and the elders clothed in sackcloth fell upon their faces.

[17] And David said to God, "*Was it* not I *that* gave orders to number the people? And I am the guilty one; I have greatly sinned; but these sheep, what have they done? O Lord God, let Your hand be upon me, and upon my father's house, and not on Your people for destruction, O Lord!"

[18] And the angel of the Lord told Gad to tell David, that he should go up to erect an altar to the Lord, on the threshing floor of Ornan the Jebusite.

[19] And David went up according to the word of Gad, which he spoke in the name of the Lord.

[20] And Ornan turned and saw the king; and he hid himself and his four sons with him. Now Ornan was threshing wheat.

21 And David came to Ornan, and Ornan came forth from the threshing floor, and bowed down to David with his face to the ground.

22 And David said to Ornan, "Give me your place of the threshing floor, and I will build upon it an altar to the Lord: give it to me for its worth in money, and the plague shall cease from *among* the people."

23 And Ornan said to David, "Take it to yourself, and let my lord the king do what is right in his eyes: see, I have given the calves for a burnt offering, and the plough for wood, and the wheat for a grain offering; I have given all."

24 And King David said to Ornan, "No, but I will surely buy it for its worth in money—for I will not take your property for the Lord, to offer a burnt offering to the Lord without cost *to myself*."

25 And David gave to Ornan six hundred shekels of gold for the site.

26 And David built there an altar to the Lord, and offered up burnt offerings and peace offerings. And he cried to the Lord, and He answered him by fire out of heaven on the altar of burnt offerings, and *the fire* consumed the burnt offering.

27 And the Lord spoke to the angel; and he put up the sword into its sheath.

28 At that time when David saw that the Lord answered him in the threshing floor of Ornan the Jebusite, he also sacrificed there.

29 And the tabernacle of the Lord which Moses made in the wilderness, and the altar of burnt offerings, *were* at that time in the high place at Gibeon.

30 And David could not go before it to inquire of God; for he was afraid of the sword of the angel of the Lord.

1 CHRONICLES CHAPTER 22

David Prepares to Build the Temple

1 And David said, "This is the house of the Lord God, and this *is* the altar for burnt offering for Israel."

2 And David gave orders to gather all the strangers that were in the land of Israel; and he appointed stone hewers to hew polished stones to build the house to God.

3 And David prepared much iron for the nails of the doors and the gate; the hinges also and bronze in abundance, there was no weighing *of it.*

4 And cedar trees without number; for the Sidonians and the Tyrians brought cedar trees in abundance to David.

5 And David said, "My son Solomon *is* a tender child, and the house *for me* to build to the Lord *is* for superior magnificence for a name and for a glory throughout all the earth; I will make preparation for it." And David prepared abundantly before his death.

6 And he called Solomon his son, and commanded him to build the house for the Lord God of Israel.

7 And David said to Solomon, "*My* child, it was in my heart to build a house to the name of the Lord God.

8 But the word of the Lord came to me, saying, 'You have shed blood abundantly, and have carried on great wars; you shall not build a house to My name, because you have shed much blood upon the earth before Me.

9 Behold, a son shall be born to you, he shall be a man of rest; and I will give him rest from all his enemies round about; for his name *shall be* Solomon, and I will give peace and quietness to Israel in his days.

10 He shall build a house to My name; and he shall be a son to Me, and I will be a Father to him; and I will establish the throne of his kingdom in Israel forever.'

11 And now, my son, the Lord shall be with you, and prosper *you*; and you shall build a house to the Lord your God, as He spoke concerning you.

12 Only may the Lord give you wisdom and prudence, and strengthen you over Israel, both to keep and to do the law of the Lord your God.

13 Then will He prosper *you*, if you take heed to do the commandments and judgments which the Lord commanded Moses for Israel; be courageous and strong; fear not, nor be terrified.

14 And behold, I, according to my poverty, have prepared for *the* house of *the* Lord a hundred thousand talents of gold, and a million talents of silver, and bronze and iron without measure, for it is abundant; and I have prepared timber and stones; and you therefore add to these.

15 And *of them that are* with you, add to the multitude of workmen; *let there be* stonecutters and masons, and carpenters, and every skillful *workman* in every work;

16 in gold and silver, bronze and iron, *of which* there is no number. Arise and begin working, and the Lord *be* with you."

17 And David charged all the chief men of Israel to help Solomon his son, *saying,*

18 "*Is* not the Lord with you? And He has given you rest round about, for He has given into your hands the inhabitants of the land; and the land is subdued before the Lord, and before His people.

19 Now set your hearts and souls to seek after the Lord your God; arise, and build a sanctuary to your God, to carry in the ark of the covenant of the Lord, and the holy vessels of God, into the house that is to be built to the name of the Lord."

1 CHRONICLES CHAPTER 23

The Divisions of the Levites

1 And David was old and full of days, and he made Solomon his son king over Israel in his place.

2 And he assembled all the chief men of Israel, and the priests, and the Levites.

3 And the Levites numbered *themselves* from thirty years old and upward; and their number by their polls amounted to thirty-eight thousand men.

4 Of the overseers over the works of the house of the Lord *there were* twenty-four thousand, and *there were* six thousand scribes and judges;

5 and four thousand gatekeepers, and four thousand to praise the Lord with instruments which he made to praise the Lord.

6 And David divided them *into* daily courses, for the sons of Levi, for Gershon, Kohath, and Merari.

7 And for *the family of* Gershon, Laadan, and Shimei.

8 The sons of Laadan *were* Jehiel the chief, Zetham, and Joel—three *in all.*

9 The sons of Shimei *were* Shelomith, Haziel, and Haran, three *in all*: these *were* the chiefs of the families of Laadan.

10 And to the sons of Shimei *were* Jahath, Zina, Jeush, and Beriah: these *were* the four sons of Shimei.

11 And Jahath was the chief, and Zizah; but Jeush and Beriah did not multiply sons, and they became *only* one reckoning according to the house of their father.

12 The sons of Kohath *were* Amram, Izhar, Hebron, and Uzziel—four *in all.*

13 The sons of Amram *were* Aaron and Moses; and Aaron was appointed for the consecration of the most holy things, he and his sons forever, to burn incense before the Lord, to minister and bless in His name forever.

14 And *as for* Moses the man of God, his sons were reckoned to the tribe of Levi.

15 The sons of Moses *were* Gershon, and Eliezer.

16 Of the sons of Gershon, Shebuel *was* the chief.

17 And the sons of Eliezer were Rehabiah the chief; and Eliezer had no other sons; but the sons of Rehabiah were very greatly multiplied.

18 Of the sons of Izhar, Shelomith *was* the chief.

19 Of the sons of Hebron, Jeriah *was* the chief, Amariah the second, Jahaziel the third, and Jekameam the fourth.

20 Of the sons of Uzziel, Michah *was* the chief, and Jesshiah the second.

21 The sons of Merari *were* Mahli and Mushi. The sons of Mahli *were* Eleazar, and Kish.

22 And Eleazar died, and he had no sons, but daughters. And the sons of Kish, their brothers, took them *as wives.*

23 The sons of Mushi *were* Mahli, Eder, and Jeremoth—three *in all.*

24 These *are* the sons of Levi according to the houses of their fathers; chiefs of their families according to their numbering, according to the number of their names, according to their polls, doing the works of service of the house of the Lord, from twenty years old and upward.

25 For David said, "The Lord God of Israel has given rest to His people, and has taken up His dwelling place in Jerusalem forever."

26 And the Levites did not bear the tabernacle, or any of the vessels for its service.

27 For by the last words of David was the number of the Levites *taken* from twenty years old and upward.

28 For he appointed them to wait on Aaron, to minister in the house of the Lord, over the courts, and over the chambers, and over the purification of all the holy things, and over the works of the service of the house of God;

29 and for the showbread, and for the fine flour of the meat offering, and for the unleavened cakes, and for the fried cake, and for the dough, and for every measure;

30 and to stand in the morning to praise and give thanks to the Lord, and so in the evening;

31 and *to be* over all the burnt offerings that were offered up to the Lord on the Sabbaths, and at the new moons, and at the feasts, by number, according to the order *given* to them, continually before the Lord.

32 And they are to keep the charge of the tabernacle of witness, and the charge of the holy place, and the charges of the sons of Aaron their brothers, to minister in the house of the Lord.

1 CHRONICLES CHAPTER 24

The Divisions of the Priests

1 And *they numbered* the sons of Aaron in *their* division, Nadab, Abihu, Eleazar, and Ithamar.

2 And Nadab and Abihu died before their father, and they had no sons, so Eleazar and Ithamar the sons of Aaron ministered as priests.

3 And David distributed them, even Zadok of the sons of Eleazar, and Ahimelech of the sons of Ithamar, according to their numbering, according to their service, according to the houses of their fathers.

4 And there were found *among* the sons of Eleazar more chiefs of the mighty ones, than of the sons of Ithamar. And he divided them, sixteen heads of families to the sons of Eleazar, eight according to *their* families to the sons of Ithamar.

5 And he divided them according to their lots, one with the other; for there were those who had charge of the holy things, and those who had charge of the *house* of the Lord among the sons of Eleazar, and among the sons of Ithamar.

6 And Shemaiah the son of Nethanel, the scribe, *of the family* of Levi, wrote them down before the king, and the princes, and Zadok the priest, and Ahimelech the son of Abiathar *were present*; and the heads of the families of the priests and the Levites, each of a household *were assigned*, one to Eleazar, and one to Ithamar.

7 And the first lot came out to Jehoiarib, the second to Jedaiah,

8 the third to Harim, the fourth to Seorim,

9 the fifth to Malchijah, the sixth to Mijamin,

10 the seventh to Hakkoz, the eighth to Abijah,

11 the ninth to Jeshua, the tenth to Shecaniah,

12 the eleventh to Eliashib, the twelfth to Jakim,

13 the thirteenth to Huppah, the fourteenth to Jeshebeab,

14 the fifteenth to Bilgah, the sixteenth to Immer,

¹⁵ the seventeenth to Hezir, the eighteenth to Aphses,

¹⁶ the nineteenth to Pethahiah, the twentieth to Jehezekel,

¹⁷ the twenty-first to Jachin, the twenty-second to Gamul,

¹⁸ the twenty-third to Delaiah, the twenty-fourth to Maaziah.

¹⁹ This *is* their numbering according to their service to go into the house of the Lord, according to their appointment by the hand of Aaron their father, as the Lord God of Israel had commanded *him*.

Other Levites

²⁰ And the rest of the sons of Levi: of the sons of Amram, Shubael; of the sons of Shubael, Jehdeiah.

²¹ Concerning Rehabiah, the chief *was* Isshiah,

²² and for Isshiah, Shelomoth; for the sons of Shelomoth, Jahath.

²³ *Of* the sons of Hebron, *Jeriah was the chief*, Amariah the second, Jahaziel the third, Jekameam the fourth.

²⁴ Of the sons of Uzziel, Michah; *of* the sons of Michah, Shamir.

²⁵ The brother of Michah, Isshiah, the son of Issiah, Zechariah.

²⁶ The sons of Merari *were* Mahli and Mushi; the sons of Ozia,

²⁷ *That is, the sons* of Merari by Ozia, his sons *were* Beno, Zaccur, and Ibri.

²⁸ To Mahli *were born* Eleazar, and Ithamar; and Eleazar died, and had no sons.

²⁹ Of Kish: the son of Kish, Jerahmeel.

³⁰ And the sons of Mushi *were* Mahli, Eder, and Jerimoth. These *were* the sons of the Levites according to the houses of their families.

³¹ And they also received lots as their brothers the sons of Aaron before the king; Zadok also, and Ahimelech, and the chiefs of the families of the priests and of the Levites, principal heads of families, even as their younger brothers.

1 CHRONICLES CHAPTER 25

The Musicians

¹ And King David and the captains of the army appointed to their services the sons of Asaph, and of Heman, and of Jeduthun, who *should* prophesy with harps, lutes, and cymbals; and their number was according to their polls serving in their ministrations.

² The sons of Asaph: Zaccur, Joseph, Nethaniah, and Asharelah; the sons of Asaph *were* next *to* the king.

³ To Jeduthun *were reckoned* the sons of Jeduthun, Gedaliah, Zeri, Jeshaiah, Shimei, Hashabiah, and Mattithiah, six after their father Jeduthun, sounding loudly on the harp thanksgiving and praise to the Lord.

⁴ To Heman *were reckoned* the sons of Heman, Bukkiah, Mattaniah, Uzziel, Shebuel, Jerimoth, Hananiah, Hanani, Eliathah, Giddalti, Romamti-Ezer, Joshbekashah, Mallothi, Hothir, and Mahazioth.

⁵ All these *were* the sons of Heman the king's chief player in the praises of God, to lift up the horn. And God gave to Heman fourteen sons, and three daughters.

⁶ All these sang hymns with their father in the house of God, with cymbals, lutes, and harps, for the service of the house of God, near the king, and Asaph, and Jeduthun, and Heman.

⁷ And the number of them after their brothers, those instructed to sing to God, everyone that understood *singing* was two hundred and eighty-eight.

⁸ And they also cast lots for the daily courses, for the great and the small *of them*, of the perfect ones and the learners.

⁹ And the first lot of his sons and of his brothers came forth to Asaph the son of Joseph, *namely*, Gedaliah; the second Heneia, his sons and his brothers *being* twelve.

¹⁰ The third Zaccur, his sons and his brothers *were* twelve;

¹¹ the fourth Jizri, his sons and his brothers *were* twelve;

¹² the fifth Nethaniah, his sons and his brothers, twelve;

¹³ the sixth Bukkiah, his sons and his brothers, twelve;

¹⁴ the seventh Jesharelah, his sons and his brothers, twelve;

¹⁵ the eighth Jeshaiah, his sons and his brothers, twelve;

¹⁶ the ninth Mattaniah, his sons and his brothers, twelve;

¹⁷ the tenth Shimei, his sons and his brothers, twelve;

¹⁸ the eleventh Azarel, his sons and his brothers, twelve;

¹⁹ the twelfth Hashabiah, his sons and his brothers, twelve;

²⁰ the thirteenth Shubael, his sons and his brothers, twelve;

²¹ the fourteenth Mattithiah, his sons and his brothers, twelve;

²² the fifteenth Jerimoth, his sons and his brothers, twelve;

²³ the sixteenth Hananiah, his sons and his brothers, twelve;

²⁴ the seventeenth Joshbekashah, his sons and his brothers, twelve;

²⁵ the eighteenth Hanani, his sons and his brothers, twelve;

²⁶ the nineteenth Mallothi, his sons and his brothers, twelve;

²⁷ the twentieth Eliathah, his sons and his brothers, twelve;

²⁸ the twenty-first Hothir, his sons and his brothers, twelve;

²⁹ the twenty-second Giddalti, his sons and his brothers, twelve;

³⁰ the twenty-third Mahazioth, his sons and his brothers, twelve;

³¹ the twenty-fourth Romamti-Ezer, his sons and his brothers, twelve.

1 CHRONICLES CHAPTER 26

The Gatekeepers

¹ And for the divisions of the gates: the sons of the Korahites *were* Meshelemiah, of the sons of Asaph.

² And Meshelemiah's firstborn son *was* Zechariah, the second Jadiael, the third Zebadiah, the fourth Jathniel,

3 the fifth Elam, the sixth Jehohanan, the seventh Eliehoenai, the eighth Obed-Edom.

4 And to Obed-Edom *there were born* sons, Shemaiah the firstborn, Jehozabad the second, Joah the third, Sacar the fourth, Nethanel the fifth,

5 Ammiel the sixth, Issachar the seventh, and Peulthai the eighth; for God blessed him.

6 And to Shemaiah his son were born the sons of his firstborn, chiefs over the house of their father, for they were mighty.

7 The sons of Shemaiah *were* Othni, Rephael, Obed, Elzabad, and Achiud, mighty men, *along with* Elihu, Sabachia, and Isbacom.

8 All *these were* of the sons of Obed-Edom, they and their sons and their brothers, doing mightily in service; sixty-two in all *were born* to Obed-Edom.

9 And Meshelemiah *had* eighteen sons and brothers, mighty men.

10 And to Hosah of the sons of Merari *there were born* sons, keeping the dominion; though he was not the firstborn, yet his father made him chief of the second division.

11 Hilkiah the second, Tebaliah the third, Zechariah the fourth; all these *were* the sons and brothers of Hosah, thirteen.

12 To these *were assigned* the divisions of the gates, to the chiefs of the mighty men the daily courses, even their brothers, to minister in the house of the Lord.

13 And they cast lots for the small as well as for the great, for the several gates, according to their families.

14 And the lot for the east gate fell to Shelemiah, and Zechariah; the sons of Soaz cast lots for Milchiah and the lot came out northward.

15 To Obed-Edom *they gave by lot* the south, opposite the house of Esephim.

16 *They gave the lot* for the second to Hosah westward, after the gate of the chamber by the ascent, watchman opposite watchman.

17 Eastward *were* six *watchmen* in the day; northward four by the day; southward four by the day; and two at the Esephim,

18 to relieve guard, also for Hosah westward after the chamber gate, three. *There was* a ward over against the ward of the ascent eastward, six *men* in a day, and four for the north, and four for the south, and at the Esephim two to relieve guard, and four by the west, and two to relieve guard at the pathway.

19 These *are* the divisions of the porters for the sons of Korah, and to the sons of Merari.

Treasuries and Other Duties

20 And the Levites their brothers *were* over the treasuries of the house of the Lord, and over the treasures of the hallowed things.

21 These *were* the sons of Laadan, the sons of the Gershonite: to Laadan *belonged* the heads of the families; *the son* of Laadan the Gershonite *was* Jehieli.

22 The sons of Jehieli *were* Zetham and Joel; brothers *who were* over the treasures of the house of the Lord.

23 To Amram and Issaar belonged Hebron, and Uzziel.

24 And Shebuel the *son* of Gershom, the *son* of Moses, *was* over the treasures.

25 And Rehabiah *was* son to his brother Eliezer, and *so was* Jeshaiah, Joram, Zichri, and Shelomith.

26 This Shelomith and his brothers *were* over all the sacred treasures, which David the king and the heads of families consecrated, *and* the captains of thousands and captains of hundreds, and princes of the host,

27 things which he took out of cities and from the spoils, and consecrated some of them, so that the building of the house of God should not need *supplies*;

28 and over all the holy things of God dedicated by Samuel the prophet, and Saul the son of Kish, and Abner the son of Ner, and Joab the son of Zeruiah, whatsoever they sanctified *was* by the hand of Shelomith and his brothers.

29 For the Izharites, Chenaniah, and *his* sons *were over* the outward ministration over Israel, to record and to judge.

30 For the Hebronites, Hashabiah and his brothers, a thousand and seven hundred mighty men, *were* over the charge of Israel beyond the Jordan westward, for all the service of the Lord and work of the king.

31 Of the *family* of Hebron Jerijah *was* chief, even of the Hebronites according to their generations, according to their families. In the fortieth year of his reign they were numbered, and there were found mighty men among them in Jazer of Gilead.

32 And his brothers *were* two thousand seven hundred mighty men, chiefs of their families, and King David set them over the Reubenites, and the Gadites, and the half-tribe of Manasseh, for every ordinance of the Lord, and business of the king.

1 CHRONICLES CHAPTER 27

The Military Divisions

1 Now the sons of Israel according to their number, heads of families, captains of thousands and captains of hundreds, and scribes ministering to the king, and for every affair of the king according to *their* divisions, *for* every ordinance of coming in and going out monthly, for all the months of the year, one division of them *was* twenty-four thousand.

2 And over the first division of the first month *was* Jashobeam the son of Zabdiel; in his division *were* twenty-four thousand.

3 Of the sons of Perez *one* was chief of all the captains of the army for the first month.

4 And over the division of the second month *was* Dodai an Ahohite, and over his division *was* Mikloth also chief; and in

his division *were* twenty-four thousand, chief men of the army.

⁵ The third for the third month *was* Benaiah the son of Jehoiada the chief priest; and in his division *were* twenty-four thousand.

⁶ This Benaiah *was* more mighty than the thirty, and over the thirty; and Ammizabad his son *was* over his division.

⁷ The fourth for the fourth month *was* Asahel the brother of Joab, and Zebadiah his son, and his brothers; and in his division *were* twenty-four thousand.

⁸ The fifth chief for the fifth month *was* Shamhuth the Izrahite; and in his division *were* twenty-four thousand.

⁹ The sixth for the sixth month *was* Ira the son of Ikkesh the Tekoite; and in his division *were* twenty-four thousand.

¹⁰ The seventh for the seventh month *was* Helez of Pelonite of the children of Ephraim; and in his division *were* twenty-four thousand.

¹¹ The eighth for the eighth month *was* Sibbechai the Hushathite, *belonging* to Zarai: and in his division *were* twenty-four thousand.

¹² The ninth for the ninth month *was* Abiezer of Anathoth, of the land of Benjamin; and in his division *were* twenty-four thousand.

¹³ The tenth for the tenth month *was* Maharai the Netophathite, *belonging* to Zarai; and in his division *were* twenty-four thousand.

¹⁴ The eleventh for the eleventh month *was* Benaiah of Pirath, of the sons of Ephraim; and in his division *were* twenty-four thousand.

¹⁵ The twelfth for the twelfth month *was* Heldai the Netophathite, *belonging* to Othniel; and in his division *were* twenty-four thousand.

¹⁶ And over the tribes of Israel, the chief for Reuben *was* Eliezer the son of Zichri; for Simeon, Shephatiah the son of Maachah;

¹⁷ for Levi, Hashabiah the son of Kemuel; for Aaron, Zadok;

¹⁸ for Judah, Elihu of the brothers of David; for Issachar, Omri the son of Michael;

¹⁹ for Zebulun, Ishmaiah the son of Obadiah: for Naphtali, Jerimoth the son of Azriel;

²⁰ for Ephraim, Hoshea the son of Azaziah; for the half-tribe of Manasseh, Joel the son of Pedaiah:

²¹ for the half-tribe of Manasseh in the land of Gilead, Iddo the son of Zechariah; for the sons of Benjamin, Jaasiel the son of Abner;

²² for Dan, Azarel the son of Jeroham; these *are* the chiefs of the tribes of Israel.

²³ But David did not take their number from twenty years old and under, because the Lord said that he would multiply Israel as the stars of the heaven.

²⁴ And Joab the son of Zeruiah began to number the people, but did not finish the work, for wrath came upon Israel; and the number was not recorded in the book of the chronicles of King David.

²⁵ And over the king's treasures *was* Azmaveth the son of Adiel; and over the treasures in the country, and in the towns, and in the villages, and in the towers, *was* Jehonathan the son of Uzziah.

²⁶ And over the farmers who tilled the ground *was* Ezri the son of Chelub.

²⁷ And over the fields *was* Shimei the Ramathite; and over the treasures of wine in the fields *was* Zabdi the son of Sephni.

²⁸ And over the olive trees, and over the sycamores in the plain country *was* Baal-Hanan the Gederite; and over the stores of oil *was* Joash.

²⁹ And over the oxen that fed in Sharon *was* Satrai the Sharonite; and over the oxen in the valleys *was* Shaphat the son of Adlai.

³⁰ And over the camels *was* Obil the Ishmaelite; and over the donkeys *was* Jehdeiah of Merathon.

³¹ And over the sheep *was* Jaziz the Hagrite. All these *were* superintendents of King David's property.

³² And Jehonathan, David's uncle on his father's side, *was* a counselor, a wise man; and Jehiel the son of Hachmoni *was* with the king's sons.

³³ Ahithophel *was* the king's counselor, and Hushai the chief friend of the king.

³⁴ And after Ahithophel was Jehoiada the son of Benaiah, then Abiathar; and Joab *was* the king's commander-in-chief.

1 CHRONICLES CHAPTER 28

Solomon Instructed to Build the Temple

¹ And David assembled all the chief *men* of Israel, the chief of the judges, and all the chief *men* of the courses *of attendance* on the person of the king, and the captains of thousands and hundreds, and the treasurers, and the masters of his property, and of his sons, together with the eunuchs, and the mighty men, and the warriors of the army, at Jerusalem.

² And David stood in the midst of the assembly, and said, "Hear me, my brothers, and my people. It was in my heart to build a house of rest for the ark of the covenant of the Lord, and a place for the feet of our Lord, and I prepared *materials* suitable for the building;

³ but God said, 'You shall not build Me a house to call My name upon it, for you are a man of war, and have shed blood.'

⁴ Yet the Lord God of Israel chose me out of the whole house of my father to be king over Israel forever; and He chose Judah as the kingly *house*, and out of the house of Judah *He chose* the house of my father; and among the sons of my father He preferred me, that I should be king over all Israel.

⁵ And of all my sons, (for the Lord has given me many sons) He has chosen Solomon my son, to set him on the throne of the kingdom of the Lord over Israel.

⁶ And God said to me, 'Solomon your son shall build My house and My court; for I have chosen him to be My son, and I will be to him a Father.

⁷ And I will establish his kingdom forever, if he continues to keep My commandments, and My judgments, as *it is* this day.'

⁸ And now *I charge you* before the whole assembly of the Lord, and in the audience of our God, keep and seek all the commandments of the Lord our God, that you may inherit the good land, and leave it for your sons to inherit after you forever.

⁹ "And now, *my* son Solomon, know the God of your fathers, and serve Him with a perfect heart and a willing soul; for the Lord searches all hearts, and knows every thought: if you seek Him, He will be found by you; but if you should forsake Him, He will forsake you forever.

¹⁰ See now, for the Lord has chosen you to build Him a house for a sanctuary; be strong and do *it*."

¹¹ And David gave Solomon his son the plan of the temple, and its buildings, and its treasuries, and its upper chambers, and the inner store rooms, and the place of the atonement,

¹² and the plan which he had in his mind of the courts of the house of the Lord, and of all the chambers round about, *designed* for the treasuries of the house of God, and of the treasuries of the holy things, and of the chambers for resting;

¹³ and *the plan* of the courses of the priests and Levites, for all the work of the service of the house of the Lord, and of the stores of vessels for ministration of the service of the house of the Lord.

¹⁴ And *he gave him* the account of their weight, both of the gold and silver *vessels.*

¹⁵ He gave him the weight of the lampstands, and of the lamps.

¹⁶ He gave him likewise the weight of the tables of showbread, of each table of gold, and likewise of the *tables of* silver.

¹⁷ Also of the flesh-hooks, and vessels for drink offering, and golden bowls. And the weight of the gold and silver *articles,* and censers, *and* bowls, according to the weight of each.

¹⁸ And he showed him the weight *of the utensils* of the altar of incense, *which was* of pure gold, and the plan of the chariot of the cherubim that spread out their wings, and overshadowed the ark of the covenant of the Lord.

¹⁹ David gave all to Solomon in the Lord's handwriting, according to the knowledge given to him of the work of the pattern.

²⁰ And David said to Solomon his son, "Be strong, and of good courage, and do *it*: fear not, neither be terrified; for the Lord my God *is* with you; He will not forsake you, and will not fail you, until you have finished all the work of the service of the house of the Lord. And behold the pattern of the temple, even His house, and its treasury, and the upper chambers, and the inner store rooms, and the place of propitiation, and the plan of the house of the Lord.

²¹ And see, *here are* the courses of the priests and Levites for all the service of the house of the Lord, and *there shall be* with you *men* for every workmanship, and everyone of ready skill in every art; also the chief men and all the people, *ready* for all your commands."

1 CHRONICLES CHAPTER 29

Offerings for Building the Temple

¹ And David the king said to all the congregation, "Solomon my son, whom the Lord has chosen, *is* young and tender, and the work *is* great; for *it is* not for man, but for the Lord God.

² I have prepared according to all *my* might for the house of my God, gold, silver, bronze, iron, wood, onyx stones, and costly and variegated stones for setting, and every precious stone, and much Parian *marble.*

³ Moreover, because I took pleasure in the house of my God, I have gold and silver which I have procured for myself, and behold, I have given them to the house of my God over and above, beyond what I have prepared for the holy house.

⁴ Three thousand talents of gold of Ophir, and seven thousand talents of fine silver, for the overlaying of the walls of the sanctuary;

⁵ *for you to use* the gold for *things of* gold, and the silver for things of silver, and for every work by the hand of the stonecutters. And who is willing to dedicate himself in work this day for the Lord?"

⁶ Then the heads of families, and the princes of the children of Israel, and the captains of thousands and captains of hundreds, and the overseers of the works, and the king's builders, offered willingly.

⁷ And they gave for the works of the house of the Lord five thousand talents of gold, and ten thousand gold *pieces,* and ten thousand talents of silver, and eighteen thousand talents of bronze, and a hundred thousand talents of iron.

⁸ And those who had *precious* stones gave them into the treasuries of the house of the Lord by the hand of Jehiel the Gershonite.

⁹ And the people rejoiced because of the willingness, for they offered willingly to the Lord with a full heart; and King David rejoiced greatly.

David's Praise to God

¹⁰ And King David blessed the Lord before the congregation, saying, "Blessed are You, O Lord God of Israel, our Father, from everlasting to everlasting.

¹¹ Yours, O Lord, *is* the greatness, and the power, and the glory, and the victory, and the might; for You are Lord of all things that are in heaven and on earth; before Your face every king and nation is troubled.

¹² From You *come* wealth and glory. You, O Lord, rule over all, the Lord of all dominion, and in Your hand *is* strength and rule; and *You are* almighty with Your hand to increase and establish all things.

¹³ "And now, O Lord, we give thanks to You, and praise Your glorious name.

¹⁴ But who am I, and what *is* my people, that we have been able to be thus forward *in offering* to You? For all things *are* Yours, and of Your own have we given You,

¹⁵ for we are strangers before You, and sojourners, as all our fathers *were*; our days upon the earth *are* as a shadow, and there is no abiding.

¹⁶ "O Lord our God, as for all this abundance which I have prepared that a house should be built to Your holy name, it is of Your hand, and all *is* Yours.

¹⁷ And I know, O Lord, that You are He that searches the hearts, and You love righteousness. I have willingly offered all these things in simplicity of heart. And now I have seen with joy Your people, who are present here, willingly offering to You.

¹⁸ O Lord God of Abraham, Isaac, and Israel our fathers, preserve these things in the thoughts of the heart of Your people forever, and direct their hearts toward You.

¹⁹ And to Solomon my son give a good heart, to perform Your commandments, and *to observe* Your testimonies, and Your ordinances, and to accomplish the building of Your house."

²⁰ And David said to the whole congregation, "Bless the Lord our God!" And all the congregation blessed the Lord God of their fathers, and they bowed their knees and worshipped the Lord, and *bowed down* to the king."

²¹ And David sacrificed to the Lord, and offered up burnt offerings to the Lord on the morning after the first day, a thousand calves, a thousand rams, a thousand lambs, and their drink offerings, and sacrifices in abundance for all Israel.

²² And they ate and drank joyfully that day before the Lord. And they made Solomon the son of David king a second time, and anointed him king before the Lord, and Zadok to the priesthood.

²³ And Solomon sat upon the throne of his father David, and was highly honored; and all Israel obeyed him.

²⁴ The princes, and the mighty men, and all the sons of King David his father were subject to him.

²⁵ And the Lord magnified Solomon over all Israel, and gave him royal glory, such as was not upon any king before him.

²⁶ And David the son of Jesse reigned over Israel forty years;

²⁷ seven years in Hebron, and thirty-three years in Jerusalem.

²⁸ And he died in a good old age, full of days, in wealth, and glory; and Solomon his son reigned in his place.

²⁹ And the rest of the acts of David, the former and the latter, are written in the history of Samuel the seer, and in the history of Nathan the prophet, and in the history of Gad the seer,

³⁰ concerning all his reign, and his power, and the times which went over him, and over Israel, and over all the kingdoms of the earth.

THE BOOK OF SECOND CHRONICLES

Solomon Requests Wisdom

¹ And Solomon the son of David was established over his kingdom, and the Lord his God was with him, and increased him exceedingly.

² And Solomon spoke to all Israel, to the captains of thousands, and to the captains of hundreds, and to the judges, and to all the rulers over Israel, even the heads of the families.

³ And Solomon and all the congregation went to the high place that was in Gibeon, where God's tabernacle of witness was, which Moses the servant of the Lord made in the wilderness.

⁴ But David had brought up the ark of God out of the city of Kirjath Jearim; for David had prepared a place for it, for he had pitched a tabernacle for it in Jerusalem.

⁵ And the bronze altar which Bezaleel the son of Uri, the son of Hur had made, was there before the tabernacle of the Lord. And Solomon and the congregation inquired *of the Lord* there.

⁶ And Solomon brought *sacrifices* there to the bronze altar that was before the Lord in the tabernacle, and offered upon it a thousand burnt offerings.

⁷ In that night God appeared to Solomon, and said to him, "Ask what I shall give you."

⁸ And Solomon said to God, "You have dealt very mercifully with my father David, and have made me king in his place.

⁹ And now, O Lord God, let Your name be established upon David my father; for You have made me king over a people as numerous *as* the dust of the earth.

¹⁰ Now give me wisdom and understanding, I pray, that I may go out and come in before this people: for who shall judge this, Your great people?"

¹¹ And God said to Solomon, "Because this was in your heart, and you have not asked for great wealth, nor glory, nor the life of your enemies, and you have not asked for long life; but have asked for yourself wisdom and understanding, that you might judge My people, over whom I have made you king;

¹² I give you this wisdom and understanding; and I will give you wealth, and riches, and glory, so that there shall not have been *any* like you among the kings before you, neither shall there be such after you."

¹³ And Solomon came from the high place that was in Gibeon to Jerusalem, *from* before the tabernacle of witness, and reigned over Israel.

¹⁴ And Solomon collected chariots and horsemen; and he had fourteen hundred chariots, and twelve thousand horsemen; and he set them in the cities of chariots, and the people *were* with the king in Jerusalem.

¹⁵ And the king made silver and gold in Jerusalem *to be* as stones, and cedars in Judea as sycamores in the plain for multitude.

¹⁶ And Solomon imported horses from Egypt, and the charge of the king's merchants for going *was as follows*, and they traded,

¹⁷ and went and brought out of Egypt a chariot for six hundred *pieces* of silver, and a horse for a hundred and fifty *pieces* of silver. And so they brought for all the kings of the Hittites, and for the kings of Syria, by their means.

2 CHRONICLES CHAPTER 2

Solomon Prepares to Build the Temple

¹ And Solomon said that he would build a house to the name of the Lord, and a house for his kingdom.

² And Solomon gathered seventy thousand men that bore burdens, and eighty thousand hewers of stone in the mountain, and *there were* three thousand six hundred superintendents over them.

³ And Solomon sent to Hiram king of Tyre, saying, "Whereas you dealt *favorably* with David my father, and sent him cedars to build for himself a house to dwell in,

⁴ behold, I also his son am building a house to the name of the Lord my God, to consecrate it to Him, to burn incense before Him, and *to offer* showbread continually, and to offer up burnt offerings continually morning and evening, and on the Sabbaths, and at the new moons, and at the feasts of the Lord our God: this *is* a perpetual *statute* for Israel.

⁵ And the house which I am building *is to be* great: for the Lord our God *is* great beyond all gods.

⁶ And who will be able to build Him a house? For the heaven and heaven of heavens cannot contain His glory. And who am I, that I should build Him a house, except only to burn incense before Him?

⁷ And now send me a man wise and skilled to work in gold, and in silver, and in bronze, and in iron, and in purple, and in scarlet, and in blue, and one that knows how to grave together with the craftsmen who are with me in Judah and in Jerusalem, which materials my father David prepared.

⁸ And send me from Lebanon cedar wood, and wood of juniper, and pine; for I know that your servants are skilled in cutting timber in Lebanon: and behold, your servants shall go with my servants,

⁹ to prepare timber for me in abundance; for the house which I am building *must be* great and glorious.

¹⁰ And behold, I have given freely to your servants that work and cut the wood, grain for food, *even* twenty thousand measures of wheat, and twenty thousand measures of barley, and twenty thousand measures of wine, and twenty thousand measures of oil."

¹¹ And Hiram king of Tyre answered in writing, and sent to Solomon, saying, "Because the Lord loved His people, He made you king over them."

¹² And Hiram said, "Blessed *be* the Lord God of Israel, who made heaven and earth, who has given to King David a wise son, and one endowed with knowledge and understanding, who shall build a house for the Lord, and a house for his kingdom.

¹³ And now I have sent you a wise and understanding man *who belonged* to Hiram my father,

¹⁴ (his mother *was* of the daughters of Dan, and his father *was* a Tyrian), skilled to work in gold, and in silver, and in brass, and in iron, and in stones and wood; and to weave with purple, and blue, and fine linen, and scarlet; and to engrave, and to understand every device, whatsoever you shalt give him *to do* with your craftsmen, and the craftsmen of my lord David your father.

¹⁵ And now, the wheat and the barley and the oil and the wine, which my lord mentioned, let him send to his servants.

¹⁶ And we will cut timber out of Lebanon according to all your needs, and we will bring it on rafts to the Sea of Joppa, and you shall bring it to Jerusalem."

¹⁷ And Solomon gathered all the foreigners that were in the land of Israel, after the numbering with which David his father numbered them; and there were found a hundred and fifty-three thousand six hundred.

¹⁸ And he made of them seventy thousand burden-bearers, and eighty thousand hewers of stone, and three thousand six hundred taskmasters over the people.

2 CHRONICLES CHAPTER 3

Solomon Builds the Temple

¹ And Solomon began to build the house of the Lord in Jerusalem on Mount Moriah, where the Lord appeared to his father David, in the place which David had prepared in the threshing floor of Ornan the Jebusite.

² And he began to build in the second month, in the fourth year of his reign.

³ And thus Solomon began to build the house of God: the length in cubits–even the first measurement from end to end, was sixty cubits, and the breadth twenty cubits.

⁴ And the porch in front of the house, its length in front of the breadth of the house *was* twenty cubits, and its height a hundred and twenty cubits: and he gilded it within with pure gold.

⁵ And he lined the great house with cedar wood, and gilded it with pure gold, and carved upon it palm trees and chains.

⁶ And he garnished the house with precious stones for beauty; and he gilded it with gold of the gold from Parvaim.

⁷ And he gilded the house, and its *inner* walls, and the doorposts, and the roofs, and the doors with gold; and he carved cherubim on the walls.

⁸ And he built the Holy of Holies, its length was according to the front *of the other house*, the breadth of the house *was* twenty cubits, and the length twenty cubits; and he gilded *it* with pure gold for cherubim, to *the amount of* six hundred talents.

⁹ And the weight of the nails, *even* the weight of each was fifty shekels of gold; and he gilded the upper chamber with gold.

¹⁰ And he made two cherubim in the Most Holy Place, woodwork, and he gilded them with gold.

¹¹ And the wings of the cherubim were twenty cubits in length; and one wing of five cubits touched the wall of the house. And the other wing of five cubits touched the wing of the other cherub.

¹² (This verse omitted in LXX)

¹³ And the wings of these cherubim expanded were of the length of twenty cubits; and they stood upon their feet, and their faces were toward the house.

¹⁴ And he made the veil of blue, and purple, and scarlet, and fine linen, and wove cherubim in it.

¹⁵ Also he made in front of the house two pillars, in height thirty-five cubits, and their chapters of five cubits.

¹⁶ And he made chains, *as* in the oracle, and put *them* on the heads of the pillars; and he made a hundred pomegranates, and put them on the chains.

¹⁷ And he set up the pillars in front of the temple, one on the right hand and the other on the left. And he called the name of the one on the right hand 'Stability,' and the name of the one on the left 'Strength.'

2 CHRONICLES CHAPTER 4

Furnishings of the Temple

¹ And he made a bronze altar, the length of it twenty cubits, and the breadth twenty cubits, and the height ten cubits.

² And he made the molten sea, in diameter ten cubits, entirely round, and the height of it five cubits, and the circumference thirty cubits.

³ And beneath it the likeness of calves, they compassed it round about: ten cubits compass the laver round about, they cast the calves two rows in their casting,

⁴ wherein they made them twelve calves—three looking northwards, three westwards, three southwards, and three eastwards; and the sea was upon them above, *and* their hind parts were inward.

⁵ And its thickness was a handbreadth, and its brim as the brim of a cup, graven with flowers of lilies, holding three thousand measures; and he finished it.

⁶ And he made ten lavers, and set five on the right hand, and five on the left, to wash in them the instruments of the burnt offerings, and to rinse *the vessels* in them; and the sea *was* for the priests to wash in.

⁷ And he made the ten golden lampstands according to their pattern, and he put them in the temple, five on the right hand, and five on the left.

⁸ And he made ten tables, and put them in the temple, five on the right hand, and five on the left. And he made a hundred golden bowls.

⁹ Also he made the priests' court, and the great court, and doors to the court, and their panels *were* overlaid with bronze. ¹⁰ And he set the sea at the corner of the house on the right, as it were, facing the east.

¹¹ And Huram made the fleshhooks and the firepans, and the grate of the altar, and all its instruments. And Hiram finished doing all the work which he wrought for King Solomon in the house of God:

¹² two pillars, and upon them an embossed work for the chapiters on the heads of the two pillars, and two nets to cover the heads of the chapiters which are on the heads of the pillars;

¹³ and four hundred golden bells for the two nets, and two rows of pomegranates in each net, to cover the two embossed rims of the chapiters which are upon the pillars.

¹⁴ And he made the ten bases, and he made the lavers upon the bases;

¹⁵ and the one sea, and the twelve calves under it;

¹⁶ and the foot-baths, and the buckets, and the caldrons, and the fleshhooks, and all their furniture (which Hiram made, and brought to King Solomon in the house of the Lord) of pure bronze.

¹⁷ In the country round about the Jordan the king cast them, in the clay ground in the house of Succoth, and between *that and* Zeredah.

¹⁸ So Solomon made all these vessels in great abundance, for the quantity of bronze failed not.

¹⁹ And Solomon made all the vessels of the house of the Lord, and the golden altar, and the tables, and upon them *were to be* the loaves of showbread;

²⁰ also the lampstands, and the lamps to give light according to the pattern, and in front of the oracle, of pure gold.

²¹ And their snuffers, and their lamps *were made*, and *he made* the bowls, and the censers, and the fire-pans, of pure gold.

²² And *there was* the inner door of the house *opening* into the Holy of Holies, and *he made* the inner doors of the temple of gold. So all the work which Solomon wrought for the house of the Lord was finished.

2 CHRONICLES CHAPTER 5

¹ And Solomon brought in the holy things of his father David, the silver, the gold, and the *other* vessels, and put them in the treasury of the house of the Lord.

The Ark Brought into the Temple

2 Then Solomon assembled all the elders of Israel, and all the heads of the tribes, *even* the leaders of the families of the children of Israel, to Jerusalem, to bring up the ark of the covenant of the Lord out of the city of David (this *is* Zion).

3 And all Israel was assembled *unto* the king in the feast, this *is* the seventh month.

4 And all the elders of Israel came; and all the Levites took up the ark,

5 and the tabernacle of witness, and all the holy vessels that were in the tabernacle; and the priests and the Levites brought it up.

6 And King Solomon, and all the elders of Israel, and the religious of them, and they of them that were gathered before the ark, *were* sacrificing calves and sheep, which could not be numbered or reckoned for multitude.

7 And the priests brought in the ark of the covenant of the Lord into its place, into the oracle of the house, *even* into the Holy of Holies, under the wings of the cherubim.

8 And the cherubim stretched out their wings over the place of the ark, and the cherubim covered the ark, and its poles above.

9 And the poles projected, and the heads of the poles were seen from the holy place in front of the oracle, they were not seen outside. And they are there to this day.

10 There was nothing in the ark except the two tablets which Moses placed *there* in Horeb, which God gave in covenant with the children of Israel, when they went out of the land of Egypt.

11 And it came to pass, when the priests came out of the holy place (for all the priests that were found were sanctified, they were not *then* arranged according to their daily course),

12 that all the singing Levites *assigned* to the sons of Asaph, to Heman, to Jeduthun, and to his sons, and to his brothers, of them that were clothed in linen garments, with cymbals and lutes and harps, *were* standing before the altar, and with them a hundred and twenty priests, blowing trumpets.

13 And there was one voice in the trumpeting and in the psalm singing, and in the loud utterance with one voice to give thanks and praise the Lord. And when they raised their voice together with trumpets and cymbals, and instruments of music, and said, "Give thanks to the Lord, for *He is* good, for His mercy *endures* forever." Then the house was filled with the cloud of the glory of the Lord.

14 And the priests could not stand to minister because of the cloud; for the glory of the Lord filled the house of God.

2 CHRONICLES CHAPTER 6

Dedication of the Temple

1 Then Solomon said, "The Lord said that He would dwell in thick darkness.

2 But I have built a house to Your name, holy to You, and prepared *for You* to dwell in forever."

3 And the king turned his face, and blessed all the congregation of Israel. And all the congregation of Israel stood by.

4 And he said, "Blessed *be* the Lord God of Israel; He has even fulfilled with His hands as He spoke with His mouth to my father David, saying,

5 'From the day when I brought up My people out of the land of Egypt, I chose no city of all the tribes of Israel, to build a house that My name should be there; neither did I choose a man to be a leader over My people Israel.

6 But I have chosen Jerusalem that My name should be there; and I have chosen David to be over My people Israel.'

7 And it came into the heart of David my father, to build a house for the name of the Lord God of Israel.

8 But the Lord said to my father David, 'Whereas it came into your heart to build a house for My name, you did well that it came into your heart.

9 Nevertheless you shall not build the house; for your son who shall come forth out of your loins, he shall build the house for My name.'

10 And the Lord has confirmed this word, which He spoke; and I have been raised up in the place of my father David, and I sit upon the throne of Israel as the Lord said, and I have built the house for the name of the Lord God of Israel;

11 and I have set there the ark in which *is* the covenant of the Lord, which He made with Israel."

12 And he stood before the altar of the Lord in the presence of all the congregation of Israel, and spread out his hands.

13 For Solomon *had* made a bronze scaffold, and set it in the midst of the court of the sanctuary; the length of it *was* five cubits, and the breadth of it five cubits, and the height of it three cubits. And he stood upon it, and fell upon his knees before the whole congregation of Israel, and spread abroad his hands toward heaven,

14 and said, "Lord God of Israel, there is no God like You in heaven, or on the earth; keeping covenant and mercy with Your servants that walk before You with *their* whole heart.

15 Even as You have kept *them* with Your servant David my father, as You have spoken to him in words– you have both spoken with Your mouth, and have fulfilled *it* with Your hands, as it is this day.

16 And now, Lord God of Israel, keep with Your servant David my father the things which You have spoken to him, saying, 'There shall not fail you a man before Me sitting on the throne of Israel, if only your sons will take heed to walk according to the ways of My statutes, as you have walked before Me.'

17 And now, O Lord God of Israel, let Your word be confirmed, I pray, which You have spoken to Your servant David.

18 "For will God indeed dwell with men upon the earth? If the heaven and the heaven of heavens cannot contain You, what then is this house which I have built?

¹⁹ Yet You shall have respect to the prayer of Your servant, and to my petition, O Lord God, so as to respond to the petition and the prayer which Your servant prays before You this day;

²⁰ so that Your eyes should be open over this house by day and by night, towards this place, in which You said that Your name should be called, so as to hear the prayer which Your servant prays towards this house.

²¹ And You shall hear the supplication of Your servant, and of Your people Israel, whatsoever prayers they shall make towards this place, and You shall hear from Your dwelling place out of heaven; indeed, You shall hear, and be merciful.

²² If a man sin against his neighbor, and he bring an oath upon him so as to make him swear, and he should come and swear before the altar in this house;

²³ then shall You hear out of heaven, and do, and judge Your servants, to recompense the transgressor, and to return his ways upon his head, and to justify the righteous, to recompense him according to his righteousness.

²⁴ "And if Your people Israel should be put to the worse before the enemy, if they should sin against You, and *then* turn and confess to Your name, and pray and make supplication before You in this house;

²⁵ then shall You hear out of heaven and shall be merciful to the sins of Your people Israel, and You shall restore them to the land which You gave to them and to their fathers.

²⁶ "When heaven is restrained, and there is no rain, because they shall have sinned against You, and *when* they shall pray towards this place, and praise Your name, and shall turn from their sins, because You shall afflict them;

²⁷ then shall You hear from heaven, and You shall be merciful to the sins of Your servants, and of Your people Israel; for You shall show them the good way in which they shall walk; and You shall send rain upon Your land, which You gave to Your people for an inheritance.

²⁸ "If there should be famine upon the land, if there should be death, a pestilent wind and blight; if there should be locusts and caterpillars, and if the enemy should harass them before their cities; in whatever plague and whatever distress *they may be*;

²⁹ then whatever prayer and whatever supplication shall be made by any man and all Your people Israel, if a man should know his own plague and his own sickness, and should spread forth his hands toward this house;

³⁰ then shall You hear from heaven, out of Your prepared dwelling place, and shall be merciful, and shall recompense to the man according to his ways, as You shall know his heart; for You alone know the heart of the children of men;

³¹ that they may reverence all Your ways all the days which they live upon the face of the land, which You gave to our fathers.

³² And every stranger who is not himself of Your people Israel, and who shall come from a distant land because of Your great name, and Your mighty hand, and Your outstretched arm; when they shall come and worship toward this place–

³³ then shall You hear out of heaven, out of Your prepared dwelling place, and shall do according to all that the stranger shall call upon You for; that all the nations of the earth may know Your name, and that they may fear You, as Your people Israel *do*, and that they may know that Your name is called upon this house which I have built.

³⁴ "And if Your people shall go forth to war against their enemies by the way by which You shall send them, and shall pray to You toward this city which You have chosen, and *toward* the house which I have built to Your name;

³⁵ then shall You hear out of heaven their prayer and their supplication, and maintain their cause.

³⁶ "Whereas if they shall sin against You, (for there is no man who will not sin) and You shall smite them, and deliver them up before their enemies, and they that take them captive shall carry them away into a land of enemies, to a land far off or near;

³⁷ and *if* they shall repent in their land where they were carried captive, and shall also turn and make supplication to You in their captivity, saying, 'We have sinned, we have transgressed, we have wrought unrighteously';

³⁸ and *if* they shall turn to You with all their heart and all their soul in the land of them that carried them *away* captive, and shall pray toward their land which You gave to their fathers, and the city which You have chosen, and the house which I built to Your name–

³⁹ then shall You hear out of heaven, out of Your prepared dwelling place, their prayer and their supplication, and You shall execute justice, and shall be merciful to Your people that sinned against You.

⁴⁰ And now, O Lord, I pray, let Your eyes be opened, and Your ears be attentive to the petition *made in* this place.

⁴¹ "And now, O Lord God, arise into Your resting place, You, and the ark of Your strength; let Your priests, O Lord God, clothe themselves with salvation, and Your sons rejoice in prosperity.

⁴² O Lord God, do not turn away the face of Your anointed: remember the mercies of Your servant David."

2 CHRONICLES CHAPTER 7

¹ And when Solomon had finished praying, then the fire came down from heaven, and devoured the burnt offerings and the sacrifices; and the glory of the Lord filled the house.

² And the priests could not enter into the house of the Lord at that time, for the glory of the Lord filled the house.

³ And all the children of Israel saw the fire descending, and the glory of the Lord was upon the house; and they fell upon their face to the ground on the pavement, and worshipped, and praised the Lord; for *it is* good *to do so*, because His mercy *endures* forever.

⁴ And the king and all the people *were* offering sacrifices before the Lord.

5 And King Solomon offered a sacrifice of twenty-two thousand calves, and a hundred and twenty thousand sheep. So the king and all the people dedicated the house of God.

6 And the priests were standing at their watches, and the Levites with instruments of music of the Lord, belonging to King David, to give thanks before the Lord, for His mercy *endures* forever, with the hymns of David, by their ministry: and the priests were blowing the trumpets before them, and all Israel was standing.

7 And Solomon consecrated the middle of the court that was in the house of the Lord; for he offered there the burnt offerings and the fat of the peace offerings, for the bronze altar which Solomon had made was not sufficient to receive the burnt offerings, and the meat offerings, and the fat.

8 And Solomon kept the feast at that time for seven days, and all Israel with him, a very great assembly, from the entering in of Hamath, and as far as the river of Egypt.

9 And on the eighth day he kept a solemn assembly; for he kept a feast of seven days as the dedication of the altar.

10 And on the twenty-third day of the seventh month he dismissed the people to their tents, rejoicing, and with a glad heart, because of the good deeds which the Lord had done to David, and to Solomon, and to Israel His people.

11 So Solomon finished the house of the Lord, and the king's house. And in whatever Solomon wished in his heart to do in the house of the Lord and in his own house, he prospered.

12 And the Lord appeared to Solomon by night, and said to him, "I have heard your prayer, and I have chosen this place to Myself for a house of sacrifice.

13 If I should restrain the heaven and there should be no rain, and if I should command the locust to devour the trees, and if I should send pestilence upon My people;

14 then if My people, on whom My name is called, should repent, and pray, and seek My face, and turn from their evil ways, I also will hear from heaven, and I will be merciful to their sins, and I will heal their land.

15 And now My eyes shall be open, and My ears attentive to the prayer of this place.

16 And now I have chosen and sanctified this house, that My name should be there forever; and My eyes and My heart shall be there always.

17 And if you will walk before Me as David your father *did*, and will do according to all that I have commanded you, and will keep My ordinances and My judgments;

18 then will I establish the throne of your kingdom, as I covenanted with David your father, saying, 'There shall not fail you a man ruling in Israel.'

19 But if you should turn away, and forsake My ordinances and My commandments, which I have set before you, and go and serve other gods, and worship them;

20 then will I remove them from the land which I gave them; and this house which I have consecrated to My name I will remove out of My sight, and I will make it a proverb and a byword among all nations.

21 And *as for* this lofty house, everyone that passes by it shall be amazed, and shall say, 'Why has the Lord done *thus* to this land, and to this house?'

22 And *men* shall say, 'Because they forsook the Lord God of their fathers, who brought them out of the land of Egypt, and they attached themselves to other gods, and worshiped them, and served them; and therefore He has brought upon them all this evil.'"

2 CHRONICLES CHAPTER 8

Solomon's Additional Achievements

1 And it came to pass after twenty years, in which Solomon built the house of the Lord, and his own house,

2 that Solomon rebuilt the cities which Hiram had given to Solomon, and caused the children of Israel to dwell in them.

3 And Solomon came to Hamath Zobah, and fortified it.

4 And he built Tadmor in the wilderness, and all the strong cities which he built in Hamath.

5 And he built Beth Horon the Upper, and Beth Horon the Lower, strong cities–they had walls, gates, and bars;

6 and Baalath, and all the strong cities which Solomon had, and all his chariot cities, and cities of horsemen, and all things that Solomon desired according to his desire of building, in Jerusalem, and in Lebanon, and in all his kingdom.

7 *As for* all the people that were left of the Hittites and the Amorites and the Perizzites and the Hivites and the Jebusites, who were not of Israel,

8 but were of the children of them whom the children of Israel did not destroy, that were left after them in the land, even them did Solomon make tributaries to this day.

9 But Solomon did not make any of the children of Israel servants in his kingdom; for behold, *they were* warriors and rulers, and mighty *men*, and captains of chariots and horsemen.

10 And these are the chiefs of the officers of King Solomon, two hundred and fifty overseeing the work among the people.

11 And Solomon brought up the daughter of Pharaoh from the City of David to the house which he had built for her; for he said, "My wife shall not dwell in the City of David, the king of Israel, for *the place* is holy into which the ark of the Lord has entered."

12 Then Solomon offered up to the Lord burnt offerings on the altar which he had built to the Lord before the temple,

13 according to the daily rate, to offer up *sacrifices* according to the commandments of Moses, on the Sabbaths, and at the new moons, and at the feasts, three times in the year, at the feast of unleavened bread, and at the feast of weeks, and at the feast of tabernacles.

14 And he established, according to the order of his father David, the courses of the priests, and *that* according to their public ministrations. And the Levites *were appointed* over

their charges, to praise and minister before the priests according to the daily order. And the porters were appointed according to their courses to the different gates; for thus *were* the commandments of David the man of God.

¹⁵ They did not transgress the commandments of the king concerning the priests and the Levites with regard to everything else, and with regard to the treasures.

¹⁶ Now all the work had been prepared from the day when the foundation was laid, until Solomon finished the house of the Lord.

¹⁷ Then Solomon went to Ezion Geber, and to Elath near the sea in the land of Edom.

¹⁸ And Hiram sent ships by the hand of his servants, and servants skilled in naval affairs; and they went with the servants of Solomon to Ophir, and brought from there four hundred and fifty talents of gold, and they came to King Solomon.

2 CHRONICLES CHAPTER 9

Solomon and the Queen of Sheba

¹ Now the queen of Sheba heard *of* the name of Solomon, and she came to Jerusalem with a very large entourage, to test Solomon with hard questions, and *she had* camels bearing spices in abundance, and gold, and precious stones. And she came to Solomon, and told him all that was in her mind.

² And Solomon answered all her questions; and there did not pass one word from Solomon which he did not tell her.

³ And the queen of Sheba saw the wisdom of Solomon, and the house which he had built,

⁴ and the food on his tables, and the sitting of his servants, and the standing of his ministers, and their garments; and his cupbearers, and their apparel; and the burnt offerings which he offered up in the house of the Lord; and she marveled.

⁵ And she said to the king, "*It was* a true report which I heard in my land concerning your words, and concerning your wisdom. ⁶ Yet I did not believe the reports until I came, and my eyes have seen; and behold, not *even* half of the abundance of your wisdom was told to me! You have exceeded the report which I heard.

⁷ Blessed *are* your men, blessed *are* these your servants, who stand before you continually, and hear your wisdom.

⁸ Blessed be the Lord your God, who took pleasure in you, to set you upon His throne as king, to the Lord your God; forasmuch as the Lord your God loved Israel to establish them forever, therefore He has set you over them as king, to execute judgment and justice."

⁹ And she gave the king a hundred and twenty talents of gold, and spices in very great abundance, and precious stones; and there were not *any where else* such spices as those which the queen of Sheba gave King Solomon.

¹⁰ And the servants of Solomon and the servants of Hiram brought gold to Solomon out of Ophir, and pine timber, and precious stones.

¹¹ And the king made of the pine timber steps to the house of the Lord, and to the king's house, and harps and lutes for the singers; and such were not seen before in the land of Judah.

¹² And King Solomon gave to the queen of Sheba all that she requested, even *much more than* she brought to King Solomon. And she returned to her *own* land.

Solomon's Great Wealth

¹³ And the weight of the gold that was brought to Solomon in one year was six hundred and sixty-six talents of gold,

¹⁴ besides what the men who were regularly appointed and the merchants brought, and all the kings of Arabia and princes of the land: all brought gold and silver to King Solomon.

¹⁵ And King Solomon made two hundred shields of hammered gold; there were six hundred *shekels* of pure gold to one shield.

¹⁶ And three hundred buckles of hammered gold; *the weight* of three hundred gold shekels went to one buckler. And the king placed them in the house of the Forest of Lebanon.

¹⁷ And the king made a great throne of ivory, and he gilded it with pure gold.

¹⁸ And *there were* six steps to the throne, riveted with gold, and elbows on either side of the seat of the throne, and two lions standing by the elbows;

¹⁹ and twelve lions standing there on the six steps on each side. There was not the like in any *other* kingdom.

²⁰ And all King Solomon's vessels were of gold, and all the vessels of the house of the Forest of Lebanon were covered with gold: silver was not regarded as anything in the days of Solomon.

²¹ For a ship went for the king to Tarshish with the servants of Hiram. Once every three years vessels came from Tarshish to the king, laden with gold, silver, ivory, and apes.

²² And Solomon exceeded all *other* kings both in riches and wisdom.

²³ And all the kings of the earth sought the presence of Solomon, to hear his wisdom, which God had put in his heart. ²⁴ And everyone brought their gifts–silver vessels and golden vessels, clothing, myrrh, spices, horses and mules, a set rate every year.

²⁵ And Solomon had four thousand mares for chariots, and twelve thousand horsemen; and he put them in the chariot cities, and with the king in Jerusalem.

²⁶ And he ruled over all the kings from the river, even to the land of the Philistines, and to the borders of Egypt.

²⁷ And the king made gold and silver in Jerusalem as stones, and cedars as the sycamore trees in the plain for abundance.

²⁸ And Solomon imported horses from Egypt, and from every *other* country.

Death of Solomon

[29] And the rest of the acts of Solomon, the first and the last, behold, these are written in the words of Nathan the prophet, and in the words of Ahijah the Shilonite, and in the visions of Joel the seer concerning Jeroboam the son of Nebat.

[30] And Solomon reigned over all Israel forty years.

[31] And Solomon fell asleep, and they buried him in the city of David his father. And Rehoboam his son reigned in his place.

2 CHRONICLES CHAPTER 10

The Revolt Against Rehoboam

[1] And Rehoboam went to Shechem, for all Israel went to Shechem to make him king.

[2] And it came to pass when Jeroboam the son of Nebat heard *it*, (now he was in Egypt, for he had fled there from the face of King Solomon, and Jeroboam dwelt in Egypt) that Jeroboam returned out of Egypt.

[3] And they sent and called him. And Jeroboam and all the congregation came to Rehoboam, saying,

[4] "Your father made our yoke grievous. Now then, lighten the burden of your father's grievous rule, and of his heavy yoke which he put upon us, and we will serve you."

[5] And he said to them, "Go away for three days, and *then* come to me." So the people departed.

[6] And King Rehoboam assembled the elders that stood before his father Solomon in his lifetime, saying, "How do you counsel *me* to return an answer to this people?"

[7] And they spoke to him, saying, "If you would this day befriend this people, and be kind to them, and speak to them good words, then will they be your servants forever."

[8] But he forsook the advice of the old men, who took counsel with him, and he took counsel with the young men who had been brought up with him, who stood before him.

[9] And he said to them, "What do you advise that I should answer this people, who spoke to me, saying, 'Lighten the burden which your father laid upon us?'"

[10] And the young men that had been brought up with him spoke to him, saying, "Thus shall you speak to the people that spoke to you, saying, 'Your father made our yoke heavy, therefore lighten *some of it* for us'; thus shall you say: 'My little finger *shall be* thicker than my father's loins.

[11] And whereas my father chastised you with a heavy yoke, I will also add to your yoke. My father chastised you with whips, and I will chastise you with scorpions.'"

[12] And Jeroboam and all the people came to Rehoboam on the third day, as the king had spoken, saying, "Return to me on the third day."

[13] And the king answered harshly. And King Rehoboam forsook the counsel of the old men,

[14] and spoke to them according to the counsel of the young men, saying, "My father made your yoke heavy, but I will add to it; my father chastised you with whips, but I will chastise you with scorpions."

[15] And the king would not listen to the people, for there was a change *of their minds* from God, saying, "The Lord has confirmed His word, which he spoke by the hand of Ahijah the Shilonite concerning Jeroboam the son of Nebat, and *concerning* all Israel";

[16] for the king did not listen to them. And the people answered the king, saying, "What portion have we in David, or *what* inheritance *have we* in the son of Jesse? To your tents, O Israel! See now to your own house, O David!" So all Israel went to their tents.

[17] But the men of Israel, even those who dwelt in the cities of Judah, *remained* and made Rehoboam king over them.

[18] And King Rehoboam sent Hadoram to them, who was over the tribute. And the children of Israel stoned him with stones, and he died. And King Rehoboam hastened to mount *his* chariot, *and* to flee to Jerusalem.

[19] So Israel rebelled against the house of David until this day.

2 CHRONICLES CHAPTER 11

[1] And Rehoboam came to Jerusalem. And he assembled Judah and Benjamin, a hundred and eighty thousand young men fit for war, and he waged war with Israel to recover the kingdom to Rehoboam.

[2] Then the word of the Lord came to Shemaiah the man of God, saying,

[3] "Speak to Rehoboam the *son* of Solomon, and to all Judah and Benjamin, saying,

[4] 'Thus says the Lord: "You shall not go up, and you shall not war against your brothers: return, everyone to his house; for this thing is from Me."'" So they listened to the word of the Lord, and returned from going against Jeroboam.

Rehoboam Fortifies the Cities

[5] And Rehoboam dwelt in Jerusalem, and he built walled cities in Judea.

[6] And he built Bethlehem, Etam, Tekoa,

[7] Beth Zur, Sochoh, Adullam,

[8] Gath, Mareshah, Ziph,

[9] Adoraim, Lachish, Azekah,

[10] Zorah, Aijalon, and Hebron, which belong to Judah and Benjamin, walled cities.

[11] And he fortified them with walls, and placed in them captains, and stores of provisions, oil and wine,

[12] shields and spears in every city, and he fortified them very strongly, and he had Judah and Benjamin on his side .

Priests and Levites Move to Judah

[13] And the priests and the Levites who were in all Israel were gathered to him out of all the coasts.

14 For the Levites left the tents of their possession, and went to Judah to Jerusalem, because Jeroboam and his sons had rejected them so that they should not minister to the Lord.

15 And he made for himself priests of the high places, and for the idols, and for the vanities, and for the calves which Jeroboam made.

16 And he cast out from the tribes of Israel those who set their heart to seek the Lord God of Israel. And they came to Jerusalem, to sacrifice to the Lord God of their fathers.

17 And they strengthened the kingdom of Judah; and *Judah* strengthened Rehoboam the *son* of Solomon for three years, for he walked three years in the ways of David and Solomon.

The Family of Rehoboam

18 And Rehoboam took to himself for a wife, Mahalath daughter of Jerimoth the son of David, and Abihail daughter of Eliah the son of Jesse.

19 And she bore him sons: Jeush, Shamariah, and Zaham.

20 And afterwards he took to himself Maachah, granddaughter of Absalom; and she bore him Abijah, Attai, Ziza, and Shelomith.

21 And Rehoboam loved Maachah the daughter of Absalom more than all his wives and all his concubines; for he had eighteen wives and sixty concubines. And he fathered twenty-eight sons, and sixty daughters.

22 And he made Abijah the son of Maachah chief, *even a* leader among his brothers, for he intended to make him king.

23 And he was exalted beyond all his *other* sons in all the coasts of Judah and Benjamin, and in the strong cities; and he gave them provisions in great abundance; and he desired many wives.

2 CHRONICLES CHAPTER 12

Egypt Attacks Judah

1 And it came to pass when the kingdom of Rehoboam was established, and when he had grown strong, *that* he forsook the commandments of the Lord, and all Israel with him.

2 And it came to pass in the fifth year of the reign of Rehoboam, *that* Shishak king of Egypt came up against Jerusalem, because they had sinned against the Lord,

3 with twelve hundred chariots, and sixty thousand horses. And there was no number of the multitude that came with him from Egypt: Libyans, *the* Sukkiim, and *the* Ethiopians.

4 And they obtained possession of the strong cities, which were in Judah, and came to Jerusalem.

5 And Shemaiah the prophet came to Rehoboam, and to the princes of Judah that were gathered to Jerusalem for fear of Shishak, and said to them, "Thus says the Lord: 'You have left Me, and I will leave you in the hand of Shishak.'"

6 And the elders of Israel and the king were ashamed, and said, "The Lord *is* righteous."

7 And when the Lord saw that they repented, then the word of the Lord came to Shemaiah, saying, "They have repented; I will not destroy them, but I will set them in safety for a little while, and My wrath shall not be poured out on Jerusalem.

8 Nevertheless they shall be servants, and know My service, and the service of the kings of the earth."

9 So Shishak king of Egypt went up against Jerusalem, and took the treasures that were in the house of the Lord, and the treasures that were in the king's house: he took all, and he took the golden shields which Solomon had made.

10 And King Rehoboam made bronze shields in their place. And Shishak set over him captains of footmen, as keepers of the gate of the king.

11 And it came to pass, when the king went into the house of the Lord, the guards and the footmen went in, and those that returned to meet the footmen.

12 And when he repented, the anger of the Lord turned from him, and did not destroy him utterly; for there were good things in Judah.

13 So King Rehoboam strengthened *himself* in Jerusalem, and reigned. And Rehoboam was forty-one years old when he began to reign, and he reigned seventeen years in Jerusalem, in the city which the Lord chose out of all the tribes of the children of Israel, to call His name there; and his mother's name was Naamah the Ammonitess.

14 And he did evil, for he did not set his heart on seeking the Lord.

15 And the acts of Rehoboam, the first and the last, behold, are they not written in the book of Shemaiah the prophet, and Iddo the seer, with his achievements?

16 And Rehoboam made war with Jeroboam all *his* days. And Rehoboam died with his fathers, and was buried in the city of David; and Abijah his son reigned in his place.

2 CHRONICLES CHAPTER 13

Abijah Reigns in Judah

1 In the eighteenth year of the reign of Jeroboam, Abijah began to reign over Judah.

2 He reigned three years in Jerusalem. And his mother's name *was* Maachah, daughter of Uriel of Gibeah. And there was war between Abijah and Jeroboam.

3 And Abijah set the battle in array with an army, with mighty men of war, *even* four hundred thousand mighty men. And Jeroboam set the battle in array against him with eight hundred thousand, *they were* mighty warriors of the army.

4 And Abijah rose up from Mount Zemaraim, which is in Mount Ephraim, and said, "Hear me, Jeroboam and all Israel:

5 *Is it* not for you to know that the Lord God of Israel has given a king over Israel forever to David, and to his sons, by a covenant of salt?

⁶ Yet Jeroboam the *son* of Nebat, the servant of Solomon *the son* of David, has risen up, and has revolted from his master.

⁷ And there are gathered to him pestilent men, transgressors, and he has risen up against Rehoboam the *son* of Solomon, while Rehoboam was young and fearful in heart, and he could not withstand him.

⁸ And now you profess to resist the kingdom of the Lord in the hand of the sons of David, and you *are* a great multitude, and with you are golden calves, which Jeroboam made you, as gods.

⁹ Did you not cast out the priests of the Lord, the sons of Aaron, and the Levites, and make for yourselves priests of the people of any *other* land? Whoever came to consecrate himself with a calf of the herd and seven rams, he then became a priest to that which is no god.

¹⁰ But we have not forsaken the Lord our God, and His priests, the sons of Aaron, and the Levites, ministers unto the Lord; and in their daily courses

¹¹ they sacrifice to the Lord burnt offerings, morning and evening, and compound incense, and *set* the showbread on the pure table; and *there is* the golden lampstand, and the lamps for burning, to light in the evening; for we keep the charge of the Lord God of our fathers; but you have forsaken Him.

¹² And behold, the Lord and His priests are with us at our head, and the signal trumpets to sound an alarm over us. Children of Israel, do not fight against the Lord God of our fathers; for you shall not prosper."

¹³ Now Jeroboam had caused an ambush to come round upon him from behind; and he *himself* was before Judah, and the ambush behind.

¹⁴ And Judah looked back, and behold, the battle *was* against them, ahead and behind. And they cried to the Lord, and the priests sounded with the trumpets.

¹⁵ And the men of Judah shouted. And it came to pass, when the men of Judah shouted, that the Lord struck Jeroboam and Israel before Abijah and Judah.

¹⁶ And the children of Israel fled from before Judah; and the Lord delivered them into their hands.

¹⁷ And Abijah and his people struck them with a great slaughter; and there fell slain of Israel five hundred thousand mighty men.

¹⁸ So the children of Israel were brought low in that day, and the children of Judah prevailed, because they trusted on the Lord God of their fathers.

¹⁹ And Abijah pursued after Jeroboam, and he took from him the cities, Bethel and her towns, and Jeshanah and her towns, and Ephron and her towns.

²⁰ And Jeroboam did not recover strength again all the days of Abijah. And the Lord struck him, and he died.

²¹ But Abijah strengthened himself, and took to himself fourteen wives, and he fathered twenty-two sons, and sixteen daughters.

²² And the rest of the acts of Abijah, and his deeds, and his sayings, are written in the book of the prophet Iddo.

CHRONICLES CHAPTER 14

¹ And Abijah rested with his fathers, and they buried him in the city of David; and Asa his son reigned in his place. In the days of Asa the land of Judah had rest for ten years.

Asa Reigns in Judah

² And he did that which was good and right in the sight of the Lord his God.

³ And he removed the altars of the strange *gods*, and the high places, and broke the pillars in pieces, and cut down the groves;

⁴ and he told Judah to seek earnestly the Lord God of their fathers, and to perform the law and the commandments.

⁵ And he removed from all the cities of Judah the altars and the idols, and established in quietness

⁶ fortified cities in the land of Judah; for the land was quiet, and he had no war in these years; for the Lord gave him rest.

⁷ And he said to Judah, "Let us fortify these cities, and make walls, and towers, and gates, and bars; we shall prevail over the land, for as we have sought out the Lord our God, He has sought out us, and has given us rest round about, and prospered us."

⁸ And Asa had a force of armed men bearing shields and spears in the land of Judah, *even* three hundred thousand, and in the land of Benjamin two hundred and eighty thousand targeteers and archers; all these were mighty warriors.

⁹ And Zerah the Ethiopian went out against them, with a force of a million, and three hundred chariots; and came to Mareshah.

¹⁰ And Asa went out to meet him, and set the battle in array in the valley north of Mareshah.

¹¹ And Asa cried to the Lord his God, and said, "O Lord, it is not impossible with You to save by many or by few: strengthen us, O Lord our God; for we trust in You, and in Your name we have come up against this great multitude. O Lord our God, let not man prevail against You."

¹² And the Lord struck the Ethiopians before Judah, and the Ethiopians fled.

¹³ And Asa and his people pursued them to Gerar; and the Ethiopians fell, so that they could not recover themselves; for they were crushed before the Lord, and before His army; and they took many spoils.

¹⁴ And they destroyed their towns roundabout Gerar; for the terror of the Lord was upon them; and they plundered all their cities, for they had much spoil.

¹⁵ Also they destroyed the tents of cattle, and the Alimazons, and took many sheep and camels, and returned to Jerusalem.

2 CHRONICLES CHAPTER 15

The Reforms of Asa

[1] And the Spirit of the Lord came upon Azariah the son of Oded.

[2] And he went out to meet Asa, and all Judah and Benjamin, and said, "Hear me, Asa, and all Judah and Benjamin. The Lord *is* with you, while you are with Him; and if you seek Him out, He will be found by you; but if you forsake Him, He will forsake you.

[3] And Israel *has been* a long time without the true God, and without a priest to expound *the truth*, and without the law.

[4] But He shall turn them to the Lord God of Israel, and He will be found of them.

[5] And in that time there is no peace to one going out, or to one coming in, for the terror of the Lord is upon all that inhabit the land.

[6] And nation shall fight against nation, and city against city; for God has confounded them with every *kind of* affliction.

[7] But be strong, and let not your hands be weakened, for there is a reward for your work."

[8] And when *Asa* heard these words, and the prophesy of Oded the prophet, then he strengthened himself, and cast out the abominations from all the land of Judah and Benjamin, and from the cities which Jeroboam possessed, in Mount Ephraim, and he renewed the altar of the Lord, which was before the temple of the Lord.

[9] And he assembled Judah and Benjamin, and the strangers that dwelt with him, of Ephraim, and of Manasseh, and of Simeon; for many of Israel were joined to him, when they saw that the Lord his God was with him.

[10] And they assembled at Jerusalem in the third month, in the fifteenth year of the reign of Asa.

[11] And they sacrificed to the Lord in that day of the spoils which they brought, seven hundred calves and seven thousand sheep.

[12] And they entered into a covenant, that they should seek the Lord God of their fathers with all their heart and with all their soul.

[13] And that whoever should not seek the Lord God of Israel should die, whether young or old, whether man or woman.

[14] And they swore to the Lord with a loud voice, and with trumpets, and with cornets.

[15] And all Judah rejoiced concerning the oath; for they swore with all their heart, and they sought Him with all their desires, and He was found of them. And the Lord gave them rest round about.

[16] And he removed Maachah his mother from being priestess to Asherah; and he cut down the idol, and burned it in the Brook of Kidron.

[17] But they did not remove the high places; they still existed in Israel. Nevertheless the heart of Asa was perfect all of his days.

[18] And he brought in the holy things of David his father, and the holy things of the house of God, silver, and gold, and vessels.

[19] And there was no war *waged* with him until the thirty-fifth year of the reign of Asa.

2 CHRONICLES CHAPTER 16

Asa's Treaty with Syria

[1] And in the thirty-eighth year of the reign of Asa, the king of Israel went up against Judah, and built Ramah, so as not to allow any to go out or come in to Asa king of Judah.

[2] And Asa took silver and gold out of the treasures of the house of the Lord, and of the king's house, and sent *them* to the son of Hadad king of Syria, who dwelt in Damascus, saying,

[3] "Make a covenant between me and you, and between my father and your father: behold, I have sent you gold and silver. Come, turn away Baasha king of Israel from me, and let him depart from me."

[4] And the son of Hadad listened to King Asa, and sent the captains of his army against the cities of Israel. And they attacked Ijon, Dan, and Abel Maim, and all the country round about Naphtali.

[5] And it came to pass when Baasha heard *it, that* he left off building Ramah, and put a stop to his work.

[6] Then King Asa took all Judah, and took the stones of Ramah, and its timber, *with* which Baasah *had* built; and he built with them Geba and Mizpah.

[7] And at that time Hanani the prophet came to Asa king of Judah, and said to him, "Because you have trusted on the king of Syria, and did not trust on the Lord your God, therefore the army of Syria has escaped out of your hand.

[8] Were not the Ethiopians and Libyans a great force, in courage, in horsemen, and in great numbers? And did He not deliver them into your hands, because you trusted in the Lord?

[9] For the eyes of the Lord run to and fro throughout all the earth, to strengthen every heart that is perfect toward Him. In this you have done foolishly; from now on there shall be war with you."

[10] And Asa was angry with the prophet, and put him in prison, for he was angry at this. And Asa oppressed some of the people at that time.

[11] And behold, the acts of Asa, the first and the last, *are* written in the book of the kings of Judah and Israel.

[12] And Asa was diseased *in* his feet in the thirty-ninth year of his reign, until he was very ill, but in his disease he did not seek the Lord, but rather the physicians.

[13] And Asa slept with his fathers, and died in the fortieth year of his reign.

[14] And they buried him in the tomb which he had dug for himself in the city of David, and they laid him on a bed, and

filled *it* with spices and *all* kinds of perfumes of the apothecaries; and they made for him a very great funeral.

2 CHRONICLES CHAPTER 17

Jehoshaphat Reigns in Judah

[1] And Jehoshaphat his son reigned in his place, *and* he strengthened himself against Israel.

[2] And he put garrisons in all the strong cities of Judah, and appointed captains in all the cities of Judah, and in the cities of Ephraim, which Asa his father had taken.

[3] And the Lord was with Jehoshaphat, for he walked in the first ways of his father, and did not seek to idols;

[4] but he sought the Lord God of his father, and walked in the commandments of his father, and not according to the works of Israel.

[5] And the Lord prospered the kingdom in his hand; and all Judah gave gifts to Jehoshaphat; and he had great wealth and glory.

[6] And his heart was exalted in the way of the Lord; and he removed the high places and the groves from the land of Judah.

[7] And in the third year of his reign, he sent his chief men and his mighty men, Obadiah, Zechariah, Nethaneel and Michaiah, to teach in the cities of Judah.

[8] And with them *were* the Levites, Shemaiah, Nethaniah, Zebadiah, Asahel, Shemiramoth, Jehonathan, Adonijah, Tobijah and Tobadonijah, Levites, and with them Elishama and Jehoram, the priests.

[9] And they taught in Judah, and *there was* with them the Book of the Law of the Lord, and they passed through the cities of Judah, and taught the people.

[10] And the terror of the Lord was upon all the kingdoms of the land round about Judah, and they made no war against Jehoshaphat.

[11] And *some* of the Philistines brought to Jehoshaphat gifts, and silver, and presents; and the Arabians brought him seven thousand seven hundred rams.

[12] And Jehoshaphat increased in greatness exceedingly, and built fortresses in Judea, and strong cities.

[13] And he had many works in Judea. And the mighty men of war, *the men* of strength, *were* in Jerusalem.

[14] And this *is* their number according to the houses of their fathers; even the captains of thousands in Judah *were*: Adnah the chief, and with him mighty men of strength, three hundred thousand.

[15] And after him, Jehohanan the captain, and with him two hundred eighty thousand.

[16] And after him Amasiah the *son* of Zichri, who was zealous for the Lord; and with him two hundred thousand mighty men of strength.

[17] And out of Benjamin *there was* a mighty man of strength, even Eliada, and with him two hundred thousand archers and targeteers.

[18] And after him Jehozabad, and with him a hundred and eighty thousand mighty men of war.

[19] These were the king's servants besides those whom the king put in the strong cities in all Judea.

2 CHRONICLES CHAPTER 18

Micaiah Warns Ahab

[1] And Jehoshaphat had great wealth and glory, and he connected himself by marriage with the house of Ahab.

[2] And he went down after some years to Ahab in Samaria. And Ahab slaughtered for him sheep and calves, in abundance, and for the people with him, and he much desired him to go up with him to Ramoth of the country of Gilead.

[3] And Ahab king of Israel said to Jehoshaphat king of Judah, "Will you go with me to Ramoth of the country of Gilead?" And he said to him, "As I *am*, so also *are* you, as your people, *so* also *are* my people with you for the war."

[4] And Jehoshaphat said to the king of Israel, "Please inquire of the Lord today."

[5] And the king of Israel gathered the prophets, four hundred men, and said to them, "Shall I go to Ramoth Gilead to battle, or shall I refrain?" And they said, "Go up, and God shall deliver *it* into the hands of the king."

[6] And Jehoshaphat said, "Is there not still a prophet of the Lord here, that we may inquire of Him?"

[7] And the king of Israel said to Jehoshaphat, "There is yet one man by whom to inquire of the Lord, but I hate him, for he does not prophesy concerning me for good, for all his days *are* for evil: this *is* Micaiah the son of Imla." And Jehoshaphat said, "Let not the king say such things!"

[8] And the king called a eunuch, and said, "*Fetch* quickly Micaiah the son of Imla."

[9] And the king of Israel and Jehoshaphat king of Judah were sitting each on his throne, and clothed in their robes, sitting in the open space at the entrance of the gate of Samaria; and all the prophets were prophesying before them.

[10] And Zedekiah son of Chenaanah made for himself iron horns, and said, "Thus says the Lord: 'With these you shall thrust Syria until they are destroyed.'"

[11] And all the prophets prophesied so, saying, "Go up to Ramoth Gilead, and you shall prosper; and the Lord shall deliver it into the hands of the king."

[12] And the messenger that went to call Micaiah spoke to him, saying, "Behold, the prophets have spoken favorably concerning the king with one accord; therefore, please let your words be as *the words* of one of them, and speak good things."

[13] And Micaiah said, "*As* the Lord lives, whatever God shall say to me, that will I speak."

[14] And he came to the king, and the king said to him, "Micaiah, shall I go up to Ramoth Gilead to battle, or shall I

refrain?" And he said, "Go up, and you shall prosper, and they shall be given into your hands."

15 And the king said to him, "How often shall I solemnly charge you that you speak to me nothing but truth in the name of the Lord?"

16 And he said, "I saw Israel scattered on the mountains, as sheep without a shepherd. And the Lord said, 'These have no commander; let each return to his home in peace.'"

17 And the king of Israel said to Jehoshaphat, "*See*, did I not say to you that he would not prophesy good concerning me, but evil?"

18 But he said, "Not so. Hear the word of the Lord: I saw the Lord sitting on His throne, and all the host of heaven stood by on His right hand and on His left.

19 And the Lord said, 'Who will deceive Ahab king of Israel, that he may go up, and fall in Ramoth Gilead?' And one spoke this way, and another spoke that way.

20 And there came forth a spirit, and stood before the Lord, and said, 'I will deceive him.' And the Lord said, 'How?'

21 And he said, 'I will go forth, and will be a lying spirit in the mouth of all his prophets.' And *the Lord* said, 'You shall deceive *him*, and shall prevail: go forth, and do so.'

22 And now, behold, the Lord has put a false spirit in the mouth of these your prophets, and the Lord has spoken evil against you."

23 Then Zedekiah the son of Chenaanah drew near, and struck Micaiah on the cheek, and said to him, "By what way did the Spirit of the Lord pass from me to speak to you?"

24 And Micaiah said, "Behold, you shall see in that day, when you shall go from chamber to chamber to hide yourself."

25 And the king of Israel said, "Take Micaiah, and carry him back to Amon the governor of the city, and to Joash the captain, the king's son;

26 and you shall say, 'Thus said the king: "Put this fellow into the prison house, and let him eat the bread of affliction, and *drink* the water of affliction, until I return in peace."'"

27 And Micaiah said, "If you do at all return in peace, the Lord has not spoken by me." And he said, "Hear, all you people."

Ahab Dies in Battle

28 So the king of Israel, and Jehoshaphat king of Judah, went up to Ramoth Gilead.

29 And the king of Israel said to Jehoshaphat, "Disguise me, and I will enter into the battle; but you put on my robes." So the king of Israel disguised himself, and entered into the battle.

30 Now the king of Syria had commanded the captains of the chariots that were with him, saying, "Fight against neither small nor great, but only against the king of Israel."

31 And it came to pass, when the captains of the chariots saw Jehoshaphat, that they said, "It is the king of Israel." And they compassed him round about to fight against him.

And Jehoshaphat cried out, and the Lord delivered him; and God turned them away from him.

32 And it came to pass, when the captains of the chariots saw that it was not the king of Israel, that they turned away from him.

33 And a man drew a bow with a good aim, and struck the king of Israel between the lungs and the breastplate. And *Ahab* said to the charioteer, "Turn your hand, drive me out of the battle, for I am wounded."

34 And the battle turned in that day; and the king of Israel remained on the chariot against Syria until evening, and he died at sunset.

2 CHRONICLES CHAPTER 19

1 And Jehoshaphat king of Judah returned to his house at Jerusalem.

2 And Jehu the prophet, the son of Hanani went out to meet him, and said to him, "King Jehoshaphat, do you help a sinner, or act friendly towards one hated of the Lord? Therefore wrath has come upon you from the Lord.

3 Nevertheless *some* good things have been found in you, forasmuch as you did remove the groves from the land of Judah, and you directed your heart to seek after the Lord."

The Reforms of Jehoshaphat

4 And Jehoshaphat dwelt in Jerusalem. And he again went out among the people from Beersheba to Mount Ephraim, and turned them back to the Lord God of their fathers.

5 And he appointed judges in all the strong cities of Judah, city by city.

6 And he said to the judges, "Consider what you do, for you judge not for man, but for the Lord, and with you are matters of judgment.

7 And now let the fear of the Lord be upon you, and be wary, and do *your duty*; for there is no unrighteousness with the Lord our God, neither *is it for Him* to be a respector of persons, or to take bribes."

8 Moreover Jehoshaphat appointed in Jerusalem some of the priests and Levites, and heads of houses of Israel, for the judgment of the Lord, and to judge the inhabitants of Jerusalem.

9 And he commanded them, saying, "Thus shall you do in the fear of the Lord, in truth and with a perfect heart.

10 Whatsoever man of your brothers that dwell in their cities *shall bring* the cause that comes before you, between blood *and* blood, and between precept and commandment, and ordinances and judgments, you shall even decide for them; so they shall not sin against the Lord, and there shall not be wrath upon you, and upon your brothers. Thus you shall do, and you shall not sin.

11 And behold, Amariah the priest is head over you in every matter of the Lord; and Zebadiah the son of Ishmael is head over the house of Judah in every matter of the king; and the

scribes and Levites are before you: be strong and active, and the Lord shall be with the upright."

2 CHRONICLES CHAPTER 20

Invasion from the East

[1] And it came about after this, *that* the children of Moab and the children of Ammon, and with them *some* of the Mineans, came up against Jehoshaphat to battle.

[2] And they came and told Jehoshaphat, saying, "A great multitude is coming against you from Syria, from beyond the sea; and behold, they are in Hazazon Tamar, which is En Gedi."

[3] And Jehoshaphat was alarmed, and set his face to seek the Lord earnestly, and he proclaimed a fast in all Judah.

[4] And Judah gathered themselves together to seek after the Lord; even from all the cities of Judah they came to seek the Lord.

Jehoshaphat's Prayer and Victory

[5] And Jehoshaphat stood up in the assembly of Judah in Jerusalem, in the house of the Lord, in front of the new court. [6] And he said, "O Lord God of my fathers, are You not God in heaven above, and are You not Lord of all the kingdoms of the nations? And *is there* not in Your hand the might of dominion, and there is no one who can resist You?

[7] Are You not the Lord that destroyed the inhabitants of this land before the face of Your people Israel, and gave it to Your beloved descendants of Abraham forever?

[8] And they dwelt in it, and built in it a sanctuary to Your name, saying,

[9] 'If there should come upon us evils, sword, judgment, pestilence, *or* famine, we will stand before this house, and before You, (for Your name *is* upon this house) and we will cry to You because of the affliction, and You shall hear, and deliver.'

[10] And now, behold, the children of Ammon and Moab and Mount Seir, with regard to whom You did not permit Israel to pass through their border, when they had come out of the land of Egypt, (for they turned away from them, and did not destroy them)–

[11] yet now, behold, they make attempts against us, to come forth to cast us out from our inheritance which You have given to us.

[12] O Lord our God, will You not judge them? For we have no strength to resist this great multitude that has come against us; and we do not know what we shall do to them, but our eyes are toward You."

[13] And all of Judah was standing before the Lord, and their children, and their wives.

[14] Then the Spirit of the Lord came upon Jahaziel the *son of* Zechariah, of the sons of Benaiah, of the sons of Jeiel, of the sons of Matthaniah the Levite, of the sons of Asaph, in the assembly.

[15] And he said, "Hear, all Judah, and you inhabitants of Jerusalem, and King Jehoshaphat; Thus says the Lord to you, even you: 'Do not fear, neither be alarmed, before all this great multitude; for the battle is not yours, but God's.

[16] Tomorrow go down against them. Behold, they come up by the Ascent of Ziz, and you shall find them at the extremity of the river of the Wilderness of Jeruel.

[17] It is not for you to fight. Understand these things, and see the deliverance of the Lord with you, Judah and Jerusalem: fear not, neither be afraid to go forth tomorrow to meet them; and the Lord shall be with you.'"

[18] And Jehoshaphat bowed with his face *to the ground* with all Judah and the inhabitants of Jerusalem, *and* they fell before the Lord, to worship the Lord.

[19] And the Levites of the children of Kohath, and *those* of the sons of Korah, rose up to praise the Lord God of Israel with a loud voice on high.

[20] And they rose early in the morning and went out to the Wilderness of Tekoa. And as they went out, Jehoshaphat stood and cried, and said, "Hear me, O Judah, and you inhabitants of Jerusalem; put your trust in the Lord God, and your trust shall be honored; trust in His prophet, and you shall prosper."

[21] And he took counsel with the people, and set appointed men to sing psalms and praises, to give thanks, and sing the holy songs of praise in going forth before the army. And they said, "Give thanks to the Lord, for His mercy *endures* forever."

[22] And when they began the praise and thanksgiving, the Lord caused the children of Ammon to fight against Moab, and *the inhabitants of* Mount Seir that came out against Judah; and they were defeated.

[23] Then the children of Ammon and Moab rose up against the inhabitants of Mount Seir, to destroy and consume them. And when they had made an end of *destroying* the inhabitants of Seir, they rose up against one another so that they were utterly destroyed.

[24] And Judah came to the watchtower of the wilderness, and looked, and saw the multitude, and behold, *they were* all fallen dead upon the earth; not one escaped.

[25] And Jehoshaphat and his people went out to plunder them, and they found much cattle, and furniture, and spoils, and precious things. And they plundered them, and they were three days gathering the spoil, for it was abundant.

[26] And it came to pass on the fourth day they were gathered to the Valley of Blessing; for there they blessed the Lord. Therefore they called the name of the place the Valley of Blessing, until this day.

[27] And all the men of Judah returned to Jerusalem, and Jehoshaphat led them with great joy; for the Lord gave them joy over their enemies.

[28] And they entered into Jerusalem with lutes and harps and trumpets, *going* into the house of the lord.

²⁹ And the terror of the Lord was upon all the kingdoms of the land, when they heard that the Lord fought against the enemies of Israel.

³⁰ And the kingdom of Jehoshaphat was at peace; and his God gave him rest round about.

³¹ And Jehoshaphat reigned over Judah, being thirty-five years *old* when he began to reign, and he reigned twenty-five years in Jerusalem; and his mother's name was Azubah, daughter of Shilhi.

³² And he walked in the ways of his father Asa, and did not turn aside from doing that which was right in the sight of the Lord. ³³ Nevertheless the high places still remained; and as yet the people did not direct their heart to the Lord God of their fathers.

³⁴ And the rest of the acts of Jehoshaphat, the first and the last, behold, they are written in the history of Jehu *the son* of Hanani, who ¹wrote the book of the kings of Israel.

³⁵ And afterwards Jehoshaphat king of Judah entered into an alliance with Ahaziah king of Israel, (now this was an unrighteous man)

³⁶ by acting *with* and going to him, to build ships to go to Tarshish. And he built ships in Ezion Geber.

³⁷ But Eliezer the *son* of Dodavah of Mareshah prophesied against Jehoshaphat, saying, "Because you have allied yourself with Ahaziah, the Lord has broken your work, and your vessels have been wrecked." And they could not go to Tarshish.

2 CHRONICLES CHAPTER 21

Jehoram Reigns in Judah

¹ And Jehoshaphat slept with his fathers, and was buried in the city of David; and Jehoram his son reigned in his place.

² And he had brothers, the six sons of Jehoshaphat: Azariah, Jehiel, Zechariah, Azaryahu, Michael, and Shephatiah; all these *were* the sons of Jehoshaphat king of Judah.

³ And their father gave them many gifts, silver and gold and arms, together with fortified cities in Judah; but he gave the kingdom to Jehoram, for he *was* the firstborn.

⁴ And Jehoram entered upon his kingdom, and strengthened himself, and killed all his brothers with the sword, and also *others* of the princes of Israel.

⁵ Jehoram was thirty-two years old when he succeeded to his kingdom, and he reigned eight years in Jerusalem.

⁶ And he walked in the way of the kings of Israel, as did the house of Ahab; for one of Ahab's daughters was his wife; and he did that which was evil in the sight of the Lord.

⁷ Nevertheless the Lord would not utterly destroy the house of David, because of the covenant which He made with

---

¹ kate,grayen. 3rd person singular. LXX credits Jehu with writing the Book of Kings.

David, and as He said to him that He would give a light to him and his sons forever.

⁸ In those days Edom revolted from Judah, and they made a king over themselves.

⁹ And Jehoram went with the princes, and all the cavalry with him. And it came to pass that he arose by night, and attacked Edom that compassed him about, and the captains of the chariots, and the people fled to their tents.

¹⁰ And Edom revolted from Judah until this day. Then Libnah at that time revolted from *under* his hand, because he forsook the Lord God of his fathers.

¹¹ For he built high places in the cities of Judah, and caused the inhabitants of Jerusalem to commit harlotry, and led Judah astray.

¹² And there came to him *a message* in writing from Elijah the prophet, saying, "Thus says the Lord God of your father David: 'Because you have not walked in the way of your father Jehoshaphat, nor in the ways of Asa king of Judah,

¹³ but have walked in the ways of the kings of Israel, and have caused Judah and its inhabitants in Jerusalem to play the harlot, as the house of Ahab caused *Israel* to play the harlot, and you have slain your brothers, the sons of your father, who were better than yourself.

¹⁴ Behold, the Lord shall strike you with a great plague among your people, and your sons, and your wives, and all your possessions;

¹⁵ and you *shall be afflicted* with a grievous disease, with a disease of the bowels, until your bowels have fallen out, day by day, because of the sickness.'"

¹⁶ So the Lord stirred up the Philistines against Jehoram, and the Arabians, and those who bordered on the Ethiopians;

¹⁷ and they went up against Judah, and prevailed against them, and took away all the possessions which they found in the house of the king, and his sons, and his daughters; and there was no son left to him except Jehoahaz, the youngest of his sons.

¹⁸ And after all these things the Lord struck him in the bowels with an incurable disease.

¹⁹ And it continued from day to day. And after two years had passed by, his bowels fell out from the disease, and he died in great agony. And his people performed no funeral, like the funeral of his fathers.

²⁰ He was thirty-two years old when he began to reign, and he reigned eight years in Jerusalem. And he departed without honor, and was buried in the city of David, but not in the tombs of the kings.

2 CHRONICLES CHAPTER 22

Ahaziah Reigns in Judah

¹ And the inhabitants of Jerusalem made Jehoahaz his youngest son king in his place, for the band of robbers that came against them, even the Arabians and the

Alimazonians, had slain all the elder ones. So Jehoahaz son of Jehoram king of Judah reigned.

² Jehoahaz began to reign when he was twenty years old, and he reigned one year in Jerusalem; and his mother's name was Athaliah, the granddaughter of Omri.

³ And he walked in the way of the house of Ahab; for his mother was his counselor to do evil.

⁴ And he did that which was evil in the sight of the Lord as the house of Ahab *had done*; for they were his counselors after the death of his father, to his destruction.

⁵ And he walked in their counsels, and he went with Jehoram son of Ahab king of Israel to war against Hazael king of Syria to Ramoth Gilead. And the archers struck Joram.

⁶ And Joram returned to Jezreel to be healed of the wounds in which the Syrians struck him with in Ramoth, when he fought against Hazael king of Syria. And Ahaziah son of Jehoram, king of Judah, went down to see Jehoram the son of Ahab at Jezreel because he was sick.

⁷ And destruction from God came upon Ahaziah in *his* coming to Jehoram; for when he had come, Jehoram went out with him against Jehu the son of Nimshi, the anointed of the Lord against the house of Ahab.

⁸ And it came to pass, when Jehu was taking vengeance on the house of Ahab, that he found the princes of Judah and the brothers of Ahaziah, ministering to Ahaziah, and he killed them.

⁹ And he gave orders to search for Ahaziah. And they took him while he was healing his wounds in Samaria, and they brought him to Jehu, and he killed him. And they buried him, for they said, "He is the son of Jehoshaphat, who sought the Lord with all his heart." So there was none in the house of Ahaziah to secure their power in the kingdom.

Athaliah Seizes the Throne

¹⁰ And Athaliah the mother of Ahaziah saw that her son was dead, and she arose and destroyed all the royal heirs in the house of Judah.

¹¹ But Jehoshabeath, the daughter of the king, took Joash the son of Ahaziah and rescued him secretly out of the midst of the sons of the king that were put to death, and she placed him and his nurse in a bedchamber. So Jehoshabeath daughter of King Jehoram, sister of Ahaziah, wife of Jehoida the priest, hid him, and she *even* hid him from Athaliah, and she did not slay him.

¹² And he was hidden with them in the house of God for six years; and Athaliah reigned over the land.

2 CHRONICLES CHAPTER 23

¹ And in the eighth year Jehoiada strengthened *himself*, and took the captains of hundreds, Azariah the son of Jehoram, Ishmael the son of Jehohanan, Azariah the son of Obed,

Maaseiah the son of Adaiah, and Elishaphat the son of Zechariah, with him unto the house of the Lord.

² And they went round about Judah, and gathered the Levites out of all the cities of Judah, and heads of the families of Israel, and they came to Jerusalem.

³ And all the congregation of Judah made a covenant with the king in the house of God. And he showed them the king's son, and said to them, "Behold, let the king's son reign, as the Lord said concerning the house of David.

⁴ Now this *is* the thing which you shall do: let a third part of you, *even* of the priests and of the Levites, enter in on the Sabbath, even into the gates of the entrances;

⁵ and let a third part be in the house of the king; and another third at the middle gate. And all the people in the courts of the Lord's house.

⁶ And let no one enter into the house of the Lord except the priests and the Levites, and the servants of the Levites; they shall enter in, because they are holy; and let all the people keep the watch of the Lord.

⁷ And the Levites shall compass the king round about, every man's weapon in his hand; and whoever *else* goes into the house shall die; but they shall be with the king when he goes out, and when he comes in."

Joash Crowned King of Judah

⁸ And the Levites and all Judah did according to all that the priest Jehoiada commanded them, and they took each his men from the beginning of the Sabbath to the end of the Sabbath, for Jehoiada the priest did not dismiss the courses.

⁹ And Jehoiada gave to the men the swords, and the shields, and the arms, which *had* belonged to King David, in the house of God.

¹⁰ And he set the whole people, every man with his arms, from the right side of the house to the left side of the altar and the house, over against the king round about.

¹¹ And he brought out the king's son, and put on him the crown and the Testimony, and Jehoiada the priest and his sons proclaimed him king, and anointed him, saying, "Long live the king!"

Death of Athaliah

¹² And Athaliah heard the sound of the people running, and acknowledging and praising the king; and she went in to the king into the house of the Lord.

¹³ And she looked, and behold, the king *stood* in his place, and the princes and trumpets were at the entrance, and the princes were round the king. And all the people of the land rejoiced, and sounded the trumpets, and there were the singers singing with instruments, and singing hymns of praise. So Athaliah tore her clothes, and cried, "You surely are plotting against *me*!"

¹⁴ And Jehoiada the priest went forth and charged the captains of hundreds, even the captains of the army, and said to them, "Thrust her forth outside the house, *and whoever* follows her, and let her be slain with the sword."

For the priest said, "Let her not be slain in the house of the Lord."

[15] So they brought her *outside*; and she went through the horsemen's gate of the house of the king, and they killed her there.

[16] And Jehoiada made a covenant between himself and the people and the king, that the people should be the Lord's.

[17] And all the people of the land went into the house of Baal and they tore it down, and its altars, and they ground his images to powder, and they killed Mattan the priest of Baal before his altars.

[18] And Jehoiada the priest committed the works of the house of the Lord into the hand of the priests and Levites, and he re-established the courses of the priests and Levites which David appointed over the house of the Lord, and *he appointed them* to offer burnt offerings to the Lord, as it is written in the law of Moses, with gladness, and with songs by the hand of David.

[19] And the porters stood at the gates of the house of the Lord, that no one unclean in any respect should enter in.

[20] And he took the heads of families, and the mighty men, and the chiefs of the people, and all the people of the land, and they conducted the king into the house of the Lord. And he went through the inner gate into the king's house, and they seated the king on the throne of the kingdom.

[21] And all the people of the land rejoiced; and the city was quiet; and they killed Athaliah.

2 CHRONICLES CHAPTER 24

Joash Repairs the Temple

[1] Joash was seven years old when he began to reign, and he reigned forty years in Jerusalem; and his mother's name was Zibiah of Beersheba.

[2] And Joash did that which was right in the sight of the Lord all the days of Jehoiada the priest.

[3] And Jehoiada took to himself two wives, and they bore sons and daughters.

[4] And it came to pass afterward that it came into the heart of Joash to repair the house of the Lord.

[5] And he gathered the priests and the Levites, and said to them, "Go out into the cities of Judah, and collect money from all Israel to repair the house of the Lord from year to year, and make haste to speak *of it*." But the Levites did not act quickly.

[6] So King Joash called Jehoiada the chief, and said to him, "Why have you not looked after the Levites, so that they should bring from Judah and Jerusalem that which was prescribed by Moses the man of God, when he assembled Israel at the tabernacle of witness?

[7] For Athaliah was a transgressor, and her sons tore down the house of God; for they offered the holy things of the house of the Lord to the Baals."

[8] And the king said, "Let a box be made, and let it be put at the gate of the house of the Lord outside."

[9] And let *men* proclaim in Judah and in Jerusalem, that *the people* should bring to the Lord, as Moses the servant of God spoke concerning Israel in the wilderness."

[10] And all the princes and all the people gave, and brought in, and cast into the box until it was filled.

[11] And it came to pass, when they brought in the box to the officers of the king by the hand of the Levites, and when they saw that the money was more than sufficient, then came the king's scribe, and the officer of the high priest, and emptied the box, and restored it to its place. Thus they did day by day, and collected much money.

[12] And the king and Jehoiada the priest gave it to the workmen employed in the service of the house of the Lord, and they hired masons and carpenters to repair the house of the Lord, also smiths and iron workers to repair the house of the Lord.

[13] So the workmen labored, and the works prospered in their hands, and they established the house of the Lord on its foundation, and strengthened *it*.

[14] And when they had finished *it*, they brought to the king and to Jehoiada the remainder of the money, and they made vessels for the house of the Lord, vessels of service for burnt offerings, and gold and silver *censers*: and they offered up burnt offerings in the house of the Lord continually all the days of Jehoiada.

Apostasy of Joash

[15] And Jehoiada grew old, being full of days, and he died, being a hundred and thirty years old at his death.

[16] And they buried him with the kings in the city of David, because he had dealt well with Israel, and with God and his house.

[17] And it came to pass after the death of Jehoiada, *that* the princes of Judah went in, and bowed down to the king. Then the king listened to them.

[18] And they forsook the house of the Lord God of their fathers, and served wooden images and idols. And there was wrath upon Judah and Jerusalem in that day.

[19] Yet He sent prophets to them, to turn them to the Lord; but they would not listen; and He testified to them, but they did not obey.

[20] And the Spirit of God came upon Zechariah the son of Jehoiada the priest, and he stood up above the people and said, "Thus says the Lord: 'Why do you transgress the commandments of the Lord? So shall you not prosper; for you have forsaken the Lord, and He will forsake you.'"

[21] And they conspired against him, and stoned him by command of King Joash in the court of the Lord's house.

[22] So Joash remembered not the kindness which his father Jehoiada had exercised towards him, but killed his son. And as he died, he said, "The Lord look upon *it*, and judge."

Death of Joash

²³ And it came to pass after the end of the year, *that* the army of Syria went up against him, and came against Judah and Jerusalem. And they killed all the chiefs among the people, and all their spoils they sent to the king of Damascus.

²⁴ For the army of Syria came with few men, yet God gave into their hands a very large army, because they had forsaken the God of their fathers; and He brought judgments on Joash.

²⁵ And after they had departed from him, when they had left him with grievous diseases, then his servants conspired against him because of the blood of the son of Jehoiada the priest, and struck him on his bed, and he died, and they buried him in the city of David, but they did not bury him in the tomb of the kings.

²⁶ And they that conspired against him were Zabad the son of Shimeath the Ammonitess, and Jehozabad the son of Shimrith the Moabitess.

²⁷ And all his sons, and the five came to him. And the other *matters*, behold, they are written in the book of the kings. And Amaziah his son reigned in his place.

2 CHRONICLES CHAPTER 25

Amaziah Reigns in Judah

¹ Amaziah began to reign when he was twenty-five years old, and he reigned twenty-nine years in Jerusalem; and his mother's name *was* Jehoaddan of Jerusalem.

² And he did that which was right in the sight of the Lord, but not with a perfect heart.

³ And it came to pass, when the kingdom was established in his hand, that he killed his servants who had slain his father the king.

⁴ But he did not kill their sons, according to the covenant of the law of the Lord, as it is written, *and* as the Lord commanded, saying, "The fathers shall not die for the children, and the sons shall not die for the fathers, but they shall die each for his own sin."

The War Against Edom

⁵ And Amaziah assembled the house of Judah, and appointed them according to the houses of their families for captains of thousands and captains of hundreds in all Judah and Jerusalem. And he numbered them from twenty years old and upwards, and found of them three hundred thousand able to go out to war, holding spear and shield.

⁶ Also he hired out of Israel a hundred thousand mighty *men* for a hundred talents of silver.

⁷ And there came a man of God to him, saying, "O king, let not the army of Israel go with you; for the Lord is not with Israel, *even* all the sons of Ephraim.

⁸ For if you shall undertake to strengthen *yourself* with these, then the Lord shall put you to flight before the enemies; for it is of the Lord both to strengthen and to put to flight."

⁹ And Amaziah said to the man of God, "But what shall I do *for* the hundred talents which I have given to the army of Israel?" And the man of God said, "The Lord can give you much more than these."

¹⁰ And Amaziah separated from the army that came to him from Ephraim, that they might go away to their place; and they were very angry with Judah, and they returned to their place with great wrath.

¹¹ And Amaziah strengthened *himself*, and took his people, and went to the Valley of Salt, and killed ten thousand of the children of Seir there.

¹² And the children of Judah took ten thousand prisoners, and they carried them to the top of the rock, and cast them headlong from the top of the rock, and they were all dashed to pieces.

¹³ And the men of the army whom Amaziah sent back so that they should not go with him to battle, *went* and attacked the cities of Judah, from Samaria to Beth Horon; and they killed three thousand among them, and took much spoil.

¹⁴ And it came to pass after Amaziah had returned from attacking Edom, that he brought home the gods of the children of Seir, and set them up for himself as gods, and bowed down before them, and he sacrificed to them.

¹⁵ And the anger of the Lord came upon Amaziah, and He sent him a prophet who said to him, "Why have you sought the gods of the people, which have not rescued their own people out of your hand?"

¹⁶ And it came to pass when the prophet was speaking to him, that he said to him, "Have I made you the king's counselor? Take heed lest you be scourged!" And the prophet became silent, and said, "I know that *God* is determined to destroy you, because you have done this thing, and have not listened to my counsel."

Israel Defeats Judah

¹⁷ And Amaziah king of Judah took counsel, and sent to Joash the son of Jehoahaz, son of Jehu, king of Israel, saying, "Come, and let us look one another in the face."

¹⁸ And Joash king of Israel sent to Amaziah king of Judah, saying, "The thistle that was in Lebanon sent to the cedar that was in Lebanon, saying, 'Give your daughter to my son as wife'; but behold, your wild beasts of the field that are in Lebanon shall come. And the wild beasts did come, and trod down the thistle.

¹⁹ You have said, 'Behold, I have defeated Edom,' and your stout heart exalts you. Now stay at home; for why do you implicate yourself in mischief, that you should fall, and Judah with you?"

²⁰ Nevertheless Amaziah would not listen, for it was of the Lord to deliver him into *the enemy's* hands, because he sought after the gods of the Edomites.

21 So Joash king of Israel went up; and they saw one another, he and Amaziah king of Judah, in Beth Shemesh, which is of Judah.

22 And Judah was put to flight before Israel, and they fled, every man to his tent.

23 Then Joash king of Israel captured Amaziah king of Judah, *son* of Joash, son of Jehoahaz, in Beth Shemesh, and brought him to Jerusalem; and he pulled down *part* of the wall of Jerusalem from the gate of Ephraim to the Corner Gate, four hundred cubits.

24 And *he took* all the gold and the silver, and all the vessels that were found in the house of the Lord and with Obed-Edom, and the treasures of the king's house, and the hostages, and he returned to Samaria.

Death of Amaziah

25 And Amaziah the *son* of Joash king of Judah lived after the death of Joash the *son* of Jehoahaz king of Israel fifteen years.

26 And the rest of the acts of Amaziah, the first and the last, behold, are they not written in the book of the kings of Judah and Israel?

27 And at the time when Amaziah departed from the Lord, then they formed a conspiracy against him, and he fled from Jerusalem to Lachish. And they sent after him to Lachish, and killed him there.

28 And they took him up on horses, and buried him with his fathers in the city of David.

2 CHRONICLES CHAPTER 26

Uzziah Reigns in Judah

1 Then all the people of the land took Uzziah, who was sixteen years old, and they made him king in the place of his father Amaziah.

2 He built Elath, he restored it to Judah, after the king slept with his fathers.

3 Uzziah began to reign at the age of sixteen years, and he reigned fifty-two years in Jerusalem; and his mother's name was Jecholiah of Jerusalem.

4 And he did that which was right in the sight of the Lord, according to all that Amaziah his father did.

5 And he sought the Lord in the days of Zechariah, who understood the fear of the Lord; and in his days he sought the Lord, and the Lord prospered him.

6 And he went out and fought against the Philistines, and pulled down the walls of Gath, and the walls of Jabneh, and the walls of Ashdod, and he built cities *near* Ashdod, and among the Philistines.

7 And the Lord strengthened him against the Philistines, and against the Arabians that dwelt on the rock, and against the Meunites.

8 And the Meunites gave gifts to Uzziah; and his fame spread as far as the entering in of Egypt, for he strengthened *himself* exceedingly.

9 And Uzziah built towers in Jerusalem, both at the Corner Gate, and at the Valley Gate, and at the corner buttress of the wall; and he fortified them.

10 And he built towers in the wilderness, and dug many wells, for he had many cattle in the low country and in the plain; and vinedressers in the mountain country and in Carmel, for he was a farmer.

11 And Uzziah had a host of warriors that went out orderly to war, and returned orderly in number; and their number was *made* by the hand of Jeiel the scribe, and Maaseiah the officer, by the hand of Hananiah the king's deputy.

12 The whole number of the chiefs of families of the mighty men of war *was* two thousand six hundred;

13 and with them was a warrior force *of* three hundred thousand and seven thousand five hundred; these waged war mightily to help the king against *his* enemies.

14 And Uzziah prepared for them, *even* for all the army, shields, spears, helmets, breastplates, bows, and slings for stones.

15 And he made in Jerusalem machines invented by a wise contriver, to be upon the towers and upon the corners, to cast darts and great stones. And *the fame* of their preparation was heard from a great distance; for he was marvelously helped, till he became strong.

The Penalty for Uzziah's Pride

16 And when he was strong, his heart was lifted up to his destruction; and he transgressed against the Lord his God, and went into the temple of the Lord to burn incense on the altar of incense.

17 And Azariah the priest went in after him, and with him eighty priests of the Lord, mighty men.

18 And they withstood Uzziah the king, and said to him, "*It is* not for you, Uzziah, to burn incense to the Lord, but only for the priests, the sons of Aaron, who are consecrated to sacrifice: Leave the sanctuary, for you have departed from the Lord; and this shall not be for glory to you from the Lord God."

19 And Uzziah was angry, and in his hand *was* the censer to burn incense in the temple. And when he was angry with the priests, then the leprosy rose up in his forehead before the priests in the house of the Lord, over the altar of incense.

20 And Azariah the chief priest, and the *other* priests, turned *to look* at him, and behold, he *was* leprous in his forehead; and they got him out of there quickly, for he also hastened to go out, because the Lord had rebuked him.

21 And Uzziah the king was a leper until the day of his death, and he dwelt *as* a leper in a separate house; for he was cut off from the house of the Lord; and Jotham his son *was set* over his kingdom, judging the people of the land.

22 And the rest of the acts of Uzziah, the first and the last, *are* written by Isaiah the prophet.

[23] And Uzziah slept with his fathers, and they buried him with his fathers in the field of the burial *place* of the kings, for they said, "He is a leper"; and Jotham his son reigned in his place.

2 CHRONICLES CHAPTER 27

Jotham Reigns in Judah

[1] Jotham *was* twenty-five years old when he began to reign, and he reigned sixteen years in Jerusalem; and his mother's name *was* Jerushah, daughter of Zadok.

[2] And he did that which was right in the sight of the Lord, according to all that his father Uzziah had done; but he did not go into the temple of the Lord. And still the people corrupted themselves.

[3] He built the high gate of the house of the Lord, and he built extensively on the wall of Ophel.

[4] In the mountain of Judah, and in the woods, *he built* both dwelling places and towers.

[5] He fought against the king of the children of Ammon, and prevailed against him. And the children of Ammon gave him a hundred talents of silver each year, and ten thousand measures of wheat, and ten thousand *measures* of barley. These the king of the children of Ammon brought to him annually.

[6] So Jotham grew strong, because he prepared his ways before the Lord his God.

[7] And the rest of the acts of Jotham, and his war, and his deeds, behold, *they are* written in the book of the kings of Judah and Israel.

[8] (This verse omitted in LXX)

[9] And Jotham slept with his fathers, and was buried in the city of David; and Ahaz his son reigned in his place.

2 CHRONICLES CHAPTER 28

Ahaz Reigns in Judah

[1] Ahaz was twenty-five years old when he began to reign, and he reigned sixteen years in Jerusalem. And he did not do what was right in the sight of the Lord, as David his father.

[2] But he walked in the ways of the kings of Israel, for he made graven images.

[3] And *he sacrificed* to their idols in the valley of the Son of Hinnom, and passed his children through the fire, according to the abominations of the heathen, whom the Lord cast out from before the children of Israel.

[4] And he burnt incense upon the high places, and upon the roofs, and under every shady tree.

Syria and Israel Defeat Judah

[5] And the Lord his God delivered him into the hand of the king of Syria. And *the king* attacked him, and took a great multitude of prisoners captive, and carried him to Damascus. Also *God* delivered him into the hands of the king of Israel, who defeated him with a great slaughter.

[6] And Pekah the son of Remeliah king of Israel, killed in Judah in one day a hundred and twenty thousand mighty men, because they had forsaken the Lord God of their fathers.

[7] And Zichri, a mighty man of Ephraim, killed Maaseiah the king's son, and Azrikam the chief of his house, and Elkanah the king's deputy.

[8] And the children of Israel took captive of their brothers three hundred thousand women, sons, and daughters, and they plundered them of much property, and brought the spoils to Samaria.

Israel Returns the Captives

[9] And there was a prophet of the Lord there whose name *was* Oded. And he went out to meet the army that was coming to Samaria, and said to them, "Behold, the wrath of the Lord God of your fathers *is* upon Judah, and He has delivered them into your hands, but you have killed them in wrath, and it has reached even to heaven.

[10] And now you talk of keeping the children of Judah and Jerusalem for servants and handmaidens. Behold, am I not with you to testify for the Lord your God?

[11] And now listen to me, and restore the prisoners of your brothers whom you have taken: for the fierce anger of the Lord *is* upon you."

[12] And the chiefs of the sons of Ephraim rose up, Azariah the son of Johanan, Berechiah the son of Meshillemoth, Jehizkiah the son of Shallum, and Amasa the son of Hadlai, against those that came from the war,

[13] and said to them, "You shall not bring the prisoners here to us, for our sins against the Lord *are already* upon us, *and* you mean to add to our sins, and to our trespass: for our sin *is* great, and the fierce anger of the Lord *is* upon Israel."

[14] So the warriors left the prisoners and the spoils before the princes and all the congregation.

[15] And the men who were called by name rose up, and took hold of the prisoners, and clothed all the naked from the spoils, and gave them garments and shoes, and gave them *food* to eat, and *oil* to anoint themselves *with*, and they let everyone that was weak *to ride on* donkeys, and placed them in Jericho, the city of palm trees, with their brothers; and they returned to Samaria.

Assyria Refuses to Help Judah

[16] At that time King Ahaz sent to the king of Assyria to help him, and on this occasion,

[17] because the Edomites had attacked *him* and attacked Judah, and taken a number of prisoners.

[18] Also the Philistines had made an attack on the cities of the plain country, and the cities of the south of Judah, and had taken Beth Shemesh, and (the things in the house of the Lord, and the things in the house of the king, and of the

princes, and they gave *these* to the king) Aijalon, Gederoth, Sochoh and her villages, Timnah and her villages, and Gimzo and her villages. And they dwelt there.

¹⁹ For the Lord humbled Judah because of Ahaz king of Judah, because he grievously departed from the Lord.

²⁰ And Tiglath-Pileser king of Assyria came against him, and he afflicted him.

Apostasy and Death of Ahaz

²¹ And Ahaz took the things *that were* in the house of the Lord, and the things in the house of the king, and of the princes, and gave them to the king of Assyria; but he was no help to him,

²² but only *troubled him* in his affliction. And he departed yet again from the Lord, and King Ahaz said,

²³ "I will seek after the gods of Damascus that attack me." And he said, "Forasmuch as the gods of the king of Syria themselves strengthen them, therefore will I sacrifice to them, and they will help me." But they became a stumbling block to him, and to all Israel.

²⁴ And Ahaz removed the vessels of the house of the Lord, and cut them in pieces, and shut the doors of the house of the Lord, and made for himself altars in every corner in Jerusalem.

²⁵ And in every single city in Judah he made high places to burn incense to strange gods. And they provoked the Lord God of their fathers.

²⁶ And the rest of his acts and his deeds, the first and the last, behold, *they are* written in the book of the kings of Judah and Israel.

²⁷ And Ahaz slept with his fathers, and was buried in the city of David; for they did not bring him into the tombs of the kings of Israel; and Hezekiah his son reigned in his place.

2 CHRONICLES CHAPTER 29

Hezekiah Reigns in Judah

¹ And Hezekiah began to reign at the age of twenty-five years, and he reigned twenty-nine years in Jerusalem: and his mother's name was Abijah, daughter of Zechariah.

² And he did that which was right in the sight of the Lord, according to all that his father David had done.

Hezekiah Cleanses the Temple

³ And it came to pass, when he was established over his kingdom, in the first month, he opened the doors of the house of the Lord, and repaired them.

⁴ And he brought in the priests and the Levites, and put them on the east side,

⁵ and said to them, "Hear, you Levites: Now sanctify yourselves, and sanctify the house of the Lord God of your fathers, and cast out the impurity from the holy places.

⁶ For our fathers have revolted, and done that which was evil before the Lord our God, and have forsaken Him, and have turned away their face from the tabernacle of the Lord, and have turned *their* back.

⁷ And they have shut up the doors of the temple, and put out the lamps, and have not burned incense, and have not offered burnt offerings in the holy *place* to the God of Israel.

⁸ And the Lord was very angry with Judah and Jerusalem, and made them an astonishment, and a desolation, and a hissing, as you see with your eyes.

⁹ And behold, your fathers have been struck with the sword, and your sons and your daughters and your wives are in captivity in a land not their own, as it is even now.

¹⁰ Therefore it is now in my heart to make a covenant, a covenant with the Lord God of Israel, that He may turn away His fierce wrath from us.

¹¹ And now, do not be negligent in *your duty*, for the Lord has chosen you to stand before Him to minister, and to be ministers and burners of incense to Him."

¹² Then the Levites rose up, Mahath the son of Amasai, and Joel the son of Azariah, of the sons of Kohath: and of the sons of Merari, Kish the son of Abdi, and Azariah the son of Jehalelel; and of the sons of Gershon, Joah the son of Zimmah, and Joadam: these *were* the sons of Joah.

¹³ And of the sons of Elizaphan: Shimri, and Jehiel. And of the sons of Asaph: Zechariah and Mattaniah;

¹⁴ and of the sons of Heman: Jeiel and Shimei; and of the sons of Jeduthun: Shemaiah and Uzziel.

¹⁵ And they gathered their brothers, and they purified themselves according to the king's command by the order of the Lord, to purify the house of the Lord.

¹⁶ And the priests entered into the house of the Lord, to purify *it*, and they cast out all the uncleanness that was found in the house of the Lord, even into the court of the house of the Lord. And the Levites received *it* to cast into the Brook of Kidron outside.

¹⁷ And *Hezekiah* began on the first day, on the new moon of the first month, to purify, and on the eighth day of the month they entered into the temple of the Lord. And they purified the house of the Lord in eight days. And on the thirteenth day of the first month they finished *the work*.

¹⁸ And they went in to King Hezekiah and said, "We have purified all the things in the house of the Lord, the altar of burnt offering, and its vessels, and the table of showbread, and its vessels;

¹⁹ and all the vessels which King Ahaz polluted in his reign, in his apostasy, we have prepared and purified; behold, they are before the altar of the Lord."

Hezekiah Restores Temple Worship

²⁰ And King Hezekiah rose early in the morning, and gathered the chief men of the city, and went up to the house of the Lord.

²¹ And he brought seven calves, seven rams, seven lambs, and seven kids of goats for a sin-offering, for the kingdom, and for the holy things, and for Israel. And he told the priests, the sons of Aaron, to go up to the altar of the Lord.

22 And they killed the calves, and the priests received the blood, and poured it on the altar. And they killed the rams, and poured the blood upon the altar. Also they killed the lambs, and poured the blood on the altar.

23 And they brought the goats for a sin offering before the king and the congregation, and laid their hands upon them.

24 And the priests killed them, and offered their blood as a propitiation on the altar; and they made atonement for all Israel; for the king said, "The burnt offering, and the sin offering *are* for all Israel."

25 And he stationed the Levites in the house of the Lord with cymbals, and lutes, and harps, according to the commandment of King David, and of Gad the king's seer, and Nathan the prophet; for by the commandment of the Lord the order *was* in the hand of the prophets.

26 And the Levites stood with the instruments of David, and the priests with the trumpets.

27 And Hezekiah told *them* to offer up the burnt offering on the altar. And when they began to offer the burnt offering, they began to sing to the Lord, and the trumpets *accompanied* the instruments of David king of Israel.

28 And all the congregation worshipped, and the psalm-singers *were* singing, and the trumpets sounding, until the whole burnt sacrifice had been completely offered.

29 And when they had done offering *it*, the king and all that were present bowed down and worshipped.

30 And King Hezekiah and the princes told the Levites to sing hymns to the Lord in the words of David, and of Asaph the prophet. And they sang hymns with gladness, and fell down and worshipped.

31 Then Hezekiah answered and said, "Now *that* you have consecrated yourselves to the Lord, bring near and offer sacrifices of praise in the house of the Lord." And the congregation brought sacrifices and thank offerings into the house of the Lord; and everyone who was ready in his heart *brought* burnt offerings.

32 And the number of the burnt offerings which the congregation brought, was seventy calves, a hundred rams, and two hundred lambs: all these *were* for a burnt offering to the Lord.

33 And the consecrated calves were six hundred, *and* the sheep three thousand.

34 But the priests were few, and could not slay the burnt offering, so their brothers the Levites helped them, until the work was finished, and until the priests had purified themselves; for the Levites *more* zealously purified *themselves* than the priests.

35 And the burnt offering *was* abundant, with the fat of the complete peace offering, and the drink offerings of the whole burnt sacrifice. So the service was established in the house of the Lord.

36 And Hezekiah and all the people rejoiced, because God had prepared the people: for the thing was done suddenly.

2 CHRONICLES CHAPTER 30

Hezekiah Keeps the Passover

1 And Hezekiah sent to all Israel and Judah, and wrote letters to Ephraim and Manasseh, that they should come into the house of the Lord to Jerusalem, to keep the Passover to the Lord God of Israel.

2 For the king, and the princes, and all the congregation in Jerusalem, designed to keep the Passover in the second month.

3 For they could not keep it at that time, because a sufficient number of priests had not purified themselves, and the people were not gathered to Jerusalem.

4 And the proposal pleased the king and the congregation.

5 And they established a decree that a proclamation should go through all Israel, from Beersheba to Dan, that they should come and keep the Passover to the Lord God of Israel at Jerusalem; for the multitude had not done it lately according to the Scripture.

6 And the posts went with the letters from the king and the princes to all Israel and Judah, according to the command of the king, saying, "Children of Israel, return to the Lord God of Abraham, Isaac, and Israel, and bring back them that have escaped, *even* those that were left of the hand of the king of Assyria.

7 And do not be as your fathers and your brothers, who revolted from the Lord God of their fathers, and He gave them up to desolation, as you see.

8 And now do not harden your hearts, as your fathers *did*; give glory to the Lord God, and enter into His sanctuary, which He has sanctified forever, and serve the Lord your God, and He shall turn away *His* fierce anger from you.

9 For when you turn to the Lord, your brothers and your children shall be pitied before all that have carried them captives, and He will restore *you* to this land; for the Lord our God is merciful and gracious, and will not turn away His face from you, if we return to Him."

10 So the posts went through from city to city in Mount Ephraim and Manasseh, and as far as Zebulun; and they laughed them to scorn, and mocked them.

11 But the men of Asher, and *some* of Manasseh and of Zebulun, were ashamed, and came to Jerusalem and Judah.

12 And the hand of the Lord was *present* to give them one heart to come, to do according to the commands of the king and of the princes, by the word of the Lord.

13 And a great multitude were gathered to Jerusalem to keep the Feast of Unleavened Bread in the second month, a very great congregation.

14 And they arose, and took away the altars that were in Jerusalem, and all on which they burnt incense to false *gods* they tore down and cast into the Brook Kidron.

15 Then they killed the Passover *lambs* on the fourteenth day of the second month. And the priests and the Levites

repented, and purified *themselves*, and brought burnt offerings into the house of the Lord.

¹⁶ And they stood at their post, according to their ordinance, according to the commandment of Moses the man of God; and the priests received the blood from the hand of the Levites.

¹⁷ For a great part of the congregation was not sanctified; and the Levites were *ready* to kill the Passover for everyone who could not sanctify himself to the Lord.

¹⁸ For the greatest part of the people of Ephraim, Manasseh, Issachar, and Zebulun, had not purified *themselves*, but ate the Passover contrary to the Scripture. On this account also Hezekiah prayed concerning them, saying,

¹⁹ "The good Lord be merciful with regard to every heart that sincerely seeks the Lord God of their fathers, and *is* not *purified* according to the purification of the sanctuary."

²⁰ And the Lord listened to Hezekiah, and healed the people."

²¹ And the children of Israel who were present in Jerusalem kept the Feast of Unleavened Bread seven days with great joy; and they continued to sing hymns to the Lord daily, and the priests and the Levites *played* on instruments to the Lord.

²² And Hezekiah encouraged all the Levites, and those that had good understanding of the Lord, and they completely kept the Feast of Unleavened Bread seven days, offering peace offerings, and confessing to the Lord God of their fathers.

²³ And the congregation purposed together to keep another seven days. And they kept *another* seven days with gladness.

²⁴ For Hezekiah set apart for Judah, *even* for the congregation, a thousand calves and seven thousand sheep; and the princes set apart for the people a thousand calves and ten thousand sheep, and the holy things of the priests abundantly.

²⁵ And all the congregation rejoiced, the priests and the Levites, and all the congregation of Judah, and those that were present of Jerusalem, and the strangers that came from the land of Israel, and those that dwelt in Judah.

²⁶ And there was great joy in Jerusalem. From the days of Solomon the son of David king of Israel there was not such a feast in Jerusalem.

²⁷ Then the priests the Levites rose up and blessed the people, and their voice was heard, and their prayer came *up* to His holy dwelling place, *even* into heaven.

2 CHRONICLES CHAPTER 31

The Reforms of Hezekiah

¹ And when all these things were finished, all Israel that were found in the cities of Judah went out, and broke in pieces the pillars, and cut down the groves, and tore down the high places and the altars out of all Judea and Benjamin, also of Ephraim and Manasseh, until they had utterly destroyed them all. And all Israel returned, everyone to his inheritance, and to their cities.

² And Hezekiah appointed the courses of the priests and the Levites, and the courses of each one according to his ministry, to the priests and to the Levites, for the burnt offering, and for the peace offering, and to praise, and to give thanks, and to minister in the gates, *and* in the courts of the house of the Lord.

³ And the king's proportion out of his substance *was appointed* for the burnt offerings, the morning and the evening *offering*, and the burnt offerings for the Sabbaths, and for the new moons, and for the feasts that were ordered in the Law of the Lord.

⁴ And they told the people who dwelt in Jerusalem, to give the portion of the priests and the Levites, that they might be strong in the ministry of the house of the Lord.

⁵ And as he gave the command, Israel brought abundantly their firstfruits of grain, wine, oil, honey, and every fruit of the field. And the children of Israel and Judah brought tithes of everything abundantly.

⁶ And those who dwelt in the cities of Judah themselves also brought tithes of calves and sheep, and tithes of goats, and consecrated them to the Lord their God, and they brought them and laid them in heaps.

⁷ In the third month the heaps began to be piled, and in the seventh month they were finished.

⁸ And Hezekiah and the princes came and saw the heaps, and blessed the Lord, and His people Israel.

⁹ Then Hezekiah inquired of the priests and the Levites concerning the heaps.

¹⁰ And Azariah the priest, the chief over the house of Zadok, spoke to him, and said, "From the time that the firstfruits began to be brought into the house of the Lord, we have eaten and drunk, and have plenty left; for the Lord has blessed His people, and we have this great amount left."

¹¹ And Hezekiah told them yet farther to prepare chambers for the house of the Lord; and they prepared *them*,

¹² and they brought there the firstfruits and the tithes faithfully. And Cononiah the Levite was superintendent over them, and Shimei his brother was next.

¹³ And Jehiel, Azaziah, Nahath, Asahel, Jerimoth, Jozabad, Eliel, Ismachiah, Mahath, and Benaiah and his sons, were appointed by Cononiah and Shimei his brother, as Hezekiah the king, and Azariah who was over the house of the Lord commanded.

¹⁴ And Kore, the *son* of Imnah the Levite, the porter eastward, *was* over the gifts, to distribute the firstfruits of the Lord, and the most holy things,

¹⁵ by the hand of Eden, Benjamin, Jeshua, Shemaiah, Amariah, and Shecaniah, by the hand of the priests faithfully, to give to their brothers according to the courses, to the great as well as the small;

16 besides the increase of males from three years old and upward, to everyone entering into the house of the Lord, *a portion* according to a daily rate, for service in the daily courses of their order.

17 This *is* the distribution of the priests according to the houses of their families; and the Levites in their daily courses from twenty years old and upward *were* in *their* order,

18 to assign stations for all the increase of their sons and their daughters, for the whole number, for they faithfully sanctified the holy place.

19 As for the sons of Aaron that executed the priests' office–even those from their cities, the men in each several city who were named expressly–*were appointed* to give a portion to every male among the priests, and to everyone reckoned among the Levites.

20 And Hezekiah did so through all Judah, and did that which was good and right before the Lord his God.

21 And in every work which he began in service in the house of the Lord, and in the law, and in the ordinances, he sought his God with all his soul, and wrought, and prospered.

2 CHRONICLES CHAPTER 32

Sennacherib Boasts Against the Lord

1 And after these things and this faithful dealing, Sennacherib king of the Assyrians came to Judah, and he encamped against the fortified cities, and intended to take them for himself.

2 And Hezekiah saw that Sennacherib had come, and *that* his face *was set* to fight against Jerusalem.

3 And he took counsel with his elders and his mighty *men* to stop the wells of water which were outside the city; and they helped him.

4 And he collected many people, and stopped the wells of water, and the river that flowed through the city, saying, "Lest the king of Assyria come, and find much water, and strengthen *himself*."

5 And Hezekiah strengthened *himself*, and built all the wall that had been pulled down, and the towers, and another wall outside, and fortified the strong place of the City of David, and prepared arms in abundance.

6 And he appointed captains of war over the people, and they were gathered to *meet* him to the open place of the gate of the valley, and he encouraged them, saying,

7 "Be strong and courageous, and do not fear, neither be dismayed before the king of Assyria, and before all the nation that *is* with him: for *there are* more with us than with him.

8 With him *are* arms of flesh, but with us *is* the Lord our God to save *us*, and to fight our battle." And the people were encouraged at the words of Hezekiah king of Judah.

9 And afterward Sennacherib king of the Assyrians sent his servants to Jerusalem; and *he went* himself against Lachish, and all his army with him, and sent to Hezekiah king of Judah, and to all Judah that *was* in Jerusalem, saying,

10 "Thus says Sennacherib king of the Assyrians: 'On what do you trust, that you will remain in the siege in Jerusalem?

11 Does not Hezekiah deceive you, to deliver you to death and famine and thirst, saying, "The Lord our God will deliver us out of the hand of the king of Assyria?"

12 Is not this Hezekiah who has taken down his altars and his high places and has spoken to Judah and the inhabitants of Jerusalem, saying, "You shall worship before this altar and burn incense upon it?"

13 Do you not know what I and my fathers have done to all the nations of the countries? Could the gods of the nations of all the earth rescue their people out of my hand?

14 Who is there among all the gods of those nations whom my fathers utterly destroyed, *worthy of trust*? Could they deliver their people out of my hand, that your God should deliver you out of my hand?

15 Now then, do not let Hezekiah deceive you, and let him not make you confident in any way, and do not believe him, for no god of any kingdom or nation is in any way able to deliver his people out of my hand, or the hand of my fathers; therefore your God shall not deliver you out of my hand.'"

16 And his servants continued to speak against the Lord God, and against His servant Hezekiah.

17 And he wrote a letter to reproach the Lord God of Israel, and spoke concerning Him, saying, "As the gods of the nations of the earth have not delivered their people out of my hand, so the God of Hezekiah shall by no means deliver His people out of my hand."

18 And he cried with a loud voice in the Jews' language to the people of Jerusalem on the wall, *calling them* to assist them, and pull down *the walls*, that they might take the city.

19 And he spoke against the God of Jerusalem, even as against the gods of the nations of the earth, the works of the hands of men.

Sennacherib's Defeat and Death

20 And King Hezekiah and Isaiah the prophet the son of Amoz prayed concerning these things, and they cried to heaven.

21 And the Lord sent an angel, and He destroyed every mighty man and warrior, and leader and captain in the camp of the king of Assyria; and he returned with shame of face to his own land and came into the house of his god. And *some* of his own offspring killed him with the sword.

22 So the Lord delivered Hezekiah and the inhabitants of Jerusalem out of the hand of Sennacherib king of Assyria, and out of the hand of all *his enemies*, and gave them rest round about.

23 And many brought gifts to the Lord to Jerusalem, and presents to Hezekiah king of Judah; and he was exalted in the eyes of all the nations after these things.

Hezekiah Humbles Himself

[24] In those days Hezekiah was sick, even unto death, and he prayed to the Lord. And *God* heeded him, and gave him a sign.

[25] But Hezekiah did not recompense the Lord according to the favor shown him, but his heart was lifted up. And wrath came upon him, and upon Judah and Jerusalem.

[26] And Hezekiah humbled himself after the exaltation of his heart, he and the inhabitants of Jerusalem; and the wrath of the Lord did not come upon them in the days of Hezekiah.

[27] And Hezekiah had wealth and very great glory. And he made for himself treasuries of gold, silver, and precious stones, also for spices and stores for arms, and for precious vessels;

[28] and cities for the produce of grain, wine, and oil; and stalls and mangers for every *kind of* cattle, and folds for flocks;

[29] and cities which he built for himself, and store of sheep and oxen in abundance, for the Lord gave him a very great store.

[30] The same Hezekiah stopped up the course of the water of Upper Gihon, and brought the water down straight south of the City of David. And Hezekiah prospered in all his works.

[31] Notwithstanding, in regard to the ambassadors of the princes of Babylon, who were sent to him, to inquire of him *concerning* the wonders which came upon the land, the Lord left him, to test him, to know what was in his heart.

Death of Hezekiah

[32] And the rest of the acts of Hezekiah, and his kindness, behold, they are written in the prophecy of Isaiah the son of Amoz the prophet, and in the book of the kings of Judah and Israel.

[33] And Hezekiah slept with his fathers, and they buried him in a high place among the tombs of the sons of David. And all Judah and the inhabitants of Jerusalem gave him glory and honor at his death. And Manasseh his son reigned in his place.

2 CHRONICLES CHAPTER 33

Manasseh Reigns in Judah

[1] Manasseh was twelve years old when he began to reign, and he reigned fifty-five years in Jerusalem.

[2] And he did that which was evil in the sight of the Lord, according to all the abominations of the heathen, whom the Lord destroyed from before the face of the children of Israel.

[3] And he returned and built the high places, which his father Hezekiah had pulled down, and set up images to the Baals, and made groves, and worshipped all the host of heaven, and served them.

[4] And he built altars in the house of the Lord, concerning which the Lord had said, "In Jerusalem shall be My name forever."

[5] And he built altars to all the host of heaven in the two courts of the house of the Lord.

[6] He also caused his children to pass through the fire in the valley of the Son of Hinnom; and he practiced witchcraft, divination, and sorceries, and appointed those who had divining spirits, and enchanters, and wrought abundant wickedness before the Lord, to provoke Him.

[7] And he set the graven *image*, the molten *statue*, the idol which he made, in the house of God, of which God had said to David and to Solomon his son, "In this house, and Jerusalem, which I have chosen out of all the tribes of Israel, I will put My name forever;

[8] and I will not again remove the foot of Israel from the land which I gave to their fathers, if only they will take heed to do all things which I have commanded them, according to all the law and the ordinances and the judgments *given* by the hand of Moses."

[9] So Manasseh led Judah and the inhabitants of Jerusalem astray, to do evil beyond all the nations which the Lord cast out from before the children of Israel.

Manasseh Restored

[10] And the Lord spoke to Manasseh and to his people, but they would not listen.

[11] And the Lord brought upon them the captains of the armies of the king of Assyria, and they took Manasseh in bonds, and bound him in fetters, and brought him to Babylon.

[12] And when he was afflicted, he sought the face of the Lord his God, and was greatly humbled before the face of the God of his fathers;

[13] and he prayed to Him. And He heeded him, and listened to his cry, and brought him back to Jerusalem to his kingdom. And Manasseh knew that the Lord *was* God.

[14] And afterward he built a wall outside the City of David, from the southwest southward in the valleys and at the entrance through the Fish Gate, as men go out by the gate round about, even as far as Ophel. And he raised it much, and set captains of the army in all the fortified cities in Judah.

[15] And he removed the strange gods, and the graven *image* out of the house of the Lord, and all the altars which he had built in the mount of the house of the Lord, and in Jerusalem, and outside the city.

[16] And he repaired the altar of the Lord, and offered upon it a sacrifice of peace offering and thank offering, and he told Judah to serve the Lord God of Israel.

[17] Nevertheless the people still sacrificed on the high places, only to the Lord their God.

Death of Manasseh

¹⁸ And the rest of the acts of Manasseh, and his prayer to God, and the words of the seers that spoke to him in the name of the God of Israel,

¹⁹ behold, *they are* in the account of his prayer. And *God* listened to *his prayer.* And all his sins, and his backslidings, and the spots on which he built the high places, and set there groves and graven images, before he repented, behold, they are written in the books of the seers.

²⁰ And Manasseh slept with his fathers, and they buried him in the garden of his house; and Amon his son reigned in his place.

²¹ Amon was twenty-two years old when he began to reign, and he reigned two years in Jerusalem.

²² And he did that which was evil in the sight of the Lord, as his father Manasseh had done. And Amon sacrificed to all the idols which his father Manasseh had made, and served them.

²³ And he was not humbled before the Lord as his father Manasseh was humbled; for his son Amon abounded in transgression.

²⁴ And his servants conspired against him, and killed him in his house.

²⁵ And the people of the land killed the men who had conspired against King Amon; and the people of the land made Josiah his son king in his place.

2 CHRONICLES CHAPTER 34

Josiah Reigns in Judah

¹ Josiah was eight years old when he began to reign, and he reigned thirty-one years in Jerusalem.

² And he did that which was right in the sight of the Lord, and walked in the ways of his father David, and he did not turn aside to the right hand or to the left.

³ And in the eighth year of his reign, and he still *being* a youth, he began to seek the Lord God of his father David. And in the twelfth year of his reign he began to purge Judah and Jerusalem from the high places, and the groves, and the ornaments for the altars, and the molten images.

⁴ And he pulled down the altars of the Baals that were in his presence, and the high places that were above them; and he cut down the groves, and the graven images, and broke in pieces the molten images, and reduced them to powder, and cast *it* upon the surface of the tombs of those who *had* sacrificed to them.

⁵ And he burnt the bones of the priests upon the altars, and purged Judah and Jerusalem.

⁶ And *he did so* in the cities of Manasseh, Ephraim, Simeon, and Naphtali, and the places round about them.

⁷ And he pulled down the altars and the groves, and he cut the idols in small pieces, and cut off all the high places from all the land of Israel, and returned to Jerusalem.

Hilkiah Finds the Book of the Law

⁸ And in the eighteenth year of his reign, after having cleansed the land and the house, he sent Shaphan the son of Azaliah, Maaseiah the governor of the city, and Joah son of Joahaz the recorder, to repair the house of the Lord his God.

⁹ And they came to Hilkiah the high priest, and gave the money that was brought into the house of God, which the Levites who kept the gate collected of the hand of Manasseh and Ephraim, and of the princes, and of everyone that was left in Israel, and of the children of Judah and Benjamin, and of the inhabitants of Jerusalem.

¹⁰ And they gave it into the hand of the workmen, who were appointed in the house of the Lord, and they gave it to the workmen who wrought in the house of the Lord, to repair and strengthen the house.

¹¹ They gave *it* also to the carpenters and builders, to buy squared stones, and timber for beams to cover the houses which the kings of Judah had destroyed.

¹² And the men *were* faithfully *engaged* in the works. And over them were superintendents, Jahath and Obadiah, Levites of the sons of Merari, and Zechariah and Meshullam, of the sons of Kohath, *appointed* to oversee; and every Levite, and everyone that understood *how* to play on musical instruments.

¹³ And *overseers were* over the burden bearers, and over all the workmen in the respective works; and of the Levites *were appointed* scribes, judges, and porters.

¹⁴ And when they brought forth the money that had been brought into the house of the Lord, Hilkiah the priest found *the* Book of the Law of the Lord *given* by the hand of Moses.

¹⁵ Then Hilkiah answered and said to Shaphan the scribe, "I have found *the* Book of the Law in the house of the Lord." And Hilkiah gave the book to Shaphan.

¹⁶ And Shaphan brought in the book to the king, and moreover he gave an account to the king, *saying*, "*This is* all the money given into the hand of your servants that work.

¹⁷ And they have collected the money that was found in the house of the Lord, and given it into the hand of the overseers, and into the hand of them that do the work."

¹⁸ And Shaphan the scribe brought word to the king, saying, "Hilkiah the priest has given me a book." And Shaphan read it before the king.

¹⁹ And it came to pass, when the king heard the words of the Law, that he tore his clothes.

²⁰ And the king commanded Hilkiah, Ahikam the son of Shaphan, Abdon the son of Micah, Shaphan the scribe, and Asaiah the servant of the king, saying,

²¹ "Go, inquire of the Lord for me, and for everyone that is left in Israel and Judah, concerning the words of the book that was found; for great is the wrath of the Lord *which* has been kindled amongst us, because our fathers have not heeded the words of the Lord, to do according to all the things written in this book."

²² And Hilkiah went, and *the others* whom the king told, to Huldah the prophetess, the wife of Shallum, son of Tokhath, son of Hasrah, who kept the commandments. And she dwelt in Jerusalem in the Second *Quarter*: and they spoke to her accordingly.

²³ And she said to them, "Thus has the Lord God of Israel said: 'Tell the man who sent you to Me,

²⁴ Thus says the Lord: "Behold, I bring evil upon this place, *even* all the words that are written in the book that was read before the king of Judah;

²⁵ because they have forsaken Me, and burnt incense to strange gods, that they might provoke Me by all the works of their hands; and My wrath is kindled against this place, and it shall not be quenched."

²⁶ And concerning the king of Judah, who sent you to seek the Lord, thus shall you say to him; Thus says the Lord God of Israel: "*As for* the words which you have heard,

²⁷ forasmuch as your heart was ashamed, and you were humbled before Me when you heard My words against this place, and against the inhabitants of it, and you were humbled before Me, and you tore your clothes, and wept before Me; I also have heard, says the Lord.

²⁸ Behold, I *will* gather you to your fathers, and you shall be gathered to your grave in peace, and your eyes shall not look upon all the evils which I am bringing upon this place, and upon the inhabitants of it."'" And they brought back word to the king.

Josiah Restores True Worship

²⁹ And the king sent and gathered the elders of Judah and Jerusalem.

³⁰ And the king went up to the house of the Lord, *he* and all Judah, and the inhabitants of Jerusalem, and the priests, and the Levites, and all the people great and small; and he read in their ears all the words of the Book of the Covenant that were found in the house of the Lord.

³¹ And the king stood at a pillar, and made a covenant before the Lord, to walk before the Lord, to keep His commandments and testimonies, and His ordinances, with all *his* heart and with all *his* soul, so as to perform the words of the covenant that were written in this book.

³² And he caused all that were found in Jerusalem and Benjamin to stand; and the inhabitants of Jerusalem made a covenant in the house of the Lord God of their fathers.

³³ And Josiah removed all the abominations out of the whole land which belonged to the children of Israel, and caused all that were found in Jerusalem and in Israel, to serve the Lord their God all his days. He did not depart from following the Lord God of his fathers.

2 CHRONICLES CHAPTER 35

Josiah Keeps the Passover

¹ And Josiah kept a Passover to the Lord his God; and sacrificed the Passover on the fourteenth day of the first month.

² And he appointed the priests at their charges, and encouraged them for the services of the house of the Lord.

³ And he told the Levites that were able *to act* in all Israel, that they should consecrate themselves to the Lord. And they put the holy ark in the house which Solomon the son of David king of Israel built. And the king said, "You must not carry anything on your shoulders; now then minister to the Lord your God, and to His people Israel.

⁴ And prepare yourselves according to the houses of your families, and according to your daily courses, according to the writing of David king of Israel, and *the order* by the hand of his son Solomon.

⁵ And stand in the house according to the divisions of the houses of your families for your brothers the sons of the people; *so* also let there be for the Levites a division of the house of their family.

⁶ And kill the Passover *lamb*, and prepare *it* for your brothers, to do according to the word of the Lord, by the hand of Moses."

⁷ And Josiah gave as an offering to the children of the people, sheep, lambs, and kids of the young of the goats, all for the Passover, *even for* all that were found, in number *amounting to* thirty thousand, and three thousand calves, these *were* of the substance of the king.

⁸ And his princes gave an offering to the people, and to the priests, and to the Levites: and Hilkiah and Zechariah and Jehiel the chief men gave to the priests of the house of God, they even gave for the Passover sheep, lambs, and kids, two thousand six hundred, and three hundred calves.

⁹ And Conaniah, Benaiah, Shemaiah, Nethaneel his brother, Hashabiah, Jeiel, and Jozabad, heads of the Levites, gave an offering to the Levites for the Passover, of five thousand sheep and five hundred calves.

¹⁰ And the service was duly ordered, and the priests stood in their place, and the Levites in their divisions, according to the command of the king.

¹¹ And they killed the Passover *offerings*, and the priests sprinkled the blood from their hand, and the Levites skinned *the animals*.

¹² And they prepared the burnt offering to give to them, according to the division by the houses of families, *even* to the sons of the people, to offer to the Lord, as it is written in the Book of Moses.

¹³ And thus *they did* till the morning. And they roasted the Passover with fire according to the ordinance; and boiled the holy *pieces* in copper vessels and caldrons, and *the feast* went on well, and they quickly served all the children of the people.

¹⁴ And after they had prepared for themselves and for the priests, for the priests *were engaged* in offering the burnt offerings and the fat until night, then the Levites prepared for themselves, and for their brothers the sons of Aaron.

15 And the sons of Asaph the psalm-singers *were* at their post according to the commands of David, and Asaph, Heman, and Jeduthun, the prophets of the king. Also, the chiefs and the porters of the several gates—it was not for them to stir from the service of the holy things, for their brothers the Levites prepared for them.

16 So all the service of the Lord was duly ordered and prepared in that day, for keeping the Passover, and offering the whole burnt sacrifices on the altar of the Lord, according to the command of King Josiah.

17 And the children of Israel that were present kept the Passover at that time, and the Feast of Unleavened Bread for seven days.

18 And there was no Passover like it in Israel from the days of Samuel the prophet, or any king of Israel; they did not keep such a Passover as Josiah, and the priests, and the Levites, and all Judah and Israel that were present, and the inhabitants of Jerusalem, kept to the Lord.

19 In the eighteenth year of the reign of Josiah this Passover was kept, after all these things that Josiah did in the house. And King Josiah burnt those who had in them a divining spirit, and the wizards, and the images, and the idols, and the sodomites which were in the land of Judah and in Jerusalem, that he might confirm the words of the law that were written in the book which Hilkiah the priest found in the house of the Lord. There was no *king* like him before him, who turned to the Lord with all his heart, and all his soul, and all his strength, according to all the Law of Moses, and after him there rose up none like him. Nevertheless the Lord did not turn from the anger of His fierce wrath, wherewith the Lord was greatly angry against Judah, for all the provocations in which Manasseh had provoked Him. And the Lord said, "I will even remove Judah also from My presence, as I have removed Israel, and I have rejected the city which I chose, *even* Jerusalem, and the house of which I said, 'My name shall be there.'"

Josiah Dies in Battle

20 And Pharaoh Necho king of Egypt went up against the king of the Assyrians to the River Euphrates, and King Josiah went to meet him.

21 And he sent messengers to him, saying, "What have I to do with you, O king of Judah? I have not come today to war against you; and God has told me to make haste; beware of the God that is with me, lest He destroy you."

22 However, Josiah did not turn his face from him, but *rather* strengthened himself to fight against him, and did not listen to the words of Necho by the mouth of God, and he came to fight in the plain of Megiddo.

23 And the archers shot at King Josiah. And the king said to his servants, "Take me away, for I am severely wounded."

24 And his servants lifted him out of the chariot, and put him in the second chariot which he had, and brought him to Jerusalem. And he died, and was buried with his fathers; and all Judah and Jerusalem lamented over Josiah.

25 And Jeremiah mourned over Josiah, and all the chief men and chief women uttered a lamentation over Josiah until this day. And they made it an ordinance for Israel, and behold, it is written in the lamentations.

26 And the rest of the acts of Josiah, and his hope, are written in the law of the Lord.

27 And his acts, the first and the last, behold, *they are* written in the book of the kings of Israel and Judah.

2 CHRONICLES CHAPTER 36

The Reign and Captivity of Jehoahaz

1 And the people of the land took Jehoahaz the son of Josiah, and anointed him, and made him king over Jerusalem in the place of his father.

2 Jehoahaz *was* twenty-three years old when he began to reign, and he reigned three months in Jerusalem; and his mother's name was Amital, daughter of Jeremiah of Libnah. And he did that which was evil in the sight of the Lord, according to all that his fathers had done. And Pharaoh Necho bound him in Diblath in the land of Emath, that he might not reign in Jerusalem.

3 And the king brought him over to Egypt, and imposed a tribute on the land, a hundred talents of silver and a talent of gold.

4 And Pharaoh Necho made Eliakim the son of Josiah king over Judah in the place of his father Josiah, and changed his name *to* Jehoiakim. And Pharaoh Necho took his brother Jehoahaz and brought him into Egypt, and he died there; but *he* had given the silver and gold to Pharaoh. At that time the land began to be taxed to give the money at the command of Pharaoh; and everyone as he could borrowed the silver and the gold of the people of the land, to give to Pharaoh Necho.

The Reign and Captivity of Jehoiakim

5 Jehoiakim was twenty-five years old when he began to reign, and he reigned eleven years in Jerusalem; and his mother's name *was* Zechora, daughter of Neriah of Ramah. And he did that which was evil in the sight of the Lord, according to all that his fathers did. In his days came Nebuchadnezzar king of Babylon into the land, and he served him three years, and *then* revolted from him. And the Lord sent against them the Chaldeans, and plundering parties of Syrians, and plundering parties of the Moabites, and of the children of Ammon, and of Samaria. But after this they departed, according to the word of the Lord by the hand of His servants the prophets. Nevertheless the wrath of the Lord was upon Judah, so that they should be removed from His presence, because of the sins of Manasseh in all that he did, and for the innocent blood which Jehoiakim shed, for he had filled Jerusalem with innocent blood; yet the Lord would not utterly destroy them.

[6] And Nebuchadnezzar king of Babylon came up against him, and bound him with bronze fetters, and carried him away to Babylon.

[7] And he carried away a part of the vessels of the house of the Lord to Babylon, and put them in his temple in Babylon.

[8] And the rest of the acts of Jehoiakim, and all that he did, behold, *are* not these things written in the book of the chronicles of the kings of Judah? And Jehoiakim slept with his fathers, and was buried with his fathers; and Jeconiah his son reigned in his place.

The Reign and Captivity of Jeconiah

[9] Jeconiah *was* eight years old when he began to reign, and he reigned three months and ten days in Jerusalem, and did that which was evil in the sight of the Lord.

[10] And at the turn of the year, King Nebuchadnezzar sent, and brought him to Babylon, with the precious vessels of the house of the Lord, and made Zedekiah his father's brother king over Judah and Jerusalem.

Zedekiah Reigns in Judah

[11] Zedekiah *was* twenty-one years old when he began to reign, and he reigned eleven years in Jerusalem.

[12] And he did that which was evil in the sight of the Lord his God; he was not ashamed before the prophet Jeremiah, nor because of the word of the Lord;

[13] in that he rebelled against King Nebuchadnezzar, which he adjured him by God *not to do*; but he stiffened his neck, and hardened his heart, so as not to return to the Lord God of Israel.

[14] And all the great men of Judah, and the priests, and the people of the land transgressed abundantly in the abominations of the heathen, and polluted the house of the Lord which *was* in Jerusalem.

The Fall of Jerusalem

[15] And the Lord God of their fathers sent by the hand of His prophets; rising early and sending His messengers, for He had compassion on His people, and His sanctuary.

[16] Nevertheless they sneered at His messengers, and despised His words, and mocked His prophets, until the wrath of the Lord rose up against His people, till there was no remedy.

[17] And He brought the king of the Chaldeans against them, and killed their young men with the sword in the house of His sanctuary, and did not spare Zedekiah, and had no mercy upon their virgins, and they led away their old men; He delivered all things into their hands.

[18] And all the vessels of the house of God, the great and the small, and the treasures of the house of the Lord, and all the treasures of the king and the great men; he brought all to Babylon.

[19] And he burned the house of the Lord, and broke down the wall of Jerusalem, and burned its palaces with fire, and *utterly destroyed* every beautiful vessel.

[20] And he carried away the remnant to Babylon; and they were servants to him and to his sons until *the establishment of* the kingdom of the Medes,

[21] that the word of the Lord by the mouth of Jeremiah might be fulfilled, until the land should enjoy its Sabbaths in resting, *and* Sabbath keeping all the days of its desolation, till the accomplishment of seventy years.

The Proclamation of Cyrus

[22] In the first year of Cyrus king of the Persians, after the fulfillment of the word of the Lord by the mouth of Jeremiah, the Lord stirred up the spirit of Cyrus king of the Persians, and told him to make proclamation in writing throughout all his kingdom, saying,

[23] "Thus says Cyrus king of the Persians to all the kingdoms of the earth: The Lord God of heaven has given me *power*, and He has commanded me to build a house to Him in Jerusalem, in Judea. Who *is there* among you of all His people? His God shall be with him, and let him go up."

THE BOOK OF EZRA

End of the Babylonian Captivity

[1] Now in the first year of Cyrus king of the Persians, that the word of the Lord by the mouth of Jeremiah might be fulfilled, the Lord stirred up the spirit of Cyrus king of the Persians, and he issued a proclamation through all his kingdom, and that in writing, saying,

[2] "Thus says Cyrus king of the Persians: The Lord God of heaven has given me all the kingdoms of the earth, and He has given me a command to build Him a house in Jerusalem that is in Judea.

[3] Who *is* there among you of all His people? For his God shall be with him, and he shall go up to Jerusalem that is in Judea, and let him build the house of the God of Israel: He *is* the God that is in Jerusalem.

[4] And *let* every *Jew* that is left *go* from every place where he sojourns, and the men of his place shall help him with silver and gold, with goods and livestock, together with the freewill offering for the house of God that is in Jerusalem."

[5] Then the chiefs of the families of Judah and Benjamin arose, and the priests, and the Levites, all whose spirit the Lord stirred up to go up to build the house of the Lord that *is* in Jerusalem.

[6] And all that were round about strengthened their hands with vessels of silver, with gold, with goods, with livestock, and with presents, besides the freewill offerings.

[7] And King Cyrus brought out the vessels of the house of the Lord, which Nebuchadnezzar had brought from Jerusalem, and put in the house of his god.

[8] And Cyrus king of the Persians brought them out by the hand of Mithradath the treasurer, and he numbered them to Sheshbazzar, the chief man of Judah.

9 And this *is* their number: thirty gold platters, and a thousand silver platters, twenty-nine knives, thirty golden goblets,

10 four hundred and ten double silver *vessels*, and a thousand other vessels.

11 All the gold and silver vessels were five thousand four hundred, *even* all that went up with Sheshbazzar from the *place of* transportation, from Babylon to Jerusalem.

EZRA CHAPTER 2

List of the Returned Exiles

1 And these *are* the people of the land that went up, of the number of prisoners who were removed, whom Nebuchadnezzar king of Babylon carried away to Babylon, and they returned to Judah and Jerusalem, every man to his city.

2 *Those* who came with Zerubbabel *were*: Jeshua, Nehemiah, Seraiah, Reelaiah, Mordecai, Bilshan, Mispar, Bigvai, Rehum, *and* Baanah. The number of the people of Israel:

3 the children of Phares, two thousand one hundred and seventy-two;

4 the children of Shephatiah, three hundred and seventy-two;

5 the children of Arah, seven hundred and seventy-five;

6 the children of Pahath-Moab, belonging to the sons of Jeshua *and* Joab, two thousand eight hundred and twelve;

7 the children of Elam, a thousand two hundred and fifty-four;

8 the children of Zatthu, nine hundred and forty-five;

9 the children of Zacchai, seven hundred and sixty;

10 the children of Banui, six hundred and forty-two;

11 the children of Babai, six hundred and twenty-three;

12 the children of Azgad, a thousand two hundred and twenty-two;

13 the children of Adonikam, six hundred and sixty-six;

14 the children of Bigvai, two thousand and fifty-six;

15 the children of Adin, four hundred and fifty-four;

16 the children of Ater *the son* of Hezekiah, ninety eight;

17 the children of Bezai, three hundred and twenty-three;

18 the children of Jorah, a hundred and twelve;

19 the children of Hashum, two hundred and twenty-three;

20 the children of Gibbar, ninety-five;

21 the children of Bethlehem, a hundred and twenty-three;

22 the children of Netophah, fifty-six;

23 the children of Anathoth, a hundred and twenty-eight;

24 the children of Azmaveth, forty-three;

25 the children of Kirjath Arim, Chephirah, and Beeroth, seven hundred and forty-three;

26 the children of Ramah and Gibeah, six hundred and twenty-one;

27 the men of Michmas, a hundred and twenty-two;

28 the men of Bethel and Ai, four hundred and twenty-three;

29 the children of Nebo, fifty-two;

30 the children of Magbish, a hundred and fifty-six;

31 the children of Elamar, a thousand two hundred and fifty-four;

32 the children of Elam, three hundred and twenty;

33 the children of Lod and Ono, seven hundred and twenty-five;

34 the children of Jericho, three hundred and forty-five.

35 the children of Senaah, three thousand six hundred and thirty.

36 And the priests, the sons of Jedaiah, of the house of Jeshua, nine hundred and seventy-three;

37 the children of Immer, a thousand and fifty-two;

38 the children of Pashur, a thousand two hundred and forty-seven;

39 the children of Harim, a thousand and seven.

40 And the Levites, the sons of Jeshua and Kadmiel, belonging to the sons of Hodaviah, seventy-four.

41 The sons of Asaph, *the* singers: a hundred and twenty-eight.

42 The children of the gatekeepers, the children of Shallum, the children of Ater, the children of Talmon, the children of Akkub, the children of Hatita, the children of Shobai, a hundred and thirty-nine *in* all.

43 The Nethinim: the children of Ziha, the children of Hasupha, the children of Tabbaoth,

44 the children of Keros, the children of Siaha, the children of Padon,

45 the children of Labanah, the children of Hagabah, the sons of Akkub,

46 the children of Hagab, the children of Shalmai, the children of Hanan,

47 the children of Giddel, the children of Gahar, the children of Reaiah,

48 the children of Rezin, the children of Nekoda, the children of Gazzam,

49 the children of Uzzo, the children of Paseah, the children of Besai,

50 the children of Asnah, the children of Meunim, the children of Nephusim,

51 the children of Bakbuk, the children of Hakupha, the children of Harhur,

52 the children of Bazluth, the children of Mehida, the children of Harsha,

53 the children of Barkos, the children of Sisera, the children of Tamah,

54 the children of Neziah, the children of Hatipha.

55 The children of the servants of Solomon: the children of Sotai, the children of Sophereth, the children of Peruda,

56 the children of Jaala, the children of Darkon, the children of Giddel,

[57] the children of Shephatiah, the children of Hattil, the children of Pochereth, the children of Zebaim, the children of Ami.

[58] All the Nethinim, and the sons of Abdeselma *were* three hundred and ninety-two.

[59] And these *are* they that went up from Tel Melah, Tel Harsha, Cherub, Addan, and Immer; but they were not able to identify the house of their fathers, and their descendants, whether they were of Israel;

[60] the children of Delaiah, the children of Bua, the children of Tobiah, the children of Nekoda, six hundred and fifty-two.

[61] And of the children of the priests, the children of Labeia, the children of Akkus, the children of Barzillai, who took a wife of the daughters of Barzillai the Gileadite, and was called by their name.

[62] These sought their genealogy *as though* they had been reckoned, but they were not found; and they were removed from the priesthood, *as defiled.*

[63] And the Tirshatha told them that they should not eat of the most holy things, until a priest should arise with the Urim and Thummim.

[64] And all the congregation together *were* about forty-two thousand three hundred and sixty;

[65] besides their male and female servants, *and* these were seven thousand three hundred and thirty-seven. And *among* these were two hundred men and women singers.

[66] Their horses *were* seven hundred and thirty-six, their mules, two hundred and forty-five.

[67] Their camels, four hundred and thirty-five; their donkeys, six thousand seven hundred and twenty.

[68] And *some* of the chiefs of families, when they went into the house of the Lord that was in Jerusalem, offered willingly for the house of God, to establish it on its prepared place.

[69] According to their ability they gave into the treasury of the work pure gold, sixty-one thousand pieces, and five thousand pounds of silver, and one hundred priests' garments.

[70] So the priests, the Levites, and some of the people, and the singers, and the porters, and the Nethinim, dwelt in their cities, and all Israel in their cities.

EZRA CHAPTER 3

Worship Restored at Jerusalem

[1] And the seventh month came, and the children of Israel *were* in their cities, and the people assembled as one man at Jerusalem.

[2] Then stood up Jeshua the *son* of Jozadak, and his brothers the priests, and Zerubbabel the *son* of Shealtiel, and his brothers, and they built the altar of the God of Israel, to offer upon it burnt offerings, according to the things that were written in the law of Moses the man of God.

[3] And they set up the altar on its place, for there was a fear upon them because of the people of the land. And the burnt offerings was offered up upon it to the Lord morning and evening.

[4] And they kept the Feast of Tabernacles, according to that which was written, and *offered* burnt offerings daily, in number according to the ordinance, the exact daily rate.

[5] And after this the perpetual burnt offering, and *offering* for the season of new moon, and for all the hallowed feasts to the Lord, and for everyone that offered a freewill offering to the Lord.

[6] On the first day of the seventh month they began to offer burnt offerings to the Lord, but the foundation of the house of the Lord was not laid.

[7] And they gave money to the stone masons and carpenters, and food and drink, and oil, to the Sidonians, and Tyrians, to bring cedar trees from Lebanon to the sea of Joppa, according to the grant of Cyrus king of the Persians to them.

[8] And in the second year of their coming to the house of God in Jerusalem, in the second month, began Zerubbabel the *son* of Shealtiel, and Jeshua the *son* of Jozadak, and the rest of their brothers the priests and the Levites, and all who came from the captivity to Jerusalem, and they appointed the Levites, from twenty years old and upward, over the workmen in the house of the Lord.

[9] And Jeshua and his sons and brothers stood, *with* Kadmiel and his sons, the sons of Judah, over them that performed the works in the house of God; the sons of Henadad *with* their sons and their brothers the Levites.

[10] And they laid a foundation for building the house of the Lord; and the priests in their robes stood with trumpets and the Levites the sons of Asaph with cymbals, to praise the Lord, according to the order of David king of Israel.

[11] And they answered *each other* with praise and thanksgiving to the Lord, *saying,* "For *it is* good, for His mercy to Israel *endures* forever." And all the people shouted with a loud voice to praise the Lord at the laying the foundation of the house of the Lord.

[12] But many of the priests and the Levites, and the elder men, heads of families, who had seen the former house on its foundation, and *who saw* this house with their eyes, wept with a loud voice; but the multitude shouted with joy to raise a song.

[13] And the people did not distinguish the voice of the glad shout from the voice of the weeping of the people, for the people shouted with a loud voice, and the voice was heard, even from far away.

EZRA CHAPTER 4

Resistance to Rebuilding the Temple

[1] And they that afflicted Judah and Benjamin heard, that the children of the captivity were building a house to the Lord God of Israel.

2 And they drew near to Zerubbabel, and to the heads of families, and said to them, "We will build with you; for as you *do*, we seek *to serve* our God, and we do sacrifice to Him from the days of Esarhaddon king of Assyria, who brought us here." 3 Then Zerubbabel and Jeshua and the rest of the heads of the families of Israel said to them, "*It is* not for us and you to build a house to our God, for we ourselves will build together to the Lord our God, as Cyrus the king of the Persians commanded us."

4 And the people of the land weakened the hands of the people of Judah, and hindered them in building,

5 and *continued* hiring *people* against them, plotting to frustrate their counsel, all the days of Cyrus king of the Persians, and until the reign of Darius king of the Persians.

6 And in the reign of Ahasuerus, even in the beginning of his reign, they wrote a letter against the inhabitants of Judah and Jerusalem.

7 And in the days of Artaxerxes, Tabel wrote peaceably to Mithradath and to the rest of his fellow servants: the tax collector wrote to Artaxerxes king of the Persians a writing in the Syrian tongue, and *the same* interpreted.

8 Rehum the chancellor and Shimshai the scribe wrote an epistle against Jerusalem to King Artaxerxes, *saying,*

9 "Thus has judged Rehum the chancellor, and Shimshai the scribe, and the rest of our fellow servants, the Dinaites, the Apharsathchites, the Tarpelites, the people of Persia, the Erech, the Babylonians, the Shushan, the Dehavites,

10 and the rest of the nations whom the great and noble Osnapper removed, and settled them in the cities of Samaria, and the rest *of them* beyond the river."

11 This *is* the contents of the letter which they sent to him: "To King Artaxerxes, from your servants the men *of the region* beyond the river:

12 Be it known to the king, that the Jews who came up to us from you, have come to Jerusalem, the rebellious and wicked city which they are building, and its walls are set in order, and they have established the foundations of it.

13 Now then let it be known to the king, that if that city be built up, and its walls completed, you shall have no tribute, neither will they pay *any tribute*; and this *shall* hinder kings.

14 And it is not lawful for us to see the dishonor of the king. Therefore have we sent and made known *the matter* to the king,

15 that examination may be made in your fathers' book of record. And you shall find, and you shall know that this city *is* rebellious, and does harm to kings and countries, and there are in the midst of it from very old time refuges for *runaway* slaves. Therefore this city has been made desolate.

16 We therefore declare to the king, that if this city is rebuilt, and its walls are set up, you shall have no peace."

17 Then the king sent to Rehum the chancellor, and Shimshai the scribe, and the rest of their fellow servants who dwelt in Samaria, and the rest beyond the river, *saying,* "Peace"; and he said,

18 "The tax collector whom you sent to us has been called before me.

19 And a decree has been made by me, and we have examined, and found that city of old time exalts itself against kings, and that rebellions and desertions take place within it.

20 And there were powerful kings in Jerusalem, and they ruled over all the *country* beyond the river, and abundant revenues and tribute were given to them.

21 Now therefore make a decree to stop the work of those men, and that city shall no more be built.

22 *See* that you be careful of the decree, *not* to be remiss concerning this matter, lest at any time destruction should abound to the harm of kings."

23 Then the tax collector of King Artaxerxes read *the letter* before Rehum the chancellor, and Shimshai the scribe, and his fellow servants. And they went in haste to Jerusalem and through Judah, and caused them to cease with horses and an *armed* force.

24 Thus the work of the house of God in Jerusalem ceased, and it was at a standstill until the second year of the reign of Darius king of the Persians.

EZRA CHAPTER 5

Restoration of the Temple Resumed

1 And Haggai the prophet, and Zechariah the *son* of Iddo, prophesied to the Jews in Judah and Jerusalem in the name of the God of Israel.

2 Then Zerubbabel the *son* of Shealtiel, and Jeshua the son of Jehozadak rose up, and began to build the house of God that was in Jerusalem, and with them *were* the prophets of God assisting them.

3 At the same time Tattenai the governor on this side the river, and Shethar-Boznai, and their fellow servants came to them, and spoke thus to them: "Who has ordained a decree for you to build this house, and to *provide* this preparation?"

4 Then they spoke thus to them: "What are the names of the men that build this city?"

5 But the eyes of God were upon the captivity of Judah, and they did not cause them to cease till the decree was brought to Darius; and then was sent by the tax collector concerning this.

6 *This is* the copy of a letter which Tattenai, the governor of the part on this side the river, and Shethar-Boznai, and their fellow servants the Apharsachaeans, who were on this side of the river, sent to King Darius.

7 They sent an account to him, and thus it was written in it: "All peace to King Darius.

8 Be it known to the king, that we went into the land of Judea, to the house of the great God; and it is building with choice stones, and they are laying beams in the walls, and that work is prospering, and goes on favorably in their hands.

⁹ Then we asked those elders, and thus we said to them, 'Who gave you the order to build this house, and to *provide* this preparation?'

¹⁰ And we asked them their names, *in order* to declare *them* to you, so as to write to you the names of their leading men.

¹¹ And they answered us thus, saying, 'We *are* the servants of the God of heaven and earth, and we *are* building the house which had been built many years before this, and a great king of Israel built it, and established it for them.

¹² But after that our fathers provoked the God of heaven, *and* He gave them into the hands of Nebuchadnezzar the Chaldean, king of Babylon, and he destroyed this house, and carried the people away captive to Babylon.

¹³ And in the first year of King Cyrus, Cyrus the king made a decree that this house of God should be built.

¹⁴ And the gold and silver vessels of the house of God, which Nebuchadnezzar brought out from the house that was in Jerusalem, and carried them into the temple of the king, those King Cyrus brought out from the temple of the king, and gave to Sheshbazzar the treasurer, who was over the treasury,

¹⁵ and said to him, "Take all the vessels, and go, put them in the house that is in Jerusalem in their place."

¹⁶ Then that Sheshbazzar came, and laid the foundations of the house of God in Jerusalem. And from that time even until now it has been building, and has not been finished.'

¹⁷ And now, if it *seems* good to the king, let a search be made in the treasure house of the king at Babylon, that you may know whether *it is so*, that a decree was made by King Cyrus to build that house of God that was in Jerusalem, and let the king send to us when he has learned concerning this *matter*."

EZRA CHAPTER 6

The Decree of Darius

¹ Then Darius the king made a decree, and caused a search to be made in the record offices, where the treasure is stored in Babylon.

² And there was found in the city, in the palace, a volume, and this was the record written in it:

³ In the first year of King Cyrus, Cyrus the king made a decree concerning the holy house of God that was in Jerusalem, *saying*, "Let the house be built, and the place where they offer the sacrifices (Also he appointed its elevation, in height sixty cubits; its breadth was of sixty cubits).

⁴ And *let there be* three strong layers of stone, and one layer of timber; and the expense shall be paid out of the house of the king.

⁵ And the silver and the gold vessels of the house of God, which Nebuchadnezzar carried off from the house that was in Jerusalem, and carried to Babylon, let them also be given, and be carried to the temple that is in Jerusalem, and put in the place where they were set in the house of God.

⁶ Now, you rulers beyond the river, Shethar-Boznai, and their fellow servants the Apharsachaeans, who *are* on the other side of the river, give *these things*, keeping far from that place.

⁷ Now let alone the work of the house of God; let the rulers of the Jews and the elders of the Jews build that house of God on its place.

⁸ Also a decree has been given by me, to do through the elders of those Jews, to build that house of God: that is, out of the king's property, *even* the tributes beyond the river, let there be money to cover the expenses carefully granted to those men, so that they may not be hindered.

⁹ And whatever need *there may be*, you shall give both the young of bulls and rams, and lambs for burnt offerings to the God of heaven, *and* wheat, salt, wine, and oil—let it be given them according to the word of the priests that are in Jerusalem, day by day whatsoever they shall ask;

¹⁰ that they may offer sacrifices of sweet aroma to the God of heaven, and that they may pray for the life of the king and his sons.

¹¹ And a decree has been made by me, that every man who shall alter this word, timber shall be pulled down from his house, and let him be lifted up and slain upon it, and his house shall be confiscated.

¹² And may the God whose name dwells there, overthrow every king and people who shall stretch out his hand to alter or destroy the house of God which is in Jerusalem. I, Darius have made a decree; let it be diligently *attended to*."

The Temple Completed and Dedicated

¹³ Then Tattenai the governor on this side beyond the river, Shethar-Boznai, and his fellow servants, according to that which King Darius sent, so they did diligently.

¹⁴ And the elders of the Jews and the Levites built, at the prophecy of Haggai the prophet, and Zechariah the son of Iddo; and they built up, and finished *it*, by the decree of the God of Israel, and by the decree of Cyrus, and Darius, and Artaxerxes, kings of the Persians.

¹⁵ And they finished this house by the third day of the month *of* Adar, which is the sixth year of the reign of Darius the king.

¹⁶ And the children of Israel, the priests, and the Levites, and the rest of the children of the captivity kept the dedication of the house of God with gladness.

¹⁷ And they offered for the dedication of the house of God a hundred calves, two hundred rams, four hundred lambs, twelve kids of the goats for a sin offering for all Israel, according to the number of the tribes of Israel.

¹⁸ And they set the priests in their divisions, and the Levites in their separate orders, for the services of God in Jerusalem, according to the writing of the Book of Moses.

The Passover Celebrated

19 And the children of the captivity kept the Passover on the fourteenth day of the first month.

20 For the priests and Levites were purified, all were clean to a man, and they slaughtered the Passover *lambs* for all the children of the captivity, and for their brothers the priests, and for themselves.

21 And the children of Israel ate the Passover, *even* they that were of the captivity, and everyone who separated himself to them from the uncleanness of the nations of the land, to seek the Lord God of Israel.

22 And they kept the Feast of Unleavened Bread seven days with gladness, because the Lord made them glad, and He turned the heart of the king of Assyria to them, to strengthen their hands in the works of the house of the God of Israel.

EZRA CHAPTER 7

The Arrival of Ezra

1 Now after these things, in the reign of Artaxerxes king of the Persians, came up Ezra, the son of Seraiah, the son of Azariah, the son of Hilkiah,

2 the son of Shallum, the son of Zadok, the son of Ahitub,

3 the son of Amariah, the son of Azaria, the son of Maraioth,

4 the son of Zerahiah, the son of Uzzi, the son of Bukki,

5 the son of Abishua, the son of Phinehas, the son of Eleazar, the son of Aaron the first priest—

6 this Ezra came up out of Babylon; and he was a skilled scribe in the Law of Moses, which the Lord God of Israel had given. And the king granted him *leave*, for the hand of the Lord his God was upon him in all things which he sought.

7 And *some* of the children of Israel, and *some* of the priests, and of the Levites, and the singers, and the gatekeepers, and the Nethinim, came up to Jerusalem, in the seventh year of Artaxerxes the king.

8 And they came to Jerusalem in the fifth month (this *was* the seventh year of the king).

9 For in the first *day* of the first month he began the going up from Babylon, and in the first day of the fifth month, they came to Jerusalem, for the good hand of his God was upon him.

10 For Ezra had determined in his heart to seek the law, and to do and teach the ordinances and judgments in Israel.

The Letter of Artaxerxes to Ezra

11 And this *is* the copy of the order which Artaxerxes gave to Ezra the priest, the scribe, of the book of the words of the commandments of the Lord, and of His ordinances to Israel.

12 "Artaxerxes, king of kings, to Ezra, the scribe of the law of the Lord God of heaven, Let the order and the answer be accomplished.

13 A decree is made by me, that everyone who is willing in my kingdom of the people of Israel, and of the priests and Levites, to go to Jerusalem, *be permitted* to go with you.

14 *One* has been sent from the king and his seven counselors, to visit Judea and Jerusalem, according to the law of their God which is in your hand.

15 And for the house of the Lord *there has been sent* silver and gold, which the king and the counselors have freely given to the God of Israel, who dwells in Jerusalem.

16 And all the silver and gold, whatsoever you shall find in all the land of Babylon, with the freewill offering of the people, and the priests that offer freely for the house of God which is in Jerusalem.

17 And as for everyone that arrives *there*, speedily order him by this letter *to bring* calves, rams, lambs, and their grain offerings, and their drink offerings; and you shall offer them on the altar of the house of your God which is in Jerusalem.

18 And whatever seems good to you and to your brothers to do with the rest of the silver and the gold, do as it is pleasing to your God.

19 And deliver the vessels that are given to you for the service of the house of God, before God in Jerusalem.

20 "And as to the rest of the needs of the house of your God, you shall give from the king's treasure houses,

21 and from me, whatever seems *good* to you to give. I, King Artaxerxes have made a decree for all the treasuries that are in the *country* beyond the river, that whatsoever Ezra the priest and scribe of the God of heaven may require of you, let it be done diligently,

22 to *the amount of* a hundred talents of silver, and a hundred measures of wheat, and a hundred baths of wine, and a hundred baths of oil, and salt without reckoning.

23 Let whatever is in the decree of the God of heaven be done. Take heed lest anyone make an attack against the house of the God of heaven, lest at any time there shall be wrath against the realm of the king and his sons.

24 Also this has been declared to you, with respect to all the priests, and Levites, the singers, porters, Nethinim and ministers of the house of God, let no tribute be *paid* to you; you shall not have power to oppress them.

25 "And you, Ezra, as the wisdom of God *is* in your hand, appoint scribes and judges, that they may judge for all the people beyond the river, all that know the law of the Lord your God; and you shall make it known to him that does not know.

26 And whosoever shall not obey the law of God, and the law of the king readily, judgment shall be taken upon him, whether for death or for chastisement, or for a fine of his property, or casting into prison."

27 "Blessed *be* the Lord God of our fathers, who has put it thus into the heart of the king, to glorify the house of the Lord which is in Jerusalem;

28 and has given me favor in the eyes of the king, and of his counselors, and all the rulers of the king, the exalted ones." And I was strengthened according to the good hand of God

upon me, and I gathered chief men of Israel to go up with me.

EZRA CHAPTER 8

Heads of Families Who Returned with Ezra

[1] And these *are* the heads of their families, the leaders that went up with me in the reign of Artaxerxes the king of Babylon:

[2] Of the sons of Phinehas, Gershom; of the sons of Ithamar, Daniel; of the sons of David; Hattush.

[3] Of the sons of Shecaniah, and the sons of Parosh; Zechariah; and with him a company *of* a hundred and fifty *men*.

[4] Of the sons of Pahath-Moab, Eliehoenai the son of Zerahiah, and with him two hundred males.

[5] And of the sons of Zatho, Shechaniah the son of Jahaziel, and with him three hundred males.

[6] And of the sons of Adin, Ebed the son of Jonathan, and with him fifty males.

[7] And of the sons of Elam, Jeshaiah the son of Athaliah, and with him seventy males.

[8] And of the sons of Shephatiah, Zebadiah the son of Michael, and with him eighty males.

[9] And of the sons of Joab, Obadiah the son of Jehiel, and with him two hundred and eighteen males.

[10] And of the sons of Banni, Shelomith the son of Josiphiah, and with him a hundred and sixty males.

[11] And of the sons of Bebai, Zechariah the son of Bebai, and with him twenty-eight males.

[12] And of the sons of Azgad, Johanan the son of Hakkatan, and with him a hundred and ten males.

[13] And of the sons of Adonikam *were the* last, and these *were* their names, Eliphelet, Jeiel, and Shemaiah, and with them sixty males.

[14] And of the sons of Bigvai, Uthai and Zabbud, and with him seventy males.

Servants for the Temple

[15] And I gathered them to the river that comes to Ahava, and we encamped there three days. And I reviewed the people and the priests, and found none of the sons of Levi there.

[16] And I sent men of understanding to Eliezar, Ariel, Shemaiah, Elnathan, Jarib, Elnathan, Nathan, Zechariah, Meshullam, Joiarib, and to Elnathan.

[17] And I forwarded them to the rulers with the money of the place, and I put words in their mouth to speak to their brothers the Nethinim with the money of the place, that they should bring us singers for the house of our God.

[18] And they came to us, as the good hand of our God was upon us, even a man of understanding of the sons of Mahli, the son of Levi, the son of Israel, and at the commencement came his sons and his brothers, eighteen *men*.

[19] And Hashabiah, and Jeshaiah, of the sons of Merari, his brothers and his sons, twenty *men*.

[20] And of the Nethinim; whom David and the princes had appointed for the service of the Levites, *there were* two hundred and twenty Nethinim; all were gathered by *their* names.

Fasting and Prayer for Protection

[21] And I proclaimed there a fast, at the River Ahava, that *we* should humble ourselves before our God, to seek from Him the right way for us, and for our children, and for all our property.

[22] For I was ashamed to ask of the king a guard and horsemen to save us from the enemy in the way; for we had spoken to the king, saying, "The hand of our God *is* upon all that seek Him, for good; but His power and His wrath *are* upon all that forsake Him."

[23] So we fasted, and asked of our God concerning this; and He heard *our* prayer.

Gifts for the Temple

[24] And I gave charge to twelve of the chiefs of the priests, to Sherebiah, to Hashabiah, and ten of their brothers with them.

[25] And I weighed to them the silver, and the gold, and the vessels of the firstfruits of the house of our God, which the king, and his counselors, and his princes, and all Israel that were found, had dedicated.

[26] I even weighed into their hands six hundred and fifty talents of silver, and a hundred silver vessels, and a hundred talents of gold;

[27] and twenty golden bowls, *weighing* about a thousand drachmas, and superior vessels of fine shining brass, *precious* as gold.

[28] And I said to them, "You *are* holy to the Lord; and the vessels *are* holy; and the silver and the gold are freewill offerings to the Lord God of our fathers.

[29] Be watchful and keep them, until you weigh *them* before the chief priests and the Levites, and the chiefs of families in Jerusalem, at the chambers of the house of the Lord."

[30] So the priests and the Levites took the weight of the silver, and the gold, and the vessels, to bring to Jerusalem into the house of our God.

The Return to Jerusalem

[31] And we departed from the river of Ahava on the twelfth day of the first month, to come to Jerusalem. And the hand of our God was upon us, and He delivered us from the hand of the enemy and adversary in the way.

[32] And we came to Jerusalem, and stayed there three days.

[33] And it came to pass on the fourth day that we weighed the silver and the gold and the vessels in the house of our God, into the hand of Meremoth the son of Uriah the priest, and with him *was* Eleazar the son of Phinehas, and with

them Jozabad the son of Jeshua, and Noadiah the son of Binnui, the Levites.

³⁴ All things *were reckoned* by number and weight, and the whole weight was written *down*.

³⁵ At that time the children of the banishment that came from the captivity offered burnt offerings to the God of Israel, twelve calves for all Israel, ninety-six rams, seventy-seven lambs, twelve goats for a sin offering; all burnt offerings to the Lord.

³⁶ And they gave the king's mandate to the king's lieutenants, and the governors beyond the river: and they honored the people and the house of God.

EZRA CHAPTER 9

Intermarriage with Pagans

¹ And when these things were finished, the princes drew near to me, saying, "The people of Israel, and the priests, and the Levites, have not separated themselves from the people of the lands in their abominations, *even* the Cannanite, the Hittite, the Perizzite, the Jebusite, the Ammonite, the Moabite, and the Moserite and the Amorite.

² For they have taken of their daughters for themselves and their sons, and the holy seed has passed among the nations of the lands, and the hand of the rulers *has been* first in this transgression."

³ And when I heard this thing, I tore my clothes, and trembled, and plucked *some* of the hairs of my head and of my beard, and sat down mourning.

⁴ Then there assembled to me all that followed the word of the God of Israel, on account of the transgression of the captivity; and I remained mourning until the evening sacrifice.

⁵ And at the evening sacrifice I rose up from my humiliation; and when I had tore my clothes, then I trembled, and I bowed myself on my knees, and spread out my hands to the Lord God,

⁶ and I said, "O Lord, I am ashamed and confounded, O my God, to lift up my face to You; for our transgressions have abounded over our head, and our trespasses have increased even to heaven.

⁷ From the days of our fathers we have been in a great trespass until this day; and because of our iniquities we, and our kings, and our children, have been delivered into the hand of the kings of the Gentiles by the sword, by captivity, by spoil, and with shame of our face, as at this day.

⁸ And now our God has dealt mercifully with us, so as to leave us *a remnant* to escape, and to give us an establishment in the place of His sanctuary, to enlighten our eyes, and give us a measure of revival in our bondage.

⁹ For we are slaves, yet in our bondage the Lord our God has not deserted us; and He has extended favor to us in the sight of the kings of the Persians, to revive us, that they should raise up the house of our God, and restore the desolate places of it, and to give us a wall in Judah and Jerusalem.

¹⁰ What shall we say, O our God, after this? For we have forsaken Your commandments,

¹¹ which You have given us by the hand of Your servants the prophets, saying, 'The land, into which you go to inherit it, is a land subject to disturbance by the removal of the people of the nations for their abominations, wherewith they have filled it from one end to the other by their impurity.

¹² And now do not give your daughters to their sons, and do not take of their daughters for your sons, neither shall you ever seek their peace or their goods, that you may be strong, and eat the good of the land, and allot it as an inheritance to your children forever.'

¹³ And after all that has come upon us because of our evil deeds, and our great trespass, *it is clear* that there is none such as our God, for You have lightly visited our iniquities, and have given us deliverance;

¹⁴ whereas we have repeatedly broken Your commandments, and intermarried with the people of the lands. Be not very angry with us to *our* utter destruction, so that there should be no remnant or survivor.

¹⁵ O Lord God of Israel, You *are* righteous, for we are left as a remnant, as it is this day. Behold, we *are* before You in our trespasses, for we cannot stand before You on this account."

EZRA CHAPTER 10

Confession of Improper Marriages

¹ So when Ezra had prayed, and when he had confessed, weeping and praying before the house of God, a very great assembly of Israel came together to him, men and women and youths; for the people wept, and wept aloud.

² And Shechaniah the son of Jehiel, of the sons of Elam, answered and said to Ezra, "We have broken covenant with our God, and have taken strange wives of the nations of the land. Yet now there is patience *of hope* to Israel concerning this thing.

³ Now then let us make a covenant with our God, to put away all the wives, and their offspring, as you advise:

⁴ arise, and alarm them with the commands of our God; and let *it* be done according to the law. Rise up, for the matter *is* upon you; and we *are* with you. Be strong and do it."

⁵ Then Ezra arose, and caused the rulers, the priests, the Levites, and all Israel, to swear that they would do according to this word. And they swore.

⁶ And Ezra rose up from before the house of God, and went to the treasury of Johanan the son of Eliashib. And when he came there, he ate no bread, and drank no water, for he mourned over the unfaithfulness *of those* of the captivity.

⁷ And they made a proclamation throughout Judah and Jerusalem to all the children of the captivity, that they should assemble at Jerusalem, *saying,*

8 "Everyone who shall not arrive within three days, as *is* the counsel of the rulers and the elders, all his belongings shall be forfeited, and he shall be separated from the congregation of the captivity."

9 So all the men of Judah and Benjamin assembled at Jerusalem within the three days. This *was* the ninth month. On the twentieth day of the month all the people sat down in the street of the house of the Lord, because of their alarm concerning the word, and because of the storm.

10 And Ezra the priest arose, and said to them, "You have broken covenant, and have taken strange wives, to add to the trespass of Israel.

11 Now therefore give praise to the Lord God of our fathers, and do that which is pleasing in His sight, and separate yourselves from the peoples of the land, and from the strange wives."

12 Then all the congregation answered and said, "This your word *is* powerful upon us, to do it.

13 But the people *are* numerous, and the season *is* stormy, and there is no power to stand outside, and the work is more than enough for *just* one day or for two; for we have greatly sinned in this matter.

14 Let now our rulers stand, and for all those in our cities who have taken strange wives, let them come at appointed times, and with them elders from every city, and judges, to turn away the fierce wrath of our God from us concerning this matter.

15 Only Jonathan the son of Asahel, and Jahaziah the son of Tikvah *were* with me concerning this; and Meshullam and Shabbethai the Levite helped them."

16 And the children of the captivity did thus. And Ezra the priest, and heads of families according to *their* house were separated, and all by their names, for they returned in the first day of the tenth month to search out the matter.

17 And they made an end with all the men who had taken strange wives by the first day of the first month.

Pagan Wives Put Away

18 And there were found *some* of the sons of the priests who had taken strange wives: of the sons of Jeshua the son of Jozadek, and his brothers: Maaseiah, Eliezer, Jarib, and Gedaliah.

19 And they pledged themselves to put away their wives, and *offered* a ram of the flock for a trespass offering because of their trespass.

20 And of the sons of Immer: Hanani and Zebadiah.

21 And of the sons of Harim: Maaseiah, Elijah, Shemaiah, Jehiel, and Uzziah.

22 And of the sons of Pashur: Elioenai, Maaseiah, Ishmael, Nethanel, Jozabad, and Elasah.

23 And of the Levites: Jozabad, Shimei, Kelaiah (he *is* Kelita,) Pethahiah, Judah, and Eliezer.

24 And of the singers: Eliashib; and of the porters: Shallum, Telem, and Uri.

25 Also of Israel: of the sons of Parosh: Ramiah, Jeziah, Malchiah, Mejamin, Eleazar, Asabia, and Benaiah.

26 And of the sons of Elam: Matthaniah, Zechariah, Jehiel, Abdi, Jeremoth, and Eliah.

27 And of the sons of Zattu: Elioenai, Eliashib, Matthaniah, Jeremoth, Zabad, and Aziza.

28 And of the sons of Babai: Jehohanan, Hananiah, Zabbai, and Athlai.

29 And of the sons of Bani: Meshullam, Malluch, Adaiah, Jashub, Sheal, and Ramoth.

30 And of the sons of Pahath-Moab: Adna, Chelal, Benaiah, Maaseiah, Mattaniah, Bezalel, Binnui, and Manasseh.

31 And of the sons of Harim: Eliezer, Ishijah, Malchijah, Shemaiah, Shimeon,

32 Benjamin, Malluch, and Shemariah.

33 And of the sons of Hashum: Matthenai, Matthattah, Zadab, Eliphelet, Jeremai, Manasseh, and Shimei.

34 And of the sons of Bani: Maadai, Amram, Uel,

35 Banaia, Bedeiah, Cheluh,

36 Vaniah, Meremoth, Eliashib,

37 Matthaniah, and Matthenai.

38 And *so* did the children of Binnui, and the children of Shimei, 39 and Shelemiah, Nathan, and Adaiah,

40 Machnadebai, Shashai, Sharai,

41 Azarel, Shelemiah, Shemariah,

42 Shallum, Amariah, and Joseph.

43 Of the sons of Nebo: Jeiel, Mattithiah, Zabad, Zebina, Jaddai, Joel, and Benaiah.

44 All these had taken strange wives, and had begotten sons of them.

THE BOOK OF NEHEMIAH

Nehemiah Prays for His People

1 The words of Nehemiah the son of Hachaliah. And it came to pass in the month of Chislev, of the twentieth year, that I was in Shushan the palace.

2 And Hanani, one of my brothers, came, he and *some* men of Judah; and I asked them concerning those that had escaped, who had been left of the captivity, and concerning Jerusalem.

3 And they said to me, "The remnant, *even* those that are left of the captivity, *are* there in the land, in great distress and reproach; and the walls of Jerusalem *are* thrown down, and its gates are burned with fire."

4 And it came to pass, when I heard these words, *that* I sat down and wept, and mourned for *several* days, and continued fasting and praying before the God of heaven.

5 And I said, "I pray, O Lord God of heaven, the mighty *One*, the great and terrible, keeping Your covenant and mercy to them that love Him, and to those that keep His commandments.

6 Let now Your ear be attentive, and Your eyes open, that You may hear the prayer of Your servant, which I pray before You at this time, *both* this day and night, for the children of Israel Your servants, and make confession for the sins of the children of Israel, which we have sinned against You—both I and the house of my father have sinned.

7 We have altogether broken *our covenant* with You, and we have not kept the commandments, and the ordinances, and the judgments, which You commanded Your servant Moses.

8 Remember, I pray, the word in which You charged Your servant Moses, saying, 'If you break *your* covenant *with Me*, I will disperse you among the nations,

9 But if you turn again to Me, and keep My commandments, and do them; if you should be scattered to the uttermost *parts* of heaven, yet will I gather them from there, and I will bring them into the place which I have chosen as a dwelling for My name.'

10 Now they *are* Your servants and Your people, whom You have redeemed by Your great power, and by Your mighty hand.

11 Do not *turn away*, I pray, O Lord, but let Your ear be attentive to the prayer of Your servant, and to the prayer of Your servants, who desire to fear Your name, and prosper Your servant this day, and cause him to find mercy in the sight of this man." (For I was the king's cupbearer).

NEHEMIAH CHAPTER 2

Nehemiah Sent to Judah

1 And it came to pass in the month of Nisan of the twentieth year of King Artaxerxes, that the wine was before me. And I took the wine, and gave *it* to the king; and there was not another before him.

2 And the king said to me, "Why is your countenance sad, and you do not control yourself? And now this is nothing but sadness of heart." Then I was very much alarmed,

3 and I said to the king, "Let the king live forever. Why should not my countenance be sad, when the city, even the home of the tombs of my fathers, has been laid waste, and her gates have been devoured with fire?"

4 And the king said to me, "What is your request?" So I prayed to the God of heaven.

5 And I said to the king, "If *it pleases* the king, and if your servant has found favor in your sight, *I ask* that *you* would send him into Judah, to the city of the tombs of my fathers; then will I rebuild it."

6 And the king, and his concubine that sat next to him, said to me, "For how long will your journey be, and when will you return?" And *the proposal* was pleasing before the king, and he sent me away, and I appointed him a time.

7 And I said to the king, "If *it pleases* the king, let him give me letters to the governors beyond the river, so as to permit me to pass, till I come to Judah;

8 and a letter to Asaph the keeper of the garden which belongs to the king, that he may give me timber to cover the gates, and for the wall of the city, and for the house into which I shall enter." And the king gave to me, according as the good hand of God *was upon me.*

9 And I came to the governors beyond the river, and I gave them the king's letters. (Now the king had sent with me captains of the army and horsemen).

10 And Sanballat the Horonite heard *it*, and Tobiah the servant, the Ammonite, and it was grievous to them that a man had come to seek the welfare of the children of Israel.

Nehemiah Views the Wall of Jerusalem

11 So I came to Jerusalem, and was there three days.

12 And I rose up by night, I and a few men with me; and I told no man what God put into my heart to do with Israel; and there was no beast with me, except the beast which I rode upon.

13 And I went forth by the gate of the valley by night, and to the mouth of the Well of Fig Trees, and to the Refuse Gate; and I mourned over the wall of Jerusalem which they were destroying, and her gates were devoured with fire.

14 And I passed on to the Fountain Gate, and to the king's pool; and there was no room for the beast to pass under me.

15 And I went up by the wall of the brook by night, and mourned over the wall, and passed through the gate of the valley, and returned.

16 And the sentinels did not know why I went, nor what I was doing; and until that time I did not tell it to the Jews, or to the priests, or to the nobles, or to the captains, or to the rest *of the men* who did the work.

17 Then I said to them, "You see this evil, in which we are, how Jerusalem is desolate, and her gates have been set on fire. Come, and let us build throughout the wall of Jerusalem, and we shall no longer be a reproach."

18 And I told them of the hand of God which was good upon me, also about the words of the king which he spoke to me. And I said, "Let us arise and build." And their hands were strengthened for the good *work.*

19 And Sanballat the Horonite, and Tobiah the servant, the Ammonite, and Gesham the Arabian, heard *it*, and they laughed us to scorn, and came to us, and said, "What *is* this thing that you are doing? Are you revolting against the king?"

20 And I answered them, and said to them, "The God of heaven, He shall prosper us, and we His servants are pure, and we will build; but you have no part, nor right, nor memorial, in Jerusalem."

NEHEMIAH CHAPTER 3

Rebuilding the Wall

1 Then Eliashib the high priest rose up with his brothers the priests, and built the Sheep Gate; they sanctified it, and set

up the doors of it; even to the Tower of the Hundred they sanctified *it*, to the Tower of Hananel.

[2] And *they built* by the side of the men of Jericho, and by the side of the sons of Zacchur, the son of Imri.

[3] And the sons of Hassenaah built the Fish Gate; they roofed it, and covered in its doors, and bolts, and bars.

[4] And next to them *the order* reached to Meremoth the son of Urijah, the son of Koz, and next to them Meshullam son of Berechiah the son of Meshezebel took *his* place; and next to them Zadok the son of Baana took *his* place.

[5] And next to them the Tekoites took *their* place; but the Adorim did not put their shoulders to their service.

[6] And Jehoiada the son of Paseah, and Meshullam son of Besodeiah, repaired the old gate; they covered it in, and set up its doors, and its bolts, and its bars.

[7] And next to them Melatiah the Gibeonite, and Jadon the Meronothite, the men of Gibeon and Mizpah, made repairs to the throne of the governor on this side the river.

[8] And next to him Uzziel the son of Harhaiah of the smiths, carried on the repairs. And next to them Hananiah the son of one of the perfumers made repairs, and they finished Jerusalem to the broad wall.

[9] And next to them repaired Rephaiah the son of Hur, the ruler of half the district round about Jerusalem.

[10] And next to them repaired Jedaiah the son of Harumaph, and *that* in front of his house. And next to him repaired Hattush son of Hashabniah.

[11] And next *to him* repaired Malchijah son of Harim, and Hashub son of Pahath-Moab, even to the Tower of the Ovens.

[12] And next to him repaired Shallum the son of Hallohesh, the ruler of half the district round about Jerusalem, he and his daughters.

[13] Hanun and the inhabitants of Zanoah repaired the gate of the valley; they built it, and set up its doors, and its bolts, and its bars, and a thousand cubits of the wall as far as the Refuse Gate.

[14] And Malchijah the son of Rechab, the ruler of the district round about Beth-Haccerem, repaired the Refuse Gate, he and his sons; and they covered it, and set up its doors, and its bolts, and its bars.

[15] But Shallun the son of Col-Hozeh repaired the gate of the fountain, the ruler of part of Mizpah. He built it, and covered it, and set up its doors and its bars, and the wall of the pool of the skins by the meadow of the king, and as far as the steps that lead down from the City of David.

[16] After him repaired Nehemiah son of Azbuk, ruler of half the district round about Beth Zur, as far as the garden of David's Tomb, and as far as the artificial pool, and as far as the house of the mighty men.

[17] After him repaired the Levites, *even* Rehum the son of Bani. Next to him repaired Hashabiah, ruler of half the district round about Keilah, in his district.

[18] And after him repaired his brothers, Bavai son of Henadad, ruler of half the district round about Keilah.

[19] And next to him repaired Ezer the son of Jeshua, ruler of Mizpah, another portion of the tower of ascent, where it meets the corner.

[20] After him repaired Baruch the son of Zabbai, a second portion, from the corner as far as the door of the house of Eliashib the high priest.

[21] After him repaired Meremoth the son of Urijah the son of Koz, a second part from the door of the house of Eliashib, to the end of the house of Eliashib.

[22] And after him repaired the priests, the men of Ecchechar.

[23] And after him repaired Benjamin and Hasshub over against their house. And after him repaired Azariah son of Maaseiah the son of Ananiah, *the parts* near to his house.

[24] After him repaired Binnui the son of Henadad, another portion from the house of Azariah as far as the corner and to the turning,

[25] of Palal the son of Uzai, opposite the corner, and *where is* also the tower that projects from the king's house, even the upper one of the prison house. And after him *repaired* Pedaiah the son of Parosh.

[26] And the Nethinim dwelt in Ophel, as far as the garden of the Water Gate eastward, and *there is* the projecting tower.

[27] And after them the Tekoites repaired, another portion opposite the great projecting tower, even as far as the wall of Ophel.

[28] The priests repaired above the Horse Gate, *every* man over against his own house.

[29] And after him repaired Zadok the son of Immer repaired opposite his own house. And after him repaired Shemaiah son of Shechaniah, keeper of the East Gate.

[30] After him repaired Hananiah son of Shelemiah, and Hanun, the sixth son of Zalaph, another portion. After him Meshullam the son of Berechiah repaired over against his treasury.

[31] After him repaired Malchijah the son of Sarephi as far as the house of the Nethinim, and the merchants over against the Gate of Miphkad, and as far as the steps of the corner.

[32] And between *that and* the Sheep Gate the smiths and merchants repaired.

NEHEMIAH CHAPTER 4

Hostile Plots Thwarted

[1] Now it came to pass, when Sanaballat heard that we were building the wall, that it was grievous to him, and he was very angry, and railed against the Jews.

[2] And he said before his brothers (that is, the army of the Samaritans), "*Is it true* that these Jews are building their city? Do they indeed offer sacrifices? Will they prevail? And will they restore the stones this day, after they have been burned and made a heap of rubbish?"

[3] And Tobiah the Ammonite came near to him, and said to them, "Do they sacrifice or eat in their place? Shall not a fox go up and pull down their wall of stones?

4 "Hear, O our God, for we have become a scorn; and return their reproach upon their own heads, and make them a scorn in a land of captivity,

5 and do not cover *their* iniquity."

6 (This verse omitted in LXX)

7 But it came to pass, when Sanaballat and Tobiah, and the Arabians, and the Ammonites, heard that the building of the walls of Jerusalem was advancing, and that the breaches began to be stopped, that it appeared very grievous to them.

8 And all of them assembled together, to come to fight against Jerusalem, and to destroy it utterly.

9 So we prayed to our God and set watchmen against them day and night, because of them.

10 And Judah said, "The strength of the enemies is broken, yet *there is* much rubbish, and we shall not be able to build the wall.

11 And they that afflicted us said, 'They shall not know, and they shall not see, until we come into the midst of them, and kill them, and cause the work to cease.'"

12 And it came to pass, when the Jews who lived near them came, that they said to us, "They are coming up against us from every quarter."

13 So I set *men* in the lowest part of the place behind the wall in the secret places, I even set the people according to their families, with their swords, their spears, and their bows.

14 And I looked, and arose, and said to the nobles, and to the captains, and to the rest of the people, "Do not be afraid of them; remember our great and terrible God, and fight for your brothers, your sons, your daughters, your wives, and your houses."

15 And it came to pass, when our enemies heard that it was made known to us, and God had frustrated their counsel, that we all returned to the wall, *every* man to his work.

16 So it was, from that day on, *that* half of them that had been driven forth, did the work, and half of them kept guard; and *there were* spears, shields, bows, and breastplates, and rulers behind the whole house of Judah,

17 even of them that were building the wall. And those who carried the burdens *were* under arms: *each* with one hand performing his work, and with the other held his weapon.

18 And the builders *worked with* each man having his sword girded at his side, and so they built; and the trumpeter with his trumpet next to him.

19 And I said to the nobles, and to the rulers, and to the rest of the people, "The work *is* great and abundant, and we are dispersed upon the wall, each at a great distance from his brother.

20 In whatever place you shall hear the sound of the trumpet, gather yourselves to us there; and our God shall fight for us."

21 So we *continued* laboring at the work. And half of them held the spears from the rising of the morning until the stars appeared.

22 And at that time I said to the people, "Let every man with his servant stay at night in the midst of Jerusalem, and let the night be a watch-time to you, and the day a work-time."

23 And I was *there*, and the watchmen behind me, and there was not a man of us that put off his garments.

NEHEMIAH CHAPTER 5

Nehemiah Deals with Oppression

1 And the cry of the people and their wives *was* great against their brothers the Jews.

2 And some said, "We *are* numerous with our sons and our daughters; so we will take grain, and eat, and live."

3 And some said, "*As to* our fields and vineyards and houses, let us pledge *them*, and we will take grain, and eat."

4 And some said, "We have borrowed money for the king's tributes—our fields, and our vineyards, and houses *are* pledged.

5 And now our flesh *is* as the flesh of our brothers, our children *are* as their children. Yet behold, we are reducing our sons and our daughters to slavery, and some of our daughters are enslaved; and there is no power of our hands, for our fields and our vineyards *belong* to the nobles."

6 And I was very angry as I heard their cry and these words.

7 And my heart took counsel within me, and I contended against the nobles, and the princes, and I said to them, "Should every man demand of his brother what you demand?" And I appointed against them a great assembly,

8 and I said to them, "We of our free will have redeemed our brothers the Jews that were sold to the Gentiles; and do you sell your brothers? And shall they be delivered to us?" And they were silent, and found no answer.

9 And I said, "The thing which you do is not good; you will not so walk in the fear of our God because of the reproach of the Gentiles our enemies.

10 Both my brothers, and my acquaintances, and I, have lent them money and grain. Let us now leave off this usury!

11 Restore to them, I pray, as at this day, their fields, and their vineyards, and their olive yards, and their houses, and bring forth to them grain and wine and oil of the money."

12 And they said, "We will restore, and we will not exact of them; we will do thus as you say." Then I called the priests, and bound them by oath to do according to this word.

13 And I shook out my garment, and said, "So may God shake out every man who shall not keep to this word, from his house, and from his labors, he shall be even thus shaken out, as an outcast and empty." And all the congregation said, "Amen," and they praised the Lord; and the people did this thing.

The Generosity of Nehemiah

14 From the day that he charged me to be their ruler in the land of Judah, from the twentieth year even to the thirty-

second year of Artaxerxes, twelve years, neither I nor my brothers ate the *provisions* extorted from them.

¹⁵ But as for the former acts of extortion in which *those who were* before me oppressed them, they even took of them their last money, forty shekels for bread and wine; and the *very* outcasts of them exercised authority over the people; but I did not so, because of the fear of God.

¹⁶ Also in the work of the wall I did not treat them with rigor, I did not buy land; and all that were gathered together *came* there to the work.

¹⁷ And the Jews, to *the number of* a hundred and fifty men, besides those coming to us from the nations round about, *were* at my table.

¹⁸ And there came *to me* for one day one calf, and I had six choice sheep and a goat; and every ten days wine in abundance of all sorts. Yet with these I did not require the bread of extortion, because the bondage was heavy upon this people.

¹⁹ Remember me, O God, for good, *in* all that I have done to this people.

NEHEMIAH CHAPTER 6

Conspiracy Against Nehemiah

¹ Now it came to pass, when Sanballat, Tobiah, and Geshem the Arabian, and the rest of our enemies, heard that I had built the wall, and *that* there were no breaks left in it (though at that time I had not set up the doors on the gates),

² that Sanballat and Geshem sent to me, saying, "Come and let us meet together in the villages in the plain of Ono." But they *were* plotting to do me harm.

³ So I sent messengers to them, saying, "I am doing a great work, and I shall not be able to come down, lest the work should cease; as soon as I have finished it, I will come down to you."

⁴ And they sent to me *again* with the same request, and I sent them *word* accordingly.

⁵ Then Sanballat sent his servant to me with an open letter in his hand.

⁶ And in it was written, "It has been reported among the Gentiles that you and the Jews are planning to revolt. Therefore you are building the wall, and you will be a king to them.

⁷ And moreover you have appointed prophets to yourself, that you might dwell in Jerusalem as a king over Judah; and now these words will be reported to the king. Now then, come, let us take counsel together."

⁸ And I sent to him, saying, "It has not happened according to these words, *even* as you say, for you frame them falsely out of your own heart."

⁹ For all were trying to alarm us, saying, "Their hands shall be weakened from this work, and it shall not be done." Now therefore I have strengthened my hands.

¹⁰ And I came into the house of Shemaiah the son of Delaiah the Son of Mehetabel, and he was shut up; and he said, "Let us assemble together in the house of God, in the midst of it, and let us shut the doors of it; for they are coming by night to slay you."

¹¹ And I said, "Who is the man that shall enter into the house, that he may live?"

¹² And I observed, and behold, God had not sent him, for the prophecy was a fable *devised* against me:

¹³ and Tobiah and Sanballat had hired a multitude against me, that I might be frightened, and do this, and sin, and become to them an ill name, that they might reproach me.

¹⁴ Remember, O God, Tobiah and Sanballat, according to these their deeds, and the prophetess Noadiah, and the rest of the prophets who tried to alarm me.

The Wall Completed

¹⁵ So the wall was finished on the twenty-fifth day of Elul, in fifty-two days.

¹⁶ And it came to pass, when all our enemies heard *of it*, that all the nations round about us feared, and great alarm fell upon them, and they knew that it was of our God that this work should be finished.

¹⁷ And in those days letters came to Tobiah from many nobles of Judah, and those of Tobiah came to them.

¹⁸ For many in Judah were bound to him by oath, because he was son-in-law of Shechaniah the son of Arah; and Jehohanan his son had taken the daughter of Meshullam the son of Berechiah for a wife.

¹⁹ And they reported his words to me, and carried out my words to him: and Tobiah sent letters to terrify me.

NEHEMIAH CHAPTER 7

¹ And it came to pass, when the wall was built, and I had set up the doors, and the porters and the singers and the Levites were appointed,

² that I gave charge to my brother, and Hanani the ruler of the palace, over Jerusalem; for he was a true man, and one that feared God beyond many.

³ And I said to them, "The gates of Jerusalem shall not be opened till sunrise; and while they are still watching, let the doors be shut, and bolted; and set watches of them that dwell in Jerusalem, *every* man at his post, and *every* man over against his house."

The Captives Who Returned to Jerusalem

⁴ Now the city *was* wide and large, and the people *were* few in it, and the houses were not built.

⁵ And God put *it* into my heart, and I gathered the nobles and the rulers and the people into companies; and I found a register of the company that came up first, and I found written in it as follows:

⁶ Now these *are* the children of the country, that came up from captivity, of the number which Nebuchadnezzar king of

Babylon carried away, and they returned to Jerusalem and to Judah, *every* man to his city.

7 Those who came with Zerubbabel *were* Jeshua, Nehemiah, Azariah, Raamiah, Nahamani, Mordecai, Bilshan, Mispereth, Ezra, Bigvai, Nehum, Baanah, and Masphar, men of the people of Israel.

8 The children of Parosh, two thousand one hundred and seventy-two.

9 The children of Shephatiah, three hundred and seventy-two.

10 The children of Arah, six hundred and fifty-two.

11 The children of Pahath-Moab, with the children of Jeshua and Joab, two thousand six hundred and eighteen.

12 The children of Elam, a thousand two hundred and fifty-four. 13 The children of Zattu, eight hundred and forty-five.

14 The children of Zaccai, seven hundred and sixty.

15 The children of Binnui, six hundred and forty-eight.

16 The children of Bebai, six hundred and twenty-eight.

17 The children of Azgad, two thousand three hundred and twenty-two.

18 The children of Adonikam, six hundred and sixty-seven.

19 The children of Bagvai, two thousand and sixty-seven.

20 The children of Adin, six hundred and fifty-five.

21 The children of Ater, *the son* of Hezekiah, ninety-eight.

22 The children of Hashum, three hundred and twenty-eight.

23 The children of Bezai, three hundred and twenty-four.

24 The children of Hariph, a hundred and twelve; the children of Asen, two hundred and twenty-three.

25 The children of Gibeon, ninety-five.

26 The children of Bethlehem, a hundred and twenty-three; the children of Netopha, fifty-six.

27 The children of Anathoth, a hundred and twenty-eight.

28 The men of Beth Azmaveth, forty-two.

29 The men of Kirjath Jearim, Chephirah, and Beeroth, seven hundred and forty-three.

30 The men of Ramah and Geba, six hundred and twenty.

31 The men of Michmas, a hundred and twenty-two.

32 The men of Bethel and Ai, a hundred and twenty-three.

33 The men of Nebo, a hundred and fifty-two.

34 The men of Elam, one thousand two hundred and fifty-two. 35 The children of Harim, three hundred and twenty.

36 The children of Jericho, three hundred and forty-five.

37 The children of Lod and Ono, seven hundred and twenty-one.

38 The children of Senaah, three thousand nine hundred and thirty.

39 The priests: the sons of Jedaiah, of the house of Jeshua, nine hundred and seventy-three.

40 The children of Immer, one thousand and fifty-two.

41 The children of Pashhur, one thousand two hundred and forty-seven.

42 The children of Harim, a thousand and seventeen.

43 The Levites: the children of Jeshua the son of Kadmiel, with the children of Uduia, seventy-four.

44 The singers: the children of Asaph, a hundred and forty-eight.

45 The porters: the children of Shallum, the children of Ater, the children of Talmon, the children of Akkub, the children of Hatita, the children of Shobai, a hundred and thirty-eight.

46 The Nethinim: the children of Sea, the children of Hasupha, the children of Tabaoth,

47 the children of Keros, the children of Siaha, the children of Padon,

48 the children of Lebana, the children of Hagaba, the children of Salmai,

49 the children of Hanan, the children of Giddel, the children of Gahar,

50 the children of Reaiah, the children of Rezin, the children of Nekoda,

51 the children of Gazzam, the children of Uzza, the children of Paseah,

52 the children of Besai, the children of Meunim, the children of Nephishesim,

53 the children of Bakbuk, the children of Hakupha, the children of Harhur,

54 the children of Bazluth, the children of Mehida, the children of Harsha,

55 the children of Barkos, the children of Sisera, the children of Tamah,

56 the children of Neziah, the children of Hatipha.

57 The children of the servants of Solomon: the children of Sotai, the children of Sophereth, the children of Perida,

58 the children of Jaala, the children of Darkon, the children of Giddel,

59 the children of Shephatiah, the children of Hattil, the children of Pochereth, the children of Zebaim the children of Amon.

60 All the Nethinim, and children of the servants of Solomon, *were* three hundred and ninety-two.

61 And these went up from Tel Melah, Tel Harsha, Cherub, Addon, and Immer; but they could not declare the houses of their families, or their descendants, whether they were of Israel.

62 The children of Delaiah, the children of Tobiah, the children of Nekoda, six hundred and forty-two.

63 And of the priests: the children of Habaiah, the children of Hakkoz, the children of Barzillai, for they took wives of the daughters of Barzillai the Gileadite, and they were called by their name.

64 These sought the pedigree of their company, and it was not found, and they were removed *as polluted* from the priesthood.

65 And the governor said that they should not eat of the most holy things, until a priest should stand up to give light.

66 And all the congregation was about forty-two thousand three hundred and sixty,

67 besides their male and female servants, these were seven thousand three hundred and thirty seven. And the men and women singers *were* two hundred and forty-five.

68 (This verse omitted in LXX)

69 *Their* donkeys *were* two thousand seven hundred.

70 And some of the heads of families gave into the treasury to Nehemiah for the work a thousand pieces of gold, fifty bowls, and thirty priests' *garments*.

71 And *some* of the heads of families gave into the treasuries of the work, twenty thousand pieces of gold, and two thousand three hundred pounds of silver.

72 And the rest of the people gave twenty thousand pieces of gold, and two thousand two hundred pounds of silver, and sixty-seven priests' *garments*.

73 And the priests, and Levites, and porters, and singers, and *some* of the people, and the Nethinim, and all Israel, dwelt in their cities.

NEHEMIAH CHAPTER 8

Ezra Reads the Law

1 And the seventh month arrived, and the children of Israel *were settled* in their cities. And all the people were gathered as one man to the broad place before the Water Gate, and they told Ezra the scribe to bring the Book of the Law of Moses, which the Lord commanded Israel.

2 So Ezra the priest brought the law before the congregation both of men and women, and everyone who had understanding *was present* to hear, on the first day of the seventh month.

3 And he read in it from sunrise until midday, before the men and the women; and they understood *it*, and the ears of all the people *were attentive* to the Book of the Law.

4 And Ezra the scribe stood on a wooden stage, and there stood next to him Mattithiah, Shema, Hanani, Urijah, Hilkiah, and Maaseiah, on his right hand; and at his left *stood* Pedaiah, Mishael, Malchijah, Hashum, Hashbadana, Zechariah, and Meshullam.

5 And Ezra opened the book before all the people, for he was above the people; and it came to pass when he had opened it, *that* all the people stood.

6 And Ezra blessed the Lord, the great God; and all the people answered, and said, "Amen," lifting up their hands. And they bowed down and worshipped the Lord with their face to the ground.

7 And Jeshua, Bani and Sherebiah instructed the people in the law, and the people *stood* in their place.

8 And they read in the Book of the Law of God, and Ezra taught, and instructed them distinctly in the knowledge of the Lord, and the people understood from the reading.

9 And Nehemiah and Ezra the priest and scribe, and the Levites, and they that instructed the people, spoke and said to all the people, "It is a holy day to the Lord our God; do not mourn, nor weep." For all the people wept when they heard the words of the Law.

10 And *the governor* said to them, "Go, eat the fat, and drink the sweet, and send portions to them that have nothing; for this day is holy to our Lord: and faint not, for the Lord is our strength."

11 And the Levites caused all the people to be silent, saying, "Be silent, for *it is* a holy day, and do not be grieved."

12 So all the people departed to eat and drink, to send portions and rejoice greatly, for they understood the words which he made known to them.

13 And on the second day the heads of families assembled with all the people, *also* the priests and Levites, to Ezra the scribe, to attend to all the words of the Law.

14 And they found written in the law which the Lord commanded Moses, that the children of Israel should dwell in booths, in the feast in the seventh month,

15 and that they should sound with trumpets in all their cities, and in Jerusalem. And Ezra said, "Go forth to the mountain, and bring olive branches, and branches of cypress trees, and branches of myrtle, and branches of palm trees, and branches of *every* thick tree, to make booths, according to that which was written."

16 And the people went forth, and brought *them*, and made booths for themselves, each one upon his roof, and in their courts, and in the courts of the house of God, and in the streets of the city, and as far as the gate of Ephraim.

17 And all the congregation who had returned from the captivity made booths, and dwelt in booths, for the children of Israel *had* not done so from the days of Joshua the son of Nun until that day. And there was great joy.

18 And *Ezra* read in the Book of the Law of God daily, from the first day even to the last day; and they kept the feast seven days; and on the eighth day *was* a solemn assembly, according to the ordinance.

NEHEMIAH CHAPTER 9

The People Confess Their Sins

1 Now on the twenty-fourth day of this month the children of Israel assembled with fasting, and in sackcloth, and with ashes on their head.

2 And the children of Israel separated themselves from every stranger, and stood and confessed their sins, and the iniquities of their fathers.

3 And they stood in their place, and read in the Book of the Law of the Lord their God; and they confessed *their sins* to the Lord, and worshipped the Lord their God.

4 *And* there stood upon the stairs, of the Levites, Jeshua, and the sons of Kadmiel, Shebaniah the son of Sarabia, sons of Chenani; and they cried with a loud voice to the Lord their God.

5 And the Levites, Jeshua and Kadmiel, said, "Rise up, bless the Lord our God forever and ever; and let them bless Your glorious name, and exalt it with all blessing and praise."

6 And Ezra said, "You are the only true Lord; You have made the heaven, and the heaven of heavens, with all their

host, the earth, and everything in it, the seas, and everything in them; and You give life to all things, and the hosts of heaven worship You.

7 You are the Lord God, You chose Abram, and brought him out of the land of the Chaldeans, and gave him the name of Abraham.

8 And You found his heart faithful before You, and made a covenant with him to give to him and to his descendants the land of the Canaanites, the Hittites, the Amorites, the Perizzites, the Jebusites, and the Girgashites; and You have confirmed Your words, for You *are* righteous.

9 "And You saw the affliction of our fathers in Egypt, and You heard their cry at the Red Sea.

10 And You showed signs and wonders in Egypt, on Pharaoh and all his servants, and on all the people of his land; for You knew that they behaved insolently against them; and You made Yourself a name, as it is this day.

11 And You divided the sea before them, and they passed through the midst of the sea on dry land; and You cast them that were about to pursue them into the deep, as a stone into the mighty waters.

12 And You guided them by day by a pillar of cloud, and by night by a pillar of fire, to light the way for them in which they should walk.

13 Also You came down upon Mount Sinai, and You spoke to them out of heaven, and gave them right judgments, and laws of truth, ordinances, and good commandments.

14 And You made known to them Your holy Sabbath; You enjoined upon them commandments, and ordinances, and a law, by the hand of Your servant Moses.

15 And You gave them bread from heaven for their food, and You brought them water from a rock for their thirst; and You told them to go in to inherit the land over which You stretched out Your hand to give to them.

16 "But they and our fathers behaved proudly, and hardened their neck, and did not heed Your commandments,

17 and refused to listen, and did not remember Your wonders which You worked among them. And they hardened their neck, and appointed a leader to return to their slavery in Egypt. But You, O God, *are* merciful and compassionate, longsuffering, and abundant in mercy, and You did not forsake them.

18 And still farther they even made for themselves a molded calf, and said, 'These *are* the gods that brought us up out of Egypt'; and they worked great provocations.

19 Yet You in Your great mercy did not forsake them in the wilderness; You did not turn away from them the pillar of the cloud by day, to guide them in the way, nor the pillar of fire by night, to enlighten for them the way in which they should walk.

20 And You gave Your good Spirit to instruct them, and You did not withhold Your manna from their mouth, and gave them water in their thirst.

21 And You sustained them forty years in the wilderness; You did not allow anything to fail them. Their garments did not wear out, and their feet were not bruised.

22 Moreover, You gave them kingdoms, and divided nations to them; and they inherited the land of Sihon, king of Hesbron, and the land of Og king of Bashan.

23 And You multiplied their children as the stars of heaven, and brought them into the land of which You spoke to their fathers;

24 And they inherited it; and You destroyed from before them the inhabitants in the land of the Canaanites, and You gave into their hands them and their kings, and the nations of the land, to do unto them as it pleased them.

25 And they took lofty cities, and inherited houses full of all good things, wells *already* dug, vineyards and olive yards, and every fruit tree in abundance. So they ate, and were filled, and grew fat, and delighted themselves in Your great goodness.

26 "But they turned, and revolted from You, and cast Your law behind their backs; and they killed Your prophets, who testified against them to turn them back to You, and they worked great provocations.

27 Then You gave them into the hand of them that afflicted them, and they did afflict them. And they cried to You in the time of their affliction, and You heard them from heaven, and in Your great mercy You gave them deliverers, and saved them from the hand of them that afflicted them.

28 But when they rested, they did evil again before You, so You left them in the hands of their enemies, and they ruled over them; and they cried again to You, and You heard from heaven, and delivered them in Your great mercy.

29 And You testified against them, to bring them back to Your law; but they did not listen, and sinned against Your commandments and Your judgments, which if a man does, he shall live in them; and they turned their back, and hardened their neck, and did not hear.

30 Yet You had patience with them for many years, and testified to them by Your Spirit by the hand of Your prophets: but they did not hear; so You gave them into the hand of the nations of the land.

31 But You in Your many mercies did not appoint them to destruction, and did not forsake them; for You are strong, and merciful, and compassionate.

32 "And now, O our God, the powerful, the great, the mighty, and the terrible, keeping Your covenant and Your mercy, let not all this trouble seem little in Your sight which has come upon us, and our kings, and our princes, and our priests, and our prophets, and our fathers, and upon all Your people, from the days of the kings of Assyria even to this day.

33 For You *are* righteous in all the things that come upon us; and You have dealt faithfully, but we have greatly sinned.

34 And our kings, and our princes, and our priests, and our fathers, have not performed Your law, and have not given heed to Your commandments, and *have not kept* Your testimonies which You testified to them.

35 And they did not serve You in Your kingdom, and in Your great goodness which You gave to them, and in the large and fat land which You furnished before them, and they did not turn from their evil ways.

36 Behold, we are servants this day, and *as for* the land which You gave to our fathers, to eat the fruit of it and the good things of it, behold, we are servants upon it;

37 and its produce *is* abundant for the kings whom You appointed over us because of our sins; and they have dominion over our bodies, and over our cattle, as it pleases them, and we are in great affliction.

38 "And in regard to all these circumstances we make a covenant, and write *it,* and our princes, our Levites, *and* our priests, set their seal to *it.*"

NEHEMIAH CHAPTER 10

The People Who Sealed the Covenant

1 And over them that sealed were Nehemiah the governor, son of Hacaliah, and Zedekiah,

2 Seraiah, Azariah, and Jeremiah,

3 Pashur, Amariah, Malchijah,

4 Hattush, Shebaniah, Malluch,

5 Harim, Meremoth, Obadiah,

6 Daniel, Ginnethon, Baruch,

7 Meshullam, Abijah, Mijamin,

8 Maaziah, Bilgai, Shemaiah; these *were* priests.

9 And the Levites: Jeshua the son of Azaniah, Binnui of the sons of Henadad, Kadmiel

10 and his brothers, Shebaniah, Hodijah, Kelita, Pelaiah, Hanan,

11 Micha, Rehob, Hashabiah,

12 Zacchur, Sherebiah, Shebaniah,

13 Hodijah, the sons of Beninu.

14 The heads of the people: Parosh, Pahath-Moab, Elam, Zattu,

15 the sons of Bunni, Azgad, Bebai,

16 Adonijah, Bigvai, Adin,

17 Ater, Hezekiah, Azzur,

18 Hodijah, Hashum, Bezai,

19 Hariph, Anathoth, Nebai,

20 Magpiash, Meshullam, Hezir,

21 Meshezebel, Zadok, Jaddua,

22 Pelatiah, Hanan, Anaiah,

23 Hoshea, Hananiah, Hasshub,

24 Hallohesh, Pilha, Shobek,

25 Rehum, Hashabnah, Maaseiah,

26 Ahijah, Hanan, Anan,

27 Malluch, Harim, *and* Baanah.

28 And the rest of the people, the priests, the Levites, the porters, the singers, the Nethinim, and everyone who drew off from the nations of the land to the law of God, their wives, their sons, their daughters, everyone who had knowledge and understanding,

29 were urgent with their brothers, and bound them under a curse, and entered into a curse, and into an oath, to walk in the law of God, which was given by the hand of Moses, the servant of God; to keep and to do all the commandments of the Lord, and His judgments, and His ordinances.

30 And that "We will not," *they said,* "give our daughters to the people of the land, nor will we take their daughters to our sons.

31 And *as for* the people of the land who bring wares and all *manner of* merchandise to sell on the Sabbath day, we *will* not buy from them on the Sabbath or on the holy day; and we will leave the seventh year, and the exaction of every debt.

32 "And we will impose ordinances upon ourselves, to levy on ourselves a third of a shekel yearly for the service of the house of our God;

33 the showbread, and the continual grain offering, and for the continual burnt offering, of the Sabbaths, of the new moon, for the feast, and for the holy things, and the sin offerings, to make atonement for Israel, and for the works of the house of our God.

34 And we cast lots for the office of wood-bearing, *we* the priests, and the Levites, and the people, to bring *wood* into the house of our God, according to the house of our families, at certain set times, year by year, to burn on the altar of the Lord our God, as it is written in the law;

35 and to bring the firstfruits of our land, and the firstfruits of the fruit of every tree, year by year, into the house of the Lord;

36 the firstborn of our sons, and of our cattle, as it is written in the law, and the firstborn of our herds and of our flocks, to bring to the house of our God, for the priests that minister in the house of our God.

37 And the firstfruits of our grain, and the fruit of every tree, of wine, and of oil, will we bring to the priests to the treasury of the house of God; and a tithe of our land to the Levites; for the Levites themselves shall receive tithes in all the cities of the land we cultivate.

38 And the priest, the son of Aaron, shall be with the Levites in the tithe of the Levite: and the Levites shall bring up *their* tithe to the house of our God, into the treasuries of the house of God.

39 For the children of Israel and the children of Levi shall bring into the treasuries the firstfruits of the grain, and wine, and oil; to where the holy vessels *are,* and the priests, and the ministers, and the porters, and the singers: and we will not forsake the house of our God."

NEHEMIAH CHAPTER 11

The People Dwelling in Jerusalem

¹ And the chiefs of the people dwelt in Jerusalem. And the rest of the people cast lots, to bring one of *every* ten to dwell in Jerusalem the holy city, and nine-tenths in the *other* cities.

² And the people blessed all the men that volunteered to dwell in Jerusalem.

³ Now these *are* the chiefs of the province who dwelt in Jerusalem, and in the cities of Judah; *every* man dwelt in his possession in their cities: Israel, the priests, and the Levites, and the Nethinim, and the children of the servants of Solomon.

⁴ And there dwelt in Jerusalem *some* of the children of Judah, and of the children of Benjamin. Of the children of Judah; Athaiah son of Uzziah, the son of Zechariah, the son of Amariah, the son of Shephatiah, the son of Mahalalel, and *some* of the sons of Perez;

⁵ and Maaseiah son of Baruch, son of Col-Hozeh, son of Hazaiah, son of Adaiah, son of Joarib, son of Zechariah, son of Shiloni.

⁶ All the sons of Perez who dwelt in Jerusalem *were* four hundred and sixty-eight men of might.

⁷ And these *were* the children of Benjamin: Sallu son of Meshullam, son of Joed, son of Pedaiah, son of Kolaiah, son of Maaseiah, son of Ithiel, son of Jeshaiah.

⁸ And after him Gabbai, Sallai, nine hundred and twenty-eight.

⁹ And Joel son of Zichri *was* overseer over them: and Judah son of Senuah was second in the city.

¹⁰ Of the priests: both Jedaiah son of Joiarib, and Jachin.

¹¹ Seraiah, son of Hilkiah, son of Meshullam, son of Zadok, son of Maraioth, son of Ahitub, was over the house of God.

¹² And their brothers doing the work of the house were eight hundred and twenty-two; and Adaiah son of Jeroham, son of Pelaliah, son of Amzi, son of Zechariah, son of Pashhur, son of Malchijah,

¹³ and his brothers, chiefs of families, two hundred and forty-two: and Amashai son of Azarel, son of Meshillemoth, son of Immer,

¹⁴ and his brothers, mighty men of war, a hundred and twenty-eight: and *their* overseer *was* Zabdiel son of *one of the* great men.

¹⁵ And of the Levites: Shemaiah, son of Hasshub,

¹⁶ (This verse omitted in LXX)

¹⁷ Matthaniah son of Micha, and Jobeb son of Samui,

¹⁸ two hundred and eighty-four.

¹⁹ And the porters: Akkub, Talmon, and their brothers, a hundred and seventy-two.

²⁰ (This verse omitted in LXX)

²¹ (This verse omitted in LXX)

²² And the overseer of the Levites *was* the son of Bani, son of Uzzi, son of Hashabiah, the son of Micha. Of the sons of Asaph the singers *some were* over the house of God,

²³ for so was the king's commandment concerning them.

²⁴ And Pethahiah son of Baseza was in attendance on the king in every matter for the people,

²⁵ and with regard to villages in their country district. And *some* of the children of Judah dwelt in Kirjath Arba,

²⁶ and in Jeshua,

²⁷ and in Beersheba.

²⁸ (This verse omitted in LXX)

²⁹ (This verse omitted in LXX)

³⁰ And their villages *were* Lachish and her lands: and they pitched their tents in Beersheba.

³¹ And the children of Benjamin *dwelt* from Gibeah *to* Michmash.

³² (This verse omitted in LXX)

³³ (This verse omitted in LXX)

³⁴ (This verse omitted in LXX)

³⁵ (This verse omitted in LXX)

³⁶ And of the Levites there were divisions to Judah *and* to Benjamin.

NEHEMIAH CHAPTER 12

The Priests and Levites

¹ Now these *are* the priests and the Levites that went up with Zerubbabel the son of Shealtiel and Jeshua: Seraiah, Jeremiah, Ezra,

² Amaria, Malluch, *and*

³ Shechaniah.

⁴ (This verse omitted in LXX)

⁵ (This verse omitted in LXX)

⁶ (This verse omitted in LXX)

⁷ These *were* the chiefs of the priests, and their brothers in the days of Jeshua.

⁸ And the Levites *were:* Jeshua, Binnui, Kadmiel, Sherebiah, Judah, *and* Mattaniah, who *was* over the bands,

⁹ and his brothers *were appointed* to the daily courses.

¹⁰ And Jeshua fathered Joiakim, and Joiakim fathered Eliashib, and Eliashib *fathered* Joiada,

¹¹ and Joiada fathered Jonathan, and Jonathan fathered Jaddua.

¹² And in the days of Joiakim, his brothers the priests and the heads of families *were:* of Seraiah, Meraiah; of Jeremiah, Hananiah;

¹³ of Ezra, Meshullam; of Amariah, Jehohanan;

¹⁴ of Malluch, Jonathan; of Shebaniah, Joseph;

¹⁵ of Harim, Adna; of Meraioth, Helkai;

¹⁶ of Iddo, Zechariah; of Ginnethon, Meshullam;

¹⁷ of Abijah, Zichri; of Minjamin, Moadiah; of Piltai, *one*;

¹⁸ of Bilgah, Shammua; of Shemaiah, Jonathan;

¹⁹ of Joiarib, Matthenai; of Jedaiah, Uzzi;

²⁰ of Sallai, Kallai; of Amok, Eber;

²¹ of Hilkiah, Hashabiah; *and* of Jedaiah, Nathanel.

²² The Levites in the days of Eliashib, Joiada, Joa, Johanan, and Jaddua, *were* recorded heads of families. Also the priests, in the reign of Darius the Persian.

²³ And the sons of Levi, heads of families, *were* written in the Book of the Chronicles, even to the days of Johanan son of Eliashib.

²⁴ And the heads of the Levites *were* Hashabiah, Sherebiah, and Jeshua; and the sons of Kadmiel, and their brothers over against them, were to sing hymns of praise, according to the commandment of David the man of God, course by course.

²⁵ When I gathered the porters,

²⁶ *it was* in the days of Joiakim son of Jeshua, son of Josadak, and in the days of Nehemiah; and Ezra the priest *was* the scribe.

Nehemiah Dedicates the Wall

²⁷ And at the dedication of the wall of Jerusalem they sought the Levites in their places, to bring them to Jerusalem, to keep a feast of dedication and gladness with thanksgiving, and they sounded cymbals with songs, and *had* psalteries and harps.

²⁸ And the sons of the singers were assembled both from the neighborhood round about to Jerusalem, and from the villages,

²⁹ and from the country, for the singers built themselves villages by Jerusalem.

³⁰ And the priests and the Levites purified themselves, and they purified the people, and the porters, and the wall.

³¹ And they brought up the princes of Judah on the wall, and they appointed two great *companies* for thanksgiving, and they passed on the right hand on the wall of the Refuse Gate.

³² And after them went Hoshaiah, and half the princes of Judah,

³³ and Azariah, Ezra, Meshullam,

³⁴ Judah, Benjamin, Shemaiah and Jeremiah.

³⁵ And *some* of the sons of the priest with trumpets, Zechariah son of Jonathan, son of Shemaiah, son of Matthaniah, son of Micaiah, son of Zacchur, son of Asaph:

³⁶ and his brothers, Shemaiah, Azarel, Milalai, Gilalai, Maai, Nathanel, Judah, and Hanani, to praise with the hymns of David the man of God; and Ezra the scribe *was* before them,

³⁷ at the gate, to praise before them, and they went up by the steps of the City of David, in the ascent of the wall, above the house of David, even to the Water Gate

³⁸ (This verse omitted in LXX)

³⁹ of Ephraim, and to the Fish Gate, and by the Tower of Hananel, and as far as the Sheep Gate.

⁴⁰ (This verse omitted in LXX)

⁴¹ (This verse omitted in LXX)

⁴² And the singers were heard, and were numbered.

⁴³ And in that day they offered great sacrifices, and rejoiced; for God had made them very joyful: and their wives and their children rejoiced; and the joy in Jerusalem was heard from afar off.

Temple Responsibilities

⁴⁴ And in that day they appointed men over the treasuries, for the treasures, the firstfruits, and the tithes, and *for the* chiefs of the cities who were assembled among them, *to furnish* portions for the priests and Levites; for *there was* joy in Judah over the priests and over the Levites that waited.

⁴⁵ And they kept the charges of their God, and the charges of the purification, and *ordered* the singers and the porters, according to the commandments of David and his son Solomon.

⁴⁶ For in the days of David, Asaph was originally first of the singers, and *they sang* hymns and praises to God.

⁴⁷ And all Israel in the days of Zerubbabel, and in the days of Nehemiah, gave the portions of the singers and the porters, a daily rate; and consecrated them to the Levites, and the Levites consecrated them to the sons of Aaron.

NEHEMIAH CHAPTER 13

¹ In that day they read in the Book of Moses in the ears of the people; and it was found written in it, that the Ammonites and Moabites should not enter into the congregation of God forever;

² because they did not meet the children of Israel with bread and water, but hired Balaam against them to curse them, but our God turned the curse into a blessing.

³ And it came to pass, when they heard the law, that they were separated, *even* every alien in Israel.

The Reforms of Nehemiah

⁴ And before this time Eliashib the priest dwelt in the treasury of the house of our God, connected with Tobiah;

⁵ and he made himself a great treasury, and there they were formerly in the habit of bestowing the offerings, and the frankincense, and the vessels, and the tithe of the grain, and the wine, and the oil, the ordered portion of the Levites, and singers, and porters; and the firstfruits of the priests.

⁶ But in all this *time* I was not in Jerusalem; for in the thirty-second year of Artaxerxes king of Babylon I came to the king, and after a certain time I made my request of the king;

⁷ and I came to Jerusalem, and I understood the evil which Eliashib had done in the case of Tobiah, in making for him a treasury in the court of the house of God.

⁸ And it appeared very evil to me; so I cast forth all the furniture of the house of Tobiah from the treasury.

⁹ And I gave orders, and they purified the treasuries; and I restored the vessels into the house of God, *and* the offerings, and the frankincense.

¹⁰ And I understood that the portion of the Levites had not been given; and they had fled everyone to his field, the Levites and the singers doing the work.

[11] And I contended with the commanders, and said, "Why has the house of God been abandoned?" And I assembled them, and set them in their place.

[12] And all Judah brought a tithe of the wheat and the wine and the oil into the treasuries,

[13] to the charge of Shelemiah the priest, and Zadok the scribe, and Pedaiah of the Levites. And next to them *was* Hanan the son of Zaccur, son of Matthaniah; for they were accounted faithful. *It was* their office to distribute to their brothers.

[14] Remember me, O God, in this, and let not my kindness be forgotten which I have wrought in *regard to* the house of the Lord God.

[15] In those days I saw in Judah *men* treading wine-presses on the Sabbath, and carrying sheaves, and loading donkeys with wine, grapes, figs, and every *kind of* burden, and bringing them into Jerusalem on the Sabbath day.

[16] And I testified in the day of their sale. Also there dwelt in it *men* bringing fish, and selling every *kind of* merchandise to the children of Judah and in Jerusalem on the Sabbath.

[17] And I strove with the free children of Judah, and said to them, "What *is* this evil thing which you do, and profane the Sabbath day?

[18] Did not your fathers *commit* this same *trespass,* and our God brought upon them and upon us and upon this city all these evils? And do you bring additional wrath upon Israel by profaning the Sabbath?"

[19] And it came to pass, when the gates were set up in Jerusalem, before the Sabbath, that I spoke, and they shut the gates; and I gave orders that they should not be opened till after the Sabbath. And I set *some* of my servants at the gates, that none should bring *in* burdens on the Sabbath day.

[20] So all *the merchants* lodged, and carried on traffic outside of Jerusalem once or twice.

[21] Then I testified against them, and said to them, "Why do you lodge in front of the wall? If you do so again, I will stretch out my hand upon you." From that time on they did not come on the Sabbath.

[22] And I told the Levites who were purifying themselves, and came and kept the gates, that they should sanctify the Sabbath day. Remember me, O God, for these things, and spare me according to the abundance of Your mercy.

[23] And in those days I saw the Jews who had married women of Ashdod, of Ammon, *and* of Moab.

[24] And their children spoke half in the language of Ashdod, and did not know how to speak in the Jewish language.

[25] And I strove with them and cursed them; and I struck some of them, and plucked off their hair, and made them swear by God, *saying,* "You shall not give your daughters to their sons, and you shall not take of their daughters to your sons.

[26] Did not Solomon king of Israel sin thus? Yet there was no king like him among many nations, and he was beloved of God, and God made him king over all Israel; yet strange women turned him aside.

[27] So we will not hearken to you to do all this evil, to break covenant with our God, to marry strange wives."

[28] And Elishub the high priest, *one* of the sons of Joiada, son-in-law of Sanballat the Horonite, I chased away from me.

[29] Remember them, O God, for their *false* connection with the priesthood, and *the breaking* the covenant of the priesthood, and *for defiling* the Levites.

[30] So I purged them from all foreign connection, and established courses for the priests and the Levites, *every* man according to his work.

[31] And the offering of the wood-bearers *was* at certain set times, and in the *times of the* firstfruits. Remember me, O my God, for good.

THE BOOK OF ESTHER

Mordecai's Dream

[In the second year of reign of Artaxerxes the great king, on the first *day* of Nisan, Mordecai the *son* of Jair, the *son* of Shimei, the *son* of Kish, of the tribe of Benjamin, a Jew dwelling in the city of Susa, a great man, serving in the king's palace, saw a vision.

Now he was of the captivity which Nebuchaznezzar king of Babylon had carried captive from Jerusalem, with Jeconiah the king of Judea. And this *was* his dream: Behold, voices and a noise, thunders and an earthquake, and tumult upon the earth. And behold, two great serpents came forth, both ready for conflict, and there came from them a great voice, and by their voice of every nation was prepared for battle, even to fight against the nation of the just. And behold, a day of darkness and blackness, tribulation and anguish, affliction and great tumult upon the earth. And all the righteous nation was troubled, fearing their own afflictions; and they prepared to die, and cried to God. And from their cry there came as it were a great river from a little fountain, *even* much water. And light and the sun arose, and the lowly were exalted, and devoured the honorable.

And Mordecai, who had seen this vision and what God designed to do, having awoke, kept in his heart, and desired by all means to interpret it, even till night. And Mordecai rested quiet in the palace with Gabatha and Tharrha, the king's two chamberlains, eunuchs who guarded the palace.

And he heard their reasonings and searched out their plans, and learned that they were preparing to lay hands on King Artaxerxes. And he informed the king concerning them. And the king examined the two chamberlains, and they confessed, and were executed. And the king wrote these things for a memorial; also Mordecai wrote concerning these matters. And the king commanded Mordecai to attend in the palace, and gave him gifts for this service. And Haman the son of Hammedatha the Agagite was honorable in the sight of the king, and he endeavored to hurt Mordecai and his people, because of the two eunuchs of the king.]

ESTHER CHAPTER 1

¹ And it came to pass after these things in the days of Artaxerxes (this Artaxerxes ruled over a hundred and twenty-seven provinces from India),

² in those days, when King Artaxerxes was on the throne in the city of Susa,

³ in the third year of his reign, he made a feast for his friends, and the other nations, and to the nobles of the Persians and Medes, and the chief of the satraps.

⁴ And after this, after he had shown to them the wealth of his kingdom, and the abundant glory of his wealth during a hundred and eighty days,

⁵ when the days of the marriage feast were completed, the king made a banquet for the nations who were present in the city six days, in the court of the king's house,

⁶ *which was* adorned with *hangings* of fine linen and flax on cords of fine linen and purple, fastened to golden and silver studs, on pillars of Parian marble and stone. *There were* golden and silver couches on a pavement of emerald stone, and of pearl, and of Parian stone, and open-worked coverings variously flowered, *having* roses worked round about;

⁷ gold and silver cups, and a small cup of carbuncle set out of the value of thirty thousand talents, abundant and sweet wine, which the king himself drank.

⁸ And this banquet was not according to the appointed law; but so the king would have it: and he charged the stewards to perform his will and that of the company.

⁹ Also Vashti the queen made a banquet for the women in the palace where King Artaxerxes *dwelt*.

The King Deposes Queen Vashti

¹⁰ Now on the seventh day the king, being merry, told Mehuman, Biztha, Harbona, Bigtha, Zethar, Abagtha, and Carcas, the seven eunuchs, servants of King Artaxerxes,

¹¹ to bring the queen in to him, to enthrone her, and crown her with the diadem, and to show her to the princes, and her beauty to the nations, for she was beautiful.

¹² But Queen Vashti would not heed the word to come with the chamberlains; so the king was grieved and angered.

¹³ And he said to his friends, "Thus has Vashti spoken: pronounce therefore upon this *case* law and judgment."

¹⁴ So Carshena, Shethar, and Malisear, the princes of the Persians and Medes, who were near the king, who sat chief *in rank* by the king, drew near to him,

¹⁵ and reported to him according to the laws how it was proper to do to Queen Vashti, because she had not done the things commanded of the king by the eunuchs.

¹⁶ And Memucan said to the king and to the princes, "Queen Vashti has not wronged the king only, but also all the king's rulers and princes;

¹⁷ for he has told them the words of the queen, and how she disobeyed the king. As then, *he said*, she refused *to obey* King Artaxerxes,

¹⁸ so this day shall the other women of the chiefs of the Persians and Medes, having heard what she said to the king, dare in the same way to dishonor their husbands.

¹⁹ If then it seem good to the king, let him make a royal decree, and let it be written according to the laws of the Medes and Persians, and let him not alter *it*. And let not the queen come in to him anymore, and let the king give her royalty to a woman better than she.

²⁰ And let the law of the king which he shall have made, be widely proclaimed in his kingdom. And so shall all the women give honor to their husbands, from the poor, even to the rich."

²¹ And the saying pleased the king and the princes; and the king did as Memucan had said,

²² and sent into all his kingdom through the several provinces, according to their language, in order that men might be feared in their own houses.

ESTHER CHAPTER 2

Esther Becomes Queen

¹ And after this the king's anger subsided, and he no longer made mention of Vashti, bearing in mind what she had said, and how he had condemned her.

² Then the servants of the king said, "Let there be sought for the king chaste *and* beautiful young virgins.

³ And let the king appoint local governors in all the provinces of his kingdom, and let them select fair *and* chaste young women, *and bring them* to the city Susa, into the women's apartment, and let them be consigned to the king's eunuch, the keeper of the women. And let things for purification and other attendance be given *to them*.

⁴ And let the woman who shall please the king be queen instead of Vashti." And the thing pleased the king; and he did so.

⁵ Now there was a Jew in the city Susa, and his name was Mordecai, the *son* of Jair, *the son* of Shimei, *the son* of Kish, of the tribe of Benjamin;

⁶ who had been brought a prisoner from Jerusalem, which Nebuchadnezzar king of Babylon had carried into captivity.

⁷ And he had a foster child, daughter of Aminadab his father's brother, and her name *was* Esther. And when her parents were dead, he brought her up for a wife for himself. And the woman was beautiful.

⁸ And because the king's ordinance was published, many young women were gathered to the city Susa under the hand of Hegai; and Esther was brought to Hegai the keeper of the women.

⁹ Now the young woman pleased him, and she found favor in his sight; and he hastened to give her the things for purification, and her portion, and the seven maidens

appointed her out of the palace. And he treated her and her maidens well in the women's apartment.

¹⁰ But Esther revealed neither her family nor her relatives, for Mordecai had charged her not to tell.

¹¹ But Mordecai used to walk every day by the women's court, to see what would become of Esther.

¹² Now this was the time for a virgin to go into the king, when she should have fulfilled twelve months; for so are the days of purification fulfilled, six months while they are anointing themselves with oil of myrrh, and six months with spices and women's purifications.

¹³ And then *the young woman* goes in to the king; and *the officer* to whoever he shall give the command, will bring her to come in with him from the women's apartment to the king's chamber.

¹⁴ She enters in the evening, and in the morning she departs to the second women's apartment, where Hegai the king's eunuch *is* keeper of the women. And she does not go in to the king again, unless she should be called by name.

¹⁵ And when the time was fulfilled for Esther, the daughter of Aminadab, the brother of Mordecai's father to go in to the king, she neglected nothing which the eunuch, the women's keeper, commanded; for Esther found grace in the sight of all that looked upon her.

¹⁶ So Esther went in to King Artaxerxes in the twelfth month, which is Adar, in the seventh year of his reign.

¹⁷ And the king loved Esther, and she found favor beyond all the *other* virgins, and he put on her the queen's crown.

¹⁸ And the king made a banquet for all his friends and great men for seven days, and he highly celebrated the marriage of Esther; and he made a release to those who were under his dominion.

¹⁹ But Mordecai served in the palace.

²⁰ Now Esther had not revealed her relatives; for so Mordecai commanded her, to fear God, and perform His commandments, as when she was with him: and Esther did not change her manner of life.

²¹ And two of the king's eunuchs, the chiefs of the bodyguard, were grieved, because Mordecai was promoted; and they sought to kill King Artaxerxes.

²² And the matter became known to Mordecai, and he made it known to Esther, and she declared to the king the matter of the conspiracy.

²³ And the king examined the two eunuchs, and hanged them. And the king gave orders to make a note for a memorial in the royal records of the good offices of Mordecai, as a commendation.

ESTHER CHAPTER 3

Haman's Conspiracy

¹ And after this King Artaxerxes highly honored Haman, *son* of Hammedatha, the Agagite, and exalted him, and set his seat above all his friends.

² And everyone in the palace bowed down to him, for so the king had given orders to do; but Mordecai did not bow down to him.

³ And those in the king's palace said to Mordecai, "Mordecai, why do you transgress the commands of the king?"

⁴ *Thus* they spoke daily to him, but he did not listen to them; so they told it to Haman that Mordecai resisted the commands of the king; and Mordecai had shown to them that he was a Jew.

⁵ And when Haman understood that Mordecai did not bow down to him, he was greatly enraged,

⁶ and took counsel to utterly destroy all the Jews who were under the rule of Artaxerxes.

⁷ And he made a decree in the twelfth year of the reign of Artaxerxes, and cast lots daily and monthly, to slay in one day the race of Mordecai. And the lot fell on the fourteenth *day* of the month, which is Adar.

⁸ And he spoke to King Artaxerxes, saying, "There is a nation scattered among the nations in all your kingdom, and their laws differ from *those of* all the *other* nations; and they disobey the laws of the king. Therefore it is not fitting for the king to let them alone.

⁹ If it seems good to the king, let him make a decree to destroy them, and I will remit into the king's treasury ten thousand talents of silver."

¹⁰ And the king took off his ring, and gave it into the hands of Haman, to seal the decrees against the Jews.

¹¹ And the king said to Haman, "Keep the silver, and treat the nation as you will."

¹² So the king's recorders were called in the first month, on the thirteenth *day*, and they wrote as Haman commanded to the captains and governors in every province, from India even to Ethiopia, to a hundred and twenty-seven provinces, and to the rulers of the nations according to their *many* languages, in the name of King Artaxerxes.

¹³ And *the message* was sent by posts throughout the kingdom of Artaxerxes, to utterly destroy the race of the Jews on the first day of the twelfth month, which is Adar, and to plunder their goods. And the following is the copy of the letter:

"The great King Artaxerxes writes thus to the rulers and inferior governors of a hundred and twenty-seven provinces, from India even to Ethiopia, who hold authority under *him*. Ruling over many nations, and having obtained dominion over the whole world, I was minded, (not elated by the confidence of power but ever conducting *myself* with great moderation and with gentleness) to make the lives of *my* subjects continually tranquil, desiring both to maintain the kingdom quite and orderly to *its* utmost limits, and to restore the peace desired by all men. But when I had inquired of my counselors how this should be brought to pass, Haman, who excels in sound judgment among us, and has been manifestly well inclined without wavering and with unshaken fidelity, and has obtained the second post in the kingdom, informed us that a certain ill-disposed people is mixed up with all the tribes throughout the world, opposed in their laws to every *other* nation, and continually neglecting the commands of the kings, so that the united government blamelessly administered by us is not quietly established.

"Having then conceived that this nation alone *of all others* is continually set in opposition to every man, introducing as a change a foreign code of laws, and injuriously plotting to accomplish the worst of evils against our interests, and against the happy establishment of the monarchy; we have accordingly appointed those who are signified to you in the letters written by Haman, who is set over *the public* affairs and is our second governor, to utterly destroy them all with their wives and children by the swords of the enemies, without pitying or sparing any, on the fourteenth day of the twelfth month (which is Adar) of the present year; that the people aforetime and now ill-disposed *to us* having been violently consigned to death in one day, may hereafter secure to us continually a well- constituted and quiet *state of* affairs."

¹⁴ And the copies of the letters were published in every province; and an order was given to all the nations to be ready against that day.

¹⁵ And the business was hastened, and *that* at Susa. And the king and Haman began to drink, but the city was troubled.

ESTHER CHAPTER 4

Esther Agrees to Help the Jews

¹ But Mordecai, having perceived what was done, tore his clothes, and put on sackcloth, and sprinkled dust upon himself. And having rushed forth through the open street of the city, he cried with a loud voice, "A nation that has done no wrong is going to be destroyed!"

² And he came to the king's gate, and stood; for it was not lawful for him to enter into the palace, wearing sackcloth and ashes.

³ And in every province where the letters were published, *there was* crying and lamentation and great mourning on the part of the Jews: they spread for themselves sackcloth and ashes.

⁴ And the queen's maids and chamberlains went in and told her: and when she had heard what was done, she was disturbed; and she sent to clothe Mordecai, and take away his sackcloth; but he would not consent.

⁵ So Esther called for her eunuch Hathach, who waited upon her; and she sent to learn the truth from Mordecai.

⁶ (This verse omitted in LXX)

⁷ And Mordecai showed him what was done, and the promise which Haman had made the king of ten thousand talents *to be paid* into the treasury, that he might destroy the Jews.

⁸ And he gave him the copy *of the writing* that was published in Susa concerning their destruction, to show to

Esther. And he told him to command her to go in and make supplication to the king, and to beg him for the people, "remembering," *he said*, "the days of your low estate, how you were nursed by my hand—because Haman, who holds the next place to the king, has spoken against us for death. Call upon the Lord, and speak to the king concerning us, to deliver us from death!"

⁹ So Hathach went in and told her all these words.

¹⁰ And Esther said to Hathach, "Go to Mordecai, and say,

¹¹ 'All the nations of the empire know, that whoever, man or woman, shall go in to the king into the inner court uncalled, that person cannot live. Only to whomsoever the king shall stretch out *his* golden scepter, he shall live; and I have not been called to go into the king, for these thirty days.'"

¹² And Hathach reported to Mordecai all the words of Esther.

¹³ Then Mordecai said to Hathach, "Go, and say to her, 'Esther, do not say to yourself that you alone will escape in the kingdom, more than all the *other* Jews.

¹⁴ For if you shall refuse to heed on this occasion, help and protection will be to the Jews from another quarter; but you and your father's house will perish. And who knows if you have been made queen for this *very* occasion.'"

¹⁵ And Esther sent the *man* that came to her to Mordecai, saying,

¹⁶ "Go and assemble the Jews that are in Susa, and fast for me, and do not eat or drink for three days, night and day. And I also and my maidens will fast, and then I will go in to the king, contrary to the law, even if I must die."

¹⁷ So Mordecai went and did all that Esther commanded him.

Mordecai's Prayer

And he sought the Lord, making mention of all the works of the Lord; and he said, "Lord God, *great* King that rules over all *people*, for all things are in Your power, and there is no one that shall oppose You in Your purpose to save Israel. For You have made the heaven and the earth, and every wonderful thing in the *earth* under heaven. And You are Lord of all, and there is no one who shall resist You, the Lord. You know all things: You know, O Lord, that it is not in the insolence, nor haughtiness, nor love of glory, that I have done this, to refuse to bow down to the haughty Haman. For I would gladly have kissed the soles of his feet for the safety of Israel.

"But I have done this, that I might not set the glory of man above the glory of God: and I will not worship anyone except You, my Lord, and I will not do these things in haughtiness.

"And now, O Lord God, O King, the God of Abraham, spare Your people, for *our enemies* are looking upon us for *our* destruction, and they have desired to destroy Your ancient inheritance. Do not overlook Your peculiar people, whom you have redeemed for Yourself out of the land of Egypt. Hearken to my prayer, and be propitious to Yours in gladness, that we may live and sing praises to Your name,

O Lord; and do not utterly destroy the mount of them that praise You, O Lord."

And all Israel cried with *all* their might, for their death *was* before their eyes. And Queen Esther found refuge in the Lord, being taken, *as it were*, in the agony of death.

Esther's Prayer

And having taken off her glorious apparel, she put on garments of distress and morning. And instead of grand perfumes, she put dung and ashes on her head, and she greatly brought down her body, and she filled every place of her glad adorning with the *torn* curls of her hair. And she sought the Lord God of Israel, and said, "O my Lord, You alone are our king. Help me, *I who am* destitute, and have no helper but You, for my danger *is* close at hand. I have heard from my birth, in the tribe of my kindred, that You, O Lord, took Israel out of all the nations, and our fathers out of all their kindred for a perpetual inheritance, and have wrought for them all that You have said. And now we have sinned before You, and You have delivered us into the hands of our enemies, because we honored their gods. You are righteous, O Lord. But now they have not been contented with the bitterness of our slavery, but have laid their hands on the hands of their idols, *in order* to abolish the decree of Your mouth, and to utterly destroy Your inheritance, and to stop the mouth of them that praise You, and to extinguish the glory of Your house and Your altar, and to open the mouth of the Gentiles, to *speak* the praises of vanities, and *in order* that a mortal king should be admired forever.

"O Lord, do not resign Your scepter to them that are not, and let them not laugh at our fall, but turn their counsel against themselves, and make an example of him who has begun *to injure* us. Remember *us*, O Lord, manifest Yourself in the time of our affliction, and encourage me, O King of gods, and ruler of all dominion. Put harmonious speech into my mouth before the lion, and turn his heart to hate him that fights against us, to the utter destruction of him and of them that consent with him. But deliver us by Your hand, and help *I who am* destitute, and have no one but You, O Lord. You know all things, and know that I hate the glory of transgressors, and that I abhor the manners of the uncircumcised, and of every stranger. You know my necessity, for I abhor the symbol of my proud station, which is upon my head in the days of my splendor. I abhor it as a menstrual cloth, and I wear it not in the days of my tranquility. And Your maid has not eaten *at* the table of Haman, and I have not honored the banquet of the king, neither have I drunk the wine of libations. Neither has Your maid rejoiced since the day of my promotion until now, except in You, O Lord God of Abraham. O God, who has power over all, listen to the voice of the desperate, and deliver us from the hand of them that devise mischief, and deliver me from my fear."

ESTHER CHAPTER 5

Esther's Banquet

1 And it came to pass on the third day, when she had ceased praying, that she put off her mean dress, and put on her glorious apparel. And being splendidly arrayed, *and* having called upon God the Overseer and Preserver of all things, she took her two maids, and she leaned upon one, as a delicate female, and the other followed bearing her train. And she *was* blooming in the perfection of her beauty; and her face *was* cheerful and benevolent, but her heart *was* straitened for fear.

And having passed through all the doors, she stood before the king. And he was sitting upon his royal throne, and he had put on all his glorious apparel, *covered* all over with gold and precious stones, and was very terrible. And having raised his face resplendent with glory, he looked with intense anger. And the queen fell, and changed her color as she fainted; and she bowed herself upon the head of the maid that went before *her*. But God changed the spirit of the king's demeanor, and in intense feeling he sprang from off his throne, and took her into his arms, until she recovered. And he comforted her with peaceable words, and said to her, "What is *the matter*, Esther? I *am* your brother; be of good cheer, you shall not die, for our command is openly declared *to you;* Draw near."

2 And having raised the golden scepter he laid it upon her neck, and embraced her, and said, "Speak to me." And she said to him, "I saw you, *my lord*, as an angel of God, and my heart was troubled for fear of your glory; for you, *my lord*, are to be wondered at, and your face *is* full of grace." And while she was speaking, she fainted and fell. Then the king was troubled, and all his servants comforted her.

3 And the king said, "What do you wish, Esther? And what is your request? *Ask* even to the half of my kingdom, and it shall be yours."

4 And Esther said, "Today is my great day: if then it seems good to the king, let both him and Haman come to the feast which I will prepare this day."

5 And the king said, "Bring Haman here quickly, that we may perform the word of Esther." So they both came to the feast of which Esther had spoken.

6 And at the banquet the king said to Esther, "What is *your request*, Queen Esther? *Speak*, and you shall have all that you require."

7 And she said, "My request and my petition *is this*:

8 if I have found favor in the sight of the king, let the king and Haman come again tomorrow to the feast which I shall prepare for them, and tomorrow I will do the same."

9 So Haman went out from the king very glad *and* merry; but when Haman saw Mordecai the Jew in the court, he was greatly enraged.

10 And having gone into his own house, he called his friends, and his wife Zeresh.

[11] And he showed them his wealth, and the glory with which the king had invested him, and how he had caused him to take precedence and bear chief rule in the kingdom.

[12] And Haman said, "The queen has called no one to the feast with the king but me, and I am invited tomorrow.

[13] But these things do not please me while I *still* see Mordecai the Jew in the court."

[14] And Zeresh his wife and his friends said to him, "Let there be a gallows made for you of fifty cubits, and in the morning speak to the king, and let Mordecai be hanged on the gallows. But go in to the feast with the king, and be merry." And the saying pleased Haman, and the gallows was prepared.

ESTHER CHAPTER 6

The King Honors Mordecai

[1] But the Lord removed sleep from the king that night; and he told his servant to bring in the books, the registers of daily events, to read to him.

[2] And he found the records written concerning Mordecai, how he had told the king concerning the two eunuchs of the king, when they were keeping guard, and sought to lay hands on Artaxerxes.

[3] And the king said, "What honor or favor have we done for Mordecai?" And the king's servants said, "You have not done anything for him."

[4] And while the king was inquiring about the kindness *shown to* Mordecai, behold, Haman *was* in the court. And the king said, "Who *is* in the court?" Now Haman had come in to speak to the king, that he should hang Mordecai on the gallows, which he had prepared.

[5] And the king's servants said, "Behold, Haman stands in the court." And the king said, "Call him."

[6] And the king said to Haman, "What shall I do to the man whom I wish to honor?" And Haman said within himself, "Whom would the king honor but myself?"

[7] And he said to the king, "As for the man whom the king wishes to honor,

[8] let the king's servants bring the robe of fine linen which the king puts on, and the horse on which the king rides,

[9] and let him give *it* to one of the king's noble friends, and let him array the man whom the king loves. And let him mount him on the horse, and proclaim through the streets of the city, saying, 'Thus shall it be to every man whom the king honors.'"

[10] Then the king said to Haman, "You have well said: so do to Mordecai the Jew, who waits in the palace, and let not a word of what you have spoken be neglected."

[11] So Haman took the robe and the horse, and clothed Mordecai, and mounted him on the horse, and went through the street of the city, and proclaimed, saying, "Thus shall it be to every man whom the king wishes to honor."

[12] And Mordecai returned to the palace. But Haman went home mourning, and covered his head.

[13] And Haman related the events that had befallen him to Zeresh his wife, and to *his* friends. And his friends and his wife said to him, "If Mordecai *is* of the race of the Jews, *and* you have begun to be humbled before him, you will surely fall, and you will not be able to withstand him, for the living God *is* with him."

[14] While they were yet speaking, the eunuchs arrived, and hastened to bring Haman to the banquet which Esther had prepared.

ESTHER CHAPTER 7

Haman Hanged Instead of Mordecai

[1] So the king and Haman went in to drink with the queen.

[2] And the king said to Esther at the banquet on the second day, "What is it, Queen Esther? And what *is* your request, and what *is* your petition? And it shall be *done* for you, up to half of my kingdom."

[3] And she answered and said, "If I have found favor in the sight of the king, let *my* life be granted to my petition, and my people to my request.

[4] For both I and my people have been sold for destruction, and pillage, and slavery; *both* we and our children as bondmen and bondwomen. And I did not consent to it, for the slanderer *is* not worthy of the king's palace."

[5] And the king said, "Who *is* this that has dared to do this thing?"

[6] And Esther said, "The adversary *is* Haman, this wicked man." Then Haman was troubled before the king and the queen.

[7] And the king rose up from the banquet to go into the garden. And Haman began to plead with the queen; for he saw that harm was determined against him.

[8] And the king returned from the garden; and Haman had fallen upon the bed, begging the queen. And the king said, "Will you even force *my* wife in my house?" And when Haman heard it, his countenance changed.

[9] And Harbonah, one of the eunuchs, said to the king, "Behold, Haman has also prepared a gallows for Mordecai, who spoke concerning the king, and a gallows of fifty cubits high has been set up on Haman's premises." And the king said, "Let him be hanged on it!"

[10] So Haman was hanged on the gallows that had been prepared for Mordecai; and then the king's wrath was appeased.

ESTHER CHAPTER 8

Esther Saves the Jews

¹ And in that day King Artaxerxes gave to Esther all that belonged to Haman the slanderer. And Mordecai was called by the king; for Esther had shown that he was related to her.

² And the king took the ring which he had taken away from Haman, and gave it to Mordecai. And Esther appointed Mordecai over all that had been Haman's.

³ And she spoke yet again to the king, and fell at his feet, and beseeched *him* to do away with the evil plan of Haman, and all that he had done against the Jews.

⁴ Then the king stretched out to Esther the golden scepter; and Esther arose to stand near the king.

⁵ And Esther said, "If it seems good to you, and *if* I have found favor *in your sight*, let an order be sent that the letters sent by Haman may be reversed, that were written for the destruction of the Jews, who are in your kingdom.

⁶ For how shall I be able to look upon the affliction of my people, and how shall I be able to survive the destruction of my relatives?"

⁷ And the king said to Esther, "If I have given and freely granted you all that was Haman's, and hanged him on a gallows, because he laid his hands upon the Jews, what do you yet further seek?

⁸ Write also in my name, as it seems good to you, and seal *it* with my ring; for whatever *orders* are written at the command of the king, and sealed with my ring, it is not lawful to revoke them."

⁹ So the scribes were called in the first month, which is Nisan, on the twenty-third day of the same year. And *orders* were written concerning the Jews, whatever *the king had* commanded to the local governors and chiefs of the satraps, from India even to Ethiopia, a hundred and twenty-seven satraps, according to the several provinces, according to their dialects.

¹⁰ And they were written by order of the king, and sealed with his ring, and they sent the letters by couriers.

¹¹ In it he charged them to use their *own* laws in every city, and to help each other, and to treat their adversaries, and those who attacked them, as they pleased,

¹² on one day in all the kingdom of Artaxerxes, on the thirteenth *day* of the twelfth month, which is Adar.

The King's Letter

¹³ And the following is the copy of the letter of the orders: "The great King Artaxerxes sends greeting to the rulers of *the* provinces *in* a hundred and twenty-seven satraps, from India to Ethiopia, even to those who are faithful to our interests. Many who have been frequently honored by the most abundant kindness of their benefactors have conceived ambitious designs, and not only endeavor to hurt our subjects, but moreover, not being able to bear prosperity, they also endeavor to plot against their own benefactors.

"And they not only would utterly abolish gratitude from among men, but also, elated by the boastings of men who are strangers to all that is good, they suppose that they shall escape the sin-hating vengeance of the ever-seeing God. And oftentimes *evil* exhortation has made partakers of the guilt of shedding innocent blood, and has involved in irremediable calamities, many of those who were appointed to offices of authority, who had been entrusted with the management of their friends' affairs. While *men*, by the false sophistry of an evil disposition, have deceived the simple candor of the ruling powers. And it is possible to see *this*, not so much from more ancient traditionary accounts, as it is immediately in your power *to see it* by examining what things have been wickedly perpetrated by the baseness of men holding power in an unworthy manner. And *it is right* to take heed with regard to the future, that we may maintain the government in undisturbed peace for all men, adopting *needful* changes, and ever judging those cases which come under *our* notice, with truly equitable decision. For whereas Haman, a Macedonian, the son of Hammedatha, in reality an alien from the blood of the Persians, and differing widely from our mild course of government, having been hospitably entertained by us, obtained so large a share of our universal kindness, as to be called our father, and to continue the person next to the royal throne, reverenced by all.

"*He, however*, overcome by the pride *of his station*, endeavored to deprive us of our dominion, and our life; having by various and subtle artifices demanded for destruction both Mordecai, our deliverer and perpetual benefactor, and Esther, the blameless consort of *our* kingdom, with their whole nation. For by these methods, the thought, having surprised us in a defenseless rate, to transfer the dominion of the Persians to the Macedonians.

"But we find that the Jews, who have been consigned to destruction by the most abominable of men, are not malefactors, but living according to the most just laws, and being the sons of the living God, the Most High and Mighty, who maintains the kingdom, to us as well as to our forefathers, in the most excellent order.

"You will therefore do well in refusing to obey the letters sent by Haman the son of Hammedatha, because he that has done these things has been hanged with his whole family at the gates of Susa, Almighty God having swiftly returned to him a worthy recompense.

"*We beseech you*, therefore, having openly published a copy of this letter in every place, to give the Jews permission to use their own lawful customs, and to strengthen them, that on the thirteenth *day* of the twelfth month *of* Adar, on that same day, they may defend themselves against those who attacked them in a time of affliction. For in the place of the destruction of the chosen race, Almighty God has granted them this *time of* gladness. Therefore you also among your *notable* feasts, keep a distinct day with all festivity, that both now and hereafter it may be a day of deliverance to us and those who are well disposed toward the Persians, but to those that plotted against us a memorial of destruction. And every city and province collectively, which shall not do accordingly, shall be consumed with vengeance by spear and fire. It shall be made not only inaccessible to men, but also most hateful to wild beasts and birds forever. And let the copies be posted in conspicuous places throughout the kingdom, and let all the Jews be ready against this day, to fight against their enemies."

¹⁴ So the horsemen went forth with haste to perform the king's commands; and the ordinance was also published in Susa.

Mordecai Honored
¹⁵ And Mordecai went forth clothed in the royal apparel, and wearing a golden crown, and a diadem of fine purple linen. And the people in Susa saw *it* and rejoiced.

¹⁶ And the Jews had light and gladness,

¹⁷ in every city and province wherever the ordinance was published: wherever the proclamation took place, the Jews had joy and gladness, feasting and mirth. And many of the Gentiles were circumcised, and became Jews, for fear of the Jews.

ESTHER CHAPTER 9

Destruction of the Enemies of the Jews
¹ Now in the twelfth month, on the thirteenth day of the month which is Adar, the letters written by the king arrived.

² In that day the adversaries of the Jews perished: for no one resisted, through fear of them.

³ For the chiefs of the satraps, and the princes and the royal scribes honored the Jews; for the fear of Mordecai was upon them.

⁴ For the order of the king was in force, that he should be celebrated in all the kingdom.

⁵ (This verse omitted in LXX)

⁶ And in the city Susa the Jews killed five hundred men:

⁷ Also Parshandatha, Dalphon, Aspatha,

⁸ Poratha, Adalia, Aridatha,

⁹ Parmashta, Ruphaeus, Aridai, and Vajezatha,

¹⁰ the ten sons of Haman the son of Hammedatha the Agagite, the enemy of the Jews, and they plundered *their property* on the same day.

¹¹ And the number of them that perished in Susa was rendered to the king.

¹² And the king said to Esther, "The Jews have slain five hundred men in the city Susa. And what have they done in the rest of the country? What then is your petition, that it may be *done* for you?"

¹³ And Esther said to the king, "Let it be granted to the Jews so to treat them tomorrow as to hang the ten sons of Haman."

¹⁴ And he permitted it to be so done; and he gave up to the Jews of the city the bodies of the sons of Haman, to hang.

¹⁵ And the Jews assembled in Susa on the fourteenth *day* of Adar, and killed three hundred men, but plundered no property.

¹⁶ And the rest of the Jews who were in the kingdom assembled, and helped one another, and obtained rest from their enemies; for they destroyed fifteen thousand of them on the thirteenth *day* of Adar, but took no spoil.

¹⁷ And they rested on the fourteenth of the same month, and kept it as a day of rest with joy and gladness.

The Feast of Purim
¹⁸ And the Jews in the city Susa assembled also on the fourteenth *day* and rested; and they kept also the fifteenth with joy and gladness.

¹⁹ Because of this the Jews dispersed in every foreign land to keep the fourteenth of Adar *as* a holy day with joy, sending portions each to his neighbor.

²⁰ And Mordecai wrote these things in a book, and sent them to the Jews, as many as were in the kingdom of Artaxerxes, both them that were near and them that were afar off,

²¹ to establish these *as* joyful days, and to keep the fourteenth and fifteenth of Adar;

²² for on these days the Jews obtained rest from their enemies. And *as to* the month, which was Adar, in which a change was made for them, from mourning to joy, and from sorrow to a good day, to spend the whole of it *in* good days of feasting and gladness, sending portions to their friends, and to the poor.

²³ And the Jews consented *to this* accordingly as Mordecai wrote to them,

²⁴ *showing* how Haman the son of Hammedatha the Macedonian fought against them, how he made a decree and cast lots to utterly destroy them;

²⁵ also how he went in to the king, telling *him* to hang Mordecai. But all the calamities he tried to bring upon the Jews came upon himself, and he was hanged, and his children.

²⁶ Therefore these days were called Purim, because of the name Pur; (for in their language they are called Phrurae) because of the words of this letter, and *because of* all they suffered on this account, and all that happened to them.

²⁷ And *Mordecai* established it, and the Jews took upon themselves, and upon their descendants, and upon those that were joined to them *to observe it*, neither would they on any account behave differently. But these days *were to be* a memorial kept in every generation, and city, and family, and province.

²⁸ "And these days of the Phrurae," *they said*, "shall be kept forever, and their memorial shall not fail in any generation."

²⁹ And Queen Esther, the daughter of Aminadab, and Mordecai the Jew, wrote all that they had done, and the confirmation of the letter of Purim.

³⁰ (This verse omitted in LXX)

³¹ And Mordecai and Esther the queen appointed *a fast* for themselves privately, even at that time also having formed their plan against their own health.

32 And Esther established it by a command forever, and it was written for a memorial.

ESTHER CHAPTER 10

1 And the king levied *a tax* upon *his* kingdom both by land and sea.

2 And *as for* his strength and valor, and the wealth and glory of his kingdom, behold, they are written in the book of the Persians and Medes, for a memorial.

3 And Mordecai was second to King Artaxerxes, and was a great man in the kingdom, and honored by the Jews, and passed his life beloved of all his nation.

Mordecai Recalls His Dream

And Mordecai said, "These things have been done by God. For I remember the dream which I had concerning these matters. For not one particular of them has failed. There was the little fountain, which became a river, and there was a light, and the sun, and much water. The river is Esther, whom the king married, and made queen. And the two serpents are Haman and myself. And the nations are those that combined to destroy the name of the Jews. But *as for* my nation, this is Israel, *even* they that cried to God, and were delivered: for the Lord delivered His people, and the Lord rescued us out of all these calamities; and God wrought such signs and great wonders as have not been done among the nations."

Therefore did He ordain two lots, one for the people of God, and one for all the *other* nations. And these two lots came for an appointed season, and for a day of judgment before God, and for all the nations. And God remembered His people, and vindicated His inheritance.

And they shall observe these days, in the month *of* Adar, on the fourteenth and on the fifteenth day of the month, with an assembly, and joy and gladness before God, throughout the generations forever among His people Israel. In the fourth year of the reign of Ptolemy and Cleopatra, Dositheus, who said that he was a priest and a Levite, and Ptolemy his son, brought in the published letter of Purim, which they said existed, and *which* Lysimachus the son of Ptolemy who was in Jerusalem, had interpreted.

THE BOOK OF JOB

Job and His Family

1 There was a certain man in the land of Uz, whose name *was* Job; and that man was true, blameless, righteous, and godly, abstaining from everything evil.

2 And he had seven sons and three daughters.

3 And his possessions consisted of seven thousand sheep, three thousand camels, five hundred yoke of oxen, five hundred female donkeys in the pastures, and a very great household, and he had a great many servants on the earth; and that man was *most* noble of the men of the east.

4 And his sons, visiting one another, prepared a banquet every day, taking with them also their three sisters to eat and drink with them.

5 And when the days of the banquet were completed, Job sent and purified them, having risen up in the morning, and offered sacrifices for them, according to their number, and one calf for a sin offering for their souls; for Job said, "Lest perhaps my sons have thought evil, and cursed God in their minds." Thus, then Job did continually.

Satan Attacks Job's Character

6 And it came to pass one day, that behold, the angels of God came to stand before the Lord, and the devil came with them.

7 And the Lord said to the devil, "From where have you come?" And the devil answered the Lord and said, "I have come from compassing the earth, and walking up and down in the world."

8 And the Lord said to him, "Have you diligently considered My servant Job, that there is none like him on *all* the earth, a blameless man, true, godly, abstaining from everything evil?"

9 Then the devil answered, and said before the Lord, "Does Job worship the Lord for nothing?

10 Have You not made a hedge about him, and about his household, and all his possessions round about? And have You not blessed the works of his hands, and multiplied his possessions upon the land?

11 But put forth Your hand, and touch all that he has, and he will [1]curse You to *Your* face."

12 Then the Lord said to the devil, "Behold, I give all that he has into your hand, but touch not himself." So the devil went out from the presence of the Lord.

Job Loses His Property and Children

13 And it came to pass on a certain day, that Job's sons and his daughters were drinking wine in the house of their elder brother.

14 And behold, there came a messenger to Job, and said to him, "The oxen were plowing, and the donkeys were feeding near them;

15 when the spoilers came and took them for prey, and killed the servants with the sword; and I alone have escaped, *and have* come to tell you."

16 While he was yet speaking, there came another messenger, and said to Job, "Fire has fallen from heaven,

---

[1] ευλογησει. The Greek word actually means to bless. E.W. Bullinger, the Hebrew scholar says of this: "One of the 18 emendations of the Sopherim, by which the primitive Hebrew text, kalal (to curse), was changed to barak (to bless). Dr. Daniel Wallace concurs: "The Hebrew verb is *barak*, which means 'to bless.' Here is a case where the writer or a scribe has substituted the word 'curse' with the word 'bless,' to avoid having the expression 'curse God.'"

and burned up the sheep, and likewise have devoured the shepherds; and I alone have escaped, *and have* come to tell you."

[17] While he was yet speaking, there came another messenger, and said to Job, "The horsemen formed three companies against us, and surrounded the camels, and took them for prey, and killed the servants with the sword; and I alone have escaped, *and have* come to tell you."

[18] While he was yet speaking, another messenger came and said to Job, "While your sons and your daughters were eating and drinking with their older brother,

[19] suddenly a great wind came from across the desert, and caught the four corners of the house, and the house fell upon your children, and they are dead; and I alone have escaped, *and have* come to tell you."

[20] So Job arose and tore his clothes, and shaved his head, and fell on the ground and worshipped,

[21] and said, "I myself came forth naked from my mother's womb, and naked shall I return there; the Lord has given, and the Lord has taken away. As it seemed good to the Lord, so has it come to pass; blessed be the name of the Lord."

[22] In all these events that befell him, Job did not sin before the Lord, and did not impute wrong to God.

JOB CHAPTER 2

Satan Attacks Job's Health

[1] And it came to pass on a certain day, that the angels of God came to stand before the Lord, and the devil came among them to stand before the Lord.

[2] And the Lord said to the devil, "From where have you come?" Then the devil said to the Lord, "I have come from going throughout the world, and walking about the whole earth."

[3] And the Lord said to the devil, "Have you then observed My servant Job, that there is none like him upon the earth, a harmless, true, blameless, and godly man; abstaining from all evil? And yet he cleaves to innocence, although you have incited *Me* to destroy his substance without cause?"

[4] And the devil answered and said to the Lord, "Skin for skin! All that a man has he will give as a ransom for his life.

[5] Ah, but put forth Your hand, and touch his bones and his flesh—surely he will curse You to *Your* face!"

[6] And the Lord said to the devil, "Behold, I deliver him up to you; only spare his life."

[7] So the devil went out from the Lord, and struck Job with sore boils from *his* feet to *his* head.

[8] And he took a potsherd to scrape away the discharge, and sat upon a dung heap outside the city.

[9] And when much time had passed, his wife said to him, "How long will you hold out, saying, 'Behold, I wait yet a little while, expecting the hope of my deliverance?' For behold, your memorial is abolished from the earth, even your sons and daughters, the pangs and pains of my womb which I bore in vain with sorrows; and you yourself sit down to spend the nights in the open air among the corruption of worms, and I am a wanderer and a servant from place to place and house to house, waiting for the setting of the sun, that I may rest from my labors, and my pangs which now beset me: but curse the Lord, and die."

[10] But he looked at her, and said to her, "You have spoken like one of the foolish women. If we have received good things of the hand of the Lord, shall we not endure evil things?" In all these things that happened to him, Job did not sin with his lips before God.

Job's Three Friends

[11] Now his three friends, having heard of all the evil that had come upon him, came to him each from his own country: Eliphaz the king of the Temans, Bildad sovereign of the Shuhites, and Zophar, king of the Minaeans. And they came to him with one accord, to comfort *him*, and to visit him.

[12] And when they saw him from a distance they did not know him; and they cried with a loud voice, and wept, and everyone tore his garment, and sprinkled dust upon their heads,

[13] and they sat down beside him seven days and seven nights, and not one of them spoke; for they saw that his affliction was dreadful, and very great.

JOB CHAPTER 3

Job Deplores His Birth

[1] After this Job opened his mouth, and cursed the day *of his birth*,

[2] saying,

[3] "Let the day perish in which I was born, and that night in which they said, 'Behold a male child!'

[4] Let that night be darkness, and let not the Lord regard it from above, neither let light come upon it.

[5] But let darkness and the shadow of death seize it; let blackness come upon it.

[6] Let that day and night be cursed, let darkness carry them away; let it not come into the days of the year, neither let it be numbered with the days of the months.

[7] But let that night be pain, and let not mirth come upon it, nor joy.

[8] But let him that curses that day curse it, even he that is ready to attack the Great Whale.

[9] Let the stars of that night be darkened; let it remain *dark*, and not come into light; and let it not see the morning star arise:

[10] because it did not shut up the gates of my mother's womb, for so it would have removed sorrow from my eyes.

[11] For why did I not die in the belly? And why did I not come forth from the womb and die immediately?

¹² And why did the knees support me? And *why* did I suck the breasts?

¹³ Now I should have lain down and been quiet, I should have slept and been at rest,

¹⁴ with kings and counselors of the earth, who gloried in *their* swords;

¹⁵ or with rulers, whose gold was abundant, who filled their houses with silver:

¹⁶ or I *should have been* as an untimely birth proceeding from his mother's womb, or as infants who never saw light.

¹⁷ There the ungodly have burnt out the fury of rage; there the wearied in body rest.

¹⁸ And the men of old time have together ceased to hear the voice of the oppressor.

¹⁹ The small and great are there, and the servant that feared his lord.

²⁰ For why is light given to those who are in bitterness, and life to those souls which are in grief?

²¹ Who long for death, and do not obtain it, digging *for it* as *for* treasures;

²² and would be very joyful if they should gain it?

²³ Death is rest to such a man, for God has hedged him in.

²⁴ For my groaning comes before my food, and I weep, being beset with terror.

²⁵ For the terror of which I meditated has come upon me, and that which I had feared has befallen me.

²⁶ I was not at peace, nor quiet, nor had I rest; yet wrath has come upon me."

JOB CHAPTER 4

Eliphaz: Job Has Sinned

¹ Then Eliphaz the Temanite answered and said,

² "Have you been often spoken to in distress? But who shall endure the force of your words?

³ For seeing you have instructed many, and have strengthened the hands of the weak one,

⁴ and have supported the failing with words, and have imparted courage to feeble knees.

⁵ Yet now that pain has come upon you, and touched you, you are troubled.

⁶ Is not your fear *founded* in folly, your hope also, and the mischief of your way?

⁷ Remember then who has perished, being pure? Or when were the true-hearted utterly destroyed?

⁸ Accordingly, as I have seen men plowing barren places, and they that sow them will reap sorrows for themselves.

⁹ They shall perish by the command of the Lord, and shall be utterly consumed by the breath of His wrath.

¹⁰ The strength of the lion, and the voice of the lioness, and the exulting cry of serpents are quenched.

¹¹ The old lion has perished for lack of food, and the lions' whelps have forsaken one another.

¹² "But if there had been any truth in your words, none of these evils would have come upon you. Shall not my ear receive excellent *revelations* from Him?

¹³ But as *when* terror falls upon men, with dread and a sound in the night,

¹⁴ horror and trembling seized me, and caused all my bones greatly to shake.

¹⁵ And a spirit came before my face; and my hair and flesh quivered.

¹⁶ I arose and did not perceive it. I looked, and there was no form before my eyes: but I only heard a breath and a voice, saying,

¹⁷ 'What, shall a mortal be pure before the Lord? Or a man be blameless in regard to his works?

¹⁸ Since he does not trust in his servants, and perceives perverseness in his angels.

¹⁹ But as *for* them that dwell in houses of clay, of whom we also are formed of the same clay, He strikes them like a moth.

²⁰ And from the morning to evening they no longer exist— they have perished, because they cannot help themselves.

²¹ For He blows upon them, and they are withered: they have perished for lack of wisdom.'

JOB CHAPTER 5

Job Is Corrected by God

¹ "But call, if anyone will listen to you, or if you shall see any of the holy angels.

² For wrath destroys the foolish one, and envy slays him that has gone astray.

³ And I have seen foolish ones taking root, but suddenly their dwelling place was devoured.

⁴ Let their children be far from safety, and let them be crushed at the doors of vile men, and let there be no deliverer.

⁵ For what they have collected, the just shall eat; but they shall not be delivered out of calamities—let their strength be utterly exhausted.

⁶ For labor cannot by any means come out of the earth, nor shall trouble spring out of the mountains;

⁷ yet man is born to labor, and even so the vulture's young seek the high places.

⁸ Nevertheless I will beseech the Lord, and will call upon the Lord, the Sovereign of all;

⁹ who does great and untraceable things, glorious things also, and marvelous, of which there is no number:

¹⁰ who gives rain upon the earth, sending water on the earth:

¹¹ who exalts the lowly, and raises up them that are lost:

¹² frustrating the counsels of the crafty, and their hands shall not perform the truth:

¹³ who takes the wise in their wisdom, and subverts the counsel of the crafty.

[14] In the day darkness shall come upon them, and let them grope in the noonday even as in the night.

[15] And let them perish in war, and let the weak escape from the hand of the mighty.

[16] And let the weak have hope, but the mouth of the unjust be stopped.

[17] But blessed is the man whom the Lord has reproved; and do not reject the chastening of the Almighty,

[18] for He causes a man to be in pain, and restores him again: He bruises, and His hands heal.

[19] Six times He shall deliver you out of distresses, and in the seventh, harm shall not touch you.

[20] In famine He shall deliver you from death, and in war He shall free you from the power of the sword.

[21] He shall hide you from the scourge of the tongue, and you shall not be afraid of coming evils.

[22] You shall laugh at the unrighteous and the lawless, and you shall not be afraid of wild beasts.

[23] For the wild beasts of the field shall be at peace with you.

[24] Then shall you know that your house shall be at peace, and the provision for your tabernacle shall not fail.

[25] And you shall know that your descendants *shall be* abundant, and your children shall be like the herbs of the field.

[26] And you shall come to the grave like ripe grain reaped in its season, or as a sheaf of grain collected in its season.

[27] Behold, we have thus sought out these matters; these are what we have heard—but reflect within yourself, if you have done anything *wrong*."

JOB CHAPTER 6

Job: My Complaint is Just

[1] But Job answered and said,

[2] "Oh that one would indeed weigh the wrath that is upon me, and take up my grief in a balance together!

[3] And surely they would be heavier than the sand by the seashore: but, as it seems, my words are vain.

[4] For the arrows of the Lord are in my body, whose violence drinks up my blood: whenever I am going to speak, they pierce me.

[5] What then? Will the wild donkey bray for nothing, if he is not seeking food? Or again, will the ox low at the manger, when he has *his* fodder?

[6] Shall bread be eaten without salt? Or again, is there taste in empty words?

[7] For my wrath cannot cease, for I perceive my food as the smell of a lion *to be* loathsome.

[8] Oh, that He would grant *my desire*, and my petition might come, and the Lord would grant my hope!

[9] Let the Lord begin to wound me, but let Him not utterly destroy me.

[10] Let the grave be my city, upon the walls of which I have leaped: I will not shrink from it, for I have not denied the holy words of my God.

[11] For what is my strength, that I continue? What is my time, that my soul endures?

[12] Is my strength the strength of stones? Or is my flesh of brass?

[13] Or have I not trusted in Him? But help is *far* from me.

[14] "Mercy has rejected me; and the visitation of the Lord has disregarded me.

[15] My nearest relations have not regarded me, they have passed me by like a failing brook, or like a wave.

[16] They who used to reverence me, now have come against me like snow or congealed ice.

[17] When it has melted at the approach of heat, it is not known what it was.

[18] Thus I also have been deserted of all, and I am ruined, and have become an outcast.

[19] Behold the ways of the Temanites, you that mark the paths of the Sabaeans.

[20] They too that trust in cities and riches shall come to shame.

[21] But you also have come to me without pity; so that beholding my wounds you are afraid.

[22] What? Have I made any demand of you? Or do I ask for strength from you,

[23] to deliver me from enemies, or to rescue me from the hand of the mighty ones?

[24] "Teach me, and I will be silent: if in anything I have erred, tell me.

[25] But as it seems, the words of a true man are vain, because I do not ask strength of you.

[26] Neither will your reproof cause me to cease my words, for neither will I endure the sound of your speech.

[27] Even because you attack the fatherless, and insult your friend.

[28] But now, having looked upon your countenances, I will not lie.

[29] Sit down now, and let there not be unrighteousness, and unite again with the just.

[30] For there is no injustice in my tongue; and does not my throat meditate understanding?

JOB CHAPTER 7

Job: My Suffering Is Without End

[1] "Is not the life of man upon earth a state of trial? And his existence as that of a hireling by the day?

[2] Or as a servant that fears his master, and one who has grasped a shadow? Or as a hireling waiting for his pay?

[3] So have I also endured months of vanity, and nights of pain have been appointed to me.

[4] Whenever I lie down, I say, 'When *will it be* day?' And whenever I rise up, again *I say*, 'When *will it be* evening?' And I am full of pains from evening to morning.

⁵ And my body is covered with loathsome worms; and I waste away, scraping off clods of dust from my eruption.

⁶ And my life is lighter than a word, and has perished in vain hope.

⁷ Remember then that my life is breath, and my eye shall not yet again see good.

⁸ The eye of him that sees me shall not see me again: your eyes are upon me, and I am no more.

⁹ I *am* as a cloud that is cleared away from the sky: for if a man should go down to the grave, he shall not come up again.

¹⁰ And he shall surely not return to his own house, neither shall his place know him any more.

¹¹ "Then neither will I refrain my mouth; I will speak being in distress; being in anguish I will disclose the bitterness of my soul.

¹² Am I a sea, or a serpent, that you have set a watch over me?

¹³ I said that my bed should comfort me, and I would privately counsel with myself on my couch.

¹⁴ You scare me with dreams, and terrify me with visions.

¹⁵ You will separate life from my spirit; and yet *keep* my bones from death.

¹⁶ For I shall not live forever, that I should patiently endure: depart from me, for my life is vain.

¹⁷ For what is man, that You have magnified him? Or that You give heed to him?

¹⁸ Will You visit him till the morning, and judge him till *the time of* rest?

¹⁹ How long do You not let me alone, nor let me go, until I shall swallow down my spittle?

²⁰ If I have sinned, what shall I be able to do, O You that understand the mind of men? why have You made me as Your accuser, and why am I a burden to You?

²¹ Why have You not forgotten my iniquity, and purged my sin? But now I shall depart to the earth, and in the morning I am no more."

JOB CHAPTER 8

Bildad: Job Should Repent

¹ Then Bildad the Shuhite answered and said,

² "How long will you speak these things, *how long shall* the breath of your mouth be abundant in words?

³ Will the Lord be unjust when He judges; or will He that has made all things pervert justice?

⁴ If your sons have sinned before Him, He has cast them away because of their transgression.

⁵ But you be early in prayer to the Lord Almighty.

⁶ If you are pure and true, He will listen to your supplication, and will restore to you the habitation of righteousness.

⁷ Though then your beginning should be small, yet your end should be unspeakably great.

⁸ For ask of the former generation, and search diligently among the race of our fathers:

⁹ (for we are of yesterday, and know nothing; for our life upon the earth is a shadow)

¹⁰ shall not these teach you, and report *to you*, and bring out words from *their* heart?

¹¹ "Does the rush flourish without water, or shall the flag grow up without moisture?

¹² When it is yet on the root, and *though* it has not been cut down, does not any herb wither before it has received moisture?

¹³ Thus then shall be the end of all that forget the Lord: for the hope of the ungodly shall perish.

¹⁴ For his house shall be without inhabitants, and his tent shall prove a spider's web.

¹⁵ If he should prop up his house, it shall not stand: and when he has taken hold of it, it shall not remain.

¹⁶ For it is moist under the sun, and his branch shall come forth out of his dung heap.

¹⁷ He lies down upon a gathering of stones, and shall live in the mist of flints.

¹⁸ If *God* should destroy him, his place shall deny him. Have you not seen such things,

¹⁹ that such is the overthrow of the ungodly? And out of the earth another shall grow.

²⁰ For the Lord will by no means reject the harmless man; but He will not receive any gift of the ungodly.

²¹ But He will fill with laughter the mouth of the sincere, and their lips with thanksgiving.

²² But their adversaries shall clothe themselves with shame; and the habitation of the ungodly shall perish."

JOB CHAPTER 9

Job: There Is No Mediator

¹ Then Job answered and said,

² "Truly I know it is so, for how shall a mortal man be righteous before the Lord?

³ For if he would enter into judgment with Him, *God* would not listen to him, so that he should answer to one of His charges of a thousand.

⁴ For He is wise in mind, and mighty, and great: who has hardened himself against Him and endured?

⁵ Who wears out the mountains, and *men* do not know; who overturns them in anger.

⁶ Who shakes the *earth* under heaven from its foundations, and its pillars totter.

⁷ Who commands the sun, and it does not rise; and He seals up the stars.

⁸ Who alone has stretched out the heavens, and walks on the sea as on firm ground.

⁹ Who makes Pleias, and Hesperus, and Arcturus, and the chambers of the south.

¹⁰ Who does great and unsearchable things; glorious also and excellent things, innumerable.

¹¹ If ever He should go beyond me, I shall not see Him: if He should pass by me, neither thus have I known it.

¹² If He would take away, who shall turn Him back? Or who shall say to Him, 'What have You done?'

¹³ For *if* He has turned away *His* anger, the whales under heaven have stooped under Him.

¹⁴ Oh then that He would listen to me, or judge my cause.

¹⁵ For though I am righteous, He will not listen to me: I will intreat His judgment.

¹⁶ And if I should call and He should not hear, I cannot believe that He has listened to my voice.

¹⁷ Let Him not crush me with a dark storm: but He has made my bruises many without cause.

¹⁸ For He allows me not to take breath, but He has filled me with bitterness.

¹⁹ For indeed He is strong in power: who then shall resist His judgment?

²⁰ For though I should seem righteous, my mouth will be profane, and though I should seem blameless, I shall be proved perverse.

²¹ For even if I have sinned, I know it not in my soul: but my life is taken away.

²² Therefore I said, 'Wrath slays the great and mighty man.'

²³ For the worthless die, but the righteous are laughed to scorn.

²⁴ For they are delivered into the hands of the unrighteous man: He covers the faces of the judges *of the earth:* but if it is not He, who else could it be?

²⁵ But my life is swifter than a post: *my days* have fled away, and they did not know.

²⁶ Or again, is there a trace of *their* path *left* by ships? Or is there one of the flying eagle as it seeks its prey?

²⁷ And if I should say, 'I will forget to speak, I will bow down my face and groan';

²⁸ I quake in all my limbs, for I know that You will not leave me alone as innocent.

²⁹ But since I am ungodly, why have I not died?

³⁰ For if I should wash myself with snow, and purge myself with pure hands,

³¹ You had thoroughly plunged me in filth, and my garment has abhorred me.

³² For You are not a man like me, with whom I could contend, that we might come together to judgment.

³³ Would that *He* our mediator were *present,* and a reprover, and one who should hear *the cause* between both.

³⁴ Let Him remove His rod from me, and let not His fear terrify me.

³⁵ So shall I not be afraid, but I will speak: for I am not thus conscious of guilt."

JOB CHAPTER 10

Job: I Loathe My Life

¹ Weary in my soul, I will pour my words with groans upon Him: I will speak in the bitterness of my soul, being constrained.

² And I will say to the Lord, "Do not teach me to be impious; and why have You so judged me?

³ Is it good before You if I am unrighteous? For You have disowned the work of Your hands, and attended to the counsel of the ungodly.

⁴ Or do You see as a mortal sees? Or will You look as a man sees?

⁵ Or is Your life human, or Your years *the years* of a man,

⁶ that You have inquired into my iniquity, and searched out my sins?

⁷ For You know that I have not committed iniquity, but who is he that can deliver out of Your hands?

⁸ Your hands have formed me and made me; afterwards You changed Your mind, and struck me.

⁹ Remember that You have made me as clay, and You turn me again into dust.

¹⁰ Have You not poured me out like milk, and curdled me like cheese?

¹¹ And You clothed me with skin and flesh, and framed me with bones and sinews.

¹² And You bestowed upon me life and mercy, and Your oversight has preserved my spirit.

¹³ Having these things in Yourself, I know that You can do all things; for nothing is impossible for You.

¹⁴ And if I should sin, You watch me, and You have not cleared me from iniquity.

¹⁵ Or if I should be ungodly, woe is me: and if I should be righteous, I cannot lift myself up, for I am full of dishonor.

¹⁶ For I am hunted like a lion for slaughter; for again You have changed and are terribly destroying me;

¹⁷ renewing against me my torture: and You have dealt with me in great anger, and You have brought trials upon me.

¹⁸ Why then did You bring me out of the womb? And why did I not die, and no eye see me,

¹⁹ and I become as if I had not been? For why was I not carried from the womb to the grave?

²⁰ Is not the time of my life short? Allow me to rest a little,

²¹ before I go to where I shall not return, to a land of darkness and gloominess; to a land of perpetual darkness, where there is no light, neither *can anyone* see the life of mortals."

JOB CHAPTER 11

Zophar Speaks: Job's Guilt Deserve Punishment

¹ Then Zophar the Minaean answered and said,

² "He that speaks much, should also listen in turn: or does the fluent speaker think himself to be righteous? Blessed is the short-lived offspring of woman.

3 Be not a speaker of many words, for is there none to answer you?

4 For do not say, 'I am pure in my works, and blameless before Him.'

5 But oh that the Lord would speak to you, and open His lips to you!

6 Then shall He declare to you the power of wisdom, for it shall be double of that which is with you; and then shall you know, that a just recompense of your sins has come to you from the Lord.

7 Will you find out the traces of the Lord? Or have you come to the end of that which the Almighty has made?

8 Heaven is high, and what will you do? And there are deeper things than those in hell; what do you know?

9 Or longer than the measure of the earth, or the breadth of the sea.

10 And if He should overthrow all things, who will say to Him, 'What have You done?'

11 For He knows the works of transgressors, and when He sees wickedness, He will not overlook it.

12 But man vainly buoys himself up with words, and a mortal born of woman is like a donkey in the desert.

13 For if you have made your heart pure, and lifted up *your* hands towards Him;

14 if there is any iniquity in your hands, put if far from you, and do not let injustice dwell in your tents.

15 For thus shall your countenance shine again as pure water; and you shall divest yourself of uncleanness, and shall not fear.

16 And you shall forget trouble, as a wave that has passed by; and you shall not be scared.

17 And your prayer *shall be* as the morning star, and life shall arise to you as from the noonday.

18 And you shall be confident, because you have hope, and peace shall dawn to you from out of anxiety and care.

19 For you shall be at ease, and there shall be no one to fight against you, and many shall charge, and make supplication to you.

20 But safety shall fail them, for their hope is destruction, and the eyes of the ungodly shall waste away."

JOB CHAPTER 12

Job Answers His Critics

1 And Job answered and said,

2 "So then you *alone* are men, and wisdom shall die with you? 3 *But* I also have a heart as well as you.

4 For a righteous and blameless man has become a subject for mockery.

5 For it had been ordained that he should fall under others at the appointed time, and that his houses should be spoiled by transgressors: however do not let anyone trust that, being evil, he shall be *held* guiltless,

6 even as many as provoke the Lord, as if there were indeed to be no inquisition made of them.

7 But ask now the beasts, if they may speak to you, and the birds of the air, if they may declare to you.

8 Tell the earth, if it may speak to you, and the fish of the sea shall explain to you.

9 Who then has not known in all these things, that the hand of the Lord has made them?

10 Seeing that the life of all living things is in His hand, and the breath of every man.

11 For the ear tests words, and the palate tastes meats.

12 In length of time is wisdom, and in long life knowledge.

13 With Him are wisdom and power, with Him counsel and understanding.

14 If He should cast down, who will build up? If He should shut up against man, who shall open?

15 If He should withhold the water, He will dry the earth: and if He should let it loose, He overthrows and destroys it.

16 With Him are strength and power: He has knowledge and understanding.

17 He leads counselors away captive, and maddens the judges of the earth.

18 He seats kings upon thrones, and binds their waist with a belt.

19 He sends away priests into captivity, and overthrows the mighty ones of the earth.

20 He changes the lips of the trusty, and He knows the understanding of the elders.

21 He pours dishonor upon princes, and heals the lowly.

22 Revealing deep things out of darkness: and He has brought into light the shadow of death.

23 Causing the nations to wander, and destroying them: overthrowing the nations, and leading them away.

24 Perplexing the minds of the princes of the earth, and He causes them to wander in a way, they have not known, *saying,*

25 Let them grope *in* darkness, and *let there be* no light, and let them wander as a drunken man.

JOB CHAPTER 13

1 "Behold, my eye has seen these things, and my ear has heard *them.*

2 And I know all that you know, too; and I have no less understanding than you.

3 Nevertheless I will speak to the Lord, and I will reason before Him, if He will.

4 But you are all bad physicians, and healers of diseases.

5 Oh that you would be silent, and it would be wisdom to you in the end.

6 But hear now the reasoning of my mouth, and attend to the judgment of my lips.

7 Do you not speak before the Lord, and utter deceit before Him?

8 Or will you draw back? But you yourselves become judges.

9 For *it would be* good if He would thoroughly search you: for though doing all things *in your power* you should attach yourselves to Him,

10 He will surely not reprove you, but if you should secretly show partiality,

11 shall not His whirlpool sweep around you, and terror from Him fall upon you?

12 And your glorying shall prove in the end to you like ashes, and your body *like a body* of clay.

13 "Be silent, that I may speak, and cease from my anger,

14 while I may take my flesh in my teeth, and put my life in my hand.

15 Though the Mighty One should lay *His* hand upon me, forasmuch as He has begun, verily I will speak, and plead before Him.

16 And this shall turn to me for salvation, for fraud shall have no entrance before Him.

17 Hear, hear my words, for I will declare in your hearing.

18 Behold, I am near my judgment: I know that I shall appear evidently just.

19 For who is he that shall plead with me, that I should now be silent, and expire?

Job's Despondent Prayer

20 "But grant me two things: then I will not hide myself from Your face.

21 Withhold *Your* hand from me, and let not Your fear terrify me.

22 Then shall You call, and I will listen to You: or You shall speak, and I will give You an answer.

23 How many are my sins and my transgressions? Teach me what they are.

24 Why do You hide Yourself from me, and regard me *as* Your enemy?

25 Will You be startled *at me*, as *at* a leaf shaken by the wind? Or will You set Yourself against me as against grass borne upon the breeze?

26 For You have written evil things against me, and You have compassed me with the sins of my youth.

27 And You have placed my foot in the stocks, and You have watched all my works, and have penetrated my heels.

28 *I am as* that which grows old like a bottle, or like a moth-eaten garment.

JOB CHAPTER 14

1 "For a mortal born of a woman is short-lived, and full of wrath.

2 Or he falls like a flower that has bloomed, and he departs like a shadow, and cannot continue.

3 Have You not taken account even of him, and caused him to enter into judgment before You?

4 For who shall be pure from uncleanness? Not even one;

5 if even his life should be *but* one day upon the earth, and his months are numbered by him: You have appointed *him* for a time, and he shall by no means exceed it.

6 Depart from him, that he may be quiet, and take pleasure in his life, *though* as a hireling.

7 For there is hope for a tree, even if it should be cut down, *that* it shall blossom again, and its branch shall not fail.

8 For though its root should grow old in the earth, and its stem die in the rock,

9 it will blossom from the scent of water, and will produce a crop, as one newly planted.

10 But a man that has died is utterly gone, and when a mortal has fallen, he is no more.

11 For the sea wastes in *length of* time, and a river fails, and is dried up.

12 And man that has lain down *in death* shall certainly not rise again till the heaven be dissolved, and they shall not awake from their sleep.

13 "Oh that You had kept me in the grave, and had hidden me until Your wrath should cease, and You should set me a time in which You would remember me!

14 For if a man should die, shall he live again, having accomplished the days of his life? I will wait till I live again.

15 Then shall You call, and I will answer You: but do not reject the work of Your hands.

16 But You have numbered my steps: and not one of my sins shall escape You.

17 And You have sealed up my transgressions in a bag, and marked if I have been guilty of any transgression unawares.

18 And truly a mountain falling will utterly be destroyed, and a rock shall be worn out of its place.

19 The waters wear the stones, and waters falling headlong *overflow* a heap of the earth; so You destroy the hope of man.

20 You drive him to an end, and he is gone: You set Your face against him, and send him away;

21 and though his children be multiplied, he does not know; and if they be few, he is not aware.

22 But his flesh is in pain, and his soul mourns."

JOB CHAPTER 15

Eliphaz Accuses Job of Folly

1 Then Eliphaz the Temanite answered and said,

2 "Will a wise man give for an answer a *mere* breath of wisdom? And does he fill up the pain of his belly,

3 reasoning with improper words, and with words in which is no profit?

4 Have you not cast off fear, and accomplished such words before the Lord?

5 You are guilty by the words of your mouth, neither have you discerned the words of the Almighty.

⁶ Let your own mouth reprove you, and not me, and your lips shall testify against you.

⁷ What! Are you the first man that was born? Or were you established before the hills?

⁸ Or have you heard the ordinance of the Lord? Or has God used you as *His* counselor? Has wisdom come *only* to you?

⁹ For what you know, do we not *also* know? Or what you understand, do we not as well?

¹⁰ Truly among us are both the old and the aged man, more advanced in days than your father.

¹¹ You have been scourged for but a few of your sins; you have spoken haughtily and extravagantly.

¹² What has your heart dared? Or what have your eyes *aimed at,*

¹³ that you have vented *your* rage before the Lord, and delivered such words from *your* mouth?

¹⁴ For who, being a mortal, *is such* that he shall be blameless? Or *who that is* born of a woman, that he should be just?

¹⁵ Forasmuch as He does not trust His saints, and the heaven is not pure before Him.

¹⁶ Alas then, abominable and unclean is man, drinking iniquity as a draught.

¹⁷ "But I will tell you, listen to me; I will tell you now what I have seen;

¹⁸ things wise men say, and their fathers have not hidden.

¹⁹ To them alone the earth was given, and no stranger came upon them.

²⁰ All the life of the ungodly *is spent* in care, and the years granted to the oppressor are numbered.

²¹ And his terror is in his ears: just when he seems to be at peace, his overthrow will come.

²² Let him not trust that he shall return from darkness, for he has been already made over to the power of the sword.

²³ And he has been appointed to be food for vultures, and he knows within himself that he is doomed to be a carcass: and a dark day shall carry him away as with a whirlwind.

²⁴ Distress also and anguish shall come upon him: he shall fall as a captain in the first rank.

²⁵ For he has lifted his hands against the Lord, and he has hardened his neck against the Almighty Lord.

²⁶ And he has run against Him with insolence, on the thickness of the back of his shield.

²⁷ For he has covered his face with his fat, and made layers of fat upon his thighs.

²⁸ And let him lodge in desolate cities, and enter into houses without inhabitant: and what they have prepared, others shall carry away.

²⁹ Neither shall he grow rich, nor shall his substance remain: he shall not cast a shadow upon the earth.

³⁰ And he shall by no means escape the darkness: let the wind blast his blossom, and let his flower fall off.

³¹ Let him not think that he shall endure, for his end shall be vanity.

³² His harvest shall perish before the time, and his branch shall not flourish.

³³ And let him be gathered as the unripe grape before the time, and let him fall as the blossom of the olive.

³⁴ For death is the witness of an ungodly man, and fire shall burn the houses of them that receive gifts.

³⁵ And he shall conceive sorrows, and his end shall be vanity, and his belly shall bear deceit."

JOB CHAPTER 16

Job Reproaches His Pitiless Friends

¹ But Job answered and said,

² "I have heard many such things: miserable comforters are you all!

³ What! Is there any reason in vain words? Or what will hinder you from answering?

⁴ I also will speak as you do—if indeed your soul were in my *soul's* place, then would I insult you with words, and I would shake my head at you!

⁵ And might that there were strength in my mouth, and I would not spare the movement of my lips.

⁶ "For if I should speak, I shall not feel the pain of my wound, and if I should be silent, how shall I be wounded any less?

⁷ But now He has made me weary, and a worn out fool, and He has laid hold of me.

⁸ My falsehood has become a testimony, and has risen up against me: it has confronted me to my face.

⁹ In His anger He has cast me down; He has gnashed His teeth upon me: the weapons of His robbers have fallen upon me.

¹⁰ He has attacked me with the keen glances of His eyes; with His sharp *spear* He has struck me *down* upon my knees, and they have run upon me with one accord.

¹¹ For the Lord has delivered me into the hands of unrighteous men, and thrown me upon the ungodly.

¹² When I was at peace He distracted me: He took me by the hair of the head, and plucked it out: He set me up as a mark. ¹³ They surrounded me with spears, aiming at my reins: without sparing me they poured out my gall upon the ground. ¹⁴ They overthrew me with fall upon fall: they ran upon me in *their* might.

¹⁵ They sewed sackcloth upon my skin, and my strength has been spent on the ground.

¹⁶ My belly has been parched from wailing, and darkness is on my eyelids.

¹⁷ Yet there was no injustice on my hands, and my prayer is pure.

¹⁸ "Earth, do not cover over the blood of my flesh, and let my cry have no place.

¹⁹ And now, behold, my witness is in heaven, and my Advocate is on high.

²⁰ Let my supplication come to the Lord, and let my eye weep before Him.

²¹ Oh that a man might plead before the Lord, even as the son of man with his neighbor!

²² But my years are numbered and *their end* has come, and I shall go by the way by which I shall not return.

JOB CHAPTER 17

Job Prays for Relief

¹ "I perish, carried away by the wind, and I seek for burial, and do not obtain it.

² Weary, I intreat; and what have I done? And strangers have stolen my goods.

³ Who is this? Let him join hands with me.

⁴ For You have hid their heart from wisdom, therefore You shall not exalt them.

⁵ He shall promise mischief to *his* companions: but *their* eyes have failed for their children.

⁶ "But You have made me a byword among the nations, and I have become a scorn to them.

⁷ For my eyes are dimmed through pain; I have been grievously beset by all.

⁸ Wonder has seized true men upon this, and let the just rise up against the transgressor.

⁹ But let the faithful hold on his own way, and let him that is pure of hands take courage.

¹⁰ "How do you all strengthen *yourselves* and come now, for I do not find truth in you.

¹¹ My days have passed in groaning, and my heart strings are broken.

¹² I have turned the night into day: the light is short because of darkness.

¹³ For if I remain, Hades is my habitation: and my bed has been made in darkness.

¹⁴ I have called upon death to be my father, and corruption *to be* my mother and sister.

¹⁵ Where then is yet my hope? Or where shall I see my good?

¹⁶ Will they go down with me to Hades, or shall we go down together to the tomb?"

JOB CHAPTER 18

Bildad: The Wicked are Punished

¹ Then Bildad the Shuhite answered and said,

² "How long will you continue? Gain understanding, and afterward we also may speak.

³ For why have we been silent before you like brutes?

⁴ Anger has possessed you: for what if you should die; would *the earth* under heaven be desolate? Or shall the mountains be overthrown from their foundations?

⁵ But the light of the ungodly shall be quenched, and their flame shall not go up.

⁶ His light *shall be* darkness in *his* habitation, and his lamp shall be put out with him.

⁷ Let the meanest of men spoil his goods, and let his counsel deceive *him*.

⁸ His foot also has been caught in a snare, and let it be entangled in a net.

⁹ And let snares come upon him: he shall strengthen those that thirst for his destruction.

¹⁰ His snare is hid in the earth, and that which shall take him is by the path.

¹¹ Let pains destroy him round about, and let many *enemies* come about him,

¹² vex him with distressing hunger: and destruction has been prepared for him.

¹³ Let the soles of his feet be devoured, and death shall consume his beauty.

¹⁴ And let health be utterly banished from his tent, and let distress seize upon him with a charge from the king.

¹⁵ It shall dwell in his tent in his night: his excellency shall be sown with brimstone.

¹⁶ His roots shall be dried up from beneath, and his crop shall fall away from above.

¹⁷ Let his memorial perish from the earth, and his name shall be publicly cast out.

¹⁸ Let *one* drive him from light into darkness.

¹⁹ He shall not be known among his people, nor his house preserved on the earth.

²⁰ But strangers shall dwell in his possessions: the last groaned for him, and wonder seized the first.

²¹ These are the houses of the unrighteous, and this is the place of them that do not know the Lord."

JOB CHAPTER 19

Job Trusts in His Redeemer

¹ Then Job answered and said,

² "How long will you torment my soul, and destroy me with words? Only know that the Lord has dealt with me thus.

³ You speak against me; you do not feel for me, but bear hard upon me.

⁴ Surely I have erred in truth, (but the error abides with myself) in having spoken words which it was not right *to speak*; and my words err, and are unreasonable.

⁵ But alas! For you magnify yourselves against me, and insult me with reproach.

⁶ Know then that it is the Lord that has troubled *me*, and He has raised up high His fortress against me.

⁷ Behold, I laugh at reproach; I will not speak: or I will cry out, but judgment is nowhere.

⁸ I am fenced round about, and can by no means escape: He has set darkness before my face.

⁹ And He has stripped me of my glory, and has taken the crown from my head.
¹⁰ He has torn me round about, and I am gone, and He has cut off my hope like a tree.
¹¹ And He has dreadfully handled me in anger, and has counted me for an enemy.
¹² His troops also came upon me with one accord, liars in wait compassed my ways.
¹³ "My brothers have stood far from me; they have acknowledged strangers *rather* than me: and my friends have become pitiless.
¹⁴ My relatives have not acknowledged me, and they that knew my name have forgotten me.
¹⁵ *As for* my household, and my maidservants, I was a stranger in their sight.
¹⁶ I called my servant, but he gives no answer; and my mouth begged *him*.
¹⁷ And I sought after my wife, and earnestly begged the sons of my concubines.
¹⁸ But they rejected me forever; whenever I rise up, they speak against me.
¹⁹ They that saw me abhorred me: the very persons whom I had loved rose up against me.
²⁰ My flesh is corrupt under my skin, and my bones are held in my teeth.
²¹ "Pity me, pity me, O my friends; for it is the hand of the Lord that has touched me.
²² Why do you persecute me as also the Lord *does*, and are not satisfied with my flesh?
²³ "For oh that my words were written, and that they were recorded in a book forever,
²⁴ with an iron pen and lead, or engraved in the rocks!
²⁵ For I know that He who shall deliver me on the earth is eternal,
²⁶ *and* to raise up upon the earth my skin that endures these *sufferings*: for these things have been accomplished to me of the Lord;
²⁷ which I am conscious of in myself, which my eye has seen, and not another, but all have been fulfilled to me in my bosom.
²⁸ But if you shall also say, 'What shall we say before him,' and so find the root of the matter in him?
²⁹ Beware of deceit for yourselves; for wrath will come upon transgressors; and then shall they know where their substance is."

JOB CHAPTER 20

Zophar Speaks: Wickedness Receives Just Retribution
¹ Then Zophar the Minaean answered and said,
² "I did not suppose that you would answer this way: neither do you understand more than I.
³ I will hear my shameful reproach, and the spirit of my understanding answers me.

⁴ Have you *not* known these things of old, from the time that man was set upon the earth?
⁵ But the rejoicing of the ungodly *is* death, and the joy of transgressors *is* destruction:
⁶ although his gifts should go up to heaven, and his sacrifice reach the clouds.
⁷ For when he shall seem to be established, then he shall utterly perish, and those that knew him shall say, 'Where is he?'
⁸ Like a dream that has fled away, he shall not be found; and he has fled like a vision of the night.
⁹ The eye has looked upon him, but shall not *see him* again; and his place shall no longer perceive him.
¹⁰ Let *his* inferiors destroy his children, and let his hands kindle the fire of sorrow.
¹¹ His bones have been filled with the *vigor of* his youth, and it shall lie down with him in the dust.
¹² Though evil be sweet in his mouth, though he will hide it under his tongue;
¹³ though he will not spare it, and will not leave it, but will keep it in the midst of his throat:
¹⁴ yet he shall by no means be able to help himself; the gall of an asp is in his belly.
¹⁵ *His* wealth unjustly collected shall be vomited up; a messenger of *wrath* shall drag him out of his house.
¹⁶ And let him suck the poison of serpents, and let the serpent's tongue slay him.
¹⁷ Let him not see the milk of the pastures, nor the supplies of honey and butter.
¹⁸ He has labored unprofitably and in vain, for wealth of which he shall not taste: it is as a lean thing, unfit for food, which he cannot swallow.
¹⁹ For he has broken down the houses of many mighty men, and he has plundered a house, though he did not build it.
²⁰ There is no security to his possessions; he shall not be saved by his desire.
²¹ There is nothing remaining of his provisions, therefore his goods shall not flourish.
²² But when he shall seem to be satisfied, he shall be afflicted; and all distress shall come upon him.
²³ If by any means he would fill his belly, let *God* send upon him the fury of wrath; let Him bring a torrent of pains upon him.
²⁴ And he shall by no means escape from the power of the sword; let the bronze bow wound him.
²⁵ And let the arrow pierce through his body; and let the stars be against his dwelling-place: let terrors come upon him.
²⁶ And let all darkness wait for him: an unfanned fire shall consume him, and let a stranger plague his house.
²⁷ And let the heavens reveal his iniquities, and the earth rise up against him.
²⁸ Let destruction bring his house to an end; let a day of wrath come upon him.

²⁹ This is the portion of an ungodly man from the Lord, and the possession of his goods *appointed him* by the all-seeing *God*."

JOB CHAPTER 21

Job's Discourse on the Wicked

¹ But Job answered and said,

² "Listen, listen to my words, that I may not have this consolation from you.

³ Raise me, and I will speak; then you shall not laugh me to scorn.

⁴ What! Is my reproof from man? And why should I not be angry?

⁵ Look upon me and wonder, laying your hand upon your cheek.

⁶ For even when I remember, I am alarmed, and pains seize my flesh.

⁷ Why do the ungodly live, and grow old even in wealth?

⁸ Their seed is according to *their* desire, and their children are in *their* sight.

⁹ Their houses are prosperous, and safe from fear, neither is the rod of the Lord upon them.

¹⁰ Their cow does not cast her calf, and their *beast* with young is safe, and does not miscarriage.

¹¹ And they remain as an unfailing flock, and their children play before *them*, taking up the psaltery and harp;

¹² and they rejoice at the voice of a song.

¹³ And they spend their days in wealth, and fall asleep in the rest of the grave.

¹⁴ Yet *such a man* says to the Lord, 'Depart from me; I desire not to know Your ways.'

¹⁵ What is the Mighty One, that we should serve Him? And what profit is there that we should approach Him?

¹⁶ For their good things were in *their* hands, but He does not regard the works of the ungodly.

¹⁷ "Nevertheless, the lamp of the ungodly also shall be put out, and destruction shall come upon them, and pangs of vengeance shall seize them.

¹⁸ And they shall be as chaff before the wind, or as dust which the storm has taken up.

¹⁹ Let his substance fail to *supply* his children: God shall recompense him, and he shall know it.

²⁰ Let his eyes see his own destruction, and let him not be saved by the Lord.

²¹ For his desire is in his house with him, and the number of his months has been suddenly cut off.

²² "Is it not the Lord who teaches understanding and knowledge? And does He not judge murders?

²³ One shall die in his perfect strength, and wholly at ease and prosperous;

²⁴ and his inwards are full of fat, and his marrow is diffused *throughout him*.

²⁵ And another dies in bitterness of soul, not eating any good thing.

²⁶ But they lie down in the dust together, and corruption covers them.

²⁷ So I know you, that you presumptuously attack me,

²⁸ so that you will say, 'Where is the house of the prince? And where is the covering of the tabernacles of the ungodly?'

²⁹ Ask those that go by the way, and do not disown their tokens.

³⁰ For the wicked hastens to the day of destruction: they shall be led away for the day of His vengeance.

³¹ Who will tell him his way to his face, since he has done it? Who shall recompense him?

³² And he has been led away to the tombs, and he has watched over the heaps.

³³ The stones of the valley have been sweet to him, and every man shall depart after him, and *there are* innumerable *ones* before him.

³⁴ How then do you comfort me in vain? Since I have no rest from your molestation."

JOB CHAPTER 22

Eliphaz Accuses Job of Wickedness

¹ Then Eliphaz the Temanite answered and said,

² "Is it not the Lord that teaches understanding and knowledge?

³ For what does it matter to the Lord, if you were blameless in your works? Or is it profitable that you should perfect your way?

⁴ Will you maintain and plead your own cause? And will He enter into judgment with you?

⁵ Is not your wickedness abundant, and your sins innumerable?

⁶ And you have taken *the* security of your brothers for nothing, and have taken away the clothing of the naked.

⁷ Neither have you given water to the thirsty to drink, but have taken away the morsel of the hungry.

⁸ And you have accepted the persons of some; and you have established those *that were already settled* on the earth.

⁹ But you have sent widows away empty, and have afflicted orphans.

¹⁰ Therefore snares have surrounded you, and disastrous war has troubled you.

¹¹ The light has proved darkness to you, and water has covered you on your lying down.

¹² Does not He that dwells in the high places observe? And has He not brought down the proud?

¹³ And you have said, 'What does the Mighty One know? Does He judge in the dark?'

¹⁴ A cloud is His hiding place, and He shall not be seen; and He passes through the circle of heaven.

15 Will you not mark the old way, which righteous men have trodden?

16 Who were seized before their time—their foundations are as an overflowing stream.

17 Who say, 'What will the Lord do to us? Or what will the Almighty bring upon us?'

18 Yet He filled their houses with good things, but the counsel for the wicked is far from Him.

19 The righteous have seen it, and laughed, and the blameless one has derided them.

20 Verily their substance has been utterly destroyed, and the fire shall devour what is left of their *property*.

21 "Be firm, I pray, if you can endure; then your fruit shall prosper.

22 And receive a declaration from His mouth, and lay up His words in your heart.

23 And if you shall turn and humble yourself before the Lord, you have thus removed unrighteousness far from your habitation.

24 You shall lay up for yourself *treasure* in a heap on the rock; and Ophir *shall be* as the rock of the torrent.

25 So the Almighty shall be your helper from enemies, and He shall bring you forth *as* pure as silver that has been tried by fire.

26 Then shall you have boldness before the Lord, looking up cheerfully to heaven.

27 And He shall hear you when you pray to Him, and He shall grant you power to pay your vows.

28 And He shall establish to you again a habitation of righteousness, and there shall be light upon your paths.

29 Because you have humbled yourself, and you shall say, 'Man has behaved proudly, but He shall save him that is of lowly eyes.'

30 He shall deliver the innocent, and do you save yourself by your pure hands.

JOB CHAPTER 23

Job Proclaims God's Righteous Judgments

1 Then Job answered and said,

2 "Yes, I know that pleading is out of my reach; and His hand has been made heavy upon my groaning.

3 Oh, that I knew where I might find Him, and come to an end *of the matter*!

4 And I would plead my own cause, and He would fill my mouth with arguments.

5 And I would know the remedies which He would speak to me, and I would perceive what He would tell me.

6 Though He should come on me in His great strength, then He would not threaten me;

7 for truth and reproof are from Him, and He would bring forth my judgment to an end.

8 For if I shall go first, and exist no longer, still what do I know *concerning* the latter end?

9 When He worked on the left hand, then I did not observe it: His right hand shall encompass me but I shall not see it.

10 For He already knows my way, and He has tried me as gold.

11 And I will go forth according to His commandments, for I have kept His ways; and I shall not turn aside from His commandments,

12 neither shall I transgress; but I have hid His words in my bosom.

13 And if He too has thus judged, who is he that has contradicted, for He has both willed a thing and done it.

14 (This verse omitted in the LXX)

15 Therefore am I troubled at Him; and when I was reproved, I thought of Him. Therefore let me take good heed before Him: I will consider, and be terrified of Him.

16 But the Lord has softened my heart, and the Almighty has troubled me.

17 For I knew not that darkness would come upon me, and thick darkness has covered me before my face.

JOB CHAPTER 24

Job Complains of Violence on the Earth

1 "But why have the seasons been hidden from the Lord,

2 while the ungodly have passed over the bound, carrying off the flock with the shepherd?

3 They have led away the donkey of the fatherless, and taken the widow's ox for a pledge.

4 They have turned aside the weak from the right way, and the meek of the earth have hidden themselves together.

5 And they have departed like donkeys in the field, having gone forth on my account according to their own order. His bread is sweet to His little ones.

6 They have reaped a field that was not their own before the time; the poor have labored in the vineyards of the ungodly without pay and without food.

7 They have caused many naked to sleep without clothes, and they have taken away the covering of their body.

8 They are wet with the showers of the mountains; they have embraced the rock, because they had no shelter.

9 They have snatched the fatherless from the breast, and have afflicted the outcast.

10 And they have wrongfully caused *others* to sleep without clothing, and taken away the morsel of the hungry.

11 They have unrighteously laid wait in narrow places, and have not known the righteous way.

12 Who have cast forth the poor from the city and their own houses, and the soul of the children has groaned aloud.

13 "Why then has He not visited these? Forasmuch as they were upon the earth, and took no notice, and they knew not the way of righteousness, neither have they walked in their *appointed* paths?

14 But having known their works, He delivered them into darkness; and in the night one will be as a thief.

[15] And the eye of the adulterer has watched for the darkness, saying, 'Eye shall not see me, and he puts a covering on his face.'

[16] In darkness he digs through houses; by day they conceal themselves securely; they do not know the light.

[17] For the morning is to them all as the shadow of death, for each will be conscious of the terror of the shadow of death.

[18] He is swift on the face of the water; let his portion be cursed on the earth, and let their plants be laid bare.

[19] *Let them be* withered upon the earth, for they have plundered the sheaves of the fatherless.

[20] Then is his sin brought to remembrance, and he vanishes like a vapor of dew; but let what he has done be recompensed to him, and let every unrighteous one be crushed like rotten wood.

[21] For he has not treated the barren woman well, and has had no pity on the feeble woman.

[22] "And in wrath he has overthrown the helpless; therefore when he has arisen, a man will not feel secure of his own life.

[23] When he has fallen sick, let him not hope to recover, but let him perish by disease.

[24] For his exaltation has hurt many; but he has withered as mallows in the heat, or as an ear of corn falling off of itself from the stalk.

[25] But if not, who is he that says I speak falsely, and will make my words of no account?"

JOB CHAPTER 25

Bildad: How Can Man Be Righteous?

[1] Then Bildad the Shuhite answered and said,

[2] "What beginning or fear is His—even He that makes all things in the highest?

[3] For let none think that there is a respite for robbers: and upon whom will there not come a snare from Him?

[4] For how shall a mortal be righteous before the Lord? Or who that is born of a woman shall purify himself?

[5] If He gives an order to the moon, then it will not shine; and the stars are not pure before Him.

[6] But alas! Man is corrupt, and the son of man a worm."

JOB CHAPTER 26

Job: Man's Frailty and God's Majesty

[1] But Job answered and said,

[2] "To whom do you attach yourself, or who are you going to assist? Is it not He that has much strength, and He who has a strong arm?

[3] To whom have you given counsel? Is it not to Him who has all wisdom? Who will you follow? Is it not the One who has the greatest power?

[4] To whom have you uttered words? And whose breath is it that has come forth from you?

[5] Shall giants be born from under the water and the inhabitants thereof?

[6] Hell is naked before Him, and destruction has no covering.

[7] He stretches out the north wind upon nothing, and He hangs the earth upon nothing;

[8] binding water in His clouds, and the cloud does not break under it.

[9] He keeps back the face of His throne, stretching out His cloud upon it.

[10] He has encompassed the face of the water by an appointed ordinance, until the end of light and darkness.

[11] The pillars of heaven are prostrate and astonished at His rebuke.

[12] He has calmed the sea with *His* might, and by *His* wisdom the whale has been overthrown.

[13] And the barriers of heaven fear Him, and by a command He has slain the apostate dragon.

[14] Behold, these are parts of His way; and we will hearken to Him at the least intimation of His word: but who knows the strength of His thunder, when He shall employ it?"

JOB CHAPTER 27

Job Maintains His Integrity

[1] And Job further continued and said in his discourse,

[2] "As God lives, who has thus judged me; and the Almighty, who has embittered my soul;

[3] verily, while my breath is yet in me, and the breath of God which remains to me is in my nostrils,

[4] my lips shall not speak evil words, neither shall my soul meditate unrighteous thoughts.

[5] Far be it from me that I should justify you till I die! For I will not let go my innocence,

[6] but holding fast to my righteousness, I will by no means let it go: for I am not conscious to myself of having done anything amiss.

[7] But on the contrary, let my enemies be as the overthrow of the ungodly, and they that rise up against me as the destruction of transgressors.

[8] For what is the hope of the ungodly, that he holds to it? Will he indeed trust in the Lord and be saved?

[9] Will God hear his prayer? Or when distress has come upon him,

[10] has he any confidence before Him? Or will *God* hear him as he calls upon Him?

[11] Yet now I will tell you what is in the hand of the Lord: I will not lie concerning the things which are with the Almighty. [12] Behold, you all know that you are adding vanity to vanity.

[13] "This is the portion of an ungodly man from the Lord, and the possession of oppressors shall come upon them from the Almighty.

14 And if their children are many, they shall be for slaughter: and if they grow up, they shall beg.

15 And they that survive of him shall utterly perish, and no one shall pity their widows.

16 Even if he should gather silver as dust, and prepare gold as clay,

17 all these things shall the righteous gain, and the true-hearted shall possess His wealth.

18 And his house is gone like moths, and like a spider's web.

19 The rich man shall lie down, and shall not continue: he has opened his eyes, and he is no more.

20 Pains have come upon him as water, and darkness has carried him away by night.

21 And a burning wind shall catch him, and he shall depart, and it shall utterly drive him out of his place.

22 And *God* shall cast *trouble* upon him, and not spare: he flees desperately from out of His hand.

23 He shall cause *men* to clap their hands against them, and shall hiss him out of his place.

JOB CHAPTER 28

Job's Discourse on Wisdom

1 "For there is a place for the silver, where it comes, and a place for the gold, where it is refined.

2 For iron comes out of the earth, and brass is hewn out like stone.

3 He has set a bound to darkness, and he searches out every limit: a stone is darkness, and the shadow of death.

4 There is a cutting off the torrent by reason of dust, so they that forget the right way are weakened; they are removed from among men.

5 *As for* the earth, out of it shall come bread; under it has been turned up as it were fire.

6 Her stones are the place of the sapphire, and her dust supplies man with gold.

7 *There* is a path, the fowl has not known it, neither has the eye of the vulture seen it.

8 Neither have the sons of the proud trodden it, a lion has not passed upon it.

9 He has stretched forth his hand on the sharp *rock*, and turned up mountains by the roots;

10 and he has interrupted the whirlpools of rivers, and my eye has seen every precious thing.

11 And he has laid bare the depths of rivers, and has brought his power to light.

12 But where has wisdom been discovered? And where is the place of understanding?

13 A mortal has not known its way, neither indeed has it been discovered among men.

14 The depth has said, 'It is not in me,' and the sea has said, 'It is not with me.'

15 One shall not give fine gold instead of it, neither shall silver be weighed in exchange for it.

16 Neither shall it be compared with the gold of Ophir, with the precious onyx and sapphire.

17 Gold and crystal shall not be equaled to it, neither shall vessels of gold be its exchange.

18 Coral and fine pearl shall not be mentioned, but esteem wisdom above the most precious things.

19 The topaz of Ethiopia shall not be equaled to it; it shall not be compared with pure gold.

20 Where then is wisdom found? And of what kind is the place of understanding?

21 It has escaped the notice of every man, and has been hidden from the birds of the sky.

22 Destruction and Death have said, 'We have heard the report of it.'

23 God has well ordered the way of it, and He knows the place of it.

24 For He surveys the whole *earth* under heaven, knowing the things in the earth;

25 all that He has made; the weight of the winds, the measures of the water.

26 When He made *them*, thus He saw and numbered them, and made a way for the pealing of the thunder.

27 Then He saw it, and declared it: He prepared it, and traced it out.

28 And He said to man, 'Behold, godliness is wisdom: and to abstain from evil is understanding.'"

JOB CHAPTER 29

Job Finishes His Defense

1 And Job continued and said in his discourse,

2 "Oh that I were as in months past, in the days when God preserved me!

3 As when His lamp shone over my head; when by His light I walked through darkness.

4 As when I steadfastly pursued my ways, when God took care of my house.

5 When I was very fruitful, and my children were about me;

6 when my ways were moistened with butter, and the mountains flowed for me with milk.

7 When I went forth early in the city, and the seat was placed for me in the streets.

8 The young men saw me, and hid themselves: and all the old men stood up.

9 And the great men ceased speaking, and laid their finger on their mouth.

10 And they that heard me blessed me, and their tongue stuck to the roof of their mouth.

11 For the ear heard, and blessed me; and the eye saw me, and turned aside.

12 For I saved the poor out of the hand of the oppressor, and helped the fatherless who had no helper. **13** Let the blessing of the perishing one come upon me; indeed, the mouth of the widow has blessed me.

14 Also I put on righteousness, and clothed myself with judgment like a mantle.

15 I was the eye of the blind, and the foot of the lame.

16 I was the father of the helpless, and I searched out the cause which I did not know.

17 And I broke the fangs of the wicked; I plucked the spoil out of the midst of their teeth.

18 And I said, 'My age shall continue as the stem of a palm tree; I shall live a long while.'

19 My root was spread out by the water, and the dew would lodge on my crop.

20 My glory was fresh in me, and my bow prospered in my hand.

21 Men heard me, and gave heed, and they were silent at my counsel.

22 At my word they did not speak again, and they were very glad whenever I spoke to them.

23 As the thirsty earth expecting the rain, so they *waited for* my speech.

24 Were I to laugh at them, they would not believe it; and the light of my face has not failed.

25 I chose out their way, and sat as chief, and dwelt as a king in the midst of warriors, as one comforting mourners.

JOB CHAPTER 30

1 "But now the youngest have laughed me to scorn; now they reprove me in their turn, whose fathers I set at nought; whom I did not deem worthy *to be with* my shepherd dogs.

2 Yea, why did I have the strength of their hands? For them the full term *of life* was lost.

3 *One is* childless from want and famine, *such as* they that fled but lately the distress and misery of drought.

4 Who compass the salty places on the sounding *shore*, who had salt *herbs* for their food, and were dishonorable and of no repute, in need of every good thing; who also ate roots of trees by reason of great hunger.

5 Thieves have risen up against me,

6 whose houses were the caves of the rocks, who lived under the wild shrubs.

7 They will cry out among the rustling *bushes*.

8 *They are* sons of fools and vile men, *whose* name and glory *are* quenched from off the earth.

9 But now I am their music, and they have me for a byword.

10 And they withdrew from me and abhorred me, and spared not to spit in my face.

11 For He has opened His quiver and afflicted me: they also have cast off the restraint of my presence.

12 They have risen up against me on the right hand of their offspring; they have stretched out their foot, and directed against me the ways of their destruction.

13 My paths are ruined, for they have stripped off my garments: He has shot at me with His weapons.

14 And He has pleaded against me as He wills—I am overwhelmed with pains.

15 My pains return upon me; my hope is gone like the wind, and my safety as a cloud.

16 Even now my life shall be poured forth upon me, and days of anguish seize me.

17 And by night my bones are confounded; and my sinews are relaxed.

18 With great force *my disease* has taken hold of my garment—it has compassed me as the collar of my coat.

19 And You have counted me as clay; my portion in dust and ashes.

20 "And I have cried to You, but You do not hear me: but they stood still, and observed me.

21 They attacked me also without mercy: You have scourged me with a strong hand.

22 And You have put me to grief, and have cast me away from safety.

23 For I know that death will destroy me: for the earth is the house *appointed* for every mortal.

24 Oh, that I might lay hands upon myself, or at least ask another, and he should do this for me!

25 Yet I wept over every helpless man; I groaned when I saw a man in distress.

26 But I, when I waited for good things, behold, days of evil came upon me all the more.

27 My belly boiled, and would not cease—the days of poverty prevented me.

28 I went mourning without restraint, and I have stood and cried out in the assembly.

29 I have become a brother of monsters, and a companion of ostriches.

30 And my skin has been greatly blackened, and my bones are burned with heat.

31 My harp also has been turned into mourning, and my song into my weeping.

JOB CHAPTER 31

1 "I made a covenant with my eyes, and I will not think upon a virgin.

2 Now what portion has God given from above? And is there an inheritance given from the Mighty One from on high?

3 Alas! Destruction to the unrighteous, and rejection to them that do iniquity!

4 Will He not see my way, and number all my steps?

5 But if I had gone with scorners, and if my foot too has hastened to deceit

6 (for I am weighed in a just balance, and the Lord knows my innocence);

7 if my foot has turned aside out of the way, or if my heart has followed my eye, and if I too have touched gifts with my hands;

8 then let me sow, and let others eat; and let me be uprooted on the earth.

9 If my heart has gone forth after another man's wife, and if I laid wait at her doors;

10 then let my wife also please another, and let my children be brought low.

11 For the rage of anger is not to be controlled, in the case of defiling another man's wife.

12 For it is a fire burning on every side, and whoever it attacks, it utterly destroys.

13 And if I also despised the judgment of my servant or my maid, when they pleaded with me;

14 what then shall I do if the Lord should try me? And if also He should at all visit me, can I make an answer?

15 Were not they formed too, as I also was formed in the womb? Indeed, we were formed in the same womb.

16 But the helpless did not miss whatever need they had, and I did not cause the eye of the widow to fail.

17 And if I also ate my food alone, and did not impart *of it* to the orphan;

18 (for I nourished them as a father from my youth and guided *them* from my mother's womb).

19 And if I too overlooked the naked as he was perishing, and did not clothe him;

20 and if the poor did not bless me, and their shoulders were not warmed with the fleece of my lambs;

21 if I lifted my hand against an orphan, trusting that my strength was far superior *to his*:

22 then let my shoulder start from the blade bone, and my arm be crushed off from the elbow.

23 For the fear of the Lord constrained me, and I cannot bear up by reason of His burden.

24 If I made gold my treasure, and if I too trusted the precious stone;

25 and if I also rejoiced when my wealth was abundant, and if I laid my hand on innumerable *treasures*

26 (do we not see the shining sun eclipsed, and the moon waning? For they have not *power* to *continue*);

27 and if my heart was secretly deceived, and if I have laid my hand upon my mouth and kissed it:

28 let this also then be reckoned to me as the greatest iniquity: for I *should* have lied against the Lord Most High.

29 And if I too was glad at the fall of my enemies, and my heart said, 'Aha!'

30 Then let my ear hear my curse, and let me be a byword among my people in my affliction.

31 And if my handmaids have often said, 'Oh that we might be satisfied with his flesh' (whereas I was very kind:

32 for the stranger did not lodge without, and my door was opened to everyone that came);

33 or if also having sinned unintentionally, I hid my sin

34 (for I did not stand in awe of a great multitude, so as not to declare boldly before them); and if I also permitted a poor man to go out of my door with an empty bosom—

35 (Oh that I had a hearer!) And if I had not feared the hand of the Lord; and as to the written charge which I had against anyone,

36 I would place it as a chaplet on my shoulders, and read it.

37 And if I did not read it and return it, having taken nothing from the debtor:

38 If at any time the land groaned against me, and if its furrows mourned together;

39 and if I ate its strength alone without price, and if I too grieved the heart of the owner of the soil, by taking from *him*,

40 then let the thistles come up to me instead of wheat, and a bramble instead of barley." And Job ceased speaking.

JOB CHAPTER 32

Elihu Contradicts Job's Friends

1 And his three friends also ceased any longer to answer Job, for Job was righteous before them.

2 Then Elihu the son of Barachiel, the Buzite, of the kindred of Ram, of the land of Uz, was angered: and he was very angry with Job, because he justified himself before the Lord.

3 And he was also very angry with his three friends, because they were not able to return answers to Job, yet set him down for an ungodly man.

4 But Elihu had waited to give an answer to Job, because they were older than he was.

5 And Elihu saw that there was no answer in the mouth of the three men, and he was angered in his wrath.

6 And Elihu the Buzite the son of Barachiel answered and said, "I am younger in age, and you are older, therefore I kept silent, fearing to declare to you my own knowledge.

7 And I said, 'It is not time that speaks, though in many years men know wisdom':

8 but there is a spirit in mortals, and the inspiration of the Almighty is that which teaches.

9 The long-lived are not wise as such, neither do the aged know judgment.

10 Therefore I said, 'Hear me, and I will tell you what I know.'

11 Give ear to my words; for I will speak in your hearing, until you have tried the matter with words:

12 I have paid close attention to you; and behold, not one of you convinced Job, or answered his words—

13 lest you should say, 'We have found that we have added wisdom to the Lord.'

14 And you have commissioned a man to speak such words.

15 "They were afraid, they answered no longer; they gave up their speaking.

16 I waited, (for I had not spoken) because they stood still, and they did not speak."

17 And Elihu continued, and said, "I will again speak,

18 for I am full of words, for the spirit within me destroys me.

19 And my belly is as a skin of sweet wine, bound up and ready to burst; or as a blacksmith's laboring bellows.

20 I will speak, that I may open my lips and relieve myself.

21 For truly I will not be awed because of man, nor indeed will I be confounded before a mortal.

22 For I know not how to respect persons: and if otherwise, even the moths would eat me.

JOB CHAPTER 33

Elihu Contradicts Job

1 "But please, Job, hear my words, and listen to my speech.

2 For behold, I have opened my mouth, and my tongue has spoken.

3 My heart *shall be found* pure by my words; and the understanding of my lips shall meditate purity.

4 The Divine Spirit is that which formed me, and the breath of the Almighty *is* that which teaches me.

5 If you can, give me an answer: wait therefore; stand against me, and I will stand against you.

6 You are formed out of the clay as I also: we have been formed out of the same substance.

7 My fear shall not terrify you, neither shall my hand be heavy upon you.

8 "But you have said in my ears, (I have heard the voice of your words) because you say, 'I am pure,' not having sinned;

9 'I am blameless, for I have not transgressed.

10 Yet He has discovered a charge against me, and He has reckoned me as an adversary.

11 And He has put my foot in the stocks, and has watched all my ways.'

12 "For how do you say, 'I am righteous, yet He has not listened to me?' For He that is above mortals is eternal.

13 But you say, 'Why has He not heard every word of my cause?'

14 For when the Lord speaks once, or a second time,

15 *sending* a dream, or in the meditation of the night (as when a dreadful alarm happens to fall upon men, while sleeping on the bed),

16 then He opens the understanding of men: He scares them with such fearful visions;

17 to turn a man from unrighteousness, and He delivers his body from a fall.

18 He spares also his soul from death, and does not allow him to fall in war.

19 "And again, He chastens him with sickness on his bed, and the multitude of his bones are pained.

20 And he shall not be able to take any grain, though his soul shall desire food;

21 until his flesh shall be consumed, and he shall show his bones bare.

22 His soul also draws near to death, and his life is in Hades.

23 "Though there should be a thousand messengers of death, not one of them shall wound him: if he should

purpose in his heart to turn to the Lord, and declare to man his fault, and show his folly;

24 He will support him, that he should not perish, and will restore his body as *fresh* plaster upon a wall; and He will fill his bones with marrow.

25 And He will make his flesh tender as that of a babe, and He will restore him among men in his full strength.

26 And he shall pray to the Lord, and his prayer shall be accepted by Him; he shall enter with a cheerful countenance, with a full expression *of praise*: for He will render to men their due.

27 Even then a man shall blame himself, saying, 'What kind of things have I done? And He has not punished me according to the full amount of my sins.

28 Deliver my soul, that it may not go to destruction, and my life shall see the light.'

29 Behold, all these things, the Mighty One works in a threefold manner with a man.

30 And He has delivered my soul from death, that my life may praise Him in the light.

31 Give ear, Job, and hear me: be silent, and I will speak.

32 If you have words, answer me: speak, for I desire you to be justified.

33 If not, listen to me: be silent, and I will teach you."

JOB CHAPTER 34

Elihu Proclaims God's Justice

1 And Elihu continued and said,

2 "Hear me, you wise men; hear me, you that have knowledge.

3 For the ear tests words, and the mouth tastes food.

4 Let us choose judgment to ourselves: let us know among ourselves what is right.

5 For Job has said, 'I am righteous: the Lord has removed my judgment.

6 And He has erred in my judgment: my wound is severe, apart from *any* unrighteousness of my own.'

7 What man is like Job, drinking scorning like water?

8 *Saying,* 'I have not sinned, nor committed ungodliness, nor had fellowship with workers of iniquity, to go with the ungodly.' 9 For you should not say, 'There shall be no visitation of a man,' whereas *there is* a visitation on him from the Lord.

10 "Therefore listen to me, you that are wise in heart: far be it from me to sin before the Lord, and to pervert righteousness before the Almighty.

11 Indeed, He renders to a man accordingly as each of them does, and in a man's path He will find him.

12 And do you think that the Lord will do wrong, or will the Almighty who made the earth pervert judgment?

13 And who is He that made *the whole world* under heaven, and all things in it?

14 For if He would confine, and restrain His Spirit with Himself; **15** all flesh would die together, and every mortal would return to the earth from where he was formed.

16 Take heed lest He rebuke you: hear this, listen to the voice of words.

17 Behold then the One that hates iniquities, and that destroys the wicked, who is forever just.

18 He is ungodly that says to a king, 'You are a transgressor,' *or that says* to princes, 'O most ungodly one.'

19 *Such a one* as would not reverence the face of an honorable man, neither knows how to give honor to the great, so that they should be respected.

20 But it shall turn out *as* vanity to them, to cry and beseech a man; for they dealt unlawfully, the poor being turned aside *from their right.*

21 For He surveys the works of men, and none of what they do has escaped Him.

22 Neither shall there be a place for the workers of iniquity to hide themselves.

23 For He will not lay upon a man more *than what is right.*

24 For the Lord looks down upon all men, who comprehends unsearchable things, glorious also and excellent things without number.

25 Who discovers their works, and will bring night about upon them, and they shall be brought low.

26 And He destroys the ungodly, for they are seen before Him.

27 Because they turned aside from the law of God, and did not regard His commands,

28 so as to bring before Him the cry of the needy; for He will hear the cry of the poor.

29 And He will give quiet, and who will condemn? And He will hide His face, and who shall see Him? Whether it be done against a nation or against a man, also:

30 causing a hypocrite to be king, because of the waywardness of the people.

31 "For there is one that says to the Mighty One, 'I have received *blessings*; I will not take a pledge:

32 I will see apart from myself—show me if I have done unrighteousness; I will not do so anymore.'

33 Will He take vengeance for it on you, whereas you will put it far *from you*? For you shall choose, and not I; and whatever you know, speak thus.

34 Because the wise in heart shall say this, and a wise man listens to my word.

35 But Job has not spoken with understanding, his words are not *uttered* with knowledge.

36 How is it that you learn, Job: no longer giving answers as the foolish:

37 that we add not to our sins: for iniquity will be reckoned against us, if we speak many words before the Lord."

JOB CHAPTER 35

Elihu Condemns Self-Righteousness

1 And Elihu resumed and said,

2 "What is this that you think is right? Who are you that you have said, 'I am righteous before the Lord?'

3 I will answer you, and your three friends.

4 "Look up to the sky and see; and consider the clouds, how high *they are* above you.

5 If you have sinned, what will you do?

6 And if you have also transgressed much, what can you perform?

7 And suppose you are righteous, what will you give Him? Or what shall He receive from your hand?

8 Your ungodliness *may affect* a man such as you; or your righteousness a son of man.

9 Those that are oppressed of a multitude will be ready to cry out; they will call for help because of the arm of many.

10 But none said, 'Where is God that made me, who appoints the night watches;

11 who makes me to differ from the four-footed beasts of the earth, and from the birds of the sky?'

12 There they shall cry, and none shall hear, even because of the insolence of wicked men.

13 For the Lord desires not to look on error, for He is the Almighty One.

14 He beholds them that perform lawless deeds, and He will save me: and do you plead before Him, if you can praise Him, as it is *possible* even now?

15 For He is not now regarding His wrath, nor has He noticed severely any trespass.

16 Yet Job vainly opens his mouth, in ignorance he multiplies words."

JOB CHAPTER 36

Elihu Proclaims God's Goodness

1 And Elihu further continued, and said,

2 "Bear with me yet a little while, that I may teach you: for there is yet speech in me.

3 Having fetched my knowledge from afar, and according to my works,

4 I will speak just things truly, and you shall not unjustly receive unjust words.

5 But know that the Lord will not cast off an innocent man: being mighty in strength of wisdom,

6 He will not by any means preserve the life of the ungodly, and He will grant the judgment of the poor.

7 He will not turn away His eyes from the righteous, but *they shall be* with kings on the throne, and He will establish them in triumph, and they shall be exalted.

8 But they that are bound in fetters shall be held in cords of poverty.

9 And He shall recount to them their works, and their transgressions, for such will act with violence.

[10] But He will listen to the righteous, and He has said that they shall turn from unrighteousness.

[11] If they should hear and serve Him, they shall spend their days in prosperity, and their years in honor.

[12] But He does not preserve the ungodly; because they are not willing to know the Lord, and because, when reproved, they were disobedient.

[13] "And the hypocrites in heart will array wrath *against themselves*; they will not cry, because He has bound them.

[14] Therefore let their soul die in youth, and their life be wounded by messengers *of death*.

[15] Because they afflicted the weak and helpless, and He will vindicate the judgment of the meek.

[16] And He has also enticed you out of the mouth of the enemy: [17] *there is* a deep gulf and a rushing stream beneath it, and your table came down full of fatness. Judgment shall not fail from the righteous,

[18] but there shall be wrath upon the ungodly, by reason of the ungodliness of the bribes which they received for iniquities.

[19] Let not your mind willingly turn you aside from the petition of the feeble that are in distress.

[20] And draw not forth all the mighty men by night, so that the people should go up instead of them.

[21] But take heed, lest you do that which is wrong: for of this you have chosen rather than poverty.

[22] "Behold, the Mighty One shall prevail by His strength, for who is as powerful as He?

[23] And who is he that examines His works? Or who can say, 'He has done injustice?'

[24] "Remember that His works are great *beyond* those which men have attempted.

[25] Every man has seen in himself, how many mortals are wounded.

[26] Behold, the Mighty One is great, and we shall not know *Him*: the number of His years is infinite.

[27] And the drops of rain are numbered by Him, and shall be poured out in rain to form a cloud.

[28] The ancient heavens shall flow, and the clouds overshadow innumerable mortals: He has fixed a time to cattle, and they know the order of rest. Yet by all these things your understanding is not astonished, neither is your mind disturbed in your body.

[29] And though one should understand the outspreadings of the clouds, or the measure of His tabernacle;

[30] behold, He will stretch His bow against him, and He covers the bottom of the sea.

[31] For by them He will judge the nations: He will give food to him that has strength.

[32] He has hidden the light in His hands, and given charge concerning it to the interposing cloud.

[33] The Lord will declare concerning this to His friend: *but there is* a portion also for unrighteousness.

JOB CHAPTER 37

[1] "At this also my heart is troubled, and moved out of its place.

[2] Hear a report by the anger of the Lord's wrath, and a discourse shall come out of His mouth.

[3] His dominion is under the whole heaven, and His light is at the extremities of the earth.

[4] After Him shall be a cry with a loud voice; He shall thunder with the voice of His excellency, yet He shall not cause men to pass away, for one shall hear His voice.

[5] The Mighty One shall thunder wonderfully with His voice: for He has done great things which we did not know;

[6] for He says to the snow, 'Fall on the earth,' and the stormy rain, and the storm of the showers of His might.

[7] He seals up the hand of every man, that every man may know his own weakness.

[8] And the wild beasts come in under the covert, and rest in their lair.

[9] Troubles come on out of the secret chambers, and cold from the mountain tops.

[10] And from the breath of the Mighty One He will send frost; and He guides the water in whatever way He pleases.

[11] And if a cloud obscures what is precious to Him, His light will disperse the cloud.

[12] And He will carry round the encircling clouds by His governance, to perform their works: whatsoever He shall command them,

[13] this has been appointed by Him on the earth, whether for correction, or for His land, or if He shall find him *an object* for mercy.

[14] "Listen to this, O Job: stand still, and be admonished of the power of the Lord.

[15] We know that God has disposed His works, having made light out of darkness.

[16] And He knows the divisions of the clouds, and the signal overthrows of the ungodly.

[17] But your robe is warm, and there is quiet upon the land.

[18] Will you establish with Him foundations for the ancient heavens? They are *as* strong as a cast iron mirror.

[19] Therefore teach me what shall we say to Him? And let us cease from saying much.

[20] Have I a book or a scribe by me, that I may stand and put man to silence?

[21] But the light is not visible to all: it shines afar off in the heavens, as that which is from Him in the clouds.

[22] From the north come the clouds shining like gold: in these are the glory and honor of the Almighty;

[23] and we do not find another His equal in strength: as for Him that judges justly, do you not think that He listens?

[24] Therefore men shall fear Him, and the wise also in heart shall fear Him."

JOB CHAPTER 38

The Lord Answers Job

¹ And after Elihu had ceased from speaking, the Lord spoke to Job through the whirlwind and clouds, *saying,*

² "Who is this that hides counsel from Me, and confines words in *his* heart, and thinks to conceal *them* from Me?

³ Gird your loins like a man, and I will ask you, and you shall answer Me!

⁴ "Where were you when I founded the earth? Tell me now, if you have knowledge.

⁵ Who set the measures of it, if you know? Or who stretched a line upon it?

⁶ On what are its rings fastened? And who is He that laid the cornerstone upon it?

⁷ When the stars were made, all My angels praised Me with a loud voice.

⁸ And I shut up the sea with gates, when it rushed out, coming forth out its mother's womb.

⁹ And I made a cloud its clothing, and swathed it in mist.

¹⁰ And I set boundaries for it, surrounding it with bars and gates.

¹¹ And I said to it, 'To this point you shall come, but you shall not go beyond, but your waves shall be confined within you.'

¹² "Or did I order the morning light in your time; and did the morning star *then first* see his appointed place;

¹³ to lay hold of the extremities of the earth, to cast out the ungodly out of it?

¹⁴ Or did you take *the* clay of the ground, and form a living creature *with it*, and set it with the power of speech upon the earth?

¹⁵ Have you removed light from the ungodly, and crushed the arm of the proud?

¹⁶ Or have you gone to the source of the sea, and walked in the tracks of the deep?

¹⁷ And do the gates of death open to you out of fear; and did the porters of hell quake when they saw you?

¹⁸ And have you been instructed in the breadth of the *whole earth* under heaven? Tell me now, what is the extent of it?

¹⁹ "And in what land does the light dwell? And where is the place of darkness?

²⁰ If you could bring Me to their uttermost boundaries, and if also you know their paths;

²¹ I know then that you were born at that time, and the number of your years is great.

²² But have you gone to the treasuries of snow? And have you seen the treasuries of hail?

²³ And is there a store of them, for you against the time of your enemies, for the day of wars and battle?

²⁴ And from where does the frost proceed? Or where is the south wind dispersed over the whole world under heaven?

²⁵ And who prepared a course for the violent rain, and a way for the thunders;

²⁶ to rain upon the land where there is no man, the wilderness, where there is not a man in it; so as to feed the untrodden and uninhabited land,

²⁷ and cause it to send forth a crop of green herbs?

²⁸ Who is the rain's father? And who has generated the drops of dew?

²⁹ And out of whose womb comes the ice? And who has produced the frost in the sky,

³⁰ which descends like flowing water? Who has terrified the face of the ungodly?

³¹ "And do you understand the band of Pleiades, and have you opened the barrier of Orion?

³² Or will you reveal Mazuroth in his season, and the evening star with his rays? Will you guide them?

³³ Do you know the changes of heaven, or the events which take place together under heaven?

³⁴ And will you call a cloud by your voice, and will it obey you with a violent shower of much rain?

³⁵ And will you send lightnings, and they shall go? And shall they say to you, 'What is *your pleasure*?'

³⁶ And who has given to women skill in weaving, or knowledge of embroidery?

³⁷ And who is he that numbers the clouds in wisdom, and has bowed the heaven down to the earth?

³⁸ For it is spread out as dusty earth, and I have cemented it as one hewn stone to another.

³⁹ "And will you hunt a prey for the lions? And satisfy the desires of the serpents?

⁴⁰ For they fear in their lairs, crouching, and lying in wait in the woods.

⁴¹ And who has prepared food for the raven? For its young ones wander and cry to the Lord, in search of food.

JOB CHAPTER 39

¹ "*Say* if you know the time of the bringing forth of the wild goats of the rock, and if you have marked the birth pangs of the hinds:

² and if you have numbered the full months of their being with young, and if you have relieved their pangs:

³ and have reared their young without fear; and will you loosen their pangs?

⁴ Their young will break forth; they will be multiplied with offspring: *their young* will go forth, and will not return to them.

⁵ And who is he that sent forth the wild donkey free? And who loosed his bands?

⁶ Whereas I made his habitation the wilderness, and the salt land his coverts.

⁷ He laughs to scorn the multitude of the city, and does not hear the chiding of the tax-gatherer.

⁸ He will survey the mountains as his pasture, and he seeks after every green thing.

⁹ And will the unicorn be willing to serve you, or to lie down at your manger?

10 And will you bind his yoke with thongs, or will he plow valleys for you in the plain?

11 And do you trust him, because his strength is great? And will you commit your works to him?

12 And will you believe that he will return to you your seed, and bring it in to your threshing floor?

13 The peacock has a beautiful wing: if the stork and the ostrich conceive, *it is worthy* of notice,

14 for the ostrich will leave her eggs in the ground, and warm them on the dust,

15 and has forgotten that the foot will scatter them, and the wild beasts of the field trample them.

16 She has hardened herself against her young ones, so as to not bereave herself: she labors in vain without fear.

17 For God has withheld wisdom from her, and not given her a portion in understanding.

18 In her season she will lift herself on high; she will scorn the horse and his rider.

19 "Have you invested the horse with strength, and clothed his neck with terror?

20 And have you clad him in perfect armor, and made his breast glorious with courage?

21 He paws exulting in the plain, and goes forth in strength into the plain.

22 He laughs to scorn a king as he meets him, and will by no means turn back from the sword.

23 The bow and sword resound against him, and his rage will swallow up the ground;

24 and he will not believe until the trumpet sounds.

25 And when the trumpet sounds, he says, 'Aha!' And afar off, he smells the war with prancing and neighing.

26 And does the hawk remain steady by your wisdom, having spread out her wings unmoved, looking toward the region of the south?

27 And does the eagle rise at your command, and the vulture remain sitting over his nest,

28 on a crag of a rock, and in a secret *place*?

29 From there he seeks food, his eyes observe from afar.

30 And his young ones roll themselves in blood, and wherever the carcasses may be, immediately they are found."

JOB CHAPTER 40

1 And the Lord God answered Job and said,

2 "Will *anyone* pervert judgment with the Mighty One? And he that reproves God, let him answer it."

3 And Job answered and said to the Lord,

4 "Why do I yet plead? Being rebuked even while reproving the Lord: hearing such things, whereas I am nothing: and what shall I answer to these *arguments*? I will lay my hand upon my mouth.

5 I have spoken once, but I will not do so a second time."

6 And the Lord yet again answered and spoke to Job out of the cloud, *saying*,

7 "Gird up now your loins like a man; and I will ask you, and you shall answer Me.

8 Do not set aside My judgment: and do you think that I have dealt with you in any other way, than that you might appear to be righteous?

9 Have you an arm like the Lord's? Or can you thunder with a voice like His?

10 Assume now a lofty bearing and power; and clothe yourself with glory and honor.

11 And send forth messengers with wrath, and lay low every haughty one.

12 Bring down also the proud man, and consume at once the ungodly.

13 And hide them together in the earth, and fill their faces with shame.

14 *Then* will I confess that your right hand can save *you*.

15 "But now look at the wild beasts among you; they eat grass like oxen.

16 Behold now, his strength is in his loins, and his force is in the navel of his belly.

17 He sets up his tail like a cypress, and his nerves are wrapped together.

18 His sides are sides of brass, and his backbone is as cast iron.

19 This is the chief of the creation of the Lord; made to be played with by His angels.

20 And when he has gone up to a steep mountain, he causes joy to the quadrupeds in the deep.

21 He lies under trees of every kind, by the papyrus, *the* reed, and *the* bulrush.

22 And the great trees make a shadow over him with their branches, and so do the bushes of the field.

23 If there should be a flood, he will not perceive it; he trusts that the Jordan will rush up into his mouth.

24 *Yet one* shall take him in his sight; one shall catch him with a cord, and pierce his nose.

JOB CHAPTER 41

1 "But will you catch the serpent with a hook, and put a halter about his nose?

2 Or will you fasten a ring in his nostril, and bore his lip with a clasp?

3 Will he address you with a petition? Softly, with the voice of a suppliant?

4 And will he make a covenant with you? And will you take him for a perpetual servant?

5 And will you play with him as with a bird? Or bind him as a sparrow for a child?

6 And do the nations feed upon him, and the nations of the Phoenicians share him?

7 And all the ships come together would not be able to bear the mere skin of his tail, neither *shall they carry* his head in fishing vessels.

⁸ But you shall lay your hand upon him once, remembering the war that is waged by his mouth; and let it not be done anymore.

⁹ Have you not seen him? And have you not wondered at the things said *of him*?

¹⁰ Do you not fear because preparation has been made by Me? For who is there that resists Me?

¹¹ Or who will resist Me, and stand their ground, since the whole world under heaven is Mine?

¹² I will not be silent because of him: though because of his power one shall pity his antagonist.

¹³ Who will open the face of his garment? And who can enter within the fold of his breastplate?

¹⁴ Who will open the doors of his face? Terror is round about his teeth.

¹⁵ His inwards are as bronze plates, and the texture of his skin as a smyrite stone.

¹⁶ One *part* cleaves fast to another, and the air cannot come between them.

¹⁷ They will remain united each to the other: they are closely joined, and cannot be separated.

¹⁸ At his sneezing a light shines, and his eyes are as the appearance of the morning star.

¹⁹ Out of his mouth proceed as it were burning lamps, and as it were hearths of fire are cast abroad.

²⁰ Out of his nostrils proceeds smoke of a furnace burning with fire of coals.

²¹ His breath is as live coals, and a flame goes out of his mouth.

²² And power is lodged in his neck, before him destruction runs.

²³ The flesh also of his body is joined together: if one pours violence upon him, he shall not be moved.

²⁴ His heart is firm as a stone, and it stands like an unyielding anvil.

²⁵ And when he turns, *he is* a terror to the four-footed wild beasts which leap upon the earth.

²⁶ If spears should come against him, men will effect nothing, *neither with* the spear or the breast plate.

²⁷ For he considers iron as chaff, and brass as rotten wood.

²⁸ The bow of brass shall not wound him, he deems a slinger as grass.

²⁹ Mauls are counted as stubble; and he laughs to scorn the waving of the firebrand.

³⁰ His lair is *formed of* sharp points, and all the gold of the sea under him is an immense *quantity* of clay.

³¹ He makes the deep boil like a bronze caldron, and he regards the sea as a pot of ointment,

³² and the lowest part of the deep as a captive: he reckons the deep as his range.

³³ There is nothing upon the earth like him, formed to be played with by My angels.

³⁴ He beholds every high thing, and he is king of all that are in the waters."

JOB CHAPTER 42

Job's Repentance and Restoration

¹ Then Job answered and said to the Lord,

² "I know that You can do all things, and nothing is impossible with You.

³ For who is he that hides counsel from You? Or who keeps back his words, and thinks to hide them from You? And who will tell me what I did not know, great and wonderful things which I did not understand?

⁴ But hear me, O Lord, that I also may speak: and I will ask You, and You shall teach me.

⁵ I have heard the report of You by the ear before; but now my eye has seen You.

⁶ Therefore I have counted myself vile, and have fainted: and I esteem myself dust and ashes."

⁷ And it came to pass after the Lord had spoken all these words to Job, that the Lord said to Eliphaz the Temanite, "You have sinned, and your two friends, for you have not said anything true before Me, as My servant Job has.

⁸ Now then take seven bulls, and seven rams, and go to My servant Job, and he shall offer a burnt offering for you. And My servant Job shall pray for you, for I will only accept him: for but his sake, I would have destroyed you, for you have not spoken the truth against My servant Job."

⁹ So Eliphaz the Temanite, and Bildad the Shuhite, and Zophar the Minaean, went and did as the Lord commanded them: and He pardoned their sin for the sake of Job.

¹⁰ And the Lord prospered Job. And when he prayed also for his friends, He forgave them *their* sin: and the Lord gave Job twice as much, even double of what he had before.

¹¹ And all his brothers and sisters heard all that had happened to him, and they came to him, and so did all that had known him from the first; and they ate and drank with him, and comforted him, and wondered at all that the Lord had brought upon him: and each one gave him a lamb, and four drachmas of gold, even of unstamped *gold*.

¹² And the Lord blessed the latter end of Job more than the beginning: and his livestock consisted of fourteen thousand sheep, six thousand camels, one thousand yoke of oxen, and one thousand female donkeys of the pastures.

¹³ And there were born to him seven sons and three daughters.

¹⁴ And he called the first Jemimah, and the second Keziah, and the third was Keren-Happuch.

¹⁵ And there were not found in comparison with the daughters of Job, fairer *women* than they in all the world: and their father gave them an inheritance among their brothers.

¹⁶ And Job lived after his affliction one hundred and seventy years: and all the years he lived were two hundred and forty: and Job saw his sons and his sons' sons, *to* the fourth generation.

[17] And Job died, an old man and full of days. And it is written that he will rise again with those whom the Lord raises up. This man is described in the Syriac book as living in the land of Uz, on the borders of Edom and Arabia: and his name before was Jobab; and having taken an Arabian wife, he fathered a son whose name was Ennon. And he himself was the son of his father Zare, one of the sons of Esau, and of his mother Bosorrha, so that he was the fifth from Abraham. And these were the kings who reigned in Edom, which country he also ruled over: first, Balak, the son of Beor, and the name of his city was Dennaba: but after Balak, Jobab, who is called Job, and after him Asom, who was governor out of the country of Teman: and after him Adad, the son of Barad, who destroyed Midian in the plain of Moab; and the name of his city was Gethaim. And his friends who came to him were Eliphaz, of the children of Esau, king of the Temanites, Bildad sovereign of the Sauchaeans, and Zophar king of the Minaeans.

THE BOOK OF PSALMS

PSALM 1

[1] Blessed is the man who has not walked in the counsel of the ungodly, and has not stood in the way of sinners, and has not sat in the seat of evil men.

[2] But his pleasure is in the law of the Lord; and in His law will he meditate day and night.

[3] And he shall be as a tree planted by the brooks of waters, which shall yield its fruit in its season, and its leaf shall not fall off; and whatsoever he shall do shall prosper.

[4] Not so *for* the ungodly—not so; but rather as the chaff which the wind scatters away from the face of the earth.

[5] Therefore the ungodly shall not rise in the judgment, nor sinners in the counsel of the just.

[6] For the Lord knows the way of the righteous; but the way of the ungodly shall perish.

PSALM 2

[1] Why did the nations rage, and the people imagine vain things?

[2] The kings of the earth stood up, and the rulers gathered themselves together, against the Lord, and against His Christ;

[3] *saying,* "Let us break through Their bonds, and cast away Their yoke from us."

[4] He that dwells in the heavens shall laugh them to scorn, and the Lord shall mock them.

[5] Then shall He speak to them in His anger, and trouble them in His fury.

[6] But I have been made King by Him on Zion His holy mountain,

[7] declaring the ordinance of the Lord: "The Lord has said to Me, 'You are My Son, today I have begotten You.

[8] Ask of Me, and I shall give You the nations *for* Your inheritance, and the ends of the earth *for* Your possession.

[9] You shall rule them with a rod of iron; You shall dash them in pieces as a potter's vessel.'"

[10] Now therefore understand, you kings: be instructed, all you that judge the earth.

[11] Serve the Lord with fear, and rejoice in Him with trembling.

[12] Accept correction, lest at any time the Lord be angry, and you should perish from the righteous way. Whenever His wrath shall be suddenly kindled, blessed are all they that trust in Him.

PSALM 3

[1] A Psalm of David, when he fled from the presence of his son Absalom.

O Lord, why are they that afflict me multiplied? Many rise up against me.

[2] Many say concerning my soul, "There is no deliverance for him in his God." Selah.

[3] But You, O Lord, are my helper; my glory, and the One that lifts up my head.

[4] I cried to the Lord with my voice, and He heard me out of His holy mountain. Selah.

[5] I laid down and slept; I awoke, for the Lord will help me.

[6] I will not be afraid of ten thousands of people, who have set themselves against me all around.

[7] Arise, O Lord; deliver me, my God; for You have struck all who were my enemies without cause; You have broken the teeth of sinners.

[8] Deliverance is the Lord's, and Your blessing is upon Your people.

PSALM 4

[1] For the end, A Song of David among the Psalms.

When I called upon *Him,* the God of my righteousness heard me; You have made room for me in tribulation; pity me, and hear my prayer.

[2] O you sons of men, how long *will you be* slow to hear? Why do you love vanity, and seek falsehood? Selah.

[3] But know that the Lord has done wondrous things for His holy one: the Lord will hear me when I cry to Him.

[4] Be angry, and do not sin; be vexed upon your beds for what you say in your hearts. Selah.

[5] Offer the sacrifice of righteousness, and trust in the Lord.

[6] Many say, 'Who will show us good things?' The light of Your countenance, O Lord, has been manifested towards us.

[7] You have put gladness into my heart: they have been satisfied with the fruit of their grain and wine and oil.

[8] I will both lie down in peace and sleep; for You alone, O Lord, have caused me to dwell securely.

PSALM 5

[1] For the end, A Psalm of David, concerning her that inherits.
Give ear to my words, O Lord, attend to my cry.

[2] Attend to the voice of my supplication, my King, and my God; for to You, O Lord, will I pray.

[3] In the morning You shall hear my voice: in the morning will I wait upon You, and will look up.

[4] For You are not a God that desires iniquity; neither shall the worker of wickedness dwell with You.

[5] Neither shall the transgressors continue in Your sight. You hate, O Lord, all them that work iniquity.

[6] You will destroy all that speak falsehood: the Lord abhors the bloody and deceitful man.

[7] But I will enter into Your house in the multitude of Your mercy; I will worship in Your fear toward Your holy temple.

[8] Lead me, O Lord, in Your righteousness because of my enemies; make my way plain before Your face.

[9] For there is no truth in their mouth; their heart is vain; their throat is an open tomb; with their tongues they have used deceit.

[10] Judge them, O God; let them fail of their counsels: cast them out according to the abundance of their ungodliness; for they have provoked You, O Lord.

[11] But let all that trust in You be glad in You: they shall rejoice forever, and You shall dwell among them; and all that love Your name shall rejoice in You.

[12] For You, O Lord, shall bless the righteous: You have compassed us as with a shield of favor.

PSALM 6

[1] For the end, A Psalm of David among the Hymns for the eighth.
O Lord, do not rebuke me in Your wrath, neither chasten me in Your anger.

[2] Pity me, O Lord; for I am weak: heal me, O Lord; for my bones are vexed.

[3] My soul also is grievously vexed: but You, O Lord, how long?

[4] Return, O Lord, deliver my soul: save me for Your mercy's sake.

[5] For in death no man remembers You; and who will give You thanks in Hades?

[6] I am wearied with my groaning; I shall wash my bed every night; I shall water my couch with tears.

[7] My eye is troubled because of my wrath; I am worn out because of all my enemies.

[8] Depart from me, all you that work iniquity; for the Lord has heard the voice of my weeping.

[9] The Lord has hearkened to my petition; the Lord has accepted my prayer.

[10] Let all my enemies be put to shame and greatly troubled: let them be turned back and grievously put to shame speedily.

PSALM 7

[1] A Psalm of David, which he sang to the Lord because of the words of Cush the Benjamite.
O Lord my God, in You have I trusted: save me from all them that persecute me, and deliver me,

[2] lest at any time *the enemy* seize my soul as a lion, while there is none to ransom, nor to save.

[3] O Lord my God, if I have done this; (if there is unrighteousness in my hands)

[4] if I have recompensed with evil those who recompensed me *with good*; may I then perish empty by means of my enemies.

[5] Let the enemy persecute my soul, and take it; and let him trample my life on the ground, and lay my glory in the dust. Selah.

[6] Arise, O Lord, in Your wrath; be exalted in the utmost boundaries of my enemies: awake, O Lord my God, according to the decree which You did command.

[7] And the congregation of the nations shall compass You: and for this cause do You return on high.

[8] The Lord shall judge the nations: judge me, O Lord, according to my righteousness, and according to my innocence that is in me.

[9] Oh let the wickedness of sinners come to an end; and *then* You shall direct the righteous, O God that searches the hearts and minds.

[10] My help is righteous, *coming* from God, who saves the upright in heart.

[11] God is a righteous Judge, and strong, and patient, not inflicting vengeance every day.

[12] If you will not repent, He will furbish His sword; He has bent His bow, and made it ready.

[13] And on it He has fitted the instruments of death; He has completed His arrows for the raging ones.

[14] Behold, *the wicked* has travailed with unrighteousness; he has conceived trouble, and has brought forth iniquity.

[15] He has opened a pit, and dug it up, and he shall fall into the ditch which he has made.

[16] His trouble shall return on his own head, and his unrighteousness shall come down on his own crown.

[17] I will give thanks to the Lord according to His righteousness; I will sing to the name of the Lord Most High.

PSALM 8

[1] For the end, concerning the winepresses, A Psalm of David.
O Lord, our Lord, how wonderful is Your name in all the earth! For Your magnificence is exalted above the heavens.

415

² Out of the mouth of babes and infants You have perfected praise, because of Your enemies; that You might put down the enemy and avenger.

³ For I will regard the heavens, the work of Your fingers; the moon and stars, which You have established.

⁴ What is man, that You are mindful of him? Or the son of man, that You visit him?

⁵ You made him a little lower than the angels, You have crowned him with glory and honor;

⁶ and You have set him over the works of Your hands; You have put all things under his feet:

⁷ sheep and all oxen—yea, and the cattle of the field;

⁸ the birds of the sky, and the fish of the sea, the *creatures* passing through the paths of the sea.

⁹ O Lord our Lord, how wonderful is Your name in all the earth!

PSALM 9

¹ For the end, A Psalm of David, concerning the secrets of the Son.
I will give thanks to You, O Lord, with my whole heart; I will recount all Your wonderful works.

² I will be glad and exalt in You: I will sing to Your name, O Most High.

³ When my enemies are turned back, they shall be feeble and perish at Your presence.

⁴ For You have maintained my cause and my right; You sat on the throne, that judges in righteousness.

⁵ You have rebuked the nations, and the ungodly one has perished; You have blotted out their name forever, even forever and ever.

⁶ The swords of the enemy have failed utterly; and you have destroyed cities: their memorial has been destroyed with a noise,

⁷ but the Lord endures forever; He has prepared His throne for judgment.

⁸ And He will judge the world in righteousness, He will judge the nations in uprightness.

⁹ The Lord also has become a refuge for the poor, a seasonable help, in affliction.

¹⁰ And let them that know Your name hope in You—for You, O Lord, have not failed them that diligently seek You.

¹¹ Sing praises to the Lord, who dwells in Zion: declare His dealings among the nations.

¹² For He remembered them, *in* making inquisition for blood; He has not forgotten the supplication of the poor.

¹³ Have mercy upon me, O Lord; look upon my affliction *which I suffer* from my enemies, You that lift me up from the gates of death:

¹⁴ that I may declare all Your praises in the gates of the daughter of Zion: I will rejoice in Your salvation.

¹⁵ The heathen are caught in the destruction which they planned: in the very snare which they hid is their foot taken.

¹⁶ The Lord is known as executing judgments: the sinner is taken in the works of his hands. Selah.

¹⁷ Let sinners be driven away into Hades, *even* all the nations that forget God.

¹⁸ For the poor shall not be forgotten forever; the patience of the needy ones shall not perish forever.

¹⁹ Arise, O Lord, let not man prevail: let the heathen be judged before You.

²⁰ Appoint, O Lord, a lawgiver over them: let the heathen know that they are men. Selah.

PSALM 10

¹¹ Why do You stand afar off, O Lord? *Why* do You overlook *us* in times of need, in affliction?

² While the ungodly one acts proudly, the poor is hotly pursued; *the wicked* are taken in the crafty counsels which they imagine.

³ Because the sinner praises himself for the desires of his heart; and the unjust one blesses himself.

⁴ The sinner has provoked the Lord: according to the abundance of his pride he will not seek after *Him*; God is not before him.

⁵ His ways are profane at all times; Your judgments are removed from before him: he will gain the mastery over all his enemies.

⁶ For he has said in his heart, "I shall not be moved," *continuing* without adversity from generation to generation.

⁷ Whose mouth is full of cursing, and bitterness, and fraud: under his tongue are trouble and pain.

⁸ He lies in wait with rich *men* in secret places, in order to slay the innocent: his eyes are set against the poor.

⁹ He lies in wait in secret as a lion in his den: he lies in wait to ravish the poor, to ravish the poor when he draws him *after him*: he will bring him down in his snare.

¹⁰ He will bow down and fall when he has mastered the poor.

¹¹ For he has said in his heart, God has forgotten; He has turned away His face so as never to look.

¹² Arise, O Lord God; let Your hand be lifted up: do not forget the poor.

¹³ Why has the wicked provoked God? For he has said in his heart, "He will not require *it.*"

¹⁴ You see *it*; for You observe trouble and wrath, to deliver them into Your hands; the poor has been left to You; You are a helper to the orphan.

¹⁵ Break the arm of the sinner and wicked man: his sin shall be sought for, and shall not be found.

¹⁶ The Lord shall reign forever, even forever and ever: you Gentiles shall perish out His land.

---

¹ In the Septuagint, Psalms 9 and 10 are combined, and the Psalm numbers differ from this point on. The Apostles' Bible follows the traditional Psalm divisions, to avoid confusion.

[17] The Lord has heard the desire of the poor: Your ear has inclined to the preparation of their heart;

[18] to plead for the orphan and afflicted, that man may no more boast upon the earth.

PSALM 11

[1] For the end, A Psalm of David.

In the Lord I have put my trust: how will you say to my soul, "Flee to the mountains as a sparrow?"

[2] For behold, the sinners have bent their *bow*, they have prepared their arrows for the quiver, to shoot secretly at the upright in heart.

[3] For they have pulled down what You framed, but what has the righteous done?

[4] The Lord is in His holy temple; as for the Lord, His throne is in heaven: His eyes look upon the poor, His eyelids test the sons of men.

[5] The Lord tests the righteous and the ungodly: and he that loves unrighteousness hates his own soul.

[6] He shall rain upon sinners snares, fire, and brimstone, and a stormy blast *shall be* the portion of their cup.

[7] For the Lord *is* righteous, and loves righteousness; His face beholds uprightness.

PSALM 12

[1] For the end, A Psalm of David, upon the eighth.

Save me, O Lord; for the godly man has failed; for truth is diminished from among the children of men.

[2] Everyone has spoken vanity to his neighbor: their lips are deceitful, they have spoken with a double heart.

[3] Let the Lord destroy all the deceitful lips, and the tongue that speaks great words;

[4] who have said, "We will magnify our tongue; our lips are our own: who is Lord of us?"

[5] "Because of the misery of the poor, and because of the sighing of the needy, now will I arise," says the Lord, "I will set *them* in safety; I will speak *to them* openly."

[6] The oracles of the Lord are pure oracles; as silver tried in the fire, proved *in* a furnace of earth, purified seven times.

[7] You, O Lord, shall keep us, and shall preserve us, from this generation, and forever.

[8] The ungodly walk around; according to Your greatness You have greatly exalted the sons of men.

PSALM 13

[1] For the end, A Psalm of David.

How long, O Lord, will You forget me? Forever? How long will You turn away Your face from me?

[2] How long shall I take counsel in my soul, *having* sorrows in my heart daily? How long shall my enemy be exalted over me?

[3] Look on me, give ear to me, O Lord my God: lighten my eyes, lest I sleep in death;

[4] lest at any time my enemy say, "I have prevailed against him": my persecutors will exalt if ever I should be moved.

[5] But I have hoped in Your mercy; my heart shall rejoice in Your salvation.

[6] I will sing to the Lord who has dealt bountifully with me, and I will sing psalms to the name of the Lord Most High.

PSALM 14

[1] For the end, A Psalm of David.

The fool has said in his heart, "There is no God." They have corrupted *themselves*, and have become abominable in their devices; there is none that does good, there is not so much as one.

[2] The Lord looked down from heaven upon the sons of men, to see if there were any that understood, or sought after God.

[3] They have all gone out of the way, they have together become corrupt, there is none that does good, no not one. Their throat is an open tomb; with their tongues they have used deceit. The poison of asps is under their lips: whose mouth is full of cursing and bitterness; their feet are swift to shed blood: destruction and misery are in their ways; and the way of peace they have not known: there is no fear of God before their eyes.

[4] Will not all the workers of iniquity know, who eat up my people as they would eat bread? They have not called upon the Lord.

[5] There were they alarmed with fear, where there was no fear; for God is in the righteous generation.

[6] You have shamed the counsel of the poor, because the Lord is his hope.

[7] Who will bring the salvation of Israel out of Zion? When the Lord brings back the captivity of His people, let Jacob rejoice, and Israel be glad.

PSALM 15

[1] A Psalm of David.

O Lord, who shall sojourn in Your tabernacle? And who shall dwell in Your holy mountain?

[2] He that walks blameless, and works righteousness, who speaks truth in his heart.

[3] Who has not spoken craftily with his tongue, neither has done evil to his neighbor, nor taken up a reproach against them that dwell nearest to him.

[4] In his sight an evil worker is set at nought, but he honors them that fear the Lord. He swears to his neighbor, and does not disappoint *him*.

[5] He has not lent his money on usury, and has not received bribes against the innocent. He that does these things shall never be moved.

PSALM 16

[1] A prayer of David.
Keep me, O Lord; for I have hoped in You.

[2] I said to the Lord, "You are my Lord; my goodness is nothing apart from You."

[3] On behalf of the saints that are in His land, He has magnified all His pleasure in them.

[4] Their weaknesses have been multiplied; afterward they hastened. I will by no means assemble their bloody meetings, neither will I make mention of their names with my lips.

[5] The Lord is the portion of my inheritance and of my cup: You are He that restores my inheritance to me.

[6] The lines have fallen to me in the best places; indeed, I have a most excellent heritage.

[7] I will bless the Lord who has instructed me; my reins too have chastened me even till night.

[8] I foresaw the Lord always before my face; for He is on my right hand, that I should not be moved.

[9] Therefore my heart rejoiced and my tongue exalted; moreover also my flesh shall rest in hope:

[10] because You will not leave my soul in Hades, neither will You allow Your Holy One to see corruption.

[11] You have made known to me the ways of life; You will fill me with joy with Your countenance: at Your right hand *there are* delights forever.

PSALM 17

[1] A Prayer of David.
Hearken, O Lord of my righteousness, attend to my petition; give ear to my prayer not *uttered* with deceitful lips.

[2] Let my judgment come forth from Your presence; let my eyes behold righteousness.

[3] You have tested my heart; You have visited *me* in the night; You have tried me as with fire, and unrighteousness has not been found in me; *I am purposed* that my mouth shall not speak *amiss.*

[4] As for the works of men, by the words of Your lips I have guarded *myself from* hard ways.

[5] Direct my steps in Your paths, that my steps shall not slip.

[6] I have cried, for You heard me, O God: incline Your ear to me, and listen to my words.

[7] Show the marvels of Your mercies, You that save them that trust in You.

[8] Keep me as the apple of Your eye from those that resist Your right hand; You shall screen me by the covering of Your wings,

[9] from the face of the ungodly that have afflicted me; my enemies have compassed about my soul.

[10] They have enclosed *themselves with* their own fat; their mouths have spoken pride.

[11] They have now cast me out and compassed me round about. They have set their eyes *so as* to bow them down to the ground.

[12] They laid wait for me as a lion ready for prey, and like a lion's whelp dwelling in secret *places.*

[13] Arise, O Lord, prevent them, and cast them down; deliver my soul from the ungodly; *draw* Your sword,

[14] because of the enemies of Your hand. O Lord, destroy them from the earth; scatter them in their life, though their belly has been filled with Your hidden *treasures;* they have been satisfied with uncleanness, and have left the remnant *of their possessions* to their babes.

[15] But I shall appear in righteousness before Your face: I shall be satisfied when Your glory appears.

PSALM 18

[1] For the end, *A Psalm* of David, the servant of the Lord; *the words* which he spoke to the Lord, *even* the words of this song, in the day in which the Lord delivered him out the hand of all his enemies, and out the hand of Saul. And he said:
I will love You, O Lord, my strength.

[2] The Lord is my firm support, and my refuge, and my deliverer; my God is my helper, I will hope in Him; *He is* my defender, and the horn of my salvation, and my helper.

[3] I will call upon the Lord with praises, and I shall be saved from my enemies.

[4] The pangs of death compassed me, and the torrents of ungodliness troubled me exceedingly.

[5] The pangs of hell came round about me: the snares of death prevented me.

[6] And when I was afflicted I called upon the Lord, and cried to my God: He heard my voice out of His holy temple, and my cry shall enter before Him, into His ears.

[7] Then the earth shook and quaked, and the foundations of the mountains were disturbed, and were shaken, because God was angry with them.

[8] There went up a smoke in His wrath, and fire burst into a flame at His presence; coals were kindled at it.

[9] And He bowed the heaven, and came down: and thick darkness was under His feet.

[10] And He rode upon a cherub and flew; He flew on the wings of the wind.

[11] And He made darkness His secret place; round about Him was His tabernacle, *even* dark water in the clouds of the air.

[12] At the brightness before Him the clouds passed, hail and coals of fire.

[13] The Lord also thundered from heaven, and the Most High uttered His voice.

[14] And He sent forth *His* weapons, and scattered them; and multiplied lightnings, and routed them.

¹⁵ And the springs of waters appeared, and the foundations of the world were exposed, at Your rebuke, O Lord, at the blasting of the breath of Your wrath.

¹⁶ He sent from on high and took me, He drew me to Himself out of many waters.

¹⁷ He will deliver me from my mighty enemies, and from them that hate me; for they are stronger than I.

¹⁸ They prevented me in the day of my affliction: but the Lord was my support against *them.*

¹⁹ And He brought me out into a wide place; He shall deliver me, because He has pleasure in me.

²⁰ And the Lord shall recompense me according to my righteousness; even according to the purity of my hands shall He recompense me.

²¹ For I have kept the way of the Lord and have not wickedly departed from my God.

²² For all His judgments were before me, and His ordinances did not depart from me.

²³ And I shall be blameless before Him, and shall keep myself from my iniquity.

²⁴ And the Lord shall recompense me according to my righteousness, and according to the purity of my hands before His eyes.

²⁵ With the holy, You shall be holy; and with the blameless, You shall be blameless.

²⁶ And with the excellent, You shall be excellent; and with the perverse, You shall be shrewd.

²⁷ For You shall save the lowly people, and shall humble the eyes of the proud.

²⁸ For You, O Lord, shall light my lamp: my God, You shall lighten my darkness.

²⁹ For by You shall I be delivered from a troop; and by my God I will pass over a wall.

³⁰ *As for* my God, His way is perfect: the oracles of the Lord are tried in the fire; He is a protector of all them that hope in Him.

³¹ For who is God but the Lord? And who is a God except our God?

³² *It is* God that girds me with strength, and has made my way blameless;

³³ who strengthens my feet as hare's feet, and sets me upon high places.

³⁴ He instructs my hands for war; and You have made my arms *as* a bronze bow.

³⁵ And You have made me secure in my salvation; and Your right hand has helped me, and Your correction has upheld me to the end; yes, Your correction itself shall instruct me.

³⁶ You have made room for my goings under me, and my footsteps did not fail.

³⁷ I will pursue my enemies, and overtake them; and I will not turn back until they are consumed.

³⁸ I will dash them to pieces and they shall not be able to stand: they shall fall under my feet.

³⁹ For You have girded me with strength for war; You have beaten down under me all that rose up against me.

⁴⁰ And You has made my enemies turn their backs before me; and You have destroyed them that hated me.

⁴¹ They cried, but there was no deliverer: *even* to the Lord, but He did not listen to them.

⁴² I will grind them as the mud of the streets; and I will beat them small as dust before the wind.

⁴³ Deliver me from the strife of the people; You shall make me head of the Gentiles: a people whom I did not know served me,

⁴⁴ at the hearing of the ear they obeyed me: the foreigners lied to me.

⁴⁵ The foreigners grew old, and fell away lame from their paths.

⁴⁶ The Lord lives; and blessed *be* my God; and let the God of my salvation be exalted.

⁴⁷ *It is* God that avenges me, and has subdued the nations under me;

⁴⁸ my deliverer from angry enemies; You shall set me on high above them that rise up against me; You shall deliver me from the unrighteous man.

⁴⁹ Therefore shall I confess to You, O Lord, among the Gentiles, and sing unto Your name.

⁵⁰ *God* magnifies the deliverances of His king; and deals mercifully with David His anointed, and His descendants, forever.

PSALM 19

¹ For the end, A Psalm of David.
The heavens declare the glory of God; and the firmament proclaims the work of His hands.

² Day to day utters speech, and night to night proclaims knowledge.

³ There are no speeches or words, in which their voices are not heard.

⁴ Their voice is gone out into all the earth, and their words to the ends of the world.

⁵ In the sun He has set His tabernacle; and He came forth as a bridegroom out of His chamber; He will exalt as a giant to run His course.

⁶ His going forth is from the extremity of heaven, and His circuit to the *other* end of heaven; and no one shall be hidden from His heat.

⁷ The law of the Lord is perfect, converting souls; the testimony of the Lord is faithful, instructing babes.

⁸ The ordinances of the Lord are right, rejoicing the heart; the commandment of the Lord is bright, enlightening the eyes.

⁹ The fear of the Lord is pure, enduring forever and ever: the judgments of the Lord are true, *and* justified altogether.

¹⁰ To be desired more than gold, and much precious stone; sweeter also than honey and the honeycomb.

¹¹ For Your servant keeps to them; in the keeping of them *there is* great reward.

¹² Who will understand *his* transgressions? Purge me from my secret *sins.*

¹³ And spare Your servant *from the attack* of strangers; if they do not gain the dominion over me, then shall I be blameless, and I shall be clear from great sin.

¹⁴ So shall the sayings of my mouth, and the meditation of my heart, be pleasing continually before You, O Lord my helper, and my redeemer.

PSALM 20

¹ For the end, A Psalm of David.
May the Lord hear you in the day of trouble; the name of the God of Jacob defend you.

² May He send you help from the sanctuary, and aid you out of Zion.

³ May He remember all your sacrifices, and accept your burnt offerings. Selah.

⁴ May He grant you according to your heart, and fulfill all your desires.

⁵ We will rejoice in Your salvation, and in the name of our God shall we be magnified: May the Lord fulfill all your petitions.

⁶ Now I know that the Lord has saved His Christ; He shall hear Him from His holy heaven: the salvation of His right hand is mighty.

⁷ Some *glory* in chariots, and some in horses: but we will glory in the name of the Lord our God.

⁸ They are overthrown and fallen; but we are risen, and have been set upright.

⁹ O Lord, save the king: and hear us in whatever day we call upon You.

PSALM 21

¹ For the end, A Psalm of David.
O Lord, the king shall rejoice in Your strength; and in Your salvation he shall greatly exalt.

² You have granted him the desire of his soul, and have not withheld from him the request of his lips. Selah.

³ For You have blessed him with blessings of goodness; You have set upon his head a crown of precious stone.

⁴ He asked life of You, and You gave him length of days forever and ever.

⁵ His glory is great in Your salvation; You will crown him with glory and majesty.

⁶ For You will give him a blessing forever and ever; You will gladden him with joy with Your countenance.

⁷ For the king trusts in the Lord, and through the mercy of the Highest he shall not be moved.

⁸ Let Your hand be found by all Your enemies; let Your right hand find all that hate You.

⁹ You shall make them as a fiery oven at the time of Your presence; the Lord shall trouble them in His anger, and fire shall devour them.

¹⁰ You shall destroy their fruit from the earth, and their seed from *among* the sons of men.

¹¹ For they intended evil against You; they imagined a device which they shall by no means be able to perform.

¹² For You shall make them *turn their* back in Your latter end; You will prepare their face.

¹³ Be exalted, O Lord, in Your strength; we will sing and praise Your mighty acts.

PSALM 22

¹ For the end, concerning the morning aid, A Psalm of David.
O God, my God, attend to me; why have You forsaken me? The account of my transgressions is far from my salvation.

² O my God, I will cry to You by day, but You will not hear; and by night, and *it shall* not *be reckoned* to me as folly.

³ But You, O praise of Israel, dwell in a sanctuary.

⁴ Our fathers hoped in You; they hoped, and You delivered them.

⁵ They cried to You, and were saved; they hoped in You, and were not ashamed.

⁶ But I am a worm, and not a man; a reproach of men, and the scorn of the people.

⁷ All that saw Me mocked Me; they spoke with *their* lips, they shook the head, *saying,*

⁸ "He hoped in the Lord; let Him deliver Him, let Him save Him, because He takes pleasure in Him."

⁹ For You are He that drew Me out of the womb; My hope from My mother's breasts.

¹⁰ I was cast on You from the womb; You are My God from My mother's belly.

¹¹ Be not far from Me, for affliction is near; for there is no helper.

¹² Many bulls have compassed Me; fat bulls have beset Me round about.

¹³ They have opened their mouth against Me, as a ravening and roaring lion.

¹⁴ I am poured out like water, and all My bones are loosened; My heart in the midst of My belly has become like melting wax.

¹⁵ My strength is dried up like a potsherd; and My tongue is glued to My throat; and You have brought Me down to the dust of death.

¹⁶ For many dogs have compassed Me; the assembly of the evildoers has enclosed Me; they pierced My hands and My feet.

¹⁷ They counted all My bones; and they observed and looked upon Me.

¹⁸ They parted My garments *among* themselves, and cast lots for My clothing.

¹⁹ But You, O Lord, be not far from Me; be ready for My aid.

²⁰ Deliver My soul from the sword; My only begotten *soul* from the power of the dog.

21 Save Me from the lion's mouth; and *regard* My lowliness from the horns of the unicorns.

22 I will declare Your name to My brothers; in the midst of the congregation will I sing praise to You.

23 You that fear the Lord, praise Him; all you descendants of Jacob, glorify Him; let all the house of Israel fear Him.

24 For He has not despised nor been angry at the supplication of the poor; nor turned away His face from Me; but when I cried to Him, He heard Me.

25 My praise is of You in the great congregation; I will pay My vows before them that fear Him.

26 The poor shall eat and be satisfied; and they shall praise the Lord that seek Him; their heart shall live forever.

27 All the ends of the earth shall remember and turn to the Lord, and all the families of the nations shall worship before Him.

28 For the kingdom is the Lord's; and He is the governor of the nations.

29 All the fat ones of the earth have eaten and worshipped; all that go down to the earth shall fall down before Him; my soul also lives to him.

30 And my descendants shall serve him; the generation that is coming shall be reported to the Lord.

31 And they shall report His righteousness to the people that shall be born, whom the Lord has made.

PSALM 23

1 A Psalm of David.
The Lord is my shepherd, I shall not want.

2 In a place of green grass, there He has made me dwell; He has nourished me by the water of rest.

3 He has restored my soul; He has guided me into the paths of righteousness, for His name's sake.

4 Yea, though I walk in the midst of the shadow of death, I shall fear no evil; for You are with me; Your rod and Your staff, they comfort me.

5 You have prepared a table before me in the presence of my enemies; You have anointed my head with oil; and Your cup cheers me like the best *wine*.

6 Your mercy shall follow me all the days of my life; and I shall dwell in the house of the Lord forever.

PSALM 24

1 A Psalm of David on the first day of the week.
The earth is the Lord's and all its fullness; the world, and all that dwell in it.

2 He has founded it upon the seas, and prepared it upon the rivers.

3 Who shall go up to the mountain of the Lord, and who shall stand in His holy place?

4 He that is innocent in his hands and pure in his heart; who has not lifted up his soul to vanity, nor sworn deceitfully to his neighbor.

5 He shall receive a blessing from the Lord, and mercy from God his Savior.

6 This is the generation of them that seek Him, that seek the face of the God of Jacob. Selah.

7 Lift up your gates, you princes, and be lifted up, you everlasting doors; and the King of glory shall come in.

8 Who is this King of Glory? The Lord strong and mighty, the Lord mighty in battle!

9 Lift up your gates, you princes; and be lifted up, you everlasting doors; and the King of glory shall come in.

10 Who is this King of glory? The Lord of hosts, He is this King of glory!

PSALM 25

1 A Psalm of David.
To You, O Lord, have I lifted up my soul.

2 O my God, I have trusted in You; let me not be confounded, neither let my enemies laugh me to scorn.

3 For none of them that wait on You shall in any way be ashamed; let them be ashamed that transgress without cause.

4 Show me Your ways, O Lord; and teach me Your paths.

5 Lead me in Your truth, and teach me; for You are God my Savior; and I have waited on You all the day.

6 Remember Your compassions, O Lord, and Your mercies, for they are from everlasting.

7 Do not remember the sins of my youth, nor *my sins* of ignorance; remember me according to Your mercy, for Your goodness' sake, O Lord.

8 Good and upright is the Lord; therefore will He instruct sinners in the way.

9 The meek will He guide in judgment; the meek will He teach His ways.

10 All the ways of the Lord are mercy and truth to them that seek His covenant and His testimonies.

11 For Your name's sake, O Lord, be merciful to my sin; for it is great.

12 Who is the man that fears the Lord? He shall instruct him in the way which he has chosen.

13 His soul shall dwell in prosperity; and his descendants shall inherit the earth.

14 The Lord is the strength of them that fear Him; and His covenant is to manifest *truth* to them.

15 My eyes are continually toward the Lord; for He shall draw my feet out of the snare.

16 Look upon me, and have mercy upon me; for I am an only child and poor.

17 The afflictions of my heart have been multiplied; deliver me from my distresses.

18 Look upon my affliction and my trouble, and forgive all my sins.

19 Look upon my enemies; for they have been multiplied, and they have hated me with an unjust hatred.

20 Keep my soul, and deliver me; let me not be ashamed; for I have hoped in You.

21 The harmless and upright joined themselves to me; for I waited for You, O Lord.

22 Deliver Israel, O God, out of all his afflictions.

PSALM 26

1 *A Psalm* of David.

Judge me, O Lord; for I have walked in my innocence; and hoping in the Lord I shall not be moved.

2 Examine me, O Lord, and test me; purify as with fire my mind and my heart.

3 For Your mercy is before my eyes; and I am well pleased with Your truth.

4 I have not sat with the council of vanity, and shall by no means enter in with transgressors.

5 I have hated the assembly of evildoers; and will not sit with the ungodly.

6 I will wash my hands in innocence, and go about Your altar, O Lord;

7 to hear the voice of praise, and to declare all Your wonderful works.

8 O Lord, I have loved the beauty of Your house, and the place of the tabernacle of Your glory.

9 Do not destroy my soul together with the ungodly, nor my life with bloody men;

10 in whose hands *are* iniquities, *and* their right hand is filled with bribes.

11 But I have walked in my innocence; redeem me, and have mercy upon me.

12 My foot stands in an even place; in the congregations will I bless You, O Lord.

PSALM 27

1 *A Psalm* of David, before he was anointed.

The Lord is my light and my Savior; whom shall I fear? The Lord is the defender of my life; of whom shall I be afraid?

2 When evildoers drew near against me to eat up my flesh, my persecutors and my enemies, they fainted and fell.

3 Though an army should set itself in array against me, my heart shall not be afraid; Though war should rise up against me, in this am I confident.

4 One thing have I asked of the Lord, this will I earnestly seek; that I should dwell in the house of the Lord all the days of my life, that I should behold the fair beauty of the Lord, and survey His temple.

5 For in the day of my afflictions He hid me in His tabernacle; He sheltered me in the secret place of His tabernacle; He set me high upon a rock.

6 And now, behold, He has lifted up my head over my enemies; I went round and offered in His tabernacle the sacrifice of joy; I will sing, *I will* sing psalms unto the Lord.

7 Hear, O Lord, my voice which I have uttered aloud; pity me, and hearken to me.

8 My heart said to You, "I have diligently sought Your face"; Your face, O Lord, I will seek.

9 Do not turn Your face away from me, do not turn away from Your servant in anger; be my helper, O God my Savior, do not forsake me; do not overlook me.

10 For my father and my mother have forsaken me, but the Lord has taken me to Himself.

11 Teach me, O Lord, in Your way, and guide me in a right path, because of my enemies.

12 Do not deliver me over to the desire of them that afflict me; for unjust witnesses have risen up against me, and injustice has lied within herself.

13 I believe that I shall see the goodness of the Lord in the land of the living.

14 Wait on the Lord; be of good courage, and let your heart be strengthened; yes, *I say*, wait on the Lord!

PSALM 28

1 *A Psalm* of David.

To You, O Lord, have I cried; my God, do not be silent toward me; lest You be silent toward me, and so I should be likened to them that go down to the pit.

2 Hear the voice of my supplication, when I pray to You, when I lift up my hands toward Your holy temple.

3 Do not draw away my soul with sinners, and do not destroy me with the workers of iniquity, who speak peace with their neighbors, but evil are in their hearts.

4 Give them according to their works, and according to the wickedness of their endeavors; give them according to the works of their hands; render to them what they deserve.

5 Because they have not attended to the works of the Lord, even to the works of His hands, You shall pull them down, and shall not build them up.

6 Blessed be the Lord, for He has heard the voice of my petition.

7 The Lord is my helper and my defender; my heart has hoped in Him, and I am helped; my flesh has revived, and willingly will I give praise to Him.

8 The Lord is the strength of His people, and the saving defender of His anointed.

9 Save Your people *O Lord*, and bless Your inheritance; take care of them, and lift them up forever.

PSALM 29

1 A Psalm of David, *on the occasion* of the solemn assembly of the Tabernacle.

Bring to the Lord, you sons of God, bring to the Lord young rams; bring to the Lord glory and honor.

2 Bring to the Lord the glory *due* to His name; worship the lord in His holy court.

³ The voice of the Lord is upon the waters; the God of glory has thundered; the Lord is upon many waters.

⁴ The voice of the Lord is mighty; the voice of the Lord is full of majesty.

⁵ The voice of the Lord breaks the cedars; the Lord will break the cedars of Lebanon.

⁶ And He will beat them small, *even* Lebanon itself, like a calf; and the beloved one is as a young unicorn.

⁷ The voice of the Lord divides the flames of fire.

⁸ The voice of the Lord shakes the wilderness; the Lord will shake the wilderness of Kadesh.

⁹ The voice of the Lord strengthens the deer, and will uncover the thickets; and in His temple everyone speaks *of His* glory.

¹⁰ The Lord will dwell on the waterflood; and the Lord will sit as King forever.

¹¹ The Lord will give strength to His people; the Lord will bless His people with peace.

PSALM 30

¹ For the end, A Psalm and Song at the dedication of the house of David.
I will exalt You, O Lord; for You have lifted me up, and not caused my enemies to rejoice over me.

² O Lord my God, I cried to You, and You healed me.

³ O Lord, You have brought up my soul from Hades, You have delivered me from *among* them that go down to the pit.

⁴ Sing to the Lord, you His saints, and give thanks for the remembrance of His holiness.

⁵ For anger is in His wrath, but life in His favor; weeping may endure for a night, but joy comes in the morning.

⁶ And I said in my prosperity, "I shall never be moved."

⁷ O Lord, in Your good pleasure You added strength to my beauty; but You turned away Your face, and I was troubled.

⁸ To You, O Lord, will I cry; and to my God will I make supplication.

⁹ What profit is there in my blood, when I go down to destruction? Shall the dust give praise to You? Or shall it declare Your truth?

¹⁰ The Lord heard, and had compassion upon me; the Lord has become my helper.

¹¹ You have turned my mourning into joy for me; You have removed my sackcloth, and have clothed me with gladness;

¹² that my glory may sing praise to You, and I may not be pierced *with sorrow*. O Lord my God, I will give thanks to You forever.

PSALM 31

¹ For the end, A Psalm of David, *an utterance* of extreme fear.
O Lord, I have hoped in You; let me never be ashamed; deliver me in Your righteousness and rescue me.

² Incline Your ear to me; make haste to rescue me; be to me my protecting God, and a fortress of defense to save me.

³ For You are my strength and my refuge; and You shall guide me for Your name's sake, and maintain me.

⁴ You shall bring me out of the snare which they have hidden for me; for You, O Lord, are my defender.

⁵ Into Your hands I commit my spirit; You have redeemed me, O Lord God of truth.

⁶ You have hated them that idly persist in vanities; but I have hoped in the Lord.

⁷ I will exalt and be glad in Your mercy; for You have looked upon my affliction; You have saved my soul from distresses.

⁸ And You have not shut me up into the hands of the enemy; You have set my feet in a wide place.

⁹ Pity me, O Lord, for I am afflicted; my eye is troubled with indignation, my soul and my belly.

¹⁰ For my life is spent with grief, and my years with groanings; my strength has been weakened through poverty, and my bones are troubled.

¹¹ I became a reproach among all my enemies, but exceedingly so to my neighbors, and a fear to my acquaintances; they that saw me outside fled from me.

¹² I have been forgotten as a dead man out of mind; I have become as a broken vessel.

¹³ For I heard the slander of many that dwelt round about; when they were gathered together against me, they took counsel to take my life.

¹⁴ But I hoped in You, O Lord; I said, "You are my God."

¹⁵ My times are in Your hands; deliver me from the hand of my enemies,

¹⁶ and from them that persecute me. Make Your face to shine upon Your servant; save me in Your mercy.

¹⁷ O Lord, let me not be ashamed, for I have called upon You; let the ungodly be ashamed, and brought down to Hades.

¹⁸ Let the deceitful lips become dumb, which speak iniquity against the righteous with pride and scorn.

¹⁹ How abundant is the multitude of Your goodness, O Lord, which You have laid up for them that fear You! You have wrought *it* out for them that hope on You, in the presence of the sons of men.

²⁰ You will hide them in the secret of Your presence from the plots of man; You will screen them in a tabernacle from the strife of tongues.

²¹ Blessed *be* the Lord, for He has magnified His mercy in a fortified city.

²² But I said in my extreme fear, "I am cast out from the sight of Your eyes"; therefore You listened, O Lord, to the voice of my supplication when I cried to You.

²³ Love the Lord, all you His saints; for the Lord seeks *those that are* truthful, and He recompenses them that deal very proudly.

²⁴ Be of good courage, and let your heart be strengthened, all you that hope in the Lord.

PSALM 32

[1] *A Psalm* of instruction by David. Blessed *are they* whose transgressions are forgiven, and who sins are covered.

[2] Blessed is the man to whom the Lord will not impute sin, and in whose mouth there is no guile.

[3] Because I kept silence, my bones waxed old, from my crying all the day.

[4] For day and night Your hand was heavy upon me; I became thoroughly miserable while a thorn was fastened in *me*. Selah.

[5] I acknowledged my sin, and hid not my iniquity; I said, I will confess my iniquity to the Lord; and You forgave the ungodliness of my heart. Selah.

[6] Therefore shall every holy one pray to You in a fit time; only in the deluge of many waters they shall not come near to Him.

[7] You are my refuge from the affliction that encompasses me; my joy, to deliver me from them that have compassed me. Selah.

[8] I will instruct you and guide you in the way you should go; I will fix My eyes upon you.

[9] Be not as the horse and mule, which have no understanding; *but you must* constrain their jaws with bit and bridle, lest they should come near to you.

[10] Many are the scourges of the sinner; but he that hopes in the Lord, mercy shall surround him.

[11] Be glad in the Lord, and exalt, you righteous; and shout for joy, all you that are upright in heart!

PSALM 33

[1] *A Psalm* of David.
Rejoice in the Lord, O you righteous; praise from the upright is beautiful.

[2] Praise the Lord on the harp; make melody to Him on a psaltery of ten strings.

[3] Sing to Him a new song; play skillfully with a loud noise.

[4] For the word of the Lord is right; and all His works are faithful.

[5] He loves mercy and judgment; the earth is full of the mercy of the Lord.

[6] By the word of the Lord the heavens were established; and all the host of them by the breath of His *mouth*.

[7] Who gathers the waters of the sea as *in* a bottle; who lays up the deeps in treasuries.

[8] Let all the earth fear the Lord; and let all that dwell in the world be moved because of Him.

[9] For He spoke, and they were made; He commanded, and they were created.

[10] The Lord frustrates the counsels of the nations; He brings to nought the reasonings of the people, and brings to nought the counsels of princes.

[11] But the counsel of the Lord endures forever, the thoughts of His heart from generation to generation.

[12] Blessed is the nation whose God is the Lord; the people whom He has chosen for His own inheritance.

[13] The Lord looks out of heaven; He beholds all the sons of men.

[14] He looks *down* from His dwelling place on all the inhabitants of the earth;

[15] who fashioned their hearts alone; who understands all their works.

[16] A king is not saved by reason of a great army; and a giant shall not be delivered by the greatness of his strength.

[17] A horse is a vain *hope* for safety; neither shall he be delivered by the greatness of his power.

[18] Behold, the eyes of the Lord are on them that fear Him, those that hope in His mercy;

[19] to deliver their souls from death, and to keep them alive in famine.

[20] Our soul waits on the Lord; for He is our helper and defender.

[21] For our heart shall rejoice in Him, and we have hoped in His holy name.

[22] Let Your mercy, O Lord, be upon us, according as we have hoped in You.

PSALM 34

[1] *A Psalm* of David, when he changed his countenance before Abimelech; and he let him go, and he departed.
I will bless the Lord at all times; His praise shall be continually in my mouth.

[2] My soul shall boast in the Lord; let the meek hear, and rejoice.

[3] Magnify the Lord with me, and let us exalt His name together.

[4] I sought the Lord diligently, and He heard me, and delivered me from all my sojournings.

[5] Draw near to Him, and be enlightened; and your faces shall by no means be ashamed.

[6] This poor man cried, and the Lord heard him, and delivered him out of all his afflictions.

[7] The angel of the Lord will encamp around those that fear Him, and will deliver them.

[8] Taste and see that the Lord is good; blessed is the man who hopes in Him. [9] Fear the Lord, all you His saints; for there is no lack to them that fear Him.

[10] The rich have become poor and hungry; but they that seek the Lord diligently shall not lack any good thing. Selah.

[11] Come, you children, hear me; I will teach you the fear of the Lord.

[12] What man is there that desires life, loving to see good days?

[13] Keep your tongue from evil, and your lips from speaking guile.

[14] Turn away from evil, and do good; seek peace, and pursue it.

¹⁵ The eyes of the Lord are on the righteous, and His ears *are open* to their prayer;

¹⁶ but the face of the Lord is against them that do evil, to destroy their memorial from the earth. The righteous cried, and the Lord listened to them,

¹⁷ and delivered them out of all their afflictions.

¹⁸ The Lord is near to them that are of a contrite heart; and will save the lowly in spirit.

¹⁹ Many are the afflictions of the righteous; but out of them all the Lord shall deliver them.

²⁰ He keeps all their bones; not one of them shall be broken.

²¹ The death of sinners is evil; and they that hate righteousness will go wrong.

²² The Lord will redeem the souls of His servants; and none of those that hope in Him shall go wrong.

PSALM 35

¹ *A Psalm* of David.
Judge, O Lord, those that injure me, fight against them that fight against me.

² Take hold of shield and buckler, and arise for my help.

³ Bring forth a sword, and stop *the way* against them that persecute me; say to my soul, "I am your salvation."

⁴ Let them that seek my soul be ashamed and confounded; let them that devise evils against me be turned back and put to shame.

⁵ Let them be as dust before the wind, and an angel of the Lord afflicting them.

⁶ Let their way be dark and slippery, and an angel of the Lord persecuting them.

⁷ For without cause they have hid for me their destructive snare; without a cause they have reproached my soul.

⁸ Let a snare which they do not know come upon them; and the net which they hid take them; and let them fall into the very same snare.

⁹ But my soul shall exalt in the Lord; it shall delight in His salvation.

¹⁰ All my bones shall say, "O Lord, who is like You? Delivering the poor out of the hand of them that are stronger than he, yea, the poor and needy one from them that spoil him."

¹¹ Unjust witnesses arose, and asked me of things I did not know.

¹² They rewarded me evil for good, and bereavement to my soul.

¹³ But I, when they troubled me, put on sackcloth, and humbled my soul with fasting; and my prayer shall return to my *own* bosom.

¹⁴ I behaved agreeably towards them as *if it had been* our neighbor *or* brother; I humbled myself as one mourning and sad of countenance.

¹⁵ Yet they rejoiced against me, and plagues were plentifully brought against me, and I did not know *it*; they were scattered, but did not repent.

¹⁶ They tempted me, they sneered at me most contemptuously, they gnashed their teeth upon me.

¹⁷ O Lord, when will You look upon me? Deliver my soul from their mischief, my only begotten one from the lions.

¹⁸ I will give thanks to You even in a great congregation; in an abundant people I will praise You.

¹⁹ Let not them that are my enemies rejoice against me without a cause; who hate me for nothing, and wink with their eyes.

²⁰ For to me they spoke peaceably, but imagined deceits in *their* anger.

²¹ And they opened wide their mouth upon me; they said "Aha, aha, our eyes have seen *it*."

²² You have seen *it*, O Lord; do not keep silence; O Lord, do not withdraw *Yourself* from me.

²³ Awake, O Lord, and attend to my judgment, *even* to my cause, my God and my Lord.

²⁴ Judge me, O Lord, according to Your righteousness, O Lord my God; and let them not rejoice against me.

²⁵ Let them not say in their hearts, "Aha, aha, *it is pleasing* to our soul"; neither let them say, "We have devoured him."

²⁶ Let them be confounded and ashamed together that rejoice at my afflictions; let them be clothed with shame and confusion that speak great swelling words against me.

²⁷ Let them that rejoice in my righteousness exalt and be glad; and let them say continually, "The Lord be magnified, who desires the peace of His servant."

²⁸ And my tongue shall meditate on Your righteousness, *and* on Your praise all the day.

PSALM 36

¹ For the end, *A Psalm*, by David the servant of the Lord.
The transgressor, that he may sin, says within himself, *that* he has no fear of God.

² For he has dealt craftily before him, to discover his iniquity and hate it.

³ The words of his mouth are transgression and deceit; he is not inclined to understand *how* to do good.

⁴ He devises iniquity on his bed; he gives himself to every evil way; and does not abhor evil.

⁵ O Lord, Your mercy is in the heavens; and Your truth *reaches* to the clouds.

⁶ Your righteousness is as the mountains of God, Your judgments are as a great deep; O Lord, You will preserve men and beasts.

⁷ How have You multiplied Your mercy, O God! So the children of men shall trust in the shelter of Your wings.

⁸ They shall be fully satisfied with the fatness of Your house; and You shall cause them to drink of the full stream of Your delights.

9 For with You is the fountain of life; in Your light we shall see light.

10 Extend Your mercy to them that know You; and Your righteousness to the upright in heart.

11 Let not the foot of pride come against me, and let not the hand of sinners move me.

12 There the workers of iniquity have fallen; they are cast out, and shall not be able to stand.

PSALM 37

1 A *Psalm* of David.

Do not fret because of evildoers, neither be envious of them that do iniquity.

2 For they shall soon be withered as the grass, and shall soon fall away as the green herbs.

3 Hope in the Lord, and do good; and dwell on the land, and you shall be fed with the wealth of it.

4 Delight *yourself* in the Lord, and He shall grant you the desires of your heart.

5 Disclose Your way to the Lord, and trust in Him; and He shall bring *it* to pass.

6 And He shall bring forth your righteousness as the light, and your judgment as the noonday.

7 Submit yourself to the Lord, and make supplication to Him; do not fret because of him that prospers in his way, at the man that does unlawful deeds.

8 Cease from anger, and forsake wrath; do not fret, so as not to do evil.

9 For evildoers shall be destroyed; but they that wait on the Lord, they shall inherit the land.

10 And yet a little while, and the sinner shall not be, and you shall seek for his place, and shall not find *it*.

11 But the meek shall inherit the earth; and shall delight *themselves* in the abundance of peace.

12 The sinner will watch for the righteous, and gnash his teeth upon him.

13 But the Lord shall laugh at him; for He foresees that his day will come.

14 Sinners have drawn their swords; they have bent their bow, to cast down the poor and needy, *and* to slay the upright in heart.

15 Let their sword enter into their *own* heart, and their bows be broken.

16 A little is better to the righteous than the abundant wealth of sinners.

17 For the arms of sinners shall be broken; but the Lord supports the righteous.

18 The Lord knows the ways of the upright; and their inheritance shall be forever.

19 They shall not be ashamed in an evil time; and in days of famine they shall be satisfied.

20 For the sinners shall perish; and the enemies of the Lord at the moment of their being honored and exalted have utterly vanished like smoke.

21 The sinner borrows, and will not pay again; but the righteous has compassion, and gives.

22 For those that bless Him shall inherit the earth; and they that curse Him shall be utterly destroyed.

23 The steps of a man are rightly ordered by the Lord; and He will take pleasure in his way.

24 When he falls, he shall not be ruined; for the Lord supports his hand.

25 I was *once* young, indeed I am now old; yet I have not seen the righteous forsaken, nor his descendants seeking bread.

26 He is merciful, and lends continually; and his descendants shall be blessed.

27 Turn aside from evil, and do good; and dwell forever.

28 For the Lord loves judgment, and will not forsake His saints; they shall be preserved forever; the blameless shall be avenged, but the descendants of the ungodly shall be utterly destroyed.

29 But the righteous shall inherit the earth, and dwell upon it forever.

30 The mouth of the righteous will meditate wisdom, and his tongue will speak of judgment.

31 The law of his God is in his heart; and his steps shall not slide.

32 The sinner watches the righteous, and seeks to slay him.

33 But the Lord will not leave him in his hands, nor by any means condemn him when he is judged.

34 Wait on the Lord, and keep His way, and He shall exalt you to inherit the land; when the wicked are destroyed, you shall see *it*.

35 I saw the ungodly very highly exalting himself, and lifting himself up like the cedars of Lebanon.

36 Yet I passed by, and lo! He was not; and I sought him, but his place was not found.

37 Maintain innocence, and behold uprightness; for there is a remnant to the peaceable man.

38 But the transgressors shall be utterly destroyed together; the remnants of the ungodly shall be utterly destroyed.

39 But the salvation of the righteous is of the Lord; and He is their defender in the time of affliction.

40 And the Lord shall help them, and deliver them; and He shall rescue them from sinners, and save them, because they have hoped in Him.

PSALM 38

1 A Psalm of David for remembrance concerning the Sabbath day.

O Lord, do not rebuke me in Your wrath, neither chasten me in Your anger.

2 For Your weapons are fixed on me, and You have pressed Your hand heavily upon me.

3 For there is no health in my flesh because of Your anger; there is no peace to my bones because of my sins.

4 For my transgressions have gone over my head; they have pressed heavily upon me like a weighty burden.

5 My wounds have become foul and corrupt, because of my foolishness.

6 I have been wretched and bowed down continually; I went with a mourning countenance all the day.

7 For my soul is filled with mockings; and there is no health in my flesh.

8 I have been afflicted and brought down exceedingly; I have roared for the groaning of my heart.

9 But all my desire is before You; and my groaning is not hidden from You.

10 My heart is troubled, my strength has failed me; and the light of my eyes is not with me.

11 My friends and my neighbors drew near before me, and stood still; and my nearest of kin stood afar off.

12 While they pressed hard upon me that sought my soul; and they that sought my hurt spoke vanities, and devised deceits all the day.

13 But I, as a deaf man, did not hear; and was as a dumb man not opening his mouth.

14 And I was as a man that does not hear, and who has no reproofs in his mouth.

15 For I hoped in You, O Lord; You will hear, O Lord my God.

16 For I said, "Lest my enemies rejoice against me"; for when my feet were moved, they spoke boastfully against me.

17 For I am ready for plagues, and my grief is continually before me.

18 For I will declare my iniquity, and be distressed for my sin.

19 But my enemies live, and are mightier than I; and they that hate me unjustly are multiplied.

20 They that reward evil for good slandered me; because I followed righteousness.

21 Do not forsake me, O Lord my God; do not depart from me.

22 Draw near to my help, O Lord of my salvation.

PSALM 39

1 For the end, A Song of David, to Jeduthun.
I said, "I will take heed to my ways, that I do not sin with my tongue"; I set a guard on my mouth, while the sinner stood in my presence.

2 I was dumb, and humbled myself, and kept silence from good *words*; and my grief was renewed.

3 My heart grew hot within me, and a fire would kindle in my meditation; I spoke with my tongue,

4 "O Lord, make me to know my end, and the number of my days, what it is; that I may know what I lack·

5 Behold, You have made my days old; and my existence *is* as nothing before You; indeed, every man living *is* altogether vanity. Selah.

6 Surely man walks in a shadow; surely he is disquieted in vain; he lays up treasures, and does not know for whom he shall gather them.

7 And now what *is* my expectation? *Is it* not the Lord? And my ground *of hope* is with You. Selah.

8 Deliver me from all my transgressions; You have made me a reproach to the foolish.

9 I was dumb, and did not open my mouth; for You are He that made me.

10 Remove Your scourge from me; I have fainted by reason of the strength of Your hand.

11 You chasten man with rebukes for iniquity, and You make his life to consume away like a spider's web; surely every man is disquieted in vain. Selah.

12 O Lord, listen to my prayer and my supplication; attend to my tears; be not silent, for I am a sojourner in the land, and a stranger, as all my fathers *were*.

13 Spare me, that I may be refreshed, before I depart, and be no more."

PSALM 40

1 For the end, A Psalm of David.
I waited patiently for the Lord; and He attended to me, and heard my supplication.

2 And He brought me up out of a pit of misery, and from miry clay; and He set my feet upon a rock, and established my steps.

3 And He put a new song into my mouth, *even* a hymn to our God; many shall see *it* and fear, and shall hope in the Lord.

4 Blessed *is* the man whose hope is in the name of the Lord, and *who* has not regarded vanities, nor turned aside to lies.

5 O Lord my God, You have multiplied Your wonderful works, and in Your thoughts there is none who shall be likened to You; I declared and spoke *of them*; they exceeded in number.

6 Sacrifice and offering You did not desire; but a body You have prepared for me; burnt offering and *sacrifice* for sin You did not require.

7 Then I said, "Behold, I have come; in the volume of the book it is written of me,

8 I desired to do Your will, O my God, and Your law in the midst of my heart."

9 I have preached righteousness in the great congregation; lo! I will not refrain my lips; O Lord, You know my righteousness.

10 I have not hid Your truth within my heart, and I have declared Your salvation; I have not hid Your mercy and Your truth from the great congregation.

11 But You, O Lord, do not remove Your compassion far from me; Your mercy and Your truth have helped me continually.

12 For innumerable evils have encompassed me; my transgressions have taken hold of me, and I could not see;

they are multiplied more than the hairs of my head; and my heart has failed me.

[13] Be pleased, O Lord, to deliver me; O Lord, draw near to help me.

[14] Let those that seek my soul, to destroy it, be ashamed and confounded together; let those that wish me evil be turned backward and put to shame.

[15] Let those that say to me, "Aha, aha," quickly receive shame for their reward.

[16] Let all those that seek You, O Lord, exalt and rejoice in You; and let them that love Your salvation say continually, "The Lord be magnified!"

[17] But I am poor and needy; the Lord will take care of me; You are my helper, and my defender, O my God; do not delay.

PSALM 41

[1] For the end, A Psalm of David. Blessed *is the man* who thinks on the poor and needy; the Lord shall deliver him in an evil day.

[2] May the Lord preserve him and keep him alive, and bless him on the earth, and not deliver him into the hands of his enemy.

[3] May the Lord help him upon the bed of his pain; You have made all his bed in his sickness.

[4] I said, "O Lord, have mercy upon me; heal my soul; for I have sinned against You."

[5] My enemies have spoken evil against me, *saying*, "When shall he die, and his name perish?"

[6] And if he came to see *me*, his heart spoke vainly; he gathered iniquity to himself; he went forth and spoke in like manner.

[7] All my enemies whispered against me; against me they devised my hurt.

[8] They denounced a wicked word against me, *saying*, "Now that he lies, shall he not rise up again?"

[9] For even the man of my peace, in whom I trusted, who ate my bread, lifted up *his* heel against me.

[10] But You, O Lord, have compassion upon me, and raise me up, and I shall repay them.

[11] By this I know that You have delighted in me, because my enemy shall not rejoice over me.

[12] But You helped me because of *my* innocence, and have established me before You forever.

[13] Blessed *be* the Lord God of Israel from everlasting to everlasting. Amen and Amen.

PSALM 42

[1] For the end, *A Psalm* of instruction, for the sons of Korah.
As the deer earnestly desires the fountains of water, so my soul earnestly longs for You, O God.

[2] My soul has thirsted for the living God; when shall I come and appear before God?

[3] My tears have been bread to me day and night, while they said to me daily, "Where is your God?"

[4] I remembered these things, and poured out my soul in me, for I will go to the place of Your wondrous tabernacle, *even* to the house of God, with a voice of exaltation and thanksgiving and of the sound of those who keep festival.

[5] Why are you downcast, O my soul? And why do you trouble me? Hope in God; for I will give thanks to Him; *He is* the salvation of my countenance.

[6] O my God, my soul has been troubled within me; therefore will I remember You from the land of the Jordan, and of the Hermonites, from the little hill.

[7] Deep calls to deep at the sound of Your waterfalls; all Your billows and Your waves have gone over me.

[8] By day the Lord will command His mercy, and manifest *it* by night; with me *is* prayer to the God of my life.

[9] I will say to God, "You are my helper; why have You forgotten me? Why do I mourn, while the enemy oppresses *me*?"

[10] While my bones were breaking, they that afflicted me reproached me; while they said to me daily, "Where is your God?"

[11] Why are you cast down, O my soul? And why do you trouble me? Hope in God; for I will give thanks to Him; *He is* the health of my countenance, and my God.

PSALM 43

[1] A Psalm of David.
Judge me, O God, and plead my cause, against an ungodly nation; deliver me from the unjust and crafty;

[2] for You are my strength; why have You cast me off? And why do I go mourning, while the enemy oppresses *me*?

[3] Send forth Your light and Your truth; they have led me, and brought me to Your holy mountain, and to Your tabernacle.

[4] And I will go in to the altar of God, to God who gladdens my youth; I will give thanks to You on the harp, O God, my God.

[5] Why are you cast down, O my soul? And why do you trouble me? Hope in God; for I will give thanks to Him, *who is* the health of my countenance, *and* my God.

PSALM 44

[1] For the end, A Psalm for instruction, for the sons of Korah.
O God, we have heard with our ears, our fathers have told us, the deeds which You did in their days, in the days of old.

[2] Your hand utterly destroyed the heathen, and You planted them; You afflicted the nations, and cast them out.

[3] For they did not inherit the land by their *own* sword, and their *own* arm did not deliver them; but Your right hand, and

Your arm, and the light of Your countenance, because You were well pleased with them.

⁴ You are indeed my King and my God, who commanded deliverance for Jacob.

⁵ In You will we push down our enemies, and in Your name will we bring to nought them that rise up against us.

⁶ For I will not trust in my bow, and my sword shall not save me.

⁷ For You have saved us from them that afflicted us, and have put to shame them that hated us.

⁸ In God will we make our boast all the day, and to Your name will we give thanks forever. Selah.

⁹ But now You have cast off, and put us to shame; and You will not go forth with our hosts.

¹⁰ You have turned us back before our enemies; and they that hated us spoiled for themselves.

¹¹ You made us as sheep *intended* for food; and You scattered us among the nations.

¹² You have sold Your people without price, and there was no profit by their exchange.

¹³ You have made us a reproach to our neighbors, a scorn and derision to them that are round about us.

¹⁴ You have made us a proverb among the Gentiles, a shaking of the head among the nations.

¹⁵ All the day my shame is before me, and the confusion of my face has covered me,

¹⁶ because of the voice of the slanderer and reviler; because of the enemy and avenger.

¹⁷ All these things have come upon us; but we have not forgotten You, neither have we dealt unrighteously in Your covenant.

¹⁸ And our heart has not gone back; but You have turned aside our paths from Your way.

¹⁹ For You have laid us low in a place of affliction, and the shadow of death has covered us.

²⁰ If we have forgotten the name of our God, and if we have spread out our hands to a strange god; shall not God search these things out?

²¹ for He knows the secrets of the heart.

²² For Your sake we are killed all the day long; we are accounted as sheep for slaughter.

²³ Awake, why do You sleep, O Lord? Arise, and do not cast *us* off forever.

²⁴ Why do You turn Your face away, *and* forget our poverty and our affliction?

²⁵ For our soul has been brought down to the dust; our belly has cleaved to the earth.

²⁶ Arise, O Lord, and help us; redeem us for Your name's sake.

PSALM 45

¹ For the end, for alternate *strains* by the sons of Korah; for instruction, A song concerning the beloved.

My heart has uttered a good matter; I declare my works to the king; my tongue is the pen of a quick writer.

² You are more beautiful than the sons of men; grace has been shed forth on Your lips; therefore God has blessed You forever.

³ Gird Your sword upon Your thigh, O Mighty One, in Your comeliness, and in Your beauty;

⁴ and bend *Your bow*, and prosper, and reign, because of truth and meekness and righteousness; and Your right hand shall guide You wonderfully.

⁵ Your weapons are sharpened, O Mighty One, (the nations shall fall under You) *they are* in the heart of the king's enemies.

⁶ Your throne, O God, is forever and ever; the scepter of Your kingdom is the scepter of righteousness.

⁷ You have loved righteousness, and hated iniquity; therefore God, Your God, has anointed You with the oil of gladness beyond Your companions.

⁸ Myrrh, aloes, and cassia *emanate* from Your garments, *and* out of the ivory palaces,

⁹ with which kings' daughters have gladdened You for Your honor; the queen stood by on Your right hand, clothed in vesture wrought with gold, and arrayed in many colors.

¹⁰ Hear, O daughter, and see, and incline your ear; forget also your people, and your father's house.

¹¹ Because the King has desired your beauty; for He is your Lord.

¹² And the daughter of Tyre shall adorn Him with gifts; the rich of the people of the land shall supplicate your favor.

¹³ All her glory *is that* of the daughter of the king of Heshbon, robed in golden fringed garments,

¹⁴ in embroidered *clothing*; virgins shall be brought to the king after her; her fellows shall be brought to You.

¹⁵ They shall be brought with gladness and exaltation; they shall be led into the king's temple.

¹⁶ Instead of Your fathers children are born to You; You shall make them princes over all the earth.

¹⁷ They shall make mention of Your name from generation to generation; therefore shall the nations give thanks to You forever, even forever and ever.

PSALM 46

¹ For the end, for the sons of Korah; A Psalm concerning secret things.

God is our refuge and strength, a help in the afflictions that have come heavily upon us.

² Therefore will we not fear when the earth is troubled, and the mountains are removed into the depths of the seas.

³ Their waters have roared and been troubled, the mountains have been troubled by His might. Selah.

⁴ The flowings of the river gladden the city of God; the Most High has sanctified His tabernacle.

⁵ God is in the midst of her; she shall not be moved; God shall help her with His countenance.

6 The nations were troubled, the kingdoms tottered; He uttered His voice, the earth shook.

7 The Lord of hosts is with us; the God of Jacob is our helper. Selah.

8 Come, and behold the works of the Lord, what wonders He has achieved on the earth.

9 Putting an end to wars as to the ends of the earth; He will crush the bow, and break in pieces the weapon, and burn the bucklers with fire.

10 Be still, and know that I am God; I will be exalted among the nations, I will be exalted in the earth.

11 The Lord of hosts is with us; the God of Jacob is our helper.

PSALM 47

1 For the end, A Psalm for the sons of Korah.
Clap your hands, all you nations; shout to God with a voice of exaltation.

2 For the Lord Most High is awesome; *He is* a great King over all the earth.

3 He has subdued the peoples under us, and the nations under our feet.

4 He has chosen out His inheritance for us, the beauty of Jacob which He loved. Selah.

5 God has gone up with a shout, the Lord with a sound of a trumpet.

6 Sing praises to our God, sing praises; sing praises to our King, sing praises.

7 For God is King of all the earth; sing praises with understanding.

8 God reigns over the nations; God sits upon the throne of His holiness.

9 The rulers of the people are assembled with the God of Abraham; for God's mighty ones of the earth have been greatly exalted.

PSALM 48

1 A Psalm of praise for the sons of Korah on the second *day* of the week.
Great is the Lord, and greatly to be praised in the city of our God, in His holy mountain.

2 The city of the great King is well planted *on* the mountains of Zion, with the joy of the whole earth, *on* the sides of the north.

3 God is known in her palaces, when He undertakes to help her.

4 For behold, the kings of the earth were assembled, they came together.

5 They saw, and so they wondered; they were troubled, they were moved.

6 Trembling took hold of them; there were the pangs as of a woman in travail.

7 You will break the ships of Tarshish with a vehement wind.

8 As we have heard, so have we also seen, in the city of the Lord of hosts, in the city of our God; God has founded it forever. Selah.

9 We have thought of Your mercy, O God, in the midst of Your people.

10 According to Your name, O God, so is also Your praise to the ends of the earth; Your right hand is full of righteousness.

11 Let Mount Zion rejoice, let the daughters of Judah rejoice, because of Your judgments, O Lord.

12 Go round about Zion, and encompass her; count her towers.

13 Mark well her strength, and observe her palaces; that you may tell the next generation.

14 For this is our God forever and ever; He will be our guide forevermore.

PSALM 49

1 For the end, A Psalm for the sons of Korah.
Hear these words, all you nations, give ear, all you that dwell upon the earth;

2 both the sons of mean men, and sons of *great* men; the rich and poor *man* together.

3 My mouth shall speak of wisdom, and the meditation of my heart shall bring *forth* understanding.

4 I will incline my ear to a parable; I will open my riddle on the harp.

5 Why should I fear in the evil day? The iniquity of my heel shall surround me.

6 They that trust in their strength, and boast themselves in the multitude of their wealth—

7 a brother does not redeem, shall a man redeem? He shall not give to God a ransom for himself,

8 or the price for the redemption of his soul, though he labor forever,

9 and live to the end, *so* that he should not see corruption.

10 When he shall see wise men dying, the fool and the senseless one shall perish together; and they shall leave their wealth to strangers.

11 And their tombs are their houses forever, *even* their tabernacles to all generations; they have called their lands after their own names.

12 And man being in honor, does not understand; he is compared to the senseless cattle, and is likened unto them.

13 This their way is an offense to them; yet afterwards men will commend their sayings. Selah.

14 They have laid *them* as sheep in Hades; death shall feed on them; and the upright shall have dominion over them in the morning, and their help shall fail in Hades from their glory.

15 But God shall deliver my soul from the power of Hades, when He shall receive me. Selah.

16 Do not fear when a man is enriched, and when the glory of his house is increased.

17 For he shall take nothing when he dies; neither shall his glory descend with him.

18 For his soul shall be blessed in his life; he shall give thanks to you when you do well to him.

19 *Yet* he shall go in to the generation of his fathers; he shall never see light.

20 Man that is in honor, does not understand; he is compared to the senseless cattle, and is likened unto them.

PSALM 50

1 A Psalm of Asaph.
The God of gods, the Lord, has spoken, and called the earth from the rising of the sun to its going down.

2 Out of Zion *comes* the excellence of His beauty.

3 God, our God, shall come manifestly, and shall not keep silent; a fire shall be kindled before Him, and round about Him there shall be a very great tempest.

4 He shall summon the heaven above, and the earth, that He may judge His people.

5 Assemble His saints to Him, those that have engaged in a covenant with Him upon sacrifices.

6 And the heavens shall declare His righteousness; for God is Judge. Selah.

7 "Hear, My people, and I will speak to you, O Israel; and I will testify to you; I am God, your God.

8 I will not reprove you on account of your sacrifices; for your burnt offerings are before Me continually.

9 I will take no bulls out of your house, nor male goats out of your flocks.

10 For all the wild beasts of the thicket are Mine, the cattle on the mountains, and oxen.

11 I know all the birds of the sky; and the beauty of the field is Mine.

12 If I should be hungry, I will not tell you; for the world is Mine, and all its fullness.

13 Will I eat the flesh of bulls, or drink the blood of goats?

14 Offer to God the sacrifice of praise; and pay your vows to the Most High.

15 And call upon Me in the day of affliction; and I shall deliver you, and you shall glorify Me." Selah.

16 But to the sinner God has said, "Why do you declare My ordinances, and take up My covenant in your mouth?

17 Seeing you have hated instruction, and have cast My words behind *you.*

18 If you saw a thief, you ran along with him, and have cast in your lot with adulterers.

19 Your mouth has multiplied wickedness, and your tongue has framed deceit.

20 You sat and spoke against your brother, and scandalized your mother's son.

21 These things you did, and I kept silent; you thought wickedly that I should be like you, *but* I will reprove you, and set *your offenses* before you.

22 Now consider these things, all you that forget God, lest *I* tear *you,* and there be none to deliver.

23 The sacrifice of praise will glorify Me; and that is the way in which I will show to him the salvation of God."

PSALM 51

1 For the end, A Psalm of David, when Nathan the prophet came to him, when he had gone in to Bathsheba.   Have mercy upon me, O God, according to Your great mercy; and according to the multitude of Your compassions, blot out my transgression.

2 Wash me thoroughly from my iniquity, and cleanse me from my sin.

3 For I am conscious of my iniquity; and my sin is continually before me.

4 Against You alone have I sinned, and done evil before You; that You might be justified in Your words, and might overcome when You are judged.

5 For behold, I was conceived in iniquities, and in sins did my mother conceive me.

6 For behold, You love truth; You have manifested to me the secret and hidden things of Your wisdom.

7 You shall sprinkle me with hyssop, and I shall be purified; You shall wash me, and I shall be made whiter than snow.

8 You shall cause me to hear gladness and joy; my afflicted bones shall rejoice.

9 Turn away Your face from my sins, and blot out all my iniquities.

10 Create in me a clean heart, O God; and renew a steadfast spirit in my inward parts.

11 Do not cast me away from Your presence; and do not remove Your Holy Spirit from me.

12 Restore to me the joy of Your salvation; establish me with Your directing Spirit.

13 *Then* will I teach transgressors Your ways; and ungodly men shall turn to You.

14 Deliver me from blood-guiltiness, O God, the God of my salvation; *and* my tongue shall joyfully declare Your righteousness.

15 O Lord, You shall open my lips; and my mouth shall declare Your praise.

16 For if You desired sacrifice, I would have given *it;* You will not take pleasure in burnt offerings.

17 Sacrifice to God is a broken spirit; a broken and humbled heart God will not despise.

18 Do good, O Lord, to Zion in Your good pleasure; and let the walls of Jerusalem be built.

19 Then shall You be pleased with a sacrifice of righteousness, offering, and whole burnt sacrifices; then shall they offer calves upon Your altar.

PSALM 52

¹ For the end, *A Psalm* of instruction by David, when Doeg the Edomite came and told Saul, and said to him, "David has gone to the house of Abimelech." Why do you, O mighty man, boast of iniquity in your mischief?

² All the day your tongue has devised unrighteousness; like a sharpened razor you have worked deceit.

³ You have loved wickedness more than goodness; unrighteousness better than to speak righteousness. Selah.

⁴ You have loved all words of destruction, *and* a deceitful tongue.

⁵ Therefore may God destroy you forever, may He pluck you up and utterly remove you from *your* dwelling, and your root from the land of the living. Selah.

⁶ And the righteous shall see and fear, and shall laugh at him, and say,

⁷ "Behold, the man who did not make God his help; but trusted in the abundance of his wealth, and strengthened himself in his vanity."

⁸ But I am as a fruitful olive in the house of God; I have trusted in the mercy of God forever, even forevermore.

⁹ I will give thanks to You forever, for You have done *it*; and I will wait on Your name; for *it is* good before the saints.

PSALM 53

¹ For the end, *A Psalm* of David upon Mahalath, of instruction.
The fool has said in his heart, "There is no God." They have corrupted *themselves,* and have become abominable in iniquities; there is none that does good.

² God looked down from heaven upon the sons of men, to see if there were any that understood, or sought after God.

³ They have all gone out of the way, they have together become unprofitable; there is none that does good, there is not even one.

⁴ Will none of the workers of iniquity know, who devour my people as they would eat bread? They have not called upon God. There were they greatly afraid, where there was no fear;

⁵ for God has scattered the bones of the men-pleasers; they were ashamed, for God has despised them.

⁶ Who will bring the salvation of Israel out of Zion? When the Lord turns the captivity of His people, Jacob shall rejoice, and Israel shall be glad.

PSALM 54

¹ For the end, among Hymns of instruction by David, when the Ziphites came and said to Saul, "Is not David hiding with us?"
Save me, O God, by Your name, and judge me by Your might.

² O God, hear my prayer; hearken to the words of my mouth.

³ For strangers have risen up against me, and mighty men have sought my life; they have not set God before them. Selah.

⁴ Behold, God assists me; and the Lord is the helper of my soul.

⁵ He shall return evil to my enemies; utterly destroy them in Your truth.

⁶ I will willingly sacrifice to You; I will give thanks to Your name, O Lord; for *it is* good.

⁷ For You have delivered me out of all *my* afflictions, and my eye has seen *its desire* upon my enemies.

PSALM 55

¹ For the end, among Hymns of instruction by David.
Listen, O God, to my prayer; and do not disregard my supplication.

² Attend to me, and give heed to me; I was grieved in my meditation, and troubled;

³ because of the voice of the enemy, and because of the oppression of the sinner; for they brought iniquity against me, and were wrathfully angry with me.

⁴ My heart was troubled within me; and the fear of death fell upon me.

⁵ Fear and trembling came upon me, and darkness covered me.

⁶ And I said, "O, that I had wings as *those* of a dove! Then would I fly away, and be at rest."

⁷ Lo! I have fled afar off, and lodged in the wilderness. Selah.

⁸ I waited for Him that would deliver me from my distressed spirit, and from the tempest.

⁹ Destroy, O Lord, and divide their tongues, for I have seen iniquity and gainsaying in the city.

¹⁰ Day and night he shall go round about it upon its walls; iniquity and sorrow and unrighteousness *are* in the midst of it;

¹¹ and usury and craft have not failed from its streets.

¹² For if an enemy had reproached me, I would have endured it; and if one who hated *me* had spoken vauntingly against me, I would have hid myself from him.

¹³ But you, O like-minded man, my guide, and my acquaintance,

¹⁴ who in companionship with me sweetened *our* food; we walked in the house of God in concord.

¹⁵ Let death come upon them, and let them go down alive into Hades, for iniquity is in their dwellings, in the midst of them.

¹⁶ I cried to God, and the Lord hearkened to me.

¹⁷ Evening and morning and at noon I will declare and make known *my needs;* and He shall hear my voice.

¹⁸ He shall deliver my soul in peace from them that draw near to me; for they were with me in many *cases.*

[19] God shall hear, and bring them low, *even* He that has existed from eternity. Selah. For they suffer no recourse, and *therefore* they have not feared God.

[20] He has reached forth his hand for retribution; they have profaned His covenant.

[21] They were scattered at the anger of His countenance, and his heart drew near to them. His words were smoother than oil, yet they are darts.

[22] Cast your cares upon the Lord, and He shall sustain you; He shall never permit the righteous to be moved.

[23] But You, O God, shall bring them down to the pit of destruction; bloody and crafty men shall not live out half their days; but I will hope in You, O Lord.

PSALM 56

[1] For the end, concerning the people that were removed from the sanctuary, by David for a memorial, when the Philistines caught him in Gath.
Have mercy upon me, O God; for man has trodden me down; all the day long his warring has afflicted me.

[2] My enemies have trodden me down all the day from the dawning of the day; for there are many warring against me.

[3] They shall be afraid, but I will trust in You.

[4] In God (I will praise *His* word); all the day long have I hoped in God; I will not fear; what shall man do to me?

[5] All the day long they have abominated my words; all their devices *are* against me for evil.

[6] They will dwell near and hide *themselves*; they will watch my steps, accordingly as I have waited patiently in my soul.

[7] You will by no means save them; You will bring down the people in wrath.

[8] O God, I have declared my life to You; You have set my tears before You, even according to Your promise.

[9] My enemies shall be turned back, in the day that I shall call upon You; behold, I know that You are my God.

[10] In God, (I will praise *His* word); in the Lord (I will praise *His* word).

[11] I have hoped in God; I will not be afraid; what shall man do to me?

[12] The vows of Your praise, O God, which I will pay, are upon me.

[13] For You have delivered my soul from death, and my feet from sliding, that I should be well-pleasing before God in the land of the living.

PSALM 57

[1] For the end. Do not destroy; by David, for a memorial, when he fled from the presence of Saul, to the cave.
Have mercy on me, O God, have mercy on me; for my soul has trusted in You; and in the shadow of Your wings will I hope, until the iniquity has passed away.

[2] I will cry to God Most High; the God who has benefited me. Selah.

[3] He sent from heaven and saved me; He reproached them that trampled on me; God has sent forth His mercy and His truth;

[4] and He has delivered my soul from the midst of *the lion's* whelps; I lay down to sleep, *though* troubled. *As for* the sons of men, their teeth are spears and arrows, and their tongue a sharp sword.

[5] Be exalted, O God, above the heavens; and Your glory above all the earth.

[6] They have prepared snares for my feet, and have bowed down my soul; they have dug a pit before my face, and fallen into it *themselves*. Selah.

[7] My heart, O God, *is* ready, my heart *is* ready; I will sing; yes, I will sing psalms.

[8] Awake, my glory; awake, psaltery and harp; I will awake early.

[9] O Lord, I will give thanks to You among the nations; I will sing to You among the Gentiles.

[10] For Your mercy has been magnified, even to the heavens, and Your truth to the clouds.

[11] Be exalted, O God, above the heavens; and Your glory above all the earth.

PSALM 58

[1] For the end. Do not destroy; by David, for a memorial.
If you do indeed speak righteousness, *then* do you judge rightly, you sons of men?

[2] For you work iniquities in *your* hearts in the earth; your hands plot unrighteousness.

[3] Sinners have gone astray from the womb; they go astray from the belly; they speak lies.

[4] Their venom is like *that* of a serpent; as *that* of a deaf asp, and that stops her ears;

[5] which will not hear the voice of charmers, nor *heed* the charm prepared skillfully by the wise.

[6] God has crushed their teeth in their mouth; God has broken the teeth of the lions.

[7] They shall utterly pass away like water running through; he shall bend his bow till they shall fail.

[8] They shall be destroyed as melted wax; the fire has fallen, and they have not seen the sun.

[9] Before your pots you can feel the white thorn, He shall swallow you up as living, as in His wrath.

[10] The righteous shall rejoice when he sees the vengeance of the ungodly; he shall wash his hands in the blood of the sinner.

[11] And a man shall say, Verily then there is a reward for the righteous; verily there is a God that judges them in the earth.

PSALM 59

[1] For the end. Do not destroy; by David for a memorial, when Saul sent, and watched his house to kill him.

Deliver me from my enemies, O God; and ransom me from those that rise up against me.

2 Deliver me from the workers of iniquity, and save me from bloody men.

3 For behold, they have hunted after my soul; violent men have set upon me; neither *is it* my iniquity, nor my sin, O Lord.

4 Without iniquity I ran and directed *my course aright*; awake to help me, and behold.

5 And You, Lord God of hosts, the God of Israel, draw near to visit all the heathen; do not pity any that work iniquity. Selah.

6 They shall return at evening, and hunger like a dog, and go round about the city.

7 Behold, they shall utter a voice with their mouth, and a sword is in their lips; for who, *they say*, has heard?

8 But You, O Lord, shall laugh them to scorn; You will utterly set at nought all the heathen.

9 I will keep my strength, *looking* to You; for You, O God, are my helper.

10 *As for* my God, His mercy shall go before me; my God will show me *vengeance* on my enemies.

11 Do not slay them, lest they forget Your law; scatter them by Your power; and bring them down, O Lord, my defender.

12 *For* the sin of their mouth, *and* the word of their lips, let them be taken in their pride.

13 And for *their* cursing and falsehood shall utter destruction be denounced; *they shall fall* by the wrath of utter destruction, and shall not be; so shall they know that the God of Jacob is Lord to the ends of the earth. Selah.

14 They shall return at evening, and be hungry as a dog, and go round about the city.

15 They shall be scattered here and there for food; and if they are not satisfied, they shall murmur.

16 But I will sing to Your strength, and in the morning will I rejoice *in* Your mercy; for You have been my supporter, and my refuge in the day of my affliction.

17 *You are* my helper; to You, my God, shall I sing; You are my supporter, O my God, *and* my mercy.

PSALM 60

1 For the end, for them that shall yet be changed; for an inscription by David for instruction, when he *had* burned Mesopotamia of Syria, and Syria of Zobah; and Joab *had* returned and struck twelve thousand *in* the Valley of Salt.
O God, You have rejected and destroyed us; You have been angry, yet *You* have pitied us.

2 You have shaken the earth, and troubled it; heal its breaches, for it has been shaken.

3 You have shown Your people hard things; You have made us drink the wine of astonishment.

4 You have given a token to them that fear You, that they might flee from the bow. Selah.

5 That Your beloved ones may be delivered; save with Your right hand, and hear me.

6 God has spoken in His holiness; I will rejoice, and divide Shechem, and measure out the Valley of Tents.

7 Gilead is Mine, and Manasseh is Mine; and Ephraim is the strength of My head;

8 Judah is My king; Moab is the caldron of My hope; over Edom will I stretch out My shoe; the Philistines have been subjected to Me.

9 Who will lead me into the fortified city? Who will guide me as far as Edom?

10 Will not You, O God, who has cast us off? And will not You, O God, go forth with our forces?

11 Give us help from trouble; for vain is the deliverance of man.

12 In God will we do valiantly; and He shall bring to nought them that harass us.

PSALM 61

1 For the end, among the Hymns of David.
O God, hear my supplication; attend to my prayer.

2 From the ends of the earth have I cried to You, when my heart was in trouble; You lifted me up on a rock; You guided me;

3 because You were my hope, a tower of strength from the face of the enemy.

4 I will dwell in Your tabernacle forever; I will shelter myself under the shadow of Your wings. Selah.

5 For You, O God, have heard my prayers; You have given an inheritance to them that fear Your name.

6 You shall add days to the days of the king; *You shall lengthen* his years to all generations.

7 He shall endure forever before God. Which of them shall seek out His mercy and truth?

8 So shall I sing to Your name forever and ever, that I may daily perform my vows.

PSALM 62

1 For the end, A Psalm of David to Jeduthun.
Shall not my soul be subjected to God? For from Him is my salvation.

2 For He is my God, and my savior; my helper, I shall not be greatly moved.

3 How long will you assault a man? You are all slaughtering as with a bowed wall and a broken hedge.

4 They only took counsel to set at nought my honor. I ran in thirst; with their mouth they blessed, but with their heart they cursed. Selah.

5 Nevertheless, my soul is subjected to God; for of Him *is* my patient hope.

6 For He *is* my God and my Savior; my helper, I shall not be moved.

[7] In God *is* my salvation and my glory; *He is* the God of my help, and my hope is in God.

[8] Hope in Him, all you congregation of the people; pour out your hearts before Him, for God is our helper. Selah.

[9] But the sons of men are vain; the sons of men are false, so as to be deceitful in the balances; they are all alike, *formed* out of vanity.

[10] Do not trust in unrighteousness, and do not lust after robberies. If wealth should flow in, do not set your heart upon it.

[11] God has spoken once, *and* I have heard these two things, that power is of God;

[12] and mercy is Yours, O Lord; for You will recompense everyone according to his works.

PSALM 63

[1] A Psalm of David, when he was in the Wilderness of Edom.

O God, my God, I cry to You early; my soul has thirsted for You: how often has my flesh *longed* after You, in a barren and trackless and dry land!

[2] Thus have I appeared before You in the sanctuary, that I might see Your power and Your glory.

[3] For Your mercy is better than life: my lips shall praise You.

[4] Thus will I bless You during my life: I will lift up my hands in Your name.

[5] Let my soul be filled as with marrow and fatness; and *my* joyful lips shall praise Your name.

[6] For I have remembered You on my bed; in the early seasons I have meditated on You.

[7] For You have been my helper, and in the shelter of Your wings will I rejoice.

[8] My soul has kept very close behind You: Your right hand has upheld me.

[9] But they vainly sought after my soul; they shall go into the lowest parts of the earth.

[10] They shall be delivered up to the power of the sword; they shall be portions for jackals.

[11] But the king shall rejoice in God; everyone that swears by Him shall be praised; for the mouth of them that speak unjust things has been stopped.

PSALM 64

[1] For the end, A Psalm of David.

Hear my prayer, O God, when I make my petition to You; deliver my soul from fear of the enemy.

[2] You have sheltered me from the conspiracy of them that do wickedly; from the multitude of them that work iniquity;

[3] who have sharpened their tongues as a sword; they have bent their bow maliciously;

[4] to shoot in secret at the blameless; they will shoot him suddenly, and will not fear.

[5] They have set up for themselves an evil matter, they have given counsel to hide snares; they have said, "Who shall see them?"

[6] They have searched out iniquity; they have wearied themselves with searching diligently, a man shall approach and the heart is deep,

[7] and God shall be exalted, their wounds were *caused by* the weapon of the foolish children,

[8] and their tongues have set him at nought, all that saw them were troubled;

[9] and every man was alarmed, and they related the works of God, and understood His deeds.

[10] The righteous shall rejoice in the Lord, and hope in Him, and all the upright in heart shall be praised.

PSALM 65

[1] For the end, A Psalm *and* Song of David.

Praise becomes You, O God, in Zion; and to You shall the vow be performed.

[2] Hear my prayer; to You all flesh shall come.

[3] The words of transgressors have overpowered us; but You pardon our sins.

[4] Blessed *is* he whom You have chosen and adopted; he shall dwell in Your courts; we shall be filled with the good things of Your house; Your temple is holy.

[5] *You are* wonderful in righteousness. Hearken to us, O God our Savior; the hope of all the ends of the earth, and of them *that are* on the sea afar off;

[6] who establish the mountains in Your strength, being girded about with power;

[7] who trouble the depth of the sea, the sounds of its waves.

[8] The nations shall be troubled, and they that inhabit the ends *of the earth* shall be afraid of the signs; You will cause the outgoings of morning and evening to rejoice.

[9] You have visited the earth, and saturated it; You have abundantly enriched it. The river of God is filled with water; You have prepared their food, for thus is the preparation *of it.*

[10] Saturate her furrows, multiply her fruits; *the crop* springing up shall rejoice in its drops.

[11] You will bless the crown of the year *because* of Your goodness; and Your plains shall be filled with fatness.

[12] The mountains of the wilderness shall be enriched; and the hills shall gird themselves with joy.

[13] The rams of the flock are clothed *with wool,* and the valleys shall abound in grain; they shall cry aloud; yes, they shall sing hymns.

PSALM 66

[1] For the end, A Song of Psalm of resurrection.

Shout unto God, all the earth.

[2] O sing praises to His name; give glory to His praise.

³ Say unto God, "How awesome are Your works!" Through the greatness of Your power Your enemies shall submit themselves to You.

⁴ Let all the earth worship You, and sing to You; let them sing to Your name. Selah.

⁵ Come and behold the works of God; *He is* mighty in *His* counsels beyond the children of men,

⁶ who turns the sea into dry land; they shall go through the river on foot; there shall we rejoice in Him,

⁷ who by His power is Lord over the ages, His eyes look upon the nations; let not them that provoke *Him* be exalted in themselves. Selah.

⁸ Bless our God, you Gentiles, and make the voice of his praise to be heard;

⁹ who quickens my soul in life, and does not allow my feet to be moved.

¹⁰ For You, O God, have proved us; You have tried us with fire as silver is tried.

¹¹ You have brought us into the snare; You have laid afflictions on our back.

¹² You have caused men to ride over our heads; we went through the fire and water; but You brought us out into *a place of* refreshment.

¹³ I will go into Your house with burnt offerings; I will pay You my vows,

¹⁴ which my lips framed, and my mouth uttered in my affliction.

¹⁵ I will offer to You whole burnt sacrifices full of marrow, with incense and rams; I will sacrifice to You oxen with goats. Selah.

¹⁶ Come *and* hear, and I will tell, all You that fear God, how great things He has done for my soul.

¹⁷ I cried to Him with my mouth, and exalted Him with my tongue.

¹⁸ If I have regarded iniquity in my heart, let not the Lord hearken *to me.*

¹⁹ Therefore God has hearkened to me; He has attended to the voice of my prayer.

²⁰ Blessed be God, who has not turned away my prayer, nor His mercy from me.

PSALM 67

¹ For the end, A Psalm of David among the Hymns.
God be merciful to us, and bless us; *and* cause His face to shine upon us. Selah.

² That *men* may know Your way on the earth, Your salvation among all nations.

³ Let the nations, O God, give thanks to You; let all the nations give thanks to You.

⁴ Let the nations rejoice and exalt, for You shall judge the people in equity, and shall guide the nations on the earth. Selah.

⁵ Let the people, O God, give thanks to You; let all the people give thanks to You.

⁶ The earth has yielded her fruit; let God, our God, bless us.

⁷ Let God bless us, and let all the ends of the earth fear Him.

PSALM 68

¹ For the end, A Psalm of a Song by David.
Let God arise, and let His enemies be scattered; and let them that hate Him flee from before Him.

² As smoke vanishes, let them vanish: as wax melts before the fire, so let the sinners perish from before God.

³ But let the righteous rejoice; let them exalt before God: let them be delighted with joy.

⁴ Sing to God, sing praises to His name: make a way for Him that rides upon the west (the Lord is His name) and rejoice before Him. They shall be troubled before the face of Him,

⁵ *who is* the Father of the orphans, and Judge of the widows; *such is* God in His holy place.

⁶ God settles the solitary in a house; leading forth prisoners mightily, also them that act provokingly, *even* them that dwell in tombs.

⁷ O God, when You went forth before Your people, when You went through the wilderness; Selah.

⁸ The earth quaked; yes, the heavens dropped *water* at the presence of the God of Sinai, at the presence of the God of Israel.

⁹ O God, You will grant to Your inheritance a gracious rain; for it was weary, but You have refreshed it.

¹⁰ Your creatures dwell in it; You have in Your goodness prepared for the poor.

¹¹ The Lord God will give a word to them that preach *it* in a great company.

¹² The king of the forces of the beloved *will* even *grant them* for the beauty of the house to divide the spoils.

¹³ Even if you should lie among the lots, *you shall have* the wings of a dove covered with silver, and her breast with yellow gold.

¹⁴ When the heavenly One scatters kings upon it, they shall be made snow-white in Zalmon.

¹⁵ The mountain of God is a rich mountain; a swelling mountain, a rich mountain.

¹⁶ Why do you conceive *evil*, you swelling mountains? *This is* the mountain which God has delighted to dwell in; yes, the Lord will dwell *in it* forever.

¹⁷ The chariots of God are ten thousand fold, thousands of rejoicing ones; the Lord is among them, in Sinai, in the holy place.

¹⁸ You have ascended on high, You have led captivity captive, You have received gifts among men, yea, for *they were* rebellious, that You might dwell among them.

¹⁹ Blessed be the Lord God, blessed be the Lord daily; and the God of our salvation shall prosper us. Selah.

²⁰ Our God is the God of salvation; and to the Lord belong the issues from death.

21 But God shall crust the heads of His enemies; the hairy crown of them that go on in their trespasses.

22 The Lord said, "I will bring again from Bashan, I will bring *My people* again through the depths of the sea."

23 That your foot may be dipped in blood, *and* the tongue of your dogs *be stained* with that of *your* enemies.

24 Your goings, O God, have been seen; the goings of my God, the King, in the sanctuary.

25 The princes went first, next before the players on instruments, in the midst of damsels playing on timbrels.

26 Praise God in the congregations, the Lord from the fountains of Israel.

27 There is Benjamin the younger *one* in ecstasy, the princes of Judah their rulers, the princes of Zebulun, the princes of Naphtali.

28 O God, command Your strength; strengthen, O God, that which You have done in us.

29 Because of Your temple at Jerusalem shall kings bring presents to You.

30 Rebuke the wild beasts of the reed; let the crowd of bulls with the heifers of the nations *be rebuked*, so that they who have been proved with silver may not be shut out; scatter the nations that wish for wars.

31 Ambassadors shall arrive out of Egypt; Ethiopia shall hasten *to stretch out* her hand readily to God.

32 Sing to God, you kingdoms of the earth; sing psalms to the Lord. Selah.

33 Sing to God that rides on the heaven of heavens, eastward: lo, He will utter a mighty sound with His voice.

34 Give glory to God: His excellency is over Israel, and His power is in the clouds.

35 God is wonderful in His holy *places*, the God of Israel; He will give power and strength to His people; blessed be God.

PSALM 69

1 For the end, *A Psalm* of David, for alternate *strains*.
Save me, O God; for the waters have come in to my soul.

2 I am stuck fast in deep mire, and there is no standing: I have come in to the depths of the sea, and a storm has overwhelmed me.

3 I am weary *of* crying, my throat has become hoarse; my eyes have failed by my waiting on my God.

4 Those that hate me without a cause are more than the hairs of my head. My enemies that persecute me unrighteously have become strong. Then I restored that which I did not take away.

5 O God, You know my foolishness; and my transgressions are not hidden from You.

6 Let not them that wait on You, O Lord of hosts, be ashamed on my account; let not them that seek You, be ashamed on my account, O God of Israel.

7 For I have suffered reproach for Your sake; shame has covered my face.

8 I became a stranger to my brothers, and a stranger to my mother's children.

9 For the zeal of Your house has eaten me up; and the reproaches of them that reproached You have fallen upon me.

10 And I bowed down my soul with fasting, and that was made my reproach.

11 And I put on sackcloth for my covering; and I became a proverb to them.

12 Those that sit in the gate talked against me, and those that drank wine sang against me.

13 But I *will cry* to You, O Lord, in my prayer; O God, it is a propitious time: in the multitude of Your mercy hear me, in the truth of Your salvation.

14 Save me from the mire, that I may not sink down; let me be delivered from them that hate me, and from the deep waters.

15 Do not let the floodwater drown me, nor let the deep swallow me up; neither let the well shut its mouth upon me.

16 Hear me, O Lord; for Your mercy is good: according to the multitude of Your compassions, look upon me.

17 And do not turn away Your face from Your servant; for I am afflicted; hear me speedily.

18 Draw near to my soul and redeem it: deliver me because of my enemies.

19 For You know my reproach, and my shame, and my confusion; all that afflict me are before You.

20 My soul has waited for reproach and misery; and I waited for one to grieve with me, but there was none; and for one to comfort me, but I found none.

21 They gave *me* also gall for my food, and made me drink vinegar for my thirst.

22 Let their table before them be for a snare, and for a recompense, and for a stumbling block.

23 Let their eyes be darkened that they should not see; and bow down their back continually.

24 Pour out Your wrath upon them, and let the fury of Your anger take hold of them.

25 Let their habitation be made desolate; and let there be no inhabitant in their tents;

26 because they persecuted him whom You have smitten; and they have added to the grief of my wounds.

27 Add iniquity to their iniquity; and let them not come into Your righteousness.

28 Let them be blotted out of the book of the living, and let them not be written with the righteous.

29 I am poor and sorrowful; but the salvation of Your countenance has helped me.

30 I will praise the name of my God with a song, I will magnify Him with praise;

31 and *this* shall please God more than a young calf having horns and hoofs.

32 Let the poor see and rejoice; seek the Lord diligently, and you shall live.

³³ For the Lord hears the poor, and does not despise His prisoners.

³⁴ Let the heavens and the earth praise Him, the sea, and all things moving in them.

³⁵ For God will save Zion, and the cities of Judah shall be built; and *men* shall dwell there, and inherit it.

³⁶ And the descendants of His servants shall possess it, and those that love His name shall dwell in it.

PSALM 70

¹ For the end, by David for a remembrance, that the Lord may save me.
Draw near, O God, to my help.

² Let them be ashamed and confounded that seek my soul; let them be turned backward and put to shame, *those* that wish me evil.

³ Let them that say to me, "Aha, aha," be turned back and put to shame immediately.

⁴ Let all that seek You rejoice and be glad in You: and let those that love Your salvation say continually, "Let God be magnified."

⁵ But I am poor and needy; O God, help me: You are my helper and deliverer, O Lord; do not delay.

PSALM 71

¹ By David, *A Psalm sung by* the sons of Jonadab, and the first that were taken captive.
O Lord, I have hoped in You; let me never be put to shame.

² In Your righteousness deliver me and rescue me: incline Your ear to me, and save me.

³ Be to me a protecting God, and a stronghold to save me; for You are my fortress and my refuge.

⁴ Deliver me, O my God, from the hand of the sinner, from the hand of the transgressor and unjust man.

⁵ For You are my support, O Lord; O Lord, *You are* my hope from my youth.

⁶ On You have I been stayed from the womb: from the belly of my mother You have been my protector: of You is my praise *offered* continually.

⁷ I have become as it were a wonder to many, but You are *my* strong helper.

⁸ Let my mouth be filled with praise, that I may sing hymns *to* Your glory *and* Your majesty all the day.

⁹ Do not cast me off at the time of old age; do not forsake me when my strength fails.

¹⁰ For my enemies have spoken against me; and they that lay wait for my soul have taken counsel together,

¹¹ saying, "God has forsaken him: persecute him, and take him; for there is none to deliver *him*."

¹² O God, be not far from me; O my God, draw near to my help.

¹³ Let those that plot *evil* against my soul be ashamed and utterly fail; let those that seek my hurt be clothed with shame and dishonor.

¹⁴ But I will hope continually, and will praise You more and more.

¹⁵ My mouth shall declare Your righteousness openly, *and* Your salvation all the day; for I am not acquainted with the affairs *of men*.

¹⁶ I will go on in the might of the Lord: O Lord, I will make mention of Your righteousness only.

¹⁷ O God, You have taught me from my youth, and until now will I declare Your wonders;

¹⁸ even until I am old and advanced in years. O God, do not forsake me; until I have declared Your *mighty* arm to all the generation that is to come;

¹⁹ even Your power and Your righteousness, O God, up to the highest *heavens, even* the mighty works which You have done; O God, who is like You?

²⁰ What many and great afflictions have You shown me! Yet You turned and revived me, and brought me again from the depths of the earth.

²¹ You multiplied Your righteousness, and turned and comforted me, and brought me again out of the depths of the earth.

²² I will also therefore give thanks to You, O God, *because of* Your truth, on an instrument of music; I will sing psalms to You on the harp, O Holy One of Israel.

²³ My lips shall rejoice when I sing to You; and my soul, which You have redeemed.

²⁴ Moreover also my tongue shall dwell all the day upon Your righteousness; when they shall be ashamed and confounded that seek my hurt.

PSALM 72

¹ For Solomon.
O God, give Your judgment to the king, and Your righteousness to the king's son;

² *that he may* judge Your people with righteousness, and Your poor with judgment.

³ Let the mountains and the hills raise peace to Your people.

⁴ He shall judge the poor of the people in righteousness, and save the children of the needy; and shall bring low the false accuser.

⁵ And He shall continue as long as the sun, and before the moon forever.

⁶ He shall come down as rain upon a fleece, and as drops falling upon the earth.

⁷ In His days shall righteousness spring up; and abundance of peace till the moon be removed.

⁸ And He shall have dominion from sea to sea, and from the River to the ends of the earth.

⁹ The Ethiopians shall fall down before Him, and His enemies shall lick the dust.

10 The kings of Tarshish, and the isles, shall bring presents: the kings of the Arabians and Sheba shall offer gifts.

11 And all kings shall worship Him; all the Gentiles shall serve Him.

12 For He has delivered the poor from the oppressor; and the needy who had no helper.

13 He shall spare the poor and needy, and shall deliver the souls of the needy.

14 He shall redeem their souls from oppression and injustice, and their name *shall be* precious before Him.

15 And He shall live, and the gold of Arabia shall be given to Him, and *men* shall pray for Him continually; *and* all the day shall they praise Him.

16 There shall be an establishment on the earth on the tops of the mountains; its fruit shall be exalted above Lebanon, and those of the city shall flourish as grass of the earth.

17 Let His name be blessed forever; His name shall endure longer than the sun, and all the tribes of the earth shall be blessed in Him: all nations shall call Him blessed.

18 Blessed is the Lord God of Israel, who alone does wonders.

19 And blessed is His glorious name forever, even forever and ever; and all the earth shall be filled with His glory. Amen, and Amen.

20 The hymns of David the son of Jesse are ended.

PSALM 73

1 A Psalm of Asaph.
How good is God to Israel, to the upright in heart!

2 But my feet were almost overthrown; my goings very nearly slipped.

3 For I was jealous of the transgressors, beholding the tranquility of sinners.

4 For there is no sign of reluctance in their death, and *they have* firmness under their affliction.

5 They are not in the troubles of *other* men; and they shall not be scourged with *other* men.

6 Therefore pride has possessed them; they have clothed themselves with their injustice and ungodliness.

7 Their injustice shall go forth as out of fatness; they have fulfilled their intention.

8 They have taken counsel and spoken in wickedness; they have uttered unrighteousness proudly.

9 They have set their mouth against heaven, and their tongue has gone through upon the earth.

10 Therefore shall my people return here, and full days shall be found with them.

11 And they said, "How does God know? And is there knowledge in the Most High?"

12 Behold, these *are* the sinners, and they that prosper always; they have possessed wealth.

13 And I said, "Verily in vain have I justified my heart, and washed my hands in innocence."

14 For I was plagued all the day, and my reproof *was* every morning.

15 If I said, "I will speak thus"; behold, I *should* have broken covenant with the generation of Your children.

16 And I undertook to understand this, *but* it is too hard for me,

17 until I go into the sanctuary of God, *and so* understand the latter end.

18 Surely You have appointed *judgments* to them because of their crafty dealings; You have cast them down when they were lifted up.

19 How have they become desolate! Suddenly they have failed; they have perished because of their iniquity.

20 As the dream of one awakening, O Lord, in Your city You will despise their image.

21 For my heart has rejoiced, and my heart has been gladdened.

22 But I *was* vile and did not know: I became brutish before You.

23 Yet I am continually with You. You have taken hold of my right hand.

24 You have guided me by Your counsel, and You have taken me to Yourself with glory.

25 For whom have I in heaven *but You*? And what have I desired upon the earth besides You?

26 My heart and my flesh have failed; *but* God *is the strength* of my heart, and God is my portion forever.

27 For behold, they that remove themselves far from You shall perish; You have destroyed everyone that goes a whoring from You.

28 But it is good for me to cleave close to God, to put my trust in the Lord; that I may proclaim all Your praises in the gates of the daughter of Zion.

PSALM 74

1 *A Psalm* of instruction, of Asaph.
Why have You rejected *us*, O God, forever? *Why* has Your wrath been kindled against the sheep of Your pasture?

2 Remember Your congregation which You have purchased from the beginning; You ransomed the rod of Your inheritance, this Mount Zion where You have dwelt.

3 Lift up Your hands against their pride continually; *because of* all that the enemy has done wickedly in Your holy places.

4 And they that hate You have boasted in the midst of Your feast; they have set up their standards for signs,

5 ignorantly as it were in the entrance above;

6 they cut down its doors at once with axes as in a wood of trees; they have broken it down with hatchet and stone cutter.

7 They have burned Your sanctuary with fire to the ground; they have profaned the habitation of Your name.

8 They have said in their heart, *even* all their kindred together, "Come, let us abolish the feasts of the Lord from the earth."

[9] We have not seen our signs; there is no longer a prophet; and *God* will not know us anymore.

[10] How long, O God, shall the enemy reproach? Shall the enemy provoke Your name forever?

[11] Why do You turn away Your hand, and Your right hand from the midst of Your bosom forever?

[12] But God is our King from of old; He has wrought salvation in the midst of the earth.

[13] You established the sea in Your might, You broke to pieces the heads of the dragons in the water.

[14] You broke to pieces the heads of the dragon; You gave him *as* meat to the Ethiopian nations.

[15] You broke open the fountains and torrents; You dried up mighty rivers.

[16] The day is Yours, and the night is Yours; You have prepared the sun and the moon.

[17] You have made all the borders of the earth; You have made summer and spring.

[18] Remember this Your creation; an enemy has reproached the Lord, and a foolish people have provoked Your name.

[19] Do not deliver to the wild beasts a soul that gives praise to You: do not forget forever the souls of Your poor.

[20] Look upon Your covenant; for the dark *places* of the earth are filled with the habitations of iniquity.

[21] Let not the afflicted and ashamed one be rejected; the poor and needy shall praise Your name.

[22] Arise, O God, plead Your cause; remember Your reproaches that come from the foolish one all the day.

[23] Do not forget the voice of Your enemies; let the pride of them that hate You continually ascend before You.

PSALM 75

[1] For the end, Do not destroy, A Psalm of a Song of Asaph. We will give thanks to You, O God, we will give thanks, and call upon Your name.

[2] I will declare all Your wonderful works. When I shall take a set time, I will judge righteously.

[3] The earth is dissolved, and all that dwell in it; I have strengthened its pillars. Selah.

[4] I said unto the transgressors, "Do not transgress"; and to the sinners, "Do not lift up the horn.

[5] Do not lift up your horn on high; do not speak unrighteousness against God."

[6] For *good comes* neither from the east, nor from the west, nor from the desert mountains.

[7] For God is the judge; He puts one down, and raises up another.

[8] For *there is* a cup in the hand of the Lord, full of unmingled wine; and He has turned *it* from side to side, but its dregs have not been wholly poured out; all the sinners of the earth shall drink *them*.

[9] But I will exalt forever; I will sing praises to the God of Jacob.

[10] And I will break all the horns of sinners; but the horns of the righteous one shall be exalted.

PSALM 76

[1] For the end, among the Hymns, A Psalm of Asaph; a Song for the Assyrian.
God is known in Judah; His name is great in Israel.

[2] And His place has been in peace, and His dwelling place in Zion.

[3] There He broke the power of the bows, the shield, and the sword, and the battle. Selah.

[4] You wonderfully shine forth from the everlasting mountains.

[5] All the simple ones in heart were troubled; all the men of wealth have slept their sleep, and have found nothing in their hands.

[6] At Your rebuke, O God of Jacob, the riders on horses slumbered.

[7] *For* You are to be feared; and who shall withstand You, because of Your anger?

[8] You caused judgment to be heard from heaven; the earth feared, and was still,

[9] when God arose to judgment, to save all the meek in heart. Selah.

[10] For the inward thought of man shall give thanks to You, and the memorial of his inward thought shall keep a feast to You.

[11] Vow, and pay *your vows* to the Lord our God; all that are round about Him shall bring gifts,

[12] *even* to Him that is awesome, and that takes away the spirits of princes; to Him that is awesome among the kings of the earth.

PSALM 77

[1] For the end, for Idithun, A Psalm of Asaph.
I cried to the Lord with my voice, yes, my voice *was* addressed to God; and He listened to me.

[2] In the day of my affliction I earnestly sought the Lord; *even* with my hands by night before Him, and I was not deceived; my soul refused to be comforted.

[3] I remembered God, and rejoiced; I poured out my complaint, and my soul fainted. Selah.

[4] All my enemies set a watch *against me;* I was troubled, and did not speak.

[5] I considered the days of old, and remembered ancient ears.

[6] And I meditated; I communed with my heart by night, and diligently searched my spirit, *saying,*

[7] "Will the Lord cast off forever? And will He be well pleased no more?

[8] Will He cut off His mercy forever, even forever and ever?

[9] Will God forget to pity? Or will He shut up His compassions in His wrath?" Selah.

10 And I said, "Now I have begun; this is the change of the right hand of the Most High."

11 I remembered the works of the Lord; for I will remember Your wonders from the beginning.

12 And I will meditate on all Your works, and will consider Your doings.

13 O God, Your way is in the sanctuary; who is a great God as our God?

14 You are the God that performs wonders; You have made known Your power among the nations.

15 You have redeemed Your people, the sons of Jacob and Joseph, with Your outstretched arm. Selah.

16 The waters saw You, O God, the waters saw You, and feared; and the depths were troubled.

17 *There was* an abundant sound of waters; the clouds uttered a voice; for Your arrows went abroad.

18 The voice of Your thunder was abroad, and around Your lightnings appeared to the world; the earth trembled and quaked.

19 Your way is in the sea, and Your paths in many waters, and Your footsteps cannot be known.

20 You guided Your people like sheep by the hand of Moses and Aaron.

PSALM 78

1 *A Psalm* of instruction, of Asaph. Give heed, O my people, to my law; incline your ear to the words of my mouth.

2 I will open my mouth in parables; I will utter dark sayings *which have been* from the beginning.

3 All which we have heard and known, and our fathers have declared to us.

4 They were not hid from their children to a second generation; *the fathers* declaring the praises of the Lord, and His mighty acts, and His wonders which He has done.

5 And He raised up a testimony in Jacob, and appointed a law in Israel, which He commanded our fathers, to make it known to their children;

6 that another generation might know, even the sons which should be born; and they should arise and declare them to their children,

7 that they might set their hope on God, and not forget the works of God, but diligently seek His commandments.

8 That they should not be as their fathers, a perverse and provoking generation; a generation which did not set its heart right, and its spirit was not steadfast with God.

9 The children of Ephraim, bending and shooting *with* the bow, turned *back* in the day of battle.

10 They did not keep the covenant of God, and would not walk in His law.

11 And they forgot His benefits, and His miracles which He *had* shown them;

12 the miracles which He did before their fathers, in the land of Egypt, in the plain of Zoan.

13 He divided the sea, and led them through; He made the waters to stand as *in* a bottle.

14 And He guided them with a cloud by day, and all the night with a light of fire.

15 He split a rock in the wilderness, and made them drink as in a great deep.

16 And He brought water out of the rock, and caused the waters to flow down as rivers.

17 And they sinned even more against Him; they provoked the Most High in the wilderness.

18 And they tempted God in their hearts, in asking meat for *the desire of* their souls.

19 They spoke also against God, and said, "Will God be able to prepare a table in the wilderness?

20 Forasmuch as He struck the rock, and the waters flowed, and the torrents ran abundantly; will He be able also to give bread, or prepare a table for His people?"

21 Therefore the Lord heard, and was provoked: and fire was kindled in Jacob, and wrath went up against Israel.

22 Because they believed not in God, and trusted not in His salvation.

23 Yet He commanded the clouds from above, and opened the doors of heaven,

24 and rained upon them manna to eat, and gave them the bread of heaven.

25 Man ate angels' bread; He sent them provision to the full.

26 He removed the south wind from heaven; and by His might He brought in the south west wind.

27 And He rained upon them flesh like dust, and feathered birds like the sand on the seashore.

28 And they fell into the midst of their camp, round about their tents.

29 So they ate, and were completely filled; and He gave them their desire.

30 They were not disappointed of their desire, *but* when their food was yet in their mouth,

31 then the indignation of God rose up against them, and slew the fattest of them, and overthrew the choice men of Israel.

32 In the midst of all this they sinned even more, and did not believe His miracles.

33 And their days were consumed in vanity, and their years with anxiety.

34 When He slew them, they sought Him; and they returned and sought diligently after God.

35 And they remembered that God was their Helper, and the Most High God was their Redeemer.

36 Yet they loved Him *only* with their mouth, and lied to Him with their tongue.

37 For their heart *was* not right with Him, neither were they steadfast in His covenant.

38 But He is compassionate, and will forgive their sins, and will not destroy *them;* indeed, He will frequently turn away His wrath, and will not kindle all His anger.

39 And He remembered that they are flesh; a wind that passes away, and does not return.

40 How often did they provoke Him in the wilderness, *and* anger Him in a dry land!

41 Yes, they turned back, and tempted God, and provoked the Holy One of Israel.

42 They did not remember His hand, the day in which He delivered them from the hand of the oppressor.

43 How He had worked His signs in Egypt, and His wonders in the field of Zoan;

44 and had changed their rivers into blood, and their streams, that they should not drink.

45 He sent the dog-fly against them, and it devoured them; and the frog, and it spoiled them.

46 And He gave their fruit to the canker worm, and their labors to the locust.

47 He killed their vines with hail, and their sycamores with frost.

48 And He gave up their cattle to hail, and their substance to the fire.

49 He sent out against them the fury of His anger, wrath, and indignation, and affliction, a message by evil angels.

50 He made a way for His wrath; He did not spare their souls from death, but consigned their cattle to death;

51 and He struck down every firstborn in the land of Egypt; the firstfruits of their labors in the tents of Ham.

52 And He removed His people like sheep; He led them as a flock in the wilderness.

53 And He guided them with hope, and they did not fear; but the sea covered their enemies.

54 And He brought them in to the mountain of His sanctuary, this mountain which His right hand had purchased.

55 And He cast out the nations from before them, and made them to inherit by a line of inheritance, and made the tribes of Israel to dwell in their tents.

56 Yet they tempted and provoked the Most High God, and did not keep His testimonies.

57 And they turned back, and broke covenant, even as also their fathers; they became like a crooked bow.

58 And they provoked Him with their high places, and moved Him to jealousy with their graven images.

59 God heard and lightly regarded *them*, and greatly despised Israel.

60 And He rejected the tabernacle of Shiloh, His tent where He dwelt among men.

61 And He gave their strength into captivity, and their beauty into the enemy's hand.

62 And He gave His people to the sword; and disdained His inheritance.

63 Fire devoured their young men; and their virgins did not mourn.

64 Their priests fell by the sword; and their widows shall not be wept for.

65 So the Lord awakened as one out of sleep, *and* as a mighty man who has been heated with wine.

66 And He beat back His enemies; He brought on them a perpetual reproach.

67 And He rejected the tabernacle of Joseph, and chose not the tribe of Ephraim;

68 but chose the tribe of Judah, the Mount Zion which He loved.

69 And He built His sanctuary as *the place* of unicorns; He founded it forever on the earth.

70 He chose David also His servant, and took him up from the flocks of sheep.

71 He took him from following the ewes great with young, to be the shepherd of Jacob His servant, and Israel His inheritance.

72 So he tended them in the innocence of his heart; and guided them by the skillfulness of his hands.

PSALM 79

1 A Psalm of Asaph.

O God, the heathen have come into Your inheritance; they have polluted Your holy temple; they have made Jerusalem a storehouse of fruits.

2 They have given the dead bodies of Your servants *to be* food for the birds of the sky, the flesh of Your holy ones for the wild beasts of the earth.

3 They have shed their blood as water, round about Jerusalem; and there was none to bury *them*.

4 We have become a reproach to our neighbors, a scorn and derision to them *that are* round about us.

5 How long, O Lord? Will You be angry forever? Shall Your jealousy burn like fire?

6 Pour out Your wrath upon the heathen that have not known You, and upon the kingdoms which have not called upon Your name.

7 For they have devoured Jacob, and laid his place waste.

8 Remember not our old transgressions; let Your tender mercies come speedily to meet us; for we are greatly impoverished.

9 Help us, O God our Savior; for the glory of Your name, O Lord, deliver us; and be merciful to our sins, for Your name's sake.

10 Why should the heathen say, "Where is their God?" And let the avenging of Your servant's blood that has been shed be known among the heathen before our eyes.

11 Let the groaning of the prisoners come in before You; according to the greatness of Your power, preserve the sons of the slain.

12 Repay to our neighbors sevenfold into their bosom their reproach, with which they have reproached You, O Lord.

13 For we are Your people and the sheep of Your pasture; we will give You thanks forever; we will declare Your praise throughout all generations.

PSALM 80

[1] For the end, for alternate *strains*, a testimony of Asaph, A Psalm concerning the Assyrian.
Attend, O Shepherd of Israel, who guides Joseph like a flock; You who sit upon the cherubim, manifest Yourself;
[2] before Ephraim and Benjamin and Manasseh, stir up Your power, and come to deliver us.
[3] Turn us, O God, and cause Your face to shine, and we shall be delivered.
[4] O Lord God of hosts, how long will You be angry with the prayer of Your servant?
[5] You will feed us with the bread of tears; and will cause us to drink tears by measure.
[6] You have made us a strife to our neighbors; and our enemies have mocked us.
[7] Turn us, O Lord God of hosts, and cause Your face to shine; and we shall be saved. Selah.
[8] You have transplanted a vine out of Egypt; You have cast out the heathen, and planted it.
[9] You made a way before it, and caused its roots to strike, and the land was filled *with it*.
[10] Its shadow covered the mountains, and its shoots *equaled* the choice cedars.
[11] It sent forth its branches to the sea, and its shoots to the river.
[12] Why have You broken down its hedge, while all that pass by the way pluck it?
[13] The boar out of the wood has laid it waste, and the wild beast has devoured it.
[14] O God of hosts, turn, we pray; look on *us* from heaven, and behold and visit this vine;
[15] and restore that which Your right hand has planted, and look on the son of man whom You have strengthened for Yourself.
[16] *It is* burned with fire and dug up; they shall perish at the rebuke of Your presence.
[17] Let Your hand be upon the man of Your right hand, and upon the son of man whom You have strengthened for Yourself.
[18] So will we not depart from You: You shall revive us, and we shall call upon Your name.
[19] Turn us, O Lord God of hosts, and cause Your face to shine; and we shall be saved.

PSALM 81

[1] For the end, A Psalm for Asaph, concerning the winepresses.
Rejoice in God our helper; shout aloud to the God of Jacob.
[2] Take a psalm, and produce the timbrel, the pleasant psaltery with the harp.
[3] Blow the trumpet at the new moon, in the glorious day of your feast.
[4] For *this* is an ordinance for Israel, and a statute of the God of Jacob.

[5] He made it *to be* a testimony in Joseph, when he came forth out of the land of Egypt; he heard a language which he did not understand.
[6] He removed his back from burdens; his hands slaved in making the baskets.
[7] You called upon Me in trouble, and I delivered you; I heard you in the secret place of the storm; I proved you at the Water of Strife. Selah.
[8] Hear, My people, and I will speak to you, O Israel; and I will testify to you; if you will hearken to Me;
[9] there shall be no new god in you; neither shall you worship a strange god.
[10] For I am the Lord your God, that brought you out of the land of Egypt; open your mouth wide, and I will fill it.
[11] But My people did not obey My voice; and Israel gave no heed to Me.
[12] So I let them go after the ways of their own hearts; they will go on in their own ways.
[13] If My people had listened to Me, if Israel had walked in My ways,
[14] I would have put down their enemies very quickly, and would have laid My hand upon those that afflicted them.
[15] The Lord's enemies *would have* lied to Him; but their time shall be forever.
[16] And He fed them with the fat of wheat; and satisfied them with honey out of the rock.

PSALM 82

[1] A Psalm of Asaph.
God stands in the assembly of gods; and in the midst *of them* will judge gods.
[2] How long will you judge unrighteously, and accept the persons of sinners? Selah.
[3] Judge the orphan and poor; do justice to the low and needy.
[4] Rescue the needy, and deliver the poor out of the hand of the sinner.
[5] They do not know, nor understand; they walk on in darkness; all the foundations of the earth shall be shaken.
[6] I have said, "You are gods; and all *of you* children of the Most High.
[7] But you die as men, and fall as one of the princes."
[8] Arise, O God, judge the earth; for You shall inherit all nations.

PSALM 83

[1] A Song of a Psalm of Asaph.
O God, who shall be compared to You? Be not silent, neither be still, O God.
[2] For behold, Your enemies have made a noise; and they that hate You have lifted up the head.
[3] Against Your people they have craftily imagined an *evil* plan, and have taken counsel against Your saints.

[4] They have said, "Come, and let us utterly destroy them out of the nation; and let the name of Israel be remembered no more."

[5] For they have taken counsel together with one consent; they have made a confederacy against You;

[6] even the tents of the Edomites, and the Ishmaelites; Moab, and the Hagrites;

[7] Gebal, and Ammon, and Amalek; the Philistines also, with them that dwell at Tyre.

[8] Behold, Assyria too has come with them; they have become a help to the children of Lot. Selah.

[9] Do to them as to Midian, and to Sisera; as to Jabin at the Brook of Kishon.

[10] They were utterly destroyed at Endor; they became as dung on the earth.

[11] Make their princes as Oreb and Zeeb, and Zebah and Zalmunna; *even* all their princes,

[12] who said, "Let us take to ourselves the altar of God as an inheritance."

[13] O my God, make them as a wheel, as stubble before the face of the wind.

[14] As fire which shall burn up the wood, as the flame may consume the mountains;

[15] so shall You persecute them with Your tempest, and trouble them in Your anger.

[16] Fill their faces with dishonor; so shall they seek Your name, O Lord.

[17] Let them be ashamed and troubled forevermore; yes, let them be confounded and destroyed.

[18] And let them know that Your name is Lord; that You alone are Most High over all the earth.

PSALM 84

[1] For the end, A Psalm for the sons of Korah, concerning the winepresses. How lovely is Your tabernacle, O Lord of hosts!

[2] My soul longs and faints for the courts of the Lord; my heart and my flesh have exalted in the living God.

[3] Yea, the sparrow has found himself a home, and the turtledove a nest for herself, where she may lay her young, *even* Your altars, O Lord of hosts my King, and my God.

[4] Blessed are they that dwell in Your house; they will praise You forevermore. Selah.

[5] Blessed is the man whose help is from You, O Lord; in his heart he has purposed to go up

[6] the Valley of Weeping, to the place which He has appointed, for *there* the Lawgiver shall grant blessings.

[7] They shall go from strength to strength; the God of gods shall be seen in Zion.

[8] O Lord God of hosts, hear my prayer; hearken, O God of Jacob. Selah.

[9] Behold, O God our defender, and look upon the face of Your anointed.

[10] For one day in Your courts is better than thousands. I would rather be a doorkeeper in the house of God, than dwell in the tents of sinners.

[11] For the Lord loves mercy and truth; God will give grace and glory; the Lord will not withhold good things from them that walk in innocence.

[12] O Lord of hosts, blessed is the man that trusts in You!

PSALM 85

[1] For the end, A Psalm for the sons of Korah. O Lord, You have taken pleasure in Your land; You have turned back the captivity of Jacob.

[2] You have forgiven Your people their transgressions; You have covered all their sins. Selah.

[3] You have caused all Your wrath to cease; You have turned from Your fierce anger.

[4] Turn us, O God of our salvation, and turn Your anger away from us.

[5] Will You be angry with us forever? Will You continue Your wrath from generation to generation?

[6] O God, turn and revive us; and Your people shall rejoice in You.

[7] Show us Your mercy, O Lord, and grant us Your salvation.

[8] I will hear what the Lord God will say concerning me; for He shall speak peace to His people, and to His saints, and to those that turn their heart toward Him.

[9] Moreover His salvation is near to them that fear Him; that glory may dwell in our land.

[10] Mercy and truth have met together; righteousness and peace have kissed *each other.*

[11] Truth has sprung out of the earth; and righteousness has looked down from heaven.

[12] For the Lord shall give that which is good; and our land shall yield its fruit.

[13] Righteousness shall go before Him; and shall make His footsteps *our* pathway.

PSALM 86

[1] A Prayer of David.

O Lord, incline Your ear, and hearken to me; for I am poor and needy.

[2] Preserve my soul, for I am holy; save Your servant, O God, who trusts in You.

[3] Pity me, O Lord; for to You will I cry all the day.

[4] Make glad the soul of Your servant; for to You, O Lord, have I lifted up my soul.

[5] For You, O Lord, are kind and gentle, and abundant in mercy to all that call upon You.

[6] Give ear to my prayer, O Lord; and attend to the voice of my supplication.

[7] In the day of my trouble I cried to You; and You heard me.

[8] There is none like You, O Lord, among the gods; and there are no *works* like Your works.

⁹ All nations whom You have made shall come and shall worship before You, O Lord; and shall glorify Your name.

¹⁰ For You are great, and work wondrous things; You alone are the great God.

¹¹ Guide me, O Lord, in Your way, and I will walk in Your truth; let my heart rejoice, that I may fear Your name.

¹² I will give You thanks, O Lord my God, with all my heart; and I will glorify Your name forever.

¹³ For Your mercy is great toward me; and You have delivered my soul from the depths of hell.

¹⁴ O God, transgressors have risen up against me, and an assembly of violent *men* have sought my life; and have not set You before them.

¹⁵ But You, O Lord God, are compassionate and merciful, longsuffering, and abundant in mercy and true.

¹⁶ Look upon me, and have mercy upon me; give Your strength to Your servant, and save the son of Your maidservant.

¹⁷ Show me a sign for good; and let them that hate me see *it* and be ashamed; because You, O Lord, have helped me, and comforted me.

PSALM 87

¹ A Psalm of a Song for the sons of Korah.
His foundations are in the holy mountains.

² The Lord loves the gates of Zion, more than all the tabernacles of Jacob.

³ Glorious things have been spoken of you, O city of God. Selah.

⁴ I will make mention of Rahab and Babylon to them that know me; behold, also the Philistines, and Tyre, and the people of the Ethiopians; these were born there.

⁵ A man shall say, "Zion *is my* mother"; and *such* a man was born in her; and the Highest Himself has founded her.

⁶ The Lord shall recount *it* in the writing of the people, and of these princes that were born in her.

⁷ The dwelling of all within you is *as the dwelling* of those that rejoice.

PSALM 88

¹ A song of a Psalm for the sons of Korah for the end, upon Mahaleth for responsive *strains*, of instruction for Heman the Israelite.
O Lord God of my salvation, I have cried by day and in the night before You.

² Let my prayer come in before You; incline Your ear to my supplication, O Lord.

³ For my soul is filled with troubles, and my life has drawn near to Hades.

⁴ I have been accounted with them that go down to the pit; I became as a man without help;

⁵ free among the dead, as the slain ones cast out, who sleep in the tomb; whom You remember no more; and they are rejected from Your hand.

⁶ They laid me in the lowest pit, in darkness, and in the shadow of death.

⁷ Your wrath has pressed heavily upon me, and You have brought upon me all Your billows. Selah.

⁸ You have removed my acquaintances far from me; they have made me an abomination to themselves; I have been delivered up, and have not gone forth.

⁹ My eyes are dimmed from poverty; but I cried out to You, O Lord, all the day; I spread forth my hands to You.

¹⁰ Will You work wonders for the dead? Or shall physicians raise *them* up, that they shall praise You?

¹¹ Shall anyone declare Your mercy in the grave? And Your truth in destruction?

¹² Shall Your wonders be known in darkness? And Your righteousness in a forgotten land?

¹³ But I cried out to You, O Lord; and in the morning shall my prayer come before You.

¹⁴ Why, O Lord, do You reject my prayer, *and* turn Your face away from me?

¹⁵ I am poor and in troubles from my youth; and having been exalted, I was brought low and into despair.

¹⁶ Your wrath has passed over me; and Your terrors have greatly disquieted me.

¹⁷ They surrounded me like water; all the day they beset me together.

¹⁸ You have put far from me *every* friend, and my acquaintances because of *my* wretchedness.

PSALM 89

¹ *A Psalm* of instruction for Ethan the Israelite.
I will sing of Your mercies, O Lord, forever; I will declare Your truth with my mouth to all generations.

² For You have said, "Mercy shall be built up forever"; Your truth shall be established in the heavens.

³ I made a covenant with My chosen ones, I swore unto David My servant.

⁴ I will establish your descendants forever, and build up your throne to all generations. Selah.

⁵ The heavens shall declare Your wonders, O Lord; and Your truth in the assembly of the saints.

⁶ For who in the heavens shall be compared to the Lord? And who shall be likened to the Lord among the sons of God?

⁷ God is glorified in the council of the saints; great and terrible toward all that are round about Him.

⁸ O Lord God of hosts, who is like You? You are mighty, O Lord, and Your truth is round about You.

⁹ You rule the power of the sea; and You calm the tumult of its waves.

¹⁰ You have brought down the proud as one that is slain; and with the arm of Your power You have scattered Your enemies.

¹¹ The heavens are Yours, and the earth is Yours; You have founded the world, and the fullness of it.

¹² You have created the north and the west; Tabor and Hermon shall rejoice in Your name.

¹³ Yours is the mighty arm; let Your hand be strengthened, let Your right hand be exalted.

¹⁴ Justice and judgment are the establishment of Your throne; mercy and truth shall go before Your face.

¹⁵ Blessed are the people that knows the joyful sound; they shall walk, O Lord, in the light of Your countenance.

¹⁶ And in Your name shall they rejoice all the day; and in Your righteousness shall they be exalted.

¹⁷ For You are the boast of their strength; and in Your good pleasure shall our horn be exalted,

¹⁸ for *our* help is of the Lord; and of the Holy One of Israel, our King.

¹⁹ Then You spoke in a vision to Your children, and said, "I have laid help on a mighty one; I have exalted one chosen out of My people.

²⁰ I have found David My servant; I have anointed him by *My* holy mercy.

²¹ For My hand shall support him; and My arm shall strengthen him.

²² The enemy shall have no advantage against him; and the son of transgression shall not hurt him again.

²³ And I will hew down his foes before him, and put to flight those that hate him.

²⁴ But My truth and My mercy shall be with him; and in My name shall his horn be exalted.

²⁵ And I will set his hand in the sea, and his right hand in the rivers.

²⁶ He shall call upon Me, *saying*, 'You are my Father, my God, and the helper of my salvation.'

²⁷ And I will make him *My* firstborn, higher than the kings of the earth.

²⁸ I will keep My mercy with him forever, and My covenant *shall be* firm with him.

²⁹ And I will establish his descendants forever and ever, and his throne as the days of heaven.

³⁰ If his children should forsake My law, and not walk in My judgments;

³¹ if they should profane My ordinances, and not keep My commandments;

³² I will visit their transgressions with a rod, and their sins with scourges.

³³ But My mercy I will not utterly remove from him, nor wrong My truth.

³⁴ Neither will I by any means profane My covenant; and I will not make void the things that proceed out of My lips.

³⁵ Once have I sworn by My holiness, that I will not lie to David.

³⁶ His descendants shall endure forever, and his throne as the sun before Me;

³⁷ and as the moon *that is* established forever, and as the faithful witness in heaven." Selah.

³⁸ But You have cast off and set at nought, You have rejected Your anointed.

³⁹ You have overthrown the covenant of Your servant; You have profaned his sanctuary, *casting it* to the ground.

⁴⁰ You have broken down all his hedges; You have made his strongholds a terror.

⁴¹ All that go by the way have spoiled him; he has become a reproach to his neighbors.

⁴² You have exalted the right hand of his enemies; You have made all his enemies to rejoice.

⁴³ You have turned back the help of his sword, and have not helped him in the battle.

⁴⁴ You have deprived him of glory; You have broken down his throne to the ground.

⁴⁵ You have shortened the days of his throne; You have poured shame upon him. Selah.

⁴⁶ How long, O Lord? Will You turn away, forever? Shall Your anger flame out like fire?

⁴⁷ Remember what my being is; for have You created all the sons of men in vain?

⁴⁸ What man is there who shall live, and not see death? Shall *anyone* deliver his soul from the hand of Hades? Selah.

⁴⁹ Where are Your ancient mercies, O Lord, which You swore to David in Your truth?

⁵⁰ Remember, O Lord, the reproach of Your servants, which I have borne in my bosom, *even the reproach* of many nations;

⁵¹ with which Your enemies have reviled, O Lord; with which they have reviled the recompense of Your anointed.

⁵² Blessed be the Lord forever. Amen and Amen.

PSALM 90

¹ A Prayer of Moses the man of God. Lord, You have been our refuge in all generations.

² Before the mountains existed, and *before* the earth and the world were formed, even from everlasting to everlasting, You are *God*.

³ Do not turn man back to *his* low place, whereas You said, "Return, you sons of men."

⁴ For a thousand years in Your sight are like yesterday which is past, and like a watch in the night.

⁵ Years shall be vanity to them; let the morning pass away as grass.

⁶ In the morning let it flower, and pass away; in the evening let it droop, let it be withered and dried up.

⁷ For we have perished in Your anger, and in Your wrath we have been troubled.

⁸ You have set our transgressions before You; our age is in the light of Your countenance.

[9] For all our days are gone, and we have passed away in Your wrath; our years have spun out their tale as a spider.

[10] *As for* the days of our years, in them are seventy years; and if *men should be* in strength, eighty years; and the greater part of them would be labor and trouble; for weakness overtakes us, and we shall be chastened.

[11] Who knows the power of Your wrath?

[12] And *who knows how* to number *his days* because of the fear of Your wrath? So manifest Your right hand, and those that are instructed in wisdom in the heart.

[13] Return, O Lord! How long? And have compassion concerning Your servants.

[14] We have been satisfied in the morning with Your mercy; and we did exalt and rejoice;

[15] let us rejoice in all our days, in return for the days in which You afflicted us, the years in which we saw evil.

[16] And look upon Your servants, and upon Your works; and guide their children.

[17] And let the brightness of the Lord our God be upon us; and establish for us the works of our hands.

PSALM 91

[1] Praise of a Song, by David.

He that dwells in the help of the Highest, shall sojourn under the shelter of the God of heaven.

[2] He shall say to the Lord, "You are my helper and my refuge; my God"; I will trust in Him.

[3] For He shall deliver you from the snare of the fowler, from *every* troublesome matter.

[4] He shall overshadow you with His shoulders, and You shall trust under His wings; His truth shall cover you with a shield.

[5] You shall not be afraid of terror by night; nor of the arrow flying by day;

[6] *nor* of the *evil* thing that walks in darkness; *nor* of calamity, and the evil spirit at noonday.

[7] A thousand shall fall at your side, and ten thousand at your right hand; but it shall not come near you.

[8] Only with your eyes shall you observe and see the reward of sinners.

[9] For You, O Lord, are my hope; You, my soul, have made the Most High your refuge.

[10] No evils shall come upon you, and no scourge shall draw near to your dwelling.

[11] For He shall give His angels charge over you, to keep you in all your ways.

[12] They shall bear you up on their hands, lest at any time you dash your foot against a stone.

[13] You shall tread on the asp and basilisk; and you shall trample on the lion and dragon.

[14] For he has hoped in Me, and I will deliver him; I will protect him, because he has known My name.

[15] He shall call upon Me, and I will hearken to him; I am with him in affliction; and I will deliver him, and glorify him.

[16] I will satisfy him with length of days, and show him My salvation.

PSALM 92

[1] A Psalm of a Song for the Sabbath day.

It is a good thing to give thanks to the Lord, and to sing praises to Your name, O Most High;

[2] to proclaim Your mercy in the morning, and Your truth by night,

[3] on a psaltery of ten strings, with a song on the harp.

[4] For You, O Lord, have made me glad with Your work; and in the operations of Your hands will I rejoice.

[5] How have Your works been magnified, O Lord! Your thoughts are very deep.

[6] A foolish man will not know, and a senseless man will not understand this.

[7] When the sinners spring up as the grass, and all the workers of iniquity have watched; *it is* that they may be utterly destroyed forever.

[8] But You, O Lord, are Most High forever.

[9] For behold, Your enemies shall perish; and all the workers of iniquity shall be scattered.

[10] But my horn shall be exalted *as the horn* of a unicorn; and my old age with rich mercy.

[11] And my eye has seen my enemies, and my ear shall hear the wicked that rise up against me.

[12] The righteous shall flourish as a palmtree; he shall be increased as the cedar in Lebanon.

[13] They that are planted in the house of the Lord shall flourish in the courts of our God.

[14] Then shall they be increased in a fine old age; and they shall be prosperous; that they may declare

[15] that the Lord my God is righteous, and there is no iniquity in Him.

PSALM 93

[1] For the day before the Sabbath, when the land was *first* inhabited, the praise of a Song by David.

The Lord reigns; He has clothed Himself with honor; the Lord has clothed and girded Himself with strength; for He has established the world, which shall not be moved.

[2] Your throne is prepared of old; You are from everlasting.

[3] The rivers have lifted up, O Lord, the rivers have lifted up their voices,

[4] at the voices of many waters; the billows of the sea are wonderful; the Lord is wonderful in high places.

[5] Your testimonies are made very sure; holiness becomes Your house, O Lord, forever.

PSALM 94

[1] A Psalm of David for the fourth *day* of the week.

The Lord is a God of vengeance; the God of vengeance has declared Himself.

² Be exalted, You that judge the earth; render a reward to the proud.

³ How long shall sinners, O Lord, how long shall sinners boast?

⁴ They will utter and speak unrighteousness; all the workers of iniquity shall speak *so*.

⁵ They have afflicted Your people, O Lord, and hurt Your heritage.

⁶ They have slain the widow and fatherless, and murdered the stranger.

⁷ And they said, "The Lord shall not see, neither shall the God of Jacob understand."

⁸ Understand now, you simple among the people; and you fools, at length be wise.

⁹ He that planted the ear, does He not hear? Or He that formed the eye, does not He perceive?

¹⁰ He that chastises the heathen, shall He not punish, *even* He that teaches man knowledge?

¹¹ The Lord knows the thoughts of men, that they are vain.

¹² Blessed is the man whom You shall chasten, O Lord, and shall teach him out of Your law;

¹³ to give him rest from evil days, until the pit is dug for the wicked.

¹⁴ For the Lord will not cast off His people, neither will He forsake His inheritance;

¹⁵ until righteousness return to judgment, and all the upright in heart shall follow it. Selah.

¹⁶ Who will rise up for me against the transgressors? Or who will stand up with me against the workers of iniquity?

¹⁷ If the Lord had not helped me, my soul would soon have sojourned in Hades.

¹⁸ If I said, "My foot has been moved";

¹⁹ Your mercy, O Lord, has helped me. O Lord, according to the multitude of my griefs within my heart, Your consolation has soothed my soul.

²⁰ Shall the throne of iniquity have fellowship with You, which frames mischief by an ordinance?

²¹ They will hunt for the soul of the righteous, and condemn innocent blood.

²² But the Lord was my refuge; and my God the helper of my hope.

²³ And He will recompense to them their iniquity and their wickedness; the Lord our God shall utterly destroy them.

PSALM 95

¹ The praise of a Song by David. Come, let us rejoice in the Lord; let us make a joyful noise to God our Savior.

² Let us come before His presence with thanksgiving, and make a joyful noise to Him with psalms.

³ For the Lord is a great God, and a great King over all gods; for the Lord will not cast off His people.

⁴ For the ends of the earth are in His hands; and the heights of the mountains are His.

⁵ For the sea is His, and He made it; and His hands formed the dry land.

⁶ Come, let us worship and fall down before Him, and weep before the Lord that made us.

⁷ For He is our God; and we are the people of His pasture, and the sheep of His hand.

⁸ Today, if you will hear His voice, harden not your hearts, as in the provocation, according to the day of trial in the wilderness;

⁹ where your fathers tested Me, and tried Me, and saw My works.

¹⁰ Forty years was I grieved with this generation, and said, "They do always err in their heart, and they have not known My ways.

¹¹ So I swore in My wrath, They shall not enter into My rest."

PSALM 96

¹ When the house was built after the Captivity, a Song of David.
Sing to the Lord a new song; sing to the Lord, all the earth.

² Sing to the Lord, bless His name; proclaim His salvation from day to day.

³ Proclaim His glory among the Gentiles, His wonderful works among all people.

⁴ For the Lord is great, and greatly to be praised; He is to be feared above all gods.

⁵ For all the gods of the heathen are demons; but the Lord made the heavens.

⁶ Thanksgiving and beauty are before Him; holiness and majesty are in His sanctuary.

⁷ Bring to the Lord, you families of the Gentiles, bring to the Lord glory and honor.

⁸ Bring to the Lord the glory *due* His name; take offerings, and go into His courts.

⁹ Worship the Lord in His holy court; let all the earth tremble before Him.

¹⁰ Say among the heathen, "The Lord reigns"; for He has established the world so that it shall not be moved; He shall judge the people in righteousness.

¹¹ Let the heavens rejoice, and the earth exalt; let the sea be moved, and all its fullness.

¹² The plains shall rejoice, and all things in them; then shall all the trees of the wood exalt before the presence of the Lord;

¹³ for He comes, for He comes to judge the earth; He shall judge the world in righteousness, and the people with His truth.

PSALM 97

¹ For David, when his land was established.
The Lord reigns, let the earth exalt, let many islands rejoice.

2 Clouds and darkness are round about Him; righteousness and judgment are the establishment of His throne.

3 Fire shall go before Him, and burn up His enemies round about.

4 His lightnings light the world; the earth saw, and trembled.

5 The mountains melted like wax at the presence of the Lord, at the presence of the Lord of the whole earth.

6 The heavens have declared His righteousness, and all the people have seen His glory.

7 Let all that worship graven images be ashamed, who boast of their idols; worship Him, all you His angels.

8 Zion heard and rejoiced; and the daughters of Judah rejoiced, because of Your judgments, O Lord.

9 For You are Lord Most High over all the earth; You are greatly exalted above all gods.

10 You that love the Lord, hate evil; the Lord preserves the souls of His saints; He shall deliver them from the hand of sinners.

11 Light has sprung up for the righteous, and gladness for the upright in heart.

12 Rejoice in the Lord, you righteous; and give thanks for a remembrance of His holiness.

PSALM 98

1 A Psalm of David.
Sing to the Lord a new song; for the Lord has done wonderful works, His right hand, and His holy arm, have wrought salvation for Him.

2 The Lord has made known His salvation, He has revealed His righteousness in the sight of the nations.

3 He has remembered His mercy to Jacob, and His truth to the house of Israel; all the ends of the earth have seen the salvation of our God.

4 Shout to God, all the earth! Sing and rejoice, and sing psalms!

5 Sing to the Lord with a harp, and *with* the voice of a psalm.

6 With trumpets, and with the sound of a horn, make a joyful noise to the Lord before the king.

7 Let the sea be moved, and all its fullness; the world, and those that dwell in it.

8 The rivers shall clap their hands together; the mountains shall exalt.

9 For He has come to judge the earth; He shall judge the world in righteousness, and the nations in uprightness.

PSALM 99

1 A Psalm of David.
The Lord reigns; let the people tremble! *It is He* that sits upon the cherubim, let the earth be moved.

2 The Lord is great in Zion, and is high above all the people.

3 Let them give thanks to Your great name; for it is holy, and to be feared!

4 And the king's honor loves judgment; You have prepared equity, You have established judgment and justice in Jacob.

5 Exalt the Lord our God, and worship *at* His footstool; for He is holy.

6 Moses and Aaron among His priests, and Samuel among them that call upon His name; they called upon the Lord, and He heard them.

7 He spoke to them in a pillar of cloud; they kept His testimonies, and the ordinances which He gave them.

8 O Lord our God, You heard them; O God, You became propitious to them, though You took vengeance on all their devices.

9 Exalt the Lord our God, and worship at His holy mountain; for the Lord our God is holy.

PSALM 100

1 A Psalm for Thanksgiving.
Make a joyful noise to the Lord, all the earth.

2 Serve the Lord with gladness; come before His presence with exaltation.

3 Know that the Lord, He is God; He made us, and not we ourselves; *we are* His people, and the sheep of His pasture.

4 Enter into His gates with thanksgiving, and into His courts with praise; give thanks to Him, praise His name.

5 For the Lord is good, His mercy is everlasting; and His truth *endures* from generation to generation.

PSALM 101

1 A Psalm of David.
I will sing to You, O Lord, of mercy and judgment; I will sing a psalm,

2 and I will be wise in a blameless way. When will You come to me? I walked in the innocence of my heart, in the midst of my house.

3 I have not set before my eyes any unlawful thing; I have hated transgressors.

4 A perverse heart has not cleaved to me; I have not known an evil man, forasmuch as he turns away from me.

5 He that secretly speaks against his neighbor have I driven from *me*; he that is proud in look and insatiable in heart— with him I have not eaten.

6 My eyes *shall be* upon the faithful of the land, that they may dwell with me; he that walked in a perfect way, the same ministered to me.

7 He that is proud did not dwell in the midst of my house; the unjust speaker did not prosper in my sight.

8 Early did I slay all the sinners of the land, that I might destroy all that work iniquity out of the city of the Lord.

PSALM 102

1 A Prayer for the Poor; when he is deeply afflicted, and pours out his supplication before the Lord.

Hear my prayer, O Lord, and let my cry come to You.

2 Do not hide Your face from me in the day of my trouble; incline Your ear to me; in the day *when* I shall call upon You, speedily hear me.

3 For my days have vanished like smoke, and my bones have been parched like a stick.

4 I am blighted like grass, and my heart is dried up; for I have forgotten to eat my bread.

5 By reason of the voice of my groaning, my bones has cleaved to my flesh.

6 I have become like a pelican of the wilderness;

7 I have become like an owl in a ruined house. I have watched, and have become as a sparrow dwelling alone on a roof.

8 All the day long my enemies have reproached me; and they that praised me have sworn against me.

9 For I have eaten ashes like bread, and mingled my drink with weeping;

10 because of Your anger and Your wrath; for You have lifted me up, and dashed me down.

11 My days have declined like a shadow; and I am withered like grass.

12 But You, O Lord, endure forever, and Your memorial from generation to generation.

13 You shall arise, and have mercy upon Zion; for *it is* time to have mercy upon her, for the appointed time has come.

14 For Your servants have taken pleasure in her stones, and they shall pity her dust.

15 So the nations shall fear Your name, O Lord, and all kings Your glory.

16 For the Lord shall build up Zion, and shall appear in His glory.

17 He has had regard to the prayer of the lowly, and has not despised their petition.

18 Let this be written for another generation; and the people that shall be created shall praise the Lord.

19 For He has looked out from the height of His sanctuary; the Lord looked upon the earth from heaven;

20 to hear the groaning of the fettered ones, to loosen the sons of the slain;

21 to proclaim the name of the Lord in Zion, and His praise in Jerusalem;

22 when the people have gathered together, and the kings, to serve the Lord.

23 He answered him in the way of His strength; tell me the fewness of my days.

24 Do not take me away in the midst of my days; Your years *are* through all generations.

25 In the beginning You, O Lord, laid the foundation of the earth; and the heavens are the works of Your hands.

26 They shall perish, but You remain; and *they all* shall grow old like a garment; and as a vesture shall You fold them, and they shall be changed.

27 But You are the same, and Your years shall not fail.

28 The children of Your servants shall dwell *securely*, and their descendants shall prosper forever.

PSALM 103

1 *A Psalm* of David.
Bless the Lord, O my soul; and all *that is* within me, *bless* His holy name.

2 Bless the Lord, O my soul, and forget not all His praises;

3 who forgives all your transgressions, who heals all your diseases;

4 who redeems your life from corruption; who crowns you with mercy and compassion;

5 who satisfies your desire with good things; *so that* your youth shall be renewed like *that* of the eagle.

6 The Lord executes mercy and judgment for all that are injured.

7 He made known His ways to Moses, *and* His will to the children of Israel.

8 The Lord is compassionate and gracious, longsuffering, and full of mercy.

9 He will not always be angry; neither will He be wrathful forever.

10 He has not dealt with us according to our sins, nor recompensed us according to our iniquities.

11 For as the heaven is high above the earth, *so* has the Lord increased His mercy toward them that fear Him.

12 As far as the east is from the west, *so far* has He removed our transgressions from us.

13 As a father pities *his* children, the Lord pities them that fear Him.

14 For He knows our frame; *He* remembers that we are dust.

15 *As for* man, his days are like grass; as a flower of the field, so shall he flourish.

16 For the wind passes over it, and it shall not be; and it shall know its place no more.

17 But the mercy of the Lord is from generation to generation upon them that fear Him, and His righteousness to *the* children's children;

18 to them that keep His covenant, and remember His commandments, to do them.

19 The Lord has prepared His throne in the heaven; and His kingdom rules over all.

20 Bless the Lord, all you His angels, mighty in strength, who do His bidding, *ready* to hearken to the voice of His words.

21 Bless the Lord, all you His hosts; *you* ministers of His that do His will.

22 Bless the Lord, all His works, in every place of His dominion; bless the Lord, O my soul.

PSALM 104

1 *A Psalm* of David.

450

Bless the Lord, O my soul. O Lord my God, You are very great; You have clothed Yourself with praise and honor;

2 who cover Yourself with light as with a garment; spreading out the heaven as a curtain.

3 Who covers His chambers with waters; who makes the clouds His chariot; who walks on the wings of the wind.

4 Who makes His angels spirits, and His ministers a flaming fire.

5 Who establishes the earth on her sure foundation; it shall not ever be moved.

6 The deep, like a garment, is His covering; the waters shall stand on the hills.

7 At Your rebuke they shall flee; at the voice of Your thunder they shall be alarmed.

8 They go up to the mountains, and down to the plains, to the place which You founded for them.

9 You have set a boundary which they shall not pass, neither shall they turn again to cover the earth.

10 He sends forth His fountains among the valleys; the waters shall run between the mountains.

11 They shall give drink to all the wild beasts of the field; the wild donkeys shall take *of them* to *quench* their thirst.

12 By them shall the birds of the sky lodge; they shall utter a voice out of the midst of the rocks.

13 He waters the mountains from His chambers; the earth shall be satisfied with the fruit of Your works.

14 He makes grass to grow for the cattle, and green herbs for the service of men, to bring bread out of the earth;

15 and wine makes glad the heart of man, to make his face cheerful with oil; and bread strengthens man's heart.

16 The trees of the plain shall be full of *sap; even* the cedars of Lebanon which He has planted.

17 There the sparrows shall build their nests; and the house of the heron takes the lead among them.

18 The high mountains are a refuge for the goats, *and* the rock for the rabbits.

19 He appointed the moon for seasons; the sun knows its going down.

20 You made the darkness, and it was night; in it all the wild beasts of the forest will be abroad;

21 *even* the young lions roar after their prey, and they seek meat for themselves from God.

22 The sun arises, and they shall be gathered together, and shall lie down in their dens.

23 Man shall go forth to his work, and to his labor till evening.

24 How great are Your works, O Lord! In wisdom have You done them all; the earth is filled with Your creation.

25 *So is* this great and wide sea; there are things creeping innumerable, small animals and great.

26 There go the ships; *and* this dragon whom You have made to play in it.

27 All wait upon You, to give them *their* food in due season.

28 When You have given *it to* them, they will gather *it*; and when You have opened Your hand, they shall all be filled with good.

29 But when You have turned away Your face, they shall be troubled; You will take away their breath, and they shall fail, and return to their dust.

30 You shall send forth Your Spirit, and they shall be created; and You shall renew the face of the earth.

31 Let the glory of the Lord be forever; the Lord shall rejoice in His works;

32 who looks upon the earth, and makes it tremble; who touches the mountains, and they smoke.

33 I will sing to the Lord while I live; I will sing praise to my God while I exist.

34 Let my meditation be sweet to Him, and I will rejoice in the Lord.

35 Let the sinners fail from off the earth, and transgressors, so that they shall be no more. Bless the Lord, O my soul.

PSALM 105

1 Alleluia.
Give thanks to the Lord, and call upon His name; declare His works among the heathen.

2 Sing to Him, yes, sing praises to Him; tell of all His wonderful works.

3 Glory in His holy name; let the heart of them that seek the Lord rejoice.

4 Seek the Lord, and be strengthened; seek His face continually.

5 Remember His wonderful works that He has done; His wonders, and the judgments of His mouth;

6 *you* children of Abraham, His servants, *you* children of Jacob, His elect.

7 He is the Lord our God; His judgments are in all the earth.

8 He has remembered His covenant forever, the word which He commanded for a thousand generations;

9 which He established as a covenant to Abraham, and *He remembered* His oath to Isaac.

10 And He established it to Jacob for an ordinance, and to Israel for an everlasting covenant;

11 saying, "To you will I give the land of Canaan, the line of your inheritance";

12 when they were few in number, very few, and sojourners in it.

13 And they went from nation to nation, and from *one* kingdom to another people.

14 He allowed no man to wrong them; and He rebuked kings for their sakes;

15 *saying*, "Do not touch My anointed ones; and do My prophets no harm."

16 Moreover He called for a famine upon the land; He broke the whole support of bread.

17 He sent a man before them; Joseph was sold for a slave.

18 They hurt his feet with fetters; his soul came into iron,

¹⁹ until the time that his cause came on; the word of the Lord tried him as fire.

²⁰ The king sent and loosed him; *even* the prince of the people, and let him go free.

²¹ He made him master over his house, and ruler of all his substance;

²² to chastise his rulers at his pleasure, and to teach his elders wisdom.

²³ Israel also came into Egypt, and Jacob sojourned in the land of Ham.

²⁴ And He increased His people greatly, and made them stronger than their enemies.

²⁵ And He turned their heart to hate His people, to deal craftily with His servants.

²⁶ He sent forth Moses His servant, *and* Aaron whom He had chosen.

²⁷ He established among them His signs, and *His* wonders in the land of Ham.

²⁸ He sent forth darkness, and made it dark; yet they rebelled against His words.

²⁹ He turned their waters into blood, and slew their fish.

³⁰ Their land produced frogs abundantly, in the chambers of their kings.

³¹ He spoke, and the dog-fly came, and lice in all their coasts.

³² He turned their rain into hail, *and sent* flaming fire in their land.

³³ And He struck their vines and their fig trees; and broke every tree of their coast.

³⁴ He spoke, and the locust came, and caterpillars innumerable,

³⁵ and devoured all the grass in their land, and devoured the fruit of the ground.

³⁶ He also struck every firstborn of their land, the firstfruits of all their labor.

³⁷ And He brought them out with silver and gold; and there was not a feeble one among their tribes.

³⁸ Egypt rejoiced at their departing; for the fear of them fell upon them.

³⁹ He spread out a cloud for a covering to them, and fire to give them light by night.

⁴⁰ They asked, and the quail came, and He satisfied them with the bread of heaven.

⁴¹ He split the rock, and the waters flowed; rivers ran in dry places.

⁴² For He remembered His holy word, which *He promised* to Abraham His servant.

⁴³ And He brought out His people with exaltation, and His elect with joy;

⁴⁴ and He gave them the lands of the heathen; and they inherited the labors of the people;

⁴⁵ that they might keep His ordinances, and diligently seek His law.

PSALM 106

¹ Alleluia.

Give thanks to the Lord, for He is good; for His mercy *endures* forever.

² Who shall tell the mighty acts of the Lord? *Who* shall cause all His praises to be heard?

³ Blessed are they that keep judgment, and do righteousness at all times.

⁴ Remember us, O Lord, with the favor *You have* toward Your people; visit us with Your salvation;

⁵ that we may behold the good of Your elect, that we may rejoice in the gladness of Your nation, that we may glory with Your inheritance.

⁶ We have sinned with our fathers, we have transgressed, we have done unrighteously.

⁷ Our fathers in Egypt did not understand Your wonders, and did not remember the multitude of Your mercy; but provoked *Him* as they went up by the Red Sea.

⁸ Yet He saved them for His name's sake, that He might cause His mighty power to be known.

⁹ And He rebuked the Red Sea, and it was dried up; so He led them through the deep as through the wilderness.

¹⁰ And He saved them out of the hand of them that hated *them*, and redeemed them out of the hand of the enemy.

¹¹ The water covered those that oppressed them; there was not one of them left.

¹² Then they believed His words, and celebrated His praise.

¹³ They made haste, they forgot His works; they did not wait for His counsel.

¹⁴ And they lusted exceedingly in the wilderness, and tempted God in the dry *land*.

¹⁵ And He gave them their request, and sent fullness into their souls.

¹⁶ They provoked Moses also in the camp, and Aaron the holy one of the Lord.

¹⁷ The earth opened and swallowed up Dathan, and closed upon the congregation of Abiram.

¹⁸ And a fire was kindled in their congregation, and a flame burned up the sinners.

¹⁹ And they made a calf in Horeb, and worshipped the graven image,

²⁰ and they changed their glory into the likeness of a calf that feeds on grass.

²¹ They forgot God that saved them, who had done great deeds in Egypt;

²² wondrous *works* in the land of Ham, and awesome things at the Red Sea.

²³ So He said that He would have destroyed them, had not Moses His chosen one stood before Him in the breach, to turn *Him* away from the fierceness of His anger, so that He should not destroy them.

²⁴ Moreover they despised the desirable land, and did not believe His word.

²⁵ And they murmured in their tents; they did not listen to the voice of the Lord.

26 So He lifted up His hand against them, to cast them down in the wilderness;

27 and to cast down their descendants among the nations, and to scatter them in the countries.

28 They were joined also to Baal of Peor, and ate the sacrifices of the dead. And they provoked Him with their deeds;

29 and destruction was multiplied among them.

30 Then Phinehas stood up and made atonement, and the plague ceased.

31 And it was counted to him for righteousness, to all generations forever.

32 They provoked Him also at the Water of Strife, and Moses was hurt for their sakes;

33 for they provoked his spirit, and he spoke *unadvisedly* with his lips.

34 They did not destroy the nations which the Lord told them *to destroy*,

35 but were mingled with the heathen, and learned their works.

36 And they served their graven images; and it became an offense to them.

37 And they sacrificed their sons and their daughters to demons,

38 and shed innocent blood, the blood of their sons and daughters, whom they sacrificed to the idols of Canaan; and the land was defiled with blood,

39 and was polluted with their works; and they went a whoring by their own deeds.

40 So the Lord was very angry with His people, and He abhorred His inheritance.

41 And He delivered them into the hands of *their* enemies; and they that hated them ruled over them.

42 And their enemies oppressed them, and they were brought down under their hands.

43 Many a time He delivered them; but they provoked Him by their counsel, and they were brought low by their iniquities.

44 You the Lord looked upon their affliction, when You heard their petition.

45 And He remembered His covenant, and relented according to the multitude of His mercy.

46 And He caused them to be pitied in the sight of all who carried them captive.

47 Save us, O Lord our God, and gather us from among the heathen, that we may give thanks to Your holy name, that we may glory in Your praise.

48 Blessed be the Lord God of Israel from everlasting to everlasting; and all the people shall say, "Amen, Amen."

PSALM 107

1 Alleluia.

Give thanks to the Lord, for He is good; for His mercy *endures* forever.

2 Let the redeemed of the Lord say *so*, whom He has redeemed from the hand of the enemy;

3 and gathered them out of the countries, from the east, west, north, and south.

4 They wandered in the wilderness in a dry land; they found no way to a city of habitation.

5 Hungry and thirsty, their soul fainted in them.

6 Then they cried to the Lord in their affliction, and He delivered them out of their distresses.

7 And He guided them into a straight path, that they might go to a city of habitation.

8 Let them acknowledge to the Lord His mercies, and His wonderful works to the children of men.

9 For He satisfies the empty soul, and fills the hungry *soul* with good things,

10 *even* them that sit in darkness and the shadow of death, fettered in poverty and irons;

11 because they rebelled against the words of God, and provoked the counsel of the Most High.

12 So their heart was brought low with troubles; they were weak, and there was no helper.

13 Then they cried to the Lord in their affliction, and He saved them out of their distresses.

14 And He brought them out of darkness and the shadow of death, and broke their chains in pieces.

15 Let them acknowledge to the Lord His mercies, and His wonders to the children of men.

16 For He broke to pieces the bronze gates, and crushed the iron bars.

17 He helped them out of the way of their iniquity; for they were brought low because of their iniquities.

18 Their soul abhorred all food; and they drew near to the gates of death.

19 Then they cried to the Lord in their affliction, and He saved them out of their distresses.

20 He sent His word, and healed them, and delivered them out of their destructions.

21 Let them acknowledge to the Lord His mercies, and His wonderful works to the children of men.

22 And let them offer to Him the sacrifice of praise, and proclaim His works with exaltation.

23 They that go down to the sea in ships, doing business in many waters;

24 these have seen the works of the Lord, and His wonders in the deep.

25 He speaks, and the stormy wind arises, and its waves are lifted up.

26 They go up to the heavens, and go down to the depths; their soul melts because of troubles.

27 They are troubled, they stagger as a drunkard, and all their wisdom is swallowed up.

28 Then they cry to the Lord in their affliction, and He brings them out of their distresses.

29 And He commands the storm, and it is calmed into a gentle breeze, and its waves are still.

³⁰ And they are glad, because they are quiet; and He guides them to their desired haven.

³¹ Let them acknowledge to the Lord His mercies, and His wonderful works to the children of men.

³² Let them exalt Him in the congregation of the people, and praise Him in the seat of the elders.

³³ He turns rivers into a desert, and streams of water into a dry land;

³⁴ a fruitful land into saltness, for the wickedness of them that dwell in it.

³⁵ He turns a wilderness into pools of water, and a dry land into streams of water.

³⁶ And there He causes the hungry to dwell, and they establish for themselves cities of habitation.

³⁷ And they sow fields, and plant vineyards, and they yield a fruitful harvest.

³⁸ And He blesses them, and they multiply exceedingly, and He does not diminish the number of their cattle.

³⁹ Again they become few, and are brought low, by the pressure of evils and pain.

⁴⁰ Contempt is poured upon their princes, and He causes them to wander in a desert, and in a trackless land.

⁴¹ But He helps the poor out of poverty, and makes *him* families as a flock.

⁴² The upright shall see and rejoice; and all iniquity shall stop her mouth.

⁴³ Who is wise, and will observe these things, and understand the mercies of the Lord?

PSALM 108

¹ Song of a Psalm by David.
O God, my heart is ready, my heart is ready; I will sing and sing psalms with my glory.

² Awake, psaltery and harp; I will awake early.

³ I will give thanks to You, O Lord, among the people; I will sing praises to You among the Gentiles.

⁴ For Your mercy is great above the heavens, and Your truth *reaches* to the clouds.

⁵ Be exalted, O God, above the heavens; and Your glory above all the earth.

⁶ That Your beloved may be delivered; save with Your right hand, and hear me. God has spoken in His sanctuary.

⁷ I will be exalted, and will divide Shechem, and will measure out the Valley of Tents.

⁸ Gilead is Mine; and Manasseh is Mine; and Ephraim is the helmet for My head; Judah is My king;

⁹ Moab is the caldron of My hope; over Edom will I cast My sandal; the Philistines are made subject to Me.

¹⁰ Who will bring me into the fortified city? Or who will lead me to Edom?

¹¹ Will not You, O God, who have rejected us? And will not You, O God, go forth with our armies?

¹² Give us help from tribulation; for vain is the help of man.

¹³ Through God we shall do valiantly; and He will tread down our enemies.

PSALM 109

¹ For the end, A Psalm of David.
O God, do not pass over my praise in silence;

² for the mouth of the sinner and the mouth of the crafty have been opened against me; they have spoken against me with a crafty tongue.

³ And they have surrounded me with words of hatred; and fought against me without a cause.

⁴ Instead of loving me, they falsely accused me; but I continued to pray.

⁵ And they rewarded me evil for good, and hatred for my love.

⁶ Set a sinner against him; and let an accuser stand at his right hand.

⁷ When he is judged, let him go forth condemned; and let his prayer become sin.

⁸ Let his days be few; and let another take his office of overseer.

⁹ Let his children be orphans, and his wife a widow.

¹⁰ Let his children wander without a dwelling place and beg; let them be cast out of their habitations.

¹¹ Let *his* creditor exact all that belongs to him; and let strangers spoil his labors.

¹² Let him have no helper; neither let there be anyone to have compassion on his fatherless children.

¹³ Let his children be *given up* to utter destruction; in one generation let his name be blotted out.

¹⁴ Let the iniquity of his fathers be remembered before the Lord; and let not the sin of his mother be blotted out.

¹⁵ Let them be before the Lord continually; and let their memorial be blotted out from the earth.

¹⁶ Because he did not remember to show mercy, but persecuted the needy and poor man, *that* he might even slay the broken in heart.

¹⁷ He loved cursing also, and it shall come upon him; and he did not take pleasure in blessing, so it shall be removed far from him.

¹⁸ Yes, he put on cursing as a garment, and it has come as water into his bowels, and as oil into his bones.

¹⁹ Let it be to him as a garment which he puts on, and as a girdle with which he girds himself continually.

²⁰ This is the dealing of the Lord with those who falsely accuse me, and of them that speak evil against my soul.

²¹ But You, O Lord, my Lord, deal *mercifully* with me, for Your name's sake; for Your mercy is good.

²² Deliver me, for I am poor and needy; and my heart is troubled within me.

²³ I am removed as a shadow in its going down; I am tossed up and down like locusts.

²⁴ My knees are weakened through fasting, and my flesh is feeble from lack of fatness.

²⁵ I became also a reproach to them, *when* they saw me they shook their heads.

²⁶ Help me, O Lord my God; and save me according to Your mercy.

²⁷ And let them know that this is Your hand, and *that* You, O Lord, have done it.

²⁸ Let them curse, but You shall bless; let them that rise up against me be ashamed, but let Your servant rejoice.

²⁹ Let those that falsely accuse me be clothed with shame, and let them cover themselves with their shame as with a mantle.

³⁰ I will give thanks to the Lord abundantly with my mouth; and in the midst of many I will praise Him.

³¹ For He stood on the right hand of the poor, to save *me* from them that persecute my soul.

PSALM 110

¹ A Psalm of David.
The Lord said to my Lord, "Sit at My right hand, until I make Your enemies Your footstool."

² The Lord shall send out the rod of Your strength out of Zion; rule in the midst of Your enemies!

³ With You is dominion in the day of Your power, in the splendors of Your saints; I have begotten You from the womb before the morning.

⁴ The Lord has sworn and will not relent, "You are a priest forever, after the order of Melchizedek."

⁵ The Lord at Your right hand has dashed in pieces kings in the day of His wrath.

⁶ He shall judge among the nations, He shall fill up *the number of* corpses, He shall crush the heads of many on the earth.

⁷ He shall drink of the brook in the way; therefore shall He lift up the head.

PSALM 111

¹ Alleluia.
I will give You thanks, O Lord, with my whole heart, in the council of the upright, and *in* the congregation.

² The works of the Lord are great, sought out according to all His will.

³ His work is *worthy of* thanksgiving and honor; and His righteousness endures forever and ever.

⁴ He has caused His wonderful works to be remembered; the Lord is merciful and compassionate.

⁵ He has given food to them that fear Him; He will remember His covenant forever.

⁶ He has declared to His people the power of His works, to give them the inheritance of the heathen.

⁷ The works of His hands are truth and judgment; all His commandments are sure;

⁸ established forever and ever, done in truth and uprightness.

⁹ He sent redemption to His people; He commanded His covenant forever; holy and fearful is His name.

¹⁰ The fear of the Lord is the beginning of wisdom, and all that act accordingly have a good understanding; His praise endures forever and ever.

PSALM 112

¹ Alleluia.
Blessed is the man that fears the Lord; he will delight greatly in His commandments.

² His descendants shall be mighty in the earth; the generation of the upright shall be blessed.

³ Glory and riches shall be in his house; and his righteousness endures forevermore.

⁴ To the upright light has sprung up in darkness; he is pitiful, and merciful, and righteous.

⁵ The good man is he that pities and lends; he will direct his affairs with judgment.

⁶ For he shall not be moved forever; the righteous shall be in everlasting remembrance.

⁷ He shall not be afraid of *any* evil report; his heart is ready to trust in the Lord.

⁸ His heart is established, he shall not fear, till he shall see *his desire* upon his enemies.

⁹ He has dispersed abroad; he has given to the poor; his righteousness endures forever; his horn shall be exalted with honor.

¹⁰ The sinner shall see and be angry, he shall gnash his teeth, and consume away; the desire of the sinner shall perish.

PSALM 113

¹ Alleluia.
Praise the Lord, you servants *of His*, praise the name of the Lord.

² Let the name of the Lord be blessed, now and forevermore.

³ From the rising of the sun to its setting, the name of the Lord is to be praised.

⁴ The Lord is high above all the nations; His glory is above the heavens.

⁵ Who is as the Lord our God? Who dwells in the high places,

⁶ and *yet* looks upon the low things in heaven, and on the earth;

⁷ who lifts up the poor from the earth, and raises up the needy from the dunghill;

⁸ to set him with princes, *even* with the princes of His people;

⁹ who settles the barren *woman* in a house, *as a* mother rejoicing over children.

PSALM 114

¹ Alleluia.

At the going forth of Israel from Egypt, of the house of Jacob from a barbarous people,

² Judah became His sanctuary, *and* Israel His dominion.

³ The sea saw and fled; Jordan was turned back.

⁴ The mountains skipped like rams, and the hills like lambs.

⁵ What *ailed* you, O sea, that you fled? And you, O Jordan, that you were turned back?

⁶ *You* mountains, that you skipped like rams, and *you* hills, like lambs?

⁷ The earth trembled at the presence of the Lord, at the presence of the God of Jacob;

⁸ who turned the rock into pools of water, and the flint into fountains of water.

PSALM 115

¹ Not to us, O Lord, not to us, but to Your name give glory, because of Your mercy and Your truth;

² lest at any time the nations should say, "Where is their God?"

³ But our God has done in heaven and on earth, whatsoever He has pleased.

⁴ The idols of the nations are silver and gold, the works of men's hands.

⁵ They have a mouth, but they cannot speak; they have eyes, but they cannot see;

⁶ they have ears, but they cannot hear; they have noses, but they cannot smell;

⁷ they have hands, but they cannot handle; they have feet, but they cannot walk; they cannot speak through their mouth.

⁸ Let those that make them become like them, and all who trust in them.

⁹ The house of Israel trusts in the Lord; He is their helper and defender.

¹⁰ The house of Aaron trusts in the Lord; He is their helper and defender.

¹¹ They that fear the Lord trust in the Lord; He is their helper and defender.

¹² The Lord has remembered us, and blessed us; He has blessed the house of Israel, He has blessed the house of Aaron.

¹³ He has blessed them that fear the Lord, both small and great.

¹⁴ *May* the Lord add *blessings* to you and to your children.

¹⁵ Blessed are you of the Lord, who made the heaven and the earth.

¹⁶ The heaven of heavens *belongs* to the Lord; but He has given the earth to the sons of men.

¹⁷ The dead shall not praise You, O Lord, nor any that go down to Hades. ¹⁸ But we, the living, will bless the Lord, now and forever.

PSALM 116

¹ Alleluia.

I am well pleased, because the Lord will hearken to the voice of my supplication.

² Because He has inclined His ear to me, therefore will I call upon Him while I live.

³ The pangs of death compassed me; the dangers of hell found me; I found affliction and sorrow.

⁴ Then I called on the name of the Lord—O Lord, deliver my soul.

⁵ The Lord is merciful and righteous; behold, our God has pity.

⁶ The Lord preserves the simple; I was brought low, and He delivered me.

⁷ Return to your rest, O my soul; for the Lord has dealt bountifully with you.

⁸ For He has delivered my soul from death, my eyes from tears, and my feet from falling.

⁹ I shall be well-pleasing before the Lord in the land of the living. Alleluia.

¹⁰ I believed, therefore I have spoken; but I was greatly afflicted.

¹¹ And I said in my amazement, "Every man is a liar."

¹² What shall I render to the Lord for all the things in which He has rewarded me?

¹³ I will take the cup of salvation, and call upon the name of the Lord.

¹⁴ I will pay my vows to the Lord, in the presence of all His people.

¹⁵ Precious in the sight of the Lord is the death of His saints.

¹⁶ O Lord, I am Your servant; I am Your servant, and the son of Your maid; You have burst my bonds.

¹⁷ I will offer to You the sacrifice of praise, and will call upon the name of the Lord.

¹⁸ I will pay my vows unto the Lord, in the presence of all His people,

¹⁹ in the courts of the Lord's house, in the midst of you, O Jerusalem.

PSALM 117

¹ Alleluia.

Praise the Lord, all you nations; praise Him, all you peoples.

² For His mercy has been abundant toward us; and the truth of the Lord endures forever.

PSALM 118

¹ Alleluia.

Give thanks to the Lord; for *He is* good; for His mercy *endures* forever.

² Let now the house of Israel say that *He is* good; for His mercy *endures* forever.

3 Let now the house of Aaron say that *He is* good; for His mercy *endures* forever.

4 Let now all that fear the Lord say that *He is* good; for His mercy *endures* forever.

5 I called on the Lord out of affliction; and He hearkened to me, *and brought me* into a wide place.

6 The Lord is my helper; and I will not fear, what shall man do to me?

7 The Lord is my helper; and I shall see *my desire* upon my enemies.

8 *It is* better to trust in the Lord than to trust in man.

9 *It is* better to hope in the Lord, than to hope in princes.

10 All the nations surrounded me; but in the name of the Lord I repulsed them.

11 They completely compassed me about; but in the name of the Lord I repulsed them.

12 They compassed me about as bees *do* a honeycomb, and they burst into flame as fire among thorns; but in the name of the Lord I repulsed them.

13 I was thrust, and sorely shaken, that I might fall; but the Lord helped me.

14 The Lord is my strength and my song, and has become my salvation.

15 The voice of exaltation and salvation is in the tabernacles of the righteous; the right hand of the Lord has done mightily.

16 The right hand of the Lord has exalted me; the right hand of the Lord has done powerfully.

17 I shall not die, but live, and recount the works of the Lord.

18 The Lord has sorely chastened me; but He has not given me up to death.

19 Open to me the gates of righteousness; I will go into them, and give praise to the Lord.

20 This is the gate of the Lord; the righteous shall enter by it.

21 I will give thanks to You; because You have heard me, and have become my salvation.

22 The stone which the builders rejected has become the chief cornerstone.

23 This was the Lord's doing; and it is marvelous in our eyes.

24 This is the day that the Lord has made; let us exalt and rejoice in it.

25 O Lord, save now; O Lord, send now prosperity.

26 Blessed is he that comes in the name of the Lord; we have blessed you out of the house of the Lord.

27 God is the Lord, and He has shined upon us; celebrate the feast with thick *branches, binding the victims* even to the horns of the altar.

28 You are my God, and I will give You thanks; You are my God, and I will exalt You. I will give thanks to You, for You have heard me, and have become my salvation.

29 Give thanks to the Lord; for He is good; for His mercy *endures* forever!

PSALM 119

1 Alleluia.
Blessed are the blameless in the way, who walk in the law of the Lord.

2 Blessed are they that search out His testimonies; they will diligently seek Him with the whole heart.

3 For they that work iniquity have not walked in His ways.

4 You have commanded *us* diligently to keep Your precepts.

5 O that my ways were directed to keep Your statutes.

6 Then shall I not be ashamed, when I have respect to all Your commandments.

7 I will give You thanks with uprightness of heart, when I have learned the judgments of Your righteousness.

8 I will keep Your statutes; O do not utterly forsake me!

9 How shall a young man direct his way? By keeping Your words.

10 With my whole heart have I diligently sought You; cast me not away from Your commandments.

11 I have hidden Your oracles in my heart, that I might not sin against You.

12 Blessed are You, O Lord; teach me Your statutes.

13 With my lips have I declared all the judgments of Your mouth.

14 I have delighted in the way of Your testimonies, *as much* as in all riches.

15 I will meditate on Your commandments, and consider Your ways.

16 I will meditate on Your statutes; I will not forget Your words.

17 Render a recompense to Your servant; *so* shall I live, and keep Your words.

18 Unveil my eyes, and I shall perceive the wondrous things of Your law.

19 I am a stranger in the earth; do not hide Your commandments from me.

20 My soul has longed exceedingly for Your judgments at all times.

21 You have rebuked the proud; cursed are they that turn aside from Your commandments.

22 Remove from me reproach and contempt; for I have sought out Your testimonies.

23 For princes sat and spoke against me; but Your servant was meditating on Your statutes.

24 For Your testimonies are my meditation, and Your statutes are my counselors.

25 My soul has cleaved to the ground; revive me according to Your word.

26 I declared my ways, and You heard me; teach me Your statutes.

27 Instruct me in the ways of Your statutes; and I will meditate on Your wondrous works.

28 My soul has slumbered for sorrow; strengthen me with Your words.

29 Remove from me the way of iniquity; and be merciful to me by Your law.

30 I have chosen the way of truth; and have not forgotten Your judgments.

31 I have cleaved to Your testimonies, O Lord; do not put me to shame.

32 I ran the way of Your commandments, when You enlarged my heart.

33 Teach me, O Lord, the way of Your statutes, and I will seek it out continually.

34 Instruct me, and I will search out Your law, and will keep it with my whole heart.

35 Guide me in the path of Your commandments; for I have delighted in it.

36 Incline my heart to Your testimonies, and not to covetousness.

37 Turn away my eyes that I may not behold vanity; revive me in Your way.

38 Confirm Your oracle to Your servant, that he may fear You.

39 Take away my reproach which I have feared; for Your judgments are good.

40 Behold, I have desired Your commandments; revive me in Your righteousness.

41 And let Your mercy come upon me, O Lord; *even* Your salvation, according to Your word.

42 And *so* I shall render an answer to them that reproach me; for I have trusted in Your words.

43 And do not take the word of truth utterly out of my mouth; for I have hoped in Your judgments.

44 So shall I keep Your law continually, *even* forever and ever.

45 I walked also at large; for I sought out Your commandments.

46 And I spoke of Your testimonies before kings, and was not ashamed.

47 And I meditated on Your commandments, which I loved exceedingly.

48 And I lifted up my hands to Your commandments which I loved; and I meditated in Your statutes.

49 Remember Your words to Your servant, upon which You have made me hope.

50 This has comforted me in my affliction; for Your word has revived me.

51 The proud have transgressed exceedingly; but I did not swerve from Your law.

52 I remembered Your judgment of old, O Lord; and was comforted.

53 Despair took hold upon me, because of the sinners who forsake Your law.

54 Your statutes were my sons in the place of my sojourning.

55 I remembered Your name, O Lord, in the night, and kept Your law.

56 This I had, because I diligently sought Your statutes.

57 You are my portion, O Lord; I said that I would keep Your law.

58 I sought out Your favor with my whole heart; have mercy upon me according to Your word.

59 I thought on Your ways, and turned my feet to Your testimonies.

60 I prepared myself, (and was not terrified) to keep Your commandments.

61 The snares of sinners entangled me; but I did not forget Your law.

62 At midnight I arose, to give thanks to You for the judgments of Your righteousness.

63 I am a companion of all them that fear You, and of them that keep Your commandments.

64 O Lord, the earth is full of Your mercy; teach me Your statutes.

65 You have wrought kindly with Your servant, O Lord, according to Your word.

66 Teach me kindness, instruction, and knowledge; for I have believed Your commandments.

67 Before I was afflicted, I transgressed; therefore have I kept Your word.

68 Good are You, O Lord; therefore in Your goodness teach me Your statutes.

69 The injustice of the proud has been multiplied against me; but I will search out Your commandments with all my heart.

70 Their heart has been curdled like milk; but I have meditated on Your law.

71 *It is* good for me that You have afflicted me; that I might learn Your statutes.

72 The law of Your mouth is better to me than thousands of *coins of* gold and silver.

73 Your hands have made me, and fashioned me; instruct me, that I may learn Your commandments.

74 They that fear You will see me and rejoice; for I have hoped in Your words.

75 I know, O Lord, that Your judgments are righteousness, and *that* You in truthfulness have afflicted me.

76 Let, I pray, Your mercy be to comfort me, according to Your word to Your servant.

77 Let Your compassions come to me, that I may live; for Your law is my meditation.

78 Let the proud be ashamed; for they transgressed against me unjustly; but I will meditate on Your commandments.

79 Let those that fear You, and those that know Your testimonies, turn to me.

80 Let my heart be blameless regarding Your statutes, that I may not be ashamed.

81 My soul faints for Your salvation; I have hoped in Your words.

82 My eyes failed *from searching* for Your word, saying, "When will You comfort me?"

83 For I have become as a bottle in the frost; *yet* I have not forgotten Your statutes.

[84] How many are the days of Your servant? When will You execute judgment for me on them that persecute me?

[85] Transgressors told me *idle tales*; but not according to Your law, O Lord.

[86] All Your commandments are truth; they persecuted me unjustly; help me!

[87] They nearly made an end of me in the earth; but I did not forsake Your commandments.

[88] Revive me according to Your mercy; so shall I keep the testimonies of Your mouth.

[89] Your word, O Lord, abides in heaven forever.

[90] Your truth *endures* to all generations; You have founded the earth, and it abides.

[91] The day continues by Your arrangement; for all things are Your servants.

[92] Were it not that Your law is my meditation, then I should have perished in my affliction.

[93] I will never forget Your statutes; for with them You have revived me.

[94] I am Yours, save me; for I have sought out Your statutes.

[95] Sinners laid wait for me to destroy me; *but* I understood Your testimonies.

[96] I have seen an end of all perfection; *but* Your commandment is very broad.

[97] How I have loved Your law, O Lord! It is my meditation all the day.

[98] You have made me wiser than my enemies *in* Your commandment; for it is mine forever.

[99] I have more understanding than all my teachers; for Your testimonies are my meditation.

[100] I understand more than the aged; because I have sought out Your commandments.

[101] I have kept back my feet from every evil way, that I might keep Your words.

[102] I have not departed from Your judgments; for You have instructed me.

[103] How sweet are Your oracles to my taste! More so than honey to my mouth!

[104] I gain understanding by Your commandments; therefore I have hated every way of unrighteousness.

[105] Your law is a lamp unto my feet, and a light unto my paths.

[106] I have sworn and determined to keep the judgments of Your righteousness.

[107] I have been very greatly afflicted, O Lord; revive me, according to Your word.

[108] Accept, O Lord, the freewill offerings of my mouth, and teach me Your judgments.

[109] My soul is continually in Your hands; and I have not forgotten Your law.

[110] Sinners spread a snare for me; but I did not err from Your commandments.

[111] I have inherited Your testimonies forever; for they are the joy of my heart.

[112] I have inclined my heart to perform Your statutes forever, in return *for Your mercies*.

[113] I have hated transgressors; but I have loved Your law.

[114] You are my helper and my supporter; I have hoped in Your words.

[115] Depart from me, You evildoers; for I will search out the commandments of my God.

[116] Uphold me according to Your word, and revive me; and make me not ashamed of my hope.

[117] Help me, and I shall be saved; and I will meditate on Your statutes continually.

[118] You have rejected all that depart from Your statutes; for their inner thoughts are unrighteousness.

[119] I have reckoned all the sinners of the earth as transgressors; therefore have I loved Your testimonies.

[120] Penetrate my flesh with Your fear; for I am afraid of Your judgments.

[121] I have done judgment and justice; deliver me not up to them that injure me.

[122] Receive Your servant for good; let not the proud accuse me falsely.

[123] My eyes have failed for Your salvation, and for the word of Your righteousness.

[124] Deal with Your servant according to Your mercy, and teach me Your statutes.

[125] I am Your servant; instruct me, and I shall know Your testimonies.

[126] *It is* time for the Lord to work; they have utterly broken Your law.

[127] Therefore have I loved Your commandments more than gold, or topaz.

[128] Therefore I directed myself *according* to all Your commandments; I have hated every unjust way.

[129] Your testimonies are wonderful; therefore my soul has sought them out.

[130] The manifestation of Your words will enlighten, and instruct the simple.

[131] I opened my mouth, and drew breath; for I earnestly longed after Your commandments.

[132] Look upon me and have mercy upon me, after the manner of them that love Your name.

[133] Order my steps according to Your word; and do not let any iniquity have dominion over me.

[134] Deliver me from the false accusation of men; so will I keep Your commandments.

[135] Cause Your face to shine upon Your servant; and teach me Your statutes. [136] My eyes have been bathed in streams of water, because I did not keep Your law.

[137] Righteous are You, O Lord, and upright are Your judgments.

[138] You have commanded righteousness and perfect truth, *as* Your testimonies.

[139] Your zeal has quite wasted me; because my enemies have forgotten Your words.

[140] Your word *has been* very fully tried; and Your servant loves it.

[141] I am young and despised; *yet* I have not forgotten Your statutes.

[142] Your righteousness is an everlasting righteousness, and Your law is truth.

[143] Afflictions and distresses found me; *but* Your commandments *were* my meditation.

[144] Your testimonies *are* an everlasting righteousness; instruct me, and I shall live.

[145] I cried with my whole heart; hear me, O Lord; I will search out Your statutes.

[146] I cried to You; save me, and I will keep Your testimonies.

[147] I arose before the dawn, and cried; I hoped in Your words.

[148] My eyes prevented the dawn, that I might meditate on Your oracles.

[149] Hear my voice, O Lord, according to Your mercy; revive me according to Your judgment.

[150] They have drawn near who persecuted me unlawfully; and they are far removed from Your law.

[151] You are near, O Lord; and all Your ways are truth.

[152] I have known of old concerning Your testimonies, that You have founded them forever.

[153] Look upon my affliction, and rescue me; for I have not forgotten Your law.

[154] Plead my cause, and ransom me; revive me because of Your word.

[155] Salvation is far from sinners; for they have not searched out Your statutes.

[156] Your mercies, O Lord, are many; revive me according to Your judgment.

[157] Many are they that persecute me and oppress me; *but* I have not declined from Your testimonies.

[158] I beheld men acting foolishly, and I pined away; for they did not keep Your oracles.

[159] Behold, I have loved Your commandments, O Lord; revive me in Your mercy.

[160] The beginning of Your words is truth; and all the judgments of Your righteousness *endure* forever.

[161] Princes persecuted me without a cause, but my heart feared because of Your words.

[162] I will rejoice because of Your oracles, as one that finds much spoil.

[163] I hate and abhor unrighteousness; but I love Your law.

[164] Seven times in a day have I praised You because of the judgments of Your righteousness.

[165] Great peace have they that love Your law; and there is no stumbling block to them.

[166] I have waited for Your salvation, O Lord, and have loved Your commandments.

[167] My soul has kept Your testimonies, and loved them exceedingly.

[168] I have kept Your commandments and Your testimonies; for all my ways are before You, O Lord.

[169] Let my supplication come near before You, O Lord; instruct me according to Your oracle.

[170] Let my petition come in before You, O Lord; deliver me according to Your word.

[171] Let my lips utter a hymn, when You shall have taught me Your statutes.

[172] Let my tongue utter Your oracles; for all Your commandments are righteous.

[173] Let Your hand be *prompt* to save me; for I have chosen Your commandments.

[174] I have longed after Your salvation, O Lord; and Your law is my meditation.

[175] My soul shall live, and shall praise You; and Your judgments shall help me.

[176] I have gone astray like a lost sheep; seek Your servant; for I have not forgotten Your commandments.

PSALM 120

[1] A Song of Degrees.
In my affliction I cried to the Lord, and He listened to me.

[2] Deliver my soul, O Lord, from unjust lips, and from a deceitful tongue.

[3] What should be given to you, and what should be added to you, for *your* crafty tongue?

[4] Sharpened weapons of the mighty, with coals of the desert.

[5] Woe is me, that my sojourning is prolonged; I have dwelled among the tents of Kedar.

[6] My soul has long been a sojourner;

[7] I was peaceable among them that hated peace; when I spoke to them, they warred against me without a cause.

PSALM 121

[1] A Song of Degrees.
I lifted up my eyes to the mountains—from where my help shall come.

[2] My help *shall come* from the Lord, who made the heaven and the earth.

[3] Let not your foot be moved; and let not your keeper slumber.

[4] Behold, He that keeps Israel shall not slumber nor sleep.

[5] The Lord shall keep you: the Lord is your shelter upon your right hand.

[6] The sun shall not burn you by day, neither the moon by night.

[7] May the Lord preserve you from all evil; the Lord shall keep your soul.

[8] The Lord shall keep your coming in, and your going out, from this time forth and forever.

PSALM 122

[1] A Song of Degrees.

I was glad when they said to me, "Let us go into the house of the Lord."

[2] Our feet stood in your courts, O Jerusalem.

[3] Jerusalem is built as a city whose fellowship is complete.

[4] For from there the tribes went up, the tribes of the Lord, as a testimony for Israel, to give thanks unto the name of the Lord.

[5] For there are set thrones for judgment, *even* thrones for the house of David.

[6] Pray now for the peace of Jerusalem: and *let there be* prosperity to them that love you.

[7] Let peace, I pray, be within your host, and prosperity in your palaces.

[8] For the sake of my brothers and my neighbors, I have indeed spoken peace concerning you.

[9] Because of the house of the Lord our God, I have diligently sought your good.

PSALM 123

[1] A Song of Degrees.

Unto You who dwells in heaven have I lifted up my eyes.

[2] Behold, as the eyes of servants *are directed* to the hands of their masters, *and* as the eyes of a maidservant to the hands of her mistress; so our eyes *are directed* to the Lord our God, until He has mercy upon us.

[3] Have pity upon us, O Lord, have pity upon us; for we are exceedingly filled with contempt.

[4] For our soul has been exceedingly filled *with it: let* the reproach *be* to them that are at ease, and contempt to the proud.

PSALM 124

[1] A Song of Degrees.

If it had not been that the Lord was among us, let Israel now say;

[2] if it had not been that the Lord was among us, when men rose up against us;

[3] verily they would have swallowed us up alive, when their wrath was kindled against us:

[4] verily the water would have drowned us, our soul would have gone under the torrent.

[5] Yes, our soul would have gone under the overwhelming water.

[6] Blessed be the Lord, who has not given us for a prey to their teeth.

[7] Our soul has been delivered as a sparrow from the snare of the fowlers: the snare is broken, and we are delivered.

[8] Our help is in the name of the Lord, who made heaven and earth.

PSALM 125

[1] A Song of Degrees.

They that trust in the Lord *shall be* as Mount Zion: he that dwells in Jerusalem shall never be moved.

[2] The mountains are round about her, and *so* the Lord is round about His people, from this time forth and forever.

[3] For the Lord will not allow the rod of sinners to be upon the lot of the righteous; lest the righteous should stretch forth their hands to iniquity.

[4] Do good, O Lord, to them *that are* good, and to them *that are* upright in heart.

[5] But them that turn aside to crooked ways the Lord will lead away with the workers of iniquity; *but* peace *shall be* upon Israel.

PSALM 126

[1] A Song of Degrees.

When the Lord turned the captivity of Zion, we became as those that are comforted.

[2] Then was our mouth filled with joy, and our tongue with exaltation; then would they say among the Gentiles, "The Lord has done great things among them."

[3] The Lord has done great things for us, we became joyful.

[4] Turn, O Lord, our captivity, as the streams in the south.

[5] They that sow in tears shall reap in joy.

[6] They went on and wept as they cast their seeds; but they shall surely come with exaltation, bringing their sheaves *with them*.

PSALM 127

[1] A Song of Degrees.

Except the Lord build the house, they that build labor in vain: except the Lord keep the city, the watchman watches in vain.

[2] It is vain for you to rise early; you rise up after resting, you that eat the bread of grief; while He gives sleep to His beloved.

[3] Behold, the inheritance of the Lord, children, the reward of the fruit of the womb.

[4] As arrows in the hand of a mighty man; so are the children of those who were outcasts.

[5] Blessed is the man who shall satisfy his desire with them; they shall not be ashamed when they shall speak to their enemies in the gates.

PSALM 128

[1] A Song of Degrees.

Blessed are all they that fear the Lord; who walk in His ways.

[2] You shall eat the labors of your hands. Blessed are you, and it shall be well with you.

[3] Your wife shall be as a fruitful vine on the sides of your house; your children as young olive-plants round about your table.

[4] Behold, thus shall the man be blessed that fears the Lord.

[5] May the Lord bless you out of Zion; and may you see the prosperity of Jerusalem all the days of your life.

[6] And may you see your children's children. Peace be upon Israel.

PSALM 129

[1] A Song of Degrees.
Many a time have they warred against me from my youth, let Israel now say:

[2] Many a time have they warred against me from my youth: and yet they did not prevail against me.

[3] The sinners wrought upon my back: they prolonged their iniquity.

[4] The righteous Lord has cut in pieces the necks of sinners.

[5] Let all that hate Zion be put to shame and turned back.

[6] Let them be as the grass of the housetops, which withers before it is plucked up.

[7] Wherewith the reaper does not fill his hand, nor he that makes up the sheaves, his bosom.

[8] Neither do they that go by say, "The blessing of the Lord be upon you; we have blessed you in the name of the Lord."

PSALM 130

[1] A Song of Degrees.
Out of the depths have I cried to You, O Lord.

[2] O Lord, hear my voice; let Your ears be attentive to the voice of my supplication.

[3] If You, O Lord, should mark iniquities, O Lord, who shall stand?

[4] For with You is forgiveness;

[5] for Your name's sake have I waited for You, O Lord, my soul has waited for Your word.

[6] My soul has hoped in the Lord; from the morning watch till night.

[7] Let Israel hope in the Lord: for with the Lord is mercy, and with Him is abundant redemption.

[8] And He shall redeem Israel from all his iniquities.

PSALM 131

[1] A Song of Degrees.
O Lord, my heart is not exalted, neither have my eyes been *haughtily* raised: neither have I exercised myself in great *matters*, nor in things too wonderful for me.

[2] *I shall have sinned* if I have not been humble, but have exalted my soul; according to *the relation of* a weaned child to his mother, so will You recompense my soul.

[3] Let Israel hope in the Lord, from this time forth and forever.

PSALM 132

[1] A Song of Degrees.
Lord, remember David, and all his meekness:

[2] how he swore to the Lord, *and* vowed to the God of Jacob, *saying*,

[3] "I will not go into the tabernacle of my house; I will not go up to the couch of my bed;

[4] I will not give sleep to my eyes, nor slumber to my eyelids, nor rest to my temples,

[5] until I find a place for the Lord, a tabernacle for the God of Jacob."

[6] Behold, we heard of it in Ephratha; we found it in the fields of the wood.

[7] Let us enter into His tabernacles: let us worship at His footstool.

[8] Arise, O Lord, into Your rest; You, and the ark of Your holiness.

[9] Your priests shall clothe themselves with righteousness; and Your saints shall rejoice.

[10] For the sake of Your servant David do not turn away the face of Your Anointed.

[11] The Lord has sworn *in* truth to David, and He will not annul it, *saying*, "Of the fruit of your body will I set *a king* upon your throne.

[12] If your children will keep My covenant, and these My testimonies which I shall teach them, their children also shall sit upon your throne forever."

[13] For the Lord has elected Zion, He has chosen her for a habitation for Himself, *saying*,

[14] "This is My rest forever: here will I dwell; for I have chosen it.

[15] I will surely bless her provision: I will satisfy her poor with bread.

[16] I will clothe her priests with salvation; and her saints shall greatly rejoice.

[17] There will I cause to spring up a horn to David: I have prepared a lamp for My Anointed.

[18] His enemies will I clothe with shame; but upon Himself shall My holiness flourish."

PSALM 133

[1] A Song of Degrees.
See now! What is so good, or what so pleasant, as for brothers to dwell together?

[2] *It is* as ointment on the head, that ran down to the beard, *even* the beard of Aaron; that ran down to the fringe of his clothing.

[3] As the dew of Hermon that comes down on the mountains of Zion; for there, the Lord has commanded the blessing, even life forevermore.

PSALM 134

[1] A Song of Degrees.
Behold now, bless the Lord, all the servants of the Lord, who stand in the house of the Lord, in the courts of the house of our God.
[2] Lift up your hands by night in the sanctuaries, and bless the Lord.
[3] May the Lord, who made heaven and earth, bless you out of Zion.

PSALM 135

[1] Alleluia.
Praise the name of the Lord; praise the Lord, *you His* servants,
[2] who stand in the house of the Lord, in the courts of the house of our God.
[3] Praise the Lord; for the Lord is good: sing praises to His name; for *it is* good.   [4] For the Lord has chosen Jacob for Himself, *and* Israel for His peculiar treasure.
[5] For I know that the Lord is great, and our Lord is above all gods;
[6] all that the Lord willed, He did in heaven, and on the earth, in the sea, and in all the deep.
[7] Who brings up clouds from the extremity of the earth; He has made lightnings for the rain; He brings *the* winds out of His treasures.
[8] Who struck the firstborn of Egypt, both of man and beast.
[9] He sent signs and wonders into the midst of you, O Egypt, on Pharaoh, and on all his servants.
[10] Who struck many nations, and slew mighty kings;
[11] Sihon king of the Amorites, and Og king of Bashan, and all the kingdoms of Canaan,
[12] and gave their land *for* an inheritance, an inheritance to Israel His people.
[13] O Lord, Your name *endures* forever, and Your memorial to all generations.
[14] For the Lord shall judge His people, and comfort Himself concerning His servants.
[15] The idols of the heathen are silver and gold, the works of men's hands.
[16] They have a mouth, but they cannot speak; they have eyes, but they cannot see;
[17] they have ears, but they cannot hear; for there is no breath in their mouth.
[18] Let those who make them be made like them; and all those who trust in them.
[19] O house of Israel, bless the Lord: O house of Aaron, bless the Lord:
[20] O house of Levi, bless the Lord: you that fear the Lord, bless the Lord.
[21] Blessed in Zion is the Lord, who dwells in Jerusalem.

PSALM 136

[1] Alleluia.

Give thanks to the Lord: for He is good: for His mercy *endures* forever.
[2] Give thanks to the God of gods; for His mercy *endures* forever.
[3] Give thanks to the Lord of lords: for His mercy *endures* forever.
[4] To Him who alone has wrought great wonders; for His mercy *endures* forever.
[5] To Him who made the heavens by understanding; for His mercy *endures* forever.
[6] To Him who established the earth on the waters; for His mercy *endures* forever.
[7] To Him who alone made great lights; for His mercy *endures* forever.
[8] The sun to rule by day; for His mercy *endures* forever.
[9] The moon and the stars to rule the night; for His mercy *endures* forever.
[10] To Him who struck Egypt with their firstborn; for His mercy *endures* forever.
[11] And brought Israel out of the midst of them; for His mercy *endures* forever;
[12] with a strong hand, and an outstretched arm; for His mercy *endures* forever.
[13] To Him who parted the Red Sea; for His mercy *endures* forever;
[14] and brought Israel through the midst of it; for His mercy *endures* forever;
[15] and overthrew Pharaoh and his army in the Red Sea; for His mercy *endures* forever.
[16] To Him who led His people through the wilderness; for His mercy *endures* forever.
[17] To Him who struck down great kings; for His mercy *endures* forever;
[18] and slew mighty kings; for His mercy *endures* forever:
[19] Sihon king of the Amorites; for His mercy *endures* forever;
[20] and Og king of Bashan; for His mercy *endures* forever;
[21] and gave their land *for* an inheritance; for His mercy *endures* forever;
[22] even an inheritance to Israel His servant; for His mercy *endures* forever.
[23] For the Lord remembered us in our low estate; for His mercy *endures* forever;
[24] and redeemed us from our enemies; for His mercy *endures* forever.
[25] Who gives food to all flesh; for His mercy *endures* forever.
[26] Give thanks to the God of heaven; for His mercy *endures* forever.

PSALM 137

[1] For David, *A Psalm* of Jeremiah.
By the rivers of Babylon, there we sat; and wept when we remembered Zion.

² We hung our harps on the willows in the midst of it.

³ For there they that had taken us captive asked of us the words of a song; and they that had carried us away *asked* a hymn, *saying*, "Sing us *one* of the songs of Zion."

⁴ How should we sing the Lord's song in a strange land?

⁵ If I forget you, O Jerusalem, let my right hand forget *its skill.*

⁶ May my tongue cleave to my throat, if I do not remember you; if I do not prefer Jerusalem as the chief of my joy.

⁷ Remember, O Lord, the children of Edom in the day of Jerusalem; who said, "Raze *it,* raze *it,* even to its foundations."

⁸ Wretched daughter of Babylon! Blessed *shall he be* who shall reward you as you have rewarded us.

⁹ Blessed *shall he be* who shall seize and dash your infants against the rock.

PSALM 138

¹ A Psalm for David, of Aggaeus and Zacharias.
I will give You thanks, O Lord, with my whole heart; and I will sing psalms to You before the angels; for You have heard all the words of my mouth.

² I will worship toward Your holy temple, and give thanks to Your name, on account of Your mercy and Your truth; for You have magnified Your holy name above all things.

³ In whatsoever day I shall call upon You, hear me speedily; You shall abundantly provide me with Your power in my soul.

⁴ Let all the kings of the earth, O Lord, give thanks unto You; for they have heard all the words of Your mouth.

⁵ And let them sing in the ways of the Lord; for great is the glory of the Lord.

⁶ For the Lord is on high, and *yet* regards the lowly; and He knows high things from afar off.

⁷ Though I should walk in the midst of affliction, You will revive me; You have stretched forth Your hands against the wrath of my enemies, and Your right hand has saved me.

⁸ O Lord, You shall recompense *them* on my behalf: Your mercy, O Lord, *endures* forever: do not overlook the works of Your hands.

PSALM 139

¹ For the end, A Psalm of David.
O Lord, You have proved me, and known me.

² You know my sitting down and my rising up; You understand my thoughts long before.

³ You have traced my path and my bed, and have foreseen all my ways.

⁴ For there is no unrighteous word on my tongue: behold, O Lord, You have known all things,

⁵ the last and the first: You have fashioned me, and laid Your hand upon me.

⁶ The knowledge of You is too wonderful for me; it is very difficult, I cannot *attain* to it.

⁷ Where shall I go from Your Spirit? And to where shall I flee from Your presence?

⁸ If I should go up to heaven, You are there: if I should go down to hell, You are present.

⁹ If I should spread my wings *to fly* straight forward, and sojourn at the extremity of the sea, *it would be vain,*

¹⁰ for even there Your hand would guide me, and Your right hand would hold me.

¹¹ When I said, "Surely the darkness will cover me; even the night *was* light in my luxury."

¹² For darkness will not be darkness with You; but night will be light as day. As its darkness, so shall its light *be to You.*

¹³ For You, O Lord, have possessed my reins; You have helped me from my mother's womb.

¹⁴ I will give You thanks; for You are fearfully wondrous; wondrous are Your works; and my soul knows *it* well.

¹⁵ My bones, which You made in secret, were not hidden from You, nor my substance, in the lowest parts of the earth.

¹⁶ Your eyes saw my unformed *substance,* and all *men* shall be written in Your book; they shall be formed by day, though *there should for a time* be no one among them.

¹⁷ But Your friends, O God, have been greatly honored by me; their rule has been greatly strengthened.

¹⁸ I will number them, and they shall be multiplied beyond the sand; I awake, and am still with You.

¹⁹ Oh that You would slay the wicked, O God. Depart from me, you men of blood!

²⁰ For you will say concerning *their* thoughts, *that* they shall take your cities in vain.

²¹ Have I not hated them, O Lord, that hate You? And *have I not* wasted away because of Your enemies?

²² I have hated them with perfect hatred; they were counted as my enemies.

²³ Prove me, O God, and know my heart; examine me, and know my paths;

²⁴ and see if *there is any* way of iniquity in me, and lead me in an everlasting way.

PSALM 140

¹ For the end, A Psalm of David. Rescue me, O Lord, from the evil man; deliver me from the unjust man.

² Who have devised injustice in their hearts; all the day they prepared war.

³ They have sharpened their tongue as *the tongue* of a serpent; the poison of asps is under their lips. Selah.

⁴ Keep me, O Lord, from the hand of the sinner; rescue me from unjust men; who have purposed to overthrow my goings.

⁵ The proud have hid a snare for me, and have stretched out ropes *for* snares for my feet; they set a stumbling block for me near the path. Selah.

⁶ I said to the Lord, "You are my God"; hearken, O Lord, to the voice of my supplication.

⁷ O Lord God, the strength of my salvation; You have covered my head in the day of battle.

⁸ Deliver me not, O Lord, to the sinner, according to my desire; they have devised *mischief* against me; do not forsake me, lest they should be exalted. Selah.

⁹ *As for* the head of them that surround me, the mischief of their lips shall cover them.

¹⁰ Coals of fire shall fall upon them on the earth; and You shall cast them down in afflictions; they shall not bear up *under them.*

¹¹ A *slandering* man shall not prosper on the earth: evils shall hunt the unrighteous man to destruction.

¹² I know that the Lord will maintain the cause of the poor, and the right of the needy ones.

¹³ Surely the righteous shall give thanks to Your name: the upright shall dwell in Your presence.

PSALM 141

¹ A Psalm of David.
O Lord, I have cried to You; hear me: attend to the voice of my supplication, when I cry to You.

² Let my prayer be set forth before You as incense; the lifting up of my hands *as* an evening sacrifice.

³ Set a watch, O Lord, on my mouth, and a strong door about by lips.

⁴ Do not incline my heart to evil things, to employ pretexts for sins, with men who work iniquity: and let me not unite with their choice ones.

⁵ The righteous shall chasten me with mercy, and reprove me: but let not the oil of the sinner anoint my head: for yet shall my prayer also be in their pleasures.

⁶ Their mighty ones have been swallowed up near the rock: they shall hear my words, for they are sweet.

⁷ As a lump of earth is crushed upon the ground, our bones have been scattered by the *mouth of* the grave.

⁸ For my eyes are upon You, O Lord God: I have hoped in You; do not take my life away.

⁹ Keep me from the snare which they have set for me, and from the stumbling blocks of them that work iniquity.

¹⁰ Sinners shall fall by their own net: I am alone until I shall escape.

PSALM 142

¹ *A Psalm* of instruction for David, when he was in the cave—A Prayer.
I cried to the Lord with my voice; with my voice I made supplication to the Lord.

² I will pour out my supplication before Him. I will declare before Him my affliction.

³ When my spirit was fainting within me, then You knew my paths; in the very way in which I was walking, they hid a snare for me.

⁴ I looked on *my* right hand, and behold, for there was none that noticed me; refuge failed me; and there was none that cared for my soul.

⁵ I cried unto You, O Lord, and said, "You are my hope, my portion in the land of the living."

⁶ Attend to my supplication, for I am brought very low; deliver me from them that persecute me; for they are stronger than I.

⁷ Bring my soul out of prison, that I may give thanks to Your name, O Lord; the righteous shall wait for me, until You recompense me.

PSALM 143

¹ A Psalm of David, when his son pursued him.
O Lord, attend to my prayer; hearken to my supplication in Your truth; hear me in Your righteousness.

² And do not enter into judgment with Your servant, for in Your sight shall no *man* living be justified.

³ For the enemy has persecuted my soul; he has brought my life down to the ground; he has made me to dwell in a dark *place*, as those that have been long dead.

⁴ Therefore my spirit was grieved in me; my heart was troubled within me.

⁵ I remembered the days of old; and I meditated on all Your doings: *yes*, I meditated on the works of Your hands.

⁶ I spread forth my hands to You; my soul *thirsts* for You, as a dry land. Selah.

⁷ Hear me speedily, O Lord; my spirit has failed; do not hide Your face from me, lest I be like them that go down to the pit.

⁸ Cause me to hear Your mercy in the morning; for I have hoped in You; make known to me, O Lord, the way in which I should walk; for I have lifted up my soul to You.

⁹ Deliver me from my enemies, O Lord; for I have fled to You for refuge.

¹⁰ Teach me to do Your will; for You are my God; Your good Spirit shall guide me in the straight *way*.

¹¹ You shall revive me, O Lord, for Your name's sake; in Your righteousness You shall bring my soul out of affliction.

¹² And in Your mercy You will destroy my enemies, and will destroy all those that afflict my soul; for I am Your servant.

PSALM 144

¹ *A Psalm* of David concerning Goliath. Blessed *be* the Lord my God, who instructs my hands for battle, *and* my fingers for war.

² My mercy, and my refuge; my helper, and my deliverer; my protector, in whom I have trusted; who subdues my people under me.

[3] Lord, what is man, that You are made known to him? Or the son of man, that You take account of him?

[4] Man is likened unto vanity: his days pass as a shadow.

[5] O Lord, bow Your heavens, and come down: touch the mountains, and they shall smoke.

[6] Send lightning, and You shall scatter them: send forth Your arrows, and You shall discomfit them.

[7] Send forth Your hand from on high; rescue me, and deliver me out of great waters, out of the hand of strange children;

[8] whose mouth has spoken vanity, and their right hand is a right hand of iniquity.

[9] O God, I will sing a new song to You: I will play to You on an instrument of ten strings.

[10] *Even* to Him who gives salvation to kings: who redeems His servant David from the hurtful sword.

[11] Deliver me, and rescue me from the hand of strange children, whose mouth has spoken vanity, and their right hand is a right hand of iniquity:

[12] whose children are as plants, strengthened in their youth: their daughters are beautiful, sumptuously adorned after the likeness of a temple.

[13] Their garners are full, and bursting with one kind of store after another; their sheep are prolific, multiplying in their streets.

[14] Their oxen are fat: there is no falling down of a hedge, nor going out, nor cry in their folds.

[15] Men bless the people to whom this lot belongs, *but* blessed are the people whose God is the Lord.

PSALM 145

[1] David's *Psalm of* praise.
I will exalt You, my God, my king; and I will bless Your name forever and ever.

[2] Every day will I bless You, and I will praise Your name forever and ever.

[3] The Lord is great, and greatly to be praised; and there is no end to His greatness.

[4] Generation after generation shall praise Your works, and tell of Your power.

[5] And they shall speak of the glorious majesty of Your holiness, and recount Your wonders.

[6] And they shall speak of the power of Your awesome *acts*; and recount of Your greatness.

[7] They shall utter the memory of the abundance of Your goodness, and shall exalt in Your righteousness.

[8] The Lord is compassionate, and merciful; long suffering, and abundant in mercy.

[9] The Lord is good to those that wait *on Him*; and His compassions are over all His works.

[10] Let all Your works, O Lord, give thanks to You; and let Your saints bless You.

[11] They shall speak of the glory of Your kingdom, and talk of Your dominion;

[12] to make known to the sons of men Your power, and the glorious majesty of Your kingdom.

[13] Your kingdom is an everlasting kingdom, and Your dominion *endures* throughout all generations. The Lord is faithful in His words, and holy in all His works.

[14] The Lord supports all that are falling, and sets up all that are broken down.

[15] The eyes of all wait upon You; and You give *them* their food in due season.

[16] You open Your hands, and fill every living thing with pleasure.

[17] The Lord is righteous in all His ways, and holy in all His works.

[18] The Lord is near to all that call upon Him, to all that call upon Him in truth.

[19] He will perform the desire of them that fear Him: and He will hear their supplication, and save them.

[20] The Lord preserves all that love Him: but all sinners He will utterly destroy.

[21] My mouth shall speak the praise of the Lord: and let all flesh bless His holy name forever and ever.

PSALM 146

[1] Alleluia, *A Psalm* of Aggaeus and Zacharias.
Praise the Lord, O my soul!.

[2] While I live will I praise the Lord: I will sing praises to my God as long as I exist.

[3] Trust not in princes, nor in the children of men, in whom there is no safety.

[4] His breath shall go forth, and he shall return to his earth; in that day all his thoughts shall perish.

[5] Blessed is he whose helper is the God of Jacob, whose hope is in the Lord his God:

[6] who made heaven, and earth, and the sea, and all things in them; who keeps truth forever;

[7] who executes judgment for the wronged: who gives food to the hungry. The Lord looses the fettered ones.

[8] The Lord gives wisdom to the blind; the Lord sets up the broken down; the Lord loves the righteous; the Lord preserves the strangers;

[9] He will relieve the orphan and widow: but will utterly remove the way of sinners.

[10] The Lord shall reign forever, *even* your God, O Zion, to all generations.

PSALM 147

[1] Alleluia, *A Psalm* of Aggaeus and Zacharias.
Praise the Lord! For singing psalms is a good thing; let praise be sweetly sung to our God.

[2] The Lord builds up Jerusalem; and He will gather together the dispersed of Israel.

[3] He heals the brokenhearted, and binds up their wounds.

[4] He numbers the multitudes of stars; and calls them all by name.

[5] Great is our Lord, and great is His strength; and His understanding is infinite.

[6] The Lord lifts up the meek; but brings sinners down to the ground.

[7] Begin *the song* with thanksgiving to the Lord; sing praises on the harp to our God;

[8] who covers the heaven with clouds, who prepares rain for the earth, who causes grass to spring up on the mountains, *and green herb for the service of men*;

[9] and gives cattle their food, and to the young ravens that call upon Him.

[10] He will not take pleasure in the strength of a horse; neither is He well-pleased with the legs of a man.

[11] The Lord takes pleasure in them that fear Him, and in all that hope in His mercy.

[12] Praise the Lord, O Jerusalem; praise your God, O Zion.

[13] For He has strengthened the bars of your gates; He has blessed your children within you.

[14] He makes your borders peaceful, and fills you with the flour of wheat.

[15] He sends His oracle to the earth; His word will run swiftly.

[16] He gives snow like wool; He scatters the mist like ashes.

[17] Casting *forth* His ice like morsels; who shall stand before His cold?

[18] He shall send out His word, and melt them; He shall blow *with* His wind, and the waters shall flow.

[19] He sends His word to Jacob, His ordinances and judgments to Israel.

[20] He has not done so to any *other* nation; and He has not shown them His judgments.

PSALM 148

[1] Alleluia, *A Psalm* of Aggaeus and Zacharias.
Praise the Lord from the heavens; praise Him in the highest.

[2] Praise Him, all His angels: praise Him, all His hosts.

[3] Praise Him, sun and moon; praise Him, all you stars and light.

[4] Praise Him, you heavens of heavens, and the water that is above the heavens.

[5] Let them praise the name of the Lord; for He spoke, and they were made; He commanded, and they were created.

[6] He has established them forever, even forever and ever; He has made an ordinance, and it shall not pass away.

[7] Praise the Lord from the earth, you serpents, and all the depths.

[8] Fire, hail, snow, ice, and stormy wind; the things that perform His word.

[9] Mountains, and all hills; fruitful trees, and all cedars;

[10] wild beasts, and all cattle; reptiles, and winged birds;

[11] kings of the earth, and all peoples; princes, and all judges of the earth;

[12] young men and virgins, old men with youths;

[13] let them praise the name of the Lord, for His name alone is exalted; His praise is above the earth and heaven,

[14] and He shall exalt the horn of His people, *there is* a hymn for all His saints, *even* of the children of Israel, a people who draw near to Him.

PSALM 149

[1] Alleluia.
Sing to the Lord a new song; His praise is in the assembly of the saints.

[2] Let Israel rejoice in Him that made him; and let the children of Zion exalt in their King.

[3] Let them praise His name in the dance; let them sings praises to Him with timbrel and psaltery.

[4] For the Lord takes pleasure in His people; and will exalt the meek with salvation.

[5] The saints shall rejoice in glory; and shall exalt on their beds.

[6] The high praises of God shall be in their mouth, and two-edged swords in their hands;

[7] to execute vengeance on the nations, *and* punishments among the peoples;

[8] to bind their kings with fetters, and their nobles with manacles of iron; to execute on them the judgment written: this honor have all His saints.

PSALM 150

[1] Alleluia.
Praise God in His holy places; praise Him in the firmament of His power.

[2] Praise Him on *account of* His mighty acts; praise Him according to His abundant greatness.

[3] Praise Him with the sound of a trumpet; praise Him with psaltery and harp.

[4] Praise Him with timbrel and dance; praise Him with stringed instruments and the organ.

[5] Praise Him with melodious cymbals; praise Him with loud cymbals.

[6] Let everything that has breath praise the Lord.

PSALM 151

[1] *This Psalm is a genuine one of David, though supernumerary, composed when he fought in single combat with Goliath.*
I was small among my brothers, and youngest in my father's house: I tended my father's sheep.

[2] My hands formed a musical instrument, and my fingers tuned a psaltery.

[3] And who shall tell my Lord? The Lord Himself, He Himself hears.

4 He sent forth His angel, and took me from my father's sheep, and He anointed me with the oil of His anointing.

5 My brothers were handsome and tall; but the Lord did not take pleasure in them.

6 I went forth to meet the Philistine; and he cursed me by his idols.

7 But I drew his own sword, and beheaded him, and removed the reproach from the children of Israel.

THE BOOK OF PROVERBS

1 The Proverbs of Solomon son of David, who reigned in Israel:

2 to know wisdom and instruction, and to perceive words of understanding;

3 to receive also hard sayings, and to understand true justice, and how to direct judgment;

4 that he might give prudence to the simple, and to the young man discernment and understanding.

5 For by the hearing of these a wise man will be wiser, and a man of understanding will gain direction;

6 and will understand a parable, and an enigma; the saying of the wise also, and riddles.

7 The fear of the Lord is the beginning of wisdom; and *there is* good understanding to all that practice it: and godliness toward God is the beginning of discernment; but the ungodly will nullify wisdom and instruction.

8 Hear, my son, the instruction of your father, and do not reject the rules of your mother.

9 For you shall receive a crown of grace for your head, and a chain of gold around your neck.

10 *My* son, let not ungodly men lead you astray, neither shall you consent *to them.*

11 If they should exhort you, saying, "Come with us, partake in blood, and let us unjustly hide the just man in the earth:

12 and let us swallow him alive, as Hades would, and remove the memorial of him from the earth:

13 let us seize on his valuable property, and let us fill our houses with spoils:

14 but cast in your lot with us, and let us all provide a common purse, and let us have one pouch";

15 do not go in the way with them, let your foot turn aside from their paths;

16 (This verse omitted in LXX)

17 for nets are not spread for *the* birds without cause.

18 For they that are concerned in murder store up evils for themselves; and the overthrow of transgressors is evil.

19 These are the ways of all that perform lawless deeds; for by ungodliness they destroy their own life.

20 Wisdom sings aloud in passages, and in the broad places speaks boldly.

21 And she makes proclamation on the top of the walls, and sits by the gates of princes; and at the gates of the city boldly says,

22 So long as the simple cleave to justice, they shall not be ashamed: but the foolish being lovers of haughtiness, having become ungodly have hated knowledge, and have become subject to reproofs.

23 Behold, I will bring forth to you the utterance of my breath, and I will instruct you in my speech.

24 Since I called, and you did not hear, and I spoke at length, and you gave no heed;

25 but you disdained my counsels, and disregarded my reproofs;

26 therefore I also will laugh at your destruction; and I will rejoice against you when ruin comes upon you:

27 yes, when dismay suddenly comes upon you, and your overthrow shall arrive like a tempest; and when tribulation and distress shall come upon you, or when ruin shall come upon you.

28 For it shall be that when you call upon me, I will not listen to you: wicked men shall seek me, but shall not find me.

29 For they hated wisdom, and did not choose the word of the Lord:

30 neither would they attend to my counsels, but derided my reproofs.

31 Therefore shall they eat the fruits of their own way, and shall be filled with their own ungodliness.

32 For because they wronged the simple, they shall be slain; and an inquisition shall ruin the ungodly.

33 But he that listens to me shall dwell in confidence, and shall rest securely from all evil.

PROVERBS 2

1 *My* son, if you will receive the utterance of my commandment, and hide it within you;

2 your ear shall hearken to wisdom; you shall also apply your heart to understanding, and shall apply it to the instruction of your son.

3 For if you shall call to wisdom, and utter your voice for understanding;

4 and if you shall seek it as silver, and search diligently for it as for treasures;

5 then shall you understand the fear of the Lord, and find the knowledge of God.

6 For the Lord gives wisdom, and from His presence come knowledge and understanding,

7 and He treasures up salvation for them that walk uprightly: He will protect their way;

8 that He may guard the righteous ways: and He will preserve the way of them that fear Him.

9 Then shall you understand righteousness and judgment, equity *and* every good path.

10 For if wisdom shall come into your understanding, and discernment shall seem pleasing to your soul,

11 *then* good counsel shall guard you, and holy understanding shall keep you;

¹² to deliver you from the evil way, and from the man that speaks nothing faithfully.

¹³ Alas *for those* who forsake right paths, to walk in ways of darkness;

¹⁴ who rejoice in evils, and delight in wicked perverseness;

¹⁵ whose paths are crooked, and their courses winding;

¹⁶ to remove you far from the straight way, and to estrange you from a righteous purpose. *My* son, let not evil counsel overtake you,

¹⁷ *of her* who has forsaken the instruction of her youth, and has forgotten the covenant of God.

¹⁸ For she has fixed her house near death, and guided her wheels near Hades with the giants.

¹⁹ None that go by her shall return, neither shall they take hold of right paths, for they have not apprehended of the years of life.

²⁰ For had they gone in good paths, they would have easily found the paths of righteousness.

²¹ For the upright shall dwell in the earth, and the holy shall be left behind in it.

²² The paths of the ungodly shall perish out of the earth, and transgressors shall be driven away from it.

PROVERBS 3

¹ *My* son, forget not my laws, but let your heart keep my words:

² for length of days, and years of life, and peace, shall they add to you.

³ Let not mercy and truth forsake you; but bind them about your neck:

⁴ so shall you find favor; and provide things honest in the sight of the Lord, and of men.

⁵ Trust in God with all your heart; and be not exalted in your own wisdom.

⁶ In all your ways acquaint yourself with her, that she may rightly direct your paths.

⁷ Do not be wise in your own conceit; but fear God, and depart from all evil.

⁸ Then shall there be health to your body, and good keeping to your bones.

⁹ Honor the Lord with your just labors, and give Him the firstfruits of your righteousness,

¹⁰ that your storehouses may be completely filled with grain, and that your presses may burst forth with wine.

¹¹ *My* son, do not despise the chastening of the Lord, nor faint when you are rebuked by Him:

¹² for whom the Lord loves He rebukes, and scourges every son whom He receives.

¹³ Blessed is the man who has found wisdom, and the mortal who knows prudence.

¹⁴ For it is better to traffic for her, than for treasures of gold and silver.

¹⁵ And she is more valuable than precious stones: no evil thing shall resist her. She is well known to all that approach her, and no precious thing is equal to her in value.

¹⁶ For length of days and years of life are in her right hand, and in her left hand are wealth and glory.

Out of her mouth proceeds righteousness, and she carries law and mercy upon her tongue.

¹⁷ Her ways are good ways, and all her paths are peaceful.

¹⁸ She is a tree of life to all that lay hold of her, and she is a secure help to all that stay themselves on her, as on the Lord.

¹⁹ God by wisdom founded the earth, and by understanding He prepared the heavens.

²⁰ By His knowledge were the depths broken up, and the clouds dropped water.

²¹ *My* son, let *them* not pass from *you*, but keep my counsel and understanding:

²² that your soul may live, and that there may be grace around your neck; and it shall be health to your flesh, and safety to your bones:

²³ that you may go confidently in peace in all your ways, and that your foot may not stumble.

²⁴ For if you rest, you shall not be afraid; and if you sleep, you shall slumber sweetly.

²⁵ And you shall not be afraid of alarm coming upon you, neither of approaching attacks of ungodly men.

²⁶ For the Lord shall be over all your ways, and He shall establish your foot, that you not be moved.

²⁷ Do not refrain from doing good to the poor, whenever your hand may have power to help *them*.

²⁸ Do not say, "Come back another time, tomorrow I will give"; while you are able *today* to do *him* good; for you know not what the next day will bring forth.

²⁹ Do not devise evil against your friend, living near you and trusting in you.

³⁰ Do not quarrel with a man without a cause, lest he do you some harm.

³¹ Do not procure the reproaches of bad men, neither shall you covet their ways.

³² For every transgressor is unclean before the Lord, neither does he sit among the righteous.

³³ The curse of God is in the houses of the ungodly, but the habitations of the just are blessed.

³⁴ The Lord resists the proud, but He gives grace to the humble.

³⁵ The wise shall inherit glory, but the ungodly have exalted *their own* dishonor.

PROVERBS 4

¹ Hear, my children, the instruction of a father, and give attention to know understanding.

² For I give you a good gift; do not forsake my law.

³ For I also was a son obedient to my father, and loved in the sight of my mother:

[4] who spoke and instructed me, *saying*, "Let our speech be fixed in your heart, keep our commandments, do not forget them:

[5] and do not neglect the speech of my mouth.

[6] And do not forsake it, and it shall cleave to you: love it, and it shall keep you.

[7] (This verse omitted in LXX)

[8] "Secure it, and it shall exalt you: honor it, that it may embrace you;

[9] that it may give unto your head a crown of grace, and may cover you with a crown of delight."

[10] Hear, *my* son, and receive my words, and the years of your life shall be increased, that the resources of your life may be many.

[11] For I teach you the ways of wisdom; and I cause you to go in right paths.

[12] For when you go, your steps shall not be hindered; and when you run, you shall not be distressed.

[13] Take hold of my instruction; do not let it go, but keep it for yourself, for your life.

[14] Do not go in the ways of the ungodly, neither covet the ways of transgressors.

[15] In whatever place they shall pitch their camp, do not go there; but turn from them, and pass away.

[16] For they cannot sleep, unless they have done evil: their sleep is taken away, and they do not rest.

[17] For these live upon the bread of ungodliness, and are drunken with *the* wine of transgression.

[18] But the ways of the righteous shine like light; they go forth and shine, until the day has fully come.

[19] But the ways of the ungodly are like darkness; they do not know how they stumble.

[20] *My* son, attend to my speech, and incline your ear to my words,

[21] that your fountains may not fail you; keep them in *your* heart.

[22] For they are life to those that find them, and health to all *their* flesh.

[23] Keep your heart with the utmost care, for out of these are the issues of life.

[24] Remove from yourself a deceitful mouth, and put unjust lips far away from yourself.

[25] Let your eyes look right on, and let your eyelids assent *to* just *things*.

[26] Make straight paths for your feet, and order your ways rightly.

[27] Do not turn aside to the right hand, nor to the left, but turn away your foot from an evil way:

for God knows the ways on the right hand, but those on the left are crooked:

and He will make your ways straight, and will guide your steps in peace.

PROVERBS 5

[1] *My* son, attend to my wisdom, and incline your ear to my words;

[2] that you may keep good understanding, and the discretion of my lips gives you a charge. Pay no attention to a worthless woman,

[3] for honey drops from the lips of a harlot, who for a season pleases your palate;

[4] but afterwards you will find her more bitter than gall, and sharper than a two-edged sword.

[5] For the feet of folly lead those who deal with her down to the grave with death, and her steps are not established.

[6] For she does not travel upon the paths of life; but her ways are slippery, and not easily known.

[7] Now then *my* son, hear me, and do not make my words of no effect.

[8] Remove your way far from her; do not draw near to the doors of her house:

[9] lest you give away your life to others, and your substance to the merciless;

[10] lest strangers be filled with your strength, and your labors come into the houses of strangers;

[11] And you repent at last, when the flesh of your body is consumed,

[12] and you shall say, "How have I hated instruction, and my heart avoided reproofs!

[13] I did not hear the voice of him that instructed me, and taught me, neither did I incline my ear.

[14] I was almost in all evil in the midst of the congregation and assembly."

[15] Drink waters out of your own vessels, and out of your own springing wells.

[16] Do not let waters out of your fountain be spilled by you, but let your waters go into your streets.

[17] Let them be yours alone, and let no stranger partake with you.

[18] Let your fountain of water be *truly* your own, and rejoice with the wife of your youth.

[19] Let *your* loving deer and your graceful colt company with you, and let her be considered your own, and be with you at all times, for ravished with her love you shall be greatly increased.

[20] Do not be intimate with a strange woman, neither fold yourself in the arms of a woman not your own.

[21] For the ways of a man are before the eyes of God, and He looks on all his paths.

[22] Iniquities ensnare a man, and everyone is bound in the chains of his own sins.

[23] Such a man dies with the uninstructed, and he is cast forth from the abundance of his own substance, and has perished through folly.

PROVERBS 6

[1] *My* son, if you become surety for your friend, you shall deliver your hand to an enemy.

2 For a man's own lips become a strong snare to him, and he is caught with the lips of his own mouth.

3 *My* son, do what I command you, and deliver yourself; for on your friend's account you have come into the power of evil men: Do not faint, but stir up even your friend for whom you have become surety.

4 Do not give sleep to your eyes, nor slumber with your eyelids;

5 that you may deliver yourself as a doe out of the toils, and as a bird out of a snare.

6 Go to the ant, O sluggard; and see, and emulate his ways, and become wiser than he.

7 For whereas he has no leader, nor anyone to compel him, and is under no master,

8 he prepares food for himself in the summer, and lays up abundant supplies in harvest.
Or go to the bee, and learn how diligent she is, and how earnestly she is engaged in her work;
whose labors kings and private men use for health, and she is desired and respected by all:
though weak in body, she is advanced by honoring wisdom.

9 How long will you lie, O sluggard? And when will you awake out of sleep?

10 You sleep a little, and you rest a little, and you slumber a short time, and you fold your arms over your breast a little.

11 Then poverty comes upon you as an evil traveler, and your need as a swift courier.
But if you be diligent, your harvest shall arrive as a fountain, and poverty shall flee away as a bad courier.

12 A foolish man and a transgressor goes in ways that are not good.

13 And the same winks with the eye, and makes a sign with his foot, and teaches with the beckonings of his fingers.

14 *His* perverse heart devises evils: at all times such a one causes troubles to a city.

15 Therefore his destruction shall come suddenly, overthrow and irretrievable ruin.

16 For he rejoices in all things which God hates, and he is ruined by reason of impurity of soul.

17 The eye of the haughty, an unjust tongue, hands shedding innocent blood,

18 a heart devising evil thoughts, and feet hastening to do evil, *are hateful to God*.

19 An unjust witness kindles falsehoods, and brings on quarrels between brothers.

20 *My* son, keep the laws of your father, and do not reject the ordinances of your mother:

21 but bind them upon your soul continually, and hang them as a chain about your neck.

22 Whenever you walk, lead this along and let it be with you, that it may talk with you when you wake.

23 For the commandment of the law is a lamp and a light; a way of life; reproof also and correction:

24 to keep you continually from a married woman, and from the flattery of a strange tongue.

25 Let not the desire of beauty overcome you, neither be caught by her eyes, or captivated with her eyelids.

26 For the value of a harlot is as much as of one loaf of bread, and a woman hunts for the precious souls of men.

27 Shall anyone bind fire in his bosom, and not burn his garments?

28 Or will anyone walk on coals of fire, and not burn his feet?

29 So is he that goes in to a married woman; he shall not be held guiltless, neither anyone that touches her.

30 It is not to be wondered at if one should be caught stealing, for he steals that when hungry, he may satisfy his soul:

31 but if he should be caught, he shall repay sevenfold, and shall deliver himself by giving all his goods.

32 But the adulterer through lack of understanding procures destruction to his soul.

33 He endures both pain and disgrace, and his reproach shall never be wiped off.

34 For the soul of her husband is full of jealousy: he will not spare in the day of vengeance.

35 He will not forego his enmity for any ransom: neither will he be reconciled by many gifts.

PROVERBS 7

1 *My* son, keep my words, and hide my commandments with you. *My* son, honor the Lord, and you shall be strong; and fear none but Him.

2 Keep my commandments, and you shall live; and *keep* my words as the pupils of *your* eyes.

3 And bind them on your fingers, and write *them* on the table of your heart.

4 Say that wisdom is your sister, and gain prudence as an acquaintance for yourself;

5 that she may keep you from the strange and wicked woman, if she should assail you with flattering words.

6 For she looks from a window out of her house into the streets, at one whom she may see of the senseless ones, a young man devoid of understanding,

7 passing by the corner in the passages near her house,

8 and speaking, in the dark of the evening,

9 when there happens *to be* the stillness of night and of darkness:

10 and the woman meets him having the appearance of a harlot, that causes the hearts of young men to flutter.

11 And she is fickle and rebellious, and her feet do not abide at home.

12 For at one time she wanders outside, and at another time she lies in wait in the streets, at every corner.

13 Then she caught him, and kissed him, and with an impudent face said to him,

14 "I have a peace offering; today I pay my vows:

15 therefore I came forth to meet you, desiring your face; and I have found you.

16 I have spread my bed with sheets, and I have covered it with double tapestry from Egypt.

17 I have sprinkled my couch with saffron, and my house with cinnamon.

18 Come, and let us enjoy love until the morning; come, and let us embrace in love.

19 For my husband is not at home, and has gone on a long journey,

20 having taken in his hand a bundle of money: after many days he will return to his house."

21 So with much conversation she convinced him to go astray, and with the snares of her lips forced him from *the right path.*

22 And he followed her, being gently led on, as that of an ox led to the slaughter, and as a dog to bonds, or as a deer shot in the liver with an arrow:

23 and he hastens as a bird into a snare, not knowing that he is running for his life.

24 Now then *my* son, listen to me, and attend to the words of my mouth.

25 Let not your heart turn aside to her ways,

26 for she has wounded and cast down many, and those whom she has slain are innumerable.

27 Her house is the way to hell, leading down to the chambers of death.

PROVERBS 8

1 You shall proclaim wisdom, that understanding may be obedient to you.

2 For she is on lofty heights, and stands in the midst of the ways.

3 For she sits by the gates of princes, and sings in the entrances, *saying,*

4 "You, O men, I exhort"; and utter my voice to the sons of men.

5 O you simple, understand prudence, and you that are untaught, take in knowledge.

6 Listen to me, for I will speak solemnly, and I will proclaim the truth from my lips.

7 For my mouth shall meditate truth, and false lips are an abomination before me.

8 All the words of my mouth are in righteousness; there is nothing in them wrong or perverse.

9 They are all evident to those that understand, and right to those that find knowledge.

10 Receive instruction, and not silver; and knowledge rather than choice gold.

11 For wisdom is better than precious stones; and no valuable substance is of equal worth with it.

12 I, wisdom, have dwelt *with* counsel and knowledge, and I have called upon understanding.

13 The fear of the Lord hates unrighteousness, insolence, pride, and the ways of wicked men; and I hate the perverse ways of bad men.

14 Counsel and safety are mine; prudence is mine, and strength is mine.

15 By me kings reign, and princes decree justice.

16 By me nobles become great, and monarchs by me rule over the earth.

17 I love those that love me, and they that seek me shall find me.

18 Wealth and glory belong to me; yes, abundant possessions and righteousness.

19 *It is* better to have my fruit than *to have* gold and precious stones; and my produce is better than choice silver.

20 I walk in ways of righteousness, in the midst of the paths of judgment;

21 that I may divide substance to them that love me, and may fill their treasures with good things.

If I declare to you the things that happen daily, I will remember also to recount the things of old.

22 The Lord made me the beginning of His ways for His works.

23 He established me in the beginning, before time was, before He made the earth.

24 Even before He made the depths, before the fountains of water came forth;

25 before the mountains were settled, and before all hills, He begot me.

26 The Lord made countries and uninhabited *lands,* and the highest inhabited parts of the world.

27 When He prepared the heaven, I was present with Him; and when He prepared His throne upon the winds;

28 and when He strengthened the clouds above, and when He secured the fountains of the earth;

29 and when He strengthened the foundations of the earth;

30 I was by Him, suiting myself to Him, I was that in which He took delight; and daily I rejoiced in His presence continually.

31 For He rejoiced when He had completed the world, and rejoiced among the sons of men.

32 Now then, *my* son, hear me: blessed is the man who shall listen to me, and the mortal who shall keep my ways;

33 (This verse omitted in LXX)

34 watching daily at my doors, waiting at the posts of my entrances.

35 For my outgoings are the outgoings of life, and *in them* is prepared favor from the Lord.

36 But they that sin against me act wickedly against their own souls, and they that hate me love death.

PROVERBS 9

1 Wisdom has built a house for herself, and set up seven pillars.

2 She has killed her beasts; she has mingled her wine in a bowl, and prepared her table.

3 She has sent forth her servants, calling with a loud proclamation to the feast, saying,

⁴ "Whoever is foolish, let him turn aside to me": and to them that want understanding she says,

⁵ "Come, eat of my bread, and drink wine which I have mingled for you."

⁶ Forsake folly, that you may reign forever; and seek wisdom, and improve understanding by knowledge.

⁷ He that reproves evil *men* shall get dishonor to himself, and he that rebukes an ungodly *man* shall disgrace himself.

⁸ Do not rebuke evil men, lest they should hate you: rebuke a wise man, and he will love you.

⁹ Give an opportunity to a wise man, and he will be wiser: instruct a just man, and he will receive more *instruction*.

¹⁰ The fear of the Lord is the beginning of wisdom, and the counsel of saints is understanding:
for to know the law is *the character* of a sound mind.

¹¹ For in this way you shall live long, and years of your life shall be added to you.

¹² Son, if you are wise for yourself, you shall also be wise for your neighbors; and if you should prove wicked, you alone will bear the evil.
He that stays himself upon falsehoods, attempts to rule the winds, and the same will pursue birds in their fight;
for he has forsaken the ways of his own vineyard, and he has caused the axles of his own cart to go astray;
and he goes through a dry desert, and *a land* appointed to drought, and he gathers barrenness with his hands.

¹³ A foolish and bold woman, who does not know modesty, comes to want a morsel.

¹⁴ She sits at the doors of her house, on a seat openly in the streets,

¹⁵ calling to passers by, and to those that are going right on their ways;

¹⁶ saying, "Whoever is *the* most senseless of you, let him turn aside to me"; and I exhort those that want prudence, saying,

¹⁷ "Take and enjoy secret bread, and the sweet water of theft."

¹⁸ But he knows that mighty men die by her, and he falls into *the* snare of hell.
But flee, do not remain in *that* place, neither fix your eye upon her, for thus shall you go through strange water;
but abstain from strange water, and do not drink from a strange fountain, that you may live long, and years of life may be added to you.

PROVERBS 10

¹ A wise son makes *his* father glad, but a foolish son is a grief to his mother.

² Treasures shall not profit the lawless, but righteousness shall deliver from death.

³ The Lord will not famish a righteous soul, but He will overthrow the life of the ungodly.

⁴ Poverty brings a man low, but the hands of the vigorous make rich.

A son who is instructed shall be wise, and shall use the fool for a servant.

⁵ A wise son is saved from heat, but a lawless son is blighted of the winds in harvest.

⁶ The blessing of the Lord is upon the head of the just, but untimely grief shall cover the mouth of the ungodly.

⁷ The memory of the just is praised, but the name of the ungodly *man* is extinguished.

⁸ A wise man in heart will receive commandments, but he that is unguarded in his lips shall be overthrown in his perverseness.

⁹ He that walks simply, walks confidently, but he that perverts his ways shall be known.

¹⁰ He that winks with his eyes deceitfully procures griefs for men, but he that reproves boldly is a peacemaker.

¹¹ *There is* a fountain of life in the hand of a righteous man, but destruction shall cover the mouth of the ungodly.

¹² Hatred stirs up strife, but affection covers all that do not love strife.

¹³ He that brings forth wisdom from his lips strikes the fool with a rod.

¹⁴ The wise will hide discretion, but the mouth of the hasty draws near to ruin.

¹⁵ The wealth of rich men is a strong city, but poverty is the ruin of the ungodly.

¹⁶ The works of the righteous produce life, but the fruits of the ungodly produce sins.

¹⁷ Instruction keeps the right ways of life, but instruction unchastened goes astray.

¹⁸ Righteous lips cover enmity, but those that spead slander are most foolish.

¹⁹ By a multitude of words you shall not escape sin, but if you refrain your lips you will be prudent.

²⁰ The tongue of the just is choice silver, but the heart of the ungodly shall fail.

²¹ The lips of the righteous know sublime *truths*, but the foolish die in want.

²² The blessing of the Lord is upon the head of the righteous; it enriches him, and grief of heart shall not be added to it.

²³ A fool does mischief in sport, but wisdom brings forth prudence for a man.

²⁴ The ungodly is engulfed in destruction, but the desire of the righteous is acceptable.

²⁵ When the storm passes by, the ungodly vanishes away; but the righteous turns aside and escapes forever.

²⁶ As a sour grape is hurtful to the teeth, and smoke to the eyes, so iniquity hurts those that practice it.

²⁷ The fear of the Lord adds *length* of days, but the years of the ungodly shall be shortened.

²⁸ Joy rests long with the righteous, but the hope of the ungodly shall perish.

²⁹ The fear of the Lord is a stronghold of the saints, but ruin comes to them that work wickedness.

30 The righteous shall never fail, but the ungodly shall not dwell in the earth.

31 The mouth of the righteous drops wisdom, but the tongue of the unjust shall perish.

32 The lips of just men drop grace, but the mouth of the ungodly is perverse.

PROVERBS 11

1 False balances are an abomination to the Lord, but a just weight is acceptable unto Him.

2 Wherever pride enters, there will also be disgrace, but the mouth of the lowly meditates wisdom.

3 When a just man dies he leaves regret, but the destruction of the ungodly is speedy, and causes joy.

4 (This verse omitted in LXX)

5 Righteousness traces out blameless paths, but ungodliness encounters unjust dealing.

6 The righteousness of upright men delivers them, but transgressors are caught in their own destruction.

7 At the death of a just man his hope does not perish, but the boast of the ungodly perishes.

8 A righteous man escapes from a snare, and the ungodly man is delivered up in his place.

9 In the mouth of ungodly men is a snare to citizens, but the understanding of righteous men is prosperous.

10 In the prosperity of righteous men a city prospers:

11 but by the mouth of ungodly men it is overthrown.

12 A man void of understanding sneers at *his fellow* citizens, but a sensible man is quiet.

13 A double-tongued man discloses the secret counsels of an assembly, but he that is faithful in spirit conceals matters.

14 They that have no guidance fall like leaves, but in much counsel there is safety.

15 A bad man does harm wherever he meets a just man, and he hates the sound of safety.

16 A gracious wife brings glory to her husband, but a woman hating righteousness is a theme of dishonor. The slothful come to want, but the diligent support themselves with wealth.

17 A merciful man does good to his own soul, but the merciless destroys his own body.

18 An ungodly man performs unrighteous works, but the descendants of the righteous is a reward of truth.

19 A righteous son is born for life, but the persecution of the ungodly *ends* in death.

20 Perverse ways are an abomination to the Lord, but all those that are blameless in their ways are acceptable to Him.

21 He that unjustly strikes hands shall not be unpunished, but he that sows righteousness shall receive a faithful reward.

22 As an ornament in a swine's snout, so is beauty to an ill-minded woman.

23 All the desire of the righteous is good, but the hope of the ungodly shall perish.

24 There are *some* who scatter their own, and make it more, and there are some also who gather, yet have less.

25 Every sincere soul is blessed, but a passionate man is not graceful.

26 May he that hoards grain leave it to the nation: but blessing be on the head of him that gives it.

27 He that devises good *counsels* seeks good favor, but as for him that seeks after evil, *evil* shall overtake him.

28 He that trusts in wealth shall fall, but he that helps righteous men shall rise.

29 He that does not deal graciously with his own house shall inherit the wind, and the fool shall be servant to the wise man.

30 Out of the fruit of righteousness grows a tree of life, but the souls of transgressors are cut off before their time.

31 If the righteous are scarcely saved, where shall the ungodly and the sinner appear?

PROVERBS 12

1 He that loves instruction loves knowledge, but he that hates correction is a fool.

2 He that has found favor with the Lord is *made* better, but a transgressor shall be passed over in silence.

3 A man shall not prosper by wickedness, but the roots of the righteous shall not be taken up.

4 A virtuous woman is a crown to her husband, but as a worm in wood, so a bad woman destroys her husband.

5 The thoughts of the righteous *are true* judgments, but ungodly men devise deceits.

6 The words of ungodly men are crafty, but the mouth of the upright shall deliver them.

7 When the ungodly is overthrown, he vanishes away, but the houses of the just remain.

8 The mouth of an understanding man is praised by a man, but he that is dull of heart is had in derision.

9 Better is a man in dishonor serving himself, than one honoring himself and wanting bread.

10 A righteous man has pity for the lives of his cattle, but the bowels of the ungodly are unmerciful.

11 He that tills his own land shall be satisfied with bread; but they that pursue vanities are void of understanding. He that enjoys himself in banquets of wine, shall leave dishonor in his own strongholds.

12 The desires of the ungodly are evil, but the roots of the godly are firmly set.

13 For the sin of his lips a sinner falls into snare, but a righteous man escapes from them. He whose looks are gentle shall be pitied, but he that contends in the gates will afflict souls.

14 The soul of a man shall be filled with good from the fruits of his mouth, and the recompense of his lips shall be given to him.

15 The ways of fools are right in their own eyes, but a wise man heeds counsel.

16 A fool declares his wrath the same day, but a prudent man hides his own disgrace.

17 A righteous man declares the open truth, but an unjust witness is deceitful.

18 Some wound as they speak, like swords, but the tongues of the wise heal.

19 True lips establish testimony, but a hasty witness has an unjust tongue.

20 *There is* deceit in the heart of him that imagines evil, but they that love peace shall rejoice.

21 No injustice will please a just man, but the ungodly will be filled with mischief.

22 Lying lips are an abomination to the Lord, but he that deals faithfully is accepted by Him.

23 An understanding man is a throne of wisdom, but the heart of fools shall meet with curses.

24 The hand of chosen men shall easily obtain rule, but the deceitful shall be for a prey.

25 A terrible word troubles the heart of a righteous man, but a good message rejoices him.

26 A just arbitrator shall be his own friend, but mischief shall pursue sinners, and the way of ungodly men shall lead them astray.

27 A deceitful man shall catch no game, but a blameless man is a precious possession.

28 In the ways of righteousness is life, but the ways of those that remember injuries *lead* to death.

PROVERBS 13

1 A wise son is obedient to his father, but a disobedient son will be destroyed.

2 A good *man* shall eat of the fruits of righteousness, but the lives of transgressors shall perish before their time.

3 He that keeps his own mouth keeps his own life, but he that is hasty with his lips shall bring terror upon himself.

4 Every slothful man desires, but the hands of the active are diligent.

5 A righteous man hates an unjust word, but an ungodly man is ashamed, and will have no confidence.

6 (This verse omitted in LXX)

7 There are *some* who, having nothing, enrich themselves, and there are some who bring themselves down in *the midst of* much wealth.

8 A man's own wealth is the ransom of his life, but the poor does not endure threatening.

9 The righteous always have light, but the light of the ungodly is quenched. Crafty souls go astray in sins, but just men have pity, and are merciful.

10 A bad man does evil with insolence, but they that are judges of themselves are wise.

11 Wealth gotten hastily with iniquity is diminished, but he that gathers for himself with godliness shall be increased. The righteous *man* is merciful, and lends.

12 Better is he that begins to help heartily, than he that promises and leads *another* to hope; for a good desire is a tree of life.

13 He that slights a matter shall be slighted of it, but he that fears the commandment has health *of soul*.
To a crafty son there shall be nothing good, but a wise servant shall have his way prosperous.

14 The law of the wise is fountain of life, but the man void of understanding shall die by a snare.

15 Sound discretion gives favor, and to know the law is the part of a sound understanding, but the ways of scorners lead to destruction.

16 Every prudent man acts with knowledge, but the fool displays his own mischief.

17 A rash king shall fall into mischief, but a wise messenger shall deliver him.

18 Instruction removes poverty and disgrace, but he that attends to reproofs shall be honored.

19 The desires of the godly gladden the soul, but the works of the ungodly are far from knowledge.

20 If you walk with wise men you shall be wise, but he that walks with fools shall be known.

21 Evil shall pursue sinners, but good shall overtake the righteous.

22 A good man shall inherit children's children, and the wealth of ungodly men is laid up for the just.

23 The righteous shall spend many years in wealth, but the unrighteous shall perish suddenly.

24 He that spares the rod hates his son, but he that loves carefully chastens him.

25 A just *man* eats and satisfies his soul, but the souls of the ungodly are in want.

PROVERBS 14

1 Wise women build houses, but a foolish one digs *hers* down with her hands.

2 He that walks uprightly fears the Lord, but he that is perverse in his ways shall be dishonored.

3 Out of the mouth of fools comes a rod of pride, but the lips of the wise preserve them.

4 Where no oxen are, the cribs are clean, but where there is abundant produce, the strength of the ox is apparent.

5 A faithful witness does not lie, but an unjust witness kindles falsehoods.

6 You shall seek wisdom with bad men, and shall not find it, but discretion is easily available with the prudent.

7 All things are adverse to a foolish man, but wise lips are the weapons of discretion.

8 The wisdom of the prudent will understand their ways, but the folly of fools leads astray.

9 The houses of transgressors will need purification, but the houses of the just are acceptable.

10 If a man's mind is intelligent, his soul is sorrowful; and when he rejoices, he has no fellowship with pride.

11 The houses of ungodly men shall be utterly destroyed, but the tent of the upright shall stand.

12 There is a way which seems to be right with men, but the ends of it reach to the depths of hell.

13 Grief mingles not with mirth, and joy in the end comes to grief.

14 A stout-hearted *man* shall be filled with his own ways, and a good man with his own thoughts.

15 The simple believes every word, but the sensible man considers his steps.

16 A wise man fears, and departs from evil, but the fool trusts in himself, and joins himself with the transgressor.

17 A passionate man acts inconsiderately, but a sensible man bears up under many things.

18 Fools shall have mischief for their portion, but the prudent shall quickly take hold of understanding.

19 Evil men shall fall before the good, and the ungodly shall attend at the gates of the righteous.

20 Friends will hate poor friends, but the friends of the rich are many.

21 He that dishonors the needy, sins, but he that has pity on the poor is most blessed.

22 They that go astray devise evils, but the good devise mercy and truth.
The framers of evil do not understand mercy and truth, but compassion and faithfulness are with the framers of good.

23 With everyone who is careful there is abundance, but the pleasure-taking and indolent shall be in want.

24 A prudent man is the crown of the wise, but the occupation of fools is evil.

25 A faithful witness shall deliver a soul from evil, but a deceitful *man* kindles falsehoods.

26 In the fear of the Lord is strong confidence, and he leaves his children a support.

27 The commandment of the Lord is a fountain of life, and it causes men to turn aside from the snare of death.

28 In a populous nation is the glory of a king, but in the failure of people is the ruin of a prince.

29 A man slow to wrath abounds in wisdom, but a man of impatient spirit is very foolish.

30 A meek-spirited man is a healer of the heart, but passion is a corruption to the bones.

31 He that oppresses the needy provokes his Maker, but he that honors Him has pity upon the poor.

32 The ungodly shall be driven away in his wickedness, but he who is secure in his own holiness is just.

33 There is wisdom in the good heart of a man, but in the heart of fools it is not discerned.

34 Righteousness exalts a nation, but sins, *however,* diminish *them.*

35 An understanding servant is acceptable to a king, and by his good behavior he removes disgrace.

PROVERBS 15

1 Anger slays even wise men, yet a submissive answer turns away wrath; but a grievous word stirs up anger.

2 The tongue of the wise knows what is good, but the mouth of the foolish speaks evil things.

3 The eyes of the Lord behold both the evil and the good in every place.

4 The wholesome tongue is a tree of life, and he that keeps it shall be filled with understanding.

5 A fool scorns his father's instruction, but he that keeps his commandments is more prudent.
In abounding righteousness is great strength, but the ungodly shall utterly perish from the earth.

6 In the houses of the righteous is much strength, but the fruits of the ungodly shall perish.

7 The lips of the wise are bound by discretion, but the hearts of the foolish are not safe.

8 The sacrifices of the ungodly are an abomination to the Lord, but the prayers of them that walk honestly are acceptable to Him.

9 The ways of an ungodly man are an abomination to the Lord, but He loves those that follow after righteousness.

10 The instruction of the simple is known by them that pass by, but they that hate reproofs die disgracefully.

11 Hell and destruction are manifest to the Lord, how shall not the hearts of men be, also?

12 An uninstructed person will not love those that reprove him, neither will he associate with the wise.

13 When the heart rejoices, the countenance is cheerful, but when it is in sorrow, the countenance is sad.

14 An upright heart seeks discretion, but the mouth of the uninstructed will experience evils.

15 The eyes of the wicked are always looking for evil things, but the good are always quiet.

16 Better is a small portion with the fear of the Lord, than great treasures without the fear *of the Lord.*

17 Better is an entertainment of herbs with friendliness and kindness, than a feast of calves, with enmity.

18 A passionate man stirs up strife; but *he that is* slow to anger appeases even a rising one.
A man slow to anger will extinguish quarrels, but an ungodly man rather stirs *them* up.

19 The ways of sluggards are strewn with thorns, but those of the diligent are made smooth.

20 A wise son gladdens his father, but a foolish son sneers at his mother.

21 The ways of a foolish man are void of sense, but a wise man walks straight.

22 They that do not honor councel put off deliberation, but counsel abides in the hearts of counselors.

23 A bad man will by no means obey counsel, neither will he say anything seasonable, or of good report.

24 The thoughts of the wise are ways of life, that he may turn aside and escape from hell.

25 The Lord pulls down the houses of scorners, but He establishes the border of the widow.

26 An unrighteous thought is an abomination to the Lord, but the sayings of the pure are held in honor.

27 He who takes bribes destroys himself, but he that hates them is safe.

By alms and by faithful dealings sins are purged away, but by the fear of the Lord everyone departs from evil.

28 The hearts of the righteous meditate faithfulness, but the mouth of the ungodly answers evil things.

The ways of righteous men are acceptable with the Lord, and through them even enemies become friends.

29 God is far from the ungodly, but He hears the prayers of the righteous. Better are small receipts with righteousness, than abundant fruits with unrighteousness.

Let the heart of a man think justly, that his steps may be rightly ordered of God.

30 The eye that sees rightly rejoices the heart, and a good report fattens the bones.

31 (This verse omitted in LXX)

32 He that rejects instruction hates himself, but he who heeds rebuke loves his soul.

33 The fear of the Lord is instruction and wisdom, and the highest honor will correspond therewith.

PROVERBS 16

1 (This verse omitted in LXX)

2 All the works of the humble man are manifest with God, but the ungodly shall perish in an evil day.

3 (This verse omitted in LXX)

4 (This verse omitted in LXX)

5 Everyone that is proud in heart is unclean before God, and he that unjustly strikes hand to hand shall not be held guiltless.

6 (This verse omitted in LXX)

7 The beginning of a good way is to do justly, and it is more acceptable with God than to offer sacrifices.

8 He that seeks the Lord shall find knowledge with righteousness, and they that rightly seek Him shall find peace.

9 All of the works of the Lord *are done* with righteousness, and the ungodly *man* is kept for the evil day.

10 *There is* an oracle upon the lips of a king, and his mouth shall not err in judgment.

11 The poise of the balance is righteousness with the Lord, and His works are righteous measures.

12 An evildoer is an abomination to a king, for the throne of rule is established by righteousness.

13 Righteous lips are acceptable to a king, and he loves right words.

14 The anger of a king is a messenger of death, but a wise man will pacify him.

15 The son of a king is in the light of life, and they that are in favor with him are as a cloud of latter rain.

16 The brood of wisdom is more to be chosen than gold, and the brood of prudence more to be chosen than silver.

17 The paths of life turn aside from evil, and the ways of righteousness are length of life.

He that receives instruction shall be in prosperity, and he that regards reproofs shall be made wise.

He that keeps his ways preserves his own soul, and he that loves his life will spare his mouth.

18 Pride goes before destruction, and a haughty spirit before a fall.

19 Better is a meek-spirited man with lowliness, than one who divides spoils with the proud.

20 *He who is* skillful in business finds good, but he that trusts in God is most blessed.

21 *Men* call the wise and understanding evil, but they that are pleasing in speech shall hear more.

22 Understanding is a fountain of life to its possessors, but the instruction of fools is evil.

23 The heart of the wise will discern the *things which proceed* from his own mouth, and on his lips he will wear knowledge.

24 Good words are *like* honeycombs, and the sweetness thereof is a healing of the soul.

25 There are ways that seem right to a man, but the end of them looks to the depth of hell.

26 A man who labors, labors for himself, and drives from him his own ruin.

27 But the perverse bears destruction upon his own mouth: a foolish man digs up evil for himself, and treasures fire on his own lips.

28 A perverse man spreads mischief, and will kindle a torch of deceit with mischief, and he separates friends.

29 A transgressor tries *to ensnare* friends, and leads them in ways *that are* not good.

30 And the man that fixes his eyes devises perverse things, and marks out with his lips all evil: he is a furnace of wickedness.

31 Old age is a crown of glory, when it is found in the ways of righteousness.

32 A man slow to anger is better than a strong man, and he that governs *his* temper better than he that takes a city.

33 All *evils* come upon the ungodly into their bosoms, but all good things *come* from the Lord.

PROVERBS 17

1 Better is a morsel with pleasure in peace, than a house *full* of many good things and unjust sacrifices, with strife.

2 A wise servant shall have rule over foolish masters, and shall divide portions among brothers.

³ As silver and gold are tried in a furnace, so are choice hearts with the Lord.

⁴ A bad man listens to the tongue of transgressors, but a righteous man pays no attention to lying lips.

⁵ He that laughs at the poor provokes Him that made him, and he that rejoices at the destruction of another shall not be held guiltless;

but he that has compassion shall find mercy.

⁶ Children's children are the crown of old men; and their fathers are the glory of children.

Every ornament of wealth belongs to the faithful; but to the unfaithful, not even a farthing.

⁷ Faithful lips will not suit a fool; nor lying lips a just man.

⁸ Instruction is to them that use it a gracious reward; and wherever it may turn, it shall prosper.

⁹ He that conceals injuries seeks love, but he that hates to hide *them* separates friends and kindred.

¹⁰ A threat breaks down the heart of a wise man, but a fool, though scourged, does not understand.

¹¹ Every bad man stirs up strife, but the Lord will send out an unmerciful messenger against him.

¹² Care may befall a man of understanding, but fools will meditate evils.

¹³ Whoever rewards evil for good, evil shall not be removed from his house.

¹⁴ Rightful rule gives power to words, but sedition and strife precede poverty.

¹⁵ He that pronounces the unjust just, and the just unjust, is unclean and abominable before God.

¹⁶ Why does the fool have wealth? For a senseless man cannot purchase wisdom.

He that exalts his own house seeks ruin, and he that turns aside from instruction shall fall into mischief.

¹⁷ A friend loves at all times, and let brothers be useful in distress, for on this account are they born.

¹⁸ A foolish man applauds and rejoices over himself, as he also that becomes surety would make himself responsible for his own friends.

¹⁹ He who loves sin rejoices in strife,

²⁰ and the hard-hearted man finds no good. A man of a changeful tongue will fall into mischief,

²¹ and the heart of a fool is grief to its possessor. A father rejoices not over an uninstructed son, but a wise son gladdens his mother.

²² A glad heart promotes health, but the bones of a sorrowful man dry up.

²³ The ways of a man who unjustly receives gifts in his bosom do not prosper, and an ungodly man perverts the ways of righteousness.

²⁴ The countenance of a wise man is sensible, but the eyes of a fool go to the ends of the earth.

²⁵ A foolish son *is a cause of* anger to his father, and grief to her that bore him.

²⁶ *It is* not right to punish a righteous man, nor *is it* holy to plot against righteous princes.

²⁷ He that forbears to utter a harsh word is discreet, and a patient man is wise.

²⁸ Wisdom shall be imputed to a fool who asks after wisdom, and he who holds his peace shall seem to be sensible.

PROVERBS 18

¹ A man who wishes to separate from friends seeks excuses, but at all times he will be liable to reproach.

² A senseless man feels no need of wisdom, for he is rather led by folly.

³ When an ungodly man comes into a depth of evils, he despises *them*; but dishonor and reproach come upon him.

⁴ A word in the heart of a man is a deep water, and a river and fountain of life spring forth.

⁵ *It is* not good to accept the person of the ungodly, nor is it holy to pervert justice in judgment.

⁶ The lips of a fool bring him into troubles, and his bold mouth calls for death.

⁷ A fool's mouth is ruin to him, and his lips are a snare to his soul.

⁸ Fear casts down the slothful, and the souls of the effeminate shall hunger.

⁹ A man who does not help himself by his labor is brother to him that destroys himself.

¹⁰ The name of the Lord is of majestic power; and the righteous run to it *and* are exalted.

¹¹ The wealth of a rich man is a strong city, and its glory casts a broad shadow.

¹² Before ruin a man's heart is exalted, and before honor it is humble.

¹³ Whoever answers a word before he hears *a cause*, it is folly and reproach to him.

¹⁴ A wise servant calms a man's anger, but who can endure a faint-hearted man?

¹⁵ The heart of the sensible man purchases discretion, and the ears of the wise seek understanding.

¹⁶ A man's gift enlarges him, and seats him among princes.

¹⁷ A righteous man accuses himself at the beginning of his speech, but when he has entered upon the attack, the adversary is reproved.

¹⁸ A silent *man* quells strife, and determines among the mighty.

¹⁹ A brother helped by a brother is as a strong and high city, and is as strong as a well-founded palace.

²⁰ A man fills his belly with the fruits of his mouth, and he shall be satisfied with the fruits of his lips.

²¹ Life and death are in the power of the tongue, and they that rule it shall eat the fruits thereof.

²² He that has found a good wife has found favor, and has received favor from God.

He that puts away a good wife, puts away a good thing, and he that keeps an adulteress is foolish and ungodly.

²³ (This verse omitted in LXX)

24 (This verse omitted in LXX)

PROVERBS 19

1 (This verse omitted in LXX)

2 (This verse omitted in LXX)

3 The folly of a man destroys his ways, and in his heart he blames God.

4 Wealth acquires many friends, but the poor is deserted even of the friend he has.

5 A false witness shall not be unpunished, and he that accuses unjustly shall not escape.

6 Many court the favor of kings, but every bad man becomes a reproach to *another* man.

7 Everyone who hates his poor brother shall also be far from friendship.

Good understanding will draw near to them that know it, and a sensible man will find it.

He that does much harm perfects wickedness, and he that uses provoking words shall not escape.

8 He that procures wisdom loves himself, and he that keeps wisdom shall find good things.

9 A false witness shall not go unpunished, and whosoever shall kindle mischief shall perish by it.

10 Delight does not suit a fool, nor *is it seemly* if a servant should begin to rule with haughtiness.

11 A merciful man is long suffering, and his triumph overtakes transgressors.

12 The threatening of a king is like the roaring of a lion, but as dew on the grass, so is his favor.

13 A foolish son is a disgrace to his father; vows *paid out* of the hire of a harlot are not pure.

14 Fathers divide house and substance to their children, but a wife is suited to a man by the Lord.

15 Fear restrains the effeminate man, and the soul of the idle person shall hunger.

16 He that keeps the commandment keeps his own soul, but he that despises his ways shall perish.

17 He that has pity on the poor lends to the Lord, and He will recompense to him according to his gift.

18 Chasten your son, for so he shall be hopeful; and do not be exalted in your soul to haughtiness.

19 A malicious man shall be severely punished, and if he commit injury, he shall also lose his life.

20 Hear, son, the instruction of your father, that you may be wise in your latter days.

21 *There are* many thoughts in a man's heart, but the counsel of the Lord abides forever.

22 Mercy is a fruit to a man, and a poor man is better than a rich liar.

23 The fear of the Lord is life to a man; and he shall lodge without fear in places where knowledge is not seen.

24 He that unjustly hides his hands in his bosom, will not even bring them up to his mouth.

25 When a criminal is scourged, a simple man is made wiser, but if you rebuke a wise man, he will understand discretion.

26 He that dishonors his father, and drives away his mother, shall be disgraced and shall be exposed to reproach.

27 A son who ceases to attend to the instruction of a father will meditate on evil sayings.

28 He that becomes surety for a foolish child will despise the ordinance, and the mouth of ungodly men shall drink down judgment.

29 Scourges are preparing for the intemperate, and punishments likewise for fools.

PROVERBS 20

1 Wine is a mocker, and strong drink full of violence; and every fool is entangled with them.

2 The threat of a king does not differ from the rage of a lion; and he that provokes him sins against his own soul.

3 *It is* an honor to a man to turn aside from railing, but every fool is entangled with such matters.

4 A sluggard when reproached is not ashamed; so also he who borrows grain in harvest.

5 Counsel in a man's heart is deep water, but a prudent man will draw it out.

6 A man is valuable and a merciful man precious, but it is hard to find a faithful man.

7 He that walks blameless in justice shall leave his children blessed.

8 Whenever a righteous king sits on the throne, no evil thing can stand before his presence.

9 Who will boast that he has a pure heart? Or who will boldly say that he is pure from sins?

10 Diverse weights and diverse measures are an abomination in the eyes of the Lord, and so is he that makes them.

11 A youth *when in company* with a godly man, will be restrained in his devices, and then his way will be straight.

12 The ear hears, and the eye sees; even both of them are the Lord's work.

13 Love not to speak ill, lest you be cut off: open your eyes, and be filled with bread.

14 (This verse omitted in LXX)

15 (This verse omitted in LXX)

16 (This verse omitted in LXX)

17 (This verse omitted in LXX)

18 (This verse omitted in LXX)

19 (This verse omitted in LXX)

20 The lamp of him that reviles father or mother shall be put out, and his eyes shall see darkness.

21 A portion hastily gotten at first shall not be blessed in the end.

22 Do not say, "I will avenge myself on my enemy," but wait on the Lord, that He may help you.

23 A double weight is an abomination to the Lord, and a deceitful balance is not good in His sight.

24 A man's steps are directed by the Lord: how then can a mortal understand His ways?

25 It is a snare to a man hastily to consecrate some of his own property: for *in that case* repentance comes after vowing.

26 A wise king utterly crushes the ungodly, and will bring a wheel upon them.

27 The spirit of man is a light of the Lord, who searches the inmost parts of the belly.

28 Mercy and truth are a guard to a king, and will surround his throne with righteousness.

29 Wisdom is an ornament to young men, and gray hairs are the glory of old men.

30 Bruises and contusions befall bad men, and plagues *shall come* in the inward parts of their belly.

PROVERBS 21

1 As a rush of water, so is the king's heart in God's hand: He turns it wherever He wishes.

2 Every man appears righteous in his own eyes, but the Lord directs the hearts.

3 To do justly and to speak truth are more pleasing to God than the blood of sacrifices.

4 A high-minded man is bold-hearted in his pride, and the lamp of the ungodly is sin.

5 (This verse omitted in LXX)

6 He that gathers treasures with a lying tongue pursues vanity on the snares of death.

7 Destruction shall lodge with the ungodly, for they refuse to do justly.

8 To the crooked, God sends crooked ways, but *as for the* pure, his work is right.

9 *It is* better to dwell in a corner on the housetop, than in plastered rooms with unrighteousness, and in an open house.

10 The soul of the ungodly shall not be pitied by any man.

11 When an intemperate man is punished the simple becomes wiser, and a wise man will gain knowledge.

12 A righteous man understands the hearts of the ungodly, and despises the ungodly for their wickedness.

13 He that stops his ears from hearing the poor, himself also shall cry, and there shall be none to hear *him*.

14 A secret gift calms anger, but he that forbears to give stirs up strong wrath.

15 *It is* the joy of the righteous to execute judgment, but a holy man is abominable with evildoers.

16 A man that wanders from the path of righteousness shall rest in the congregation of giants.

17 A poor man loves pleasure, and desires wine and oil in abundance;

18 and a transgressor is the abomination of a righteous man.

19 *It is* better to dwell in a wilderness than with a quarrelsome and talkative and passionate woman.

20 A desirable treasure will rest on the mouth of the wise, but foolish men will swallow it up.

21 The way of righteousness and mercy will find life and glory.

22 A wise man assaults strong cities, and demolishes the fortress in which the ungodly trusted.

23 He that keeps his mouth and his tongue keeps his soul from trouble.

24 A bold and self-willed and insolent man is called a pest, and he that remembers injuries is a transgressor.

25 Desires kill the lazy, for his hands do not choose to do anything.

26 An ungodly man entertains evil desires all the day, but the righteous is unsparingly merciful and compassionate.

27 The sacrifices of the ungodly are an abomination to the Lord, for they offer them unrighteously.

28 A false witness shall perish, but an obedient man will speak cautiously.

29 An ungodly man hardens his face, but the upright man himself understands his ways.

30 There is no wisdom, there is no courage, there is no counsel to the ungodly.

31 A horse is prepared for the day of battle, but help comes from the Lord.

PROVERBS 22

1 A fair name is better than much wealth, and good favor is above silver and gold.

2 The rich and the poor meet together, but the Lord made them both.

3 An intelligent man seeing a bad man severely punished is himself instructed, but fools pass by and are punished.

4 The fear of the Lord is the offspring of wisdom, wealth, glory, and life.

5 Thistles and snares are in crooked paths, but he that keeps his soul shall avoid them.

6 (This verse omitted in LXX)

7 The rich will rule over the poor, and servants will lend to their own masters.

8 He that sows wickedness shall reap evils, and shall fully receive the punishment of his deeds.
God loves a cheerful and liberal giver; but a man shall fully prove the folly of his works.

9 He that has pity on the poor shall himself be maintained, for he has given of his own bread to the poor.
He that gives liberally secures victory and honor, however he takes away *the* life of them that posses them.

10 Cast out a pestilent person from the council, and strife shall go out with him; for when he sits in the council he dishonors all.

11 The Lord loves holy hearts, and all blameless persons are acceptable to Him.

A king rules with his lips.

[12] But the eyes of the Lord preserve discretion, but the transgressor despises wise words.

[13] The sluggard makes excuses, and says, "*There is* a lion in the road, and murderers in the streets."

[14] The mouth of a transgressor is a deep pit, and he that is hated of the Lord shall fall into it.

Evil ways are before a man, and he does not like to turn away from them, but it is needful to turn aside from a perverse and bad way.

[15] Folly is bound up in the heart of a child, but the rod and instruction *will drive it* far from him.

[16] He that oppresses the poor, increases his own wealth, yet gives to the rich to lessen it.

[17] Incline your ear to the words of wise men; hear also my word, and apply your heart,

[18] that you may know that they are good, and if you take them to heart, they shall give you delight and be on your lips;

[19] that your hope may be in the Lord, and He may make your way known to you.

[20] And record them repeatedly for yourself on the table of your heart, for counsel and knowledge.

[21] I therefore teach you truth, and knowledge good to hear, that you may answer words of truth to them that question you.

[22] Do no violence to the poor, for he is needy, neither dishonor the helpless man in the gates.

[23] For the Lord will plead his cause, and you shall deliver your soul in safety.

[24] Have no fellowship with a furious man, neither lodge with a passionate man,

[25] lest you learn of his ways, and ensnare your soul.

[26] Do not become surety out of respect for a person.

[27] For if those do not have anything to pay, they will take the bed that is under you.

[28] Do not remove the old landmarks, which your fathers placed.

[29] It is fit that an observant man and *one* diligent in his business should attend on kings, and not attend on slothful men.

PROVERBS 23

[1] If you sit to eat at the table of a prince, consider attentively the things set before you;

[2] and apply your hand, knowing that it behooves you to prepare such *meats*; but if you are very insatiable,

[3] do not desire his provisions; for these belong to a false life.

[4] If you are poor, do not measure yourself with a rich man, but refrain yourself in your wisdom.

[5] If you should fix your eye upon him, he will disappear; for wings like an eagle's are prepared for him, and he returns to the house of his master.

[6] Do not eat with an envious man, neither desire his meats;

[7] so he eats and drinks as if anyone should swallow a hair, and do not bring him in to yourself, nor eat your morsel with him;

[8] for he will vomit it up, and spoil your fair words.

[9] Say nothing in the ears of a fool, lest at any time he sneer at your wise words.

[10] Do not remove the ancient landmarks, and do not encroach upon the possession of the fatherless;

[11] for the Lord is their redeemer; He is mighty, and will plead their cause with you.

[12] Apply your heart to instruction, and prepare your ears for words of discretion.

[13] Do not refrain from chastening a child, for if you beat him with the rod, he shall not die.

[14] For you shall beat him with the rod, and shall deliver his soul from death.

[15] Son, if your heart is wise, you shall also gladden my heart;

[16] and your lips shall converse with my lips, if they are right.

[17] Let not your heart envy sinners, but be in the fear of the Lord all the day.

[18] For if you should keep these things, you shall have posterity; and your hope shall not be removed.

[19] Hear, *my* son, and be wise, and rightly direct the thoughts of your heart.

[20] Do not be a winebibber, neither continue long at feasts, and purchases of flesh;

[21] for every drunkard and whoremonger shall be poor, and every sluggard shall clothe himself with tatters and ragged garments.

[22] Listen, *my* son, to your father who begot you, and do not despise *your mother* because she has grown old.

[23] (This verse omitted in LXX)

[24] A righteous father brings up *his children* well, and his soul rejoices over a wise son.

[25] Let your father and your mother rejoice over you, and let her that bore you be glad.

[26] My son, give me your heart, and let your eyes observe my ways.

[27] For a strange house is a vessel full of holes, and a strange well is narrow.

[28] For such a one shall perish suddenly, and every transgressor shall be cut off.

[29] Who *has* woe? Who has trouble? Who has quarrels? And who complains and disputes? Who has bruises without a cause? Whose eyes are livid?

[30] *Are not those* of them that stay long at wine? Are not those of them that haunt *the places* where banquets are? Be not drunk with wine; but converse with just men, and converse with them openly.

[31] For if you should set your eyes on bowls and cups, you shall afterwards go more naked than a pestle.

[32] But at last *such a one* stretches himself out as one smitten by a serpent, and venom is diffused through him as by a horned serpent.

³³ Whenever your eyes shall behold a strange woman, then your mouth shall speak perverse things.

³⁴ And you shall lie as in the midst of the sea, and as a pilot in a great storm.

³⁵ And you shall say, "They struck me, and I was not pained; and they mocked me, and I did not know: when will it be morning, that I may go and seek those with whom I may go in company?"

PROVERBS 24

¹ *My* son, do not envy bad men, nor desire to be with them.

² For their heart meditates falsehoods, and their lips speak of mischief.

³ A house is built by wisdom, and is set up by understanding.

⁴ By discretion the chambers are filled with all precious and excellent wealth.

⁵ A wise man is better than a strong man, and a man who has prudence than a large estate.

⁶ War is carried on with wise counsel, and aid is supplied to the heart of a counselor.

⁷ Wisdom and good understanding are in the gates of the wise; the wise do not turn aside from the mouth of the Lord,

⁸ but deliberate in council. Death befalls uninstructed *men.*

⁹ The fools also dies in sins, and uncleanness *attaches* to a pestilent man.

¹⁰ He shall be defiled in the evil day, and in the day of affliction, until he is utterly consumed.

¹¹ Deliver them that are led away to death, and redeem them that are appointed to be slain; do not spare *your help.*

¹² But if you should say, "I do not know this man"; know that the Lord knows the hearts of all; and He that gave breath to all, He knows all things, who renders to every man according to his works.

¹³ *My* son, eat honey, for the honeycomb is good, that your mouth may be sweetened.

¹⁴ Thus shall you perceive wisdom in your soul: for if you find it, your end shall be good, and hope shall not fail you.

¹⁵ Do not bring an ungodly man into the dwelling of the righteous: neither be deceived by the feeding of the belly.

¹⁶ For a righteous man will fall seven times and rise *again,* but in calamities the ungodly shall be without strength.

¹⁷ If your enemy should fall, do not rejoice over him, neither be elated at his overthrow.

¹⁸ For the Lord will see it, and it will not please Him, and He will turn away His wrath from him.

¹⁹ Do not rejoice over evildoers, neither be envious of sinners.

²⁰ For the evil man shall have no posterity, and the light of the wicked shall be put out.

²¹ *My* son, fear God and the king, and do not disobey either of them.

²² For they will suddenly punish the ungodly, and who can know the vengeance *inflicted* by both?

A son that keeps the commandment shall escape destruction, for *such a one* has fully received it.

Let no falsehood be spoken from the mouth of a king, and from his tongue let no falsehood proceed.

The king's tongue is a sword, and not one of flesh; and whosoever shall be given up to it shall be destroyed:

for if his wrath should be provoked, he destroys men with cords,

and devours men's bones, and burns them up as a flame, so that they are not even fit to be eaten by the young eagles.

My son, honor my words, and receive them, and repent.

²³ And this thing I say to you that are wise, for you to learn: It is not good to show partiality in judgment.

²⁴ He that says of the ungodly, "He is righteous," shall be cursed by peoples, and hateful among the nations.

²⁵ But they that reprove him shall appear more excellent, and blessing shall come upon them;

²⁶ and men will kiss the lips that answer well.

²⁷ Prepare your works for your going forth, and prepare yourself for the field; and come after me, and you shall rebuild your house.

²⁸ Do not be a false witness against your fellow citizen, neither exaggerate with your lips.

²⁹ Do not say, "As he has treated me, so will I treat him, and I will avenge myself on him for that in which he has injured me."

³⁰ A foolish man is like a field, and a senseless man like a vineyard.

³¹ If you let him alone, he will altogether remain barren and covered with weeds; and he becomes destitute, and his stone walls are broken down.

³² Afterwards I reflected, I looked that I might receive instruction.

³³ The sluggard says, "I slumber a little, and I sleep a little, and for a little while I fold my arms across my breast."

³⁴ But if you do this, your poverty will come speedily; and your need like a swift courier.

PROVERBS 25

¹ These are the proverbs of Solomon, which the friends of Hezekiah king of Judea transcribed.

² The glory of God obscures a matter, but the glory of a king honors business. ³ Heaven is high, and earth is deep, and a king's heart is unsearchable.

⁴ Beat the drossy silver, and it shall be made entirely pure.

⁵ Slay the ungodly from before the king, and his throne shall prosper in righteousness.

⁶ Do not be boastful in the presence of the king, and do not remain in the places of princes;

⁷ for *it is* better for you that it should be said, "Come up to me," than that one should humble you in the presence of the prince; speak of that which your eyes have seen.

⁸ Do not enter hastily into a quarrel, lest you repent at last.

9 Whenever your friend shall reproach you, retreat backward, do not despise *him*;

10 lest your friend continue to reproach you, so your quarrel and enmity shall not depart, but shall be to you like death. Favor and friendship set a man free, which you shall keep for yourself, lest you be made liable to reproach; but take heed to your ways peaceably.

11 As a golden apple in a necklace of sardius, so *is it* to speak a wise word.

12 In an earring of gold a precious sardius is also set; so is a wise word to an obedient ear.

13 As the falling of snow in the time of harvest is good against heat, so a faithful messenger *refreshes* those that send him; for he helps the souls of his employers.

14 As winds and clouds and rains are conspicuous things, so is he that boasts of a false gift.

15 In long suffering is prosperity to kings, and a soft tongue breaks the bones.

16 Having found honey, eat *only* what is enough, lest haply you be filled, and vomit it up.

17 Enter sparingly into your friend's house, lest he be wearied with your company, and hate you.

18 *As* a club, and a dagger, and a pointed arrow, so also is a man who bears false witness against his friend.

19 The way of the wicked and the foot of the transgressor shall perish in an evil day.

20 As vinegar is bad for a sore, so trouble befalling the body afflicts the heart. As a moth in a garment, and a worm in wood, so the grief of a man hurts the heart.

21 If your enemy hungers, feed him; if he thirsts, give him drink;

22 for so doing you shall heap coals of fire upon his head, and the Lord shall reward you with good.

23 The north wind raises clouds; so an impudent face provokes the tongue.

24 *It is* better to dwell on a corner of the rooftop than in a house shared with a scolding woman.

25 As cold water is agreeable to a thirsting soul, so is a good message from a far away land.

26 As if one should stop a well, and corrupt a spring of water, so is it unseemly for a righteous man to fall before an ungodly man.

27 *It is* not good to eat too much honey, but it is right to honor glorious words.

28 As a city whose walls are broken down, and which is unfortified, so is a man who does anything without counsel.

PROVERBS 26

1 As dew in harvest, and as rain in summer, so honor is not *seemly* for a fool.

2 As birds and sparrows fly, so a curse shall not come upon anyone without a cause.

3 As a whip for a horse, and a goad for a donkey, so is a rod for a simple nation.

4 Do not answer a fool according to his folly, lest you become like him.

5 But answer a fool according to his folly, lest he seem wise in his own eyes.

6 He that sends a message by a foolish messenger procures for himself a reproach from his own ways.

7 *As well* remove walking from the legs, as transgression from the mouth of fools.

8 He that binds up a stone in a sling is like one that gives honor to a fool.

9 Thorns grow in the hand of a drunkard, and slavery in the hand of fools.

10 All the flesh of fools is afflicted, for their fury is brought to destruction.

11 As when a dog returns to his own vomit, and becomes abominable, so is a fool who returns in his wickedness to his own sin. There is a shame which leads to sin, and a shame which procures glory and grace.

12 I have seen a man who thought himself to be wise; but a fool had more hope than he.

13 A lazy *man* when sent on a journey says, "*There is* a lion in the road, and *there are* murderers in the streets."

14 As a door turns on the hinge, so does a lazy *man* on his bed.

15 A lazy *man*, having hid his hand in his bosom, will not be able to bring it up to his mouth.

16 A lazy *man* thinks himself wiser than one who most satisfactorily brings back a message.

17 As he that lays hold of a dog's tail, so is he that meddles in another man's strife.

18 As those who need correction put forth *fair* words to men, and he that first falls in with the proposal will be overthrown;

19 so are all that lay wait for their own friends, and when they are discovered, say, "I was only joking."

20 With much wood a fire increases, but where there is not a double-minded man, strife ceases.

21 A hearth is for coals, and wood for fire, and a contentious man for the tumult of strife.

22 The words of the crafty are soft; but they pierce the inmost recesses of the soul.

23 Silver given with deceit should be considered as a potsherd; smooth lips disguise a wicked heart.

24 A weeping enemy promises all things with his lips, but in his heart he contrives deceit.

25 Though your enemy intreat you with a loud voice, do not believe him, for in his heart there is seven-fold wickedness.

26 He that conceals enmity frames deceit, but being easily discerned, exposes his own sins in the public assemblies.

27 He that digs a pit for his neighbor shall fall into it, and he that rolls a stone, rolls it upon himself.

28 A lying tongue hates the truth, and an flattering mouth works ruin.

PROVERBS 27

[1] Do not boast of tomorrow, for you do not know what the next day shall bring forth.

[2] Let your neighbor praise you, and not your own mouth—a stranger, and not your own lips.

[3] A stone is heavy and sand cumbersome, but a fool's wrath is heavier than both.

[4] Wrath is cruel and anger sharp, but nothing can withstand envy.

[5] Open rebukes are better than secret love.

[6] More faithful are the wounds of a friend than the spontaneous kisses of an enemy.

[7] A satisfied soul scorns *the* honeycomb, but to a hungry soul even bitter things appear sweet.

[8] As when a bird flies down from its own nest, so is a man brought into bondage, when removed from his country.

[9] The heart delights in ointments and wines and perfumes, but the soul is broken by calamities.

[10] Do not forsake your own friend or your father's friend, nor go to your brother's house in the day of your calamity; better is a friend *that is* near than a brother far off.

[11] Son, be wise, that your heart may rejoice, and remove from yourself reproachful words.

[12] A wise man, when evils are approaching, hides himself, but fools pass on, and will be punished.

[13] Take away the man's garment, (for a scorner has passed by) whoever lays waste another's goods.

[14] Whosoever shall bless a friend in the morning with a loud voice, shall appear not unlike one who curses him.

[15] On a stormy day drops of rain drive a man out of his house, so also does a contentious woman *drive a man* out of his own house.

[16] The north wind is sharp, though it is called by an honorable name.

[17] Iron sharpens iron, and a man sharpens his friend's countenance.

[18] He that plants a fig tree shall eat of its fruits; so he that waits on his own master shall be honored.

[19] As faces do not resemble *other* faces, so neither do the thoughts of men.

[20] Hell and destruction are never full, neither are the eyes of men ever satisfied.

He that fixes his eye is an abomination to the Lord, and the uninstructed do not restrain their tongue.

[21] Fire is the trial for silver and gold, and a man is tried by the mouth of them that praise him.

The heart of the transgressor seeks after mischief, but an upright heart seeks knowledge.

[22] Though you scourge a fool, disgracing him in the midst of the council, you will *still* in no way remove his folly from him.

[23] Do you thoroughly know the number of your flock, and pay attention to your herds?

[24] For a man has not strength and power forever; neither does he transmit it from generation to generation.

[25] Take care of the herbage in the field, and you shall cut grass, and gather the mountain hay;

[26] that you may have sheep's *wool* for clothing; pay attention to the land, that you may have lambs.

[27] My son, you have from me words very useful for your life, and for the life of your servants.

PROVERBS 28

[1] The ungodly *man* flees when no one pursues, but the righteous is confident as a lion.

[2] Contentions are raised by the sins of the wicked, but a wise man shall extinguish them.

[3] A bold man oppresses the poor by ungodly deeds.

As a deluge of rain is indeed unprofitable,

[4] so they that forsake the law applaud iniquity;

but they that love the law fortify themselves with a wall.

[5] Evil men will not understand judgment, but they that seek the Lord will understand everything.

[6] A poor man walking in truth is better than a rich liar.

[7] A wise son keeps the law, but he that keeps up debauchery dishonors his father.

[8] He that increases his wealth by usury and *unjust* gains, gathers it for him that pities the poor.

[9] He that turns away his ear from hearing the law, even he has made his prayer abominable.

[10] He that causes upright men to err in an evil way, himself shall fall into destruction.

Transgressors also shall pass by prosperity, but shall not enter into it.

[11] A rich man is wise in his own conceit, but a poor man with understanding shall condemn him.

[12] For helping the righteous there is great glory, but in the places of the ungodly men are entrapped.

[13] He that covers his own ungodliness shall not prosper, but he that blames *himself* shall be loved.

[14] Blessed is the man who religiously fears always, but the hard of heart shall fall into evils.

[15] A hungry lion and a thirsty wolf *is he*, who, being poor, rules over a poor nation.

[16] A king in need of revenues is a great oppressor, but he that hates injustice shall live long.

[17] He that becomes surety for a man charged with murder shall be in exile, and not in safety.

Chasten your son, and he shall love you, and give honor to your soul: he shall not obey a sinful nation.

[18] He that walks righteously shall be helped, but he that walks in crooked ways shall be entangled.

[19] He that tills his own land shall have plenty of bread, but he that follows idleness shall have plenty of poverty.

[20] A man worthy of credit shall be much blessed, but the wicked shall not escape punishment.

²¹ He who does not regard the persons of the righteous is not good: such a one will sell a man for a morsel of bread.

²² An envious man makes haste to be rich, and does not know that the merciful man shall have mastery over him.

²³ He that reproves a man's ways shall have more favor than he that flatters with the tongue.

²⁴ He that casts off father or mother, and thinks he does not sin, the same is partaker with an ungodly man.

²⁵ A faithless man judges rashly, but he that trusts in the Lord will act carefully.

²⁶ He who puts confidence in his bold heart is a fool: but he that walks in wisdom shall be safe.

²⁷ He that gives to the poor shall not be in need, but he that turns away his eye *from him* shall be in great distress. ²⁸ In the places of ungodly *men* the righteous mourn, but in their destruction the righteous shall be multiplied.

PROVERBS 29

¹ Better is a man of reproach than a stiff-necked man, for when the latter is suddenly set on fire, there shall be no remedy.

² When the righteous are praised, the people will rejoice, but when the ungodly rule, men mourn.

³ When a man loves wisdom, his father rejoices, but he that keeps harlots will waste wealth.

⁴ A righteous king establishes a country, but a transgressor destroys it.

⁵ He that prepares a net to catch his own friend, entangles his own feet in it.

⁶ A great snare is spread for a sinner, but the righteous shall be in joy and gladness.

⁷ A righteous man knows how to judge for the poor, but the ungodly does not understand knowledge, and the poor man does not have an understanding mind.

⁸ Lawless men burn down a city, but wise men turn away wrath.

⁹ A wise man shall judge nations, but a worthless man being angry laughs and does not fear.

¹⁰ Bloody men hate one who is holy, but the upright will vindicate his soul.

¹¹ A fool shows all his mind, but the wise reserves his in part.

¹² When a king hearkens to falsehoods, all his subjects are transgressors.

¹³ When the creditor and debtor meet together, the Lord oversees them both.

¹⁴ When a king judges the poor in truth, his throne shall be established for a memorial.

¹⁵ Stripes and reproofs give wisdom, but an erring child disgraces his parents.

¹⁶ When the ungodly abound, transgressions are multiplied, but when they fall, the righteous are warned.

¹⁷ Chasten your son, and he shall give you rest, and he shall give honor to your soul.

¹⁸ There shall be no interpreter to a sinful nation, but he that observes the law is blessed.

¹⁹ A stubborn servant will not be reproved by words: for even if he understands, still he will not obey.

²⁰ If you see a man hasty in his words, know that there is more hope for a fool than for him.

²¹ He that lives wantonly from a child shall be a servant, and in the end shall grieve over himself.

²² A furious man stirs up strife, and a passionate man digs up sin.

²³ Pride brings a man low, but the Lord upholds the humble-minded with honor.

²⁴ He who is partner with a thief hates his own soul; and so do they, having heard an oath spoken, do not tell of it.

²⁵ *Those* who fear and reverence men have been overthrown, but he that trusts in the Lord shall rejoice. Ungodliness causes a man to fall, but he that trusts in the Lord shall be safe.

²⁶ Many court the favor of princes, but justice comes to a man from the Lord.

²⁷ A righteous man is an abomination to an unrighteous man, and a straight course is an abomination to the sinner.

PROVERBS 30

¹ Thus says the man to them that trust in God; and *then* I conclude.

² For I am the most simple of all men, and there is not in me the wisdom of men.

³ God has taught me wisdom, and I know the knowledge of the Holy One.

⁴ Who has ascended up to heaven, and come down? Who has gathered the winds in His bosom? Who has wrapped up the waters in a garment? Who has dominion of all the ends of the earth? What is His name? Or what is the name of His children?

⁵ For all the words of God are tried in the fire, and He defends those that reverence Him.

⁶ Do not add to His words, lest He reprove you, and you be found a liar.

⁷ Two things I ask of you: do not take favor from me before I die.

⁸ Remove vanity and falsehood far from me, and give me neither wealth nor poverty, but appoint *to* me what is needful and sufficient:

⁹ lest I be filled and become false, and say, "Who sees me?" Or be poor and steal, and swear vainly by the name of God.

¹⁰ Do not deliver a servant into the hands of his master, lest he curse you, and you be utterly destroyed.

¹¹ A wicked generation curse their father, and do not bless their mother.

¹² A wicked generation judge themselves to be righteous, but do not cleanse their way.

¹³ A wicked generation have lofty eyes, and exalt themselves with their eyebrows.

¹⁴ A wicked generation have teeth like swords, and grinders like cleavers, so as to destroy and devour the lowly from the earth, and the poor of them from among men.

¹⁵ The leech had three dearly beloved daughters, and these three did not satisfy her; and the fourth was not contented so as to say, "Enough."

¹⁶ The grave, and the love of a woman, and the earth not filled with water; water also and fire will not say, "It is enough."

¹⁷ The eye that laughs to scorn a father, and dishonors the old age of a mother, let the ravens of the valleys pick it out, and let the young eagles devour it.

¹⁸ Moreover there are three things impossible for me to comprehend, and a fourth which I know not:

¹⁹ the track of a flying eagle; and the ways of a serpent on a rock; and the paths of a ship passing through the sea; and the ways of a man in *his* youth.

²⁰ Such is the way of an adulterous woman, who having washed herself from what she has done, says she has done nothing amiss.

²¹ By three things the earth is troubled, and for four it cannot bear:

²² if a servant should reign, or a fool be filled with food;

²³ or if a maid-servant should cast out her own mistress, and if a hateful woman should marry a good man.

²⁴ There are four things upon the earth which are very small, yet these are wiser than the wise:

²⁵ the ants, which not having strength, and yet prepare their food in summer;

²⁶ the rabbits also are a feeble race, who make their houses in the rocks.

²⁷ The locusts have no king, and yet *they* march orderly at one command.

²⁸ And the lizard, which supports itself by its hands, and is easily taken, and dwells in the fortresses of kings.

²⁹ And there are three things which go well, and a fourth which passes along finely:

³⁰ A young lion, which is stronger than all other beasts, which does not turn away, nor fears any beast;

³¹ and a rooster, which struts boldly among the hens, and the goat leading the herd; and a king addressing a nation.

³² If you abandon yourself to mirth, and stretch forth your hand in a quarrel, you shall be disgraced.

³³ Churn the milk, and there shall be butter, and if you wring one's nose, there shall come out blood; so if you use provoking language, there will come forth quarrels and strife.

PROVERBS 31

¹ My words have been dictated by God—they are the prophecy of a king, whom his mother instructed.

² What will you keep, my son? What? The words of God? My firstborn son, I speak to you: what? Son of my womb? What? Son of my vows?

³ Do not give your wealth to women, nor your understanding and your life for that which will bring sorrow.
Do all things with counsel; drink wine with counsel.

⁴ Princes are prone to anger: therefore let them not drink wine;

⁵ lest by drinking they forget wisdom, and become incapable of administering justice to the oppressed.

⁶ Give strong drink to those that are in sorrow, and wine to drink to those in pain,

⁷ that they may forget their distress, and may not remember their troubles anymore.

⁸ Open your mouth with the word of God, and administer justice to all fairly.

⁹ Open your mouth and judge justly, and plead the cause of the poor and weak.

¹⁰ Who can find a virtuous woman? For such a one is indeed more valuable than precious stones.

¹¹ The heart of her husband trusts in her; such a one shall stand in no need of fine spoils.

¹² For she employs all her living for her husband's good.

¹³ Gathering wool and flax, she makes it useful with her hands.

¹⁴ She is like a ship trading from a distance—so she procures her livelihood.

¹⁵ And she rises by night, and gives food to her household, and work to her maids.

¹⁶ She views a farm, and buys it; and with the fruit of her hands she plants a possession.

¹⁷ She girds herself tight about the waist, and strengthens her arms for work.

¹⁸ And she finds by experience that working is good, and her lamp does not go out all night.

¹⁹ She reaches forth her arms to needful works, and applies her hands to the spindle.

²⁰ And she opens her hands to the needy, and reaches out fruit to the poor.

²¹ Her husband is not anxious about those at home when he tarries anywhere abroad: for all her household are well clothed.

²² She makes for her husband clothes of double texture, and garments for herself of fine linen and scarlet.

²³ And her husband becomes a distinguished *person* in the gates, when he sits in council with the elders of the land.

²⁴ She makes fine linens, and sells sashes to the Canaanites; she opens her mouth sparingly and with propriety, and controls her tongue.

²⁵ She clothes herself with majesty and excellence, and rejoices in *her* latter days.

²⁶ But she opens her mouth wisely, and according to law.

²⁷ The ways of her household are careful, and she does not eat the bread of idleness.

²⁸ And her kindness to them sets up her children for them, and they grow rich, and her husband praises her.

29 Many daughters have possessed wealth, many have acted valiantly, but you have exceeded *them all*, you have surpassed all.

30 Charms are false, and woman's beauty is vain: for it is a wise woman that is blessed, and let her praise the fear the Lord.

31 Give her of the fruit of her lips; and let her husband be praised in the gates.

THE BOOK OF ECCLESIASTES

The Vanity of Life

1 The words of the Preacher, the son of David, king of Israel in Jerusalem.

2 "Vanity of vanities," said the Preacher, "vanity of vanities; all is vanity.

3 What advantage *is there* to a man in all his labor that he takes under the sun?

4 A generation goes, and a generation comes; but the earth abides forever."

5 And the sun arises, and the sun goes down and draws toward its place;

6 arising there it proceeds southward, and goes round toward the north. The wind goes round and round, and the wind returns to its circuits.

7 All the rivers run into the sea; and yet the sea is not filled. To the place from which the rivers come, there they return again. 8 All things are full of labor; a man will not be able to speak *of them*. Neither shall the eye be satisfied with seeing, neither shall the ear be filled with hearing.

9 What is that which has been? The very thing which shall be. And what is that which has been done? The very thing which shall be done; and there is nothing new under the sun.

10 *Who is he* that shall speak and say, "Behold, this is new?" It has already been in the ages that have passed before us.

11 There is no remembrance of former things; neither to the things that have been last shall their memorial be with them that shall at the last *time*.

The Grief of Wisdom

12 I, the Preacher, was king over Israel in Jerusalem.

13 And I applied my heart to seek out and examine by wisdom concerning all things that are done under heaven, for God has given to the sons of men a burdensome task to be afflicted with.

14 I beheld all the works that were done under the sun; and indeed, all is vanity and grasping for the wind.

15 That which is crooked cannot be made straight; and what is lacking cannot be numbered.

16 I spoke in my heart, saying, "Behold, I have attained, and acquired wisdom beyond all who were before me in Jerusalem." Also I applied my heart to know wisdom and knowledge.

17 And my heart knew much—wisdom, knowledge, parables and understanding: I perceived that this also is grasping for the wind.

18 For in the abundance of wisdom is abundance of knowledge; and he that increases knowledge will increase sorrow.

ECCLESIASTES CHAPTER 2

The Vanity of Pleasure

1 I said in my heart, "Come now, I will test you with mirth, therefore enjoy pleasure." And behold, this is also vanity.

2 I said to laughter, "It is madness!" And to mirth, "Why do you do this?"

3 And I examined whether my heart would excite my flesh as *with* wine, (though my heart guided *me* in wisdom,) and *I desired* to lay hold of mirth, until I should see of what sort that good is, which the sons of men are to pursue under the sun, all the days of their life.

4 I enlarged my work; I built myself houses; I planted myself vineyards.

5 I made for myself gardens and orchards, and planted in them every kind of fruit tree.

6 I made myself pools of water, to water from them the timber-bearing wood.

7 I acquired servants and maidens, and servants were born to me in the house. Also I had abundant possessions of flocks and herds, beyond all who were before me in Jerusalem.

8 Moreover I collected for myself both silver and gold, and the peculiar treasures of kings and provinces. I procured for myself singing men and singing women, and delights of the sons of men, a butler and female cupbearers.

9 So I became great, and advanced beyond all that were before in Jerusalem. Also my wisdom was established to me.

10 And whatever my eyes desired, I did not withhold from them, I did not withhold my heart from all my mirth; for my heart rejoiced in all my labor; and this was my portion of all my labor.

11 And I looked on all my works which my hands had done, and on my labor which I labored to perform, and behold, all was vanity and grasping for the wind, and there is no advantage under the sun.

12 Then I looked back to view wisdom, and madness, and folly; for who is the man who will follow after counsel, in all things where in he employs it?

13 And I saw that wisdom excels folly, as much as light excels darkness.

14 The wise man's eyes are in his head; but the fool walks in darkness. And I perceived, even I, that one event shall happen to them all.

[15] And I said in my heart, "As the event of the fool is, so shall it be to me, even to me." And to what purpose have I gained wisdom? Moreover, I said in my heart, "This is also vanity, because the fool speaks of his abundance."

[16] For there is no remembrance of the wise man with the fool forever; forasmuch as now *in* the coming days all things are forgotten. And how shall the wise man die with the fool?

[17] So I hated life, because the work that was done under the sun was evil before me. For all is vanity and grasping for the wind.

[18] And I hated all of my labor which I had toiled under the sun, because I must leave it to the man who will come after me.

[19] And who knows whether he will be wise, or a fool? And whether he will have power over all my labor in which I labored, and in which I grew wise under the sun? This is also vanity.

[20] So I went about to dismiss from my heart all my labor in which I had labored under the sun.

[21] For there is *such* a man that his labor is in wisdom, and in knowledge, and in fortitude; *yet* this man shall give his portion to one who has not labored for it. This is also vanity and a great evil.

[22] For it happens to a man in all his labor, and in the purpose of his heart in which he labors under the sun.

[23] For all his days *are* sorrowful, and vexation of spirit is his; in the night also his heart rests not. This is also vanity.

[24] A man has nothing good to eat, and to drink, and to show his soul *as* good in his trouble. This also I saw, that it is from the hand of God.

[25] For who shall eat, or who shall drink, without Him?

[26] For *God* has given wisdom, knowledge, and joy to the man who is good in His sight, but He has given to the sinner trouble, to add and to heap up, that He may give to him that is good before God; for this is also vanity and grasping for the wind.

ECCLESIASTES CHAPTER 3

Everything Has Its Time

[1] To everything there is a season, and a time for every purpose under heaven.

[2] A time to be born, and a time to die; a time to plant, and a time to root up what was planted;

[3] a time to kill, and a time to heal; a time to pull down, and a time to build up;

[4] a time to weep, and a time to laugh; a time to mourn, and a time to dance;

[5] a time to throw stones, and a time to gather stones together; a time to embrace, and a time to refrain from embracing;

[6] a time to seek, and a time to lose; a time to keep, and a time to cast away;

[7] a time to tear, and a time to sew; a time to be silent, and a time to speak;

[8] a time to love, and a time to hate; a time of war, and a time of peace.

The God-Given Task

[9] What advantage *has* he that works in those things in which he labors?

[10] I have seen all the trouble, which God has given to the sons of men to be burdened with.

[11] All the things which He has made are beautiful in His time. He has also set the whole world in their heart, that man might not find out the work which God has done from the beginning, even to the end.

[12] I know that there is no good in them, except *for a man* to rejoice, and to do good in his life.

[13] Also, every man who shall eat and drink, and see good in all his labor, *this* is a gift of God.

[14] I know that whatsoever things God has done, they shall be forever. It is impossible to add to it, and it is impossible to take away from it; and God has done *it*, that *men* should fear at His presence.

[15] That which has been is now; and whatever things *are appointed* to be have already been; and God will seek out that which is past.

[16] And moreover I saw under the sun: *in* the place of judgment, wickedness *was* there; and in the place of righteousness, there was godliness.

[17] And I said in my heart, "God will judge the righteous and the ungodly"; for there is a time there for every action and for every work.

[18] I said in my heart, concerning the speech of the sons of men, "God will judge them," and that to show that they are beasts.

[19] Also to them is the event of the sons of men, and the event of the brute; one event befalls them. As is the death of the one, so also the death of the other; and there is one breath to all; and what has the man more than the brute? Nothing; for all is vanity.

[20] All *go* to one place; all were formed of the dust, and all will return to dust.

[21] And who has seen the spirit of the sons of men, whether it ascends upward? And the spirit of the beast, whether it descends downward to the earth?

[22] And I saw that there was no good, but that wherein a man shall rejoice in his works, for it is his portion, for who shall bring him to see anything of that which shall be after him?

ECCLESIASTES CHAPTER 4

[1] So I returned, and saw all the oppressions that were done under the sun. And behold, the tears of the oppressed, and they had no comforter; and on the side of them that oppressed them was power; but they had no comforter.

2 And I praised all the dead that had already died more than the living, as many as are alive until now.

3 Better also than both these is he who has not yet been, who has not seen all the evil work that is done under the sun.

The Vanity of Selfish Toil

4 And I saw all labor, and all the diligent work, that this is a man's envy from his neighbor. This also is vanity and grasping for the wind.

5 The fool folds his hands together, and eats his own flesh.

6 Better is a handful of rest than two handfuls of trouble and grasping for the wind.

7 So I returned, and saw vanity under the sun.

8 There is one *alone*, and there is not a second; yes, he has neither son nor brother: yet there is no end to all his labor; neither is his eye satisfied with wealth. And for whom do I labor, and deprive my soul of good? This is also vanity, and an evil trouble.

The Value of a Friend

9 Two *are* better than one, *seeing* they have a good reward for their labor.

10 For if they fall, the one will lift up his companion. But woe to him that is alone when he falls, and there is not a second to lift him up.

11 Again if two should lie together, they also have warmth. But how shall one be warmed who is *alone*?

12 And if one should prevail against *him*, the two shall withstand him; and a threefold cord cannot easily be broken.

13 Better is a poor and wise child than an old and foolish king, who knows not how to take heed any longer.

14 For he shall come forth out of the house of the prisoners to reign, because *he* also that was in his kingdom has become poor.

15 I beheld all the living who were walking under the sun, with the second youth who shall stand up in each one's place.

16 There is no end to all the people, to all who were before them; and the last shall not rejoice in him; for this also is vanity and grasping for the wind.

ECCLESIASTES CHAPTER 5

Fear God. Keep Your Vows

1 Keep your foot, whenever you go to the house of God; and *when you are* near to hear, let your sacrifice *be* better than the gift of fools; for they do not know they are doing evil.

2 Do not be hasty with your mouth, and do not let your heart be swift to utter anything before God; for God is in heaven above, and you *are* on earth; therefore let your words be few.

3 For through the multitude of trial a dream comes; and a fool's voice is with a multitude of words.

4 Whenever you shall vow a vow to God, do not delay in paying it; for *He has* no pleasure in fools. Pay, therefore, whatsoever you have vowed.

5 *It is* better that you should not vow, than that you should vow and not pay.

6 Do not allow your mouth to lead your flesh to sin; and do not say in the presence of God, "It was an error"; lest God be angry at your voice, and destroy the works of your hands.

7 For in a multitude of dreams and in many words there is vanity; rather fear God.

8 If you should see the oppression of the poor, and the wresting of judgment and of justice in the land, do not marvel at the matter; for *there is* a high one to watch over him that is high, and high ones over them.

9 Also the abundance of the earth is for everyone. The king *is dependent on* the tilled field.

10 He that loves silver shall not be satisfied with silver; nor he who has loved gain, in the abundance thereof. This also is vanity.

11 In the multitude of good they are increased that eat it, and what virtue has the owner, but the right of beholding *it* with his eyes?

12 The sleep of a servant is sweet, whether he eats little or much; but the full stomach of the rich man does not allow him to sleep.

13 There is an infirmity which I have seen under the sun, *namely*, wealth kept for its owner to his *own* hurt.

14 And that wealth shall perish in an evil trouble, and *the man* begets a son, and there is nothing in his hand.

15 As he came forth naked from his mother's womb, he shall return back as he came, and he shall receive nothing for his labor, that it should go *with him* in his hand.

16 And this is also an evil infirmity; for as he came, so also shall he return. And what is his gain, for which he labors in vain?

17 Indeed, all his days are in darkness, and in mourning, and much sorrow, and infirmity, and wrath.

18 Behold, I have seen good, that it is a fine thing *for a man* to eat and to drink, and to see good in all his labor in which he may labor under the sun; *all* the number of the days of his life which God has given to him; for it is his portion.

19 And *as for* every man to whom God has given wealth and possessions, and has given to him power to eat thereof, and to receive his portion, and to rejoice in his labor; this is the gift of God.

20 For he shall not much remember the days of his life; for God troubles him in the joy of his heart.

ECCLESIASTES CHAPTER 6

1 There is an evil which I have seen under the sun, and it is abundant with man.

2 A man to whom God shall give wealth, and substance, and honor, and he lacks nothing for his soul of all things that he

shall desire, yet God shall not give him power to eat of it, for a stranger shall devour it. This is vanity, and an evil infirmity.

3 Though a man should father a hundred *children*, and live many years, however abundant the days of his years shall be, yet *if* his soul shall not be satisfied with good, and also he have no burial; I said, "An untimely birth is better than he."

4 For he came in vanity, and departs in darkness, and his name shall be covered in darkness.

5 Moreover he has not seen the sun, nor known rest. There is *no more rest* to this one than another.

6 Though he has lived to the return of a thousand years, yet he has seen no good. Do not all go to one place?

7 All the labor of a man is for his mouth, and yet the appetite shall not be satisfied.

8 For *what* advantage has the wise man over the fool, since *even* the poor knows how to walk in the direction of life?

9 The sight of the eyes is better than that which wanders in soul. This is also vanity, and grasping for the wind.

10 If anything has been, its name has already been called. And it is known what man is; neither can he contend with him who is stronger than he.

11 For there are many things which increase vanity. What advantage has a man?

12 For who knows *what is* good for a man in his life, *during* the number of the life of the days of his vanity? And he has spent them as a shadow; for who shall tell a man what shall be after him under the sun?

ECCLESIASTES CHAPTER 7

The Value of Practical Wisdom

1 A good name is better than good oil; and the day of death than the day of birth.

2 *It is* better to go to the house of mourning, than to go to the banquet house. Since this is the end of every man, and the living man will apply good *warning* to his heart.

3 Sorrow is better than laughter; for by the sadness of the countenance the heart will be made better.

4 The heart of the wise is in the house of mourning; but the heart of fools is in the house of mirth.

5 *It is* better to hear a reproof of a wise man, than for a man to hear the song of fools.

6 As the sound of thorns under a caldron, so is the laughter of fools. This is also vanity.

7 For oppression makes a wise man mad, and destroys his noble heart.

8 The end of a matter is better than the beginning thereof; the patient is better than the high-minded.

9 Do not be hasty in your spirit to be angry; for anger will rest in the bosom of fools.

10 Do not say, "What has happened, that the former days were better than these?" For you do not inquire wisely concerning this.

11 Wisdom is good with an inheritance; and *there is* an advantage *by it* to them that see the sun.

12 For wisdom in its shadow is as the shadow of silver, and the excellence of the knowledge of wisdom will give life to him that has it.

13 Behold the works of God; for who shall be able to straighten him whom God has made crooked?

14 In the day of prosperity live joyfully, and consider in the day of adversity. Consider, *I say*, God also has caused the one to agree with the other for *this* reason, that man should find nothing after him.

15 I have seen all things in the days of my vanity; there is a just man perishing in his justice, and there is an ungodly man remaining in his wickedness.

16 Do not be overrighteous, neither be very wise, lest you be confounded.

17 Do not be very wicked, and do not be stubborn, lest you should die before your time.

18 It is good for you to restrain yourself by this; also by this you shall not defile your hand; for to them that fear God all things shall come forth *well*.

19 Wisdom will help the wise man more than ten mighty men which are in the city.

20 For there is not a righteous man in the earth who will do good, and not sin.

21 Also take no heed to all the words which ungodly men shall speak, lest you hear your servant cursing you.

22 For many times he shall trespass against you, and repeatedly shall he afflict your heart; for thus also have you cursed others.

23 All these things have I proved in wisdom. I said, "I will be wise"; but it was far from me.

24 *That which is* far beyond what was, and a great depth, who shall find it out?

25 I and my heart went round about to know, and to examine, and to seek wisdom, and the account *of things*, and to know the folly and trouble and madness of the ungodly man.

26 And I find her *to be*, and I will pronounce *to be* more bitter than death, the woman which is a snare, and her heart nets, *who has* a band in her hands. *He that is* good in the sight of God shall be delivered from her; but the sinner shall be caught by her.

27 "Behold, this have I found," said the Preacher, *seeking* by one at a time to find out the account,

28 which my soul sought after, though I did not find; for I have found one man of a thousand; but a woman in all these I have not found.

29 But behold, this have I found, that God made man upright; but they have sought out many devices.

ECCLESIASTES CHAPTER 8

1 Who knows the wise? And who knows the interpretation of a saying? A man's wisdom will lighten his

countenance; but a man of shameless countenance will be hated.

Obey Authorities for God's Sake

[2] Observe the commandment of the king, and *that* because of the word of the oath of God.

[3] Do not be hasty; you shall go forth out of his presence. Do not stand in an evil matter; for he will do whatsoever he shall please,

[4] even as a king having power; and who will say to him, "What are you doing?"

[5] He that keeps the commandment shall not know an evil thing; and the heart of the wise knows the time of judgment.

[6] Because for every matter there is a time and judgment; for the knowledge of a man is great to him.

[7] For there is no one that knows what is going to be; for who shall tell him how it shall be?

[8] There is no man that has power over the spirit to retain the spirit; and there is no power in the day of death; and there is no discharge in the day of the battle; neither shall wickedness deliver those who are given to it.

[9] So I saw all this, and I applied my heart to every work that has been done under the sun; all the things in which man has power over man, to afflict him.

Death Comes to All

[10] And then I saw the ungodly carried into the tombs, and *that* out of the holy place. And they departed, and were praised in the city, because they had done thus. This also is vanity.

[11] Because there is no contradiction made on the part of those who are quick to do evil, therefore the heart of the children of men is fully determined in them to do evil.

[12] He that has sinned has done evil from that time, and from long beforehand. Nevertheless I know, that it is well with them that fear God, that they may fear before Him.

[13] But it shall not be well with the ungodly, and he shall not prolong his days, *which are but* a shadow; forasmuch as he does not fear before God.

[14] There is a vanity which is done upon the earth; that there are righteous persons to whom it happens according to the doing of the ungodly; and there are ungodly men, to whom it happens according to the doing of the just. This is also vanity.

[15] Then I praised mirth, because there is no good for a man under the sun, but to eat, and drink, and be merry. And this shall attend him in his labor all the days of his life, which God has given him under the sun.

[16] On this I set my heart to know wisdom, and to perceive the trouble that was done upon the earth; even though one sees no sleep day or night.

[17] And I beheld all the works of God, that a man shall not be able to discover the work which is done under the sun. Whatever things a man shall endeavor to seek, however a man may labor to seek it, yet he shall not find it. Moreover, *though* a wise man may speak of knowing it, he shall not be able to find it; for I applied all this to my heart, and my heart has seen all this.

ECCLESIASTES CHAPTER 9

[1] *I saw* that the righteous, the wise, and their works, are in the hand of God. Indeed, there is no man that knows either love or hatred, *though* all are before their face.

[2] Vanity is in all. There is one event to the righteous, and to the wicked; to the good, and to the bad; both to the pure, and to the impure; both to him that sacrifices, and to him that does not sacrifice. As is the good, so is the sinner; as is the swearer, even so is he that fears an oath.

[3] There is this evil in all that is done under the sun, that there is one event to all, so that the heart of the sons of men is filled with evil, and madness is in their heart during their life, and after that *they go* to the dead.

[4] For who is he that has fellowship with all the living? There is hope *for him*; for a living dog is better than a dead lion.

[5] For the living will know that they shall die; but the dead know nothing, and there is no longer any reward to them, for their memory is lost.

[6] Also their love and their hatred and their envy have now perished, for there is no portion for them anymore, forever in all that is done under the sun.

[7] Go, eat your bread with joy, and drink your wine with a merry heart; for now God has approved your works.

[8] Let your garments be always white; and do not let oil be lacking on your head.

[9] And see life with the wife whom you love, all the days of the life of your vanity, which are given to you under the sun; for that is your portion in your life, and in your labor in which you labor under the sun.

[10] Whatsoever your hand shall find to do, do with all your might; for there is no work nor device nor knowledge nor wisdom in Hades, where you are going.

[11] I returned, and saw under the sun, that the race is not to the swift, nor the battle to the strong, nor yet bread to the wise, nor yet wealth to men of understanding, nor yet favor to men of knowledge; for time and chance will happen to them all.

[12] For surely man also does not know his time; as fish that are taken in an evil net, and as birds that are caught in a snare, even thus the sons of men are snared at an evil time, when it falls suddenly upon them.

Wisdom Superior to Folly

[13] This I also saw *to be* wisdom under the sun, and it is great before me.

[14] *Suppose there were* a little city, and few men in it; and there should come against it a great king, and surround it, and build great mounds against it;

[15] and should find in it a poor wise man, and he should save the city through his wisdom: yet no man would remember that poor man.

[16] And I said, "Wisdom is better than power"; yet the wisdom of the poor man is despised, and his words are not listened to.

[17] The words of the wise are heard in quiet more than the cry of them that rule in folly.

[18] Wisdom is better than weapons of war; and one sinner will destroy much good.

ECCLESIASTES CHAPTER 10

[1] Pestilent flies will corrupt a preparation of sweet ointment; *and* a little wisdom is more precious than great glory of folly.

[2] A wise man's heart is at his right hand, but a fool's heart at his left.

[3] And whenever a fool walks down the road, his heart will fail him, and all that he thinks of is folly.

[4] If the spirit of the ruler rises up against you, do not leave your place; for soothing will put an end to great offenses.

[5] There is an evil which I have seen under the sun, as an error that has proceeded from the ruler.

[6] The fool has been set in very high places, while rich men would sit in a low one.

[7] I have seen servants upon horses, and princes walking as servants on the earth.

[8] He that digs a pit shall fall into it; and him that breaks down a hedge a serpent shall bite.

[9] He that quarries stones may be hurt by them; and he that splits wood may be endangered by them.

[10] If the ax-head should fall off, then the man troubles his countenance, and he must put forth more strength; and *in that case* skill is of no advantage to a man.

[11] If a serpent bite when there is no *charmer's* whisper, then there is no advantage to the charmer.

[12] The words of a wise mouth are gracious, but the lips of a fool will swallow him up.

[13] The beginning of the words of his mouth is folly, and the end of his talk mischievous madness.

[14] A fool moreover multiplies words. No man knows what has been, nor what will be. Who shall tell him what will come after him?

[15] The labor of fools will afflict them, *as that of one* who knows not to go to the city.

[16] Woe to you, O city, whose king is young, and your princes eat in the morning!

[17] Blessed are you, O land, whose king is a son of nobles, and whose princes shall eat seasonably, for strength, and shall not be ashamed.

[18] By slothful neglect a building will be brought low, and by idleness of the hands the house will fall to pieces.

[19] Men prepare bread for laughter, and wine and oil that the living should rejoice; but to money all things will humbly yield obedience.

[20] Even in your conscience, do not curse the king; and do not curse the rich in your bedchamber; for a bird of the air shall carry your voice, and that which has wings shall report your speech.

ECCLESIASTES CHAPTER 11

The Value of Diligence

[1] Send forth your bread upon the face of the water, for you shall find it after many days.

[2] Give a portion to seven, and also to eight; for you do not know what evil there shall be upon the earth.

[3] If the clouds are filled with rain, they pour *it* out upon the earth; and if a tree fall southward, or if it fall northward, in the place where the tree shall fall, there it shall be.

[4] He that observes the wind does not sow; and he that looks at the clouds will not reap.

[5] Among whom none knows what is the way of the wind. As the bones *are hid* in the womb of a pregnant *woman*, so you shall not know the works of God, *even* all things whatsoever He shall do.

[6] In the morning sow your seed, and in the evening let not your hand be slack; for you do not know what sort shall prosper whether this or that, or whether both shall be good alike.

[7] Moreover the light is sweet, and it is good for the eyes to see the sun.

[8] For even if a man should live many years, *and* rejoice in them all; yet let him remember the days of darkness; for they shall be many. All that comes is vanity.

Seek God Early in Life

[9] Rejoice, O young man, in your youth; and let your heart cheer in the days of your youth, and walk in the ways of your heart blameless, but not in the sight of your eyes: yet know that for all these things God will bring you into judgment.

[10] Therefore remove sorrow from your heart, and put away evil from your flesh; for youth and folly are vanity.

ECCLESIASTES CHAPTER 12

[1] And remember your Creator in the days of your youth, before the days of evil come, and the years overtake *you* in which you shall say, "I have no pleasure in them."

[2] While the sun and light are not darkened, nor the moon and the stars; nor the clouds return after the rain;

[3] in the day when the keepers of the house shall tremble, and the mighty men shall become bent, and the grinding *women* cease because they have become few, and those looking out at the windows grow dim;

[4] and they shall shut the doors in the marketplace, because of the weakness of the voice of her that grinds *at the mill*; and he shall rise up at the voice of the sparrow, and all the daughters of song shall be brought low;

492

5 and they shall look up, and fears *shall be* in the way, and the almond tree shall blossom, and the locust shall increase, and the caper shall be scattered, because man has gone to his eternal home, and the mourners have gone about the market.

6 *Remember Him* before the silver cord is *let go*, or the choice gold is broken, or the pitcher is broken at the fountain, or the wheel is run down to the cistern;

7 *before* the dust also return to the earth as it was, and the spirit return to God who gave it.

8 "Vanity of vanities," said the Preacher; "All is vanity."

The Whole Duty of Man

9 And because the Preacher was wise above *others, so it was* that he taught men excellent knowledge, and the ear will trace out the parables.

10 The Preacher sought diligently to find out acceptable words, and a correct writing, *even* words of truth.

11 The words of the wise are as goads, and as nails firmly fastened, which have been given from one shepherd by agreement.

12 And moreover, my son, guard yourself by means of them; of making many books there is no end; and much study is a weariness of the flesh.

13 Hear the end of the matter, the sum: Fear God, and keep His commandments; for this is man's all.

14 For God will bring every work into judgment, with everything that has been overlooked, whether good or evil.

SONG OF SOLOMON

1 The song of songs, which is Solomon's.

2 Let him kiss me with the kisses of his mouth: for your breasts are better than wine.

3 And the smell of your ointments is better than all spices: your name is ointment poured forth; therefore do the young maidens love you.

4 They have drawn you: we will run after you, for the smell of your ointments: the king has brought me into his closet: let us rejoice and be glad in you; we will love your breasts more than wine: righteousness loves you.

5 I am dark, but beautiful, you daughters of Jerusalem, as the tents of Kedar, as the curtains of Solomon.

6 Do not look upon me, because I am dark, because the sun has looked unfavorably upon me: my mother's sons strove with me; they made me keeper in the vineyards; I have not kept my own vineyard.

7 Tell me, *you* whom my soul loves, where you tend your flock, where you cause *them* to rest at noon, lest I become as one that is veiled by the flocks of your companions.

8 If you do not know yourself, you fair one among women, go forth by the footsteps of the flocks, and feed your little goats by the shepherd's tents.

9 I have likened you, my companion, to my horses in the chariots of Pharaoh.

10 How beautiful are your cheeks, as those of a dove, your neck as chains!

11 We will make you figures of gold with studs of silver.

12 So long as the king was at table, my spikenard gave forth its smell.

13 My kinsman is to me a bundle of myrrh; he shall lie between my breasts.

14 My kinsman is to me a cluster of camphor in the vineyards of En Gedi.

15 Behold, you are fair, my companion; behold, you are fair; your eyes are doves.

16 Behold, you are fair, my kinsman, yea, beautiful, overshadowing our bed.

17 The beams of our house are cedars, our ceilings are of cypress.

SONG OF SOLOMON CHAPTER 2

1 I am a flower of the plain, a lily of the valleys.

2 As a lily among thorns, so is my companion among the daughters.

3 As the apple among the trees of the wood, so is my kinsman among the sons. I desired his shadow, and sat down, and his fruit was sweet in my throat.

4 Bring me into the wine house; set love before me.

5 Strengthen me with perfumes, stay me with apples: for I am wounded with love.

6 His left *hand shall be* under my head, and his right hand shall embrace me.

7 I have charged you, you daughters of Jerusalem, by the powers and by the virtues of the field, that you do not rouse or wake my love, until he please.

8 The voice of my kinsman! Behold, he comes leaping over the mountains, bounding over the hills.

9 My kinsman is like a gazelle or a young hart on the mountains of Bethel: behold, he is behind our wall, looking through the windows, peeping through the lattices.

10 My kinsman answers, and says to me, "Rise up, come, my companion, my fair one, my dove.

11 For behold, the winter is past, the rain is gone, it has departed.

12 The flowers are seen in the land; the time of pruning has arrived; the voice of the turtle dove has been heard in our land.

13 The fig tree has put forth its young figs, the vines put forth the tender grape, they yield a smell: arise, come, my companion, my fair one, my dove; yea, come."

14 *You are* my dove, in the shelter of the rock, near the wall: show me your face, and cause me to hear your voice; for your voice is sweet, and your countenance is beautiful.

15 Take us the little foxes that spoil the vines: for our vines put forth tender grapes.

[16] My kinsman is mine, and I am his: he feeds *his flock* among the lilies.

[17] Until the day dawn, and the shadows depart, turn, my kinsman, be like to a gazelle or young hart on the mountains of the ravines.

SONG OF SOLOMON CHAPTER 3

[1] By night on my bed I sought him whom my soul loves: I sought him, but did not find him; I called him, but he did not hear me.

[2] I will rise now, and go about in the city, in the market places, and in the streets, and I will seek him whom my soul loves: I sought him, but I did not find him.

[3] The watchmen who go their rounds in the city found me. I *said*, "Have you seen him whom my soul loves?"

[4] It *was* as a little *while* after I parted from them, that I found him whom my soul loves: I held him, and did not let him go, until I brought him into my mother's house, and into the chamber of her that conceived me.

[5] I have charged you, O daughters of Jerusalem, by the powers and by the virtues of the field, that you do not rouse nor awake my love, until he please.

[6] Who is this that comes up from the wilderness as pillars of smoke, perfumed with myrrh and frankincense, with all powders of the perfumer?

[7] Behold Solomon's bed; sixty mighty men of the mighty ones of Israel are round about it.

[8] They all hold a sword, being expert in war: every man has his sword upon his thigh because of fear by night.

[9] King Solomon made himself a litter of woods of Lebanon.

[10] He made the pillars of it silver, the bottom of it gold, the covering of it scarlet, in the midst of it a pavement of love, for the daughters of Jerusalem.

[11] Go forth, you daughters of Zion, and behold King Solomon, with the crown with which his mother crowned him, in the day of his wedding, and in the day of the gladness of his heart.

SONG OF SOLOMON CHAPTER 4

[1] Behold, you are fair, my companion; behold, you are fair; your eyes are doves, beside your veil: your hair is as flocks of goats, that have appeared from Gilead.

[2] Your teeth are as flocks of shorn *sheep*, that have gone up from the washing; all of them bearing twins, and there is not a barren one among them.

[3] Your lips are as a thread of scarlet, and your speech is comely: like the rind of a pomegranate is your cheek without your veil.

[4] Your neck is as the tower of David, that was built for an armory: a thousand shields hang upon it, and all darts of mighty men.

[5] Your two breasts are as two twin fawns, that feed among the lilies.

[6] Until the day dawn, and the shadows depart, I will go my way to the mountain of myrrh, and to the hill of frankincense.

[7] You are all fair, my companion, and there is no spot in you.

[8] Come from Lebanon, my bride, come from Lebanon: you shall come and pass from the top of Faith, from the top of Senir and Hermon, from the lions' dens, from the mountains of the leopards.

[9] My sister, my spouse, you have ravished my heart; you have ravished my heart with one of your eyes, with one chain of your neck.

[10] How beautiful are your breasts, my sister, my spouse! How much more beautiful are your breasts than wine, and the smell of your garments than all spices!

[11] Your lips drop honeycomb, my spouse: honey and milk are under your tongue; and the smell of your garments is as the smell of Lebanon.

[12] My sister, my spouse is a garden enclosed; a garden enclosed, a fountain sealed.

[13] Your shoots are a garden of pomegranates, with the fruit of choice berries; camphor, with spikenard:

[14] spikenard and saffron, calamus and cinnamon; with all woods of Lebanon, myrrh, aloes, with all chief spices:

[15] a fountain of a garden, and a well of water springing up from Lebanon.

[16] Awake, O north wind; and come, O south; and blow through my garden, and let my spices flow out.

SONG OF SOLOMON CHAPTER 5

[1] Let my kinsman come down into his garden, and eat the fruit of his choice berries. I have come into my garden, my sister, my spouse: I have gathered my myrrh with my spices; I have eaten my bread with my honey; I have drunk my wine with my milk. Eat, O friends, and drink; yes, brothers, drink abundantly.

[2] I sleep, but my heart is awake: the voice of my kinsman knocks at the door, *saying*, "Open, open to me, my companion, my sister, my dove, my perfect one: for my head is filled with dew, and my locks with the drops of the night."

[3] I have put off my coat; how shall I put it on? I have washed my feet, how shall I defile them?

[4] My kinsman put forth his hand by the hole of the door, and my belly moved for him.

[5] I rose up to open to my kinsman; my hands dropped myrrh, my fingers choice myrrh, on the handles of the lock.

[6] I opened to my kinsman; my kinsman was gone: my soul failed at his speech: I sought him, but did not find him; I called him, but he did not answer me.

[7] The watchman that make their rounds in the city found me, they struck me, they wounded me; the keepers of the walls took away my veil from me.

[8] I have charged you, O daughters of Jerusalem, by the powers and the virtues of the field: if you should find my

kinsman, what are you to say to him? That I am wounded with love.

[9] What is your kinsman *more* than *another* kinsman, O fairest among women? What is your kinsman *more* than *another* kinsman, that you have so charged us?

[10] My kinsman is white and ruddy, chosen out from myriads.

[11] His head is as very fine gold, his locks are flowing, black as a raven.

[12] His eyes are as doves, by the pools of waters, washed with milk, sitting by the pools.

[13] His cheeks are as bowls of spices pouring forth perfumes: his lips are lilies, dropping choice myrrh.

[14] His hands are as turned gold set with beryl: his belly is an ivory tablet on a sapphire stone.

[15] His legs are marble pillars set on golden sockets: his form is as Lebanon, choice as the cedars. His throat is most sweet, and altogether desirable. This is my kinsman, and this is my companion, O daughters of Jerusalem.

SONG OF SOLOMON CHAPTER 6

[1] Where has your kinsman gone, O fairest among women? Where has your kinsman turned aside? *Tell us,* and we will seek him with you.

[2] My kinsman has gone down to his garden, to the beds of spice, to feed *his flock* in the gardens, and to gather lilies.

[3] I am my kinsman's, and my kinsman is mine, who feeds among the lilies.

[4] You are fair, my companion, as Pleasure, beautiful as Jerusalem, terrible as armies set in array.

[5] Turn away your eyes from before me, for they have ravished me: your hair is as flocks of goats which have appeared from Gilead.

[6] Your teeth are as flocks of shorn *sheep,* that have gone up from the washing, all of them bearing twins, and there is none barren among them: your lips are as a thread of scarlet, and your speech is comely.

[7] Your cheek is like the rind of a pomegranate, *being seen* without your veil.

[8] There are sixty queens, and eighty concubines, and maidens without number.

[9] My dove, my perfect one is one; she is the only one of her mother; she is the choice of her that bore her. The daughters saw her, and the queens will pronounce her blessed, yes, and the concubines, and they will praise her.

[10] Who is this that looks forth as the morning, fair as the moon, choice as the sun, terrible as *armies* set in array?

[11] I went down to the garden of nuts, to look at the fruits of the valley, to see if the vine flowered, if the pomegranates blossomed.

[12] There I will give you my breasts: my soul did not know it: it made me as the chariots of Aminadab.

[13] Return, return, O Shulamite; return, return, and we will look at you. What will you see in the Shulamite? She comes as bands of armies.

SONG OF SOLOMON CHAPTER 7

[1] Your steps are beautiful in shoes, O daughter of the prince: the joints of your thighs are like chains, the work of the craftsman.

[2] Your navel is as a turned bowl, not wanting liquor; your belly is as a heap of wheat set about with lilies.

[3] Your two breasts are as two twin fawns.

[4] Your neck is as an ivory tower; your eyes are as pools in Heshbron, by the gates of the daughter of many: your nose is as the tower of Lebanon, looking toward Damascus.

[5] Your head upon you is as Carmel, and the curls of your hair like scarlet; the king is bound in the galleries.

[6] How beautiful are you, and how sweet are you, my love!

[7] This is your greatness in your delights: you were made like a palm tree, and your breasts to cluster.

[8] I said, "I will go up to the palm tree, I will take hold of its high boughs." And now shall your breasts be as clusters of the vine, and the smell of your nose as apples;

[9] and your throat as good wine, going well with my kinsman, suiting my lips and teeth.

[10] I am my kinsman's, and his desire is toward me.

[11] Come, my kinsman, let us go forth into the field; let us lodge in the villages.

[12] Let us go early into the vineyards; let us see if the vine has flowered, if the blossoms have appeared, if the pomegranates have blossomed; there will I give you my breasts.

[13] The mandrakes have given a smell, and at our doors are all kinds of choice fruits, new and old. O my kinsman, I have kept *them* for you.

SONG OF SOLOMON CHAPTER 8

[1] I would that you, O my kinsman, were he that nursed at the breasts of my mother; *if* I should find you outside, I would kiss you; I would not be despised.

[2] I would take you, I would bring you into my mother's house, and into the chamber of her that conceived me; I would make you to drink of spiced wine, of the juice of my pomegranates.

[3] His left hand *should be* under my head, and his right hand should embrace me.

[4] I have charged you, you daughters of Jerusalem, by the virtues of the field, that you do not stir up, nor awaken my love, until he please.

[5] Who is this that comes up all white, leaning on her kinsman? I raised you up under an apple tree; there your mother brought you forth; there she that bore you brought you forth.

[6] Set me as a seal upon your heart, as a seal upon your arm; for love is strong as death; jealousy is cruel as the grave, her shafts are shafts of fire, *even* the flames thereof.

[7] Much water will not be able to quench love, and rivers shall not drown it; if a man would give all his substance for love, men would utterly despise it.

[8] Our sister is little, and has no breasts; what shall we do for our sister, in the day when she shall be spoken for?

[9] If she is a wall, let us build upon her silver bulwarks; and if she is a door, let us carve for her cedar panels.

[10] I am a wall, and my breasts are as towers; I was in their eyes as one that found peace.

[11] Solomon had a vineyard in Baal Hamon; he leased his vineyard to keepers; everyone was to bring for its fruit a thousand pieces of silver.

[12] My vineyard, even mine, is before me; Solomon *shall have* a thousand, and they that keep its fruit two hundred.

[13] You that dwell in the gardens, the companions hearken to your voice: make me hear it. Make haste, my kinsman, and be like a doe or a fawn on the mountains of spices.

THE BOOK OF ISAIAH

[1] The vision which Isaiah the son of Amoz saw, which he saw concerning Judah, and Jerusalem, in the reign of Uzziah, Jotham, Ahaz, and Hezekiah, who reigned over Judah.

The Wickedness of Judah

[2] Hear, O heaven, and hearken, O earth! For the Lord has spoken, *saying*, "I have begotten and reared up children, but they have rebelled against Me.

[3] The ox knows his owner, and the donkey his master's crib; but Israel does not know Me, and the people have not regarded Me."

[4] Alas, sinful nation, a people full of sins, an evil seed, lawless children; you have forsaken the Lord, and provoked the Holy One of Israel.

[5] Why should you be smitten anymore, transgressing more and more? The whole head is pained, and the whole heart sad.

[6] From the feet to the head, there is no soundness in them; neither wound, nor bruise, nor festering ulcer *are healed*; it is not possible to apply a plaister, nor oil, nor bandages.

[7] Your land is desolate, your cities are burned with fire; strangers devour your land in your presence, and it is made desolate, overthrown by strange nations.

[8] The daughter of Zion shall be deserted as a tent in a vineyard, and as a storehouse of fruits in a garden of cucumbers, as a besieged city.

[9] And if the Lord of Sabaoth had not left us a seed, we would have become like Sodom, and been made like Gomorrah.

[10] Hear the word of the Lord, you rulers of Sodom; attend to the law of God, you people of Gomorrah.

[11] "Of what *value* to Me is the abundance of your sacrifices?" Says the Lord. "I am full of burnt offerings of rams; and I delight not in the fat of lambs, and the blood of bulls and goats;

[12] neither shall you come *with these* to appear before Me; for who has required these things at your hands? You shall no more tread My court.

[13] Though you bring fine flour, *it is* futile; incense is an abomination to Me; I cannot bear your new moons, and your Sabbaths, and the great day;

[14] *your* fasting, and rest from work, your new moons also, and your feasts My soul hates; you have become loathsome to Me; I will no longer pardon your sins.

[15] When you stretch forth your hands, I will turn away My eyes from you; and though you make many supplications, I will not hearken to you; for your hands are full of blood.

[16] Wash, and be clean; remove your iniquities from your souls before My eyes; cease from your iniquities;

[17] learn to do well; diligently seek judgment, deliver him that is suffering wrong, plead for the orphan, and obtain justice for the widow.

[18] "And come, let us reason together," says the Lord; "and though your sins be as purple, I will make them white as snow; and though they be as scarlet, I will make *them* white as wool.

[19] And if you are willing, and hearken to Me, you shall eat the good of the land;

[20] but if you be not willing, nor hearken to Me, a sword shall devour you; for the mouth of the Lord has spoken this."

The Degenerate City

[21] How has the faithful city of Zion, *once* full of judgment, become a harlot! Where righteousness lodged, but now murderers.

[22] Your silver is worthless, your wine merchants mix the wine with water.

[23] Your princes are rebellious, companions of thieves, loving bribes, seeking after rewards; not pleading for orphans, and not heeding the cause of widows.

[24] Therefore thus says the Lord, the Lord of hosts, "Woe to the mighty *men* of Israel; for My wrath shall not cease against My adversaries, and I will execute judgment on My enemies.

[25] And I will bring My hand upon you, and purge you completely, and I will destroy the rebellious, and I will take away all transgressors from you.

[26] And I will establish your judges as before, and your counselors as at the beginning; and afterward you shall be called the city of righteousness, the faithful mother city of Zion."

[27] For her captives shall be saved with judgment, and with mercy.

[28] And the transgressors and the sinners shall be crushed together, and they that forsake the Lord shall be utterly consumed.

29 For they shall be ashamed of their idols, which they delighted in, and they have been made ashamed of the gardens which they coveted.

30 For they shall be as a terebinth tree that has cast its leaves, and as a garden that has no water.

31 And their strength shall be as a thread of tow, and their works as sparks, and the transgressors and the sinners shall be burned up together, and there shall be none to quench *them*.

ISAIAH CHAPTER 2

The Future House of God

1 The word which came to Isaiah the son of Amoz concerning Judah, and concerning Jerusalem.

2 For in the last days the mountain of the Lord shall be glorious, and the house of God *shall be* on the top of the mountains, and it shall be exalted above the hills; and all nations shall come to it.

3 And many nations shall go and say, "Come, and let us go up to the mountain of the Lord, and to the house of the God of Jacob; and He will tell us His way, and we will walk in it"; for out of Zion shall go forth the law, and the word of the Lord out of Jerusalem.

4 And He shall judge among the nations, and shall rebuke many people; and they shall beat their swords into plowshares, and their spears into sickles; and nation shall not take up sword against nation, neither shall they learn to war anymore.

Judgment Pronounced on Arrogance

5 And now, O house of Jacob, come, *and* let us walk in the light of the Lord.

6 For He has forsaken His people the house of Israel, because their land is filled as at the beginning with divinations, as the *land* of the Philistines, and many strange children were born to them.

7 For their land is filled with silver and gold, and there was no number of their treasures; their land also is filled with horses, and there was no number of chariots.

8 And the land is filled with abominations, *even* the works of their hands; and they have worshipped *the works* which their fingers made.

9 And the mean man bowed down, and the great man was humbled; and I will not pardon them.

10 Now therefore enter into the rocks, and hide yourselves in the earth, for fear of the Lord, and by reason of the glory of His might, when He shall arise to strike mightily the earth.

11 For the eyes of the Lord are high, but man is low; and the haughtiness of men shall be brought low, and the Lord alone shall be exalted in that day.

12 For the day of the Lord of hosts shall be upon everyone that is proud and haughty, and upon everyone that is high and lifted up, and they shall be brought down;

13 and upon every cedar of Lebanon, of them that are high and lifted up, and upon every oak of Bashan,

14 and upon every high mountain, and upon every high hill,

15 and upon every high tower, and upon every high wall,

16 and upon every ship of the sea, and upon every display of fine ships.

17 And every man shall be brought low, and the pride of men shall fall; and the Lord alone shall be exalted in that day.

18 And they shall hide all *idols* made with hands,

19 having carried *them* into the caves, and into the clefts of the rocks, and into the caverns of the earth, for fear of the Lord, and by reason of the glory of His might, when He shall arise to strike mightily the earth.

20 For in that day a man shall cast forth his silver and gold abominations, which they made, *in order* to worship vanities and bats;

21 to enter into the caverns of the solid rock, and into the clefts of the rocks, for fear of the Lord, and by reason of the glory of His might, when He shall arise to strike mightily the earth.

ISAIAH CHAPTER 3

Judgment on Judah and Israel

1 Behold now, the Lord, the Lord of hosts, will take away from Jerusalem and from Judah the mighty man and mighty woman, the strength of bread, and the strength of water,

2 the great and mighty man, the warrior and the judge, the prophet, the counselor, and the elder,

3 the captain of fifty also, and the honorable counselor, and the skillful artisan, and the intelligent hearer.

4 And I will make youths their princes, and mockers shall have dominion over them.

5 And the people shall fall, man upon man, and *every* man upon his neighbor; the child shall insult the elder man, and the base *toward* the honorable.

6 For a man shall lay hold of his brother, as one of his father's household, saying, "You have clothing, you be our ruler, and let my food be under your *power*."

7 And he shall answer in that day, and say, "I will not be your ruler; for I have no bread in my house, nor clothing; I will not be the ruler of this people."

8 For Jerusalem is ruined, and Judah has fallen, and their tongues *have spoken* with iniquity, disobedient *as they are* towards the Lord.

9 Wherefore now their glory has been brought low, and the shame of their countenance has withstood them, and they have proclaimed their sin as Sodom, and made it manifest.

10 Woe to their soul, for they have devised an evil counsel against themselves, saying against themselves, "Let us bind the just, for he is burdensome to us; therefore shall they eat the fruits of their works."

[11] Woe to the transgressor! Evils shall happen to him according to the works of his hands.

[12] "O My people, your exactors strip you, and extortioners rule over you; O My people, they that pronounce you blessed lead you astray, and pervert the path of your feet."

[13] But now the Lord will stand up for judgment, and will enter into judgment with His people.

[14] The Lord Himself shall enter into judgment with the elders of the people, and with their rulers; "but why have you set My vineyard on fire, and *why is* the spoil of the poor in your houses?

[15] Why do you wrong My people, and shame the face of the poor?"

[16] Thus says the Lord, "Because the daughters of Zion are haughty, and have walked with an outstretched neck, and winking with their eyes, and jingling with their feet, at the same time drawing their garments in trains, and at the same time sporting with their feet;

[17] therefore the Lord will humble the chief daughters of Zion, and the Lord will expose their form in that day."

[18] And the Lord will take away the glory of their garments, the curls and the fringes, and the crescents,

[19] and the chains, and the ornaments of their faces,

[20] and the array of glorious ornaments, and the armlets, and the bracelets, and the wreathed work, and the finger rings, and the ornaments for the right hand,

[21] and the earrings, and the garments with scarlet borders,

[22] and the garments with purple grounds, and the shawls to be worn in the house, and the Spartan transparent dresses,

[23] and those made of fine linen, and the purple *ones*, and the scarlet *ones*, and the fine linen, interwoven with gold and purple, and the light coverings for couches.

[24] And instead of a sweet smell there shall be dust; and instead of a sash, you shall gird yourself with a rope; and instead of a golden ornament for your head, you shall have baldness on account of your works; and instead of a tunic with a scarlet ground, you shall gird yourself with sackcloth.

[25] And your most beautiful son whom you love shall fall by the sword; and your mighty men shall fall by the sword, and shall be brought low.

[26] And the stores of your ornaments shall mourn, and you shall be left alone, and shall be leveled to the ground.

ISAIAH CHAPTER 4

[1] And seven women shall take hold of one man, saying, "We will eat our own bread, and wear our own clothes; only let your name be called upon us, *and* take away our reproach."

TheFuture Glory of the Survivors in Zion

[2] And in that day God shall shine gloriously in counsel on the earth, to exalt and glorify the remnant of Israel.

[3] And it shall be, *that* the remnant left in Zion, and the remnant left in Jerusalem, *even* all that are appointed to life in Jerusalem, shall be called holy.

[4] For the Lord shall wash away the filth of the sons and daughters of Zion, and He shall purge out the blood from the midst of them, with the spirit of judgment, and the spirit of burning.

[5] And He shall come, and it shall be with regard to every place in Mount Zion, yea, all the region round about it shall a cloud overshadow by day, and *there shall be* as it were the smoke and light of fire burning by night; and upon all the glory shall be a defense.

[6] And it shall be for a shadow from the heat, and as a shelter and a hiding place from inclemency *of weather* and from rain.

ISAIAH CHAPTER 5

God's Disappointing Vineyard

[1] Now I will sing to *my* Beloved a song of my Beloved concerning His vineyard. *My* Beloved had a vineyard on a high hill in a fertile place.

[2] And I made a hedge round it, and dug a trench, and planted a choice vine, and built a tower in the midst of it, and dug a place for the wine vat in it; and I waited *for it* to bring forth grapes, and it brought forth thorns.

[3] And now, you inhabitants of Jerusalem, and *every* man of Judah, judge between Me and My vineyard.

[4] What shall I do anymore to My vineyard, that I have not done to it? Whereas I expected *it* to bring forth grapes, but it has brought forth thorns.

[5] And now I will tell you what I will do to My vineyard; I will take away its hedge, and it shall be for a spoil; and I will pull down its walls, and it shall be *left* to be trodden down.

[6] And I will forsake My vineyard; and it shall not be pruned, nor dug, and thorns shall come up upon it as on barren land; and I will command the clouds to rain no rain upon it.

[7] For the vineyard of the Lord of hosts is the house of Israel, and the men of Judah *His* beloved plant; I expected *it* to bring forth judgment, and it brought forth iniquity; and not righteousness, but a cry.

Social Injustice Denounced

[8] Woe *to them* that join house to house, and add field to field, that they may take away something of their neighbor's; will you dwell alone upon the land?

[9] For these things have reached the ears of the Lord of hosts; for though many houses should be built, many and fair houses shall be desolate, and there shall be no inhabitants in them.

[10] For where ten yoke of oxen plow *the land* shall yield one jar full, and he that sows six homers shall produce three measures.

[11] Woe *to them* that rise up in the morning, and follow strong drink; who wait *at it till* evening; for the wine shall inflame them.

12 For they drink wine with harp, and psaltery, and drums, and pipes; but they do not regard the works of the Lord, and do not consider the works of His hands.

13 Therefore my people have been taken captive, because they do not know the Lord; and there has been a multitude of dead *bodies*, because of hunger and of thirst for water.

14 Therefore hell has enlarged its desire and opened its mouth without ceasing; and her glorious and great, and her rich and her pestilent men shall go down *into it*.

15 And the mean man shall be brought low, and the great man shall be disgraced, and the lofty eyes shall be brought low.

16 But the Lord of hosts shall be exalted in judgment, and the holy God shall be glorified in righteousness.

17 And they that were spoiled shall be fed as bulls, and lambs shall feed on the waste places of them that are taken away.

18 Woe *to them* that draw sins to them as with a long rope, and iniquities as with a thong of the heifer's yoke;

19 who say, "Let him speedily hasten what he will do, that we may see *it*; and let the counsel of the Holy One of Israel come, that we may know *it*."

20 Woe *to them* that call evil good, and good evil; who make darkness light, and light darkness; who make bitter sweet, and sweet bitter.

21 Woe *to them* that are wise in their own conceit, and knowing in their own sight.

22 Woe to the strong of you that drink wine, and the mighty that mingle strong drink;

23 who justify the ungodly for rewards, and take away the righteousness of the righteous.

Foreign Invasion Predicted

24 Therefore as stubble shall be burned by a coal of fire, and shall be consumed by a violent flame, their root shall be as chaff, and their flower shall go up as dust; for they rejected the law of the Lord of hosts, and insulted the word of the Holy One of Israel.

25 Therefore the Lord of hosts was greatly angered against His people, and He reached forth His hand upon them, and struck them. And the mountains were troubled, and their carcasses were as dung in the midst of the streets; yet for all this His anger has not been turned away, but His hand is yet raised.

26 Therefore shall He lift up a signal to the nations that are afar, and shall whistle for them from the end of the earth; and behold, they are coming very quickly.

27 They shall not hunger nor be weary, neither shall they slumber nor sleep; neither shall they loose their sashes from their loins, neither shall they break their sandal straps be broken.

28 Whose arrows are sharp, and their bows bent; their horses' hoofs are counted as solid rock; their chariot wheels are as a storm.

29 They rage as lions, and draw near as a lion's whelps; and he shall seize, and roar as a wild beast, and he shall cast *them* forth, and there shall be none to deliver them.

30 And he shall roar on account of them in that day, as the sound of the swelling sea; and they shall look to the land, and behold, *there shall be* thick darkness in their perplexity.

ISAIAH CHAPTER 6

A Vision of God in the Temple

1 And it came to pass in the year in which King Uzziah died, *that* I saw the Lord sitting on a high and exalted throne, and the house was full of His glory.

2 And seraphim stood round about Him; each one had six wings; and with two they covered *their* face, and with two they covered *their* feet, and with two they flew.

3 And one cried to the other, and they said, "Holy, holy, holy *is the* Lord of hosts; the whole earth is full of His glory."

4 And the doorpost shook at the voice they uttered, and the house was filled with smoke.

5 And I said, "Woe is me, for I am pricked to the heart; for being a man, and having unclean lips, I dwell in the midst of a people having unclean lips; and I have seen with my eyes the King, the Lord of hosts."

6 Then one of the seraphim was sent to me, and he had in his hand a coal which he had taken off the altar with the tongs;

7 and he touched my mouth and said, "Behold, this has touched your lips, and will take away your iniquities, and will purge off your sins."

8 And I heard the voice of the Lord, saying, "Whom shall I send, and who will go to this people?" And I said, "Behold, *here* am I, send me." And He said, "Go, and say to this people,

9 'You shall hear indeed, but you shall not understand; and you shall see indeed, but you shall not perceive.'

10 For the heart of this people has become dull, and their ears are hard of hearing, and they have closed their eyes; lest they should see with their eyes, and hear with their ears, and understand with their heart, and be converted, and I should heal them."

11 And I said, "How long, O Lord?" And He said, "Until cities are deserted by reason of them not being inhabited, and the houses by reason of there being no men, and the land shall be left desolate."

12 And after this God shall remove the men far off, and they that are left upon the land shall be multiplied.

13 And yet there shall be a tenth upon it, and again it shall be for a spoil, as a terebinth tree, and as an acorn when it falls out of its husk.

ISAIAH CHAPTER 7

Isaiah Reassures King Ahaz

¹ And it came to pass in the days of Ahaz *the son* of Jotham, the son of Uzziah, king of Judah, that Rezin king of Aram, and Pekah son of Remaliah, king of Israel, came up against Jerusalem to war against it, but they could not take it.

² And a message was brought to the house of David, saying, "Aram has conspired with Ephraim." And his soul was amazed, and the soul of his people, as in a wood a tree is moved by the wind.

³ And the Lord said to Isaiah, "Go forth to meet Ahaz; you, and your son Jashub who is left, to the pool of the upper way of the fuller's field.

⁴ And you shall say to him, 'Take care to be quiet, and fear not, neither let your soul be disheartened because of these two smoking firebrands; for when My fierce anger is over, I will heal again.

⁵ And *as for* the son of Aram, and the son of Remaliah, forasmuch as they have devised an evil counsel, *saying,*

⁶ "We will go up against Judah, and having conferred with them we will turn them away to our side, and we will make the son of Tabel king over it";

⁷ thus says the Lord of hosts: "This counsel shall not abide, nor come to pass.

⁸ But the head of Aram is Damascus, and the head of Damascus *is* Rezin; and yet within sixty-five years the kingdom of Ephraim shall cease from *being* a people.

⁹ And the head of Ephraim is Samaria, and the head of Samaria the son of Romaliah; but if you do not believe, neither will you at all understand.'"

The Emmanuel Prophecy

¹⁰ And the Lord again spoke to Ahaz, saying,

¹¹ "Ask for yourself a sign of the Lord your God, in the depth or in the height."

¹² And Ahaz said, "I will not ask, neither will I tempt the Lord."

¹³ And he said, "Hear now, O house of David; is it a little thing for you to contend with men? And how do you contend against the Lord?

¹⁴ Therefore the Lord Himself shall give you a sign; behold, a virgin shall conceive in the womb, and shall bring forth a son, and you shall call His name Emmanuel.

¹⁵ Butter and honey shall He eat, before He knows either to prefer evil *or* choose the good.

¹⁶ For before the child shall know good or evil, He *shall* refuse evil, to choose the good; and the land shall be forsaken which you are afraid of because of the two kings.

¹⁷ But God shall bring upon you, and upon your people, and upon the house of your father, days which have never come, from the day that Ephraim took away from Judah the king of the Assyrians."

¹⁸ And it shall come to pass in that day that the Lord shall call for the flies, which shall rule over a part of the river of Egypt, and for the bee which is in the land of the Assyrians.

¹⁹ And they all shall enter into the clefts of the land, and into the holes of the rocks, and into the caves, and into every ravine.

²⁰ In that day the Lord shall shave with a hired razor the head of the king of Assyria beyond the river, and the hairs of the feet, and will remove the beard.

²¹ And it shall come to pass in that day, *that* a man shall rear a heifer, and two sheep.

²² And it shall come to pass from their drinking an abundance of milk, *that* everyone that is left on the land shall eat butter and honey.

²³ And it shall come to pass in that day, *for* every place where there shall be a thousand vines at a thousand shekels, they shall become barren land and thorns.

²⁴ *Men* shall enter there with arrow and bow; for all the land shall be *barren* ground and thorns.

²⁵ And every mountain shall be certainly plowed; and no fear shall come there; for there shall be from *among* the *barren* ground and thorns on which the cattle shall feed, and oxen shall tread.

ISAIAH CHAPTER 8

Assyria Will Invade the Land

¹ And the Lord said to me, "Take to yourself a volume of a great new *book*, and write in it with a man's pen concerning the making a rapid plunder of spoils; for it is close at hand.

² And make for Me witnesses *among* faithful men, Uriah, and Zechariah the son of Berechiah."

³ And I went in to the prophetess; and she conceived, and bore a son. And the Lord said to me, "Call his name, Spoil Quickly, Plunder Speedily.

⁴ For before the child shall know *how* to call *his* father or *his* mother, *one* shall take the power of Damascus and the spoils of Samaria before the king of the Assyrians."

⁵ And the Lord spoke to me yet again, *saying,*

⁶ "Because this people chooses not the water of Siloam that goes softly, but wills to have Rezin, and the son of Remaliah *to be* king over you;

⁷ therefore behold, the Lord shall bring upon you the water of the river, strong and abundant, *even* the king of the Assyrians, and his glory; and he shall come up over every valley of yours, and shall walk over every wall of yours;

⁸ and he shall take away from Judah *every* man who shall be able to lift up his head, *and everyone* able to accomplish anything; and his camp shall fill the breadth of your land, O Immanuel."

⁹ Know, you Gentiles, and be conquered; listen, even to the extremity of the earth; be conquered, after you strengthened yourselves; for even if you should again strengthen yourselves, you shall again be conquered.

¹⁰ And whatever counsel you shall take, the Lord shall bring it to nought; and whatever word you shall speak, it shall not stand among you; for God is with us.

[11] Thus says the Lord, "With a strong hand they revolt from the course of the way of this people, saying,

[12] 'Let them not say, "*It is* hard,"' for whatsoever this people says, is hard; but do not fear their fear, neither be dismayed."

[13] Sanctify the Lord Himself; and He shall be your fear.

[14] And if you shall trust in Him, He shall be to you for a sanctuary; and you shall not come against *Him* as against a stumbling stone, neither as against the falling of a rock; but the houses of Jacob are in a snare, and those who dwell in Jerusalem are in a pit.

[15] Therefore many among them shall be weak and fall, and be crushed; and they shall draw near, and men shall be taken securely.

[16] Then those who seal themselves, that they may not learn the law, shall be made manifest.

[17] And *one* shall say, "I will wait for God, who has turned away His face from the house of Jacob, and I will trust in Him."

[18] Behold I and the children which God has given me; and they shall be *for* signs and wonders in the house of Israel from the Lord of hosts, who dwells in Mount Zion.

[19] And if they should say to you, "Seek those who have in them a divining spirit, and those that speak from out of the ground"—those that speak vain words, who speak out of their belly; shall not a nation diligently seek their God? Why do they look to the dead concerning the living?

[20] For He has given the law for a help, that they should not speak according to this word, concerning which there are no gifts to give for it.

[21] And famine shall come sorely upon you, and it shall come to pass, *that* when you shall be hungry, you shall be grieved, and you shall speak evil of the prince and of your fathers' ordinances; and they shall look up to heaven above,

[22] and they shall look on the earth below, and behold severe distress, and darkness, affliction, and anguish, and darkness so that *no one* can see; and he that is in anguish shall not be distressed only for a season.

ISAIAH CHAPTER 9

The Righteous Reign of the Coming King

[1] Drink this first. Act quickly, O land of Zebulun, land of Naphtali, and the rest *that inhabit* the seacoast, and *the land* beyond the Jordan, Galilee of the Gentiles.

[2] O people walking in darkness, behold a great light; you that dwell in the region *and* shadow of death, a light shall shine upon you.

[3] The multitude of the people which you have brought down in your joy, they shall even rejoice before you as they that rejoice in harvest, and as they that divide the spoil.

[4] Because the yoke that was laid upon them has been taken away, and the rod that was on their neck; for he has broken the rod of the exactors, as in the day of Midian.

[5] For they shall compensate for every garment that has been acquired by deceit, and *all* garments with restitution; and they shall be willing, *even* if they were burned with fire.

[6] For a Child is born to us, and a Son is given to us, whose government is upon His shoulder; and His name is called The Messenger of Great Counsel; for I will bring peace upon the princes, and health to Him.

[7] His government shall be great, and of His peace there is no end; *it shall be* upon the throne of David, and *upon* His kingdom, to establish it, and to support *it* with judgment and with righteousness, from this time forward and forevermore. The zeal of the Lord of hosts shall perform this.

The Punishment of Samaria

[8] The Lord has sent death upon Jacob, and it has come upon Israel.

[9] And all the people of Ephraim, and those that dwelt in Samaria shall know, who say in their pride and lofty heart,

[10] "The bricks are fallen down, but come, let us hew stones, and cut down sycamores and cedars, and let us build for ourselves a tower."

[11] And God shall dash them down that rise up against Him on Mount Zion, and He shall scatter His enemies;

[12] *even* Syria from the rising of the sun, and the Greeks from the setting of the sun, who devour Israel with open mouth. For all this *His* anger is not turned away, but still *His* hand is exalted.

[13] But the people did not turn until they were smitten, and they did not seek the Lord.

[14] So the Lord took away from Israel the head and tail, great and small, in one day;

[15] the old man, and them that respect persons, this is the head; and the prophet teaching unlawful things, he is the tail.

[16] And they that pronounce this people blessed shall mislead them; and they mislead them that they may devour them.

[17] Therefore the Lord shall not take pleasure in their young men, neither shall He have pity on their orphans or on their widows; for they are all transgressors and wicked, and every mouth speaks unjustly. For all this *His* anger is not turned away, but *His* hand is yet exalted.

[18] And iniquity shall burn as fire, and shall be devoured by fire as dry grass; and it shall burn in the thickets of the wood, and shall devour all that is round about the hills.

[19] The whole earth is set on fire because of the fierce anger of the Lord, and the people shall be as men burned by fire; no man shall pity his brother.

[20] But *one* shall turn aside to the right hand, for he shall be hungry; and shall eat on the left, and a man shall by no means be satisfied with eating the flesh of his own arm.

[21] For Manasseh shall eat *the flesh* of Ephraim, and Ephraim *the flesh* of Manasseh; for they shall besiege Judah together. For all this *His* anger is not turned away, but *His* hand is yet exalted.

ISAIAH CHAPTER 10

[1] "Woe to them that write wickedness; for when they write, they write wickedness,

[2] perverting the cause of the poor, violently seizing the judgment of the needy ones of My people, that the widow may be a prey to them, and the orphan a spoil.

[3] And what will they do in the day of visitation? For affliction shall come to you from afar; and to whom will you flee for help? And where will you leave your glory,

[4] that you may not fall into captivity? For all this *His* wrath is not turned away, but *His* hand is yet exalted.

Arrogant Assyria Also Judged

[5] "Woe to the Assyrians; the rod of My wrath and anger are in their hands.

[6] I will send My wrath against a sinful nation, and I will command My people to take plunder and spoil, and to trample the cities, and to make dust out of them.

[7] But he does not mean so, neither did he devise thus in his heart; but his mind shall change, and *that* to destroy nations not a few.

[8] And if they should say to him, 'You alone are ruler';

[9] then shall he say, 'Have I not taken the country above Babylon and Chalanes, where the tower was built? And have I *not* taken Arabia, and Damascus, and Samaria?'

[10] As I have taken them, I will also take all the kingdoms; howl, you idols in Jerusalem, and in Samaria.

[11] For as I did to Samaria and her idols, so will I also do to Jerusalem and her idols."

[12] And it shall come to pass, when the Lord has finished doing all things on Mount Zion and Jerusalem, *that* I will visit upon the proud heart, *even* upon the ruler of the Assyrians, and upon the boastful haughtiness of his eyes.

[13] For he said, I will act in strength, and in the wisdom of *my* understanding I will remove the boundaries of nations, and will spoil their strength.

[14] And I will shake the inhabited cities; and I will take with My hand all the world as a nest; and I will even take them as eggs that have been left; and there is none that shall escape Me, or contradict Me.

[15] Shall the ax glorify itself without him that chops with it? Or shall the saw lift itself up without him that uses it, as if one should lift a rod or staff? But it shall not be so;

[16] but the Lord of hosts shall send dishonor upon your honor, and burning fire shall be kindled upon your glory.

[17] And the light of Israel shall be for a fire, and He shall sanctify him with burning fire, and it shall devour the wood as grass.

[18] In that day the mountains shall be consumed, and the hills, and the forests, and *fire* shall devour *both* soul and body; and he that flees shall be as one fleeing from a burning flame.

[19] And they that are left of them shall be a *small* number, and a child shall write them.

The Returning Remnant of Israel

[20] And it shall come to pass in that day *that* the remnant of Israel shall no more join themselves with, and the saved of Jacob shall no more trust in them that injured them; but they shall trust in the Holy God of Israel, in truth.

[21] And the remnant of Jacob shall *trust* in the mighty God.

[22] And though the people of Israel be as the sand of the sea, a remnant of them shall be saved.

[23] He will finish the work, and cut it short in righteousness; because the Lord will make a short work in all the world.

[24] Therefore thus says the Lord of hosts: "Be not afraid, My people who dwell in Zion, of the Assyrians, because he shall smite you with a rod; for I am bringing a stroke upon you, that *you* may see the way of Egypt.

[25] For yet a little while, and the indignation shall cease; but My wrath shall be against their counsel."

[26] And God will stir up *enemies* against them, according to the stroke of Midian in the place of affliction; and His wrath shall be by the way of the sea, *even* to the way that leads to Egypt.

[27] And it shall come to pass in that day, *that* his yoke shall be taken away from your shoulder, and his fear from you, and the yoke shall be destroyed from off your shoulders.

[28] For he shall arrive at the city of Aiath, and shall pass on to Migron, and shall lay up his stores in Michmash.

[29] And he shall pass by the valley, and shall arrive at Aiath; fear shall seize upon Ramah, the city of Saul.

[30] The daughter of Gallim shall flee; Laish shall hear; one shall hear in Anathoth.

[31] Madmenah also is amazed, and the inhabitants of Gebim.

[32] Exhort *them* today to remain in the way; exhort, *beckoning* the mountain with your hand, the daughter of Zion, even you hills that are in Jerusalem.

[33] Behold, the Lord, the Lord of hosts, will mightily confound the glorious ones; and the haughty in pride shall be crushed, and the lofty shall be brought low;

[34] and the lofty ones shall fall by the sword, and Lebanon shall fall with his lofty ones.

ISAIAH CHAPTER 11

The Reign of Jesse's Offspring

[1] And there shall come forth a Rod out of the root of Jesse, and a blossom shall come up from *his* root;

[2] and the Spirit of God shall rest upon Him, the spirit of wisdom and understanding, the spirit of counsel and strength, the spirit of knowledge and godliness shall fill Him;

[3] the spirit of the fear of God. He shall not judge according to appearance, nor reprove according to report;

4 but He shall judge the cause of the lowly, and shall reprove the lowly of the earth; and He shall smite the earth with the word of His mouth, and with the breath of His lips shall He destroy the ungodly one.

5 And He shall have His loins girded with righteousness, and His sides clothed with truth.

6 And the wolf shall feed with the lamb, and the leopard shall lie down with the kid; and the young calf and bull and lion shall feed together; and a little child shall lead them.

7 And the ox and bear shall feed together; and their young shall be together; and the lion shall eat straw like the ox.

8 And an infant shall put his hand into the holes of asps, and on the nest of young asps.

9 And they shall not be hurt, nor shall they be able to destroy anyone on My holy mountain; for the whole *world* is filled with the knowledge of the Lord, as much water covers the seas.

10 And in that day there shall be a Root of Jesse, and He that shall arise to rule over the Gentiles; in Him shall the Gentiles trust, and His rest shall be glorious.

11 And it shall be in that day, *that* the Lord shall again show His hand, to be zealous for the remnant that is left of the people, which shall be left by the Assyrians, and *that* from Egypt, and from the country of Babylon, and from Ethiopia, and from the Elamites, and from the rising of the sun, and out of Arabia.

12 And He shall lift up a standard for the nations, and He shall gather the lost ones of Israel, and He shall gather the dispersed of Judah from the four corners of the earth.

13 And the envy of Ephraim shall be taken away, and the enemies of Judah shall perish; Ephraim shall not envy Judah, and Judah shall not afflict Ephraim.

14 And they shall fly in the ships of the Philistines; they shall at the same time spoil the sea, and them *that come* from the east, and Edom; and they shall lay their hands on Moab first; but the children of Ammon shall first obey *them*.

15 And the Lord shall make desolate the sea of Egypt; and He shall lay His hand on the river with a strong wind, and He shall smite the seven channels, so that men shall pass through it dry-shod.

16 And there shall be a passage for His people that are left in Egypt; and it shall be to Israel as the day when he came forth out of the land of Egypt.

ISAIAH CHAPTER 12

1 And in that day you shall say, "I *will* bless You, O Lord; for You were angry with me, but You have turned aside Your wrath, and have pitied me."

2 Behold, my God is my Savior; I will trust in Him, and not be afraid; for the Lord is my glory and my praise, and has become my salvation.

3 Therefore draw water with joy out of the wells of salvation.

4 And in that day you shall say, "Sing to the Lord, call aloud upon His name, proclaim His glorious *deeds* among the Gentiles; make mention that His name is exalted.

5 Sing praise to the name of the Lord; for He has done great *things*; declare this in all the earth.

6 Exalt and rejoice, you that dwell in Zion; for the Holy One of Israel is exalted in the midst of her."

ISAIAH CHAPTER 13

Proclamation Against Babylon

1 The vision which Isaiah son of Amoz saw against Babylon.

2 "Lift up a standard on the mountain of the plain, exalt the voice to them, beckon with the hand, open *the gates*, you rulers.

3 I give command, and I bring them; giants are coming to fulfill My wrath, rejoicing at the same time and insulting."

4 A voice of many nations on the mountains, *even like to that* of many nations; a voice of kings and nations gathered together; the Lord of hosts has given command to a war-like nation,

5 to come from a land afar off, from the utmost foundation of heaven; the Lord and His warriors *are coming* to destroy all the world.

6 Howl, for the day of the Lord is near, and destruction from God shall arrive.

7 Therefore every hand shall become powerless, and every soul of man shall be dismayed.

8 The elders shall be troubled, and pangs shall seize them, as of a woman in labor; and they shall mourn one to another, and shall be amazed, and shall change their countenance as a flame.

9 For behold, the day of the Lord is coming which cannot be escaped, *a day* of wrath and anger, to make the world desolate, and to destroy sinners out of it.

10 For the stars of heaven, and Orion, and all the host of heaven, shall not give their light; and it shall be dark at sunrise, and the moon shall not give her light.

11 "And I will command evils for the whole world, and *will visit* their sins on the ungodly; and I will destroy the pride of transgressors, and will bring low the pride of the haughty.

12 And they that are left shall be more precious than gold tried in the fire; and a man shall be more precious than the stone that is in Ophir."

13 For the heaven shall be enraged, and the earth shall be shaken from her foundation, because of the fierce anger of the Lord of hosts, in the day in which His wrath shall come on.

14 And they that are left shall be as a fleeing fawn, and as a stray sheep, and there shall be none to gather *them*; so that a man shall turn back to his people, and a man shall flee to his own land.

15 For whosoever shall be taken shall be overcome; and they that are gathered together shall fall by the sword.

¹⁶ And they shall dash their children before their eyes; and they shall spoil their houses, and shall take their wives.

¹⁷ "Behold, I will stir up the Medes against you, who do not regard silver, neither have they need of gold.

¹⁸ They shall break the bows of the young men; and they shall have no mercy on your children; nor shall their eyes spare your children.

¹⁹ And Babylon, which is called glorious by the king of the Chaldeans, shall be as *when* God overthrew Sodom and Gomorrah.

²⁰ It shall never be inhabited, neither shall any enter into it for many generations; neither shall the Arabians pass through it; nor shall shepherds at all rest in it.

²¹ But wild beasts shall rest there; and the houses shall be filled with howling; and monsters shall rest there, and demons shall dance there,

²² and satyrs shall dwell there; and hedgehogs shall make their nests in their houses. It will come soon, and will not tarry."

ISAIAH CHAPTER 14

Mercy on Jacob

¹ And the Lord will have mercy on Jacob, and will yet choose Israel, and they shall rest on their land; and the stranger shall be added to them; yes, they shall be added to the house of Jacob.

² And the Gentiles shall take them, and bring them into their place; and they shall inherit them, and they shall be multiplied upon the land for servants and handmaidens; and they that took them captives shall become captives *to them*; and they that had lordship over them shall be under *their* rule.

³ And it shall come to pass in that day, *that* the Lord shall give you rest from your sorrow and vexation, *and from* your hard servitude in which you served them.

⁴ And you shall take up this lamentation against the king of Babylon: "How has the extortioner ceased, and the taskmaster ceased!

⁵ The Lord has broken the yoke of sinners, *and* the yoke of princes.

⁶ Having smitten a nation in wrath with an incurable plague, smiting a nation with a wrathful plague, which did not spare, he rested in quiet.

⁷ All the earth cries aloud with joy;

⁸ the trees of Lebanon also rejoice against you, and the cedars of Lebanon, *saying*, 'From the time that you have been laid low, no one has come up to cut us down.'

⁹ Hell from beneath is provoked to meet you; all the great ones that have ruled over the earth have risen up together against you, they that have raised up from their thrones all the kings of the nations.

¹⁰ All shall answer and say to you, 'You also have been taken, even as we; and you are numbered amongst us.

¹¹ Your glory has come down to Hades, and your great mirth; under you they shall spread corruption, and the worm shall be your covering.'

The Fall of Lucifer

¹² "How has Lucifer, that rose of the morning, fallen from heaven! He that sent *orders* to all the nations is crushed to the earth.

¹³ But you have said in your heart, 'I will go up to heaven, I will set my throne above the stars of heaven; I will sit on a lofty mount, on the lofty mountains toward the north;

¹⁴ I will go up above the clouds; I will be like the Most High.'

¹⁵ "But now you shall go down to hell, even to the foundations of the earth!

¹⁶ They that see you shall marvel at you, and say, 'Is this is the man that troubled the earth, that made kings to shake?

¹⁷ Who made the whole world desolate, and destroyed its cities; he loosed not those who were in captivity.'

¹⁸ All the kings of the nations lie in honor, *every* man in his house.

¹⁹ But you shall be cast forth on the mountains, as a loathsome carcass, with many dead who have been pierced with swords, going down to the grave.

²⁰ As a garment defiled with blood shall not be pure, so neither shall you be pure; because you have destroyed My land, and have slain My people; you shall not endure forever; *you are* an evil seed.

²¹ Prepare your children to be slain for the sins of their father; that they may not arise, and inherit the earth, nor fill the earth with wars.

Babylon Destroyed

²² "And I will rise up against them," says the Lord of hosts, "and I will destroy their name, and remnant, and seed"; thus says the Lord.

²³ "And I will make the region of Babylon a desert, so that hedgehogs shall dwell *there*, and it shall come to nothing; and I will make it a pit of clay for destruction."

Assyria Destroyed

²⁴ Thus says the Lord of hosts: "As I have said, so it shall be; and as I have purposed, so *the matter* shall remain;

²⁵ *even* to destroy the Assyrians upon My land, and upon My mountains; and they shall be for trampling; and their yoke shall be taken away from them, and their glory shall be taken away from their shoulders."

²⁶ This is the purpose which the Lord has purposed upon the whole earth; and this the hand that is uplifted against all the nations.

²⁷ For what the Holy God has purposed, who shall frustrate? And who shall turn back His uplifted hand?

Philistia Destroyed

²⁸ In the year in which King Ahaz died, this word came:

²⁹ "Do not rejoice, all you Philistines, because the yoke of him that struck you is broken; for out of the seed of the serpent shall come forth the young asps, and their young shall come forth *as* flying serpents,

³⁰ and the poor shall be fed by him, and poor men shall rest in peace; but he shall destroy your offspring with hunger, and shall destroy your remnant.

³¹ Howl, you gates of cities; let the cities be troubled and cry, *even* all the Philistines; for smoke is coming from the north, and there is no *possibility* of living."

³² And what shall the kings of the nations answer? That the Lord has founded Zion, and by Him the poor of the people shall be saved.

ISAIAH CHAPTER 15

Proclamation Against Moab

¹ The word against the land of Moab. By night the land of Moab shall be destroyed; for by night the wall of the land of Moab shall be destroyed.

² Grieve for yourselves; for even Dibon, where your altar is, shall be destroyed; there shall you go up to weep, over Nebo of the land of Moab; howl; baldness shall be on every head, *and* all arms *shall be* wounded.

³ Gird yourselves with sackcloth in her streets; and lament upon her roofs, and in her streets, and in her ways; howl, all of you, with weeping.

⁴ For Heshbon and Elealeh have cried; their voice was heard to Jahaz; therefore the loins of the region of Moab cry aloud; her soul shall know.

⁵ The heart of the region of Moab cries within her to Segor; for it is *as* a heifer of three years old; and on the Ascent of Luith they shall go up to you weeping by the way of Aroniim; she cries, "Destruction, and trembling."

⁶ The water of Nimrim shall be desolate, and its grass shall fail; for there shall be no green grass.

⁷ Shall *Moab* even thus be delivered? "For I *will* bring the Arabians upon the valley, and they shall take it.

⁸ For the cry has reached the border of the region of Moab, *even* of Eglaim; and her howling *has gone* as far as the Well of Elim.

⁹ And the water of Dimon shall be filled with blood; for I will bring Arabians upon Dimon, and I will take away the descendants of Moab, and Ariel, and the remnant of Adamah."

ISAIAH CHAPTER 16

Moab Destroyed

¹ "I will send as it were reptiles on the land; is *not* the mount of the daughter of Zion a desolate rock?

² For you shall be as a young bird taken away from a bird that has flown; *even* you shall be *so*, O daughter of Moab; and then do you, O Arnon,

³ take farther counsel, and continually make a shelter from grief; they flee in darkness at midday; they are amazed; do not be led captive.

⁴ The fugitives of Moab shall sojourn with you; they shall be to you a shelter from the face of the pursuer; for your alliance has been taken away, and the oppressing ruler has perished from off the earth.

⁵ And a throne shall be established with mercy; and one shall sit upon it with truth in the tabernacle of David, judging, and earnestly seeking judgments, and hastening righteousness."

⁶ We have heard of the pride of Moab; he is very proud. I have cut off his pride; your prophecy shall not be thus, *no* not thus.

⁷ Moab shall howl; for all shall howl in the land of Moab; but you shall care for them that dwell in Hareseth, and you shall not be ashamed.

⁸ The plains of Heshbon shall mourn, the vine of Sibmah; swallowing up the nations, trample her vines, even to Jazer; you shall not come together; wander in the desert; they that were sent are deserted, for they have gone over to the sea.

⁹ Therefore will I weep as with the weeping of Jazer for the vine of Sibmah; Heshbon and Elealeh have cast down your trees; for I will trample on your harvest and on your vintages, and all *your plants* shall fall.

¹⁰ And gladness and rejoicing shall be taken away from the vineyards; and they shall not at all tread wine into the vats; for *the* vintage has ceased.

¹¹ Therefore my belly shall sound as a harp for Moab, and you have repaired my inward parts as a wall.

¹² And it shall be to your shame (for Moab is wearied at the altars), that he shall go in to the idols thereof to pray, but they shall by no means be able to deliver him.

¹³ This is the word which the Lord spoke against Moab, when He spoke.

¹⁴ "And now I say, in three years, of the years of a hireling, the glory of Moab shall be dishonored *with* all his great wealth; and he shall be left few in number, and not honored."

ISAIAH CHAPTER 17

Proclamation Against Syria and Israel

¹ The word against Damascus. "Behold, Damascus shall be taken away from among cities, and shall become a ruin;

² abandoned forever, to *be* a fold and resting place for flocks, and there shall be none to go after them.

³ And she shall no longer be a strong place for Ephraim to flee to, and there shall no longer be a kingdom in Damascus, or a remnant of Syrians; for you are no better

than the children of Israel, *even* than their glory"; thus says the Lord of hosts.

⁴ "There shall be in that day a failure of the glory of Jacob, and the riches of his glory shall be shaken.

⁵ And it shall be as if one should gather standing grain, and reap the grain off the ears; and it shall be as if one should gather heads of grain in a rich valley;

⁶ and *as if* there should be left stubble therein, or the berries of an olive tree, two or three on the topmost bough, or *as if* four or five should be left on their branches"; thus says the Lord, the God of Israel.

⁷ In that day a man shall trust in Him that made him, and his eyes shall have respect to the Holy One of Israel.

⁸ And they shall not at all trust in their altars, nor in the works of their hands, which their fingers made; and they shall not look to the trees, nor to their abominations.

⁹ In that day your cities shall be deserted, as the Amorites and the Evaens deserted *theirs*, because of the children of Israel; and they shall be desolate.

¹⁰ Because you have forsaken God your Savior, and have not been mindful of the Lord your Helper; therefore shall you plant a false plant, and a false seed.

¹¹ In the day in which you shall plant you shall be deceived; but if you sow in the morning, *the seed* shall spring up for a crop in the day in which you shall obtain an inheritance, and as a man's father, you shall obtain an inheritance for your sons.

¹² Woe *to* the multitude of many nations, as the swelling sea, so shall you be confounded; and the force of many nations shall sound like water;

¹³ many nations like much water, as when much water rushes violently; and they shall drive him away, and pursue him afar, as the dust of chaff when men winnow before the wind, and as a storm whirling the dust of the wheel.

¹⁴ Toward evening, and there shall be grief; before the morning, and he shall not be. This is the portion of them that spoiled you, and the inheritance to them that robbed you of your inheritance.

ISAIAH CHAPTER 18

Proclamation Against Ethiopia

¹ Woe to you, you wings of the land of ships, beyond the rivers of Ethiopia.

² He sends messengers by the sea, and paper letters on the water; for swift messengers shall go to a lofty nation, and to a strange and harsh people. Who is beyond it? A nation not looked for, and trodden down.

³ Now all the rivers of the land shall be inhabited as an inhabited country; their land shall be as when a signal is raised from a mountain; it shall be audible as the sound of a trumpet.

⁴ For thus said the Lord to me: "There shall be security in My city, as the light of noonday heat, and it shall be as a cloud of dew in the day of harvest."

⁵ Before the reaping time, when the flower has been completely formed, and the unripe grape has put forth its flower and blossomed, then shall He take away the little clusters with pruning hooks, and shall take away the small branches, and cut them off;

⁶ And He shall leave *them* together to the birds of the sky, and to the wild beasts of the earth; and the fowls of the sky shall be gathered upon them, and all the beasts of the land shall come upon them.

⁷ In that time shall presents be brought to the Lord of hosts from a people afflicted and peeled, and from a people great from henceforth and forever; a nation hoping and *yet* trodden down, which is in a part of a river of His land, to the place where is the name of the Lord of hosts, the Mount Zion.

ISAIAH CHAPTER 19

Proclamation Against Egypt

¹ The vision of Egypt. Behold, the Lord sits on a swift cloud, and shall come to Egypt. And the idols of Egypt shall be moved at His presence, and their hearts shall faint within them.

² And the Egyptians shall be stirred up against the Egyptians; and a man shall fight against his brother, and a man against his neighbor, city against city, and law against law.

³ And the spirit of the Egyptians shall be troubled within them. "I will frustrate their counsel; and they shall inquire of their gods and their images, and them that speak out of the earth, and them that have in them a divining spirit.

⁴ And I will deliver Egypt into the hands of men, of cruel masters; and cruel kings shall rule over them"; thus says the Lord of hosts.

⁵ And the Egyptians shall drink the water that is by the sea, but the river shall fail, and be dried up.

⁶ And the streams shall fail, and the canals of the river; and every reservoir of water shall be dried up, in every marsh also of reed and papyrus.

⁷ And all the green herbs round about the river, and everything sown by the side of the river, shall be blasted with the wind and dried up.

⁸ And the fishermen shall groan, and all that cast a hook into the river shall groan; they also that cast nets, and the anglers shall mourn.

⁹ And shame shall come upon them that work fine flax, and them that make fine linen.

¹⁰ And they that work at them shall be in pain, and all that brew beer shall be grieved, and be pained in their souls.

¹¹ And the princes of Tanis shall be fools; *as for* the king's wise counselors, their counsel shall be turned into folly; how

will you say to the king, "We are sons of wise men, sons of ancient kings?"

¹² Where are your wise men now? And let them declare to you, and say, "What has the Lord of hosts purposed upon Egypt?"

¹³ The princes of Tanis have failed, and the princes of Memphis are lifted up *with pride*, and they shall cause Egypt to wander by tribes.

¹⁴ For the Lord has prepared for them a spirit of error, and they have caused Egypt to err in all their works, as one staggers who is drunken and vomits also.

¹⁵ And there shall be no work to the Egyptians, which shall make head or tail, or beginning or end.

¹⁶ But in that day the Egyptians shall be as women, in fear and in trembling because of the hand of the Lord of hosts, which He shall bring upon them.

¹⁷ And the land of the Jews shall be for a terror to the Egyptians; whosoever shall name it to them, they shall fear, because of the counsel which the Lord of hosts has purposed concerning it.

Egypt, Assyria, and Israel Blessed

¹⁸ In that day there shall be five cities in Egypt speaking the language of Canaan, and swearing by the name of the Lord of hosts; one city shall be called the City of Asedek.

¹⁹ In that day there shall be an altar to the Lord in the land of the Egyptians, and a pillar to the Lord by its border.

²⁰ And it shall be for a sign to the Lord forever in the land of Egypt; for they shall presently cry to the Lord by reason of them that afflict them, and He shall send them a man who shall save them; He shall judge and save them.

²¹ And the Lord shall be known to the Egyptians, and the Egyptians shall know the Lord in that day; and they shall offer sacrifices, and shall vow vows to the Lord, and pay *them*.

²² And the Lord shall strike the Egyptians with a stroke, and shall completely heal them; and they shall return to the Lord, and He shall hear them, and thoroughly heal them.

²³ In that day there shall be a way from Egypt to the Assyrians, and the Assyrians shall enter into Egypt, and the Egyptians shall go to the Assyrians, and the Egyptians shall serve the Assyrians.

²⁴ In that day shall Israel be third with the Egyptians and the Assyrians, blessed in the land which the Lord of hosts has blessed,

²⁵ saying, "Blessed be My people that are in Egypt, and that are among the Assyrians, and Israel My inheritance."

ISAIAH CHAPTER 20

The Sign Against Egypt and Ethiopia

¹ In the year that Tartan came to Ashdod, when he was sent by Sargon king of the Assyrians, and warred against Ashdod, and took it;

² then the Lord spoke to Isaiah the son of Amoz, saying, "Go and take the sackcloth off your loins, and loose your sandals from off your feet, and do thus, going naked and barefoot."

³ And the Lord said, "As My servant Isaiah has walked naked and barefoot three years, there shall be three years for signs and wonders to the Egyptians and Ethiopians;

⁴ for thus shall the king of the Assyrians lead the captivity of Egypt and the Ethiopians, young men and old, naked and barefoot, having the shame of Egypt exposed.

⁵ And the Egyptians, being defeated, shall be ashamed of the Ethiopians, in whom they had trusted; for they were their glory.

⁶ And they that dwell in this island shall say in that day, 'Behold, we trusted to flee to them for help, who could not save themselves from the king of the Assyrians; and how shall we be saved?'"

ISAIAH CHAPTER 21

¹ The vision of the desert. As though a whirlwind should pass through the desert, coming from a desert, *even* from such a land,

² *so* a fearful and a grievous vision was declared to me; he that is treacherous deals treacherously, the transgressor transgresses. The Elamites are upon me, and the ambassadors of the Persians come against me; now will I groan and comfort myself.

³ Therefore are my loins filled with feebleness, and pangs have seized me as a travailing woman; I dealt wrongfully that I might not hear; I hastened that I might not see.

⁴ My heart wanders, and transgression overwhelms me; my soul is occupied with fear.

⁵ Prepare the table; eat, drink. Arise, you princes, and prepare *your* shields.

⁶ For thus said the Lord to me: "Go and station a watchman for yourself, and declare whatever you shall see."

⁷ And I saw two mounted horsemen, and a rider on a donkey, and a rider on a camel.

⁸ "Listen with great attention, and call Uriah to the watchtower"; the Lord has spoken. I stood continually during the day, and I stood in the camp all night;

⁹ and behold, he comes riding in a chariot and pair; and he answered and said, "Babylon is fallen, is fallen; and all her images and her idols have been crushed to the ground."

¹⁰ Hear, you that are left, and you that are in pain, hear what things I have heard of the Lord of hosts, *which* the God of Israel has declared to us.

¹¹ The vision of Edom. Call to me out of Seir; guard the bulwarks.

¹² I watch in the morning and the night, if you would inquire, inquire, and dwell by me.

¹³ You may lodge in the forest in the evening, or in the way of Dedan.

[14] You that dwell in the country of Tema, bring water to meet him that is thirsty;

[15] meet the fugitives with bread, because of the multitude of the slain, and because of the multitude of them that lose their way, and because of the multitude of swords, and because of the multitude of bent bows, and because of the multitude of them that have fallen in war.

[16] For thus said the Lord to me, "Yet a year, as the year of a hireling, *and* the glory of the sons of Kedar shall fail";

[17] and the remnant of the strong bows of the sons of Kedar shall be small; for the Lord God of Israel has spoken *it*.

ISAIAH CHAPTER 22

Proclamation Against Jerusalem

[1] The word of the valley of Zion. What has happened to you, that you now are all going up to the housetops, which do not help you?

[2] The city is filled with shouting; your slain are not slain with swords, nor are your dead those who have died in battle.

[3] All your princes have fled, and *your* captives are tightly bound, and the mighty *men* in you have fled far away.

[4] Therefore I said, "Let me alone, I will weep bitterly; labor not to comfort me for the breach of the daughter of my people."

[5] For *it is* a day of trouble, and of destruction, and of treading down, and *there is* perplexity *sent* from the Lord of hosts; they wander in the valley of Zion; they wander from the least to the greatest on the mountains.

[6] And the Elamites took *their* quivers, and *there were* men mounted on horses, and *there was* a gathering for battle.

[7] And it shall be *that* your choice valleys shall be filled with chariots, and horsemen shall block up your gates.

[8] And they shall uncover the gates of Judah, and they shall look in that day on the choice houses of the city.

[9] And they shall uncover the secret places of the houses of the citadel of David; and they saw that they were many, and that one *had* turned the water of the old pool into the city;

[10] and that they *had* pulled down the houses of Jerusalem, to fortify the wall of the city.

[11] And you procured for yourselves water between the two walls within the ancient pool; but you did not look to Him that made it from the beginning, and did not regard Him that created it.

[12] And the Lord, the Lord of hosts, called in that day for weeping, and lamentation, and baldness, and for girding with sackcloth;

[13] but they engaged in joy and gladness, slaying calves, and killing sheep, so as to eat flesh, and drink wine; saying, "Let us eat and drink; for tomorrow we die."

[14] And these things are revealed in the ears of the Lord of hosts; for this sin shall not be forgiven you, until you die.

The Judgment on Shebna

[15] Thus says the Lord of hosts: "Go into the chamber, to Shebna the treasurer, and say to him, 'Why are you here?

[16] And what have you to do here, that you have hewn yourself a tomb, and made yourself a tomb on high, and have graven for yourself a dwelling in the rock?'

[17] Behold now, the Lord of hosts casts forth and will utterly destroy *such* a man, and will take away your robe and your glorious crown,

[18] and will cast you into a great and unmeasured land, and there you shall die; and He will bring your fair chariot to shame, and the house of your prince to be trodden down.

[19] And you shall be removed from your stewardship, and from your place.

[20] "And it shall come to pass in that day, that I will call My servant Eliakim the son of Hilkiah;

[21] and I will put on him your robe, and I will grant him your crown with power, and I will give your stewardship into his hands; and he shall be as a father to them that dwell in Jerusalem, and to them that dwell in Judah.

[22] And I will give him the glory of David; and he shall rule, and there shall be none to speak against him; and I will give him the key of the house of David *upon* his shoulder. And he shall open, and there shall be none to shut; and he shall shut, and there shall be none to open.

[23] And I will make him a ruler in a sure place, and he shall be for a glorious throne in his father's house.

[24] And everyone that is glorious in the house of his father shall trust in him, from the least to the greatest; and they shall depend upon him in that day."

[25] Thus says the Lord of hosts: "The man that is fastened in the sure place shall be removed and be taken away, and shall fall; and the glory that is upon him shall be utterly destroyed; for the Lord has spoken it."

ISAIAH CHAPTER 23

Proclamation Against Tyre

[1] The word concerning Tyre. Howl, you ships of Carthage; for she has perished, and *men* no longer arrive from the land of the Citians; she is led captive.

[2] To whom have the inhabitants of the island become like, the merchants of Phoenice, passing over the sea

[3] in great waters, a generation of merchants? As when the harvest is gathered in, *so are* these traders with the nations.

[4] Be ashamed, O Sidon; the sea has said, yea, the strength of the sea has said, "I have not travailed, nor brought forth, nor have I brought up young men, nor reared virgins."

[5] Moreover when it shall be heard in Egypt, sorrow shall seize them for Tyre.

[6] Depart to Carthage. Howl, you that dwell in this island.

[7] Was not this your pride from the beginning, before she was given up?

8 Who has devised this counsel against Tyre. Is she inferior? Or has she no strength? Her merchants were the glorious princes of the earth.

9 The Lord of hosts has purposed to bring down all the pride of the glorious ones, and to disgrace every glorious thing on the earth.

10 Till your land; for ships no more come out of Carthage.

11 And your hand prevails no more by sea, which troubled kings; the Lord of hosts has given a command concerning Canaan, to destroy the strength thereof.

12 And *men* shall say, "You shall no longer at all continue to insult and injure the daughter of Sidon; and if you depart to the Citians, neither there shall you have rest.

13 And *if you depart* to the land of the Chaldeans, this also is laid waste by the Assyrians, for her wall is fallen."

14 Howl, you ships of Carthage; for your stronghold is destroyed.

15 And it shall come to pass in that day, *that* Tyre shall be left seventy years, as the time of a king, as the time of a man; and it shall come to pass after seventy years, *that* Tyre shall be as the song of a harlot.

16 Take a harp, go about, O city, you harlot that have been forgotten; play well on the harp, sing many *songs*, that you may be remembered.

17 And it shall come to pass after the seventy years, *that* God will visit Tyre, and she shall be again restored to her primitive state, and she shall be a mart for all the kingdoms of the world on the face of the earth.

18 And her trade and her gain shall be holiness to the Lord; it shall not be gathered for them, but for those that dwell before the Lord, *even* all her trade, to eat and drink and be filled, and for a covenant *and* a memorial before the Lord.

ISAIAH CHAPTER 24

Impending Judgment on the Earth

1 Behold, the Lord is about to lay waste the world, and will make it desolate, and will lay bare its surface, and scatter them that dwell in it.

2 And the people shall be as the priest, and the servant as the master, and the maid as the mistress; the buyer shall be as the seller, the lender as the borrower, and the debtor as his creditor.

3 The earth shall be completely laid waste, and the earth shall be utterly spoiled; for the mouth of the Lord has spoken these things.

4 The earth mourns, and the world is ruined, the lofty ones of the earth are mourning.

5 And she has sinned by reason of her inhabitants; because they have transgressed the law, and changed the ordinances, *even* the everlasting covenant.

6 Therefore a curse shall consume the earth, because its inhabitants have sinned; therefore the inhabitants of the earth shall be poor, and few men shall be left.

7 The wine shall mourn, the vine shall mourn, all the merry-hearted shall sigh.

8 The mirth of timbrels has ceased, the sound of the harp has ceased.

9 They are ashamed, they have not drunk wine; strong drink has become bitter to them that drink *it*.

10 All the city has become desolate; one shall shut his house so that none shall enter.

11 There is a howling for the wine everywhere; all the mirth of the land has ceased, all the mirth of the land has departed.

12 And cities shall be left desolate, and houses being left shall fall to ruin.

13 All this shall be in the land in the midst of the nations, as if one should strip an olive tree, so shall they strip them, but when the vintage is done,

14 these shall cry aloud. But they that are left on the land shall rejoice together in the glory of the Lord; the water of the sea shall be troubled.

15 Therefore shall the glory of the Lord be in the isles of the sea; the name of the Lord shall be glorious.

16 O Lord God of Israel, from the ends of the earth we have heard wonderful things, *and there is* hope for the godly; but they shall say, "Woe to the despisers, that abhor the law."

17 Fear, and a pit, and a snare, are upon you that dwell on the earth.

18 And it shall come to pass, *that* he that flees from the fear shall fall into the pit; and he that comes up out of the pit shall be caught by the snare; for windows have been opened in heaven, and the foundations of the earth shall be shaken,

19 the earth shall be utterly confounded, and the earth shall be completely perplexed.

20 It reels as a drunkard and one oppressed with wine, and the earth shall be shaken as a storehouse of fruits; for iniquity has prevailed upon it, and it shall fall, and shall not be able to rise.

21 And God shall bring *His* hand upon the host of heaven, and upon the kings of the earth.

22 And they shall gather the multitude thereof into prisons, and they shall shut them into a stronghold; after many generations they shall be visited.

23 And the brick shall decay, and the wall shall fall; for the Lord shall reign from out of Zion, and out of Jerusalem, and shall be glorified before *His* elders.

ISAIAH CHAPTER 25

Praise to God

1 O Lord God, I will glorify You, I will sing to Your name; for You have done wonderful things, *even* an ancient *and* faithful counsel. Amen.

2 For You have reduced cities to a heap of ruins—cities *made* strong that their foundations should not fall; the city of ungodly men shall not be built forever.

³ Therefore shall the poor people bless You, and cities of injured men shall bless You.

⁴ For You have been a helper to every lowly city, and a shelter to them that were disheartened by reason of poverty; You shall deliver them from wicked men; *You have been* a shelter for them that thirst, and a refreshing air to injured men.

⁵ *We were* as faint-hearted men thirsting in Zion, by reason of ungodly men to whom You delivered us.

⁶ And the Lord of hosts shall make *a feast* for all the nations; on this mount they shall drink gladness, they shall drink wine;

⁷ they shall anoint themselves with ointment in this mountain. Impart all these things to the nations; for this is *God's* counsel upon all the nations.

⁸ Death has prevailed and swallowed *men* up; but again the Lord God has taken away every tear from every face. He has taken away the reproach of *His* people from all the earth; for the mouth of the Lord has spoken it.

⁹ And in that day they shall say, "Behold, our God in whom we have trusted, and He shall save us; this *is* the Lord; we have waited for Him, and we have exalted, and will rejoice in our salvation."

¹⁰ God will give rest on this mountain, and the country of Moab shall be trodden down, as they tread the floor with wagons.

¹¹ And He shall spread forth His hands, even as He also brings down *man* to destroy *him*; and He shall bring low his pride *regarding that* in which he has laid his hands.

¹² And He shall bring down the height of the refuge of the wall, and it shall come down, even to the ground.

ISAIAH CHAPTER 26

A Song of Salvation

¹ In that day they shall sing this song in the land of Judah; Behold a strong city; and He shall make salvation *its* wall and bulwark.

² Open the gates, let the nation enter that keeps righteousness, and keeps truth,

³ supporting truth, and keeping peace; for on You, O Lord,

⁴ they have trusted with confidence forever, the great, eternal God;

⁵ who has humbled and brought down them that dwell on high; You shall cast down strong cities, and bring them to the ground.

⁶ And the feet of the meek and lowly shall trample them.

⁷ The way of the godly is made straight; the way of the godly is also prepared.

⁸ For the way of the Lord is judgment; we have hoped in Your name, and on the remembrance *of You,*

⁹ which our soul longs for; my spirit seeks You very early in the morning, O God, for Your commandments are a light on the earth; learn righteousness, you that dwell upon the earth.

¹⁰ For the ungodly one is put down; no one who will not learn righteousness on the earth, shall be able to do the truth; let the ungodly be taken away, that he may not see the glory of the Lord.

¹¹ O Lord, Your arm is exalted, yet they did not know it; but when they know, they shall be ashamed; jealously shall seize upon an untaught nation, and now fire shall devour the adversaries.

¹² O Lord our God, give us peace, for You have rendered to us all things.

¹³ O Lord our God, take possession of us; O Lord, we know no other beside You; we name Your name.

¹⁴ But the dead shall not see life, neither shall physicians by any means raise *them* up; therefore You have brought *wrath* upon *them*, and slain *them*, and have taken away all their males. Bring more evils upon them, O Lord;

¹⁵ bring more evils on the glorious ones of the earth.

¹⁶ Lord, in affliction I remembered You; Your chastening was to us with small affliction.

¹⁷ And as a woman in labor draws near to be delivered, *and* cries out in her pain; so have we been to Your beloved.

¹⁸ We have conceived, O Lord, because of Your fear, and have been in pain, and have brought forth the breath of Your salvation, which we have wrought upon the earth; we shall not fall, but all that dwell upon the land shall fall.

¹⁹ The dead shall rise, and those that are in the tombs shall be raised up, and those that are in the earth shall rejoice; for the dew from You is healing to them; but the land of the ungodly shall perish.

²⁰ Go, my people, enter into your closets, shut your door, hide yourself for a short season, until the anger of the Lord has passed away.

²¹ For behold, the Lord is bringing wrath from *His* holy place on those that dwell upon the earth; the earth also shall disclose her blood, and shall not cover her slain.

ISAIAH CHAPTER 27

¹ In that day God shall bring *His* holy and great and strong sword upon the dragon, even the serpent that flees, upon the dragon, the crooked serpent; He shall destroy the dragon.

The Restoration of Israel

² In that day *there shall be* a fair vineyard, *and* a desire to commence *a song* concerning it.

³ I am a strong city, a city in a siege; in vain shall I water it; for it shall be taken by night, and by day the wall shall fall.

⁴ There is no woman that has not taken hold of it; who will set me to watch stubble in the field? Because of this enemy I have set her aside; therefore on this account the Lord has done all that He has appointed.

⁵ I am burned up; they that dwell in her shall cry, "Let us make peace with Him, let us make peace";

⁶ they that are coming are the children of Jacob. Israel shall bud and blossom, and the world shall be filled with his fruit.

⁷ Shall he himself be stricken this way, even as he has struck? And as he slew, shall he be thus slain?

⁸ Fighting and reproaching he will dismiss them; did you not meditate with a harsh spirit, to slay them with a wrathful spirit?

⁹ "Therefore shall the iniquity of Jacob be taken away; and this is his blessing, when I have taken away his sin; when they have broken to pieces all the stones of the altars as fine dust, and their trees shall not remain, and their idols shall be cut off, as a thicket afar off."

¹⁰ The flock that dwelt *there* shall be left, as a deserted flock; and *the ground* shall be for a long time for pasture, and there shall flocks lie down to rest.

¹¹ And after a time there shall be in it no green thing because of *the grass* being parched. Come here, you woman that comes from a sight; for it is a people of no understanding; therefore He that made them shall have no pity upon them, and He that formed them shall have no mercy *upon them*.

¹² And it shall come to pass in that day *that* God shall fence *men* off from the channel of the river as far as the Brook of Egypt; but gather one by one the children of Israel.

¹³ And it shall come to pass in that day *that* they shall blow the great trumpet, and the lost ones in the land of the Assyrians shall come, and the lost ones in Egypt, and shall worship the Lord on the holy mountain in Jerusalem.

ISAIAH CHAPTER 28

Woe to Ephraim and Jerusalem

¹ Woe to the crown of pride, the hirelings of Ephraim, the flower that has fallen from the glory of the top of the fertile mountain, they that are drunken without wine.

² Behold, the anger of the Lord is strong and severe, as descending hail where there is no shelter, violently descending; as a great body of water sweeping away the soil, He shall make rest for the land.

³ The crown of pride, the hirelings of Ephraim, shall be beaten down with the hands and with the feet.

⁴ And the fading flower of the glorious hope on the top of the high mountain shall be as the early fig; he that sees it, before he takes it into his hand, will desire to swallow it down.

⁵ In that day the Lord of hosts shall be the crown of hope, the woven *crown* of glory, to the remnant of the people.

⁶ They shall be left in the spirit of judgment for judgment, and for the strength of them that hinder slaying.

⁷ For these have trespassed through wine; they have erred through strong drink; the priest and the prophet are mad through strong drink, they are swallowed up by reason of wine, they have staggered through drunkenness; they have erred; this is *their* vision.

⁸ A curse shall devour this counsel, for this *is their* counsel for the sake of covetousness.

⁹ To whom have we reported evils? And to whom have we reported a message? *Even to those* that are weaned from the milk, who are drawn from the breast.

¹⁰ Receive affliction on affliction, hope upon hope; yet a little, *and* yet a little,

¹¹ by reason of the contemptuous *words* of the lips, by means of another language; for they shall speak to this people, saying to them,

¹² "This is the rest to him that is hungry, and this is the calamity"; but they would not hear.

¹³ Therefore the oracle of God shall be to them affliction on affliction, hope on hope, yet a little, *and* yet a little, that they may go and fall backward; and they shall be crushed and shall be in danger, and shall be taken.

¹⁴ Therefore hear the word of the Lord, you afflicted men, and you princes of this people that is in Jerusalem.

¹⁵ Because you have said, "We have made a covenant with Hades, and agreements with death; if the rushing storm should pass, it shall not come upon us; we have made falsehood our hope, and by falsehood shall we be protected."

A Cornerstone in Zion

¹⁶ Therefore thus says the Lord, *even* the Lord, "Behold, I lay for the foundations of Zion a costly stone, a choice cornerstone *and* precious, for its foundations; and he that believes *on Him* shall by no means be ashamed.

¹⁷ And I will cause judgment *to be* for hope, and My compassion shall be for *just* measures, and you that trust vainly in falsehood *shall fall*; for the storm shall by no means pass by you,

¹⁸ except it also take away your covenant of death, and your trust in Hades shall by no means stand; if the rushing storm should come upon you, you shall be beaten down by it.

¹⁹ Whenever it shall pass by, it shall overtake you; morning by morning it shall pass by in the day, and in the night there shall be an evil hope."

²⁰ Learn to hear, you that are distressed; we cannot fight, but we are ourselves too weak for you to be gathered.

²¹ The Lord shall rise up as *against* a mountain of ungodly *men*, and shall be in the valley of Gibeon; He shall perform His works with wrath, *even* a work of bitterness, and His wrath shall deal strangely, and His destruction shall be strange.

²² Therefore do not rejoice, neither let your bands be made strong; for I have heard of works finished and cut short by the Lord of hosts, which He will execute upon all the earth.

²³ Listen, and hear my voice; give ear, and hear my words.

²⁴ Will the plowman plow all the day? Or will he prepare the seed beforehand, before he tills the ground?

[25] Does he not, when he has leveled the surface, then sow the small black poppy, or cummin, and afterward sow wheat, barley, millet, and grain in your borders?

[26] So you shall be chastened by the judgment of your God, and shall rejoice.

[27] For the black poppy is not cleansed with harsh treatment, nor will a wagon wheel pass over the cummin; but the black poppy is threshed with a rod, and the cummin shall be eaten with bread;

[28] "For I will not be angry with you forever, neither shall the voice of My anger crush you."

[29] And these signs came forth from the Lord of hosts. Take counsel, exalt vain comfort.

ISAIAH CHAPTER 29

Woe to Jerusalem

[1] "Alas for the city of Ariel, which David besieged. Gather your fruits year by year; eat, for you shall eat with Moab.

[2] For I will grievously afflict Ariel; and her strength and her wealth shall be Mine.

[3] And I will compass you round about like David, and will raise a mound about you, and set up towers around you.

[4] And your words shall be brought down to the earth, and your words shall sink down to the earth, and your voice shall be as they that speak out of the earth, and your voice shall be lowered to the ground.

[5] "But the wealth of the ungodly shall be as dust from a wheel, and the multitude of them that oppress you as flying chaff, and it shall be suddenly as a moment,

[6] from the Lord of Hosts; for there shall be a visitation with thunder, and earthquake, and a loud noise, a rushing tempest, and a devouring flame of fire.

[7] And the wealth of all the nations together, as many as have fought against Ariel, and all they that war against Jerusalem, and all who are gathered against her, and they that distress her, shall be as one that dreams in sleep by night.

[8] And as men drink and eat in sleep, and when they have arisen, the dream is vain. And as a thirsty man dreams as if he drank, and having arisen is still thirsty, and his soul has desired in vain, so shall be the wealth of all the nations, as many as have fought against Mount Zion."

[9] Faint, and be amazed, and be overpowered, not with strong drink, nor with wine.

[10] For the Lord has made you to drink a spirit of deep sleep; and He shall close their eyes, and *the eyes* of their prophets and of their rulers, who see secret things.

[11] And all these things shall be to you as the words of this sealed book, which if they shall give to a learned man, saying, "Read this," he shall then say, "I cannot read *it*, for it is sealed."

[12] And this book shall be given into the hands of a man that is unlearned, and *one* shall say to him, "Read this"; and he shall say, "I am unlearned."

[13] And the Lord has said, "This people draw near to Me with their mouth, and they honor Me with their lips, but their heart is far from Me; and in vain do they worship Me, teaching the commandments and doctrines of men.

[14] Therefore behold, I will proceed to remove this people, and I will remove them; and I will destroy the wisdom of the wise, and I will hide the understanding of the prudent."

[15] Woe to them that deepen their counsel, and not by the Lord. Woe to them that take secret counsel, and whose works are in darkness, and they say, "Who has seen us? And who shall know us, or what we do?"

[16] Shall you not be counted as clay of the potter? Shall the thing formed say to him that formed it, "You did not form me?" Or the work to the maker, "You have not made me wisely?"

[17] *Is it* not yet a little while, and Lebanon shall be changed as the mountains of Carmel, and Carmel shall be reckoned as a forest?

[18] And in that day the deaf shall hear the words of the book, and they that are in darkness, and they that are in mist; the eyes of the blind shall see,

[19] and the poor shall rejoice with joy because of the Lord, and they that had no hope among men shall be filled with joy.

[20] The lawless man has been brought down, and the proud man has perished, and they that transgress mischievously have been utterly destroyed;

[21] and they that cause men to sin by a word; and men shall make all that reprove in the gates an offense, because they have unjustly turned aside the righteous.

[22] Therefore thus says the Lord concerning the house of Jacob, whom He set apart from Abraham: "Jacob shall not now be ashamed, neither shall he now change his countenance.

[23] But when their children shall have seen My works, they shall sanctify My name for My sake, and they sanctify the Holy One of Jacob, and shall fear the God of Israel.

[24] And they that erred in spirit shall know understanding, and the murmurers shall learn obedience, and the stammering tongues shall learn to speak peace."

ISAIAH CHAPTER 30

Futile Confidence in Egypt

[1] "Woe to the apostate children," says the Lord; "you have framed counsel, not by Me, and covenants not by My Spirit, to add sins to sins;

[2] *even* they that proceed to go down into Egypt, for they have not inquired of Me, that they might be helped by Pharaoh, and protected by the Egyptians.

3 For the protection of Pharaoh shall be to you a disgrace, and *there shall be* a reproach to them that trust in Egypt.

4 For there are princes in Tannis, evil messengers.

5 In vain shall they labor *in seeking* for a people which shall not profit them for help, but *shall be* for a shame and reproach."

6 The vision against the beasts of the south. In affliction and distress, *where are* the lion and lion's whelp, from there also *come* asps, and the young of flying asps, *there shall they be* who bore their wealth on donkeys and camels to a nation which shall not profit them.

7 The Egyptians shall help you utterly in vain; tell them, "This your consolation is vain."

8 Now then sit down and write these words on a tablet, and in a book; for these things shall be for *many long* days, even forever.

9 For the people are disobedient, false children, who would not hear the law of God;

10 who say to the prophets, "Do not report to us"; and to them that see visions, "Do not speak *them* to us, but speak and report to us deceitful *things*;

11 and turn us aside from this way; remove from us this path, and remove from us the oracle of Israel."

12 Therefore thus says the Holy One of Israel: "Because you have refused to obey these words, and have trusted in falsehood; and because you have murmured, and been confident in this respect;

13 therefore shall this sin be to you as a wall suddenly falling when a strong city has been taken, of which the fall is very close at hand.

14 And its fall shall be as the breaking of an earthen vessel, *as* small fragments of a pitcher, so that you should not find among them a sherd, with which you might take up fire, and with which you should draw a little water."

15 Thus says the Lord, the Holy Lord of Israel; "When you shall turn and mourn, then you shall be saved; and you shall know where you were, when you trusted in vanities; *then* your strength became vain, yet you would not obey.

16 But you said, 'We will flee upon horses'; therefore shall you flee; and *you said*, 'We will be aided by swift riders'; therefore shall they that pursue you be swift.

17 A thousand shall flee because of the voice of one, and many shall flee on account of the voice of five; until you are left as a signal-post upon a mountain, and as one bearing an ensign upon a hill."

God Will Be Gracious

18 And the Lord will again wait, that He may pity you, and will therefore be exalted that He may have mercy upon you; because the Lord your God is a Judge; blessed are they that wait on Him.

19 For the holy people shall dwell in Zion; and *whereas* Jerusalem has wept bitterly, *saying*, "Pity me"; He shall pity you; when He heard the voice of your cry, He listened to you. 20 And *though* the Lord shall give you the bread of affliction and scant water, yet they that cause you to err shall no longer draw near to you; for your eyes shall see those that cause you to err,

21 and your ears shall hear the words of them that went after you to lead you astray, who say, "This *is* the way, let us walk in it, whether to the right or to the left."

22 And you shall pollute the plated idols, and you shall grind to powder the gilt ones, and shall scatter them as the water of a removed *woman*, and you shall thrust them forth as dung.

23 Then shall there be rain to the seed of your land; and the bread of the fruit of your land shall be plenteous and rich; and your cattle shall feed in that day in a fertile and spacious place.

24 Your bulls and your oxen that till the ground shall eat chaff mixed with winnowed barley.

25 And there shall be upon every lofty mountain and upon every high hill, water running in that day, when many shall perish, and when the towers shall fall.

26 And the light of the moon shall be as the light of the sun, and the light of the sun shall be sevenfold in the day when the Lord shall heal the breach of His people, and shall heal the pain of your wound.

27 Behold, the name of the Lord comes after a *long* time, burning wrath; the word of His lips is with glory, a word full of anger, and the anger of His wrath shall devour like fire.

28 And His breath, as rushing water in a valley, shall reach as far as the neck, and be divided, to confound the nations for *their* vain error; error also shall pursue them, and overtake them.

29 "Must you always rejoice, and go into My holy places continually, as they that keep a feast? And must you go with a flute, as those that rejoice, into the mountain of the Lord, to the God of Israel?"

30 And the Lord shall make His glorious voice to be heard, and the wrath of His outstretched arm, to make a display with wrath and anger and devouring flame; He shall lighten terribly, and *His wrath shall be* as water and violent hail.

31 For by the voice of the Lord the Assyrians shall be overcome, *even* by the stroke in which He shall strike them.

32 And it shall happen to him from every side, *that* they from whom their hope of assistance was, in which he trusted, themselves shall war against Him in turn with drums and with harps.

33 For you shall be required before *your* time; has it been prepared for you also to reign? No, God has *prepared for you* a deep trench, wood piled, fire and much wood; the wrath of the Lord *shall be* as a trench kindled with sulphur.

ISAIAH CHAPTER 31

Alliance with Egypt is Futile

1 Woe to them that go down to Egypt for help, who trust in horses and chariots, for they are many; and in horses, *which*

are a great multitude; and have not trusted in the Holy One of Israel, and have not sought the Lord.

² Therefore He has wisely brought evils upon them, and His word shall not be frustrated; and He shall rise up against the houses of wicked men, and against their vain hope,

³ *even* an Egyptian, a man, and not God; the flesh of horses, and there is no help *in them*; but the Lord shall bring His hand upon them, and the helpers shall fail, and all shall perish together.

God Will Deliver Jerusalem

⁴ For thus said the Lord unto me: "As a lion roars, or a lion's whelp over prey which he has taken, and cry over it, until the mountains are filled with his voice, and *the animals* are awe-struck and tremble at the fierceness of his wrath; so the Lord of hosts shall descend to fight upon Mount Zion, *even* upon her mountains.

⁵ As birds flying, so shall the Lord of hosts defend; He shall defend Jerusalem, and He shall rescue, and save and deliver."

⁶ Turn, you children of Israel, who devise a deep and sinful counsel.

⁷ For in that day men shall renounce their silver idols and *their* golden idols, which their hands have made.

⁸ And the Assyrian shall fall; not the sword of a great man, nor the sword of a mean man shall devour him; neither shall he flee from the face of the sword; but the young men shall be overthrown;

⁹ for they shall be compassed with rocks as with a trench, and shall be overcome; and he that flees shall be taken. Thus says the Lord: "Blessed is he that has a seed in Zion, and household friends in Jerusalem."

ISAIAH CHAPTER 32

Government with Justice Predicted

¹ For behold, a righteous king shall reign, and princes shall govern with judgment.

² And a man shall hide his words, and be hidden, as from rushing water, and shall appear in Zion as a rushing river, glorious in a thirsty land.

³ And they shall no longer trust in men, but they shall incline their ears to hear.

⁴ And the heart of the weak ones shall attend to hear, and the stammering tongues shall soon learn to speak peace.

⁵ And they shall no longer tell a fool to rule, and your servants shall no longer say, "Be silent."

⁶ For the fool shall speak foolish words, and his heart shall meditate vanities, and to perform lawless deeds and to speak error against the Lord, to scatter hungry souls, and He will cause the thirsty souls to be empty.

⁷ For the counsel of the wicked will devise iniquity, to destroy the poor with unjust words, and ruin the cause of the poor in judgment.

⁸ But the godly have devised wise *measures*, and this counsel shall stand.

Complacent Women Warned of Disaster

⁹ Rise up, you rich women, and hear my voice; you confident daughters, listen to my words.

¹⁰ Remember for a full year in pain, yet with hope; the vintage has been cut off; it has ceased, it shall by no means come again.

¹¹ Be amazed, be pained, you confident ones; strip, bare yourselves, gird your loins

¹² and beat your breasts, because of the pleasant field, and the fruit of the vine.

¹³ *As for* the land of my people, the thorn and grass shall come upon *it*, and joy shall be removed from every house.

¹⁴ *As for* the rich city, the houses are deserted; they shall abandon the wealth of the city, *and* the pleasant houses; and the villages shall be caves forever, the joy of wild donkeys, shepherds' pastures;

¹⁵ until the Spirit shall come upon you from on high, and Carmel shall be desert, and Carmel shall be counted for a forest.

The Peace of God's Reign

¹⁶ Then judgment shall abide in the wilderness, and righteousness shall dwell in Carmel.

¹⁷ And the works of righteousness shall be peace; and righteousness shall ensure rest, and *the righteous* shall be confident forever.

¹⁸ And His people shall inhabit a city of peace, and dwell in *it* in confidence, and they shall rest with wealth.

¹⁹ And if the hail should come down, it shall not come upon you; and they that dwell in the forests shall be in confidence, as those in the plain country.

²⁰ Blessed are they that sow by every water, where the ox and the donkey tread.

ISAIAH CHAPTER 33

A Prophecy of Deliverance from Foes

¹ Woe to those that afflict you; but no one makes you miserable; and he that deals treacherously with you does not deal treacherously; those that deal treacherously shall be taken and given up, and like a moth on a garment, so shall they be spoiled.

² Lord, have mercy upon us; for we have trusted in You; the descendants of the rebellious has gone to destruction, but our deliverance was in a time of affliction.

³ By reason of the terrible sound, the nations were dismayed for fear of You, and the heathen were scattered.

⁴ And now shall the spoils of Your small and great be gathered, as if one should gather locusts, so shall they mock You.

5 The God who dwells on high is holy; Zion is filled with judgment and righteousness.

6 They shall be delivered up to the law; our salvation is our treasure; there is wisdom and knowledge and godliness toward the Lord; these are the treasures of righteousness.

7 Behold now, these shall be terrified with fear of you; those whom you feared shall cry out because of you; messengers shall be sent, bitterly weeping, entreating for peace.

8 For the ways of these shall be made desolate; the terror of the nations has been made to cease, and the covenant with these is taken away, and you shall by no means deem them men.

9 The land mourns; Lebanon is ashamed; Sharon has become a marsh; Galilee shall be laid bare, and Carmel.

Impending Judgment on Zion

10 "Now will I arise," says the Lord, "now will I be glorified; now will I be exalted.

11 Now shall you see, now shall you perceive; the strength of your breath shall be vain; fire shall devour you.

12 And the nations shall be burned up, as a thorn in the field is cast out and burned up.

13 They that are afar off shall hear what I have done; they that draw near shall know My strength."

14 The sinners in Zion have departed; trembling shall seize the ungodly. Who will tell you that a fire is kindled? Who will tell you of the eternal place?

15 He that walks in righteousness, speaking rightly, hating transgression and iniquity, and shaking his hands from gifts, stopping his ears that he should not hear the judgment of blood, shutting his eyes that he should not see injustice.

16 He shall dwell in a high cave of a strong rock; bread shall be given to him, and his water shall be sure.

The Land of the Majestic King

17 You shall see a king with glory; your eyes shall behold a land from afar.

18 Your soul shall meditate terror. Where are the scribes? Where are the counselors? Where is he that numbers them that are growing up,

19 *both* the small and great people? With whom he did not take counsel, neither did he understand *a people* of deep speech, so that a despised people should not hear, and there is no understanding to him that hears.

20 Behold the city of Zion, our refuge; your eyes shall behold Jerusalem, a rich city, tabernacles which shall not be shaken, neither shall the pins of her tabernacle be moved forever, neither shall her cords be at all broken;

21 for the name of the Lord is great to you; you shall have a place, *even* rivers and wide and spacious channels; you shall not go this way, neither shall a vessel with oars go *thereby.*

22 For my God is great; the Lord our judge shall not pass me by; the Lord is our Prince, the Lord is our King; the Lord, He shall save us.

23 Your cords are broken, for they had no strength; your food has given way, it shall not spread the sails, it shall not bear a signal, until it is given up for plunder; therefore shall many lame men take spoil.

24 And the people dwelling among them shall by no means say, "I am in pain"; for their sin shall be forgiven them.

ISAIAH CHAPTER 34

Judgment on the Nations

1 Draw near, you nations; and hearken, you princes; let the earth hear, and they that are in it; the world, and the people therein.

2 For the wrath of the Lord is upon all nations, and *His* anger upon the number of them, to destroy them, and give them up to slaughter.

3 And their slain shall be cast forth, and their corpses; and their stench shall come up, and the mountains shall be made wet with their blood.

4 And all the powers of the heavens shall melt, and the sky shall be rolled up like a scroll; and all the stars shall fall like leaves from a vine, and as leaves fall from a fig tree.

5 "My sword has been made drunk in heaven; behold, it shall come down upon Edom, and with judgment upon the people doomed to destruction."

6 The sword of the Lord is filled with blood, it is glutted with fat, with the blood of goats and lambs, and with the fat of goats and rams; for the Lord has a sacrifice in Bozrah, and a great slaughter in Edom.

7 And the mighty ones shall fall with them, and the rams and the bulls; and the land shall be soaked with blood, and shall be filled with their fat.

8 For it is the day of the judgment of the Lord, and the year of the recompense of Zion in judgment.

9 And her valleys shall be turned into pitch, and her land into sulphur; and her land shall be as pitch burning night and day; 10 and it shall never be quenched, and her smoke shall go up; it shall be made desolate throughout her generations,

11 and for a long time birds and hedgehogs, and ibises and ravens shall dwell in it; and the measuring line of desolation shall be cast over it, and satyrs shall dwell in it.

12 Her princes shall be no more, for her kings and her great men shall be destroyed.

13 And thorns shall spring up in their cities, and in her strongholds; and they shall be habitations of monsters, and a court of ostriches.

14 And demons shall meet with satyrs, and they shall cry one to the other; there shall the satyrs rest, having found for themselves *a place of* rest.

15 There has the hedgehog made its nest, and the earth has safely preserved its young; there have the deer met, and seen one another's faces.

[16] They passed by in *full* number, and not one of them perished; they did not seek one another; for the Lord commanded them, and His Spirit gathered them.

[17] And He shall cast lots for them, and His hand has portioned out *their* pasture, *saying*, "You shall inherit *the land* forever; they shall rest on it *throughout* all generations."

ISAIAH CHAPTER 35

The Return of the Redeemed to Zion

[1] Be glad, you thirsty desert; let the wilderness rejoice, and flower as the lily.

[2] And the desert places of the Jordan shall blossom and rejoice; the glory of Lebanon has been given to it, and the honor of Carmel; and my people shall see the glory of the Lord, and the majesty of God.

[3] Be strong, you relaxed hands and feeble knees.

[4] Comfort one another, you fainthearted; be strong, do not fear; behold, our God renders judgment, and He will render *it*; He will come and save us.

[5] Then shall the eyes of the blind be opened, and the ears of the deaf shall hear.

[6] Then shall the lame man leap as a deer, and the tongue of the stammerers shall speak plainly; for water has burst forth in the desert, and a channel *of water* in a thirsty land. [7] And the dry land shall become pools, and a fountain of water shall *be poured* into the thirsty land; there shall there be a joy of birds, ready habitations and marshes.

[8] There shall be there a pure way, and it shall be called a holy way; and there shall not pass by there any unclean person, neither shall there be there an unclean way; but the dispersed shall walk on it, and they shall not go astray.

[9] And there shall be no lion there, neither shall any evil beast go up upon it, nor at all be found there; but the redeemed and gathered on the Lord's behalf shall walk in it,

[10] and shall return, and come to Zion with joy, and everlasting joy *shall be* over their head; for on their head *shall be* praise and exaltation, and joy shall take possession of them; sorrow and pain, and groaning have fled away.

ISAIAH CHAPTER 36

Sennacherib Threatens Jerusalem

[1] Now it came to pass in the fourteenth year of the reign of Hezekiah, *that* Sennacherib, king of the Assyrians, came up against the strong cities of Judah, and took them.

[2] And the king of the Assyrians sent Rabshakeh out of Lachish to Jerusalem, to King Hezekiah with a large force; and he stood by the conduit of the upper pool in the way of the fuller's field.

[3] And there went forth to him Eliakim the manager, the *son* of Hilkiah, and Shebna the scribe, and Joah the *son* of Asaph, the recorder.

[4] And Rabshakeh said to them, "Say to Hezekiah, Thus says the great king, the king of the Assyrians: 'Why are you secure?

[5] Is war carried on with counsel and *mere* words of the lips? And now on whom do you trust, that you rebel against me?

[6] Behold, you trust on this bruised staff of reed, on Egypt; *as soon* as a man leans upon it, it shall go into his hand, and pierce it; so is Pharaoh king of Egypt and all that trust in him.'

[7] But if you say, 'We trust in the Lord our God';

[8] yet now make an agreement with my lord the king of the Assyrians, and I will give you two thousand horses, if you shall be able to set riders upon them.

[9] And how can you *then* turn to the face of the satraps? They that trust in the Egyptians for horse and rider are *our* servants. [10] And now, Have we come up against this land to fight against it without the Lord? The Lord said to me, 'Go up against this land, and destroy it.'"

[11] Then Eliakim, Shebna and Joah said to him, "Speak to your servants in the Syrian language; for we understand *it*; and do not speak to us in the Jewish language; and why do you speak in the ears of the men on the wall?"

[12] And Rabshakeh said to them, "Has my lord sent me to your master or to you, to speak these words? *Has he* not *sent* me to the men that sit on the wall, that they may eat dung, and drink *their* urine together with you?"

[13] And Rabshakeh stood and cried with a loud voice in the Jewish language, and said, "Hear the words of the great king, the king of the Assyrians:

[14] Thus says the king: 'Let not Hezekiah deceive you with words; he will not be able to deliver you.

[15] And let not Hezekiah say to you that God will deliver you, and this city will not at all be delivered into the hand of the king of the Assyrians.'

[16] Do not listen to Hezekiah. Thus says the king of the Assyrians: 'If you wish to be blessed, come out to me; and you shall all eat *of* his own vine and his *own* fig trees, and you shall drink water out of your own cisterns;

[17] until I come and take you to a land, like your own land, a land of grain and wine, and bread and vineyards.

[18] Let not Hezekiah deceive you, saying, "God will deliver you." Have the gods of the nations delivered each one his own land out of the hand of the king of the Assyrians?

[19] Where is the god of Hamath, and Arpad? And where is the god of Sepharvaim? Have they been able to deliver Samaria out of my hand?

[20] Which is the god of all these nations that has delivered his land out of my hand, that God should deliver Jerusalem out of my hand?'"

[21] And they were silent, and none answered him a word, because the king had commanded that none should answer.

[22] And Eliakim the *son* of Hilkiah, the manager, and Shebna the scribe, and Joah the *son* of Asaph the recorder, came in to Hezekiah, having torn their clothes, and they reported to him the words of Rabshakeh.

ISAIAH CHAPTER 37

Isaiah Assures Deliverance

¹ And it came to pass, when King Hezekiah heard *it, that* he tore his clothes, and put on sackcloth, and went up to the house of the Lord.

² And he sent Eliakim the manager, and Shebna the scribe, and the elders of the priests clothed with sackcloth, to Isaiah the son of Amoz, the prophet. And they said to him, thus says Hezekiah:

³ "Today is a day of affliction, and reproach, and rebuke, and anger; for the pangs have come upon the travailing *woman*, but she has not the strength to bring forth.

⁴ May the Lord your God hear the words of Rabshakeh, which the king of the Assyrians has sent, to reproach the living God, even to reproach with the words which the Lord your God has heard; therefore you shall pray to your Lord for these that are left."

⁵ So the servants of King Hezekiah came to Isaiah.

⁶ And Isaiah said to them, "Thus shall you say to your master, Thus says the Lord: 'Be not afraid at the words which you have heard, in which the ambassadors of the king of the Assyrians have reproached Me.

⁷ Behold, I *will* send a blast upon him, and he shall hear a report, and return to his own country, and he shall fall by the sword in his own land."

⁸ So Rabshakeh returned, and found the king of the Assyrians besieging Libnah; for he had heard that he had departed from Lachish.

⁹ And Tirhakah king of the Ethiopians went forth to attack him. And when he heard it, he turned aside, and sent messengers to Hezekiah, saying,

¹⁰ Thus shall you say to Hezekiah king of Judah: "Do not let your God in whom you trust deceive you, saying, 'Jerusalem shall not be delivered into the hand of the king of the Assyrians.'

¹¹ Have you not heard what the kings of the Assyrians have done, how they have destroyed the whole earth? And shall you be delivered?

¹² Have the gods of the nations which my fathers destroyed delivered them, *be it* Gozan, Haran, or Rezeph, which are in the land of Telassar?

¹³ Where are the kings of Hamath? And where *is the king of* Arpad? And where *is the king* of the city of Sepharvaim, *and of* Ivah?"

¹⁴ And Hezekiah received the letter from the messengers, and read it, and went up to the house of the Lord, and opened it before the Lord.

¹⁵ And Hezekiah prayed to the Lord, saying,

¹⁶ "O Lord of hosts, God of Israel, who sits upon the cherubim, You alone are God of every kingdom of the world; You have made heaven and earth.

¹⁷ Incline Your ear, O Lord, hearken, O Lord; open Your eyes, O Lord, look, O Lord; and behold the words of Sennacherib, which he has sent to reproach the living God.

¹⁸ For truly, O Lord, the kings of the Assyrians have laid waste the whole world, and the countries thereof,

¹⁹ and have cast their idols into the fire; for they were not gods, but the work of men's hands, wood and stone; and they have cast them away.

²⁰ But now, O Lord our God, deliver us from his hands, that every kingdom of the earth may know that You alone are God."

²¹ And Isaiah the son of Amoz was sent to Hezekiah, and said to him, thus says the Lord, the God of Israel: "I have heard your prayer to Me concerning Sennacherib king of the Assyrians.

²² This is the word which God has spoken concerning him: 'The virgin daughter of Zion has despised you, and mocked you; the daughter of Jerusalem has shaken her head at you.

²³ Whom have you reproached and provoked? And against whom have you lifted up your voice? And have you not lifted up your eyes on high against the Holy One of Israel?

²⁴ For you have reproached the Lord by messengers; for you have said, "With the multitude of chariots have I ascended to the height of mountains, and to the sides of Lebanon, and I have cropped the height of his cedars and the beauty of his cypresses, and I entered into the height of the forest region;

²⁵ and I have made a bridge, and dried up the waters, and every pool of water."

²⁶ Have you not heard of these things which I have done of old? I appointed *them* from ancient times; but now have I manifested *My purpose* of desolating nations in *their* strongholds, and them that dwell in strong cities.

²⁷ I weakened *their* hands, and they withered; and they became as dry grass on the housetops, and as grass.

²⁸ But now I know your dwelling place, and your going out, and your coming in.

²⁹ And your wrath in which you have been enraged, and your rage has come up before Me; therefore I will put a hook in your nose, and a bit in your lips, and I will turn you back by the way which you came.'"

³⁰ "And this shall be a sign to you: eat this year what you have sown; and the second year that which is left; and the third year sow, and reap, and plant vineyards, and eat the fruit thereof.

³¹ And they that are left in Judah shall take root downward, and bear fruit upward;

³² for out of Jerusalem there shall be a remnant, and the saved ones out of Mount Zion; the zeal of the Lord of hosts shall perform this.

³³ "Therefore thus says the Lord concerning the king of the Assyrians: 'He shall not enter into this city, nor cast a weapon against it, nor bring a shield against it, nor make a rampart around it.

34 But by the way in which he came, by it shall he return, and shall not enter into this city,' says the Lord,

35 'for I will protect this city to save it for My own sake, and for My servant David's sake.'"

Sennacherib's Defeat and Death

36 And the angel of the Lord went forth, and killed out of the camp of the Assyrians a hundred and eighty-five thousand; and they arose in the morning and found a *multitude* of dead bodies.

37 And Sennacherib king of the Assyrians turned and departed, and dwelt in Nineveh.

38 And while he was worshipping Nisroch his country's god in the house, Adrammelech and Sharezer his sons struck him with swords; and they escaped into Armenia; and Esarhaddon his son reigned in his place.

ISAIAH CHAPTER 38

Hezekiah's Life Extended

1 And it came to pass at that time, *that* Hezekiah was sick, even unto death. And Isaiah the prophet, the son of Amoz, came to him, and said to him, "Thus says the Lord: 'Give orders concerning your house; for you shall die, and not live.'" 2 And Hezekiah turned his face to the wall, and prayed to the Lord, saying,

3 "Remember, O Lord, how I have walked before You in truth, with a true heart, and have done that which was pleasing in Your sight." And Hezekiah wept bitterly.

4 And the word of the Lord came to Isaiah, saying, "Go and say to Hezekiah,

5 'Thus says the Lord, the God of David your father: "I have heard your prayer, and have seen your tears; behold, I *will* add to your days fifteen years.

6 And I will deliver you and this city out of the hand of the king of the Assyrians; and I will defend this city.

7 And this *shall be* a sign to you from the Lord, that God will do this thing:

8 Behold, I will turn back the shadow of the degrees *of the sundial* by ten degrees on the house of your father. I will turn back the sun the ten degrees.'" So the sun went back the ten degrees by which the shadow had gone down.

9 *This was* the prayer of Hezekiah king of Judah, when he had been sick, and had recovered from his sickness:

10 "I said in the end of my days, I shall go to the gates of the grave; I shall part with the remainder of my years.

11 I said, I shall no more see the salvation of God in the land of the living; I shall no more see the salvation of Israel on the earth; I shall no more see man.

12 *My life* has failed from among my kindred; I have parted with the remainder of my life; it has gone forth and departed from me, as one that has pitched a tent takes it down *again*; my breath was with me as a weaver's web, when she that weaves draws near to cut off *the* thread.

13 In that day I was given up as to a lion until the morning; so has He broken all my bones; for I was so given up from day *even* to night.

14 As a swallow, so will I cry, and as a dove, so do I mourn; for my eyes have failed from looking to the height of heaven to the Lord, who has delivered me,

15 and removed the sorrow of my soul.

16 "O Lord, for it was told You concerning this; and You have revived my breath; and I am comforted, and live.

17 For You have chosen my soul, that it should not perish; and You have cast all *my* sins behind me.

18 For they that are in the grave shall not praise You, neither shall the dead bless You, neither shall they that are in Hades hope for Your mercy.

19 The living shall bless You, as I also *do*; for from this day shall I beget children, who shall declare Your righteousness,

20 O God of my salvation; and I will not cease *from* blessing You with the psaltery all the days of my life before the house of God."

21 Now Isaiah had said to Hezekiah: "Take a cake of figs, and mash them, and apply them as a plaster, and you shall be well."

22 And Hezekiah said, "This is a sign to Hezekiah, that I shall go up to the house of God."

ISAIAH CHAPTER 39

The Babylonion Envoys

1 At that time Merodach-Baladan, the son of Baladan, the king of Babylon, sent letters and ambassadors and gifts to Hezekiah; for he had heard that he had been sick, *even unto* death, and had recovered.

2 And Hezekiah was pleased that they came, and he showed them the house of *his* spices, and of silver, gold, myrrh, incense, ointment, and all the houses of his treasures, and all that he had in his stores. And there was nothing in his house, nor in all his dominion, which Hezekiah did not show *them*.

3 And Isaiah the prophet came to King Hezekiah, and said to him, "What did these men say, and from where did they come to you?" And Hezekiah said, "They have come to me from a land afar off, from Babylon."

4 And Isaiah said, "What have they seen in your house?" And Hezekiah said, "They have seen everything in my house; and there is nothing in my house which they have not seen, even all the *possessions* in my treasuries."

5 And Isaiah said to him, "Hear the word of the Lord of hosts:

6 'Behold, the days are coming when they shall take all the *things that are* in your house, and all that your fathers have gathered until this day, *and they* shall go to Babylon, and they shall not leave one thing.'" And God said,

7 "They shall also take of your children whom you shall father, and they shall make them eunuchs in the house of the king of the Babylonians."

8 And Hezekiah said to Isaiah, "The word of the Lord is good, which He has spoken; let there be peace and righteousness in my days."

ISAIAH CHAPTER 40

God's People Are Comforted

1 "Comfort, yes, comfort My people," says *your* God.

2 Speak, you priests, to the heart of Jerusalem; comfort her, for her humiliation is accomplished, her sin is put away; for she has received of the Lord's hand double *for* her sins.

3 The voice of one crying in the wilderness, "Prepare the way of the Lord, make straight the paths of our God.

4 Every valley shall be filled, and every mountain and hill shall be brought low; and all the crooked *ways* shall become straight, and the rough *places* smooth.

5 And the glory of the Lord shall appear, and all flesh shall see the salvation of God; for the Lord has spoken *it*."

6 The voice of one saying, "Proclaim"; and I said, "What shall I proclaim? All flesh is grass, and all the glory of man as the flower of grass.

7 (This verse omitted in LXX)

8 The grass withers, and the flower fades; but the word of our God abides forever."

9 O you that brings glad tidings to Zion, go up on the high mountain; lift up your voice with strength, you that brings glad tidings to Jerusalem; lift it up, fear not; say unto the cities of Judah, "Behold your God!"

10 Behold the Lord! The Lord is coming with strength, and *His* arm is with power; behold, His reward is with Him, and *His* work before Him.

11 He shall tend His flock as a shepherd, and He shall gather the lambs with His arm, and He shall soothe them that are with young.

12 Who has measured the water in His hand, and the heaven with a span, and all the earth in a handful? Who has weighed the mountains in scales, and the forests in a balance?

13 Who has known the mind of the Lord? And who has been His counselor, to instruct Him?

14 Or with whom has He taken counsel, and he has instructed Him? Or who has taught Him judgment, or who has taught Him the way of understanding;

15 since all the nations are counted as a drop in a bucket, and as the turning of a balance, *and* shall be counted as spittle?

16 And Lebanon is not enough to burn, nor all beasts enough for a burnt offering;

17 and all the nations are as nothing, and counted as nothing.

18 To whom have you compared the Lord? And with what likeness have you compared Him?

19 Has not the carpenter made an image, or the goldsmith having melted gold, guilded it over, *and* made it a likeness *of Him*?

20 For the carpenter chooses out a wood that will not rot, and will wisely inquire how he shall set up his image, and *that so* that it should not be moved.

21 Will you not know? Will you not hear? Has it not been told to you from the beginning? Have you not known the foundations of the earth?

22 *It is* He that comprehends the circle of the earth, and the inhabitants in it are as grasshoppers; He that set up the heaven as a chamber, and stretched *it* out as a tent to dwell in;

23 He that appoints princes to rule as nothing, and has made the earth as nothing.

24 For they shall not plant, neither shall they sow, neither shall their root be fixed in the ground; He has blown upon them, and they have withered, and a storm shall carry them away like sticks.

25 "Now then to whom have you compared Me, that I may be exalted?" says the Holy One.

26 Lift up your eyes on high, and see, who has displayed all these things? *Even* He that brings forth His host by number; He shall call them all by name by *means of His* great glory, and by the power of His might; nothing has escaped you.

27 For do not say, O Jacob, and why have you spoken, O Israel, *saying*, "My way is hid from God, and my God has taken away *my* judgment, and has departed?"

28 And now, have you not known? Have you not heard? The eternal God, the God that formed the ends of the earth, shall not hunger, neither shall He be weary, and there is no searching of His understanding.

29 He gives strength to the hungry, and sorrow to them that are not suffering.

30 For the young *men* shall hunger, and the youths shall be weary, and the choice *men* shall be powerless;

31 but they that wait on God shall renew *their* strength; they shall put forth new feathers like eagles; they shall run, and not be weary; they shall walk, and not faint.

ISAIAH CHAPTER 41

Israel Assured of God's Help

1 "Hold a feast to Me; you islands; for the princes shall renew *their* strength; let them draw near and speak together; then let them declare judgment.

2 Who raised up righteousness from the east, *and* called it to His feet, so that it should go? *Who* shall appoint *it* as an adversary of Gentiles, and shall dismay kings, and bury their swords in the earth, and cast forth their bows and arrows as sticks?

³ And he shall pursue them; the way of his feet shall proceed in peace.

⁴ Who has performed and done these things? He has called it who called it from the generations of old; I God, the first and to *all* futurity, I AM."

⁵ The nations saw, and feared; the ends of the earth drew near, and came together,

⁶ everyone judging for his neighbor and *that* to assist his brother; and one will say,

⁷ "The carpenter has become strong, and the coppersmith that plates with the hammer, *and* forges also"; sometimes he will say, "It is a piece well joined"; they have fastened them with nails; they will fix them, and they shall not be moved.

⁸ "But you, O Israel, are My servant Jacob, and he whom I have chosen, the descendants of Abraham, whom I have loved;

⁹ whom I have taken hold of from the ends of the earth, and from the high places of it I have called you, and said to you, 'You are My servant; I have chosen you, and I have not forsaken you.'

¹⁰ Do not fear; for I am with you; do not be led astray; for I am your God, who has strengthened you; and I have helped you, and have established you with My righteous right hand.

¹¹ Behold, all your adversaries shall be ashamed and confounded; for they shall be as if they were not; and all your opponents shall perish.

¹² You shall seek them, and you shall not find the men who shall insolently rage against you; for they shall be as if they were not, and they that war against you shall not be.

¹³ For I am your God, who holds your right hand, who says to you,

¹⁴ 'Do not fear, O Jacob, *and you* Israel, few in number; *for* I have helped you,' says your God, He that redeems you, O Israel.

¹⁵ Behold, I have made you as new saw-shaped threshing wheels of a wagon; and you shall thresh the mountains, and beat the hills to powder, and make *them* as chaff;

¹⁶ and you shall winnow *them*, and the wind shall carry them away, and a tempest shall scatter them; but you shall rejoice in the holy ones of Israel.

¹⁷ "And the poor and the needy shall rejoice; for *when* they shall seek water, and there shall be none, *and* their tongue is parched with thirst, I the Lord God, I the God of Israel will hear, and will not forsake them;

¹⁸ but I will open rivers on the mountains, and fountains in the midst of plains; I will make the desert pools of water, and a thirsty land watercourses.

¹⁹ I will plant in the dry land the cedar and box, the myrtle and cypress, and white poplar;

²⁰ that they may see, and know, and perceive, and understand together, that the hand of the Lord has done these *works*, and the Holy One of Israel has displayed *them*.

²¹ "Your judgment draws near," says the Lord God; "your counsel has drawn near," says the King of Jacob.

²² Let them draw near, and declare to you what things shall come to pass; or tell *us* what things were of old, and we will apply *our* understanding, and we shall know what are the last and the future things;

²³ tell us, declare to us the things that are coming on at the last *time*, and we shall know that you are gods; do good, and do evil, and we shall wonder, and see at the same time

²⁴ where you are, and where your works are; they have chosen you an abomination out of the earth.

²⁵ "But I have raised up him that *comes* from the north, and him that *comes* from the rising of the sun; they shall be called by My name; let the princes come, and as potter's clay, and as a potter treading clay, so shall you be trodden down.

²⁶ For who will declare the things from the beginning, that we may know also the former things, and we will say that they are true? There is no one that speaks beforehand, nor anyone that hears your words.

²⁷ I will give dominion to Zion, and will comfort Jerusalem by the way.

²⁸ For from among the nations, behold, *there was* no one; and of their idols there was none to declare *anything*; and if I should ask them, 'Where are you from?' They could not answer Me.

²⁹ For *these* are your makers, *as you think*, and they that cause you to err in vain.

ISAIAH CHAPTER 42

The Servant of the Lord

¹ Jacob is My servant, I will help him; Israel is My elect, My soul has accepted him; I have put My Spirit upon him; he shall bring forth judgment to the Gentiles.

² He shall not cry, nor lift up *his voice*, nor shall his voice be heard outside.

³ A bruised reed he shall not break, and smoking flax he shall not quench; but he shall bring forth judgment to truth.

⁴ He shall shine out, and shall not be discouraged, until he has set judgment on the earth; and in his name shall the Gentiles trust."

⁵ Thus says the Lord God, who made the heaven, and established it; who settled the earth, and the things in it, and gives breath to the people in it, and spirit to them that tread on it:

⁶ "I, the Lord God, have called you in righteousness, and will hold your hand, and will strengthen you; and I have given you for the covenant of a race, for a light of the Gentiles;

⁷ to open the eyes of the blind, to bring the bound and them that sit in darkness out of bonds and the prison house.

⁸ I am the Lord God; that is My name; I will not give My glory to another, nor My praises to graven images.

⁹ Behold, the ancient things have come to pass, and *so will* the new things which I tell you; yes, before I declare *them* they are made known to you."

¹⁰ Sing to the Lord a new song; you *who are* His dominion, glorify His name from the ends of the earth; you that go down to the sea, and sail upon it; the islands, and they that dwell in them.
¹¹ Rejoice, you wilderness, and the villages thereof, the hamlets, and the inhabitants of Kedar; the inhabitants of the rock shall rejoice, they shall shout from the top of the mountains.
¹² They shall give glory to God, *and* shall proclaim His praises in the islands.
¹³ The Lord God of hosts shall go forth, and crush the war; He shall stir up jealousy, and shall shout mightily against His enemies.
¹⁴ "I have been silent; shall I also always be silent and forbear; I have endured like a travailing *woman*; I will *now* amaze and wither at once.
¹⁵ I will make desolate mountains and hills, and will dry up all their grass; and I will make the rivers islands, and dry up the pools.
¹⁶ And I will bring the blind by a way that they did not know, and I will cause them to tread paths which they have not known; I will turn darkness into light for them, and crooked things into straight. These things will I do, and I will not forsake them.
¹⁷ But they are turned back; be utterly ashamed, you that trust in graven *images*, who say to the molten *images*, 'You are our gods.'
¹⁸ "Hear, you deaf, and look up, you blind, to see.
¹⁹ And who is blind, but My servants? And *who is* deaf, but those that rule over them? Yes, the servants of God have been made blind.
²⁰ You have often seen, and have not taken heed; *your* ears have been opened, and you have not heard."
²¹ The Lord God has taken counsel, that He might be justified, and might magnify *His* praise.
²² And I beheld, and the people were spoiled and plundered; for *there is* a snare in the secret chambers everywhere, and in the houses also, where they have hidden them; they became a spoil, and there was no one that delivered the prey, and there was none who said, "Restore."
²³ Who *is there* among you that will give ear to these things? Hearken to the things which are coming to pass.
²⁴ For what did He give Jacob up to spoil, and Israel to them that plundered him? Did not God *do it* against whom they sinned? *And* they would not walk in His ways, nor obey His law.
²⁵ So He brought upon them the fury of His wrath; and the war, and those that burned round about them, prevailed against them; yet none of them knew *it*, neither did they take *it* to heart.

ISAIAH CHAPTER 43

The Redeemer of Israel

¹ And now thus says the Lord God that made you, O Jacob, and formed you, O Israel: "Do not fear; for I have redeemed you, I have called you *by* your name; you are Mine.
² And if you pass through water, I am with you; and the rivers shall not overflow you; and if you go through the fire, you shall not be burned; the flame shall not burn you.
³ For I am the Lord your God, the Holy One of Israel, that saves you; I have made Egypt and Ethiopia your ransom, and *have given* Seba for you.
⁴ Since you became precious in My sight, you have become glorious, and I have loved you; and I will give men for you, and princes for your life.
⁵ Do not fear; for I am with you; I will bring your descendants from the east, and will gather you from the west.
⁶ I will say to the north, 'Give them up'; and to the south, 'Do not keep them back'; bring My sons from the *land* afar off, and My daughters from the ends of the earth;
⁷ *even* all who are called by My name; for I have prepared him for My glory, and I have formed him, and have made him;
⁸ and I have brought forth the blind people; for *their* eyes are as if they were blind, and those that have ears are deaf.
⁹ All the nations are gathered together, and princes shall be gathered out of them; who will declare these things? Or who will declare to you things from the beginning? Let them bring forth their witnesses, and be justified; and let them hear, and declare the truth.
¹⁰ "Be My witnesses, and I *too am* a witness," says the Lord God, "and My servant whom I have chosen; that you may know, and believe, and understand that I am *He*; before Me there was no other God, and after Me there shall be none.
¹¹ I am God; and beside Me there is no savior.
¹² I have declared, and have saved; I have reproached, and there was no strange *god* among you; you are My witnesses, and I am the Lord God,
¹³ even from the beginning; and there is none that can deliver out of My hands; I will work, and who shall turn it back?"
¹⁴ Thus says the Lord God that redeems you, the Holy One of Israel: "For your sakes I will send to Babylon, and I will stir up all that flee, and the Chaldeans shall be bound in ships.
¹⁵ I am the Lord God, your Holy One, who has appointed for Israel your king."
¹⁶ Thus says the Lord, who makes a way in the sea, and a path in the mighty water;
¹⁷ who brought forth chariots and horse, and a mighty multitude; but they have laid down, and shall not rise; they are extinct, as quenched flax:
¹⁸ "Do not remember the former things, and do not consider the ancient things.
¹⁹ Behold, I *will* do new things, which shall presently spring forth, and you shall know them; and I will make a way in the wilderness, and rivers in the dry land;

[20] the beasts of the field shall bless Me, the owls and young ostriches; for I have given water in the wilderness, and rivers in the dry land, to give drink to My chosen race,

[21] My people whom I have preserved to tell forth My praises.

Pleading with Unfaithful Israel

[22] "I have not now called you, O Jacob; neither have I made you weary, O Israel.

[23] You have not brought Me the sheep of your burnt offering; neither have you glorified Me with your sacrifices. I have not caused you to serve with sacrifices, neither have I wearied you with frankincense.

[24] Neither have you purchased for Me victims for silver, neither have I desired the fat of your sacrifices; but you stood before Me in your sins, and in your iniquities.

[25] "I, *even* I, am He that blots out your transgressions for My own sake, and your sins; and I will remember *them* no more.

[26] Put Me in rememberance, and let us contend *together*; confess your transgressions first, that you may be justified.

[27] Your fathers first, and your princes have transgressed against Me.

[28] And the princes have defiled My sanctuaries; so I gave Jacob *to enemies* to destroy, and Israel to reproach.

ISAIAH CHAPTER 44

God's Blessing on Israel

[1] "But now hear, O Jacob My servant; and Israel, whom I have chosen.

[2] Thus says the Lord God that made you, and He that formed you from the womb: 'You shall yet be helped; do not fear, My servant Jacob; and *My* beloved Israel, whom I have chosen.

[3] For I will give water to the thirsty that walk in a dry land; I will put My Spirit upon your descendants, and My blessings upon your children;

[4] and they shall spring up as grass between brooks, and as willows on *the banks of* running water.'

[5] One shall say, 'I am God's'; and another shall call himself by the name of Jacob; and another shall write with his hand, 'I am God's,' and shall call himself by the name of Israel.

[6] "Thus says God, the King of Israel, and the God of hosts that delivered him: 'I am the First and I am the Last; beside Me there is no God.

[7] Who is like Me? Let him stand, and call, and declare, and prepare for Me from the time that I made man forever; and let them tell you the things that are coming before they arrive.

[8] Do not hide yourselves, nor go astray; have you not heard from the beginning, and *have I not* told you? You are witnesses if there is a God beside Me.'"

Idolatry is Foolishness

[9] But they that framed *false gods* did not then hearken; and they that engraved *images* are all vain, performing their own desires, which shall not profit them, but they shall be ashamed

[10] that form a god, and all that engrave worthless things;

[11] and all by whom they were made have withered; yes, let all the deaf be gathered from *among* men, and let them stand together; and let them be ashamed and confounded together;

[12] For the blacksmith sharpens the iron; he fashions *the idol* with an ax, and fixes it with an awl, and fashions it with the strength of his arm; and he will be hungry and weak, and will drink no water.

[13] The carpenter, having chosen a piece of wood, marks it out with a rule, and fits it with glue, and makes it as the form of a man, and as the beauty of a man, to set it up in the house.

[14] He cuts wood out of the forest, which the Lord planted, *even* a pine tree, and the rain made it grow,

[15] that it might be for men to burn; and having taken part of it he warms himself; yes, they burn part of it, and bake loaves on it; and *of* the rest they make for themselves gods, and they worship them.

[16] Half of it he burns in the fire, and with half of it he bakes loaves on the coals; and having roasted flesh on it he eats, and is satisfied, and having warmed himself he says, "I am comfortable, for I have warmed myself, and have seen the fire."

[17] And the rest he makes a graven god, and worships and prays, saying, "Deliver me; for you are my god."

[18] They have no understanding to perceive; for they have been blinded so that they should not see with their eyes, nor perceive with their heart.

[19] And one has not considered in his mind, nor known in his understanding, that he has burned up half of it in the fire, and baked loaves on its coals and has roasted and eaten flesh, and of the rest of it he has made an abomination, and they worship it.

[20] Know that their heart is ashes, and they err, and no one is able to deliver his soul; see, you will not say, "*There is a* lie in my right hand."

Israel is not Forgotten

[21] "Remember these things, O Jacob and Israel; for you are My servant; I have formed you *to be* My servant; and do not forget Me, O Israel.

[22] For behold, I have blotted your transgressions out as a cloud, and your sin as darkness; turn to Me, and I will redeem you."

[23] Rejoice, you heavens; for God has had mercy upon Israel; sound the trumpet, you foundations of the earth; you mountains, shout *with* joy, you hills, and all the trees therein; for God has redeemed Jacob, and Israel shall be glorified.

24 Thus says the Lord that redeems you, and who formed you from the womb: "I am the Lord that performs all things; I stretched out the heaven alone, and established the earth.

25 Who else will frustrate the tokens of those that have divining spirits, and prophecies from the heart of *man*? Turning the wise back, and making their counsel foolishness;

26 and confirming the word of His servant, and verifying the counsel of His messengers; who says to Jerusalem, 'You shall be inhabited'; and to the cities of Edom, 'You shall be built, and her desert places shall spring forth.'

27 Who says to the deep, 'You shall be dried up, and I will dry up the rivers.'

28 Who bids Cyrus, 'Be wise, and he shall perform all My will'; who says to Jerusalem, 'You shall be built, and I will lay the foundation of My holy house.'"

ISAIAH CHAPTER 45

Cyrus, God's Instrument

1 "Thus says the Lord God to My anointed Cyrus, whose right hand I have held, that nations might be obedient before him; and I will break through the strength of kings; I will open doors before him, and cities shall not be closed.

2 I will go before you, and I will level mountains; I will break to pieces the bronze doors, and burst the iron bars.

3 And I will give you the treasures of darkness, I will open to you hidden, unseen *treasures*, that you may know that I, the Lord your God, that call you by name, am the God of Israel.

4 For the sake of My servant Jacob, and Israel My elect, I will call you by your name, and accept you; but you have not known Me.

5 For I am the Lord God, and there is no other God beside Me; I strengthened you, and you have not known Me.

6 That they that *come* from the east, and they that *come* from the west may know that there is no God but Me. I am the Lord God, and there is no other.

7 I am He that prepared light, and formed darkness; who makes peace, and creates calamity; I am the Lord God, that does all these things.

8 "Let the heavens rejoice from above, and let the clouds rain righteousness; let the earth bring forth, and blossom *with* mercy, and bring forth righteousness likewise; I am the Lord that created you.

9 "What excellent thing have I prepared as clay of the potter? Will the plowman plow the earth all day? Shall the clay say to the potter, 'What are you doing that you do not work, nor have hands?' Shall the thing formed answer Him that formed it?

10 As though one should say to *his* father, 'What will you beget me?' And to his mother, 'What are you bringing forth?'

11 "For thus says the Lord God, the Holy One of Israel, who has formed the things that are to come: Inquire of Me concerning My sons, and concerning the works of My hands, ask of Me.

12 I have made the earth, and man upon it; with My hand I have established the heavens; I have given commandment to all the stars.

13 I have raised him up *to be* a king with righteousness, and all his ways are right; he shall build My city, and shall turn the captivity of My people, not for ransoms, nor for rewards," says the Lord of hosts.

The Lord, the Only Savior

14 Thus says the Lord of hosts: "Egypt has labored *for you*; and the merchandise of the Ethiopians, and the Sabeans, men of stature, shall pass over to you, and shall be your servants; and they shall follow after you bound with chains, and shall pass over to you, and shall bow down to you, and they shall pray to you; for God is in you." There is no God beside You."

15 For you are God, the God of Israel, the Savior, yet we did not know.

16 All that are opposed to Him shall be ashamed and confounded, and shall walk in shame. "Dedicate yourselves to Me, you islands!"

17 Israel is saved by the Lord with an everlasting salvation; they shall not be ashamed nor confounded forever.

18 Thus says the Lord that made the heaven, the very God that created the earth, and made it; He marked it out, He did not create it in vain, but formed it to be inhabited: "I am the Lord, and there is no other.

19 I have not spoken in secret, nor in a dark place of the earth; I did not say to the descendants of Jacob, 'Seek vanity'; I, even I, am the Lord, speaking righteousness, and proclaiming truth.

20 "Assemble yourselves and come; take counsel together, you that escape from the nations. They that set up wood, *even* their graven image, have no knowledge, nor do they who pray to gods that do not save.

21 If they will declare, let them draw near, that they may know together, who has caused these things to be heard from the beginning; then was it told you. I am God, and there is no other beside Me; a just *God* and a Savior; there is none besides Me.

22 Turn to Me, and you shall be saved, you that *come* from the end of the earth; I am God, and there is none other.

23 By Myself I swear, righteousness shall surely proceed out of My mouth; My words shall not be frustrated; that to Me every knee shall bow, and every tongue shall swear by God,

24 saying, 'Righteousness and glory shall come to Him; and all that remove them from their borders shall be ashamed.

25 By the Lord shall they be justified, and in God shall all the descendants of the children of Israel be glorified.'"

ISAIAH CHAPTER 46

Idols Cannot Save Babylon

[1] Bel has fallen, Nebo is broken to pieces, their graven images have gone to the wild beasts and the cattle; you take them packed up as a burden to the weary, exhausted, hungry, and *at the same time* helpless man;

[2] who will not be able to save themselves from war, but they themselves are led *away* captive.

[3] "Hear Me, O house of Jacob, and all the remnant of Israel, who are borne *by Me* from the womb, and taught *by Me* from infancy, *even* unto old age.

[4] I am *He*; and until you have grown old, I am *He*; I bear you, I have made, and I will relieve, I will take up and save you.

[5] "To whom have you compared Me? See *and* consider, you that go astray.

[6] They that furnish gold out of a purse, and silver by weight, will weigh it in a scale, and they hire a goldsmith and make idols, and bow down, and worship them.

[7] They bear it upon the shoulder, and go; and if they put it upon its place, it remains, it cannot move; and whosoever shall cry to it, it cannot hear; it cannot save him from trouble.

[8] "*Therefore* remember these things, and groan; repent, you that have gone astray, return in your heart;

[9] and remember the former things of old; for I am God, and there is none besides Me,

[10] declaring beforehand the latter events before they come to pass, and they are accomplished together; and I said, 'All My counsel shall stand, and I will do all things that I have planned';

[11] calling a bird from the east, and from a land afar off, for the things which I have planned; I have spoken, and brought *him*; I have created and made *him*, I have brought him, and prospered his way.

[12] "Listen to Me, you senseless ones, that are far from righteousness;

[13] I have brought near My righteousness, and I will not be slow with the salvation that is from Me; I have given salvation in Zion to Israel for glory.

ISAIAH CHAPTER 47

The Humiliation of Babylon

[1] "Come down, sit on the ground, O virgin daughter of Babylon; sit on the ground, O daughter of the Chaldeans; for you shall no more be called tender and luxurious.

[2] Take a millstone, grind meal; remove your veil, uncover your white hairs, make bare the leg, pass through the rivers.

[3] Your shame shall be uncovered, your reproaches shall be brought to light; I will exact of you due vengeance, I will no longer deliver you to men."

[4] Your deliverer is the Lord of hosts, the Holy One of Israel is His name.

[5] "Sit down, you that are pierced with woe, go into darkness, O daughter of the Chaldeans; you shall no more be called the strength of a kingdom.

[6] I have been provoked with My people; you have defiled My inheritance; I gave them into your hand, but you did not extend mercy to them; you made the yoke of the aged man very heavy,

[7] and said, 'I shall be a princess forever'; you did not perceive these things in your heart, nor did you remember the latter end.

[8] "But now hear these words, you luxurious one, that sits *at ease*, that is secure, that says in her heart, 'I am, and there is not another; I shall not sit *as* a widow, neither shall I know bereavement.'

[9] But now these two things shall come upon you suddenly in one day, the loss of children and widowhood shall come suddenly upon you, for your sorcery, for the strength of your enchantments,

[10] for your trusting in wickedness; for you said, 'I am, and there is not another'; know therefore the understanding of these things and your harlotry shall be your shame; for you said in your heart, 'I am, and there is not another.'

[11] And destruction shall come upon you, and you shall not be aware; *there shall be a* pit, and you shall fall into it; and grief shall come upon you, and you shall not be able to be clear; and destruction shall come suddenly upon you, and you shall not know.

[12] "Stand now with your enchantments, and with the abundance of your sorcery, which you have learned from your youth; if you can be profited.

[13] You are wearied in your counsels. Let now the astrologers of the heaven stand and deliver you, let them that see the stars tell you what is about to come upon you.

[14] Behold, they all shall be burned up as sticks in the fire; neither shall they at all deliver their life from the flame. Because you have coals of fire, sit upon them;

[15] these shall be your help. You have wearied yourself with traffic from your youth; every man has wandered to his own home, but you shall have no deliverance.

ISAIAH CHAPTER 48

Israel Refined for God's Glory

[1] "Hear these *words*, you house of Jacob, who are called by the name of Israel, and have come forth out of Judah, who swear by the name of the Lord God of Israel, making mention *of it, but* not with truth, nor with righteousness;

[2] maintaining also the name of the holy city, and staying themselves on the God of Israel; the Lord of hosts is His name. "The former things I have already declared;

3 and they that have proceeded out of My mouth, and it became well known; I wrought suddenly, and *the events* came to pass.

4 I know that you are stubborn, and your neck is an iron sinew, and your forehead bronze.

5 And I told you of old what *would be* before it came upon you; I made it known to you, lest you should say, '*My* idols have done *it* for me'; and should say, '*My* graven and molten images have commanded me.'

6 You have heard all this, but you have not known; yet I have made known to you the new things which hereafter shall come to pass, and you did not say,

7 'Now they come to pass, and not formerly'; and you did not hear of them in former days; do not say, 'Yes, I know them.'

8 You have neither known, nor understood, neither from the beginning have I opened your ears; for I knew that you would surely deal treacherously, and would be called a transgressor even from the womb.

9 For My own sake will I show you My wrath, and will bring before you My glorious acts, that I may not utterly destroy you.

10 Behold, I have sold you, *but* not for silver; but I have rescued you from the furnace of affliction.

11 For My own sake I will do *this* for you, because My name is profaned; and I will not give My glory to another.

God's Ancient Plan to Redeem Israel

12 "Hear Me, O Jacob, and Israel whom I call; I am the first, and I endure forever.

13 My hand also has founded the earth, and My right hand has fixed the sky; I will call them, and they shall stand together.

14 And all shall be gathered, and shall hear. Who has told them these things? Out of love to you I have fulfilled your desire on Babylon, to abolish the descendants of the Chaldeans.

15 I have spoken, I have called, I have brought him, and made his way prosperous.

16 Draw near to Me, and hear these words; from the beginning I have not spoken in secret; when it took place I was there." And now the Lord, *even* the Lord, and His Spirit, has sent me.

17 Thus says the Lord that delivered you, the Holy One of Israel: "I am your God, I have shown you how you should find the way in which you should walk.

18 And if you had hearkened to My commandments, *then* would your peace have been like a river, and your righteousness as a wave of the sea.

19 Your descendants also would have been as the sand, and the offspring of your belly as the dust of the ground; neither now shall you by any means be utterly destroyed, neither shall your name perish from before Me."

20 Go forth of Babylon, you that flee from the Chaldeans; utter aloud a voice of joy, and let this be made known, proclaim it to the end of the earth; say, "The Lord has delivered His servant Jacob."

21 And if they shall thirst, He shall lead them through the desert; He shall bring forth water to them out of the rock; the rock shall be split, and the water shall flow forth, and my people shall drink.

22 "There is no rejoicing," says the Lord, "for the ungodly."

ISAIAH CHAPTER 49

The Servant, the Light to the Gentiles

1 "Hearken to Me, you islands; and attend, you Gentiles; after a long time it shall come to pass," says the Lord. "From my mother's womb He has called my name;

2 and He has made my mouth as a sharp sword, and He has hid me under the shadow of His hand; He has made me as a choice shaft, and He has hid me in His quiver;

3 and said to me, 'You are My servant, O Israel, and in you I will be glorified.'

4 Then I said, 'I have labored in vain, I have given my strength for vanity and for nothing; therefore is my judgment with the Lord, and my labor before my God.'"

5 And now thus says the Lord, who formed me from the womb to be His own servant, to gather Jacob to Him and Israel. I shall be gathered and glorified before the Lord, and my God shall be my strength.

6 And He said to me, "*It is* a great thing for you to be called My servant, to establish the tribes of Jacob, and to recover the dispersion of Israel; behold, I have given you for the covenant of a race, for a light of the Gentiles, that you should be for salvation to the end of the earth."

7 Thus says the Lord that delivered you, the God of Israel: "Sanctify him that despises his life, him that is abhorred by the nations that are the servants of princes; kings shall behold him, and princes shall arise, and shall worship him, for the Lord's sake; for the Holy One of Israel is faithful, and I have chosen you."

8 Thus says the Lord: "In an acceptable time have I heard you, and in a day of salvation have I helped you; and I have formed you, and given you for a covenant of the nations, to establish the earth, and to cause to inherit the desert heritages;

9 saying to them that are in bonds, 'Go forth'; and *bidding* them that are in darkness, 'show themselves.' They shall be fed in all the ways, and in all the paths *shall be* their pasture.

10 They shall not hunger, neither shall they thirst; neither shall the heat nor the sun strike them; but He that has mercy on them shall comfort *them*, and by fountains of waters shall He lead them.

11 And I will make every mountain a passage, and every path a pasture to them.

12 Behold, these shall come from afar; *and* these from the north and the west, and others from the land of the Persians.

[13] "Rejoice, you heavens; and let the earth be glad; let the mountains break forth *with* joy; for the Lord has had mercy on His people, and has comforted the lowly ones of His people."

God Will Remember Zion

[14] But Zion said, "The Lord has forsaken me," and, "The Lord has forgotten me."

[15] "Will a woman forget her child, so as not to have compassion upon the offspring of her womb? But if a woman should even forget these, yet I will not forget you," says the Lord.

[16] "Behold, I have painted your walls on My hands, and you are continually before Me.

[17] And you shall soon be built by those by whom you were destroyed, and they that made you desolate shall go forth from you.

[18] Lift up your eyes round about, and look on them all. Behold, they are gathered together, and have come to you. *As* I live, says the Lord, you shall clothe yourself with them all as with an ornament, and put them on, as a bride in her attire.

[19] For your deserted and marred and ruined *places* shall now be too narrow by reason of the inhabitants, and they that devoured you shall be removed far from you.

[20] For your sons whom you have lost shall say in your ears, The place *is too* narrow for me; make room for me that I may dwell.

[21] And you shall say in your heart, 'Who has begotten me these? Whereas I *was* childless, and a widow; but who has brought up these for me? And I was left alone; but from where did these come to me?'"

[22] Thus says the Lord, *even* the Lord: "Behold, I lift up My hand to the nations, and I will lift up My signal to the islands; and they shall bring your sons in *their* bosom, and shall bear your daughters on *their* shoulders.

[23] And kings shall be your nursing fathers, and their princesses your nurses, they shall bow down to you on the face of the earth, and shall lick up the dust of your feet; and you shall know that I am the Lord, and they that wait on Me shall not be ashamed.

[24] "Will anyone take spoils from a giant? And if one should take *a man* captive unjustly, shall he be delivered?

[25] For thus says the Lord: 'If one should take a giant captive, he shall take spoils, and he who takes *them* from a mighty *man* shall be delivered; for I will plead your cause, and I will deliver your children.

[26] And they that afflicted you shall eat their own flesh; and they shall drink their own blood as new wine, and shall be drunk; and all flesh shall perceive that I am the Lord that delivers you, and that upholds the strength of Jacob.'"

ISAIAH CHAPTER 50

The Servant, Israel's Hope

[1] Thus says the Lord: "Of what kind is your mother's bill of divorcement, by which I put her away? Or to which debtor have I sold you? Behold, you are sold for your sins, and for your iniquities have I put your mother away.

[2] Why did I come, and there was no man? *Why* did I call, and there was none to obey? Is not My hand strong to redeem? Or can I not deliver? Behold, by My rebuke I will dry up the sea, and make rivers a wilderness; and their fish shall be dried up because there is no water, and shall die of thirst.

[3] I will clothe the sky with darkness, and will make its covering as sackcloth."

[4] The Lord, *even* God, gives me the tongue of instruction, to know when it is fit to speak a word; He has appointed for me early, He has given me an ear to hear;

[5] and the instruction of the Lord, even the Lord, opens my ears, and I do not disobey, nor dispute.

[6] I gave my back to scourges, and my cheeks to blows; and I did not turn away my face from the shame of spitting;

[7] but the Lord God became my helper; therefore I was not ashamed, but I set my face as a solid rock; and I know that I shall never be ashamed,

[8] for He that has justified me draws near. Who is he that pleads with me? Let him stand up against me at the same time; yea, who is he that pleads with me? Let him draw near to me.

[9] Behold, the Lord, the Lord will help me; who will hurt me? Behold, all you shall grow as old as a garment, and a moth shall devour you.

[10] Who is among you that fears the Lord? Let him heed the voice of His servant; you that walk in darkness, and have no light, trust in the name of the Lord, and stay upon God.

[11] Behold, you all kindle a fire, and feed a flame; walk in the light of your fire, and in the flame which you have kindled. This has happened to you for my sake; you shall lie down in sorrow.

ISAIAH CHAPTER 51

The Lord Comforts Zion

[1] "Listen to Me, all you that follow after righteousness, and seek the Lord; look to the solid rock, which you have hewn, and to the hole of the pit which you have dug.

[2] Look to Abraham your father, and to Sarah who bore you; for he was alone when I called him, and blessed him, and loved him, and multiplied him.

[3] "And now I will comfort you, O Zion; and I have comforted all her desert places; and I will make her desert places as a garden, and her western places as the garden of the Lord; they shall find in her gladness and exaltation, thanksgiving and the voice of praise.

4 "Hear Me, hear Me, My people; and you kings, listen to Me; for a law shall proceed from Me, and My judgment *shall be* for a light of the nations.

5 My righteousness speedily draws near, and My salvation shall go forth as light, and on My arm shall the Gentiles trust; the isles shall wait for Me, and on My arm shall they trust.

6 Lift up your eyes to the sky, and look on the earth beneath; for the sky was darkened like smoke, and the earth shall grow old like a garment, and the inhabitants shall die in like manner; but My righteousness shall not fail.

7 "Hear Me, you that know judgment, the people in whose heart is My law; do not fear the reproach of men, and do not be overcome by their contempt.

8 For as a garment will be devoured by time, and as wool will be devoured by a moth, *so shall they be consumed*; but My righteousness shall be forever, and My salvation for all generations."

9 Awake, awake, O Jerusalem, and put on the strength of your arm; awake as in the early time, as the ancient generation.

10 Are you not *the One* that dried the sea, the water, *even* the abundance of the deep; that made the depths of the sea a way of passage for the delivered and redeemed?

11 For by *the help of* the Lord they shall return, and come to Zion with joy and everlasting exaltation, for praise and joy shall come upon their head; pain, grief, and groaning have fled away.

12 "I, *even* I, am He that comforts you; consider who you are, that you were afraid of mortal man, and of the son of man, who have withered as grass.

13 And you have forgotten God who made you, who made the sky and founded the earth; and you were continually afraid because of the wrath of him that afflicted you; for *whereas* he counseled to take you away, yet now where is the wrath of him that afflicted you?

14 For in your deliverance he shall not halt, nor tarry;

15 for I am your God, that troubles the sea, and causes its waves to roar; the Lord of hosts is My name.

16 I will put My words into your mouth, and I will shelter you under the shadow of My hand, with which I fixed the sky, and founded the earth; and *the Lord* shall say to Zion, 'You are My people.'"

God's Fury Removed

17 Awake, awake, stand up, O Jerusalem, that have drunk at the hand of the Lord the cup of His fury; for you have drunk out and drained the cup of calamity, the cup of wrath;

18 and there was none to comfort you of all the children whom you bore; and there was none to take hold of your hand, not even of all the children whom you have reared.

19 Therefore these things are against you; who shall sympathize with you in your grief? Downfall and destruction, famine and sword; who shall comfort you?

20 Your sons are the perplexed ones, that sleep at the top of every street as a half-boiled beet; they that are full of the anger of the Lord, caused to faint by the Lord God.

21 Therefore hear, you afflicted one, and drunken, *but* not with wine;

22 thus says the Lord God that judges His people: "Behold, I have taken out of your hand the cup of calamity, the cup of My wrath; and you shall not drink it anymore.

23 And I will give it into the hands of them that injured you, and them that afflicted you; who said to your soul, 'Bow down, that we may pass over'; and you laid your body to the ground to them passing by outside."

ISAIAH CHAPTER 52

God Redeems Jerusalem

1 Awake, awake, O Zion; put on your strength, and put on your glory, O Jerusalem the holy city; for the uncircumcised and unclean shall pass through you no more.

2 Shake off the dust and arise; sit down, O Jerusalem; put off the band of your neck, captive daughter of Zion.

3 For thus says the Lord: "You have been sold for nothing; and you shall not be ransomed with silver."

4 Thus says the Lord: "My people went down at first to Egypt to sojourn there; and were carried away forcibly to the Assyrians.

5 And now why are you here? Thus says the Lord: Because My people were taken for nothing, wonder and howl. Thus says the Lord: On account of you My name is continually blasphemed among the Gentiles.

6 "Therefore shall My people know My name in that day, for I am He that speaks. I am at hand,

7 like beauty on the mountains—like the feet of one preaching glad tidings of peace, like one preaching good news." For I will proclaim your salvation, saying, "O Zion, your God shall reign." 8 For the voice of them that guard you is exalted, and with the voice together they shall rejoice; for eyes shall look to eyes, when the Lord shall have mercy upon Zion.

9 Let the waste places of Jerusalem break forth *in* joy together, because the Lord has had mercy upon her, and has delivered Jerusalem.

10 And the Lord shall reveal His holy arm in the sight of all the nations; and all the ends of the earth shall see the salvation that *comes* from our God.

11 Depart! Depart, go out from there, and touch not the unclean thing! Go out from the midst of her; separate yourselves, you that bear the vessels of the Lord.

12 For you shall not go forth with haste, neither go by flight; for the Lord shall go first in advance of you; and the God of Israel shall be *the One* that brings up your rear.

The Suffering Servant

[13] "Behold, My servant shall understand, and be exalted, and glorified exceedingly."

[14] As many shall be amazed at You, so shall Your face be without glory from men; and Your glory *shall not be honored* by the sons of men.

[15] Thus shall many nations wonder at Him; and kings shall keep their mouths shut; for they to whom no report was brought concerning Him shall see; and they who have not heard, shall consider.

ISAIAH CHAPTER 53

[1] O Lord, who has believed our report? And to whom has the arm of the Lord been revealed?

[2] We brought a report as *of* a child before Him; *He is* as a root in a thirsty land; He has no form, nor comeliness; and we saw Him, but He had no form nor beauty.

[3] But His appearance was without honor, and inferior to that of the sons of men; *He was* a man in suffering, and acquainted with the bearing of sickness, for His face has turned from *us*; He was dishonored, and not esteemed.

[4] He bears our sins, and is pained for us; yet we accounted Him to be in trouble, and in suffering, and in affliction.

[5] But He was wounded on account of our sins, and was bruised because of our iniquities; the chastisement of our peace was upon Him; *and* by His stripes we are healed.

[6] All we like sheep have gone astray; everyone has wandered in his way; and the Lord has delivered Him up for our sins.

[7] And He, because of His affliction, opened not His mouth; He was led as a sheep to the slaughter, and as a lamb before the shearer is silent, so He opened not His mouth.

[8] In *His* humiliation His judgment was taken away; who shall declare His generation? For His life is taken away from the earth; because of the iniquities of My people He was led to death.

[9] And I will give the wicked for His burial, and the rich for His death; for He practiced no iniquity, nor craft with His mouth.

[10] The Lord also is pleased to purge Him from His stroke. If you give an offering for sin, Your soul shall see a long-lived seed;

[11] the Lord also is pleased to take away from the travail of His soul, to show Him light, and to form *Him* with understanding; to justify the just one who serves many well; and He shall bear their sins.

[12] Therefore He shall inherit many, and He shall divide the spoils of the mighty; because His soul was delivered to death; and He was numbered among the transgressors; and He bore the sins of many, and was delivered up because of their transgressions.

ISAIAH CHAPTER 54

The Eternal Covenant of Peace

[1] Rejoice, you barren that do not bear; break forth and cry, you that does not travail; for more are the children of the desolate than of her that has a husband; for the Lord has said,

[2] "Enlarge the place of your tent, and of your curtains; fix *the pins*, do not spare, lengthen your cords, and strengthen your pins;

[3] spread forth *your tent* yet to the right and the left; for your descendants shall inherit the Gentiles, and you shall make the desolate cities to be inhabited.

[4] "Do not fear, because you have been put to shame, neither be confounded, because you were reproached; for you shall forget your former shame, and shall no more at all remember the reproach of your widowhood.

[5] For *it is* the Lord that made you; the Lord of hosts is His name; and He that delivered you, He is the God of Israel, *and* shall be called *so* by the whole earth.

[6] The Lord has not called you as a deserted and faint-hearted woman, nor as a woman hated from *her* youth," says your God.

[7] "For a little while I left you; but with great mercy will I have compassion upon you.

[8] In a little wrath I turned away My face from you; but with everlasting mercy will I have compassion upon you," says the Lord, your Redeemer.

[9] "From the time of the water of Noah this is My *purpose*; as I swore to him at that time, *saying* of the earth, 'I will no more be angry with you, neither when you are threatened,

[10] shall the mountains depart, nor shall your hills be removed; so neither shall My mercy fail you, nor shall the covenant of your peace be at all removed; for the Lord *who is* gracious to you has spoken *it*.'

[11] "Afflicted and outcast, you have not been comforted; behold, I *will* prepare carbuncle *for* your stones, and sapphire for your foundations;

[12] and I will make your buttresses jasper, and your gates crystal, and your border precious stones.

[13] And *I will* cause all your sons *to be* taught of God, and your children *to be* in great peace.

[14] And you shall be built in righteousness; abstain from injustice, and you shall not fear; and trembling shall not come near to you.

[15] Behold, strangers shall come to you by Me, and shall sojourn with you, and shall run to you for refuge.

[16] Behold, I have created you, not as the coppersmith blowing coals, and bringing out a vessel *fit* for work; but I have created you, not for ruin, that *I* should destroy *you*.

[17] I will not allow any weapon formed against you to prosper; and every voice that shall rise up against you for judgment, you shall vanquish them all; and your adversaries shall be *condemned* thereby. There is an inheritance to them that serve the Lord, and you shall be righteous before Me," says the Lord.

ISAIAH CHAPTER 55

An Invitation to Abundant Life

1 "You that thirst, go to the water, and all that have no money, go *and* buy; and eat *and drink* wine and milk without money or price.

2 Why do you value at the price of money, and *give* your labor for that which will not satisfy? Hearken to Me, and you shall eat of *all* that is good, and your soul shall feast itself on good things.

3 Listen with your ears, and follow My ways; obey Me, and your soul shall live in prosperity; and I will make with you an everlasting covenant, the sure mercies of David.

4 Behold, I have made him a testimony among the Gentiles, a prince and commander to the Gentiles.

5 Nations which know you not shall call upon you, and peoples which are not acquainted with you shall flee to you for refuge, for the sake of the Lord your God, the Holy One of Israel; for He has glorified you."

6 Seek the Lord, and when you find Him, call upon Him; and when He draws near to you,

7 let the ungodly leave his ways, and the transgressor his counsels; and let him return to the Lord, and he shall find mercy; for He shall abundantly pardon your sins.

8 "For My counsels are not as your counsels, nor are My ways as your ways," says the Lord.

9 "But as the heaven is distant from the earth, so are My ways distant from your ways, and your thoughts from My mind.

10 For as the rain shall come down, or snow from heaven, and shall not return until it has saturated the earth, and it bring forth and bud, and give seed to the sower, and bread for food;

11 so shall My word be, whatever shall proceed out of My mouth, it shall by no means return to Me void, until all the things which I willed have been accomplished; and I will make your ways prosperous, and *will effect* My commands.

12 For you shall go forth with joy, and shall be taught with gladness; for the mountains and the hills shall exalt to welcome you with joy, and all the trees of the field shall applaud with their branches.

13 And instead of the bramble shall come up the cypress, and instead of the nettle shall come up the myrtle; and the Lord shall be for a name, and for an everlasting sign, and shall not fail."

ISAIAH CHAPTER 56

Salvation for the Gentiles

1 Thus says the Lord: "Keep justice, and do righteousness; for My salvation is about to come, and My mercy shall be revealed.

2 Blessed is the man that does these things, and the man that holds by them, and keeps the Sabbaths, from profaning them, and keeps his hands from doing unrighteousness."

3 Let not the stranger who attaches himself to the Lord, say, "Surely the Lord will separate me from His people"; and let not the eunuch say, "I am a dry tree."

4 Thus says the Lord to the eunuchs: "As many as shall keep My Sabbaths, and choose the things which I take pleasure in, and take hold of My covenant;

5 I will give to them in My house and within My walls an honorable place, better than sons and daughters; I will give them an everlasting name, and it shall not fail."

6 "And *I will give it* to the strangers that attach themselves to the Lord, to serve Him, and to love the name of the Lord, to be to Him servants and handmaids; and *as for* all that keep My Sabbaths, from profaning *them*, and that take hold of My covenant,

7 I will bring them to My holy mountain, and gladden them in My house of prayer; their burnt offerings and their sacrifices shall be acceptable upon My altar; for My house shall be called a house of prayer for all nations,"

8 says the Lord that gathers the dispersed of Israel; "for I will gather to him a congregation."

9 All you beasts of the field, come, devour, all you beasts of the forest.

10 See how they are all blinded; they have not known; *they are* dumb dogs *that* will not bark; dreaming of rest, loving to slumber.

11 Yes, they are insatiable dogs, that know not what it is to be filled, and they are wicked, having no understanding; all have followed their own ways, each according to his *will*.

ISAIAH CHAPTER 57

Israel's Futile Idolatry

1 See how the just man has perished, and no one lays *it* to heart; and righteous men are taken away, and no one considers; for the righteous has been removed out of the way of injustice.

2 His burial shall be in peace; he has been removed out of the way.

3 "But draw nearby, you lawless children, the seed of adulterers and the harlot.

4 Against whom have you been rioting? And against whom have you opened your mouth, and against whom have you loosed your tongue? Are you not children of perdition? A lawless seed?

5 Who call upon idols under the leafy trees, slaying your children in the valleys among the rocks?

6 That is your portion, this is your lot; and to them have you poured forth drink offerings, and to these have you offered meat offerings. Shall I not therefore be angry for these things?

7 On a lofty and high mountain, there is your bed, and from there you carried up your meat offerings;

8 and behind the posts of your door did you placed your memorials. Did you think that if you should depart from Me, you would gain? You have loved those that lay with you;

9 and you have multiplied your whoredom with them, and you have increased the number of them that are far from you, and have sent ambassadors beyond your borders, and have been debased, even to hell.

10 You have wearied yourself with your many ways; yet you did not say, 'I will cease to strengthen myself'; for you have done these things; therefore you have not supplicated Me.

11 "Through dread of whom have you feared, and lied against Me, and have not remembered, nor considered Me, nor regarded Me; yea, though when I see you I pass them by, yet you have not feared Me.

12 And I will declare your righteousness, and your sins, which shall not profit you.

13 When you cry out, let them deliver you in your affliction; for all these the wind shall take, and the tempest shall carry *them* away; but they that cleave to Me shall possess the land, and shall inherit My holy mountain."

Healing for the Backslider

14 And they shall say, "Clear the ways before him, and take up the stumbling blocks out of the way of My people."

15 Thus says the Most High, who dwells on high forever, Holy in the holies is His name, the Most High resting in the holies, and giving patience to the faint-hearted, and giving life to the broken-hearted:

16 "I will not take vengeance on you forever, neither will I always be angry with you; for My Spirit shall go forth from Me, and I have created all breath.

17 On account of sin for a little while I grieved him and struck him, and turned away My face from him; and he was grieved, and he went on sorrowful in his ways.

18 I have seen his ways, and healed him, and comforted him, and given him true comfort;

19 peace upon peace to them that are far off, and to them that are close by"; and the Lord has said, "I will heal them."

20 But the unrighteous shall be tossed as troubled waves, and shall not be able to rest.

21 "There is no peace," says *my* God, "for the wicked."

ISAIAH CHAPTER 58

Fasting that Pleases God

1 "Cry aloud, and spare not; lift up your voice as with a trumpet, and declare to My people their sins, and to the house of Jacob their iniquities.

2 They seek Me day by day, and desire to know My ways, as a people that had done righteousness, and had not forsaken the judgment of their God; they now ask of Me righteous judgment, and desire to draw near to God,

3 saying, 'Why have we fasted, and You did not see? *Why* have we afflicted our souls, and You did not know it?' In fact, in the days of your fasts you find your pleasures, and all them that are under your power you wound.

4 If you fast for quarrels and strife, and strike the lowly with *your* fists, why do you fast to Me as *you do* this day, so that your voice may be heard in crying?

5 I have not chosen this fast, nor *such* a day for a man to afflict his soul; although you should bend down your neck as a ring, and spread under you sackcloth and ashes, neither thus shall you call a fast acceptable.

6 "I have not chosen such a fast," says the Lord; "but do you loose every burden of iniquity, do you untie the knots of hard bargains, set the bruised free, and cancel every unjust account?

7 Break your bread to the hungry, and lead the unsheltered poor to your house; if you see one naked, clothe *him*, and you shall not disregard the relations of your own seed.

8 Then shall your light break forth as the morning, and your health shall speedily spring forth; and your righteousness shall go before you, and the glory of God shall surround you.

9 Then shall you cry, and God shall hearken to you; while you are yet speaking He will say, 'Behold, I am here.' If you remove from you the band, and the stretching forth of the hands, and murmuring speech;

10 and *if* you give bread to the hungry from your heart, and satisfy the afflicted soul; then shall your light spring up in darkness, and your darkness *shall be* as noon day;

11 and your God shall be with you continually, and you shall be satisfied according as your soul desires; and your bones shall be made fat, and shall be as a well-watered garden, and as a fountain *from* which the water has not failed.

12 And your old waste *places* shall be built up, and your foundations shall last through all generations; and you shall be called a repairer of breaches, and you shall cause your paths between to be in peace.

13 "If you turn away your foot from the Sabbath, so as not to do your pleasure on the holy days, and shall call the Sabbaths delightful, holy to God; *if* you shall not lift up your foot to work, nor speak a word in anger out of your mouth,

14 then shall you trust on the Lord; and He shall bring you up to the good places of the land, and feed you with the heritage of Jacob your father; for the mouth of the Lord has spoken this."

ISAIAH CHAPTER 59

Separated from God

1 Has the hand of the Lord no power to save? Or has He made His ear heavy, so that He should not hear?

2 But rather, your iniquities separate between you and God, and because of your sins has He turned away *His* face from you, so as not to have mercy *upon you.*

³ For your hands are defiled with blood, and your fingers with sins; your lips also have spoken iniquity, and your tongue meditates unrighteousness.

⁴ None speaks justly, neither is there true judgment; they trust in vanities, and speak empty *words*; for they conceive trouble, and bring forth iniquity.

⁵ They have hatched vipers' eggs, and weave a spider's web; and he that is going to eat of their eggs, having broken one, has found a viper therein.

⁶ Their web shall not become a garment, nor shall they at all clothe themselves with their works; for their works are works of iniquity.

⁷ And their feet run to wickedness, *and are* swift to shed blood; their thoughts also are thoughts of murder; destruction and misery are in their ways;

⁸ and the way of peace they do not know, neither is there judgment in their ways; for their paths by which they go are crooked, and they do not know peace.

⁹ Therefore has judgment departed from them, and righteousness shall not overtake them; while they waited for light, darkness came upon them; while they waited for brightness, they walked in perplexity.

¹⁰ They shall feel for the wall as blind *men*, and shall feel *for it* as if they had no eyes; and they shall feel at noonday as at midnight; they shall groan as dying men.

¹¹ They shall proceed together as a bear and as a dove; we have waited for judgment, and there is no salvation, it is gone far from us.

¹² For our iniquity is great before You, and our sins have risen up against us; for our iniquities are in us, and we know our unrighteous deeds.

¹³ We have sinned, and dealt falsely, and revolted from our God; we have spoken unrighteous words, and have been disobedient; we have conceived and uttered from our heart unrighteous words.

¹⁴ And we have turned back judgment, and righteousness has departed afar off; for truth is consumed in their ways, and they could not pass by a straight *path*.

¹⁵ And truth has been taken away, and they have turned aside *their* mind from understanding. And the Lord saw it, and it displeased Him that there was no judgment.

¹⁶ And He looked, and there was no man, and He observed, and there was none to help; so He defended them with His arm, and established *them* with *His* mercy.

¹⁷ And He put on righteousness as a breastplate, and placed the helmet of salvation on His head; and He clothed himself with the garment of vengeance, and with His cloak,

¹⁸ as one about to render a recompense, *even* reproach to His adversaries.

¹⁹ So shall they of the west fear the name of the Lord, and they *that come* from the rising of the sun *shall fear* His glorious name; for the wrath of the Lord shall come as a mighty river, it shall come with fury.

²⁰ And the deliverer shall come for Zion's sake, and shall turn away ungodliness from Jacob.

²¹ "And this shall be My covenant with them," said the Lord: "My Spirit which is upon you, and the words which I have put in your mouth, shall never fail from your mouth, nor from the mouth of your descendants, for the Lord has spoken it, from this time and forevermore!"

ISAIAH CHAPTER 60

The Gentiles Bless Zion

¹ Be enlightened, be enlightened, O Jerusalem, for your light is come, and the glory of the Lord is risen upon you!

² Behold, darkness shall cover the earth, and *there shall be* deep darkness on the nations; but the Lord shall appear upon you, and His glory shall be seen upon you.

³ And kings shall walk in your light, and nations in your brightness.

⁴ "Lift up your eyes round about, and behold your children gathered; all your sons have come from far, and your daughters shall be borne on *men's* shoulders.

⁵ Then shall you see, and fear, and be amazed in your heart; for the wealth of the sea shall come round to you, and of nations and peoples; and herds of camels shall come to you,

⁶ and the camels of Midian and Ephah shall cover you; all from Saba shall come bearing gold, and shall bring frankincense, and they shall proclaim the salvation of the Lord.

⁷ And all the flocks of Kedar shall be gathered, and the rams of Nebaioth shall come; and acceptable sacrifices shall be offered on My altar, and My house of prayer shall be glorified. ⁸ Who are these *that* fly as clouds, and as doves with young ones to Me?

⁹ The isles have waited for Me, and the ships of Tarshish among the first, to bring your children from afar, and their silver and their gold with them, and *that* for the sake of the holy name of the Lord, and because the Holy One of Israel is glorified.

¹⁰ "And strangers shall build your walls, and their kings shall wait upon you; for by reason of My wrath I have struck you, and by reason of mercy I have loved you.

¹¹ And your gates shall be opened continually; they shall not be shut, day or night; to bring in to you the power of the Gentiles, and their kings as captives.

¹² For the nations and the kings which will not serve you shall perish; and those nations shall be made utterly desolate.

¹³ And the glory of Lebanon shall come to you, with the cypress, and pine, and cedar together, to glorify My holy place.

¹⁴ And the sons of them that afflicted you, and of them that provoked you, shall come to you in fear; and you shall be called Zion, the city of the Holy One of Israel.

[15] "Because you have become desolate and hated, and there was no helper, therefore I will make you a perpetual gladness, a joy of many generations.

[16] And you shall drink the milk of the Gentiles, and shall eat the wealth of kings; and shall know that I am the Lord that saves you and delivers you, the Holy One of Israel.

[17] "And for brass I will bring you gold, and for iron I will bring you silver, and instead of wood I will bring you brass, and instead of stones, iron; and I will make your princes peaceable, and your overseers righteous.

[18] And injustice shall no more be heard in your land, nor destruction nor misery in your coasts; but your walls shall be called Salvation, and your gates Sculptured Work.

God the Glory of His People

[19] "And you shall no more have the sun for a light by day, nor shall the rising of the moon lighten your night; but the Lord shall be your everlasting light, and God your glory.

[20] For the sun shall no more set, nor shall the moon be eclipsed; for the Lord shall be your everlasting light, and the days of your mourning shall be completed.

[21] Your people also shall be all righteous; they shall inherit the land forever, preserving that which they have planted, *even* the works of their hands, for glory.

[22] The little one shall become thousands, and the least a great nation; I the Lord will gather them in *due* time."

ISAIAH CHAPTER 61

The Good News of Salvation

[1] "The Spirit of the Lord is upon Me, because He has anointed Me; He has sent Me to preach the gospel to the poor, to heal the brokenhearted, to proclaim liberty to the captives, and recovery of sight to the blind;

[2] to declare the acceptable year of the Lord, and the day of recompense; to comfort all that mourn;

[3] that there should be given to them that mourn in Zion glory instead of ashes, the oil of joy to the mourners, the garment of glory for the spirit of heaviness; and they shall be called generations of righteousness, the planting of the Lord for glory."

[4] And they shall build the old waste places, they shall raise up those that were before made desolate, and shall renew the desert cities, *even* those that had been desolate for *many* generations.

[5] And strangers shall come and feed your flocks, and aliens *shall be your* plowmen and vinedressers.

[6] But you shall be called priests of the Lord, the ministers of God; you shall eat the strength of nations, and shall be admired because of their wealth.

[7] Thus shall they inherit the land a second time, and everlasting joy shall be upon their head.

[8] "For I am the Lord who loves righteousness, and hate robberies of injustice; and I will give their labor to the just, and will make an everlasting covenant with them.

[9] And their descendants shall be known among the Gentiles, and their offspring in the midst of peoples; everyone that sees them shall take notice of them, that they are a seed blessed of God;

[10] and they shall greatly rejoice in the Lord." Let my soul rejoice in the Lord; for He has clothed me with the robe of salvation, and the garment of joy; He has put a turban on me as on a bridegroom, and adorned me with ornaments as a bride.

[11] And as the earth putting forth her flowers, and as a garden its seed; so shall the Lord, *even* the Lord, cause righteousness to spring forth, and exaltation before all nations.

ISAIAH CHAPTER 62

Assurance of Zion's Salvation

[1] "For Zion's sake I will not hold My peace, and for Jerusalem's sake I will not rest, until her righteousness go forth as light, and My salvation burn as a torch."

[2] And the Gentiles shall see your righteousness, and kings your glory; and one shall call you *by* a new name, which the Lord shall name.

[3] And you shall be a crown of beauty in the hand of the Lord, and a royal diadem in the hand of your God.

[4] And you shall no more be called 'Forsaken'; and your land shall no more be called 'Desert'; for you shall be called 'My Pleasure,' and your land Inhabited; for the Lord has taken pleasure in you, and your land shall be inhabited.

[5] And as a young man lives with a virgin, so shall your sons dwell in *you*; and it shall come to pass *that* as a bridegroom will rejoice over a bride, so will the Lord rejoice over you.

[6] And on your walls, O Jerusalem, have I set watchmen all day and all night, who shall never cease making mention of the Lord, for there is none like You.

[7] When He shall have re-established, and made Jerusalem a praise on the earth.

[8] For the Lord has sworn by His glory, and by the might of His arm, *saying*, "I will no more give your grain and your provisions to your enemies; nor shall strangers anymore drink your wine, for which you have labored.

[9] But they that have gathered them shall eat them, and they shall praise the Lord; and they that have gathered *the grapes* shall drink thereof in My holy courts.

[10] "Go through My gates, and make a way for My people; and cast the stones out of the way; lift up a standard for the Gentiles.

[11] For behold, the Lord has proclaimed to the end of the earth, say to the daughter of Zion, 'Behold, your Savior has come to you, having His reward and His work before His face.'

[12] And one shall call them the holy people, the redeemed of the Lord; and you shall be called a city sought out, and not forsaken."

ISAIAH CHAPTER 63

Vengeance on Edom

[1] Who is this that has come from Edom, *with* red garments from Bosor? Thus fair in his apparel, with mighty strength? I speak of righteousness and saving judgment.

[2] Why are your garments red, and your clothing as *if fresh* from a trodden winepress?

[3] "I am full of trodden *grapes*, and of the nations there is not a man with Me; and I trampled them in My fury, and dashed them to pieces as earth, and brought down their blood to the earth.

[4] For the day of recompense has come upon them, and the year of redemption is at hand.

[5] And I looked, and there was no helper; and I observed, and none upheld; therefore My arm delivered them, and My anger drew near.

[6] And I trampled them in My anger, and brought down their blood to the earth."

God's Mercy Remembered

[7] I remembered the mercy of the Lord, the praises of the Lord in all things in which He recompenses us. The Lord is a good judge to the house of Israel; He deals with us according to His mercy, and according to the abundance of His righteousness.

[8] And He said, "Is it not My people?" The children surely will not be rebellious; and He became to them deliverance

[9] out of all their affliction; not an ambassador, nor a messenger, but *He H*imself saved them, because He loved them and spared them; He Himself redeemed them, and took them up, and lifted them up all the days of old.

[10] But they disobeyed, and provoked His Holy Spirit; so He turned to be an enemy, He Himself contended against them.

[11] Then he remembered the days of old, *saying*, "Where is He that brought up from the sea the shepherd of the sheep? Where is He that put His Holy Spirit in them?

[12] Who led Moses with His right hand, the arm of His glory? He forced the water *to separate* from before him, to make Himself an everlasting name.

[13] He led them through the deep, as a horse through the wilderness, and they did not faint."

[14] And as cattle through a plain; the Spirit came down from the Lord, and guided them; thus You led Your people, to make Yourself a glorious name.

A Prayer of Penitence

[15] Turn from heaven, and look from Your holy habitation and *from* Your glory; where is Your zeal and Your strength? Where is the abundance of Your mercy and of Your compassions, that You have withheld Yourself from us?

[16] For You are our Father; and *though* Abraham did not know us, and Israel did not acknowledge us, yet do You, O Lord, our Father, deliver us; Your name has been upon us from the beginning.

[17] Why have You caused us to err, O Lord, from Your way? *And* have hardened our hearts, that we should not fear You? Return for Your servants' sake, for the sake of the tribes of Your inheritance,

[18] that we may inherit a small part of Your holy mountain.

[19] We have become as at the beginning, when You did not rule over us, and Your name was not called upon us.

ISAIAH CHAPTER 64

[1] If you would open the heaven, trembling will take hold upon the mountains from You, and they shall melt,

[2] as wax melts before the fire; and fire shall burn up the enemies, and Your name shall be manifest among the adversaries; at Your presence the nations shall be troubled,

[3] whenever You shall work gloriously; trembling from You shall take hold upon the mountains.

[4] From of old we have not heard, neither have our eyes seen a God besides You, and Your works which You will perform to them that wait for mercy.

[5] For *these blessings* shall happen to them that work righteousness, and they shall remember Your ways; behold, You were angry and we have sinned; therefore we have erred,

[6] and we have all become as unclean, and all our righteousness is as a filthy rag; and we have fallen as leaves because of our iniquities; thus the wind shall carry us *away*.

[7] And there is none that calls upon Your name, or that remembers to take hold of You; for You have turned Your face away from us, and have delivered us up because of our sins.

[8] And now, O Lord, You are our Father, and we are the clay, all *of us are* the work of Your hands.

[9] Do not be very angry with us, and do not remember our sins forever; but now look on *us*, for we are all Your people.

[10] The city of Your holiness has become desolate, Zion has become as a wilderness, Jerusalem a curse.

[11] The house, our sanctuary, and the glory which our fathers blessed, has been burned with fire; and all our glorious things have gone to ruin.

[12] And for all these things You, O Lord, have withheld Yourself, and have been silent, and have brought us very low.

ISAIAH CHAPTER 65

The Righteousness of God's Judgment

[1] "I became manifest to them that did not ask for Me; I was found by them that did not seek Me. I said, 'Behold, I am *here*,' to a nation who did not call on My name.

2 I have stretched forth My hands all day long to a disobedient and gainsaying people, to them that walked in a way that was not good, but according to their sins.

3 This is the people that provokes Me continually in My presence; they offer sacrifices in gardens, and burn incense on bricks to demons, which do not exist.

4 They lie down to sleep in the tombs and in the caves for the sake of dreams, *even* they that eat swine's flesh, and the broth of *their* sacrifices; all their vessels are defiled;

5 who say, 'Depart from me, do not draw near to me, for I am pure.' This is the smoke of My wrath, a fire burns with it continually.

6 Behold, it is written before Me; I will not be silent until I have recompensed into their bosom,

7 their sins and *the sins* of their fathers," says the Lord, "who have burned incense on the mountains, and reproached Me on the hills; I will recompense their works into their bosom."

8 Thus says the Lord: "As the new wine shall be found in the cluster, and they shall say, 'Do not destroy it, for a blessing is in it'; so will I do for the sake of him that serves Me, for his sake I will not destroy *them* all.

9 And I will lead forth the descendants *that came* of Jacob and of Judah, and they shall inherit My holy mountain; and My elect and My servants shall inherit it, and shall dwell there.

10 And there shall be in the forest folds of flocks, and the Valley of Achor *shall* be for a resting place of herds for My people, who have sought Me.

11 But you are they that have left Me, and forget My holy mountain, and prepare a table for the demon, and fill up the drink offering to Fortune.

12 I will deliver you up to the sword, you shall all fall by slaughter; for I called you, and you did not listen; I spoke, and you refused to hear; and you did evil in My sight, and chose the things in which I do not delight."

13 Therefore thus says the Lord: "Behold, My servants shall eat, but you shall hunger; behold, My servants shall drink, but you shall thirst; behold, My servants shall rejoice, but you shall be ashamed;

14 behold, My servants shall exalt with joy, but you shall cry for the sorrow of your heart, and shall howl for the grief of your spirit.

15 For you shall leave your name for a loathing to My chosen, and the Lord shall destroy you; but My servants shall be called by a new name,

16 which shall be blessed on the earth; for they shall bless the true God; and they that swear upon the earth shall swear by the true God; for they shall forget the former affliction, it shall not come into their mind.

The Glorious New Creation

17 "For there shall be a new heaven and a new earth; and they shall not at all remember the former, neither shall they at all come into their mind.

18 But they shall find in her joy and exaltation; for behold, I make Jerusalem a rejoicing, and My people a joy.

19 And I will rejoice in Jerusalem, and will be glad in My people; and there shall no more be heard in her the voice of weeping, or the voice of crying.

20 "Neither shall there be there anymore a *child that dies* untimely, or an old man who has not fulfilled his days; for the youth shall be a hundred years *old*, and the sinner who dies at a hundred years shall also be accursed;

21 and they shall build houses, and they shall dwell in *them*; and they shall plant vineyards, and shall eat its fruit.

22 They shall by no means build, and others inhabit; and they shall by no means plant, and others eat; for as the days of the tree of life shall be the days of My people, they shall long enjoy the fruits of their labors.

23 My elect shall not toil in vain; neither shall they beget children to be cursed; for they are a seed blessed of God, and their offspring with them.

24 "And it shall come to pass, *that* before they call, I will listen to them; while they are yet speaking, I will say, 'What is it?'

25 Then wolves and lambs shall feed together, and the lion shall eat straw like the ox, and earth *shall be* the serpent's bread. They shall not injure nor destroy on My holy mountain," says the Lord.

ISAIAH CHAPTER 66

True Worship and False

1 Thus says the Lord: "Heaven is My throne, and the earth is My footstool; what kind of a house will you build for Me? And of what kind *is to be* the place of My rest?

2 For all these things are Mine," says the Lord; "and to whom will I have respect, but to the humble and meek, and the *man* that trembles *at* My words?

3 "But the transgressor that sacrifices a calf to Me, is as he that kills a dog; and he that offers fine flour, as *one that offers* swine's blood; he that gives frankincense for a memorial, is as a blasphemer. Yet they have chosen their own ways, and their soul has delighted in their abominations.

4 I also will choose their mockeries, and will recompense their sins upon them; because I called them, and they did not hearken to Me; I spoke, and they did not listen; and they did evil before Me, and chose the things in which I did not delight."

5 Hear the words of the Lord, you that tremble at His word; speak, our brothers, to them that hate you and abominate you, that the name of the Lord may be glorified, and may appear their joy; but they shall be ashamed.

6 A voice of a cry from the city, a voice from the temple, a voice of the Lord rendering recompense to *His* adversaries.

7 Before she that travailed has brought forth, before the birth pains came on, she escaped *it* and brought forth a male.

8 Who has heard such a thing? And who has seen after this manner? Has the earth travailed in one day? Or has even a nation been born at once, that Zion has travailed, and brought forth her children?

9 "But I have raised this expectation, yet you have not remembered Me," says the Lord. "Behold, have not I made the bearing and barren woman?" Says your God.

10 Rejoice, O Jerusalem, and all you that love her hold in her a general assembly; rejoice greatly with her, all that *now* mourn over her;

11 that you may feed and be satisfied with the consolation of her bosom; that you may drink deeply, and delight yourselves with the abundance of her glory.

12 For thus says the Lord: "Behold, I turn toward them as a river of peace, and as a torrent bringing upon them in a flood the glory of the Gentiles; their children shall be borne upon the shoulders, and comforted on the knees.

13 As if his mother should comfort one, so will I also comfort you; and you shall be comforted in Jerusalem."

14 And you shall see, and your heart shall rejoice, and your bones shall thrive like grass; and the hand of the Lord shall be known to them that fear Him, and He shall threaten the disobedient.

15 For behold, the Lord will come as fire, and His chariots as a storm, to render His vengeance with wrath, and His rebuke with a flame of fire.

16 For with the fire of the Lord all the earth shall be judged, and all flesh with His sword; many shall be slain by the Lord.

17 "They that sanctify themselves and purify themselves in the gardens, and eat swine's flesh in the porches, and the abominations, and the mouse, shall be consumed together," says the Lord.

18 "And I *know* their works and their imagination. I am going to gather all nations and tongues; and they shall come, and see My glory.

19 And I will leave a sign upon them, and I will send forth them that have escaped of them to the nations, to Tarshish, Pul, Lud, Mosoch, and to Tubal, and to Greece, and to the isles afar off, to those who have not heard of My name, nor seen My glory; and they shall declare My glory among the Gentiles. 20 And they shall bring your brothers out of all nations for a gift to the Lord with horses, and chariots, in litters *drawn by* mules with awnings, to the holy city Jerusalem," said the Lord, "as though the children of Israel should bring their sacrifices to Me with psalms into the house of the Lord.

21 And I will take of them priests and Levites, says the Lord.

22 "For as the new heaven and the new earth, which I make, remain before Me," says the Lord, "so shall your descendants and your name continue.

23 And it shall come to pass from month to month, and from Sabbath to Sabbath, *that* all flesh shall come to worship before Me in Jerusalem," says the Lord.

24 "And they shall go forth, and see the carcasses of the men that have transgressed against Me; for their worm shall not die, and their fire shall not be quenched; and they shall be a spectacle to all flesh."

THE BOOK OF JEREMIAH

1 The word of God which came to Jeremiah the *son of* Hilkiah, *one* of the priests who dwelt at Anathoth in the land of Benjamin:

2 as the word of God came to him in the days of Josiah son of Amon king of Judah, in the thirteenth year of his reign.

3 And it was in the days of Joakim, son of Josiah king of Judah, until the eleventh year of Zedekiah king of Judah, *even* until the captivity of Jerusalem in the fifth month.

The Prophet is Called

4 And the word of the Lord came to him, *saying,*

5 "Before I formed you in the womb I knew you; and before you came forth from the womb, I sanctified you; I have ordained you a prophet to the nations."

6 And I said, "Ah, Lord God! Behold, I know not *how* to speak, for I am a youth."

7 And the Lord said to me: "Do not say, 'I am a youth,' for you shall go to all to whomsoever I shall send you, and according to all *the words* that I shall command you, you shall speak.

8 Do not be afraid of them; for I am with you, to deliver you," says the Lord.

9 And the Lord stretched forth His hand to me, and touched my mouth. And the Lord said to me, "Behold, I have put My words into your mouth.

10 "Behold, I have appointed you this day over nations and over kingdoms, to root out, and to pull down, and to destroy, and to rebuild, and to plant."

11 And the word of the Lord came to me, saying, "What do you see?" And I said, "A rod of an almond tree."

12 And the Lord said to me, "You have seen well, for I have watched over My words, to perform them."

13 And the word of the Lord came to me a second time, saying, "What do you see?" And I said, "A caldron on the fire; and it is facing the north."

14 And the Lord said to me, "From the north shall flame forth evils upon all the inhabitants of the land.

15 For behold, I am calling together all the kingdoms of the earth from the north," says the Lord. "And they shall come, and shall set each one his throne at the entrance of the gates of Jerusalem, and against all the walls round about her, and against all the cities of Judah.

16 And I will speak to them in judgment concerning all their wickedness, because they have forsaken Me, and sacrificed to strange gods, and worshipped the works of their own hands.

17 "Gird up your loins, and stand up, and speak all *the words* that I shall command you. Do not be afraid of them, nor terrified at their presence, for I am with you, to deliver you," says the Lord.

[18] "Behold, I have made you this day as a strong city, and as a bronze wall, strong *against* all the kings of Judah and its princes, and the people of the land.

[19] And they shall fight against you, but they shall by no means prevail against you; because I am with you, to deliver you," says the Lord.

JEREMIAH CHAPTER 2

God's Case Against Israel

[1] And He said, "Thus says the Lord,

[2] I remember the kindness of your youth, and the love of your betrothal,

[3] in following the Holy One of Israel," says the Lord. "Israel was holiness unto the Lord, *and* the firstfruits of His increase. All that devoured him shall offend; evils shall come upon them," says the Lord.

[4] Hear the word of the Lord, O house of Jacob, and every family of the house of Israel.

[5] Thus says the Lord: "What trespass have your fathers found in Me, that they have revolted far from Me, and gone after vanities, and have become vain?

[6] And they did not say, 'Where is the Lord, who brought us up out of the land of Egypt, who guided us in the wilderness, in an untried and trackless land, in a land in which no man has entered, and no man has dwelt in?'

[7] And I brought you to Carmel, that you should eat its fruits, and its goods; and you went in, and defiled My land, and made My heritage an abomination.

[8] The priest did not say, 'Where is the Lord?' And they that held by the law did not know Me. The shepherds also sinned against Me, and the prophets prophesied by Baal, and went after that which did not profit.

[9] "Therefore I will yet plead with you, and with your children's children.

[10] For go to the isles of Kittim, and see; and send to Kedar, and observe accurately, and see if there has ever been such a thing;

[11] if the nations have changed their gods, though they are not gods. But My people have changed their glory *for that* which will not profit them.

[12] The heaven is amazed at this, and is very exceedingly horrorstruck," says the Lord.

[13] "For My people have committed two evils: they have forsaken Me, the fountain of living waters, and hewn out for themselves broken cisterns, which will not be able to hold water.

[14] "Is Israel a servant, or a home-born slave? Why has he become a spoil?

[15] The lions roared at him, and uttered their voice, which have made his land a wilderness; and his cities are broken down, that they should not be inhabited.

[16] Also the children of Memphis and Tahpanhes have known you, and mocked you.

[17] Has not your forsaking Me brought these things upon you?" Says the Lord your God.

[18] "And now what have you to do with the way of Egypt, to drink the water of Gihon? And what have you to do with the way of the Assyrians, to drink the water of rivers?

[19] Your apostasy shall correct you, and your wickedness shall reprove you. Know then, and see, that your forsaking Me *has been* bitter to you," says the Lord your God; "and I have taken no pleasure in you," says the Lord your God.

[20] "For of old you have broken your yoke, and burst your bonds; and you have said, 'I will not serve You, but will go upon every high hill, and under every shady tree, there will I indulge in my fornication.'

[21] Yet I planted you a fruitful vine, entirely of the right sort—how are you a strange vine turned to bitterness!

[22] Though you should wash yourself with lye, and use much soap, *still* you are stained by your iniquities before Me," says the Lord.

[23] "How will you say, 'I am not polluted, and have not gone after Baal?' Behold your ways in the burial ground, and know what you have done: her voice has howled in the evening;

[24] she has extended her ways over the waters of the desert; she was hurried along by the lusts of her soul; she is given up *to them*; who will turn her back? None that seek her shall be weary; at *the time of* her humiliation they shall find her.

[25] Withdraw your foot from a rough way, and your throat from thirst: but she said 'I will strengthen myself'—for she loved strangers, and went after them.

[26] "As is the shame of a thief when he is caught, so shall the children of Israel be ashamed; they, and their kings, and their princes, and their priests, and their prophets.

[27] They said to a tree, 'You are my father'; and to a stone, 'You have begotten me'; and they have turned *their* backs to Me, and not their faces. Yet in the time of their afflictions they will say, 'Arise, and save us.'

[28] And where are your gods which you have made for yourself? Will they arise and save *you* in the time of your affliction? For according to the number of your cities were your gods, O Judah; and according to the number of the streets of Jerusalem they sacrificed to Baal.

[29] "Why do you speak unto Me? You all have been ungodly, and you all have transgressed against Me," says the Lord.

[30] "In vain have I chastened your children; you did not receive correction. A sword has devoured your prophets as a destroying lion; yet you did not fear.

[31] Therefore hear the word of the Lord: thus says the Lord, 'Have I been a wilderness or a dry land to Israel? Why have My people said, "We will not be ruled over, and will not come to You anymore?"

[32] Will a bride forget her attire, or a virgin her ornaments? But My people have forgotten Me days without number!

[33] What fair device will you yet employ in your ways, so as to seek love? *It shall* not *be* so; moreover you have done wickedly in corrupting your ways;

34 and in your hands have been found the blood of innocent souls; I have not found them in holes, but on every oak.

35 Yet you said, "I am innocent: only let His wrath be turned away from me." Behold, I *will* plead with you, in that you say, 'I have not sinned.'

36 For you have been so exceedingly contemptuous as to repeat your ways; but you shall be ashamed of Egypt, as you were ashamed of Assyria.

37 For you shall go forth from here also with your hands upon your head; for the Lord has rejected your hope, and you shall not prosper in it.

JEREMIAH CHAPTER 3

Israel is Shameless

1 "If a man divorce his wife, and she depart from him, and become another man's, shall she return to him anymore? Shall not that woman be utterly defiled? But you have played the harlot with many shepherds, and have returned to Me," says the Lord·

2 Lift up your eyes *and look* straight ahead, and see where you have not been utterly defiled. You have sat for them by the wayside as a deserted crow, and have defiled the land with your fornications and your wickedness.

3 And you retained many shepherds for a stumbling block to yourself. You had a whore's face; you became shameless toward all.

4 Have you not called Me as it were a home, and the father and guide of your youth?

5 Will *God's anger* continue forever, or be preserved to the end? Behold, you have spoken and done these bad things, as you were able."

A Call to Repentance

6 And the Lord said to me in the days of Josiah the king, "Have you seen what things the house of Israel has done to Me? They have gone on every high mountain, and under every shady tree, and have committed fornication there.

7 And I said after she had committed all these acts of fornication, 'Turn again to Me.' Yet she did not return. And faithless Judah saw her faithlessness.

8 And I saw that (for all the sins of which she was convicted, wherein the house of Israel committed adultery, and I put her away, and gave into her hands a certificate of divorce) yet faithless Judah did not fear, but went and also committed fornication herself.

9 And her fornication was nothing accounted of; and she committed adultery with wood and stone.

10 And for all these things faithless Judah did not turn to Me with all her heart, but falsely."

11 And the Lord said to me, "Israel has justified himself more than faithless Judah.

12 Go and read these words toward the north, and you shall say: 'Return to Me, O house of Israel,' says the Lord; 'and I will not set My face against you: for I am merciful,' says the Lord, 'and I will not be angry with you forever.

13 Nevertheless, know your iniquity, that you have sinned against the Lord your God, and have scattered your ways to strangers under every shady tree, but you did not listen to My voice,' says the Lord.

14 'Turn, you children that have revolted,' says the Lord; 'for I will rule over you. And I will take you, one of a city, and two of a family, and I will bring you in to Zion.

15 And I will give you shepherds after My heart, and they shall certainly tend you with knowledge.

16 And it shall come to pass that when you are multiplied and increased upon the land,' says the Lord, 'in those days they shall say no more, "The ark of the Covenant of the Holy One of Israel." It shall not come to mind; it shall not be named; neither shall it be visited; nor shall *this* be done anymore.

17 In those days and at that time they shall call Jerusalem the throne of the Lord; and all the nations shall be gathered to it: and they shall not walk anymore after the imaginations of their evil heart.

18 In those days the house of Judah shall come together to the house of Israel, and they shall come, together, from the land of the north, and from all the countries, to the land, which I caused their fathers to inherit.'"

19 And I said, "So be it, Lord, for *You said* 'I will set you among children, and will give you a choice land, the inheritance of the Almighty God of the Gentiles.'" And *He* said, "You shall call me Father; and you shall not turn away from Me.

20 But as a wife acts treacherously against her husband, so has the house of Israel dealt treacherously against Me," says the Lord.

21 A voice from the lips was heard, *even* of weeping and supplication of the children of Israel; for they have dealt unrighteously in their ways, they have forgotten God, their Holy One.

22 "Turn, you children that are given to turning, and I will heal your bruises." Behold, we will be Your servants; for You are the Lord our God.

23 Truly the hills and the strength of the mountains were a lying refuge; but by the Lord our God is the salvation of Israel.

24 But shame has consumed the labors of our fathers from our youth; their sheep and their calves, and their sons and their daughters.

25 We have lain down in our shame, and our disgrace has covered us. Because we and our fathers have sinned before our God, from our youth until this day; and we have not obeyed the voice of the Lord our God."

JEREMIAH CHAPTER 4

1 "If Israel will return to Me," says the Lord, "he shall return: and if he will remove his abominations out of his mouth, and fear before Me, and swear,

2 'The Lord lives,' in truth, in judgment, and in righteousness,' then shall nations bless by him, and by him they shall praise God in Jerusalem."

3 For thus says the Lord to the men of Judah, and to the inhabitants of Jerusalem: "Break up fresh ground for yourselves, and do not sow among thorns.

4 Circumcise yourselves to your God, and circumcise your hardness of heart, you men of Judah, and inhabitants of Jerusalem, lest My wrath go forth as fire, and burn, and there be none to quench it, because of the evil of your doings.

An Imminent Invasion

5 "Declare in Judah, and let it be heard in Jerusalem. Say, 'Sound the trumpet in the land'; cry aloud: say, 'Gather yourselves together, and let us enter into the fortified cities.'

6 Gather up *your wares* and flee to Zion. Hasten, do not delay: for I will bring evils from the north, and great destruction.

7 The lion has gone up from his lair, he has roused *himself* to the destruction of the nations, and has gone forth out of his place, to make the land desolate; and the cities shall be destroyed, so as to be without inhabitant.

8 For these things gird yourselves with sackcloth and lament, and howl; for the anger of the Lord has not turned away from you.

9 And it shall come to pass in that day," says the Lord, "that the heart of the king shall perish, and the heart of the princes; and the priests shall be amazed, and the prophets shall wonder."

10 And I said, "Ah, Lord God! Surely You have deceived this people and Jerusalem, saying, 'There shall be peace'; whereas behold, the sword has reached even to their soul."

11 At that time it will be said to this people and to Jerusalem, "*There is* a spirit of error in the wilderness: the way of the daughter of My people is not to purity, nor to holiness.

12 *But* a spirit of full vengeance shall come upon Me; and now I declare My judgments against them."

13 Behold, he shall come up as a cloud, and his chariots as a tempest. His horses are swifter than eagles. Woe unto us, for we are in misery!

14 Cleanse your heart from wickedness, O Jerusalem, that you may be saved; how long will your grievous thoughts be within you?

15 For a voice of a messenger shall come from Dan, and distress out of Mount Ephraim shall be heard of.

16 "Remind the nations: behold, they have come. Proclaim *it* in Jerusalem, that bands are approaching from a land afar off, and have uttered their voice against the cities of Judah.

17 As keepers of a field, they have surrounded her; because you," says the Lord, "have neglected Me.

18 Your ways and your devices have brought these things upon you; this is your wickedness, for *it is* bitter, for it has reached to your heart."

19 I am pained in my bowels, my bowels, and the sensitive powers of my heart. My soul is in great commotion, my heart is torn. I will not be silent, for my soul has heard the sound of a trumpet, the cry of war, and of distress: it calls on destruction.

20 For all the land is distressed. Suddenly *my* tabernacle is distressed, my curtains have been torn in two.

21 How long shall I see fugitives, and hear the sound of the trumpet?

22 "For the princes of My people have not known Me, they are foolish and unwise children. They are wise to do evil, but *how* to do good they have not known."

23 I looked upon the earth, and behold, *it was* not; and to the sky, and there was no light in it.

24 I beheld the mountains, and they trembled, and *I saw* all the hills in commotion.

25 I looked, and behold, there was no man, and all the birds of the sky were scared.

26 I saw, and behold, Carmel was desert, and all the cities were burnt with fire at the presence of the Lord, and at the presence of His fierce anger they were utterly destroyed.

27 Thus says the Lord: "The whole land shall be desolate; but I will not make a full end.

28 For these things let the earth mourn, and let the sky be dark above. For I have spoken, and I will not relent; I have purposed, and I will not turn back from it.

29 The whole land has recoiled from the noise of the horseman and the bent bow; they have gone into the caves, and have hidden themselves in the groves, and have gone up upon the rocks: every city was abandoned, no man dwelt in them.

30 And what will you do? Though you clothe yourself with scarlet, and adorn yourself with golden ornaments; though you adorn your eyes with paint, your beauty *shall be* in vain. Your lovers have rejected you, they seek your life.

31 For I have heard your groaning as the voice of a woman in travail, as of her that brings forth her first child; the voice of the daughter of Zion shall fail through weakness, and she shall lose the strength of her hands, *saying*, 'Woe is me, for my soul faints because of the slain!'

JEREMIAH CHAPTER 5

The Utter Corruption of God's People

1 "Run about in the streets of Jerusalem and see, and know, and seek in her broad places, if you can find *one*, if there is anyone that executes judgment, and seeks faithfulness, and I will pardon them," says the Lord.

2 "The Lord lives," they say; do they not therefore swear falsely?

³ O Lord, Your eyes are upon faithfulness. You have scourged them, but they have not grieved; You have consumed them; but they would not receive correction. They have made their faces harder than a rock; and they would not return.

⁴ Then I said, "It may be they are poor; for they are weak, for they do not know the way of the Lord, or the judgment of God.

⁵ I will go to the rich men, and will speak to them; for they have known the way of the Lord, and the judgment of God." But, behold, with one consent they have broken the yoke, they have burst the bonds.

⁶ Therefore has a lion out of the forest smitten them, and a wolf has destroyed them, even to *their* houses, and a leopard has watched against their cities. All that go forth from them shall be hunted, for they have multiplied their ungodliness, they have strengthened themselves in their backslidings.

⁷ "In what *way* shall I forgive you for these things? Your sons have forsaken Me, and sworn by them that are not gods. And I fed them to the full, and they committed adultery, and lodged in harlots' houses.

⁸ They became as wanton horses—each one neighed after his neighbor's wife.

⁹ Shall I not punish them for these things?" says the Lord. "And shall not My soul be avenged on such a nation as this?"

¹⁰ "Go up upon her battlements and break *them* down, but do not make a full end; leave her buttresses; for they are the Lord's.

¹¹ For the house of Israel have indeed dealt treacherously against Me," says the Lord. "The house of Judah also

¹² have lied to their Lord, and they have said, 'These things are not so; no evils shall come upon us; and we shall not see sword or famine.

¹³ Our prophets became wind, and the word of the Lord was not in them.'

¹⁴ Therefore thus says the Lord Almighty: "Because you have spoken this word, behold, I have made My words in your mouth fire, and this people wood, and it shall devour them.

¹⁵ Behold, I *will* bring upon you a nation from afar, O house of Israel," says the Lord; "a nation the sound of whose language you shall not understand.

¹⁶ *They are* all mighty men;

¹⁷ and they shall devour your harvest and your bread, and shall devour your sons, and your daughters. And they shall devour your sheep, and your calves, and devour your vineyards, and your fig trees, and your olive yards. And they shall utterly destroy your strong cities, in which you trusted, with the sword.

¹⁸ "And it shall come to pass in those days," says the Lord your God, "that I will not utterly destroy you.

¹⁹ And it shall come to pass, when you shall say, 'Why has the Lord our God done all these things to us?' That you shall say to them, 'Because you served strange gods in your land, so shall you serve strangers in a land that is not yours.'

²⁰ "Proclaim these things to the house of Jacob, and let them be heard in the house of Judah.

²¹ Hear now these things, O foolish and senseless people; who have eyes and do not see, and have ears and do not hear:

²² Will you not fear Me?" says the Lord. "And will you not fear before Me, who has set the sand as a boundary for the sea, *as* a perpetual ordinance, and it shall not pass over it. Yes, it shall rage, but not prevail; and its waves shall roar, but not pass over it.

²³ But this people have a disobedient and rebellious heart; and they have turned aside and gone back.

²⁴ And they have not said in their heart, 'Let us fear now the Lord our God, who gives us the early and latter rain, according to the season of the fulfillment of the ordinance of harvest, and has preserved *it* for us.'

²⁵ Your transgressions have turned away these things, and your sins have removed good things from you.

²⁶ For among My people were found ungodly men; and they have set snares to destroy men, and have caught *them*.

²⁷ As a snare which has been set is full of birds, so are their houses full of deceit: therefore have they grown great, and become rich.

²⁸ They have transgressed *the rule of* judgment; they have not judged the cause of the orphan, nor have they judged the cause of the widow.

²⁹ Shall I not punish for these things?" says the Lord, "and shall not My soul be avenged on such a nation as this?

³⁰ "Shocking and horrible deeds have been done in the land; ³¹ the prophets utter unrighteous prophecies, and the priests have clapped their hands, and My people have loved it! And what will you do for the future?

JEREMIAH CHAPTER 6

Impending Destruction from the North

¹ "Strengthen yourselves, you children of Benjamin, *to flee* out of the midst of Jerusalem, and sound an alarm with the trumpet in Tekoa, and set up a signal over Beth Haccerem; for evil threatens from the north, and a great destruction is coming.

² And *your* pride shall be taken away, O daughter of Zion.

³ The shepherds and their flocks shall come to her; and they shall pitch *their* tents against her round about, and shall feed *their flocks,* each with his hand."

⁴ "Prepare yourselves for war against her; rise up, and let us go up against her at noon. Woe to us, for the day has gone down, and the shadows of the day fail.

⁵ Rise, and let us go up against her by night, and destroy her foundations."

[6] For thus says the Lord: "Cut down her trees, array a numerous force against Jerusalem. O false city, she is full of oppression.

[7] As a cistern cools water, so her wickedness cools her, ungodliness and misery shall be heard in her, *as* continually before her.

[8] You shall be chastened, O Jerusalem, with pain and the scourge, lest My soul depart from you; lest I make you a desert land, which shall not be inhabited.

[9] For thus says the Lord: 'Glean, glean thoroughly as a vine the remnant of Israel: turn back *your hands* as a grape-gatherer to his basket.'

[10] "To whom shall I speak and testify, that he may hear? Behold, your ears are uncircumcised, and they shall not be able to hear. Behold, the word of the Lord has become a reproach to them, they will not at all desire it.

[11] And I allowed My wrath to come to full, yet I kept *it* in, and did not utterly destroy them. I will pour it out on the children outside, and on the assembly of young men together; for man and woman shall be taken together, the old man with him that is full of days.

[12] And their houses shall be turned to others, *with* their fields and their wives together; for I will stretch out My hand upon the inhabitants of this land," says the Lord.

[13] "For from the least of them even to the greatest they have all committed iniquity; from the priest even to the false prophet they have all dealt falsely.

[14] And they healed the breach of My people *imperfectly*, making light *of it*, and saying, 'Peace, peace,' and where is peace?

[15] They were ashamed because they failed; yet they were not ashamed as those who were *truly* ashamed, and they knew not their own disgrace; therefore shall they *utterly* fall when they do fall, and in the time of visitation shall they perish," says the Lord.

[16] Thus says the Lord: "Stand in the ways and see, and ask for the old paths of the Lord; and see what is the good way and walk in it, and you shall find purification for your souls. But they said, 'We will not walk *in them*.'

[17] I have set watchmen over you, *saying*, 'Hear the sound of the trumpet.' But they said, 'We will not hear.'

[18] Therefore have the nations heard, and they that feed their flocks.

[19] Hear, O earth; behold, I will bring evils upon this people, *even* the fruit of their rebellions; for they have not heeded My words, and they have rejected My law.

[20] Why do you bring Me frankincense from Sheba, and cinnamon from a land afar off? Your burnt offerings are not acceptable, and your sacrifices have not been pleasing to Me.

[21] Therefore thus says the Lord: 'Behold, I *will* bring weakness upon this people, and the fathers and sons shall be weak together; the neighbor and his friend shall perish.'

[22] Thus says the Lord: 'Behold, a people come from the north, and nations shall be stirred up from the end of the earth.

[23] They shall lay hold of bow and spear; *the people* are fierce, and will have no mercy; their voice is as the roaring sea; they shall array themselves for war against you as fire on horses and chariots, O daughter of Zion.'"

[24] We have heard the report of them; our hands are weakened. Anguish has seized us, the pangs as of a woman in travail.

[25] "Do not go forth into the field, and do not walk in the ways, for the sword of the enemy lingers round about.

[26] O daughter of My people, gird yourself with sackcloth; sprinkle *yourself* with ashes; make for yourself lamentation, *as* the mourning for a beloved *son*; for misery will come suddenly upon you.

[27] "I have caused you to be tried among tried nations, and you shall know Me when I have tested their way.

[28] *They are* all disobedient, walking perversely. *They are* brass and iron; they are all corrupted.

[29] The bellows have failed from the fire, the lead has failed. The silversmith works at his trade in vain; their wickedness is not consumed.

[30] Call them reprobate silver, because the Lord has rejected them."

JEREMIAH CHAPTER 7

[1] (This verse omitted in LXX)

Trusting in Lying Words

[2] Hear the word of the Lord, all Judea.

[3] Thus says the Lord God of Israel: "Correct your ways and your devices, and I will cause you to dwell in this place.

[4] Trust not in yourselves with lying words, for they shall not profit you at all, saying, 'It is the temple of the Lord, the temple of the Lord.'

[5] For if you thoroughly correct your ways and your practices, and do indeed execute judgment between a man and his neighbor;

[6] and do not oppress the stranger, and the orphan, and the widow, and do not shed innocent blood in this place, and do not go after strange gods to your hurt;

[7] then will I cause you to dwell in this place, in the land which I gave to your fathers of old, and forever.

[8] But seeing you have trusted in lying words, whereby you shall not be profited;

[9] and you murder, and commit adultery, and steal, and swear falsely, and burn incense to Baal, and have gone after strange gods whom you do not know,

[10] so that it is evil with you; yet have you come, and stood before Me in the house which is called by My name, and you have said, 'We have refrained from doing all these abominations.'

11 Is My house, which is called by My name, a den of robbers in your eyes? And behold, I have seen *it*," says the Lord.

12 "For go to My place which is in Shiloh, where I caused My name to dwell before, and see what I did to it because of the wickedness of My people Israel.

13 And now, because you have done all these deeds, and I spoke to you, but you did not listen to Me; and I called you, but you did not answer.

14 Therefore I also will do to the house which is called by My name, in which you trust, and to the place which I gave to you and to your fathers, as I did to Shiloh.

15 And I will cast you out of My sight, as I cast away your brothers, all the descendants of Ephraim.

16 "Therefore do not pray for this people, and do not intercede for them to be pitied. Yes, do not pray, and do not approach Me for them, for I will not listen.

17 Do you not see what they do in the cities of Judah, and in the streets of Jerusalem?

18 Their children gather wood, and their fathers kindle a fire, and their women knead dough, to make cakes to the host of heaven; and they have poured out drink offerings to strange gods, that they might provoke Me to anger.

19 Do they provoke Me to anger?" says the Lord. "Do they not *provoke* themselves, that their faces may be ashamed?

20 Therefore thus says the Lord: 'Behold, My anger and wrath shall be poured out upon this place, and upon the men, and upon the cattle, and upon every tree of their field, and upon the fruits of the land; and it shall burn, and not be quenched.'"

21 Thus says the Lord: "Gather your burnt offerings with your grain offerings, and eat flesh.

22 For I did not speak to your fathers, nor did I command them in the day that I brought them up out of the land of Egypt, concerning burnt offerings and sacrifice;

23 but I commanded them this thing, saying, 'Hear My voice, and I will be your God, and you shall be My people. And walk in all My ways which I shall command you, that it may be well with you.'

24 But they did not obey Me, and their ear did not hear, instead they walked in the imaginations of their evil heart, and went backward, and not forward.

25 From the day that their fathers went forth out of the land of Egypt, even until this day, and I sent to you all My servants the prophets, by day and early in the morning. Yes, I have sent *them*,

26 but they did not listen to Me, and their ear did not hear; and they made their neck harder than their fathers.

27 Therefore you shall speak this word to them:

Judgment on Obscene Religion

28 "This is the nation that has not heeded the voice of the Lord, nor received correction; truth has failed from their mouth.

29 Cut off your hair, and cast it away, and take up a lamentation on your lips; for the Lord has reprobated and rejected the generation that does these things.

30 For the children of Judah have done evil before Me," says the Lord; "they have set their abominations in the house which is called by My name, to defile it.

31 And they have built the altar of Tophet, which is in the valley of the son of Hinnom, to burn their sons and their daughters with fire; which I did not command them *to do*, neither did I design it in My heart.

32 "Therefore behold, the days are coming," says the Lord, "when they shall no more say, 'The altar of Tophet,' and, 'the valley of the son of Hinnom,' but 'The Valley of Slaughter'; and they shall bury in Tophet, for need of room.

33 And the dead bodies of this people shall be for food to the birds of the sky, and to the wild beasts of the earth; and there shall be none to drive *them* away.

34 And I will destroy out of the cities of Judah, and the streets of Jerusalem, the voice of them that make merry, and the voice of them that rejoice, the voice of the bridegroom, and the voice of the bride; for the whole land shall become a desolation.

JEREMIAH CHAPTER 8

1 "At that time," says the Lord, "they shall bring out the bones of the kings of Judah, and the bones of his princes, and the bones of the priests, and the bones of the prophets, and the bones of the inhabitants of Jerusalem, out of their graves;

2 and they shall spread them out to the sun, and the moon, and to all the stars, and to all the host of heaven, which they have loved, and which they have served, and after which they have walked, and to which they have held, and which they have worshipped. They shall not be mourned for, neither shall they be buried; but they shall be for an example on the face of the earth,

3 because they chose death rather than life, even to all the remnant that are left of that family, in every place where I shall drive them out."

The Peril of False Teaching

4 "For thus says the Lord: shall not he that falls arise? Or he that turns away, shall he not turn back again?

5 Why have My people turned away with a shameless revolting, and strengthened themselves in their willfulness, and refused to return?

6 Pay attention, and listen: will they not say, 'There is no man that repents of his wickedness', saying, 'What have I done?' The runner has failed from his course, as a tired horse in his neighing.

7 Even the stork in the heaven knows her time, *also* the turtledove and wild swallow; the sparrows observe the times of their coming in; but My people do not know the judgments of the Lord.

[8] "How will you say, 'We are wise,' and, 'the law of the Lord is with us?' In vain have the scribes used a false pen.

[9] The wise men are ashamed, and alarmed, and taken; because they have rejected the word of the Lord; what wisdom is there in them?

[10] Therefore will I give their wives to others, and their fields to *new* inheritors; and they shall gather their fruits," says the Lord.

[11] (This verse omitted in LXX)

[12] (This verse omitted in LXX)

[13] There are no grapes on the vines, and there are no figs on the fig trees, and the leaves have fallen off.

[14] Why do we sit still? Assemble yourselves, and let us enter into the strong cities, and let us be cast out there: for God has cast us out, and made us drink water of gall, because we have sinned against Him.

[15] We assembled for peace, but there was no prosperity; for a time of healing, but there was anxiety.

[16] We shall hear the neighing of His swift horses out of Dan. The whole land quaked at the sound of the neighing of His horses; and He shall come, and devour the land and its fullness; the city, and them that dwell in it.

[17] "For behold, I send forth against you deadly serpents, which cannot be charmed, and they shall bite you

[18] mortally with the pain of your distressed heart.

[19] Behold, *there is* a sound of the cry of the daughter of My people from a land afar off. Is not the Lord in Zion? Is there not a king there? Because they have provoked Me with their graven *images*, and with strange vanities."

[20] The summer is gone, the harvest is past, and we are not saved.

[21] For the breach of the daughter of my people I have been saddened: in my perplexity pangs have seized upon me as of a woman in travail.

[22] And is there no balm in Gilead, or is there no physician there? Why has not the healing of the daughter of my people taken place?

JEREMIAH CHAPTER 9

[1] Who will give water to my head, and a fountain of tears to my eyes? Then would I weep for this my people day and night, *even* for the slain of the daughter of my people.

[2] Who would give me a most distant lodge in the wilderness, that I might leave my people, and depart from them? For they all commit adultery, an assembly of treacherous men.

[3] "And they have bent their tongue like a bow; falsehood and not faithfulness has prevailed upon the earth; for they have gone on from evil to evil, and have not known Me," says the Lord.

[4] "Beware, each *of you*, of his neighbor, and do not trust in your brother, for everyone will surely supplant, and every friend will walk craftily.

[5] Everyone will mock his friend; they will not speak truth; their tongue has learned to speak falsehoods; they have committed iniquity, they have not ceased, so as to return.

[6] *There is* usury upon usury, and deceit upon deceit: they would not know Me," says the Lord.

[7] Therefore thus says the Lord: "Behold, I will try them with fire, and prove them; for I will do *thus* because of the wickedness of the daughter of My people.

[8] Their tongue is a wounding arrow; the words of their mouth are deceitful. *One* speaks peaceably to his neighbor, but in himself retains enmity.

[9] Shall I not punish them for these things?" says the Lord. "And shall not My soul be avenged on such a people as this?

[10] Take up a lamentation for the mountains, and a mournful dirge for the paths of the wilderness, for they are desolate from a lack of men; they did not hear the sound of life from the birds of the sky, nor the cattle. They were amazed, they are gone.

[11] And I will remove the inhabitants of Jerusalem, and make it a dwelling place of dragons; and I will utterly waste the cities of Judah, so that they shall not be inhabited."

[12] Who is the wise man, that he may understand this? And he that has the word of the mouth of the Lord *addressed* to him, let him tell you why the land has been destroyed, *and* has been ravaged by fire like a desert, so that no one passes through it.

[13] And the Lord said to me, "Because they have forsaken My law, which I set before them, and have not heeded My voice, [14] but went after the lusts of their evil heart, and after the idols which their fathers taught them *to worship.*

[15] Therefore thus says the Lord God of Israel: behold, I will feed them with trouble and will cause them to drink water of gall:

[16] and I will scatter them among the nations, to them whom neither they nor their fathers knew; and I will send a sword upon them, until I have consumed them with it."

[17] Thus says the Lord: "Call the mourning women, and let them come; and send to the wise women, and let them utter their voice;

[18] and let them take up a lamentation for you, and let your eyes pour down tears, and your eyelids drop water.

[19] For a voice of lamentation has been heard in Zion, *saying*, 'How we have become wretched! We are greatly ashamed, for we have forsaken the land, and have abandoned our tabernacles!'"

[20] Hear the word of God, you women, and let your ears receive the words of His mouth, and teach your daughters a lamentation, and a dirge to *every* woman her neighbor.

[21] For death has come up through your windows, it has entered into our land, to destroy the infants outside, and the young men from the streets.

[22] And the carcasses of the men shall be for an example on the face of the field of your land, like grass after the mower, and there shall be none to gather *them.*

²³ Thus says the Lord: "Let not the wise man boast in his wisdom, and let not the strong man boast in his strength, and let not the rich man boast in his wealth;

²⁴ but let him that boasts, boast in this: that he understands and knows that I am the Lord that exercises mercy, and judgment, and righteousness upon the earth; for in these things I delight," says the Lord.

²⁵ "Behold, the days are coming," says the Lord, "when I will visit upon all the circumcised their uncircumcision:

²⁶ on Egypt, on Idumea, on Edom, on the children of Ammon, on the children of Moab, and on everyone that shaves his face round about, *even* them that dwell in the wilderness; for all the Gentiles are uncircumcised in flesh, and all the house of Israel are uncircumcised *in* their hearts."

JEREMIAH CHAPTER 10

Idols and the True God

¹ Hear the word of the Lord, which He has spoken to you, O house of Israel.

² Thus says the Lord: "Do not learn the ways of the heathen, and do not be alarmed at the signs of the sky, for they are alarmed at them, *falling* on their faces.

³ For the customs of the nations are vain; it is a tree cut out of the forest, the work of the carpenter, or a molten image.

⁴ *They are* beautified with silver and gold, they fix them with hammers and nails;

⁵ they will set them up that they may not move.

⁶ It is wrought silver, they will not walk, it is forged silver

⁷ (This verse omitted in LXX)

⁸ (This verse omitted in LXX)

⁹ *brought* from Tarshish, gold will come from Uphaz, and the work of goldsmiths. *They are* all the works of craftsmen, they will clothe themselves with blue and scarlet.

¹⁰ They must certainly be borne, for they cannot ride *of themselves*. Do not fear them, for they cannot do any evil, and there is no good in them.

¹¹ "Thus shall you say to them: 'Let the gods which have not made heaven and earth perish from off the earth, and from under this sky.'"

¹² It is the Lord that made the earth by His strength, who set up the world by His wisdom, and by His understanding stretched out the sky,

¹³ and set abundance of waters in the sky, and brought up clouds from the ends of the earth. He made lightnings for the rain, and brought forth light out of His treasures.

¹⁴ Every man is deprived of knowledge, every goldsmith is confounded because of his graven images; for he has cast false gods, there is no breath in them.

¹⁵ They are vain works, wrought in mockery; in the time of their visitation they shall perish.

¹⁶ Such is not the portion of Jacob; for He that formed all things, He is his inheritance; the Lord is His name.

¹⁷ He has gathered your substance from abroad, dwelling in chosen places.

¹⁸ For thus says the Lord: "Behold, I *will* overthrow the inhabitants of this land with affliction, that your plague may be discovered."

¹⁹ Alas for your ruin! Your plague is grievous. And I said, "Surely this is your wound, and it has overtaken you."

²⁰ Your tabernacle is in a ruinous state, it has perished; and all your curtains have been torn asunder. My children and my cattle are no more; there is no longer any place for my tent, *nor* place for my curtains.

²¹ For the shepherds have become foolish, and have not sought the Lord; therefore the whole pasture has failed, and *the sheep* have been scattered.

²² Behold, there comes a sound of a noise, and a great earthquake from the land of the north, to make the cities of Judah a desolation, and a resting place for ostriches.

²³ I know, O Lord, that man's way is not his own; neither shall a man go, and direct his own steps.

²⁴ Chasten us, O Lord, but with judgment; and not in wrath, lest You make us few *in number*.

²⁵ Pour out Your wrath upon the nations that have not known You, and upon the families that have not called upon Your name; for they have devoured Jacob, and consumed him, and have made his pasture desolate.

JEREMIAH CHAPTER 11

The Broken Covenant

¹ The word that came to Jeremiah from the Lord, saying,

² "Hear the words of this covenant, and you shall speak to the men of Judah, and to the inhabitants of Jerusalem.

³ And you shall say to them, Thus says the Lord God of Israel: 'Cursed is the man who shall not heed the words of this covenant

⁴ which I commanded your fathers, in the day that I brought them up out of the land of Egypt, out of the iron furnace, saying, "Obey My voice, and do all things that I shall command you; so shall you be My people, and I will be your God,

⁵ that I may confirm My oath which I swore to your fathers, to give them a land flowing *with* milk and honey, as *it is* this day."'" Then I answered and said, "So be it, O Lord."

⁶ And the Lord said to me, "Read these words in the cities of Judah, and in the streets of Jerusalem, saying, 'Hear the words of this covenant, and do them.'"

⁷ (This verse omitted in LXX)

⁸ But they did not do them.

⁹ And the Lord said to me, "A conspiracy has been found among the men of Judah, and among the inhabitantsof Jerusalem.

¹⁰ They have turned *aside* to the iniquities of their forefathers, who refused to hear My words, and behold, they have gone after strange gods, to serve them. And the house

of Israel and the house of Judah have broken My covenant which I made with their fathers.

[11] Therefore thus says the Lord: 'Behold, I bring evils upon this people, out of which they shall not be able to come forth; and they shall cry to Me, but I will not listen to them.

[12] And the cities of Judah and the inhabitants of Jerusalem shall go, and cry to the gods to whom they burn incense; which shall not deliver them in the time of their troubles.

[13] For according to the number of your cities were your gods, O Judah; and according to the number of the streets of Jerusalem have you set up altars to burn incense to Baal.

[14] "So do not pray for this people, and do not intercede for them with supplication and prayer; for I will not hear in the day in which they call upon Me, in the day of their affliction.

[15] Why has *My* beloved done abominable *things* in My house? Will prayers and holy offerings take away your wickedness from you, or shall you escape by these things?

[16] The Lord has called your name a fair olive tree, of a pleasant shade in appearance, at the noise of its being lopped, fire was kindled against it; great is the affliction *coming* upon you. Her branches have become good for nothing.

[17] And the Lord that planted you has pronounced evils against you, because of the iniquity of the house of Israel and the house of Judah, whatsoever they have done against themselves to provoke Me to anger by burning incense to Baal."

[18] O Lord, teach me, and I shall know: then I saw their practices.

[19] But I, as an innocent lamb led to the slaughter, did not know. Against me they devised an evil device, saying, "Come and let us put wood into his bread, and let us utterly destroy him from off the land of the living, and let his name not be remembered any more."

[20] O Lord, *You* that judges righteously, and who tests the heart and the most secret parts, let me see Your vengeance *taken* upon them, for to You I have declared my cause.

[21] Therefore thus says the Lord concerning the men of Anathoth, that seek my life, that say, "You shall not prophesy at all in the name of the Lord, but if you do, you shall die by our hands."

[22] "Behold, I will visit them. Their young men shall die by the sword, and their sons and their daughters shall die of famine. [23] And there shall be no remnant of them, for I will bring evil upon the inhabitants of Anathoth, in the year of their visitation.

JEREMIAH CHAPTER 12

Jeremiah Complains to God

[1] Righteous are You, O Lord, that I may make my defense to You: yet I will speak to You *of* judgments. Why *is it* that the way of the ungodly prospers? *And why* are all that deal very treacherously flourishing?

[2] You have planted them, and they have taken root; they have begotten children, and become fruitful; You are near to their mouth, but far from their mind.

[3] But You, O Lord, know me; You have tested my heart before You; purify them for the day of their slaughter.

[4] How long shall the land mourn, and the grass of the field wither, because the wickedness of them that dwell in it? The beasts and birds are utterly destroyed, because *the people* said, "God shall not see our ways."

[5] Your feet run, and they cause you to faint; how will you prepare *to ride* upon horses? And you have been confident in the land of your peace? How will you do in the roaring of the Jordan?

[6] For even your brothers and the house of your father, even they have dealt treacherously with you; and they have cried out, they are gathered together in pursuit of you. Do not trust in them, though they shall speak fair *words* to you.

[7] "I have forsaken My house, I have left My heritage; I have given My beloved one into the hands of her enemies.

[8] My inheritance has become to Me as a lion in a forest; she has uttered her voice against Me; therefore have I hated her.

[9] Is not My inheritance to Me *like* a hyena's cave, or a cave round about her? Go, gather together all the wild beasts of the field, and let them come to devour her.

[10] Many shepherds have destroyed My vineyard, they have defiled My portion, they have made My desirable portion a trackless wilderness.

[11] It is made a complete ruin: for My sake the whole land has been utterly ruined, because there is none that takes *the matter* to heart.

[12] The ravagers have come to every passage in the wilderness: for the sword of the Lord will devour from one end of the land to the other—no flesh has any peace.

[13] Sow wheat, and reap thorns; their portions shall not profit them. Be ashamed of your boasting, because of *your* reproach before the Lord.

[14] "For thus says the Lord concerning all the evil neighbors that touch My inheritance, which I have divided to My people Israel: 'Behold, I *will* draw them away from their land, and I will cast out Judah from the midst of them.

[15] And it shall come to pass, after I have cast them out, *that* I will return and have mercy upon them, and will cause them to dwell everyone in his inheritance, and everyone in his land.

[16] And it shall be, if they will indeed learn the way of My people, to swear by My name, *saying*, "The Lord lives"; as they taught My people to swear by Baal; then shall *that nation* be built in the midst of My people.

[17] But if they will not return, then will I cut off that nation with utter ruin and destruction.'"

JEREMIAH CHAPTER 13

Symbol of the Linen Sash

[1] Thus says the Lord: "Go and procure for yourself a linen sash, and put it around your waist, but do not put it in water."

[2] So I procured the sash according to the word of the Lord, and put it around my waist.

[3] And the word of the Lord came to me, saying,

[4] "Take the sash that is around your waist, and get up, and go to the Euphrates, and hide it there in a hole of the rock."

[5] So I went, and hid it by the Euphrates, as the Lord commanded me.

[6] And it came to pass after many days, that the Lord said to me, "Arise, go to the Euphrates, and take the sash from there, which I commanded you to hide there."

[7] So I went to the river Euphrates, and dug, and took the sash out of the place where I had buried it. And behold, it was ruined, utterly good for nothing.

[8] And the word of the Lord came to me, saying, "Thus says the Lord:

[9] 'Thus will I ruin the pride of Judah, and the pride of Jerusalem;

[10] *even* this great pride *of the men* that will not listen to My words, and have gone after strange gods, to serve them, and to worship them. And they shall be as this sash, which is profitable for nothing.

[11] For as a sash clings about the waist of a man, so have I caused the house of Israel, and the whole house of Judah to cling to Me; that they might be to Me a famous people, and a praise, and a glory. But they did not listen to Me.

[12] "And you shall say to this people, 'Every bottle shall be filled with wine. And it shall come to pass, if they shall say to you, "Shall we not certainly know that every bottle shall be filled with wine?" That you shall say to them,

[13] "Thus says the Lord: 'Behold, I *will* fill the inhabitants of this land, and their kings, the sons of David that sit upon their throne, and the priests, and the prophets, and Judah and all the inhabitants of Jerusalem, with strong drink.

[14] And I will scatter them, a man and his brother, and their fathers and their sons together. I will not have compassion,' says the Lord, 'and I will not spare, neither will I pity *to save them* from destruction.'"

[15] Hear, and give ear, and do not be proud; for the Lord has spoken.

[16] Give glory to the Lord your God, before He causes darkness, and before your feet stumble on the dark mountains, and you shall wait for light, and behold the shadow of death, and they shall be brought into darkness.

[17] But if you will not hear it, your soul shall weep in secret because of pride, and your eyes shall pour down tears, because the Lord's flock is sorely bruised.

[18] Say to the king and the princes, "Humble yourselves, and sit down; for your crown of glory is removed from your head."

[19] The cities toward the south were shut up, and there was none to open *them*. Judah is removed *into captivity*; they have suffered a complete removal.

[20] Lift up your eyes, O Jerusalem, and behold them that come from the north; where is the flock that was given you, the sheep of your glory?

[21] What will you say when they shall visit you, for you have taught them lessons to rule over you; shall not pangs seize you as a woman in travail?

[22] And if you should say in your heart, "Why have these things happened to me?" Because of the abundance of your iniquity have your skirts been discovered, that your heels might be exposed.

[23] If the Ethiopian shall change his skin, or the leopard its spots, then shall you be able to do good, having learned *to do* evil.

[24] So I scattered them as sticks carried by the wind into the wilderness.

[25] "Thus is your lot, and the reward of your disobedience to Me," says the Lord. "As you have forgotten Me, and trusted in lies,

[26] I also will expose your skirts upon your face, and your shame shall be seen;

[27] your adultery also, and your neighing, and the looseness of your fornication. On the hills and in the fields I have seen your abominations. Woe to you, O Jerusalem, for you have not been purified so as to follow Me; how long yet *shall it be*?

JEREMIAH CHAPTER 14

Sword, Famine, and Pestilence

[1] And the word of the Lord came to Jeremiah concerning the drought.

[2] "Judah has mourned, and her gates are emptied, and are darkened upon the earth; and the cry of Jerusalem has gone up.

[3] And her nobles have sent their little ones to the water: they came to the wells, and found no water: and brought back their vessels empty.

[4] And the labors of the land failed, because there was no rain: the plowmen were ashamed; they covered their heads.

[5] And the deer gave birth in the field, but left because there was no grass.

[6] The wild donkeys stood by the forests, and snuffed up the wind; their eyes failed, because there was no grass."

[7] Our sins have risen up against us. O Lord, do for us for Your name's sake; for our sins are many before You; for we have sinned against You.

[8] O Lord, *You are* the hope of Israel, and deliver *us* in times of trouble; why have You become as a sojourner upon the land, or as one born in the land, yet turning aside for a resting place?

[9] Will You be as a man asleep, or as a *strong* man that cannot save? Yet You are among us, O Lord, and we are called by Your name; do not forget us.

[10] Thus says the Lord to this people: "They have loved to wander, and they have not spared, therefore God has not prospered them; now will He remember their iniquity."

[11] And the Lord said to me, "Do not pray for this people, for *their* good:

[12] for though they fast, I will not hear their supplication; and though they offer burnt offerings and sacrifices, I will take no pleasure in them: for I will consume them with the sword, and with famine, and with pestilence."

[13] And I said, "Ah, Lord *God*! Behold, their prophets prophesy, and say, 'You shall not see the sword, nor shall famine be among you; for I will give truth and peace on the land, and in this place.'"

[14] Then the Lord said to me, "The prophets prophesy lies in My name. I have not send them, commanded them, nor spoken to them: for they prophesy to you false visions, divinations, and worthless things, and devices of their own heart.

[15] Therefore thus says the Lord concerning the prophets that prophesy lies in My name, and I have not sent them, who say, 'Sword and famine shall not be upon this land'; they shall die by a grievous death, and the prophets shall be consumed by famine.

[16] And the people to whom they prophesy, they also shall be cast out in the streets of Jerusalem, because of the sword and famine; and there shall be none to bury them. Their wives also, and their sons, and their daughters *shall die thus*; and I will pour out their wickedness upon them.

[17] "And you shall speak this word to them: 'Let your eyes shed tears day and night, and let them not cease; for the daughter of My people has been sorely bruised, and her plague is very grievous.

[18] If I go forth into the plain, then behold the slain by the sword! And if I enter into the city, then behold the distress of famine! For priest and prophet have gone to a land which they did not know.'"

[19] Have You utterly rejected Judah? And has Your soul departed from Zion? Why have You stricken us, and there is no healing for us? We waited for peace, but there was no prosperity; for a time of healing, and behold trouble!

[20] We know our sins, O Lord, *and* the iniquities of our fathers, for we have sinned before You.

[21] Refrain for Your name's sake; do not destroy the throne of Your glory. Remember, *O Lord, and* do not break Your covenant with us.

[22] Is there anyone among the idols of the Gentiles that can give rain? And will the sky yield His fullness *at their bidding*? Are You not He? We will even wait on You, O Lord, for You have made all these things.

JEREMIAH CHAPTER 15

The Lord Will Not Relent

[1] And the Lord said to me, "Even if Moses and Samuel stood before My face, My soul would not be *favorable* toward them: dismiss this people, and let them go forth.

[2] And it shall be, if they say to you, 'Where shall we go forth?' Then you shall say to them, 'Thus says the Lord: As many as are for death, to death; and as many as are for famine, to famine; and as many as are for the sword, to the sword; and as many as are for captivity, to captivity.'

[3] And I will punish them with four kinds *of death*," says the Lord; "the sword to slay, the dogs to tear, the wild beasts of the earth, and the birds of the sky to devour and destroy.

[4] And I will deliver them up for distress to all the kingdoms of the earth, because of Manasseh son of Hezekiah king of Judah, for all that he did in Jerusalem.

[5] "Who will spare you, O Jerusalem? And who will fear for you? Or who will turn back *to ask* about your welfare?

[6] You have turned away from Me," says the Lord; "you will go back. Therefore I will stretch out My hand, and I will destroy you, and will spare them no more.

[7] And I will completely scatter them; in the gates of My people they are bereaved of children. They have destroyed My people because of their iniquities.

[8] Their widows have been multiplied more than the sand of the sea. I have brought young men against the mother, *and* distress at noonday. I have suddenly cast trembling and anxiety upon her.

[9] She that bore seven is spent; her soul has fainted under trouble; her sun has gone down while it is yet noon; she is ashamed and disgraced. I will give the remnant of them to the sword before their enemies."

[10] Woe is me, *my* mother! You have born me as some man of strife, and at variance with the whole earth. I have not helped *others*, nor has anyone helped me; my strength has failed among them that curse me.

[11] Be it so, O Lord, in their prosperity; surely I stood before You in the time of their calamities, and in the time of their affliction, for *their* good against the enemy.

[12] "Will iron be known? Whereas your strength is a bronze covering.

[13] Yes, I will give your treasures for a spoil as a recompense, because of all your sins, and *that* in all your borders.

[14] And I will enslave you to your enemies round about, in a land which you have not known; for a fire has been kindled out of My wrath; it shall burn upon you."

[15] O Lord, remember me, and visit me, and vindicate me before them that persecute me. Do not bear long with them; know how I have met with reproach for Your sake, from those who nullify Your words.

[16] Consume them, and Your word shall be to me for the joy and gladness of my heart. For Your name has been called upon me, O Lord Almighty.

[17] I have not sat in the assembly of them as they mocked, but I feared because of Your power. I sat alone, for I was filled with bitterness.

[18] Why do those that grieve me prevail against me? My wound is severe; when shall I be healed? It has indeed become to me as deceitful water that has no faithfulness.

The Lord Reassures Jeremiah

[19] Therefore thus says the Lord: "If you will return, then will I restore you, and you shall stand before My face. And if you will bring forth the precious from the worthless, you shall be as My mouth; and they shall return to you; but you shall not return to them.

[20] And I will make you to this people as a strong bronze wall; and they shall fight against you, but they shall by no means prevail against you.

[21] For I am with you, to save you, and to deliver you out of the hand of wicked *men*; and I will ransom you out of the hand of pestilent *men*.

JEREMIAH CHAPTER 16

Jeremiah's Celibacy and Message

[1] "And you shall not take a wife," says the Lord God of Israel.

[2] "And there shall be no son born to you, nor daughter in this place.

[3] For thus says the Lord concerning the sons and daughters that are born in this place, and concerning their mothers that have born them, and their fathers that have begotten them in this land:

[4] 'They shall die a grievous death. They shall not be lamented *over*, nor buried; they shall be for an example on the face of the earth; and they shall be for the wild beasts of the land, and for the birds of the sky. They shall fall by the sword, and shall be consumed with famine.'

[5] "Thus says the Lord: 'Do not enter into their mourning feast, and do not go to lament, nor mourn for them, for I have removed My peace from this people.

[6] They shall not bewail them, nor make cuttings for them, and they shall not shave themselves *for them*.

[7] And there shall be no bread broken in mourning for them in consolation over the dead; they shall not give one to drink a cup for consolation over his father or his mother.

[8] You shall not enter into the banquet house, to sit with them to eat and to drink.

[9] For thus says the Lord God of Israel: "Behold, I *will* make the voice of joy to cease out of this place before your eyes, and the voice of gladness, the voice of the bridegroom, and the voice of the bride.

[10] "And it shall come to pass, when you report to this people all these words, and they shall say to you, 'Why has the Lord pronounced all these evils against us? What is our unrighteousness? And what is our sin which we have sinned before the Lord our God?'

[11] Then you shall say to them, 'Because your fathers forsook Me,' says the Lord, 'and went after strange gods and served them, and worshipped them, and forsook Me, and did not keep My law.'

[12] (And you sinned worse than your fathers—for behold, you walk everyone after the lusts of your own evil heart, so as not to listen to Me).

[13] Therefore I will cast you off from this good land into a land which neither you nor your fathers have known. And you shall serve their other gods, who shall have no mercy upon you.

God Will Restore Israel

[14] "Therefore behold, the days are coming," says the Lord, "when they shall no more say, 'The Lord lives, that brought up the children of Israel out of the land of Egypt';

[15] but, 'The Lord lives, who brought up the house of Israel from the land of the north, and from all countries in which they were thrust out.' And I will restore them to their own land, which I gave to their fathers.

[16] "Behold, I *will* send many fishermen," says the Lord, "and they shall fish them; and afterward I will send many hunters, and they shall hunt them upon every mountain, and upon every hill, and out of the holes of the rocks.

[17] For My eyes are upon all their ways; and their iniquities have not been hidden from My eyes.

[18] And I will recompense double for their iniquity and their sins, whereby they have profaned My land with the carcasses of their abominations, and with their iniquities, whereby they have trespassed against My inheritance."

[19] O Lord, You are my strength and my help, and my refuge in days of evil. To You the Gentiles shall come from the ends of the earth, and shall say, "How worthless *were the* idols *which* our fathers procured for themselves, and there is no help in them."

[20] Will a man make gods for himself, whereas these are no gods?

[21] "Therefore behold, I will at this time manifest My hand to them, and will make known to them My power; and they shall know that My name is the Lord."

JEREMIAH CHAPTER 17

[1] (This verse omitted in LXX)
[2] (This verse omitted in LXX)
[3] (This verse omitted in LXX)
[4] (This verse omitted in LXX)

Judah's Sin and Punishment

[5] "Cursed is the man who trusts in man, and will lean his arm of flesh upon him, while his heart departs from the Lord.

[6] And he shall be as the wild tamarisk in the desert. he shall not see when good comes; but he shall dwell in barren *places*, and in the wilderness, in a salty land which is not inhabited.

[7] But blessed is the man who trusts in the Lord, and whose hope is the Lord.

[8] And he shall be as a thriving tree by the waters, and he shall cast forth his root toward a moist place. He shall not fear when heat comes, and there shall be shady branches upon him; he shall not fear in a year of drought, and he shall not fail to bear fruit.

[9] "The heart is deep beyond all things, and it constitutes the man, and who can know him?

[10] I, the Lord, search the hearts, and test the mind, to give to everyone according to his ways, and according to the fruits of his doings.

[11] "The partridge utters her voice; she gathers *eggs* which she did not lay. *So is a man* gaining his wealth unjustly: in the midst of his days *his riches* shall leave him, and at his latter end he will be a fool."

[12] An exalted throne of glory is our sanctuary.

[13] O Lord, the hope of Israel, let all that have left You be ashamed, let them that have revolted be written on the earth, because they have forsaken the fountain of life, the Lord.

Jeremiah Prays for Deliverance

[14] Heal me, O Lord, and I shall be healed. Save me, and I shall be saved; for You are my boast.

[15] Behold, they say to me, "Where is the word of the Lord? Let it come."

[16] But I have not been weary of following You, nor have I desired the day of man. You know the *words* that proceed out of my lips; *they* are before Your face.

[17] Be not a stranger to me, *but* spare me in the evil day.

[18] Let them that persecute me be ashamed, but let me not be ashamed. Let them be alarmed, but let me not be alarmed. Bring upon them the evil day, crush them with double destruction.

Hallow the Sabbath Day

[19] Thus says the Lord: "Go and stand in the gates of the children of your people, by which the kings of Judah enter, and by which they go out, and in all the gates of Jerusalem.

[20] And you shall say to them: 'Hear the word of the Lord, you kings of Judah, and all Judea, and all Jerusalem, *all* who go in at these gates:

[21] thus says the Lord: "Take heed to your souls, and take up no burdens on the Sabbath day, and do not go forth *through* the gates of Jerusalem;

[22] and carry forth no burdens out of your houses on the Sabbath day, and you shall do no work. Sanctify the Sabbath day, as I commanded your fathers.

[23] But they would not obey, and would not listen, but stiffened their neck more than their fathers *did*, so as not to hear Me, and not to receive correction.

[24] "And it shall come to pass, if you will hearken to Me," says the Lord, "to carry in no burdens through the gates of this city on the Sabbath day, and to sanctify the Sabbath day, so as to do no work *upon it*,

[25] that there shall enter through the gates of this city kings and princes sitting on the throne of David, and riding on their chariots and horses, they, and their princes, the men of Judah, and the inhabitants of Jerusalem. And this city shall be inhabited forever.

[26] And *men* shall come out of the cities of Judah, and from round about Jerusalem, and out of the land of Benjamin, and out of the plain country, and from the hill country, and from the south, bringing burnt offerings, sacrifices, incense, manna, and frankincense, and bringing praise to the house of the Lord.

[27] But it shall come to pass, that if you will not listen to Me and sanctify the Sabbath day, to bear no burdens, nor go in *with them by* the gates of Jerusalem on the Sabbath day, then will I kindle a fire in its gates, and it shall devour the streets of Jerusalem, and shall not be quenched."

JEREMIAH CHAPTER 18

The Potter and the Clay

[1] The word that came from the Lord to

[2] Jeremiah, saying, "Arise, and go down to the potter's house, and there you shall hear My words."

[3] So I went down to the potter's house, and behold, he was making a vessel on the stones.

[4] And the vessel which he was making with his hands fell *apart*. So he made it into another vessel, as it seemed good to him.

[5] And the word of the Lord came to me, saying,

[6] "O house of Israel, can I not do with you as this potter? Behold, as the clay *is in* the potter's *hand*, so are you in My hands.

[7] *If* I shall pronounce a decree upon a nation, or upon a kingdom, to cut them off, and to destroy *them*;

[8] and that nation turn from all their sins, then will I relent of the disasters which I purposed to do to them.

[9] And *if* I shall pronounce a decree upon a nation and kingdom, to rebuild and to plant *it*;

[10] and they do evil before Me, so as not to heed My voice, then will I relent of the good which I spoke of, to do it to them.

[11] "And now, say to the men of Judah, and to the inhabitants of Jerusalem, 'Behold, I prepare disasters against you, and devise a plan against you: let everyone turn now from his evil way, and amend your practices.'"

[12] And they said, "We will act like men, for we will pursue our perverse ways, and we will every one perform the lusts of his evil heart."

God's Warning Rejected

[13] Therefore thus says the Lord: "Inquire now among the nations, who has heard such horrible things as *what* the virgin of Israel has done?

¹⁴ Will fertilizing streams fail *to flow* from a rock, or snow *fail* from Lebanon? Will water violently impelled by the wind turn aside?

¹⁵ For My people have forgotten Me, they have offered incense in vain, and they fail in their ways, *leaving* the ancient tracks, to enter upon impassable paths;

¹⁶ to make their land a desolation, and a perpetual hissing. All that go through it shall be amazed, and shall shake their heads.

¹⁷ I will scatter them before their enemies like an east wind. I will show them the day of their destruction."

Jeremiah Persecuted

¹⁸ Then they said, "Come, and let us devise a plan against Jeremiah; for the law shall not perish from the priest, nor counsel from the wise, nor the word from the prophet. Come, and let us attack him with the tongue, and we will hear all his words."

¹⁹ Hear me, O Lord, and hear the voice of my pleading.

²⁰ Forasmuch as evil is rewarded for good; for they have spoken words against my soul, and they have hidden the punishment they *meant* for me. Remember that I stood before Your face, to speak good concerning them, to turn away Your wrath from them.

²¹ Therefore deliver up their sons to famine, and gather them to the power of the sword. Let their women be childless and widows, and let their men be cut off by death, and their young men fall by the sword in war.

²² Let there be a cry in their houses: You shall bring upon them robbers suddenly— for they have formed a plan to take me, and have hidden snares for me.

²³ And You, O Lord, know all their deadly counsel against me: provide no atonement for their iniquities, and do not blot out their sins from before You. Let their weakness come before You; deal with them in the time of Your wrath.

JEREMIAH CHAPTER 19

The Broken Earthen Bottle

¹ Then the Lord said to me, "Go and get an earthen bottle, the work of the potter, and you shall bring *some* of the elders of the people, and of the priests.

² And you shall go forth to the burial place of the sons of their children, which is at the entrance of the Potsherd Gate; and proclaim there all these words which I shall speak to you.

³ And you shall say to them, 'Hear the word of the Lord, you kings of Judah, and men of Judah, and inhabitants of Jerusalem, and they that enter in by these gates. Thus says the Lord God of Israel: "Behold, I *will* bring such a catastrophe upon this place, that the ears of everyone that hears it shall tingle.

⁴ "Because they forsook Me, and profaned this place, and burned incense in it to strange gods, which they and their fathers did not know; and the kings of Judah have filled this place with innocent blood,

⁵ and built high places for Baal, to burn their children in the fire, which things I did not command, neither did I design *them* in My heart.

⁶ Therefore, behold, the days are coming," says the Lord, "when this place shall no more be called Tophet, or the fall and burial place of the son of Hinnom, but the burial place of slaughter.

⁷ And I will destroy the counsel of Judah and the counsel of Jerusalem in this place; and I will cast them down with the sword before their enemies, and by the hands of them that seek their lives. And I will give their dead bodies for food to the birds of the sky, and to the wild beasts of the earth.

⁸ And I will bring this city to desolation and *make it* a hissing: everyone that passes by it shall scowl, and hiss because of all her plagues.

⁹ And they shall eat the flesh of their sons, and the flesh of their daughters; and they shall eat, everyone the flesh of his neighbor in the blockade, and in the siege with which their enemies shall besiege them.

¹⁰ "And you shall break the bottle in the sight of the men that go forth with you,

¹¹ and you shall say, 'Thus says the Lord: "Thus will I break in pieces this people, and this city, even as an earthen vessel is broken in pieces which cannot be mended again.

¹² Thus will I do to this place," says the Lord, "and to the inhabitants of it, that this city may be given up, as one that is falling to ruin.

¹³ And the houses of Jerusalem, and the houses of the kings of Judah shall be as a ruinous place, because of their uncleanness in all the houses, in which they burnt incense upon their roofs to all the host of heaven, and poured *out* drink offerings to strange gods.'"'

¹⁴ And Jeremiah came from Tophet, where the Lord had sent him to prophesy; and he stood in the court of the Lord's house. And said to all the people, "Thus says the Lord:

¹⁵ 'Behold I bring upon this city, and upon all the cities belonging to it, and upon the villages of it, all the doom which I have spoken against it, because they have hardened their neck, *that they might not* hearken to My commands.'"

JEREMIAH CHAPTER 20

The Word of God to Pashur

¹ Now Pashur the son of Immer, the priest, who also had been appointed chief of the house of the Lord, heard Jeremiah prophesying these words.

² And he struck him, and cast him into the dungeon which was by the gate of the upper house that was set apart, which was by the house of the Lord.

³ And Pashur brought Jeremiah out of the dungeon. And Jeremiah said to him, "*The Lord* has not called your name Pashur, but Exile.

⁴ For thus says the Lord: 'Behold, I *will* give you up to captivity with all your friends, and they shall fall by the sword of their enemies, and your eyes shall see *it*. And I will give you and all Judah into the hands of the king of Babylon, and they shall carry them captives, and cut them to pieces with swords.

⁵ And I will give all the strength of this city, and all the labors of it, and all the treasures of the king of Judah, into the hands of his enemies, and they shall bring them to Babylon.

⁶ And you and all who live in your house shall go into captivity, and you shall die in Babylon, and there you and all your friends shall be buried, to whom you have prophesied lies.'"

Jeremiah's Unpopular Ministry

⁷ You have deceived me, O Lord, and I have been deceived. You have been strong, and have prevailed. I have become a laughing stock, I am continually mocked every day.

⁸ For I will laugh with my bitter speech, I will call upon rebellion and misery; for the word of the Lord has become a reproach to me and a mockery all my days.

⁹ Then I said, "I will by no means name the name of the Lord, and I will no longer speak in His name." But it was a burning fire flaming in my bones, and I am utterly weakened on all sides, and cannot bear *up*.

¹⁰ For I have heard the reproach of many gathering round, *saying*, "Conspire, and let us conspire together against him, *even* all his friends. Watch his intentions, if perhaps he shall be deceived, and we shall prevail against him, and we shall be avenged on him."

¹¹ But the Lord was with me as a mighty man of war; therefore they persecuted *me*, but could not perceive *anything against me*. They were greatly confounded, for they did not perceive their disgrace, which shall never be forgotten.

¹² O Lord, *You* who tests the righteous, *and* who understands the mind and heart, let me see Your vengeance upon them: for to You I have revealed my cause.

¹³ Sing to the Lord, sing praises to Him: for He has rescued the soul of the poor from the hand of evildoers.

¹⁴ Cursed be the day in which I was born! Let the day not be blessed in which my mother bore me!

¹⁵ Cursed be the man who brought the glad tidings to my father, saying, "A male child has been born to you."

¹⁶ Let that man rejoice as the cities which the Lord overthrew in wrath, and did not repent: let him hear crying in the morning, and loud lamentation at noon;

¹⁷ because he did not slay me in the womb, and my mother did not become my tomb, and her womb always enlarged with me. ¹⁸ Why is it that I came forth from the womb to see troubles and distresses, and my days are spent in shame?

JEREMIAH CHAPTER 21

Jeremiah's Doom is Sealed

¹ The word that came from the Lord to Jeremiah, when King Zedekiah sent to him Pashur, the son of Melchiah, and Zephaniah, son of Maaseiah the priest, saying,

² "Inquire of the Lord for us, for the king of Babylon has risen up against us. Perhaps the Lord will do according to all His wonderful works, and *the king* shall depart from us."

³ And Jeremiah said to them, "Thus shall you say to Zedekiah, king of Judah:

⁴ 'Thus says the Lord: "Behold, I *will* turn back the weapons of war with which you fight against the Chaldeans that have besieged you from outside the wall, and I will gather them into the midst of this city.

⁵ And I will fight against you with an outstretched hand and with a strong arm, with wrath and great anger.

⁶ And I will strike all the inhabitants of this city, *both* men and cattle, with grievous pestilence, and they shall die.

⁷ And after this," says the Lord, "I will give Zedekiah king of Judah, and his servants, and the people that are left in this city from the pestilence, and from the famine, and from the sword, into the hands of their enemies that seek their lives, and they shall cut them in pieces with the edge of the sword. I will not spare them, and I will not have compassion upon them."'

⁸ "And you shall say to this people, 'Thus says the Lord: "Behold, I have set before you the way of life, and the way of death.

⁹ He that remains in this city shall die by the sword, and by famine; but he that goes forth to defect to the Chaldeans that have besieged you shall live, and his life shall be as a prize to him, and he shall live.

¹⁰ For I have set My face against this city for evil, and not for good: it shall be delivered into the hands of the king of Babylon, and he shall consume it with fire."'

Message to the House of David

¹¹ O house of the king of Judah, hear the word of the Lord.

¹² O house of David, thus says the Lord: "Administer judgment in the morning, and act rightly, and rescue the spoiled one from the hand of him that wrongs him, lest My anger be kindled like fire, and it burn, and there be none to quench *it*.

¹³ "Behold, I am against you that dwell in the valley of Sor; in the plain country, *even against* them that say, 'Who shall alarm us? Or who shall enter into our dwellings?'

¹⁴ And I will kindle a fire in its forest, and it shall devour all things round about it.'"

JEREMIAH CHAPTER 22

¹ Thus says the Lord: "Go down to the house of the king of Judah, and you shall speak this word *to him* there,

2 and you shall say, 'Hear the word of the Lord, O king of Judah, who sits on the throne of David; you, your house, your people, and those that go in at these gates.

3 Thus says the Lord: "Execute judgment and justice, rescue the spoiled out of the hand of him that wrongs him; and do not oppress the stranger, the orphan, or widow, and do not sin, and shed no innocent blood in this place.

4 For if you will indeed perform this word, then shall there enter in by the gates of this house kings sitting upon the throne of David, and riding on chariots and horses; they, their servants, and their people.

5 But if you will not perform these words, by Myself have I sworn," says the Lord, "that this house shall be *brought* to desolation."""

6 For thus says the Lord concerning the house of the king of Judah: "You are Gilead to Me, *and* the head of Lebanon. Yet surely I will make you a desert, *even* cities that shall not be inhabited;

7 and I will bring upon you a destroying man, and his axe; and they shall cut down your choice cedars, and cast *them* into the fire.

8 And nations shall pass through this city, and each shall say to his neighbor, 'Why has the Lord done thus to this great city?'

9 And they shall say, 'Because they forsook the covenant of the Lord their God, and worshipped strange gods, and served them.'"

10 Weep not for the dead, nor lament for him: weep bitterly for him that goes away; for he shall return no more, nor see his native land.

Message to the Sons of Josiah

11 For thus says the Lord concerning Shallum the son of Josiah, who reigns in the place of Josiah his father, who has gone forth out of this place: "He shall not return here anymore. 12 But in that place where I have carried him captive, there shall he die, and shall see this land no more."

13 "Woe to him that builds his house by unrighteousness, and his upper chambers by injustice, who uses his neighbor's service without wages, and gives him nothing for his work.

14 You have built for yourself a well-proportioned house, *with* airy chambers, fitted with windows, and paneled with cedar, and painted with vermilion.

15 Shall you reign because you are provoked with your father Ahaz? They shall not eat, and they shall not drink: it is better for you to execute justice and righteousness.

16 They did not understand, they did not judge the cause of the afflicted, nor the cause of the poor—is not this your not knowing Me?" says the Lord.

17 "Behold, your eyes are not good, nor your heart, but *they go* after your covetousness, and after the innocent blood to shed it, and after acts of injustice and slaughter, to commit them."

18 Therefore thus says the Lord concerning Jehoiakim son of Josiah, king of Judah, even concerning this man: "They shall not lament for him, *saying,* 'Ah brother!' Neither shall they weep for him, *saying,* 'Alas Lord.'

19 He shall be buried with the burial of a donkey; he shall be dragged roughly along and cast outside the gate of Jerusalem.

20 "Go up to Lebanon and cry; and utter your voice to Bashan, and cry aloud to the extremity of the sea: for all your lovers are destroyed.

21 I spoke to you on *occasion of* your trespass, but you said, 'I will not listen.' This *has been* your way from your youth, you have not listened to My voice.

22 The wind shall tend all your shepherds, and your lovers shall go into captivity; for then shall you be ashamed and disgraced because of all your lovers.

23 O inhabitant of Lebanon, making your nest in the cedars, you shall groan heavily, when pangs as of a travailing woman have come upon you.

Message to Jeconiah

24 "As I live," says the Lord, "though Jeconiah son of Jehoiakim king of Judah were the signet ring upon My right hand, yet would I pluck you off;

25 and I will deliver you into the hands of them that seek you life, before whom you are afraid, into the hands of the Chaldeans.

26 And I will cast you out, and your mother that bore you, into a land where you were not born; and there you shall die.

27 But they shall by no means return to the land which they long for in their souls.

28 Jeconiah is dishonored as a good for nothing vessel; for he is thrown out and cast forth into a land which he did not know.

29 "O earth, earth, hear the word of the Lord!

30 Write this man down as childless; for by no means shall his descendants ever grow up to sit on the throne of David, *or be as* a prince yet in Judah."

JEREMIAH CHAPTER 23

Restoration After Exile

1 Woe to the shepherds that destroy and scatter the sheep of their pasture!

2 Therefore thus says the Lord against them that tend My people: "You have scattered My sheep, and driven them out, and you have not visited them: behold, I *will* take vengeance upon you according to your evil practices.

3 And I will gather in the remnant of My people in every land, where I have driven them out, and will set them in their pasture; and they shall increase and be multiplied.

4 And I will raise up shepherds to them, who shall feed them, and they shall fear no more, nor be alarmed," says the Lord.

The Righteous Branch of David

5 "Behold, the days are coming," says the Lord, "when I will raise up to David a righteous branch, and a king shall reign and understand, and shall execute judgment and righteousness on the earth.

6 In his days both Judah shall be saved, and Israel shall dwell securely. And this is His name, which the Lord shall call Him, Josedek among the prophets.

7 "Therefore behold, the days are coming," says the Lord, "when they shall no more say, 'The Lord lives, who brought up the house of Israel out of the land of Egypt';

8 but, 'The Lord lives, who has gathered the whole seed of Israel from the north land, and from all the countries where He had driven them out, and has restored them into their own land.'"

False Prophets of Hope Denounced

9 My heart is broken within me; all my bones are shaken. I have become as a broken down man, and as a man overcome with wine, because of the Lord, and because of the excellence of His glory.

10 For because of these things the land mourns; the pastures of the wilderness are dried up; and their course has become evil, and so *also* their strength.

11 "For priest and prophet are defiled, and I have seen their iniquities in My house.

12 Therefore let their way be slippery and dark to them, and they shall be tripped up and fall in it; for I will bring evils upon them, in the year of their visitation.

13 And in the prophets of Samaria I have seen lawless deeds; they prophesied by Baal, and led My people Israel astray.

14 Also in the prophets of Jerusalem I have seen horrible things: as they committed adultery, and walked in lies, and strengthened the hands of many, that they should not return each from his evil way. They have all become to Me as Sodom, and its inhabitants as Gomorrah.

15 Therefore thus says the Lord: 'Behold, I will feed them with pain, and give them bitter water to drink; for from the prophets of Jerusalem has defilement gone forth *into* all the land.'"

16 Thus says the Lord Almighty: "Do not listen to the words of the prophets, for they frame a vain vision for themselves; they speak from their own heart, and not from the mouth of the Lord.

17 They say to them that reject the word of the Lord, 'There shall be peace to you'; and to all that walk after their own lusts, and to everyone that walks in the error of his heart, they have said, 'No evil shall come upon you.'"

18 For who has stood in the counsel of the Lord, and seen His word? Who has hearkened, and heard?

19 Behold, *there is* an earthquake from the Lord, and anger proceeds to a convulsion, it shall come violently upon the ungodly.

20 And the Lord's wrath shall return no more, until He has accomplished it, and until He has established it, according to the purpose of His heart. At the end of the days they shall understand it.

21 "I have not sent these prophets, yet they ran: neither did I speak to them, yet they prophesied.

22 But if they had stood in My counsel, and if they had hearkened to My words, then would they have turned My people from their evil practices.

23 "I am a God close at hand," says the Lord, "and not a God afar off.

24 Shall anyone hide himself in secret places, and I not see him? Do I not fill heaven and earth?" Says the Lord.

25 "I have heard what the prophets say, what they prophesy in My name, saying falsely, 'I have seen a night vision.'

26 How long shall *these things* be in the heart of the prophets that prophesy lies, when they prophesy the purposes of their own heart?

27 Who devise that *men* may forget My law by their dreams, which they have told everyone to his neighbor, as their fathers forgot My name in *the worship of* Baal.

28 The prophet who has a dream, let him tell his dream; and *he* in whom is My word *spoken* to him, let him tell My word truly. What is the chaff to the wheat? So are My words," says the Lord.

29 "Behold, are not My words as fire?" says the Lord; "and as an axe cutting the rock?

30 "Behold, I am therefore against the prophets," says the Lord God, "that steal My words everyone from his neighbor.

31 Behold, I am against the prophets that put forth prophecies of mere words, and slumber their sleep.

32 Therefore behold, I am against the prophets that prophesy false dreams, and have not told them *truly*, and have caused My people to err by their lies, and by their errors; yet I did not send them, nor have I commanded them. Therefore, they shall not profit this people at all.

33 "And if this people, or the priest, or the prophet, should ask, 'What is the burden of the Lord?' Then you shall say to them, 'You are the burden,' and I will dash you down," says the Lord.

34 "*As for* the prophet and the priests and the people, who shall say, 'The burden of the Lord,' I will even take vengeance on that man, and on his house.

35 Thus shall you say everyone to his neighbor, and everyone to his brother, 'What has the Lord answered?' And, 'What has the Lord said?'

36 And the burden of the Lord you shall mention no more; for his own word shall be a man's burden.

37 "But what," *you say*, "has the Lord our God spoken?"

38 Therefore thus says the Lord our God: "Because you have spoken this word, 'The burden of the Lord,' and I sent to you, saying, you shall not say, 'The burden of the Lord';

39 therefore behold, I *will* seize and dash you down and the city which I gave to you and your fathers.

⁴⁰ And I will bring upon you an everlasting reproach, and everlasting disgrace, which shall not be forgotten."

JEREMIAH CHAPTER 24

The Good and the Bad Figs

¹ The Lord showed me two baskets of figs, lying in front of the temple of the Lord, after Nebuchadnezzar king of Babylon had carried Jeconiah son of Joakim king of Judah captive, *along* with the princes, the craftsmen, the prisoners, and the rich men out of Jerusalem, and had brought them to Babylon.

² The one basket was *full* of very good figs, as the early figs; and the other basket was *full* of very bad figs, which could not be eaten, for they were so bad.

³ And the Lord said to me, "What do you see, Jeremiah?" And I said, "Figs; the good figs, very good; and the bad, very bad, which cannot be eaten, for they are so bad."

⁴ And the word of the Lord came to me, saying,

⁵ "Thus says the Lord, the God of Israel: 'Like these good figs, so will I acknowledge the Jews that have been carried away captive, whom I have sent forth out of this place into the land of the Chaldeans for good.

⁶ And I will fix My eyes upon them for good, and I will restore them into this land for good; and I will build them up, and not pull them down, and I will plant them, and not pluck them up.

⁷ And I will give them a heart to know Me, that I am the Lord: and they shall be to Me a people, and I will be to them a God: for they shall turn to Me with all their heart.

⁸ 'And as the bad figs, which cannot be eaten, they are so bad'; thus says the Lord: 'So will I deliver Zedekiah king of Judah, and his nobles, and the remnant of Jerusalem, them that are left in this land, and those that dwell in the land of Egypt.

⁹ And I will cause them to be dispersed into all the kingdoms of the earth, and they shall be for a reproach, and a proverb, and an *object of* hatred, and a curse, in every place where I have driven them out.

¹⁰ And I will send against them famine, and pestilence, and the sword, until they are consumed from off the land which I have given them.'"

JEREMIAH CHAPTER 25

Seventy Years of Desolation

¹ The word that came to Jeremiah concerning all the people of Judah in the fourth year of Jehoiakim, son of Josiah, king of Judah;

² which he spoke to all the people of Judah, and to the inhabitants of Jerusalem, saying,

³ "In the thirteenth year of Josiah, son of Amon, king of Judah, even until this day for twenty-three years, I have spoken to you, rising early and speaking,

⁴ and I sent to you My servants the prophets, sending them early; (but you would not listen, nor incline your ear to hear) saying,

⁵ 'Turn, everyone of you, from his evil way, and from your evil practices, and you shall dwell in the land which I gave to you and your fathers, forever and ever.

⁶ Do not go after strange gods, to serve them, and to worship them, lest you provoke Me by the works of your hands, to do you harm.'

⁷ But you hearkened not to Me.

⁸ "Therefore thus says the Lord: 'Since you did not believe My words,

⁹ behold I *will* send and take a family from the north, and will bring them against this land, and against the inhabitants of it, and against all the nations round about it. And I will utterly destroy them, and make them a horror, and a hissing, and an everlasting reproach.

¹⁰ And I will destroy from *among* them the voice of joy, and the voice of gladness, the voice of the bridegroom, and the voice of the bride, the scent of ointment, and the light of a candle.

¹¹ And all the land shall be a desolation; and they shall serve among the Gentiles seventy years.

¹² 'And when the seventy years are fulfilled, I will take vengeance on that nation, and will make them a perpetual desolation.

¹³ And I will bring upon that land all My words which I have spoken against it, *even* all things that are written in this book.'"

¹⁴ (This verse omitted in LXX)

The Cup of God's Wrath

¹⁵ "Thus said the Lord God of Israel: 'Take the cup of this unmixed wine from My hand, and you shall cause all the nations to drink, to whom I send you.

¹⁶ And they shall drink, and vomit, and be mad, because of the sword which I send among them.'"

¹⁷ So I took the cup out of the Lord's hand, and caused the nations to whom the Lord sent me to drink:

¹⁸ Jerusalem, and the cities of Judah, and the kings of Judah, and his princes, to make them a desert place, a desolation, and a hissing.

¹⁹ And Pharaoh king of Egypt, and his servants, and his nobles, and all his people;

²⁰ and all the mixed multitude, and all the kings of the Philistines, *namely* Ashkelon, Gaza, Ekron, and the remnant of Ashdod,

²¹ and Edom, and the land of Moab, and the children of Ammon,

²² and the kings of Tyre, and the kings of Sidon, and the kings in the *country* beyond the sea,

²³ and Dedan, Tema, Buz, and everyone that is shaved round about the face,

²⁴ and all the mixed multitude dwelling in the wilderness,

25 and all the kings of Elam, and all the kings of the Persians, 26 and all the kings from the north, the far and the near, each one with his brother, and all the kingdoms which are on the face of the earth.

27 "And you shall say to them, 'Thus said the Lord Almighty: "Drink, and be drunk; and you shall vomit and fall, and shall by no means rise, because of the sword which I send among you."'

28 And it shall come to pass, when they refuse to take the cup out of your hand, to drink it, that you shall say, 'Thus said the Lord: "You shall surely drink.

29 For I am beginning to afflict the city which is called by My name, and you shall by no means be held guiltless: for I am calling a sword upon all that dwell upon the earth."

30 "And you shall prophesy against them these words, and shall say: 'The Lord shall speak from on high, from His sanctuary He will utter His voice. He will pronounce a declaration on His place; and these shall answer like men gathering grapes. And destruction is coming on them that dwell on the earth,

31 even upon the extreme part of the earth; for the Lord has a controversy with the nations, He is pleading with all flesh, and the ungodly are given to the sword," says the Lord.

32 "Thus said the Lord: 'Behold, evils are proceeding from nation to nation, and a great whirlwind goes forth from the end of the earth.

33 And the slain of the Lord shall be in the day of the Lord from one end of the earth even to the other end of the earth. They shall not be buried; they shall be as dung on the face of the earth.

34 "Howl, O you shepherds, and cry; lament, you rams of the flock: for your days have been completed for slaughter, and you shall fall as the choice rams.

35 And flight shall perish from the shepherds, and safety from the rams of the flock.

36 A voice of the crying of the shepherds, and a moaning of the sheep and the rams: for the Lord has destroyed their pastures.

37 And the peaceful dwellings that remain shall be destroyed before the fierceness of My anger.

38 He has forsaken His lair, as a lion: for their land has become desolate before the great sword."

JEREMIAH CHAPTER 26

Jeremiah's Prophecies in the Temple

1 In the beginning of the reign of King Jehoiakim son of Josiah, there came this word from the Lord:

2 "Thus said the Lord: 'Stand in the court of the Lord's house, and you shall declare to all the Jews, and to all that come to worship in the house of the Lord, all the words which I commanded you to speak to them; do not leave out one word.

3 Perhaps they will listen, and turn from their evil ways; then I will cease from the evils which I purpose to do to them, because of their evil practices.'

4 And you shall say, 'Thus said the Lord: "If you will not listen to Me, to walk in My statutes which I set before you,

5 to listen to the words of My servants the prophets, whom I sent to you early in the morning; yes, I sent them, but you did not listen to Me;

6 then will I make this house as Shiloh, and I will make this city a curse to all the nations of all the earth."'"

7 And the priests, and the false prophets, and all the people heard Jeremiah speaking these words in the house of the Lord.

8 And it came to pass, when Jeremiah had ceased speaking all that the Lord had ordered him to speak to all the people, that the priests and the false prophets and all the people grabbed hold of him, saying,

9 "You shall surely die, because you have prophesied in the name of the Lord, saying, 'This house shall be as Shiloh, and this city shall be made quite destitute of inhabitants.'" And all the people assembled against Jeremiah in the house of the Lord.

10 And the princes of Judah heard this word, and they went up out of the house of the king to the house of the Lord, and sat in the entrance of the new gate.

11 Then the priests and the false prophets said to the princes and to all the people, "The judgment of death is due to this man, because he has prophesied against this city, as you have heard with your ears."

12 Then Jeremiah spoke to the princes, and to all the people, saying, "The Lord sent me to prophesy against this house and against this city, all the words which you have heard.

13 And now amend your ways and your works, and listen to the voice of the Lord, and the Lord shall relent from the doom which He has pronounced against you.

14 And behold, I am in your hands; do to me as seems best to you.

15 But be certain of this: that if you kill me, you shall bring innocent blood upon yourselves, and upon this city, and upon its inhabitants; for in truth the Lord has sent me to you to speak all these words in your ears."

16 Then the princes and all the people said to the priests and to the false prophets; "Judgment of death is not due to this man; for he has spoken to us in the name of the Lord our God."

17 And there rose up men of the elders of the land, and said to all the assembly of the people,

18 "Micah the Moreshite lived in the days of Hezekiah king of Judah, and said to all the people of Judah, 'Thus says the Lord; Zion shall be plowed as a field, and Jerusalem shall become a desolation, and the mountain of the house shall be a thicket of trees.'

19 Did Hezekiah and all Judah in any way kill him? Was it not that they feared the Lord, and they made supplication

before the Lord, and the Lord relented from the doom which He *had* pronounced against them? But we have wrought great evil against our own souls."

20 And there was *another* man prophesying in the name of the Lord, Urijah the son of Shemaiah, of Kirjath Jearim; and he prophesied concerning this land according to all the words of Jeremiah.

21 And King Jehoiakim and all the princes heard all his words, and sought to kill him; and Urijah heard *it* and went to Egypt.

22 And the king sent men to Egypt,

23 and they brought him out, and brought him into the king; and he struck him with the sword, and cast him into the tomb of the children of his people.

24 Nevertheless the hand of Ahikam son of Shaphan was with Jeremiah, to prevent his being delivered into the hands of the people, or from being killed.

JEREMIAH CHAPTER 27

The Sign of the Yoke

1 (This verse omitted in LXX)

2 "Thus says the Lord: 'Make for yourself bonds and yokes, and put *them* about your neck,

3 and you shall send them to the king of Edom, to the king of Moab, to the king of the children of Ammon, to the king of Tyre, and to the king of Sidon, by the hands of their messengers that come to meet them at Jerusalem to Zedekiah king of Judah.

4 And you shall commission them to say to their masters, "Thus says the Lord God of Israel: 'Thus shall you say to your masters:

5 "I have made the earth by My great power, and by My outstretched arm, and I will give it to whomsoever it shall seem *good* in My eyes.

6 I have given the earth to Nebuchadnezzar king of Babylon to serve him, and the wild beasts of the field to labor for him.

7 (This verse omitted in LXX)

8 "And the nation and kingdom, all that shall not put their neck under the yoke of the king of Babylon, with sword and famine will I visit them," says the Lord, "until they are consumed by his hand.

9 And do not listen to your false prophets, nor to them that divine to you, nor to them that foretell events by dreams to you, nor to your soothsayers, nor your sorcerers, that say, 'You shall by no means work for the king of Babylon';

10 for they prophesy lies to you, to remove you far from your land.

11 But the nation which shall put its neck under the yoke of the king of Babylon, and serve him, I will even leave it upon its land, and it shall serve him, and dwell in it."''"

12 I spoke also to Zedekiah king of Judah according to all these words, saying, "Put your neck into *the yoke*, and serve the king of Babylon."

13 (This verse omitted in LXX)

14 "These men prophesy unrighteous *words* to you,

15 for I did not send them, says the Lord; "and they prophesy *in* My name unjustly, that I might destroy you, and you should perish, and your prophets, who unrighteously prophesy lies to you.

16 "I spoke to you, and to all this people, and to the priests, saying, 'Thus says the Lord: "Do not listen to the words of the prophets that prophesy to you, saying, 'Behold, the vessels of the Lord's house shall return from Babylon'—for they prophesy unrighteous *words* to you.

17 I did not send them.

18 If they are prophets, and if the word of the Lord is in them, let them meet Me, for thus has the Lord spoken."

19 "And as for the remaining vessels,

20 which the king of Babylon did not take, when he carried Jeconiah prisoner out of Jerusalem,

21 (This verse omitted in LXX)

22 they shall go into Babylon," says the Lord.

JEREMIAH CHAPTER 28

Hananiah Opposes Jeremiah and Dies

1 And it came to pass in the fourth year of Zedekiah king of Judah, in the fifth month, *that* Hananiah the false prophet, the son of Azur, from Gibeon, spoke to me in the house of the Lord, in the sight of the priests and all the people, saying,

2 "Thus says the Lord: I have broken the yoke of the king of Babylon.

3 Yet two full years, and I will return into this place the vessels of the house of the Lord,

4 *with* Jeconiah, and the captivity of Judah; for I will break the yoke of the king of Babylon."

5 Then Jeremiah spoke to Hananiah in the sight of all the people, and in the sight of the priests that stood in the house of the Lord,

6 and Jeremiah said, "May the Lord indeed do thus; may He confirm your word which you prophesy, to return the vessels of the house of the Lord, and all the captivity, out of Babylon to this place.

7 Nevertheless hear the word of the Lord which I speak in your ears, and in the ears of all the people:

8 The prophets that were before me and before you of old, also prophesied over much country, and against great kingdoms, concerning war.

9 *As for* the prophet that has prophesied for peace, when the word has come *to pass*, they shall know the prophet whom the Lord has truly sent."

10 Then Hananiah took the yokes from the neck of Jeremiah in the sight of all the people, and broke them to pieces.

11 And Hananiah spoke in the presence of all the people, saying, "Thus said the Lord: Thus will I break the yoke of the king of Babylon from the necks of all the nations." And Jeremiah went his way.

¹² And the word of the Lord came to Jeremiah, after Hananiah had broken the yokes off his neck, saying,

¹³ "Go and speak to Hananiah, saying, 'Thus says the Lord: You have broken the yokes of wood, but I will make yokes of iron in their place.

¹⁴ For thus said the Lord: I have put a yoke of iron on the neck of all the nations, that they may serve the king of Babylon.'"

¹⁵ And Jeremiah said to Hananiah, "The Lord has not sent you; and you have caused this people to trust in unrighteousness.

¹⁶ Therefore thus said the Lord: 'Behold, I *will* cast you off from the face of the earth—this year you shall die!'"

¹⁷ So he died in the seventh month.

JEREMIAH CHAPTER 29

Jeremiah's Letter to the Exiles in Babylon

¹ And these are the words of the book which Jeremiah sent from Jerusalem to the elders of the captivity, and to the priests, and to the false prophets, even an epistle to Babylon for the captivity, and to all the people:

² (after the departure of Jeconiah the king, *with* the queen, the eunuchs, every freeman and bondsman, and craftsman, out of Jerusalem)

³ by the hand of Elasah son of Shaphan, and Gemariah son of Hilkiah, (whom Zedekiah king of Judah sent to *Nebuchadnezzar* king of Babylon, to Babylon) saying,

⁴ "Thus said the Lord God of Israel concerning the captivity which I caused to be carried away from Jerusalem:

⁵ 'Build houses, and inhabit *them*; and plant gardens, and eat the fruits thereof;

⁶ and take for yourselves wives, and bear sons and daughters; and take wives for your sons, and give your daughters to husbands, and be multiplied, and not diminished.

⁷ And seek the peace of the land into which I have carried you captive, and you shall pray to the Lord for the people: for in its peace you shall *have* peace.'

⁸ 'For thus says the Lord: Let not the false prophets that are among you persuade you, and let not your diviners persuade you, and do not heed the dreams which you dream.

⁹ For they prophesy to you unrighteous *words* in My name; and I did not send them.'

¹⁰ 'For thus said the Lord: When seventy years shall be on the verge of being accomplished at Babylon, I will visit you, and I will confirm My words to you, to bring back your people to this place.

¹¹ And I will devise for you a plan of peace, and not evil, to bestow upon you these *good things*.

¹² And pray to Me, and I will hear you; and you shall earnestly seek Me, and you shall find Me;

¹³ for you shall seek Me with your whole heart.

¹⁴ And I will appear to you.

¹⁵ Because you have said, 'The Lord has appointed for us prophets in Babylon.'

¹⁶ (This verse omitted in LXX)

¹⁷ (This verse omitted in LXX)

¹⁸ (This verse omitted in LXX)

¹⁹ (This verse omitted in LXX)

²⁰ (This verse omitted in LXX)

²¹ "Thus says the Lord concerning Ahab *the son of Kolaiah*, and concerning Zedekiah: Behold, I *will* deliver them into the hands of the king of Babylon; and he shall slay them in your sight.

²² And they shall make of them a curse in all the captivity of Judah in Babylon, saying, 'The Lord do to you as He did to Zedekiah, and as He did to Ahab, whom the king of Babylon fried in the fire';

²³ because of the iniquity which they have done in Israel, and *because* they committed adultery with the wives of their fellow citizens, and spoke a word in My name, which I did not command them *to speak*, and I am witness," says the Lord.

²⁴ "And to Shemaiah the Nehelamite you shall say,

²⁵ 'I did not send you in My name.' And to Zephaniah the priest, the son of Maaseiah, say,

²⁶ 'The Lord has made you priest in the place of Jehoida the priest, to be ruler in the house of the Lord over every prophet, and to every madman, and you shall put them in prison, and into the dungeon.

²⁷ And now, why have you together reviled Jeremiah of Anathoth, who prophesied to you?

²⁸ Did he not send for this purpose? For in the course of this month he sent to you to Babylon, saying, "It is far off: build houses, and inhabit *them*; plant gardens, and eat the fruit of them."'"

²⁹ And Zephaniah read the book in the ears of Jeremiah.

³⁰ Then the word of the Lord came to Jeremiah, saying,

³¹ "Send to the captivity, saying, 'Thus says the Lord concerning Shemaiah the Nehelamite: Since Shemaiah has prophesied to you, and I did not send him, and he has caused you to trust in iniquity,

³² therefore thus says the Lord: Behold, I will visit Shemaiah and his family; and there shall not be a man of them in the midst of you to see the good which I will do for *My* people; they shall not see *it*.'"

JEREMIAH CHAPTER 30

Restoration Promised for Israel and Judah

¹ The word that came to Jeremiah from the Lord, saying,

² "Thus says the Lord God of Israel: Write all the words which I have spoken to you in a book.

³ For behold, the days are coming, says the Lord, when I will bring back the captivity of My people Israel and Judah; and I will bring them back to the land which I gave to their fathers, and they shall be masters over it," says the Lord.

[4] And these are the words which the Lord spoke concerning Israel and Judah:

[5] "Thus said the Lord: You shall hear a sound of fear—fear, and not peace.

[6] Ask, and see if a male has ever born a child? And *ask* concerning the fear, why they shall hold their loins, and *look for* safety; for I have seen every man, and his hands are on his loins; *their* faces have turned pale.

[7] For that day is great, and there is none like it; and it is a time of Jacob's trouble, but he shall be saved out of it.

[8] In that day, said the Lord, I will break the yoke off their neck, and will burst their bonds, and they shall no longer serve strangers.

[9] But they shall serve the Lord their God; and I will raise up to them David their king."

[10] (This verse omitted in LXX)

[11] (This verse omitted in LXX)

[12] "Thus says the Lord: I have brought on *you* destruction. Your stroke is painful.

[13] There is none to judge your cause; you have been painfully treated for healing, there is no help for you.

[14] All your friends have forgotten you; they shall not ask *about you* at all, for I have struck you with the stroke of the enemy, *even* severe correction. Your sins have abounded above all your iniquity.

[15] Your sins have abounded beyond the multitude of your iniquities, *therefore* they have done these things to you.

[16] Therefore all that devour you shall be eaten, and all your enemies shall eat all their *own* flesh. And they that spoil you shall become a spoil, and I will give up to be plundered all that have plundered you.

[17] For I will bring about your healing, I will heal you of your grievous wound, says the Lord; for you are called Dispersed: she is your prey, for no one seeks after her."

[18] "Thus said the Lord: Behold, I will turn the captivity of Jacob, and will have pity upon his prisoners; and the city shall be built upon her hill, and the people shall settle after their manner.

[19] And there shall go forth from them singers, *even* the sound of men making merry, and I will multiply them, and they shall by no means be diminished.

[20] And their sons shall go in as before, and their testimonies shall be established before Me, and I will visit those that afflict them.

[21] And their mighty ones shall be over them, and their prince shall proceed of themselves; and I will gather them, and they shall return to Me; for who is this that has set his heart to return to Me?" says the Lord.

[22] (This verse omitted in LXX)

[23] For the wrathful anger of the Lord has gone forth, *even a* whirlwind of anger has gone forth: it shall come upon the ungodly.

[24] The fierce anger of the Lord shall not return, until He shall execute *it*, and until He shall establish the purpose of His heart. In the latter days you shall know these things.

JEREMIAH CHAPTER 31

The Joyful Return of the Exiles

[1] "At that time, says the Lord, I will be a God to the family of Israel, and they shall be to Me a people.

[2] Thus says the Lord: I found him warm in the wilderness with them that were slain with the sword: therefore go and do not destroy Israel."

[3] The Lord appeared to him from afar, *saying*, "I have loved you with an everlasting love; therefore with lovingkindness have I drawn you.

[4] For I will build you, and you shall be built, O virgin of Israel. You shall yet take your timbrel, and go forth with the party of them that make merry.

[5] For you have planted vineyards on the mountains of Samaria. Plant, and praise.

[6] For it is a day when those that plead on the mountains of Ephraim shall call, *saying*, 'Arise, and go up to Zion to the Lord your God.'"

[7] "For thus says the Lord to Jacob: Rejoice, and exult over the head of the nations: make proclamation, and praise. Say, 'The Lord has delivered His people, the remnant of Israel.'

[8] Behold, I bring them from the north, and I will gather them from the end of the earth to the feast of the Passover: and *the people* shall beget a great multitude, and they shall return there.

[9] They went forth with weeping, and I will bring them back with consolation, causing them to lodge by the channels of waters in a straight way, and they shall not err in it: for I have become a father to Israel, and Ephraim is My firstborn.

[10] "Hear the words of the Lord, you nations, and proclaim *them* to the islands afar off. Say, 'He that scattered Israel will also gather him, and keep him as one that feeds his flock.'

[11] For the Lord has ransomed Jacob, He has rescued him out of the hand of them *that were* stronger than he.

[12] And they shall come, and shall rejoice in the mount of Zion, and shall come to the good things of the Lord, to a land of wheat, and wine, and fruits, and cattle, and sheep. And their soul shall be as a fruitful tree; and they shall hunger no more. [13] Then shall the virgins rejoice in the assembly of youth, and the old men shall rejoice; and I will turn their mourning into joy, and will make them merry.

[14] I will expand and cheer with wine the soul of the priests, the sons of Levi, and My people shall be satisfied with My good things. Thus says the Lord."

[15] A voice was heard in Ramah, *that* of lamentation, and of weeping, and wailing— Rachel would not cease weeping for her children, because they are not.

[16] "Thus says the Lord: Let your voice cease from weeping, and your eyes from your tears; for your work shall be rewarded, and they shall return from the land of *your*

enemies. [17] *There shall be* an abiding *home* for your children.

[18] "I have heard the sound of Ephraim lamenting, *and saying*, 'You have chastened me, and I was chastened; I as a calf was not *willingly* taught: turn me, and I shall turn; for You *are* the Lord my God.

[19] For after my captivity I repented, and after I knew, I groaned for the day of shame, and showed You that I bore reproach from my youth.'

[20] Ephraim is a beloved son, a pleasing child to Me: for because My words are in him, I will surely remember him. Therefore I made haste *to help* him. I will surely have mercy upon him, says the Lord."

[21] "Prepare yourself, O Zion; execute vengeance. Look to your ways; return, O virgin of Israel, by the way in which you went, return mourning to your cities.

[22] How long, O disgraced daughter, will you turn away? For the Lord has created safety for a new plantation. Men shall go about in safety.

[23] For thus says the Lord: "They shall yet speak this word in the land of Judah, and in its cities, when I shall turn his captivity: 'Blessed be the Lord on His righteous holy mountain!'

[24] And there shall be inhabitants in the cities of Judah, and in all his land, together with the farmers, and *the shepherd* shall go forth with the flock.

[25] For I have saturated every thirsting soul, and filled every hungry soul."

[26] Therefore I awoke, and beheld; and my sleep was sweet to me.

[27] "Therefore behold, the days are coming, says the Lord, when I will sow the house of Israel and the house of Judah with the seed of man, and the seed of beast.

[28] And it shall come to pass, that as I watched over them, to pull down, and to afflict, so will I watch over them, to build, and to plant, says the Lord.

[29] In those days they shall certainly not say, 'The fathers ate a sour grape, and the children's teeth were set on edge.'

[30] But everyone shall die in his own sin; and the teeth of him that eats the sour grape shall be set on edge.

[31] "Behold, the days are coming, says the Lord, when I will make a new covenant with the house of Israel, and with the house of Judah.

[32] Not according to the covenant which I made with their fathers in the day when I took hold of their hand to bring them out of the land of Egypt; for they did not abide in My covenant, and I disregarded them, says the Lord.

[33] For this is My covenant which I will make with the house of Israel: after those days, says the Lord, I will surely put My laws into their mind, and write them on their hearts. And I will be to them a God, and they shall be to Me a people.

[34] And no more shall every man teach his neighbor, and every man his brother, saying, 'Know the Lord.' For all shall know Me, from the least of them to the greatest of them. For I will be merciful to their iniquities, and their sins I will remember no more."

[35] Thus says the Lord, who gives the sun for a light by day, the moon and the stars for a light by night, and *makes* a roaring in the sea, so that its waves roar: the Lord Almighty is His name: [36] "If these ordinances cease from before Me, says the Lord, then shall the family of Israel cease to be a nation before Me forever.

[37] Though the sky should be raised to a *greater* height, says the Lord, and though the ground of the earth should be sunk *lower* beneath, yet I will not cast off the family of Israel, says the Lord, for all that they have done.

[38] "Behold, the days are coming, says the Lord, when the city shall be built to the Lord from the tower of Hananel to the Corner Gate.

[39] And the measurement of it shall proceed in front of them as far as the hills of Gareb, and it shall be compassed with a circular wall of choice stones.

[40] And all the Asaremoth, even to the Brook Kidron, as far as the corner of the Horse Gate eastward, shall be holiness to the Lord; and it shall not fail anymore, and shall not be destroyed forever."

JEREMIAH CHAPTER 32

Jeremiah Buys a Field

[1] The word that came from the Lord to Jeremiah in the tenth year of King Zedekiah, this is the eighteenth year of King Nebuchadnezzar king of Babylon.

[2] And the army of the king of Babylon had made a rampart against Jerusalem; and Jeremiah was kept in the court of the prison, which is in the king's house.

[3] For King Zedekiah *had* shut him up, saying, "Why do you prophesy, saying, 'Thus says the Lord, Behold, I *will* give this city into the hands of the king of Babylon, and he shall take it; [4] and Zedekiah shall by no means be delivered out of the hand of the Chaldeans, for he shall certainly be given up into the hands of the king of Babylon, and his mouth shall speak to his mouth, and his eyes shall look upon his eyes;

[5] and Zedekiah shall go into Babylon, and dwell there?'"

[6] And the word of the Lord came to Jeremiah, saying,

[7] "Behold, Hanamel the son of Shallom your father's brother is coming to you, saying, 'Buy my field that is in Anathoth: for you *have* the right of redemption, to buy *it.*'"

[8] So Hanamel the son of Shallom my father's brother came to me into the court of the prison, and said, "Buy my field that is in the land of Benjamin, in Anathoth: for you *have* a right to buy it, and you are the elder." So I knew that it was the word of the Lord.

[9] And I bought the field of Hanamel the son of my father's brother, and I weighed him seventeen shekels of silver.

[10] And I wrote *it* in a book, and sealed *it*, and took the testimony of witnesses, and weighed the money on the scales. [11] And I took the book of the purchase that was sealed;

¹² and I gave it to Baruch son of Neriah, son of Mahseiah, in the sight of Hanamel my father's brother's son, and in the sight of the men that stood by and wrote in the book of the purchase, and in the sight of the Jews that were in the court of the prison.

¹³ And I charged Baruch in their presence, saying, Thus says the Lord Almighty:

¹⁴ "Take this book of the purchase, and the book that has been read; and you shall put it into an earthen vessel, that it may remain many days.

¹⁵ For thus says the Lord: There shall yet be bought fields and houses and vineyards in this land."

¹⁶ And I prayed to the Lord after I had given the book of the purchase to Baruch the son of Neriah, saying,

¹⁷ "O great Lord! You have made the heaven and the earth by Your great power, and with Your high and outstretched arm; nothing can be hidden from You;

¹⁸ granting mercy to thousands, and recompensing the sins of the fathers into the bosoms of their children after them: the Great, the Mighty God;

¹⁹ the Lord of great counsel, and mighty in deeds, the Great Almighty God, and Lord of great name. Your eyes are upon the ways of the children of men, to give to everyone according to his way;

²⁰ who has wrought signs and wonders in the land of Egypt even to this day, and in Israel, and among the inhabitants of the earth; and You made for Yourself a name, as it is this day; ²¹ and You brought out Your people Israel out of the land of Egypt with signs, and with wonders, with a mighty hand, and with an outstretched arm, and with great sights.

²² And You gave them this land, which You swore to their fathers, a land flowing with milk and honey;

²³ and they went in, and took it; but they did not heed Your voice, and did not walk in Your ordinances. They did none of the things which You commanded them, and they caused all these calamities to come upon them.

²⁴ Behold, a multitude has come against the city, to take it; and the city is given into the hands of the Chaldeans that fight against it, by the power of the sword, and the famine. As You have spoken, so has it happened.

²⁵ And You have said to me, 'Buy the field for money'; and I wrote a book, and sealed *it*, and took the testimony of witnesses: and the city was given into the hands of the Chaldeans."

God's Assurance of the People's Return

²⁶ And the word of the Lord came to me, saying,

²⁷ "I am the Lord, the God of all flesh: shall anything be hidden from Me?

²⁸ Therefore thus says the Lord God of Israel: This city shall certainly be delivered into the hands of the king of Babylon, and he shall take it:

²⁹ and the Chaldeans shall come to war against this city, and they shall burn this city with fire, and shall burn down the houses where they burnt incense on its roofs to Baal, and poured out drink offerings to other gods, to provoke Me.

³⁰ For the children of Israel and the children of Judah alone did evil in My sight from their youth.

³¹ For this city was *obnoxious* to My anger and My wrath, from the day that they built it, even to this day; that I should remove it from My presence,

³² because of all the wickedness of the children of Israel and Judah, which they have done to provoke Me, they and their kings, and their princes, and their priests, and their prophets, the men of Judah, and the inhabitants of Jerusalem.

³³ And they turned their backs to Me, and not their faces; though I taught them early in the morning, but they listened no more to receive instructions,

³⁴ and they set their abominations in the house which is called by My name, by their uncleannesses.

³⁵ And they built to Baal the altars that are in the valley of the son of Hinnom, to offer their sons and their daughters to King Moloch; which things I did not command them, neither came it into My mind that they should do this abomination, to cause Judah to sin.

³⁶ "And now thus has the Lord God of Israel said concerning this city, of which you say, 'It shall be delivered into the hands of the king of Babylon by the sword, and by famine, and banishment':

³⁷ "Behold, I *will* gather them out of every land, where I have scattered them in My anger, and My wrath, and great fury; and I will bring them back into this place, and will cause them to dwell safely:

³⁸ and they shall be to Me a people, and I will be to them a God.

³⁹ And I will give them another way, and another heart, to fear Me continually, and *that* for good to them and their children after them.

⁴⁰ And I will make with them an everlasting covenant, which I will by no means turn away from them, and I will put My fear into their heart, that they may not depart from Me.

⁴¹ And I will visit *them* to do them good, and I will plant them in this land in faithfulness, and with all My heart, and with all *My* soul.

⁴² "For thus says the Lord: As I have brought upon this people all these great evils, so will I bring upon them all the good things which I pronounced upon them.

⁴³ And there shall yet be fields bought in the land, of which you say, 'It shall be destitute of man and beast; and they are delivered into the hands of the Chaldeans.'

⁴⁴ And they shall buy fields for money, and you shall write a book, and seal *it*, and shall take the testimony of witnesses in the land of Benjamin, and round about Jerusalem, and in the cities of Judah, and in the cities of the mountain, and in the cities of the plain, and in the cities of the south: for I will turn their captivity."

JEREMIAH CHAPTER 33

Healing After Punishment

[1] And the word of the Lord came to Jeremiah the second time, when he was yet bound in the court of the prison, saying,

[2] "Thus says the Lord, who made the earth and formed it, to establish it; the Lord is His name:

[3] Cry out to Me, and I will answer you, and I will declare to you great and mighty things, which you know not.

[4] For thus says the Lord concerning the houses of this city, and concerning the houses of the king of Judah, which have been pulled down for mounds and fortifications,

[5] to fight against the Chaldeans, and to fill it with the corpses of men, whom I struck down in My anger and My wrath, and turned away My face from them, for all their wickedness:

[6] 'Behold, I bring upon her healing and a cure, and I will show *Myself* to them, and will heal her, and make both peace and security.

[7] And I will turn the captivity of Judah, and the captivity of Israel, and will build them, even as before.

[8] And I will cleanse them from all their iniquities by which they have sinned against Me, and I will not remember their sins by which they have sinned against Me, and revolted from Me.

[9] And it shall be for joy and praise, and for glory to all the people of the earth, who shall hear all the good that I will do. And they shall fear and be provoked for all the good things and for all the peace which I will bring upon them.

[10] Thus says the Lord: There shall yet be heard in this place, of which you say, It is destitute of men and cattle, in the cities of Judah, and in the streets of Jerusalem, *the places* that have been made desolate for lack of men and cattle,

[11] the voice of gladness, and the voice of joy, the voice of the bridegroom, and the voice of the bride, the voice of men saying, 'Give thanks to the Lord Almighty; for the Lord is good; for His mercy *endures* forever.' And they shall bring gifts into the house of the Lord, for I will turn all the captivity of that land as before,' says the Lord.

[12] "Thus says the Lord of hosts: There shall yet be in this place, that is desolate of man and beast, and in all its cities, resting places for shepherds causing their flocks to lie down.

[13] In the cities of the hill country, and in the cities of the valley, and in the cities of the south, and in the land of Benjamin, and in the *cities* round about Jerusalem, and in the cities of Judah, flocks shall yet pass under the hand of him that numbers *them*," says the Lord.

[14] (This verse omitted in LXX)

[15] (This verse omitted in LXX)

[16] (This verse omitted in LXX)

[17] (This verse omitted in LXX)

[18] (This verse omitted in LXX)

[19] (This verse omitted in LXX)

[20] (This verse omitted in LXX)

[21] (This verse omitted in LXX)

[22] (This verse omitted in LXX)

[23] (This verse omitted in LXX)

[24] (This verse omitted in LXX)

[25] (This verse omitted in LXX)

[26] (This verse omitted in LXX)

JEREMIAH CHAPTER 34

Death in Captivity Predicted for Zedekiah

[1] The word that came to Jeremiah from the Lord (now Nebuchadnezzar king of Babylon, and all his army, and all the country of his dominion, were fighting against Jerusalem, and against all the cities of Judah), saying,

[2] "Thus says the Lord: Go to Zedekiah king of Judah, and you shall say to him, 'Thus says the Lord: This city shall certainly be delivered into the hands of the king of Babylon, and he shall take it, and shall burn it with fire.

[3] And you shall not escape out of his hand, but shall certainly be taken, and shall be given into his hands; and your eyes shall see his eyes, and you shall enter into Babylon.

[4] But hear the word of the Lord, O Zedekiah king of Judah: Thus says the Lord:

[5] You shall die in peace; and as they wept for your fathers that reigned before you, so shall they weep for you, *saying*, "Alas, lord!" And they shall lament for you down to the grave; for I have spoken the word, says the Lord.'"

[6] And Jeremiah spoke to King Zedekiah all these words in Jerusalem.

[7] And the army of the king of Babylon fought against Jerusalem, and against the cities of Judah, and against Lachish, and against Azekah; for these fortified cities were left among the cities of Judah.

Treacherous Treatment of Slaves

[8] *This is* the word that came from the Lord to Jeremiah, after King Zedekiah had made a covenant with the people, to proclaim a release:

[9] That every man should set his servant free, and every man his maidservant, the Hebrew man and Hebrew woman, that no one from Judah should be in bondage.

[10] Then all the nobles, and all the people who had entered into the covenant, *engaging* to set free everyone of his male and female slaves, *changed their minds*,

[11] and gave them over to be male and female slaves.

[12] And the word of the Lord came to Jeremiah, saying,

[13] "Thus says the Lord: I made a covenant with your fathers in the day that I brought them out of the land of Egypt, out of the house of bondage, saying,

[14] 'When six years are accomplished, you shall set free your brother the Hebrew, who shall be sold to you; for he shall serve you six years, and *then* you shall let him go free.' But they did not listen to Me, nor incline their ear.

¹⁵ And this day they turned to do that which was right in My sight, to proclaim everyone the release of his neighbor; and they had made a covenant before Me, in the house which is called by My name.

¹⁶ But you turned and profaned My name, to bring back everyone his servant, and everyone his maid, whom you had set free *and* at their own disposal, to be to you male and female slaves.

¹⁷ Therefore thus said the Lord: You have not listened to Me, to proclaim a release everyone to his neighbor. Behold; I proclaim a release to you, to the sword, and to the pestilence, and to the famine; and I will give you up to dispersion *among* all the kingdoms of the earth.

¹⁸ And I will give the men that have transgressed My covenant, who have not kept My covenant, which they made before Me, the calf which they prepared to sacrifice with it,

¹⁹ the princes of Judah, and the men in power, and the priests, and the people.

²⁰ I will even give them to their enemies, and their carcasses shall be food for the birds of the sky and for the wild beasts of the earth.

²¹ And I will give Zedekiah king of Judah, and their princes, into the hands of their enemies, and the host of the king of Babylon *shall come upon* them that run away from them.

²² Behold, I *will* give command, says the Lord, and will bring them back to this land; and they shall fight against it, and take it, and burn it with fire, and the cities of Judah; and I will make them desolate without inhabitants."

JEREMIAH CHAPTER 35

The Rechabites Commended

¹ The word that came to Jeremiah from the Lord in the days of Jehoiakim, king of Judah, saying,

² "Go to the house of the Rechabites, and you shall bring them to the house of the Lord, into one of the courts, and give them wine to drink."

³ So I brought forth Jaazaniah the son of Jeremiah the son of Habazziniah, and his brothers, and his sons, and all the family of the Rechabites.

⁴ And I brought them into the house of the Lord, into the chamber of the sons of Hanan, the son of Ananias, the son of Godolias, a man of God, who dwells near the house of the princes that are over the house of Maaseiah the son of Shallum, who kept the court.

⁵ And I set before them a jar of wine, and cups, and I said, "Drink *some* wine."

⁶ But they said, "We will by no means drink wine, for our father Jonadab the son of Rechab commanded us, saying, 'You shall by no means drink wine, *neither* you, nor your sons, forever.

⁷ Neither shall you build houses, nor sow any seed, nor shall you have a vineyard; for you shall dwell in tents all your days, that you may live many days upon the land in which you sojourn.'

⁸ And we heeded the voice of Jonadab our father, so as to drink no wine all our days—we, our wives, our sons, and our daughters;

⁹ and so as to build no houses to dwell in. And we have had no vineyard, nor field, nor seed.

¹⁰ But we have dwelt in tents, and have obeyed, and done according to all that Jonadab our father commanded us.

¹¹ And it came to pass, when Nebuchadnezzar came up against the land, that we said we would come in; and we entered into Jerusalem, for fear of the army of the Chaldeans, and for fear of the army of the Assyrians; and we dwelt there."

¹² And the word of the Lord came to me, saying,

¹³ "Thus says the Lord: Go, and say to the men of Judah, and to them that dwell in Jerusalem, 'Will you not receive correction, and listen to My words?

¹⁴ The sons of Jonadab the son of Rechab have kept the word which he commanded his children, that they should drink no wine; and they have not drunk; but I spoke to you early, and you would not listen.

¹⁵ And I sent to you My servants the prophets, saying, 'Turn, everyone from his evil way, and amend your practices, and do not go after other gods to serve them, and you shall dwell upon the land which I gave to you and to your fathers.' But you have not inclined your ears, and you would not listen.

¹⁶ But the sons of Jonadab the son of Rechab have kept the command of their father; but this people have not obeyed Me.

¹⁷ Therefore thus says the Lord: Behold, I *will* bring upon Judah and upon the inhabitants of Jerusalem all the evils which I pronounced against them."

¹⁸ "Therefore thus says the Lord: Since the sons of Jonadab the son of Rechab have obeyed the command of their father, to do as their father commanded them,

¹⁹ there shall never lack a man of the sons of Jonadab the son of Rechab to stand before My face while the earth remains."

JEREMIAH CHAPTER 36

The Scroll Read in the Temple

¹ In the fourth year of Jehoiakim son of Josiah king of Judah, the word of the Lord came to me, saying,

² "Take a scroll of a book, and write upon it all the words which I spoke to you against Jerusalem, and against Judah, and against all the nations, from the day when I spoke to you, from the days of Josiah king of Judah, even to this day.

³ Perhaps the house of Judah will hear all the evils which I purpose to do to them; that they may turn from their evil way; and *so* I will be merciful to their iniquities and their sins."

4 So Jeremiah called Baruch the son of Neriah. And he wrote from the mouth of Jeremiah all the words of the Lord, which He had spoken to him, on a roll of a book.

5 And Jeremiah commanded Baruch, saying, "I am in prison; I cannot enter into the house of the Lord.

6 So you shall read this scroll in the ears of the people in the house of the Lord, on the day of fasting; and in the ears of all Judah that come out of their cities, you shall read to them.

7 Perhaps their supplication will come before the Lord, and they will turn from their evil way; for great is the wrath and the anger of the Lord, which He has pronounced against this people."

8 And Baruch did according to all that Jeremiah commanded him—reading in the book the words of the Lord in the Lord's house.

9 And it came to pass in the eighth year of King Jehoiakim, in the ninth month, that all the people in Jerusalem and the house of Judah proclaimed a fast before the Lord.

10 And Baruch read in the book the words of Jeremiah in the house of the Lord, in the house of Gemariah son of Shaphan the scribe, in the upper court, in the entrance of the new gate of the house of the Lord, and in the ears of all the people.

11 And Michaiah the son of Gemariah the son of Shaphan heard all the words of the Lord, *read* from out of the book.

12 And he went down to the king's house, into the house of the scribe. And behold, there were sitting there all the princes, Elishama the scribe, and Delaiah the son of Shemaiah, and Jonathan the son of Achbor, and Gemariah the son of Shaphan, and Zedekiah the son of Hananiah, and all the princes.

13 And Michaiah reported to them all the words which he had heard Baruch reading in the ears of the people.

14 And all the princes sent Jehudi, the son of Nethaniah, the son of Shelemiah, the son of Cushi, to Baruch, saying, "Take in your hand the scroll in which you read in the ears of the people, and come." So Baruch took the scroll, and went down to them.

15 And they said to him, "Read *it* again in our ears." And Baruch read *it*.

16 And it came to pass, when they heard all the words, *that* they took counsel each with his neighbor, and said, "Let us by all means tell the king all these words."

17 And they asked Baruch, saying, "Where did you write all these words?"

18 And Baruch said, "Jeremiah told me from his *own* mouth all these words, and I wrote them in a book."

19 And they said to Baruch, "Go and hide, you and Jeremiah; let no man know where you *are*."

20 And they went in to the king into the court, and gave the scroll *to one* to keep in the house of Elishama; and they told the king all these words.

21 And the king sent Jehudi to bring the scroll. And he took it out of the house of Elishama, and Jehudi read *the scroll* in the ears of the king, and in the ears of all the princes who stood round the king.

22 Now the king was sitting in the winter house, and *there was* a fire on the hearth before him.

23 And it came to pass when Jehudi had read three or four leaves, he cut them off with a penknife, and cast *them* into the fire that was on the hearth, until the whole scroll was consumed in the fire that was on the hearth.

24 And the king and his servants that heard all these words did not seek *the Lord*, and did not tear their clothes.

25 But Elnathan and Gemariah suggested to the king that he should burn the scroll.

26 And the king commanded Jerahmeel the king's son, and Shelemiah the son of Abdeel, to take Baruch and Jeremiah, but they were hidden.

27 Then the word of the Lord came to Jeremiah, after the king had burnt the scroll, *and* all the words which Baruch had written by the mouth of Jeremiah, saying,

28 "Again take another scroll, and write all the words that were on the scroll which King Jehoiakim has burned.

29 And you shall say, 'Thus says the Lord: You have burned this scroll, saying, "Why have you written in here, saying, 'The king of Babylon shall certainly come in, and destroy this land, and man and beast shall fail from off it?'"

30 Therefore thus says the Lord concerning Jehoiakim king of Judah: He shall not have *a man* to sit on the throne of David, and his carcass shall be cast out in the heat by day, and in the frost by night.

31 And I will visit him, and his family, and his servants; and I will bring upon him, and upon the inhabitants of Jerusalem, and upon the land of Judah, all the evils which I spoke of to them; and they did not heed."

32 And Baruch took another scroll, and wrote upon it by the mouth of Jeremiah all the words of the book which Jehoiakim had burned. And there were yet more words added to it like the former.

JEREMIAH CHAPTER 37

Zedekiah's Vain Hope

1 And Zedekiah the son of Josiah reigned instead of Jehoiakim, whom Nebuchadnezzar appointed to reign over Judah.

2 And he and his servants and the people of the land would not listen to the words of the Lord, which He spoke by Jeremiah.

3 And King Zedekiah sent Jehucal son of Shelemiah and Zephaniah the priest, son of Maaseiah, to Jeremiah, saying, "Pray now for us to the Lord."

4 Now Jeremiah came and went through the midst of the city, for they *had* not put him into the house of the prison.

5 And Pharaoh's army had come forth out of Egypt; and the Chaldeans heard the report of them, and they went up from Jerusalem.

6 And the word of the Lord came to Jeremiah, saying,

7 "Thus says the Lord: Thus shall you say to the king of Judah who sent to you, to seek Me: 'Behold, the army of Pharaoh which has come forth to help you shall return to the land of Egypt.

8 And the Chaldeans themselves shall turn again, and fight against this city, and take it, and burn it with fire.

9 For thus says the Lord: Do not assume in your hearts, saying, 'The Chaldeans will certainly depart from us': for they shall not depart.

10 And though you should strike the whole army of the Chaldeans that fight against you, and there should be left a few wounded *men*, these should rise up each in his place, and burn this city with fire.'"

Jeremiah Imprisoned

11 And it came to pass, when the army of the Chaldeans had gone up from Jerusalem for fear of Pharaoh's army,

12 that Jeremiah went forth from Jerusalem to go into the land of Benjamin, to buy *some property* from there among the people.

13 And he was in the gate of Benjamin, and *there was* a man there with whom he lodged, Irajah the son of Shelemiah, the son of Hananiah; and he caught Jeremiah, saying, "You are fleeing to the Chaldeans!"

14 And he said, "*That's a* lie! I am not fleeing to the Chaldeans!" But he would not listen to him. So Irajah caught Jeremiah, and brought him to the princes.

15 And the princes were very angry with Jeremiah, and struck him, and sent him into the house of Jonathan the scribe, for they had turned *his house* into a prison.

16 So Jeremiah came into the dungeon, and into the cells, and he remained there many days.

17 Then Zedekiah sent, and called him. And the king asked him secretly, saying, "Is there a word from the Lord?" And he said, "There is. You shall be delivered into the hands of the king of Babylon."

18 And Jeremiah said to the king, "How have I wronged you, or your servants, or this people, that you have put me in prison?

19 And where are your prophets who prophesied to you saying, 'The king of Babylon shall not come against this land?'

20 Now therefore, my lord the king, let my supplication come before your face; and why do you send me back to the house of Jonathan the scribe? And by no means let me die there."

21 Then the king commanded, and they cast him into the prison, and gave him a loaf a day out of the place where they bake, until the bread failed out of the city. So Jeremiah continued in the court of the prison.

JEREMIAH CHAPTER 38

Jeremiah in the Cistern

1 And Shephatiah the son of Mattan, and Gedaliah the son of Pashhur, and Jehucal the son of Shelemiah, heard the words which Jeremiah spoke to the people, saying,

2 "Thus says the Lord: He that remains in this city shall die by the sword, and by famine. But he that goes out to the Chaldeans shall live; and his life shall be to him as a found treasure, and he shall live.

3 For thus says the Lord: This city shall certainly be delivered into the hands of the army of the king of Babylon, and they shall take it."

4 And they said to the king, "Let that man be slain, for he weakens the hands of the fighting men that are left in the city, and the hands of all the people, speaking to them according to these words; for this man does not prophesy peace to this people, but evil."

5 Then the king said, "Behold, he is in your hands." (For the king could not resist them).

6 And they cast him into the dungeon of Malchiah the king's son, which was in the court of the prison; and they let him down into the pit: and there was no water in the pit, but mire. And he was in the mire.

Jeremiah Rescued my Ebed-Melech

7 And Ebed-Melech the Ethiopian heard (now he was in the king's household) that they *had* put Jeremiah into the dungeon; and the king was in the Gate of Benjamin.

8 And he went forth to him, and spoke to the king and said,

9 "You have wrought evil in what you have done to slay this man with hunger, for there is no more bread in the city."

10 And the king commanded Ebed-Melech, saying, "Take with you thirty men from here, and bring him up out of the dungeon, lest he die."

11 So Ebed-Melech took the men and went into the underground *part of the* king's house, and took from there old rags and old ropes, and threw them down to Jeremiah into the dungeon.

12 And he said, "Put these under the ropes." And Jeremiah did so.

13 And they pulled him up with the ropes, and lifted him out of the dungeon. And Jeremiah remained in the court of the prison.

Zedekiah Consults Jeremiah Again

14 Then the king sent, and called *Jeremiah* to himself into the house of Aselisel, which was in the house of the Lord. And the king said to him, "I will ask you a question, and I pray you hide nothing from me."

15 And Jeremiah said to the king, "If I tell you, will you not certainly put me to death? And if I give you counsel, you will by no means listen to me."

16 And the king swore to him, saying, "*As* the Lord lives, who gave us this soul, I will not slay you, neither will I give you into the hands of these men."

[17] And Jeremiah said to him, Thus says the Lord: "If you will indeed go forth to the captains of the king of Babylon, your soul shall live, and this city shall certainly not be burned with fire; and you shall live, and your house.

[18] But if you will not go forth, *then* this city shall be delivered into the hands of the Chaldeans, and they shall burn it with fire, and you shall by no means escape."

[19] And the king said to Jeremiah, "I consider the Jews that have gone over to the Chaldeans, lest they deliver me into their hands, and they mock me."

[20] And Jeremiah said, "They shall by no means deliver you up. Hear the word of the Lord which I speak to you; and it shall be well with you, and your soul shall live.

[21] But if you will not go forth, this is the word which the Lord has shown me."

[22] And behold, all the women that are left in the house of the king of Judah were brought forth to the princes of the king of Babylon. And they said, "The men who were at peace with you have deceived you, and will prevail against you; and they shall cause your foot to slide and fail, they have turned back from you.

[23] And they shall bring forth your wives and your children to the Chaldeans; and you shall by no means escape, for you shall be taken by the hand of the king of Babylon, and this city shall be burned."

[24] Then the king said to him, "Let no man know *any* of these words, and certainly shall not die.

[25] And if the princes shall hear that I have spoken to you, and they come to you, and say to you, 'Tell us, what did the king say to you? Do not hide *it* from us, and we will by no means kill you, and what did the king say to you?'

[26] Then you shall say to them, 'I brought my supplication before the presence of the king, that he would not send me back into the house of Jonathan, that I should die there.'"

[27] And all the princes came to Jeremiah, and asked him. And he told them according to all these words which the king had commanded him. And they were silent, because the word of the Lord was not heard.

[28] And Jeremiah remained in the court of the prison, until the time when Jerusalem was taken.

JEREMIAH CHAPTER 39

The Fall of Jerusalem

[1] And it came to pass in the ninth month of Zedekiah king of Judah, *that* Nebuchadnezzar king of Babylon came up against Jerusalem, he and all his army, and they besieged it.

[2] And in the eleventh year of Zedekiah, in the fourth month, on the ninth day of the month, the city was penetrated.

[3] And all the leaders of the king of Babylon went in, and sat in the middle gate, Marganasar, Samagoth, Nabusachar, Nabusaris, Nagargas, Naserrabamath, and the rest of the leaders of the king of Babylon,

[4] (This verse omitted in LXX)

[5] (This verse omitted in LXX)

[6] (This verse omitted in LXX)

[7] (This verse omitted in LXX)

[8] (This verse omitted in LXX)

[9] (This verse omitted in LXX)

[10] (This verse omitted in LXX)

[11] (This verse omitted in LXX)

[12] (This verse omitted in LXX)

[13] (This verse omitted in LXX)

[14] and they sent and took Jeremiah out of the court of the prison, and committed him to Gedaliah the son of Ahikam, the son of Shaphan. And they brought him out, and he sat in the midst of the people.

[15] And the word of the Lord came to Jeremiah in the court of the prison, saying,

[16] "Go and say to Ebed-Melech the Ethiopian, 'Thus said the Lord God of Israel: Behold, I *will* bring My words upon this city for evil, and not for good.

[17] But I will save you in that day, and I will by no means deliver you into the hands of the men before whom you are afraid.

[18] For I will surely save you, and you shall by no means fall by the sword; and you shall find your life, because you trusted in Me, says the Lord.'"

JEREMIAH CHAPTER 40

Jeremiah with Gedaliah the Governor

[1] The word that came from the Lord to Jeremiah, after that Nabuzaradan the captain of the guard had let him go out of Ramah, when he had taken him in chains in the midst of the captivity of Judah, *even* those who were carried to Babylon.

[2] And the chief captain of the guard took him, and said to him, "The Lord your God has pronounced all these evils upon this place;

[3] and the Lord has done it; because you sinned against Him, and did not heed His voice.

[4] Behold, I have loosed you from the chains that were upon your hands. If it seems good to you to go with me to Babylon, then will I set my eyes upon you.

[5] But if not, depart. Return to Gedaliah the son of Ahikam, the son of Shaphan, whom the king of Babylon has appointed governor in the land of Judah, and dwell with him in the midst of the people in the land of Judah. Or go to wherever places seems good in your sight to go." And the captain of the guard made him presents, and let him go.

[6] And he came to Gedaliah, to Mizpah, and dwelt among his people that were left in the land.

[7] And all the leaders of the army that were in the country, they and their men, heard that the king of Babylon had appointed Gedaliah *governor* in the land, and they committed to him the men and their wives whom *Nebuchadnezzar had* not taken to Babylon.

8 And there came to Gedaliah at Mizpah—Ishmael, the son of Nethaniah, and Johanan son of Kareah, and Seraiah the son of Tanhumeth, and the sons of Ephai the Netophathite, and Jezaniah son of a Maachathite, they and their men.

9 And Gedaliah swore to them and to their men, saying, "Do not be afraid before the children of the Chaldeans; dwell in the land, and serve the king of Babylon, and it shall be well with you.

10 And behold, I dwell in your presence at Mizpah, to stand before the Chaldeans who shall come against you. And gather grapes, and fruits, and oil, and put *them* into your vessels, and dwell in the cities which you have obtained possession of."

11 And all the Jews that were in Moab, and among the children of Ammon, and those *that were* in Edom, and those *that were* in all *the rest of* the country, heard that the king of Babylon *had* granted a remnant to Judah, and that he had appointed over them Gedaliah the son of Ahikam.

12 And they came to Gedaliah into the land of Judah, to Mizpah, and gathered grapes, and very much summer fruit, and oil.

13 And Johanan the son of Kareah, and all the leaders of the army, who were in the fields, came to Gedaliah at Mizpah,

14 and said to him, "Do you indeed know that King Baalis son of Ammon has sent Ismael to you, to kill you?" But Gedaliah did not believe them.

15 And Johanan said to Gedaliah secretly in Mizpah, "I will go now and kill Ishmael, and let no man know *it*; lest he kill you, and all the Jews that are gathered to you be dispersed, and the remnant of Judah perish."

16 But Gedaliah said to Johanan, "Do not do this thing, for you speak lies concerning Ishmael."

JEREMIAH CHAPTER 41

Insurrection Against Gedaliah

1 Now it came to pass in the seventh month that Ishmael the son of Nethaniah the son of Elishama of the royal family came, and ten men with him, to Gedaliah, at Mizpah. And they ate bread there together.

2 And Ishmael rose up, and the ten men that were with him, and killed Gedaliah, whom the king of Babylon had appointed *governor* over the land,

3 and all the Jews that were with him at Mizpah, and all the Chaldeans that were found there.

4 And it came to pass on the second day after he had killed Gedaliah, and no man knew,

5 that there came men from Shechem, and from Shiloh, and from Samaria, eighty men, having their beards shaven, and their clothes torn, and beating their breasts, and *they had* manna and frankincense in their hands, to bring into the house of the Lord.

6 And Ishmael went out to meet them; *and* they went on and wept. And he said to them, "Come in to Gedaliah."

7 And it came to pass, when they had entered into the midst of the city, *that* he killed them *and cast them* into a pit.

8 But ten men were found there, and they said to Ishmael, "Do not kill us, for we have treasures in the field, wheat and barley, honey and oil." So he passed by, and did not kill them in the midst of their brothers.

9 Now the pit into which Ishmael cast all whom he killed is the great pit, which King Asa had made for fear of Baasha king of Israel. Ismael filled this with the slain.

10 And Ishmael brought back all the people that were left in Mizpah, and the king's daughter, whom the captain of the guard had committed in charge to Gedaliah the son of Ahikam. And he went away beyond the children of Ammon.

11 And Johanan the son of Kareah, and all the leaders of the army that were with him, heard of all the evil deeds which Ishmael had done.

12 And they brought all their army, and went to fight against him, and found him near much water in Gibeon.

13 And it came to pass, that when all the people that were with Ishmael saw Johanan, and the leaders of the army that were with him,

14 that they returned to Johanan.

15 But Ishmael escaped with eight men and went to the children of Ammon.

16 And Johanan, and all the leaders of the army that were with him, took all the remnant of the people, whom he had brought back from Ishmael, mighty men in war, and the women, and the other *property*, and the eunuchs, whom they had brought back from Gibeon;

17 and they departed, and dwelt in Chimham, which is by Bethlehem, to go into Egypt, for fear of the Chaldeans;

18 for they were afraid of them, because Ishmael had killed Gedaliah, whom the king of Babylon had appointed in the land.

JEREMIAH CHAPTER 42

Jeremiah Advises Survivors Not to Migrate

1 Then all the leaders of the army came, and Johanan, and Azarias the son of Maasaiah, and all the people great and small,

2 to Jeremiah the prophet, and said to him, "Let now our supplication come before your face, and pray to the Lord your God for this remnant; for we are left *but a* few out of many, as your eyes see.

3 And let the Lord your God declare to us the way in which we should walk, and the thing which we should do."

4 And Jeremiah said to them, "I have heard *you.* Behold, I will pray for you to the Lord our God, according to your words; and it shall come to pass, *that* whatsoever word the Lord God shall answer, I will declare to you; I will not hide anything from you."

⁵ And they said to Jeremiah, "Let the Lord be between us for a just and faithful witness, if we do not according to every word which the Lord shall send to us.

⁶ And whether *it be* good or bad, we will obey the voice of the Lord our God, to whom we send you; that it may be well with us, because we shall obey the voice of the Lord our God."

⁷ And it came to pass after ten days, *that* the word of the Lord came to Jeremiah.

⁸ And he called Johanan, and the leaders of the army, and all the people from the least even to the greatest,

⁹ and he said to them, "Thus says the Lord:

¹⁰ If you will indeed dwell in this land, I will build you, and will not pull *you* down, and I will plant you, and by no means pluck you up; for I have ceased from the calamities which I brought upon you.

¹¹ Do not be afraid of the king of Babylon, of whom you are afraid; do not fear him, says the Lord. For I am with you, to deliver you, and save you out of their hand.

¹² And I will grant you mercy, and pity you, and will restore you to your land.

¹³ 'But if you say, "We will not dwell in this land," and so not listen to the voice of the Lord;

¹⁴ "and we will go into the land of Egypt, and we shall see no war, and shall not hear the sound of a trumpet, and we shall not hunger for bread; and there we will dwell"—

¹⁵ then hear the word of the Lord. "Thus says the Lord:

¹⁶ If you set your face toward Egypt, and go in there to dwell; then it shall be *that* the sword in which you fear shall find you in the land of Egypt, and the famine in which you have regard, shall overtake you in Egypt; and there you shall die.

¹⁷ And all the men, and all the strangers who have set their face toward the land of Egypt to dwell there, shall be consumed by the sword, and by the famine; and there shall not one of them escape from the evils which I bring upon them.

¹⁸ "For thus says the Lord: As My wrath has dropped upon the inhabitants of Jerusalem, so shall My wrath drop upon you, when you have entered into Egypt. And you shall be a desolation, and under the power of others, and a curse and a reproach; and you shall see this place no more."

¹⁹ Thus says the Lord concerning you the remnant of Judah: "Do not go into Egypt." And now know this for certain,

²⁰ that you have wrought wickedness in your hearts, when you sent for me, saying, "Pray for us to the Lord; and according to all that the Lord shall speak to you we will do."

²¹ And you have not obeyed the voice of the Lord, with which He sent me to you.

²² Now therefore you shall perish by the sword and by famine, in the place in which you desire to dwell.

JEREMIAH CHAPTER 43

Jeremiah Taken to Egypt

¹ And it came to pass, when Jeremiah ceased speaking to the people all the words of the Lord, *for* which the Lord had sent him to them,

² that Azariah son of Hoshaiah spoke, and Johanan, the son of Kareah, and all the men who had spoken to Jeremiah, saying, "You speak falsely! The Lord has not sent you to us, saying, 'Do not go into Egypt, to dwell there.

³ But Baruch the son of Neriah sets you against us, that you may deliver us into the hands of the Chaldeans, to kill us, and that we should be carried away captive to Babylon."

⁴ So Johanan, and all the leaders of the army, and all the people, refused to obey the voice of the Lord, to dwell in the land of Judah.

⁵ And Johanan, and all the leaders of the army, took all the remnant of Judah, who had returned to dwell in the land;

⁶ the mighty men, and the women, and the children that were left, and the daughters of the king, and the people which Nebuzaradan had left with Gedaliah the son of Ahikam and Jeremiah the prophet, and Baruch the son of Neriah.

⁷ And they came into Egypt, for they would not obey the voice of the Lord, and they entered into Tahpanhes.

⁸ And the word of the Lord came to Jeremiah in Tahpanhes, saying,

⁹ "Take for yourself large stones, and hide them in the entrance, at the gate of the house of Pharaoh in Tahpanhes, in the sight of the men of Judah.

¹⁰ And you shall say, 'Thus says the Lord: Behold, I *will* send, and will bring Nebuchadnezzar king of Babylon, and he shall place his throne upon these stones which you have hidden, and he shall lift up weapons against them.

¹¹ And he shall enter in, and strike the land of Egypt, *and deliver* to death *those appointed* for death; and to captivity *those appointed* for captivity; and to the sword *those appointed* for the sword.

¹² And he shall kindle a fire in the houses of their gods, and shall burn them, and shall carry them away captives; and shall search the land of Egypt, as a shepherd searches his garment; and he shall go forth in peace.

¹³ And he shall break to pieces the pillars of Heliopolis that are in On, and shall burn their houses with fire."

JEREMIAH CHAPTER 44

Denunciation of Persistent Idolatry

¹ The word that came to Jeremiah for all the Jews dwelling in the land of Egypt, and for those settled in Migdol and in Tahpanhes, and in the land of Pathura, saying,

² "Thus says the Lord God of Israel: You have seen all the evils which I have brought upon Jerusalem, and upon the cities of Judah; and behold, they are desolate without inhabitants,

³ because of their wickedness which they have done to provoke Me, *by* going to burn incense to other gods, whom you did not know.

⁴ Yet I sent to you My servants the prophets early in the morning; and I sent, saying, 'Do not do this abominable thing which I hate.'

⁵ But they would not listen to Me, and would not incline their ear to turn from their wickedness, so as not to burn incense to strange gods.

⁶ So My anger and My wrath fell *upon them*, and was kindled in the gates of Judah, and in the streets of Jerusalem; and they became a desolation and a waste, as it is this day.

⁷ And now thus says the Lord Almighty: Why do you commit *these* great evils against your souls, to cut off man and woman from you, infant and suckling from the midst of Judah, to the end that not one of you should be left;

⁸ by provoking Me with the works of your hands, to burn incense to other gods in the land of Egypt, into which you entered to dwell there, that you might be cut off, and that you might become a curse and a reproach among all the nations of the earth?

⁹ Have you forgotten the sins of your fathers, and the sins of the kings of Judah, and the sins of your princes, and the sins of your wives, which they did in the land of Judah, and in the streets of Jerusalem?

¹⁰ And have not ceased even to this day, and they have not kept My ordinances, which I set before their fathers.

¹¹ "Therefore thus says the Lord: Behold, I set My face against *you*,

¹² to destroy all the remnant that are in Egypt; and they shall fall by the sword, and by famine, and shall be consumed, small and great; and they shall be for a reproach, and for destruction, and for a curse.

¹³ And I will visit them that dwell in the land of Egypt, as I have visited Jerusalem, with sword and with famine.

¹⁴ And there shall not one be preserved of the remnant of Judah that sojourn in the land of Egypt, to return to the land of Judah, to which they hope in their hearts to return. They shall not return, but only they that escape."

¹⁵ Then all the men that knew that their wives burned incense, and all the women, a great multitude, and all the people that dwelt in the land of Egypt, in Pathros, answered Jeremiah, saying,

¹⁶ "*As for* the word which you have spoken to us in the name of the Lord, we will not listen to you.

¹⁷ For we will surely perform every word that shall proceed out of our mouth, to burn incense to the queen of heaven, and to pour drink offerings to her, as we and our fathers have done, and our kings and princes, in the cities of Judah, and in the streets of Jerusalem. And *so* we were filled with bread, and were well, and saw no evils.

¹⁸ But since we left off to burn incense to the queen of heaven, we have all been brought low, and have been consumed by the sword and by famine.

¹⁹ And when we burned incense to the queen of heaven, and poured drink offerings to her, did we make cakes to her, and pour drink offerings to her, without our husbands?"

²⁰ Then Jeremiah answered all the people, the mighty men, and the women, and all the people that returned him *these* words for an answer, saying,

²¹ "Did not the Lord remember the incense which you burned in the cities of Judah, and in the streets of Jerusalem—you, and your fathers, and your kings, and your princes, and the people of the land? Did it not enter into His heart?

²² And the Lord could no longer bear *you*, because of the wickedness of your doings, and because of your abominations which you wrought; and so your land became a desolation and a waste, and a curse, as it is this day.

²³ Because of your burning incense, and *because* of the things in which you sinned against the Lord. And you have not obeyed the voice of the Lord, and you have not walked in His ordinances, and in His law, and in His testimonies; and so these evils have come upon you."

²⁴ And Jeremiah said to the people, and to the women, "Hear the word of the Lord.

²⁵ Thus says the Lord God of Israel: You women have spoken with your mouth, and you have fulfilled *it* with your hands, saying, 'We will surely perform our vows that we have vowed, to burn incense to the queen of heaven, and to pour drink offerings to her.' Full well did you keep to your vows, and you have indeed performed *them*.

²⁶ Therefore hear the word of the Lord, all *you* Jews dwelling in the land of Egypt: Behold, I have sworn by My great name, says the Lord, My name shall no longer be in the mouth of every Jew to say, 'The Lord lives,' in all the land of Egypt.

²⁷ For I have watched over them, to hurt them, and not to do them good. And all the Jews dwelling in the land of Egypt shall perish by sword and by famine, until they are utterly consumed.

²⁸ And they that escape the sword shall return to the land of Judah few in number, and the remnant of Judah, who have continued in the land *of* Egypt to dwell there, shall know whose word shall stand.

²⁹ And this *shall be* a sign to you, that I will visit you for evil.

³⁰ Thus said the Lord: Behold, I *will* give Hophra king of Egypt into the hands of his enemy, and into the hands of one that seeks his life, as I gave Zedekiah king of Judah into the hands of Nebuchadnezzar king of Babylon, his enemy, and who sought his life."

JEREMIAH CHAPTER 45

A Word of Comfort to Baruch

¹ The word which Jeremiah the prophet spoke to Baruch son of Neriah, when he wrote these words in the book by

the mouth of Jeremiah, in the fourth year of Jehoiakim the son of Josiah king of Judah.

2 Thus says the Lord to you, O Baruch:

3 "Seeing that you have said, 'Alas! alas! For the Lord has laid a grievous trouble upon me; I lay down in groaning, *and* I find no rest.'

4 Thus you shall say to him, 'Thus says the Lord: Behold, I pull down those whom I have built up, and I pluck up those whom I have planted.

5 And will you seek great things for yourself? Seek *them* not. For behold, I bring evil upon all flesh, says the Lord; but I will give *to you* your life for a prize in every place that you go."

JEREMIAH CHAPTER 46

Judgment of Egypt

1 In the beginning of the reign of King Zedekiah, there came this word concerning the nations.

2 For Egypt, against the power of Pharaoh Necho king of Egypt, who was by the river Euphrates in Carchemish, whom Nebuchadnezzar king of Babylon struck in the fourth year of Jehoiakim king of Judah:

3 "Take up arms and spears, and draw close to battle;

4 and harness the horses. Mount, you horsemen, and stand ready in your helmets; advance the spears, and put on your breastplates.

5 Why do they fear, and turn back? Even their mighty men shall be slain; they have utterly fled, and being hemmed in they have not rallied, says the Lord.

6 Let not the swift flee, and let not the mighty man escape to the north. Those at the Euphrates have become feeble, and they have fallen.

7 Who is this *that* shall come up as a river, and as rivers roll *their* waves?

8 The waters of Egypt shall come up like a river. And he said, 'I will go up, and will cover the earth, and will destroy its inhabitants.'

9 Mount the horses, prepare the chariots; go forth, you warriors of the Ethiopians, and Libyans armed with shields; and mount, you Libyans, bend the bow.

10 And that day *shall be* to the Lord our God a day of vengeance, to take vengeance on His enemies. And the sword of the Lord shall devour, and be glutted, and be drunken with their blood; for the Lord *has* a sacrifice from the land of the north at the River Euphrates.

11 Go up to Gilead, and take balm for the virgin daughter of Egypt. In vain have you multiplied your medicines; there is no help for you.

12 The nations have heard your voice, and the land has been filled with your cry; for the warriors have fainted fighting, one against another, *and* both have fallen together."

Babylonia Will Strike Egypt

13 The words which the Lord spoke by Jeremiah, concerning the coming of the king of Babylon to strike the land of Egypt.

14 "Proclaim *it* at Migdol, and declare *it* at Memphis. Say, 'Stand up, and prepare; for the sword has devoured your yew tree.'

15 Why has Apis fled from you? Your choice calf has not remained; for the Lord has utterly weakened him.

16 And your multitude has fainted and fallen; and each one has said to his neighbor, 'Let us arise, and return into our country to our people, from the Grecian sword.'

17 Call on the name of Pharaoh Necho king of Egypt; he has passed the appointed time.

18 *As* I live, says the Lord God, he shall come, *surely* as Tabor is among the mountains, and as Carmel that is on the sea.

19 O daughter of Egypt dwelling *at home*, prepare for yourselves stuff for removing: for Memphis shall be utterly desolate, and shall be called 'Woe,' because there are no inhabitants in it.

20 "Egypt is a fair heifer, *but* destruction from the north has come upon her.

21 Also her hired *soldiers* in the midst of her are as fatted calves fed in her; for they also have turned, and fled with one accord. They did not stand, for the day of destruction had come upon them, and the time of their retribution.

22 Their voice is as *that* of a hissing serpent, for they go upon the sand. They shall come upon Egypt with axes, as men that cut wood.

23 They shall cut down her forest, says the Lord, for *their number* cannot at all be determined, for it exceeds the locust in multitude, and they are innumerable.

24 The daughter of Egypt is confounded; she is delivered into the hands of a people from the north.

25 Behold, I *will* avenge Ammon her son upon Pharaoh, and upon them that trust in him."

26 (This verse omitted in LXX)

God Will Preserve Israel

27 "But fear not, My servant Jacob, neither be alarmed, Israel; for behold, I will save you from afar, and your descendants from their captivity; and Jacob shall return, and be at ease, and sleep, and there shall be no one to trouble him.

28 Do not fear, My servant Jacob, says the Lord; for I am with you. She *that was* without fear and in luxury, has been delivered up; for I will make a full end of every nation among whom I have thrust you forth. But I will not cause you to fail. Yet will I chastise you in the way of judgment, and will not hold you entirely guiltless."

JEREMIAH CHAPTER 47

Judgment on the Philistines

¹ Thus says the Lord against the Philistines:

² "Behold, waters come up from the north, and shall become a sweeping torrent, and it shall sweep away the land, and its fullness. The city, and them that dwell in it; and men shall cry and all that dwell in the land shall howl,

³ at the sound of his rushing, at *the sound of* his hoofs, and at the rattling of his chariots, at the noise of his wheels. The fathers did not turn to their children because of the weakness of their hands,

⁴ in the day that is coming to destroy all the Philistines. And I will utterly destroy Tyre and Sidon and all the rest of their allies; for the Lord will destroy the remaining *inhabitants* of the islands.

⁵ Baldness has come upon Gaza; Ashkelon is cast away, and the remnant of the Enakim."

⁶ "How long will you strike, O sword of the Lord? How long will it be till you are quiet? Return into your sheath; rest, and be removed.

⁷ How shall it be quiet, seeing the Lord has given it a commission against Ashkelon, and against the regions on the sea coast, to awake against the remaining *countries*!"

JEREMIAH CHAPTER 48

Judgment on Moab

¹ Thus says the Lord concerning Moab: "Woe to Nebo! For it has perished. Kirjathaim is taken; Amath and Agath are put to shame.

² There is no longer any healing for Moab, *nor* glorying in Heshbon. He has devised evils against her. We have cut her off from *being* a nation, and she shall be completely still. After you shall go a sword;

³ for *there is* a voice of *men* crying out of Horonaim, destruction and great ruin.

⁴ Moab is ruined, proclaim *it* to Zoar;

⁵ for Aloth is filled with weeping; one shall go up weeping by the way of Horonaim; you have heard a cry of destruction.

⁶ "Flee, and save your lives, and you shall be as a wild donkey in the desert.

⁷ Since you have trusted in your stronghold, therefore you shall be taken; and Chemosh shall go forth into captivity, and his priests, and his princes together.

⁸ And destruction shall come upon every city, it shall by no means escape. The valley also shall perish, and the plain country shall be completely destroyed, as the Lord has said.

⁹ Set marks upon Moab, for she shall be hit with a plague, and all her cities shall become desolate; where *shall there be* an inhabitant for her?

¹⁰ Cursed is the man that does the works of the Lord carelessly, keeping back his sword from blood.

¹¹ "Moab has been at ease from a child, and trusted in his glory; he has not poured out *his liquor* from vessel to vessel, and has not gone into banishment, therefore his taste remained in him, and his smell did not depart.

¹² Therefore behold, his days are coming, says the Lord, when I shall send upon him bad leaders, and they shall lead him astray, and they shall utterly break in pieces his possessions, and shall cut off his horns.

¹³ And Moab shall be ashamed of Chemosh, as the house of Israel was ashamed of Bethel their hope, having trusted in them.

¹⁴ How will you say, 'We are strong, and men strong for war?'

¹⁵ Moab is ruined, *even* his city, and his choice young men have gone down to slaughter.

¹⁶ The day of Moab is near at hand, and his iniquity moves swiftly *to vengeance*.

¹⁷ Shake *the head* at him, all you that are round about him; all *of you* utter his name. Say, 'How is the glorious staff broken to pieces, the rod of magnificence!'

¹⁸ Come down from *your* glory, and sit down in a damp place. Dibon shall be broken, because Moab is destroyed. There has gone up against you one to ravage your stronghold.

¹⁹ Stand by the way, and look, you that dwell in Aroer; and ask him that is fleeing, and him that escapes, and say, 'What has happened?'

²⁰ Moab is put to shame, because he is broken. Howl and cry, proclaim in Arnon, that Moab has perished.

²¹ And judgment is coming against the land of Misor, upon Chelon, and Rephas, and Mophas,

²² and upon Dibon, and upon Nebo, and upon Beth Diblathaim,

²³ and upon Kirjathaim, and upon Beth Gamul, and upon Beth Meon,

²⁴ and upon Kerioth, and upon Bozrah, and upon all the cities of Moab, far and near.

²⁵ The horn of Moab is broken, and his arm is crushed.

²⁶ "Make him drunk; for he has magnified himself against the Lord. And Moab shall clap with his hand, and shall be also himself a laughing stock.

²⁷ For surely Israel was to you a laughing stock, and was found among your thefts, because you fought against him.

²⁸ The inhabitants of Moab have left the cities, and dwelt in rocks; they have become as doves nestling in rocks, at the mouth of a cave.

²⁹ And I have heard of the pride of Moab, he has greatly heightened his pride and his haughtiness, and his heart has been lifted up.

³⁰ But I know his works. Is it not enough for him? Has he not done thus?

³¹ Therefore howl for Moab on all sides; cry out against the shorn men *in* a gloomy place. I will weep for you,

³² O vine of Sibmah, as with the weeping of Jazer. Your branches are gone over the sea, they reached the cities of

Jazer; destruction has come upon your fruits, *and* upon your grape gatherers.

33 Joy and gladness have been utterly swept off the land of Moab; and *though* there was wine in your presses, in the morning they did not tred the grapes, neither in the evening did they raise the cry of joy.

34 "From the cry of Heshbron even to Elealeh their cities uttered their voice, from Zoar to Horonaim, and their tidings *as* a heifer of three years old, for the water also of Nimrim shall be dried up.

35 And I will destroy Moab, says the Lord, as he comes up to the altar, and burns incense to his gods.

36 Therefore the heart of Moab shall sound as pipes, My heart shall sound as a pipe for the shorn men; forasmuch as what *every* man has gained has perished from him.

37 They shall all have their heads shaved in every place, and every beard shall be shaved; and all hands shall beat *their breasts*, and on all loins shall be sackcloth.

38 And on all the housetops of Moab, and in his streets *shall be mourining*; for I have broken *him*, says the Lord, as a vessel, which is useless.

39 How has he changed! How has Moab turned *his* back! Moab is put to shame, and become a laughing stock, and an object of anger to all that are round about him.

40 "For thus said the Lord:

41 Kerioth is taken, and the strongholds have been taken together.

42 And Moab shall perish from being a multitude, because he has magnified himself against the Lord.

43 A snare, and fear, and the pit, are upon you, O inhabitant of Moab.

44 He that flees from the terror shall fall into the pit, and he that comes up out of the pit shall even be taken in the snare; for I will bring these things upon Moab in the year of their visitation."

45 (This verse omitted in LXX)

46 (This verse omitted in LXX)

47 (This verse omitted in LXX)

JEREMIAH CHAPTER 49

Judgment on Ammon

1 Concerning the sons of Ammon, thus says the Lord: "Are there no sons in Israel? Or have they no one to succeed *them*? Why has Milcom inherited Gilead, and why shall their people dwell in their cities?

2 Therefore behold, the days are coming, says the Lord, when I will cause a tumult of wars to be heard in Rabbah; and they shall become a waste and ruined place, and her altars shall be burned with fire; then shall Israel succeed to his dominion.

3 Howl, O Heshbron, for Ai has perished; cry, you daughters of Rabbah, gird yourselves with sackcloth, and lament; for

Milcom shall go into banishment, his priests and his princes together.

4 Why do you boast in the plains of the Enakim, you haughty daughter, that trust in *your* treasures, that say, Who shall come in to me?

5 Behold, I *will* bring terror upon you, says the Lord, from all the country round about you; and you shall be scattered, everyone right before him, and there is none to gather you."

6 (This verse omitted in LXX)

Judgment on Edom

7 Concerning Edom, thus says the Lord: "There is no longer wisdom in Teman, counsel has perished from the wise ones, their wisdom is gone,

8 their place has been deceived. Dig deep for a dwelling, you that inhabit Dedan, for he has wrought grievously. I have brought trouble upon him in the time at which I visited him.

9 For grape gatherers have come, who shall not leave to you a remnant; as thieves by night, they shall lay their hand upon *your possessions*.

10 For I have stripped Esau, I have uncovered their secret places; they shall have no power to hide themselves, they have perished, *each* by the hand of his brother, My neighbor, and it is impossible

11 for your fatherless one to be left to live, but I shall live, and the widows trust in Me.

12 "For thus says the Lord: They who were not appointed to drink the cup have drunk; and you shall by no means be cleared.

13 For by Myself I have sworn, says the Lord, that you shall be in the midst of her an impassable *land*, and a reproach, and a curse; and all her cities shall be deserted forever."

14 I have heard a report from the Lord, and He has sent messengers to the nations, *saying,* "Assemble yourselves, and come against her; rise up to war.

15 I have made you small among the nations, utterly contemptible among men.

16 Your insolence has risen up against you, the fierceness of your heart has burst the holes of the rocks, it has seized upon the strength of a lofty hill; for as an eagle he set his nest on high; from there will I bring you down.

17 And Edom shall be a desert; everyone that passes by shall hiss at it.

18 As Sodom and Gomorrah were overthrown, and they that sojourned in her, says the Lord Almighty, no man shall dwell there, nor shall any son of man inhabit there.

19 Behold, he shall come up as a lion out of the midst of the Jordan to the place of Etham; for I will speedily drive them from it, and I will set the young men against her; for who is like Me? And who will withstand Me? And who *is* this shepherd, who shall confront Me?

20 "Therefore hear the counsel of the Lord which He has framed against Edom, and his device, which he has devised against the inhabitants of Teman: surely the least of the

sheep shall be swept off; surely their dwelling shall be made desolate for them.

21 For at the sound of their fall the earth was scared, and the cry of the sea was not heard.

22 Behold, He shall look *upon her* as an eagle, and spread forth *His* wings over her strongholds; and the heart of the mighty men of Edom shall be in that day as the heart of a woman in her pangs."

Judgment on Damascus

23 Concerning Damascus: "Hamath is brought to shame, and Arpad; for they have heard an evil report. They are amazed, they are angry, they shall be utterly unable to rest.

24 Damascus is utterly weakened, she is put to flight; trembling has seized upon her.

25 How has she not left My city, they have loved the village?

26 Therefore shall the young men fall in your streets, and all your warriors shall fall, says the Lord.

27 And I will kindle a fire in the wall of Damascus, and it shall devour the streets of the son of Ader."

Judgment on Kedar and Hazor

28 Concerning Kedar, the queen of the palace, whom Nebuchadnezzar king of Babylon struck, thus says the Lord: "Arise, and go up to Kedar, and fill the sons of Kedem.

29 They shall take their tents and their sheep, they shall take for themselves their garments, and all their baggage and their camels; and summon destruction against them from every side.

30 Flee, dig very deep for a dwelling place, you that dwell in the palace; for the king of Babylon has framed a counsel, and devised a plan against you.

31 Rise up, and go up against a nation settled *and* dwelling at ease, who have no doors, nor bolts, nor bars, *who* dwell alone.

32 And their camels shall be a spoil, and the multitude of their cattle shall be destroyed; and I will scatter them as chaff with every wind, having their hair cut about their foreheads; I will bring on their overthrow from all sides," says the Lord.

33 "And the palace shall be a resting place for ostriches, and desolate forever. No man shall abide there, and no son of man shall dwell there."

Judgment on Elam

34 The prophecies of Jeremiah against the nations of Elam:

35 Thus says the Lord: "The bow of Elam is broken, *even* the chief of their power.

36 And I will bring upon Elam the four winds from the four corners of heaven, and I will disperse them toward all these winds; and there shall be no nation *to* which they shall not come, *even* the outcasts of Elam.

37 And I will put them in fear before their enemies that seek their life; and I will bring evils upon them according to My great anger; and I will send forth My sword after them, until I have utterly destroyed them.

38 And I will set My throne in Elam, and I will send forth from there king and rulers.

39 But it shall come to pass at the end of days, that I will turn the captivity of Elam," says the Lord.

JEREMIAH CHAPTER 50

Judgment on Babylon

1 The word of the Lord which He spoke against Babylon:

2 "Proclaim among the Gentiles, and cause the tidings to be heard, and do not suppress *them*. Say, 'Babylon is taken, Bel is confounded; the fearless, the luxurious Merodach is delivered up.'

3 For a nation has come up against her from the north, he shall utterly ravage her land, and there shall be none to dwell in it, neither man nor beast.

4 "In those days, and at that time, the children of Israel shall come, they and the children of Judah together; they shall proceed, weeping as they go, seeking the Lord their God.

5 They shall ask the way till *they come to* Zion, for that way shall they set their face; and they shall come and flee for refuge to the Lord their God; for the everlasting covenant shall not be forgotten.

6 "My people have been lost sheep; their shepherds thrust them out, they caused them to wander on the mountains; they went from mountain to hill, they forgot their resting place.

7 All that found them consumed them. Their enemies said, 'Let us not leave them alone, because they have sinned against the Lord. He that gathered their fathers *had a* pasture of righteousness.'

8 "Flee out of the midst of Babylon, and from the land of the Chaldeans, and go forth, and be as serpents before sleep.

9 For behold, I shall stir up against Babylon the gatherings of nations out of the land of the north, and they shall set themselves in array against her. From there shall she be taken, as the dart of an expert warrior shall not return empty.

10 And Chaldea shall be a spoil. All that spoil her shall be satisfied.

11 "Because you rejoiced, and boasted, *while* plundering My heritage; because you exulted as calves in the grass, and pushed with the horn as bulls.

12 Your mother is greatly ashamed; your mother that bore you for prosperity is confounded. *She is* the last of the nations, desolate,

13 by reason of the Lord's anger. It shall not be inhabited, but it all shall be a desolation; and everyone that passes through Babylon shall scowl, and they shall hiss at all her plagues.

14 Set yourselves in array against Babylon round about, all you that bend the bow; shoot at her, do not spare your arrows,

15 and prevail against her. Her hands are weakened, her bulwarks are fallen, and her wall is broken down; for it is vengeance from God. Take vengeance upon her; as she has done, so do to her.

16 Utterly destroy the seed out of Babylon, *and* him that holds a sickle in time of harvest; for fear of the Grecian sword, they shall return everyone to his people, and everyone shall flee to his own land.

17 "Israel is a wandering sheep; the lions have driven him out. The king of Assyria first devoured him, and afterward this king of Babylon *has gnawed* his bones.

18 Therefore thus says the Lord: Behold, I *will* take vengeance on the king of Babylon, and upon his land, as I took vengeance on the king of Assyria.

19 And I will restore Israel to his pasture, and he shall feed on Carmel and on Mount Ephraim and in Gilead, and his soul shall be satisfied.

20 In those days, and at that time, they shall seek for the iniquity of Israel, and there shall be none; and for the sins of Judah, and they shall not be found; for I will be merciful to them that are left on the land, says the Lord.

21 Go up against it roughly, and against them that dwell on it. Avenge, O sword, and destroy utterly, says the Lord, and do according to all that I command you.

22 A sound of war, and great destruction in the land of the Chaldeans!

23 How has the hammer of the whole earth been broken and crushed! How has Babylon become a desolation among the nations!

24 They shall come upon you, and you shall not know it, O Babylon, that you will even be taken captive. You are found and taken, because you resisted the Lord.

25 The Lord has opened His treasury, and brought forth the weapons of His anger; for the Lord God *has* a work in the land of the Chaldeans.

26 For her times have come. Open her storehouses; search her as a cave, and utterly destroy her; let there be no remnant of her.

27 Dry up all her fruits, and let them go down to the slaughter. Woe to them! For their day has come, and the time of their retribution.

28 A voice of men fleeing and escaping from the land of Babylon, to declare to Zion the vengeance *that comes* from the Lord our God.

29 "Summon many against Babylon, everyone that bends the bow. Camp against her round about; let none of her *people* escape. Render to her according to her works, according to all that she has done, do to her; for she has resisted the Lord, the Holy God of Israel.

30 Therefore shall her young men fall in the streets, and all her warriors shall be cast down, says the Lord.

31 Behold, I am against you, O haughty one, says the Lord; for your day has come, and the time of your retribution.

32 And your pride shall fail, and fall, and there shall be no one to set it up again. And I will kindle a fire in her forest, and it shall devour all things round about her.

33 "Thus says the Lord: The children of Israel and the children of Judah have been oppressed. All those that have taken them captive have oppressed them together, for they would not let them go.

34 But their Redeemer is strong; the Lord Almighty is His name. He will enter into judgment with His adversaries, that He may destroy the earth;

35 and He will sharpen a sword against the Chaldeans, and against the inhabitants of Babylon, and upon her nobles and upon her wise men.

36 A sword upon her warriors, and they shall be weakened. A sword upon their horses, and upon their chariots.

37 A sword upon their warriors and upon the mixed people in the midst of her; and they shall be as women. A sword upon the treasures, and they shall be scattered upon her water,

38 and they shall be ashamed; for it is a land of graven *images*; and in the islands, where they boasted.

39 Therefore shall idols dwell in the islands, and the young ostriches shall dwell in it. It shall not be inhabited anymore, forever.

40 As God overthrew Sodom and Gomorrah, and the cities bordering upon them, says the Lord: no man shall dwell there, and no son of man shall sojourn there.

41 "Behold, a people comes from the north, and a great nation, and many kings shall be stirred up from the end of the earth, holding bow and dagger.

42 *The people* are fierce, and will have no mercy; their voices shall sound as the sea, they shall ride upon horses, prepared for war, like fire, against you, O daughter of Babylon.

43 The king of Babylon heard the sound of them, and his hands grew feeble. Anguish overcame him, pangs as of a woman in travail.

44 Behold, he shall come up as a lion from Jordan to Gaethan; for I will speedily drive them from her, and I will set all the youths against her; for who is like Me? And who will resist Me? And who is this shepherd who will stand before Me?

45 Therefore hear the counsel of the Lord, which He has taken against Babylon; and His devices, which He has devised upon the Chaldeans inhabiting *it*. Surely lambs of their flock shall be destroyed. Surely pasture shall be cut off from them.

46 Or at the sound of the taking of Babylon the earth shall quake, and a cry shall be heard among the nations."

JEREMIAH CHAPTER 51

1 Thus says the Lord: "Behold, I stir up against Babylon, and against the Chaldeans dwelling there, a deadly burning wind.

2 And I will send forth against Babylon spoilers, and they shall spoil her, and shall ravage her land. Woe to Babylon round about *her* in the day of her affliction.

3 Let the archer bend his bow, and him that has armor put it on, and do not spare her young men, but destroy all her host.

4 And slain men shall fall in the land of the Chaldeans, and *men* pierced through shall fall without it.

5 For Israel and Judah have not been forsaken of their God, of the Lord Almighty; whereas their land was filled with iniquity against the holy things of Israel."

6 Flee from the midst of Babylon, and deliver everyone his soul; and do not be overthrown in her iniquity; for it is the time of her retribution from the Lord. He is rendering to her a recompense.

7 Babylon has been a golden cup in the Lord's hand, causing all the earth to be drunken. The nations have drunk of her wine; therefore they were shaken.

8 And Babylon has fallen suddenly, and is broken to pieces. Lament for her; take balm for her deadly wound, if by any means she may be healed.

9 We tried to heal Babylon, but she was not healed. Let us forsake her, and depart everyone to his own country; for her judgment has reached to the heaven, it has mounted up to the stars.

10 The Lord has brought forth His judgment. Come, and let us declare in Zion the works of the Lord our God.

11 Prepare the arrows; fill the quivers. The Lord has stirred up the spirit of the king of the Medes; for His wrath is against Babylon, to destroy it utterly; for it is the Lord's vengeance, it is the vengeance of His people.

12 Lift up a standard on the walls of Babylon, prepare the quivers, rouse the guards, prepare the weapons; for the Lord has taken *the work* in hand, and will execute what He has spoken against the inhabitants of Babylon,

13 dwelling on many waters, and amidst the abundance of her treasures. Assuredly your end has come, into your inward parts.

14 For the Lord has sworn by His arm, *saying*, "I will fill you with men as with locusts; and they that come down shall cry against you."

15 The Lord made the earth by His power, preparing the world by His wisdom, by His understanding He stretched out the heaven.

16 At *His* voice He makes a sound of water in the heaven, and brings up clouds from the extremity of the earth. He makes the lightning for rain, and brings light out of His treasuries.

17 Every man has completely lost understanding; every goldsmith is confounded because of his graven *images*; for they have cast false *gods;* there is no breath in them.

18 They are vain works, objects of scorn; in the time of their visitation they shall perish.

19 Not so is Jacob's portion; for He that formed all things, He is his inheritance; the Lord is His name.

20 "You scatter for Me the weapons of war, and I will scatter nations by you, and will destroy kings by means of you.

21 And by you I will scatter the horse and his rider; and by you I will scatter chariots and them that ride in them.

22 And by you I will scatter youth and maid; and by you I will scatter man and woman.

23 And by you I will scatter the shepherd and his flock; and by you I will scatter the farmer and his yoke of oxen; and by you I will scatter leaders and the captains.

24 "And I will recompense to Babylon and to all the Chaldeans that dwell *there* all the evil that they have done to Zion before your eyes, says the Lord.

25 Behold, I am against you, the ruined mountain, that destroys the whole earth; and I will stretch out My hand upon you, and will roll you down upon the rocks, and will make you as a burnt mountain.

26 And they shall not take from you a stone for a corner, nor a stone for a foundation; for you shall be a desolation forever, says the Lord.

27 Set up a standard in the land, sound the trumpet among the nations, consecrate the nations against her, raise up kings against her by Me, and for the people of Ashkenaz; set against her engines of war; bring up against her horses as a multitude of locusts.

28 Bring up nations against her, *even* the king of the Medes and of the whole earth, his rulers, and all his captains.

29 The earth has quaked and been troubled, because the purpose of the Lord has risen up against Babylon, to make the land of Babylon a desolation, and uninhabitable.

30 The warrior of Babylon has failed to fight; they shall sit there in the siege. Their power is broken; they have become like women; her tabernacles have been set on fire; her bars are broken.

31 One shall rush, running to meet *another* runner, and one shall *go* with tidings to meet *another* with tidings, to bring tidings to the king of Babylon, that his city is taken.

32 At the end of his passages they were taken, and his cisterns they have burned with fire, and his warriors are going forth.

33 "For thus says the Lord: The houses of the king of Babylon shall be threshed as a floor in the season; yet a little while, and her harvest shall come."

34 He has devoured me, he has torn me asunder, airy darkness has come upon me; Nebuchadnezzar king of Babylon has swallowed me up, as a dragon has he filled his belly with my delicacies.

35 My troubles and my distresses have driven me out into Babylon, shall she that dwells in Zion say; and my blood *shall be* upon the Chaldeans dwelling *there*, shall Jerusalem say.

36 Therefore thus says the Lord: "Behold, I will judge your adversary, and I will execute vengeance for you; and I will waste her sea, and dry up her fountain.

37 And Babylon shall be a desolation, and shall not be inhabited.

38 For they rose up together as lions, and as lions' whelps.

39 In their excitement I will give them a drink, and make them drunk, that they may be stupefied, and sleep an everlasting sleep, and not awake, says the Lord.

40 And bring them down as lambs to the slaughter, and rams with kids.

41 How has the boast of all the earth been taken and caught in a snare! How has Babylon become a desolation among the nations!

42 The sea has come up upon Babylon with the sound of its waves, and she is covered.

43 Her cities have become like a dry and trackless land; not so much as one *soul* shall dwell in it, neither shall a son of man lodge in it.

44 And I will take vengeance on Babylon, and bring forth out of her mouth what she has swallowed down, and the nations shall no more be gathered to her."

45 (This verse omitted in LXX)

46 (This verse omitted in LXX)

47 (This verse omitted in LXX)

48 (This verse omitted in LXX)

49 And in Babylon the slain men of all the earth shall fall.

50 Go forth of the land, you that escape, and do not stay; you that are afar off, remember the Lord, and let Jerusalem come into your mind.

51 We are ashamed, because we have heard our reproach; disgrace has covered our face; aliens have come into our sanctuary, *even* into the house of the Lord.

52 "Therefore behold, the days are coming, says the Lord, when I will take vengeance upon her graven *images;* and slain men shall fall in all her land.

53 For though Babylon should go up as the heaven, and though she should strengthen her walls with her power, from Me shall come they that shall destroy her, says the Lord."

54 A sound of a cry in Babylon, and great destruction in the land of the Chaldeans;

55 for the Lord has utterly destroyed Babylon, and cut off from her the great voice sounding as many waters; He has consigned her voice to destruction.

56 For distress has come upon Babylon, her warriors are taken, their bows are useless; for God has recompensed them.

57 "The Lord recompenses, and will make her leaders and her wise men and her captains completely drunk," says the King, the Lord Almighty is His name.

58 Thus says the Lord: "The wall of Babylon was made broad, but it shall be completely broken down, and her high gates shall be burned with fire; and the people shall not labor in vain, nor the nations fail in *their* rule."

59 The word which the Lord commanded the prophet Jeremiah to say to Seraiah son of Neriah, son of Mahseiah, when he went from Zedekiah king of Judah to Babylon, in the fourth year of his reign. And Seraiah was over the bounties.

60 And Jeremiah wrote in a book all the evils which should come upon Babylon, *even* all these words that are written against Babylon.

61 And Jeremiah said to Seraiah, "When you have come to Babylon, and shall see and read all these words;

62 then you shall say, 'O Lord God, You have spoken against this place to destroy it, and that there should be none to dwell in it, neither man nor beast; for it shall be a desolation forever.'

63 And it shall come to pass, when you shall cease from reading this book, that you shall bind a stone upon it, and cast it into the midst of the Euphrates;

64 and shall say, 'Thus shall Babylon sink, and not rise, because of the evils which I bring upon it.'"

JEREMIAH CHAPTER 52

The Destruction of Jerusalem Reviewed

1 Zedekiah was twenty-one years old when he began to reign, and he reigned eleven years in Jerusalem. And his mother's name was Hamutal, the daughter of Jeremiah, of Libnah.

2 (This verse omitted in LXX)

3 (This verse omitted in LXX)

4 And it came to pass in the ninth year of his reign, in the ninth month, on the tenth day of the month, *that* Nebuchadnezzr king of Babylon came, and all his army, against Jerusalem, and they made a rampart round it, and built a wall round about it with large stones.

5 So the city was besieged, until the eleventh year of King Zedekiah,

6 on the ninth day of the month. And *then* the famine was severe in the city, and there was no bread for the people of the land.

7 And the city was broken up, and all the men of war went out by night by the way of the gate, between the wall and the outworks, which were by the king's garden. And the Chaldeans were by the city round about; and they went by the way *leading* to the wilderness.

8 But the army of the Chaldeans pursued after the king, and overtook him beyond Jericho. And all his servants were dispersed.

9 And they took the king, and brought him to the king of Babylon to Riblah, and he judged him.

10 And the king of Babylon killed the sons of Zedekiah before his eyes; and he killed all the princes of Judah in Riblah.

11 And he put out the eyes of Zedekiah, and bound him in fetters. And the king of Babylon brought him to Babylon, and put him into the grinding-house, until the day he died.

12 And in the fifth month, on the tenth day of the month, Nabuzaradan the captain of the guard, who waited on the king of Babylon, came to Jerusalem;

13 and he burned the house of the Lord, and the king's house, and all the houses of the city, and every great house he burned with fire.

14 And the army of the Chaldeans that was with the captain of the guard pulled down all the wall of Jerusalem round about.

15 (This verse omitted in LXX)

16 But the captain of the guard left the remnant of the people to be vinedressers and farmers.

17 And the Chaldeans broke in pieces the bronze pillars that were in the house of the Lord, and the bases, and the bronze sea that was in the house of the Lord, and they took the brass thereof, and carried it away to Babylon.

18 Also the rim, and the bowls, and the flesh-hooks, and all the bronze vessels, which they ministered with;

19 and the basins, and the snuffers, and the oil-funnels, and the lampstands, and the censers, and the cups, and whatever *was* solid gold, and the silver, and whatever *was* of solid silver, the captain of the guard took away.

20 And the two pillars, and the one sea, and the twelve bronze oxen under the sea, which *things* King Solomon made for the house of the Lord; the brass of which was without weight.

21 And as for the pillars, the height of one pillar was thirty-five cubits; and a line of twelve cubits compassed it round; and the thickness of it *all* round was four fingers.

22 And *there was* a bronze chapiter upon them, and the length was five cubits, *even* the height of one chapiter; and *there was* on the chapiter round about network and pomegranates, all of brass. And correspondingly the second pillar *had* eight pomegranates to a cubit for the twelve cubits.

23 And the pomegranates were ninety-six on a side; and all the pomegranates on the network round about were a hundred.

24 And the captain of the guard took the chief priest, and the second priest, and those that kept the way;

25 and one eunuch, who was over the men of war, and seven men of renown, who were in the king's presence that were found in the city; and the scribe of the forces, who did the part of a scribe to the people of the land; and sixty men of the people of the land, who were found in the midst of the city.

26 And Nabuzaradan the captain of the king's guard took them, and brought them to the king of Babylon to Riblah.

27 And the king of Babylon struck them in Riblah, in the land of Hamath.

28 (This verse omitted in LXX)

29 (This verse omitted in LXX)

30 (This verse omitted in LXX)

31 And it came to pass in the thirty-seventh year after that Jehoiakim king of Judah had been carried away captive, in the twelfth month, on the twenty-fourth *day* of the month, *that* Evil-Merodach king of Babylon, in the year in which he began to reign, raised the head of Jehoiakim king of Judah, and shaved him, and brought him out of the house where he was kept,

32 and spoke kindly to him, and set his throne above the kings that were with him in Babylon,

33 and changed his prison garments. And he ate bread continually before him all the days that he lived.

34 And his appointed portion was given him continually by the king of Babylon from day to day, until the day that he died.

THE BOOK OF LAMENTATIONS

Jerusalem in Affliction

1 And it came to pass, after Israel was taken captive, and Jerusalem made desolate, *that* Jeremiah sat weeping, and lamented with this lamentation over Jerusalem, and said:
ALEPH. How does the city that was filled with people sit solitary! She has become as a widow: she that was magnified among the nations, and princess among the provinces, has become a slave.

2 BETH. She weeps bitterly in the night, and her tears are on her cheeks; and there is none of all her lovers to comfort her: all that were her friends have dealt deceitfully with her, they have become her enemies.

3 GIMEL. Judah has gone into captivity by reason of her affliction, and by reason of the abundance of her servitude; she dwells among the nations, she has not found rest. All her pursuers have overtaken her between her oppressors.

4 DALETH. The ways of Zion mourn, because there are none that come to the feast. All her gates are ruined. Her priests groan, her virgins are led captive, and she is in bitterness in herself.

5 HE. Her oppressors have become the head, and her enemies have prospered; for the Lord has afflicted her because of the multitude of her sins. Her young children have gone into captivity before the face of the oppressor.

6 VAU. And all her beauty has been taken away from the daughter of Zion. Her princes were as rams finding no pasture, and have gone *away* in weakness before the face of the pursuer.

7 ZAIN. Jerusalem remembered the days of her affliction, and her rejection. *She thought on* all her desirable things which were from the days of old, when her people fell into the hands of the oppressor, and there was none to help her; when her enemies saw it, they laughed at her habitation.

8 HETH. Jerusalem has sinned a great sin; therefore has she come into tribulation, all that used to honor her have afflicted her, for they have seen her shame: yea, she herself groaned, and turned backward.

9 TETH. Her uncleanness is before her feet; she did not remember her former state; she has lowered her boasting *tone*, there is none to comfort her. Behold, O Lord, my affliction, for the enemy has magnified himself.

[10] JOD. The oppressor has stretched out his hand on all her desirable things, for she has seen the Gentiles entering into her sanctuary, *concerning* whom You commanded that they should not enter into Your congregation.

[11] CHAPH. All her people groan, seeking bread: they have given their desirable things for meat, to restore their soul: behold, Lord, and look; for she has become dishonored.

[12] LAMED. All you that pass by the way, turn, and see if there is sorrow likened to my sorrow, which has happened to me. The Lord who spoke by me has afflicted me in the day of His fierce anger.

[13] MEM. He has sent fire from His lofty habitation, He has brought it into my bones: He has spread a net for my feet, He has turned me back: He has made me desolate and mourning all the day.

[14] NUN. He has watched over my sins, they are woven about my hands, they have come up on my neck. My strength has failed, for the Lord has laid pains on my hands, I shall not be able to stand.

[15] SAMECH. The Lord has cut off all my strong men from the midst of me: He has summoned against me a time for crushing my choice men: the Lord has trodden a wine press for the virgin daughter of Judah: for these things I weep.

[16] AIN. My eye has poured out water, because He that should comfort me, that should restore my soul, has been removed far from me. My sons have been destroyed, because the enemy has prevailed.

[17] PHE. Zion has spread out her hand, and there is none to comfort her: the Lord has commanded concerning Jacob, his oppressors are round about him: Jerusalem has become among them as a removed woman.

[18] TSADE. The Lord is righteous, for I have provoked His mouth. Listen, I pray, all you people, and behold my grief: my virgins and my young men have gone into captivity.

[19] KOPH. I called my lovers, but they deceived me: my priests and my elders failed in the city, for they sought food that they might restore their souls, but did not find it.

[20] RHECHS. Behold, O Lord; for I am afflicted; my belly is troubled, and my heart is turned within me; for I have been grievously rebellious; abroad the sword has bereaved me, even as death at home.

[21] CHSEN. Hear, I pray you, for I groan: there is none to comfort me: all my enemies have heard of my afflictions and rejoiced, because You have done it: You have brought on the day, You have called the time: they have become like to me.

[22] THAU. Let all their wickedness come before Your face, and strip them, as they have made a gleaning for all my sins: for my groans are many, and my heart is grieved.

LAMENTATIONS CHAPTER 2

God's Anger With Jerusalem

[1] ALEPH. How has the Lord darkened in His wrath the daughter of Zion! He has cast down the glory of Israel from heaven to earth, and has not remembered His footstool.

[2] BETH. In the day of His wrath the Lord has overwhelmed *her* as in the sea, *and* not spared. He has brought down in His fury all the beautiful things of Jacob; He has brought down to the ground the strongholds of the daughter of Judah; He has profaned her kings and her princes.

[3] GIMEL. He has broken in His fierce anger the whole horn of Israel; He has turned back His right hand from the face of the enemy, and has kindled a flame in Jacob as a fire, and it has devoured all things round about.

[4] DALETH. He has bent His bow as an opposing enemy; He has strengthened His right hand as an adversary, and has destroyed all the desirable things of my eyes in the tabernacle of the daughter of Zion; He has poured forth His anger as fire.

[5] HE. The Lord has become as an enemy; He has overwhelmed Israel as in the sea, He has overwhelmed her palaces; He has destroyed her strongholds, and has multiplied the afflicted and humbled ones to the daughter of Judah.

[6] VAU. And He has scattered His tabernacle as a vine, He has marred His feast; the Lord has forgotten the feast and the Sabbath which He appointed in Zion, and in the fury of His wrath has vexed the king, priest, and prince.

[7] ZAIN. The Lord has rejected His altar, He has cast off His sanctuary, He has broken by the hand of the enemy the wall of her palaces; they have uttered their voice in the house of the Lord as on a feast day.

[8] HETH. And He has turned to destroy the wall of the daughter of Zion; He has stretched out the measuring line, He has not turned back His hand from afflicting her; therefore the bulwark mourned, and the wall was weakened with it.

[9] TETH. Her gates have sunk into the ground; He has destroyed and broken to pieces her bars, and her king and her prince among the Gentiles. There is no law; indeed, her prophets have seen no vision from the Lord.

[10] JOD. The elders of the daughter of Zion have sat upon the ground, they have kept silence; they have cast up dust upon their heads; they have girded themselves with sackcloth; they have brought down to the ground the chief virgins in Jerusalem.

[11] CHAPH. My eyes have failed with tears, my heart is troubled, my glory is cast down to the ground, for the destruction of the daughter of my people; while the infant and suckling swoon in the streets of the city.

[12] LAMED. They said to their mothers, "Where is grain and wine?" While they fainted like wounded men in the streets of the city, while their souls were poured out into their mother's bosom.

[13] MEM. What shall I testify to you, or what shall I compare to you, O daughter of Jerusalem? Who shall save and

comfort you, O virgin daughter of Zion? For the cup of your destruction is enlarged—who shall heal you?

[14] NUN. Your prophets have seen for you false and deceptive visions, and they have not discovered your iniquity, to turn back your captivity; but they have seen for you vain burdens, and worthless visions.

[15] SAMECH. All that go by the way have clapped their hands at you; they have hissed and shaken their head at the daughter of Jerusalem. "Is this the city," they say, "the crown of joy of all the earth?"

[16] AIN. All your enemies have opened their mouth against you; they have hissed and gnashed their teeth, and said, "We have swallowed her up; surely this is the day which we looked for; we have found it, we have seen it."

[17] PHE. The Lord has done that which He purposed; He has accomplished His word, even the things which He commanded from the ancient days; He has thrown down, and has not spared, and He has caused the enemy to rejoice over you, He has exalted the horn of him that afflicted you.

[18] TSADE. Their heart cried to the Lord, "You walls of Zion, pour down tears like torrents day and night: give yourself no rest; let not the apple of your eyes cease."

[19] KOPH. Arise, rejoice in the night at the beginning of your watch: pour out your heart as water before the face of the Lord, lift up your hands to Him for the life of your infants, who faint from hunger at the top of all the streets.

[20] RHECHS. Behold, O Lord, and see for whom You have gathered thus. Shall the women eat the fruit of their womb? The cook has made a gathering: shall the infants nursing at the breasts be slain? Will You slay the priest and prophet in the sanctuary of the Lord?

[21] CHSEN. The child and old man have lain down in the street; my virgins and my young men have gone into captivity; You have slain them with the sword and with famine; in the day of Your wrath You have mangled them, You have not spared.

[22] THAU. He has called my sojourners round about to a solemn day, and there was not in the day of the wrath of the Lord any one that escaped, or was left; whereas I have strengthened and multiplied all my enemies.

LAMENTATIONS CHAPTER 3

God's Steadfast Love Endures

[1] ALEPH. I am the man that sees poverty, through the rod of His wrath upon me.

[2] He has taken me, and led me away into darkness, and not *into* light.

[3] And against me has He turned His hand all the day.

[4] He has made old my flesh and my skin; He has broken my bones.

[5] BETH. He has built against me, and compassed my head, and brought travail upon me.

[6] He has set me in dark places, as them that have long been dead.

[7] He has hedged me in, and I cannot come forth; He has made my bronze chain heavy.

[8] GIMEL. Yea, *though* I cry and shout, He shuts out my prayer.

[9] DALETH. He has built up my ways, He has hedged my paths;

[10] He has troubled me, as a female bear lying in wait; He is to me as a lion in secret places.

[11] He pursued *me* after I departed, and brought me to a stand; He has utterly ruined me.

[12] HE. He has bent His bow, and set me as a mark for the arrow.

[13] He has caused the arrows of His quiver to enter into my reins.

[14] I have become a laughing stock to all my people; and their song all the day.

[15] VAU. He has filled me with bitterness, He has drenched me with gall.

[16] And He has dashed out my teeth with gravel, He has fed me with ashes.

[17] He has also removed my soul from peace: I have forgotten prosperity.

[18] Therefore my success has perished, and my hope from the Lord.

[19] ZAIN. I remembered by reason of my poverty, and because of persecution my bitterness and gall shall be remembered;

[20] and my soul shall meditate with me.

[21] This will I lay up in my heart, therefore I will endure.

[22] HETH. *It is through* the mercies of the Lord that He has not failed me, because His compassions are not exhausted. Pity us, O Lord, early every month: for we are not brought to an end, because His compassions are not exhausted.

[23] They are new every morning: great is Your faithfulness.

[24] "The Lord is my portion," says my soul; therefore will I wait for Him.

[25] TETH. The Lord is good to them that wait for Him; the soul which shall seek Him

[26] is good, and shall wait for, and quietly expect salvation from the Lord.

[27] TETH. It is good for a man when he bears a yoke in his youth.

[28] He will sit alone, and be silent, because he has borne it upon him.

[29] (This verse omitted in LXX)

[30] JOD. He will give his cheek to him that smites him: he will be filled full with reproaches.

[31] For the Lord will not reject forever.

[32] CHAPH. For He that has brought down will pity, and that according to the abundance of His mercy.

[33] He has not answered in anger from His heart, though He has brought low the children of men.

34 LAMED. To bring down under His feet all the prisoners of the earth,

35 to turn aside the judgment of a man before the face of the Most High,

36 to condemn a man unjustly in his judgment, the Lord has not given commandment.

37 Who has thus spoken, and it has come to pass? The Lord has not commanded it.

38 Out of the mouth of the Most High there shall not come forth evil and good.

39 MEM. Why should a living man complain, a man concerning his sin?

40 NUN. Our way has been searched out and examined, and we will turn to the Lord.

41 Let us lift up our hearts with our hand to the lofty One in heaven.

42 We have sinned, we have transgressed; and You have not pardoned.

43 SAMECH. You has visited us in wrath, and driven us away; You have slain, You have not pitied.

44 You have veiled Yourself with a cloud because of prayer, that I might be blind, and be cast off.

45 AIN. You have set us *alone* in the midst of the nations.

46 All our enemies have opened their mouth against us.

47 Fear and wrath have come upon us, suspense and destruction.

48 My eye shall pour down torrents of water, for the destruction of the daughter of my people.

49 PHE. My eye is drowned *with tears*, and I will not be silent, so that there shall be no rest,

50 until the Lord look down, and behold from heaven.

51 My eye shall prey upon my soul, because of all the daughters of the city.

52 TSADE. The fowlers chased me as a sparrow; all my enemies destroyed my life in a pit without cause,

53 and laid a stone upon me.

54 Water flowed over my head: I said, "I am cut off."

55 KOPH. I called upon Your name, O Lord, out of the lowest dungeon.

56 You heard my voice; close not Your ears to my supplication. 57 You drew near to my help; in the day that I called upon You, You said to me, "Do not fear."

58 RECHS. O Lord, You have pleaded the causes of my soul; You have redeemed my life.

59 You have seen my troubles, O Lord; You have judged my cause.

60 You have seen all their vengeance; You have looked on all their devices against me.

61 CHSEN. You have heard their reproach and all their devices against me;

62 the lips of them that rose up against me, and their plots against me all the day;

63 their sitting down and their rising up: look upon their eyes.

64 You will render them a recompense, O Lord, according to the works of their hands.

65 THAU. You will give them as a covering, the grief of my heart.

66 You will persecute them in anger, and will consume them from under the heaven, O Lord.

LAMENTATIONS CHAPTER 4

The Punishment of Zion

1 ALEPH. How will the gold be tarnished, and the fine silver changed! The sacred stones have been poured forth at the top of all the streets.

2 BETH. The precious sons of Zion, who were equaled in value with gold, how are they counted as earthen vessels, the works of the hands of the potter!

3 GIMEL. Serpents have drawn out the breasts, they nurse their young; *but* the daughters of my people are incurably cruel, as an ostrich in a desert.

4 DALETH. The tongue of the sucking child cleaves to the roof of its mouth for thirst; the little children ask for bread, and there is none to break it for them.

5 HE. They that eat delicacies are desolate in the streets; they that used to be nursed in scarlet have clothed themselves with dung.

6 VAU. And the iniquity of the daughter of my people has been increased beyond the iniquities of Sodom, *the city* that was overthrown very suddenly, and none labored against her *with their* hands.

7 ZAIN. Her Nazarites were made purer than snow, they were whiter than milk, they were purified as with fire, their polishing was superior to sapphire stone.

8 HETH. Their countenance has become blacker than smoke; they are not known in the streets: their skin has cleaved to their bones; they are withered, they have become as a stick.

9 TETH. The slain with the sword were better than they that were slain with hunger; they have departed, pierced through from lack of the fruits of the field.

10 JOD. The hands of tender hearted women have boiled their own children; they became meat for them in the destruction of the daughter of my people.

11 CHAPH. The Lord has accomplished His wrath; He has poured out fierce anger, and has kindled a fire in Zion, and it has devoured her foundations.

12 LAMED. The kings of the earth, even all that dwell in the world, believed not that an enemy and oppressor would enter through the gates of Jerusalem.

13 MEM. For the sins of her prophets, and iniquities of her priests, who shed righteous blood in the midst of her,

14 NUN. Her watchmen staggered in the streets, they were defiled with blood in their weakness, they touched their clothing with it.

¹⁵ SAMECH. Depart from the unclean ones; call them: depart, depart, touch *them* not: for they are on fire, yea, they stagger. Say among the nations, "They shall no more sojourn *there*."

¹⁶ AIN. The presence of the Lord was their portion; but He will not again look upon them. They did not regard the priests; they did not pity the prophets.

¹⁷ PHE. While we yet lived our eyes failed, while we looked in vain for our help. We looked to a nation that could not save.

¹⁸ TSADE We have hunted for our little ones, that they should not walk in our streets. Our time has drawn near, our days are fulfilled, our time has come.

¹⁹ KOPH. Our pursuers were swifter than the eagles of the sky, they flew on the mountains, in the wilderness they laid wait for us.

²⁰ RECHS. The breath of our nostrils, our anointed Lord, was taken in their destructive snares, of whom we said, "In His shadow we shall live among the Gentiles."

²¹ CHSEN. Rejoice and be glad, O daughter of Edom, that dwell in the land; yet the cup of the Lord shall pass through to you: you shall be drunken, and pour forth.

²² THAU. O daughter of Zion, your iniquity has come to an end; He shall no longer carry you captive: He has visited your iniquities, O daughter of Edom; He has discovered your sins.

LAMENTATIONS CHAPTER 5

A Prayer for Restoration

¹ Remember, O Lord, what has happened to us: behold, and look on our reproach.

² Our inheritance has been turned away to aliens, our houses to strangers.

³ We have become orphans, we have no father, our mothers are as widows.

⁴ We have drunk our water for money; our wood is sold to us *for a burden* on our neck.

⁵ We have been persecuted, we have labored, we have had no rest.

⁶ Egypt gave the hand to us, Assyria to their own satisfaction.

⁷ Our fathers sinned, and are not: we have borne their iniquities.

⁸ Servants have ruled over us: there is none to ransom us out of their hand.

⁹ We shall bring in our bread with *danger of* our lives, because of the sword of the wilderness.

¹⁰ Our skin is blackened like an oven; they are convulsed, because of the storms of famine.

¹¹ They humbled the women in Zion, the virgins in the cities of Judah.

¹² Princes were hanged up by their hands; the elders were not honored.

¹³ The chosen men lifted up the voice in weeping, and the youths fainted under the wood.

¹⁴ And the elders ceased from the gate, the chosen men ceased from their music.

¹⁵ The joy of our heart has ceased; our dance is turned into mourning.

¹⁶ The crown has fallen from our head: woe to us, for we have sinned!

¹⁷ For this has grief come; our heart is sorrowful: for this our eyes are darkened.

¹⁸ Over the mountain of Zion, because it is made desolate, foxes have walked therein.

¹⁹ But You, O Lord, shall dwell forever; Your throne *shall endure* from generation to generation.

²⁰ Why will You utterly forget us, and abandon us a long time? ²¹ Turn us to You, O Lord, and we shall be turned; and renew our days as before.

²² For You have indeed rejected us; You have been very angry with us.

THE BOOK OF EZEKIEL

Ezekiel's Vision of God

¹ Now it came to pass in the thirtieth year, in the fourth month, on the fifth day of the month, that I was in the midst of the captivity by the River Chebar; and the heavens were opened, and I saw visions of God.

² On the fifth day of the month; this was the fifth year of the captivity of King Jehoiachin.

³ And the word of the Lord came to Ezekiel the priest, the son of Buzi, in the land of the Chaldeans, by the River Chebar; and the hand of the Lord was upon me.

⁴ And I looked, and behold, a sweeping wind came from the north, and a great cloud on it, and *there was* brightness round about it, and gleaming fire, and in the midst of it as it were the appearance of amber in the midst of the fire, and brightness in it.

⁵ And in the midst as it were the likeness of four living creatures. And this was their appearance: the likeness of a man was upon them.

⁶ And each one *had* four faces, and each one *had* four wings.

⁷ And their legs were straight; and their feet were winged, and *there were* sparks, like gleaming brass, and their wings were light.

⁸ And the hand of a man was under their wings on their four sides.

⁹ And their faces did not turn when they went; but each one went straight forward.

¹⁰ And the likeness of their faces was the face of a man, and the face of a lion on the right of the four; and the face of a calf on the left of the four; and the face of an eagle to the four.

[11] And the four had their wings spread out above; each one *had* two joined to one another, and two covered their bodies.

[12] And each one went straight forward: wherever the spirit was going they went, and turned not back.

[13] And in the midst of the living creatures *there was* an appearance as of burning coals of fire, as an appearance of lamps turning among the living creatures; and the brightness of fire, and out of the fire came forth lightning.

[14] (This verse omitted in LXX)

[15] And I looked, and behold, the four *each had* one wheel on the ground near the living creatures.

[16] And the appearance of the wheels was as the appearance of beryl: and the four had one likeness; and their work was as it were a wheel in a wheel.

[17] They went on their four sides; they did not turn as they went; [18] neither did their backs *turn*. And they were high. And I beheld them, and the backs of the four were full of eyes round about.

[19] And when the living creatures went, the wheels went by them: and when the living creatures lifted themselves off the earth, the wheels were lifted off.

[20] Wherever the cloud happened to be, there was the spirit ready to go. The wheels went and were lifted up with them; because the spirit of life was in the wheels.

[21] When those went, *the wheels* went; and when those stood, *the wheels* stood; and when those lifted themselves off the earth, they were lifted off with them, for the spirit of life was in the wheels.

[22] And the likeness over the heads of the living creatures was as a firmament, as the appearance of crystal, spread out over their wings above.

[23] And their wings were spread out under the firmament, reaching one to the other; two *wings* to each, covering their bodies.

[24] And I heard the sound of their wings when they went, as the sound of much water: and when they stood, their wings were let down.

[25] And lo! A voice from above the firmament

[26] that was over their head, there was as the appearance of a sapphire stone, *and* the likeness of a throne upon it. And upon the likeness of the throne was the likeness as an appearance of a man above.

[27] And I saw as it were the resemblance of amber from the appearance of the loins and upwards, and from the appearance of the loins and under I saw an appearance of fire, and the brightness thereof round about.

[28] As the appearance of the rainbow when it is in the cloud in days of rain, so was the form of brightness round about.

EZEKIEL CHAPTER 2

The Vision of the Scroll

[1] This was the appearance of the likeness of the glory of the Lord. And I saw and fell on my face, and heard the voice of One speaking. And He said to me, "Son of man, stand upon your feet, and I will speak to you."

[2] And the Spirit came upon me, and took me up, and raised me, and set me on my feet. And I heard Him speaking to me.

[3] And He said to me, "Son of Man, I send you forth to the house of Israel, to them that provoke Me; who have provoked Me, they and their fathers to this day.

[4] And you shall say to them, 'Thus says the Lord.'

[5] Whether then indeed they shall hear or fear (for they are a provoking house), yet they shall know that you are a prophet in the midst of them.

[6] "And you, son of man, do not fear them, nor be dismayed at their face (for they will madden and will rise up against you round about, and you dwell in the midst of scorpions), do not be afraid of their words, nor be dismayed at their countenance, for they are a provoking house.

[7] And you shall speak My words to them, whether they will hear or fear; for they are a provoking house.

[8] And you, son of man, hear Him that speaks to you; be not provoking, as the provoking house: open your mouth, and eat what I give you."

[9] And I looked, and behold, a hand stretched out to me, and in it *was* a volume of a book.

[10] And He unrolled it before me. And in it the front and the back were written *upon*. And there was written *in it* lamentations, and mournful songs, and woe.

EZEKIEL CHAPTER 3

[1] And He said to me, "Son of Man, eat this scroll, and go and speak to the children of Israel."

[2] So He opened my mouth, and caused me to eat the scroll. And He said to me, "Son of man,

[3] your mouth shall eat, and your belly shall be filled with this scroll that is given to you." So I ate it; and it was in my mouth as sweet as honey.

[4] And He said to me, "Son of man, go your way, and go to the house of Israel, and speak My words to them.

[5] For you are not sent to a people of hard speech, *but* to the house of Israel;

[6] neither to many nations of other speech and other tongues, nor of harsh language, whose words you would not understand; although if I *had* sent you to such, they would have listened to you.

[7] But the house of Israel will not be willing to listen to you; for they will not listen to Me; for all the house of Israel are stubborn and hard-hearted.

[8] And behold, I have made your face strong against their faces, and I will strengthen your power against their power.

[9] And it shall be continually stronger than a rock—do not be afraid of them, neither be dismayed at their faces, because they are a provoking house."

[10] And He said to me, "Son of man, receive into your heart all the words that I have spoken to you, and hear *them* with your ears.

[11] And go your way, go in to the captivity, to the children of your people, and you shall speak to them, and say to them, 'Thus says the Lord'; whether they will hear, *or* whether they will refuse."

Ezekiel at the River Chebar

[12] Then the Spirit took me up, and I heard behind me the voice *as* of a great earthquake, *saying,* "Blessed *be* the glory of the Lord from His place."

[13] And I perceived the sound of the wings of the living creatures clapping one to the other, and the sound of the wheels was near them, and the sound of the earthquake.

[14] And the Spirit lifted me, and took me up, and I went in the impulse of my spirit; and the hand of the Lord was mighty upon me.

[15] Then I passed through the air and came into the captivity, and went round *to* those that dwelt by the River Chebar who were there; and I sat there seven days, conversant in the midst of them.

[16] And after the seven days the word of the Lord came to me, saying, "Son of man,

[17] I have made you a watchman to the house of Israel; and you shall hear a word from My mouth, and shall warn them from Me.

[18] When I say to the wicked, 'You shall surely die'; and you have not warned him, to give warning to the wicked, to turn from his ways, that he should live; that wicked man shall die in his iniquity; but his blood will I require at your hand.

[19] But if you warn the wicked, and he does not turn from his wickedness, and from his way, that wicked man shall die in his iniquity, and you shall deliver your soul.

[20] And when the righteous turns away from his righteousness, and commits a trespass, and I shall bring punishment before him, he shall die, because you did not warn him: he shall even die in his sins, because his righteousness shall not be remembered; but his blood will I require at your hand.

[21] But if you warn the righteous not to sin, and he does not sin, the righteous shall surely live, because you have warned him; and you shall deliver your own soul."

[22] And the hand of the Lord came upon me; and He said to me, "Arise, and go forth into the plain, and there shall you be spoken to."

[23] And I arose, and went forth to the plain. And behold, the glory of the Lord stood there, according to the vision, and according to the glory of the Lord, which I saw by the River Chebar; and I fell on my face.

[24] Then the Spirit came upon me, and set me on my feet, and spoke to me, and said to me, "Go in, and shut yourself up in the midst of your house.

[25] And you, son of man, behold, bonds are prepared for you, and they shall bind you with them, and you shall not come forth of the midst of them.

[26] Also I will bind your tongue, and you shall be dumb, and shall not be to them a reprover; because they are a provoking house.

[27] But when I speak to you, I will open your mouth, and you shall say to them, 'Thus says the Lord': He that hears, let him hear; and he that is disobedient, let him be disobedient; for they are a provoking house."

EZEKIEL CHAPTER 4

The Siege of Jerusalem Portrayed

[1] "And you, son of man, take a brick, and set it before your face, and portray on it the city, *even* Jerusalem.

[2] And you shall besiege it, and build works against it, and throw up a mound round about it, and pitch camps against it, and set up engines round about.

[3] And take to yourself an iron pan, and you shall set it *for* an iron wall between you and the city. And you shall set your face against it, and it shall be in a siege, and you shall besiege it. This is a sign to the children of Israel.

[4] "And you shall lie upon your left side, and lay the iniquities of the house of Israel upon it, according to the number of the hundred and fifty days *during* which you shall lie upon it; and you shall bear their iniquities.

[5] For I have appointed you their iniquities for a number of days, for a hundred and ninety days: so you shall bear the iniquities of the house of Israel.

[6] And you shall accomplish this, and *then* you shall lie on your right side, and shall bear the iniquities of the house of Judah for forty days: I have appointed you a day for a year.

[7] So you shall set your face to the siege of Jerusalem, and shall strengthen your arm, and shall prophesy against it.

[8] And behold, I have prepared bonds for you, and you may not turn from your one side to the other, until the days of your siege shall be accomplished.

[9] "Take also wheat, barley, beans, lentils, millet, and grain; and you shall cast them into one earthen vessel, and shall make them into loaves for yourself; and you shall eat them a hundred and ninety days, according to the number of the days which you sleep on your side.

[10] And you shall eat your food by weight, twenty shekels a day: from time to time shall you eat them.

[11] And you shall drink water by measure, even from time to time you shall drink the sixth part of a hin.

[12] And you shall eat them *as* a barley cake; you shall bake them before their eyes in man's dung.

[13] And you shall say, 'Thus says the Lord God of Israel: Thus shall the children of Israel eat unclean things among the Gentiles.'"

[14] Then I said, "By no means, Lord God of Israel! Surely my soul has not been defiled with uncleanness, nor have I

eaten that which has died of itself, or was torn by beasts from my birth until now; neither has any corrupt flesh entered into my mouth."

¹⁵ And He said to me, "Behold, I have given you dung of oxen instead of man's dung, and you shall prepare your loaves upon it."

¹⁶ And He said to me, "Son of man, behold, I break the support of bread in Jerusalem: and they shall eat bread by weight and in poverty, and shall drink water by measure, and in a state of ruin;

¹⁷ that they may want bread and water; and a man and his brother shall be brought to ruin, and they shall pine away in their iniquities."

EZEKIEL CHAPTER 5

A Sword Against Jerusalem

¹ "And you, son of man, take a sword sharper than a barber's razor; you shall procure it for yourself, and shall bring it upon your head, and upon your beard; and you shall take a pair of scales, and shall separate the hair.

² A fourth part you shall burn in the fire in the midst of the city, at the fulfillment of the days of the siege. And you shall take a fourth part, and burn it up in the midst of it. And a fourth part you shall cut with a sword round about it. And a fourth part you shall scatter to the wind; and I will draw out a sword after them.

³ And you shall take a few of them, and wrap them in the fold of your garment.

⁴ And you shall take of these again, and cast them into the midst of the fire, and burn them up with fire. From there shall come forth fire, and you shall say to the whole house of Israel,

⁵ 'Thus says the Lord: This is Jerusalem: I have set her and the countries round about her in the midst of the nations.'

⁶ And you shall declare My ordinances to the lawless one from out of the nations; and My statutes *to the sinful one* of the countries round about her, because they have rejected My ordinances, and have not walked in My statutes.

⁷ Therefore thus says the Lord: 'Because your occasion *for sin has been taken* from the nations round about you, and you have not walked in My statutes, nor kept My ordinances, no, you have not even done according to the ordinances of the nations round about you; therefore thus says the Lord:

⁸ 'Behold, I am against you, and I will execute judgment in the midst of you in the sight of the nations.

⁹ And I will do in you things which I have not done, and the like of which I will not do again, for all your abominations.

¹⁰ Therefore the fathers shall eat *their* children in the midst of you, and children shall eat *their* fathers; and I will execute judgments in you, and I will scatter all that are left of you to the four winds.

¹¹ Therefore, *as* I live, says the Lord; surely, because you have defiled My holy things with all your abominations, I also

will reject you; My eye shall not spare, and I will have no mercy.

¹² A fourth part of you shall be cut off by pestilence, and a fourth part of you shall be consumed in the midst of you with famine; and *as for another* fourth part of you, I will scatter them to all the winds; and a fourth part of you shall fall by the sword round about you, and I will draw out a sword after them.

¹³ And My wrath and My anger shall be accomplished upon them: and you shall know that I, the Lord, have spoken in My jealousy, when I have accomplished My anger upon them.

¹⁴ And I will make you desolate, and your daughters round about you, in the sight of everyone that passes through.

¹⁵ And you shall be mourned over and miserable among the nations round about you, when I have executed judgments in you in the vengeance of My wrath. I, the Lord, have spoken.

¹⁶ And when I have sent against them shafts of famine, then they shall be consumed, and I will break the strength of your bread.

¹⁷ So I will send forth against you famine and evil beasts, and I will take vengeance upon you; and pestilence and blood shall pass through upon you; and I will bring a sword upon you round about. I, the Lord, have spoken.'"

EZEKIEL CHAPTER 6

Judgment on Idolatrous Israel

¹ And the word of the Lord came to me, saying,

² "Son of man, set your face against the mountains of Israel, and prophesy against them;

³ and you shall say, 'You mountains of Israel, hear the word of the Lord; Thus says the Lord to the mountains, and to the hills, and to the valleys, and to the forests: "Behold, I bring a sword upon you, and your high places shall be utterly destroyed.

⁴ And your altars shall be broken to pieces, and your consecrated plats; and I will cast down your slain *men* before your idols.

⁵ And I will scatter your bones round about your altars,

⁶ and in all your habitations; the cities shall be made desolate, and the high places utterly laid waste, that your altars may be destroyed, and your idols be broken to pieces, and your works be abolished.

⁷ And slain *men* shall fall in the midst of you, and you shall know that I am the Lord.

⁸ When there are *some* of you escaping from the sword among the Gentiles, and when you are scattered in the countries,

⁹ then those of you that escape among the nations where they were carried captive shall remember Me; (I have sworn *an oath* against their heart that goes a-whoring from Me,

and their eyes that go a-whoring after their practices) and they shall mourn over themselves for all their abominations.
[10] And they shall know that I, the Lord, have spoken."""
[11] Thus says the Lord: "Clap with *your* hand, and stamp with *your* foot and say, 'Aha, aha!' For all the abominations of the house of Israel; they shall fall by the sword, and by pestilence, and by famine.
[12] He that is near shall fall by the sword; and he that is far off shall die by the pestilence; and he that is in the siege shall be consumed with famine; and I will accomplish My anger upon them.
[13] Then you shall know that I am the Lord, when your slain are in the midst of your idols round about your altars, on every high hill, and under *every* shady tree, where they offered a sweet savor to all their idols.
[14] And I will stretch out My hand against them, and I will make the land desolate and ruined from the wilderness of Diblah, in all their habitations; *and* you shall know that I am the Lord."

EZEKIEL CHAPTER 7

Judgment on Israel is Near

[1] Moreover the word of the Lord came to me, saying, "Also, you, son of man, say,
[2] Thus says the Lord: 'An end has come to the land of Israel, the end has come on the four corners of the land.
[3] Now the end *has come* upon you, and I will send *judgment* upon you: and I will take vengeance on your ways, and will recompense all your abominations upon you.
[4] My eye shall not spare, nor will I have any mercy, for I will recompense your way upon you, and your abominations shall be in the midst of you; and you shall know that I am the Lord.'
[5] "For thus says the Lord; Behold, the end has come.
[6] The end has come on you,
[7] the inhabitant of the land: the time has come, the day has drawn near, not with tumult, nor with pangs.
[8] Now I will pour out My anger upon you near at hand, and I will accomplish My wrath on you: and I will judge you for your ways, and recompense all your abominations upon you.
[9] My eye shall not spare, nor will I have any mercy: for I will recompense your ways upon you, and your abominations shall be in the midst of you; and you shall know that I am the Lord that strikes *you*.
[10] "Behold, the day of the Lord! Although the rod has blossomed,
[11] pride has sprung up, and will break the staff of the wicked one, and *that* not with tumult, nor with haste.
[12] The time has come, behold the day: let not the buyer rejoice, and let not the seller mourn.
[13] For the buyer shall never again return to the seller, neither shall a man cleave with the eye *of hope* to his life.

[14] Sound the trumpet, and pass sentence on all together.
[15] *There shall be* war with the sword without, and famine and pestilence within: he that is in the field shall die by the sword, and famine and pestilence shall destroy them that are in the city.
[16] "But they that escape among them shall be delivered, and shall be upon the mountains, and I will slay all *the rest*, everyone for his iniquities.
[17] All hands shall be completely weakened, and all thighs shall be defiled with moisture.
[18] And they shall gird themselves with sackcloth, and amazement shall cover them; and shame shall be upon them, *even* upon every face, and baldness upon every head.
[19] Their silver shall be cast forth in the streets, and their gold shall be despised: their souls shall not be satisfied, and their bellies shall not be filled; for it was the punishment of their iniquities.
[20] "*As for* their choice ornaments, they employed them for pride, and they made of them images of their abominations; therefore have I made them uncleanness to them.
[21] And I will deliver them into the hands of strangers to make them a prey, and to the pests of the earth for a spoil; and they shall profane them.
[22] And I will turn away My face from them, and they shall defile My secret place, and shall go in to them unguardedly, and profane them.
[23] "And they shall work uncleanness: because the land is full of strange nations, and the city is full of iniquity.
[24] And I will turn back the boasting of their strength; and their holy things shall be defiled.
[25] And *though* propitiation shall come, and *one* shall seek peace, yet there shall be none.
[26] There shall be woe upon woe, and there shall be message upon message; and a vision shall be sought from a prophet, but the law shall perish from the priest, and counsel from the elders.
[27] The prince shall clothe himself with desolation, and the hands of the people of the land shall be made feeble. I will do to them according to their ways, and according to their judgments will I punish them; and they shall know that I am the Lord."

EZEKIEL CHAPTER 8

Abominations in the Temple

[1] And it came to pass in the sixth year, in the fifth month, on the fifth *day* of the month, I was sitting in the house, and the elders of Judah were sitting before me. And the hand of the Lord came upon me.
[2] And I looked, and behold, the likeness of a man: from his loins and downwards *there was* fire, and from his loins upwards *there was* as the appearance of amber.

³ And He stretched forth the likeness of a hand, and took me by the crown of my head. And the Spirit lifted me up between the earth and sky, and brought me to Jerusalem in a vision of God, to the porch of the gate that looks to the north, where was the pillar of the Purchaser.

⁴ And behold, the glory of the Lord God of Israel was there, according to the vision which I saw in the plain.

⁵ And He said to me, "Son of man, lift up your eyes toward the north." So I lifted up my eyes toward the north, and behold, *I looked* from the north toward the eastern gate.

⁶ And He said to me, "Son of man, have you seen what these *people* do? They commit great abominations here, so that I should keep away from My sanctuary; and you shall see even greater iniquities."

⁷ And He brought me to the porch of the court.

⁸ And He said to me, "Son of man, dig." So I dug, and behold, *there was* a door.

⁹ And He said to me, "Go in, and behold the iniquities which they practice here."

¹⁰ So I went in and looked, and I beheld vain abominations, and all the idols of the house of Israel, portrayed upon them round about.

¹¹ And seventy men of the elders of the house of Israel, and Jechoniah the son of Shaphan stood in their presence in the midst of them, and each one held his censer in his hand; and the smoke of the incense went up.

¹² And He said to me, "You have seen, son of man, what the elders of the house of Israel do, each one of them in their secret chamber; because they have said, 'The Lord does not see; the Lord has forsaken the earth.'"

¹³ And He said to me, "You shall see even greater iniquities than these."

¹⁴ And He brought me in to the porch of the house of the Lord that looks to the north; and behold *there were* women sitting there lamenting for Tammuz.

¹⁵ And He said to me, "Son of man, you have seen; but you shall yet see *evil* practices *even* greater then these."

¹⁶ And He brought me into the inner court of the house of the Lord, and at the entrance of the temple of the Lord, between the porch and the altar, were about twenty men, with their back parts toward the temple of the Lord, and their faces *turned* the opposite way; and these were worshipping the sun.

¹⁷ And He said to me, "Son of man, you have seen this. *Is it* a trivial thing to the house of Judah to practice the iniquities which they have practiced here? For they have filled the land with iniquity; and behold, these are as scorners.

¹⁸ Therefore will I deal with them in wrath: My eye shall not spare, nor will I have any mercy."

EZEKIEL CHAPTER 9

The Slaughter of the Idolaters

¹ Then He called out in my ears with a loud voice, saying, "The judgment of the city has drawn near." And each had the weapons of destruction in his hand.

² And behold, six men came from the way of the high gate that looks toward the north, and each one's axe was in his hand; and there was one man in the midst of them clothed with a long robe down to his feet, and a sapphire belt was on his loins. And they came in and stood near the bronze altar.

³ And the glory of the God of Israel that was upon them went up from the cherubim to the porch of the house. And He called the man that was clothed with the long robe, who had the belt on his loins;

⁴ and said to him, "Go through the midst of Jerusalem, and set a mark on the foreheads of the men that groan and that grieve for all the iniquities that are done in the midst of them."

⁵ And He said to the first in my hearing, "Go after him into the city, and strike: and let not your eyes spare, neither have mercy.

⁶ Utterly slay old man and youth, and virgin and infants and women: but do not go near any on whom is the mark: begin at My sanctuary." So they began with the elder men who were within in the house.

⁷ And He said to them, "Defile the house, and go out and fill the ways with dead bodies, and strike."

⁸ And it came to pass as they were striking, that I fell upon my face and cried out, and said, "Alas, O Lord! Will You destroy the remnant of Israel, in pouring out Your wrath upon Jerusalem?"

⁹ Then He said to me, "The iniquity of the house of Israel and Judah has become exceedingly great: for the land is filled with many nations, and the city is filled with iniquity and uncleanness; because they have said, 'The Lord has forsaken the earth, the Lord does not see.'

¹⁰ Therefore My eye shall not spare, neither will I have any mercy: I have recompensed their ways upon their heads."

¹¹ And behold, the man clothed with the long robe, and girded with the belt about his loins, answered and said, "I have done as You have commanded me."

EZEKIEL CHAPTER 10

The Glory Departs from the Temple

¹ Then I looked, and behold, over the firmament that was above the head of the cherubim *there was* a likeness of a throne over them, as a sapphire stone.

² And He said to the man clothed with the *long* robe, "Go in between the wheels that are under the cherubim, and fill your hands with coals of fire from between the cherubim, and scatter *them* over the city." And he went in my sight.

3 And the cherubim stood on the right hand of the house, as the man went in; and the cloud filled the inner court.

4 Then the glory of the Lord departed from the cherubim to the porch of the house; and the cloud filled the house, and the court was filled with the brightness of the glory of the Lord.

5 And the sound of the wings of the Cherubim was heard as far as the outer court, as the voice of Almighty God speaking.

6 And it came to pass, when He gave a charge to the man clothed with the sacred robe, saying, "Take fire from between the wheels from between the cherubim," that he went in, and stood near the wheels.

7 And he stretched forth his hand into the midst of the fire that was between the cherubim, and he took *of the fire*, and put *it* into the hands of the man clothed with the sacred robe. And he took *it*, and went out.

8 And I saw the cherubim *having* the likeness of men's hands under their wings.

9 And I saw, and behold, four wheels stood by the cherubim, one wheel by each cherub: and the appearance of the wheels was as the appearance of a carbuncle stone.

10 And *as for* their appearance, *there was* one likeness to the four, as if there should be a wheel in the midst of a wheel.

11 When they went, they went on their four sides; they did not turn when they went, for whichever way the first head looked, they went; and they did not turn as they went.

12 And their backs, and their hands, and their wings, and the wheels, were full of eyes round about the four wheels.

13 And these wheels were called "Gelgel" in my hearing.

14 (This verse omitted in LXX)

15 And the cherubim were the same living creatures which I saw by the River Chebar.

16 And when the cherubim went, the wheels went, and they were close to them. And when the cherubim lifted up their wings to mount up from the earth, their wheels turned not.

17 When they stood, *the wheels* stood; and when they mounted up, *the wheels* mounted up with them, because the spirit of life was in them.

18 Then the glory of the Lord departed from the house, and went up on the cherubim.

19 And the cherubim lifted up their wings, and mounted up from the earth in my sight. When they went forth, the wheels were also beside them, and they stood at the entrance of the front gate of the house of the Lord; and the glory of the God of Israel was upon them above.

20 This is the living creature which I saw under the God of Israel by the River Chebar; and I knew that they were cherubim.

21 Each one *had* four faces, and each one *had* eight wings; and under their wings was the likeness of men's hands.

22 And *as for* the likeness of their faces, these are the *same* faces which I saw under the glory of the God of Israel by the River Chebar: and they went each straight forward.

EZEKIEL CHAPTER 11

Judgment on Wicked Counselors

1 Moreover the Spirit took me up, and brought me to the front gate of the house of the Lord, that looks eastward. And behold, at the entrance of the gate were about twenty-five men; and I saw in the midst of them Jechoniah the son of Azzur, and Pelatiah the son of Benaiah, the leaders of the people.

2 And the Lord said to me, "Son of man, these are the men that devise vanities, and take evil counsel in this city;

3 who say, 'Have not the houses been newly built? This is the caldron, and we are the flesh.'

4 Therefore prophesy against them; prophesy, son of man."

5 And the Spirit of the Lord fell upon me, and said to me, "Say; Thus says the Lord: 'Thus have you said, O house of Israel: and I know the devices of your spirit.

6 You have multiplied your dead in this city, and you have filled your ways with slain men.

7 Therefore thus says the Lord: "Your dead whom you have smitten in the midst of it, these are the flesh, and this *city* is the caldron; but I will bring you forth out of the midst of it.

8 You fear the sword; and I will bring a sword upon you, says the Lord.

9 And I will bring you forth out of the midst of it, and will deliver you into the hands of strangers, and will execute judgments among you.

10 You shall fall by the sword; I will judge you on the mountains of Israel; and you shall know that I am the Lord."'"

11 (This verse omitted in LXX)

12 (This verse omitted in LXX)

13 And it came to pass, while I was prophesying, that Pelatiah the son of Benaiah died. And I fell upon my face, and cried with a loud voice, and said, "Alas, alas, O Lord! Will you utterly destroy the remnant of Israel?"

God will Restore Israel

14 And the word of the Lord came to me, saying,

15 "Son of man, your brothers, and the men of your captivity, and all the house of Israel have come to the full, to whom the inhabitants of Jerusalem said, 'Keep far away from the Lord: the land is given to us for an inheritance.'

16 Therefore say, 'Thus says the Lord: I will cast them off among the nations, and will disperse them into every land, yet will I be to them for a little sanctuary in the countries which they shall enter.

17 Therefore say, "Thus says the Lord: I will also take them from the heathen, and gather them out of the lands in which I have scattered them, and will give them the land of Israel.

18 And they shall enter in there, and shall remove all the abominations from it, and all its iniquities from it.

¹⁹ And I will give them another heart, and will put a new spirit within them; and will extract the heart of stone from their flesh, and give them a heart of flesh;

²⁰ that they may walk in My commandments, and keep My ordinances, and do them: and they shall be to Me a people, and I will be to them a God.

²¹ And as for the heart *set upon* their abominations and their iniquities, as their heart went *after them*, I have recompensed their ways on their heads, says the Lord.'"

²² Then the cherubim lifted up their wings, and the wheels beside them; and the glory of the God of Israel was over them above.

²³ And the glory of the Lord went up from the midst of the city, and stood on the mountain which was in front of the city.

²⁴ And the Spirit took me up, and brought me to the land of the Chaldeans, to the captivity, in a vision by the Spirit of God: and I went up after the vision which I saw.

²⁵ And I spoke to the captivity all the words of the Lord, which He had shown me.

EZEKIEL CHAPTER 12

Judah's Captivity Portrayed

¹ And the word of the Lord came to me, saying,

² "Son of man, you dwell in the midst of the iniquities of those who have eyes to see, and do not see; and have ears to hear, and do not hear; because they are a provoking house.

³ You therefore, son of man, prepare yourself baggage for going into captivity by day in their sight; and you shall be led into captivity from your place into another place in their sight; that they may see that they are a provoking house.

⁴ And you shall carry forth your baggage, baggage for captivity, by day before their eyes; and you shall go forth at evening, as a captive goes forth, in their sight.

⁵ Dig for yourself into the wall *of the house*, and you shall pass through it in their sight.

⁶ You shall be lifted up on *men's* shoulders, and shall go forth in secret; you shall cover your face, and shall not see the ground, because I have made you a sign to the house of Israel."

⁷ And so I did according to all that He commanded me; and I carried forth my baggage for captivity by day, and in the evening I dug through the wall for myself, and I went out secretly; I was taken up on *men's* shoulders before them.

⁸ And the word of the Lord came to me in the morning, saying,

⁹ "Son of man, has not the house of Israel, the provoking house, said to you, 'What are you doing?'

¹⁰ Say to them, Thus says the Lord God, the Prince and the Ruler in Israel, even to all the house of Israel who are in the midst of them:

¹¹ say, 'I am performing signs: as I have done, so shall it be to him; they shall go into banishment and captivity.

¹² And the prince in the midst of them shall be borne upon shoulders, and shall go forth in secret through the wall, and shall dig, so that he may go forth thereby; he shall cover his face, so that he may not be seen by *anyone*, and he himself shall not see the ground.

¹³ And I will spread out My net upon him, and he shall be caught in My snare, and I will bring him to Babylon to the land of the Chaldeans; but he shall not see it, though he shall die there.

¹⁴ And I will scatter to every wind all his assistants round about him, and all that help him; and I will draw out a sword after them;

¹⁵ And they shall know that I am the Lord, when I have scattered them among the nations; and I will disperse them into the countries.

¹⁶ And I will leave among them *a few* men in number *spared* from the sword, and from famine, and pestilence; that they may declare all their iniquities among the nations where they have gone; and they shall know that I am the Lord.'"

Judgment Not Postponed

¹⁷ And the word of the Lord came to me, saying,

¹⁸ "Son of man, eat your bread with sorrow, and drink *your* water with torment and affliction.

¹⁹ And you shall say to the people of the land, 'Thus says the Lord to the inhabitants of Jerusalem, on the land of Israel: They shall eat their bread in scarcity, and shall drink their water in desolation, that the land may be desolate with all that it contains, for all that dwell in it are ungodly.

²⁰ And their inhabited cities shall be laid utterly waste, and the land shall be desolate; and you shall know that I am the Lord.'"

²¹ And the word of the Lord came to me, saying,

²² "Son of man, what is your parable on the land of Israel, that you say, 'The days are long, *and* the vision has perished?'

²³ Therefore say to them, 'Thus says the Lord: I will even set aside this parable, and the house of Israel shall by no means use this parable *again*; for you shall say to them, "The days are at hand, and the fulfillment of every vision.

²⁴ For there shall no more be any false vision, nor anyone prophesying flatteries in the midst of the children of Israel.

²⁵ For I the Lord will speak My words; I will speak and perform *them*, and will delay no more, for in your days, O provoking house, I will speak the word, and will perform *it*, says the Lord."'"

²⁶ Moreover the word of the Lord came to me, saying,

²⁷ "Son of man, behold, the provoking house of Israel boldly say, 'The vision which this man sees is for many days, and he prophesies for times afar off.'

²⁸ Therefore say to them, 'Thus says the Lord: Henceforth none of My words shall linger, which I shall speak: I will speak and do, says the Lord.'"

EZEKIEL CHAPTER 13

False Prophets Condemned

¹ And the word of the Lord came to me, saying,

² "Son of man, prophesy against the prophets of Israel, and you shall prophesy, and shall say to them, Hear the word of the Lord:

³ Thus says the Lord: 'Woe to them that prophesy out of their own heart, and who see nothing at all.

⁴ Your prophets, O Israel, are like foxes in the deserts.

⁵ They have not continued steadfast, and they have gathered flocks against the house of Israel, they that say,

⁶ "In the day of the Lord," have not stood, seeing false *visions,* prophesying vanities, who say, "The Lord says," and the Lord has not sent them, and they began *to try* to confirm the word. ⁷ Have you not seen a false vision, and spoken vain prophecies?

⁸ 'And therefore say, Thus says the Lord: "Because your words are false, and your prophecies are vain, therefore behold, I am against you, says the Lord.

⁹ And I will stretch forth My hand against the prophets that see false *visions,* and those that utter vanities. They shall not partake of the instruction of My people, neither shall they be written in the roll of the house of Israel, and they shall not enter into the land of Israel; and they shall know that I am the Lord.

¹⁰ Because they have caused My people to err, saying, 'Peace'; and there is no peace; and one builds a wall, and they plaster it—it shall fall.

¹¹ Say to them that plaster *it,* 'It shall fall'; and there shall be a flooding rain; and I will send great stones upon their joinings, and they shall fall; and there shall be a sweeping wind, and it shall be broken.

¹² And lo! The wall has fallen; and will they not say to you, 'Where is your plaster with which you plastered *it?'*

¹³ Therefore thus says the Lord: 'I will even cause to burst forth a sweeping blast with fury, and there shall be a flooding rain in My wrath; and in *My* fury I will bring on great hailstones for complete destruction.

¹⁴ And I will break down the wall which you have plastered, and it shall fall; and I will lay it on the ground, and its foundations shall be discovered, and it shall fall; and you shall be consumed with rebukes; and you shall know that I am the Lord.

¹⁵ And I will accomplish My wrath upon the wall, and upon them that plaster it; it shall fall: and I said to you, "The wall is not, nor they that plaster it,"

¹⁶ even the prophets of Israel, who prophesy concerning Jerusalem, and who see *visions of* peace for her, and there is no peace, says the Lord.'"

¹⁷ "And you, son of man, set your face firmly against the daughters of your people, that prophesy out of their own heart; and prophesy against them.

¹⁸ And you shall say, 'Thus says the Lord: Woe to the *women* that sew pillows under every elbow, and make handkerchiefs on the head of every stature to pervert souls! The souls of My people are perverted, and they have saved souls alive.

¹⁹ And they have dishonored Me before My people for a handful of barley, and for pieces of bread, to slay the souls which should not die, and to save alive the souls which should not live, while you speak to a people hearing vain speeches.

²⁰ 'Therefore thus says the Lord God: Behold, I am against your pillows, whereby you there confound souls, and I will tear them away from your arms, and will set at liberty their souls which you pervert, to scatter them.

²¹ And I will tear your handkerchiefs, and will rescue My people out of your hands, and they shall no longer be in your hands to be confounded; and you shall know that I am the Lord.

²² Because you have perverted the heart of the righteous, whereas I did not pervert him, and *that* in order to strengthen the hands of the wicked, that he should not at all turn from his evil way and live:

²³ therefore you shall not see false *visions,* and you shall no more utter prophecies; but I will deliver My people out of your hand; and you shall know that I am the Lord.'"

EZEKIEL CHAPTER 14

God's Judgments Justified

¹ And there came to me men of the people of Israel, of the elders, and sat before me.

² And the word of the Lord came to me, saying,

³ "Son of man, these men have conceived their devices in their hearts, and have set before their faces the punishment of their iniquities: shall I indeed answer them?

⁴ Therefore speak to them, and you shall say to them, 'Thus says the Lord: Any man of the house of Israel, who shall conceive his devices in his heart, and shall set the punishment of his iniquity before his face, and shall come to the prophet; I the Lord will answer him *according to the things* in which his mind is entangled,

⁵ that he should turn aside the house of Israel, according to their hearts that are estranged from Me in their thoughts.'"

⁶ "Therefore say to the house of Israel, 'Thus says the Lord God: Be converted, and turn from your *evil* practices, and from all your sins, and turn your faces back again.

⁷ For any man of the house of Israel, or of the strangers that sojourn in Israel, who shall separate himself from Me, and conceive his imaginations in his heart, and set before his face the punishment of his iniquity, and come to the prophet to inquire of him concerning Me; I the Lord will answer him, *according to the things* in which he is entangled.

[8] And I will set My face against that man, and will make him desolate and ruined, and will cut him off from the midst of My people; and you shall know that I am the Lord.

[9] And if a prophet should cause to err and should speak, I the Lord have caused that prophet to err, and I will stretch out My hand upon him, and will utterly destroy him from the midst of My people Israel.

[10] And they shall bear their iniquity according to the trespass of him that asks; and it shall be in like manner to the prophet according to the trespass,

[11] that the house of Israel may not go astray from Me, and that they may no more defile themselves with any of their transgressions; so shall they be My people, and I will be their God,'" says the Lord.

[12] And the word of the Lord came to me, saying,

[13] "Son of man, if a land shall sin against Me by committing a trespass, then will I stretch out My hand upon it, and will break its staff of bread, and will send forth famine upon it, and cut off man and beast from it.

[14] And though these three men should be in the midst of it, Noah, Daniel, and Job, they *alone* would be delivered by their righteousness," says the Lord.

[15] "If again I bring evil beasts upon the land, and take vengeance upon it, and it is ruined, and there be no one to pass through for fear of the wild beasts;

[16] and *if* these three men should be in the midst of it, *as* I live, says the Lord, neither sons nor daughters shall be saved, but these only shall be saved, and the land shall be destroyed.

[17] "Or again if I bring a sword upon that land, and say, 'Let the sword go through the land'; and I cut off from them man and beast;

[18] though these three men were in the midst of it, as I live, says the Lord, they shall not deliver sons or daughters, but they only shall be saved themselves.

[19] "Or if again I send pestilence upon that land, and pour out My wrath upon it in blood, to destroy from off it man and beast; and should Noah, Daniel, and Job be in the midst of it,

[20] as I live, says the Lord, there shall be left *them* neither sons nor daughters; *only* they by their righteousness shall deliver their souls.

[21] "Thus says the Lord: And if I even send upon Jerusalem My four severe judgments—the sword, famine, evil beasts, and pestilence, to destroy from out of it *both* man and beast;

[22] yet behold, *there shall be* men left in it, those that escaped, who *shall* lead forth of it sons and daughters—behold, they *shall* go forth to you, and you shall see their ways and their thoughts, and you shall mourn over the evils which I have brought upon Jerusalem, *even* all the evils which I have brought upon it.

[23] And they shall comfort you, because you shall see their ways and their thoughts; and you shall know that I have not done in vain all that I have done in it," says the Lord.

The Useless Vine

[1] And the word of the Lord came to me, saying,

[2] "And you, son of man—of all the wood, of the branches that are among the trees of the forest, what shall be made of the wood of the vine?

[3] Will they take wood from it to make *it fit* for work? Will they take a peg from it to hang any vessel upon it?

[4] It is only given to the fire to be consumed; the fire consumes that which is yearly ruined of it, and it is utterly gone. Will it be useful for *any* work?

[5] Not even while it is yet whole will it be *useful* for *any* work; if the fire shall have utterly consumed it, will it still be *fit* for work?

[6] Therefore say, 'Thus says the Lord: As the vine tree among the trees of the forest, which I have given up to the fire to be consumed, so have I given up the inhabitants of Jerusalem.

[7] And I will set My face against them; they shall go forth of the fire, and *yet* fire shall devour them; and they shall know that I am the Lord, when I have set My face against them.

[8] And I will give up the land to ruin, because they have utterly transgressed, says the Lord.'"

God's Faithless Bride

[1] Moreover the word of the Lord came to me, saying,

[2] "Son of man, testify to Jerusalem *of* her iniquities;

[3] and you shall say, 'Thus says the Lord to Jerusalem: Your root and your birth are of the land of Canaan: your father was an Amorite, and your mother a Hittite.

[4] And *as for* your birth in the day in which you were born, you did not bind your breasts, and you were not washed in water, neither were you salted with salt, neither were you swathed in swaddling-bands.

[5] Nor did My eye pity you, to do for you one of all these things, to feel at all for you; but you were cast out on the face of the field, because of the deformity of your person, in the day in which you were born.

[6] 'And I passed by to you, and saw you polluted in your blood; and I said to you, "*Let there be* life out of your blood;

[7] increase"; I have made you as the springing grass of the field. So you increased and grew, and entered into great cities: your breasts were set, and your hair grew, whereas you were naked and bare.

[8] And I passed by you and saw you, and behold, *it was* your time and a time of resting; and I spread My wings over you, and covered your shame, and swore *an oath* to you; and I entered into covenant with you, says the Lord, and you became Mine.

9 And I washed you in water, and washed your blood from you, and anointed you with oil.

10 And I clothed you with embroidered *garments*, and clothed you beneath with purple, and girded you with fine linen, and clothed you with silk,

11 and decked you also with ornaments, and put bracelets on your hands, and a necklace on your neck.

12 And I put a pendant in your nose, and rings in your ears, and a crown of glory on your head.

13 So you were adorned with gold and silver; and your clothing was of fine linen, and silk, and embroidered work; you ate fine flour and oil and honey, and became extremely beautiful.

14 And your name went forth among the nations because of your beauty; because it was perfected with elegance, *and in* the comeliness which I put upon you, says the Lord.

15 'But you trusted in your beauty, and went a-whoring because of your fame, and poured out your fornication on every passer by.

16 And you took of your garments, and made for yourself idols of needlework, and went a-whoring after them; therefore you shall never come in, nor shall *the like* take place.

17 And you took your fair ornaments of My gold and of My silver, of what I gave you, and you made for yourself male images, and you committed harlotry with them.

18 And you took your embroidered garments and covered them, and you set before them My oil and My incense.

19 And *you took* My bread which I gave you, (*indeed*, I fed you with fine flour and oil and honey) and set them before them for a sweet-smelling savor; yes, it was so, says the Lord.

20 And you took your sons and your daughters, whom you bore, and sacrificed *these* to them to be destroyed. You went a-whoring as *if that were* a small thing,

21 and slain your children, and gave them up, in offering them up as a sacrifice.

22 This is beyond all your fornication, and you did not remember the days of your youth, when you were naked and bare, *and* lived, *though* defiled in your blood.

23 'And it came to pass after all your wickedness, says the Lord,

24 that you built yourself a house of fornication, and made a public place for yourself in every street;

25 and on the head of every road you set up your fornications, and defiled your beauty, and opened your feet to every passer by, and multiplied your fornication.

26 And you went a-whoring after the children of Egypt your neighbors, great of flesh; and went a-whoring, often to provoke Me to anger.

27 And if I stretch out My hand against you, then will I abolish your statutes, and deliver *you* up to the will of those that hate you, *even to* the daughters of the Philistines that turned you aside from the way in which you sinned.

28 And you went a-whoring to the daughters of Assyria, and not even then were you satisfied; indeed, you went a-whoring, and were not satisfied.

29 And you multiplied your covenants with the land of the Chaldeans; and not even with these were you satisfied.

30 Why should I make a covenant with your daughter, says the Lord, while you do all these things, the works of a harlot? And you have gone a-whoring in a threefold degree with your daughters.

31 'You have built a house of harlotry at the head of every road, and have set up your high place in every street; and you became as a harlot gathering payments.

32 An adulteress resembles you, taking rewards of her husband.

33 She has even given rewards to all that went a-whoring after her, and you have given rewards to all your lovers, yea, you loaded them with rewards, that they should come to you from every side for your fornication.

34 And there has happened in you perverseness in your fornication beyond *other* women, and they have committed fornication with you, in that you give payments over and above, and payments were not given to you; and *thus* perverseness happened in you.

35 Therefore, harlot, hear the word of the Lord:

36 Thus says the Lord: "Because you have poured forth your money, therefore your shame shall be discovered in your harlotry with your lovers, and *with* regard to all the imaginations of your iniquities, and for the blood of your children which you have given to them.

37 Therefore, behold, I *will* gather all your lovers with whom you have consorted, and all whom you have loved, with all whom you hated; and I will gather them against you round about, and will expose your wickedness to them, and they shall see all your shame.

38 And I will be avenged on you with the vengeance of an adulteress, and I will bring upon you blood of fury and jealousy.

39 And I will deliver you into their hands, and they shall break down your house of harlotry, and destroy your high place; and they shall strip you of your garments, and shall take your proud ornaments, and leave you naked and bare.

40 And they shall bring multitudes upon you, and they shall stone you with stones, and pierce you with their swords.

41 And they shall burn your houses with fire, and shall execute vengeance on you in the sight of many women; and I will turn you back from harlotry, and I will no more give *you* rewards.

42 So will I slacken My fury against you, and My jealousy shall be removed from you, and I will rest, and be angry no more.

43 Because you did not remember the days of your youth, and you grieved Me in all these things; therefore, behold, I have recompensed your ways upon your head, says the Lord; for thus have you wrought ungodliness above all your *other* iniquities.

⁴⁴ "These are all the things they have spoken against you in a proverb, saying,

⁴⁵ 'Like mother, like daughter: you are she that has rejected her husband and her children; and the sisters of your sisters have rejected their husbands and their children. Your mother was a Hittite, and *your* father an Amorite.

⁴⁶ Your elder sister who dwells on your left hand is Samaria, she and her daughters; and your younger sister, that dwells on your right hand, is Sodom and her daughters.

⁴⁷ Yet notwithstanding you have not walked in their ways, neither have you done according to their iniquities within a little, but you have exceeded them in all your ways.

⁴⁸ *As* I live, says the Lord, this Sodom and her daughters have not done as you and your daughters have done.

⁴⁹ Moreover this was the sin of your sister Sodom—pride. She and her daughters lived in pleasure, in fullness of bread *and* in abundance; this belonged to her and her daughters, and they did not help the hand of the poor and needy.

⁵⁰ And they boasted, and worked iniquities before Me: so I cut them off as I saw *fit*.

⁵¹ Also Samaria has not sinned according to half of your sins; but you have multiplied your iniquities beyond them, and you have justified your sisters in all your iniquities which you have committed.

⁵² You therefore bear your punishment, for that you have corrupted your sisters by your sins which you have committed beyond them; and you have made them *appear* more righteous than yourself: you therefore be ashamed, and bear your dishonor, in that you have justified your sisters.

⁵³ "And I will turn their captivity, *even* the captivity of Sodom and her daughters; and I will turn the captivity of Samaria and her daughters; and I will turn your captivity in the midst of them;

⁵⁴ that you may bear your punishment, and be dishonored for all that you have done in provoking Me to anger.

⁵⁵ And your sister Sodom and her daughters shall be restored as they were at the beginning, and you and your daughters shall be restored as you were at the beginning.

⁵⁶ And surely your sister Sodom was not mentioned by your mouth in the days of your pride;

⁵⁷ before your wickedness was discovered, even now you are the reproach of the daughters of Syria, and of all that are round about her, *even* of the daughters of the Philistines that compass you round about.

⁵⁸ *As for* your ungodliness and your iniquities, you have borne them, says the Lord.

An Everlasting Covenant

⁵⁹ "Thus says the Lord: I will even do to you as you have done, as you have dealt shamefully in these things to transgress My covenant.

⁶⁰ And I will remember My covenant, *made* with you in the days of your infancy, and I will establish an everlasting covenant with you.

⁶¹ Then you shall remember your ways, and you shall be utterly dishonored when you receive your elder sisters with your younger ones, and I will give them to you for building up, but not by your covenant.

⁶² And I will establish My covenant with you; and you shall know that I am the Lord,

⁶³ that you may remember, and be ashamed, and may no more be able to open your mouth for your shame, when I am reconciled to you for all that you have done, says the Lord.""

EZEKIEL CHAPTER 17

The Two Eagles and the Vine

¹ And the word of the Lord came to me, saying,

² "Son of man, relate a tale, and speak a parable to the house of Israel:

³ and you shall say, Thus says the Lord: 'A great eagle with large wings, spreading them out very far, with many claws, which has the design of entering into Lebanon—and he took the choice *branches* of the cedar;

⁴ he cropped off the ends of the tender twigs, and brought them into the land of Canaan; he laid them up in a walled city.

⁵ And he took of the seed of the land, and sowed it in a field planted by much water; he set it in a conspicuous place.

⁶ And it sprang up, and became a weak and little vine, so that its branches appeared *on* it, and its roots were under it: and it became a vine, and put forth shoots, and sent forth its branches.

⁷ "And there was another great eagle, with great wings and many claws. And behold, this vine bent itself round toward him, and its roots *were turned* towards him, and it sent forth its branches towards him, that *he* might water it together with the growth of its plantation.

⁸ It thrives in a fair field by much water, to produce shoots and bear fruit, that it might become a great vine.

⁹ "Therefore say, Thus says the Lord: 'Shall it prosper? Shall not the roots of its tender stem and its fruit be blighted? Yea, all its early shoots shall be dried up, and *that* not by a mighty arm, nor by many people, to tear it up from its roots.

¹⁰ And behold, it thrives; shall it prosper? Shall it not wither as soon as the east wind touches it? It shall be withered together with the growth of its shoots.""

¹¹ Moreover the word of the Lord came to me saying,

¹² "Son of man, say now to the provoking house, 'Do you not know you what these things were?' Say *to them*, 'Whenever the king of Babylon shall come against Jerusalem, then he shall take her king and her princes, and shall take them home to Babylon.

¹³ And he shall take of the royal seed, and shall make a covenant with him, and shall bind him with an oath; and he shall take the princes of the land,

[14] that it may become a weak kingdom, so as never to lift itself up, that he may keep his covenant, and establish it.

[15] And *if* he shall revolt from him, to send his messengers into Egypt, that *they* may give him horses and much people; shall he prosper? Shall he that acts as an adversary be preserved? And shall he that transgresses the covenant be preserved?

[16] *As* I live, says the Lord, verily in *the* place where the king is that made him king, who dishonored My oath, and who broke My covenant, shall he die with him in the midst of Babylon.

[17] And Pharaoh shall make war upon him not with a large force or great multitude, in throwing up a mound, and in building of forts, to cut off souls.

[18] Whereas he has profaned the oath so as to break the covenant, when behold, I engage his hand, and he has done all these things to him, he shall not escape.'

[19] Therefore say, Thus says the Lord: '*As* I live, surely My oath which he has profaned, and My covenant which he has transgressed, I will recompense it upon his own head.

[20] And I will spread a net upon him, and he shall be caught in its snare.

[21] In every battle of his they shall fall by the sword, and I will scatter *his* remnant to every wind, and you shall know that I the Lord have spoken it.'

Israel Exalted at Last

[22] "For thus says the Lord: I will even take of the choice *branches* of the cedar from the top *thereof*, I will crop off their hearts, and I will plant it on a high mountain;

[23] and I will hang it on a lofty mountain of Israel: yes, I will plant it, and it shall put forth shoots, and shall bear fruit, and it shall be a great cedar. And every bird shall rest beneath it, even every fowl shall rest under its shadow; its branches shall be restored.

[24] And all the trees of the field shall know that I am the Lord, who brings low the high tree, and who exalts the low tree, and who withers the green tree, and causes the dry tree to flourish. I, the Lord, have spoken, and will do *it*."

EZEKIEL CHAPTER 18

Individual Retribution

[1] And the word of the Lord came to me, saying,

[2] "Son of man, what do you mean by this parable concerning the children of Israel, saying, 'The fathers have eaten sour grapes, and the children's teeth have been set on edge?'

[3] *As* I live, says the Lord, surely this parable shall no more be spoken in Israel.

[4] For all souls are Mine; as the soul of the father, so also the soul of the son, they are Mine: the soul that sins, it shall die.

[5] But the righteous man, who executes judgment and righteousness,

[6] who shall not eat upon the mountains, and shall not at all lift up his eyes to the devices of the house of Israel, and shall not defile his neighbor's wife, and shall not draw near to her that is removed,

[7] and shall not oppress any man, *but* shall return the pledge of the debtor, and shall be guilty of no plunder, shall give his bread to the hungry, and clothe the naked;

[8] and shall not lend his money upon usury, and shall not receive usurious increase, and shall turn back his hand from injustice, shall execute righteous judgment between a man and his neighbor,

[9] and has walked in My commandments and kept My ordinances, to do them—the righteous man shall surely live, says the Lord.

[10] "And if he should have a mischievous son, shedding blood and committing sins,

[11] who has not walked in the way of his righteous father, but has even eaten upon the mountains, and has defiled his neighbor's wife,

[12] and has oppressed the poor and needy, and has committed robbery, and not restored a pledge, and has set his eyes upon idols, has worked iniquities,

[13] has lent upon usury, and taken usurious increase; he shall by no means live: he has done all these iniquities; he shall surely die; his blood shall be upon him.

[14] "And if he has a son, and *the son* should see all his father's sins which he has done, and fear, and does not do according to them,

[15] and *if he* has not eaten on the mountains, and has not set his eyes on the devices of the house of Israel, and has not defiled his neighbor's wife,

[16] and has not oppressed a man, and has not retained the pledge, nor committed robbery, has given his bread to the hungry, and has clothed the naked,

[17] and has turned back his hand from unrighteousness, has not received interest or usurious increase, has worked righteousness, and walked in My ordinances; he shall not die for the iniquities of his father, *and* he shall surely live.

[18] But if his father should grievously afflict or plunder, he has wrought enmity in the midst of My people, and shall die in his iniquity.

[19] "But you will say, 'Why has not the son borne the iniquity of the father?' Because the son has wrought judgment and mercy, has kept all My statues, and done them, he shall surely live.

[20] But the soul that sins shall die; and the son shall not bear the iniquity of the father, nor shall the father bear the iniquity of the son; the righteousness of the righteous shall be upon him, and the iniquity of the transgressor shall be upon him.

[21] "And if the transgressor shall turn away from all his iniquities which he has committed, and keep all My commandments, and do justice and mercy, he shall surely live, and shall no means die.

22 None of his trespasses which he has committed shall be remembered; in his righteousness which he has done he shall live.

23 Shall I in any way desire the death of the sinner, says he Lord, as I *desire* that he should turn from *his* evil way, and live?

24 "But when the righteous man turns away from his righteousness, and commits iniquity, according to all the transgressions which the transgressor has done, none of his righteousness which he has wrought shall be at all remembered; in his trespass in which he has trespassed, and in his sins in which he has sinned, in them shall he die.

25 "Yet you have said, 'The way of the Lord is not straight.' Hear now, all the house of Israel: will not My way be straight? Is your way straight?

26 When the righteous turns away from his righteousness and commits a trespass, and dies in the trespass he has committed, he shall *even* die in it.

27 And when the wicked man turns away from his wickedness that he has committed, and shall do judgment and justice, he has kept his soul,

28 and has turned away from all his ungodliness which he has committed: he shall surely live, he shall not die.

29 Yet the house of Israel says, 'The way of the Lord is not right.' Is not My way right, O house of Israel? Is not your way wrong?

30 "I will judge you, O house of Israel, says the Lord, each one according to his way: be converted, and turn from all your ungodliness, and the punishment for iniquity shall not befall you.

31 Cast away from yourselves all your ungodliness in which you have sinned against Me; and get yourselves a new heart and a new spirit: for why should you die, O house of Israel?

32 For I have no pleasure in the death of one who dies, says the Lord."

EZEKIEL CHAPTER 19

Israel Degraded

1 "Moreover do you take up a lamentation for the prince of Israel,

2 and say, 'Why has your mother become a whelp in the midst of lions?' In the midst of lions she has multiplied her whelps.

3 And one of her whelps sprang forth; he became a lion, and learned to take prey, he devoured men.

4 And the nations heard a report of him; he was caught in their pit, and they brought him into the land of Egypt in chains.

5 And she saw that he was driven away from her, *and* her hope for him perished, and she took another of her whelps; she made him a lion.

6 And he went up and down in the midst of lions, he became a lion, and learned to take prey, he devoured men.

7 And he prowled in his boldness and laid waste their cities, and made the land desolate, and the fullness of it, by the voice of his roaring.

8 Then the nations set against him from the surrounding regions, and they spread their nets upon him; he was taken in their pit.

9 And they put him in chains and in a cage, *and* he came to the king of Babylon; and he cast him into prison, that his voice should not be heard on the mountains of Israel.

10 "Your mother was as a vine and as a blossom on a pomegranate tree, planted by water; her fruit and her shoot abounded by reason of much water.

11 And she became a rod for a tribe of princes, and was elevated in her bulk in the midst of *other* trees, and she saw her bulk in the multitude of her branches.

12 But she was broken down in wrath, she was cast upon the ground, and the east wind dried up her choice *branches;* vengeance came upon them, and the rod of her strength was withered; fire consumed it.

13 And now they have planted her in the wilderness, in a dry land.

14 And fire has gone out of a rod of her choice *boughs,* and has devoured her; and there was no rod of strength in her. Her race has become a parable of lamentation, and it shall be for a lamentation."

EZEKIEL CHAPTER 20

Israel's Continuing Rebellion

1 And it came to pass in the seventh year, on the fifteenth day of the month, there came men of the elders of the house of Israel to inquire of the Lord, and they sat before me.

2 And the word of the Lord came to me, saying,

3 "Son of man, speak to the elders of the house of Israel, and you shall say to them, Thus says the Lord: 'Have you come to inquire of Me? *As* I live, I will not be inquired of by you,' says the Lord.

4 Shall I utterly take vengeance on them, son of man? Testify to them of the iniquities of their fathers,

5 and you shall say to them, Thus says the Lord: 'From the day that I chose the house of Israel, and became known to the descendants of the house of Jacob, and was known to them in the land of Egypt, and helped them with My hand, saying, "I am the Lord your God";

6 in that day I helped them with My hand, to bring them out of the land of Egypt into the land which I prepared for them, a land flowing with milk and honey, it is abundant beyond every land.

7 And I said to them, "Let everyone cast away the abominations of his eyes, and do not defile yourselves with the devices of Egypt: I am the Lord your God."

8 But they revolted against Me, and would not listen to Me: they would not cast away the abominations of their eyes, and would not forsake the devices of Egypt. Then I said that I would pour out My wrath upon them, to accomplish My wrath upon them in the midst of Egypt.

9 But I acted *so* that My name should not be at all profaned in the sight of the Gentiles, in the midst of whom they are, among whom I was made known to them in their sight, to bring them out of the land of Egypt.

10 "And I brought them into the wilderness.

11 And I gave them My commandments, and made known to them My ordinances, which, *if* a man shall do, he shall live by them.

12 And I gave them My Sabbaths, that they should be for a sign between Me and them, that they should know that I am the Lord that sanctifies them.

13 And I said to the house of Israel in the wilderness, 'Walk in My commandments': but they did not walk *in them*, and they rejected My ordinances, which, *if* a man shall do, he shall live by them; and they grievously profaned My Sabbaths. And I said that I would pour out My wrath upon them in the wilderness, to consume them.

14 But I acted *so* that My name should not be at all profaned before the Gentiles, before whose eyes I brought them out.

15 But I lifted up My hand against them in the wilderness once for all, that I would not bring them into the land which I gave them, a land flowing with milk and honey, it is sweeter than all lands;

16 because they rejected My ordinances, and did not walk in My commandments, but profaned My Sabbaths, and went after the imaginations of their hearts.

17 Yet My eyes spared them, so as *not* to destroy them utterly, and I did not make an end of them in the wilderness.

18 "And I said to their children in the wilderness, 'Do not walk in the customs of your fathers, and do not keep their ordinances, and have no fellowship with their practices, nor defile yourselves *with them*.

19 I *am* the Lord your God; walk in My commandments, and keep My ordinances, and do them;

20 and sanctify My Sabbaths, and let them be for a sign between Me and you, that you may know that I am the Lord your God.'

21 But they provoked Me, and their children did not walk in My commandments, and they took no heed to My ordinances, to do them, which, *if* a man shall do, he shall live by them, and they profaned My Sabbaths. Then I said that I would pour out My wrath upon them in the wilderness, to accomplish My anger upon them.

22 But I acted so that My name might not be at all profaned before the Gentiles; and I brought them out in their sight.

23 I lifted up My hand against them in the wilderness, that I would scatter them among the Gentiles, *and* disperse them in the countries;

24 because they did not keep My ordinances, and rejected My commandments, and profaned My Sabbaths, and their eyes went after the imaginations of their fathers.

25 So I gave them commandments *that were* not good, and ordinances in which they should not live.

26 And I will defile them by their *own* decrees, when I pass through upon everyone that opens the womb, that I may destroy them.

27 "Therefore, son of man, speak to the house of Israel, and you shall say to them, Thus says the Lord: 'In this too have your fathers provoked Me, in their trespasses in which they have transgressed against Me.

28 Whereas I brought them into the land concerning which I lifted up My hand to give it to them; and they looked upon every high hill, and every shady tree, and they sacrificed there to their gods, and offered there sweet-smelling savors, and there they poured out their drink offerings.'

29 And I said to them, 'What is Bamah, that you go in there?' And they called its name Bamah, until this day.

30 Therefore say to the house of Israel, Thus says the Lord: 'Do you pollute yourselves with the iniquities of your fathers, and do you go a-whoring after their abominations,

31 and *do you pollute yourselves* with the firstfruits of your gifts, in the offerings wherewith you pollute yourselves in all your imaginations, until this day; and shall I answer you, O house of Israel? *As* I live, says the Lord, I will not answer you, neither shall this thing come upon your spirit.

32 And it shall not be as you say, "We will be as the nations, and as the tribes of the earth, to worship stocks and stones."

God Will Restore Israel

33 "Therefore, *as* I live, says the Lord, I will reign over you with a strong hand, and with an outstretched arm, and with outpoured wrath.

34 I will bring you out from the nations, and will take you out of the lands in which you were dispersed, with a strong hand, and with an outstretched arm, and with outpoured wrath.

35 And I will bring you into the wilderness of the nations, and will plead with you there face to face.

36 As I pleaded with your fathers in the wilderness of the land of Egypt, so will I judge you, says the Lord.

37 And I will cause you to pass under My rod, and I will bring you in by number.

38 And I will separate from among you the ungodly and the revolters; for I will lead them forth out of their place of sojourning, and they shall not enter into the land of Israel: and you shall know that I am the Lord, *even* the Lord.

39 And *as for* you, O house of Israel, thus says the Lord, *even* the Lord: Put away each one his *evil* practices, and hereafter if you hearken to Me, then shall you no more profane My holy name by your gifts and by devices.

40 For upon My holy mountain, on the high mountain, says the Lord, *even* the Lord, there shall all the house of Israel serve Me forever. And there will I accept *you*, and there will I

have respect to your firstfruits, and the firstfruits of your offerings, in all your holy things.

⁴¹ I will accept you with a sweet-smelling savor, when I bring you out from the nations, and take you out of the countries in which you have been dispersed; and I will be sanctified among you in the sight of the nations.

⁴² And you shall know that I am the Lord, when I have brought you into the land of Israel, into the land concerning which I lifted up My hand to give it to your fathers.

⁴³ And there you shall remember your ways, and your devices in which you defiled yourselves; and you shall bewail yourselves for all your wickedness.

⁴⁴ And you shall know that I am the Lord, when I have done thus to you, that My name may not be profaned in your evil ways, and in your corrupt devices, says the Lord."

Prophecy Against the Negev

⁴⁵ And the word of the Lord came to me, saying,

⁴⁶ "Son of man, set your face against Thaman, and look toward Darom, and prophesy against the chief forest of Negev,

⁴⁷ and you shall say to the forest of Negev, 'Hear the word of the Lord; thus says the Lord: "Behold, I *will* kindle a fire in you, and it shall devour in you every green tree, and every dry tree. The flame that is kindled shall not be quenched, and every face shall be scorched with it from the south to the north.

⁴⁸ And all flesh shall know that I, the Lord, have kindled it: it shall not be quenched.""""

⁴⁹ And I said, "Not so, O Lord God! They say to me, 'Is not this that is spoken a parable?'"

EZEKIEL CHAPTER 21

¹ And the word of the Lord came to me, saying,

² "Prophesy, son of man, set your face steadfastly toward Jerusalem, and look toward their holy places, and you shall prophesy against the land of Israel,

³ and you shall say to the land of Israel, Thus says the Lord: 'Behold, I am against you, and I will draw forth My sword out of its sheath, and I will destroy out of you the transgressor and the unrighteous.

⁴ Because I will destroy out of you the unrighteous and the transgressor, *therefore* so shall My sword come forth out of its sheath against all flesh from the south to the north;

⁵ and all flesh shall know that I the Lord have drawn forth My sword out of its sheath: it shall not return anymore.'

The Drawn Sword of God

⁶ "And you, son of man, groan with the breaking of your loins; you shall even groan heavily in their sight.

⁷ And it shall come to pass, if they shall say to you, 'Why do you groan?' that you shall say, 'For the report; because it comes: and every heart shall break, and all hands shall become feeble, and all flesh and every spirit shall faint, and all thighs shall be defiled with moisture: behold, it comes, says the Lord.'"

⁸ And the word of the Lord came to me, saying,

⁹ "Son of man, prophesy, and you shall say, Thus says the Lord: 'Say, Sword, sword, be sharpened and rage,

¹⁰ that you may slay victims; be sharpened, that you may be bright, ready for slaughter, slay, set at nought, despise every tree.'

¹¹ And He made it ready for His hand to hold. The sword is sharpened, it is ready to put into the hand of the slayer.

¹² Cry out and howl, son of man, for this *sword* has come upon My people, this *sword has come* upon all the princes of Israel: they shall be as strangers: *judgment* with the sword has come upon My people; therefore clap your hands, for sentence has been passed;

¹³ and what if even the tribe be rejected? It shall not be, says the Lord God."

¹⁴ "And you, son of man, prophesy, and clap your hands, and take a second sword: the third sword is *the sword* of the slain, the great sword of the slain; and you shall strike them with amazement, lest the heart should faint,

¹⁵ and the weak ones be multiplied at every gate—they are given up to the slaughter of the sword; it is well fitted for slaughter, it is well fitted for glittering.

¹⁶ And go on, sharpen yourself on the right and on the left, wherever your face may set itself.

¹⁷ And I also will clap My hands, and let loose My fury. The Lord has spoken *it*."

¹⁸ And the word of the Lord came to me, saying,

¹⁹ "And you, son of man, appoint for yourself two ways, that the sword of the king of Babylon may enter in: the two shall go forth from one country; and *there shall be* a force at the top of the way of the city, you shall set *it* at the top of the road,

²⁰ that the sword may enter in upon Rabbah of the children of Ammon, and upon Judah, and upon Jerusalem in the midst thereof.

²¹ For the king of Babylon shall stand on the old road, at the head of the two roads, to use divination, to make bright the arrow, and to inquire of the graven images, and to examine *the victims*.

²² On his right was the divination against Jerusalem, to cast a mound, to open the mouth in shouting, to lift up the voice with crying, to cast a mound against her gates, to cast up a heap, and to build forts.

²³ And he was to them as one using divination before them, and he himself recounting his iniquities, that they might be borne in mind.

²⁴ "Therefore thus says the Lord: 'Because you have caused your iniquities to be remembered, in the discovery of your wickedness, so that your sins should be seen, in all your wickedness and in your *evil* practices; because you have caused remembrance *of them*, in these shall you be taken.'

25 And you, O profane wicked prince of Israel, whose day, and whose end, has come in a sea of iniquity, thus says the Lord: 26 'You have taken off the turban and put on the crown, it shall not have such *another* after it: you have abased that which was high, and exalted that which was low.

27 Injustice, injustice, injustice, will I make it; woe to it. Such shall it be until he comes to whom it belongs; and I will deliver *it* to him.'

28 "And you, son of man, prophesy, and you shall say, Thus says the Lord, concerning the children of Ammon, and concerning their reproach: and you shall say, 'O sword, sword, drawn for slaughter, and drawn for destruction, awake, that you may gleam.

29 While you are seeing vain *visions*, and while you are prophesying falsehoods, to bring yourself upon the necks of ungodly transgressors, the day has come, *even* an end, in a season of iniquity.

30 Turn, do not rest in this place in which you were born: in your own land will I judge you.

31 And I will pour out My wrath upon you, I will blow upon you with the fire of My wrath, and I will deliver you into the hands of barbarians skilled in working destruction.

32 You shall be fuel for fire; your blood shall be in the midst of your land; there shall be no remembrance at all of you: for I the Lord have spoken *it*.'"

EZEKIEL CHAPTER 22

The Sins of Israel

1 And the word of the Lord came to me, saying,

2 "And you, son of man, will you judge the bloody city? Yea, declare to her all her iniquities.

3 And you shall say, Thus says the Lord God: 'O city that sheds blood in the midst of her, so that her time should come, and that forms devices against herself, to defile herself;

4 in their blood which you have shed, you have transgressed; and in your devices which you have formed, you have polluted yourself; and you have brought near your days, and have brought on the time of your years; therefore have I made you a reproach to the Gentiles, and a mockery to all countries,

5 to those near you, and to those far away; and they shall mock you, *you that are* notoriously unclean, and abundant in iniquities.

6 "Behold, the princes of the house of Israel have conspired in you each one with his kindred, that they might shed blood.

7 In you they have reviled father and mother; and in you they have behaved unjustly toward the stranger; they have oppressed the orphan and widow.

8 And they have set at nought My holy things, and in you they have profaned My Sabbaths.

9 *There are* robbers in you, to shed blood in you; and in you they have eaten upon the mountains; they have wrought ungodliness in the midst of you.

10 In you they have uncovered their father's shame; and in you they have humbled her that was set apart for uncleanness.

11 They have dealt unlawfully each one with his neighbor's wife; and each one in ungodliness has defiled his daughter-in-law: and in you they have humbled each one his sister, the daughter of his father.

12 In you they have received gifts to shed blood; they have received in you interest and usurious increase; and by oppression you have brought your wickedness to the full, and have forgotten Me, says the Lord.

13 "And if I shall smite My hand at *your iniquities* which you have accomplished, which you have wrought, and at your blood that has been shed in the midst of you,

14 shall your heart endure? Shall your hands be strong in the days which I bring upon you? I the Lord have spoken, and will do *it*.

15 And I will scatter you among the nations, and disperse you in the countries, and your uncleanness shall be removed out of you.

16 And I will give heritages in you in the sight of the nations, and you shall know that I am the Lord.'"

17 And the word of the Lord came to me, saying,

18 "Son of man, behold, the house of Israel has become to Me *as it were* mixed with brass, and iron, and tin, and lead; they are mixed up in the midst of the silver.

19 Therefore say, Thus says the Lord God: 'Because you have become one mixture, therefore I will gather you into the midst of Jerusalem.

20 As silver, brass, iron, tin, and lead are gathered into the midst of the furnace, to blow fire into it, that they may be melted: so will I take *you* in My wrath, and I will gather and melt you.

21 And I will blow upon you in the fire of My wrath, and you shall be melted in the midst thereof.

22 As silver is melted in the midst of a furnace, so shall you be melted in the midst thereof; and you shall know that I, the Lord, have poured out My wrath upon you.'"

23 And the word of the Lord came to me, saying,

24 "Son of man, say to her: 'You are the land that is not rained upon, neither has rain come upon you in the day of wrath;

25 whose princes in the midst of her are as roaring lions seizing prey, devouring souls by oppression, and taking bribes; and your widows are multiplied in the midst of you.

26 Her priests also have set at nought My law, and profaned My holy things: they have not distinguished between the holy and profane, nor have they distinguished between the unclean and the clean, and have hidden their eyes from My Sabbaths, and I was profaned in the midst of them.

27 Her princes in the midst of her are as wolves ravening to shed blood, that they may get dishonest gain.

²⁸ And her prophets that daub them shall fall, that see vanities, that prophesy falsehoods, saying, "Thus says the Lord," when the Lord has not spoken;

²⁹ *and* who sorely oppress the people of the land with injustice, and commit robbery; oppressing the poor and needy, and not dealing justly with the stranger.

³⁰ And I sought from among them a man behaving uprightly, and standing before Me perfectly in the time of wrath, so that I should not utterly destroy her, but I found no one.

³¹ So I have poured out My wrath upon her in the fury of My anger, to accomplish *it*. I have recompensed their ways on their own heads," says the Lord God.

EZEKIEL CHAPTER 23

Oholah and Oholibah

¹ And the word of the Lord came to me, saying,

² "Son of man, there were two women, daughters of one mother:

³ and they went a-whoring in Egypt in their youth. There their breasts fell, *and* there they lost their virginity.

⁴ And their names were Oholah the elder, and Oholibah her sister: and they were Mine, and bore sons and daughters. And *as for* their names, Samaria was Oholah, and Jerusalem was Oholibah.

⁵ "And Oholah departed from Me and played the harlot, and doted on her lovers, on the Assyrians that were her neighbors,

⁶ clothed with purple, princes and captains; *they were* young men and choice, all horsemen riding on horses.

⁷ And she bestowed her fornication upon them; all were choice sons of the Assyrians: and on whomsoever she doted herself, with them she defiled herself in all *their* devices.

⁸ And she did not forsake her fornication with the Egyptians: for in her youth they committed fornication with her, and they deflowered her, and poured out their fornication upon her.

⁹ Therefore I delivered her into the hands of her lovers, into the hands of the children of the Assyrians, on whom she doted.

¹⁰ They uncovered her shame; they took her sons and daughters, and slew her with the sword; and she became a byword among women; and they wrought vengeance in her for the sake of the daughters.

¹¹ "Now her sister Oholibah saw *it*, and she indulged in her fondness more corruptly than she, and in her fornication more than the fornication of her sister.

¹² She doted upon the sons of the Assyrian, princes and captains, her neighbors, clothed with fine linen, horsemen riding on horses; *they were* all choice young men.

¹³ And I saw that they were defiled, *that* the two *had* one way.

¹⁴ And she increased her fornication, and she saw men painted on the wall, likenesses of the Chaldeans painted with a pencil,

¹⁵ having various belts on their loins, having also richly dyed *turbans* upon their heads; all had a princely appearance, the likeness of the children of the Chaldeans, of their native land.

¹⁶ And she doted upon them as soon as she saw them, and sent forth messengers to them into the land of the Chaldeans.

¹⁷ And the sons of Babylon came to her, into the bed of rest, and they defiled her in her fornication, and she was defiled by them, and her soul was alienated from them.

¹⁸ And she exposed her fornication, and exposed her shame. And My soul was alienated from her, even as My soul was alienated from her sister.

¹⁹ And you multiplied your fornication, so as to call to remembrance the days of your youth, in which you committed harlotry in Egypt,

²⁰ and you doted upon the Chaldeans, whose flesh is as the flesh of donkeys, and their members *as* the members of horses.

²¹ And you looked upon the iniquity of your youth, *the things* which you did in Egypt in your lodgings, where were the breasts of your youth.

²² "Therefore, Oholibah, thus says the Lord: 'Behold, I *will* stir up your lovers against you, from whom your soul is alienated, and I will bring them upon you round about,

²³ the children of Babylon, and all the Chaldeans, Pekod, and Shoa, and Koa, and all the sons of the Assyrians with them; choice young men, governors and captains, all princes and renowned, riding on horses.

²⁴ And they all shall come upon you from the north, chariots and wheels, with a multitude of nations, shields and targets; and *the enemy* shall set a watch against you round about; and I will set judgment before them, and they shall take vengeance on you with their judgements.

²⁵ And I will bring upon you My jealousy, and they shall deal with you in great wrath. They shall take away your nose and your ears, and shall cast down your remnant with the sword. They shall take your sons and your daughters, and fire shall devour your remnant.

²⁶ And they shall strip you of your clothing, and take *away* your ornaments.

²⁷ So I will turn back your ungodliness from you, and your fornication from the land of Egypt; and you shall not lift up your eyes upon them, and shall no more remember Egypt.

²⁸ Therefore thus says the Lord God: Behold, I *will* deliver you into the hands of those whom you hate, from whom your soul is alienated.

²⁹ And they shall deal with you in hatred, and shall take all *the fruits* of your labors and your toils, and you shall be naked and bare; and the shame of your fornication shall be exposed. And your ungodliness and your fornication

30 has brought this upon you, in that you played the harlot with the nations, and defiled yourself with their devices.

31 You walked in the way of your sister; and I will put her cup into your hands.

32 "Thus says the Lord: Drink your sister's cup, deep and large and full, to cause complete drunkenness.

33 And you shall be thoroughly weakened; and the cup of destruction, the cup of your sister Samaria,

34 drink it, and I will take away her feasts and her new moons; for I have spoken *it*, says the Lord.

35 Therefore thus says the Lord: Because you have forgotten Me, and have cast Me behind your back, therefore receive *the reward* of your ungodliness and your fornication.'"

36 And the Lord said to me, "Son of man, will you not judge Oholah and Oholibah, and declare to them their iniquities?

37 For they have committed adultery, and blood was on their hands, they committed adultery with their devices, and they passed through the fire to them their children which they bore to Me.

38 So long too as they did these things to Me, they defiled My sanctuary, and profaned My Sabbaths.

39 And when they sacrificed their children to their idols, they also went into My sanctuary to profane it; and whereas they did thus in the midst of My house,

40 and whereas they did thus to the men that came from afar, to whom they sent messengers, and as soon as they came, immediately you washed yourself, and painted your eyes and adorned yourself with ornaments,

41 and sat on a prepared bed, and before it *there was* a table set out, and *as for* My incense and My oil, they rejoiced in them,

42 and they raised a sound of music, and *that* with men coming from the wilderness out of a multitude of men, and they put bracelets on their hands, and a crown of glory on their heads.

43 Therefore I said, 'Do they not commit adultery with these? And has she also gone a-whoring *after* the manner of a harlot?'

44 And they went in to her, as *men* go in to a harlot; so they went in to Oholah and to Oholibah, to work iniquity.

45 And they are just men, and shall take vengeance on them with the judgment of an adulteress and the judgment of blood, for they are adulteresses, and blood is on their hands.

46 "Thus says the Lord God: Bring up a multitude upon them, and send trouble and plunder into the midst of them.

47 And stone them with the stones of a multitude, and pierce them with their swords; they shall slay their sons and their daughters, and shall burn up their houses.

48 And I will remove ungodliness out of the land, and all the women shall be instructed, and shall not do according to their ungodliness.

49 And your ungodliness shall be recompensed upon you, and you shall bear the guilt of your devices, and you shall know that I am the Lord."

EZEKIEL CHAPTER 24

Parable of the Boiling Pot

1 And the word of the Lord came to me, in the ninth year, in the tenth month, on the tenth *day* of the month, saying,

2 "Son of man, write down the name of the day, this very day, on which the king of Babylon set himself against Jerusalem, *even* from this day.

3 And speak a parable to the provoking house, and you shall say to them, Thus says the Lord: 'Set on the caldron, and pour water into it,

4 and put the pieces into it, every prime piece, the leg and shoulder taken off from the bones,

5 *which are* taken from choice cattle, and burn the bones under them; her bones are boiled and cooked in the midst of her.

6 "Therefore thus says the Lord: O bloody city, the caldron in which there is scum, and the scum has not gone out of, she has brought it forth piece by piece, no lot has fallen upon it.

7 For her blood is in the midst of her; I have set it upon a smooth rock; I have not poured it out upon the earth, so that the earth should cover it;

8 that My wrath should come up for complete vengeance to be taken; I set her blood upon a smooth rock, so as not to cover it.

9 "Therefore thus says the Lord: I will also make the firebrand great,

10 and I will multiply the wood, and kindle the fire, that the flesh may be consumed, and the liquor boiled away;

11 and that *it* may stand upon the coals, that her brass may be thoroughly heated, and be melted in the midst of her filthiness, and her scum may be consumed,

12 and her abundant scum may not come forth from her.

13 Her scum shall become shameful, because you defiled yourself; and what if you shall be purged no more until I have accomplished My wrath?

14 I the Lord have spoken; and it shall come, and I will do *it*; I will not delay, neither will I have any mercy: I will judge you," says the Lord, "according to your ways, and according to your devices. Therefore will I judge you according to your bloodshed, and according to your devices will I judge you, you unclean, notorious, and abundantly provoking one.'"

Death of Ezekiel's Wife Is a Sign

15 And the word of the Lord came to me, saying,

16 "Son of man, behold I take from you the desire of your eyes by violence. You shall by no means lament, neither shall you weep.

17 You shall groan for blood, and have mourning upon your loins; your hair shall not be braided upon you, and your

sandals *shall be* on your feet; you shall by no means be comforted by their lips, and you shall not eat the bread of men."

¹⁸ So I spoke to the people in the morning, as He commanded me in the evening, and I did in the morning as it was commanded me.

¹⁹ And the people said to me, "Will you not tell us what these things are that you do?"

²⁰ Then I said to them, "The word of the Lord came to me, saying,

²¹ 'Say to the house of Israel, Thus says the Lord: Behold, I *will* profane My sanctuary, the boast of your strength, the desire of your eyes, and for which your souls are concerned; and your sons and your daughters, whom you have left, shall fall by the sword.

²² And you shall do as I have done: you shall not be comforted at their mouth, and you shall not eat the bread of men.

²³ And your hair *shall be* upon your head, and your shoes on your feet; neither shall you lament or weep, but you shall pine away in your iniquities, and shall comfort everyone his brother.

²⁴ And Ezekiel shall be for a sign to you: according to all that I have done shall you do, when these things shall come; and you shall know that I am the Lord.'"

²⁵ "And you, son of man, *shall it* not *be* in the day when I take their strength from them, the pride of their boasting, the desires of their eyes, and the pride of their soul, their sons and their daughters,

²⁶ that in that day he that escapes shall come to you, to tell *it* to you in your ears?

²⁷ In that day your mouth shall be opened to him that escapes; you shall speak, and shall be no longer dumb; and you shall be for a sign to them, and they shall know that I am the Lord."

EZEKIEL CHAPTER 25

Judgment on Gentile Nations—Ammon

¹ And the word of the Lord came to me, saying,

² "Son of man, set your face steadfastly against the children of Ammon, and prophesy against them;

³ and you shall say to the children of Ammon: Hear the word of the Lord; thus says the Lord: 'Forasmuch as you have rejoiced against My sanctuary, because it was profaned; and against the land of Israel, because it was laid waste, and against the house of Judah, because they went into captivity;

⁴ therefore, behold, I *will* deliver you to the children of Kedem for an inheritance, and they shall lodge in you with all their belongings, and they shall pitch their tents in you; they shall eat your fruits, and they shall drink your milk.

⁵ And I will give up the city of Ammon for camels' pastures, and the children of Ammon for a pasture of sheep; and you shall know that I am the Lord.

⁶ For thus says the Lord: Because you have clapped your hands, and stamped with your foot, and heartily rejoiced against the land of Israel;

⁷ therefore I will stretch out My hand against you, and I will make you a spoil to the nations; and I will utterly destroy you from among the peoples, and I will completely cut you off from out of the countries; and you shall know that I am the Lord.'"

Moab

⁸ "Thus says the Lord; Because Moab has said, 'Behold, are not the houses of Israel and Judah like all the *other* nations?'

⁹ Therefore, behold, I will weaken the shoulder of Moab from his frontier cities, *even* the choice land, the house of Beth Jeshimoth above the fountain of the city, by the seaside.

¹⁰ I have given him the children of Kedem in addition to the children of Ammon for an inheritance, that there may be no remembrance of the children of Ammon.

¹¹ And I will execute vengeance on Moab; and they shall know that I am the Lord."

Edom

¹² "Thus says the Lord: Because of what the Edomites have done in taking vengeance on the house of Judah, and *because they* have remembered injuries, and have exacted full recompense;

¹³ therefore thus says the Lord: I will also stretch out My hand upon Edom, and will utterly destroy out of it *both* man and beast, and I will make it desolate; and they that are pursued out of Teman shall fall by the sword.

¹⁴ And I will execute My vengeance on Edom by the hand of My people Israel; and they shall deal in Edom according to My anger and according to My wrath, and they shall know My vengeance," says the Lord.

Philistia

¹⁵ "Thus says the Lord: Because the Philistines have wrought revengefully, and raised up vengeance rejoicing from their heart to destroy *the Israelites* to a man;

¹⁶ therefore thus says the Lord: Behold, I *will* stretch out My hand upon the Philistines, and will utterly destroy the Cretans, and will cut off the remnant that dwell by the seacoast.

¹⁷ And I will execute great vengeance upon them, and they shall know that I am the Lord, when I have brought My vengeance upon them."

EZEKIEL CHAPTER 26

Judgment on Tyre

[1] And it came to pass in the eleventh year, on the first *day* of the month, *that* the word of the Lord came to me, saying,

[2] "Son of man, because Tyre has said against Jerusalem, 'Aha, she is crushed—the nations are destroyed; she has turned to me; she that was full is made desolate.'

[3] Therefore thus says the Lord: 'Behold, I am against you, O Tyre, and I will bring up many nations against you, as the sea comes up with its waves.

[4] And they shall cast down the walls of Tyre, and shall cast down your towers: and I will scrape her dust from off her, and make her a bare rock.

[5] She shall be in the midst of the sea a place for repairing nets, for I have spoken *it*,' says the Lord; 'and it shall be a spoil for the nations.

[6] And her daughters *which are* in the field shall be slain with the sword, and they shall know that I am the Lord.'"

[7] For thus says the Lord: "Behold, I *will* bring up against you, O Tyre, Nebuchadnezzar king of Babylon from the north: he is a king of kings, with horses, and chariots, and horsemen, and a concourse of very many nations.

[8] He shall slay your daughters that are in the field with the sword, and shall set a watch against you, and build forts around you, and carry a rampart round against you, and set up warlike works, and array his spears against you.

[9] He shall cast down with his swords your walls and your towers.

[10] By reason of the abundance of his horses their dust shall cover you, and by reason of the sound of his horsemen and the wheels of his chariots your walls shall be shaken, when he enters into your gates, as one entering into a city from the plain.

[11] With the hoofs of his horses they shall trample all your streets. He shall slay your people with the sword, and shall bring down to the ground the support of your strength.

[12] And he shall prey upon your power, and plunder your substance, and shall cast down your walls, and break down your pleasant houses; and he shall cast your stones and your timber and your dust into the midst of your sea.

[13] And he shall destroy the multitude of your musicians, and the sound of your psalteries shall be heard no more.

[14] And I will make you a bare rock. You shall be a place to spread nets upon; you shall be built no more; for I the Lord have spoken *it*," says the Lord.

[15] For thus says the Lord God to Tyre: "Shall not the isles shake at the sound of your fall, while the wounded are groaning, while they have drawn a sword in the midst of you?

[16] And all the princes of the nations of the sea shall come down from their thrones, and shall take off their crowns from their heads, and shall take off their embroidered garments; they shall be utterly amazed; they shall sit upon the ground, and fear their *own* destruction, and shall groan over you.

[17] And they shall take up a lamentation for you, and shall say to you, 'How are you destroyed from out of the sea, O renowned city, that brought her terror upon all her inhabitants!'

[18] And the isles shall be alarmed at the day of your fall."

[19] For thus says the Lord God: "When I shall make the city desolate, as the cities that shall not be inhabited, when I have brought the deep up upon you,

[20] and great waters shall cover you, and I shall bring you down to them that go down to the pit, to the people of old time, and shall cause you to dwell in the depths of the earth, as in everlasting desolation, with them that go down to the pit, that you may not be inhabited, nor stand upon the land of life;

[21] I will make you a terror, and you shall be no more forever," says the Lord God.

EZEKIEL CHAPTER 27

Lament over Tyre

[1] And the word of the Lord came to me saying,

[2] "And you, son of man, take up a lamentation against Tyre;

[3] and you shall say to Tyre that dwells at the entrance of the sea, to the merchant of the nations coming from many islands, Thus says the Lord to Tyre: 'You have said, "I have clothed myself with my beauty."

[4] In the heart of the sea your sons have put beauty upon you for Beelim.

[5] Cedar in Senir was employed for you in building; boards of cypress timber were taken out of Lebanon, and wood to make your masts of fir.

[6] They made your oars *of wood* out of the land of Bashan; your sacred utensils they made of ivory, your shady houses of wood from the isles of Kittim.

[7] Fine linen with embroidery from Egypt supplied the couch, to put honor upon you, and to clothe you with blue and purple from the isles of Elishah; and they became your coverings.

[8] And your princes were the inhabitants of Sidon, and the Aradians were your rowers. Your wise men, O Tyre, who were in you, these were your pilots.

[9] The elders of the Biblians, and their wise men, who were in you, these helped your counsel; and all the ships of the sea and their rowers traded for you to the utmost west.

[10] "Persians and Lydians and Libyans were in your army. Your warriors hung in you shields and helmets; these gave *you* your glory.

[11] The sons of the Aradians and your army were upon the walls; there were guards in your towers. They hung their quivers on your battlements round about; these completed your beauty.

[12] "The Carthaginians were your merchants because of the abundance of all your strength; they furnished your market with silver, gold, iron, tin and lead.

[13] Greece, both the whole *world*, and the adjacent coasts, these traded with you, in the persons of men, and they gave *as* your merchandise vessels of brass.

[14] Out of the house of Togarmah horses and horsemen furnished the market.

[15] The sons of the Dedan were your merchants; from the islands they multiplied your merchandise, *even* the elephants' tusks: and to them that came to you payed you back,

[16] *even* men *as* your merchandise, from the multitude of your trading *population*, myrrh and embroidered works from Tarshish. Ramoth also and Chorchor furnished your market.

[17] Judah and the children of Israel, these were your merchants; in the sale of grain and ointments and cassia; and they gave the best honey and oil and resin, to your trading *population*.

[18] *The people of* Damascus were your merchants by reason of the abundance of all your power; wine out of Helbon, and wool from Miletus; and they brought wine into your market.

[19] Out of Uzal *came* wrought iron, and there is the sound of wheels among your trading *population*.

[20] *The people of* Dedan were your merchants, with choice cattle for chariots.

[21] Arabia and all the princes of Kedar, these were your traders with you, *bringing* camels, lambs, and rams, in which they trade with you.

[22] The merchants of Sheba and Raamah, these were your merchants, with choice spices, and precious stones; and they brought gold to your market.

[23] Haran and Canneh, these were your merchants: Assyria and Chilmad, were your merchants;

[24] bringing for merchandise blue, and choice stores bound with cords, and cypress wood.

[25] Ships were your merchants, in abundance, with your trading *population*; and you were filled and very heavily loaded in the heart of the sea.

[26] The rowers have brought you into great waters. The south wind has broken you in the heart of the sea.

[27] "Your forces and your gain, and that of your traders and your rowers, and your pilots and your counselors, and they that traffic with you, and all your warriors that are in you; and all your company in the midst of you shall perish in the heart of the sea, in the day of your fall.

[28] At the cry of your voice your pilots shall be greatly terrified;

[29] and all the rowers and the mariners shall come down from the ships, and the pilots of the sea shall stand on the land.

[30] And they shall wail over you with their voice, and cry bitterly, and put earth on their heads, and spread ashes under them.

[31] (This verse omitted in LXX)

[32] And their sons shall take up a *lament* for you, even a lamentation for Tyre, *saying*,

[33] 'How large a reward have you gained from the sea?' You have filled nations out of your abundance; and out of your mixed merchandise you have enriched all the kings of the earth.

[34] Now are you broken in the sea, your traders are in the deep water, and all your company in the midst of you; all your rowers have fallen.

[35] All the inhabitants of the islands have mourned over you, and their kings have been utterly amazed, and their countenance has wept.

[36] Merchants from the nations have hissed at you; you are utterly destroyed, and shall not be any more forever.'"

EZEKIEL CHAPTER 28

Proclamation Against the King of Tyre

[1] And the word of the Lord came to me, saying,

[2] "And you, son of man, say to the prince of Tyre, Thus says the Lord: 'Because your heart has been exalted, and you have said, "I am God, I have inhabited the dwelling of God in the heart of the sea"; yet you are a man and not God, though you have set your heart as the heart of God.

[3] Are you wiser than Daniel? Or have not the wise instructed you with their knowledge?

[4] Have you gained power for yourself by your *own* knowledge or your *own* prudence, and *gathered* gold and silver in your treasures?

[5] By your abundant knowledge and your traffic you have multiplied your power; your heart has been lifted up by your power.

[6] Therefore thus says the Lord: Since you have set your heart as the heart of God;

[7] because of this, behold, I *will* bring on you strange plagues from the nations; and they shall draw their swords against you, and against the beauty of your knowledge,

[8] and they shall bring down your beauty to destruction. And they shall bring you down; and you shall die the death of the slain in the heart of the sea.

[9] Will you indeed say, "I am God," before them that slay you? Seeing you are man, and not God.

[10] You shall perish by the hands of strangers among the multitude of the uncircumcised, for I have spoken it,'" says the Lord.

Lamentation over the King of Tyre

[11] And the word of the Lord came to me, saying,

[12] "Son of man, take up a lamentation for the prince of Tyre, and say to him, Thus says the Lord God: 'You were a seal of resemblance, and a crown of beauty.

[13] You were in the delight of the paradise of God; you were adorned with every precious stone—the sardius, topaz, emerald, carbuncle, sapphire, jasper, silver, gold, ligure,

agate, amethyst, chrysolite, beryl and onyx; and you have filled your treasures and your stores in you with gold.

¹⁴ From the day that you were created you *were* with the cherub; I set you on the holy mount of God; you were in the midst of the stones of fire.

¹⁵ You were faultless in your days, from the day that you were created, until iniquity was found in you.

¹⁶ Of the abundance of your merchandise you have filled your storehouses with iniquity, and have sinned. Therefore you have been cast down wounded from the mount of God, and the cherub has brought you out of the midst of the stones of fire.

¹⁷ Your heart was lifted up because of your beauty; your knowledge has been corrupted by your beauty: because of the multitude of your sins I have cast you to the ground, I have caused you to be put to open shame before kings.

¹⁸ Because of the multitude of your sins and the iniquities of your merchandise, I have profaned your sacred things; and I will bring fire out of the midst of you, this shall devour you; and I will make you *to be* ashes upon your land before all that see you.

¹⁹ And all that know you among the nations shall groan over you. You have gone to destruction, and you shall not exist any longer.'"

Proclamation Against Sidon

²⁰ And the word of the Lord came to me, saying,

²¹ "Son of man, set your face against Sidon, and prophesy against it,

²² and say, Thus says the Lord: 'Behold, I am against you, O Sidon; and I will be glorified in you; and you shall know that I am the Lord, when I have wrought judgments in you, and I will be sanctified in you.

²³ Blood and death *shall be* in your streets; and *men* wounded with swords shall fall in you and on every side of you; and they shall know that I am the Lord.'

²⁴ "And there shall no more be in the house of Israel a thorn of bitterness and a pricking briar proceeding from them that are round about them, who dishonored them; and they shall know that I am the Lord."

²⁵ Thus says the Lord God: "I will also gather Israel from the nations, among whom they have been scattered, and I will be sanctified among them, and before the peoples and nations; and they shall dwell upon their land, which I gave to My servant Jacob.

²⁶ Yes, they shall dwell upon it safely, and they shall build houses, and plant vineyards, and dwell securely, when I shall execute judgment on all that have dishonored them, *even* on those *that are* round about them; and they shall know that I am the Lord their God, and the God of their fathers."

EZEKIEL CHAPTER 29

Proclamation Against Egypt

¹ In the twelfth year, in the tenth month, on the first *day* of the month, the word of the Lord came to me, saying,

² "Son of man, set your face against Pharaoh king of Egypt, and prophesy against him, and against all of Egypt,

³ and say, Thus says the Lord: 'Behold, I am against you O Pharaoh, the great dragon that lies in the midst of his rivers, that says, "The rivers are mine, and I made them."

⁴ And I will put hooks in your jaws, and I will cause the fish of your river to stick to your sides, and I will bring you up out of the midst of your river;

⁵ and I will quickly cast you down, and all the fish of your river. You shall fall on the face of the plain, and shall by no means be gathered, and shall not be brought together; I have given you for food to the wild beasts of the earth and to the birds of the sky.

⁶ And all the inhabitants of Egypt shall know that I am the Lord, because you have been a staff of reed to the house of Israel.

⁷ When they took hold of you with their hand, you broke *them;* and when every hand was clapped against them, and when they leaned on you, you utterly broke them, and crushed the loins of them all.

⁸ "Therefore thus says the Lord: Behold, I *will* bring a sword upon you, and will cut off from you both man and beast;

⁹ and the land of Egypt shall be ruined and desolate; and they shall know that I am the Lord; because you say, "The rivers are mine, and I made them."

¹⁰ Therefore, behold, I am against you, and against all your rivers, and I will give up the land of Egypt to desolation, and the sword, and destruction, from Migdol and Syene even to the borders of the Ethiopians.

¹¹ Man's foot shall not pass through it, nor the foot of beast, and it shall be uninhabited for forty years.

¹² And I will cause her land to be utterly destroyed in the midst of a land that is desolate, and her cities shall be *desolate* forty years in the midst of cities that are desolate; and I will disperse Egypt among the nations, and will utterly scatter them into the countries.

¹³ "Thus says the Lord: After forty years I will gather the Egyptians from the nations among whom they have been scattered;

¹⁴ and I will turn the captivity of the Egyptians, and will cause them to dwell in the land of Pathros, in the land from where they were taken;

¹⁵ and it shall be a lowly kingdom beyond all *other* kingdoms; it shall no longer be exalted above the nations; and I will make them few in number, that they may not be great among the nations.

¹⁶ And they shall no more be to the house of Israel a confidence bringing iniquity to remembrance, when they follow after them; and they shall know that I am the Lord.'"

Babylonia Will Plunder Egypt

[17] And it came to pass in the twenty-seventh year, on the first *day* of the month, the word of the Lord came to me, saying,

[18] "Son of man, Nebuchadnezzar king of Babylon caused his army to serve a great service against Tyre; every head was bald, and every shoulder rubbed raw; yet there was no reward to him or to his army *serving* against Tyre, nor for the service which they served against it.

[19] Thus says the Lord God: Behold, I *will* give to Nebuchadnezzar king of Babylon the land of Egypt, and he shall take its plunder, and seize the spoils, and *it* shall be a reward for his army.

[20] In return for his service in which he served against Tyre, I have given him the land of Egypt. Thus says the Lord God:

[21] In that day shall a horn spring forth for all the house of Israel, and I will give you an open mouth in the midst of them; and they shall know that I am the Lord."

EZEKIEL CHAPTER 30

Lamentation for Egypt

[1] And the word of the Lord came to me, saying,

[2] "Son of man, prophesy, and say, Thus says the Lord: 'Woe, woe to the day!

[3] For the day of the Lord is near, a day of clouds; it shall be the end of the nations.

[4] And the sword shall come upon the Egyptians, and there shall be tumult in Ethiopia, and in Egypt *men* shall fall down slain together, and her foundations shall fall.

[5] Persians, Cretans, Lydians, Libyans and all the mixed multitude, and they of the children of My covenant, shall fall by the sword therein.

[6] "And the supports of Egypt shall fall; and the pride of her strength shall come down from Migdol to Syene; they shall fall by the sword in it, says the Lord.

[7] And it shall be made desolate in the midst of desolate countries, and their cities shall be *desolate* in the midst of desolate cities;

[8] and they shall know that I am the Lord, when I shall send fire upon Egypt, and *when* all that help her shall be broken.

[9] In that day shall messengers go forth hasting to destroy Ethiopia utterly, and there shall be tumult among them in the day of Egypt; for behold, it comes.

[10] "Thus says the Lord God: I will also destroy the multitude of the Egyptians by the hand of Nebuchadnezzar king of Babylon,

[11] his *hand* and his people's; *they are* plagues sent forth from the nations to destroy the land; and they all shall unsheathe their swords against Egypt, and the land shall be filled with the slain.

[12] And I will make their rivers desolate, and will destroy the land and its fulness by the hands of strangers: I the Lord have spoken.

[13] "For thus says the Lord God: I will also destroy the nobles from Memphis, and the princes of Memphis out of the land of Egypt; and they shall be no more.

[14] And I will destroy the land of Pathros, and will send fire upon Tanis, and will execute vengeance on Noph.

[15] And I will pour out My wrath upon Sin, the strength of Egypt, and I will destroy the multitude of Memphis.

[16] And I will send fire upon Egypt; and Syene shall be greatly troubled; and there shall be a breaking in Noph, and waters shall be poured out.

[17] The youths of Heliopolis and Pi Beseth shall fall by the sword, and the women shall go into captivity.

[18] And the day shall be darkened in Tahpanhes, when I have broken there the scepters of Egypt; and the pride of her strength shall perish there, and a cloud shall cover her, and her daughters shall be taken prisoners.

[19] And I will execute judgment on Egypt; and they shall know that I am the Lord."

Proclamation Against Pharaoh

[20] And it came to pass in the eleventh year, in the first month, on the seventh *day* of the month, the word of the Lord came to me, saying,

[21] "Son of man, I have broken the arms of Pharaoh, king of Egypt; and behold, it has not been bound up to be healed, to have a plaster put upon it, *or* to be strengthened to lay hold of the sword.

[22] Therefore thus says the Lord God: Behold, I am against Pharaoh king of Egypt, and I will break his strong and outstretched arms, and I will strike down his sword from out of his hand.

[23] And I will disperse the Egyptians among the nations, and will utterly scatter them among the countries.

[24] And I will strengthen the arms of the king of Babylon, and put My sword into his hand, and he shall bring it upon Egypt, and shall take her plunder and seize her spoils.

[25] Yea, I will strengthen the arms of the king of Babylon, and the arms of Pharaoh shall fail; and they shall know that I am the Lord, when I have put My sword into the hands of the king of Babylon, and he shall stretch it out over the land of Egypt.

[26] And I will disperse the Egyptians among the nations, and utterly scatter them among the countries; and they all shall know that I am the Lord."

EZEKIEL CHAPTER 31

The Lofty Cedar

[1] And it came to pass in the eleventh year, in the third month, on the first *day* of the month, the word of the Lord came to me, saying,

2 "Son of man, say to Pharaoh king of Egypt, and to his multitude: 'To whom have you compared yourself in your haughtiness?

3 Behold, the Assyrian was a cypress in Lebanon, and was fair in shoots, and high in stature; his top reached to the midst of the clouds.

4 The water nourished him, the depth made him grow tall; she led her rivers round about his plants, and she sent forth her streams to all the trees of the field.

5 Therefore was his stature exalted above all the trees of the field, and his branches spread far by the help of much water.

6 All the birds of the sky made their nests in his boughs, and under his branches all the wild beasts of the field bred; the whole multitude of nations dwelt under his shadow.

7 And he was fair in his height by reason of the multitude of his branches, for his roots were amidst much water.

8 And such cypresses *as these* were in the paradise of God; and there were no pines like his shoots, and there were no firs like his branches; no tree in the paradise of God was like him in his beauty,

9 because of the multitude of his branches. And the trees of Eden envied him.

10 "Therefore thus says the Lord: Because you have grown great, and have set your top in the midst of the clouds, and I saw when he was exalted;

11 therefore I delivered him into the hands of the prince of the nations, and he wrought his destruction.

12 And ravaging strangers from the nations have destroyed him, and have cast him down upon the mountains. His branches fell in all the valleys, and his boughs were broken in every field of the land; and all the people of the nations have gone down from their shelter, and have laid him low.

13 All the birds of the sky have settled on his fallen trunk, and all the wild beasts of the field came upon his boughs,

14 in order that none of the trees by the water should exalt themselves by reason of their size; whereas they set their top in the midst of the clouds, yet they did not continue in their high state in their place, all that drank water, all were consigned to death, to the depth of the earth, in the midst of the children of men, with them that go down to the pit.

15 "Thus says the Lord God: In the day in which he went down to Hades, the deep mourned for him; and I kept back her floods, and restrained her abundance of water; and Lebanon mourned for him, *and* all the trees of the field fainted for him.

16 At the sound of his fall the nations quaked, when I brought him down to Hades with them that go down to the pit. And all the trees of Eden comforted him in the heart, and the choice *plants* of Lebanon, all that drink water.

17 For they went down to hell with him among the slain with the sword; and his descendants, *even* those that dwelt under his shadow, perished in the midst of their life.

18 To whom are you compared? Descend, and be debased with the trees of Eden to the depth of the earth. You shall lie in the midst of the uncircumcised with those that are slain by the sword. Thus shall Pharaoh be, and the multitude of his army,' says the Lord God."

EZEKIEL CHAPTER 32

Lamentation for Pharaoh and Egypt

1 And it came to pass in the twelfth year, in the tenth month, on the first *day* of the month, *that* the word of the Lord came to me, saying,

2 "Son of man, take up a lamentation for Pharaoh king of Egypt, and say to him: 'You have become like a lion among the nations, and as a serpent that is in the sea; and you made assaults with your rivers, and troubled the waters with your feet, and trampled your rivers.

3 Thus says the Lord: I will also cast over you the nets of many nations, and will bring you up with My hook;

4 and I will stretch you upon the earth. The fields shall be covered *with you*, and I will cause all the birds of the sky to settle upon you, and I will fill *with you* all the wild beasts of the earth.

5 And I will cast your flesh upon the mountains, and will saturate *them* with your blood.

6 And the land shall be drenched with your dung, because of your multitude upon the mountains; I will fill the valleys with you.

7 And I will veil the heavens when you are extinguished, and will darken the stars thereof; I will cover the sun with a cloud, and the moon shall not give her light.

8 All the *bodies* that give light in the sky shall be darkened over you, and I will bring darkness upon the earth, says the Lord God.

9 And I will provoke to anger the heart of many people, when I shall lead you captive among the nations, to a land which you have not known.

10 And many nations shall mourn over you, and their kings shall be utterly amazed, when My sword flies in their faces, as they wait for their *own* fall from the day of your fall.

11 "For thus says the Lord God: The sword of the king of Babylon shall come upon you,

12 with the swords of mighty men; and I will cast down your strength; *they are* all destroying ones from the nations, and they shall destroy the pride of Egypt, and all her strength shall be crushed.

13 And I will destroy all her cattle from *beside* the great water; and the foot of man shall not trouble it anymore, and the step of cattle shall no more trample it.

14 Thus shall their waters then be at rest, and their rivers shall flow like oil, says the Lord,

15 when I shall give up Egypt to destruction, and the land shall be made desolate with the fullness thereof; when I shall scatter all that dwell in it, and they shall know that I am the Lord.

16 There is a lamentation, and you shall utter it; and the daughters of the nations shall utter it, *even* for Egypt, and

they shall mourn for it over all the strength thereof,' says the Lord God."

Dirge over Egypt

¹⁷ And it came to pass in the twelfth year, in the first month, on the fifteenth *day* of the month, the word of the Lord came to me, saying,

¹⁸ "Son of man, lament over the strength of Egypt, for the nations shall bring down her daughters dead to the depth of the earth, to them that go down to the pit.

¹⁹ (This verse omitted in LXX)

²⁰ They shall fall with him in the midst of them *that are* slain with the sword, and all his strength shall perish. The giants also shall say to you,

²¹ 'Go down to the depths of the pit; to whom are you superior?' Yea, go down, and lie with the uncircumcised, in the midst of them *that are* slain with the sword.

²² There are Assyria and all his company; all *his* slain have been laid there,

²³ and their graves are in the depth of the pit, and his company is set around about his tomb. All the slain that fell by the sword, who had caused the fear of them *to be* upon the land of the living.

²⁴ There is Elam and all his multitude round about his tomb; all the slain that fell by the sword, and the uncircumcised that go down to the deep of the earth, who caused their fear to be upon the land of the living, and they have received their punishment with them that go down to the pit,

²⁵ in the midst of the slain.

²⁶ "There were laid Meshech and Tubal, and all his strength round about his tomb. All his slain men, all the uncircumcised, slain with the sword, who caused their fear to be in the land of the living.

²⁷ And they are laid with the giants that fell of old, who went down to Hades with *their* weapons of war: and they laid their swords under their heads, but their iniquities were upon their bones, because they terrified all men during their life.

²⁸ And you shall lie in the midst of the uncircumcised, with them that have been slain by the sword.

²⁹ "There are laid the princes of Assyria, who yielded their strength to a wound of the sword; these are laid with the slain, with them that go down to the pit.

³⁰ There are the princes of the north, *even* all the captains of Assyria, who go down slain *to the pit*; they lie uncircumcised among the slain with the sword together with their terror and their strength, and they have received their punishment with them that go down to the pit·

³¹ "King Pharaoh shall see them, and shall be comforted over all their force, says the Lord God.

³² For I have caused his fear to be upon the land of the living, yet he shall lie in the midst of the uncircumcised with them that are slain with the sword, *even* Pharaoh, and all his multitude with him," says the Lord God.

EZEKIEL CHAPTER 33

The Watchman and His Message

¹ And the word of the Lord came to me, saying,

² "Son of man, speak to the children of your people, and you shall say to them, 'On whatsoever land I shall bring a sword, and the people of the land take a man from their territory, and set him for their watchman,

³ and he shall see the sword coming upon the land, and blow the trumpet, and sound an alarm to the people;

⁴ and he that hears the sound of the trumpet shall hear, and *yet* does not take warning, and the sword shall come upon him, and overtake him, his blood shall be upon his *own* head.

⁵ Because he heard the sound of the trumpet, and did not take warning, his blood shall be upon him. But the other, because he took warning, has delivered his soul.

⁶ But if the watchman sees the sword coming, and does not sound the trumpet, and the people do not watch; and the sword comes, and takes a soul from among them, that *soul* is taken because of its iniquity; but the blood *thereof* will I require at the watchman' hand.

⁷ And you, son of man, I have set you *as* a watchman for the house of Israel, and you shall hear a word from My mouth.

⁸ When I say to the sinner, 'You shall surely die'; *if* you do not speak to warn the wicked from his way, the wicked himself shall die in his iniquity, but his blood will I require at your hand.

⁹ But if you forewarn the wicked of his way, to turn from it, and he does not turn from his way, he shall die in his ungodliness; but you have delivered your own soul.

¹⁰ "And you, son of man, say to the house of Israel: 'Thus have you spoken, saying, "Our errors, and our iniquities weigh upon us, and we pine away in them, and how then shall we live?"

¹¹ Say to them, "Thus says the Lord: 'As I live, I do not desire the death of the ungodly, but that the ungodly should turn from his way and live: turn heartily from your way; for why will you die, O house of Israel?

¹² "Say to the children of your people, 'The righteousness of the righteous shall not deliver him, in the day in which he errs; and the iniquity of the ungodly shall not harm him, in the day in which he turns from his iniquity, but the righteous *that errs* shall not be able to deliver himself.'

¹³ When I say to the righteous, 'You shall live,' *and* he trusts in his righteousness, and shall commit iniquity, none of his righteousness shall be remembered; in his unrighteousness which he has wrought, in it shall he die.

¹⁴ And when I say to the ungodly, 'You shall surely die,' and he shall turn from his sin, and do judgment and justice,

¹⁵ and return the pledge, and repay that which he has robbed, *and* walk in the ordinances of life, so as to do no wrong; he shall surely live, and shall not die.

16 None of his sins which he has committed shall be remembered, because he has wrought judgment and righteousness; by them shall he live.

17 Yet the children of your people will say, 'The way of the Lord is not straight'; when their way is not straight.

18 When the righteous turns away from his righteousness, and shall commit iniquities, then shall he die in them.

19 And when the sinner turns from his iniquity, and shall do judgment and righteousness, he shall live by them.

20 And this is that which you said, 'The way of the Lord is *not* straight.' I will judge you, O house of Israel, everyone for his ways."

The Fall of Jerusalem

21 And it came to pass in the tenth year of our captivity, in the twelfth month, on the fifth *day* of the month, *that* one that had escaped from Jerusalem came to me, saying, "The city has been taken."

22 Now the hand of the Lord had come upon me in the evening, before he came; and He opened my mouth, when he came to me in the morning. And my mouth was open, it was no longer kept closed.

23 And the word of the Lord came to me, saying,

24 "Son of man, those that inhabit the desolate *places* on the land of Israel say, 'Abraham was *only* one, and he possessed the land; and we are more numerous; to us the land is given for a possession.'

25 (This verse omitted in LXX)

26 (This verse omitted in LXX)

27 Therefore say to them, Thus says the Lord God: 'As I live, surely those that are in the desolate places shall fall by the sword, and those that are in the open plain shall be given for food to the wild beasts of the field, and those that are in the fortified *cities* and those that are in the caves I will slay with pestilence.'

28 And I will make the land desolate, and the pride of her strength shall perish; and the mountains of Israel shall be made desolate by reason of no man passing through.

29 And they shall know that I am the Lord; and I will make their land desolate, and it shall be made desolate because of all their abominations which they have done.

30 "And *as for* you, son of man, the children of your people are they that speak concerning you by the walls, and in the porches of the houses, and they talk one to another, saying, 'Let us come together, and let us hear the *words* that proceed from the Lord.'

31 They approach you as a people that come together, and sit before you, and hear your words, but they will not do them; for *there is* falsehood in their mouth, and their heart *goes* after their pollutions.

32 And you are to them as a sound of a sweet, well-tuned psaltery, and they will hear your words, but they will not do them.

33 But whenever it shall come *to pass*, they will say, 'Behold, it is come'; and they shall know that there was a prophet in the midst of them."

EZEKIEL CHAPTER 34

Israel's False Shepherds

1 And the word of the Lord came to me, saying,

2 "Son of man, prophesy against the shepherds of Israel; prophesy, and say to the shepherds, Thus says the Lord God: 'O shepherds of Israel, do shepherds feed themselves? Do not the shepherds feed the sheep?

3 Behold, you feed on the milk, and clothe yourselves with the wool, and slay the fat, but you do not feed My sheep!

4 The weak one you have not strengthened, and the sick you have not cherished, and the bruised you have not bound up, and the stray one you have not turned back, and the lost you have not sought; and the strong you have wearied with labor.

5 And My sheep were scattered, because there were no shepherds, and they became meat to all the wild beasts of the field.

6 And My sheep were scattered on every mountain, and on every high hill; they were scattered on the face of the earth, and there was none to seek them out, nor to bring them back.

7 'Therefore, you shepherds, hear the word of the Lord:

8 "As I live, says the Lord God, surely because My sheep became a prey, and My sheep became meat to all the wild beasts of the field, because there were no shepherds, and the shepherds did not seek out My sheep, and the shepherds fed themselves, but did not feed My sheep,

9 for this cause, O shepherds,

10 thus says the Lord God: Behold, I am against the shepherds; and I will require My sheep at their hands, and will turn them back, that they shall not feed My sheep, and the shepherds shall no longer feed them; and I will deliver My sheep out of their mouth, and they shall no longer be meat for them.'

11 "For thus says the Lord God: Behold, I will seek out My sheep, and I will visit them.

12 As the shepherd seeks his flock, in the day when there is darkness and clouds, in the midst of the sheep that are separated, so will I seek out My sheep, and I will bring them back from every place where they were scattered in the day of clouds and darkness.

13 And I will bring them out from the Gentiles, and will gather them from the countries, and will bring them into their own land, and will feed them upon the mountains of Israel, and in the valleys, and in every inhabited place of the land.

14 I will feed them in a good pasture, on a high mountain of Israel; and their folds shall be there, and they shall lie down, and there shall they rest in perfect prosperity, and they shall feed in a fat pasture on the mountains of Israel.

[15] I will feed My sheep, and I will cause them to rest; and they shall know that I am the Lord"; thus says the Lord God.

[16] "I will seek that which is lost, and I will recover the stray one, and will bind up that which was broken, and will strengthen the fainting, and will guard the strong, and will feed them with judgment.

[17] "And *as for* you, you sheep, thus says the Lord God: 'Behold, I will distinguish between sheep and sheep, *and between* rams and goats.

[18] And *is it* not enough for you that you fed on the good pasture, that you trampled with your feet the remnant of your pasture? And *that* you drank the standing water, *and that* you disturbed the residue with your feet?

[19] So My sheep fed on that which you had trampled on with your feet; and they drank the water that had been disturbed by your feet.

[20] 'Therefore thus says the Lord God: Behold, I will separate between the strong sheep and the weak sheep.

[21] You thrusted with your sides and shoulders, and pushed with your horns, and you cruelly treated all the sick.

[22] Therefore I will save My sheep, and they shall no longer be for a prey; and I will judge between ram and ram.

[23] And I will raise up one shepherd over them, and he shall tend them, *even* My servant David, and he shall be their shepherd;

[24] and I the Lord will be to them a God, and David a prince in the midst of them; I the Lord have spoken it.

[25] "And I will make with David a covenant of peace, and I will utterly destroy evil beasts from off the land; and they shall dwell in the wilderness, and sleep in the forests.

[26] And I will settle them round about My mountain; and I will give you the rain, the rain of blessing.

[27] And the trees that are in the field shall yield their fruit, and the earth shall yield her strength, and they shall dwell in the confidence of peace on their land, and they shall know that I am the Lord, when I have broken their yoke; and I will deliver them out of the hand of those that enslaved them.

[28] And they shall no more be a spoil to the nations, and the wild beasts of the land shall no more at all devour them; and they shall dwell safely, and there shall be none to make them afraid.

[29] And I will raise up for them a plant of peace, and they shall no more perish with hunger upon the land, and they shall no more bear the reproach off the nations.

[30] And they shall know that I am the Lord their God, and they My people. "O house of Israel," says the Lord God,

[31] "you are My sheep, even the sheep of My flock, and I am the Lord your God," says the Lord God.

EZEKIEL CHAPTER 35

Judgment on Mount Seir

[1] And the word of the Lord came to me, saying,

[2] "Son of man, set your face against Mount Seir, and prophesy against it,

[3] and say to it, Thus says the Lord God: 'Behold, I am against you, O Mount Seir, and I will stretch out My hand against you, and I will make you a waste, and you shall be made desolate.

[4] And I will cause desolation in your cities, and you shall be desolate, and you shall know that I am the Lord.

[5] Because you have been a perpetual enemy, and have lied in wait craftily for the house of Israel, with the hand of enemies with a sword, in the time of injustice, at the last:

[6] Therefore, as I live, says the Lord God, verily you have sinned, even to bloodshed, therefore blood shall pursue you.

[7] And I will make Mount Seir a waste, and desolate, and I will destroy from off of it both men and cattle;

[8] and I will fill your hills and your valleys with the slain, and in all your plains there shall fall in you men slain with the sword.

[9] I will make you a perpetual desolation, and your cities shall not be inhabited anymore; and you shall know that I am the Lord.

[10] "Because you said, 'The two nations and the two countries shall be mine, and I shall inherit them'; whereas the Lord is there.

[11] Therefore, *as* I live, says the Lord, I will even deal with you according to your enmity, and I will be made known to you when I shall judge you;

[12] and you shall know that I am the Lord. I have heard the voice of your blasphemies, whereas you have said, 'The desert mountains of Israel are given to us for food';

[13] and you have spoken swelling words against Me with your mouth: I have heard *them*.

[14] Thus says the Lord: 'When all the earth is rejoicing, I will make you desolate.

[15] You shall be desolate, O Mount Seir, and all of Edom; and it shall be utterly consumed; and you shall know that I am the Lord their God.'"

EZEKIEL CHAPTER 36

Blessing on Israel

[1] "And you, son of man, prophesy to the mountains of Israel, and say to the mountains of Israel, 'Hear the word of the Lord: [2] Thus says the Lord God: "Because the enemy has said against you, 'Aha, the old waste places have become a possession for us';

[3] therefore prophesy, and say, Thus says the Lord God: 'Because you have been dishonored, and hated by those round about you, that you might be a possession to the remainder of the nations, and you became a byword, and a reproach to the nations.

[4] Therefore, you mountains of Israel, hear the word of the Lord: Thus says the Lord to the mountains, and to the hills, and to the streams, and to the valleys, and to *the places* that

have been made desolate and destroyed, and to the cities that have been deserted, and have become a spoil and a trampling to the nations that were left round about;

⁵ therefore, thus says the Lord: "Surely in the fire of My wrath have I spoken against the rest of the nations, and against all Edom, because they have appropriated My land to themselves for a possession with joy, disregarding the lives *of its inhabitants*, to destroy *it* by plunder."

⁶ Therefore prophesy concerning the land of Israel, and say to the mountains, and to the hills, and to the valleys, and to the forests, Thus says the Lord: "Behold, I have spoken in My jealousy and in My wrath, because you have borne the reproaches of the heathen;

⁷ therefore I will lift up My hand against the nations that are round about you; they shall bear their reproach.

⁸ "But your grapes and your fruits, O mountains of Israel, shall My people eat; for they are hoping to come.

⁹ For behold, I am for you, and I will have respect to you, and you shall be tilled and sown;

¹⁰ and I will multiply men upon you, *even* all the house of Israel to the last; and the cities shall be inhabited, and the desolate land shall be built upon.

¹¹ And I will multiply men and cattle upon you, and I will cause you to dwell as at the beginning, and I will treat you well, as in your former *times*; and you shall know that I am the Lord.

¹² And I will increase men upon you, *even* My people Israel; and they shall inherit you, and you shall be to them for a possession; and you shall no more be bereaved of them."

¹³ Thus says the Lord God: "Because they said to you, 'You devour men, and have been bereaved of your nation';

¹⁴ therefore you shall no more devour men, and you shall no more bereave your nation, says the Lord God.

¹⁵ And there shall no more be heard against you the reproach of the nations, and you shall no more bear the revilings of the peoples, says the Lord God."

The Renewal of Israel

¹⁶ And the word of the Lord came to me, saying,

¹⁷ "Son of man, the house of Israel dwelt upon their land, and defiled it by their way, and with their idols, and with their uncleannesses; and their way was before Me like the uncleanness of a removed woman.

¹⁸ So I poured out My wrath upon them,

¹⁹ and I dispersed them among the nations, and utterly scattered them through the countries. I judged them according to their way and according to their sin.

²⁰ And they went in among the nations, among which they went, and they profaned My holy name, while it was said of them, 'These are the people of the Lord, and they came forth out of His land.'

²¹ But I spared them for the sake of My holy name, which the house of Israel profaned among the nations, among whom they went.

²² "Therefore say to the house of Israel, Thus says the Lord: I do not do this, O house of Israel, for your sakes, but because of My holy name, which you have profaned among the nations, among whom you went.

²³ And I will sanctify My great name, which was profaned among the nations, which you profaned in the midst of them; and the nations shall know that I am the Lord, when I am sanctified among you before their eyes.

²⁴ And I will take you out from the nations, and will gather you out of all the lands, and will bring you into your own land;

²⁵ and I will sprinkle clean water upon you, and you shall be purged from all your uncleannesses, and from all your idols, and I will cleanse you.

²⁶ And I will give you a new heart, and will put a new spirit in you: and I will take away the heart of stone out of your flesh, and I will give you a heart of flesh.

²⁷ And I will put My Spirit in you, and will cause you to walk in My ordinances, and to keep My judgments, and do *them*.

²⁸ And you shall dwell upon the land which I gave to your fathers; and you shall be My people, and I shall be your God. ²⁹ And I will save you from all your uncleannesses; and I will call for the grain, and multiply it, and will not bring famine upon you.

³⁰ And I will multiply the fruit of the trees, and the produce of the field, that you may not bear the reproach of famine among the nations.

³¹ And you shall remember your evil ways and your practices that were not good, and you shall be hateful in your own sight for your transgressions and for your abominations.

³² Not for your sakes do I do *this*," says the Lord God, "*as it is known to you*; be ashamed and confounded for your own ways, O house of Israel!"

³³ "Thus says the Lord God: In the day in which I shall cleanse you from all your iniquities, I will also cause the cities to be inhabited, and the waste *places* shall be built upon;

³⁴ and the desolate land shall be cultivated, whereas it was desolate in the eyes of everyone that passed by.

³⁵ And they shall say, 'That desolate land has become like the garden of Eden; and the waste and desolate and ruined cities are inhabited.'

³⁶ And the nations, as many as shall have been left round about you, shall know that I the Lord have built the ruined *cities* and planted what was desolate. I the Lord have spoken, and will do *it*."

³⁷ "Thus says the Lord God: Yet *for* this will I be sought by the house of Israel, to establish them; I will multiply them, *even* men as sheep;

³⁸ as holy sheep, as the sheep of Jerusalem in her feasts; thus shall the desert cities be full of flocks of men. And they shall know that I *am* the Lord."

EZEKIEL CHAPTER 37

The Valley of Dry Bones

¹ And the hand of the Lord came upon me, and the Lord brought me forth by the Spirit, and set me in the midst of the plain, and it was full of human bones.

² And He led me round about them every way. And behold, *there were* very many on the face of the plain, and they were very dry.

³ And He said to me, "Son of man, will these bones live?" And I said, "O Lord God, *only* You know this!"

⁴ And He said to me, "Prophesy upon these bones, and you shall say to them, 'You dry bones, hear the word of the Lord.

⁵ Thus says the Lord to these bones: "Behold, I *will* bring upon you the breath of life;

⁶ and I will lay sinews upon you, and I will bring up flesh upon you, and spread skin upon you, and I will put My Spirit into you, and you shall live; and you shall know that I am the Lord.""

⁷ So I prophesied as *the Lord* commanded me. And it came to pass while I was prophesying, that behold, *there was* a rattling, and the bones approached each one to his joint.

⁸ And I looked, and behold, sinews and flesh grew upon them, and skin covered them over; but there was not breath in them.

⁹ And He said to me, "Prophesy to the wind; prophesy, son of man, and say to the wind, Thus says the Lord: 'Come from the four winds, *O breath,* and breathe upon these dead, that they may live.'"

¹⁰ So I prophesied as He commanded me, and the breath entered into them, and they lived, and stood upon their feet, a very great congregation.

¹¹ And the Lord spoke to me, saying, "Son of man, these bones are the whole house of Israel. And they say, 'Our bones have become dry, our hope has perished, we are quite spent.'

¹² Therefore prophesy and say, Thus says the Lord: 'Behold, I *will* open your tombs, and will bring you up out of your tombs, and I will bring you into the land of Israel.

¹³ And you shall know that I am the Lord, when I have opened your graves, that I may bring up My people from *their* graves.

¹⁴ And I will put My Spirit within you, and you shall live, and I will place you upon your own land; and you shall know that I *am* the Lord; I have spoken, and will do *it,*'" says the Lord.

One Kingdom, One King

¹⁵ And the word of the Lord came to me, saying,

¹⁶ "Son of man, take for yourself a rod, and write upon it, 'Judah, and the children of Israel his adherents'; and you shall take for yourself another rod, and you shall inscribe it for 'Joseph, the rod of Ephraim, and all the children of Israel that belong to him.'

¹⁷ And you shall join them together for yourself, so as that they should bind themselves into one stick; and they shall be in your hand.

¹⁸ "And it shall come to pass, when the children of your people shall say to you, 'Will you not tell us what you mean by these things?'

¹⁹ Then shall you say to them, Thus says the Lord: 'Behold, I will take the tribe of Joseph, which is in the hand of Ephraim, and the tribes of Israel that belong to him, and I will add them to the tribe of Judah, and they shall become one rod in the hand of Judah.'

²⁰ And the rods on which you wrote shall be in your hand in their presence.

²¹ And you shall say to them, Thus says the Lord God: 'Behold, I *will* take the whole house of Israel out of the midst of the nations, among whom they have gone, and I will gather them from all that are round about them, and I will bring them into the land of Israel.

²² And I will make them a nation in My land, even on the mountains of Israel; and they shall have one prince; and they shall be two nations no longer, neither shall they be divided anymore into two kingdoms;

²³ that they may no more defile themselves with their idols; and I will deliver them from all their transgressions whereby they have sinned, and I will cleanse them; and they shall be My people, and I the Lord shall be their God.

²⁴ "And My servant David *shall be* a prince in the midst of them. There shall be one shepherd of *them* all; for they shall walk in My ordinances, and keep My judgments, and do them.

²⁵ And they shall dwell in their land, which I have given to My servant Jacob, where their fathers dwelt; and they shall dwell upon it; and David My servant *shall be their* prince forever.

²⁶ And I will make with them a covenant of peace; it shall be an everlasting covenant with them; and I will establish My sanctuary in the midst of them forever.

²⁷ And My tabernacle shall be among them; and I shall be their God, and they shall be My people.

²⁸ And the nations shall know that I am the Lord that sanctifies them, when My sanctuary is in the midst of them forever."

EZEKIEL CHAPTER 38

Invasion by Gog

¹ And the word of the Lord came to me, saying,

² "Son of man, set your face against Gog, and the land of Magog, Rosh, prince of Meshech and Tubal, and prophesy against him,

³ and say to him, Thus says the Lord God: 'Behold, I am against you O Gog, prince of Rosh, Meshach and Tubal;

4 and I will gather you, and all your army, horses and horsemen, all wearing breastplates, with a great multitude, shields and helmets and swords;

5 Persians, Ethiopians, and Libyans; all with helmets and shields.

6 Gomer, and all belonging to him; the house of Togarmah, from the end of the north, and all belonging to him; and many nations with you.

7 "Prepare yourselves and be ready, you and all your multitude that is assembled with you, and you shall be to Me for a guard.

8 He shall be prepared after many days, and he shall come at the end of years, and shall come to a land that is brought back from the sword, when *the people* have been gathered from many nations against the land of Israel, which was entirely desolate; and he has come forth out of the nations, and they shall all dwell securely.

9 And you shall go up as rain, and shall arrive as a cloud to cover the land, and there shall be you, and all that are about you, and many nations with you.

10 "Thus says the Lord God: It shall also come to pass in that day, that thoughts shall rise up into your heart, and you shall devise an evil plan.

11 And you shall say, 'I will go up to the rejected land; I will come upon them that are at ease in tranquility, and dwelling in peace, all inhabiting a land in which there is no wall, nor bars, nor have they doors;

12 to seize plunder, and to take their spoil; to turn my hands against the desolate land that is *now* inhabited, and against a nation that is gathered from many nations, that have acquired property, dwelling in the midst of the land.'

13 Sheba, Dedan, and Carthaginian merchants, and all their villages shall say to you, 'You have come for plunder to take a prey, and to get spoils; you have gathered your multitude to take silver and gold, to carry off property, to take spoils.'

14 "Therefore prophesy, son of man, and say to Gog, Thus says the Lord: 'Will you not arise in that day, when my people Israel are dwelling securely,

15 and come out of your place from the farthest north, and many nations with you? All of them mounted on horses, a great gathering, and a large force?

16 And you shall come up upon My people Israel as a cloud to cover the land; it shall come to pass in the last days, that I will bring you up upon My land, that all the nations may know Me, when I am sanctified in you before them.'

17 Thus says the Lord God, to Gog: 'You are *the one* concerning whom I spoke in former times, by the hand of My servants the prophets of Israel, in those days and years, that I would bring you up against them.'

Judgment on Gog

18 "And it shall come to pass in that day, in the day when Gog shall come against the Land of Israel," says the Lord God,

19 "that My wrath and My jealousy shall arise, I have spoken in the fire of My anger, verily in that day there shall be a great shaking in the land of Israel;

20 and the fish of the sea shall quake at the presence of the Lord, and the birds of the sky and the wild beasts of the field, and all the reptiles that creep upon the earth, and all the men that are on the face of the earth; and the mountains shall be thrown down, and the valleys shall fall, and every wall on the land shall fall.

21 And I will summon against it even every fear, says the Lord; the sword of *every* man shall be against his brother.

22 And I will judge him with pestilence, and blood, and sweeping rain, and hailstones; and I will rain upon him fire and brimstone, and upon all that are with him, and upon many nations with him.

23 And I will be magnified, and sanctified, and glorified; and I will be known in the presence of many nations, and they shall know that I am the Lord."

EZEKIEL CHAPTER 39

Gog's Armies Destroyed

1 "And you, son of man, prophesy against Gog, and say, Thus says the Lord: 'Behold, I am against you, O Gog, prince of Rosh, Meshech and Tubal;

2 and I will assemble you, and guide you, and raise you up on the extremity of the north, and I will bring you up upon the mountains of Israel.

3 And I will destroy the bow out of your left hand, and your arrows out of your right hand, and I will cast you down on the mountains of Israel;

4 and you and all that belong to you shall fall, and the nations that are with you shall be given to multitudes of birds, *even* to every fowl, and I have given you to all the wild beasts of the field to be devoured.

5 You shall fall on the face of the field; for I have spoken *it*,' says the Lord.

6 And I will send a fire upon Gog, and the islands shall be securely inhabited; and they shall know that I am the Lord.

7 And My holy name shall be known in the midst of My people Israel; and My holy name shall no more be profaned: and the nations shall know that I am the Lord, the Holy *One* in Israel.

8 Behold it is come, and you shall know that it shall be, says the Lord God; this is the day concerning which I have spoken.

9 "And they that inhabit the cities of Israel shall come forth, and make a fire with the arms, the shields and the spears, and bows and arrows, and javelins, and lances, and they shall keep the fire burning with them for seven years.

10 And they shall not take any wood out of the field, neither shall they cut any out of the forests, but they shall burn the weapons with fire, and they shall plunder those that

plundered them, and spoil those that spoiled them," says the Lord.

The Burial of Gog

[11] "And it shall come to pass, *that* in that day I will give to Gog a place of renown, a tomb in Israel, the burial place of them that approach the sea. And they shall build round about the outlet of the valley, and there they shall bury Gog and all his multitude. And *the place* shall then be called the Valley of Haman Gog.

[12] And the house of Israel shall bury them, that the land may be cleansed in the space of seven months.

[13] Yea, all the people of the land shall bury them; and it shall be to them a *place* of renown in the day in which it was glorified, says the Lord.

[14] And they shall appoint men continually to go over the land, to bury them that have been left on the face of the earth, to cleanse it after the space of seven months, and they shall seek *them* out.

[15] And everyone that goes through the land, and sees a man's bone, shall set up a marker by it, until the buriers shall have buried it in the valley, the burial place of Gog.

[16] For the name of the city *shall be* Burial Place; so shall the land be cleansed.

[17] "And you, son of man, say, Thus says the Lord: Say to every winged bird, and to all the wild beasts of the field, 'Gather yourselves, and come; gather yourselves from all *places* round about to My sacrifice, which I have made for you, *even* a great sacrifice on the mountains of Israel, and you shall eat flesh, and drink blood.

[18] You shall eat the flesh of mighty men, and you shall drink the blood of princes of the earth, rams, and calves and goats; they are all fatted calves.

[19] And you shall eat fat till you are full, and shall drink wine till you are drunk, of My sacrifice which I have prepared for you. [20] And you shall be filled at My table, *eating* horse and rider, and mighty man, and every warrior,' says the Lord.

Israel Restored to the Land

[21] "And I will set My glory among you, and all the nations shall see My judgment which I have wrought, and My hand which I have brought upon them.

[22] And the house of Israel shall know that I am the Lord their God, from this day and forevermore.

[23] And all the nations shall know that the house of Israel was led captive because of their sins, because they rebelled against Me, and I turned away My face from them, and delivered them into the hands of their enemies, and they all fell by the sword.

[24] According to their uncleannesses and according to their transgressions did I deal with them, and I turned away My face from them.

[25] "Therefore thus says the Lord God: Now will I turn back captivity in Jacob, and will have mercy on the house of Israel, and I will be jealous for the sake of My holy name.

[26] And they shall bear their reproach, and the iniquity which they committed when they dwelt upon their land in peace. Yet there shall be none to terrify *them*

[27] when I have brought them back from the nations, and gathered them out of the countries of the nations; and I will be sanctified among them in the presence of the nations.

[28] And they shall know that I am the Lord their God, when I have been manifested to them among the nations.

[29] And I will no more turn away My face from them, because I have poured out My wrath upon the house of Israel," says the Lord God.

EZEKIEL CHAPTER 40

The Vision of the New Temple

[1] And it came to pass in the twenty-fifth year of our captivity, in the first month, on the tenth *day* of the month, in the fourteenth year after the taking of the city, in that day the hand of the Lord was upon me, and brought me

[2] in a vision of God into the land of Israel, and set me on a very high mountain, and upon it *there was* as it were the frame of a city before *me.*

[3] And He brought me in there, and behold, *there was* a man, and the appearance of him was as the appearance of shining brass, and in his hand was a builder's line, and a measuring reed; and he stood at the gate.

[4] And the man said to me, "Look with your eyes at him whom you have seen, son of man, and hear with your ears, and lay up in your heart all things that I show you; for you have come in here that I might show you, and you shall show all things that you see to the house of Israel."

[5] And behold, a wall round about the house outside, and in the man's hand was a reed, the measure *of it was* six cubits by the cubit, and a span. And he measured across the front wall; the breadth was equal to the reed, and the length of it equal to the reed.

The Eastern Gateway of the Temple

[6] And he entered by seven steps into the gate that looks eastward, and he measured across the porch of the gate equal to the reed.

[7] And the chamber was equal in length to the reed, and equal in breadth to the reed; and the porch between the chambers *was* six cubits; and the second chamber equal in breadth to the reed, and equal in length to the reed, and the porch *was* five cubits.

[8] And the third chamber equal in length to the reed, and equal in breadth to the reed.

[9] And the porch of the gateway *near the porch of the gate was* eight cubits; and the posts there of two cubits; and the porch of the gate was inward.

[10] And the chambers of the gate of the chamber in front *were* three on one side and three on the other, and *there*

was one measure to the three: *there was* one measure to the porches on this side and on that.

[11] And he measured the breadth of the door of the gateway, ten cubits; and the breadth of the gateway *was* thirteen cubits.

[12] And the space before the chambers was narrowed to a cubit in front of the chambers on this side and on that side; and the chamber was six cubits this way, and six cubits that way.

[13] And he measured the gate from the wall of one chamber to the wall of the other chamber. The breadth was twenty-five cubits, the one gate over against the other gate.

[14] And the open space of the porch of the gate outside was twenty cubits to the chambers round about the gate.

[15] And the open space of the gate outside to the open space of the porch of the gate within was fifty cubits.

[16] And *there were* secret windows to the chambers, and to the porches within the gate of the court round about, and in the same manner windows to the porches round about within. And on the porch *there were* palm trees on this side and on that side.

The Outer Court

[17] And he brought me into the inner court, and behold, *there were* chambers, and peristyles round about the court; thirty chambers within the ranges of columns.

[18] And the porches were behind the gates; according to the length of the gates, was the lower peristyle.

[19] And he measured the breadth of the court, from the open space of the outer gate inwards to the open space of the gate looking outwards: a hundred cubits *was the distance to the place* of the gate looking eastward. And he brought me to the north.

The Northern Gateway

[20] And behold, a gate looking northwards *belonging to* the outer court, and he measured it, both the length of it and the breadth;

[21] and the chambers, three on this side and three on that; and the posts, and the porches, and the palm trees thereof: and they were according to the measures of the gate that looks eastward: the length thereof was fifty cubits, and the breadth thereof was twenty-five cubits.

[22] And its windows, and its porches, and its palm-trees, were according to *the dimensions of* the gate looking eastward; and they went up to it by seven steps; and the porches were within.

[23] And *there was* a gate to the inner court looking toward the north gate, after the manner of the gate looking toward the east; and he measured the court from gate to gate, a hundred cubits.

The Southern Gateway

[24] And he brought me to the south side, and behold, a gate looking southwards: and he measured it, and its chambers, and its posts, and its porches, according to these dimensions.

[25] And its windows and its porches round about were according to the windows of the porch: the length thereof was fifty cubits, and the breadth thereof was twenty-five cubits.

[26] And it had seven steps, and porches within. And it *had* palm trees on the posts, one on one side, and one on the other side.

[27] And *there was* a gate opposite the gate of the inner court southward. And he measured the court from gate to gate, a hundred cubits in breadth southward.

Gateways of the Inner Court

[28] And he brought me into the inner court of the south gate; and he measured the gate according to these measures;

[29] and the chambers, and the posts, and the porches, according to these measures; and *there were* windows to it and to the porches round about: its length was fifty cubits, and *its* breadth *was* twenty-five cubits,

[30] (This verse omitted in LXX)

[31] from the porch to the outer court: and *there were* palm trees to the post *thereof*, and eight steps.

[32] And he brought me in at the gate that looks eastward, and he measured it according to these measures:

[33] and the chambers, and the posts, and the porches according to these measures: and *there were* windows to it, and porches round about: the length of it was fifty cubits, and the breadth of it *was* twenty-five cubits.

[34] And *there were* porches *opening* into the inner court, and palm trees on the posts on this side and on that side; and it *had* eight steps.

[35] And he brought me in at the northern gate, and measured *it* according to these measures:

[36] and the chambers, and the posts, and the porches; and it *had* windows round about, and *it had* its porches: the length of it was fifty cubits, and the breadth *was* twenty-five cubits.

[37] And its porches were toward the inner court; and *there were* palm trees to the posts on this side and on that side; and it *had* eight steps.

[38] Its chambers and its doorways, and its porches at the second gate *served as* a drain,

[39] that they might slay in it the sin offerings and the trespass offerings.

[40] And behind the drain for the burnt offerings at the north *gate*, two tables eastward behind the second gate; and *behind* the porch of the gate *were* two tables eastward.

[41] Four on one side and four on the other side behind the gate; *and* upon them they kill the victims, in front of the eight tables of sacrifices.

[42] And *there were* four tables of hewn stone for burnt offerings, the breadth *of them was* a cubit and a half, and the length *of them* two cubits *and* a half, and *their* height was a cubit: on them they shall place the instruments with which they slay there the burnt offerings and the victims.

43 And they shall have within a border of hewn stone round about of a span broad, and over the tables above *were* screens for covering *them* from the wet and from the heat.

44 And he brought me into the inner court, and behold, *there were* two chambers in the inner court, one behind the gate looking to the north, turning southward, and one behind the southern gate, but which looks to the north.

45 And he said to me, This chamber that looks to the south, is for the priests that keep the charge of the house.

46 And the chamber that looks to the north is for the priests that keep the charge of the altar; they are the sons of Zadok, those of the tribe of Levi who draw near to the Lord, to serve Him.

47 And he measured the court, its length *was* a hundred cubits, and the breadth a hundred cubits, on its four sides; and the altar in front of the house.

48 And he brought me into the porch of the house, and he measured the post of the porch, the breadth was five cubits on one side and five cubits on the other side; and the breadth of the door *was* fourteen cubits, and the sidepieces of the door of the porch *were* three cubits on one side, and three cubits on the other side.

49 And the length of the porch was twenty cubits, and the breadth twelve cubits; and they went up to it by ten steps; and *there were* pillars to the porch, one on this side and one on that side.

EZEKIEL CHAPTER 41

Dimensions of the Sanctuary

1 And he brought me into the temple, the porch of which he measured, six cubits the breadth on one side, and six cubits the breadth of the porch on the other side.

2 And the breadth of the gateway was ten cubits, and the sidepieces of the gateway were five cubits on this side, and five cubits on that side. And he measured the length of it, forty cubits, and the breadth *was* twenty cubits.

3 And he went into the inner court, and measured the post of the door, two cubits; and the door, six cubits; and the sidepieces of the door, seven cubits on one side, and seven cubits on the other side.

4 And he measured the length of the doors, forty cubits; and the breadth, twenty cubits, in front of the temple. And he said, This is the Holy of Holies.

5 And he measured the wall of the house, six cubits: and the breadth of *each* side *was* four cubits round about.

6 And the sides were twice ninety, side against side; and *there was* a space in the wall of the house at the sides round about, that they should be for those that take hold of them to see, that they should not at all touch the walls of the house.

7 And the breadth of the upper side *was made* according to the projection out of the wall, against the upper one round about the house, that it might be enlarged above, and that *men* might go up to the upper chambers from those below, and from the ground sills to the third story.

8 And as for the height of the house round about, *each* space between the sides was equal to a reed of six cubits;

9 and the breadth of the wall of each side without was five cubits; and the spaces that were left between the sides of the house,

10 and between the chambers, were a width of twenty cubits, the circumference of the house.

11 And the doors of the chambers were toward the space left by the one door that looked northward, and *there was* one door southward; and the breadth of the remaining open space *was* five cubits in extent round about.

12 And the partition *wall* in front of the remaining space, toward the west, was seventy cubits in breadth; the breadth of the partition wall was five cubits round about, and the length of it *was* ninety cubits.

13 And he measured in front of the house a length of a hundred cubits, and the remaining spaces and the partitions; and the walls thereof were in length a hundred cubits.

14 And the breadth in front of the house, and the remaining *spaces* before *it were* a hundred cubits.

15 And he measured the length of the partition in front of the space left by the back parts of that house; and the *spaces* left on this side and on that side were in length a hundred cubits: and the temple and the corners and the outer porch were ceiled.

16 And the windows were latticed, *giving* light round about to the three *stories*, so as to look through. And the house and the parts adjoining were planked round about, and *so was* the floor, and from the floor up to the windows, and the window *shutters* folded back in three parts for one to look through.

17 And almost all the way to the inner, and close to the outer *side*, and upon all the wall round about within and without,

18 were carved cherubim and palm trees between the cherubim, *and each* cherub *had* two faces.

19 The face of a man was toward one palm tree on this side and on that side, and the face of a lion toward another palm tree on this side and on that side; the house was carved all round.

20 From the floor to the ceiling were cherubim and palm trees carved.

21 And the holy place and the temple opened on four sides; in front of the holy places the appearance was as the look of

22 a wooden altar, the height of it three cubits, and the length two cubits, and the breadth two cubits; and it had horns, and the base of it and the sides of it were of wood. And he said to me, This is the table, which is before the face of the Lord.

23 And the temple *had* two doors, and the sanctuary *had* two doors, with two turning leaves *each*;

24 two leaves to the one, and two leaves to the other door.

25 And *there was* carved work upon them, and cherubim on the doors of the temple, and palm trees according to the

carving of the sanctuary; and *there were* stout planks in front of the porch outside.

26 And *there were* secret windows; and he measured from side to side, to the roofing of the porch; and the sides of the house were closely planked.

EZEKIEL CHAPTER 42

The Chambers for the Priests
1 And he brought me into the inner court eastward, opposite the northern gate. And he brought me in, and behold, five chambers near the vacant space, and near the northern partition,

2 a hundred cubits in length toward the north, and in breadth fifty,

3 ornamented accordingly as the gates of the inner court, and arranged accordingly as the peristyles of the outer court, *with three* porches fronting one another.

4 And in front of the chambers was a walk ten cubits in breadth, the length *reaching* to a hundred cubits; and their doors were northward.

5 And the upper walks were in like manner: for the peristyle projected from it, *even* from the range of columns below, and *there was* a space between; so *were there* a peristyle and a space between, and so *were there* two porches.

6 For they were triple, and they had not pillars like the pillars of the outer ones; therefore they projected from the lower ones and the middle ones from the ground.

7 And *there was* light outside, corresponding to the chambers of the outer court looking toward the front of the northern chambers; the length *of them was* fifty cubits.

8 For the length of the chambers looking toward the inner court was fifty cubits, and these are the ones that front the others; the whole was a hundred cubits.

9 And *there were* doors of these chambers for an outlet toward the east, so that one should go through them out of the outer court,

10 by the opening of the walk at the corner; and the south parts were toward the south, toward the remaining space, and toward the partition, and *so were* the chambers.

11 And the walk was in front of them, according to the measures of the chambers toward the north, both according to the length of them, and according to the breadth of them, and according to all their openings, and according to all their turnings, and according to their lights, and according to their doors.

12 So *were the measures* of the chambers toward the south, and according to the doors at the entrance of the walk, as it were the distance of a reed for light, and eastward as one went in by them.

13 And he said to me, "The chambers toward the north, and the chambers toward the south, in front of the empty spaces, these are the chambers of the sanctuary, in which the priests, the sons of Zadok, who draw near to the Lord, shall eat the most holy things: and there shall they lay the most holy things, and the meat offering, and the sin offerings, and the trespass offerings; because the place is holy.

14 None shall go in there except the priests, *and* they shall not go forth into the holy place into the outer court, that they that draw near *to God* may be continually holy, and may not touch their garments in which they minister, *with defilement*, for they are holy; and they shall put on other garments whenever they come in contact with the people."

Outer Dimensions of the Temple
15 So the measurement of the house within was accomplished. And he brought me forth by the way of the gate that looks eastward, and measured the plan of the house round about in order.

16 And he stood behind the gate looking eastward, and measured five hundred *cubits* with the measuring reed.

17 An he turned to the north and measured in front of the north *side* five hundred cubits with the measuring reed.

18 And he turned to the west, and measured in front of the west side, five hundred *cubits* with the measuring reed.

19 And he turned to the south, and measured in front of the south side, five hundred *cubits* by the measuring reed.

20 The *four sides he measured* by the same reed, and he marked out the house and the circumference of the parts round about, *a space* of five hundred *cubits* eastward, and a breadth of five hundred cubits, to make a division between the sanctuary and the outer wall, that *belonged to* the design of the house.

EZEKIEL CHAPTER 43

The Divine Glory Returns to the Temple
1 Moreover he brought me to the gate looking eastward, and led me forth.

2 And behold, the glory of the God of Israel came by the eastern way; and *there was* a voice of an army, as the sound of many redoubling *their shouts*, and the earth shone like light from the glory round about.

3 And the vision which I saw was like the vision which I saw when I went in to anoint the city. And the vision of the chariot which I saw was like the vision which I saw at the River Chebar; and I fell upon my face.

4 And the glory of the Lord came into the house, by the way of the gate looking eastward.

5 And the Spirit took me up, and brought me into the inner court. And behold, the house of the Lord was full of glory.

6 And I stood, and behold, *there was* a voice out of the house of one speaking to me, and a man stood near me,

7 and he said to me, "Son of man, you have seen the place of My throne, and the place of the soles of My feet, in which My name shall dwell in the midst of the house of Israel forever; and the house of Israel shall no more profane My

holy name, they and their princes, by their fornication, or by the murders of *their* princes in the midst of them;

⁸ when they set My doorway by their doorway, and My thresholds near to their thresholds; and they made My wall as it were joining Myself and them, and they profaned My holy name with their iniquities which they have done; and I destroyed them in My wrath and with slaughter.

⁹ And now let them put away from Me their fornication, and the murders of their princes, and I will dwell in the midst of them forever.

¹⁰ "And you, son of man, show the temple to the house of Israel, that they may cease from their sins; and *show* its aspect and the arrangement of it.

¹¹ And they shall bear their punishment for all the things that they have done. And you shall describe the house, and its entrances, and the plans, and all its ordinances, and you shall make known to them all the regulations of it, and describe *them* before them. And they shall keep all My commandments, and all My ordinances, and do them.

¹² And you shall show the plan of the house on the top of the mountain: all its limits round about *shall be* most holy.

¹³ "And these are the measures of the altar by the cubit of a cubit and a span, the cavity *shall be* a cubit deep, and a cubit shall be the breadth, and the border on the rim of it round about shall be a span: and this *shall be* the height of the altar

¹⁴ from the bottom at the commencement of the hollow part to this great mercy seat, from beneath was two cubits, and the breadth was a cubit; and from the little mercy seat to the great mercy seat *there were* four cubits, and the breadth was a cubit.

¹⁵ And the altar *shall be* four cubits; and from the altar and above the horns a cubit.

¹⁶ And the altar *shall be* of the length of twelve cubits, by twelve cubits *in breadth*, square upon its four sides.

¹⁷ And the mercy seat *shall be* fourteen cubits in length, by fourteen cubits in breadth on its four sides; and *there shall be* a border to it carried round about it of half a cubit; and the rim of it *shall be* a cubit round about; and the steps thereof looking eastward.'

Consecrating the Altar

¹⁸ And He said to me, "Son of man, thus says the Lord God of Israel: These are the ordinances of the altar in the day of its being made, to offer upon it burnt offerings, and to pour blood upon it.

¹⁹ And you shall appoint to the priests the Levites of the descendants of Zadok, that draw near to Me, says the Lord God, to minister to Me, a calf of the heard for a sin offering.

²⁰ And they shall take of its blood, and shall put *it* on the four horns of the altar, and upon the four corners of the propitiatory, and upon the base round about, and they shall make atonement for it.

²¹ And they shall take the calf of the sin offering, and it shall be consumed by fire in the separate place of the house, outside the sanctuary.

²² And on the second day they shall take two kids of the goats without blemish for a sin offering; and they shall make atonement for the altar, as they made atonement with the calf.

²³ And after they have finished the atonement, they shall bring an unblemished calf of the herd, and an unblemished ram of the flock.

²⁴ And you shall offer *them* before the Lord, and the priests shall sprinkle salt upon them, and shall offer them up *as* burnt offerings to the Lord.

²⁵ Seven day shall you offer a kid daily for a sin offering, and a calf of the herd, and a ram out of the flock; they shall sacrifice them unblemished for seven days.

²⁶ And they shall make atonement for the altar, and shall purge it; and they shall consecrate themselves.

²⁷ And it shall come to pass from the eighth day and onward, *that* the priests shall offer your burnt offerings on the altar, and your peace offerings; and I will accept you," says the Lord.

EZEKIEL CHAPTER 44

The Closed Gate

¹ Then he brought me back by the way of the outer gate of the sanctuary that looks eastward; and it was shut.

² And the Lord said to me, "This gate shall be shut, it shall not be opened, and no one shall pass through it; for the Lord God of Israel shall enter by it, and it shall be shut.

³ For the prince, he shall sit in it, to eat bread before the Lord; he shall go in by the way of the porch of the gate, and shall go forth by the way of the same."

Admission to the Temple

⁴ And He brought me in by the way of the gate that looks northward, in front of the house: and I looked, and behold, the house was full of the glory of the Lord. And I fell upon my face.

⁵ And the Lord said to me, "Son of man, attend with your heart, and see with *your* eyes, and hear with your ears all that I say to you, according to all the ordinances of the house of the Lord, and all the regulations thereof; and you shall attend well to the entrance of the house, according to all its outlets, in all the holy things.

⁶ And you shall say to the provoking house, to the house of Israel, Thus says the Lord God: 'Let it suffice you *to have committed* all your iniquities, O house of Israel!

⁷ That you have brought in aliens, uncircumcised in heart, and uncircumcised in flesh, to be in My sanctuary, and to profane it, when you offered bread, flesh, and blood; and you transgressed My covenant by all your iniquities;

8 and you appointed *others* to keep the charges in My sanctuary.

9 Therefore thus says the Lord God: No alien, uncircumcised in heart or uncircumcised in flesh, shall enter into My sanctuary, of all the children of strangers that are in the midst of the house of Israel.

Laws Governing Priests

10 "But as for the Levites who departed far from Me when Israel went astray from Me after their imaginations, they shall even bear their iniquity.

11 Yet they shall minister in My sanctuary, *being* porters at the gates of the house, and serving the house; they shall slay the victims and the burnt offerings for the people, and they shall stand before the people to minister to them.

12 Because they ministered to them before their idols, and it became to the house of Israel a punishment of iniquity; therefore have I lifted up My hand against them, says the Lord God.

13 And they shall not draw near to Me, to minister to Me in the priests' office, nor to approach the holy things of the children of Israel, nor *to approach* My Holy of Holies; but they shall bear their reproach for the error in which they erred.

14 They shall bring them to keep the charges of the house, for all the service of it, and for all that they shall do.

15 "The priests the Levites, the sons of Zadok, who kept the charges of My sanctuary when the house of Israel when astray from Me, these shall draw near to Me to minister to Me, and shall stand before My face, to offer sacrifice to Me, the fat and the blood, says the Lord God.

16 These shall enter into My sanctuary, and these shall approach My table, to minister to Me, and they shall keep My commandments.

17 And it shall come to pass when they enter the gates of the inner court, *that* they shall put on linen robes; and they shall not put on woolen garments when they minister at the gate of the inner court.

18 And they shall have linen turbans upon their heads, and shall have linen trousers on their bodies; and they shall not tightly gird themselves.

19 And when they go out into the outer court to the people, they shall take off their robes, in which they minister; and they shall lay them up in the chambers of the sanctuary, and shall put on other robes, and they shall not sanctify the people with their robes.

20 And they shall not shave their heads, nor shall they pluck off their hair; they shall carefully cover their heads.

21 And no priest shall drink any wine, when they go into the inner court.

22 Neither shall they take to themselves a widow for a wife, or one that is put away, but a virgin of the descendants of Israel. But if there should happen to be a priest's widow, they shall take *her*.

23 And they shall teach My people *to distinguish* between holy and profane, and they shall make known to them *the difference* between unclean and clean.

24 And these shall attend at a judgment of blood to decide it. They shall rightly observe My ordinances, and judge My judgments, and keep My statutes and My commandments in all My feasts; and they shall hallow My Sabbaths.

25 And they shall not go in to the dead body of a man to defile themselves. Only *a priest* may defile himself for a father, or for a mother, or for a son, or for a daughter, or for a brother, or for his sister, who has not been married.

26 And after he has been cleansed, let him number to himself seven days.

27 And on whatsoever day they shall enter into the inner court to minister in the holy place, they shall bring a propitiation, says the Lord God.

28 "And it shall be to them for an inheritance. I am their inheritance: and no possession shall be given them among the children of Israel; for I am their possession.

29 And these shall eat the meat offerings, and the sin offerings, and the trespass offerings; and every special offering in Israel shall be theirs.

30 *And* the firstfruits of all things, and the firstborn of all *animals* and all offerings, of all your firstfruits there shall be *a share* for the priests; and you shall give your earliest produce to the priest, to bring your blessings upon your houses.

31 And the priests shall eat no bird or beast that dies of itself, or is taken of wild beasts.

EZEKIEL CHAPTER 45

The Holy District

1 "And when you measure you land for inheritance, you shall set apart the firstfruits to the Lord, a holy space of the land, in length twenty-five thousand *reeds*, and in breadth twenty thousand; it shall be holy in all its borders round about.

2 And there shall be a sanctuary out of this, five hundred *reeds in length,* by five hundred in breadth, a square round about; and *there shall be* a vacant space *beyond* this of fifty cubits round about.

3 And out of this measurement shall you measure the length, twenty-five thousand, and the breadth twenty thousand; and in it shall be the Holy of Holies.

4 Of the land shall be *a portion* for the priests that minister in the holy place, and it shall be for them that draw near to minister to the Lord: and it shall be to them a place for houses set apart for their sacred office;

5 the length *shall be* twenty-five thousand, and the breadth twenty thousand. And the Levites that attend the house, they shall have cities to dwell in for a possession.

6 "And you shall appoint *for* the possession of the city five thousand in breadth, and in length twenty-five thousand;

after the manner of the firstfruits of the holy portion, they shall be for all the house of Israel.

7 "And the prince *shall have a portion* out of this, and out of this *there shall be a portion* for the firstfruits of the sanctuary, *and* for the possession of the city, in front of the firstfruits of the sanctuary, and in front of the possession of the city westward, and from the western parts eastward. And the length *shall be* equal to one of the parts of the western borders, and the length *shall be* to the eastern borders of the land.

8 And he shall have it for a possession in Israel. And the princes of Israel shall no more oppress My people; but the house of Israel shall inherit the land according to their tribes."

Laws Governing the Prince

9 "Thus says the Lord God: Let it suffice you, you princes of Israel; remove injustice and misery, execute judgment and justice; take away oppression from My people, says the Lord God.

10 You shall have a just balance, and a just measure, and a just bath for measure.

11 And in like manner there shall be one bath as a measure of capacity; the tenth of the homer *shall be* the bath, and the tenth of the homer shall be in fair proportion to the homer.

12 And the weights *shall be* twenty gerahs, your pound shall be five shekels, fifteen shekels and fifty shekels.

13 And these are the firstfruits which you shall offer: a sixth part of a homer of wheat, and the sixth part of it *shall consist* of an ephah of a homer of barley.

14 And *you shall give as* the appointed measure of oil one bath of oil out of ten baths; for ten baths are a homer.

15 And one sheep from the flock out of ten, as an oblation from all the tribes of Israel, for sacrifices, and for burnt offerings, and for peace offerings, to make atonement for you, says the Lord God.

16 And all the people shall give these firstfruits to the prince of Israel.

17 And through the prince shall be *offered* the burnt offerings and the meat offerings, and the drink offerings in the feasts, and at the new moons, and on the Sabbaths; and in all the feasts of the house of Israel; he shall offer the sin offerings, and the meat offerings, and the burnt offerings, and the peace offerings, to make atonement for the house of Israel.

Keeping the Feasts

18 "Thus says the Lord God: In the first month, on the first *day* of the month, you shall take a calf without blemish out of the herd, to make atonement for the holy place.

19 And the priest shall take of the blood of the atonement, and put it on the thresholds of the house, and upon the four corners of the temple, and upon the altar, and upon the thresholds of the gate of the inner court.

20 And thus shall you do in the seventh month: on the first *day* of the month you shall take a rate from each one; and you shall make atonement for the house.

21 "And in the first *month*, on the fourteenth *day* of the month, you shall have the Feast of Passover; seven days shall you eat unleavened bread.

22 And the prince shall offer it that day a calf for a sin offering for himself, and the house, and for all the people of the land.

23 And for the seven days of the feast he shall offer as burnt offerings to the Lord seven calves and seven rams without blemish daily for the seven days; and a kid of the goats daily for a sin offering, and a meat offering.

24 And you shall prepare a cake for the calf, and cakes for the ram, and a hin of oil for the cake.

25 And in the seventh month, on the fifteenth *day* of the month, you shall sacrifice in the feast in the same way seven days, as *they sacrificed* the sin offerings, and the burnt offerings, and the freewill offering, and the oil."

EZEKIEL CHAPTER 46

The Manner of Worship

1 "Thus says the Lord God: The gate that is in the inner court, that looks eastward, shall be shut the six working days; *but* let it be opened on the Sabbath day, and it shall be opened on the day of the new moon.

2 And the prince shall enter by the way of the porch of the inner gate, and shall stand at the entrance of the gate, and the priests shall prepare his burnt offerings and his peace offerings, and he shall worship at the entrance of the gate. Then shall he come forth; but the gate shall not be shut till evening.

3 And the people of the land shall worship at the entrance of that gate, both on the Sabbaths and at the new moons, before the Lord.

4 And the prince shall offer burnt offerings to the Lord on the Sabbath day, six lambs without blemish, and a ram without blemish;

5 and a freewill offering, a meat offering for the ram, and a meat offering for the lambs, the gift of his hand, and a hin of oil for the meat offering.

6 And on the day of the new moon a calf without blemish, and six lambs, and there shall be a ram without blemish;

7 and a meat offering for the ram, and there shall be a meat offering for the calf as a freewill offering, and for the lambs, according as his hand can furnish, and *there shall be* a hin of oil for the cake.

8 And when the prince goes in, he shall go in by the way of the porch of the gate, and he shall go forth by the way of the gate.

9 "And whenever the people of the land shall go in before the Lord at the feasts, he that goes in by the way of the north gate to worship shall go forth by the way of the south

gate; and he that goes in by the way of the south gate shall go forth by the way of the north gate: he shall not return by the gate by which he entered, but he shall go forth opposite it.

¹⁰ And the prince shall enter with them in the midst of them when they go in; and when they go forth, he shall go forth.

¹¹ And in the feasts and in the general assemblies the freewill oblation shall be a meat offering for the calf, and a meat offering for the ram, and for the lambs, as his hand can furnish, and a hin of oil for the meat offering.

¹² "And if the prince should prepare *as* a thanksgiving a whole burnt peace offering to the Lord, and should open for himself the gate looking eastward, and offer his burnt offering, and his peace offerings, as he does on the Sabbath day; then shall he go out, and shall shut the doors after he has gone out.

¹³ And he shall prepare daily as a burnt offering to the Lord a lamb of a year old without blemish; in the morning shall he prepare it.

¹⁴ And he shall prepare a freewill offering for it in the morning, the sixth part of a measure *of flour*, and a third part of a hin of oil to mix *with* the fine flour, *as* a freewill offering to the Lord, a perpetual ordinance.

¹⁵ You shall prepare the lamb, and the freewill offering, and the oil in the morning, *for* a perpetual whole burnt sacrifice.

¹⁶ "Thus says the Lord God: If the prince shall give a gift to one of his sons out of his inheritance, this shall be to his sons a possession *as* an inheritance.

¹⁷ But if he give a gift to one of his servants, then it shall belong to him until the year of release; and *then* he shall restore *it* to the prince; but of the inheritance of his sons the *possession* shall continue to them.

¹⁸ And the prince shall by no means take of the inheritance of the people, to oppress them: he shall give an inheritance to his sons out of his *own* possession; that My people be not scattered, everyone from his possession."

¹⁹ And he brought me into the entrance of the *place* behind the gate, into the chamber of the sanctuary belonging to the priests, that looks toward the north. And behold, there was a place set apart.

²⁰ And he said to me, "This is the place where the priests shall boil the trespass offerings and the sin offerings, and there shall they bake the meat offering always; so as not to carry *them* out into the outer court, to sanctify the people."

²¹ And he brought me into the outer court, and led me round upon the four sides of the court; and behold, there was a court on *each of* the sides of the court,

²² on *every* side a court, *even* a court for all the four *sides*, and *each* little court belonging to the court was in length forty cubits, and *in* breadth thirty cubits, *there was* one measure to the four.

²³ And *there were* chambers in them round about, round about the four, and cooking-places formed under the chambers round about.

²⁴ And he said to me, "These are the cooks' houses, where they that serve the house shall boil the sacrifices of the people."

EZEKIEL CHAPTER 47

Water Flowing from the Temple

¹ And he brought me to the entrance of the house. and behold, water issued from under the porch eastward, for the front of the house looked eastward; and the water came down from the right side, from the south to the altar.

² And he brought me out by the way of the northern gate, and he led me round by the way outside to the gate of the court that looks eastward. And behold, water came down from the right side,

³ in *the direction* in which a man went forth opposite; and *there was* a measuring line in his hand, and he measured a thousand *cubits* with the measure;

⁴ and he passed through the water; *it was* water of a fountain. And *again* he measured a thousand, and passed through the water; and the water was up to his thighs. And *again* he measured a thousand; and he passed through water up to the loins.

⁵ And *again* he measured a thousand; and he could not pass through, for *the water* rose as of a torrent which *men* cannot pass over.

⁶ And he said to me, "Have you seen *this*, son of man?" Then he brought me, and led me back to the brink of the river

⁷ as I returned. And behold, on the brink of the river *there were* very many trees on this side and on that side.

⁸ And he said to me, "This is the water that goes forth to Galilee that lies eastward, and it is gone down to Arabia, and has reached as far as to the sea to the outlet of the water; and it shall heal the waters.

⁹ And it shall come to pass, *that* every animal of living *and* moving creatures, all on which the river shall come, shall live; and there shall be there very many fish; for this water shall go there, and it shall heal *them,* and they shall live: everything on which the river shall come shall live.

¹⁰ And fishermen shall stand there from En Gedi to En Eglaim; it shall be a place to spread out nets upon; it shall be distinct; and its fish *shall be* as the fish of the great sea, a very great multitude.

¹¹ But at the outlet of the water, and the turn of it, and where it overflows *its banks*, they shall not heal at all; they are given to salt.

¹² And every fruit tree shall grow by the river, *even* on the bank of it on this side and on that side. They shall not decay upon it, neither shall their fruit fail. They shall bring forth the firstfruit of their early crop, for these their waters come forth of the sanctuary; and their fruit shall be for meat, and their foliage for health."

Borders of the Land

13 "Thus says the Lord God: You shall inherit these borders of the land; *they are* given by lot to the twelve tribes of the children of Israel.

14 And you shall inherit it, each according to his brother's portion, *even the land* concerning which I lifted up My hand to give *it* to your fathers; and this land shall fall to you by lot.

15 And these are the borders of the land that lies northward, from the Great Sea that comes down, and divides the entrance of Emaseldam;

16 Hamath, Berothah, between the coasts of Damascus and the coasts of Emathi, the habitation of Saunan, which *places* are above the coasts of Auranitis.

17 These are the borders from the sea, from the habitations of Enan, the coasts of Damascus, and the northern *coasts.*

18 And the eastern coasts between Loranitis and Damascus, and the land of Gilead, and the land of Israel, the Jordan divides to the sea that is east of the city of palm trees. These are the eastern *coasts.*

19 And the southern and southwestern *coasts are* from Tamar and the city of palm trees, to the water of Meribah Kadesh, reaching forth to the Great Sea. This part is the south and southwest.

20 This part of the great sea forms a border, till *one comes* opposite the entrance of Hamath, *even* as far as the entrance thereof. These are the parts west of Hamath.

21 "So you shall divide this land to them, *even* to the tribes of Israel.

22 You shall cast the lot upon it, for yourselves and the strangers that sojourn in the midst of you, who have begotten children in the midst of you; and they shall be to you as natives among the children of Israel; they shall eat with you in *their* inheritance in the midst of the tribes of Israel.

23 And they shall be in the tribe of proselytes among the proselytes that are with them. There shall you give them an inheritance," says the Lord God.

EZEKIEL CHAPTER 48

Division of the Land

1 "And these are the names of the tribes from the northern corner, on the side of the decent that draws a line to the entrance of Hamath the palace of Elam, the border of Damascus northward on the side of Hamath the palace; and they shall have the eastern parts as far as the sea, for Dan, one *portion.*

2 And from the borders of Dan eastward as far as the west seacoast, for Asher, one.

3 And from the borders of Asher, from the eastern parts as far as the west coasts, for Naphtali, one.

4 And from the borders of Naphtali, from the east as far as the west coasts, for Manasseh, one.

5 And from the borders of Manasseh, from the eastern parts as far as the west coasts, for Ephraim, one.

6 And from the borders of Ephraim, from the eastern parts to the west coasts, for Reuben, one.

7 And from the borders of Reuben, from the eastern parts as far as the west coasts, for Judah, one.

8 "And from the borders of Judah, from the eastern parts shall be the offering of firstfruits, in the breadth twenty-five thousand *reeds,* and in length as one of the portions *measured* from the east even to the western parts; and the sanctuary shall be in the midst of them.

9 "*As for* the firstfruits which they shall offer to the Lord, *it shall be* in length twenty-five thousand, and in breadth twenty-five thousand.

10 Out of this shall be the firstfruits of the holy things to the priests, northward twenty-five thousand, and toward the west, ten thousand, and southward twenty-five thousand. And the mountain of the sanctuary shall be in the midst of it,

11 for the priests, for the consecrated sons of Zadok, who keep the charges of the house, who erred not in the error of the children of Israel, as the Levites erred.

12 And the firstfruits shall be given to them out of the firstfruits of the land, *even* a most holy portion from the borders of the Levites.

13 "And the Levites *shall have* the *part* next to the borders of the priests, in length twenty-five thousand, and in breadth ten thousand: the whole length *shall be* twenty-five thousand, and the breadth twenty thousand.

14 No *part* of it shall be sold, nor measured *as for sale,* neither shall the firstfruits of the land be taken away; for they are holy to the Lord.

15 "But *concerning* the five thousand that remain in the breadth in the twenty-five thousand, they shall be a suburb to the city for dwelling, and for a space before it; and the city shall be in the midst thereof.

16 And these *shall be* its dimensions: from the northern side four thousand and five hundred, and from the southern side four thousand and five hundred, and from the eastern side four thousand and five hundred, and from the western side *they shall measure* four thousand five hundred.

17 And there shall be a space to the city northward two hundred and fifty, and southward two hundred and fifty, and eastward two hundred and fifty, and westward two hundred and fifty.

18 And the remainder of the length that is next to the firstfruits of the holy *portion shall be* ten thousand eastward, and ten thousand westward; and they shall be the firstfruits of the sanctuary; and the fruits thereof shall be for bread to them that labor for the city.

19 And they that labor for the city shall labor for it out of all the tribes of Israel.

20 The whole offering *shall be* a square of twenty-five thousand by twenty-five thousand: you shall separate *again part* of it, the firstfruits of the sanctuary, from the possession of the city.

21 "And the prince *shall have* the remainder on this side and on that side from the firstfruits of the sanctuary, and *there*

shall be a possession of the city, for twenty-five thousand cubits in length, to the eastern and western borders, for twenty-five thousand to the western borders, next to the portions of the prince; and the firstfruits of the holy things and the sanctuary of the house *shall be* in the midst of it.

22 And there shall be *a portion taken* from the Levites, from the possession of the city in the midst of the princes between the borders of Judah and the borders of Benjamin, and it shall be *the portion* of the princes.

23 And *as for* the rest of the tribes, from the eastern parts as far as the western, Benjamin *shall have* one *portion*.

24 And from the borders of Benjamin, from the eastern parts to the western, Simeon, one.

25 And from the borders of Simeon, from the eastern parts to the western, Issachar, one.

26 And from the borders of Issachar, from the eastern parts to the western, Zebulun, one.

27 And from the borders of Zebulun, from the east to the western parts, Gad, one.

28 And from the borders of Gad, from the eastern parts to the southwestern parts; his coasts shall even be from Tamar, and the water of Meribah Kadesh, for an inheritance, unto the Great Sea.

29 This is the land, which you shall divide by lot to the tribes of Israel, and these are their portions," says the Lord God.

30 "And these are the goings out of the city northward, four thousand and five hundred by measure.

31 And the gates of the city *shall be* after the names of the tribes of Israel: three gates northward; the gate of Reuben, one, and the gate of Judah, one, and the gate of Levi, one.

32 And eastward four thousand and five hundred: and three gates; the gate of Joseph, one, and the gate of Benjamin, one, and the gate of Dan, one.

33 And southward, four thousand and five hundred by measure; and three gates: the gate of Simeon, one, and the gate of Issachar, one, and the gate of Zebulun, one.

34 And westward, four thousand and five hundred by measure; *and* three gates: the gate of Gad, one, and the gate of Asher, one, and the gate of Naphtali, one.

35 The circumference, eighteen thousand *measures*. And the name of the city, from the day that it shall be finished, shall be THE LORD IS THERE."

THE BOOK OF DANIEL

1 In the third year of the reign of Jehoiakim king of Judah, Nebuchadnezzar king of Babylon came to Jerusalem, and besieged it.

2 And the Lord gave into his hand Jehoiakim king of Judah, and part of the vessels of the house of God: and he brought them into the land of Shinar to the house of his god; and he brought the vessels into the treasure house of his god.

3 And the king told Ashpenaz his chief eunuch, to bring in *some* of the captive children of Israel, and of the descendants of the kingdom, and of the princes;

4 young men in whom was no blemish, and beautiful in appearance, and skilled in all wisdom, and possessing knowledge, and acquainted with prudence, and who had ability to stand in the house before the king, and *the king gave commandment* to teach them the knowledge and language of the Chaldeans.

5 And the king appointed them a daily portion from the king's table, and from the wine which he drank; and *gave orders* to nourish them three years, and *that* afterwards they should stand before the king.

6 Now these were among them of the children of Judah: Daniel, Hananiah, Azariah, and Mishael.

7 And the chief of the eunuchs gave them names: to Daniel, Belteshazzar; and to Hananiah, Shadrach; and to Mishael, Meshach; and to Azariah, Abed-Nego.

8 And Daniel purposed in his heart, that he would not defile himself with the king's table, nor with the wine of his drink: and he intreated the chief of the eunuchs that he might not defile himself.

9 Now God *had* brought Daniel into favor and compassion with the chief of the eunuchs.

10 And the chief of the eunuchs said to Daniel, "I fear my lord the king, who has appointed your meat and your drink, lest he see your countenances gloomy, in comparison with the young men your equals; also shall you endanger my head to the king."

11 And Daniel said to Melzar, whom the chief of the eunuchs had appointed over Daniel, Hananiah, Mishael, *and* Azariah,

12 "Please test your servants for ten days, and let them give us vegetables to eat, and water to drink.

13 And let our countenances be seen by you, and the countenances of the children that eat *at* the king's table; and deal with your servants according as you shall see."

14 So he consented with them in this matter, and tested them for ten days.

15 And at the end of the ten days their countenances appeared fairer and stouter in flesh than the children that ate at the king's table.

16 So Melzar took away their supper and the wine they were to drink, and gave them vegetables.

17 And *as for* these four children, God gave them understanding and prudence in all learning and wisdom. And Daniel had understanding in all visions and dreams.

18 And at the end of the days, *after* which the king had given orders to bring them in, then the chief of the eunuchs brought them in before Nebuchadnezzar.

19 And the king spoke with them; and there were not found out of them all any like Daniel, Hananiah, Mishael, and Azariah: and they stood before the king.

20 And in every matter of wisdom and knowledge wherein the king questioned them, he found them ten times wiser than all the enchanters and sorcerers that were in all his kingdom.

21 And Daniel continued until the first year of King Cyrus.

DANIEL CHAPTER 2

Nebuchadnezzar's Dream

¹ In the second year of *his* reign Nebuchadnezzar dreamed a dream, and his spirit was amazed, and his sleep departed from him.

² And the king gave orders to call the enchanters, and the magicians, and the sorcerers, and the Chaldeans, to declare to the king his dreams. And they came and stood before the king.

³ And the king said to them, "I have had a dream, and my spirit is troubled to know the dream."

⁴ And the Chaldeans spoke to the king in the Syrian language, *saying*, "O king, live forever: tell the dream to your servants, and we will declare the interpretation."

⁵ The king answered the Chaldeans *and said,* "The thing has departed from me: if you do not make known to me the dream and the interpretation, you shall be destroyed, and your houses shall be spoiled.

⁶ But if you make known to me the dream, and the interpretation thereof, you shall receive from me gifts and presents and much honor: only tell me the dream, and its interpretation."

⁷ They answered the second time, and said, "Let the king tell the dream to his servants, and we will declare the interpretation."

⁸ And the king answered and said, "I know very well that you are trying to gain time, because you see that the thing has gone from me.

⁹ If then you do not tell me the dream, I know that you have conspired to utter before me a false and corrupt tale, until the time has past: now tell me my dream, and I shall know that you will also declare to me its interpretation."

¹⁰ The Chaldeans answered before the king and said, "There is no man upon the earth, who shall be able to make known the king's matter: forasmuch as no great king or ruler asks such a question of an enchanter, magician, or Chaldean.

¹¹ For the question which the king asks is difficult, and there is no one else who shall answer it before the king, but the gods, whose dwelling is not with flesh."

¹² Then the king in rage and anger commanded to destroy all the wise men of Babylon.

¹³ So the decree went forth, and they began to destroy the wise men; and they sought Daniel and his companions to destroy *them.*

God Reveals Nebuchadnezzar's Dream

¹⁴ Then Daniel answered *with* counsel and prudence to Arioch the captain of the royal guard, who was gone forth to kill the wise men of Babylon, *saying,*

¹⁵ "Why has this shameless command proceeded from the king?" So Arioch made known the matter to Daniel.

¹⁶ And Daniel intreated the king to give him time, and that he might declare to the king its interpretation.

¹⁷ So Daniel went into his house, and made known the matter to Hananiah, Mishael, and Azariah, his friends.

¹⁸ And they sought mercies from the God of heaven concerning this mystery; that Daniel and his friends might not perish with the rest of the wise men of Babylon.

¹⁹ Then the mystery was revealed to Daniel in a night vision; and Daniel blessed the God of heaven, and said,

²⁰ "May the name of God be blessed from everlasting to everlasting; for wisdom and understanding are His.

²¹ And He changes times and seasons; He appoints kings, and removes *them,* giving wisdom to the wise, and prudence to them that have understanding.

²² He reveals deep and secret *things*; knowing what is in darkness, and the light is with Him.

²³ I give thanks to You, and praise *You,* O God of my fathers, for You have given me wisdom and power, and have made known to me the things which we asked of You; and You have made known to me the king's vision."

Daniel Explains the Dream

²⁴ And Daniel came to Arioch, whom the king had appointed to destroy the wise men of Babylon, and said to him; "Do not destroy the wise men of Babylon, but bring me in before the king, and I will declare the interpretation to the king."

²⁵ Then Arioch immediately brought Daniel in before the king, and said to him, "I have found a man of the children of the captivity of Judah who will declare the interpretation to the king."

²⁶ And the king answered and said to Daniel, whose name was Belteshazzar, "Can you declare to me the dream which I saw, and its interpretation?"

²⁷ And Daniel answered before the king, and said, "The mystery of which the king asks is not *in the power* of the wise men, magicians, enchanters, *or* soothsayers to declare to the king.

²⁸ But there is a God in heaven who reveals mysteries, and He has made known to King Nebuchadnezzar what things must come to pass in the last days. Your dream, and the visions of your head upon your bed are as follows:

²⁹ O king: your thoughts upon your bed arose *as to* what must come to pass hereafter: and He that reveals mysteries has made known to you what must come to pass.

³⁰ Moreover, this mystery has not been revealed to me by reason of wisdom which is in me beyond all *others* living, but for the sake of making known the interpretation to the king, that you might know the thoughts of your heart.

³¹ "You, O king, were watching; and behold, an image. And the image was great, and its appearance *was* excellent, standing before your face; and its form was awesome.

³² *It was* an image, the head of which was of fine gold, its hands and breast and arms of silver, *its* belly and thighs of brass,

³³ its legs of iron, its feet partly of iron and partly of clay.

34 You saw until a stone was cut out of a mountain without hands, and it struck the image upon its feet of iron and clay, and utterly reduced them to powder.

35 Then once for all the clay, the iron, the brass, the silver, and the gold were ground into powder, and became as chaff from the summer threshing floor. And the violence of the wind carried them away, and no place was found for them. And the stone which had struck the image became a great mountain, and filled the whole earth.

36 "This is the dream; and we will tell its interpretation before the king.

37 You, O king, are a king of kings, to whom the God of heaven has given a powerful and strong and honorable kingdom,

38 in every place where the children of men dwell: and He has given into your hand the wild beasts of the field, and the birds of the sky and the fish of the sea, and He has made you ruler over them all.

39 You are this head of gold. And after you shall arise another kingdom inferior to yours, and a third kingdom which is the brass, which shall have dominion over all the earth;

40 and a fourth kingdom, which shall be strong as iron; as iron beats to powder and subdues all things, so shall it beat to powder and subdue.

41 And whereas you saw the feet and the toes, partly of clay, and partly of iron, the kingdom shall be divided; yet there shall be in it of the strength of iron, as you saw the iron mixed with the clay.

42 And *whereas* the toes of the feet were partly of iron and partly of clay, part of the kingdom shall be strong, and *part* of it shall be broken.

43 Whereas you saw the iron mixed with the clay, they shall be mingled with the seed of men: but they shall not cleave together, as the iron does not mix itself with clay.

44 And in the days of those kings the God of heaven shall set up a kingdom which shall never be destroyed; and His kingdom shall not be left to another people, *but* it shall beat to pieces and grind to powder all *other* kingdoms, and it shall stand forever.

45 Whereas you saw that a stone was cut out of a mountain without hands, and it beat to pieces the clay, the iron, the brass, the silver, and the gold; the great God has made known to the king what must happen hereafter: and the dream is true, and its interpretation is sure."

Daniel and His Friends Promoted

46 Then King Nebuchadnezzar fell upon his face, and worshipped Daniel, and gave orders to offer to him gifts and incense.

47 And the king answered and said to Daniel, "Truly your God is a God of gods, and Lord of kings, who reveals mysteries; for you have been able to reveal this mystery."

48 And the king promoted Daniel, and gave him great and abundant gifts, and set him over the whole province of Babylon, and *made him* chief satrap over all the wise men of Babylon.

49 And Daniel asked of the king, and he appointed Shadrach, Meshach, and Abed-Nego over the affairs of the province of Babylon; but Daniel was in the king's palace.

DANIEL CHAPTER 3

The Image of Gold

1 In the eighteenth year Nebuchadnezzar the king made a golden image, its height was sixty cubits, *and* its breadth *was* six cubits. And he set it up in the plain of Dura, in the province of Babylon.

2 And he sent forth to gather the governors, and the captains, and the heads of provinces, chiefs, and princes, and those who were in authority, and all the rulers of districts, to come to the dedication of the image.

3 So the heads of provinces, the governors, the captains, the chiefs, the great princes, those who were in authority, and all the rulers of districts, were gathered to the dedication of the image which King Nebuchadnezzar had set up. And they stood before the image.

4 Then a herald cried aloud, "To you it is commanded, you peoples, tribes, and languages,

5 at what hour you shall hear the sound of the trumpet, pipe, harp, sackbut, psaltery, and every kind of music, you shall fall down and worship the golden image which King Nebuchadnezzar has set up.

6 And whosoever shall not fall down and worship, in the same hour he shall be cast into the burning fiery furnace."

7 And it came to pass when the nations heard the sound of the trumpet, pipe, harp, sackbut, psaltery, and all kinds of music, all the nations, tribes, and languages fell down and worshipped the golden image which King Nebuchadnezzar had set up.

Daniel's Friends Disobey the King

8 Then *certain* Chaldeans came near, and accused the Jews to the king, *saying,*

9 "O king, live forever!

10 You, O king, have made a decree that every man who shall hear the sound of the trumpet, pipe, harp, sackbut, psaltery, and all kinds of music,

11 and shall not fall down and worship the golden image, shall be cast into the burning fiery furnace.

12 There are *certain* Jews whom you have appointed over the affairs of the province of Babylon--Shadrach, Meshach, *and* Abed-Nego, who have not obeyed your decree, O king: they do not serve your gods, and they do not worship the golden image which you have set up."

13 Then Nebuchadnezzar, in wrath and anger, commanded to bring Shadrach, Meshach, and Abed-Nego. And they were brought before the king.

[14] And Nebuchadnezzar answered and said to them, "Is it true, Shadrach, Meshach, *and* Abed-Nego, that you do not serve my gods, and that you do not worship the golden image which I have set up?

[15] Now then, if you are ready, whenever you shall hear the sound of the trumpet, pipe, harp, sackbut, psaltery, harmony, and every kind of music, to fall down and worship the golden image which I have made, *fine;* but if you will not worship, in the same hour you shall be cast into the burning fiery furnace; and who is the god that shall deliver you out of my hand?"

[16] Then Shadrach, Meshach *and* Abed-Nego answered and said to King Nebuchadnezzar, "We have no need to answer you concerning this matter.

[17] For our God whom we serve is in the heavens, *and He is* able to deliver us from the burning fiery furnace, and He shall rescue us from your hands, O king.

[18] But if not, let it be known to you, O king, that we *will* not serve your gods, neither *will we* worship the image which you have set up."

The Fiery Furnace

[19] Then Nebuchadnezzar was filled with wrath, and the expression of his face was changed toward Shadrach, Meshach, and Abed-Nego. And he gave orders to heat the furnace seven times *more than usual,* until it should burn to the uttermost.

[20] And he commanded mighty men to bind Shadrach, Meshach, and Abed-Nego, and to cast *them* into the burning fiery furnace.

[21] Then those men were bound with their coats, caps, and trousers, and were cast into the midst of the burning fiery furnace,

[22] forasmuch as the king's word prevailed; and the furnace was made exceedingly hot.

[23] Then these three men, Shadrach, Meshach, and Abed-Nego, fell bound into the midst of the burning furnace, and walked in the midst of the flame, singing praises to God, and blessing the Lord.

[24] Then Nebuchadnezzar heard them singing praises. And he wondered, and rose up in haste, and said to his nobles, "Did we not cast three men bound into the midst of the fire?" And they said to the king, "Yes, O king."

[25] And the king said, "But I see four men loose, and walking in the midst of the fire, and there has no harm happened to them; and the appearance of the fourth is like the Son of God."

Nebuchadnezzar Praises God

[26] Then Nebuchadnezzar drew near to the door of the burning fiery furnace, and said, "Shadrach, Meshach, *and* Abed-Nego, you servants of the Most High God, proceed forth, and come here." So Shadrach, Meshach, *and* Abed-Nego came forth out of the midst of the fire.

[27] Then were assembled the satraps, and captains, and heads of provinces, and the royal princes; and they saw the men, *and perceived* that the fire had not had power against their bodies, and the hair of their head was not burned, and their coats were not scorched, nor was the smell of fire upon them.

[28] And King Nebuchadnezzar answered and said, "Blessed be the God of Shadrach, Meshach, *and* Abed-Nego, who has sent His angel, and delivered His servants, because they trusted in Him; and they have changed the king's word, and delivered their bodies to be burned, that they might not serve nor worship any god, except their own God.

[29] Therefore I publish a decree: Every people, tribe, *or* language that shall speak reproachfully against the God of Shadrach, Meshach, *and* Abed-Nego shall be destroyed, and their houses shall be plundered, because there is no other God who shall be able to deliver thus."

[30] Then the king promoted Shadrach, Meshach, *and* Abed-Nego, in the province of Babylon, and advanced them, and gave them authority to rule over all the Jews who were in his kingdom.

DANIEL CHAPTER 4

Nebchadnezzar's Second Dream

[1] King Nebuchadnezzar, to all nations, tribes, and tongues that dwell in all the earth: Peace be multiplied to you.

[2] It seemed good to me to declare to you the signs and wonders which the Most High God has worked for me,

[3] how great and mighty *they are;* His kingdom is an everlasting kingdom, and His power to all generations.

[4] I, Nebuchadnezzar, was thriving in my house, and prospering.

[5] I saw a vision and it terrified me, and I was troubled on my bed, and the visions of my head troubled me.

[6] And I made a decree to bring in before me all the wise men of Babylon, that they might make known to me the interpretation of the dream.

[7] So the enchanters, magicians, soothsayers, *and* Chaldeans came in, and I told the dream before them; but they did not make known to me its interpretation;

[8] until Daniel came, whose name is Belteshazzar, according to the name of my god, who has within him the Holy Spirit of God, to whom I said,

[9] "O Belteshazzar, chief of the enchanters, of whom I know that the Holy Spirit of God is in you, and no mystery is too hard for you, hear the vision of my dream which I had, and tell me the interpretation of it.

[10] I had a vision upon my bed; and behold a tree in the midst of the earth, and its height was great.

[11] The tree grew large and strong, and its height reached to the sky, and its extent to the extremity of the whole earth;

[12] its leaves were fair, and its fruit abundant, and in it was food for all; and under it the wild beasts of the field took

shelter, and the birds of the sky lodged in the branches of it, and all flesh was fed by it.

[13] "I beheld in the night vision upon my bed, and behold, a watcher and a holy one came down from heaven and cried aloud, and thus he said,

[14] 'Cut down the tree, and pluck off its branches, and shake off its leaves, and scatter its fruit—let the wild beasts be removed from under it, and the birds from its branches.

[15] Only leave the stump of its roots in the earth, and *bind it* with an iron and brass band; and it shall lie in the outer grass, and in the dew of heaven, and its portion *shall be* with the wild beasts in the grass of the field.

[16] His heart shall be changed from that of a man, and the heart of a wild beast shall be given to him; and seven times shall pass over him.

[17] This decision is by the decree of the watcher, and the demand is a word of the holy ones; that the living may known that the Lord is Most High *over* the kingdom of men, and He will give it to whomever He will, and sets it over the lowest of men.'

[18] This is the vision which I, King Nebuchadnezzar saw. Now you, Belteshazzar, declare the interpretation, for none of the wise men of my kingdom are able to show me its interpretation—but you, Daniel, are able, for the Holy Spirit of God is in you."

Daniel Explains the Second Dream

[19] Then Daniel, whose name is Belteshazzar, was amazed about one hour, and his thoughts troubled him. And Belteshazzar answered and said, "*My* lord, let the dream concern those that hate you, and the interpretation of it to your enemies.

[20] The tree which you saw, which grew large and strong, whose height reached to the heavens, and its extent to all *parts* of the earth,

[21] and whose leaves were flourishing, and its fruit abundant, (and it was food for all; under it the wild beasts lodged, and the birds of the sky took shelter in its branches)

[22] is you, O king; for you have grown great and powerful, and your greatness has increased and reached to the heavens, and your dominion to the ends of the earth.

[23] "And whereas the king saw a watcher and a holy one coming down from heaven, and he said, 'Strip the tree, and destroy it; only leave the stump of its roots in the ground, and *bind it* with a band of iron and brass; and it shall lie in the outer grass, and in the dew of heaven, and its portion shall be with wild beasts, until seven times have passed over it.'

[24] This is the interpretation of it, O king, and it is a decree of the Most High, which has come upon my lord the king:

[25] and they shall drive you forth from men, and your dwelling shall be with the wild beasts, and they shall feed you with grass like an ox, and you shall have your lodging under the dew of heaven, and seven times shall pass over

you, until you know that the Most High is Lord of the kingdom of men, and gives it to whomever He chooses.

[26] "And whereas they said, 'Leave the stumps of the roots of the tree'; your kingdom shall be *assured* to you, from the time that you realize the power of the heavens.

[27] Therefore, O king, let my counsel please you, and atone for your sins by alms, and *your* iniquities by compassion on the poor; *perhaps* God will be longsuffering toward your trespasses."

Nebuchadnezzar's Humiliation

[28] All these things came upon King Nebuchadnezzar.

[29] After the twelfth month, as he walked in his palace in Babylon,

[30] the king spoke, saying, "Is not this great Babylon, which I have built for a royal residence, by the might of my power, for the honor of my glory?"

[31] While the word was yet in the king's mouth, there came a voice from heaven, *saying*, "King Nebuchadnezzar, to you it is spoken, 'The kingdom has departed from you.'

[32] And they *shall* drive you from men, and your dwelling shall be with the wild beasts of the field, and they shall feed you with grass like an ox. And seven times shall pass over you, until you know that the Most High is Lord of the kingdom of men, and He shall give it to whomever He chooses."

[33] In the same hour the word was fulfilled upon Nebuchadnezzar. And he was driven forth from men, and he ate grass like an ox, and his body was bathed with the dew of heaven, until his hair had grown like the *hair* of a lion, and his nails as birds' *claws*.

Nebuchadnezzar Praises God

[34] And at the end of the time, I, Nebuchadnezzar, lifted up my eyes to heaven, and my reason returned to me, and I blessed the Most High, and praised Him that lives forever, and gave *Him* glory; for His dominion is an everlasting dominion, and His kingdom *endures* to all generations.

[35] All the inhabitants of the earth are reputed as nothing; and He does according to His will in the host of heaven, and among the inhabitants of the earth: and there is none who shall withstand His power, and say to Him, "What have You done?"

[36] At the same time my reason returned to me, and I came to the honor of my kingdom; and my *natural* form returned to me, and my princes and my nobles sought me, and I was established in my kingdom, and more abundant majesty was added to me.

[37] Now therefore, I, Nebuchadnezzar, praise and greatly exalt and glorify the King of heaven; for all His works are true, and His paths are judgment: and all that walk in pride He is able to abase.

DANIEL CHAPTER 5

Belshazzar's Feast

[1] Belshazzar the king made a great feast for his thousand nobles, and *there was* wine before the thousand.

[2] And Belshazzar, drinking, gave orders as he tasted the wine, that they should bring the gold and silver vessels which Nebuchadnezzar his father had brought forth from the temple in Jerusalem; that the king, and his nobles, and his mistresses, and his concubines, should drink out of them.

[3] So the gold and silver vessels were brought which *Nebuchadnezzar* had taken out of the temple of God in Jerusalem; and the king, and his nobles, and his mistresses, and his concubines drank out of them.

[4] They drank wine, and praised the gods of gold, and of silver, and of brass, and of iron, and of wood, and of stone.

The Writing on the Wall

[5] In the same hour came forth fingers of a man's hand, and wrote in front of the lamp on the plaster of the wall of the king's house. And the king saw the knuckles of the hand that wrote.

[6] Then the king's countenance changed, and his thoughts troubled him, and the joints of his hips were loosed, and his knees knocked one another.

[7] And the king cried aloud to bring in the magicians, Chaldeans, *and* soothsayers. And he said to the wise men of Babylon, "Whosoever shall read this writing, and make known to me the interpretation, shall be clothed with scarlet, and *there shall be* a golden chain upon his neck, and he shall be the third ruler in my kingdom."

[8] Then all the king's wise men came in, but they could not read the writing, nor make known its interpretation to the king.

[9] And King Belshazzar was troubled, and his countenance changed upon him, and his nobles were troubled with him.

[10] Then the queen came into the banquet house, and said, "O king, live forever. Let not your thoughts trouble you, and let not your countenance be changed.

[11] There is a man in your kingdom, in whom is the Spirit of God; and in the days of your father watchfulness and understanding were found in him; and King Nebuchadnezzar your father made him chief of the enchanters, magicians, Chaldeans, *and* soothsayers.

[12] For *there is* an excellent spirit in him, and sense and understanding *is* in him, interpreting dreams *as he does*, and answering hard *questions*, and solving riddles. *It is* Daniel, and the king gave him the name of Belteshazzar. Now then let him be called, and he shall tell you the interpretation of the writing."

The Writing on the Wall Explained

[13] Then Daniel was brought in before the king, and the king said to Daniel, "Are you Daniel, of the children of the captivity of Judah, which my father the king brought *from Judah*?

[14] I have heard about you, that the Spirit of God is in you, and *that* watchfulness and understanding and excellent wisdom have been found in you.

[15] And now, the wise men, magicians, *and* soothsayers have come in before me, to read the writing, and make known to me the interpretation, but they could not tell it to me.

[16] And I have heard about you, that you are able to make *known* interpretations. Now then, if you are able to read the writing, and to make known to me its interpretation, you shall be clothed with purple, and there shall be a golden chain upon your neck, and you shall be third ruler in my kingdom."

[17] And Daniel said before the king, "Let your gifts be to yourself, and give the presents of your house to another; but I will read the writing, and will make known to you its interpretation.

[18] O king, the Most High God gave to your father Nebuchadnezzar a kingdom, and majesty, and honor, and glory.

[19] And by reason of the majesty which He gave to him, all nations, tribes, *and* languages trembled and feared before him. Whomever he wished, he executed; whomever he wished, he exalted; and whomever he wished, he abased.

[20] But when his heart was lifted up, and his spirit was emboldened to act proudly, he was deposed from his royal throne, and *his* honor was taken from him.

[21] And he was driven forth from men. And a heart was given to him after the nature of wild beasts, and his dwelling was with the wild donkeys. And they fed him with grass like an ox, and his body was bathed with the dew of heaven, until he knew that the Most High God is Lord of the kingdom of men, and will give it to whomever He chooses.

[22] And you accordingly, his son, O Belshazzar, have not humbled your heart before God: do you not know all this?

[23] And you have exalted yourself against the Lord God of heaven; and they have brought before you the vessels of His house, and you, your nobles, your mistresses, and your concubines have drunk wine out of them; and you have praised the gods of gold, silver, brass, iron, wood, and stone, which neither see, nor hear, nor know: and the God who holds your breath in His hand and owns all your ways, you have not glorified.

[24] Therefore from His presence has been sent forth the finger of a hand, and He has ordered the writing.

[25] And this is the ordered writing: Mene, Tekel, Peres.

[26] This is the interpretation of the sentence: Mene; God has numbered your kingdom, and finished it.

[27] Tekel; it has been weighed in the balance, and found wanting.

[28] Peres; your kingdom is divided, and given to the Medes and Persians."

[29] Then Belshazzar commanded, and they clothed Daniel with scarlet, and put the golden chain about his neck, and

proclaimed concerning him that he was the third ruler in the kingdom.

Belshazzar's Fall

30 In the same night Belshazzar the Chaldean king was slain.

31 And Darius the Mede succeeded to the kingdom, being sixty-two years old.

DANIEL CHAPTER 6

The Plot Against Daniel

1 And it pleased Darius, and he set over the kingdom a hundred and twenty satraps, to be in all his kingdom;

2 and over them three governors (of whom one was Daniel) for the satraps to give account to them, that the king should not be troubled.

3 And Daniel was over them, for *there was* an excellent spirit in him; and the king set him over all his kingdom.

4 Then the governors and satraps sought to find occasion against Daniel; but they found against him no occasion, nor trespass, nor error, because he was faithful.

5 And the governors said, "We shall not find occasion against Daniel, except in the ordinances of his God."

6 Then the governors and satraps stood by the king, and said to him, "King Darius, live forever!

7 All who preside over your kingdom, captains and satraps, chiefs and local governors, have taken counsel together, to establish by a royal statute, and to confirm a decree, that whosoever shall ask a petition of any god or man for thirty days, except for you, O king, shall be cast into the den of lions.

8 Now then, O king, establish the decree, and publish a writ, that the decree of the Persians and Medes may not be changed."

9 Then King Darius commanded the decree to be written.

Daniel in the Lion's Den

10 And when Daniel knew that the decree was ordered, he went into his house. And his windows were opened in his chambers toward Jerusalem, and three times in the day he knelt upon his knees, and prayed and gave thanks before his God, as he did before.

11 Then these men watched, and found Daniel praying and making supplication to his God.

12 And they came and said to the king, "O king, have you not made a decree, that if any man shall ask a petition of any god or man for thirty days, except for you, O king, shall be cast into the den of lions?" And the king said, "The word is true, and the decree of the Medes and Persians shall not pass."

13 Then they answered and said before the king, "Daniel of the sons of the captivity of Judah, has not submitted to your decree; and three times in the day he makes his requests of his God."

14 Then the king, when he heard these words, was greatly grieved for Daniel, and he set his heart on Daniel to deliver him: and he exerted himself till evening to deliver him.

15 Then those men said to the king, "Know, O king, that the law of the Medes and Persians is that we must not change any decree or statute which the king shall make."

16 Then the king commanded, and they brought Daniel, and cast him into the den of lions. But the king said to Daniel, "Your God, whom you serve continually, He shall deliver you."

17 And they brought a stone, and put it on the mouth of the den; and the king sealed *it* with his ring, and with the ring of his nobles; that the case might not be altered with regard to Daniel.

Daniel Saved from the Lions

18 And the king departed to his house, and lay down fasting, and they brought him no food; and his sleep departed from him. But God shut the mouths of the lions, and they did not molest Daniel.

19 Then the king arose very early in the morning, and went in haste to the den of lions.

20 And when he drew near to the den, he cried out with a loud voice *and said*, "Daniel, servant of the living God, has your God, whom you serve continually, been able to deliver you from the lion's mouth?"

21 And Daniel said to the king, "O king, live forever!

22 My God has sent His angel, and stopped the lions' mouths, and they have not hurt me: for uprightness was found in me before Him; and moreover before you, O king, I have committed no trespass."

23 Then the king was very glad for him, and he commanded to bring Daniel out of the den. So Daniel was taken up out of the den, and no injury was found on him, because he believed in his God.

Darius Honors God

24 And the king commanded, and they brought the men that had accused Daniel, and they were cast into the den of lions, they, their children, and their wives. And they did not reach the bottom of the den before the lions overpowered them, and utterly broke to pieces all their bones.

25 Then King Darius wrote to all nations, tribes, *and* languages, who dwell in all the earth, *saying*, "Peace be multiplied to you.

26 This decree has been set forth by me in every dominion of my kingdom, that *men must* tremble and fear before the God of Daniel; for He is the living and eternal God, and His kingdom shall not be destroyed, and His dominion is forever.

27 He helps and delivers, and works signs and wonders in the heaven and on the earth, who has rescued Daniel from the power of the lions."

²⁸ And Daniel prospered in the reign of Darius, and in the reign of Cyrus the Persian.

DANIEL CHAPTER 7

Vision of the Four Beasts

¹ In the first year of Belteshazzar, king of the Chaldeans Daniel had a dream, and visions of his head upon his bed: and he wrote down the dream.

² I, Daniel, beheld, and lo, the four winds of heaven blew violently upon the great sea.

³ And four great beasts came up out of the sea, each differing from one another.

⁴ The first *was* as a lioness, and her wings as an eagle's; I beheld until her wings were plucked, and she was lifted off from the earth, and she stood on human feet, and a man's heart was given to her.

⁵ And behold, the second beast was like a bear, and it supported itself on one side, and there were three ribs in its mouth, between its teeth. And thus they said to it, "Arise, devour much flesh."

⁶ After this one I looked, and behold, another wild beast as a leopard, and it had four wings of a bird upon it. And the wild beast had four heads, and power was given to it.

⁷ After this one I looked, and behold, a fourth beast, dreadful and terrible, and exceedingly strong, and its teeth were of iron; devouring and crushing to atoms, and it trampled the remainder with its feet. And it was altogether different from the beasts that were before it; and it *had* ten horns.

⁸ I noticed his horns, and behold, another one came up in the midst of them, a little horn, and before it three of the former horns were rooted out. And behold, *there were* eyes as the eyes of a man in this horn, and a mouth speaking great things.

Vision of the Ancient of Days

⁹ I beheld until the thrones were set, and the Ancient of Days sat; and His garment was white as snow, and the hair of His head was as pure wool; His throne was a flame of fire, *and* His wheels burning fire.

¹⁰ A stream of fire rushed forth before Him. Thousands *upon* thousands ministered to Him, and ten thousand times ten thousand attended to Him. The court was seated, and the books were opened.

¹¹ I beheld then because of the voice of the great words which that horn spoke, until the wild beast was slain and destroyed, and his body given to be burned with fire.

¹² And the dominion of the rest of the wild beasts was taken away; but a prolonging of life was given to them for an appointed time.

¹³ I beheld in the night vision, and behold, *One* like the Son of Man coming with the clouds of heaven, and He came to the Ancient of Days, and was brought near to Him.

¹⁴ And to Him was given the dominion, and the honor, and the kingdom; and all nations, tribes, and languages, shall serve Him. His dominion is an everlasting dominion, which shall not pass away, and His kingdom shall not be destroyed.

Daniel's Visions Interpreted

¹⁵ *As for* me, Daniel, my spirit in my body trembled, and the visions of my head troubled me.

¹⁶ And I drew near to one of them that stood by, and I sought to learn from him the truth of all these things. And he told me the truth, and made known to me the interpretation of the things.

¹⁷ "These four beasts are four kingdoms *that* shall rise up on the earth,

¹⁸ which shall be taken away; and the saints of the Most High shall take the kingdom, and possess it forever and ever."

¹⁹ Then I inquired carefully concerning the fourth beast; for it was different from the other beasts, exceedingly dreadful. Its teeth were of iron, and its claws of brass, devouring, and utterly breaking to pieces, and it trampled the remainder with its feet.

²⁰ And concerning its ten horns that were on its head, and the other that came up, and rooted up *some* of the former *ones*, which had eyes, and a mouth speaking great things, and his appearance was greater than the others.

²¹ I beheld, and that horn made war with the saints, and prevailed against them;

²² until the Ancient of Days came, and He gave judgment to the saints of the Most High; and the time was fulfilled, and the saints possessed the kingdom.

²³ And he said, "The fourth beast shall be the fourth kingdom on the earth, which shall excel *beyond* all *other* kingdoms, and shall devour the whole earth, and trample and destroy it.

²⁴ And his ten horns are ten kings *that* shall arise: and after them shall arise another, who shall exceed all the former ones in wickedness and he shall subdue three kings.

²⁵ And he shall speak words against the Most High, and shall wear out the saints of the Most High, and shall think to change times and law. And *power* shall be given into his hand for a time, times and half a time.

²⁶ "But the court shall be seated, and they shall remove *his* dominion to abolish it, and to destroy it utterly.

²⁷ And the kingdom and the power and the greatness of the kings that are under the whole heaven were given to the saints of the Most High; and His kingdom is an everlasting kingdom, and all powers shall serve and obey Him."

²⁸ This is the end of the matter. As for me, Daniel, my thoughts greatly troubled me, and my countenance was changed: but I kept the matter in my heart.

DANIEL CHAPTER 8

Vision of a Ram and a Goat

¹ In the third year of the reign of King Belshazzar, a vision appeared to me, Daniel, after that which appeared to me at the first.

² And I was in Susa the palace, which is in the land of Elam, and I was on the *bank of the* Ulai.

³ And I lifted up my eyes and saw, and behold, a ram standing in front of the Ulai; and he had two horns; and one was higher than the other, and the higher one came up last.

⁴ And I saw the ram butting westward, northward, and southward; and no beast could stand before him, and there was none that could deliver out of his hand; and he did according to his will, and became great.

⁵ And as I was considering *the ram*, behold, a male goat came from the southwest on the face of the whole earth, and he did not touch the earth. And the goat *had* a horn between his eyes.

⁶ And he came to the ram that had the *two* horns, which I had seen standing in front of the Ulai, and he ran at him with the violence of his strength.

⁷ And I saw him coming up close to the ram, and he was exceedingly enraged against him, and he attacked the ram, and broke both his horns: and there was no strength in the ram to withstand him, but he cast him on the ground, and trampled on him; and there was none that could deliver the ram out of his hand.

⁸ And the male goat grew exceedingly great. And when he was strong, his great horn was broken; and four other *horns* rose up in its place toward the four winds of heaven.

⁹ And out of one of them came forth one strong horn, and it grew very great toward the south, and toward the host.

¹⁰ And it magnified itself to the host of heaven; and there fell to the earth *some* of the host of heaven and of the stars, and they trampled on them.

¹¹ And *this shall be* until the Chief Captain has delivered the captivity: and by reason of *the horn* the sacrifice was disturbed, and he prospered; and the holy place shall be made desolate.

¹² And a sin offering was given for the sacrifice, and righteousness was cast down to the ground; and he did all this, and prospered.

¹³ And I heard one saint speaking, and a saint said to a certain one speaking, "How long shall the vision continue, *even* the removal of the sacrifice, and the bringing in of the sin of desolation; and *how long* shall the sanctuary and host be trampled?"

¹⁴ And he said to him, "Evening and morning *there shall be* two thousand three hundred days; and *then* the sanctuary shall be cleansed."

Gabriel Interprets the Vision

¹⁵ And it came to pass, as I, Daniel, saw the vision, and sought to understand it, that behold, there stood before me *one* having the appearance of a man.

¹⁶ And I heard the voice of a man between *the banks of* the Ulai; and he called, and said, "Gabriel, cause this man to understand the vision."

¹⁷ And he came and stood near where I stood. And when he came, I was struck with awe, and fell upon my face. But he said to me, "Understand, son of man, for the vision is yet for an appointed time."

¹⁸ And while he spoke with me, I fell upon my face to the earth. And he touched me, and set me on my feet.

¹⁹ And he said, "Behold, I will make known to you the things that shall come to pass at the end of the wrath: for the vision *is* yet for an appointed time.

²⁰ The ram which you saw that had the *two* horns is the king of the Medes and Persians.

²¹ The male goat is the king of the Greeks: and the great horn which was between his eyes, he is the first king.

²² And *as for* the one that was broken, in whose place there stood up four horns, four kings shall arise out of his nation, but not in their *own* strength.

The King of Fierce Countenance

²³ "And at the latter time of their kingdom, when their sins are coming to the full, there shall arise a king of fierce countenance, who understands riddles;

²⁴ and his power *shall be* great, and he shall destroy fearfully, and shall prosper and thrive, and shall destroy *the* mighty men, and the holy people.

²⁵ And the yoke of his chain shall prosper: *there is* underhanded treachery in his hand, and he shall magnify himself in his heart, and by deceit he shall destroy many, and shall stand up for the destruction of many, and shall crush them like eggs in his hand.

²⁶ And the vision of the evening and morning that was mentioned is true: seal up the vision; for *it is* for many days."

²⁷ And I, Daniel, fell asleep, and was sick. Then I arose, and did the king's business; and I was astonished by the vision, and there was none that understood *it*.

DANIEL CHAPTER 9

Daniel's Prayer for the People

¹ In the first year of Darius the son of Ahasuerus, of the lineage of the Medes, who reigned over the kingdom of the Chaldeans,

² I, Daniel understood by the books the number of years which was the word of the Lord to the prophet Jeremiah, *the* seventy years for the accomplishment of the desolation of Jerusalem.

³ And I set my face toward the Lord God, to seek *Him* diligently by prayer and supplications, with fasting and sackcloth.

⁴ And I prayed to the Lord my God, and confessed, and said, "O Lord, the great and wonderful God, keeping Your covenant and Your mercy to them that love You, and to them that keep Your commandments; we have sinned;

⁵ we have committed iniquity, we have transgressed, and we have departed and turned aside from Your commandments and from Your judgments.

⁶ We have not obeyed Your servants the prophets, who spoke in Your name to our kings, and our princes, and our fathers, and to all the people of the land.

⁷ To you, O Lord, *belongs* righteousness, and to us confusion of face, as it is this day; to the men of Judah, and to the inhabitants of Jerusalem, and to all Israel, to them that are near, and to them that are far off in all the earth, wherever You have scattered them, for the sin which they have committed.

⁸ In you, O Lord, is our righteousness, and to us *belongs* confusion of face, and to our kings, and to our princes, and to our fathers, forasmuch as we have sinned.

⁹ To you, O Lord our God, *belong* compassion and forgiveness, whereas we have departed *from You.*

¹⁰ Neither have we heeded the voice of the Lord our God, to walk in His laws, which He set before us by the hands of His servants the prophets.

¹¹ Moreover, all Israel has transgressed Your law, and have refused to heed Your voice; so the curse has come upon us, and the oath that is written in the law of Moses the servant of God, because we have sinned against Him.

¹² And He has confirmed His words, which He spoke against us, and against our judges who judged us; *by* bringing upon us great evils, such as have not happened under the whole heaven, according to what has happened in Jerusalem.

¹³ As it is written in the Law of Moses, all these evils have come upon us: yet we have not sought after the Lord our God, that we might turn away from our iniquities, and have understanding in all Your truth.

¹⁴ The Lord also has watched, and brought these evils upon us: for the Lord our God is righteous in all His work which He has executed, but we have not heeded His voice.

¹⁵ And now, O Lord our God, who brought Your people out of the land of Egypt with a mighty hand, and made to Yourself a name, as *it is* this day; we have sinned, we have transgressed.

¹⁶ "O Lord, Your mercy is over all: let Your wrath turn away, I pray, and Your anger from Your city Jerusalem, *even* Your holy mountain; for we have sinned, and because of our iniquities, and those of our fathers, Jerusalem and Your people have become a reproach among all that are round about us.

¹⁷ And now, O lord our God, hear the prayer of Your servant, and his supplications, and cause Your face to shine on Your desolate sanctuary, for Your *name's* sake, O Lord.

¹⁸ Incline Your ear, O my God, and hear; open Your eyes and behold our desolation, and that of the city which is called by Your name; for we do not bring our pitiful case before You on *the grounds of* our righteousness, but *because of* Your manifold compassions, O Lord.

¹⁹ O Lord, hear! O Lord, forgive! O Lord, attend! Do not delay, O my God, for Your own sake; for Your city and Your people are called by Your name."

The Seventy Weeks Prophecy

²⁰ And while I was yet speaking, and praying, and confessing my sins and the sins of my people Israel, and bringing my pitiful case before the Lord my God concerning the holy mountain;

²¹ yes, while I was yet speaking in prayer, behold the man Gabriel, whom I had seen in the vision at the beginning, *came* flying, and he touched me about the hour of the evening sacrifice.

²² And he instructed me, and spoke with me, and said, "O Daniel, I have now come forth to impart to you understanding.

²³ At the beginning of your supplication the word came forth, and I have come to tell you; for you are a man greatly beloved. Therefore consider the matter, *and* understand the vision:

²⁴ "Seventy weeks have been determined upon your people, and upon the holy city, for sin to be ended, to seal up transgressions, to blot out iniquities, to make atonement for iniquities, to bring in everlasting righteousness, to seal up vision and prophecy, and to anoint the Most Holy.

²⁵ And you shall know and understand, that from the going forth of the command for the answer and for the building of Jerusalem, until Christ the Prince, *there shall be* seven weeks, and sixty-two weeks; and then *the time* shall return, and the street shall be built, and the wall, and the times shall be exhausted.

²⁶ And after the sixty-two weeks, the Anointed One shall be killed, and there is no judgment in Him. And He shall destroy the city and the sanctuary with the prince that is to come. They shall be cut off with a flood, and to the end of the war which is rapidly completed He shall appoint *the city* to desolations.

²⁷ And one week shall establish the covenant with many. And in the midst of the week my sacrifice and drink offering shall be taken away: and on the temple *shall be* the abomination of desolations; and at the end of the time an end shall be put to the desolation."

DANIEL CHAPTER 10

Vision of the Glorious Man

¹ In the third year of Cyrus king of the Persians a thing was revealed to Daniel, whose name was called Belteshazzar; and the thing was true, and great power and understanding in the vision was given to him.

² In those days I, Daniel was mourning three full weeks.

[3] I ate no pleasant bread, and no flesh or wine entered into my mouth, neither did I anoint myself with oil, until three whole weeks were accomplished.

[4] On the twenty-fourth day of the first month, I was near the great river, that is, the Tigris.

[5] And I lifted up my eyes and looked, and behold, a man clothed in linen, and his waist was girded with gold of Ophaz.

[6] And his body was like beryl, and his face was as the appearance of lightning, and his eyes as lamps of fire, and his arms and his legs as the appearance of shining brass, and the voice of his words as the voice of a multitude.

[7] And I, Daniel alone saw the vision: and the men that were with me did not see the vision; but a great amazement fell upon them, and they fled in fear.

[8] So I was left alone, and saw this great vision, and there was no strength left in me, and my glory was turned into corruption, and I retained no strength.

[9] Yet I heard the voice of his words; and when I heard him I was cut *to the heart*, and *I fell with* my face to the earth.

Prophecies Concerning Persia and Greece

[10] And behold, a hand touched me, and it raised me on my knees.

[11] And he said to me, "O Daniel, man greatly beloved, understand the words which I speak to you, and stand upright, for I am now sent to you." And when he had spoken to me this word, I stood trembling.

[12] And he said to me, "Do not fear, Daniel: for from the first day that you set your heart to understand, and to afflict yourself before the Lord your God, your words were heard, and I have come because of your words.

[13] But the prince of the kingdom of the Persians withstood me twenty-one days; and behold, Michael, one of the princes, came to help me; and I left him there with the prince of the kingdom of the Persians.

[14] And I have come to inform you of all that shall befall your people in the last days, for the vision *refers* to *many* days yet *to come*."

[15] And when he had spoken with me according to these words, I turned my face to the ground, and was cut *to the heart*.

[16] And behold, as it were the likeness of a son of man touched my lips; and I opened my mouth, and spoke, and said to him that stood before me, "O *my* lord, at the sight of you my insides were turned within me, and I had no strength.

[17] And how shall your servant be able, O *my* lord, to speak with this my lord? And as for me, from now on strength will not remain in me, and there is no breath left in me."

[18] And there touched me again as it were the appearance of a man, and he strengthened me,

[19] and said to me, "Do not fear, man greatly beloved: peace be to you, gird yourself like a man, and be strong." And

when he had spoken with me, I received strength, and said, "Let my lord speak; for you have strengthened me."

[20] And he said, "Do you know why I have come to you? And now I will return to fight with the prince of the Persians: and I was going in, and the prince of the Greeks came.

[21] But I will tell you that which is ordained in the Scripture of Truth; and there is no one that holds with me in these matters but Michael your prince."

DANIEL CHAPTER 11

[1] "And I, in the first year of Cyrus, stood to strengthen and confirm *him*.

[2] And now I will tell you the truth. Behold, there shall yet rise up three kings in Persia: and the fourth shall be far more richer than all. And after that he is master of his wealth, he shall rise up against all the kingdoms of the Greeks.

[3] And there shall rise up a mighty king, and he shall be lord of a great empire, and shall do according to his will.

[4] And when his kingdom shall stand up, it shall be broken, and shall be divided to the four winds of heaven; but not to his posterity, nor according to his dominion which he ruled over; for his kingdom shall be plucked up, and *given* to others beside these.

Warring Kings of North and South

[5] "And the king of the south shall be strong; and one of their princes shall prevail against him, and shall obtain a great dominion.

[6] And after his years they shall associate; and the daughter of the king of the south shall come to the king of the north, to make agreements with him, but she shall not retain power of arm; neither shall his descendants stand: and she shall be delivered up, and they that brought her, and the maiden, and he that strengthened her in these times.

[7] *But* out of the flower of her root there shall arise *one in* his place, and shall come against the host, and shall enter into the strongholds of the king of the north, and shall fight against them, and prevail.

[8] Yea, he shall carry with a body of captives into Egypt their gods with their molten *images, and* all their precious vessels of silver and gold; and he shall last longer than the king of the north.

[9] And he shall enter into the kingdom of the king of the south, and shall return to his own land.

[10] And his sons shall gather a multitude among many. And one shall certainly come, and overflow, and pass through, and he shall rest, and collect his strength.

[11] "And the king of the south shall be greatly enraged, and shall come forth, and shall war with the king of the north, and he shall raise a great multitude; but the multitude shall be delivered into his hand.

[12] And he shall take the multitude, and his heart shall be exalted; and he shall cast down many thousands; but he shall not prevail.

13 For the king of the north shall return, and bring a multitude greater than the former, and at the end of the times of years an invading army shall come with a great force, and with much substance.

14 "And in those times many shall rise up against the king of the south; and the children of the spoilers of your people shall exalt themselves to establish the vision; and they shall fail.

15 And the king of the north shall come in, and cast up a mound, and take strong cities; and the arms of the king of the south shall withstand, and his chosen ones shall rise up, but there shall be no strength to stand.

16 And he that comes in against him shall do according to his will, and there is no one to stand before him; and he shall stand in the land of beauty, and it shall be consumed by his hand.

17 And he shall set his face to come in with the force of his whole kingdom, and shall cause everything to prosper with him, and he shall give him the daughter of women to corrupt her, but she shall not continue, neither be on his side.

18 And he shall turn his face to the islands, and shall take many, and cause princes to cease from their reproach: nevertheless his own reproach shall return to him.

19 Then he shall turn back his face to the strength of his own land, but he shall become weak, and fall, and not be found.

20 "And there shall arise out of his root one that shall cause a plant of the kingdom to pass over his place, earning kingly glory, and yet in those days shall he be broken, yet not openly, nor in war.

21 *One* shall stand on his place, *who* has been set at nought, and they have not put upon him the honor of the kingdom: but he shall come in prosperously, and obtain the kingdom by deceitful ways.

22 And the arms of him that overflows shall be washed away as with a flood from before him, and shall be broken, and *so shall be* the head of the covenant.

23 And because of the leagues made with him he shall work deceit; and he shall come up, and overpower them with a small nation.

24 And he shall enter with prosperity, and *that* into fertile districts; and he shall do what his fathers and his fathers' fathers have not done; he shall scatter among them plunder, and spoils, and wealth; and he shall devise plans against Egypt, even for a time.

25 And his strength and his heart shall be stirred up against the king of the south with a great force; and the king of the south shall engage in war with a great and very strong force; but *his* forces shall not stand, for they shall devise plans against him.

26 And they shall eat his provisions, and shall crush him, and he shall carry away armies as with a flood, and many shall fall down slain.

27 And *as for* both the kings, their hearts *are set* upon evil, and they shall speak lies at one table; but it shall not prosper; for yet the end is for a *fixed* time.

28 And he shall return to his land with much substance; and his heart *shall be* against the holy covenant; and he shall perform *great deeds*, and return to his own land.

The Northern King's Blasphemies

29 "At the *set* time he shall return, and shall come into the south, but the last *expedition* shall *not* be as the first.

30 For the Cyprians issuing forth shall come against him, and he shall be brought low, and shall return, and shall be incensed against the holy covenant: and he shall do *thus*, and shall return, and have intelligence with them that have forsaken the holy covenant.

31 And seeds shall spring up out of him, and they shall profane the sanctuary of strength, and they shall remove the perpetual *sacrifice*, and make the abomination of desolation.

32 And the transgressors shall bring about a covenant by deceitful ways; but a people knowing their God shall prevail, and do *valiantly*.

33 And the intelligent of the people shall understand much; yet they shall fall by the sword, and by flame, and by captivity, and by the spoil of *many* days.

34 And when they are weak they shall be helped with a little help, but many shall attach themselves to them with treachery. 35 And *some* of them that understand shall fall, to try them as with fire, and to test *them*, and that they may be manifested at the time of the end, for the matter *is* yet for an *appointed* time.

36 "And he shall do according to his will, and the king shall exalt and magnify himself against every god, and shall speak great swelling words, and shall prosper until the indignation shall be accomplished; for it is coming to an end.

37 And he shall not regard any gods of his fathers, nor the desire of women, neither shall he regard any deity: for he shall magnify himself above all.

38 And he shall honor the god of fortresses in his place: and a god whom his fathers did not know he shall honor with gold, and silver, and precious stones, and desirable things.

39 And he shall do *thus* in the strong places of refuge with a strange god, and shall increase his glory; and he shall subject many to them, and shall distribute the land in gifts.

The Northern King's Conquests

40 "And at the end of the time he shall conflict with the king of the south. And the king of the north shall come against him with chariots, and with horsemen, and with many ships; and they shall enter into the land, and he shall break in pieces, and pass on.

41 And he shall enter into the land of beauty, and many shall fail. But these shall escape out of his hand, Edom, Moab, and the chief of the children of Ammon.

42 And he shall stretch forth *his* hand over the land; and the land of Egypt shall not escape.

43 And he shall have the mastery over the secret *treasures* of gold and silver, and over all the desirable *possessions* of Egypt, and of the Libyans and Ethiopians in their strongholds.

44 But rumors and anxieties out of the east and from the north shall trouble him; and he shall come with great wrath to destroy many.

45 And he shall pitch the tabernacle of his palace between the seas in the holy mountain of beauty; *but* he shall come to his portion, and there is none to deliver him."

DANIEL CHAPTER 12

Prophecy of the End Time

1 "And at that time Michael the great prince shall stand up, that stands over the children of your people, and there shall be a time of tribulation, such tribulation as has not been from the time that there was a nation on the earth until that time. At that time your people shall be delivered, everyone that is written in the book.

2 And many of them that sleep in the dust of the earth shall awake, some to everlasting life, and some to reproach and everlasting shame.

3 And the wise shall shine as the brightness of the firmament, and *some* of the many righteous as the stars forever and ever.

4 And you, Daniel, close the words, and seal the book to the time of the end; until many are taught, and knowledge is increased."

5 And I Daniel, saw, and behold, two others stood, on one side of the bank of the river, and the other on the other side of the bank of the river.

6 And *one* said to the man clothed in linen, who was over the water of the river, "When *will be* the end of the wonders which you have mentioned?"

7 And I heard the man clothed in linen, who was over the water of the river, and he lifted up his right hand and his left hand to heaven, and swore by Him that lives forever, that *it should be* for a time, times and half a time. When the dispersion is ended, they shall know all these things.

8 And I heard, but I did not understand. And I said, "O Lord, what *will be* the end of these things?"

9 And he said, "Go, Daniel; for the words are closed and sealed up till the time of the end.

10 Many must be tested, and thoroughly whitened, and tried with fire, and sanctified; but the transgressors shall transgress: and none of the transgressors shall understand, but the wise shall understand.

11 And from the time of the removal of the perpetual sacrifice, when the abomination of desolation shall be set up, *there shall be* a thousand two hundred and ninety days.

12 Blessed is he that waits, and comes to the thousand three hundred and thirty-five days.

13 But you, go *your* way, and rest; for *there are* yet days and seasons to the fulfillment of the end; and you shall stand in your inheritance at the end of the days."

THE BOOK OF HOSEA

1 The word of the Lord which came to Hosea the son of Beeri, in the days of Uzziah, Jotham, Ahaz, and Hezekiah, kings of Judah, and in the days of Jeroboam son of Joash, king of Israel.

2 The beginning of the word of the Lord by Hosea. And the Lord said to Hosea, "Go, take to yourself a wife of fornication, and children of fornication: for the land will surely go a-whoring in departing from the Lord."

3 So he went and took Gomer, daughter of Diblaim; and she conceived, and bore him a son.

4 And the Lord said to him, "Call his name Jezreel; for yet a little *while* and I will avenge the blood of Jezreel on the house of Judah, and will make to cease the kingdom of the house of Israel.

5 And it shall be in that day, *that* I will break the bow of Israel in the valley of Jezreel."

6 And she conceived again, and bore a daughter. And He said to him, "Call her name Unpitied: for I will no more have mercy on the house of Israel, but will surely set Myself in array against them.

7 But I will have mercy on the house of Judah, and will save them by the Lord their God, and will not save them with bow, nor with sword, nor by war, nor by horses, nor by horsemen."

8 And she weaned Unpitied; and she conceived again, and bore a son.

9 And He said, "Call his name, Not my people; for you are not My people, and I am not your *God*.

10 Yet the number of the children of Israel was as the sand of the sea, which shall not be measured nor numbered; and it shall come to pass, *that* in the place where it was said to them, 'You are not My people,' even they shall be called the sons of the living God.

11 And the children of Judah shall be gathered, and the children of Israel together, and shall appoint themselves one head, and shall come up out of the land: for great *shall be* the day of Jezreel."

HOSEA CHAPTER 2

1 Say to your brother, "My people," and to your sister, "Pitied."

God's Unfaithful People

2 "Plead with your mother; plead. For she is not My wife, and I am not her husband: and I will remove her fornication out of My presence, and her adultery from between her breasts;

[3] that I may strip her naked, and make her again as she was at the day of her birth; and I will make her desolate, and make her as a dry land, and will kill her with thirst.

[4] And I will not have mercy upon her children; for they are children of fornication.

[5] And their mother went a-whoring; she that bore them disgraced *them*, for she said, 'I will go after my lovers, that give me my bread and my water, and my garments, and my linen clothes, my oil and my necessaries.'

[6] "Therefore, behold, I hedge up her way with thorns, and I will stop the ways, and she shall not find her path.

[7] And she shall follow after her lovers, and shall not overtake them; and she shall seek them, but shall not find them: and she shall say, 'I will go, and return to my former husband; for it was better with me *before* than it is now.'

[8] And she did not know that I gave her her grain, and wine, and oil, and multiplied silver to her: but she made silver and gold *images* for Baal.

[9] "Therefore I will return, and take away My grain in its season, and My wine in its time; and I will take away My wool and My linen clothes, so that she shall not cover her nakedness.

[10] And now I will expose her uncleanness before her lovers, and no one shall by any means deliver her out of My hand.

[11] And I will take away all her gladness, her feasts, and her festivals at the new moon, and her Sabbaths, and all her solemn assemblies.

[12] And I will utterly destroy her vines, and her fig trees, all things of which she said, 'These are my hire which my lovers have given me'; and I will make them a testimony, and the wild beasts of the field, and the birds of the sky, and the reptiles of the earth shall devour them.

[13] And I will recompense on her the days of Baalam, wherein she sacrificed to them, and put on her earrings, and her necklaces, and went after her lovers, and forgot Me," says the Lord.

God's Mercy on His People

[14] "Therefore, behold, I *will* cause her to err, and will make her as desolate, and will speak comfortably to her.

[15] And I will giver her possessions from there, and the valley of Achor to open her understanding; and she shall be afflicted there according to the days of her infancy, and according to the days of her coming up out of the land of Egypt.

[16] And it shall come to pass in that day, says the Lord, *that* she shall call Me, 'My husband,' and shall no longer call me 'Baalam.'

[17] And I will take away the names of Baalam out of her mouth, and their names shall be remembered no more at all.

[18] And I will make for them in that day a covenant with the wild beasts of the field, and with the birds of the sky, and with the reptiles of the earth: and I will break the bow and the sword and the battle from off the earth, and will cause you to dwell safely.

[19] And I will betroth you to Myself forever; yes, I will betroth you to Myself in righteousness, and in judgment, and in mercy, and in tender compassions;

[20] and I will betroth you to Myself in faithfulness: and you shall know the Lord.

[21] "And it shall come to pass in that day, says the Lord, I will hearken to the heaven, and it shall hearken to the earth;

[22] and the earth shall hearken to the grain, and the wine, and the oil; and they shall hearken to Jezreel.

[23] And I will sow her to Me on the earth; and will love her that was not loved, and will say to that which was not My people, 'You are My people'; and they shall say, 'You are the Lord my God.'"

HOSEA CHAPTER 3

Further Assurance of God's Redeeming Love

[1] And the Lord said to me, "Go yet, and love a woman that loves evil things, an adulteress, even as the Lord loves the children of Israel, and they have respect to strange gods, and love cakes of dried grapes."

[2] So I hired *her* to myself for fifteen *pieces* of silver, and a homer of barley, and a flagon of wine.

[3] And I said to her, "You shall wait for me many days; and you shall not commit fornication, neither shall you be for *another* man; and I *will be* for you."

[4] For the children of Israel shall abide many days without a king, and without a prince, and without a sacrifice, and without an altar, and without a priesthood, and without manifestations. [5] And afterward shall the children of Israel return, and shall seek the Lord their God, and David their king; and shall be amazed at the Lord and at His goodness in the latter days.

HOSEA CHAPTER 4

God Accuses Israel

[1] Hear the word of the Lord, you children of Israel: for the Lord *has* a controversy with the inhabitants of the land: "There is no truth, nor mercy, nor knowledge of God in the land.

[2] Cursing, and lying, and murder, and theft, and adultery bound in the land, and they mingle blood with blood.

[3] Therefore shall the land mourn, and shall be diminished with all that dwell in it, with the wild beasts of the field, and the reptiles of the earth, and with the birds of the sky, and the fish of the sea shall fail:

[4] that neither anyone may plead, nor any one reprove *another*; but My people are as a priest spoken against.

[5] Therefore they shall fall by day, and the prophet with you shall fall; I have compared your mother unto night.

[6] My people are as if they had no knowledge: because you have rejected knowledge, I also will reject you, that you shall

not minister as priest unto Me: and *as* you have forgotten the law of your God, I also will forget your children.

7 "According to their multitude, so they sinned against Me: I will turn their glory into shame.

8 They will devour the sins of My people, and will set their hearts on their iniquities.

9 And the priest shall be as the people: and I will avenge on them their ways, and I will recompense to them their counsels.

10 And they shall eat, and shall not be satisfied: they have played the harlot, and shall by no means prosper: because they have stopped listening to the Lord.

The Idolatry of Israel

11 "The heart of My people has gladly engaged in fornication and wine and strong drink.

12 They asked counsel by *means of* signs, and their staff informs them; they have gone astray in a spirit of harlotry, and have played the harlot and turned from their God.

13 They have sacrificed on the tops of the mountains, and on the hills they have sacrificed under the oak and poplar, and under the shady tree, because the shade was good; therefore your daughters shall play the harlot, and your daughters-in-law shall commit adultery.

14 And I will not visit upon your daughters when they shall commit fornication, nor your daughters-in-law when they shall commit adultery; for they themselves mingled themselves with harlots, and sacrificed with polluted ones, and the people that did not understand entangled themselves with a harlot.

15 "But you, O Israel, do not be ignorant, and do not go to Gilgal, O *men of* Judah, and do not go up to the house of On, and do not swear by the living Lord.

16 For Israel was maddened like a mad heifer: now the Lord will feed them as a lamb in a wide place.

17 Ephraim, joined with idols, has laid stumbling blocks in his own way.

18 He has chosen the Canaanites: they have grievously played the harlot: they have loved dishonor through her insolence.

19 You are a blast of wind in her wings, and they shall be ashamed because of their altars.

HOSEA CHAPTER 5

Impending Judgment on Israel and Judah

1 "Hear these things, you priests; and attend, O house of Israel; and give ear, O house of the king; for the controversy is with you, because you have been a snare in Mizpah, and as a net spread on Tabor,

2 which they that hunt the prey have fixed: but I will correct you.

3 I know Ephraim, and Israel is not far from Me: for now Ephraim has played the harlot, Israel is defiled.

4 They have not framed their counsels to return to their God, for the spirit of fornication is in them, and they have not known the Lord.

5 And the pride of Israel shall be brought low before his face; and Israel and Ephraim shall fall in their iniquities; and Judah also shall fall with them.

6 They shall go with sheep and calves diligently to seek the Lord; but they shall not find Him, for He has withdrawn Himself from them.

7 For they have forsaken the Lord; for strange children have been born to them: now shall the cankerworm devour them and their heritage.

8 "Blow the trumpet on the hills, sound aloud on the heights: proclaim in the house of On, 'Benjamin is amazed.'

9 Ephraim has come to nought in the days of reproof: in the tribes of Israel I have shown faithful *dealings*.

10 The princes of Judah have become as those that removed the landmarks; I will pour out upon them My fury as water.

11 Ephraim altogether prevailed against his adversary, he trod judgment under foot, for he began to go after vanities.

12 Therefore I *will be* as consternation to Ephraim, and as a goad to the house of Judah.

13 And Ephraim saw his disease, and Judah his pain; then Ephraim went to the Assyrians, and sent ambassadors to King Jareb, but he could not heal you, and your pain shall by no means cease from you.

14 For I am as a panther to Ephraim, and as a lion to the house of Judah. And I will tear, and go away; and I will take, and there shall be none to deliver.

15 I will go and return to My place, until they are brought to nought, and *then* shall they seek My face."

HOSEA CHAPTER 6

A Call to Repentance

1 "In their affliction they will seek Me early, saying, 'Let us go, and return to the Lord our God; for He has torn, and will heal us; He will smite, and bind us up.

2 After two days He will heal us: in the third day we shall arise, and live before Him, and shall know *Him*.

3 Let us follow on to know the Lord: we shall find Him ready as the morning, and He will come to us as the early and latter rain to the earth.'

4 "What shall I do to you, Ephraim? What shall I do to you, Judah? For your mercy is as a morning cloud, and as the early dew that goes away.

5 Therefore have I mown down your prophets; I have slain them with the word of My mouth; and My judgment shall go forth as the light.

6 For I desire mercy rather than sacrifice, and the knowledge of God rather than burnt offerings.

7 But they are as a man transgressing a covenant.

8 There the city Gilead despised Me, working vanity, troubling water.

9 And your strength *is that* of a robber: the priests have hid the way, they have murdered *the people of* Shechem; for they have wrought iniquity in the house of Israel.

10 I have seen horrible *things* there, *even* the fornication of Ephraim. Israel and Judah are defiled;

11 begin together grapes for yourself, when I return the captivity of My people.

HOSEA CHAPTER 7

1 "When I have healed Israel, then shall the iniquity of Ephraim be revealed, and the wickedness of Samaria; for they have wrought falsehood. And a thief shall come in to him, *even* a robber spoiling in his way;

2 that they may concert together as *men* singing in their heart. I remember all their wickedness; now have their own counsels compassed them about; they came before My face.

3 They gladdened kings with their wickedness, and princes with their lies.

4 "They are all adulterers, as an oven glowing with a flame for hot baking, on account of the kneading of the dough, until it is leavened.

5 *In* the days of our kings, the princes began to be inflamed with wine. He stretched out his hand with pestilent fellows.

6 Therefore their hearts are inflamed as an oven, while they rage all the night. Ephraim is satisfied with sleep; the morning has come; he is burnt up as a flame of fire.

7 They are all heated like an oven, and have devoured their judges. All their kings are fallen; there was not one among them that called on Me.

8 "Ephraim is mixed among his people; Ephraim became a cake not turned.

9 Strangers devoured his strength, but he did not know *it*; yes, gray hairs came upon him, yet he did not know *it*.

10 And the pride of Israel shall be brought down before his face; yet they have not returned to the Lord their God, neither have they diligently sought Him for all this.

Futile Reliance on the Nations

11 "And Ephraim was as a silly dove, not having a heart: he called to Egypt, and they went to the Assyrians.

12 Whenever they shall go, I will cast My net upon them; I will bring them down as the birds of the sky, I will chasten them with the rumor of their *coming* affliction.

13 "Woe to them! For they have started aside from Me: they are cowards; for they have sinned against Me; yet I redeemed them, but they spoke falsehoods against Me.

14 And their hearts did not cry to Me, but they howled on their beds; they pined for oil and wine. 1

5 They were instructed by Me, and I strengthened their arms; and they devised evils against Me.

16 They turned aside to that which is not, they became as a bent bow. Their princes shall fall by the sword, by reason of the unbridled state of their tongue. This is their setting at nought in the land of Egypt.

HOSEA CHAPTER 8

Israel's Apostasy

1 "*He shall come* into their midst as the land, as an eagle against the house of the Lord, because they have transgressed My covenant, and have sinned against My law.

2 They shall soon cry out to Me, *saying*, 'O God, we know You.'

3 For Israel has turned away from good things; they have pursued an enemy.

4 They have made kings for themselves, but not by Me: they have ruled, but they did not make it known to Me: *of* their silver and their gold they have made images to themselves, that they might be destroyed.

5 Cast off your calf, O Samaria; My anger is kindled against them: how long will they be unable to purge themselves in Israel?

6 Seeing the workman made it, and it is not God; for your calf, O Samaria, was a deceiver.

7 "For they sowed blighted *seed*, and their destruction shall await them, a sheaf of corn that avails not to make meal; and even if it should produce it, strangers shall devour it.

8 Israel is swallowed up; now he has become among the nations as a worthless vessel.

9 For they have gone up to the Assyrians; Ephraim has been strengthened against himself; they loved gifts.

10 Therefore shall they be delivered to the nations. Now I will receive them, and they shall cease a little to anoint a king and princes.

11 "Because Ephraim has multiplied altars, *his* beloved altars have become sins to him.

12 I will write down a multitude *of commands* for him; but his statutes are accounted strange things, *even* the beloved altars.

13 For if they should offer a sacrifice, and eat flesh, the Lord will not accept them. Now will He remember their iniquities, and will take vengeance on their sins; they have returned to Egypt, and they shall eat unclean things among the Assyrians.

14 And Israel has forgotten Him that made him, and they have built palaces, and Judah has multiplied walled cities, but I will send fire on his cities, and it shall devour their foundations."

HOSEA CHAPTER 9

Punishment for Israel's Sin

1 Do not rejoice, O Israel, neither make merry, as *other* nations. For you have played the harlot against your God; you have loved gifts upon every threshing floor.

2 The threshing floor and winepress did not know them, and the wine disappointed them.

3 They did not dwell in the Lord's land: Ephraim dwelt in Egypt, and they shall eat unclean things among the Assyrians.

4 They have not offered wine to the Lord, neither have their sacrifices been sweet to Him, *but* as the bread of mourning to them; all that eat them shall be defiled; for their bread for their soul shall not enter into the house of the Lord.

5 What will you do in the day of the general assembly, and in the day of the feast of the Lord?

6 Therefore, behold, they go forth from the trouble of Egypt, and Memphis shall receive them, and Machmas shall bury them. *As for* their silver, destruction shall inherit it; thorns *shall be* in their tents.

7 The days of vengeance have come, the days of your recompense have come; and Israel shall be afflicted as the prophet that is mad, as a man deranged. By reason of the multitude of your iniquities your madness has abounded.

8 The watchman of Ephraim *was* with God. The prophet is a crooked snare in all his ways: they have established madness in the house of God.

9 They have corrupted themselves according to the days of the hill. He will remember their iniquities, He will take vengeance on their sins.

10 "I found Israel as grapes in the wilderness, and I saw their fathers as an early watchman in a fig tree. They went in to Baal Peor, and were shamefully estranged, and the abominable became as the beloved.

11 Ephraim has flown away as a bird; their glories from the birth, and the travail, and the conception.

12 For even if they should rear their children, yet shall they be utterly bereaved. Therefore also there is woe to them, *though* My flesh is of them.

13 Ephraim, *even* as I saw, gave their children for a prey; yes, Ephraim *was ready* to bring out his children to slaughter."

14 Give them, O Lord: what will you give them? A miscarrying womb, and dry breasts.

15 "All their wickedness is in Gilgal. For there I hated them; because of the wickedness of their practices, I will cast them out of My house, I will not love them anymore; all their princes are disobedient.

16 Ephraim is sick, he is dried up at his roots, he shall by no means bear fruit any longer. For even if they should beget *children*, I will kill the desired *fruit* of their womb."

17 God shall reject them, because they have not obeyed Him, and they shall be wanderers among the nations.

HOSEA CHAPTER 10

Israel's Sin and Captivity

1 Israel is a vine with choice branches, her fruit is abundant: according to the multitude of her fruits she has multiplied *her* altars; according to the wealth of his land, he has set up pillars.

2 They have divided their hearts; now shall they be utterly destroyed: he shall dig down their altars, their pillars shall mourn.

3 Because now they shall say, "We have no king, because we did not fear the Lord."

4 And what should a king do for us, speaking false professions *as his* words? He will make a covenant: judgment shall spring up as a weed on the soil of the field.

5 The inhabitants of Samaria shall dwell near the calf of the house of On; for the people of it mourned for it. And as they provoked Him, they shall rejoice at His glory, because He has departed from them.

6 And having bound it for the Assyrians, they carried it away as presents to King Jareb. Ephraim shall receive a gift, and Israel shall be ashamed of his own counsel.

7 Samaria has cast off her king as a twig on the surface of the water.

8 And the altars of On, the sins of Israel shall be taken away. Thorns and thistles shall come up on their altars; and they shall say to the mountains, "Cover us"; and to the hills, "Fall on us."

9 "From the time the hills *existed* Israel has sinned. There they stood. War *waged* against the children of iniquity,

10 to chastise them. The nations shall be gathered against them, when they are chastened for their two sins,

11 Ephraim is a heifer taught to love victory, but I will come upon the fairest part of her neck: I will Mount Ephraim; I will pass over Judah in silence; Jacob shall prevail against him."

12 Sow to yourselves for righteousness, gather in for the fruit of life: light for yourselves the light of knowledge; seek the Lord till the fruits of righteousness come upon you.

13 "For have you passed over ungodliness in silence, and reaped the sins of it? You have eaten false fruit; for you has trusted in your sins, in the abundance of your power.

14 Therefore shall destruction rise up among your people, and all your strong places shall be ruined. As a prince Solomon *departed* out of the house of Jeroboam, in the days of battle they dashed the mother to the ground upon the children,

15 thus will I do to you, O house of Israel, because of the unrighteousness of your sins."

HOSEA CHAPTER 11

God's Compassion Despite Israel's Ingratitude

[1] "Early in the morning were they cast off, the king of Israel has been cast off: for Israel is a child, and I loved him, and out of Egypt have I called his children.

[2] As I called them, so they departed from My presence; they sacrificed to Baalam, and burnt incense to graven images.

[3] Yet I bound the feet of Ephraim, I took him on My arm; but they did not know that I healed them.

[4] When men were destroyed, I drew them with the bands of My love: and I will be to them as a man smiting *another* on his cheek: and I will have regard for him, *and* I will prevail with him.

[5] "Ephraim dwelt in Egypt; and *as for* the Assyrian, he was his king, because he would not return.

[6] And in his cities he did not prevail with the sword, and he ceased *to war* with his hands; and they shall eat *of the fruit* of their own devices.

[7] And his people *shall* cleave fondly to their habitation; but God shall be angry with his precious things, and shall not at all exalt him.

[8] "How shall I deal with you, O Ephraim? *How* shall I protect you, O Israel? What shall I do with you? I will make you as Admah, and as Zeboiim; My heart is turned at once, My repentance is powerfully excited.

[9] I will not act according to the fury of My wrath, I will not abandon Ephraim to be utterly destroyed: for I am God, and not man; the Holy One in your midst; and I will not enter into the city."

[10] I will go after the Lord: He shall utter *His voice* as a lion. For He shall roar, and the children of the waters shall be amazed.

[11] "They shall be amazed *and fly* as a bird out of Egypt, and as a dove out of the land of the Assyrians: and I will restore them to their houses," says the Lord.

God's Anger with Judah's Sin

[12] "Ephraim has compassed Me with falsehood, and the house of Israel and Judah with ungodliness; *but* now God knows them, and they shall be called God's holy people.

HOSEA CHAPTER 12

[1] "But Ephraim is an evil spirit, he has chased the east wind all the day. He has multiplied empty and vain things, and made a covenant with the Assyrians, and oil has gone in the way of traffic into Egypt.

[2] And the Lord *has* a controversy with Judah, in order to punish Jacob: according to His ways and according to His practices will He recompense him.

[3] He took his brother by the heel in the womb, and in his labors he had power with God.

[4] And he prevailed with the Angel and was strong. They wept, and entreated Me: they found Me in the house of On, and there *a word* was spoken to them.

[5] But the Lord God Almighty shall be his memorial.

[6] You therefore shall return to your God. Keep mercy and judgment, and draw near to your God continually.

[7] "*As for* Canaan, in his hand is a balance of unrighteousness: he has loved to tyrannize.

[8] And Ephraim said, 'Nevertheless I am rich, I have found refreshment for myself.' None of his labors shall be found *available* to him, by reason of the sins which he has committed.

[9] "But I the Lord your God brought you up out of the land of Egypt. I will yet cause you to dwell in tents, according to the days of the feast.

[10] And I will speak to the prophets, and I have multiplied visions, and by the means of the prophets I was represented." [11] If Gilead does not exist, then the chiefs in Gilead when they sacrificed were false, and their altars were as heaps on the ground of the field.

[12] And Jacob retreated into the plain of Syria, and Israel served for a wife, and waited for a wife.

[13] And the Lord brought Israel out of the land of Egypt by a prophet, and by a prophet was he preserved.

[14] Ephraim was angry and excited, therefore his blood shall be poured out upon him, and the Lord shall recompense to him his reproach.

HOSEA CHAPTER 13

Relentless Judgment on Israel

[1] According to the word of Ephraim he adopted ordinances for himself in Israel; and he established them for Baal, and died.

[2] And now they have sinned increasingly, and have made for themselves a molten image of their silver, according to the fashion of idols, the work of stonecutters accomplished for them. They say, "Sacrifice men, for the calves have come to an end."

[3] Therefore shall they be as a morning cloud, and as the early dew that passes away, as chaff blown away from the threshing floor, and as a vapor from tears.

[4] "But I am the Lord your God that establishes the heavens, and creates the earth, whose hands have framed the whole host of heaven. But I did not show them to you, that you should go after them; and I brought you up out of the land of Egypt, and you shall know no God but Me; and there is no Saviour beside Me.

[5] I tended to you as a shepherd in the wilderness, in an uninhabited land.

[6] According to their pastures, so they were completely filled; and their hearts were exalted; therefore they forgot Me.

[7] And I will be to them as a panther, and as a leopard.

8 I will meet them by the way of the Assyrians, as a female bear excited, and I will tear open their rib cage, and the lions' cubs in the thicket shall devour them there; the wild beasts of the field shall tear them to pieces.

9 "O Israel, who will aid *you* in your destruction?

10 Where is this your king? Let him even save you in all your cities. Let him judge you, of whom you said, 'Give me a king and a prince.'

11 And I gave you a king in My anger, and kept *him* back in My wrath.

12 "Ephraim *has framed* a conspiracy of unrighteousness; his sin is hidden.

13 Pains as of a woman in travail shall come upon him: he is your wise son, because he shall not stay in the destruction of *your* children.

14 I will deliver *them* out of the power of Hades, and will redeem them from death. O death, where is your punishment? O Hades, where is your sting? Comfort is hidden from My eyes."

15 Though he will cause a division among *his* brothers, the Lord shall bring upon him an east wind from the desert, and shall dry up his veins *and* quite drain his fountains. He shall dry up his land, and *spoil* all his precious vessels.

16 Samaria shall be utterly destroyed, for she has resisted her God; they shall fall by the sword, and their sucklings shall be dashed against the ground, and their women and children ripped up.

HOSEA CHAPTER 14

Israel Restored at Last

1 Return, O Israel, to the Lord your God; for the people have fallen through your iniquities.

2 Take with you words, and turn to the Lord your God. Speak to Him, that you may not receive *the reward of* unrighteousness, but that you may receive good things; and we will render in return the fruit of our lips.

3 Assyria shall never save us; we will not mount on horseback; we will no longer say to the works of our hands, Our gods. He who is in you shall pity the orphan.

4 "I will restore their dwellings, I will love them truly: for he has turned away My wrath from him.

5 I will be as dew to Israel: he shall bloom as the lily, and cast forth his roots as Lebanon.

6 His branches shall spread, and he shall be as a fruitful olive, and his smell shall be as *the smell* of Lebanon.

7 They shall return, and dwell under his shadow: they shall live and be satisfied with grain, and he shall flower like a vine. His memorial shall be to Ephraim as the wine of Lebanon.

8 "What *has* he to do anymore with idols? I have afflicted him, and I will strengthen him. I am as a leafy juniper tree. From Me is your fruit found."

9 Who is wise, and will understand these things? Or prudent, and will know them? For the ways of the Lord are straight, and the righteous shall walk in them; but the ungodly shall fall therein.

THE BOOK OF JOEL

1 The word of the Lord which came to Joel the son of Pethuel.

Lament over the Ruin of the City

2 Hear these *words*, you elders, and hear, you that inhabit the land. Have such things happened in your days, or in the days of your fathers?

3 Tell your children concerning them, and *let* your children *tell* their children, and their children another generation.

4 What the caterpillar has left, the locust has eaten, and what the locust has left, the palmerworm has eaten, and what the palmerworm has left, the cankerworm has eaten.

5 Awake, you drunkards, from your wine, and weep: mourn, all you that drink wine to drunkenness: for joy and gladness are removed from your mouth.

6 For a strong and innumerable nation has come up against My land, their teeth are *like* lion's teeth, and their back teeth *as* those of a *lion's* whelp.

7 He has ruined My vine, and utterly broken My fig trees: he has utterly searched *My vine*, and cast it down; he has peeled its branches.

8 Lament to Me more than a virgin clothed in sackcloth for the husband of her youth.

9 The grain offering and drink offering are removed from the house of the Lord: mourn, you priests that serve at the altar of the Lord.

10 For the plains languish: let the land mourn, for the grain languishes; the wine is dried up, the oil becomes scarce; 11 the farmers are consumed: mourn your property on account of the wheat and barley; for the harvest has perished from off the field.

12 The vine is dried up, and the fig trees have become few; the pomegranate, and palm tree, and apple, and all the trees of the field have dried up: for the sons of men have abolished joy."

A Call to Repentance and Prayer

13 Gird yourselves *with sackcloth*, and lament, you priests: mourn, you that serve at the altar: go in, sleep in sackcloth, you that minister to God: for the grain offering and drink offering are withheld from the house of your God.

14 Sanctify a fast, proclaim a solemn service, gather the elders and all the inhabitants of the land into the house of your God, and cry earnestly to the Lord,

15 Alas, Alas, Alas for the day! For the day of the Lord is near, and it will come as trouble upon trouble.

16 *Your* food has been destroyed before your eyes, joy and gladness from out of the house of your God.

[17] The heifers have started at their mangers, the treasures are abolished, the wine presses are broken down; for the grain is withered.

[18] What shall we store up for ourselves? The herds of cattle have mourned, because they had no pasture; and the flocks of sheep have been utterly destroyed.

[19] To You, O Lord, will I cry; for fire has devoured the fair places of the wilderness, and a flame has burnt up all the trees of the field.

[20] And the cattle of the field have looked up to You; for the fountains of waters have been dried up, and fire has devoured the fair places of the wilderness.

JOEL CHAPTER 2

The Day of the Lord

[1] Sound the trumpet in Zion, make a proclamation in My holy mountain, and let all the inhabitants of the land be confounded; for the day of the Lord is near;

[2] for a day of darkness and gloominess is near, a day of cloud and mist; a numerous and strong people shall be spread upon the mountains as the morning; there has not been one like it from the beginning, and after it there shall not be again, even to the years of many generations.

[3] Before them is a consuming fire, and behind them is a flame kindled; the land before them is as a paradise of delight, and behind them a desolate plain, and none of them shall escape.

[4] Their appearance is as the appearance of horses, and as horsemen, so shall they pursue.

[5] As the sound of chariots on the tops of mountains shall they leap, and as the sound of a flame of fire devouring stubble, and as a numerous and strong people setting themselves in array for battle.

[6] Before them shall the people be crushed; every face *shall be* as the blackness of a caldron.

[7] As warriors shall they run, and as men of war shall they mount on the walls; and each shall move in his *right* path, and they shall not turn aside from their tracks;

[8] and not one shall stand aloof from his brother: they shall go on weighed down with their arms, and they fall upon their weapons, yet shall they in no way be destroyed.

[9] They shall seize upon the city, and run upon the walls, and go up upon the houses, and enter in through the windows as thieves.

[10] Before them the earth shall be confounded, and the sky shall be shaken: the sun and the moon shall be darkened, and the stars shall withdraw their light.

[11] And the Lord shall utter His voice before His army, for His camp is very great; for the execution of His words is mighty; for the day of the Lord is great, very glorious, and who shall be able to *resist* it?

[12] "Now therefore," says the Lord your God, "turn to Me with all your heart, and with fasting, and with weeping, and with lamentation."

[13] And rend your hearts, and not your garments, and turn to the Lord your God: for He is merciful and compassionate, long suffering, and plenteous in mercy, and relenting of evil.

[14] Who knows if He will return and relent, and leave a blessing behind Him, even a grain offering and a drink offering to the Lord your God?

[15] Sound the trumpet in Zion, sanctify a fast, proclaim a *solemn* service.

[16] Gather the people, sanctify the congregation, assemble the elders, gather the infants at the breast; let the bridegroom go forth out of his chamber, and the bride out of her closet.

[17] Between the porch and the altar let the priests that minister to the Lord weep, and say, "Spare Your people, O Lord, and do not give Your heritage to reproach, that the heathen should rule over them, lest they should say among the heathen, 'Where is their God?'"

God's Response and Promise

[18] But the Lord was jealous of His land, and spared His people.

[19] And the Lord answered and said to His people, "Behold, I will send you grain, and wine, and oil, and you shall be satisfied with them: and I will no longer make you a reproach among the Gentiles.

[20] And I will chase away from you the northern *adversary*, and will drive him away into a dry land, and I will sink his face in the former sea, and his back parts in the latter sea, and his stench shall come up, and his foul odor will rise, because he has worked great things."

[21] Be of good courage, O land; rejoice and be glad, for the Lord has done great things.

[22] Be of good courage, you beasts of the plain, for the plains of the wilderness have budded, for the trees have borne their fruit, the fig tree and the vine have yielded their strength.

[23] Rejoice then and be glad, you children of Zion, in the Lord your God; for He has given you food fully, and He will rain on you the early and the latter rain, as before.

[24] And the floors shall be filled with wheat, and the presses shall overflow with wine and oil.

[25] "And I will recompense you for the years which the locust, and the caterpillar, and the palmerworm, and the cankerworm have eaten, even My great army, which I sent against you.

[26] And you shall eat abundantly, and be satisfied, and shall praise the name of the Lord your God *for the things* which He has wrought wonderfully with you, and My people shall not be put to shame.

[27] And you shall know that I am in the midst of Israel, and *that* I am the Lord your God, and *that* there is none else

beside Me; and My people shall no more be ashamed forever.

God's Spirit Poured Out

28 "And it shall come to pass afterward, that I will pour out My Spirit on all flesh; and your sons and your daughters shall prophesy, and your old men shall dream dreams, and your young men shall see visions.

29 And on My servants and on My maidservants in those days will I pour out My Spirit.

30 And I will show wonders in heaven, and upon the earth, blood, and fire, and vapors of smoke.

31 The sun shall be turned into darkness, and the moon into blood, before the coming of the great and glorious day of the Lord.

32 And it shall come to pass that whosoever shall call on the name of the Lord shall be saved: for in Mount Zion and in Jerusalem shall the saved one be as the Lord has said, and they that have glad tidings preached to them, whom the Lord has called.

JOEL CHAPTER 3

1 "For behold, in those days and at that time, when I shall have turned the captivity of Judah and Jerusalem,

2 I will also gather all the Gentiles, and bring them down to the valley of Jehoshaphat, and will plead with them there for My people and My heritage Israel, who have been dispersed among the Gentiles; and *these Gentiles* have divided My land,

3 and cast lots over My people, and have given *their* boys to harlots, and sold *their* girls for wine, and have drunk.

4 "And what have you to do with Me, O Tyre, and Sidon, and all Galilee of the Gentiles? Do you render Me a recompense? Or do you bear malice against Me? Quickly and speedily will I return your recompense on your own heads;

5 because you have taken My silver and My gold, and you have brought My choice ornaments into your temples;

6 and you have sold the children of Judah and the children of Jerusalem to the children of the Greeks, that you might expel them from their coasts.

7 Therefore, behold, I *will* raise them up out of the place where you have sold them, and I will return your recompense on your own heads.

8 And I will sell your sons and your daughters into the hands of the children of Judah, and they shall sell them into captivity to a distant nation; for the Lord has spoken *it*."

Judgment in the Valley of Jehoshaphat

9 Proclaim these things among the Gentiles; declare war, arouse the warriors, draw near and go up, all you men of war.

10 Beat your plowshares into swords, and your sickles into spears: let the weak say, 'I am strong.'

11 Gather yourselves together, and go in, all you nations round about, and gather yourselves there; let the timid become a warrior.

12 Let them be aroused, let all the nations go up to the valley of Jehoshaphat, for there will I sit to judge all the Gentiles round about.

13 Bring forth the sickles, for the vintage is come: go in, tread *the grapes*, for the press is full: cause the vats to overflow; for their wickedness is multiplied.

14 Noises have resounded in the valley of judgment, for the day of the Lord is near in the valley of judgment.

15 The sun and the moon shall be darkened, and the stars shall withdraw their light.

16 And the Lord shall cry out of Zion, and shall utter His voice from Jerusalem; and the heaven and the earth shall be shaken, but the Lord shall spare His people, and shall strengthen the children of Israel.

17 And you shall know that I am the Lord your God, who dwells in Zion My holy mountain: and Jerusalem shall be holy, and strangers shall not pass through her anymore.

The Glorious Future of Judah

18 And it shall come to pass in that day that the mountains shall drop sweet wine, and the hills shall flow with milk, and all the fountains of Judah shall flow with water, and a fountain shall go forth of the house of the Lord, and water the Valley of Flags.

19 Egypt shall be a desolation, and Edom shall be a desolate plain, because of the wrongs of the children of Judah, because they have shed righteous blood in their land.

20 But Judea shall be inhabited forever, and Jerusalem to all generations.

21 And I will make inquisition for their blood, and will by no means leave it unavenged: and the Lord shall dwell in Zion.

THE BOOK OF AMOS

Judgment on Israel's Neighbors

1 The words of Amos, which came *to him* in Accarim out of Tekoa, which he saw concerning Jerusalem, in the days of Uzziah king of Judah, and in the days of Jeroboam the son of Joash, king of Israel, two years before the earthquake.

2 And he said, "The Lord has spoken out of Zion, and has uttered His voice out of Jerusalem, and the pastures of the shepherds have mourned, and the top of Carmel is dried up."

3 And the Lord said, "For three sins of Damascus, and for four, I will not turn away from it, because they sawed with iron saws the women with child of the Gileadites.

4 And I will send a fire on the house of Hazael, and it shall devour the foundations of the son of Ader.

5 And I will break to pieces the bars of Damascus, and will destroy the inhabitants out of the plain of On, and will cut in

pieces a tribe out of the men of Harrhan; and the famous people of Syria shall be led captive," says the Lord.

[6] Thus says the Lord; "For three sins of Gaza, and for four, I will not turn away from them, because they took prisoners the captivity of Solomon, to shut *them* up into Edom.

[7] And I will send forth a fire on the walls of Gaza, and it shall devour its foundations.

[8] And I will destroy the inhabitants out of Ashdod, and a tribe shall be cut off from Ashkelon, and I will stretch out My hand upon Ekron, and the remnant of the Philistines shall perish," says the Lord.

[9] Thus says the Lord: "For three transgressions of Tyre, and for four, I will not turn away from it, because they shut up the prisoners of Solomon into Edom, and did not remember the covenant of brothers.

[10] And I will send forth a fire on the walls of Tyre, and it shall devour the foundations of it."

[11] Thus says the Lord: "For three sins of Edom, and for four, I will not turn away from them, because they pursued their brother with the sword, and destroyed the mother upon the earth, and summoned up his anger for a testimony, and kept up his fury to the end.

[12] And I will send forth a fire upon Teman, and it shall devour the foundations of her walls."

[13] Thus says the Lord: "For three sins of the children of Ammon, and for four, I will not turn away from him, because they ripped up the women with child of the Gileadites, that they might widen their coasts.

[14] And I will kindle a fire on the walls of Rabbah, and it shall devour her foundations with shouting in the day of war, and she shall be shaken in the days of her destruction:

[15] and her kings shall go into captivity, their priests and their rulers together," says the Lord.

AMOS CHAPTER 2

[1] Thus says the Lord: "For three sins of Moab, and for four, I will not turn away from it, because they burnt the bones of the king of Edom to lime.

[2] But I will send forth a fire on Moab, and it shall devour the foundations of its cities, and Moab shall perish in weakness, with a shout, and with the sound of a trumpet.

[3] And I will destroy the judge out of her, and slay all her princes with him," says the Lord.

Judgment on Judah

[4] Thus says the Lord: "For three sins of the children of Judah, and for four, I will not turn away from him, because they have rejected the law of the Lord, and have not kept His commandments, and their vain *idols* which they made, which their fathers followed, caused them to err.

[5] And I will send a fire on Judah, and it shall devour the foundations of Jerusalem."

Judgment on Israel

[6] Thus says the Lord: "For three sins of Israel, and for four, I will not turn away from him, because they sold the righteous for silver, and the poor for sandals,

[7] in which to tread on the dust of the earth, and they have smitten upon the heads of the poor, and have perverted the way of the lowly; and a son and his father have gone into the same maid, that they might profane the name of their God.

[8] And binding their clothes with cords, they have made them curtains near the altar, and they have drunk wine gained by extortion in the house of their God.

[9] "Nevertheless I cut off the Amorite from before them, whose height was as the height of a cedar, and he was strong as an oak; and I dried up his fruit from above, and his roots from beneath.

[10] And I brought you up out of the land of Egypt, and led you about in the desert forty years, that you should inherit the land of the Amorites.

[11] And I took of your sons for prophets, and of your young men for consecration. Are not these things so, you sons of Israel?" says the Lord.

[12] "But you gave the consecrated ones wine to drink, and you commanded the prophets, saying, 'Do not prophesy.'

[13] "Therefore behold, I roll under you, as a wagon full of straw is rolled.

[14] And flight shall perish from the runner, and the strong shall not hold fast his strength, and the warrior shall not save his life;

[15] and the archer shall not withstand, and he that is swift of foot shall by no means escape; and the horseman shall not save his life.

[16] And the strong shall find no confidence in power: the naked shall flee away in that day," says the Lord.

AMOS CHAPTER 3

Authority of the Prophet's Message

[1] Hear this word, O house of Israel, which the Lord has spoken concerning you, and against the whole family whom I brought up out of the land of Egypt, saying,

[2] "You especially have I known out of all the families of the earth: therefore will I take vengeance upon you for all your sins.

[3] Shall two walk together at all, if they do not know one another?

[4] Will a lion roar out of his thicket if he has no prey? Will a young *lion* utter his voice at all out of his lair, if he has taken nothing?

[5] Will a bird fall on the earth without a fowler? Will a snare be taken up from the earth without having taken anything?

[6] Shall the trumpet sound in the city, and the people not be alarmed? Shall there be evil in a city which the Lord has not wrought?

7 For the Lord God will do nothing without revealing instruction to His servants the prophets.

8 A lion shall roar, and who will not be alarmed? The Lord God has spoken, and who will not prophesy?"

9 "Proclaim it to the regions among the Assyrians, and to the regions of Egypt, and say, 'Gather yourselves to the mountain of Samaria, and behold many wonderful things in the midst of it, and the oppression that is in it.'

10 And she did not know the things that would come against her," says the Lord, "even those that store up wrong and misery in their countries.

11 Therefore thus says the Lord God: "O Tyre, your land shall be made desolate round about *you*; and he shall bring down your strength out of you, and your countries shall be spoiled.

12 Thus says the Lord: 'As when a shepherd rescues from the mouth of a lion two legs or a piece of an ear, so shall be drawn forth the children of Israel who dwell in Samaria in the presence of *a foreign* tribe, and in Damascus.'

13 Hear, O you priests, and testify to the house of Jacob," says the Lord God Almighty.

14 "For in the day that I punish Israel for their transgressions, I will also take vengeance on the altars of Bethel, and the horns of the altar shall be broken down, and they shall fall upon the ground.

15 I will crush and smite the winter house upon the summer house, and the ivory houses shall be destroyed, and many other houses also," says the Lord.

AMOS CHAPTER 4

1 Hear this word, you heifers of the land of Bashan, that are in the mountain of Samaria, that oppress the poor and trample on the needy, which say to their masters, Give us, that we may drink.

2 The Lord swears by His holiness, that behold, the days come upon you, when they shall take you with weapons, and fiery destroyers shall cast those with you into boiling caldrons.

3 "And you shall be brought forth naked in the presence of each other, and you shall be cast forth onto Mount Harmon," says the Lord.

4 "You went into Bethel and sinned, and you multiplied sin at Gilgal; and you brought your grain offerings in the morning, and your tithes every third day.

5 And they read the law outdoors, and called for public professions: proclaim aloud that the children of Israel have loved these things," says the Lord.

Israel Did Not Accept Correction

6 "And your teeth shall be idle in all your cities, and lack of bread in all your places; yet you did not return to Me," says the Lord.

7 "Also I withheld from you the rain three months before the harvest, and I will rain upon one city, and on another city I will not rain; one part shall be rained upon, and the part on which I shall not rain shall be dried up.

8 And *the inhabitants of* two or three cities shall be gathered to one city to drink water, and they shall not be satisfied; yet you have not returned to Me," says the Lord.

9 "I blasted you with parching, and with blight; you multiplied your gardens, your vineyards, and your fig trees, and the cankerworm devoured your olive trees; yet still you did not return to Me," says the Lord.

10 "I sent pestilence among you by the way of Egypt, and slew your young men with the sword, together with your horses that were taken captive; and in My wrath against you I set fire to your camps; yet not even thus did you return to Me," says the Lord.

11 "I overthrew you, as God overthrew Sodom and Gomorrah, and you became as a brand plucked out of the fire; yet not even then did you return to Me," says the Lord.

12 "Therefore thus will I do to you, O Israel: because I will do thus to you, prepare to call on your God, O Israel.

13 For behold, I am He that strengthens the thunder, and creates the wind, and proclaims His Messiah unto men, forming the morning and the darkness, and mounting on the high places of the earth; The Lord God Almighty is His name."

AMOS CHAPTER 5

A Lament for Israel's Sin

1 Hear this word of the Lord, even a lamentation, which I take up against you. The house of Israel has fallen; it shall not rise again.

2 The virgin of Israel has fallen; there is none that shall raise her up.

3 Therefore thus says the Lord God: "The city out of which there went forth a thousand, *in it* there shall be left a hundred, and *in that* out of which there went forth a hundred, there shall be left ten to the house of Israel."

4 For thus says the Lord to the house of Israel, "Seek Me, and you shall live.

5 But do not seek Bethel, and do not go into Gilgal, and do not cross over to the Well of the Oath; for Gilgal shall surely go into captivity, and Bethel shall be as that which is not."

6 But seek the Lord, and you shall live; lest the house of Joseph blaze as fire, and it devour him, and there shall be none to quench it for the house of Israel.

7 *It is He* that executes judgment in the heights *above*, and He has established justice on the earth;

8 who makes all things, and changes *them*, and turns darkness into the morning, and darkens the day into night; who calls for the water of the sea, and pours it out on the face of the earth: the Lord is His name;

9 who dispenses ruin to strength, and brings distress upon the fortress.

[10] They hated him that reproved in the gates, and abhorred holy speech.

[11] Therefore because they have smitten the poor with their fists, and you have received of them choice gifts, you have built polished houses, but you shall not dwell in them; you have planted desirable vineyards, but you shall not drink the wine of them.

[12] For I know your many transgressions, and your sins are great, trampling on the just, taking bribes, and turning aside *the judgment of* the poor in the gates.

[13] Therefore the prudent shall be silent at that time; for it is a time of evils.

[14] Seek good, and not evil, that you may live; and so the Lord God Almighty shall be with you, as you have said,

[15] "We have hated evil, and loved good"; restore judgment in the gates, so that the Lord God Almighty may have mercy on the remnant of Joseph.

[16] Therefore thus says the Lord God Almighty: "In all the streets *shall be* lamentations, and in all the ways shall it be said, 'Woe, woe!' The farmer shall be called to mourning and lamentation, and to them that are skilled in complaining.

[17] And *there shall be* lamentation in all the ways, because I will pass through the midst of you," says the Lord.

The Day of the Lord

[18] Woe to you that desire the day of the Lord! What is this day of the Lord to you? Seeing that it is darkness, and not light.

[19] As if a man should flee from the face of a lion, and a bear should meet him; and he should spring into his house, and lean his hands upon the wall, and a serpent should bite him.

[20] Is not the day of the Lord darkness, and not light? And is not this day gloom without brightness?

[21] "I hate, I reject your feasts, and I will not smell your grain offerings in your general assemblies.

[22] Even if you should bring Me your whole burnt sacrifices and grain offerings, I will not accept them, neither will I have respect to your grand peace offerings.

[23] Remove from Me the sound of your songs, and I will not hear the music of your instruments.

[24] But let judgment roll down as water, and righteousness as an impassable torrent.

[25] "Have you offered to Me victims and sacrifices, O house of Israel, forty years in the wilderness?

[26] Yea, you took up the tabernacle of Moloch, and the star of your god Rephan, the images of them which you made for yourselves.

[27] And I will carry you away beyond Damascus," says the Lord, the Almighty God is His name.

AMOS CHAPTER 6

Warnings to Zion and Samaria

[1] Woe to them that are at ease in Zion, and that trust in the mountain of Samaria; they have gathered *the harvest of* the heads of the nations, and they have gone in themselves.

[2] O house of Israel, pass by all of you, and see; and pass by from there to Hamath; and from there descend to Gath of the Philistines, the chief of all these kingdoms, see if their coasts are greater than your coasts.

[3] You who are approaching the evil day, who are drawing near and adopting false sabbaths;

[4] who sleep upon beds of ivory, and live delicately on their couches, and eat kids out of the flocks, and calves out of the midst of the stalls;

[5] who excel in the sound of musical instruments; they have regarded them as abiding, not as fleeting *pleasures*;

[6] who drink strained wine, and anoint themselves with the best ointment, and have suffered nothing on occasion of the calamity of Joseph.

[7] Therefore now shall they depart into captivity from the dominion of princes, and the neighing of horses shall be cut off from Ephraim.

[8] For the Lord has sworn by Himself, saying, "Because I abhor all the pride of Jacob, I do also hate his countries, and I will cut off his city with all who inhabit it.

[9] And it shall come to pass, if there be ten men left in one house, that they shall die.

[10] But a remnant shall be left behind, and their relations shall take them, and shall strenuously endeavor to carry forth their bones from the house; and one shall say to the heads of the house, 'Is there yet *anyone* else with you?' And he shall say, 'No one else.' And *the other* shall say, 'Be silent, that you name not the name of the Lord.'

[11] For, behold, the Lord commands, and He will smite the great house with breaches, and the little house with clefts.

[12] "Will horses run upon rocks? Will they refrain from neighing at mares? For you have turned judgment into poison, and the fruit of righteousness into bitterness.

[13] You who rejoice at vanity, who say, 'Have we not possessed horns by our own strength?'

[14] For behold, O house of Israel, I will raise up against you a nation," says the Lord of hosts, "and they shall afflict you so that you shall not enter into Hamath, and as it were to the valley of the Arabah."

AMOS CHAPTER 7

Locusts, Fire, and a Plumb Line

[1] Thus has the Lord God showed me; and behold, a swarm of locusts coming from the east. And behold, one caterpillar, King Gog.

[2] And it came to pass when he had finished devouring the grass of the land, that I said, "Lord God, be merciful; who shall raise up Jacob? For he is small in number.

[3] Relent, O Lord, of this." "And this shall not be," says the Lord.

4 Thus has the Lord showed me; and behold, the Lord called for judgment by fire, and it devoured the great deep, and devoured the Lord's portion.

5 Then I said, "O Lord, cease, I pray: who shall raise up Jacob? For he is small in number. Relent, O Lord, of this."

6 "This also shall not be," says the Lord.

7 Thus the Lord showed me; and behold, He stood upon a wall *made* with a plumb line, and in His hand was a plumb line.

8 And the Lord said to me, "What do you see, Amos?" And I said, "A plumb line." And the Lord said to me, "Behold, I appoint a plumb line in the midst of My people Israel; I will not pass by them anymore.

9 And the joyful altars shall be abolished, and the sacrifices of Israel shall be set aside; and I will rise up against the house of Jeroboam with the sword."

Amaziah Complains to the King

10 Then Amaziah the priest of Bethel sent to Jeroboam king of Israel, saying, "Amos is forming conspiracies against you in the midst of the house of Israel: the land will be utterly unable to bear all his words.

11 For thus says Amos, 'Jeroboam shall die by the sword, and Israel shall be led away captive from his land.'"

12 And Amaziah said to Amos, "Go, seer, remove yourself to the land of Judah, and live there, and you shall prophesy there:

13 but you shall no longer prophesy at Bethel—for it is the king's sanctuary, and it is the royal house."

14 And Amos answered, and said to Amaziah, "I was not a prophet, nor the son of a prophet; but I was a sheepbreeder, and a gatherer of sycamore fruits.

15 And the Lord took me from the sheep, and the Lord said to me, 'Go, and prophesy to My people Israel.'

16 And now hear the word of the Lord: "You say, 'Do not prophesy to Israel, and do not raise a tumult against the house of Jacob.'

17 Therefore thus says the Lord; 'Your wife shall be a harlot in the city, and your sons and your daughters shall fall by the sword, and your land shall be measured with the line; and you shall die in an unclean land; and Israel shall be led captive out of his land. Thus has the Lord God showed me.'"

AMOS CHAPTER 8

The Fowler's Basket

1 And behold, *The Lord showed me* a fowler's basket.

2 And He said, "What do you see, Amos?" And I said, "A fowler's basket. And the Lord said to me, "The end has come upon My people Israel; I will not pass by them anymore.

3 And the ceilings of the temple shall howl in that day," says the Lord God. "*There shall be* many a fallen one in every place; I will bring silence upon *them.*

4 Now hear this, you that oppress the poor in the morning, and drive the needy ones by tyranny from the earth,

5 saying, "When will the month pass away, and we shall sell, and the sabbath, and we shall open the treasure, to make the measure small, and to enlarge the weight, and make the balance unfair?

6 That we may buy the poor for silver, and the needy for shoes; and we will trade in every kind of fruit."

7 The Lord has sworn against the pride of Jacob, "None of your works shall ever be forgotten."

8 And shall not the land be troubled for these things, and shall not everyone who dwells in it mourn? Whereas destruction shall come up as a river, and shall descend as the river of Egypt.

9 "And it shall come to pass in that day," says the Lord God, "that the sun shall go down at noon, and the light shall be darkened on the earth by day;

10 and I will turn your feasts into mourning, and all your songs into lamentation; and I will bring up sackcloth on all loins, and baldness on every head; and I will make them as the mourning of a beloved *friend*, and those with them as a day of grief.

11 "Behold, the days are coming," says the Lord, "that I will send forth a famine on the land, not a famine of bread, nor a thirst for water, but a famine of hearing the word of the Lord.

12 And the waters shall be troubled from sea to sea, and from the north to the east shall *men* run to and fro, seeking the word of the Lord, and they shall not find it.

13 In that day shall the fair virgins and the young men faint for thirst;

14 they who swear by the propitiation of Samaria, and who say, 'Your god, O Dan, lives'; and, 'Your god, O Beersheba, lives'; and they shall fall, and shall not rise again."

AMOS CHAPTER 9

The Destruction of Israel

1 I saw the Lord standing on the altar. And He said, "Strike the mercy seat, and the porch shall be shaken; and cut through into the heads of all; and I will slay the remnant of them with the sword: he who flees shall not escape, and he who escapes shall not be delivered.

2 Though they hid themselves in hell, from there shall My hand drag them forth; and though they go up to heaven, from there will I bring them down.

3 If they hide themselves in the top of Carmel, from there will I search them out and take them; and if they should go down from My presence into the depths of the sea, there will I command the serpent, and he shall bite them.

4 And if they should go into captivity before the face of their enemies, there will I command the sword, and it shall slay them; and I will set My eyes against them for evil, and not for good."

⁵ And the Lord, the Lord God Almighty, is He that takes hold of the land, and causes it to shake, and all that inhabit it shall mourn; and its destruction shall go up as a river, and shall descend as the river of Egypt.

⁶ *It is He* that builds His ascent up to the sky, and establishes His promise on the earth; who calls the water of the sea, and pours it out on the face of the earth; the Lord Almighty is His name.

⁷ "Are not you to Me as the sons of the Ethiopians, O children of Israel?" says the Lord. "Did I not bring Israel up out of the land of Egypt, and the Philistines from Cappadocia, and the Syrians out of the deep?

⁸ Behold, the eyes of the Lord God are upon the kingdom of sinners, and I will cut it off from the face of the earth; only I will not utterly cut off the house of Jacob," says the Lord.

⁹ "For I *will* give commandment, and sift the house of Israel among all the Gentiles, as *grain* is sifted in a sieve, and yet a fragment shall by no means fall upon the earth.

¹⁰ All the sinners of My people shall die by the sword, who say, 'Calamities shall certainly not draw near, nor come upon us.'

Israel Will Be Restored

¹¹ "In that day I will raise up the tabernacle of David that is fallen, and will rebuild the ruins of it, and will set up the parts thereof that have been broken down, and will build it up as in the ancient days:

¹² that the remnant of men, and all the Gentiles upon whom My name is called, may earnestly seek Me," says the Lord who does all these things.

¹³ "Behold, the days are coming," says the Lord, "when the harvest shall overtake the vintage, and the grapes shall ripen at seed time; and the mountains shall drop sweet wine, and all the hills shall be planted.

¹⁴ And I will turn the captivity of My people Israel, and they shall rebuild the ruined cities, and shall inhabit *them*; and they shall plant vineyards, and shall drink the wine from them; and they shall form gardens, and eat the fruit of them.

¹⁵ And I will plant them on their land, and they shall no more be plucked up from the land which I have given them," says the Lord God Almighty.

THE BOOK OF OBADIAH

The Coming Judgment on Edom

¹ The vision of Obadiah. Thus says the Lord God to Edom: I have heard a report from the Lord, and He has sent forth a message to the nations.

² "Arise, and let us rise up against her to war.

³ Behold, I have made you small among the Gentiles: you are greatly dishonored. The pride of your heart has elated you, dwelling *as you do* in the holes of the rocks, *as one that* exalts his habitation, saying in his heart, 'Who will bring me down to the ground?'

⁴ If you should mount up as the eagle, and if you should make your nest among the stars, from there will I bring you down," says the Lord.

⁵ "If thieves came in to you, or robbers by night, where would you have been cast away? Would they not have stolen just enough for themselves? And if grape-gatherers went in to you, would they not leave a gleaning?

⁶ How has Esau been searched out, and how have his hidden things been detected?

⁷ They sent you to your coasts: all the men of your covenant have withstood you; your allies have prevailed against you, they have set snares under you: they have no understanding.

⁸ In that day," says the Lord, "I will destroy the wise men out of Edom, and understanding out of the mount of Esau.

⁹ And your warriors from Teman shall be dismayed, to the end that man may be cut off from the mount of Esau.

Edom Mistreated His Brother

¹⁰ "Because of the slaughter and the sin *committed against* your brother Jacob, shame shall cover you, and you shall be cut off forever.

¹¹ From the day that you stood in opposition *to him*, in the days when foreigners were taking captive his forces, and strangers entered into his gates, and cast lots on Jerusalem, you also were as one of them.

¹² And you should not have looked on the day of your brother in the day of strangers; nor should you have rejoiced against the children of Judah in the day of their destruction; neither should you have boasted in the day of their affliction.

¹³ Neither should you have gone into the gates of the people in the day of their troubles; nor yet should you have looked upon their gathering in the day of their destruction, nor should you have attacked their host in the day of their perishing.

¹⁴ Neither should you have stood at the opening of their passages, to destroy utterly those of them that were escaping; neither should you have shut up his fugitives in the day of affliction.

¹⁵ "For the day of the Lord is near upon all the Gentiles; as you have done, so shall it be done to you; your recompense shall be returned on your own head.

¹⁶ For as you have drunk upon My holy mountain, so shall all the nations drink wine; they shall drink, and go down, and be as if they were not.

¹⁷ But on Mount Zion there shall be deliverance, and there shall be a sanctuary; and the house of Jacob shall take for an inheritance those that took them for an inheritance.

¹⁸ And the house of Jacob shall be fire, and the house of Joseph a flame, and the house of Esau *shall be* for stubble; and *Israel* shall flame forth against them, and shall devour them, and there shall not be a corn field *left* to the house of Esau; because the Lord has spoken.

¹⁹ And those *that dwell* in the south shall inherit the mount of Esau, and they in the plain the Philistines: and they shall

inherit the mount of Ephraim, and the plain of Samaria, and Benjamin, and the land of Gilead.

20 And this *shall be* the domain of the captivity of the children of Israel, the land of the Canaanites as far as Zarephath; and the captives of Jerusalem *shall inherit* as far as Ephratha; they shall inherit the cities of the south.

21 And they that escape shall come up from Mount Zion, to take vengeance on the mount of Esau; and the kingdom shall be the Lord's.

THE BOOK OF JONAH

Jonah's Disobedience

1 Now the word of the Lord came to Jonah the son of Amittai, saying,

2 "Arise, and go to Nineveh, that great city, and preach in it; for the cry of its wickedness has come up before Me."

3 But Jonah rose up to flee to Tarshish from the presence of the Lord. And he went down to Joppa, and found a ship going to Tarshish: and he paid his fare, and went up into it, to sail with them to Tarshish from the presence of the Lord.

The Storm at Sea

4 And the Lord raised up a wind on the sea; and there was a great storm on the sea, and the ship was in danger of being broken.

5 And the sailors were alarmed, and cried everyone to his god. And they threw the cargo that was in the ship into the sea, that it might lighten the load. But Jonah had gone down into the hold of the ship, and was asleep, and was snoring.

6 And the shipmaster came to him, and said to him, "Why do you snore? Arise, and call upon your God, that God may save us, and we not perish."

7 And each man said to his neighbor, "Come, let us cast lots, and find out for whose sake this mischief is upon us." So they cast lots, and the lot fell upon Jonah.

8 And they said to him, "Tell us, what is your occupation, and where do you come from, and of what country and of what people are you?"

9 And he said to them, "I am a servant of the Lord; and I worship the Lord God of heaven, who made the sea, and the dry land."

Jonah Cast into the Sea

10 Then the men feared exceedingly, and said to him, "What is this that you have done?" For the men knew that he was fleeing from the face of the Lord, because he had told them.

11 And they said to him, "What shall we do to you, that the sea may be calm to us?" (For the sea rose, and lifted its waves exceedingly.)

12 And Jonah said to them, "Take me up, and cast me into the sea, and the sea shall be calm for you: for I know that for my sake this great tempest is upon you."

13 And the men tried hard to return to the land, and were not able: for the sea rose and grew more and more tempestuous against them.

14 And they cried to the Lord, and said, "Forbid it, O Lord: do not let us perish for the sake of this man's life, and do not bring righteous blood upon us: for You, O Lord, have done as You willed."

15 So they took Jonah, and cast him out into the sea: and the sea ceased from its raging.

16 And the men feared the Lord very greatly, and offered a sacrifice to the Lord, and made vows.

Jonah's Prayer and Deliverance

17 Now the Lord had commanded a great whale to swallow up Jonah; and Jonah was in the belly of the whale three days and three nights.

JONAH CHAPTER 2

1 And Jonah prayed to the Lord his God out of the belly of the whale,

2 and said, "I cried in my affliction to the Lord my God, and He heard me, even to my cry out of the belly of hell: You heard my voice.

3 For You have cast me into the depths of the heart of the sea, and the floods compassed me: all Your billows and Your waves have passed upon me.

4 And I said, I am cast out of Your presence: shall I indeed look again toward Your holy temple?

5 Water was poured around me, *even* to *my* soul. The lowest deep compassed me, my head went down

6 to the clefts of the mountains; I went down into the earth, whose bars are the everlasting barriers. Yet, O Lord my God, let my ruined life be restored.

7 When my soul was failing me, I remembered the Lord; and may my prayer come to You into Your holy temple.

8 Those that observe vanities and lies have forsaken their own mercy.

9 But I will sacrifice to You with the voice of praise and thanksgiving: all that I have vowed I will pay to You, the Lord of my salvation."

10 And the whale was commanded by the Lord, and it cast up Jonah on the dry land.

JONAH CHAPTER 3

Jonah Preaches at Nineveh

1 And the word of the Lord came to Jonah the second time, saying,

2 "Arise, go to Nineveh, that great city, and preach in it according to the former preaching which I spoke to you of."

3 And Jonah arose, and went to Nineveh, as the Lord had spoken. Now Nineveh was an exceedingly great city, of about three days' journey.

⁴ And Jonah began to enter into the city about a day's journey, and he preached, and said, "Yet three days, and Nineveh shall be overthrown."

The People of Nineveh Believe
⁵ And the men of Nineveh believed God, and proclaimed a fast, and put on sackcloth, from the greatest of them to the least of them.
⁶ And the word reached the king of Nineveh, and he arose from off his throne, and took off his robe, and put on sackcloth, and sat on ashes.
⁷ And proclamation was made, and it was commanded in Nineveh by the king and by his great men, saying, "Let not men, or cattle, or oxen, or sheep, taste any thing, nor feed, nor drink water."
⁸ So men and cattle were clothed with sackcloth, and cried earnestly to God; and they turned everyone from their evil way, and from the iniquity that was in their hands, saying,
⁹ "Who knows if God will relent, and turn from His fierce anger, and so we shall not perish?"
¹⁰ And God saw their works, that they turned from their evil ways; and God relented of the evil which He had said He would do to them; and He did not do it.

JONAH CHAPTER 4

Jonah's Anger
¹ But Jonah was very deeply grieved, and he was confounded.
² And he prayed to the Lord, and said, "O Lord, were not these my words when I was yet in my land? Therefore I made haste to flee to Tarshish; because I knew that You are merciful and compassionate, longsuffering, and abundant in lovingkindness, and relents from doing harm.
³ And now, Lord God, take my life from me; for it is better for me to die than to live."
⁴ And the Lord said to Jonah, "Are you very much grieved?"
⁵ And Jonah went out from the city, and sat over against the city; and he made for himself there a booth, and he sat under it, until he should perceive what would become of the city.
⁶ And the Lord God commanded a gourd, and it came up over the head of Jonah, to be a shadow over his head, to shade him from his calamities. And Jonah rejoiced with great joy for the gourd.
⁷ And God commanded a worm the next morning, and it struck the gourd, and it withered away.
⁸ And it came to pass at the rising of the sun, that God commanded a burning east wind; and the sun beat upon the head of Jonah, and he fainted, and despaired of his life, and said, "It is better for me to die than to live."
⁹ And God said to Jonah, "Are you very much grieved for the gourd?" And he said, "I am very much grieved, even to death."

¹⁰ And the Lord said, "You had pity on the gourd, for which you have not suffered, neither did you rear it; which came up before night, and perished before another night:
¹¹ and shall not I spare Nineveh, that great city, in which dwell more than twelve myriads of human beings, who do not know their right hand or their left hand, and also much cattle?"

THE BOOK OF MICAH

¹ And the word of the Lord came to Micah the son of Moresheth, in the days of Jotham, Ahaz, and Hezekiah, kings of Judah, concerning what he saw regarding Samaria and Jerusalem.

The Coming Judgment on Israel
² Hear *these* words, you people; and let the earth give heed, and all that are in it: and the Lord God shall be among you for a testimony, the Lord out of His holy habitation.
³ For behold, the Lord comes forth out of His place, and will come down, and will go upon the high places of the earth.
⁴ And the mountains shall be shaken under Him, and the valleys shall melt like wax before the fire, and as water rushing down a steep place.
⁵ All these *calamities* are for the transgression of Jacob, and for the sin of the house of Israel. What is the transgression of Jacob? Is it not Samaria? And what is the sin of the house of Judah? Is it not Jerusalem?
⁶ "Therefore I will make Samaria as a storehouse of the fruits of the field, and as a planting of a vineyard; and I will utterly demolish her stones, and I will expose her foundations.
⁷ And they shall cut in pieces all the graven images, and all that she has hired they shall burn with fire, and I will utterly destroy all her idols, because she has gathered of the hires of fornication, and of the hires of fornication has she amassed *wealth*."

Mourning for Israel and Judah
⁸ Therefore shall she lament and wail, she shall go barefooted, and *being* naked she shall make lamentation as *that* of serpents, and mourning as of the daughters of sirens.
⁹ For her plague has become grievous; for it has come even to Judah; and has reached to the gate of My people, even to Jerusalem.
¹⁰ You that are in Gath, do not exalt yourselves, and you Enakim, do not rebuild from *the ruins of* the house in derision: sprinkle dust *in the place of* your laughter.
¹¹ The inhabitant of Shaphir, fairly inhabiting her cities, did not come forth to mourn for the house next to her: she shall receive of you the stroke of grief.
¹² Who has begun *to act* for good to her that dwells in sorrow? For calamities have come down from the Lord upon the gates of Jerusalem,

13 even a sound of chariots and horsemen; the inhabitants of Lachish, she is the leader of sin to the daughter of Zion: for in you were found the transgressions of Israel.

14 Therefore shall he cause men to be sent forth as far as the inheritance of Gath, even vain houses; they have become vanity to the kings of Israel;

15 until they bring the heirs, O inhabitant of Lachish. The inheritance shall reach to Adullam, even the glory of the daughter of Israel.

16 Shave your hair, and make yourself bald for your delicate children; increase your widowhood as an eagle; for *your people* have gone into captivity from you.

MICAH CHAPTER 2

Woe to Evildoers

1 They meditated troubles, and wrought wickedness on their beds, and they put it in execution with the daylight; for they have not lifted up their hands to God.

2 And they desired fields, and plundered orphans, and oppressed families, and spoiled a man and his house, even a man and his inheritance.

3 Therefore thus says the Lord: "Behold, I devise disasters against this family, out of which you shall not lift up your necks, neither shall you walk upright speedily, for the time is evil.

4 In that day shall a parable be taken up against you, and a plaintive lamentation shall be uttered, saying, 'We are thoroughly miserable'; the portion of my people has been measured out with a line, and there was none to hinder him so as to turn him back; your fields have been divided.

5 Therefore you will have no one to cast a line for the lot.

6 Do not weep with tears in the assembly of the Lord, neither let *any* weep for these things; for He shall not remove the reproaches,

7 who says, "The house of Jacob has provoked the Spirit of the Lord"; are not these his practices? Are not the Lord's words right with him? And have they not proceeded correctly?

8 "Even before time My people withstood him as an enemy against his peace; they have stripped off his skin to remove hope in the conflict of war.

9 The leaders of My people shall be cast forth from their luxurious houses; they are rejected because of their evil practices; draw near to the everlasting mountains.

10 Arise, and depart; for this is not your rest because of uncleanness: you have been utterly destroyed;

11 you have fled, no one pursues *you*: *your* spirit has framed falsehood, it has dropped on you for wine and strong drink. But it shall come to pass, that out of the dropping of this people,

12 "Jacob shall be completely gathered with all *his people*: I will surely receive the remnant of Israel; I will cause them to return together, as sheep in trouble, as a flock in the midst

of their fold: they shall rush forth from among men through the breach made before them:

13 they have broken through, and passed the gate, and gone out by it, and their king has gone out before them, and the Lord shall lead them."

MICAH CHAPTER 3

Wicked Rulers and Prophets

1 And He shall say, "Hear now these words, you heads of the house of Jacob, and you remnant of the house of Israel: is it not for you to know judgment?"

2 Who hate good, and seek evil; who tear their skins off them, and their flesh off their bones:

3 even as they devoured the flesh of My people, and stripped their skins off them, and broke their bones, and divided *them* as flesh for the caldron, and as meat for the pot,

4 thus they shall cry to the Lord, but He shall not listen to them; and He shall turn away His face from them at that time, because they have done wickedly in their practices against themselves.

5 Thus says the Lord concerning the prophets that lead My people astray, that bite with their teeth, and proclaim peace to them; and *when* nothing was put into their mouth, they raised up war against them:

6 "Therefore there shall be night to you instead of a vision, and there shall be to you darkness instead of prophecy; and the sun shall go down upon the prophets, and the day shall be dark upon them.

7 And the seers of night visions shall be ashamed, and the prophets shall be laughed to scorn; and all the people shall speak against them, because there shall be none to listen to them."

8 Surely I will strengthen myself with the Spirit of the Lord, and of judgment, and of power, to declare to Jacob his transgressions, and to Israel his sins.

9 Hear now these words, you chiefs of the house of Jacob, and the remnant of the house of Israel, who hate judgment, and pervert all righteousness;

10 who build up Zion with blood, and Jerusalem with iniquity.

11 Their heads have judged for gifts, and their priests have answered for hire, and her prophets have divined for silver; and yet they have rested on the Lord, saying, "Is not the Lord among us? No evil shall come upon us." Therefore on your account Zion shall be plowed as a field, and Jerusalem shall be as a storehouse of fruits, and the mountain of the house as a grove of the forest.

MICAH CHAPTER 4

The Lord's Reign in Zion

¹ And at the last days the mountain of the Lord shall be manifest, established on the tops of the mountains, and it shall be exalted above the hills; and the peoples shall hasten to it.

² And many nations shall go, and say, "Come, let us go up to the mountain of the Lord, and to the house of the God of Jacob; and they shall show us His way, and we will walk in His paths"; for out of Zion shall go forth a law, and the word of the Lord from Jerusalem.

³ And He shall judge among many peoples, and shall rebuke strong nations afar off; and they shall beat their swords into plow shares, and their spears into sickles; and nation shall no more lift up sword against nation, neither shall they learn to war any more.

⁴ And everyone shall rest under his vine, and everyone under his fig tree; and no one shall alarm them; for the mouth of the Lord Almighty has spoken these *words*.

⁵ For all other nations shall walk everyone in his own way, but we will walk in the name of the Lord our God forever and ever.

⁶ "In that day," says the Lord, "I will gather her that is bruised, and will receive her that is cast out, and those whom I rejected.

⁷ And I will make her that was bruised a remnant, and her that was rejected a mighty nation: and the Lord shall reign over them in Mount Zion from now on, even forever.

⁸ And you, dark tower of the flock, daughter of Zion, on you the dominion shall come and enter in, even the first kingdom from Babylon to the daughter of Jerusalem."

⁹ And now, why have you known calamities? Is there no king in you? Or has your counsel perished that pangs as of a woman in labor have seized upon you?

¹⁰ Be in pain, and strengthen yourself, and draw near, O daughter of Zion, as a woman in labor: for now you shall go forth out of the city, and you shall dwell in the plain, and you shall reach even to Babylon. There shall the Lord your God deliver you, and there shall He redeem you out of the hand of your enemies.

¹¹ And now have many nations gathered against you, saying, "We will rejoice, and our eyes shall look upon Zion."

¹² But they know not the thought of the Lord, and have not understood His counsel, for He has gathered them as sheaves of the floor.

¹³ Arise, and thresh them, O daughter of Zion: for I will make your horns iron, and I will make your hoofs brass: and you shall utterly destroy many nations, and shall consecrate their abundance to the Lord, and their strength to the Lord of all the earth.

MICAH CHAPTER 5

¹ Now shall the daughter *of Zion* be completely hedged in; he has laid siege against us; they shall smite the tribes of Israel with a rod upon the cheek.

The Coming Messiah

² "And you, Bethlehem, house of Ephratha, are few in number to be reckoned among the thousands of Judah; yet out of you shall one come forth to Me, to be a ruler of Israel; and His goings forth were from the beginning, even from eternity."

³ Therefore shall He appoint them to wait till the time of her that labors. She shall bring forth, and then the remnant of their brothers shall return to the children of Israel.

⁴ And the Lord shall stand, and see, and feed His flock with power, and they shall dwell in the glory of the name of the Lord their God; for now shall they be magnified to the ends of the earth.

⁵ And she shall have peace when the Assyrian shall come into your land, and when he shall come up upon your country; and there shall be raised up against him seven shepherds, and eight attacks of men.

⁶ And they shall tend the Assyrian with a sword, and the land of Nimrod with her trench, and He shall deliver you from the Assyrian, when he shall come upon your land, and when he shall invade your coasts.

⁷ And the remnant of Jacob shall be among the Gentiles in the midst of many peoples, as dew falling from the Lord, and as lambs on the grass; that none may assemble nor resist among the sons of men.

⁸ And the remnant of Jacob shall be among the Gentiles in the midst of many nations, as a lion in the forest among cattle, and as a lion's whelp among the flocks of sheep, even as when he goes through, and selects, and carries off *his prey*, and there is none to deliver.

⁹ Your hand shall be lifted up against them that afflict you, and all your enemies shall be utterly destroyed.

¹⁰ "And it shall come to pass in that day," says the Lord, "that I will utterly destroy the horses out of the midst of you, and destroy your chariots;

¹¹ and I will utterly destroy the cities of your land, and demolish all your strongholds;

¹² and I will utterly destroy your sorceries out of your hands; and there shall be no soothsayers in you.

¹³ And I will utterly destroy your graven images, and your statues out of the midst of you; and you shall never any more worship the works of your hands.

¹⁴ And I will cut off the groves out of the midst of you, and I will abolish your cities.

¹⁵ And I will execute vengeance on the heathen in anger and wrath, because they did not obey."

MICAH CHAPTER 6

God Pleads with Israel

¹ Hear now a word: the Lord God has said, "Arise, plead with the mountains, and let the hills hear your voice."

² Hear, O you mountains, the controversy of the Lord, and you valleys; even the foundations of the earth: for the Lord has a controversy with His people, and will plead with Israel.

³ "O My people, what have I done to you? Or wherein have I grieved you? Or wherein have I troubled you? Answer Me.

⁴ For I brought you up out of the land of Egypt, and redeemed you out of the house of bondage, and sent before you Moses, and Aaron, and Miriam.

⁵ O My people, remember now, what counsel Balak king of Moab took against you, and what Balaam the son of Beor answered him, from the reeds to Gilgal; that the righteousness of the Lord might be known."

⁶ With what shall I reach the Lord, and lay hold of my God Most High? Shall I reach Him by burnt offerings, by calves of a year old?

⁷ Will the Lord accept thousands of rams, or ten thousands of fat goats? Should I give my firstborn for ungodliness, the fruit of my body for the sin of my soul?

⁸ Has it not been told you, O man, what is good? Or what does the Lord require of you, but to do justice, and love mercy, and be ready to walk with the Lord your God?

Punishment for Israel's Injustice

⁹ The Lord's voice shall be proclaimed in the city, and He shall save those that fear His name. Hear, O tribe; and who shall order the city?

¹⁰ *Is there* not fire, and the house of the wicked heaping up wicked treasures, and that with the pride of unrighteousness?

¹¹ Shall the wicked be justified by the balanced, or deceitful weights in the bag,

¹² whereby they have accumulated their ungodly wealth, and they that dwell in the city have uttered falsehoods, and their tongue has been exalted in their mouth?

¹³ "Therefore will I begin to strike you; I will destroy you in your sins.

¹⁴ You shall eat, and shall not be satisfied; and there shall be darkness upon you; and he shall depart from you, and you shall not escape; and all that shall escape shall be delivered over to the sword.

¹⁵ You shall sow, but you shall not reap; you shall press the olive, but you shall not anoint yourself with oil; and *shall make* wine, but you shall drink no wine; and the ordinances of My people shall be utterly abolished.

¹⁶ For you have kept the statues of Omri, and done all the works of the house of Ahab; and you have walked in their ways, that I might deliver you to utter destruction, and those that inhabit the city to hissing: and you shall bear the reproach of nations."

MICAH CHAPTER 7

Sorrow for israel's Sins

¹ Woe is me! For I have become as one gathering straw in harvest, and as *one gathering* grape-gleanings in the vintage, when there is no cluster for me to eat the first-ripe fruit: alas my soul!

² For the godly has perished from the earth; and there is none upright among men; they all quarrel even to blood. They grievously afflict everyone his neighbor.

³ They prepare their hands for mischief, the prince asks a *reward*, and the judge speaks flattering words; it is the desire of their soul;

⁴ therefore I will take away their goods as a devouring moth, and as one who acts by a *rigid* rule in a day of visitation. Woe, woe, your times of vengeance have come; now shall be their lamentations.

⁵ Do not trust in friends, nor confide in guides; beware of your wife, so as not to commit anything to her.

⁶ For the son dishonors his father, the daughter will rise up against her mother, the daughter-in-law against her mother-in-law: those in his house *shall be* all a man's enemies.

⁷ But I will look to the Lord; I will wait upon God my Savior: my God will hear me.

Israel's Confession and Comfort

⁸ Do not rejoice against me, mine enemy; for I have fallen, yet shall arise; for though I should sit in darkness, the Lord shall be a light to me.

⁹ I will bear the indignation of the Lord, because I have sinned against Him, until He make good my cause. He also shall maintain my right, and shall bring me out to the light, and I shall behold His righteousness.

¹⁰ And she that is my enemy shall see it, and shall clothe herself with shame, who says, "Where is the Lord your God?" My eyes shall look upon her; now shall she be for trampling as mire in the ways.

¹¹ *It is* the day of brick-making; that day shall be your utter destruction, and that day shall utterly abolish your ordinances.

¹² And your cities shall be leveled, and parted among the Assyrians; and your strong cities shall be parted from Tyre to the river, and from sea to sea, and from mountain to mountain.

¹³ And the land shall be utterly desolate together with them that inhabit it, because of the fruit of their doings.

God Will Forgive Israel

¹⁴ Tend your people with your rod, the sheep of your inheritance, those that inhabit by themselves the thicket in the midst of Carmel; they shall feed in the land of Bashan, and in the land of Gilead, as in the days of old.

¹⁵ And according to the days of your departure out of Egypt shall you see marvelous *things*.

¹⁶ The nations shall see and be ashamed; and at all their might they shall lay their hands upon their mouth, their ears shall be deafened.

¹⁷ They shall lick the dust as serpents crawling on the earth, they shall be confounded in their holes; they shall be amazed at the Lord our God, and will be afraid of you.

¹⁸ Who is a God like You, canceling iniquities, and passing over the sins of the remnant of His inheritance? And He has not kept His anger for a testimony, for He delights in mercy.

¹⁹ He will return and have mercy upon us; He will sink our iniquities, and they shall be cast into the depth of the sea, even all our sins.

²⁰ He shall give blessings truly to Jacob, and mercy to Abraham, as You swore to our fathers, according to the former days.

THE BOOK OF NAHUM

¹ The burden of Nineveh: the book of the vision of Nahum the Elkoshite.

The Consuming Wrath of God

² God is jealous, and the Lord avenges; the Lord avenges with wrath; the Lord takes vengeance on His adversaries, and He cuts off His enemies.

³ The Lord is longsuffering, and His power is great, and the Lord will not hold any guiltless. His way is in destruction and in the whirlwind, and the clouds are the dust of His feet.

⁴ He threatens the sea, and dries it up, and exhausts all the rivers: the land of Bashan and Carmel are brought low, and the flourishing *trees* of Lebanon have come to nought.

⁵ The mountains quake at Him, and the hills are shaken, and the earth recoils at His presence, even the world, and all that dwell in it.

⁶ Who shall stand before His anger? And who shall withstand in the anger of His wrath? His wrath brings kingdoms to nothing, and the rocks are thrown down by Him.

⁷ The Lord is good to them that wait on Him in the day of affliction; and He knows them that reverence Him.

⁸ But with an overrunning flood He will make an utter end: darkness shall pursue those that rise up against *Him* and His enemies.

⁹ What do you devise against the Lord? He will make a complete end: He will not take vengeance by affliction twice at the same time.

¹⁰ For *the enemy* shall be laid bare even to the foundation, and shall be devoured as twisted yew, and as stubble fully dry.

¹¹ Out of you shall proceed a device against the Lord, counseling evil things hostile *to Him.*

Good News for Judah

¹² Thus says the Lord who rules over many waters: "Even thus shall they be sent away, and the report of you shall not be heard any more.

¹³ And now will I break off his rod from you, and will burst your bonds.

¹⁴ "And the Lord shall give a command concerning you; your name shall be fruitful no longer: I will utterly destroy the graven *images* out of the house of your god, and the molten *images*: I will make your grave; for *they are* swift."

¹⁵ Behold, upon the mountains the feet of him that brings good news, and proclaims peace! O Judah, keep your feasts, pay your vows; for they shall no more pass through you to your decay.

NAHUM CHAPTER 2

The Overthrow of Nineveh

¹ It is all over with him, he has been removed, one who has been delivered from affliction has come up panting into your presence; watch the way, strengthen your loins, be very valiant in your strength.

² For the Lord has turned aside the pride of Jacob, as the pride of Israel; for they have utterly rejected them, and have destroyed their branches.

³ *They have destroyed* the arms of their power from among men, their mighty men sporting with fire; the reins of their chariots *shall be destroyed* in the day of his preparation, and the horsemen shall be thrown into confusion

⁴ in the ways, and the chariots shall clash together, and shall be entangled in each other in the broad ways; their appearance is as lamps of fire, and as gleaming lightning.

⁵ And their mighty men shall bethink themselves and flee by day; and they shall be weak as they go; and they shall hasten to her walls, and shall prepare their defenses.

⁶ The gates of the cities have been opened, and the palaces have fallen into ruin,

⁷ and the foundation has been exposed; and she has gone up, and her maid servants were led *away* as doves moaning in their hearts.

⁸ And as for Nineveh, her waters shall be as a pool of water. And they fled, and did not stand, and there was none to look back.

⁹ They plundered the silver, they plundered the gold, and there was no end of their adorning; they were loaded *with it* upon all their pleasant vessels.

¹⁰ *There is* thrusting forth, and shaking, and tumult, and heart breaking, and loosing of knees, and pangs on all loins; and the faces of all are as the blackening of a pot.

¹¹ Where is the dwelling place of the lions, and the feeding place of the young lions? Where did the lion go, that the lion's cub should enter in there, and there was none to scare *him* away?

[12] The lion seized enough prey for his cubs, and strangled for his *young* lions, and filled his lair with prey, and his dwelling place with spoil.

[13] "Behold, I am against you," says the Lord Almighty, "and I will burn up your multitude in the smoke, and the sword shall devour your lions; and I will utterly destroy your prey from off the land, and your deeds shall be heard of no more."

NAHUM CHAPTER 3

Nineveh's Complete Ruin

[1] O city of blood, wholly false, full of unrighteousness; the prey shall not be handled.

[2] The noise of whips, and the noise of the rumbling of wheels, and of the pursuing horse, and of the bounding chariot,

[3] and of the mounting rider, and of the glittering sword, and of the gleaming arms, and of a multitude of slain, and of heavy falling; and there was no end to her nations, but they shall be weak in their bodies,

[4] because of the abundance of her fornication: she is a fair harlot, and well-favored, skilled in sorcery, that sells the nations by her fornication, and peoples by her sorceries.

[5] "Behold, I am against you," says the Lord God Almighty, "and I will uncover your skirts in your presence, and I will show the nations your shame, and the kingdoms your disgrace.

[6] And I will cast abominable filth upon you according to your unclean ways, and will make you a public spectacle.

[7] And it shall be that everyone that sees you shall go down from you, and shall say, 'Wretched Nineveh!' Who shall lament for her? Where shall I seek comfort for her?"

[8] Prepare a portion, tune the chord, prepare a portion for Ammon: she that dwells among the rivers, water is round about her, whose dominion is the sea, and whose walls are water.

[9] And Ethiopia is her strength, and Egypt; and there was no limit of the flight *of her enemies*; and the Libyans became her helpers.

[10] Yet she shall go as a prisoner into captivity, and they shall dash her infants against the ground at the top of all her ways; and they shall cast lots upon all her glorious *possessions*, and all her nobles shall be bound in chains.

[11] And you will be drunk, and shall be overlooked; and you will seek strength for yourself because of your enemies.

[12] All your strongholds are as fig trees having watchers. If they be shaken, they shall fall into the mouth of the eater.

[13] Behold, your people within you are as women; the gates of your land shall surely be opened to your enemies. The fire shall devour your bars.

[14] Draw your water for a siege, and well secure your strongholds; enter into the clay, and thus be trodden in the chaff, make *the fortifications* stronger than brick.

[15] There the fire shall devour you; the sword shall utterly destroy you, it shall devour you as the locust, and you shall be pressed down as a palmerworm.

[16] You have multiplied your merchandise beyond the stars of heaven: the palmerworm has attacked it, and has flown away.

[17] Your mixed *multitude* has suddenly departed as the grasshopper, as the locust perched on a hedge in a frosty day; the sun arises, and it flies off, and does not know its place: woe to them!

[18] Your shepherds have slumbered, the Assyrian king has laid low your mighty men. Your people departed to the mountains, and there was none to receive them.

[19] There is no healing for your bruise; your wound is uncurable. All that hear the report of you shall clap their hands against you; for upon whom has not your wickedness passed continually?"

THE BOOK OF HABAKKUK

[1] The burden which the prophet Habakkuk saw.

The Prophet's Complaint

[2] How long, O Lord, shall I cry out, and You will not hear? How long shall I cry out to You, being injured, and You will not save?

[3] Why have You shown me troubles and grievances to look upon, misery and ungodliness? Judgment is before me, and the judge receives a reward.

[4] Therefore the law is frustrated, and judgment never goes forth, for the ungodly man prevails over the just; therefore perverse judgment will proceed.

[5] "Behold, you despisers, and look, and wonder marvelously, and vanish: for I work a work in your days which you will by no means believe, though a man declare it to you!

[6] Wherefore, behold, I stir up the Chaldeans, that bitter and hasty nation, that walks upon the breadth of the earth, to inherit tabernacles not his own.

[7] He is terrible and infamous; his judgment shall proceed of himself, and his dignity shall come out of himself.

[8] And his horses shall bound more swiftly than leopards, and they are fiercer than the wolves of Arabia; and his horsemen shall ride forth, and shall rush from afar; and they shall fly as an eagle *that* hastens to eat.

[9] Destruction shall come upon ungodly men, resisting with their adverse front, and he shall gather the captivity as the sand.

[10] And he shall be at his ease with kings, and princes are his toys, and he shall mock at every stronghold, and shall cast a mound, and take possession of it.

[11] Then shall he change his spirit, and he shall pass through, and make an atonement, saying, 'This strength belongs to my God.'"

[12] Are You not from everlasting, O Lord God, my Holy One? And surely we shall not die. O Lord. You have established it for judgment, and He has formed me to chasten with His correction.

[13] His eye is too pure to behold evil doings, and to look upon grievous afflictions: why do You look upon despisers? Will You be silent when the ungodly swallows up the just?

[14] And will You make men as the fish in the sea, and as the reptiles which have no guide?

[15] He has brought up destruction with a hook, and drawn one with a casting net, and caught another in his drags: therefore shall his heart rejoice and be glad.

[16] Therefore will he sacrifice to his drag, and burn incense to his casting net, because by them he has made his portion fat, and his meats choice.

[17] Therefore will he cast his net, and will not spare to slay the nations continually.

HABAKKUK CHAPTER 2

God's Reply to the Prophet's Complaint

[1] I will stand upon my watch, and mount upon the rock, and watch to see what He will say to me, and what I shall answer when I am reproved.

[2] And the Lord answered me and said, "Write the vision, and that plainly on a tablet, that he that reads it may run.

[3] For the vision is yet for a time, and it shall shoot forth at the end, and not in vain: though he should tarry, wait for him; for he will surely come, and will not tarry.

[4] If he should draw back, My soul has no pleasure in him: but the just shall live by My faith.

[5] "But the arrogant man and the scorner, the boastful man, shall not finish anything; who has enlarged his desire as the grave, and like death he is never satisfied, and he will gather to himself all the nations, and will receive to himself all the peoples.

The Woes of the Wicked

[6] "Shall not all these take up a parable against him? And a proverb to tell against him? And they shall say, 'Woe to him that multiplies to himself the possessions which are not his!' How long? And who heavily loads his yoke.

[7] For suddenly there shall arise up those that bite him, and those that plot against you shall awake, and you shall be a plunder to them.

[8] Because you have plundered many nations, all the nations that are left shall plunder you, because of the blood of men, and the sins of the land and city, and of all that dwell in it.

[9] "Woe to him that covets an evil gain for his house, that he may set his nest on high, that he may be delivered from the power of evils.

[10] You have devised shame for your house, you have utterly destroyed many nations, and your soul has sinned.

[11] For the stone shall cry out of the wall, and the beetle out of the timber shall speak.

[12] "Woe to him that builds a city with blood, and establishes a city by unrighteousness.

[13] Are not these things of the Lord Almighty? Surely many people have been exhausted in the fire, and many nations have fainted.

[14] For the earth shall be filled with the knowledge of the glory of the Lord; it shall cover them as water.

[15] "Woe to him that gives his neighbor to drink the thick lees of wine, and intoxicates him, that he may look upon their secret parts.

[16] Drink also your fill of disgrace instead of glory. Shake, O heart, and quake, the cup of the right hand of the Lord has come round upon you, and dishonor has gathered upon your glory.

[17] For the ungodliness of Lebanon shall cover you, and distress because of wild beasts shall dismay you, because of the blood of men, and the sins of the land and city, and of all that dwell in it.

[18] "What profit is the graven image, that they have graven it? One has made it a molten work, a false image; for the maker has trusted in his work, to make dumb idols.

[19] Woe to him that says to the wood, 'Awake, arise'; and to the stone, 'Arise!' For it is an image, and this is a casting of gold and silver, and there is no breath in it.

[20] But the Lord is in His holy temple: let all the earth fear before Him."

HABAKKUK CHAPTER 3

[1] A prayer of the prophet Habakkuk, with a song.

The Prophet's Prayer

[2] O Lord, I have heard Your report, and was afraid: I considered Your works, and was amazed: You shall be known between the two living creatures, You shall be acknowledged when the years draw nigh; You shall be manifested when the time is come; when my soul is troubled, You will in wrath remember mercy.

[3] God shall come from Teman, and the Holy One from the dark shady Mount Paran. Selah.

[4] His excellence covered the heavens, and the earth was full of His praise. And His brightness shall be as light; there were horns in His hands, and He caused a mighty love of His strength.

[5] Before His face shall go a report, and it shall go forth into the plains,

[6] the earth stood at His feet and trembled. He beheld, and the nations melted away. The mountains were violently burst through, the everlasting hills melted at His everlasting going forth.

[7] Because of troubles I looked upon the tents of the Ethiopians. The tabernacles also of the land of Midian shall be dismayed.

8 Were You angry, O Lord, with the rivers? Or was Your wrath against the rivers, or Your anger against the sea? For You will mount on Your horses, and Your chariots are salvation.

9 "Surely you bent your bow at scepters," says the Lord. Selah. The land of rivers shall be torn asunder.

10 The nations shall see You and be in pain, as You divided the moving waters. The deep uttered her voice, and raised her form on high.

11 The sun was exalted, and the moon stood still in her course. Your darts shall go forth at the light, at the brightness of the gleaming of Your spear.

12 You will bring low the land with threatening, and in wrath You will break down the nations.

13 You went forth for the salvation of Your people, to save Your anointed. You shall bring death on the heads of transgressors; You have brought bands upon their neck. Selah.

14 You thrust through the heads of princes with amazement, they shall tremble in it; they shall burst their bridles, they shall be as a poor man devouring in secret.

15 And You caused Your horses to enter the sea, disturbing much water.

16 I watched, and my belly trembled at the sound of the prayer of my lips, and trembling entered into my bones, and my frame was troubled within me; I will rest in the day of affliction, from going up to the people of my sojourning.

Trust and Joy in the Midst of Trouble

17 For though the fig tree shall bear no fruit, and there shall be no produce on the vines; the labor of the olive shall fail, and the fields shall produce no food. The sheep have failed from the pasture, and there are no oxen at the cribs;

18 yet I will rejoice in the Lord, I will joy in God my Savior.

19 The Lord God is my strength, and He will perfectly strengthen my feet; He sets me up on high places, that I may conquer by His song.

THE BOOK OF ZEPHANIAH

1 The word of the Lord which came to Zephaniah the son of Cushi, the son of Gedaliah, the son of Amoriah, the son of Hezekiah, in the days of Josiah son of Amon, king of Judah.

The Coming Judgment on Judah

2 "Let there be an utter cutting off from the face of the land," says the Lord.

3 "Let man and cattle be cut off; let the birds of the air and the fish of the sea be cut off; and the ungodly shall fail, and I will take away the transgressors from the face of the land," says the Lord.

4 "And I will stretch out My hand upon Judah, and upon all the inhabitants of Jerusalem; and I will remove the names of Baal out of this place, and the names of the priests;

5 and them that worship the host of heaven upon the housetops; and them that worship and swear by the Lord, and them that swear by their king;

6 and them that turn aside from the Lord, and them that do not seek the Lord, and them that do not cleave to the Lord."

7 Be fearful before the Lord God; for the day of the Lord is near; for the Lord has prepared His sacrifice, and has sanctified His guests.

8 "And it shall come to pass in the day of the Lord's sacrifice, that I will take vengeance on the princes, and on the king's house, and upon all that wear strange apparel.

9 And I will openly take vengeance on the porches in that day, *on the men* that fill the house of the Lord their God with ungodliness and deceit.

10 And there shall be in that day," says the Lord, "the sound of a cry from the gate of men slaying, and a howling from the second *gate*, and a great crashing from the hills.

11 Lament, you that inhabit the *city* that has been broken down, for all the people have become like Canaan; and all that were exalted by silver have been utterly destroyed.

12 And it shall come to pass in that day, that I will search Jerusalem with a lamp, and I will take vengeance on the men that despise the things committed to them; but they say in their hearts, 'The Lord will not do any good, neither will He do any evil.'

13 And their power shall be for a spoil, and their houses for utter desolation; and they shall build houses, but shall not dwell in them; and they shall plant vineyards, but shall not drink the wine of them."

The Great Day of the Lord

14 For the great day of the Lord is near, it is near, and hastens quickly; the sound of the day of the Lord is made bitter and harsh.

15 A mighty day of wrath is that day, a day of affliction and distress, a day of desolation and destruction, a day of gloominess and darkness, a day of clouds and vapor,

16 a day of the trumpet and cry against the strong cities, and against the high towers.

17 "And I will greatly afflict the men, and they shall walk as blind men," because they have sinned against the Lord; therefore He shall pour out their blood as dust, and their flesh as dung.

18 And their silver and their gold shall by no means be able to rescue them in the day of the Lord's wrath; but the whole land shall be devoured by the fire of His jealously; for He will bring a speedy destruction on all them that inhabit the land.

ZEPHANIAH CHAPTER 2

A Call to Repentance

1 Be gathered and closely joined together, O unchastened nation;

[2] before you become as the flower that passes away, before the anger of the Lord come upon you, before the day of the wrath of the Lord come upon you.

[3] Seek the Lord, all you meek of the earth; work righteousness, and seek justice, and answer accordingly; that you may be hid in the day of the wrath of the Lord.

Judgment on Nations

[4] For Gaza shall be utterly forsaken, and Ashkelon shall be destroyed; and Ashdod shall be cast forth at noonday, and Ekron shall be rooted up.

[5] Woe to them that dwell on the border of the sea, neighbors of the Cretans! "The word of the Lord is against you, O Canaan, land of the Philistines, and I will destroy you out of your dwelling place."

[6] And Crete shall be a pasture of flocks, and a fold of sheep.

[7] And the sea coast shall be for the remnant of the house of Judah; they shall pasture upon them in the houses of Ashkelon; they shall rest in the evening because of the children of Judah; for the Lord their God has visited them, and He will turn away their captivity.

[8] "I have heard the revilings of Moab, and the insults of the children of Ammon, wherewith they have reviled My people, and magnified themselves against My coasts.

[9] Therefore, as I live," says the Lord of hosts, the God of Israel, "Moab shall be as Sodom, and the children of Ammon as Gomorrah; and Damascus *shall be* left as a heap of the threshing floor, and desolate forever; and the remnant of My people shall plunder them, and the remnant of My nations shall inherit them."

[10] This is their punishment in return for their haughtiness, because they have reproached and magnified themselves against the Lord Almighty.

[11] The Lord shall appear against them, and shall utterly destroy all the gods of the nations of the earth; and they shall worship Him everyone from his place, *even* all the islands of the nations.

[12] "You Ethiopians also shall be slain by My sword."

[13] And He shall stretch forth His hand against the north and destroy the Assyrian, and make Nineveh a dry wilderness, even as a desert.

[14] And flocks, and all the wild beasts of the land, and chameleons shall feed in the midst thereof; and hedgehogs shall lodge in the ceilings thereof; and wild beasts shall cry in the breaches thereof, and ravens in her porches, whereas her loftiness was *as* a cedar.

[15] This is the scornful city that dwells securely, that says in her heart, "I am *it*, and there is no longer any *to be* after me." How has she become desolate, and a habitation of wild beasts! Everyone that passes through her shall hiss, and shake their hands *in contempt*.

ZEPHANIAH CHAPTER 3

The Wickedness of Jerusalem

[1] Alas the glorious and ransomed city.

[2] The dove would not obey the voice, nor receive correction; she has not trusted in the Lord, and she did not draw near to her God.

[3] Her princes within her were as roaring lions, her judges as the wolves of Arabia; they did not remain till the morning.

[4] Her prophets are insolent and scornful men: her priests profane the holy things, and sinfully transgress the law.

[5] But the righteous Lord is in the midst of her, and He will never do an unjust thing. Morning by morning He will bring out His judgment to the light, and it is not hidden, and He knows not injustice by extortion, nor injustice in strife.

[6] "I have brought down the proud with destruction; their corners are destroyed: I will make their ways completely waste, so that none shall go through. Their cities have come to an end, by reason of no man living or dwelling *in them*.

[7] I said, 'Fear Me, and receive instruction,' and you shall not be cut off from the face of the land, for all the vengeance I have brought upon her: prepare yourself; rise early: all their produce is spoiled.

Punishment and Conversion of the Nations

[8] "Therefore wait upon Me," says the Lord, "until the day when I rise up for a witness; because My judgment shall be on the gatherings of the nations, to draw to Me kings, to pour out upon them all My fierce anger; for the whole earth shall be consumed with the fire of My jealousy.

[9] For then will I turn to the peoples a tongue for her generation, that all may call on the name of the Lord, to serve Him under one yoke.

[10] From the boundaries of the rivers of Ethiopia will I receive My dispersed ones; they shall offer sacrifices to Me.

[11] In that day you shall not be ashamed of all your practices, where you have transgressed against Me: for then will I take away from you your disdainful pride, and you shall no more magnify yourself upon My holy mountain.

[12] And I will leave in you a meek and lowly people;

[13] and the remnant of Israel shall fear the name of the Lord, and shall do no iniquity, neither shall they speak vanity; neither shall a deceitful tongue be found in their mouth: for they shall feed, and lie down, and there shall be none to terrify them."

A Song of Joy

[14] Rejoice, O daughter of Zion; cry aloud, O daughter of Jerusalem; rejoice and delight yourself with all your heart, O daughter of Jerusalem.

[15] The Lord has taken away your iniquities, He has ransomed you from the hand of your enemies: the Lord, the King of Israel, is in the midst of you: you shall not see evil anymore.

[16] At that time the Lord shall say to Jerusalem, "Be of good courage, Zion; let not your hands be slack.

17 The Lord your God is in you; the Mighty One shall save you: He shall bring joy upon you, and shall refresh you with His love; and He shall rejoice over you with delight as in a day of feasting.

18 And I will gather your afflicted ones. Alas! Who has taken up a reproach against her?

19 Behold, I *will* work in you for your sake at that time," says the Lord; "and I will save her that was oppressed, and receive her that was rejected; and I will make them a praise, and honored in all the earth.

20 And *their enemies* shall be ashamed at that time, when I shall deal well with you, and at the time when I shall receive you; for I will make you honored and a praise among all the nations of the earth, when I turn back your captivity before you," says the Lord.

THE BOOK OF HAGGAI

The Command to Rebuild the Temple

1 In the second year of Darius the king, in the sixth month, on the first *day* of the month, the word of the Lord came by the hand of the prophet Haggai, saying, "Speak to Zerubbabel the son of Shealtiel, of the tribe of Judah, and to Joshua the son of Jehozadak, the high priest, saying,

2 Thus says the Lord Almighty, saying, 'This people say, "The time has not come to build the house of the Lord."'"

3 And the word of the Lord came by the hand of the prophet Haggai, saying,

4 "Is it time for you to dwell in your paneled houses, whereas this house is desolate?

5 And now thus says the Lord Almighty; Consider your ways!

6 You have sown much, but brought in little; you have eaten, and are not satisfied; you have drunk, and are not satisfied with drink, you have clothed yourselves, and have not become warm thereby: and he that earns wages has gathered *them* into a bag full of holes.

7 Thus says the Lord Almighty: "Consider your ways!

8 Go up to the mountain, and cut timber; build the house, and I will take pleasure in it, and be glorified," says the Lord.

9 "You looked for much, and there came little; and it was brought into the house, and I blew it away. Therefore thus says the Lord Almighty: 'Because My house is desolate, and you run everyone into his own house,

10 therefore shall the sky withhold dew, and the earth shall keep back her produce.

11 And I will bring a sword upon the land, and upon the mountains, and upon the grain, and upon the wine, and upon the oil, and all that the earth produces, and upon the men, and upon the cattle, and upon all the labors of their hands.'"

The People's Obedience

12 And Zerubbabel the son of Shealtiel, of the tribe of Judah, and Joshua the son of Jehozadak, the high priest, and all the remnant of the people, obeyed the voice of the Lord their God, and the words of the prophet Haggai, according as the Lord their God had sent him to them, and the people feared before the Lord.

13 And Haggai the Lord's messenger spoke among the messengers of the Lord to the people, *saying*, "I am with you," says the Lord.

14 And the Lord stirred up the spirit of Zerubbabel the son of Shealtiel, of the tribe of Judah, and the spirit of Joshua the son of Jehozadak, the high priest, and the spirit of the remnant of all the people; and they went in, and worked in the house of the Lord Almighty their God,

15 on the twenty-fourth *day* of the sixth month, in the second year of Darius the king.

HAGGAI CHAPTER 2

The Future Glory of the Temple

1 In the seventh month, on the twenty-first *day* of the month, the Lord spoke by Haggai the prophet, saying,

2 "Speak now to Zerubbabel the son of Shealtiel, of the tribe of Judah, and to Joshua the son of Jehozadak, the high priest, and to all the remnant of the people, and say *to them*,

3 'Who is left among you that saw this house in its former glory? And how do you now look upon it, as it were nothing before your eyes?

4 Yet now be strong, O Zerubbabel,' says the Lord; 'and strengthen yourself, O Joshua the high priest, the son of Jehozadak; and let all the people of the land strengthen themselves,' says the Lord, 'and work, for I am with you,' says the Lord Almighty;

5 'and My Spirit remains in the midst of you; be of good courage.'

6 "For thus says the Lord Almighty: 'Yet once I will shake the heaven, and the earth, and the sea, and the dry *land*;

7 and I will shake all nations, and the choice *portions* of all the nations shall come; and I will fill this house with glory,' says the Lord Almighty.

8 'Mine is the silver, and Mine *is* the gold,' says the Lord Almighty.

9 'For the glory of this house shall be great, the latter more than the former,' says the Lord Almighty, 'and in this place will I give peace,' says the Lord Almighty, 'even peace of soul for a possession to everyone that builds, to raise up this temple.'"

The People Are Defiled

10 On the twenty-fourth *day* of the ninth month, in the second year of Darius, the word of the Lord came to Haggai the prophet, saying,

11 "Thus says the Lord Almighty: Inquire now of the priest *concerning* the law, saying,

¹² 'If a man should take holy meat in the fold of his garment, and the fold of his garment should touch bread, or stew, or wine, or oil, or any food, shall it be holy?'" And the priests answered and said, "No."

¹³ And Haggai said, "If a defiled person who is unclean by reason of a dead body, touch any of these, shall it be defiled?" And the priests answered and said, "It shall be defiled."

¹⁴ And Haggai answered and said, "So is this people, and so is this nation before Me," says the Lord; "and so are all the works of their hands; and whosoever shall approach them, shall be defiled because of their early burdens; they shall be pained because of their toils, and you have hated him that reproved in the gates.

Promised Blessing

¹⁵ "And now consider from this day forward, before they laid a stone upon a stone in the temple of the Lord, what manner of men you were.

¹⁶ When you cast into the grain bin twenty measures of barley, and there were *only* ten measures of barley: and you went to the vat to draw out fifty measures, and there were *but* twenty.

¹⁷ I struck you with blight and with mildew, and all the works of your hands with hail; yet you returned not to Me," says the Lord.

¹⁸ "Set your hearts now *to think* from this day forward, from the twenty-fourth *day* of the ninth month, even from the day when the foundation of the temple of the Lord was laid;

¹⁹ consider in your hearts, whether *this* shall be known on the grain floor, and whether yet the vine, and the fig tree, and the pomegranate, and the olive trees that bear no fruit *are with you*: from this day will I bless *you*."

²⁰ And the word of the Lord came the second time to Haggai the prophet, on the twenty-fourth *day* of the month, saying,

²¹ "Speak to Zerubbabel the son of Shealtiel, of the tribe of Judah, and say *to him*, 'I shake the heaven, and the earth, and the sea, and the dry *land*;

²² and I will overthrow the thrones of kings, and I will destroy the power of the kings of the nations; and I will overthrow chariots and riders; and the horses and their riders shall come down, everyone by the sword striving against his brother.

²³ In that day,' says the Lord Almighty, 'I will take you, O Zerubbabel, the son of Shealtiel, My servant,' says the Lord, 'and I will make you as a seal; for I have chosen you,'" says the Lord Almighty.

THE BOOK OF ZECHARIAH

Israel Urged to Repent

¹ In the eighth month, in the second year of *the reign of* Darius, the word of the Lord came to Zechariah, the son of Berechiah, the son of Iddo, the prophet, saying,

² "The Lord has been very angry with your fathers.

³ And you shall say to them, Thus says the Lord Almighty: 'Turn to Me,' says the Lord of hosts, 'and I will turn to you,' says the Lord of hosts.

⁴ 'And do not be as your fathers, whom the prophets before charged, saying, Thus says the Lord Almighty: "Turn from your evil ways, and from your evil practices"; but they did not hear, nor heed Me,' says the Lord.

⁵ 'Where are your fathers, and the prophets? Will they live forever?

⁶ But do you receive My words and My ordinances, all that I command by My Spirit to My servants the prophets, who lived in the days of your fathers? And they answered and said, "As the Lord Almighty determined to do to us, according to our ways, and according to our practices, so has He done to us.""

First Vision: The Horsemen

⁷ On the twenty-fourth *day* in the eleventh month, this is the month of Shebat, in the second year of *the reign of* Darius, the word of the Lord came to Zechariah, the son of Berechiah, the son of Iddo the prophet, saying,

⁸ I saw by night, and behold, a man mounted on a red horse, and he stood between the shady mountains; and behind him were red horses, and gray, and spotted, and white.

⁹ And I said, "What are these, *my* lord?" And the angel who talked with me said to me, "I will show you what these *things* are."

¹⁰ And the man that stood between the mountains answered, and said to me, "These are *those* whom the Lord has sent forth to go around the earth."

¹¹ And they answered the Angel of the Lord that stood between the mountains, and said, "We have gone around all the earth, and behold, all the earth is inhabited, and is at rest."

¹² Then the Angel of the Lord answered and said, "O Lord Almighty, how long will You have no mercy on Jerusalem, and the cities of Judah, which You has disregarded these seventy years?"

¹³ And the Lord Almighty answered the angel that spoke with me *with* good and comforting words.

¹⁴ And the angel that spoke with me said to me, "Cry out and say, 'Thus says the Lord Almighty: I have been jealous for Jerusalem and Zion with great jealousy.

¹⁵ And I am very angry with the heathen that combine to attack *her*; for as I indeed was a little angry, but they combined to attack *her* for evil.

16 Therefore thus says the Lord: "I will return to Jerusalem with compassion; My house shall be rebuilt in her," says the Lord Almighty, "and a measuring line shall yet be stretched out over Jerusalem."'"

17 And the angel that spoke with me said to me, "Cry yet, and say, 'Thus says the Lord Almighty: "Yet shall cities be spread abroad through prosperity; and the Lord shall yet have mercy upon Zion, and shall choose Jerusalem."'"

Second Vision: The Horns

18 And I lifted up my eyes and looked, and behold, four horns.

19 And I said to the angel that spoke with me, "What are these things, my lord?" And he said to me, "These are the horns that have scattered Judah and Israel, and Jerusalem."

20 And the Lord showed me four craftsmen.

21 And I said, "What are these coming to do?" And he said, "These are the horns that scattered Judah, and they broke Israel in pieces, and none of them lifted up his head: and these have come forth to sharpen them for their hands, even the four horns, the nations that lifted up the horn against the land of the Lord to scatter it."

ZECHARIAH CHAPTER 2

Third Vision: The Man With a Measuring Line

1 And I lifted up my eyes and looked, and behold, a man, and in his hand a measuring line.

2 And I said to him, "Where are you going?" And he said to me, "To measure Jerusalem, to see what is the breadth of it, and what is the length of it."

3 And behold, the angel that spoke with me stood by, and another angel went forth to meet him,

4 and spoke to him, saying, "Run and speak to that young man, saying, 'Jerusalem shall be fully inhabited by reason of the abundance of men and cattle in the midst of her.'

5 'For I,' says the Lord, 'will be to her a wall of fire round about, and I will be for a glory in the midst of her.'

Future Joy of Zion and Many Nations

6 "Up, up! Flee from the land of the north," says the Lord; "for I will gather you from the four winds of heaven," says the Lord,

7 "even to Zion; deliver yourselves, you that dwell *with* the daughter of Babylon.

8 "For thus says the Lord Almighty: 'After the glory has he sent Me to the nations that spoiled you: for he that touches you is as one that touches the apple of His eye.

9 For behold, I bring My hand upon them, and they shall be a spoil to them that serve them: and you shall know that the Lord Almighty has sent Me.

10 "Rejoice and be glad, O daughter of Zion! For behold, I come, and will dwell in the midst of you," says the Lord.

11 And many nations shall flee for refuge to the Lord in that day, and they shall be for a people to Him, and they shall dwell in the midst of you; and you shall know that the Lord Almighty has sent Me to you.

12 And the Lord shall take possession of Judah, His portion in the holy land, and He will yet choose Jerusalem.

13 Let all flesh fear before the Lord, for He has risen up from His holy clouds."

ZECHARIAH CHAPTER 3

Fourth Vision: Joshua and Satan

1 And the Lord showed me Joshua the high priest standing before the Angel of the Lord, and the devil stood on his right hand to resist him.

2 And the Lord said to the devil, "The Lord rebuke you, O devil, even the Lord that has chosen Jerusalem rebuke you. Behold, is not this as a brand plucked from the fire?"

3 Now Joshua was clothed in filthy garments, and stood before the Angel.

4 And *the Lord* answered and spoke to those who stood before Him, saying, "Take away the filthy garments from him." And He said to him, "Behold, I have taken away your iniquities, and clothed you with a long robe,

5 and place a clean turban upon his head." So they placed a clean turban upon his head, and clothed him with garments. And the Angel of the Lord stood by.

The Coming Branch

6 And the Angel of the Lord testified to Joshua, saying,

7 "Thus says the Lord Almighty: 'If you will walk in My ways, and keep My commandments, then shall you judge My house; and if you will diligently keep My court, then will I give you men to walk in the midst of these that stand here.

8 Hear now O Joshua, high priest, you and your neighbors that are sitting before you—for they are diviners; for behold, I bring forth My servant the Branch.

9 And as for the stone which I have set before the face of Joshua, on the one stone are seven eyes: behold, I am digging a trench,' says the Lord Almighty, 'and I will search out all the iniquity of that land in one day.

10 In that day,' says the Lord Almighty, 'you shall call together every man his neighbor under the vine and under the fig tree.'"

ZECHARIAH CHAPTER 4

Fifth Vision: The Lampstand and Olive Trees

1 And the angel that talked with me returned, and awakened me, as when a man is awakened out of his sleep.

2 And he said to me, "What do you see?" And I said, "I am looking, and behold, a lampstand of solid gold, with a bowl

upon it, and seven lamps upon it, and seven oil funnels to the lamps upon it.

3 Two olive trees *are* above it, one on the right of the bowl, and one on the left."

4 And I inquired, and spoke to the angel that talked with me, saying, "What are these things, my lord?"

5 And the angel that talked with me answered, and spoke to me, saying, "Don't you know what these things are?" And I said, "No, my lord."

6 And he answered and spoke to me, saying, "This is the word of the Lord to Zerubbabel, saying, 'Not by mighty power, nor by strength, but by My Spirit,' says the Lord Almighty.

7 'Who are you, O great mountain, before Zerubbabel, that you should prosper? Whereas I will bring out the stone of the inheritance, its grace equal to My grace.'"

8 And the word of the Lord came to me, saying,

9 "The hands of Zerubbabel have laid the foundation of this house, and his hands shall finish it; and you shall know that the Lord Almighty has sent Me to you.

10 For who has despised the small days? Surely they shall rejoice, and shall see the plummet of tin in the hand of Zerubbabel: these are the seven eyes that look upon all the earth."

11 And I answered, and said to him, "What are these two olive trees, which are on the right and left hand of the lampstand?"

12 And I asked the second time, and said to him, "What are the two branches of the olive trees that are by the side of the two golden pipes that pour into and communicate with the golden oil funnels?"

13 And he said to me, "Don't you know what these are?" And I said, "No, my lord."

14 And he said, "These are the two anointed ones that stand by the Lord of the whole earth."

ZECHARIAH CHAPTER 5

Sixth Vision: The Flying Sickle

1 And I turned, and lifted up my eyes, and I beheld a flying sickle.

2 And he said to me, "What do you see?" And I said, "I see a flying sickle, its length *is* twenty cubits, and its width *is* ten cubits."

3 And he said to me, "This is the curse that goes out over the face of the whole earth; for every thief shall be punished with death on this side, and everyone who swears falsely shall be punished on that side."

4 "And I will bring it forth," says the Lord Almighty, "and it shall enter into the house of the thief, and into the house of him that swears falsely by My name, and it shall rest in the midst of his house, and shall consume it, and the timber of it, and the stones of it."

Seventh Vision: The Woman in a Basket

5 And the angel that talked with me went forth, and said to me, "Lift up your eyes, and see this that goes forth."

6 And I said, "What is it?" And he said, "This is the measure that goes forth." And he said, "This is their iniquity in all the earth."

7 And behold, a talent of lead lifted up; and a woman sat in the midst of the measure.

8 And he said, "This is iniquity." And he cast it into the midst of the measure, and cast the weight of lead on the mouth of it.

9 And I lifted up my eyes, and saw, and behold, two women coming forth, and the wind was in their wings; and they had stork's wings; and they lifted up the measure between the earth and the sky.

10 And I said to the angel that spoke with me, "Where are they carrying away the measure?"

11 And he said to me, "To build a house for it in the land of Babylon, and to prepare *a place for it*; and they shall set it there on its own base."

ZECHARIAH CHAPTER 6

Eighth Vision: Four Chariots

1 And I turned, and lifted up my eyes, and looked, and behold, four chariots coming out from between two mountains; and the mountains were mountains of bronze.

2 In the first chariot were red horses, and in the second chariot black horses;

3 and in the third chariot white horses; and in the fourth chariot spotted and ash-colored horses.

4 And I answered and said to the angel that talked with me, "What are these, my lord?"

5 And the angel that talked with me answered and said, "These are the four winds of heaven, and they are going forth to stand before the Lord of all the earth.

6 *As for the chariot* in which were the black horses, they went out to the land of the north; and the white went out after them; and the spotted went out to the land of the south."

7 And the ash-colored went out, and looked to go and compass the earth. And he said, Go, and compass the earth. And they compassed the earth.

8 And He cried out and spoke to me, saying, "Behold, these go out to the land of the north, and they have quieted My anger in the land of the north."

The Coronation of the Branch

9 And the word of the Lord came to me, saying,

10 "Take the things of the captivity from the chief men, and from the useful men of it, and from them that have understood it; and you shall enter in that day into the house of Josiah the son of Zephaniah that came out of Babylon.

¹¹ And you shall take silver and gold, and make crowns, and you shall put them upon the head of Joshua the son of Jehozadak the high priest;

¹² and you shall say to him, 'Thus says the Lord Almighty: "Behold the man whose name is the Branch; from His place He shall branch out, and build the house of the Lord.

¹³ And He shall receive power, and shall sit and rule upon His throne; and there shall be a priest on His right hand, and a peaceable counsel shall be between them both.

¹⁴ And the crown shall be to them that wait patiently, and to the useful men of the captivity, and to them that have known it, and for the favor of the son of Zephaniah, and for a psalm in the house of the Lord.

¹⁵ And they *that are* far from them shall come and build in the house of the Lord, and you shall know that the Lord Almighty has sent Me to you: and this shall come to pass, if you will diligently heed the voice of the Lord your God."

ZECHARIAH CHAPTER 7

Obedience Better than Fasting

¹ And it came to pass in the fourth year of Darius the king, *that* the word of the Lord came to Zechariah on the fourth day of the ninth month, which is Chislev.

² And Sherezer and Arbeseer the king and his men sent to Bethel, to entreat the favor of the Lord,

³ speaking to the priests that were in the house of the Lord Almighty, and to the prophets, saying, "The holy offering has come in here in the fifth month, as it has done already for many years."

⁴ And the word of the Lord of hosts came to me, saying,

⁵ "Speak to the whole people of the land, and to the priests, saying, 'Though you fasted or lamented in the fifth or seventh *months* (yea, behold, these seventy years) have you at all fasted to Me?

⁶ And if you eat or drink, do you not eat and drink for yourselves?

⁷ Are not these the words which the Lord spoke by the former prophets, when Jerusalem was inhabited and in prosperity, and her cities round about her, and the hill country and the low country was inhabited?'"

Disobedience Resulted in Captivity

⁸ And the word of the Lord came to Zechariah, saying,

⁹ Thus says the Lord Almighty; Judge righteous judgment, and deal mercifully and compassionately, everyone with his brother,

¹⁰ and oppress not the widow, or the fatherless, or the stranger, or the poor; and let not one of you remember in his heart the injury of his brother.

¹¹ But they refused to attend, and madly turned their back, and made their ears heavy, so that they should not hear.

¹² And they made their heart disobedient, so as not to hearken to My law, and the words which the Lord Almighty sent forth by His Spirit by the former prophets: so there was great wrath from the Lord Almighty.

¹³ Therefore it came to pass, *that* as He spoke and they did not listen, so they shall cry, and I will not listen, says the Lord Almighty.

¹⁴ And I will cast them out among all the nations, whom they know not; and the land behind them shall be made utterly destitute of any going through or returning; for they have made the choice land a desolation.

ZECHARIAH CHAPTER 8

God's Promise to Zion

¹ And the word of the Lord Almighty came, saying,

² "Thus says the Lord Almighty: 'I have been jealous for Jerusalem and for Zion with great jealousy, and I have been jealous for her with great fury.'

³ Thus says the Lord: 'I will return to Zion, and dwell in the midst of Jerusalem; and Jerusalem shall be called a true city, and the mountain of the Lord Almighty a holy mountain.'

⁴ Thus says the Lord Almighty: 'There shall yet dwell old men and old women in the streets of Jerusalem, everyone holding his staff in his hand for age.

⁵ And the broad places of the city shall be filled with boys and girls playing in its streets.'

⁶ Thus says the Lord Almighty: 'If it shall be impossible in the sight of the remnant of this people in those days, shall it also be impossible in My sight?" Says the Lord Almighty.

⁷ "Thus says the Lord Almighty: 'Behold, I *will* save My people from the east country, and the west country;

⁸ and I will bring them in, and cause *them* to dwell in the midst of Jerusalem, and they shall be to Me a people, and I will be to them a God, in truth and in righteousness.'

⁹ "Thus says the Lord Almighty: 'Let your hands be strong, *you that* hear in these days these words out of the mouth of the prophets, from the day that the house of the Lord Almighty was founded, and from the time that the temple was built.

¹⁰ For before those days the wages of men could not be profitable, and there could be no hire of cattle, and there could be no peace by reason of the affliction to him that went out, or to him that came in, for I would have let loose all men, everyone against his neighbor.

¹¹ But now I *will* not do to the remnant of this people according to the former days,'" says the Lord Almighty.

¹² "But I will show peace: the vine shall yield her fruit, and the land shall yield her produce, and the heaven shall give its dew; and I will give as an inheritance all these things to the remnant of My people.

¹³ And it shall come to pass, as you were a curse among the nations, O house of Judah, and house of Israel; so will I save you, and you shall be a blessing: be of good courage, and strengthen your hands.

[14] "For thus says the Lord Almighty: 'As I took counsel to afflict you when your fathers provoked Me,' says the Lord Almighty, 'and I did not relent,

[15] so have I prepared and taken counsel in these days to do good to Jerusalem and to the house of Judah: be of good courage.

[16] These are the things which you shall do: speak truth everyone with his neighbor; judge truth and peaceable judgment in your gates;

[17] and let none of you devise evil in his heart against his neighbor, and do not love a false oath; for all these things I hate,'" says the Lord Almighty.

Joyful Fasting

[18] And the word of the Lord Almighty came to me, saying,

[19] "Thus says the Lord Almighty: 'The fourth fast, and the fifth fast, and the seventh fast, and the tenth fast, shall be to the house of Judah for joy and gladness, and for good feasts; and you shall rejoice; therefore love the truth, and peace.'

[20] Thus says the Lord Almighty: 'Yet shall many peoples come, and the inhabitants of many cities;

[21] and the inhabitants of five cities shall come together to one city, saying, "Let us go to make supplication to the Lord, and to seek the face of the Lord Almighty"; I will go also.

[22] And many peoples and many nations shall come to seek earnestly the face of the Lord Almighty in Jerusalem, and to obtain *the* favor of the Lord.'

[23] Thus says the Lord Almighty: 'In those days *My word shall be fulfilled* if ten men of all the languages of the nations should take hold—even take hold of the hem of a Jew, saying, "We will go with you; for we have heard that God is with you."'"

ZECHARIAH CHAPTER 9

Judgment on Israel's Enemies

[1] The burden of the word of the Lord, in the land of Hadrach, and His sacrifice shall be in Damascus; for the Lord looks upon men, and upon all the tribes of Israel.

[2] And in Hamath, even in her coasts, are Tyre and Sidon, because they were very wise.

[3] And Tyre built strongholds for herself, and heaped up silver as dust, and gathered gold as the mire of the ways.

[4] And therefore the Lord will take them for a possession, and will destroy her power in the sea; and she shall be consumed with fire.

[5] Ashkelon shall see and fear; Gaza also, and shall be greatly pained, and Ekron; for she is ashamed at her trespass; and the king shall perish from Gaza, and Ashkelon shall not be inhabited.

[6] "And aliens shall dwell in Ashdod, and I will bring down the pride of the Philistines.

[7] And I will take their blood out of their mouth, and their abominations from between their teeth; and these also shall be left to our God, and they shall be as a captain of a thousand in Judah, and Ekron as a Jebusite.

[8] And I will set up a defense for My house, that they may not pass through, nor turn back, neither shall an oppressor come upon them to drive them away: for now have I seen with My eyes.

The Coming King

[9] "Rejoice greatly, O daughter of Zion; proclaim it aloud, O daughter of Jerusalem; behold, your King is coming to you, righteous, and *your* Savior; He is meek and riding on a donkey, a young foal of a donkey.

[10] And He shall destroy the chariots out of Ephraim, and the horse out of Jerusalem, and the bow of war shall be utterly destroyed; and there shall be abundance and peace out of the nations; and He shall rule over the waters as far as the sea, and the rivers to the ends of the earth.

[11] "And you, by the blood of your covenant, have sent forth your prisoners out of the waterless pit.

[12] You shall dwell in strongholds, you prisoners of the congregation: and for one day of your captivity I will recompense you double.

[13] For I have bent you, O Judah, for Myself as a bow, I have filled Ephraim; and I will raise up your children, O Zion, against the children of the Greeks, and I will handle you as the sword of a warrior."

[14] And the Lord shall be over them, and His arrow shall go forth as lightning: and the Lord Almighty shall blow with the trumpet; and shall proceed with the tumult of His threatening.

[15] The Lord Almighty shall protect them, and they shall destroy them, and overwhelm them with slingstones; and they shall swallow them down as wine, and fill the bowls as the altar.

[16] And the Lord their God shall save them in that day, even His people as a flock; for holy stones are rolled upon His land.

[17] For if He has anything good, and if He has anything fair, the young men shall have grain, and there shall be fragrant wine to the virgins.

ZECHARIAH CHAPTER 10

Restoration of Judah and Israel

[1] Ask of the Lord rain in *its* season, the early and the latter rain. The Lord has given bright signs, and will give them abundant rain, grass in the field for everyone.

[2] For the speakers have uttered grievous things, and the diviners have seen false visions, and they have spoken false dreams, they have given vain comfort; therefore have they fallen away like sheep, and been afflicted, because there was no healing.

3 "My anger was kindled against the shepherds, and I will visit the lambs; and the Lord God Almighty shall visit His flock, the house of Judah, and He shall make them as His royal horse in war.

4 And from Him he looked, and from Him He set the battle in order, and from Him came the bow in anger, and from Him shall come forth every oppressor together.

5 And they shall be as warriors treading clay in the ways in war; and they shall set the battle in array, because the Lord is with them, and the riders on horses shall be put to shame.

6 And I will strengthen the house of Judah, and save the house of Joseph, and I will settle them; because I have loved them: and they shall be as if I had not cast them off: for I am the Lord their God, and I will hear them.

7 And they shall be as the warriors of Ephraim, and their heart shall rejoice as with wine; and their children also shall see it, and be glad; and their heart shall rejoice in the Lord.

8 I will make a sign to them, and gather them in; for I will redeem them, and they shall be multiplied according to their number before.

9 And I will sow them among the people, and they that are afar off shall remember Me. They shall nourish their children, and they shall return.

10 And I will bring them again from the land of Egypt, and I will gather them in from among the Assyrians; and I will bring them into the land of Gilead and to Lebanon; and not one of them shall be left behind.

11 And they shall pass through a narrow sea, they shall smite the waves in the sea, and all the deep places of the rivers shall be dried up: and all the pride of the Assyrians shall be taken away, and the scepter of Egypt shall be removed.

12 And I will strengthen them in the Lord their God; and they shall boast in His name," says the Lord.

ZECHARIAH CHAPTER 11

Desolation of Israel

1 Open your doors, O Lebanon, and let the fire devour your cedars.

2 Let the pine howl, because the cedar has fallen; for the mighty men have been greatly afflicted. Howl, you oaks of the land of Bashan, for the thickly planted forest has been torn down.

3 There is a voice of the shepherds mourning, for their greatness is brought low; a voice of roaring lions, for the pride of the Jordan is brought down.

Prophecy of the Shepherds

4 Thus says the Lord Almighty: "Feed the sheep of the slaughter;

5 which their possessors have slain, and have not repented. And they that sold them said, 'Blessed be the Lord; for we

have become rich'; and their shepherds have suffered no sorrow for them.

6 Therefore I will no longer have mercy upon the inhabitants of the land," says the Lord; "but behold, I will deliver up the men, everyone *of them*, into the hand of his neighbor, and into the hand of his king; and they shall destroy the land, and I will not rescue out of their hand.

7 And I will tend the flock of slaughter in the land of Canaan: and I will take for Myself two rods; the one I called Beauty, and the other I called Line; and I will tend the flock.

8 And I will cut off three shepherds in one month, and My soul shall grieve over them, for their souls cried out against Me.

9 And I said, 'I will not tend you: that which dies, let it die; and that which falls off, let it fall off; and let the rest eat the flesh of his neighbor.'

10 And I will take My beautiful staff, and cast it away, that I may break My covenant which I made with all the people.

11 And it shall be broken in that day. And the Canaanites, the sheep that are kept for me, shall know that it is the word of the Lord."

12 And I will say to them, 'If it is good in your eyes, give me my price, or refuse it. And they weighed for my price thirty pieces of silver.

13 And the Lord said to me, "Drop them into the furnace, and I will see if it is good metal, as I was proved for their sakes." And I took the thirty pieces of silver, and cast them into the furnace in the house of the Lord.

14 And I cast away my second rod, even Line, that I might break the possession between Judah and Israel.

15 And the Lord said to me, "Take to yourself shepherd's implements belonging to an unskillful shepherd.

16 For behold, I will raise up a shepherd against the land: he shall not visit that which is perishing, and he shall not seek that which is scattered, and he shall not heal that which is bruised, nor guide that which is whole; but he shall devour the flesh of the choice ones, and shall dislocate the joints of their necks.

17 Alas for the vain shepherds that have forsaken the sheep! The sword shall be upon the arms of such a one, and upon his right eye; his arm shall be completely withered, and his right eye shall be utterly darkened."

ZECHARIAH CHAPTER 12

The Coming Deliverance of Judah

1 The burden of the word of the Lord for Israel. Thus says the Lord, that stretches out the sky, and lays the foundation of the earth, and forms the spirit of man within him.

2 "Behold, I *will* make Jerusalem as trembling door posts to all the nations round about, and in Judea there shall be a siege against Jerusalem.

3 And it shall come to pass in that day *that* I will make Jerusalem a trodden stone to all the nations; everyone that

tramples on it shall utterly mock at it, and all the nations of the earth shall be gathered together against it.

[4] In that day," says the Lord Almighty, "I will strike every horse with amazement, and his rider with madness: but I will open My eyes upon the house of Judah, and I will strike all the horses of the nations with blindness.

[5] And the captains of thousands of Judah shall say in their hearts, 'We shall find for ourselves the inhabitants of Jerusalem in the Lord Almighty their God.'

[6] In that day I will make the captains of thousands of Judah as a firebrand among wood, and as a torch of fire in stubble; and they shall devour on the right hand and on the left all the nations round about; and Jerusalem shall dwell again by herself, even in Jerusalem.

[7] And the Lord shall save the tabernacles of Judah as at the beginning, that the boast of the house of David, and the pride of the inhabitants of Jerusalem, may not magnify themselves against Judah.

[8] And it shall come to pass in that day, *that* the Lord shall defend the inhabitants of Jerusalem, and the weak one among them in that day shall be as David, and the house of David as the house of God, as the Angel of the Lord before them.

[9] And it shall come to pass in that day, *that* I will seek to destroy all the nations that come against Jerusalem.

[10] "And I will pour upon the house of David, and upon the inhabitants of Jerusalem, the Spirit of grace and compassion: and they shall look upon Me, because they have mocked Me, and they shall make lamentation for Him, as for a beloved *friend*, and they shall grieve intensely, as for a firstborn son.

[11] In that day the lamentation in Jerusalem shall be very great, as the mourning for the pomegranate grove cut down in the plain.

[12] And the land shall lament in separate families, the family of the house of David by itself, and their wives by themselves; the family of the house of Nathan by itself, and their wives by themselves;

[13] the family of the house of Levi by itself, and their wives by themselves; the family of Simeon by itself, and their wives by themselves.

[14] All the families that are left, each family by itself, and their wives by themselves.

ZECHARIAH CHAPTER 13

Idolatry Cut Off

[1] "In that day every place shall be opened to the house of David and to the inhabitants of Jerusalem for removal and for separation.

[2] "And it shall come to pass in that day," says the Lord of hosts, "that I will utterly destroy the names of the idols from off the land, and there shall be no longer any remembrance of them; and I will cut off the false prophets and the evil spirit from the land.

[3] And it shall come to pass, if a man will yet prophesy, that his father and his mother which gave birth to him shall say to him, 'You shall not live; for you have spoken lies in the name of the Lord.' And his father and his mother who gave him birth shall bind him as he is prophesying.

[4] "And it shall come to pass in that day, *that* the prophets shall be ashamed, everyone of his vision, when he prophesies; and they shall clothe themselves with a garment of hair, because they have lied.

[5] And one shall say, 'I am not a prophet, but I am a farmer, for a man brought me up *thus* from my youth.'

[6] And I will say to him, 'What are these wounds between your hands?' And he shall say, '*Those* with which I was wounded in the house of my friends.'

The Shepherd Savior

[7] "Awake, O sword, against My shepherds, and against the man who is My citizen," says the Lord Almighty. "Strike the shepherds, and draw out the sheep: and I will bring My hand upon the little ones.

[8] And it shall come to pass that in all the land," says the Lord, "that two-thirds in it shall be cut off and perish, but one-third shall be left in it.

[9] And I will bring the third *part* through the fire, and I will try them as silver is tried, and I will prove them as gold is proved: they shall call upon My name, and I will hear them, and say, 'This is My people'; and they shall say, 'The Lord is my God.'"

ZECHARIAH CHAPTER 14

The Day of the Lord

[1] Behold, the day of the Lord is coming, and your spoils shall be divided in you.

[2] And I will gather all the Gentiles to Jerusalem to war, and the city shall be taken, and the houses plundered, and the women ravished; and half of the city shall go forth into captivity, but the rest of My people shall not be utterly cut off from the city.

[3] And the Lord shall go forth, and fight with those Gentiles as when He fought in the day of war.

[4] And His feet shall stand in that day on the Mount of Olives, which is before Jerusalem on the east, and the Mount of Olives shall be split in two, from east to west, a very great division; half the mountain shall lean to the north, and half of it to the south.

[5] And the valley of My mountains shall be closed up, and the valley of the mountains shall be joined on to Jasod, and shall be blocked up as it was blocked up in the days of the earthquake, in the days of Uzziah king of Judah; and the Lord my God shall come, and all the saints with Him.

⁶ And it shall come to pass in that day that there shall be no light,

⁷ and there shall be for one day cold and frost, and that day *shall be* known to the Lord, and *it shall* not *be* day, nor night: but towards evening it shall be light.

⁸ And in that day living water shall come forth out of Jerusalem; half of it toward the former sea, and half of it toward the latter sea; and so shall it be in summer and spring.

⁹ And the Lord shall be king over all the earth. In that day there shall be one Lord, and His name one,

¹⁰ compassing all the earth, and the wilderness from Geba unto Rimmon south of Jerusalem. And Rama shall remain in its place. From the gate of Benjamin to the place of the first gate, to the gate of the corners, and to the tower of Hananel, as far as the king's winepresses,

¹¹ they shall dwell in the city; and there shall be no more curse, and Jerusalem shall dwell securely.

¹² And this shall be the plague with which the Lord will smite all the nations, as many as have fought against Jerusalem: their flesh shall dissolve while they are standing upon their feet, and their eyes shall melt out of their sockets, and their tongue shall dissolve in their mouth.

¹³ And there shall be in that day a great panic from the Lord upon them; and they shall lay hold every man of the hand of his neighbor, and his hand shall be clasped with the hand of his neighbor.

¹⁴ Judah also shall fight in Jerusalem; and *God* shall gather the strength of all the nations round about—gold, silver, and apparel, in great abundance.

¹⁵ And this shall be the overthrow of the horses, mules, camels, donkeys, and all the beasts that are in those camps, according to this overthrow.

The Nations Worship the King

¹⁶ And it shall come to pass, *that* whoever shall be left of all the nations that came against Jerusalem, shall come up every year to worship the King, the Lord Almighty, and to keep the Feast of Tabernacles.

¹⁷ And it shall come to pass, that whichever of all the families of the earth shall not come up to Jerusalem to worship the King, the Lord Almighty, even these shall be added to the others.

¹⁸ And if the family of Egypt shall not go up, nor come; then upon them shall be the plague with which the Lord shall strike all the nations, whichever of them shall not come up to keep the Feast of Tabernacles.

¹⁹ This shall be the sin of Egypt, and the sin of all the nations, those that shall not come up to keep the Feast of Tabernacles.

²⁰ In that day there shall be *engraved* upon the bridle of every horse, Holiness to the Lord Almighty. And the caldrons in the house of the Lord shall be as bowls before the altar.

²¹ And every pot in Jerusalem and in Judah shall be holy to the Lord Almighty, and all that sacrifice shall come and take of them, and shall cook *meat* in them. And in that day there shall be no more Canaanites in the house of the Lord Almighty.

THE BOOK OF MALACHI

¹ The burden of the word of the Lord to Israel by the hand of his messenger. Take this to heart, I pray.

Israel Preferred to Edom

² "I have loved you," says the Lord. "Yet you say, 'How have You loved us?' Was not Esau Jacob's brother?" says the Lord. "Yet I have loved Jacob,

³ and hated Esau and laid waste his borders, and made his heritage as dwellings of the wilderness?

⁴ Because one will say, 'Edom has been overthrown, but let us return and rebuild the desolate places'; thus says the Lord Almighty: 'They shall build, but I will throw down; and they shall be called "The borders of wickedness," and, "The people against whom the Lord has set Himself forever."

⁵ And your eyes shall see, and you shall say, "The Lord has been magnified upon the borders of Israel."

Polluted Offerings

⁶ "A son honors *his* father, and a servant his master: if then I am a Father, where is My honor? And if I am a Master, where is My fear?" says the Lord Almighty. "You the priests are they that despise My name. Yet you say, 'In what way have we despised Your name?'

⁷ In that you bring to My altar polluted bread; and you say, 'In what way have we polluted it?' In that you say, 'The table of the Lord is polluted, and that which was set on it you have despised.'

⁸ For if you bring a blind *victim* for sacrifices, is it not evil? And if you bring the lame or the sick, *is it* not evil? Offer it now to your ruler, and see if he will receive you, if he will accept your person," says the Lord Almighty.

⁹ "And now entreat the face of your God, and make supplication to Him. These things have been done by your hands; shall I accept you?" says the Lord Almighty.

¹⁰ "Because even among you the doors shall be shut, and one will not kindle *the fire of* My altar for nothing, I have no pleasure in you," says the Lord Almighty, "and I will not accept the sacrifice from your hands.

¹¹ For from the rising of the sun, even to the going down thereof, My name has been glorified among the Gentiles; and in every place incense is offered to My name, and a pure offering: for My name is great among the Gentiles," says the Lord Almighty.

¹² "But you profane it, in that you say, 'The table of the Lord is polluted, and His foods set on it are despised.'

¹³ And you said, 'These *services* are troublesome': therefore I have utterly rejected them with scorn," says the

Lord Almighty. And you brought in torn victims, and lame, and sick: if then you should bring an offering, shall I accept them at your hands?" says the Lord Almighty.

14 "And cursed is *the man* who had the power, and possessed a male in his flock, and whose vow is upon him, and who sacrifices a corrupt thing to the Lord: for I am a great King," says the Lord Almighty, "and My name is glorious among the nations."

MALACHI CHAPTER 2

Corrupt Priests

1 "And now, O priests, this commandment is for you.

2 If you will not hear, and if you will not take it to heart, to give glory to My name," says the Lord Almighty, "then I will send forth the curse upon you, and I will bring a curse upon your blessing: yes, I will curse it, and I will scatter your blessing, and it shall not exist among you, because you take this not to heart.

3 Behold, I turn My back upon you, and I will scatter dung upon your faces, the dung of your feasts, and I will carry you away at the same time.

4 And you shall know that I have sent this commandment to you, that My covenant might be with the sons of Levi," says the Lord Almighty.

5 "My covenant of life and peace was with him, and I gave it to him that he might reverently fear Me, and that he might be awe struck at My name.

6 The law of truth was in his mouth, and iniquity was not found in his lips: he walked before Me directing *his way* in peace, and he turned many from unrighteousness.

7 For the priest's lips should keep knowledge, and they should seek the law at his mouth; for he is the messenger of the Lord Almighty.

8 But you have turned aside from the way, and caused many to fail in *following* the law. You have corrupted the covenant of Levi," says the Lord Almighty,

9 "and I have made you despised and cast out among all the people, because you have not kept My ways, but have been partial in the law.

The Covenant Profaned by Judah

10 Have you not all one Father? Did not one God create you? Why have you forsaken every man his brother, to profane the covenant of your fathers?

11 Judah has been forsaken, and an abomination has been committed in Israel and in Jerusalem; for Judah has profaned the holy things of the Lord, which He delighted in, and has gone after other gods.

12 The Lord will utterly destroy the man that does these things, until he be even cast down from out of the tabernacles of Jacob, and from among them that offer sacrifice to the Lord Almighty.

13 "And these things which I hated, you did: you covered with tears the altar of the Lord, and with weeping and groaning because of troubles: *is it* right *for Me* to have respect for your sacrifice, or to receive *anything* from your hands with goodwill?

14 Yet you said, 'For what reason?' Because the Lord has borne witness between you and the wife of your youth, whom you have forsaken, and yet she was your partner, and the wife of your covenant.

15 And did he not do well? And *there was* the residue of his spirit. But you said, 'What does God seek but a seed?' But take heed to your own spirit, and do not forsake the wife of your youth.

16 But if you should hate *your wife* and put her away," says the Lord God of Israel, "then ungodliness shall cover your thoughts," says the Lord Almighty. "Therefore take heed to your own spirit, and do not forsake them,

17 *all* you that have provoked God with your words. But you said, 'In what way have we provoked Him?' In that you say, 'Everyone that does evil is a pleasing object in the sight of the Lord, and He takes pleasure in such; and where is the God of justice?'

MALACHI CHAPTER 3

The Coming Messenger

1 "Behold, I send forth My messenger, and he shall prepare the way before Me: and the Lord, whom you seek, shall suddenly come into His temple, even the Messenger of the covenant, whom you take pleasure in: behold, He is coming," says the Lord Almighty.

2 "And who will abide the day of His coming? Or who will withstand at His appearing? For He is coming in as the fire of a furnace and as the herb of fullers.

3 He shall sit to melt and purify as it were silver, and as it were gold; and He shall purify the sons of Levi, and refine them as gold and silver, and they shall offer to the Lord an offering in righteousness.

4 And the sacrifice of Judah and Jerusalem shall be pleasing to the Lord, according to the former days, and according to the former years.

5 And I will draw near to you in judgment; and I will be a swift witness against the witches, and against the adulteresses, and against them that swear falsely by My name, and against them that keep back the hireling's wages, and them that oppress the widow, and afflict orphans, and that wrest the judgment of the stranger, and do not fear Me," says the Lord Almighty.

6 "For I am the Lord your God, and I change not;

7 but you, the sons of Jacob, have not refrained from the iniquities of your fathers: you have perverted My statutes, and have not kept them. Return to Me, and I will return to you," says the Lord Almighty. "But you said, 'In what way shall we return?'

8 Will a man insult God? For you insult Me. But you say, 'How have we insulted You?' In that the tithes and firstfruits are with you *still*.

9 And you do surely look off from Me, and you insult Me.

10 The year is completed, and you have brought all the produce into the storehouses; but there shall be the plunder thereof in its house. Return now on this behalf," says the Lord Almighty; "*and see* if I will not open to you the torrents of heaven, and pour out My blessing upon you, until you are satisfied.

11 And I will appoint food for you, and I will not destroy the fruit of your land; and your vine in the field shall not fail," says the Lord Almighty.

12 And all nations shall call you blessed: for you shall be a desirable land," says the Lord Almighty.

13 "You have spoken grievous words against Me," says the Lord. "Yet you said, 'In what way have we spoken against You?'

14 You said, 'He that serves God labors in vain: and what have we gained in that we have kept His ordinances, and in that we have walked as suppliants before the face of the Lord Almighty?

15 And now we pronounce strangers blessed; and all they who act unlawfully are built up; and they have resisted God, and yet have been delivered.'"

The People Complain Harshly

16 Thus they spoke, *those* that feared the Lord, everyone to his neighbor: and the Lord gave heed, and listened, and He wrote a book of remembrance before him for them that feared the Lord and reverenced His name.

17 "And they shall be Mine," says the Lord Almighty, "in the day which I appoint for a peculiar possession; and I will make choice of them, as a man makes choice of his son that serves him.

18 Then shall you return, and discern between the righteous and the wicked, and between him that serves God, and him that does not serve Him.

MALACHI CHAPTER 4

The Great Day of God

1 "For behold, the day is coming, burning as an oven, and it shall consume them; and all the aliens, and all that do wickedly, shall be stubble, And the day that is coming shall set them on fire," says the Lord Almighty, "and there shall not be left of them root or branch.

2 But to you that fear My name shall the Sun of righteousness arise, and healing *shall be* in His wings: and you shall go forth, and bound as young calves let loose from bonds.

3 And you shall trample the wicked; for they shall be ashes underneath your feet in the day which I appoint," says the Lord Almighty.

4 "Remember the law of My servant Moses, accordingly as I charged him *with it* in Horeb for all Israel, even the commandments and ordinances.

5 And, behold, I will send to you Elijah the Tishbite, before the great and glorious day of the Lord comes;

6 who shall turn again the heart of the father to the son, and the heart of a man to his neighbor, lest I come and smite the earth grievously."